1. To investigate in a systematic way: examine. 2. To search into or range over for the purpose of discovery.

Microsoft®

Office 2007

BRIEF

Robert T. Grauer

Michelle Hulett | Cynthia Krebs | Maurie Wigman Lockley

Keith Mulbery | Judy Scheeren

Upper Saddle River
New Jersey 07458

Library of Congress Cataloging-in-Publication Data
Grauer, Robert T., 1945-
Exploring Microsoft Office 2007 brief / Robert T. Grauer, Michelle Hulett, Cynthia Krebs.
p. cm.
ISBN-13: 978-0-13-224004-8
ISBN-10: 0-13-224004-1
1. Microsoft Office. 2. Business--Computer programs. I. Hulett, Michelle J. II. Krebs, Cynthia. III. Title.
HF5548.4.M525G695 2007
005.5--dc22

2007025035

Vice President and Publisher: Natalie E. Anderson
Associate VP/ Executive Acquisitions Editor, Print: Stephanie Wall
Executive Acquisitions Editor, Media: Richard Keaveny
Sr. Acquisitions Editor: Melissa Sabella
Product Development Manager: Eileen Bien Calabro
Sr. Editorial Project Manager/Development: Eileen Clark
Editorial Project Manager/Assistant Editor: Jenelle J. Woodrup
Market Development Editor: Claire Hunter
Editorial Assistants: Rebecca Knauer
Executive Producer: Lisa Strite
Content Development Manager: Cathi Profitko
Project Manager, Media: Ashley Lulling
Director of Marketing: Margaret Waples
Sr. Marketing Manager: Scott Davidson
Sr. Sales Associate: Rebecca Scott
Senior Managing Editor: Cynthia Zonneveld
Associate Managing Editor: Camille Trentacoste
Production Project Manager: Lynne Breitfeller
Senior Operations Supervisor: Nick Sklitis
Production Media Project Manager: Lorena E. Cerisano
Design Director: Maria Lange
Art Director/Interior and Cover Design: Blair Brown
Cover Illustration/Photo: Courtesy of Getty Images/Laurent Hamels
Composition: GGS Book Services
Project Management: GGS Book Services
Project Manager: Kevin Bradley
Production Editor: Blair Woodcock and Andrea Shearer
Cover Printer: Phoenix Color
Printer/Binder: Banta/Menasha

10 9 8 7 6 5 4 3 2 1
ISBN-13: 978-0-13-224004-8
ISBN-10: 0-13-224004-1

Dedications

To Marion—my wife, my lover, and my best friend.

Robert Grauer

I would like to dedicate this book to the memory of my grandmother, Effie Burrell Marcum. Her love, encouragement, and belief in my abilities got me to this point and help me endure every day. And also to John. 143

Michelle Hulett

I dedicate this book to those I love in thanks for the joy and support they give me: My wonderful children: Marshall, Jaron, Jenalee, and Michelle who make it all worthwhile, and Bradley Behle—my newest son and a welcome addition to our family.

My granddaughter, Ava—her baby cuddles make life a pleasure.
My parents, Neal and Zola Mulhern, who continually do all they can to make life easier.
And to those who have gone before: my father, Reed J. Olsen, and my Grandparents Waddoups. I would like to dedicate this book to my siblings: my sister, Vicki O. Ridgway, and my brothers, Randy J. and Michael R. Olsen.
Thank you for always being there for me.

Cynthia Krebs

I would like to express appreciation for my family's patience and support as I have worked on this project. Elizabeth, Aaron, and James were extraordinarily understanding and cooperative about letting me work. I need to acknowledge Dan Bullard for his continuing source of motivation and inspiration. Most of all, I need to thank my best friend and husband, Jim, for always believing in me.

Maurie Wigman Lockley

I would like to dedicate this book to my family and close friends who provided a strong community of emotional support and patience as I completed my doctorate program and worked on this edition of the Exploring series.

Keith Mulbery

Thanks for my husband, Bill, for all the support and energy that has helped me to put ideas on paper. His encouragement made it all possible.

Thanks also to my parents who believe in learning at any age.
And, a special thanks to the following people for their contributions: Frank Lucente, colleague, friend, and mentor for sharing his tips and unique teaching style; and the students at Westmoreland County Community College who make it all worthwhile.

Judy Scheeren

About the Authors

Dr. Robert T. Grauer

Dr. Robert T. Grauer is an Associate Professor in the Department of Computer Information Systems at the University of Miami, where he has been honored with the Outstanding Teacher Award in the School of Business. He is the vision behind the Exploring Series, which is about to sell its 3 millionth copy.

Dr. Grauer has written more than 50 books on programming and information systems. His work has been translated into three foreign languages and is used in all aspects of higher education at both national and international levels.

Dr. Grauer also has been a consultant to several major corporations including IBM and American Express. He received his Ph.D. in operations research in 1972 from the Polytechnic Institute of Brooklyn.

Michelle Hulett

Michelle Hulett received a B.S. degree in CIS from the University of Arkansas and a M.B.A. from Missouri State University. She has worked for various organizations as a programmer, network administrator, computer literacy coordinator, and educator. She currently teaches computer literacy and Web design classes at Missouri State University.

When not teaching or writing, she enjoys flower gardening, traveling (Alaska and Hawaii are favorites), hiking, canoeing, and camping with her husband, John, and dog, Dakota.

Cynthia Krebs

Cynthia Krebs is a professor in the Digital Media Department at Utah Valley State College, where she has taught since 1988. In addition to teaching classes in basic computer proficiency using Microsoft Office, she teaches classes in business presentations, business graphics, and an introduction to multimedia. She has received the Teacher-of-the-Year Award in the School of Business twice during her tenure at UVSC.

She has written chapters for many texts, co-authored a text on advanced word processing, and has presented locally and nationally. A graduate of Utah State University, Cynthia lives in Springville, Utah.

She has four children and one granddaughter. When she isn't teaching or writing, she enjoys spending time with her children and spoiling her granddaughter.

Maurie Wigman Lockley

Maurie Wigman Lockley teaches desktop applications and management information systems classes at the University of North Carolina Greensboro. She has been an instructor there since 1990.

She lives in a tiny piedmont North Carolina town with her husband, daughter, and two preschool-aged grandsons. She spends her free time playing with the boys, reading, camping, playing computer games, and singing. She serves on several not-for-profit boards and is active at her church.

Dr. Keith Mulbery

Dr. Keith Mulbery is an Associate Professor in the Information Systems and Technology Department at Utah Valley State College, where he teaches computer applications, programming, and MIS classes. He has written more than 15 software textbooks and business communication test banks. In January 2001, he received the Utah Valley State College Board of Trustees Award of Excellence for authoring *MOUS Essentials Word 2000*. In addition to his series editor and authoring experience, he also served as a developmental editor on two word processing textbooks. In 2007, he received the UVSC School of Technology and Computing Scholar Award.

He received his B.S. and M.Ed. (majoring in Business Education) from Southwestern Oklahoma State University and earned his Ph.D. in Education with an emphasis in Business Information Systems at Utah State University in 2006. His dissertation topic was computer-assisted instruction using TAIT to supplement traditional instruction in basic computer proficiency courses.

Judith Scheeren

Judith Scheeren is a professor of computer technology at Westmoreland County Community College in Youngwood, Pennsylvania where she received the Outstanding Teacher award. She holds an M.S.I.S. She holds an M.S. from the University of Pittsburgh and an advanced certificate in online teaching and learning from the University of California at Hayward. She has several years of experience in the computer industry with Fortune 500 companies. She has developed and written training materials for custom applications in both the public and private sectors. She also has written books on desktop publishing.

Contributing Authors

Linda Ericksen, Office Fundamentals Chapter

Linda Ericksen is Associate Professor of Software Engineering at the University of Advancing Technology in Tempe, Arizona. She is the author of over 20 college-level computer text books on topics ranging from the Internet through many software applications, writing for major publishers such as Que, Addison-Wesley, and Course Technology. She was also the author of her own popular series for Prentice Hall, the Quick Simple Series, which featured Microsoft Office 2000.

Lynn Hogan, Windows XP Chapter

Lynn Hogan has taught computer literacy and microcomputer applications classes at Calhoun Community College for 25 years. For the past 18 years, she has served as chair of the Department of Computer Information Systems. She received Calhoun's outstanding instructor award in 2006, and currently teaches computer literacy for senior adults and web design courses. Having developed the first online computer course at Calhoun, she continues to work with the distance education program. She received an M.B.A. from the University of North Alabama and a Ph.D. from the University of Alabama.

She resides in Alabama with her husband and two daughters. Much of her free time is spent traveling to cutting horse shows and dressage shows, watching her daughters compete. In addition to working with horses, she enjoys cooking, reading, and family travel.

A Special Thank You to Maryann Barber

After being a key part of the Exploring series for 15 years, Maryann Barber has retired from authoring. Prentice Hall and Bob Grauer would like to thank her for all of her tremendous work through the years that helped make the series the success it is today. While she will be greatly missed, her contributions will be felt for many editions to come.

Brief Contents

Contents

CHAPTER ONE | Office Fundamentals: Using Word, Excel, Access, and PowerPoint 1

Microsoft Office Word 2007

CHAPTER ONE | Microsoft Word: What Will Word Processing Do for Me? 69

CHAPTER TWO | Gaining Proficiency: Editing and Formatting 131

CHAPTER THREE | Enhancing a Document: Tables and Graphics 195

MICROSOFT OFFICE EXCEL 2007

CHAPTER ONE | Introduction to Excel: What Can I Do with a Spreadsheet? 249

CHAPTER TWO | Formulas and Functions: Math Basics for Spreadsheet Use 317

CHAPTER THREE | Charts: Delivering a Message 367

Microsoft Office Access 2007

CHAPTER ONE | Introduction to Access: Finding Your Way through a Database 423

Microsoft Office PowerPoint 2007

CHAPTER ONE | Introduction to PowerPoint: Presentations Made Easy 483

WINDOWS XP | Getting Started with Windows XP 557

Acknowledgments

The success of the Exploring series is attributed to contributions from numerous individuals. First and foremost, our heartfelt appreciation to Melissa Sabella, senior acquisitions editor, for providing new leadership and direction to capitalize on the strength and tradition of the Exploring series while implementing innovative ideas into the Exploring Office 2007 edition. Scott Davidson, senior marketing manager, was an invaluable addition to the team who believes in the mission of this series passionately and did an amazing job communicating its message.

During the first few months of the project, Eileen Clark, senior editorial project manager, kept the team focused on the vision, pedagogy, and voice that has been the driving force behind the success of the Exploring series. Claire Hunter, market development editor, facilitated communication between the editorial team and the reviewers to ensure that this edition meets the changing needs of computer professors and students at the collegiate level. Keith Mulbery gave up many nights and weekends (including Thanksgiving) to jump in and help out with anything that was asked of him, including assisting with topical organization, reviewing and revising content, capturing screenshots, and ensuring chapter manuscripts adhered to series guidelines.

Jenelle Woodrup, editorial project manager/assistant editor, masterfully managed the flow of manuscript files among the authors, editorial team, and production to ensure timely publication of series. Laura Town, developmental editor, provided an objective perspective in reviewing the content and organization of selected chapters. Jenelle Woodrup, editorial project manager, provided valuable assistance in communication among team members and keeping the files moving into production. Eileen Calabro, product development manager, facilitated communication among the editorial team, authors, and production during a transitional stage. The team at GGS worked through software delays, style changes and anything else we threw at them to bring the whole thing together. Art director Blair Brown's conversations with students and professors across the country yielded a design that addressed the realities of today's students with function and style.

A special thanks to the following for the use of their work in the PowerPoint section of the text: Cameron Martin, Ph.D., Assistant to the President, Utah Valley State College, for the use of the Institutional Policies and Procedures Approval Process flowchart; Nick Finner, Paralegal Studies, Utah Valley State College, for the use of his research relating to the elderly population residing in the prisons of Utah; Ryan Phillips, Xeric Landscape and Design (XericUtah.com), for sharing Xeric's concepts for creating beautiful, drought-tolerant landscapes and for the photographs illustrating these concepts; Jo Porter, Photographer, Mapleton, Utah, for allowing the use of her beautiful engagement and wedding photographs; and David and Ali Valeti for the photographs of their baby and their family.

The following organizations and individuals generously provided data and structure from their organizational databases: Replacements, Ltd., Shweta Ponnappa, JC Raulston Arboretum at North Carolina State University, and Valerie Tyson. We deeply appreciate the ability to give students a feel for "real" data.

The new members of the Exploring author team would like to especially thank Bob Grauer for his vision in developing Exploring and his leadership in creating this highly successful series.

Maryann Barber would like to thank Bob Grauer for a wonderful collaboration and providing the opportunities through which so much of her life has changed.

The Exploring team would like to especially thank the following instructors who drew on their experience in the classroom and their software expertise to give us daily advice on how to improve this book. Their impact can be seen on every page:

Barbara Stover, Marion Technical College

Bob McCloud, Sacred Heart University

Cassie Georgetti, Florida Technical College

Dana Johnson, North Dakota State University

Jackie Lamoureux, Central New Mexico Community College

Jim Pepe, Bentley College

Judy Brown, The University of Memphis

Lancie Anthony Affonso, College of Charleston

Mimi Duncan, University of Missouri – St. Louis

Minnie Proctor, Indian River Community College

Richard Albright, Goldey-Beacom College

We also want to acknowledge all the reviewers of the Exploring 2007 series. Their valuable comments and constructive criticism greatly improved this edition:

Aaron Schorr
Fashion Institute of Technology

Alicia Stonesifer
La Salle University

Allen Alexander, Delaware
Tech & Community College

Amy Williams, Abraham
Baldwin Agriculture College

Annie Brown
Hawaii Community College

Barbara Cierny
Harper College

Barbara Hearn
Community College of Philadelphia

Barbara Meguro
University of Hawaii at Hilo

Bette Pitts
South Plains College

Beverly Fite
Amarillo College

Bill Wagner
Villanova

Brandi N. Guidry
University of Louisiana at Lafayette

Brian Powell
West Virginia University – Morgantown Campus

Carl Farrell
Hawaii Pacific University

Carl Penzuil
Ithaca College

Carole Bagley;
University of St. Thomas

Catherine Hain
Central New Mexico CC

Charles Edwards
University of Texas of the Permian Basin

Christine L. Moore
College of Charleston

David Barnes
Penn State Altoona

David Childress;
Ashland Community College

David Law, Alfred
State College

Dennis Chalupa
Houston Baptist

Diane Stark
Phoenix College

Dianna Patterson
Texarkana College

Dianne Ross
University of Louisiana at Lafayette

Dr. Behrooz Saghafi
Chicago State University

Dr. Gladys Swindler
Fort Hays State University

Dr. Joe Teng
Barry University

Dr. Karen Nantz
Eastern Illinois University.

Duane D. Lintner
Amarillo College

Elizabeth Edmiston
North Carolina Central University

Erhan Uskup
Houston Community College

Fred Hills, McClellan
Community College

Gary R. Armstrong
Shippensburg University of Pennsylvania

Glenna Vanderhoof
Missouri State

Gregg Asher
Minnesota State University, Mankato

Hong K. Sung
University of Central Oklahoma

Hyekyung Clark
Central New Mexico CC

J Patrick Fenton
West Valley College

Jana Carver
Amarillo College

Jane Cheng
Bloomfield College

Janos T. Fustos
Metropolitan State College of Denver

Jeffrey A Hassett
University of Utah

Jennifer Pickle
Amarillo College

Jerry Kolata
New England Institute of Technology

Jesse Day
South Plains College

John Arehart
Longwood University

John Lee Reardon
University of Hawaii, Manoa

Joshua Mindel
San Francisco State University

Karen Wisniewski
County College of Morris

Karl Smart
Central Michigan University

Kathryn L. Hatch
University of Arizona

Krista Terry
Radford University

Laura McManamon
University of Dayton

Laura Reid
University of Western Ontario

Linda Johnsonius
Murray State University

Lori Kelley
Madison Area Technical College

Lucy Parker,
California State University, Northridge

Lynda Henrie
LDS Business College

Malia Young
Utah State University

Margie Martyn
Baldwin Wallace

Marianne Trudgeon
Fanshawe College

Marilyn Hibbert
Salt Lake Community College

Marjean Lake
LDS Business College

Mark Olaveson
Brigham Young University

Nancy Sardone
Seton Hall University

Patricia Joseph
Slippery Rock University.

Patrick Hogan
Cape Fear Community College

Paula F. Bell
Lock Haven University of Pennsylvania

Paulette Comet
Community College of Baltimore County, Catonsville

Pratap Kotala
North Dakota State University

Richard Blamer
John Carroll University

Richard Herschel
St. Joseph's University

Richard Hewer
Ferris State University

Robert Gordon
Hofstra University

Robert Marmelstein
East Stroudsburg University

Robert Stumbur
Northern Alberta Institute of Technology

Roberta I. Hollen
University of Central Oklahoma

Roland Moreira
South Plains College

Ron Murch
University of Calgary

Rory J. de Simone
University of Florida

Ruth Neal
Navarro College

Sandra M. Brown
Finger Lakes Community College

Sharon Mulroney
Mount Royal College

Stephen E. Lunce
Midwestern State University

Steve Schwarz
Raritan Valley Community College

Steven Choy
University of Calgary

Susan Byrne
St. Clair College

Thomas Setaro
Brookdale Community College

Todd McLeod
Fresno City College

Vickie Pickett
Midland College

Vipul Gupta
St Joseph's University

Vivek Shah
Texas State University - San Marcos

Wei-Lun Chuang
Utah State University

William Dorin
Indiana University Northwest

Finally, we wish to acknowledge reviewers of previous editions of the Exploring series—we wouldn't have made it to the 7th edition without you:

Alan Moltz
Naugatuck Valley Technical Community College

Alok Charturvedi
Purdue University

Antonio Vargas
El Paso Community College

Barbara Sherman
Buffalo State College

Bill Daley
University of Oregon

Bill Morse
DeVry Institute of Technology

Bonnie Homan
San Francisco State University

Carl M. Briggs
Indiana University School of Business

Carlotta Eaton
Radford University

Carolyn DiLeo
Westchester Community College

Cody Copeland
Johnson County Community College

Connie Wells
Georgia State University

Daniela Marghitu
Auburn University

David B. Meinert
Southwest Missouri State University

David Douglas
University of Arkansas

David Langley
University of Oregon

David Rinehard
Lansing Community College

David Weiner
University of San Francisco

Dean Combellick
Scottsdale Community College

Delores Pusins
Hillsborough Community College

Don Belle
Central Piedmont Community College

Douglas Cross
Clackamas Community College

Ernie Ivey
Polk Community College

Gale E. Rand
College Misericordia

Helen Stoloff
Hudson Valley Community College

Herach Safarian
College of the Canyons

Jack Zeller
Kirkwood Community College

James Franck
College of St. Scholastica

James Gips
Boston College

Jane King
Everett Community College

Janis Cox
Tri-County Technical College

Jerry Chin
Southwest Missouri State University

Jill Chapnick
Florida International University

Jim Pruitt
Central Washington University

John Lesson
University of Central Florida

John Shepherd
Duquesne University

Judith M. Fitspatrick
Gulf Coast Community College

Judith Rice
Santa Fe Community College

Judy Dolan
Palomar College

Karen Tracey
Central Connecticut State University

Kevin Pauli
University of Nebraska

Kim Montney
Kellogg Community College

Kimberly Chambers
Scottsdale Community College

Larry S. Corman
Fort Lewis College

Lynn Band
Middlesex Community College

Margaret Thomas
Ohio University

Marguerite Nedreberg
Youngstown State University

Marilyn Salas
Scottsdale Community College

Martin Crossland
Southwest Missouri State University

Mary McKenry Percival
University of Miami

Michael Hassett
Fort Hayes State University

Michael Stewardson
San Jacinto College – North

Midge Gerber
Southwestern Oklahoma State University

Mike Hearn
Community College of Philadelphia

Mike Kelly
Community College of Rhode Island

Mike Thomas
Indiana University School of Business

Paul E. Daurelle
Western Piedmont Community College

Ranette Halverson
Midwestern State University

Raymond Frost
Central Connecticut State University

Robert Spear, Prince
George's Community College

Rose M. Laird
Northern Virginia Community College

Sally Visci
Lorain County Community College

Shawna DePlonty
Sault College of Applied Arts and Technology

Stuart P. Brian
Holy Family College

Susan Fry
Boise State Universtiy

Suzanne Tomlinson
Iowa State University

Vernon Griffin
Austin Community College

Wallace John Whistance-Smith
Ryerson Polytechnic University

Walter Johnson
Community College of Philadelphia

Wanda D. Heller
Seminole Community College

We very much appreciate the following individuals for painstakingly checking every step and every explanation for technical accuracy, while dealing with an entirely new software application:

Barbara Waxer
Bill Daley
Beverly Fite
Dawn Wood
Denise Askew
Elizabeth Lockley
James Reidel
Janet Pickard
Janice Snyder
Jeremy Harris
John Griffin
Joyce Neilsen
LeeAnn Bates
Mara Zebest
Mary E. Pascarella
Michael Meyers
Sue McCrory

Preface

The Exploring Series

Exploring has been Prentice Hall's most successful Office Application series of the past 15 years. For Office 2007 Exploring has undergone the most extensive changes in its history, so that it can truly move today's student "beyond the point and click."

The goal of Exploring has always been to teach more than just the steps to accomplish a task – the series provides the theoretical foundation necessary for a student to understand when and why to apply a skill. This way, students achieve a broader understanding of Office.

Today's students are changing and Exploring has evolved with them. Prentice Hall traveled to college campuses across the country and spoke directly to students to determine how they study and prepare for class. We also spoke with hundreds of professors about the best ways to administer materials to such a diverse body of students.

Here is what we learned

Students go to college now with a different set of skills than they did 5 years ago. The new edition of Exploring moves students beyond the basics of the software at a faster pace, without sacrificing coverage of the fundamental skills that everybody needs to know. This ensures that students will be engaged from Chapter 1 to the end of the book.

Students have diverse career goals. With this in mind, we broadened the examples in the text (and the accompanying Instructor Resources) to include the health sciences, hospitality, urban planning, business and more. Exploring will be relevant to every student in the course.

Students read, prepare and study differently than they used to. Rather than reading a book cover to cover students want to easily identify what they need to know, and then learn it efficiently. We have added key features that will bring students into the content and make the text easy to use such as objective mapping, pull quotes, and key terms in the margins.

Moving students beyond the point and click

All of these additions mean students will be more engaged, achieve a higher level of understanding, and successfully complete this course. In addition to the experience and expertise of the series creator and author Robert T. Grauer we have assembled a tremendously talented team of supporting authors to assist with this critical revision. Each of them is equally dedicated to the Exploring mission of **moving students beyond the point and click.**

Key Features of the Office 2007 revision include

- New **Office Fundamentals Chapter** efficiently covers skills common among all applications like save, print, and bold to avoid repetition in each Office application's first chapter, along with coverage of problem solving skills to prepare students to apply what they learn in any situation.

- New **Moving Beyond the Basics** introduces advanced skills earlier because students are learning basic skills faster.

- **White Pages/Yellow Pages clearly** distinguish the theory (white pages) from the skills covered in the Hands-On exercises (yellow pages) so students always know what they are supposed to be doing.

- New **Objective Mapping** enables students to skip the skills and concepts they know, and quickly find those they don't, by scanning the chapter opener page for the page numbers of the material they need.

- New **Pull Quotes e**ntice students into the theory by highlighting the most interesting points.

- New **Conceptual Animations** connect the theory with the skills, by illustrating tough to understand concepts with interactive multimedia

- New **More End of Chapter Exercises** offer instructors more options for assessment. Each chapter has approximately 12–15 exercises ranging from Multiple Choice questions to open-ended projects.

- New **More Levels of End of Chapter Exercises,** including new Mid-Level Exercises tell students what to do, but not how to do it, and Capstone Exercises cover all of the skills within each chapter.

- New **Mini Cases with Rubrics** are open ended exercises that guide both instructors and students to a solution with a specific rubric for each mini case.

Instructor and Student Resources

Instructor Chapter Reference Cards

A four page color card for every chapter that includes a:

- *Concept Summary* that outlines the KEY objectives to cover in class with tips on where students get stuck as well as how to get them un-stuck. It helps bridge the gap between the instructor and student when discussing more difficult topics.
- *Case Study Lecture Demonstration Document* which provides instructors with a lecture sample based on the chapter opening case that will guide students to critically use the skills covered in the chapter, with examples of other ways the skills can be applied.

The Enhanced Instructor's Resource Center on CD-ROM includes:

- **Additional Capstone Production Tests** allow instructors to assess all the skills in a chapter with a single project.
- **Mini Case Rubrics** in Microsoft® Word format enable instructors to customize the assignment for their class.
- **PowerPoint® Presentations** for each chapter with notes included for online students
- **Lesson Plans** that provide a detailed blueprint for an instructor to achieve chapter learning objectives and outcomes.
- **Student Data Files**
- **Annotated Solution Files**
- **Complete Test Bank**
- **Test Gen Software with QuizMaster**

TestGen is a test generator program that lets you view and easily edit testbank questions, transfer them to tests, and print in a variety of formats suitable to your teaching situation. The program also offers many options for organizing and displaying testbanks and tests. A random number test generator enables you to create multiple versions of an exam.
QuizMaster, also included in this package, allows students to take tests created with TestGen on a local area network. The QuizMaster Utility built into TestGen lets instructors view student records and print a variety of reports. Building tests is easy with Test-Gen, and exams can be easily uploaded into WebCT, BlackBoard, and CourseCompass.

Prentice Hall's Companion Web Site

www.prenhall.com/exploring offers expanded IT resources and downloadable supplements. This site also includes an online study guide for student self-study.

Online Course Cartridges

Flexible, robust and customizable content is available for all major online course platforms that include everything instructors need in one place.
www.prenhall.com/webct
www.prenhall.com/blackboard
www.coursecompass.com

my**it**lab for Microsoft Office 2007, is a solution designed by professors that allows you to easily deliver Office courses with defensible assessment and outcomes-based training.

The new *Exploring Office 2007* System will seamlessly integrate online assessment and training with the new my**it**lab for Microsoft Office 2007!

Integrated Assessment and Training

To fully integrate the new my**it**lab into the *Exploring Office 2007* System we built my**it**lab assessment and training directly from the *Exploring* instructional content. No longer is the technology just mapped to your textbook.

This 1:1 content relationship between the *Exploring* text and my**it**lab means that your online assessment and training will work with your textbook to move your students beyond the point and click.

Advanced Reporting

With my**it**lab you will get advanced reporting capabilities including a detailed student click stream. This ability to see exactly what actions your students took on a test, click-by-click, provides you with true defensible grading.

In addition, myitlab for Office 2007 will feature. . .

Project-based assessment: Test students on Exploring projects, or break down assignments into individual Office application skills.

Outcomes-based training: Students train on what they don't know without having to relearn skills they already know.

Optimal performance and uptime: Provided by world-class hosting environment.

Dedicated student and instructor support: Professional tech support is available by phone and email when you need it.

No installation required! my**it**lab runs entirely from the Web.

And much more!

www.prenhall.com/myitlab

Office Fundamentals Chapter

efficiently covers skills common among all applications like save, print, and bold to avoid repetition in each 1st application chapter.

chapter 1 | Office Fundamentals

Using Word, Excel, Access, and PowerPoint

After you read this chapter you will be able to:

1. Identify common interface components **(page 4)**.
2. Use Office 2007 Help **(page 10)**.
3. Open a file **(page 18)**.
4. Save a file **(page 21)**.
5. Print a document **(page 24)**.
6. Select text to edit **(page 31)**.
7. Insert text and change to the Overtype mode **(page 32)**.
8. Move and copy text **(page 34)**.
9. Find, replace, and go to text **(page 36)**.
10. Use the Undo and Redo commands **(page 39)**.
11. Use language tools **(page 39)**.
12. Apply font attributes **(page 43)**.
13. Copy formats with the Format Painter **(page 47)**.

Hands-On Exercises

Exercises	Skills Covered
1. IDENTIFYING PROGRAM INTERFACE COMPONENTS AND USING HELP (page 12)	• Use PowerPoint's Office Button, Get Help in a Dialog Box, and Use the Zoom Slider • Use Excel's Ribbon, Get Help from an Enhanced ScreenTip, and Use the Zoom Dialog Box • Search Help in Access • Use Word's Status Bar • Search Help and Print a Help Topic
2. PERFORMING UNIVERSAL TASKS (page 28) **Open:** chap1_ho2_sample.docx **Save as:** chap1_ho2_solution.docx	• Open a File and Save it with a Different Name • Use Print Preview and Select Options • Print a Document
3. PERFORMING BASIC TASKS (page 48) **Open:** chap1_ho3_internet_docx **Save as:** chap_ho3_internet_solution.docx	• Cut, Copy, Paste, and Undo • Find and Replace Text • Check Spelling • Choose Synonyms and Use Thesaurus • Use the Research Tool • Apply Font Attributes • Use Format Painter

Microsoft Office 2007 Software Office Fundamentals 1

chapter 3 | **Access**

Customize, Analyze, and Summarize Query Data

Creating and Using Queries to Make Decisions

After you read this chapter you will be able to:

1. Understand the order of precedence **(page 679)**.
2. Create a calculated field in a query **(page 679)**.
3. Create expressions with the Expression Builder **(page 679)**.
4. Create and edit Access functions **(page 690)**.
5. Perform date arithmetic **(page 694)**.
6. Create and work with data aggregates **(page 704)**.

Hands-On Exercises

Exercises	Skills Covered
1. **CALCULATED QUERY FIELDS (PAGE 683)** **Open:** chap3_ho1-3_realestate.accdb **Save:** chap3_ho1-3_realestate_solution.accdb **Back up as:** chap3_ho1_realestate_solution.accdb	• Copy a Database and Start the Query • Select the Fields, Save, and Open the Query • Create a Calculated Field and Run the Query • Verify the Calculated Results • Recover from a Common Error
2. **EXPRESSION BUILDER, FUNCTIONS, AND DATE ARITHMETIC (page 695)** **Open:** chap3_ho1-3_realestate.accdb (from Exercise 1) **Save:** chap3_ho1-3_realestate_solution.accdb (additional modifications) **Back up as:** chap3_ho2_realestate_solution.accdb	• Create a Select Query • Use the Expression Builder • Create Calculations Using Input Stored in a Different Query or Table • Edit Expressions Using the Expression Builder • Use Functions • Work with Date Arithmetic
3. **DATA AGGREGATES (page 707)** **Open:** chap3_ho1-3_realestate.accdb (from Exercise 2) **Save:** chap3_ho1-3_realestate_solution.accdb (additional modifications)	• Add a Total Row • Create a Totals Query Based on a Select Query • Add Fields to the Design Grid • Add Grouping Options and Specify Summary Statistics

Access 2007 677

Objective Mapping

allows students to skip the skills and concepts they know and quickly find those they don't by scanning the chapter opening page for the page numbers of the material they need.

Case Study

begins each chapter to provide an effective overview of what students can accomplish by completing the chapter.

CASE STUDY

West Transylvania College Athletic Department

The athletic department of West Transylvania College has reached a fork in the road. A significant alumni contingent insists that the college upgrade its athletic program from NCAA Division II to Division I. This process will involve adding sports, funding athletic scholarships, expanding staff, and coordinating a variety of fundraising activities.

Tom Hunt, the athletic director, wants to determine if the funding support is available both inside and outside the college to accomplish this goal. You are helping Tom prepare the five-year projected budget based on current budget figures. The plan is to increase revenues at a rate of 10% per year for five years while handling an estimated 8% increase in expenses over the same five-year period. Tom feels that a 10% increase in revenue versus an 8% increase in expenses should make the upgrade viable. Tom wants to examine how increased alumni giving, increases in college fees, and grant monies will increase the revenue flow. The Transylvania College's Athletic Committee and its Alumni Association Board of Directors want Tom to present an analysis of funding and expenses to determine if the move to NCAA Division I is feasible. As Tom's student assistant this year, it is your responsibility to help him with special projects. Tom prepared the basic projected budget spreadsheet and has asked you to finish it for him.

Case Study

Your Assignment

- Read the chapter carefully and pay close attention to mathematical operations, formulas, and functions.
- Open *chap2_case_athletics*, which contains the partially completed, projected budget spreadsheet.
- Study the structure of the worksheet to determine what type of formulas you need to complete the financial calculations. Identify how you would perform calculations if you were using a calculator and make a list of formulas using regular language to determine if the financial goals will be met. As you read the chapter, identify formulas and functions that will help you complete the financial analysis. You will insert formulas in the revenue and expenditures sections for column C. Use appropriate cell references in formulas. Do not enter constant values within a formula; instead enter the 10% and 8% increases in an input area. Use appropriate functions for column totals in both the revenue and expenditures sections. Insert formulas for the Net Operating Margin and Net Margin rows. Copy the formulas.
- Review the spreadsheet and identify weaknesses in the formatting. Use your knowledge of good formatting design to improve the appearance of the spreadsheet so that it will be attractive to the Athletic Committee and the alumni board. You will format cells as currency with 0 decimals and widen columns as needed. Merge and center the title and use an attractive fill color. Emphasize the totals and margin rows with borders. Enter your name and current date. Create a custom footer that includes a page number and your instructor's name. Print the worksheet as displayed and again with cell formulas displayed. Save the workbook as **chap2_case_athletics_solution**.

380 CHAPTER 2 | Formulas and Functions

Key Terms

are called out in the margins of the chapter so students can more effectively study definitions.

Pull Quotes

entice students into the theory by highlighting the most interesting points.

Tables

A *table* is a series of rows and columns that organize data.

A *cell* is the intersection of a row and column in a table.

A *table* is a series of rows and columns that organize data effectively. The rows and columns in a table intersect to form *cells*. The table feature is one of the most powerful in Word and is an easy way to organize a series of data in a columnar list format such as employee names, inventory lists, and e-mail addresses. The Vacation Planner in Figure 3.1, for example, is actually a 4x9 table (4 columns and 9 rows). The completed table looks impressive, but it is very easy to create once you understand how a table works. In addition to the organizational benefits, tables make an excellent alignment tool. For example, you can create tables to organize data such as employee lists with phone numbers and e-mail addresses. The Exploring series uses tables to provide descriptions for various software commands. Although you can align text with tabs, you have more format control when you create a table. (See the Practice Exercises at the end of the chapter for other examples.)

> The table feature is one of the most powerful in Word and is the basis for an almost limitless variety of documents. It is very easy to create once you understand how a table works.

Vacation Planner			
Item	Number of Days	Amount per Day (est)	Total Amount
Airline Ticket			449.00
Amusement Park Tickets	4	50.00	200.00
Hotel	5	120.00	600.00
Meals	6	50.00	300.00
Rental Car	5	30.00	150.00
Souvenirs	5	20.00	100.00
TOTAL EXPECTED EXPENSES			$1799.00

Figure 3.1 The Vacation Planner

In this section, you insert a table in a document. After inserting the table, you can insert or delete columns and rows if you need to change the structure. Furthermore, you learn how to merge and split cells within the table. Finally, you change the row height and column width to accommodate data in the table.

Inserting a Table

You can create a table from the Insert tab. Click Table in the Tables group on the Insert tab to see a gallery of cells from which you select the number of columns and rows you require in the table, or you can choose the Insert Table command below the gallery to display the Insert Table dialog box and enter the table composition you prefer. When you select the table dimension from the gallery or from the Insert Table dialog box, Word creates a table structure with the number of columns and rows you specify. After you define a table, you can enter text, numbers, or graphics in individual cells. Text

Tables | Word 2007 197

White Pages/ Yellow Pages

clearly distinguishes the theory (white pages) from the skills covered in the Hands-On exercises (yellow pages) so students always know what they are supposed to be doing.

Keyword for search

Collections to be searched

Type of clips to be included in results

Search results

Link to Microsoft Clip Organizer

Link to more clips online

CIS 101 Review Session
Test #2

Monday
7pm
Glass 102

Figure 3.18 The Clip Art Task Pane

You can access the Microsoft Clip Organizer (to view the various collections) by clicking Organize clips at the bottom of the Clip Art task pane. You also can access the Clip Organizer when you are not using Word; click the Start button on the taskbar, click All Programs, Micros Clip Organizer. Once in the Organi ous collections, reorganize the exi add new clips (with their associate the bottom of the task pane in Figu and tips for finding more relevant

Insert a Picture

In addition to the collection of clip you also can insert your own pictu ital camera attached to your compu Word. After you save the picture to on the Insert tab to locate and inser opens so that you can navigate to t insert the picture, there are many mands are discussed in the next sec

Formatting a Grap

(Remember that graphical elements should enhance a document, not overpower it.)

When you ins fined size. For very large and resized. Most t within the d

Step 2
Move and Resize the Clip Art Object

Refer to Figure 3.24 as you complete Step 2.

a. Click once on the clip art object to select it. Click **Text Wrapping** in the Arrange group on the Picture Tools Format tab to display the text wrapping options, and then select **Square**, as shown in Figure 3.24.

   You must change the layout in order to move and size the object.

b. Click **Position** in the Arrange group, and then click **More Layout Options.** Click the **Picture Position tab** in the Advanced Layout dialog box, if necessary, then click **Alignment** in the *Horizontal* section. Click the **Alignment drop-down arrow** and select **Right**. Deselect the **Allow overlap check box** in the *Options* section. Click **OK**.

c. Click **Crop** in the Size group, then hold your mouse over the sizing handles and notice how the pointer changes to angular shapes. Click the **bottom center handle** and drag it up. Drag the side handles inward to remove excess space surrounding the graphical object.

d. Click the Shape **Height box** in the Size group and type **2.77**.

   Notice the width is changed automatically to retain the proportion.

e. Save the document.

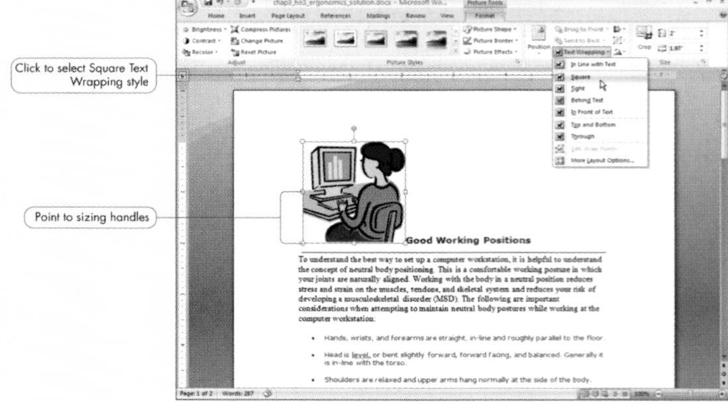

Figure 3.24 Formatting Clip Art

Step 3
Create a WordArt Object

Refer to Figure 3.25 as you complete Step 3.

a. Press **Ctrl+End** to move to the end of the document. Click the **Insert tab**, and then click **WordArt** in the Text group to display the WordArt gallery.

b. Click **WordArt Style 28** on the bottom row of the gallery.

   The Edit WordArt Text dialog box displays, as shown in Figure 3.25.

Summary

1. **Create a presentation using a template.** Using a template saves you a great deal of time and enables you to create a more professional presentation. Templates incorporate a theme, a layout, and content that can be modified. You can use templates that are installed when Microsoft Office is installed, or you can download templates from Microsoft Office Online. Microsoft is constantly adding templates to the online site for your use.
2. **Modify a template.** In addition to changing the content of a template, you can modify the structure and design. The structure is modified by changing the layout of a slide. To change the layout, drag placeholders to new locations or resize placeholders. You can even add placeholders so that elements such as logos can be included.
3. **Create a presentation in Outline view.** When you use a storyboard to determine your content, you create a basic outline. Then you can enter your presentation in Outline view, which enables you to concentrate on the content of the presentation. Using Outline view keeps you from getting buried in design issues at the cost of your content. It also saves you time because you can enter the information without having to move from placeholder to placeholder.
4. **Modify an outline structure.** Because the Outline view gives you a global view of the presentation, it helps you see the underlying structure of the presentation. You are able to see where content needs to be strengthened, or where the flow of information needs to be revised. If you find a slide with content that would be presented better in another location in the slide show, you can use the Collapse and Expand features to easily move it. By collapsing the slide content, you can drag it to a new location and then expand it. To move individual bullet points, cut and paste the bullet point or drag-and-drop it.
5. **Print an outline.** When you present, using the outline version of your slide show as a reference is a boon. No matter how well you know your information, it is easy to forget to present some information when facing an audience. While you would print speaker's notes if you have many details, you can print the outline as a quick reference. The outline can be printed in either the collapsed or the expanded form, giving you far fewer pages to shuffle in front of an audience than printing speaker's notes would.
6. **Import an outline.** You do not need to re-enter information from an outline created in Microsoft Word or another word processor. You can use the Open feature to import any outline that has been saved in a format that PowerPoint can read. In addition to a Word outline, you can use the common generic formats Rich Text Format and Plain Text Format.
7. **Add existing content to a presentation.** After you spend time creating the slides in a slide show, you may find that slides in the slide show would be appropriate in another show at a later date. Any slide you create can be reused in another presentation, thereby saving you considerable time and effort. You simply open the Reuse Slides pane, locate the slide show with the slide you need, and then click on the thumbnail of the slide to insert a copy of it in the new slide show.
8. **Examine slide show design principles.** With a basic understanding of slide show design principles you can create presentations that reflect your personality in a professional way. The goal of applying these principles is to create a slide show that focuses the audience on the message of the slide without being distracted by clutter or unreadable text.
9. **Apply and modify a design theme.** PowerPoint provides you with themes to help you create a clean, professional look for your presentation. Once a theme is applied you can modify the theme by changing the color scheme, the font scheme, the effects scheme, or the background style.
10. **Insert a header or footer.** Identifying information can be included in a header or footer. You may, for example, wish to include the group to whom you are presenting, or the location of the presentation, or a copyright notation for original work. You can apply footers to slides, handouts, and Notes pages. Headers may be applied to handouts and Notes pages.

908 CHAPTER 2 | Introduction to PowerPoint

Summary

links directly back to the objectives so students can more effectively study and locate the concepts that they need to focus on.

More End-of-Chapter Exercises with New Levels of Assessment

offer instructors more options for assessment. Each chapter has approximately 12-15 projects per chapter ranging from multiple choice to open-ended projects.

Practice Exercises

reinforce skills learned in the chapter with specific directions on what to do and how to do it.

New Mid-Level Exercises

assess the skills learned in the chapter by directing the students on what to do but not how to do it.

New Capstone Exercises

cover all of the skills with in each chapter without telling students how to perform the skills.

Mini Cases with Rubrics

are open ended exercises that guide both instructors and students to a solution with a specific rubric for each Mini Case.

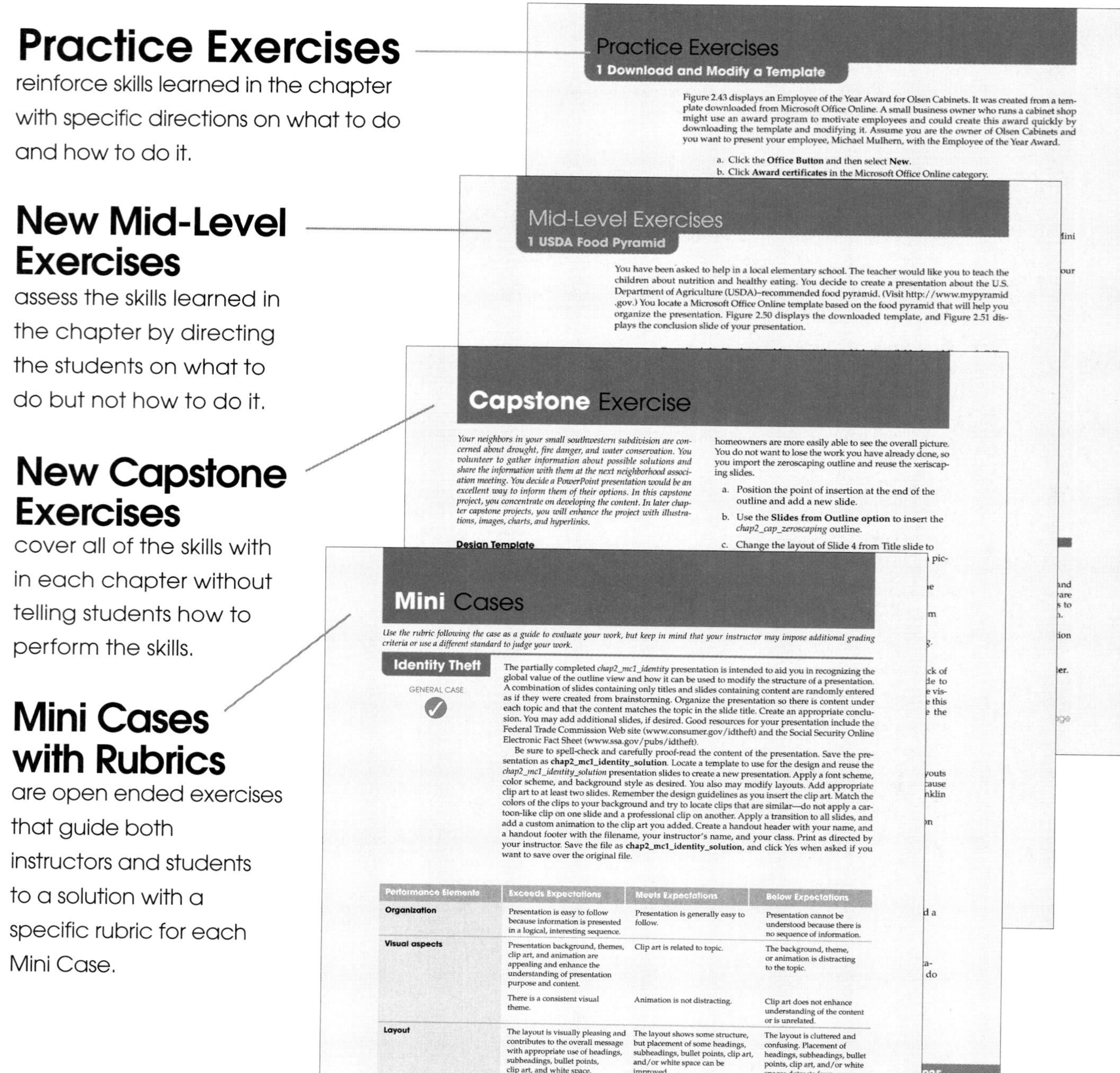

Practice Exercises

1 Download and Modify a Template

Figure 2.43 displays an Employee of the Year Award for Olsen Cabinets. It was created from a template downloaded from Microsoft Office Online. A small business owner who runs a cabinet shop might use an award program to motivate employees and could create this award quickly by downloading the template and modifying it. Assume you are the owner of Olsen Cabinets and you want to present your employee, Michael Mulhern, with the Employee of the Year Award.

a. Click the **Office Button** and then select **New**.

b. Click **Award certificates** in the Microsoft Office Online category.

Mid-Level Exercises

1 USDA Food Pyramid

You have been asked to help in a local elementary school. The teacher would like you to teach the children about nutrition and healthy eating. You decide to create a presentation about the U.S. Department of Agriculture (USDA)–recommended food pyramid. (Visit http://www.mypyramid.gov.) You locate a Microsoft Office Online template based on the food pyramid that will help you organize the presentation. Figure 2.50 displays the downloaded template, and Figure 2.51 displays the conclusion slide of your presentation.

Capstone Exercise

Your neighbors in your small southwestern subdivision are concerned about drought, fire danger, and water conservation. You volunteer to gather information about possible solutions and share the information with them at the next neighborhood association meeting. You decide a PowerPoint presentation would be an excellent way to inform them of their options. In this capstone project, you concentrate on developing the content. In later chapter capstone projects, you will enhance the project with illustrations, images, charts, and hyperlinks.

Design Template

homeowners are more easily able to see the overall picture. You do not want to lose the work you have already done, so you import the zeroscaping outline and reuse the xeriscaping slides.

a. Position the point of insertion at the end of the outline and add a new slide.

b. Use the **Slides from Outline option** to insert the *chap2_cap_zeroscaping* outline.

c. Change the layout of Slide 4 from Title slide to

Mini Cases

Use the rubric following the case as a guide to evaluate your work, but keep in mind that your instructor may impose additional grading criteria or use a different standard to judge your work.

Identity Theft

GENERAL CASE

The partially completed *chap2_mc1_identity* presentation is intended to aid you in recognizing the global value of the outline view and how it can be used to modify the structure of a presentation. A combination of slides containing only titles and slides containing content are randomly entered as if they were created from brainstorming. Organize the presentation so there is content under each topic and that the content matches the topic in the slide title. Create an appropriate conclusion. You may add additional slides, if desired. Good resources for your presentation include the Federal Trade Commission Web site (www.consumer.gov/idtheft) and the Social Security Online Electronic Fact Sheet (www.ssa.gov/pubs/idtheft).

Be sure to spell-check and carefully proof-read the content of the presentation. Save the presentation as **chap2_mc1_identity_solution**. Locate a template to use for the design and reuse the *chap2_mc1_identity_solution* presentation slides to create a new presentation. Apply a font scheme, color scheme, and background style as desired. You also may modify layouts. Add appropriate clip art to at least two slides. Remember the design guidelines as you insert the clip art. Match the colors of the clips to your background and try to locate clips that are similar—do not apply a cartoon-like clip on one slide and a professional clip on another. Apply a transition to all slides, and add a custom animation to the clip art you added. Create a handout header with your name, and a handout footer with the filename, your instructor's name, and your class. Print as directed by your instructor. Save the file as **chap2_mc1_identity_solution**, and click Yes when asked if you want to save over the original file.

Performance Elements	Exceeds Expectations	Meets Expectations	Below Expectations
Organization	Presentation is easy to follow because information is presented in a logical, interesting sequence.	Presentation is generally easy to follow.	Presentation cannot be understood because there is no sequence of information.
Visual aspects	Presentation background, themes, clip art, and animation are appealing and enhance the understanding of presentation purpose and content.	Clip art is related to topic.	The background, theme, or animation is distracting to the topic.
	There is a consistent visual theme.	Animation is not distracting.	Clip art does not enhance understanding of the content or is unrelated.
Layout	The layout is visually pleasing and contributes to the overall message with appropriate use of headings, subheadings, bullet points, clip art, and white space.	The layout shows some structure, but placement of some headings, subheadings, bullet points, clip art, and/or white space can be improved.	The layout is cluttered and confusing. Placement of headings, subheadings, bullet points, clip art, and/or white spaces detracts from readability.
Mechanics	Presentation has no errors in spelling, grammar, word usage, or punctuation.	Presentation has no more than one error in spelling, grammar, word usage, or punctuation.	Presentation readability is impaired due to repeated errors in spelling, grammar, word usage, or punctuation.
		…points are inconsistent in	Most bullet points are not parallel.

Using Word, Excel, Access, and PowerPoint

Objectives

After you read this chapter, you will be able to:

1. Identify common interface components (page 4).
2. Use Office 2007 Help (page 10).
3. Open a file (page 18).
4. Save a file (page 21).
5. Print a document (page 24).
6. Select text to edit (page 31).
7. Insert text and change to the Overtype mode (page 32).
8. Move and copy text (page 34).
9. Find, replace, and go to text (page 36).
10. Use the Undo and Redo commands (page 39).
11. Use language tools (page 39).
12. Apply font attributes (page 43).
13. Copy formats with the Format Painter (page 47).

Hands-On Exercises

Exercises	Skills Covered
1. IDENTIFYING PROGRAM INTERFACE COMPONENTS AND USING HELP (page 12)	• Use PowerPoint's Office Button, Get Help in a Dialog Box, and Use the Zoom Slider • Use Excel's Ribbon, Get Help from an Enhanced ScreenTip, and Use the Zoom Dialog Box • Search Help in Access • Use Word's Status Bar • Search Help and Print a Help Topic
2. PERFORMING UNIVERSAL TASKS (page 28) **Open:** chap1_ho2_sample.docx **Save as:** chap1_ho2_solution.docx	• Open a File and Save It with a Different Name • Use Print Preview and Select Options • Print a Document
3. PERFORMING BASIC TASKS (page 48) **Open:** chap1_ho3_internet_docx **Save as:** chap_ho3_internet_solution.docx	• Cut, Copy, Paste, and Undo • Find and Replace Text • Check Spelling • Choose Synonyms and Use Thesaurus • Use the Research Tool • Apply Font Attributes • Use Format Painter

CASE STUDY

Color Theory Design

Case Study

Natalie Trevino's first job after finishing her interior design degree is with Color Theory Design of San Diego. Her new supervisor has asked her to review a letter written to an important client and to make any changes or corrections she thinks will improve it. Even though Natalie has used word processing software in the past, she is unfamiliar with Microsoft Office 2007. She needs to get up to speed with Word 2007 so that she can open the letter, edit the content, format the appearance, re-save the file, and print the client letter. Natalie wants to successfully complete this important first task, plus she wants to become familiar with all of Office 2007 because she realizes that her new employer, CTD, makes extensive use of all the Office products.

In addition, Natalie needs to improve the appearance of an Excel workbook by applying font attributes, correcting spelling errors, changing the zoom magnification, and printing the worksheet. Finally, Natalie needs to modify a short PowerPoint presentation that features supplemental design information for CTD's important client.

Your Assignment

- Read the chapter and open the existing client letter, *chap1_case_design*.
- Edit the letter by inserting and overtyping text and moving existing text to improve the letter's readability.
- Find and replace text that you want to update.
- Check the spelling and improve the vocabulary by using the thesaurus.
- Modify the letter's appearance by applying font attributes.
- Save the file as **chap1_case_design_solution**, print preview, and print a copy of the letter.
- Open the *chap1_case_bid* workbook in Excel, apply bold and blue font color to the column headings, spell-check the worksheet, change the zoom to 125%, print preview, and print the workbook. Save the workbook as **chap1_case_bid_solution**.
- Open the *chap1_case_design* presentation in PowerPoint, spell-check the presentation, format text, and save it as **chap1_case_design_solution**.

Microsoft Office 2007 Software

Which software application should you choose? You have to start with an analysis of the output required.

Microsoft Office 2007 is composed of several software applications, of which the primary components are Word, Excel, PowerPoint, and Access. These programs are powerful tools that can be used to increase productivity in creating, editing, saving, and printing files. Each program is a specialized and sophisticated program, so it is necessary to use the correct one to successfully complete a task, much like using the correct tool in the physical world. For example, you use a hammer, not a screwdriver, to pound a nail into the wall. Using the correct tool gets the job done correctly and efficiently the first time; using the wrong tool may require redoing the task, thus wasting time. Likewise, you should use the most appropriate software application to create and work with computer data.

Choosing the appropriate application to use in a situation seems easy to the beginner. If you need to create a letter, you type the letter in Word. However, as situations increase in complexity, so does the need to think through using each application. For example, you can create an address book of names and addresses in Word to create form letters; you can create an address list in Excel and then use spreadsheet commands to manipulate the data; further, you can store addresses in an Access database table and then use database capabilities to manipulate the data. Which software application should you choose? You have to start with an analysis of the output required. If you only want a form letter as the final product, then you might use Word; however, if you want to spot customer trends with the data and provide detailed reports, you would use Access. Table 1.1 describes the main characteristics of the four primary programs in Microsoft Office 2007 to help you decide which program to use for particular tasks.

Word processing software is used primarily with text to create, edit, and format documents.

Spreadsheet software is used primarily with numbers to create worksheets.

Presentation graphics software is used primarily to create electronic slide shows.

Relational database software is used to store data and convert it into information.

Table 1.1 Office Products

Office 2007 Product	Application Characteristics
Word 2007	***Word processing software*** is used with text to create, edit, and format documents such as letters, memos, reports, brochures, resumes, and flyers.
Excel 2007	***Spreadsheet software*** is used to store quantitative data and to perform accurate and rapid calculations with results ranging from simple budgets to financial analyses and statistical analyses.
PowerPoint 2007	***Presentation graphics software*** is used to create slide shows for presentation by a speaker, to be published as part of a Web site, or to run as a stand-alone application on a computer kiosk.
Access 2007	***Relational database software*** is used to store data and convert it into information. Database software is used primarily for decision-making by businesses that compile data from multiple records stored in tables to produce informative reports.

In this section, you explore the common interface among the programs. You learn the names of the interface elements. In addition, you learn how to use Help to get assistance in using the software.

Identifying Common Interface Components

A ***user interface*** is the meeting point between computer software and the person using it.

A ***user interface*** is the meeting point between computer software and the person using it and provides the means for a person to communicate with a software program. Word, Excel, PowerPoint, and Access share the overall Microsoft Office 2007 interface. This interface is made up of three main sections of the screen display shown in Figure 1.1.

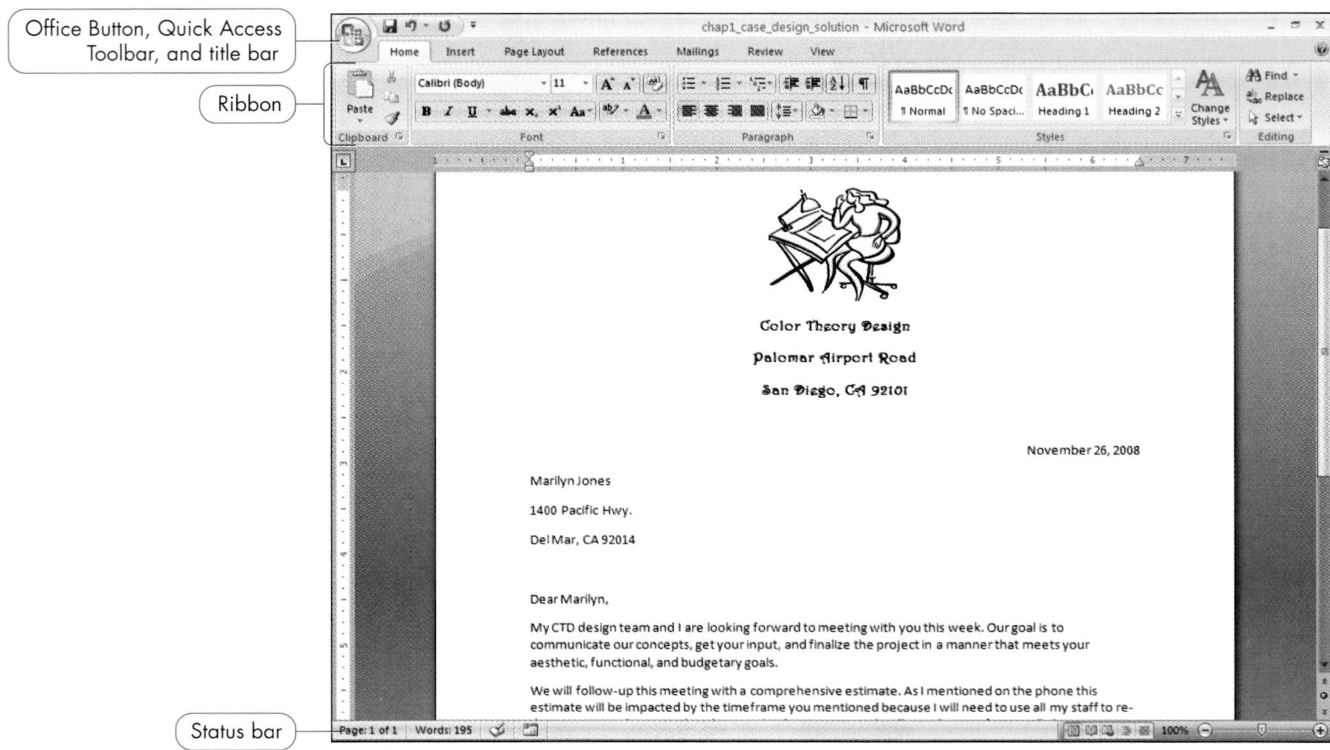

Figure 1.1 Office 2007 Interface

Use the Office Button and Quick Access Toolbar

The first section of the Office 2007 interface contains three distinct items: the Microsoft Office Button (referred to as Office Button in the Exploring series), Quick Access Toolbar, and the title bar. These three items are located at the top of the interface for quick access and reference. The following paragraphs explain each item.

Click the ***Office Button*** to display the Office menu.

The ***Office menu*** contains commands that work with an entire file or with the program.

The ***Office Button*** is an icon that, when clicked, displays the ***Office menu***, a list of commands that you can perform on the entire file or for the specific Office program. For example, when you want to perform a task that involves the entire document, such as saving, printing, or sharing a file with others, you use the commands on the Office menu. You also use the Office menu commands to work with the entire program, such as customizing program settings or exiting from the program. Some commands on the Office menu perform a default action when you click them, such as Save—the file open in the active window is saved. However, other commands open a submenu when you point to or click the command. Figure 1.2 displays the Office menu in Access 2007.

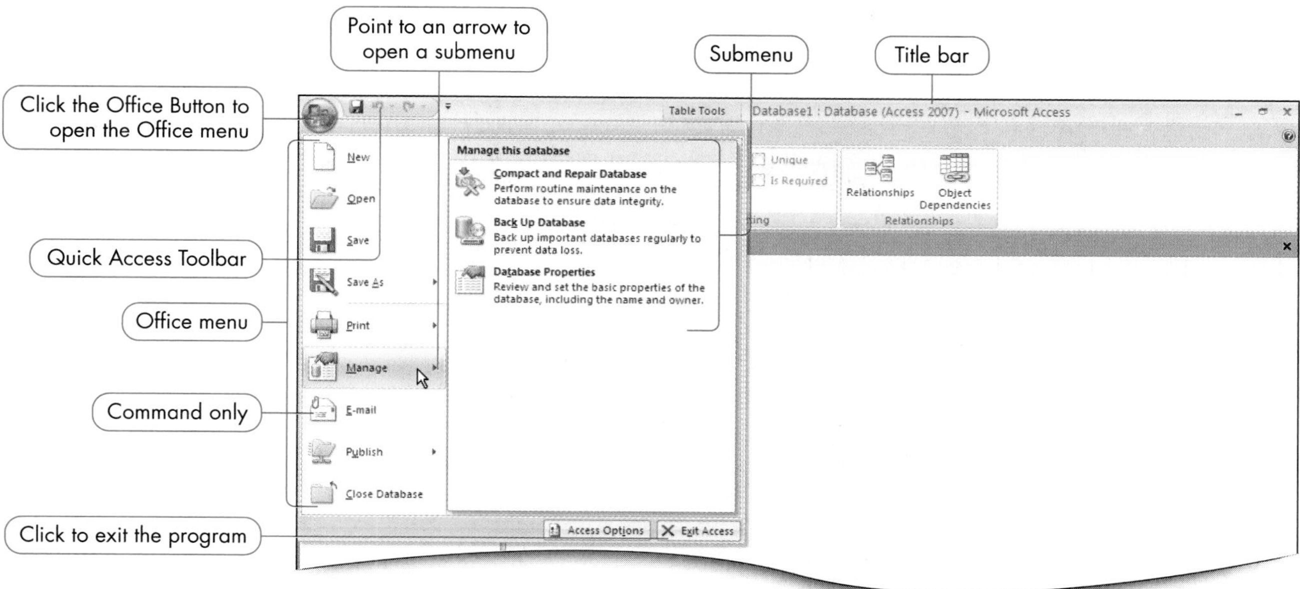

Figure 1.2 Access Office Menu

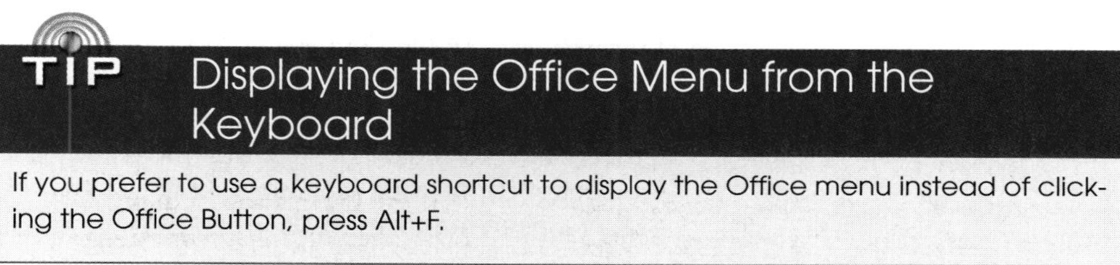

TIP **Displaying the Office Menu from the Keyboard**

If you prefer to use a keyboard shortcut to display the Office menu instead of clicking the Office Button, press Alt+F.

The ***Quick Access Toolbar*** contains buttons for frequently used commands.

The second item at the top of the window is the ***Quick Access Toolbar***, which contains buttons for frequently used commands, such as saving a file or undoing an action. This toolbar keeps buttons for common tasks on the screen at all times, enabling you to be more productive in using these frequently used commands.

TIP **Customizing the Quick Access Toolbar**

As you become more familiar with Microsoft Office 2007, you might find that you need quick access to additional commands, such as Print Preview or Spelling & Grammar. You can easily customize the Quick Access Toolbar by clicking the Customize Quick Access Toolbar drop-down arrow on the right end of the toolbar and adding command buttons from the list that displays. You also can customize the toolbar by changing where it displays. If you want it closer to the document window, you can move the toolbar below the Ribbon.

A ***title bar*** displays the program name and file name at the top of a window.

The third item at the top of the screen is the ***title bar***, which displays the name of the open program and the file name at the top of a window. For example, in Figure 1.1, *chap1_case_design_solution* is the name of a document, and *Microsoft Word* is the name of the program. In Figure 1.2, *Database1* is the name of the file, and *Microsoft Access* is the name of the program.

The ***Ribbon*** is a large strip of visual commands that enables you to perform tasks.

Familiarize Yourself with the Ribbon

The second section of the Office 2007 interface is the ***Ribbon***, a large strip of visual commands that displays across the screen below the Office Button, Quick Access Toolbar, and the title bar. The Ribbon is the most important section of the interface: It is the command center of the Microsoft Office 2007 interface, providing access to the functionality of the programs (see Figure 1.3).

> The Ribbon is the command center of the Microsoft Office 2007 interface, providing access to the functionality of the programs.

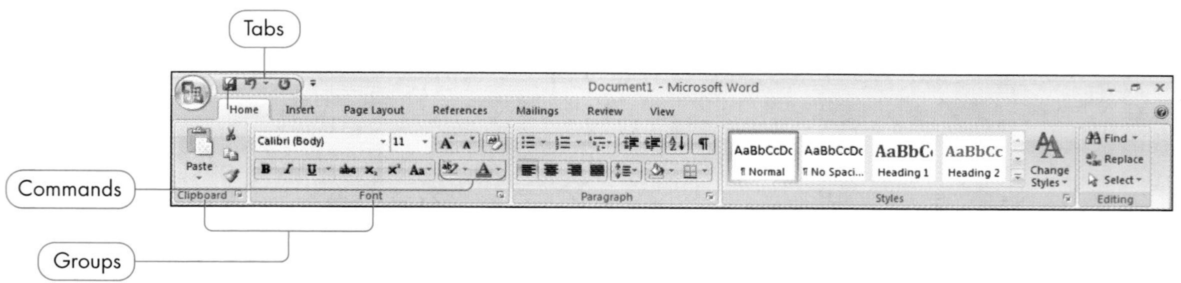

Figure 1.3 The Ribbon

The Ribbon has three main components: tabs, groups, and commands. The following list describes each component.

Tabs, which look like folder tabs, divide the Ribbon into task-oriented categories.

- ***Tabs***, which look like folder tabs, divide the Ribbon into task-oriented sections. For example, the Ribbon in Word contains these tabs: Home, Insert, Page Layout, Reference, Mailings, Review, and View. When you click the Home tab, you see a set of core commands for that program. When you click the Insert tab, you see a set of commands that enable you to insert objects, such as tables, clip art, headers, page numbers, etc.

Groups organize similar commands together within each tab.

- ***Groups*** organize related commands together on each tab. For example, the Home tab in Word contains these groups: Clipboard, Font, Paragraph, Styles, and Editing. These groups help organize related commands together so that you can find them easily. For example, the Font group contains font-related commands, such as Font, Font Size, Bold, Italic, Underline, Highlighter, and Font Color.

A ***command*** is a visual icon in each group that you click to perform a task.

- ***Commands*** are specific tasks performed. Commands appear as visual icons or buttons within the groups on the Ribbon. The icons are designed to provide a visual clue of the purpose of the command. For example, the Bold command looks like a bolded B in the Font group on the Home tab. You simply click the desired command to perform the respective task.

The Ribbon has the same basic design—tabs, groups, and commands—across all Microsoft Office 2007 applications. When you first start using an Office 2007 application, you use the Home tab most often. The groups of commands on the Home tab are designed to get you started using the software. For example, the Home tab contains commands to help you create, edit, and format a document in Word, a worksheet in Excel, and a presentation in PowerPoint. In Access, the Home tab contains groups of commands to insert, delete, and edit records in a database table. While three of the four applications contain an Insert tab, the specific groups and commands differ by application. Regardless of the application, however, the Insert tab contains commands to *insert something*, whether it is a page number in Word, a column chart in Excel, or a shape in PowerPoint. One of the best ways to develop an understanding of the Ribbon is to study its structure in each application. As you explore each program, you will notice the similarities in how commands are grouped on tabs, and you will notice the differences specific to each application.

TIP Hiding the Ribbon

If you are creating a large document or worksheet, you might find that the Ribbon takes up too much of the screen display. Microsoft enables you to temporarily hide a large portion of the Ribbon. Double-click the active tab, such as Home, to hide all the groups and commands, greatly reducing the size of the Ribbon. When you want to display the entire Ribbon, double-click the active tab. You also can press **Ctrl+F1** to minimize and maximize the Ribbon.

The Ribbon provides an extensive sets of commands that you use when creating and editing documents, worksheets, slides, tables, or other items. Figure 1.4 points out other important components of the Ribbon.

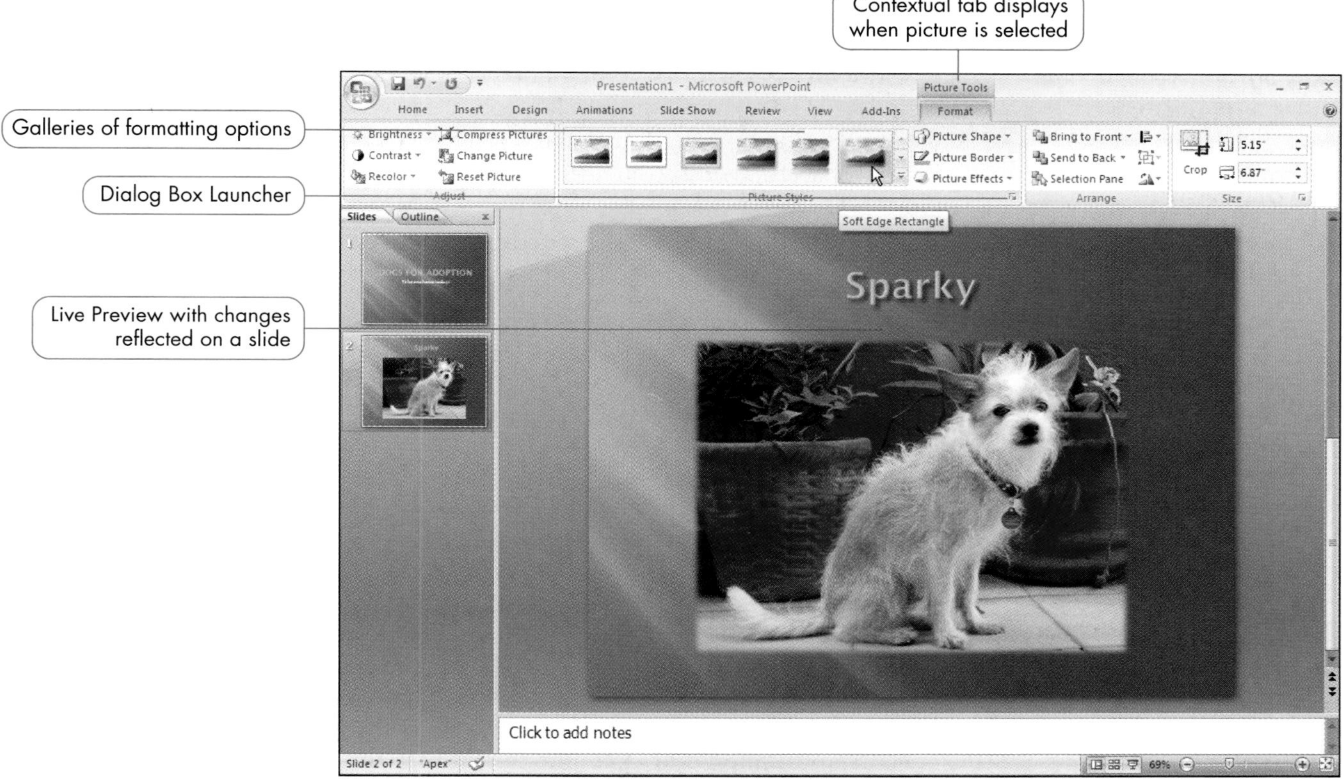

Figure 1.4 PowerPoint with Ribbon

A ***dialog box*** is a window that provides options related to a group of commands.

A ***Dialog Box Launcher*** is a small icon that, when clicked, opens a related dialog box.

A ***gallery*** is a set of options that appears as thumbnail graphics.

Live Preview provides a preview of the results for gallery options.

Figure 1.4 shows examples of four other components of the Ribbon. These components include a Dialog Box Launcher, a gallery, Live Preview, and a contextual tab. The following list describes each component:

- A ***Dialog Box Launcher*** is a small icon located on the right side of some group names that you click to open a related ***dialog box***, which is a window that provides options related to a group of commands.
- A ***gallery*** is a set of options that appear as thumbnail graphics that visually represent the option results. For example, if you create a chart in Excel, a gallery of chart formatting options provides numerous choices for formatting the chart.
- ***Live Preview*** works with the galleries, providing a preview of the results of formatting in the document. As you move your mouse pointer over the gallery

thumbnails, you see how each formatting option affects the selected item in your document, worksheet, or presentation. This feature increases productivity because you see the results immediately. If you do not like the results, keep moving the mouse pointer over other gallery options until you find a result you like.

A ***contextual tab*** is a tab that provides specialized commands that display only when the object they affect is selected.

- A ***contextual tab*** provides specialized commands that display only when the object they affect is selected. For example, if you insert a picture on a slide, PowerPoint displays a contextual tab on the Ribbon with commands specifically related to the selected image. When you click outside the picture to deselect it, the contextual tab disappears.

A ***Key Tip*** is the letter or number that displays over each feature on the Ribbon and Quick Access Toolbar and is the keyboard equivalent that you press.

TIP Using Keyboard Shortcuts

Many people who have used previous Office products like to use the keyboard to initiate commands. Microsoft Office 2007 makes it possible for you to continue to use keyboard shortcuts for commands on the Ribbon. Simply press Alt on the keyboard to display the Ribbon and Quick Access Toolbar with shortcuts called Key Tips. A ***Key Tip*** is the letter or number that displays over each feature on the Ribbon or Quick Access Toolbar and is the keyboard equivalent that you press. Notice the Key Tips that display in Figure 1.5 as a result of pressing Alt on the keyboard. Other keyboard shortcuts, such as Ctrl+C to copy text, remain the same from previous versions of Microsoft Office.

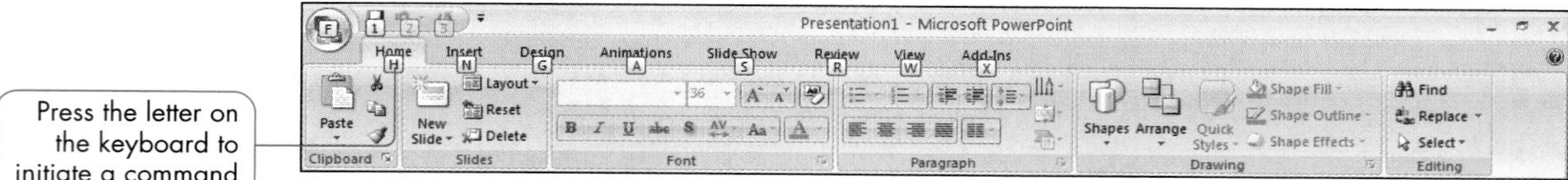

Figure 1.5 Key Tips Displayed for Ribbon and Quick Access Toolbar

Use the Status Bar

The ***status bar*** displays below the document and provides information about the open file and buttons for quick access.

The third major section of the Office 2007 user interface is the status bar. The ***status bar*** displays at the bottom of the program window and contains information about the open file and tools for quick access. The status bar contains details for the file in the specific application. For example, the Word status bar shows the current page, total number of pages, total words in the document, and proofreading status. The PowerPoint status bar shows the slide number, total slides in the presentation, and the applied theme. The Excel status bar provides general instructions and displays the average, count, and sum of values for selected cells. In each program, the status bar also includes View commands from the View tab for quick access. You can use the View commands to change the way the document, worksheet, or presentation displays onscreen. Table 1.2 describes the main characteristics of each Word 2007 view.

Table 1.2 Word Document Views

View Option	Characteristics
Print Layout	Displays the document as it will appear when printed.
Full Screen Reading	Displays the document on the entire screen to make reading long documents easier. To remove Full Screen Reading, press the Esc key on the keyboard.
Web Page	Displays the document as it would look as a Web page.
Outline	Displays the document as an outline.
Draft	Displays the document for quick editing without additional elements such as headers or footers.

The ***Zoom slider*** enables you to increase or decrease the magnification of the file onscreen.

The ***Zoom slider***, located on the right edge of the status bar, enables you to drag the slide control to change the magnification of the current document, worksheet, or presentation. You can change the display to zoom in on the file to get a close up view, or you can zoom out to get an overview of the file. To use the Zoom slider, click and drag the slider control to the right to increase the zoom or to the left to decrease the zoom. If you want to set a specific zoom, such as 78%, you can type the precise value in the Zoom dialog box when you click Zoom on the View tab. Figure 1.6 shows the Zoom dialog box and the elements on Word's status bar. The Zoom dialog box in Excel and PowerPoint looks similar to the Word Zoom dialog box, but it contains fewer options in the other programs.

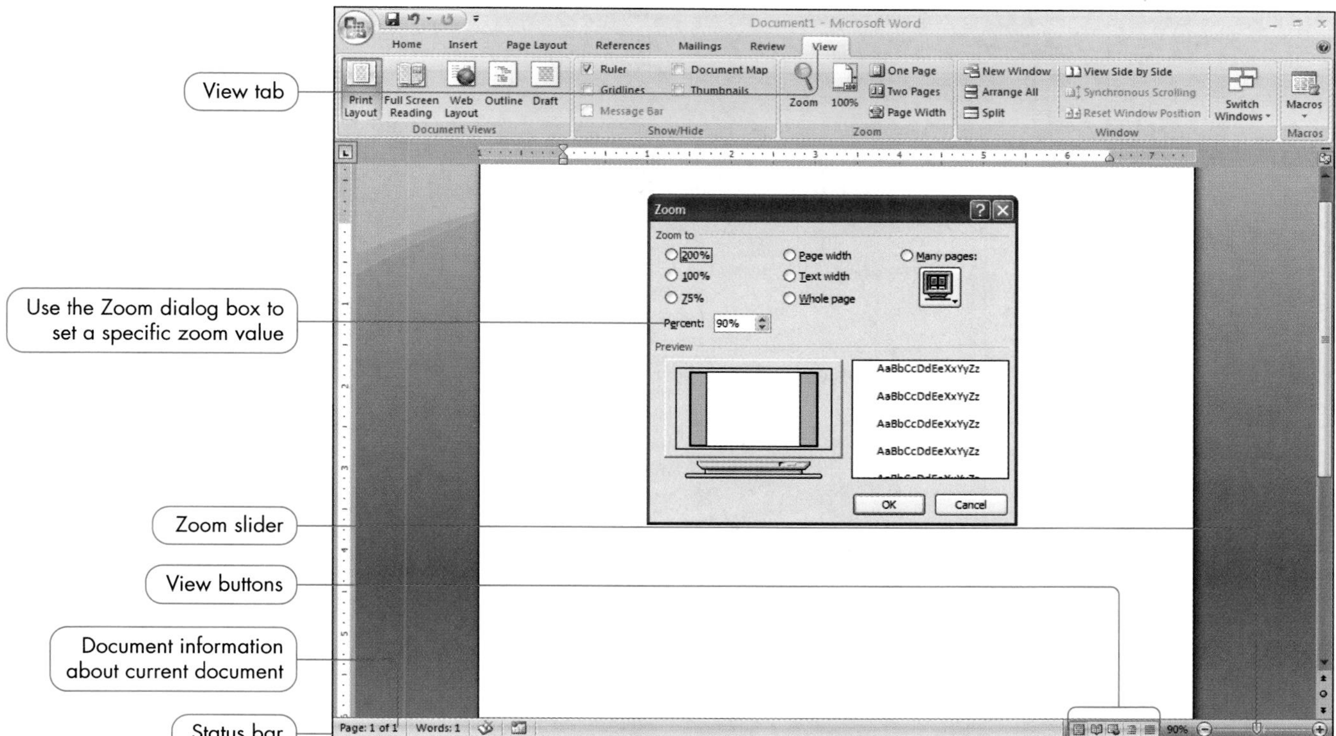

Figure 1.6 View Tab, Zoom Dialog Box, and the Status Bar in Word

Using Office 2007 Help

(Help is always available when you use any Office 2007 program.)

Have you ever started a project such as assembling an entertainment center and had to abandon it because you had no way to get help when you got stuck? Microsoft Office includes features that keep this type of scenario from happening when you use Word, Excel, Access, or PowerPoint. In fact, several methods are available to locate help when you need assistance performing tasks. Help is always available when you use any Office 2007 program. Help files reside on your computer when you install Microsoft Office, and Microsoft provides additional help files on its Web site. If you link to Microsoft Office Online, you not only have access to help files for all applications, you also have access to up-to-date products, files, and graphics to help you complete projects.

Use Office 2007 Help

To access Help, press F1 on the keyboard or click the Help button on the right edge of the Ribbon shown in Figure 1.7. If you know the topic you want help with, such as printing, you can type the key term in the Search box to display help files on that topic. Help also displays general topics in the lower part of the Help window that are links to further information. To display a table of contents for the Help files, click the Show Table of Contents button, and after locating the desired help topic, you can print the information for future reference by clicking the Print button. Figure 1.7 shows these elements in Excel Help.

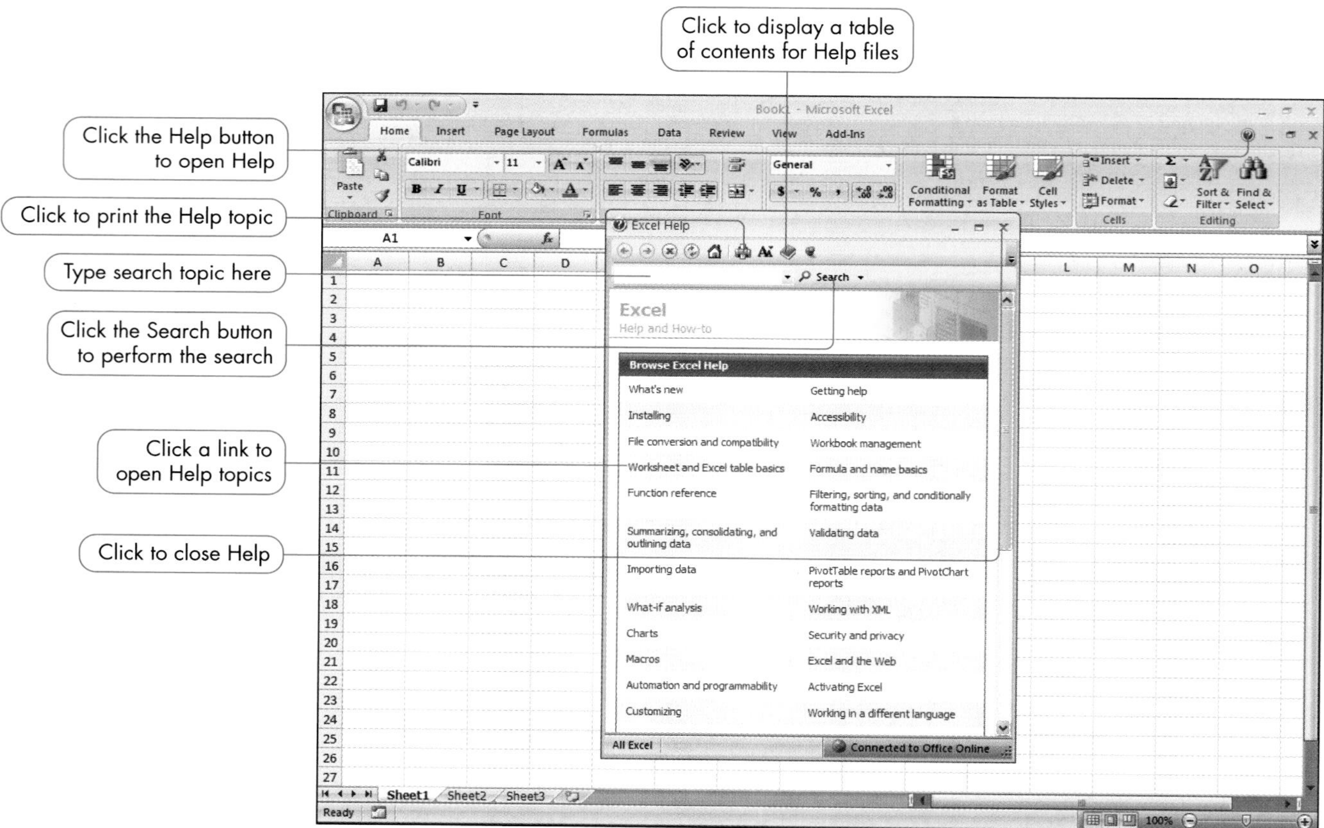

Figure 1.7 Excel Help

Use Enhanced ScreenTips

An ***Enhanced ScreenTip*** displays the name and brief description of a command when you rest the pointer on a command.

Another method for getting help is to use the Office 2007 Enhanced ScreenTips. An *Enhanced ScreenTip* displays when you rest the mouse pointer on a command. Notice in Figure 1.8 that the Enhanced ScreenTip provides the command name, a brief description of the command, and a link for additional help. To get help on the specific command, keep the pointer resting on the command and press F1 if the Enhanced ScreenTip displays a Help icon. The advantage of this method is that you do not have to find the correct information yourself because the Enhanced ScreenTip help is context sensitive.

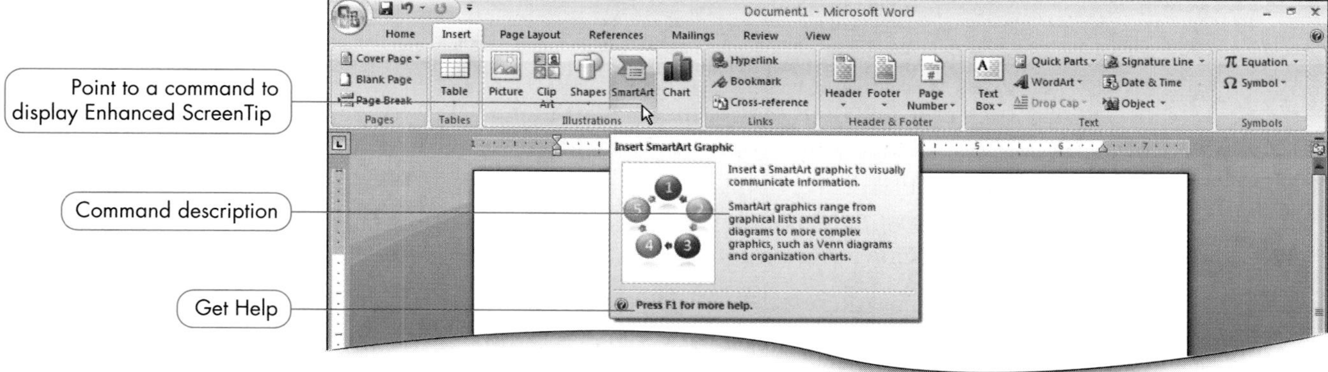

Figure 1.8 Enhanced ScreenTip

Get Help with Dialog Boxes

As you work within a dialog box, you might need help with some of the numerous options contained in that dialog box, but you do not want to close the dialog box to get assistance. For example, if you open the Insert Picture dialog box and want help with inserting files, click the Help button located on the title bar of the dialog box to display specific help for the dialog box. Figure 1.9 shows the Insert Picture dialog box with Help displayed.

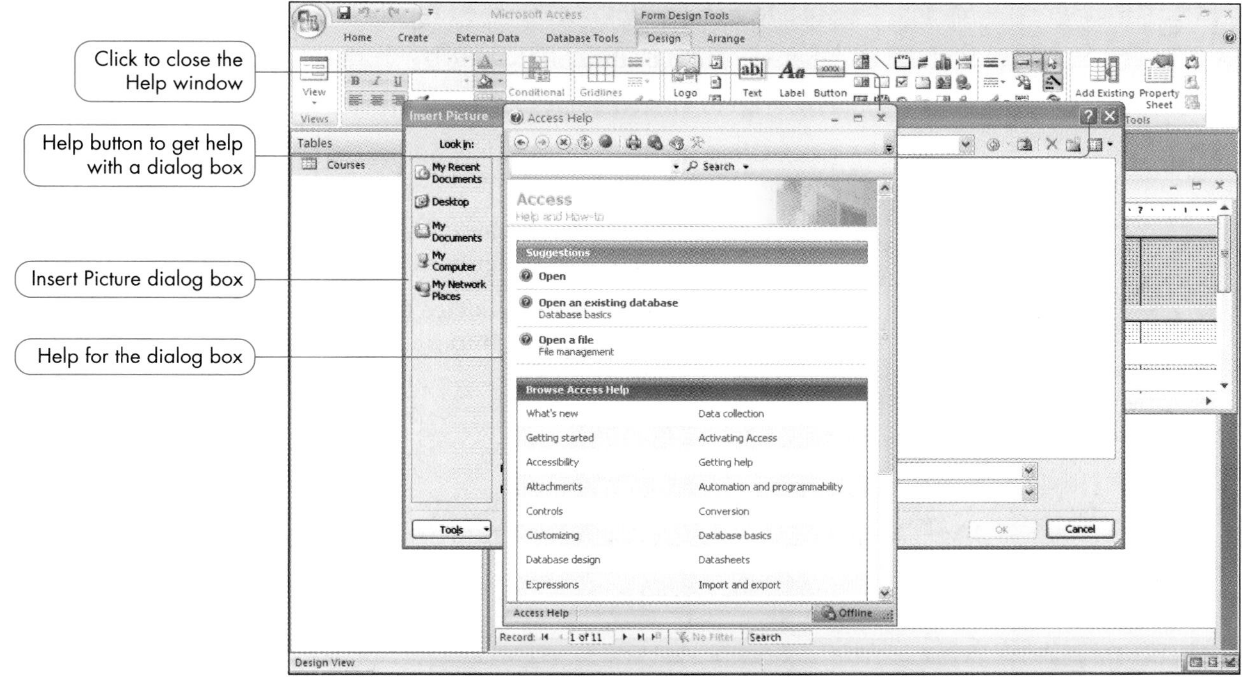

Figure 1.9 Help with Dialog Boxes

Hands-On Exercises

1 | Identifying Program Interface Components and Using Help

Skills covered: 1. Use PowerPoint's Office Button, Get Help in a Dialog Box, and Use the Zoom Slider **2.** Use Excel's Ribbon, Get Help from an Enhanced ScreenTip, and Use the Zoom Dialog Box **3.** Search Help in Access **4.** Use Word's Status Bar **5.** Search Help and Print a Help Topic

Step 1
Use PowerPoint's Office Button, Get Help in a Dialog Box, and Use the Zoom Slider

Refer to Figure 1.10 as you complete Step 1.

a. Click **Start** to display the Start menu. Click (or point to) **All Programs**, click **Microsoft Office**, then click **Microsoft Office PowerPoint 2007** to start the program.

b. Point to and rest the mouse on the Office Button, and then do the same to the Quick Access Toolbar.

   As you rest the mouse pointer on each object, you see an Enhanced ScreenTip for that object.

   TROUBLESHOOTING: If you do not see the Enhanced ScreenTip, keep the mouse pointer on the object a little longer.

c. Click the **Office Button** and slowly move your mouse down the list of menu options, pointing to the arrow after any command name that has one.

   The Office menu displays, and as you move the mouse down the list, submenus display for menu options that have an arrow.

d. Select **New**.

   The New Presentation dialog box displays. Depending on how Microsoft Office 2007 was installed, your screen may vary. If Microsoft Office 2007 was fully installed, you should see a thumbnail to create a Blank Presentation, and you may see additional thumbnails in the *Recently Used Templates* section of the dialog box.

e. Click the **Help button** on the title bar of the New Presentation dialog box.

   PowerPoint Help displays the topic *Create a new file from a template*.

f. Click **Close** on the Help Window and click the **Cancel** button in the New Presentation dialog box.

g. Click and drag the **Zoom slider** to the right to increase the magnification. Then click and drag the **Zoom slider** back to the center point for a 100% zoom.

h. To exit PowerPoint, click the **Office Button** to display the Office menu, and then click the **Exit PowerPoint button**.

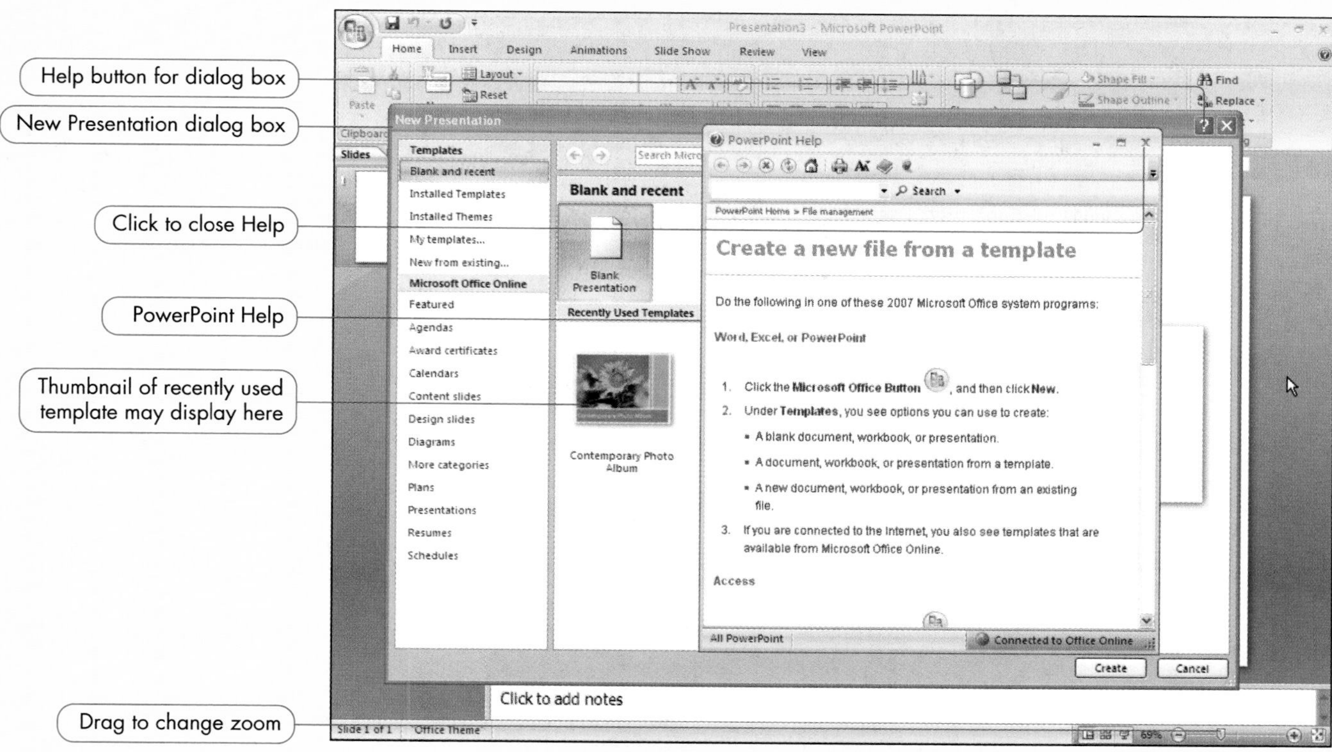

Figure 1.10 PowerPoint Help for New Presentations Dialog Box

Step 2
Use Excel's Ribbon, Get Help from an Enhanced ScreenTip, and Use the Zoom Dialog Box

Refer to Figure 1.11 as you complete Step 2.

a. Click **Start** to display the Start menu. Click (or point to) **All Programs**, click **Microsoft Office**, then click **Microsoft Office Excel 2007** to open the program.

b. Click the **Insert tab** on the Ribbon.

The Insert tab contains groups of commands for inserting objects, such as tables, illustrations, charts, links, and text.

c. Rest the mouse on **Hyperlink** in the Links group on the Insert tab.

The Enhanced ScreenTip for Hyperlinks displays. Notice the Enhanced ScreenTip contains a Help icon.

d. Press **F1** on the keyboard.

Excel Help displays the *Create or remove a hyperlink* Help topic.

TROUBLESHOOTING: If you are not connected to the Internet, you might not see the context-sensitive help.

e. Click the **Close button** on the Help window.

f. Click the **View tab** on the Ribbon and click **Zoom** in the Zoom group.

The Zoom dialog box appears so that you can change the zoom percentage.

g. Click the **200%** option and click **OK**.

The worksheet is now magnified to 200% of its regular size.

h. Click **Zoom** in the Zoom group on the View tab, click the **100%** option, and click **OK**.

The worksheet is now restored to 100%.

i. To exit Excel, click the **Office Button** to display the Office menu, and then click the **Exit Excel button**.

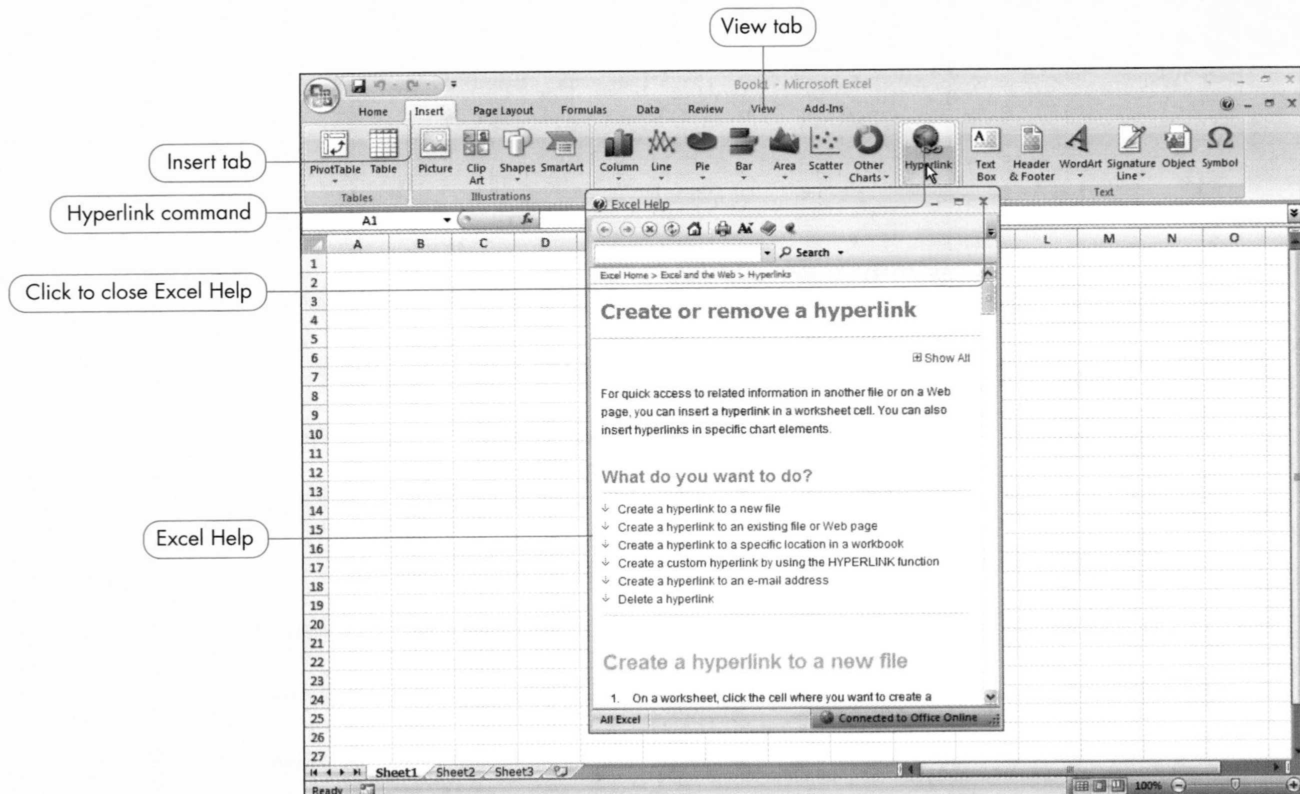

Figure 1.11 Excel Ribbon with Help

Step 3
Search Help in Access

Refer to Figure 1.12 as you complete Step 3.

a. Click **Start** to display the Start menu. Click (or point to) **All Programs**, click **Microsoft Office**, then click **Microsoft Office Access 2007** to start the program.

   Access opens and displays the Getting Started with Microsoft Access screen.

   TROUBLESHOOTING: If you are not familiar with Access, just use the opening screen that displays and continue with the exercise.

b. Press **F1** on the keyboard.

   Access Help displays.

c. Type **table** in the Search box in the Access Help window.

d. Click the **Search** button.

   Access displays help topics.

e. Click the topic **Create tables in a database**.

   The help topic displays.

f. Click the **Close** button on the Access Help window.

   Access Help closes.

g. To exit Access, click the **Office Button** to display the Office menu, and then click the **Exit Access button**.

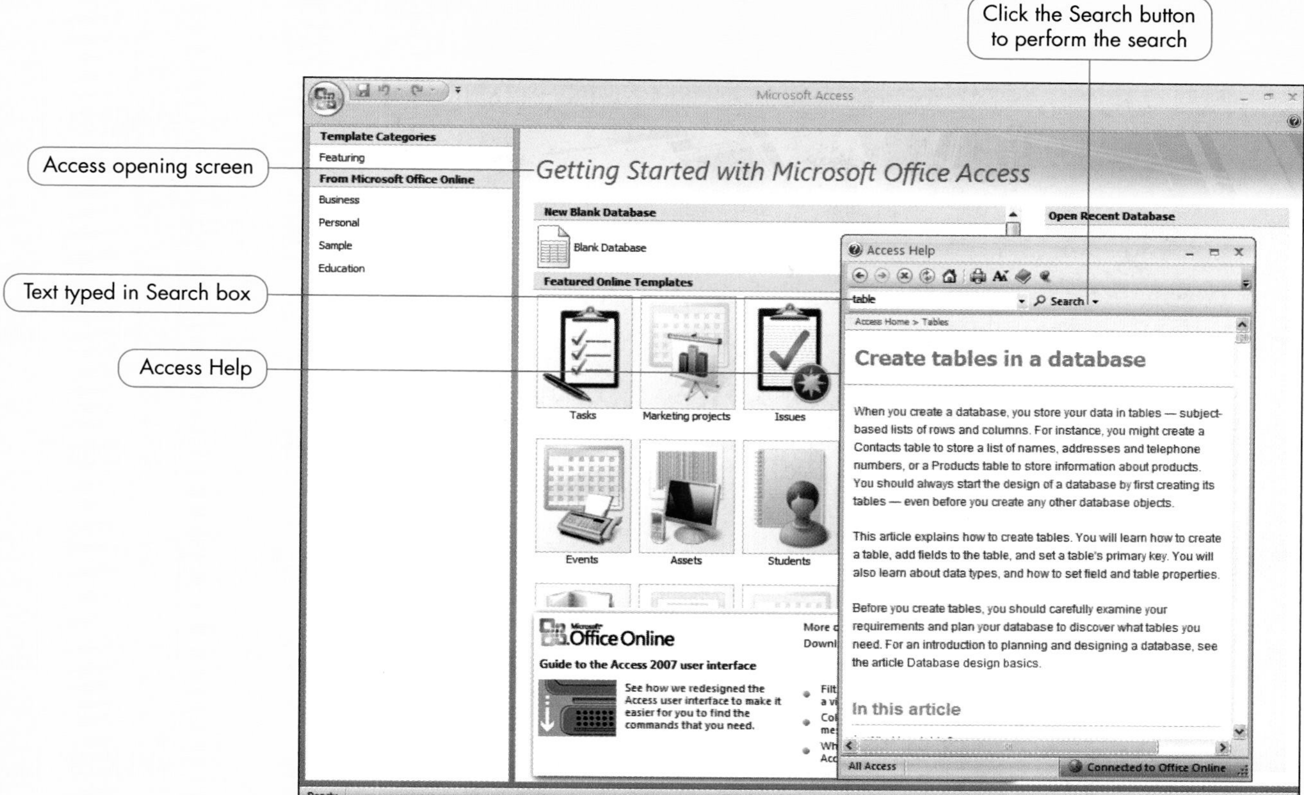

Figure 1.12 Access Help

Step 4
Use Word's Status Bar

Refer to Figure 1.13 as you complete Step 4.

a. Click **Start** to display the Start menu. Click (or point to) **All Programs**, click **Microsoft Office**, then click **Microsoft Office Word 2007** to start the program.

   Word opens with a blank document ready for you to start typing.

b. Type your first name.

   Your first name displays in the document window.

c. Point your mouse to the **Zoom slider** on the status bar.

d. Click and drag the **Zoom slider** to the right to increase the magnification.

   The document with your first name increases in size onscreen.

e. Click and drag the slider control to the left to decrease the magnification.

   The document with your first name decreases in size.

f. Click and drag the **Zoom slider** back to the center.

   The document returns to 100% magnification.

g. Slowly point the mouse to the buttons on the status bar.

   A ScreenTip displays the names of the buttons.

h. Click the **Full Screen Reading button** on the status bar.

The screen display changes to Full Screen Reading view.

i. Press **Esc** on the keyboard to return the display to Print Layout view.

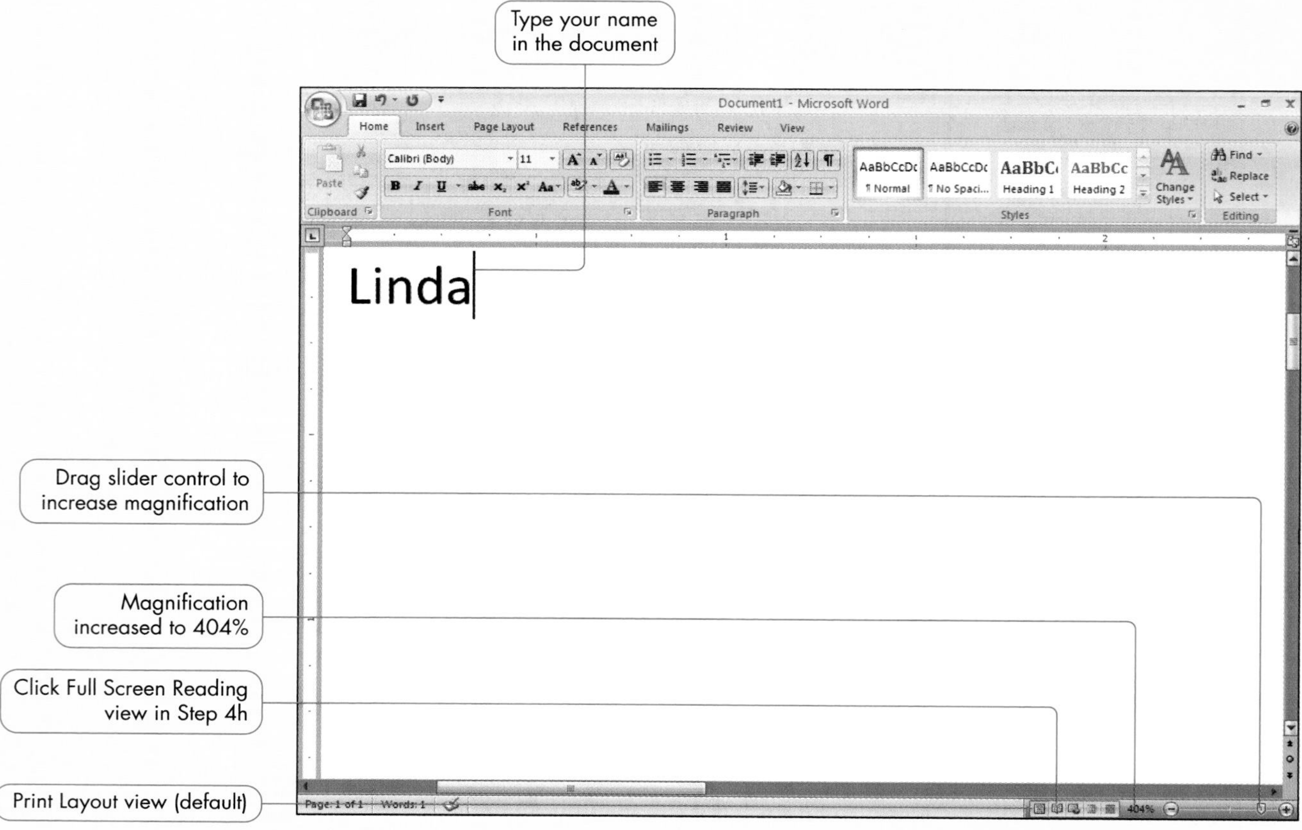

Figure 1.13 The Word Status Bar

Step 5
Search Help and Print a Help Topic

Refer to Figure 1.14 as you complete Step 5.

a. With Word open on the screen, press **F1** on the keyboard.

Word Help displays.

b. Type **zoom** in the Search box in the Word Help window.

c. Click the **Search** button.

Word Help displays related topics.

d. Click the topic **Zoom in or out of a document**.

The help topic displays.

TROUBLESHOOTING: If you do not have a printer that is ready to print, skip Step 5e and continue with the exercise.

e. Turn on the attached printer, be sure it has paper, and then click the Word Help **Print** button.

The Help topic prints on the attached printer.

f. Click the **Show Table of Contents** button on the Word Help toolbar.

The Table of Contents pane displays on the left side of the Word Help dialog box so that you can click popular Help topics, such as *What's new*. You can click a closed book icon to see specific topics to click for additional information, and you can click an open book icon to close the main Help topic.

g. Click the **Close** button on Word Help.

Word Help closes.

h. To exit Word, click the **Office Button** to display the Office menu, and then click the **Exit Word button.**

A warning appears stating that you have not saved changes to your document.

i. Click **No** in the Word warning box.

You exit Word without saving the document.

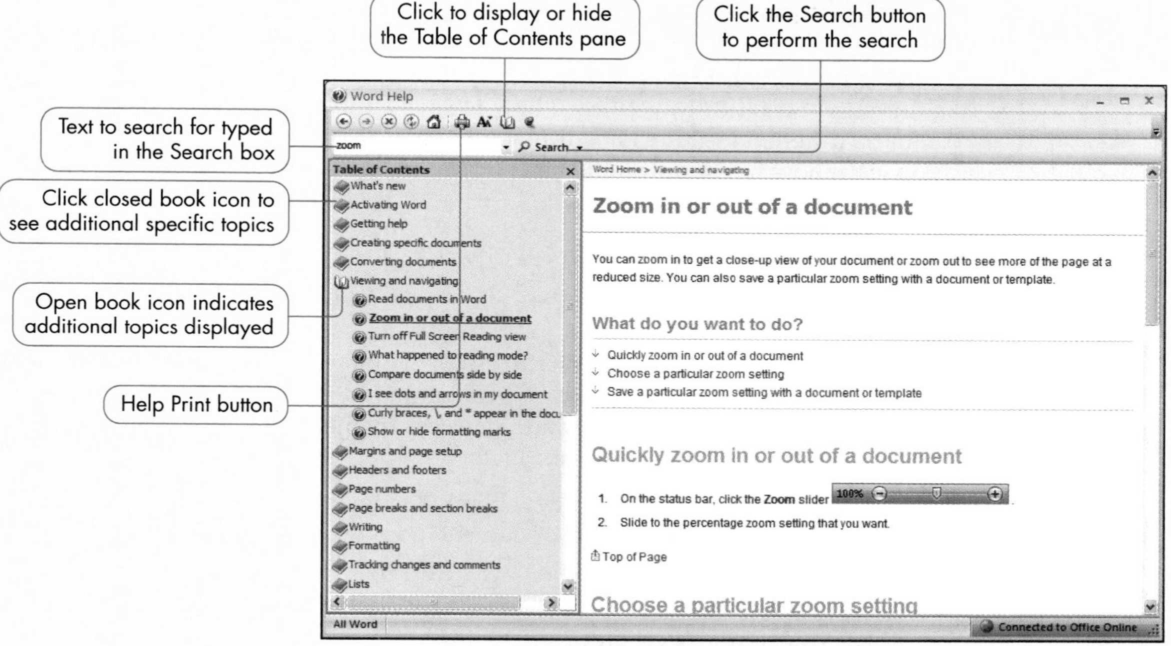

Figure 1.14 Word Help

Universal Tasks

Today, storing large amounts of information on a computer is taken for granted, but in reality, computers would not have become very important if you could not save and re-use the files you create.

One of the most useful and important aspects of using computers is the ability to save and re-use information. For example, you can store letters, reports, budgets, presentations, and databases as files to reopen and use at some time in the future. Today, storing large amounts of information on a computer is taken for granted, but in reality, computers would not have become very important if you could not save and re-use the files you create.

Three fundamental tasks are so important for productivity that they are considered universal to most every computer program, including Office 2007:

- opening files that have been saved
- saving files you create
- printing files

In this section, you open a file within an Office 2007 program. Specifically, you learn how to open a file from within the Open dialog box and how to open a file from a list of recently used files in a specific program. You also save files to keep them for future use. Specifically, you learn how to save a file with the same name, a different name, a different location, or a different file type. Finally, you print a file. Specifically, you learn how to preview a file before printing it and select print options within the Print dialog box.

Opening a File

When you start any program in Office 2007, you need to start creating a new file or open an existing one. You use the Open command to retrieve a file saved on a storage device and place it in the random access memory (RAM) of your computer so you can work on it. For example:

The ***insertion point*** is the blinking vertical line in the document, cell, slide show, or database table designating the current location where text you type displays.

- When you start Word 2007, a new blank document named Document1 opens. You can either start typing in Document1, or you can open an existing document. The ***insertion point***, which looks like a blinking vertical line, displays in the document designating the current location where text you type displays.
- When you start PowerPoint 2007, a new blank presentation named Presentation1 opens. You can either start creating a new slide for the blank presentation, or you can open an existing presentation.
- When you start Excel 2007, a new blank workbook named Book1 opens. You can either start inputting labels and values into Book1, or you can open an existing workbook.
- When you start Access 2007—unlike Word, PowerPoint, and Excel—a new blank database is not created automatically for you. In order to get started using Access, you must create and name a database first or open an existing database.

Open a File Using the Open Dialog Box

Opening a file in any of the Office 2007 applications is an easy process: Use the Open command from the Office menu and specify the file to open. However, locating the file to open can be difficult at times because you might not know where the file you want to use is located. You can open files stored on your computer or on a remote computer that you have access to. Further, files are saved in folders, and you might need to look for files located within folders or subfolders. The Open dialog box, shown in Figure 1.15, contains many features designed for file management; however, two features are designed specifically to help you locate files.

- **Look in**—provides a hierarchical view of the structure of folders and subfolders on your computer or on any computer network you are attached to. Move up or down in the structure to find a specific location or folder and then click the desired location to select it. The file list in the center of the dialog box displays the subfolders and files saved in the location you select. Table 1.3 lists and describes the toolbar buttons.
- **My Places bar**—provides a list of shortcut links to specific folders on your computer and locations on a computer network that you are attached to. Click a link to select it, and the file list changes to display subfolders and files in that location.

Table 1.3 Toolbar Buttons

Buttons	Characteristics
Previous Folder	Returns to the previous folder you viewed.
Up One Level	Moves up one level in the folder structure from the current folder.
Delete	Deletes the selected file or selected folder.
Create New Folder	Creates a new folder within the current folder.
Views	Changes the way the list of folders and files displays in the File list.

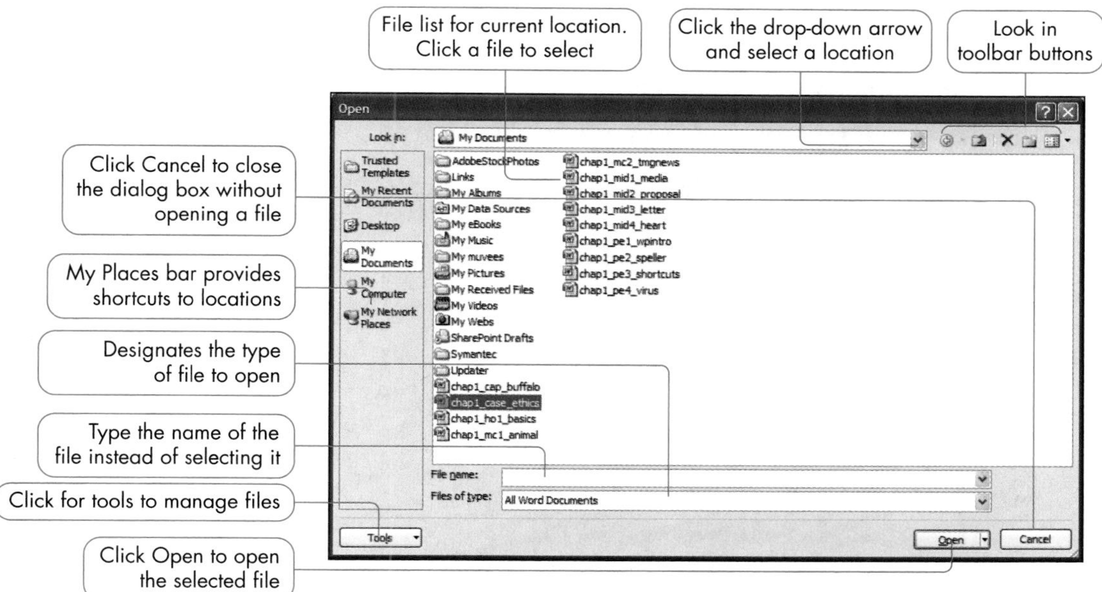

Figure 1.15 Open Dialog Box in Word

After you locate and select the file, click the Open button in the dialog box to display the file on the screen. However, if, for example, you work as part of a workgroup that shares files with each other, you might find the need to open files in a more specialized way. Microsoft Office programs provide several options for opening files when you click the drop-down arrow on the Open button. For example, if you want to keep the original file intact, you might open the file as a copy of the original. Table 1.4 describes the Open options.

Table 1.4 Open Options

Open Options	Characteristics
Open	Opens the selected file with the ability to read and write (edit).
Open Read-Only	Opens the selected file with the ability to read the contents but prevents you from changing or editing it.
Open as Copy	Opens the selected file as a copy of the original so that if you edit the file, the original remains unchanged.
Open in Browser	Opens the selected file in a Web browser.
Open with Transform	Opens a file and provides the ability to transform it into another type of document, such as an HTML document.
Open and Repair	Opens the selected file and attempts to repair any damage. If you have difficulty opening a file, try to open it by selecting Open and Repair.

Open Files Using the Recent Documents List

Office 2007 provides a quick method for accessing files you used recently. The Recent Documents list displays when the Office menu opens and provides a list of links to the last few files you used. The list changes as you work in the application to reflect only the most recent files. Figure 1.16 shows the Office menu with the Recent Documents list.

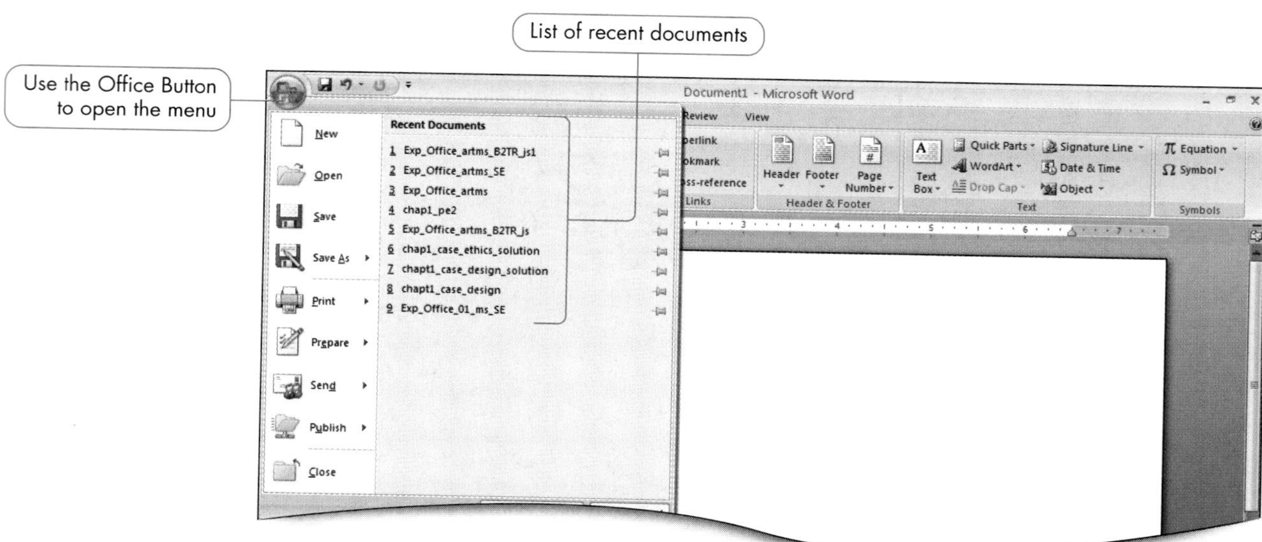

Figure 1.16 The Recent Documents List

TIP Keeping Files on the Recent Documents List

As you use the Office application and open several files, the list of Recent Documents changes; however, you can designate files to keep displayed on the Recent Documents list at all times. Notice the icon of the pushpin that displays immediately following each file name on the Recent Documents list. Just as you use pushpins to post an important notice in the real world, you use pushpins here to designate important files that you want easy access to. To pin a specific file to the Recent Documents list, click the icon of a gray pushpin. The shape of the pin changes as if pushed in, and the color of the pin changes to green designating that the file is pinned permanently on the list. However, if later you decide to remove the file from the list, you can unpin it by simply clicking the green pushpin, changing the icon back to gray, and the file will disappear from the list over time. Notice the Recent Documents list with both gray and green pushpins in Figure 1.17.

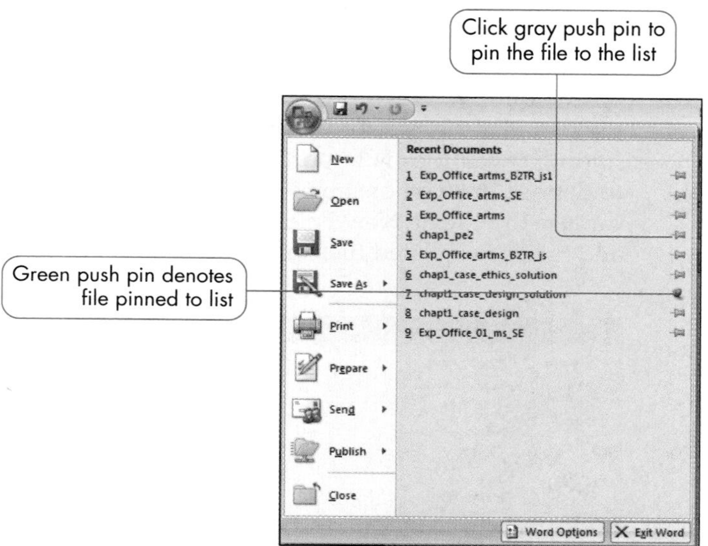

Figure 1.17 The Recent Documents List

Saving a File

As you work with any Office 2007 application and create files, you will need to save them for future use. While you are working on a file, it is stored in the temporary memory or RAM of your computer. When you save a file, the contents of the file stored in RAM are saved to the hard drive of your computer or to a storage device such as a flash drive. As you create, edit, and format a complex file such as a report, slide show, or budget, you should consider saving several versions of it as you work. For example, you might number versions or use the date in the file name to designate each version. Using this method enables you to revert to a previous version of the document if necessary. To save a file you create in Word, PowerPoint, or Excel, click the Office Button to display the Office menu. Office provides two commands that work similarly: Save and Save As. Table 1.5 describes the characteristics of these two commands.

> As you create, edit, and format a complex file such as a report, slide show, or budget, you should consider saving several versions of it as you work.

Table 1.5 Save Options

Command	Characteristics
Save	Saves the open document: • If this is the first time the document is being saved, Office 2007 opens the Save As dialog box so that you can name the file. • If this document was saved previously, the document is automatically saved using the original file name.
Save As	Opens the Save As dialog box: • If this is the first time the document is being saved, use the Save As dialog box to name the file. • If this document was saved previously, use this option to save the file with a new name, in a new location, or as a new file type preserving the original file with its original name.

When you select the Save As command, the Save As dialog box appears (see Figure 1.18). Notice that saving and opening files are related, that the Save As dialog box looks very similar to the Open dialog box that you saw in Figure 1.15. The dialog box requires you to specify the drive or folder in which to store the file, the name of the file, and the type of file you wish the file to be saved as. Additionally, because finding saved files is important, you should always group related files together in folders, so that you or someone else can find them in a location that makes sense. You can use the Create New Folder button in the dialog box to create and name a folder, and then save related files to it.

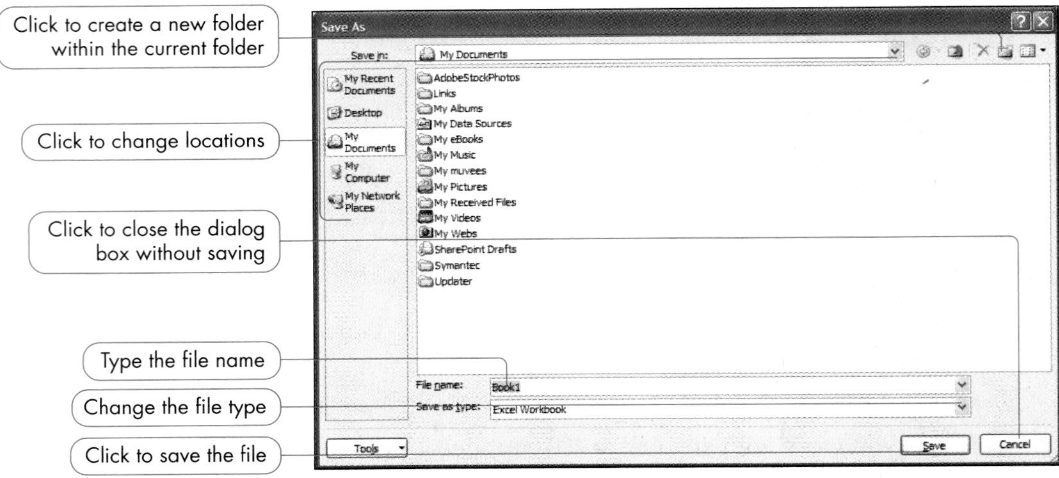

Figure 1.18 Save As Dialog Box in Excel

All subsequent executions of the Save command save the file under the assigned name, replacing the previously saved version with the new version. Pressing Ctrl+S is another way to activate the Save command. If you want to change the name of the file, use the Save As command. Word, PowerPoint, and Excel use the same basic process for saving files, which include the following options:

- naming and saving a previously unsaved file
- saving an updated file with the same name and replacing the original file with the updated one
- saving an updated file with a different name or in a different location to keep the original intact
- saving the file in a different file format

TIP Saving from the Office Menu

You should select the Save As command on the Office menu rather than pointing to the arrow that follows the command. When you point to the arrow, menu options display for saving the file in an alternative format. Always check the Save as type box in the dialog box to be sure that the correct file type is specified.

A ***macro*** is a small program that automates tasks in a file.

A ***virus checker*** is software that scans files for a hidden program that can damage your computer.

A ***template*** is a file that contains formatting and design elements.

Office 2007 saves files in a different format from previous versions of the software. Office now makes use of XML formats for files created in Word, PowerPoint, and Excel. For example, in previous versions of Word, all documents were saved with the three-letter extension .doc. Now Word saves default documents with the four-letter extension .docx. The new XML format makes use of file compression to save storage space for the user. The files are compressed automatically when saved and uncompressed when opened. Another important feature is that the XML format makes using the files you create in Office 2007 easier to open in other software. This increased portability of files is a major benefit in any workplace that might have numerous applications to deal with. The new file format also differentiates between files that contain ***macros***, which are small programs that automate tasks in a file, and those that do not. This specification of files that contain macros enables a virus checker to rigorously check for damaging programs hidden in files. A ***virus checker*** is software that scans files for a hidden program that can damage your computer. Table 1.6 lists the file formats with the four-letter extension for Word, PowerPoint, and Excel, and a five-letter extension for Access.

Table 1.6 Word, PowerPoint, Excel, and Access File Extensions

File Format	Characteristics
Word	.docx—default document format .docm—a document that contains macros .dotx—a template without macros (a ***template*** is a file that contains formatting and design elements) .dotm—a template with macros
PowerPoint	.pptx—default presentation format .pptm—a presentation that contains macros .potx—a template .potm—a template with macros .ppam—an add-in that contains macros .ppsx—a slide show .ppsm—a slide show with macros .sldx—a slide saved independently of a presentation .sldm—a slide saved independently of a presentation that contains a macro .thmx—a theme used to format a slide
Excel	.xlsx—default workbook .xlsm—a workbook with macros .xltx—a template .xltm—a template with a macro .xlsb—non-XML binary workbook—for previous versions of the software .xlam—an add-in that contains macros
Access	.accdb—default database

Access 2007 saves data differently from Word, PowerPoint, and Excel. When you start Access, which is a relational database, you must create a database and define at least one table for your data. Then as you work, your data is stored automatically. This powerful software enables multiple users access to up-to-date data. The concepts of saving, opening, and printing remain the same, but the process of how data is saved is unique to this powerful environment.

TIP Changing the Display of the My Places Bar

Sometimes finding saved files can be a time-consuming chore. To help you quickly locate files, Office 2007 provides options for changing the display of the My Places bar. In Word, PowerPoint, Excel, and Access, you can create shortcuts to folders where you store commonly used files and add them to the My Places bar. From the Open or Save As dialog box, select the location in the Look in list you want to add to the bar. With the desired location selected, point to an empty space below the existing shortcuts on the My Places bar. Right-click the mouse to display a ***shortcut menu***, which displays when you right-click the mouse on an object and provides a list of commands pertaining to the object you clicked. From the shortcut menu, choose Add (folder name)—the folder name is the name of the location you selected in the Look in box. The new shortcut is added to the bottom of the My Places bar. Notice the shortcut menu in Figure 1.19, which also provides options to change the order of added shortcuts or remove an unwanted shortcut. However, you can only remove the shortcuts that you add to the bar; the default shortcuts cannot be removed.

A ***shortcut menu*** displays when you right-click the mouse on an object and provides a list of commands pertaining to the object you clicked.

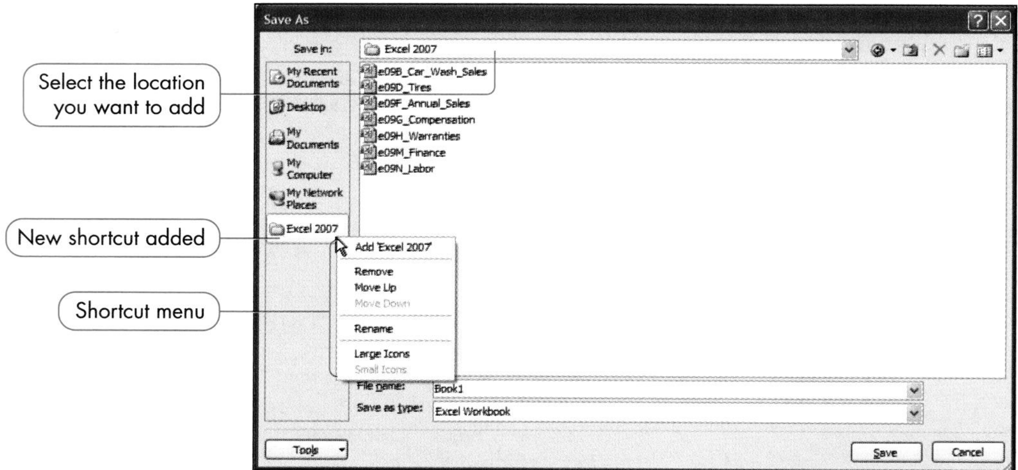

Figure 1.19 Save As Dialog Box with New Shortcut Added to My Places Bar

Printing a Document

As you work with Office 2007 applications, you will need to print hard copies of documents, such as letters to mail, presentation notes to distribute to accompany a slide show, budget spreadsheets to distribute at a staff meeting, or database summary reports to submit. Office provides flexibility so that you can preview the document before you send it to the printer; you also can select from numerous print options, such as changing the number of copies printed; or you can simply and quickly print the current document on the default printer.

Preview Before You Print

It is highly recommended that you preview your document before you print because Print Preview displays all the document elements, such as graphics and formatting, as they will appear when printed on paper. Previewing the document first enables you to make any changes that you need to make without wasting paper. Previewing documents uses the same method in all Office 2007 applications, that is, point to the arrow next to the Print command on the Office menu and select Print Preview to display the current document, worksheet, presentation, or database table in the Print Preview window. Figure 1.20 shows the Print Preview window in Word 2007.

It is highly recommended that you preview your document before you print because Print Preview displays all the document elements, such as graphics and formatting, as they will appear when printed on paper.

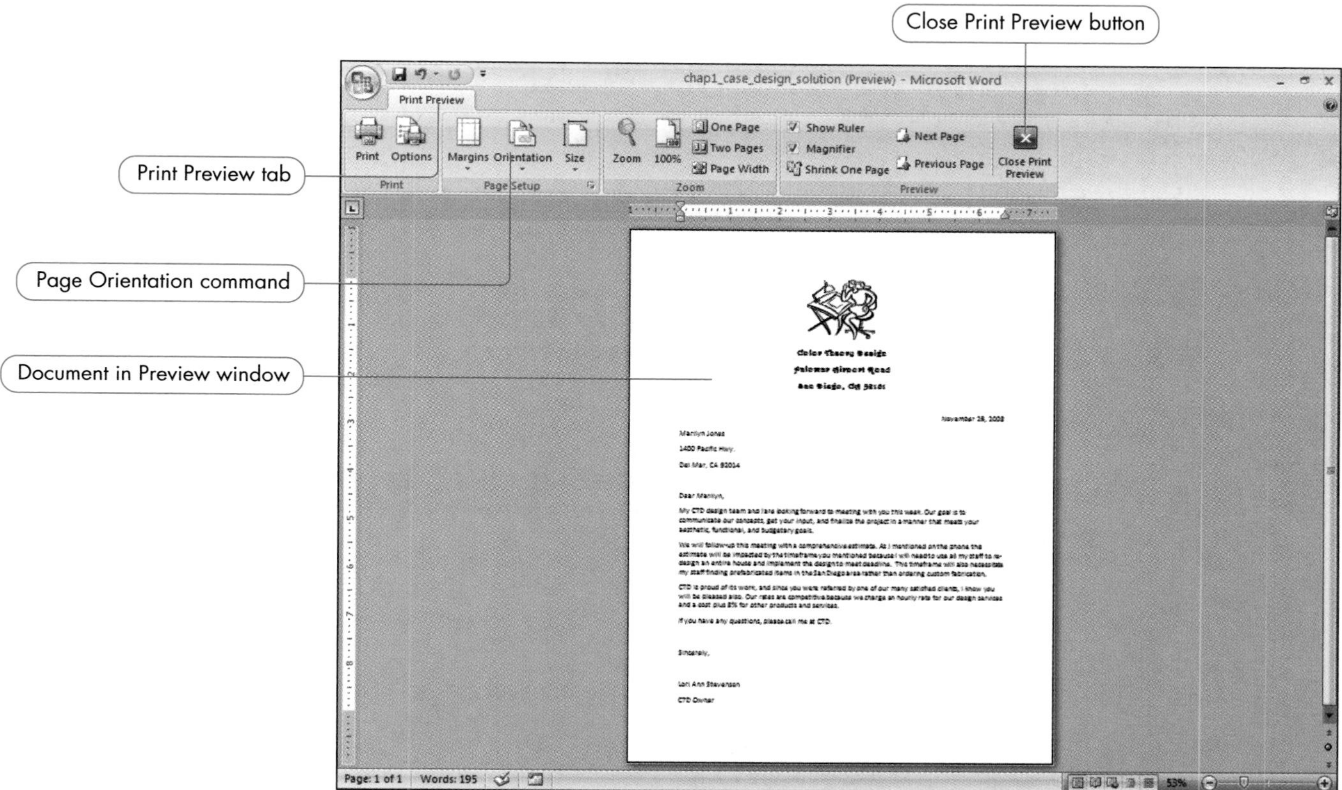

Figure 1.20 Print Preview Window

As you preview the document, you can get a closer look at the results by changing the zoom. Notice that the mouse pointer displays in the Preview window as a magnifying glass with a plus sign, so that you can simply click in the document to increase the zoom. Once clicked, the plus sign changes to a minus sign, enabling you to click in the document again to decrease the zoom. You also can use the Zoom group on the Print Preview tab or the Zoom slider on the status bar to change the view of the document.

Portrait orientation is longer than it is wide—like the portrait of a person.

Landscape orientation is wider than it is long, resembling a landscape scene.

Other options on the Print Preview tab change depending on the application that you are using. For example, you might want to change the orientation to switch from portrait to landscape. Refer to Figure 1.20. ***Portrait orientation*** is longer than it is wide, like the portrait of a person; whereas, ***landscape orientation*** is wider than it is long, resembling a landscape scene. You also can change the size of the paper or other options from the Print Preview tab.

If you need to edit the document before printing, close the Print Preview window and return to the document. However, if you are satisfied with the document and want to print, click Print in the Print group on the Print Preview tab. The Print dialog box displays. Figure 1.21 shows Word's Print dialog box.

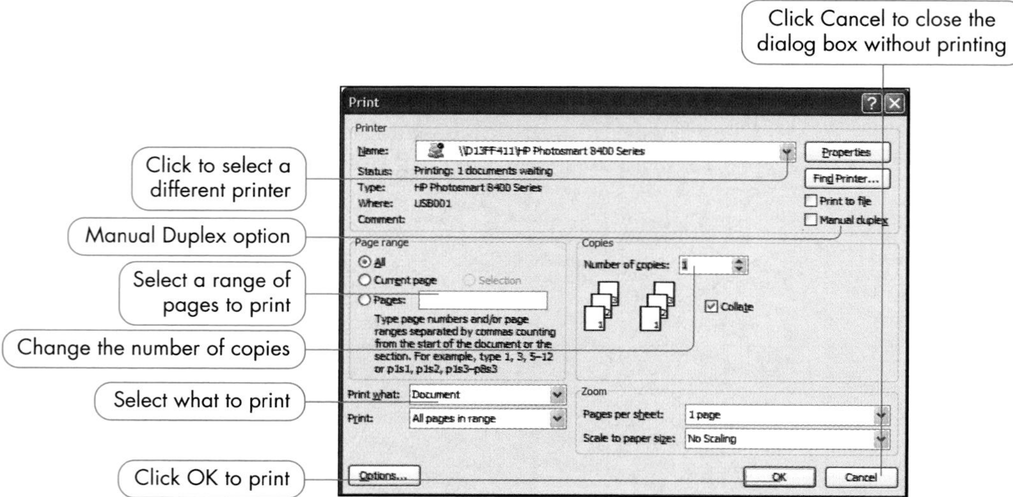

Figure 1.21 Print Dialog Box

The Print dialog box provides numerous options for selecting the correct printer, selecting what to print, and selecting how to print. Table 1.7 describes several important and often-used features of the Print dialog box.

Table 1.7 Print Dialog Box

Print Option	Characteristics
All	Select to print all the pages in the file.
Current page/slide	Select to print only the page or slide with the insertion point. This is a handy feature when you notice an error in a file, and you only want to reprint the corrected page.
Pages	Select to print only specific pages in a document. You must specify page numbers in the text box.
Number of Copies	Change the number of copies printed from the default 1 to the number desired.
Collate	Click if you are printing multiple copies of a multi-page file, and you want to print an entire first copy before printing an entire second copy, and so forth.
Print what	Select from options on what to print, varying with each application.
Selection	Select to print only selected text or objects in an Excel worksheet.
Active sheet(s)	Select to print only the active worksheet(s) in Excel.
Entire workbook	Select to print all worksheets in the Excel workbook.

As you work with other Office 2007 applications, you will notice that the main print options remain unchanged; however, the details vary based on the specific task of the application. For example, the *Print what* option in PowerPoint includes options such as printing the slide, printing handouts, printing notes, or printing an outline of the presentation.

A ***duplex printer*** prints on both sides of the page.

A ***manual duplex*** operation allows you to print on both sides of the paper by printing first on one side and then on the other.

TIP Printing on Both Sides of the Paper

Duplex printers print on both sides of the page. However, if you do not have a duplex printer, you can still print on two sides of the paper by performing a ***manual duplex*** operation, which prints on both sides of the paper by printing first on one side, and then on the other. To perform a manual duplex print job in Word 2007, select the Manual duplex option in the Print dialog box. Refer to Figure 1.21. With this option selected, Word prints all pages that display on one side of the paper first, then prompts you to turn the pages over and place them back in the printer tray. The print job continues by printing all the pages that appear on the other side of the paper.

Print Without Previewing the File

If you want to print a file without previewing the results, select Print from the Office menu, and the Print dialog box displays. You can still make changes in the Print dialog box, or just immediately send the print job to the printer. However, if you just want to print quickly, Office 2007 provides a quick print option that enables you to send the current file to the default printer without opening the Print dialog box. This is a handy feature to use if you have only one printer attached and you want to print the current file without changing any print options. You have two ways to quick print:

- Select Quick Print from the Office menu.
- Customize the Quick Access toolbar to add the Print icon. Click the icon to print the current file without opening the Print dialog box.

Hands-On Exercises

2 | Performing Universal Tasks

Skills covered: 1. Open a File and Save It with a Different Name **2.** Use Print Preview and Select Options **3.** Print a Document

Step 1
Open a File and Save It with a Different Name

Refer to Figure 1.22 as you complete Step 1.

a. Start Word, click the **Office Button** to display the Office menu, and then select **Open**.

The Open dialog box displays.

b. If necessary, click the **Look in drop-down arrow** to locate the files for this textbook to find *chap1_ho2_sample*.

TROUBLESHOOTING: If you have trouble finding the files that accompany this text, you may want to ask your instructor where they are located.

c. Select the file and click **Open**.

The document displays on the screen.

d. Click the **Office Button**, and then select **Save As** on the Office menu.

The Save As dialog box displays.

e. In the *File name* box, type **chap1_ho2_solution**.

f. Check the location listed in the **Save in** box. If you need to change locations to save your files, use the **Save in drop-down arrow** to select the correct location.

g. Make sure that the *Save as type* option is Word Document.

TROUBLESHOOTING: Be sure that you click the **Save As** command rather than pointing to the arrow after the command, and be sure that Word Document is specified in the Save as type box.

h. Click the **Save button** in the dialog box to save the file under the new name.

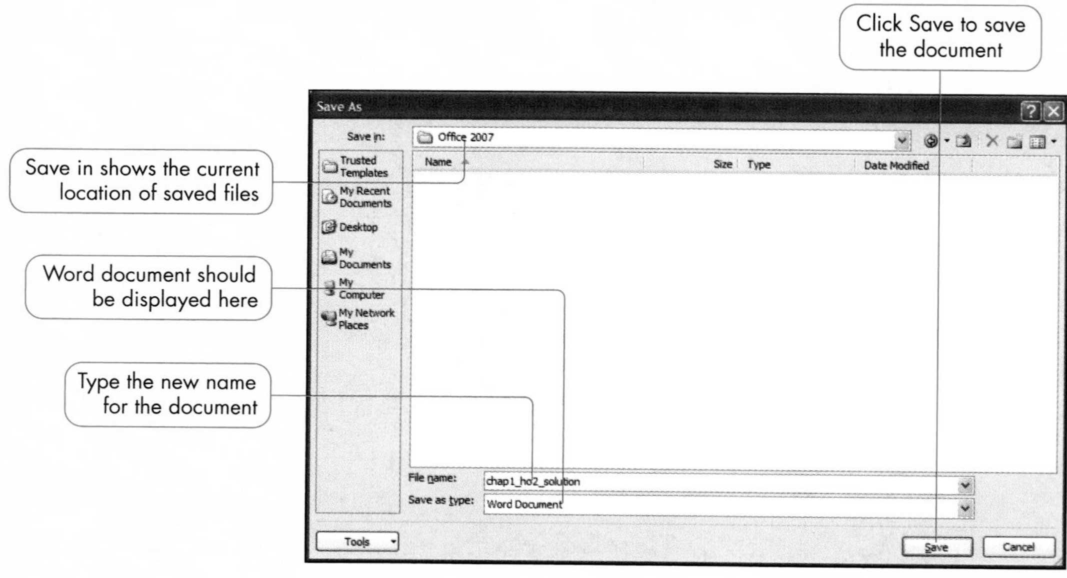

Figure 1.22 Save As Dialog Box

Step 2
Use Print Preview and Select Options

Refer to Figure 1.23 as you complete Step 2.

a. With the document displayed on the screen, click the **Office Button** and point to the arrow following **Print** on the Office menu.

The Print submenu displays.

b. Select **Print Preview**.

The document displays in the Print Preview window.

c. Point the magnifying glass mouse pointer in the document and click the mouse once.

TROUBLESHOOTING: If you do not see the magnifying glass pointer, point the mouse in the document and keep it still for a moment.

The document magnification increases.

d. Point the magnifying glass mouse pointer in the document and click the mouse again.

The document magnification decreases.

e. Click **Orientation** in the Page Setup group on the Print Preview tab.

The orientation options display.

f. Click **Landscape**.

The document orientation changes to landscape.

g. Click **Orientation** a second time, and then choose **Portrait**.

The document returns to portrait orientation.

h. Click the **Close Print Preview** button on the Print Preview tab.

i. The Print Preview window closes.

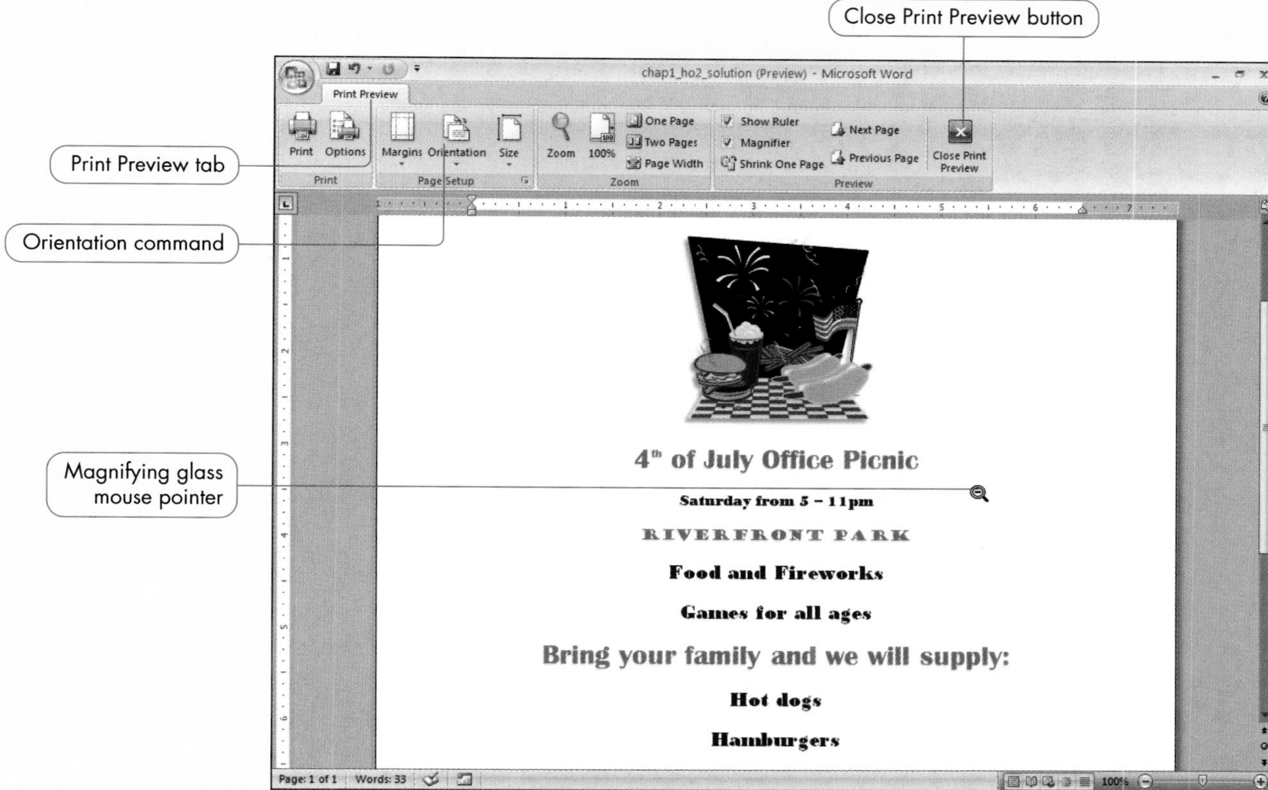

Figure 1.23 Print Preview

Step 3
Print a Document

Refer to Figure 1.24 as you complete Step 3.

a. Click the **Office Button**, and then point to the arrow next to **Print** on the Office menu.

   The print options display.

b. Select **Print**.

   The Print dialog box displays.

   TROUBLESHOOTING: Be sure that your printer is turned on and has paper loaded.

c. If necessary, select the correct printer in the **Name box** by clicking the drop-down arrow and selecting from the resulting list.

d. Click **OK**.

   The Word document prints on the selected printer.

e. To exit Word, click the **Office Button**, and then click the **Exit Word button**.

f. If prompted to save the file, choose **No**.

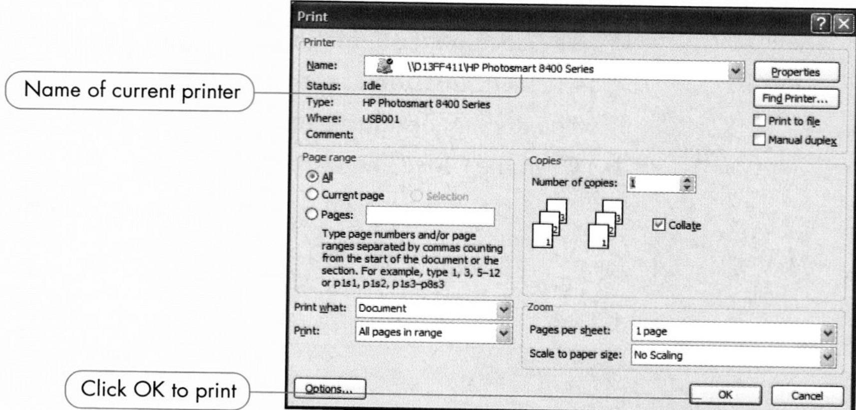

Figure 1.24 The Print Dialog Box

Basic Tasks

Many of the operations you perform in one Office program are the same or similar in all Office applications. These tasks are referred to as basic tasks and include such operations as inserting and typing over, copying and moving items, finding and replacing text, undoing and redoing commands, checking spelling and grammar, using the thesaurus, and using formatting tools. Once you learn the underlying concepts of these operations, you can apply them in different applications.

Most basic tasks in Word fall into two categories:

- editing a document
- formatting a document

Most successful writers use many word processing features to revise and edit documents, and most would agree that the revision process takes more time than the initial writing process. Errors such as spelling and grammar need to be eliminated to produce error-free writing. However, to turn a rough draft into a finished document, such as a report for a class or for a business, requires writers to revise and edit several times by adding text, removing text, replacing text, and moving text around to make the meaning clearer. Writers also improve their writing using tools to conduct research to make the information accurate and to find the most appropriate word using the thesaurus. Modern word processing applications such as Word 2007 provide these tools and more to aid the writer.

Most successful writers use many word processing features to revise and edit documents, and most would agree that the revision process takes more time than the initial writing process.

The second category of basic tasks is formatting text in a document. Formatting text includes changing the type, the size, and appearance of text. You might want to apply formatting to simply improve the look of a document, or you might want to emphasize particular aspects of your message. Remember that a poorly formatted document or workbook probably will not be read. So whether you are creating your résumé or the income statement for a corporation's annual report, how the output looks is important. Office 2007 provides many tools for formatting documents, but in this section, you will start by learning to apply font attributes and copy those to other locations in the document.

In this section, you learn to perform basic tasks in Office 2007, using Word 2007 as the model. As you progress in learning other Office programs such as PowerPoint, Excel, and Access, you will apply the same principles in other applications.

Selecting Text to Edit

Most editing processes involve identifying the text that the writer wants to work with. For example, to specify which text to edit, you must select it. The most common method used to select text is to use the mouse. Point to one end of the text you want to select (either the beginning or end) and click-and-drag over the text. The selected text displays highlighted with a light blue background so that it stands out from other text and is ready for you to work with. The ***Mini toolbar*** displays when you select text in Word, Excel, and PowerPoint. It displays above the selected text as semitransparent and remains semitransparent until you point to it. Often-used commands from the Clipboard, Font, and Paragraph groups on the Home tab are repeated on the Mini toolbar for quick access. Figure 1.25 shows selected text with the Mini toolbar fully displayed in the document.

The ***Mini toolbar*** displays above the selected text as semitransparent and repeats often-used commands.

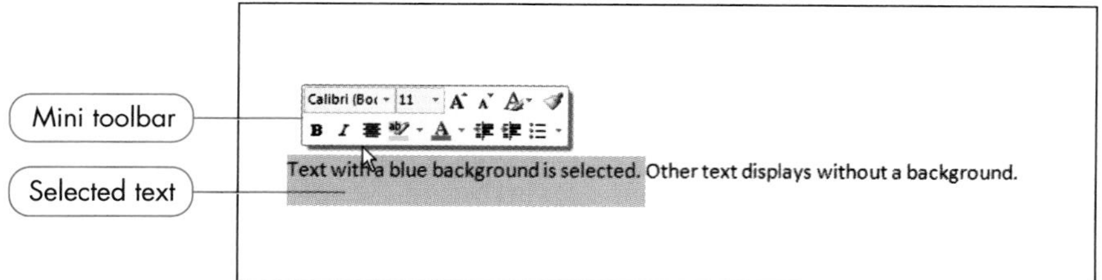

Figure 1.25 Selected Text

Sometimes you want to select only one word or character, and trying to drag over it to select it can be frustrating. Table 1.8 describes other methods used to select text.

Table 1.8 Easy Text Selection in Word

Outcome Desired	Method
Select a word	Double-click the word.
One line of text	Point the mouse to the left of the line, and when the mouse pointer changes to a right-pointing arrow, click the mouse.
A sentence	Hold down Ctrl and click in the sentence to select.
A paragraph	Triple-click the mouse in the paragraph.
One character to the left of the insertion point	Hold down Shift and press the left arrow key.
One character to the right of the insertion point	Hold down Shift and press the right arrow key.

TIP Selecting Large Amounts of Text

As you edit documents, you might need to select a large portion of a document. However, as you click-and-drag over the text, you might have trouble stopping the selection at the desired location because the document scrolls by too quickly. This is actually a handy feature in Word 2007 that scrolls through the document when you drag the mouse pointer at the edge of the document window.

To select a large portion of a document, click the insertion point at the beginning of the desired selection. Then move the display to the end of the selection using the scroll bar at the right edge of the window. Scrolling leaves the insertion point where you placed it. When you reach the end of the text you want to select, hold down Shift and click the mouse. The entire body of text is selected.

Inserting Text and Changing to the Overtype Mode

Insert is adding text in a document.

As you create and edit documents using Word, you will need to ***insert*** text, which is adding text in a document. To insert or add text, point and click the mouse in the location where the text should display. With the insertion point in the location to insert the text, simply start typing. Any existing text moves to the right, making room for the new inserted text. At times, you might need to add a large amount of text in a document, and you might want to replace or type over existing text instead of inserting text. This task can be accomplished two ways:

Overtype mode replaces the existing text with text you type character by character.

- Select the text to replace and start typing. The new text replaces the selected text.
- Switch to ***Overtype mode***, which replaces the existing text with text you type character by character. To change to Overtype mode, select the Word Options button on the Office menu. Select the option Use Overtype Mode in the Editing Options section of the Advanced tab. Later, if you want to return to Insert mode, repeat these steps to deselect the overtype mode option. Figure 1.26 shows the Word Options dialog box.

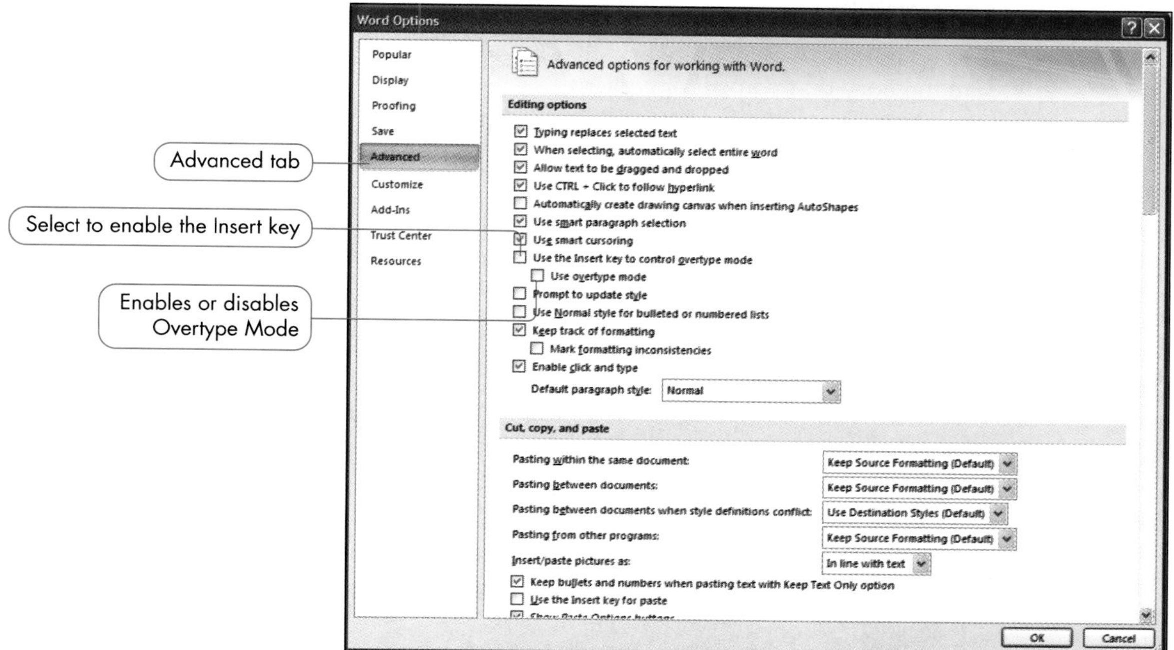

Figure 1.26 The Word Options Dialog Box

TIP Using the Insert Key on the Keyboard

If you find that you need to switch between Insert and Overtype mode often, you can enable Insert on the keyboard by clicking the Word Options button on the Office menu. Select the option Use the Insert Key to Control Overtype Mode in the Editing Options section on the Advanced tab. Refer to Figure 1.26. You can now use Insert on the keyboard to switch between the two modes, and this option stays in effect until you go back to the Word Options dialog box and deselect it.

Moving and Copying Text

As you revise a document, you might find that you need to move text from one location to another to improve the readability of the content. To move text, you must cut the selected text from its original location and then place it in the new location by pasting it there. To duplicate text, you must copy the selected text in its original location and then paste the duplicate in the desired location. To decide whether you should use the Cut or Copy command in the Clipboard group on the Home tab to perform the task, you must notice the difference in the results of each command:

Cut removes the original text or object from its current location.

Copy makes a duplicate copy of the text or object, leaving the original intact.

- ***Cut*** removes the selected original text or object from its current location.
- ***Copy*** makes a duplicate copy of the text or object, leaving the original text or object intact.

Keep in mind while you work, that by default, Office 2007 retains only the last item in memory that you cut or copied.

Paste places the cut or copied text or object in the new location.

You complete the process by invoking the Paste command. ***Paste*** places the cut or copied text or object in the new location. Notice the Paste Options button displays along with the pasted text. You can simply ignore the Paste Options button, and it will disappear from the display, or you can click the drop-down arrow on the button and select a formatting option to change the display of the text you pasted. Figure 1.27 shows the options available.

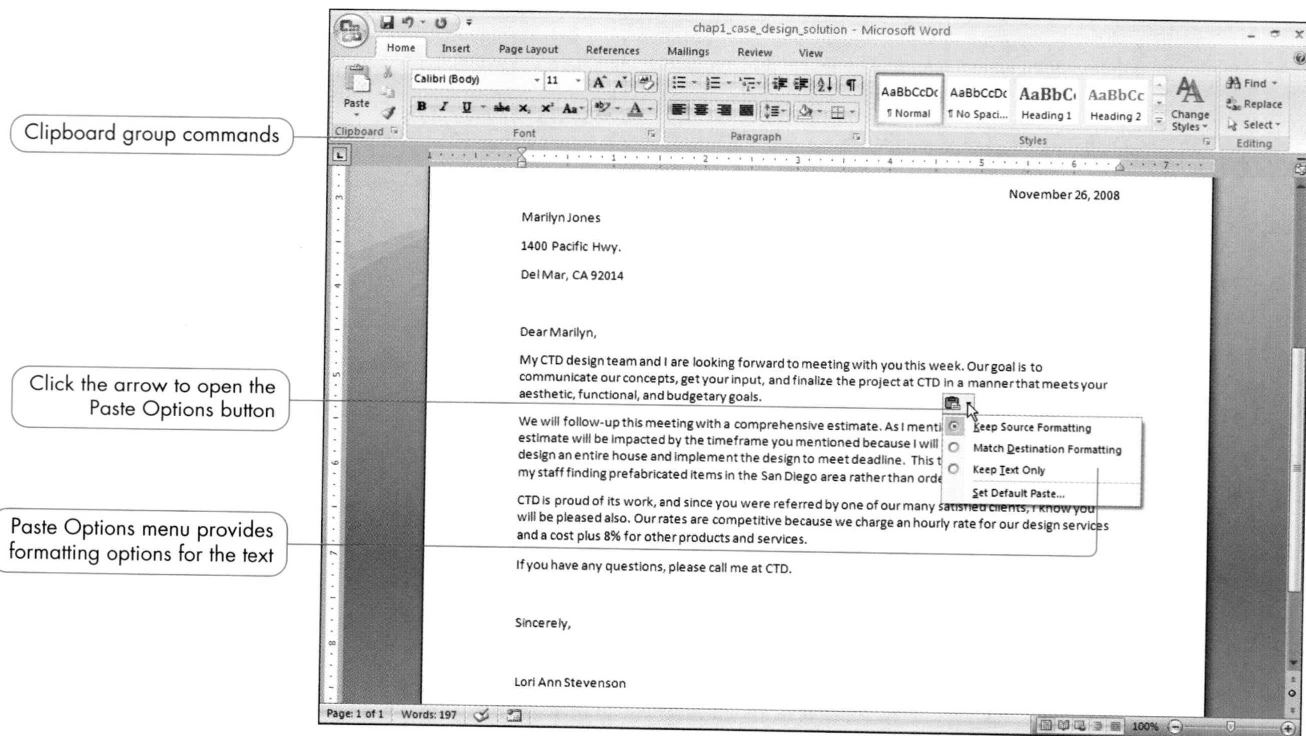

Figure 1.27 Text Pasted in the Document

TIP Moving and Copying Using Shortcuts

You can use alternative methods instead of using the commands located on the Home tab to cut, copy, and paste text. Office 2007 provides the following shortcuts:

- After selecting text, point back to the selected text and right-click the mouse. The shortcut menu displays, allowing you to choose Cut or Copy. Move the insertion point to the desired location, right-click the mouse again, and choose Paste from the shortcut menu.
- After selecting text, use the keyboard shortcut combinations Ctrl+C to copy or Ctrl+X to cut text. Move the insertion point to the new location and press Ctrl+V to paste. These keyboard shortcuts work in most Windows applications, so they can be very useful.
- After selecting text, you can move it a short distance in the document by dragging to the new location. Point to the selected text, hold down the left mouse button, and then drag to the desired location. While you are dragging the mouse, the pointer changes to a left-pointing arrow with a box attached to it. Release the mouse button when you have placed the insertion point in the desired location, and the text displays in the new location.

Use the Office Clipboard

The ***Clipboard*** is a memory location that holds up to 24 items for you to paste into the current document, another file, or another application.

Office 2007 provides an option that enables you to cut or copy multiple items to the ***Clipboard***, which is a memory location that holds up to 24 items for you to paste into the current file, another file, or another application. The Clipboard stays active only while you are using one of the Office 2007 applications. When you exit from all Office 2007 applications, all items on the Clipboard are deleted. To accumulate items on the Clipboard, you must first display it by clicking the Dialog Box Launcher in the Clipboard group on the Home tab. When the Clipboard pane is open on the screen, its memory location is active, and the Clipboard accumulates all items you cut or copy up to the maximum 24. To paste an item from the Clipboard, point to it, click the resulting drop-down arrow, and choose Paste. To change how the Clipboard functions, use the Options button shown in Figure 1.28. One of the most important options allows the Clipboard to accumulate items even when it is not open on the screen. To activate the Clipboard so that it works in the background, click the Options button in the Clipboard, and then select Collect without Showing Office Clipboard.

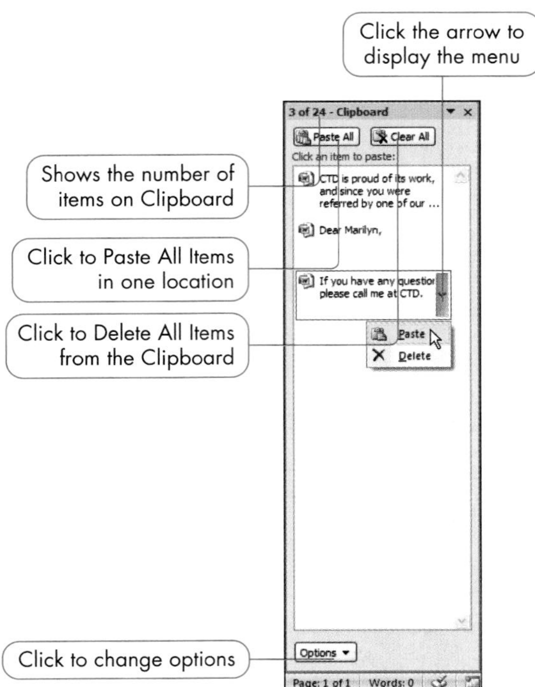

Figure 1.28 Clipboard

Finding, Replacing, and Going to Text

You can waste a great deal of time slowly scrolling through a document trying to locate text or other items. Office 2007 provides features that speed up editing by automatically finding text and objects in a document, thus making you more productive. Office 2007 provides the following three related operations that all use the Find and Replace dialog box:

Find locates a word or group of words in a document.

Replace not only finds text, it replaces a word or group of words with other text.

Go To moves the insertion point to a specific location in the document.

- The ***Find*** command enables you to locate a word or group of words in a document quickly.
- The ***Replace*** command not only finds text quickly, it replaces a word or group of words with other text.
- The ***Go To*** command moves the insertion point to a specific location in the document.

Find Text

To locate text in an Office file, choose the Find command in the Editing group on the Home tab and type the text you want to locate in the resulting dialog box, as shown in Figure 1.29. After you type the text to locate, you can find the next instance after the insertion point and work through the file until you find the instance of the text you were looking for. Alternatively, you can find all instances of the text in the file at one time. If you decide to find every instance at once, the Office application temporarily highlights each one, and the text stays highlighted until you perform another operation in the file.

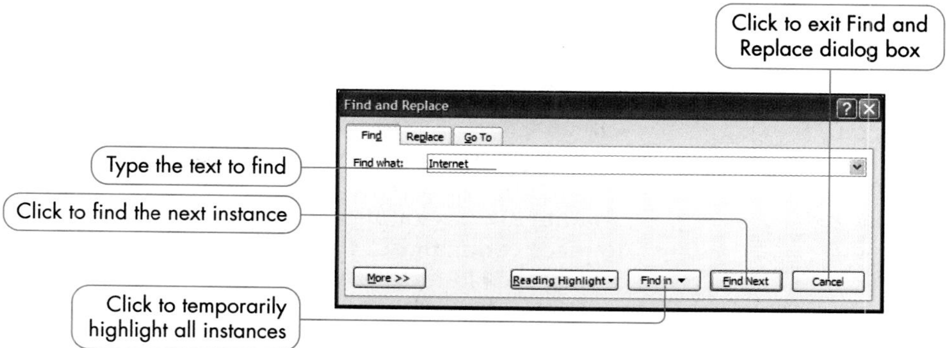

Figure 1.29 Find Tab of the Find and Replace Dialog Box

TIP Finding and Highlighting Text in Word

Sometimes, temporarily highlighting all instances of text is not sufficient to help you edit the text you find. If you want Word to find all instances of specific text in a document and keep the highlighting from disappearing until you want it to, you can use the Reading Highlight option in the Find dialog box. One nice feature of this option is that even though the text remains highlighted on the screen, the document prints normally without highlighting. Figure 1.30 shows the Find and Replace dialog box with the Reading Highlight options that you use to highlight or remove the highlight from a document.

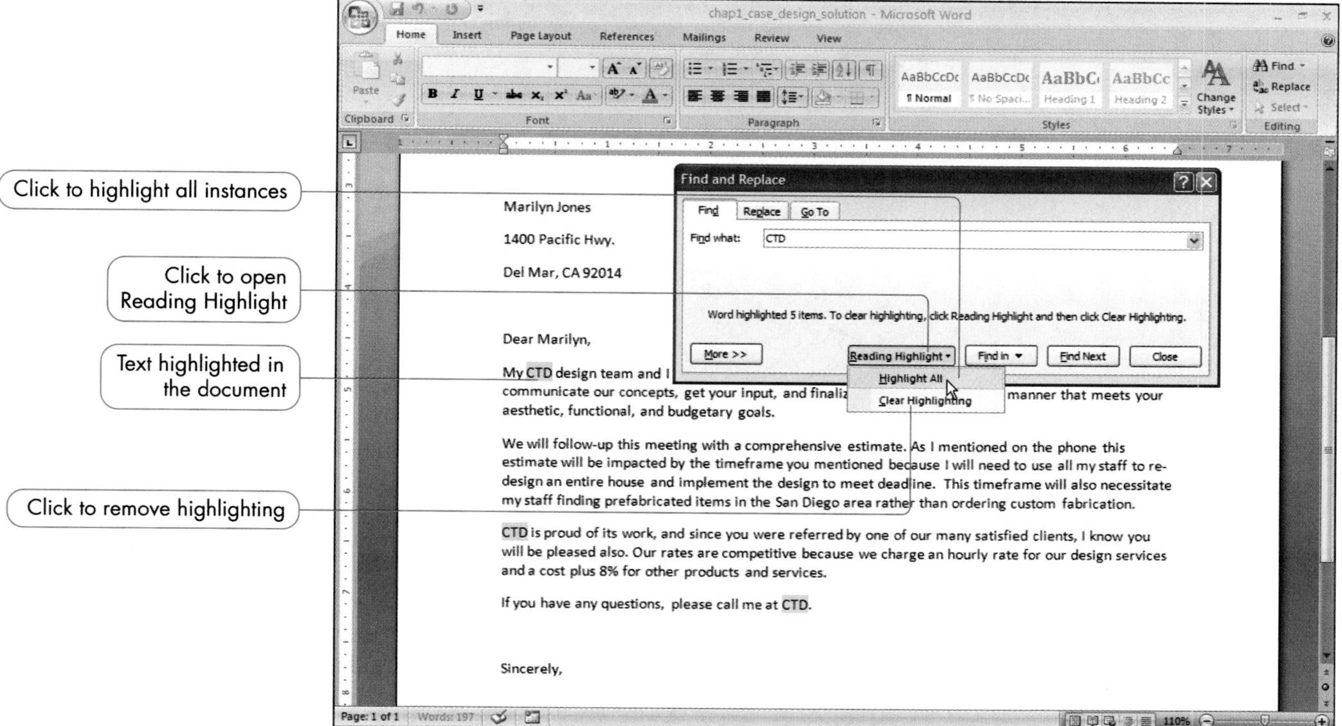

Figure 1.30 Find and Replace Dialog Box with Highlighting Options

Replace Text

While revising a file, you might realize that you have used an incorrect term and need to replace it throughout the entire file. Alternatively, you might realize that you could be more productive by re-using a letter or report that you polished and saved if you replace the previous client's or corporation's name with a new one. While you could perform these tasks manually, it would not be worth the time involved, and you might miss an instance of the old text, which could prove embarrassing. The Replace command in the Editing group on the Home tab can quickly and easily replace the old text with the new text throughout an entire file.

In the Find and Replace dialog box, first type the text to find, using the same process you used with the Find command. Second, type the text to replace the existing text with. Third, specify how you want Word to perform the operation. You can either replace each instance of the text individually, which can be time-consuming but allows you to decide whether to replace each instance one at a time, or you can replace every instance of the text in the document all at once. Word (but not the other Office applications) also provides options in the dialog box that help you replace only the correct text in the document. Click the More button to display these options. The most important one is the Find whole words only option. This option forces the application to find only complete words, not text that is part of other words. For instance, if you are searching for the word *off* to replace with other text, you would not want Word to replace the *off* in *office* with other text. Figure 1.31 shows these options along with the options for replacing text.

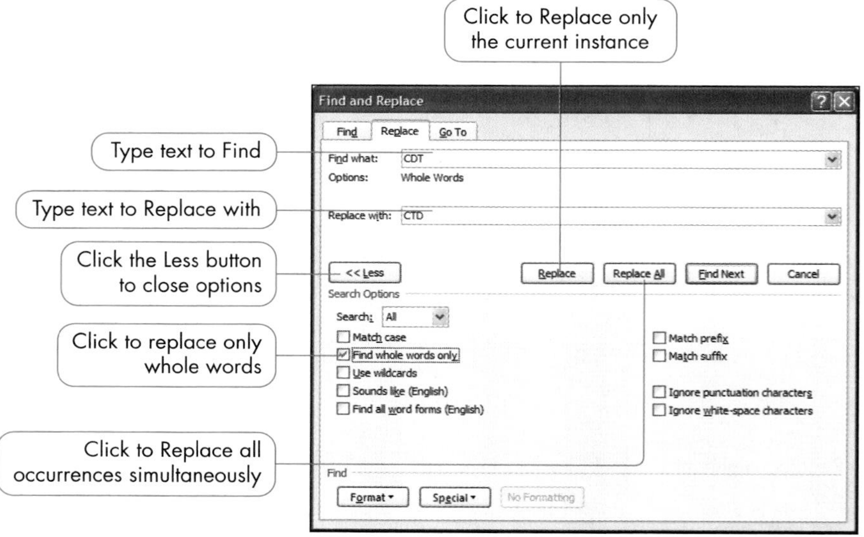

Figure 1.31 Find and Replace Dialog Box

Go Directly to a Location in a File

If you are editing a long document and want to move within it quickly, you can use the Go To command by clicking the down arrow on the Find command in the Editing group on the Home tab rather than slowly scrolling through an entire document or workbook. For example, if you want to move the insertion point to page 40 in a 200-page document, choose the Go To command and type 40 in the *Enter page number* text box. Notice the list of objects you can choose from in the Go to what section of the dialog box in Figure 1.32.

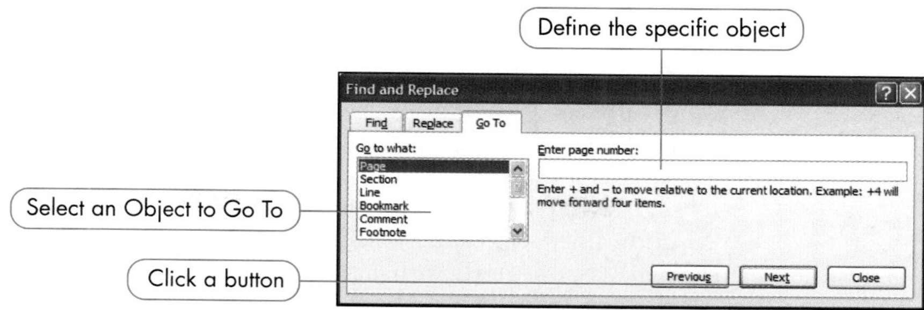

Figure 1.32 Go To Tab of the Find and Replace Dialog Box

Using the Undo and Redo Commands

The ***Undo*** command cancels your last one or more operations.

The ***Redo*** command reinstates or reverses an action performed by the Undo command.

As you create and edit files, you may perform an operation by mistake or simply change your mind about an edit you make. Office applications provide the ***Undo*** command, which can cancel your previous operation or even your last few operations. After using Undo to reverse an action or operation, you might decide that you want to use the ***Redo*** command to reinstate or reverse the action taken by the Undo command.

To undo the last action you performed, click Undo on the Quick Access Toolbar. For example, if you deleted text by mistake, immediately click Undo to restore it. If, however, you deleted some text and then performed several other operations, you can find the correct action to undo, with the understanding that all actions after that one will also be undone. To review a list of the last few actions you performed, click the Undo drop-down arrow and select the desired one from the list—Undo highlights all actions in the list down to that item and will undo all of the highlighted actions. Figure 1.33 shows a list of recent actions in PowerPoint. To reinstate or reverse an action as a result of using the Undo command, click Redo on the Quick Access Toolbar.

The ***Repeat*** command repeats only the last action you performed.

The ***Repeat*** command provides limited use because it repeats only the last action you performed. To repeat the last action, click Repeat on the Quick Access Toolbar. If the Office application is able to repeat your last action, the results will display in the document. Note that the Repeat command is replaced with the Redo command after you use the Undo command. For example, Figure 1.33 shows the Redo command after the Undo command has been used, and Figure 1.34 shows the Repeat command when Undo has not been used.

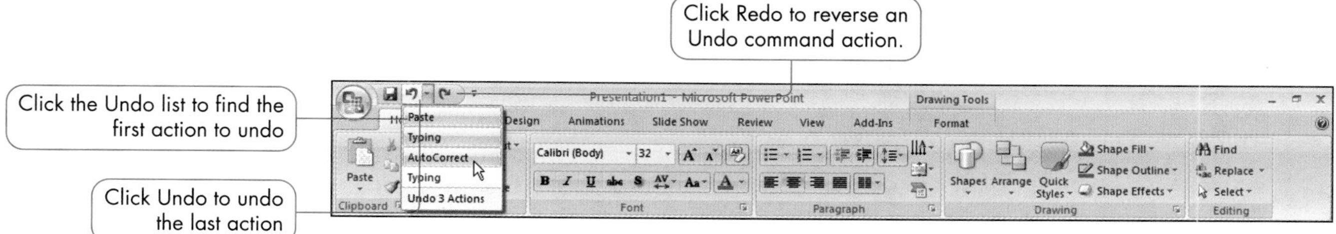

Figure 1.33 Undo and Redo Buttons

Using Language Tools

Documents, spreadsheets, and presentations represent the author, so remember that errors in writing can keep people from getting a desired job, or once on the job, can keep them from getting a desired promotion. To avoid holding yourself back, you should polish your final documents before submitting them electronically or as a hard copy. Office 2007 provides built-in proofing tools to help you fix spelling and grammar errors and help you locate the correct word or information.

Check Spelling and Grammar Automatically

By default, Office applications check spelling as you type and flag potential spelling errors by underlining them with a red wavy line. Word also flags potential grammar errors by underlining them with a green wavy line. You can fix these errors as you enter text, or you can ignore the errors and fix them all at once.

To fix spelling errors as you type, simply move the insertion point to a red wavy underlined word and correct the spelling yourself. If you spell the word correctly, the red wavy underline disappears. However, if you need help figuring out the correct spelling for the flagged word, then point to the error and right-click the mouse. The shortcut menu displays with possible corrections for the error. If you find the correction on the shortcut menu, click it to replace the word in the document. To fix grammar errors, follow the same process, but when the shortcut menu displays, you can choose to view more information to see rules that apply to the potential error. Notice the errors flagged in Figure 1.34. Note that the Mini toolbar also displays automatically.

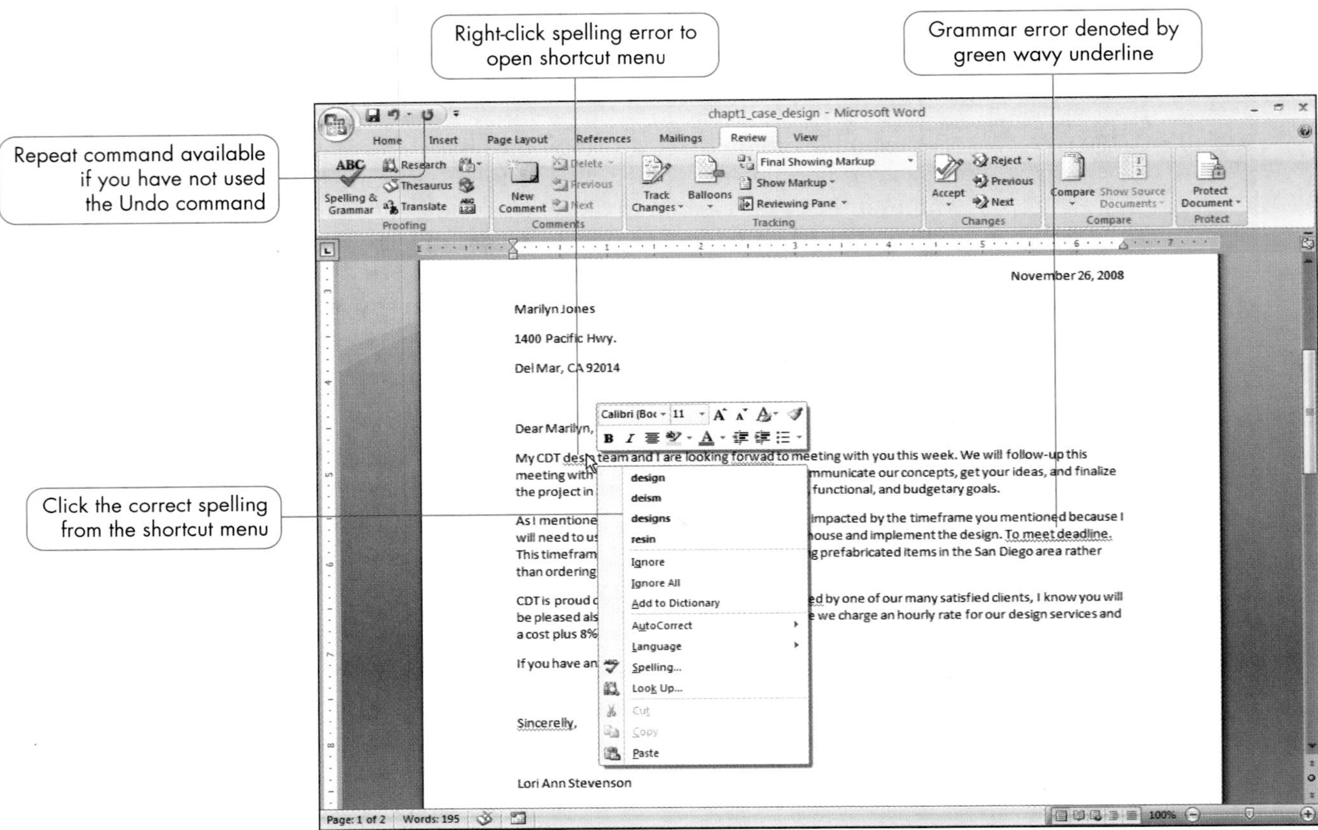

Figure 1.34 Automatic Spell and Grammar Check

Check Spelling and Grammar at Once

Some people prefer to wait until they complete typing the entire document and then check spelling and grammar at once. To check for errors, click Spelling & Grammar in Word (Spelling in Excel or PowerPoint) in the Proofing group on the Review tab. As the checking proceeds through the file and detects any spelling or grammar errors, it displays the Spelling dialog box if you are using Excel or PowerPoint, or the Spelling and Grammar dialog box in Word. You can either correct or ignore the changes that the Spelling checker proposes to your document. For example, Figure 1.35 shows the Spelling and Grammar dialog box with a misspelled word in the top section and Word's suggestions in the bottom section. Select the correction from the list and change the current instance, or you can change all instances of the error throughout the document. However, sometimes the flagged word might be a specialized term or a person's name, so if the flagged word is not a spelling error, you can ignore it once in the current document or throughout the entire document; further, you could add the word to the spell-check list so that it never flags that spelling again.

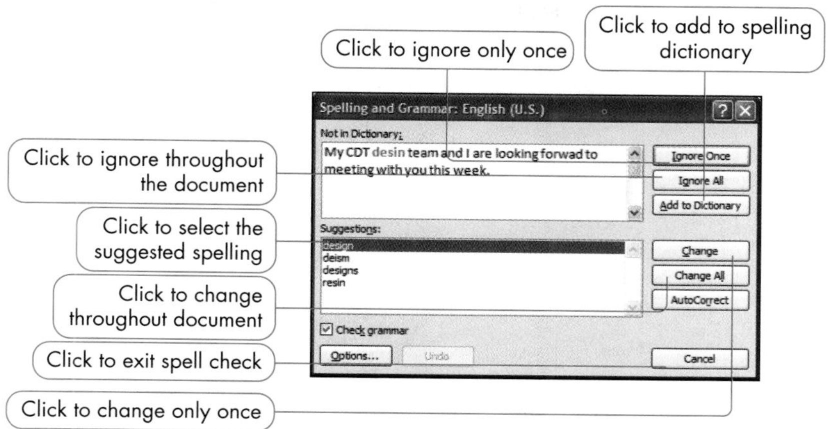

Figure 1.35 Spelling and Grammar Dialog Box

> **TIP Proofreading Your Document**
>
> The spelling and grammar checks available in Word provide great help improving your documents. However, you should not forget that you still have to proofread your document to ensure that the writing is clear, appropriate for the intended audience, and makes sense.

Use the Thesaurus

As you edit a document, spreadsheet, or presentation, you might want to improve your writing by finding a better or different word for a particular situation. For example, say you are stuck and cannot think of a better word for *big*, and you would like to find an alternative word that means the same. Word, Excel, and PowerPoint provide a built-in thesaurus, which is an electronic version of a book of synonyms. Synonyms are different words with the same or similar meaning, and antonyms are words with the opposite meaning.

The easiest method for accessing the Thesaurus is to point to the word in the file that you want to find an alternative for and right-click the mouse. When the shortcut menu displays, point to Synonyms, and the program displays a list of alternatives. Notice the shortcut menu and list of synonyms in Figure 1.36. To select one of the alternative words on the list, click it, and the word you select replaces the original word. If you do not see an alternative on the list that you want to use and you want to investigate further, click Thesaurus on the shortcut menu to open the full Thesaurus.

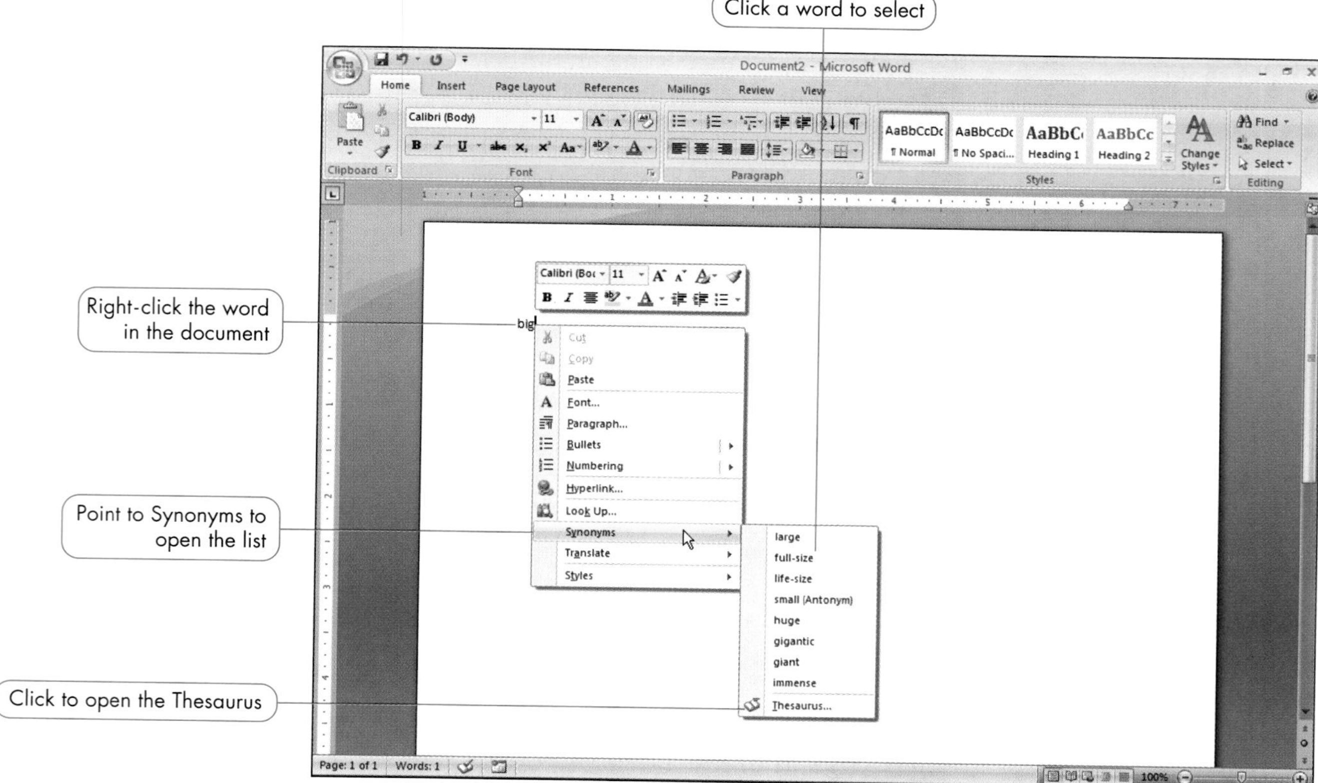

Figure 1.36 Shortcut Menu with Synonyms

An alternative method for opening the full Thesaurus is to place the insertion point in the word you want to look up, and then click the Thesaurus command in the Proofing group on the Review tab. The Thesaurus opens with alternatives for the selected word. You can use one of the words presented in the pane, or you can look up additional words. If you do not find the word you want, use the Search option to find more alternatives. Figure 1.37 shows the Thesaurus.

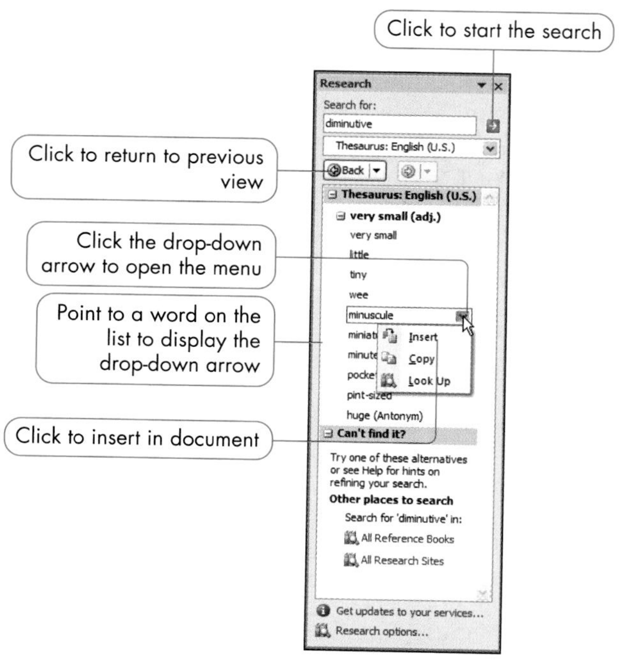

Figure 1.37 The Thesaurus

Conduct Research

As you work in Word, Excel, or PowerPoint, you might need to find the definition of a word or look up an item in the encyclopedia to include accurate information. Office 2007 provides quick access to research tools. To access research tools, click the Research button in the Proofing group on the Review tab. Notice in Figure 1.38 that you can specify what you want to research and specify where to Search. Using this feature, you can choose from reference books, research sites, and business and financial sites.

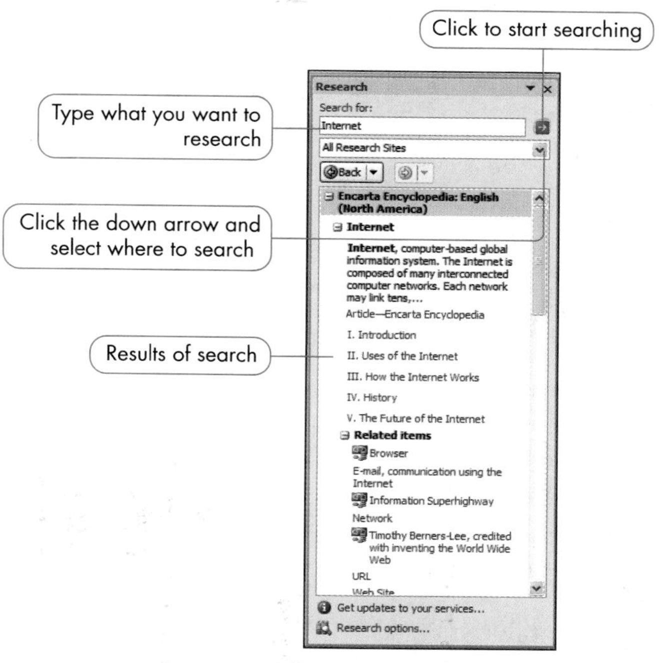

Figure 1.38 Research Task Pane

TIP Avoiding Plagiarism

If you use the research feature in Office to find information in an encyclopedia or in other locations to help you create your document, then you need to credit the source of that information. Avoid the problem of plagiarism, which is borrowing other people's words or ideas, by citing all sources that you use. You might want to check with your instructor for the exact format for citing sources.

Applying Font Attributes

Taking the time to format text helps the reader find important information in the document by making it stand out and helps the reader understand the message by emphasizing key items.

After you have edited a document, you might want to improve its visual appeal by formatting the text. ***Formatting text*** changes an individual letter, a word, or a body of selected text. Taking the time to format text helps the reader find important information in the document by making it stand out and helps the reader understand the message by emphasizing key items. You can format the text in the document by changing the following font attributes:

Formatting text changes an individual letter, a word, or a body of selected text.

- font face or size
- font attributes such as bold, underline, or italic
- font color

The Font group on the Home tab—available in Word, Excel, PowerPoint, and Access—provides many formatting options, and Office provides two methods for applying these font attributes:

- Choose the font attributes first, and then type the text. The text displays in the document with the formatting.
- Type the text, select the text to format, and choose the font attributes. The selected text displays with the formatting.

You can apply more than one attribute to text, so you can select one or more attributes either all at once or at any time. Also, it is easy to see which attributes you have applied to text in the document. Select the formatted text and look at the commands in the Font group on the Home tab. The commands in effect display with a gold background. See Figure 1.39. To remove an effect from text, select it and click the command. The gold background disappears for attributes that are no longer in effect.

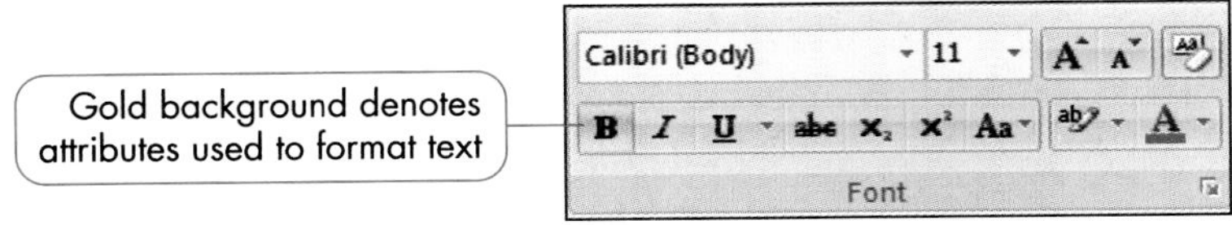

Figure 1.39 Font Group of the Home tab

Change the Font

A ***font*** is a named set of characters with the same design.

A ***font*** is a named set of characters with the same design, and Office 2007 provides many built-in fonts for you to choose from. Remember that more is not always better when applied to fonts, so limit the number of font changes in your document. Additionally, the choice of a font should depend on the intent of the document and should never overpower the message. For example, using a fancy or highly stylized font that may be difficult to read for a client letter might seem odd to the person receiving it and overpower the intended message.

(Remember that more is not always better when applied to fonts, so limit the number of font changes in your document.)

One powerful feature of Office 2007 that can help you decide how a font will look in your document is Live Preview. First, select the existing text, and then click the drop-down arrow on the Font list in the Font group on the Home tab. As you point to a font name in the list, Live Preview changes the selected text in the document to that font. Figure 1.40 shows the selected text displaying in a different font as a result of Live Preview.

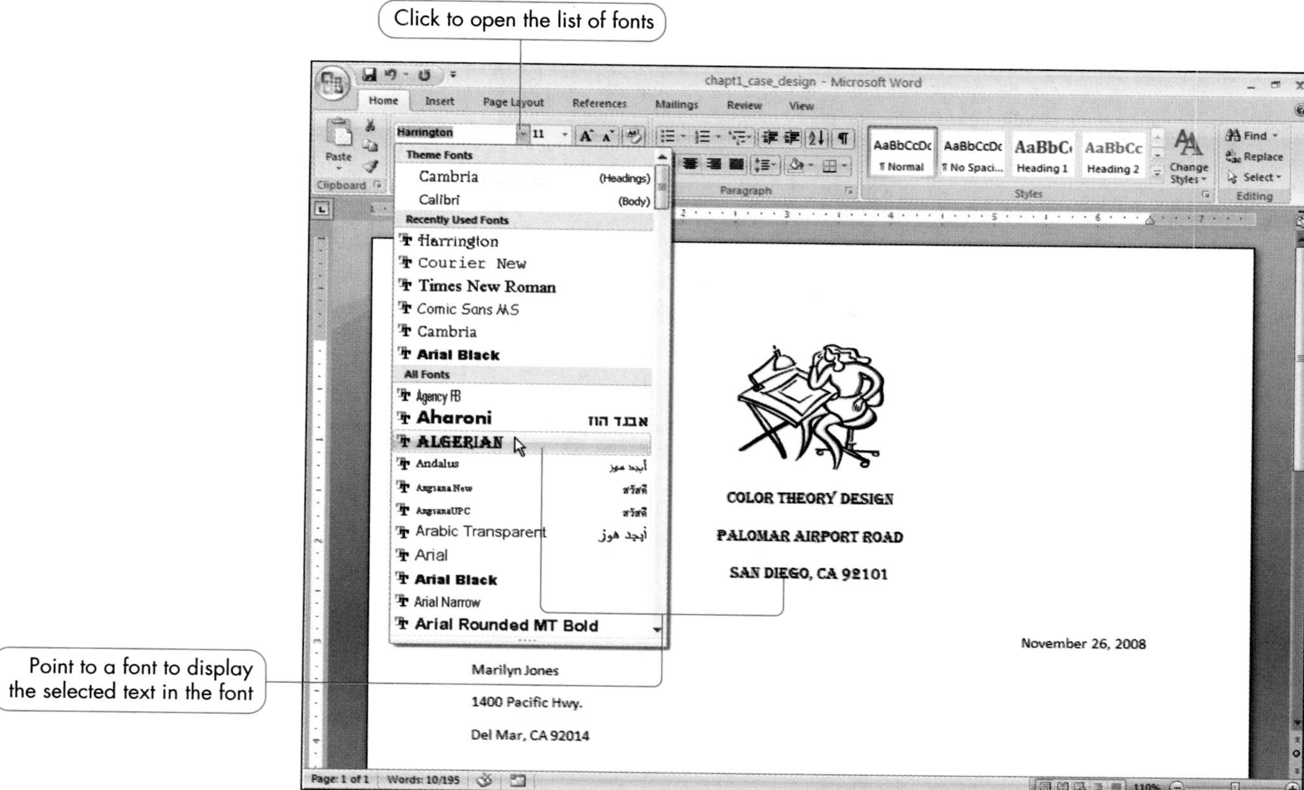

Figure 1.40 Font List

Change the Font Size, Color, and Attributes

Besides changing the font, you also can change the size, color, and other attributes of text in a document. Because these formatting operations are used so frequently, Office places many of these commands in several places for easy access:

- in the Font group on the Home tab
- on the Mini toolbar
- in the Font dialog box

Table 1.9 describes the commands that display in the Font group of the Home tab and in the Font dialog box.

Table 1.9 Font Commands

Command	Description	Example
Font	Enables you to designate the font.	Arial Comic Sans MS
Font Size	Enables you to designate an exact font size.	Size 8 Size 18
Grow Font	Each time you click the command, the selected text increases one size.	A A
Shrink Font	Each time you click the command, the selected text decreases one size.	B B
Clear Formatting	Removes all formatting from the selected text.	***Formatted*** Cleared
Bold	Makes the text darker than the surrounding text.	**Bold**
Italic	Places the selected text in italic, that is, slants the letters to the right.	*Italic*
Underline	Places a line under the text. Click the drop-down arrow to change the underline style.	Underline
Strikethrough	Draws a line through the middle of the text.	~~Strikethrough~~
Subscript	Places selected text below the baseline.	$\text{Sub}_{\text{script}}$
Superscript	Places selected text above the line of letters.	$\text{Super}^{\text{script}}$
Change Case	Changes the case of the selected text. Click the drop-down arrow to select the desired case.	lowercase UPPERCASE
Text Highlight Color	Makes selected text look like it was highlighted with a marker pen. Click the drop-down arrow to change color and other options.	Highlighted
Font Color	Changes the color of selected text. Click the drop-down arrow to change colors.	Font Color

If you have several formatting changes to make, click the Dialog Box Launcher in the Font group on the Home tab to display the Font dialog box. The Font dialog box is handy because all the formatting features display in one location, and it provides additional options such as changing the underline color. Figure 1.41 shows the Font dialog box in Word.

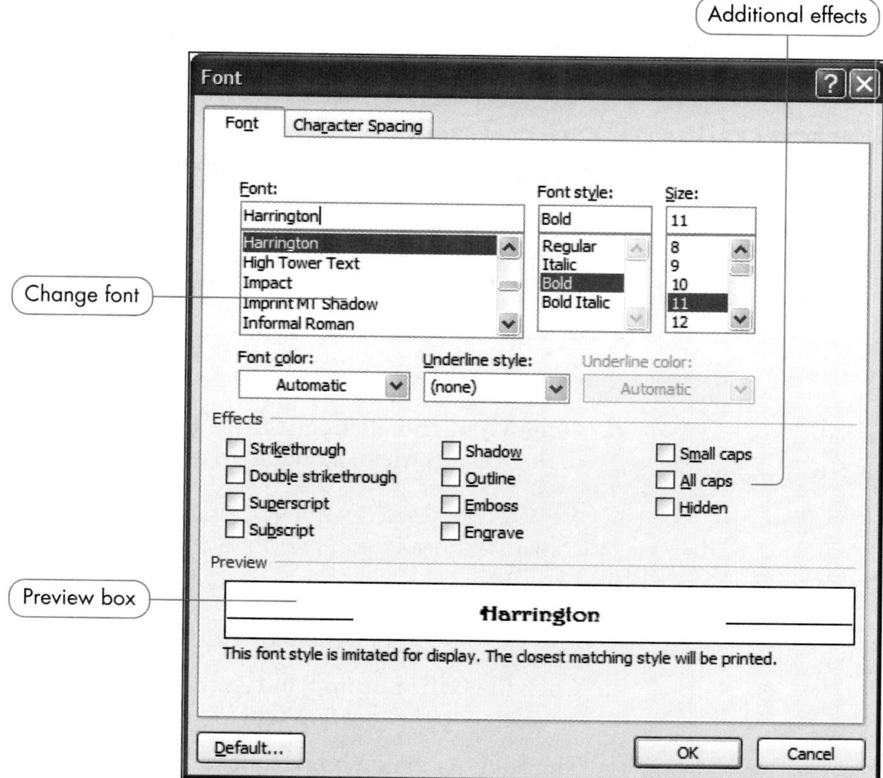

Figure 1.41 Font Dialog Box

Copying Formats with the Format Painter

The ***Format Painter*** copies the formatting of text from one location to another.

After formatting text in one part of a document, you might want to apply that same formatting to other text in a different location in the document. You could try to remember all the formatting options you selected, but that process would be time-consuming and could produce inconsistent results. Office 2007 provides a shortcut method called the ***Format Painter***, which copies the formatting of text from one location to another.

Select the formatted text you want to copy and click the Format Painter in the Clipboard group on the Home tab to copy the format. Single-click the command to turn it on to copy formatting to one location—the option turns off automatically after one copy—or double-click the command to turn it on for unlimited format copying—you must press Esc on the keyboard to turn it off.

Hands-On Exercises

3 | Performing Basic Tasks

Skills covered: 1. Cut, Copy, Paste, and Undo **2.** Find and Replace Text **3.** Check Spelling **4.** Choose Synonyms and Use Thesaurus **5.** Use the Research Tool **6.** Apply Font Attributes **7.** Use Format Painter

Step 1
Cut, Copy, Paste, and Undo

Refer to Figure 1.42 as you complete Steps 1 and 2.

a. Open Word and click the **Office Button**, click **Open**, and then using the Open dialog box features, navigate to your classroom file location.

TROUBLESHOOTING: If you have trouble finding the file, remember to use the Look in feature to find the correct location.

b. Select the file *chap1_ho3_internet* and click the **Open** button.

The Word document displays on the screen.

c. Click the **Office Button** and select **Save As**. If necessary, use the **Look in** feature to change to the location where you save files.

The Save As dialog box displays.

d. Type the new file name, **chap1_ho3_internet_solution**, be sure that *Word Document* displays in the *Save as type* box, and click **Save**.

The file is saved with the new name.

e. Click to place the insertion point at the beginning of the second sentence in the first paragraph. Type **These developments brought together**, and then press **Spacebar**.

The text moves to the right, making room for the new inserted text.

f. Press and hold down **Ctrl** as you click this sentence below the heading The World Wide Web: *The Netscape browser led in user share until Microsoft Internet Explorer took the lead in 1999.*

g. Click **Cut** in the Clipboard group on the Home tab.

The text disappears from the document.

h. Move the insertion point to the end of the last paragraph and click **Paste** in the Clipboard group on the Home tab.

The text displays in the new location.

i. Reselect the sentence you just moved and click **Copy** in the Clipboard group on the Home tab.

j. Move the insertion point to the end of the first paragraph beginning *The idea* and click the right mouse button.

The shortcut menu displays.

k. Select **Paste** from the shortcut menu.

The text remains in the original position and is copied to the second location.

l. Click **Undo** on the Quick Access Toolbar to undo the last paste.

Step 2
Find and Replace Text

Refer to Figure 1.42 to complete Step 2.

a. Press **Ctrl + Home** to move the insertion point to the beginning of the document. Click **Replace** in the Editing group on the Home tab.

   The Find and Replace dialog box displays.

b. Type **Internet** in the *Find what* box and type **World Wide Web** in the *Replace with* box.

c. Click the **Replace All** button. Click **OK** to close the information box that informs you that Word has made seven replacements. Click **Close** to close the Find and Replace dialog box.

   All instances of Internet have been replaced with World Wide Web in the document.

d. Click **Undo** on the Quick Access Toolbar.

   All instances of *World Wide Web* have changed back to *Internet* in the document.

e. Click **Replace** in the Editing group on the Home tab.

   The Find and Replace dialog box displays with the text you typed still in the boxes.

f. Click the **Find Next** button.

   The first instance of the text *Internet* is highlighted.

g. Click the **Replace** button.

   The first instance of Internet is replaced with World Wide Web, and the next instance of Internet is highlighted.

h. Click the **Find Next** button.

   The highlight moves to the next instance of Internet without changing the previous one.

i. Click the **Close** button to close the Find and Replace dialog box.

   The Find and Replace dialog box closes.

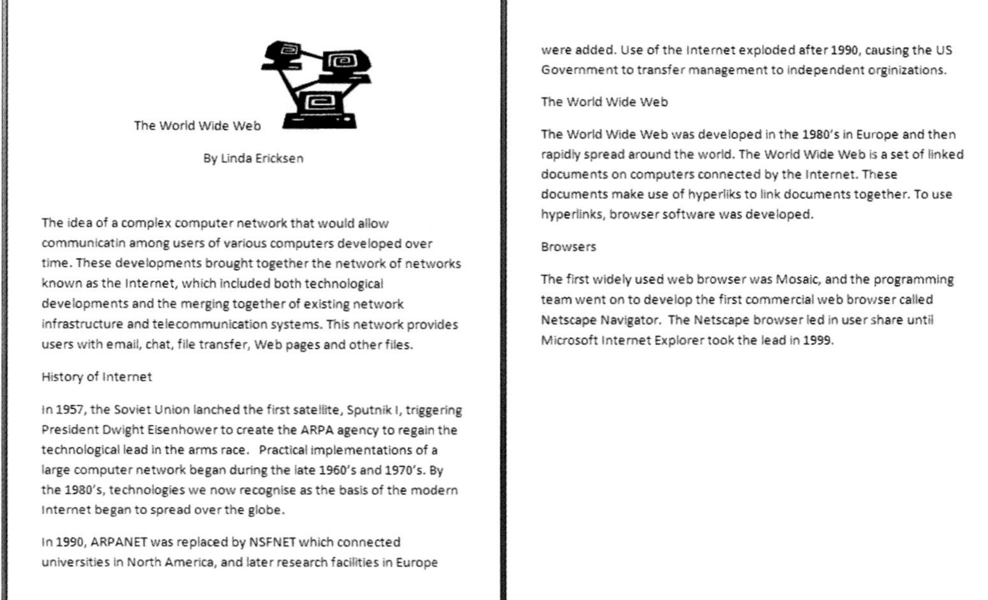

The World Wide Web

By Linda Ericksen

The idea of a complex computer network that would allow communicatin among users of various computers developed over time. These developments brought together the network of networks known as the Internet, which included both technological developments and the merging together of existing network infrastructure and telecommunication systems. This network provides users with email, chat, file transfer, Web pages and other files.

History of Internet

In 1957, the Soviet Union lanched the first satellite, Sputnik I, triggering President Dwight Eisenhower to create the ARPA agency to regain the technological lead in the arms race. Practical implementations of a large computer network began during the late 1960's and 1970's. By the 1980's, technologies we now recognise as the basis of the modern Internet began to spread over the globe.

In 1990, ARPANET was replaced by NSFNET which connected universities in North America, and later research facilities in Europe were added. Use of the Internet exploded after 1990, causing the US Government to transfer management to independent orginizations.

The World Wide Web

The World Wide Web was developed in the 1980's in Europe and then rapidly spread around the world. The World Wide Web is a set of linked documents on computers connected by the Internet. These documents make use of hyperliks to link documents together. To use hyperlinks, browser software was developed.

Browsers

The first widely used web browser was Mosaic, and the programming team went on to develop the first commercial web browser called Netscape Navigator. The Netscape browser led in user share until Microsoft Internet Explorer took the lead in 1999.

Figure 1.42 Edited Document (Shown in Full Screen Reading View)

Step 3
Check Spelling

Refer to Figure 1.43 as you complete Steps 3–5.

a. Right-click the first word in the document that displays with the red wavy underline: *communicatin*.

TROUBLESHOOTING: If the first word highlighted is the author's last name, ignore it for now. The name is spelled correctly, but if it is not listed in the spell check, then Word flags it.

The shortcut menu displays with correct alternatives.

b. Click **communication** to replace the misspelled word in the document.

The incorrect spelling is replaced, and the red wavy underline disappears.

c. Click the **Review tab**, and then click **Spelling & Grammar** in the Proofing group.

The Spelling and Grammar dialog box opens with the first detected error displayed.

d. Move through the document selecting the correct word from the suggestions provided and choosing to **Change** the errors.

e. Click **OK** to close the Spelling and Grammar checker when the process is complete.

Step 4
Choose Synonyms and Use Thesaurus

a. Place the insertion point in the word **complex** in the first sentence and right-click the mouse.

The shortcut menu displays.

b. Point to **Synonyms** on the shortcut menu.

The list of alternative words displays.

c. Click the alternative word **multifaceted**.

The new word replaces the word *complex* in the document.

d. Click in the word you just replaced, *multifaceted*, and click the **Thesaurus** button on the Review tab.

The Thesaurus displays with alternatives for **multifaceted**.

e. Scroll down the list and point to the word *comprehensive*.

A box displays around the word with a drop-down arrow on the right.

f. Click the drop-down arrow to display the menu and click **Insert**.

The word *comprehensive* replaces the word in the document.

Step 5
Use the Research Tool

Refer to Figure 1.43 to complete Step 5.

a. Place the insertion point in the Search for text box and type **browser**.

b. Click the drop-down arrow on the **Reference** list, which currently displays the Thesaurus.

The list of reference sites displays.

c. Click **Encarta Encyclopedia: English (North American)** option.

A definition of the browser displays in the results box.

d. Click the **Close** button on the Research title bar.

The Research pane closes.

The World Wide Web

By Linda Ericksen

The idea of a comprehensive computer network that would allow communication among users of various computers developed over time. These developments brought together the network of networks known as the Internet, which included both technological developments and the merging together of existing network infrastructure and telecommunication systems. This network provides users with email, chat, file transfer, Web pages and other files.

History of Internet

In 1957, the Soviet Union launched the first satellite, Sputnik I, triggering President Dwight Eisenhower to create the ARPA agency to regain the technological lead in the arms race. Practical implementations of a large computer network began during the late 1960's and 1970's. By the 1980's, technologies we now recognize as the basis of the modern Internet began to spread over the globe.

In 1990, ARPANET was replaced by NSFNET which connected universities in North America, and later research facilities in Europe were added. Use of the Internet exploded after 1990, causing the US Government to transfer management to independent organizations.

The World Wide Web

The World Wide Web was developed in the 1980's in Europe and then rapidly spread around the world. The World Wide Web is a set of linked documents on computers connected by the Internet. These documents make use of hyperlinks to link documents together. To use hyperlinks, browser software was developed.

Browsers

The first widely used web browser was Mosaic, and the programming team went on to develop the first commercial web browser called Netscape Navigator. The Netscape browser led in user share until Microsoft Internet Explorer took the lead in 1999.

Figure 1.43 Language Tools Improved the Document

Step 6
Apply Font Attributes

Refer to Figure 1.44 as you complete Steps 6 and 7.

a. Select the title of the document.

   The Mini toolbar displays.

b. Click **Bold** on the Mini toolbar, and then click outside the title.

   TROUBLESHOOTING: If the Mini toolbar is hard to read, remember to point to it to make it display fully.

   The text changes to boldface.

c. Select the title again and click the drop-down arrow on the **Font** command in the Font group on the Home tab.

   The list of fonts displays.

d. Point to font names on the list.

   Live Preview changes the font of the selected sentence to display the fonts you point to.

e. Scroll down, and then select the **Lucinda Bright** font by clicking on the name.

   The title changes to the new font.

f. With the title still selected, click the drop-down arrow on the **Font Size** command and select **16**.

   The title changes to font size 16.

g. Select the byline that contains the author's name and click the **Underline** command, the **Italic** command, and the **Shrink Font** command once. All are located in the Font group on the Home tab.

   The author's byline displays underlined, in italic, and one font size smaller.

h. Select the first heading *History of Internet* and click the **Font Color** down arrow command in the Font group on the Home tab. When the colors display, under Standard Colors, choose **Purple**, and then click outside the selected text.

   The heading displays in purple.

i. Select the heading you just formatted as purple text and click **Bold**.

Step 7
Use Format Painter

Refer to Figure 1.44 to complete Step 7.

a. Click the **Format Painter** command in the Clipboard group on the Home tab.

The pointer changes to a small paintbrush.

b. Select the second unformatted heading and repeat the process to format the third unformatted heading.

The Format Painter formats that heading as purple and bold and automatically turns off.

c. Press **Ctrl** while you click the last sentence in the document and click the **Dialog Box Launcher** in the Font group.

d. Select **Bold** in the Font style box and **Double strikethrough** in the *Effects* section of the dialog box, then click **OK**.

e. Click outside the selected sentence to remove the selection and view the effects, and then click back in the formatted text.

The sentence displays bold with two lines through the text. The Bold command in the Font group on the Home tab displays with a gold background.

f. Select the same sentence again, click **Bold** in the Font group on the Home tab, and then click outside the sentence.

The Bold format has been removed from the text.

g. Click **Save** on the Quick Access Toolbar.

The document is saved under the same name.

h. To exit Word, click the **Office Button**, and then click the **Exit Word** button.

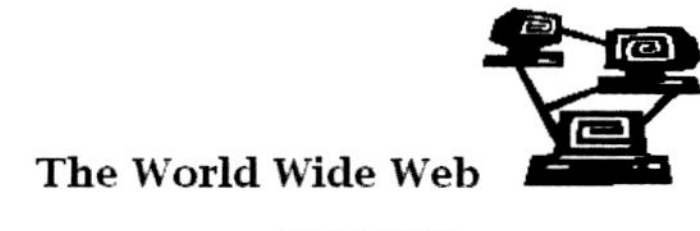

The World Wide Web

By Linda Ericksen

The idea of a big computer network that would allow communication among users of various computers developed over time. These developments brought together the network of networks known as the Internet, which included both technological developments and the merging together of existing network infrastructure and telecommunication systems. This network provides users with email, chat, file transfer, Web pages and other files.

History of Internet

In 1957, the Soviet Union launched the first satellite, Sputnik I, triggering President Dwight Eisenhower to create the ARPA agency to regain the technological lead in the arms race. Practical implementations of a large computer network began during the late 1960's and 1970's. By the 1980's, technologies we now recognize as the basis of the modern Internet began to spread over the globe.

In 1990, ARPANET was replaced by NSFNET which connected universities in North America, and later research facilities in Europe were added. Use of the Internet exploded after 1990, causing the US Government to transfer management to independent organizations.

The World Wide Web

The World Wide Web was developed in the 1980's in Europe and then rapidly spread around the world. The World Wide Web is a set of linked documents on computers connected by the Internet. These documents make use of hyperlinks to link documents together. To use hyperlinks, browser software was developed.

Browsers

The first widely used web browser was Mosaic, and the programming team went on to develop the first commercial web browser called Netscape Navigator. ~~The Netscape browser led in user share until Microsoft Internet Explorer took the lead in 1999.~~

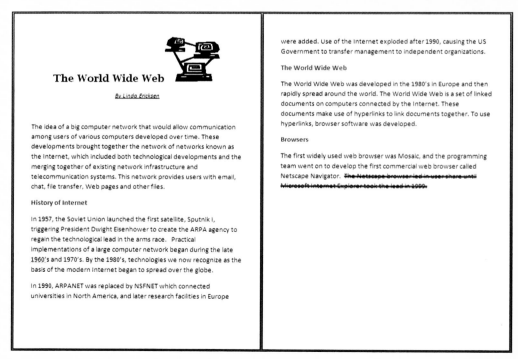

Figure 1.44 Formatted Document

Summary

1. **Identify common interface components.** You learned to identify and use the common elements of the Office 2007 interface and apply them in Word, PowerPoint, Excel, and Access. The top of the application window contains the Office Button that, when clicked, displays the Office menu. The Quick Access Toolbar provides commonly used commands, such as Save and Undo. The primary command center is the Ribbon, which contains tabs to organize major tasks. Each tab contains groups of related commands. The bottom of the window contains a status bar that gives general information, view options, and the Zoom slider.
2. **Use Office 2007 Help.** When you need help to continue working with Office 2007, you can use the Help feature from your computer or get help at Microsoft Office Online. You can position the mouse pointer on a command to see an Enhanced ScreenTip. You can click some Enhanced ScreenTips to display help. You can get context-sensitive help by clicking Help within dialog boxes.
3. **Open a file.** To retrieve a file you have previously saved, you use the Open command. When you open a file, it is copied into RAM so that you can view and work on it.
4. **Save a file.** As you create and edit documents, you should save your work for future use. Use the Save or Save As command to save a file for the first time, giving it a name and location. To continue saving changes to the same file name, use Save. To assign a new name, location, or file type, use Save As.
5. **Print a document.** Producing a perfect hard copy of the document is an important task, and you can make it easier by previewing, selecting options, and printing. You can select the printer, how many copies to print, and the pages you want to print. In addition, each program has specific print options.
6. **Select text to edit.** In order to edit text, you have to identify the body of text you want to work with by selecting it first. You can select text by using the mouse.
7. **Insert text and change to the Overtype mode.** To edit text in the document, you need to be able to insert text and to replace text by typing over it. The Insert mode inserts text without deleting existing text. The Overtype mode types over existing text as you type.
8. **Move and copy text.** You can move text from one location to another to achieve a better flow in a document, worksheet, or presentation. You can use the Copy command to duplicate data in one location and use the Paste command to place the duplicate in another location.
9. **Find, replace, and go to text.** Another editing feature that can save you time is to find text by searching for it or going directly to a specific element in the document. You can also replace text that needs updating.
10. **Use the Undo and Redo commands.** If you make a mistake and want to undo it, you can easily remedy it by using the Undo feature. Likewise, to save time, you can repeat the last action with the Redo command.
11. **Use language tools.** Office 2007 provides tools to help you create and edit error-free documents. You can use the spelling check and grammar check, the built-in thesaurus, and even conduct research all from your Word document. You can check spelling and conduct research in Excel and PowerPoint as well.
12. **Apply font attributes.** Applying font formats can help make the message clearer. For example, you can select a different font to achieve a different look. In addition, you can adjust the font size and change the font color of text. Other font attributes include bold, underline, and italic.
13. **Copy formats with the Format Painter.** You might want to copy the format of text to another location or to several locations in the document. You can easily accomplish that with the Format Painter.

Key Terms

Clipboard 35
Command 6
Contextual tab 8
Copy 34
Cut 34
Dialog box 7
Dialog Box Launcher 7
Duplex printer 27
Enhanced ScreenTip 11
Find 36
Font 44
Format Painter 47
Formatting text 43
Gallery 7
Go To 36
Group 6
Insert 32
Insertion point 18
Key Tip 8
Landscape orientation 25
Live Preview 7
Macro 23
Manual duplex 27
Mini toolbar 31
Office Button 4
Office menu 4
Overtype mode 33
Paste 34
Portrait orientation 25
Presentation graphics software 3
Quick Access Toolbar 5
Redo 39
Relational database software 3
Repeat 39
Replace 36
Ribbon 6
Shortcut menu 24
Spreadsheet software 3
Status bar 8
Tab 6
Template 23
Title bar 5
Undo 39
User interface 4
Virus checker 23
Word processing software 3
Zoom slider 9

Multiple Choice

1. Software that is used primarily with text to create, edit, and format documents is known as:
   (a) Electronic spreadsheet software
   (b) Word processing software
   (c) Presentation graphics software
   (d) Relational database software

2. Which Office feature displays when you rest the mouse pointer on a command?
   (a) The Ribbon
   (b) The status bar
   (c) An Enhanced ScreenTip
   (d) A dialog box

3. What is the name of the blinking vertical line in a document that designates the current location in the document?
   (a) A command
   (b) Overtype mode
   (c) Insert mode
   (d) Insertion point

4. If you wanted to locate every instance of text in a document and have it temporarily highlighted, which command would you use?
   (a) Find
   (b) Replace
   (c) Go To
   (d) Spell Check

5. The meeting point between computer software and the person using it is known as:
   (a) A file
   (b) Software
   (c) A template
   (d) An interface

6. Which of the following is true about the Office Ribbon?
   (a) The Ribbon displays at the bottom of the screen.
   (b) The Ribbon is only available in the Word 2007 application.
   (c) The Ribbon is the main component of the Office 2007 interface.
   (d) The Ribbon cannot be used for selecting commands.

7. Which element of the Ribbon looks like folder tabs and provides commands that are task oriented?
   (a) Groups
   (b) Tabs
   (c) Status bar
   (d) Galleries

8. Which Office 2007 element provides commands that work with an entire document or file and displays by default in the title bar?
   (a) Galleries
   (b) Ribbon
   (c) Office Button
   (d) Groups

9. If you needed the entire screen to read a document, which document view would you use?
   (a) Outline view
   (b) Draft view
   (c) Print Layout
   (d) Full Screen Reading

10. The default four-letter extension for Word documents that do not contain macros is:
    (a) .docx
    (b) .pptx
    (c) .xlsx
    (d) .dotm

11. Before you can cut or copy text, you must first do which one of the following?
    (a) Preview the document.
    (b) Save the document.
    (c) Select the text.
    (d) Undo the previous command.

12. What is the name of the memory location that holds up to twenty-four items for you to paste into the current document, another document, or another application?
    (a) My Places bar
    (b) My Documents
    (c) Ribbon
    (d) Clipboard

Multiple Choice Continued...

13. Word flags misspelled words by marking them with which one of the following?

(a) A green wavy underline
(b) Boldfacing them
(c) A red wavy underline
(d) A double-underline in black

14. Which of the following displays when you select text in a document?

(a) The Mini toolbar
(b) The Quick Access Toolbar
(c) A shortcut menu
(d) The Ribbon

15. Formatting text allows you to change which of the following text attributes?

(a) The font
(b) The font size
(c) The font type
(d) All of the above

Practice Exercises

1 Using Help and Print Preview in Access 2007

a. Open Access. Click the **Office Button**, and then select **Open**. Use the Look in feature to find the *chap1_pe1* database, and then click **Open**.
b. At the right side of the Ribbon, click the **Help** button. In the Help window, type **table** in the **Type words to search for** box. Click the **Search** button.
c. Click the topic *Create tables in a database*. Browse the content of the Help window, and then click the **Close** button in the Help window.
d. Double-click the **Courses table** in the left pane. The table opens in Datasheet view.
e. Click the **Office Button**, point to the arrow after the **Print** command, and select **Print Preview** to open the Print Preview window with the Courses table displayed.
f. Point the mouse pointer on the table and click to magnify the display. Compare your screen to Figure 1.45.
g. Click the **Close Print Preview** button on the Print Preview tab.
h. Click the **Office Button**, and then click the **Exit Access button**.

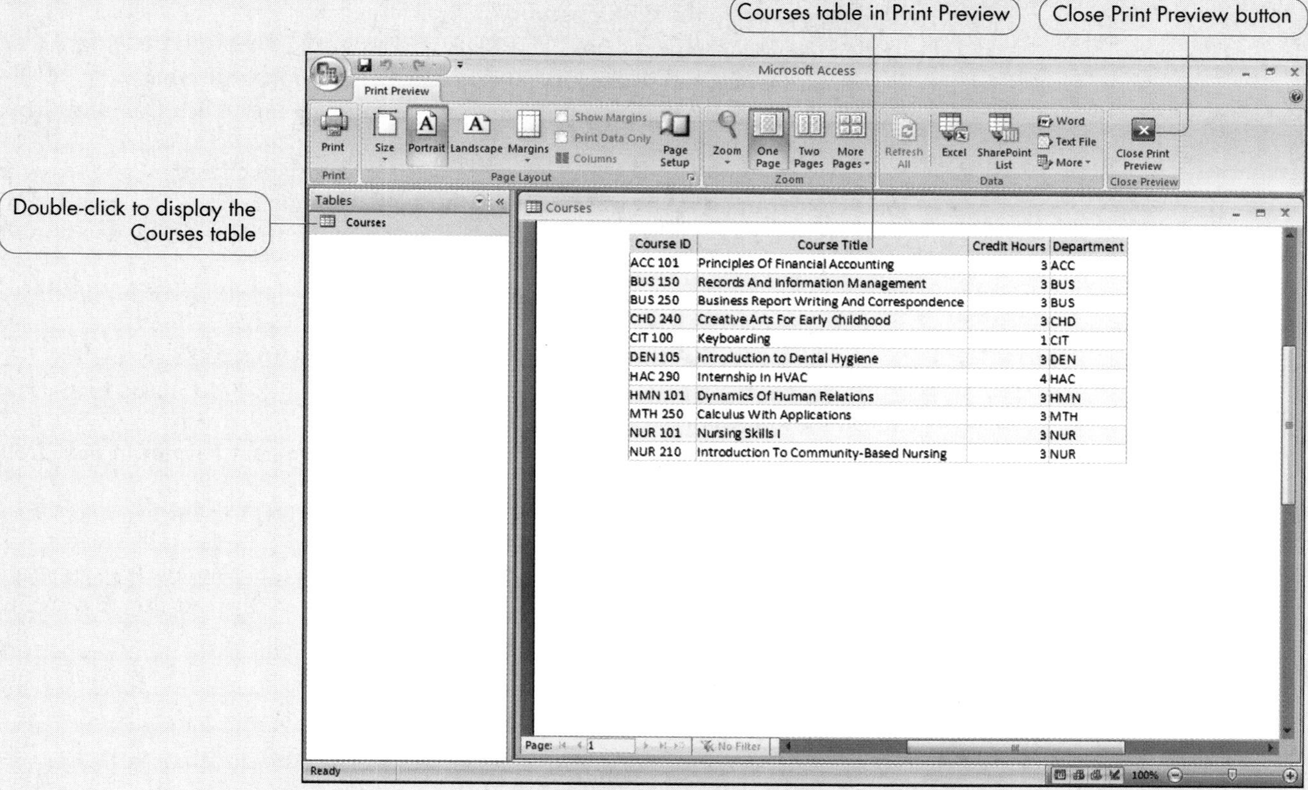

Figure 1.45 Access Print Preview

...continued on Next Page

2 Avoiding Fraud Report

As part of your Introduction to Computers course, you have prepared an oral report on phishing. You want to provide class members with a handout that summarizes the main points of your report. This handout is in the rough stages, so you need to edit it, and you also realize that you can format some of the text to emphasize the main points.

a. Start Word. Click the **Office Button**, and then select **Open**. Use the *Look in* feature to find the *chap1_pe2* document, and then click **Open**.
b. Click the **Office Button**, and then select **Save As**. In the *File name* box, type the document name, **chap1_pe2_solution**, be sure that Word document displays in the *Save as type* box, and use the *Look in* option to move to the location where you save your class files. Click **Save**.
c. In the document, click after the word Name and type **your name**.
d. Select your name, and then click **Bold** and **Italic** on the Mini toolbar—remember to point to the Mini toolbar to make it display fully. Your name displays in bold and italic.
e. Move the insertion point immediately before the title of the document and click the **Replace** button in the Editing group on the Home tab.
f. In the *Find what* box of the Find and Replace dialog box, type **internet**.
g. In the *Replace with* box of the Find and Replace dialog box, type **email**.
h. Click the **Replace All** button to have Word replace the text. Click **OK**, and then click **Close** to close the dialog boxes.
i. To format the title of the document, first select it, and then click the **Font arrow** in the Font group on the Home tab to display the available fonts.
j. Scroll down and choose the **Impact** font if you have it; otherwise, use one that is available.
k. Place the insertion point in the word *Phishng*. Right-click the word, and then click **Phishing** from the shortcut menu.
l. To emphasize important text in the list, double-click the first **NOT** to select it.
m. Click the **Font Color** arrow and select Red, and then click **Bold** in the Font group on the Home tab to apply bold to the text.
n. With the first instance of NOT selected, double-click **Format Painter** in the Clipboard group on the Home tab.
o. Double-click the second and then the third instance of **NOT** in the list, and then press **Esc** on the keyboard to turn off the Format Painter.
p. Compare your document to Figure 1.46. Save by clicking **Save** on the Quick Access Toolbar. Close the document and exit Word or proceed to the next step to preview and print the document.

...continued on Next Page

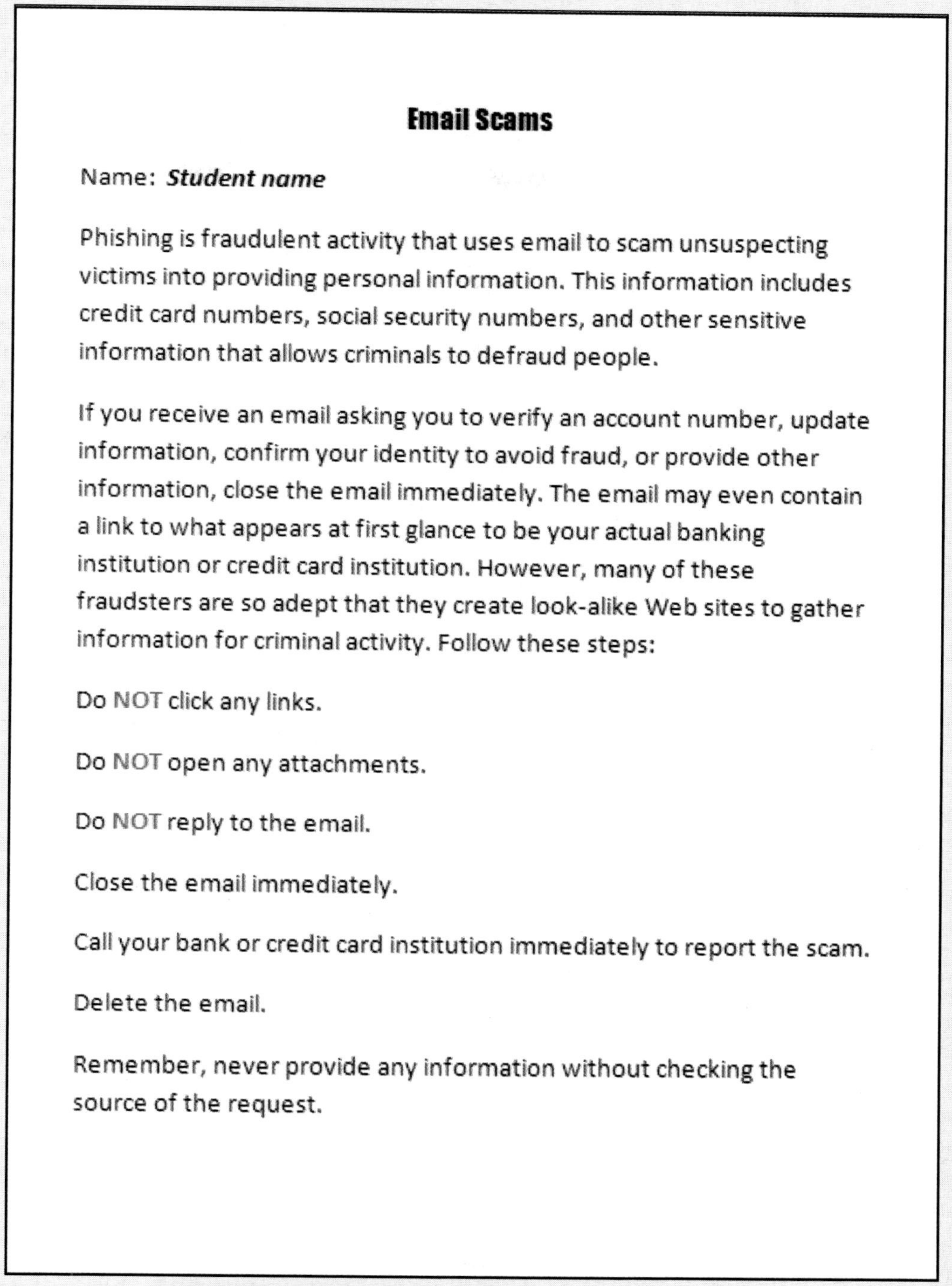

Email Scams

Name: ***Student name***

Phishing is fraudulent activity that uses email to scam unsuspecting victims into providing personal information. This information includes credit card numbers, social security numbers, and other sensitive information that allows criminals to defraud people.

If you receive an email asking you to verify an account number, update information, confirm your identity to avoid fraud, or provide other information, close the email immediately. The email may even contain a link to what appears at first glance to be your actual banking institution or credit card institution. However, many of these fraudsters are so adept that they create look-alike Web sites to gather information for criminal activity. Follow these steps:

Do NOT click any links.

Do NOT open any attachments.

Do NOT reply to the email.

Close the email immediately.

Call your bank or credit card institution immediately to report the scam.

Delete the email.

Remember, never provide any information without checking the source of the request.

Figure 1.46 Phishing Document

3 Previewing and Printing a Document

You created a handout to accompany your oral presentation in the previous exercise. Now you want to print it out so that you can distribute it.

a. If necessary, open the *chap1_pe2_solution* document that you saved in the previous exercise.
b. Click the **Office Button**, point to the arrow after the Print command, and select **Print Preview** to open the Print Preview window with the document displayed.

...continued on Next Page

c. Point the mouse pointer in the document and click to magnify the display. Click the mouse pointer a second time to reduce the display.
d. To change the orientation of the document, click **Orientation** in the Page Setup group and choose **Landscape**.
e. Click **Undo** on the Quick Access Toolbar to undo the last command, which returns the document to portrait orientation. Compare your results to the zoomed document in Figure 1.47.
f. Click **Print** on the Print Preview tab to display the Print dialog box.
g. Click **OK** to print the document.
h. Close the document without saving it.

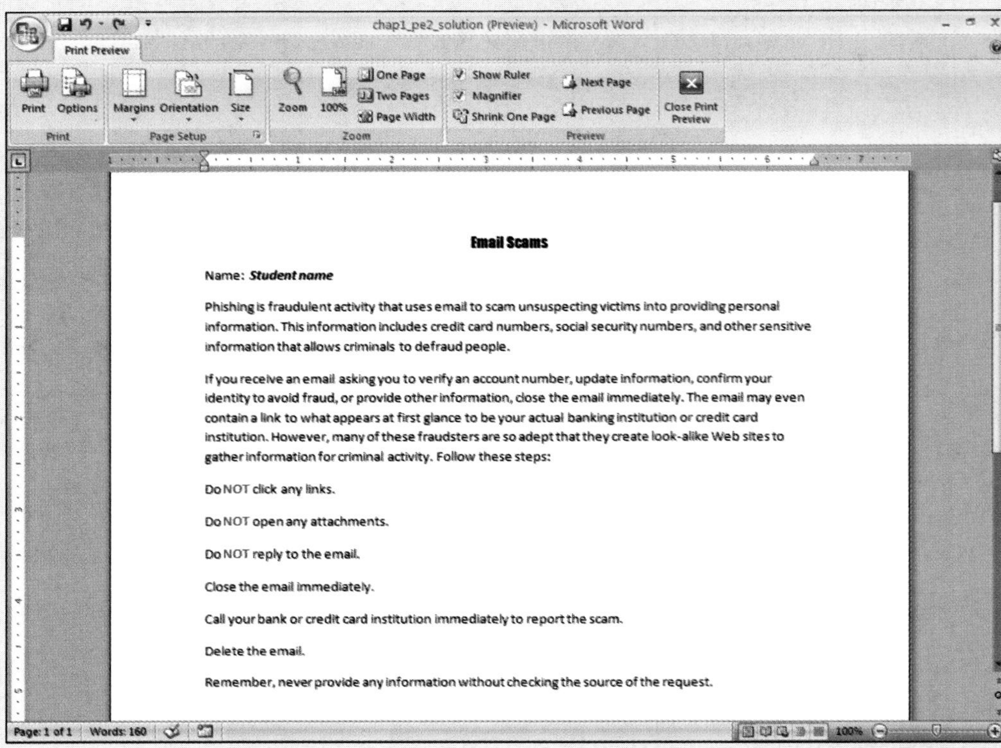

Figure 1.47 Document in Print Preview Window

4 Editing a Promotion Flyer

You work for Business Express, formerly known as Print Express, a regional company specializing in business centers that design and produce documents for local businesses and individuals. Business Express has just undergone a major transition along with a name change. Your job is to edit and refine an existing flyer to inform customers of the new changes. Proceed as follows:

a. Open Word. Click the **Office Button**, and then select **Open**. Use the *Look in* feature to find the *chap1_pe4* document.
b. Click the **Office Button** again and select **Save As**. Type the document name, **chap1_pe4_solution**, be sure that Word document displays in the *Save as type* box, and use the *Look in* option to move to the location where you save your class files.
c. Place the insertion point at the beginning of the document, and then click **Spelling & Grammar** in the Proofing group on the Review tab to open the Spelling and Grammar dialog box.
d. Click the **Change** button three times to correct the spelling errors. Click **OK** to close the completion box.

...continued on Next Page

e. Place the insertion point at the end of the first sentence of the document—just before the period. To insert the following text, press **Spacebar** and type **that offers complete business solutions**.

f. Place the insertion point in *good* in the first sentence of the third paragraph and right-click the mouse.

g. Point to **Synonyms**, and then click **first-rate** to replace the word in the document.

h. Place the insertion point in *bigger* in the last sentence of the third paragraph and click **Thesaurus** in the Proofing group on the Review tab. Point to **superior** and click the drop-down arrow that displays. Click **Insert** from the menu to replace the word in the document, and then click the **Close** button on the Thesaurus.

i. Select the last full paragraph of the document and click **Cut** in the Clipboard group on the Home tab to remove the paragraph from the document.

j. Place the insertion point at the beginning of the new last paragraph and click **Paste** in the Clipboard group on the Home tab to display the text.

k. Click **Undo** on the Quick Access Toolbar twice to undo the paste operation and to undo the cut operation—placing the text back in its original location.

l. Place the insertion point after the colon at the bottom of the document and type **your name**.

m. Compare your results to Figure 1.48, and then save and close the document.

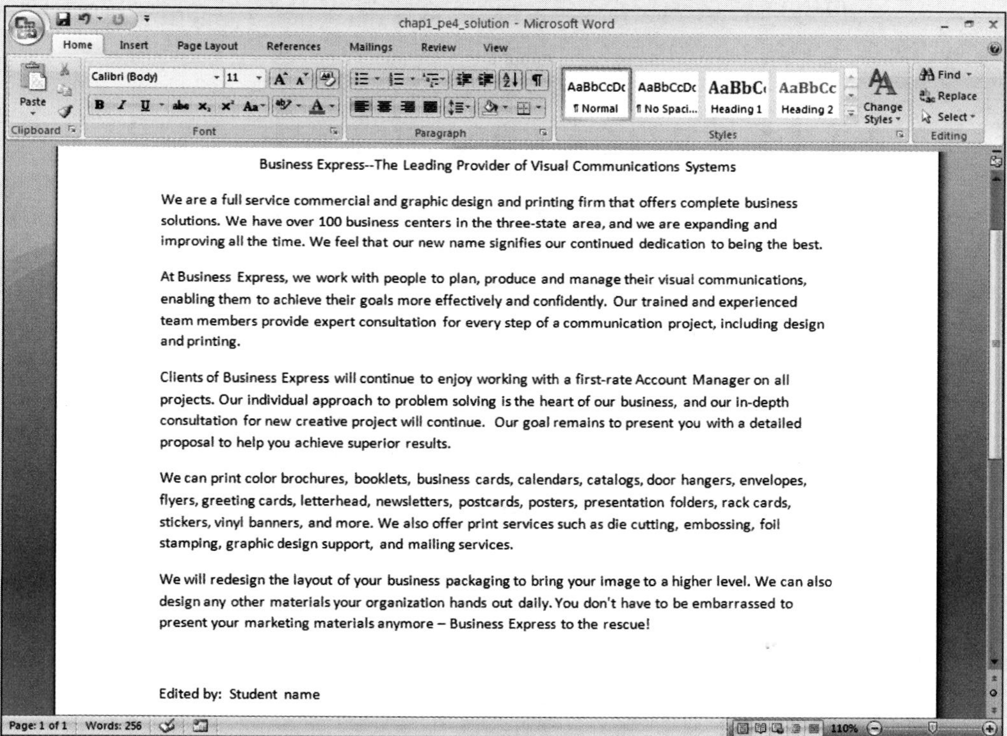

Business Express--The Leading Provider of Visual Communications Systems

We are a full service commercial and graphic design and printing firm that offers complete business solutions. We have over 100 business centers in the three-state area, and we are expanding and improving all the time. We feel that our new name signifies our continued dedication to being the best.

At Business Express, we work with people to plan, produce and manage their visual communications, enabling them to achieve their goals more effectively and confidently. Our trained and experienced team members provide expert consultation for every step of a communication project, including design and printing.

Clients of Business Express will continue to enjoy working with a first-rate Account Manager on all projects. Our individual approach to problem solving is the heart of our business, and our in-depth consultation for new creative project will continue. Our goal remains to present you with a detailed proposal to help you achieve superior results.

We can print color brochures, booklets, business cards, calendars, catalogs, door hangers, envelopes, flyers, greeting cards, letterhead, newsletters, postcards, posters, presentation folders, rack cards, stickers, vinyl banners, and more. We also offer print services such as die cutting, embossing, foil stamping, graphic design support, and mailing services.

We will redesign the layout of your business packaging to bring your image to a higher level. We can also design any other materials your organization hands out daily. You don't have to be embarrassed to present your marketing materials anymore – Business Express to the rescue!

Edited by: Student name

Figure 1.48 Business Flyer

Mid-Level Exercises

1 Updating a Training Document

Your position as trainer for a large building supply company involves training all new employees. It is your job to familiarize new employees with the services provided by Castle Home Building Supply. You distribute a list at the training session and you realize that it needs updating before the next session, so you decide to edit and format it.

a. Start Word. Open the *chap1_mid1* file and save it as **chap1_mid1_solution**.

b. Change the title font to Arial Rounded MT Bold size 16 and change the font color to dark brown.

c. Make the subtitle Arial Unicode MS and italic.

d. Cut the item *Help with permits* and make it the second item on the list.

e. In the first list item, insert **and** after the word *fair*.

f. Change the word *help* in the last list item to **Assistance**.

g. Select the list of items excluding the heading, Services Provided.

h. Bold the list and change the font size to 16.

i. Save the document and compare it to Figure 1.49.

Castle Home Building Supply

Where the Customer Comes First

Services Provided:

Fair and accurate estimates

Help with permits

Free delivery on all orders over $100

Design help

Professional Installation available

Custom work

Professional assistance

New building and renovations

Assistance with inspections

Figure 1.49 Training Document

...continued on Next Page

2 Formatting a Menu

The owner of the Bayside Restaurant wants your help formatting his menu so that it is more pleasing to customers; follow the steps below:

a. Open the *chap1_mid2* document and save it as **chap1_mid2_solution**.

b. Format the menu title as Broadway size 16.

c. Format the three headings: Appetizers, Soups and Salads, and Lunch or Dinner Anytime! as Bodoni MT Black, size 12, and change the font color to Dark Red. Remember to format the first one and use the Format Painter for the second two headings.

d. Format all the dish names, such as Nachos, using the Outline Font Effects.

e. Bold all the prices in the document.

f. Preview the document, compare to Figure 1.50, and then print it.

g. Save and close the document.

Bayside Menu - Great Food & Prices!

APPETIZERS

NACHOS: tri-color tortilla chips, melted cheddar cheese topped with tomato, onion and jalapeno **$ 9.00**

CHICKEN WINGS: baked, served with celery sticks and blue cheese dip **$ 9.00**

MOZZARELLA STICKS: baked, then served with a hearty marinara sauce **$ 9.00**

CRAB & ARTICHOKE DIP: a creamy blend of artichoke hearts, lump meat crab meat and cheese, served with toasted bread **$ 12.00**

STEAMED SHRIMP: half-pound of extra large shrimp, served with cocktail sauce **$14.00**

SOUPS and SALADS

CHILE: beef and bean chili with tortilla chips on the side **$ 7.00**

HOUSE SALAD: mixed greens and garden vegetables **$ 5.00**

LUNCH or DINNER ANYTIME!

CRAB CAKE SANDWICH: jumbo crab meat on a toasted roll served with chips and dip **$ 15.00**

CLASSIC CLUB: turkey, ham, cheddar and provolone cheese, bacon, lettuce, tomato and mayo on toasted bread, served with chips and dip **$ 10.00**

DOUBLE BURGER: half-pound Black Angus beef burger, cooked the way you order it, topped with American cheese, bacon, onion, lettuce and tomato on a toasted roll with French fries **$ 11.00**

BBQ PULLED PORK SANDWICH: pulled pork with BBQ sauce served on a toasted roll with chips **$ 10.00**

SWISS CHICKEN: breast topped with Swiss cheese, bacon and tomato with ranch dressing, served on a toasted roll and French fries **$ 10.00**

TURKEY WRAP: sliced turkey breast, lettuce, tomato and mayo, rolled on a flour tortilla, served with chips and dip **$ 10.00**

RUEBEN: corned beef, sauerkraut, Swiss cheese and Russian dressing on toasted rye, served with French fries **$ 10.00**

CHICKEN TENDERS: breaded and baked just right, served with BBQ sauce, honey mustard and French Fries **$ 10.00**

ITALIAN PIZZA: mozzarella, pepperoni, and marinara **$ 8.00**

Figure 1.50 The Formatted Menu

...continued on Next Page

3 Enhance the Insurance Letter

Your job duties at Health First Insurance, Inc., involve maintaining the correspondence. You need to update the welcome letter you send to clients to reflect the company's new name, new address, and other important elements, and then address it to a new client. Proceed as follows.

a. Open the *chap1_mid3* document and save it as **chap1_mid3_solution**.

b. Run the Spelling check to eliminate the errors.

c. Use Replace to change **University Insurance, Inc**. to **Health First Insurance, Inc**. throughout the letter.

d. Change the Address from **123 Main St**. to **1717 N. Zapata Way**.

e. Change the inside address that now has **Client name, Client Address, Client City, State and Zip Code** to **your name and complete address**. Also change the salutation to your name.

f. Move the first paragraph so that it becomes the last paragraph in the body of the letter.

g. Preview the letter to be sure that it fits on one page, compare it with Figure 1.51, and then print it.

h. Save and close the document.

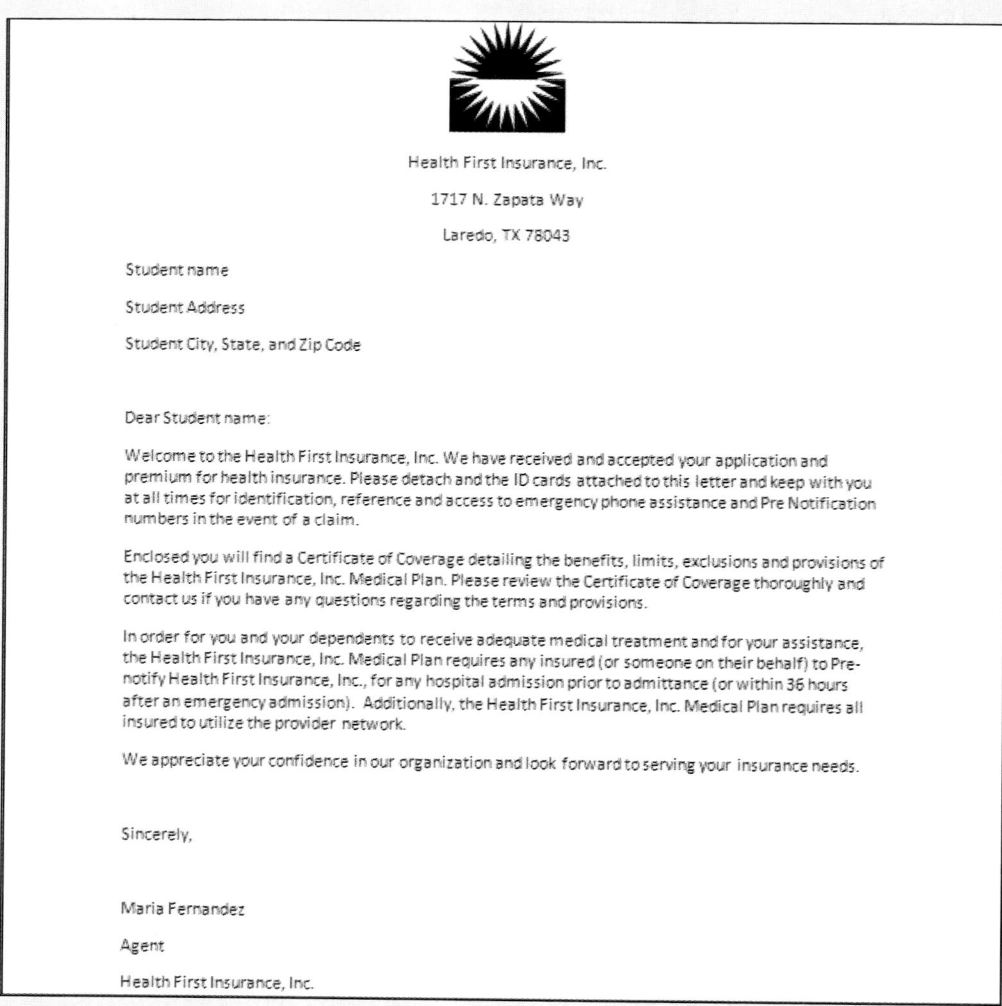

Health First Insurance, Inc.

1717 N. Zapata Way

Laredo, TX 78043

Student name

Student Address

Student City, State, and Zip Code

Dear Student name:

Welcome to the Health First Insurance, Inc. We have received and accepted your application and premium for health insurance. Please detach and the ID cards attached to this letter and keep with you at all times for identification, reference and access to emergency phone assistance and Pre Notification numbers in the event of a claim.

Enclosed you will find a Certificate of Coverage detailing the benefits, limits, exclusions and provisions of the Health First Insurance, Inc. Medical Plan. Please review the Certificate of Coverage thoroughly and contact us if you have any questions regarding the terms and provisions.

In order for you and your dependents to receive adequate medical treatment and for your assistance, the Health First Insurance, Inc. Medical Plan requires any insured (or someone on their behalf) to Pre-notify Health First Insurance, Inc., for any hospital admission prior to admittance (or within 36 hours after an emergency admission). Additionally, the Health First Insurance, Inc. Medical Plan requires all insured to utilize the provider network.

We appreciate your confidence in our organization and look forward to serving your insurance needs.

Sincerely,

Maria Fernandez

Agent

Health First Insurance, Inc.

Figure 1.51 The Updated Letter

Capstone Exercise

In this project, you work with a business plan for Far East Trading Company that will be submitted to funding sources in order to secure loans. The document requires editing to polish the final product and formatting to enhance readability and emphasize important information.

Editing the Document

This document is ready for editing, so proceed as follows:

a. Open the *chap1_cap* document. Save the document as **chap1_cap_solution**.

b. Run the Spelling and Grammar check to eliminate all spelling and grammar errors in the document.

c. Use the Thesaurus to find a synonym for the word **unique** in the second paragraph of the document.

d. Use the Go To command to move to page 3 and change the $175,000 to $250,000.

e. Move the entire second section of the document (notice the numbers preceding it) now located at the end of the document to its correct location after the first section.

f. Insert the street **1879 Columbia Ave.** before Portland in the first paragraph.

g. Copy the inserted street address to section 2.3 and place it in front of Portland there also.

h. Replace the initials **FET** with **FETC** for every instance in the document.

i. Type over 1998 in the third paragraph so that it says 2008.

Formatting the Document

Next, you will apply formatting techniques to the document. These format options will further increase the readability and attractiveness of your document.

a. Select the two-line title and change the font to Engravers MT, size 14, and change the color to Dark Red.

b. Select the first heading in the document: 1.0 Executive Summary, then change the font to Gautami, bold, and change the color to Dark Blue.

c. Use the Format Painter to make all the main numbered headings the same formatting, that is 2.0, 3.0, 4.0, and 5.0.

d. The first three numbered sections have subsections such as 1.1, 1.2. Select the heading 1.1 and format it for bold, italic, and change the color to a lighter blue—Aqua, Accents, Darker 25%.

e. Use the Format Painter to make all the numbered subsections the same formatting.

Printing the Document

To finish the job, you need to print the business plan.

a. Preview the document to check your results.

b. Print the document.

c. Save your changes and close the document.

Mini Cases

Use the rubric following the case as a guide to evaluate our work, but keep in mind that your instructor may impose additional grading criteria or use a different standard to judge your work.

A Thank-You Letter

GENERAL CASE

As the new volunteer coordinator for Special Olympics in your area, you need to send out information for prospective volunteers, and the letter you were given needs editing and formatting. Open the *chap1_mc1* document and make necessary changes to improve the appearance. You should use Replace to change the text (insert your state name), use the current date and your name and address information, format to make the letter more appealing, and eliminate all errors. Your finished document should be saved as **chap1_mc1_solution**.

Performance Elements	Exceeds Expectations	Meets Expectations	Below Expectations
Corrected all errors	Document contains no errors.	Document contains minimal errors.	Document contains several errors.
Use of character formatting features such as font, font Size, font color, or other attributes	Used character formatting options throughout entire document.	Used character formatting options in most sections of document.	Used character formatting options on a small portion of document.
Inserted text where instructed	The letter is complete with all required information inserted.	The letter is mostly complete.	Letter is incomplete.

The Information Request Letter

RESEARCH CASE

Search the Internet for opportunities to teach abroad or for internships available in your major. Have fun finding a dream opportunity. Use the address information you find on the Web site that interests you, and compose a letter asking for additional information. For example, you might want to teach English in China, so search for that information. Your finished document should be saved as **chap1_mc2_solution**.

Performance Elements	Exceeds Expectations	Meets Expectations	Below Expectations
Use of character formatting	Three or more character formats applied to text.	One or two character formats applied to text.	Does not apply character formats to text.
Language tools	No spelling or grammar errors.	One spelling or grammar error.	More than one spelling or grammar error.
Presentation	Information is easy to read and understand.	Information is somewhat unclear.	Letter is unclear.

Movie Memorabilia

DISASTER RECOVERY

Use the following rubrics to guide your evaluation of your work, but keep in mind that your instructor may impose additional grading criteria.

Open the *chap1_mc3* document that can be found in the Exploring folder. The advertising document is over-formatted, and it contains several errors and problems. For example, the text has been formatted in many fonts that are difficult to read. The light color of the text also has made the document difficult to read. You should improve the formatting so that it is consistent, helps the audience read the document, and is pleasing to look at. Your finished document should be saved as **chap1_mc3_solution**.

Performance Elements	Exceeds Expectations	Meets Expectations	Below Expectations
Type of font chosen to format document	Number and style of fonts appropriate for short document.	Number or style of fonts appropriate for short document.	Overused number of fonts or chose inappropriate font.
Color of font chosen to format document	Appropriate font colors for document.	Most font colors appropriate.	Overuse of font colors.
Overall document appeal	Document looks appealing.	Document mostly looks appealing.	Did not improve document much.

chapter 1 | **Word**

Microsoft Word

What Will Word Processing Do for Me?

After you read this chapter, you will be able to:

1. Understand Word basics **(page 72)**.
2. Use AutoText **(page 76)**.
3. View a document **(page 78)**.
4. Use the Mini toolbar **(page 80)**.
5. Set margins and specify page orientation **(page 87)**.
6. Insert page breaks **(page 88)**.
7. Add page numbers **(page 90)**.
8. Insert headers and footers **(page 91)**.
9. Create sections **(page 92)**.
10. Insert a cover page **(page 93)**.
11. Use Find and Replace commands **(page 94)**.
12. Check spelling and grammar **(page 103)**.
13. Use save and backup options **(page 104)**.
14. Select printing options **(page 107)**.
15. Customize Word **(page 108)**.

Hands-On Exercises

Exercises	Skills Covered
1. INTRODUCTION TO MICROSOFT WORD (page 81) **Open:** chap1_ho1_credit.docx **Save as:** chap1_ho1_credit_solution.docx	• Open and Save a Word Document • Modify the Document • Insert AutoText • Create an AutoText Entry • Change Document Views and Zoom
2. DOCUMENT ORGANIZATION (page 96) **Open:** chap1_ho1_credit_solution.docx (from Exercise 1) **Save as:** chap1_ho2_credit_solution.docx (additional modifications)	• Set Page Margins and Orientation • Insert a Page Break • Add a Cover Page and Insert a Document Header • Insert a Section Break • Insert a Page Number in the Footer • Use Find, Replace, and Go To
3. THE FINAL TOUCHES (page 110) **Open:** chap1_ho2_credit_solution.docx (from Exercise 2) **Save as:** chap1_ho3_credit_solution.docx (additional modifications), chap1_ho3_credit2_solution.docx, and chap1_ho3_credit_solution.doc	• Perform a Spelling and Grammar Check • Run the Document Inspector and a Compatibility Check • Save in a Compatible Format • Change Word Options • Use Print Preview Features

CASE STUDY

A Question of Ethics

You would never walk into a music store, put a CD under your arm, and walk out without paying for it. What if, however, you could download the same CD from the Web for free? Are you hurting anyone? Or what if you gave a clerk a $5 bill, but received change for a $50? Would you return the extra money? Would you speak up if it was the person ahead of you in line who received change for the $50, when you clearly saw that he or she gave the clerk $5? Ethical conflicts occur all the time and result when one person or group benefits at the expense of another.

Case Study

Your Philosophy 101 instructor assigned a class project whereby students are divided into teams to consider questions of ethics and society. Each team is to submit a single document that represents the collective efforts of all the team members. The completed project is to include a brief discussion of ethical principles followed by five examples of ethical conflicts. Every member of the team will receive the same grade, regardless of his or her level of participation; indeed, this might be an ethical dilemma, in and of itself.

Your Assignment

- Read the chapter, paying special attention to sections that describe how to format a document using page breaks, headers and footers, and page numbers.
- Open the *chap1_case_ethics* document, which contains the results of your team's collaboration, but which requires further formatting before you submit it to your professor.
- Create a cover page for the document. Include the name of the report, the team members, and your course name.
- View the document in draft view and remove any unnecessary page breaks.
- Set the margins on your document to a width and height that allows for binding the document.
- Set page numbers for each page of the document except the cover page. The page numbers should display in the center of the footer. Page numbering should begin on the page that follows the cover page.
- Perform a spelling and grammar check on the document, but proofread it also.
- Save your work in a document named **chap1_case_ethics_solution.docx**.
- Run a compatibility check, and then save it also in Word 97–2003 format, as **chap1_case_ethics_solution.doc**, in case your professor, who does not have Office 2007, requests a digital copy.

Introduction to Word Processing

Word processing software is probably the most commonly used type of software. You can create letters, reports, research papers, newsletters, brochures, and other documents with Word. You can even create and send e-mail, produce Web pages, and update blogs with Word.

Word processing software is probably the most commonly used type of software. People around the world—students, office assistants, managers, and professionals in all areas—use word processing programs such as Microsoft Word for a variety of tasks. You can create letters, reports, research papers, newsletters, brochures, and other documents with Word. You can even create and send e-mail, produce Web pages, and update blogs with Word. Figure 1.1 shows examples of documents created in Word.

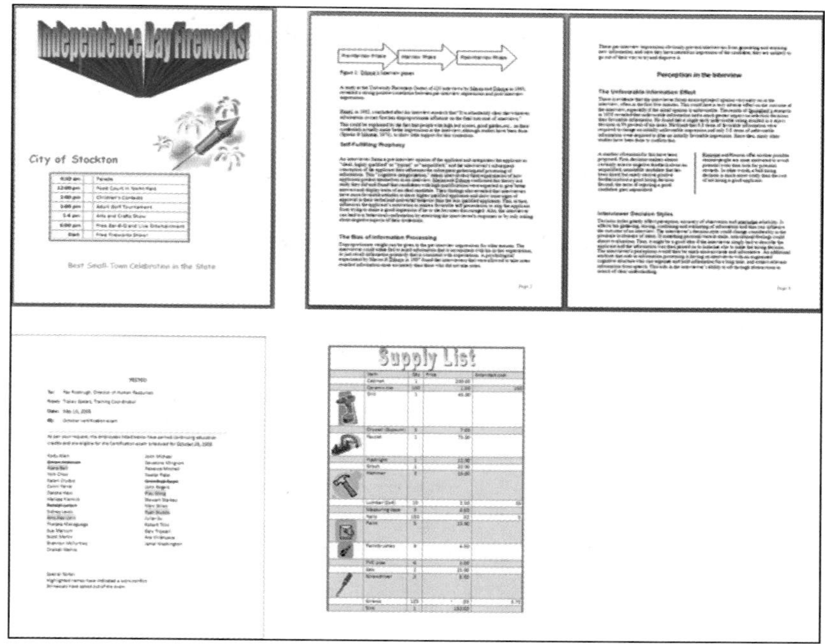

Figure 1.1 The Versatility of Microsoft Word 2007

Microsoft Word provides a multitude of features that enable you to enhance documents with only a few clicks of the mouse. You can change colors, add interesting styles of text, insert graphics, use a table to present data, track changes made to a document, view comments made about document content, combine several documents into one, and quickly create reference pages such as a table of contents, an index, or a bibliography.

This chapter provides a broad-based introduction to word processing in general and Microsoft Word in particular. All word processors adhere to certain basic concepts that must be understood to use the program effectively.

In this section, you learn about the Word interface, word-wrap, and toggles. You learn how to use the AutoText feature to insert text automatically in your document, and then you change document views and learn to use the new Mini toolbar.

Understanding Word Basics

The Exploring series authors used Microsoft Word to write this book. You will use Word to complete the exercises in this chapter. When you start Word, your screen might be different. You will not see the same document shown in Figure 1.2, nor is it likely that you will customize Word in exactly the same way. You should, however, be able to recognize the basic elements that are found in the Microsoft Word window and that are emphasized in Figure 1.2.

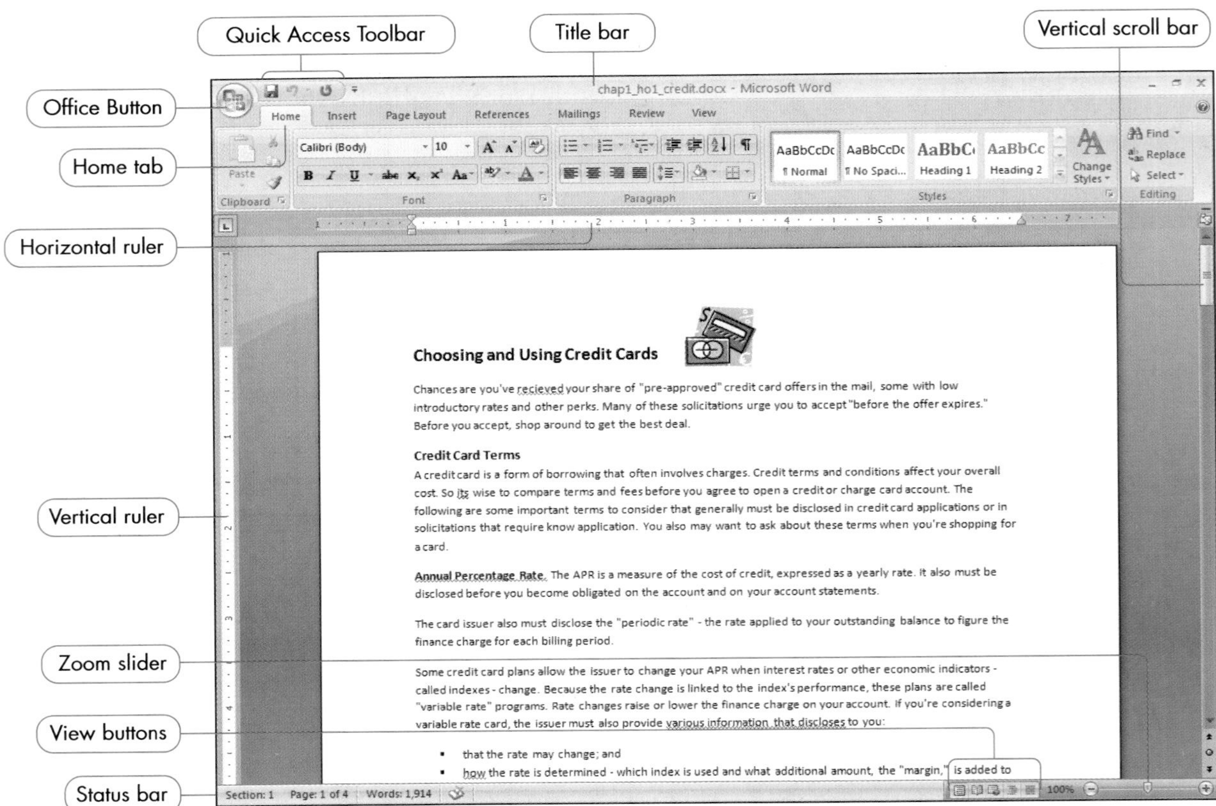

Figure 1.2 The Microsoft Word Window

Figure 1.2 displays two open windows—an application window for Microsoft Word and a document window for the specific document on which you are working. However, only one title bar appears at the top of the application window, and it reflects the application (Microsoft Word) as well as the document name (chap1_ho1_credit.docx). If you want to close the document but not the Word program, click the Office Button and select Close. To close both the document and the application, click Close in the upper-right corner.

The Quick Access Toolbar appears on the left side of the title bar. This toolbar contains commands that are used very frequently, such as Save, Undo, and Repeat. Vertical and horizontal scroll bars appear at the right and bottom of a document window. You use them to view portions of a document that do not display on the screen. Each Microsoft Office application includes the Ribbon, which contains tabs that organize commands into task-oriented groups. The active tab is highlighted, and the commands on that tab display immediately below the title bar. The tab can change according to the current task, or you can display a different tab by clicking the tab name. The tabs in Word are displayed in the Reference on the next two pages.

The status bar at the bottom of the document window displays information about the document such as the section and page where the insertion point is currently positioned, the total number of pages in the document, and the total number of words in the document. At the right side of the status bar, you find command buttons that enable you to quickly change the view and zoom level of the document.

Word Tabs | Reference

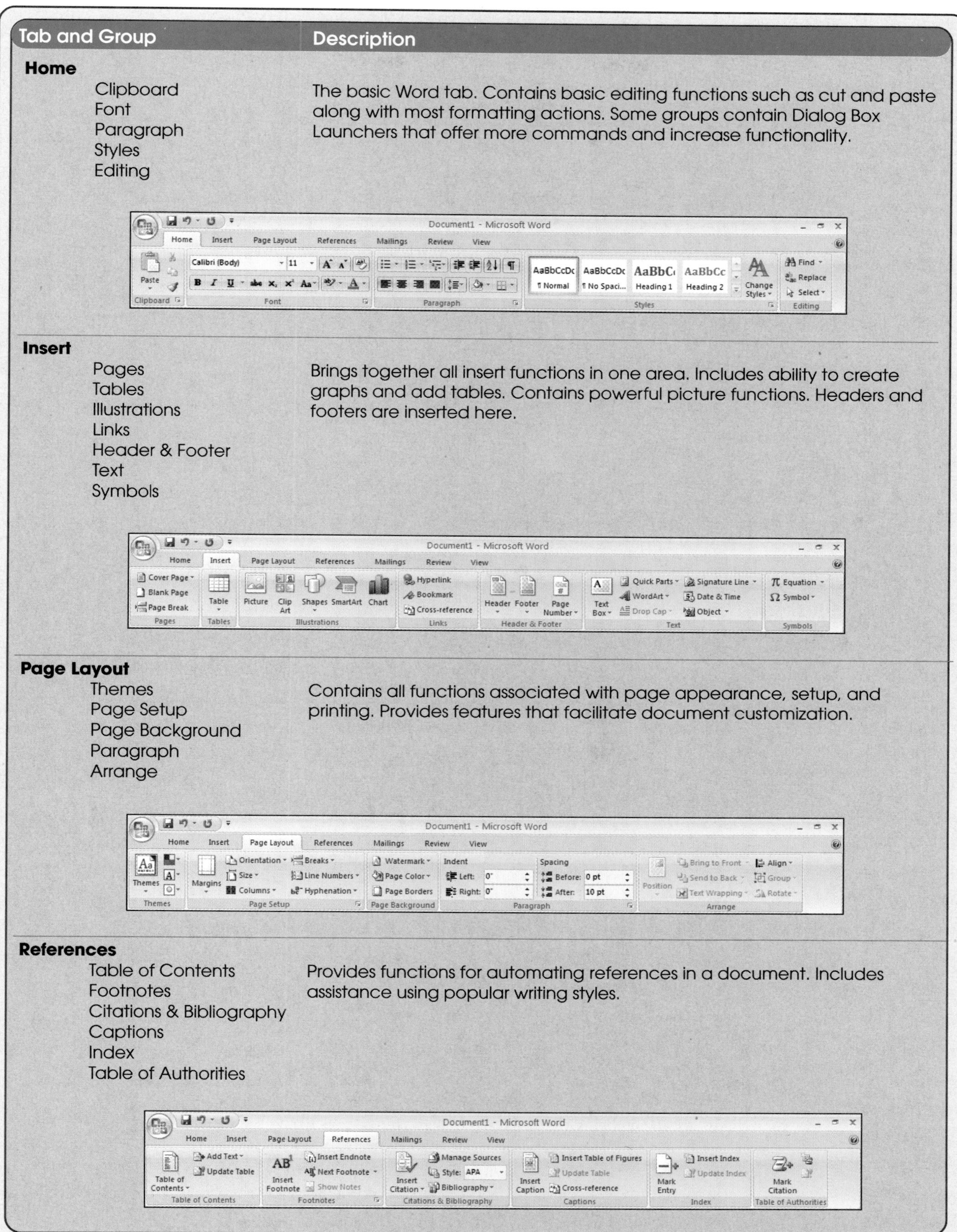

Tab and Group	Description
Home Clipboard Font Paragraph Styles Editing	The basic Word tab. Contains basic editing functions such as cut and paste along with most formatting actions. Some groups contain Dialog Box Launchers that offer more commands and increase functionality.
Insert Pages Tables Illustrations Links Header & Footer Text Symbols	Brings together all insert functions in one area. Includes ability to create graphs and add tables. Contains powerful picture functions. Headers and footers are inserted here.
Page Layout Themes Page Setup Page Background Paragraph Arrange	Contains all functions associated with page appearance, setup, and printing. Provides features that facilitate document customization.
References Table of Contents Footnotes Citations & Bibliography Captions Index Table of Authorities	Provides functions for automating references in a document. Includes assistance using popular writing styles.

Mailings

Create
Start Mail Merge
Write & Insert Fields
Preview Results
Finish

Contains commands used in the process of combining data from multiple sources and providing useful information.

Review

Proofing
Comments
Tracking
Changes
Compare
Protect

Contains all reviewing tools in Word, including spelling and grammatical check, the management of comments, sharing, and protection.

View

Document Views
Show/Hide
Zoom
Window
Macros

Contains basic and advanced view settings. Some of these options also appear below the horizontal and vertical scroll bars.

Learn About Word Wrap

A word processor is a software tool that enables you to document your thoughts or other information. Whether you are new to using a word processor or have been using one for a period of time, you will notice that certain functions seem to happen automatically. As you type, you probably don't think about how much text can fit on one line or where the sentences must roll from one line to the other. Fortunately, the word processor takes care of that for you. This function is called ***word wrap*** and enables you to type continually without pressing Enter at the end of a line within a paragraph. The only time you press Enter is at the end of a paragraph or when you want the insertion point to move to the next line.

Word wrap moves words to the next line if they do not fit on the current line.

Word wrap is closely associated with another concept, that of hard and soft returns. A ***hard return*** is created by the user when he or she presses the Enter key at the end of a line or paragraph; a ***soft return*** is created by the word processor as it wraps text from one line to the next. The locations of the soft returns change automatically as a document is edited (e.g., as text is inserted or deleted, or as margins or fonts are changed). The locations of hard returns can be changed only by the user, who must intentionally insert or delete each hard return.

A ***hard return*** is created when you press Enter to move the insertion point to a new line.

A ***soft return*** is created by the word processor as it wraps text to a new line.

The paragraphs at the top of Figure 1.3 show two hard returns, one at the end of each paragraph. It also includes four soft returns in the first paragraph (one at the end of every line except the last) and three soft returns in the second paragraph. Now suppose the margins in the document are made smaller (that is, the line is made longer), as shown in the bottom paragraphs of Figure 1.3. The number of soft returns drops to three and two (in the first and second paragraphs, respectively) as more text fits on a line and fewer lines are needed. The revised document still contains the two original hard returns, one at the end of each paragraph.

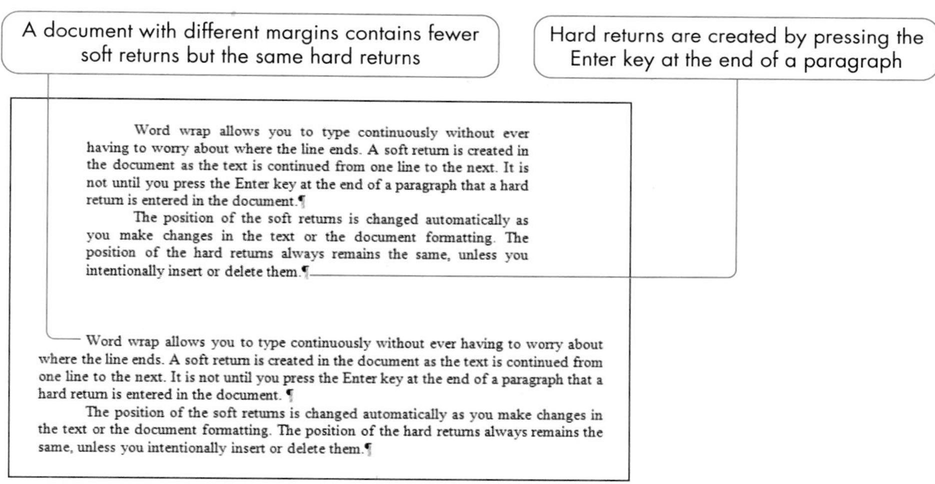

Figure 1.3 Document with Hard and Soft Returns

Use Keyboard Shortcuts to Scroll

The horizontal and vertical scrollbars frequently are used to move around in a document. However, clicking the scroll arrows does not move the insertion point; it merely lets you see different parts of the document in the document window and leaves the insertion point where it was last positioned. You can use the mouse or the keyboard to move the insertion point in a document. Table 1.1 shows useful keyboard shortcuts for moving around in a document and relocating the insertion point.

Table 1.1 Keyboard Scrolling Methods

Key	Moves the Insertion Point . . .	Key	Moves the Insertion Point . . .
Left arrow	one character to the left	Ctrl + Home	to the beginning of the document
Right arrow	one character to the right	Ctrl + End	to the end of the document
Up arrow	up one line	Ctrl + Left arrow	one word to the left
Down arrow	down one line	Ctrl + Right arrow	one word to the right
Home	to the beginning of the line	Ctrl + Up arrow	up one paragraph
End	to the end of the line	Ctrl + Down arrow	down one paragraph
PgUp	up one window or page	Ctrl + Pgup	to the top of the previous page
PgDn	down one window or page	Ctrl + PgDn	to the top of the next page

Discover Toggle Switches

Suppose you sat down at the keyboard and typed an entire sentence without pressing Shift; the sentence would be in all lowercase letters. Then you pressed the Caps Lock key and retyped the sentence, again without pressing the Shift key. This time, the sentence would be in all uppercase letters. Each time you pressed the Caps Lock key, the text you type would switch from lowercase to uppercase and vice versa.

The ***toggle switch*** is a device that causes the computer to alternate between two states.

The point of this exercise is to introduce the concept of a ***toggle switch***, a device that causes the computer to alternate between two states. Caps Lock is an example of a toggle switch. Each time you press it, newly typed text will change from uppercase to lowercase and back again. In the Office Fundamentals chapter, you read about other toggle switches. Some toggle switches are physical keys you press, such as the Insert key (which toggles to Overtype). And some toggle switches are software features such as the Bold, Italic, and Underline commands (which can be clicked to turn on and off).

The ***Show/Hide feature*** reveals where formatting marks such as spaces, tabs, and returns are used in the document.

Another toggle switch that enables you to reveal formatting applied to a document is the ***Show/Hide feature***. Click Show/Hide ¶ in the Paragraph group on the Home tab to reveal where formatting marks such as spaces, tabs, and hard returns are used in the document.

The Backspace and Delete keys delete one character immediately to the left or right of the insertion point, respectively. The choice between them depends on when you need to erase a character(s). The Backspace key is easier if you want to delete a character (or characters) immediately after typing. The Delete key is preferable during subsequent editing.

You can delete several characters at one time by selecting (clicking and dragging the mouse over) the characters to be deleted, then pressing the Delete key. You can delete and replace text in one operation by selecting the text to be replaced and then typing the new text in its place. You can also select a block of text by clicking to place the insertion point in front of the first character, holding down Shift and then clicking to the right of the last character. Double-click a word to select it, and triple-click to select a paragraph. These forms of selecting text enable you to quickly format or delete text.

Using AutoText

The ***AutoText*** feature substitutes a predefined item for specific text but only when the user initiates it.

You learned about the AutoCorrect feature in the Office Fundamentals chapter. The ***AutoText*** feature is similar in concept to AutoCorrect in that both substitute a predefined item for a specific character string or group of characters. The difference is that the substitution occurs automatically with the AutoCorrect entry, whereas you have to take deliberate action for the AutoText substitution to take place. AutoText entries can also include significantly more text, formatting, and even clip art.

Microsoft Word includes a host of predefined AutoText entries such as days of the week and months of the year. For example, if you start typing today's date, you see a ScreenTip that displays the entire date, as shown in Figure 1.4. Press Enter while the ScreenTip is visible to insert the date automatically.

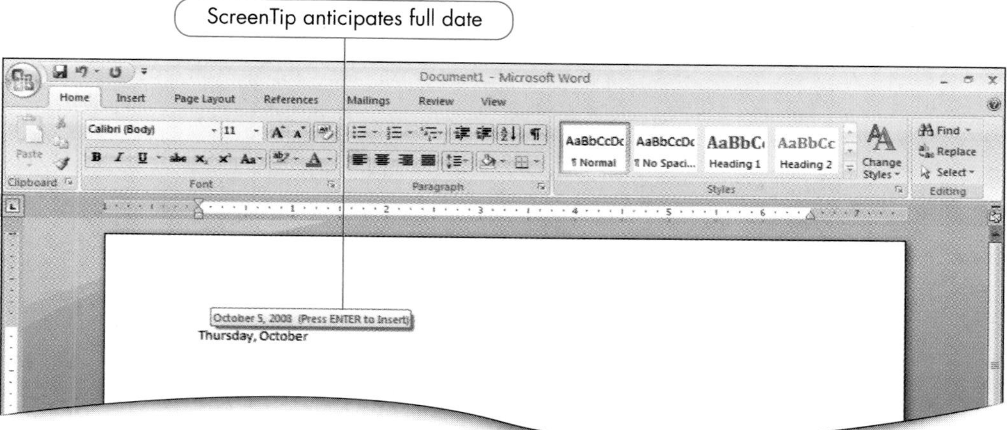

Figure 1.4 Insert AutoText

As with the AutoCorrect feature, you can define additional entries of your own. (However, you may not be able to do this in a computer lab environment.) This is advisable if you use the same piece of text frequently, such as a disclaimer, a return address, a company logo, or a cover page. You first select the text, click Quick Parts in the Text group on the Insert tab, and select Save Selection to Quick Part Gallery. In the Create New Building Block dialog box, make sure the Gallery option displays Quick Parts, and click OK. After you add entries to the Quick Parts gallery, they are included in the ***Building Blocks*** library, which contains document components you use frequently, such as those mentioned above. After you add the text to the Quick Parts gallery, you can type a portion of the entry, then press F3 to insert the remainder into your document. Figure 1.5 demonstrates the creation of the AutoText entry.

Building Blocks are document components used frequently, such as disclaimers, company addresses, or a cover page.

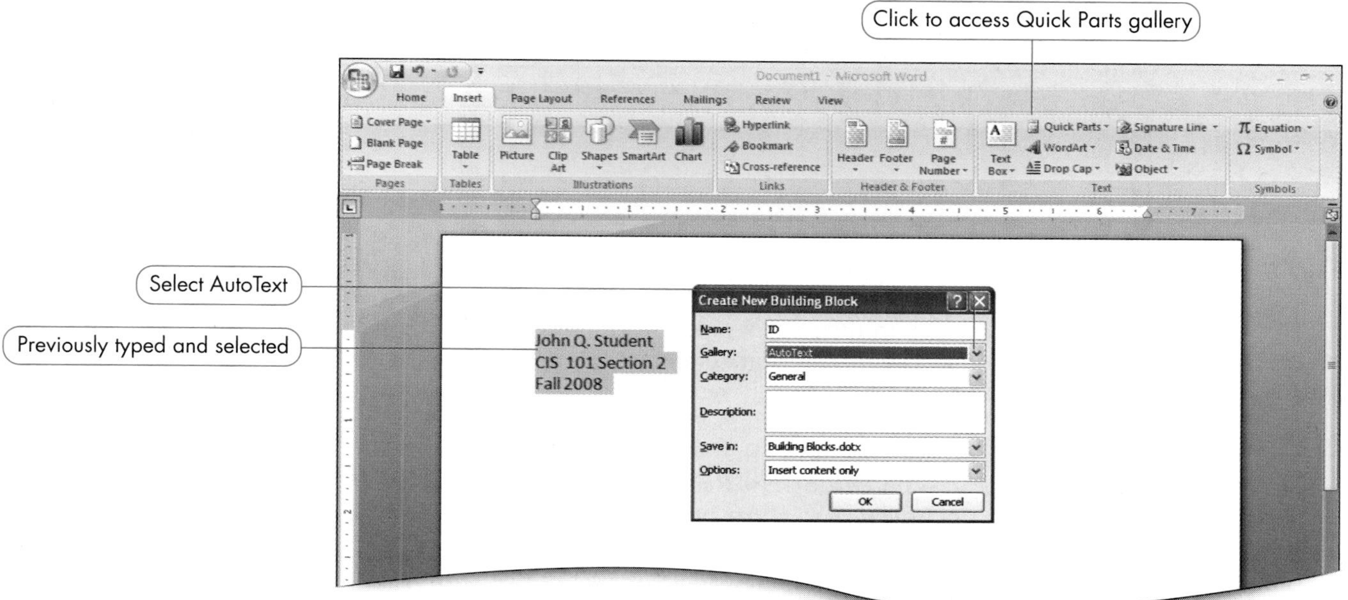

Figure 1.5 Adding an AutoText Building Block

TIP Insert the Date and Time

Some documents include the date and time they were created. A time and date stamp can help determine the most recent edition of a document, which is important if the document is updated frequently. To create a time and date stamp, display the Insert tab, click Insert Date and Time in the Text group to display the Date and Time dialog box, then choose a format. Click the *Update automatically* check box to update the date automatically if you want your document to reflect the date on which it is opened, or clear the box to retain the date on which the date was inserted (see Figure 1.6).

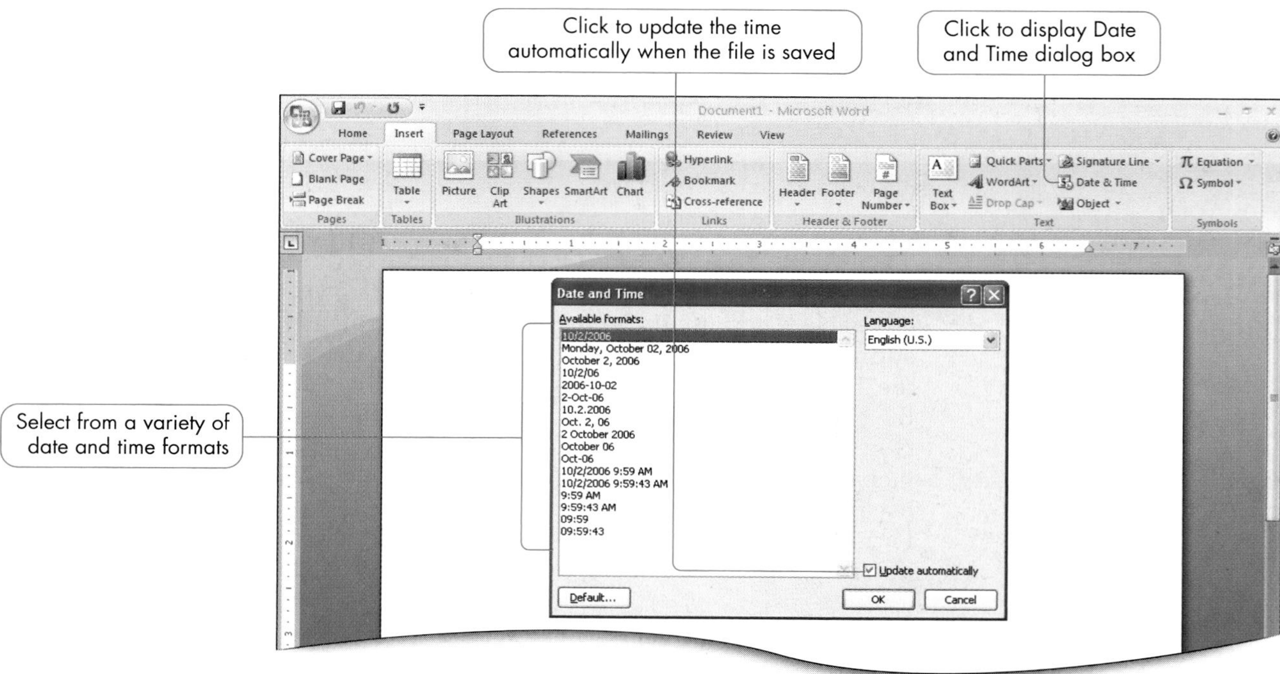

Figure 1.6 The Date and Time Dialog Box

Viewing a Document

The View tab provides options that enable you to display a document in many different ways. Each view can display your document at different magnifications, which in turn determine the amount of scrolling necessary to see remote parts of a document. The ***Print Layout view*** is the default view and is the view you use most frequently. It closely resembles the printed document and displays the top and bottom margins, headers and footers, page numbers, graphics, and other features that do not appear in other views.

Print Layout view is the default view and closely resembles the printed document.

Full Screen Reading view eliminates tabs and makes it easier to read your document.

Draft view shows a simplified work area, removing white space and other elements from view.

The ***Full Screen Reading view*** hides the Ribbon, making it easier to read your document. The ***Draft view*** creates a simple area in which to work; it removes white space and certain elements from the document, such as headers, footers, and graphics, but leaves the Ribbon. It displays information about some elements, such as page and section breaks, not easily noticed in other views. Because view options are used frequently, buttons for each also are located on the status bar, as shown in Figure 1.2.

The Zoom command displays the document on the screen at different magnifications—for example, 75%, 100%, or 200%. But this command does not affect the size of the text on the printed page. It is helpful to be able to zoom in to view details or to zoom out and see the effects of your work on a full page. When you click Zoom in the Zoom group on the View tab, a dialog box displays with several zoom options (see Figure 1.7).

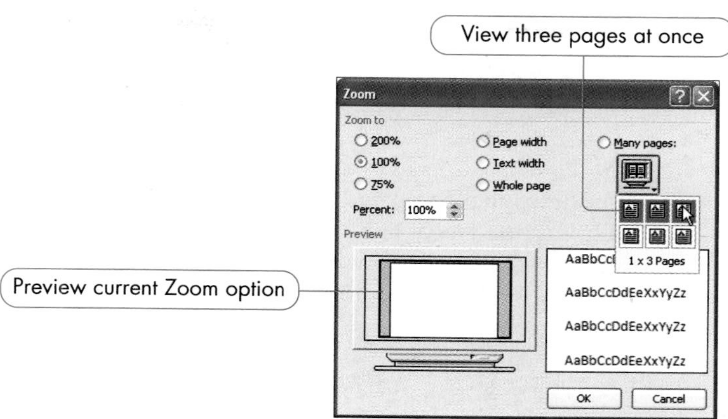

Figure 1.7 The Zoom Dialog Box

Word automatically will determine the magnification if you select one of the Zoom options—Page Width, Text Width, Whole Page, or Many Pages (Whole Page and Many Pages are available only in the Print Layout view). Figure 1.8, for example, displays a four-page document in Print Layout view. The 28% magnification is determined automatically after you specify the number of pages. If you use a wide screen, the magnification size might differ slightly.

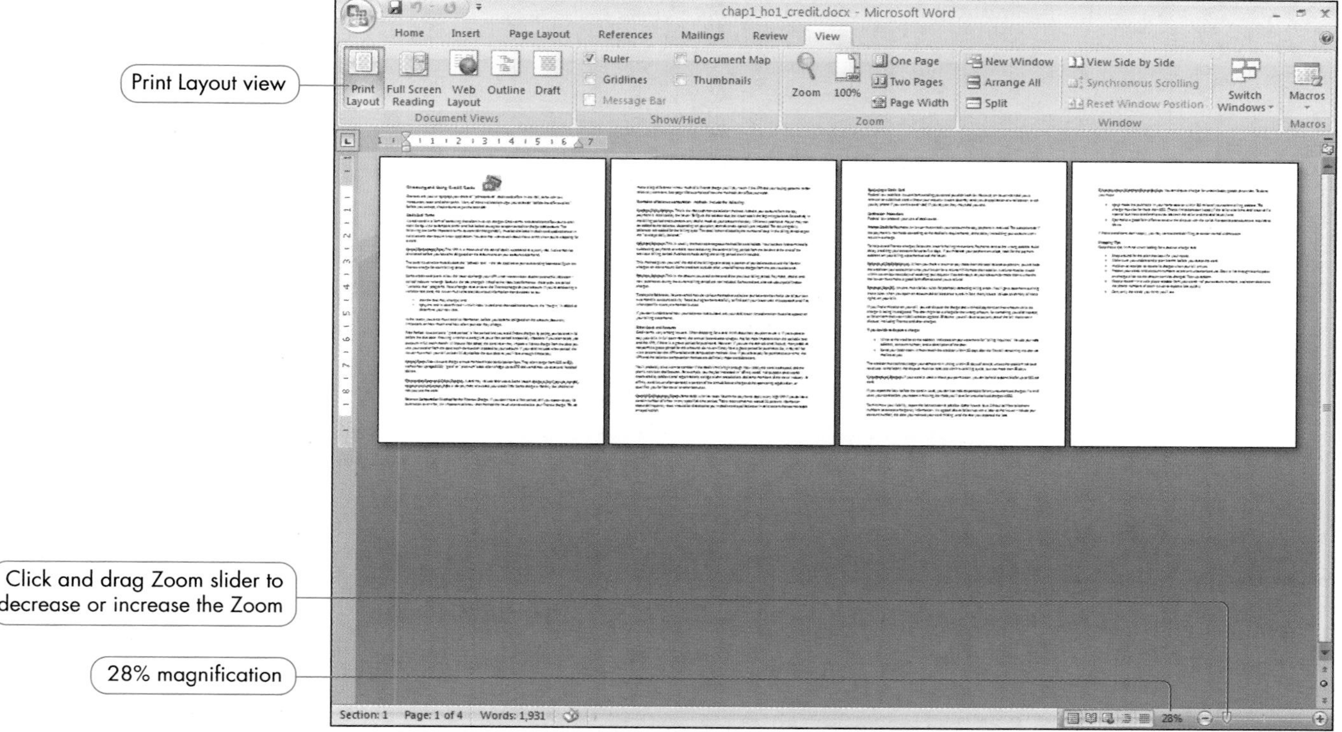

Figure 1.8 View Four Pages of Document

TIP Use the Status Bar to Change View Options

The status bar repeats commands from the View tab in a handy location for quick access. You can switch to Print Layout, Full Screen Reading, Web Page Layout, Outline, or Draft view from the buttons on the status bar. You also can use the Zoom slider to change the zoom of the current document or click the Zoom command to display the Zoom dialog box, which contains more viewing options.

The ***Outline view*** displays a structural view of the document that can be collapsed or expanded.

The ***Web Layout view*** is used when creating a Web page.

The View tab also provides access to two additional views—the Outline view and the Web Layout view. The ***Outline view*** does not display a conventional outline, but rather a structural view of a document that can be collapsed or expanded as necessary. The ***Web Layout view*** is used when you are creating a Web page.

Using the Mini Toolbar

The ***Mini toolbar*** contains frequently used formatting commands and displays when you select text.

Several formatting commands, such as Bold, Center, and Italic, are used frequently, and although they can be found on the Home tab, you can also apply them using the Mini toolbar. The ***Mini toolbar*** contains frequently used formatting commands and displays when you select text or right-click selected text. The Mini toolbar displays faintly at first, then darkens as you move the mouse pointer closer to it, as seen in Figure 1.9. If you move the mouse pointer away from it, it becomes fainter; if you do not want to use the Mini toolbar and prefer it disappear from view, press Esc when it displays. The Mini toolbar reduces the distance your mouse pointer has to travel around the screen and enables you to quickly and easily apply the most frequently used commands.

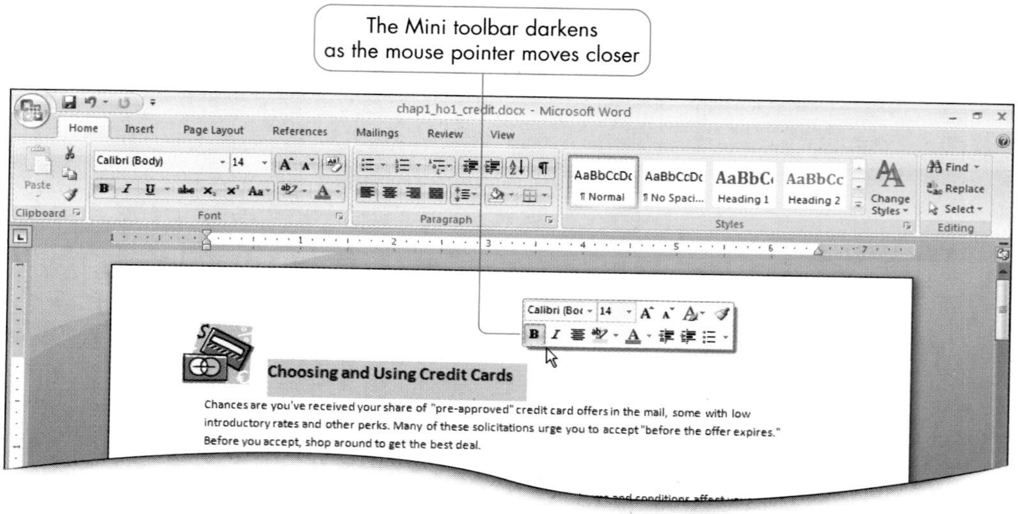

The Mini toolbar darkens as the mouse pointer moves closer

Figure 1.9 The Mini Toolbar

TIP Learning by Doing

Every chapter contains a series of hands-on exercises that enable you to apply what you learn at the computer. The exercises in this chapter are linked to one another in that you open and edit a simple document in Exercise 1, then you make additional modifications to that document in Exercises 2 and 3. The ability to save and open a document is critical, and you do not want to spend an inordinate amount of time entering text unless you are confident in your ability to retrieve it later.

Hands-On Exercises

1 | Introduction to Microsoft Word

Skills covered: 1. Open and Save a Word Document **2.** Modify the Document **3.** Insert AutoText **4.** Create an AutoText Entry **5.** Change Document Views and Zoom

Step 1
Open and Save a Word Document

Refer to Figure 1.10 as you complete Step 1.

a. Click **Start** to display the Start menu. Click (or point to) **All Programs**, click **Microsoft Office**, and then click **Microsoft Office Word 2007** to start the program.

b. Click the **Office Button** and select **Open**. Navigate to the Exploring Word folder and open the *chap1_ho1_credit* document.

   You should see the document containing the title *Choosing and Using Credit Cards*.

c. Click the **Office Button** and select **Save As.**

   The Save As dialog box displays so that you can save the document in a different location, with a different name, or as a different file type. The **Exploring Word folder** is the active folder, as shown in Figure 1.10.

> **TIP Use Save and Save As**
>
> You should practice saving your files often. If you open a document and you do not want to change its name, the easiest way to save it is to click Save on the Quick Access Toolbar. You can also click the Office Button and select Save, but many users press the Ctrl+S keyboard command to save quickly and often. The first time you save a document, use the Save As command from the Microsoft Office menu. The command displays the Save As dialog box that enables you to assign a descriptive file name (*job cover letter*, for example) and indicate where the file will be saved. Subsequent saves will be to the same location and will update the file with new changes.

d. Click the **Save in drop-down arrow**. Click the appropriate drive, such as (C:), where you want to store your completed files.

e. In the **File name** box, click once to position the insertion point at the end of the word *credit*. Type **_solution** to rename the document as *chap1_ho1_credit_solution*.

f. Click **Save** or press **Enter**. The title bar changes to reflect the new document name, *chap1_ho1_credit_solution.docx*.

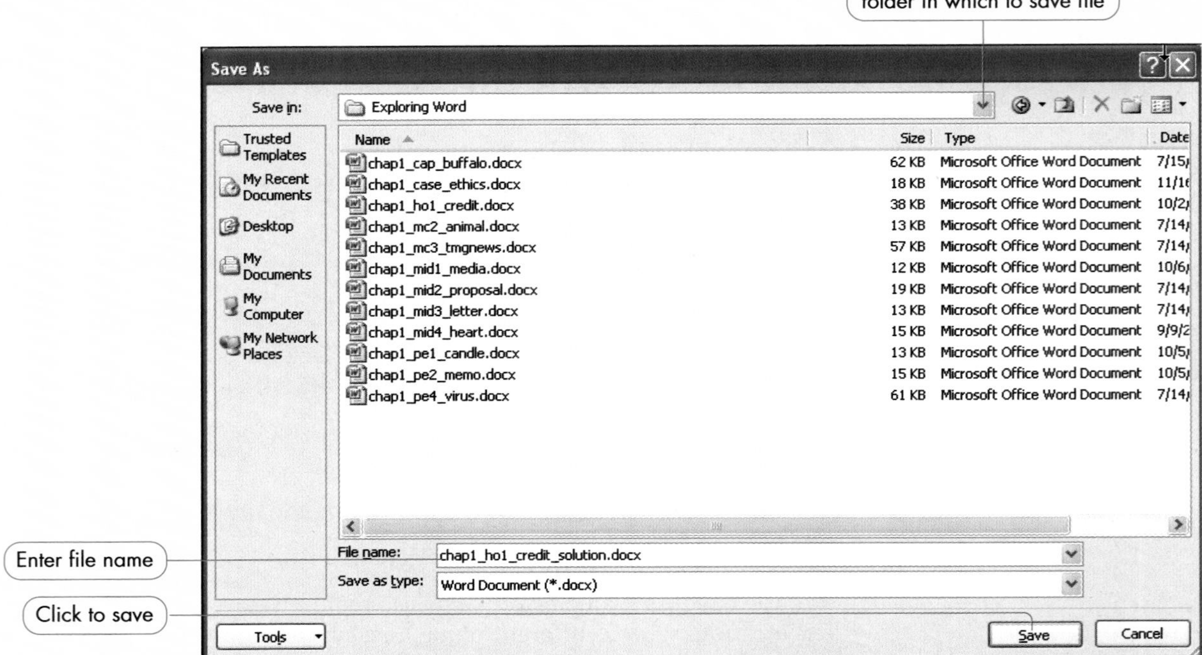

Figure 1.10 Save As Dialog Box

Step 2
Modify the Document

Refer to Figure 1.11 as you complete Step 2.

a. Use the vertical scroll bar to move down to the bottom of the third page in the document. Select the text ****Insert Text Here**** and press **Delete**.

You will add the heading and introduction to this paragraph in the next step.

b. Click **Bold** in the Font group on the Home tab to toggle the format on, if necessary, and then type **Unauthorized Charges**.

c. Click **Bold** in the Font group again to toggle the format off. Press **Spacebar** once to insert a space after the period typed in the step above. Then type **If your card is used without your permission, you can be held responsible for up to $50 per card**.

d. Press **Enter** after you complete the sentence. Select the *$50* that you just typed, and then click **Bold** on the Mini toolbar.

You completed the sentence using toggle switches, and you used the Mini toolbar to apply formatting.

e. Click **Show/Hide ¶** in the Paragraph group on the Home tab, if necessary, to display formatting marks in the document.

Notice the formatting marks display to indicate where each space, tab, and soft and hard return occurs.

f. Select the hard return character that follows the sentence typed above, as shown in Figure 1.11. Press **Delete** to delete the unnecessary hard return.

   You also can place the insertion point on either side of the formatting mark and press Delete or Backspace to remove it, depending on the location of the insertion point.

g. Click **Save** on the Quick Access Toolbar.

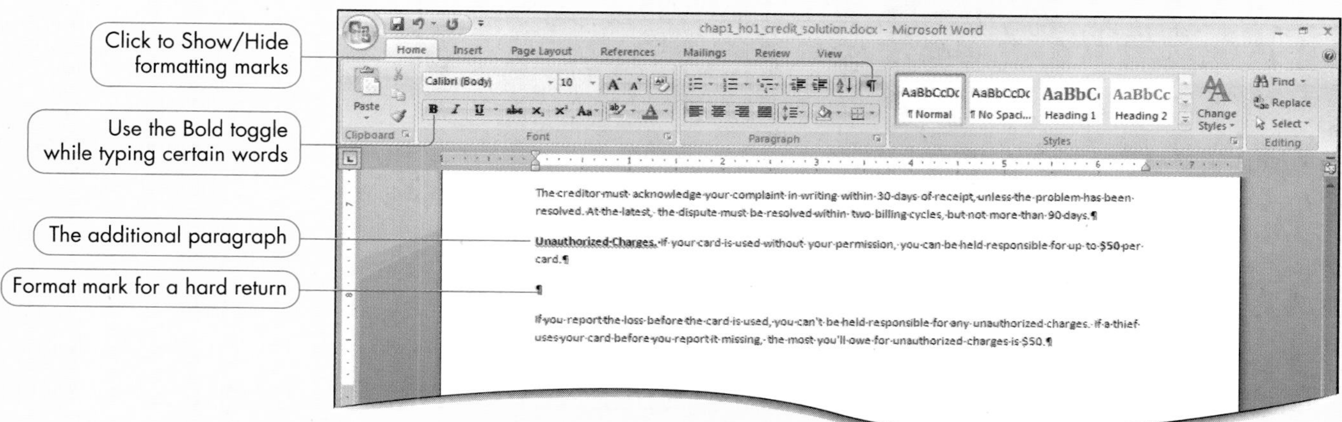

Figure 1.11 The Modified Document

Step 3
Insert AutoText

Refer to Figure 1.12 as you complete Step 3.

a. Press **Ctrl+End** to move to the end of the document and press **Enter** two times.

b. Type the first few letters of the current day of the week, such as **Tues** for *Tuesday*.

   Notice that after you type the first few letters, a ScreenTip displays the full name.

c. Press **Enter** to accept the AutoText, and then type a comma.

   Now a ScreenTip displays with the complete date—day or week, month, day, and year, as shown in Figure 1.12.

   TROUBLESHOOTING: If the complete date does not display, press **Spacebar**, then type the first few letters of the current month, such as **Oct** for October. Press **Enter** to accept the AutoText after a ScreenTip displays with the full name of the month. Then continue until a ScreenTip displays with the complete date—month, day, and year, then press **Enter** to accept and insert the date.

d. Press **Enter** to accept the date. Press **Enter** one more time to insert a hard return.

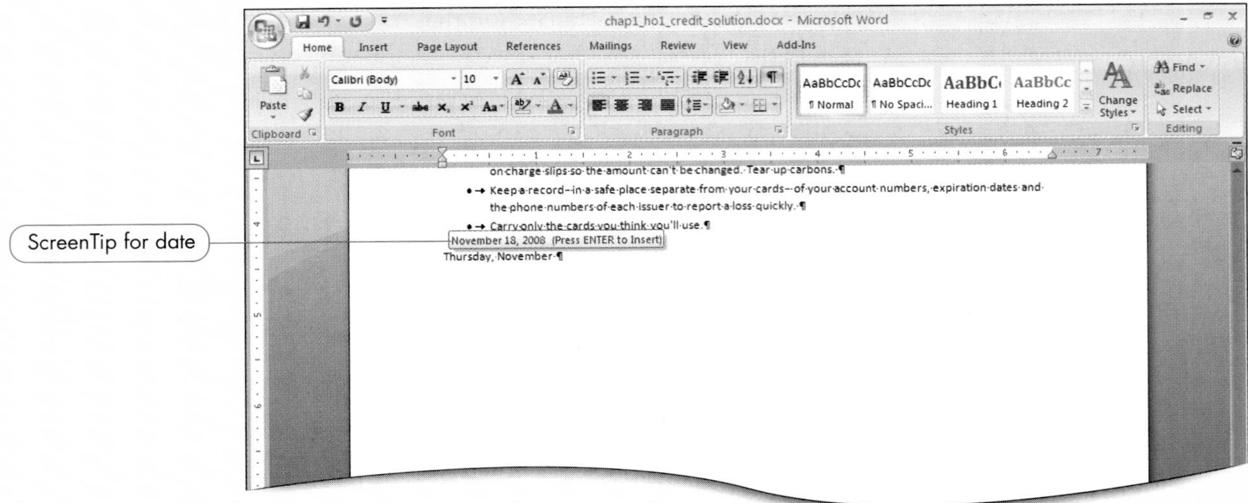

Figure 1.12 Use AutoText to Insert the Date

Step 4
Create an AutoText Entry

Refer to Figure 1.13 as you complete Step 4.

a. Type your name on the line you just added, and then select it.

b. Click the **Insert tab** and click **Quick Parts** in the Text group. Select **Save Selection to Quick Part Gallery**.

The Create New Building Block dialog box displays.

c. In the **Name box**, type your initials.

The text in this box is what you begin to type, then press F3 to insert the actual building block content.

d. Click the **Gallery drop-down arrow**. Select **AutoText**, as shown in Figure 1.13. Click **OK.**

This procedure adds an AutoText entry to the Normal template. If you are in a lab environment, you might not have permission to add this item or save the changes to the Normal template.

e. Select your name in the document, but do not select the hard return mark, and then press **Delete** to remove it. Click **Quick Parts**, and then select **Building Blocks Organizer**.

The Building Blocks Organizer dialog box opens so that you can manage building blocks.

f. Click the **Gallery** heading at the top of the Building Blocks Organizer dialog box to sort the entries.

The AutoText entries display first. You should be able to see your new entry near the top of the list.

g. Select your entry in the Name column. Click **Insert** at the bottom of the dialog box.

Your name displays at the bottom of the page.

h. Click **Undo** in the Quick Access Toolbar to remove your name. Type the first two letters of your initials, and then press **F3**.

Your name, as saved in the Building Block, displays. You now have experience inserting a Building Block using two different methods.

i. Click **Save** on the Quick Access Toolbar.

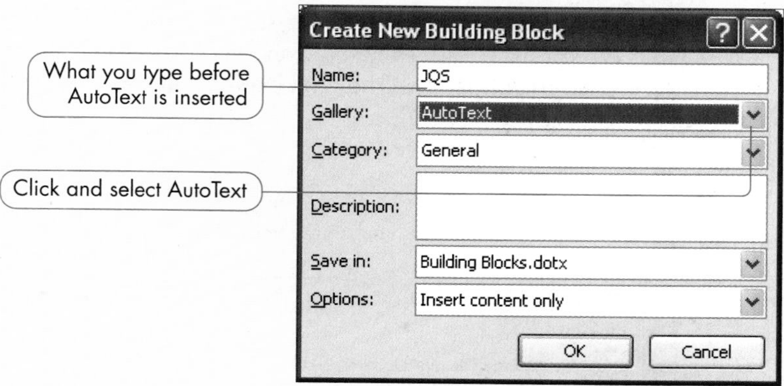

Figure 1.13 The Create New Building Block Dialog Box

Step 5
Change Document Views and Zoom

Refer to Figure 1.14 as you complete Step 5.

a. Press **Ctrl+Home** to move the insertion point to the beginning of the document. Click the **View tab** and click **Full Screen Reading** in the Document Views group.

The document looks different, pages one and two display, the Ribbon is removed, and only a few buttons display (see Figure 1.14).

TROUBLESHOOTING: If you do not see two pages, click **View Options** in the upper-right corner and select **Show Two Pages**.

b. Hover your mouse pointer over the arrow in the lower-right corner of the screen, and then click the arrow to scroll to the next set of pages. Click the arrow one more time to view the last pages.

Once you reach the end of the document, the navigation arrow moves to the lower-left side of the screen.

c. Click the left-pointing arrow twice to display the first two pages again.

TIP Return to Print Layout View

Press **Esc** to return to Print Layout view and close the Full Screen Reading view.

d. Click **Close** in the upper-right corner of the screen to return to the default view.

e. Click **Zoom** in the Zoom group on the View tab. Click the icon below **Many pages** and roll your mouse to select 1 × 3 Pages. Click **OK** to change the view and display three pages on the top of the screen and one page at the bottom.

Notice the Zoom slider in the lower-right corner of the window displays 39%. If you use a wide-screen monitor, the size might differ slightly.

f. Save the *chap1_ho1_credit_solution* document and keep it onscreen if you plan to continue with the next exercise. Close the file and exit Word if you do not want to continue with the next exercise at this time.

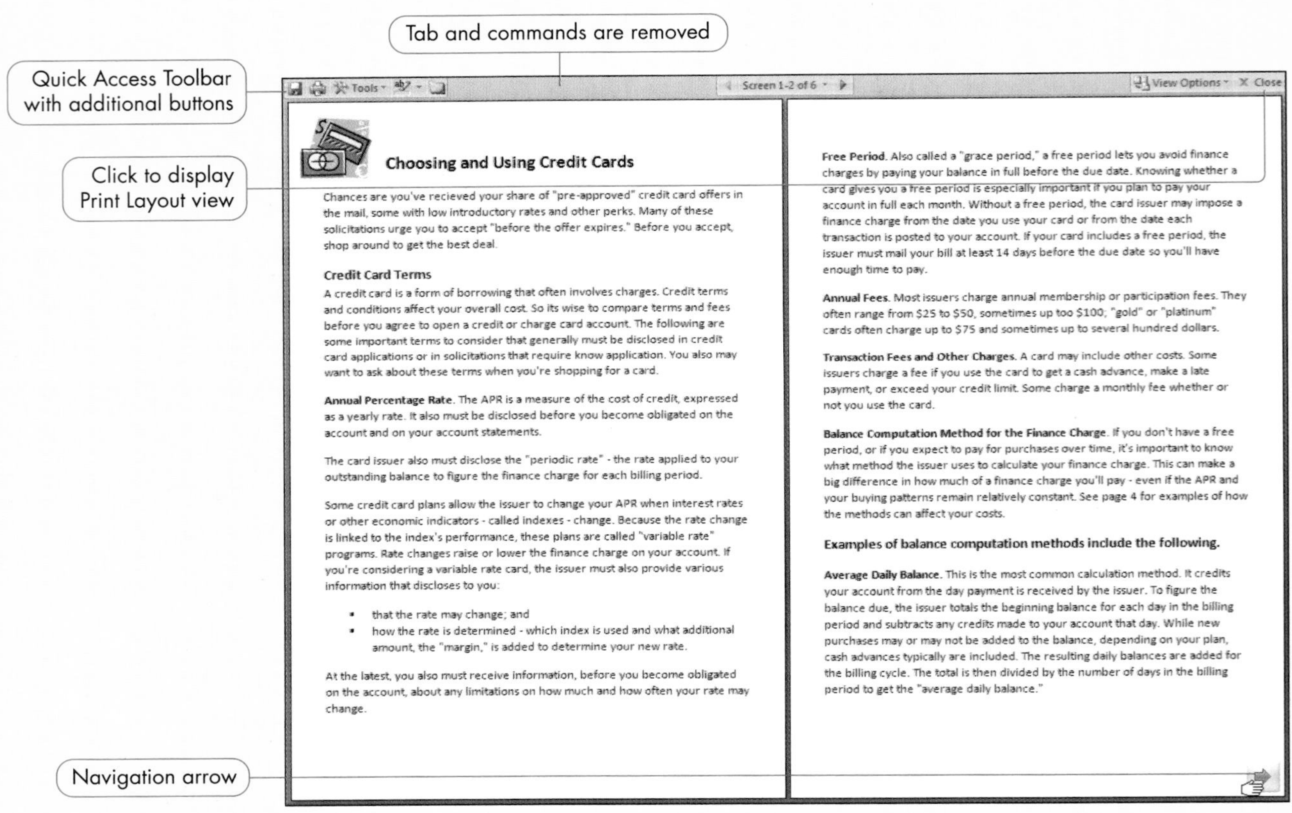

Figure 1.14 Full Screen Reading View

Document Formatting

Throughout your college and professional career, you will create a variety of documents. As you compose and edit large documents, you want to set them up so they have title pages, display a certain way when printed, or include page numbers at the top or bottom of a page. All of these options are available using features in Microsoft Word.

In this section, you make formatting changes to a Word document, such as changing the document margins and orientation. You insert page breaks, page numbers, headers and footers, sections, and cover pages. You also learn how to use the Find and Replace commands.

Setting Margins and Specifying Page Orientation

Margins are the amount of white space around the top, bottom, left, and right edges of the page.

When you create a document, you consider the content you will insert, but you also should consider how you want the document to look when you print or display it. Many of the settings needed for this purpose are found on the Page Layout tab. The first setting most people change is ***margins***. Margins determine the amount of white space from the text to the edges of the page. You should adjust margins to improve the appearance and readability of your document.

The default margins, indicated in Figure 1.15, are 1″ on the top, bottom, left, and right of the page. You can select different margin settings from the gallery that displays when you click Margins in the Page Setup group on the Page Layout tab, or you can select the Custom Margins option to enter specific settings.

> When you create a document, you consider the content you will insert, but you should also consider how you want the document to look when you print or display it. . . to have title pages, or include page numbers at the top or bottom of a page. All of these options are available using features in Microsoft Word.

When you create a short business letter, you want to increase the margins to a larger size, such as 1.5″ on all sides, so the letter contents are balanced on the printed page. When you print a long document, you might want to reduce the margins to a small amount, such as 0.3″ or 0.5″, in order to reduce the amount of paper used. If you print a formal or research paper, you want to use a 1.5″ left margin and a 1″ right margin to allow extra room for binding. The margins you choose will apply to the whole document regardless of the position of the insertion point. You can establish different margin settings for different parts of a document by creating sections. Sections are discussed later in this chapter.

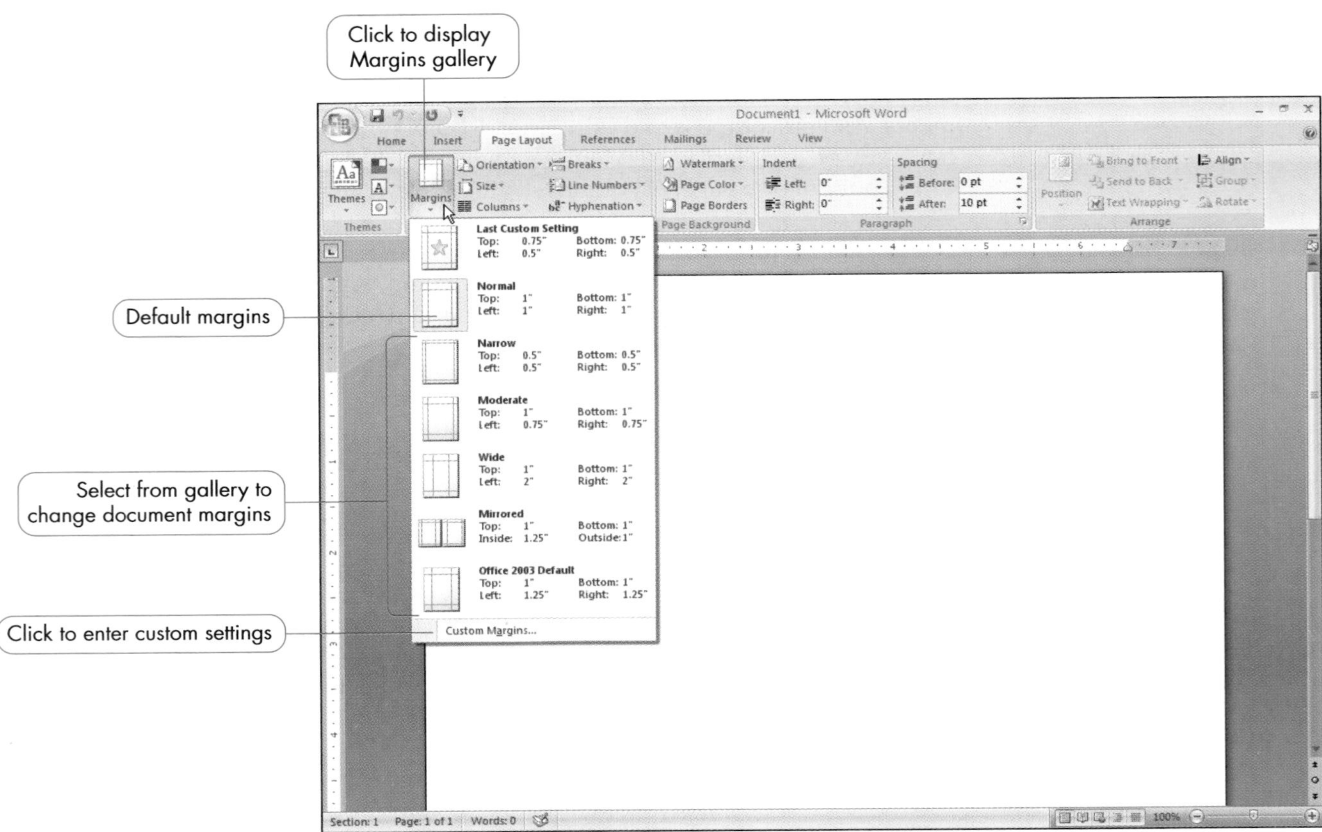

Figure 1.15 Setting Margins

Portrait orientation positions text parallel with the short side of the page.

Landscape orientation positions text parallel with the long side of the page.

Another setting to consider for a document is orientation. The Page Layout tab contains the Orientation command with two settings—portrait and landscape. ***Portrait orientation,*** the default setting, positions text parallel with the short side of the page so that the printed page is taller than it is wide. ***Landscape orientation*** flips the page 90 degrees so that text displays parallel with the longer side of the page, so that the printed page is wider than it is tall. The type of document you create and the manner in which you wish to display the information will dictate which type of orientation you use. Most documents, such as letters and research papers, use portrait orientation, but a brochure, large graphic, chart, or table might display better on a page with landscape orientation.

If you need to print a document on special paper, such as legal size (8½″ × 14″) or on an envelope, you should select the paper size before you create the document text. The Size command in the Page Setup group on the Page Layout tab contains several different document sizes from which you can choose. If you have special paper requirements, you can select More Paper Sizes to enter your own custom size. If you do not select the special size before you print, you will waste paper and find yourself with a very strange looking printout.

Inserting Page Breaks

A ***soft page break*** is inserted when text fills an entire page, then continues on the next page.

When you type more text than can fit on a page, Word continues the text on another page using soft and hard page breaks. The ***soft page break*** is a hidden marker that automatically continues text on the top of a new page when text no longer fits on the current page. These breaks adjust automatically when you add and delete text. For the most part, you rely on soft page breaks to prepare multiple-page documents. However, at times you need to start a new page before Word inserts a soft page break.

A ***hard page break*** forces the next part of a document to begin on a new page.

You can insert a ***hard page break***, a hidden marker, to force text to begin on a new page. A hard page break is inserted into a document using the Breaks command in the Page Setup group on the Page Layout tab, or Page Break in the Pages group on the Insert tab. To view the page break markers in Print Layout view, you must click Show/Hide ¶ on the Home tab, to toggle on the formatting marks, as seen in Figure 1.16. You can view the page break markers without the Show/Hide toggled on when you switch to Draft view (see Figure 1.17).

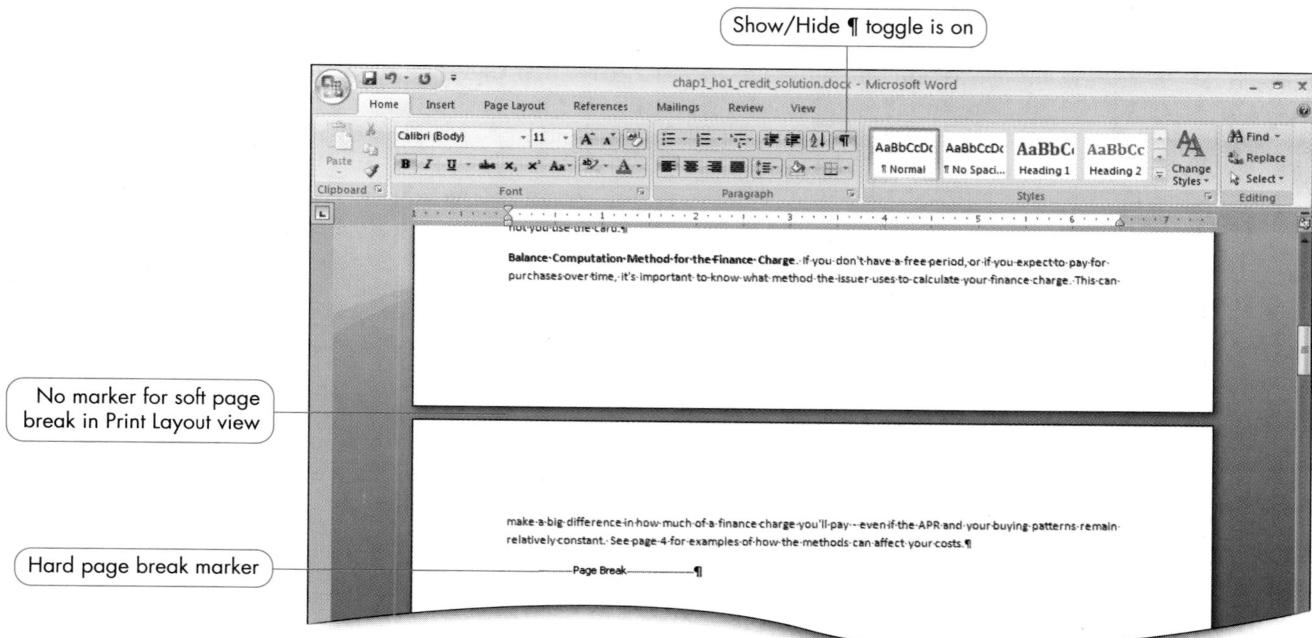

Figure 1.16 View Page Breaks in Print Layout View

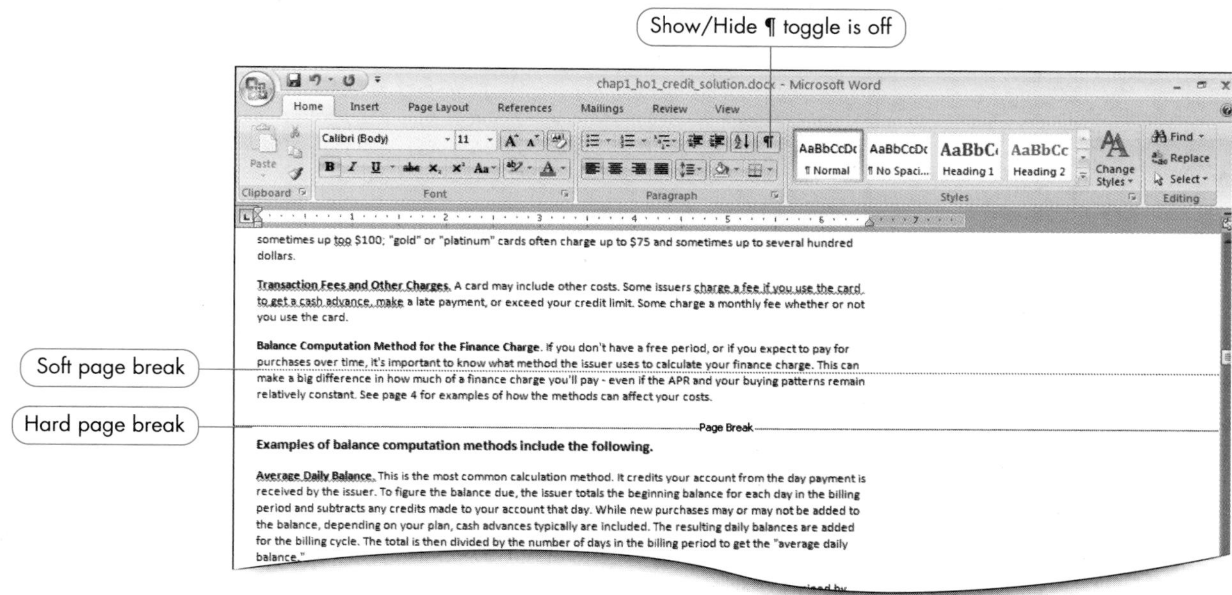

Figure 1.17 View Page Breaks in Draft View

TIP Hard Page Break Shortcut

You can use the keyboard shortcut **Ctrl+Enter** to insert a hard page break.

Adding Page Numbers

Page numbers are essential in long documents. They serve as a convenient reference point for the writer and reader. If you do not include page numbers in a long document, you will have difficulty trying to find text on a particular page or trying to tell someone where to locate a particular passage in the document. Have you ever tried to reassemble a long document that was out of order and did not have page numbers? It can be very frustrating and makes a good case for inserting page numbers in your documents.

The Page Number command in the Header & Footer group on the Insert tab is the easiest way to place page numbers into a document. When you use this feature, Word not only inserts page numbers but also automatically adjusts the page numbering when you add or delete pages. Page numbers can appear at the top or bottom of a page, and can be left-, center-, or right-aligned. Your decision on whether to place page numbers in a header or footer might be based on personal preference, whether the writing guide for your paper dictates a specific location, or if you have other information to include in a header or footer also.

Word 2007 provides several galleries with options for formatting page numbers. New to Office 2007 is the Page Margin option, which enables you to put a page number on the side of a page. This feature adds a nice element of style to a multipage document that will be distributed as a flyer or annual report. Figure 1.18 displays a few gallery options for placing a page number at the bottom of a page.

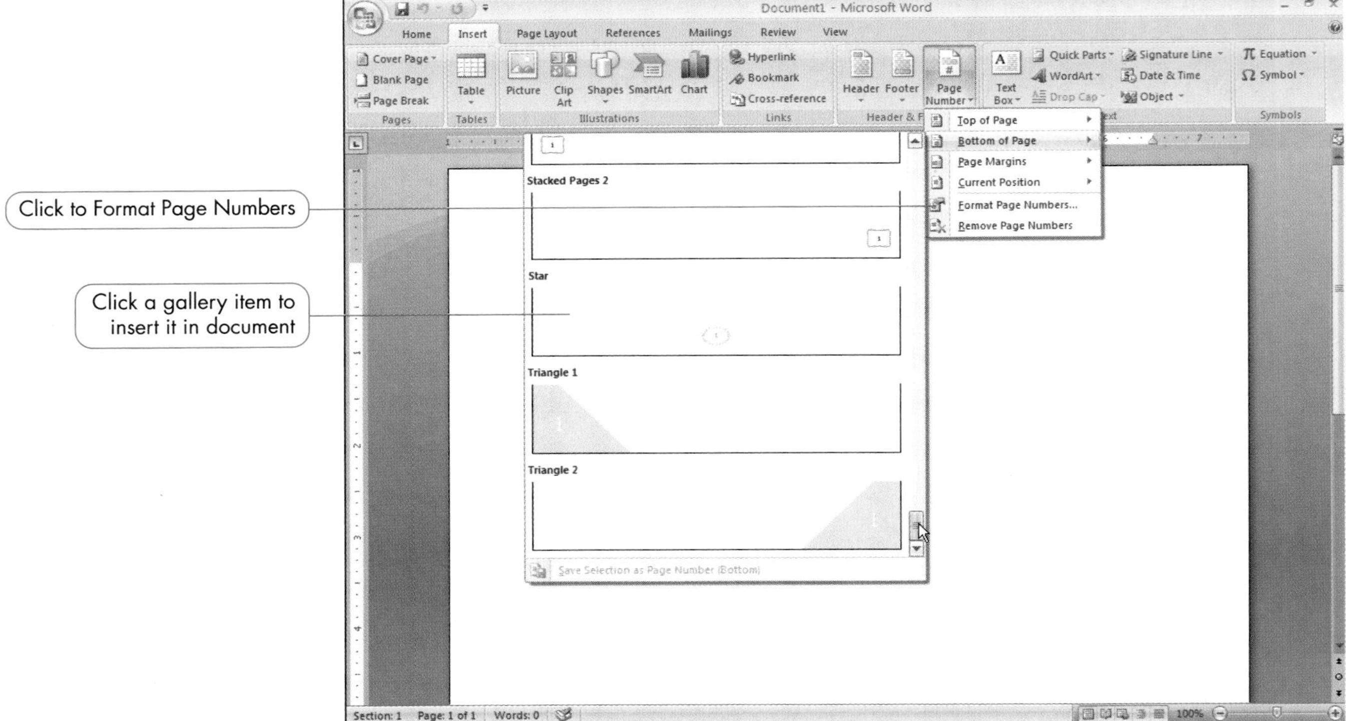

Figure 1.18 Insert Page Numbers at Bottom of Page

Word enables you to customize the number format for page numbers to use Roman rather than Arabic numerals, which often are used for preliminary or preface pages at the beginning of a book. You also can adjust the page numbering so that it starts numbering at a page other than the first. This is useful when you have a report with a cover page; you typically do not consider the cover as page one but instead begin numbering with the page that follows it. You use the Format Page Numbers command to display the Page Number Format dialog box (see Figure 1.19) where you can make these changes. If you are not satisfied with the page numbering in a document, use the Remove Page Numbers command to remove them.

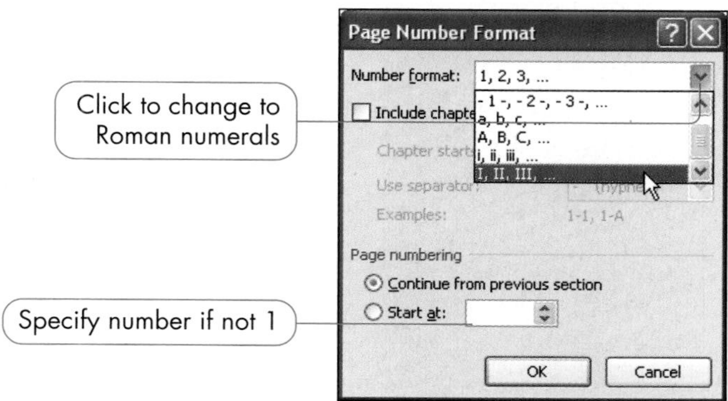

Figure 1.19 Page Number Format Dialog Box

Inserting Headers and Footers

A ***header*** is information printed at the top of document pages.

A ***footer*** is information printed at the bottom of document pages.

Headers and footers give a professional appearance to a document. A ***header*** consists of one or more lines that are printed at the top of a page. A ***footer*** is printed at the bottom of the page. A document may contain headers but not footers, footers but not headers, both headers and footers, or neither. Footers often contain the page number and a date the document was created. Headers might contain the name of an organization, author, or title of the document. Take a moment to notice the type of information you see in the headers/footers of the books or magazines you are reading.

Headers and footers are added from the Insert tab. You can create a simple header or footer by clicking Insert Page Number, depending on whether the page number is at the top or bottom of a page. Headers and footers are formatted like any other paragraph and can be center, left or right aligned. You can format headers and footers in any typeface or point size and can include special codes to automatically insert the page number, date, and time a document is printed.

The advantage of using a header or footer (over typing the text yourself at the top or bottom of every page) is that you type the text only once, after which it appears automatically according to your specifications. In addition, the placement of the headers and footers is adjusted for changes in page breaks caused by the insertion or deletion of text in the body of the document.

Headers and footers can change continually throughout a document. Once you insert one, the Header & Footer Tools tab displays and contains many options (see Figure 1.20). For instance, you can specify a different header or footer for the first page; this is advisable when you have a cover page and do not want the header (or footer) to display on that page. You also can have different headers and footers for odd and even pages. This feature is useful when you plan to print a document that will be bound as a book. Notice the different information this book prints on the footer of odd versus even pages, and how the page numbers display in the corners of each page. If you want to change the header (or footer) midway through a document, you need to insert a section break at the point where the new header (or footer) is to begin. These breaks are discussed in the next section.

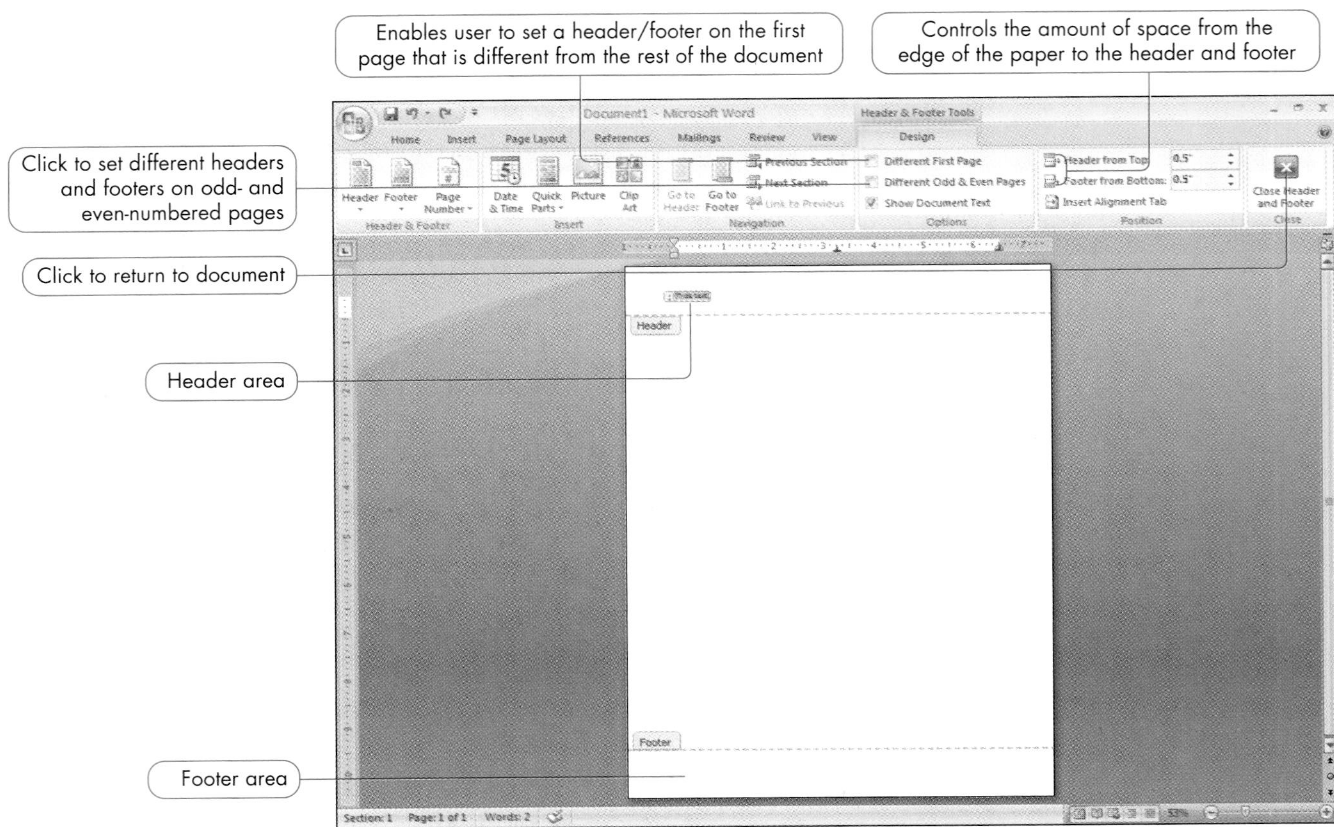
Enables user to set a header/footer on the first page that is different from the rest of the document
Controls the amount of space from the edge of the paper to the header and footer
Click to set different headers and footers on odd- and even-numbered pages
Click to return to document
Header area
Footer area

Figure 1.20 Header and Footer Tools Commands

Creating Sections

Formatting in Word occurs on three levels: character, paragraph, and section. Formatting at the section level controls headers and footers, page numbering, page size and orientation, margins, and columns. All of the documents in the text so far have consisted of a single section, and thus any section formatting applied to the entire document. You can, however, divide a document into sections and format each section independently.

A ***section break*** is a marker that divides a document into sections, thereby allowing different formatting in each section.

You determine where one section ends and another begins by clicking Breaks in the Page Setup group on the Page Layout tab. A ***section break*** is a marker that divides a document into sections. It enables you to decide how the section will be formatted on the printed page; that is, you can specify that the new section continues on the same page, that it begins on a new page, or that it begins on the next odd or even page even if a blank page has to be inserted. Formatting at the section level gives you the ability to create more sophisticated documents. You can use section formatting to do the following:

- Change the margins within a multipage letter, where the first page (the letterhead) requires a larger top margin than the other pages in the letter.
- Change the orientation from portrait to landscape to accommodate a wide table at the end of the document.
- Change the page numbering to use Roman numerals at the beginning of the document for a table of contents and Arabic numerals thereafter.
- Change the number of columns in a newsletter, which may contain a single column at the top of a page for the masthead, then two or three columns in the body of the newsletter.

Word stores the formatting characteristics of each section in the section break at the end of a section. Thus, deleting a section break also deletes the section formatting, causing the text above the break to assume the formatting characteristics of the next section.

Figure 1.21 displays a multipage view of a six-page document. The document has been divided into two sections, and the insertion point is currently on the last page of the document, which is also the first page of the second section. Note the corresponding indications on the status bar and the position of the headers and footers throughout the document.

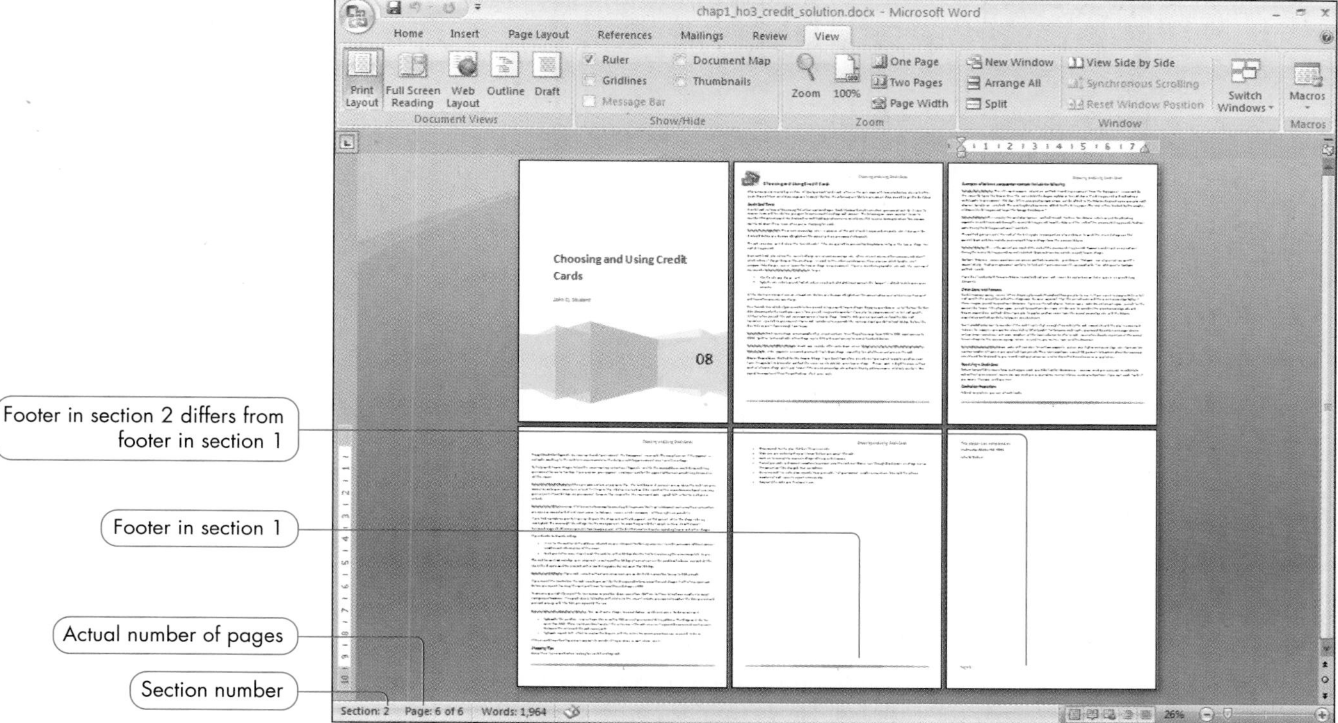

Figure 1.21 A Document with Two Sections

Inserting a Cover Page

You can use commands such as page break and keystrokes such as Ctrl+Enter, mentioned in previous sections, to create a cover page for a document. But Word 2007 offers a feature to quickly insert a preformatted cover page in your document. The Cover Page feature in the Pages group of the Insert tab includes a gallery with several designs, as seen in Figure 1.22. Each design includes building block fields, such as Document Title, Company Name, Date, and Author, which you can personalize. Additionally, the title pages already are formatted with the different first page option in the header and footer, so you don't have to change that setting after you insert the page. After you personalize and make any additional modifications of your choice, your document will include an attractive cover page.

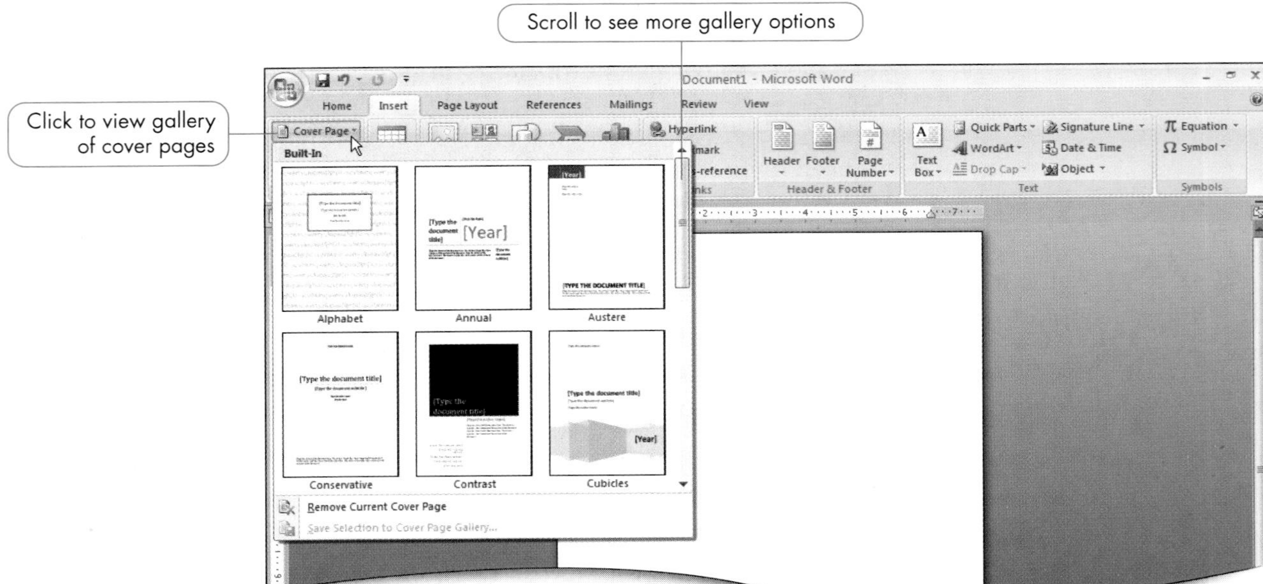

Figure 1.22 Insert a Cover Page

Using Find and Replace Commands

Even though Find and Replace have individual commands in the Editing group, on the Home tab, they share a common dialog box with different tabs for each command as well as the Go To command. The Find command locates one or more occurrences of specific text (e.g., a word or phrase). The Replace command goes one step further in that it locates the text, and then enables you to optionally replace (one or more occurrences of) that text with different text. The Go To command goes directly to a specific place (e.g., a specific page) in the document. If you use the find function and then decide you want to replace text, you can simply click the Replace tab to initiate the process. These functions are very helpful when working in a long document; you can use them to quickly locate text or jump to a different location in the document.

A ***case-sensitive search*** matches not only the text but also the use of upper- and lowercase letters.

A ***case-insensitive search*** finds a word regardless of any capitalization used.

Selective replacement lets you decide whether to replace text.

Automatic replacement makes a substitution automatically.

The search in both the Find and Replace commands is case sensitive or case insensitive. A ***case-sensitive search***, where the Match Case option is selected, matches not only the text but also the use of upper- and lowercase letters. Thus, *There* is different from *there*, and a search on one will not identify the other. A ***case-insensitive search***, where Match Case is *not* selected, is just the opposite and finds both *There* and *there*. A search also may specify whole words only to identify *there*, but not *therefore* or *thereby*. And finally, the search and replacement text also can specify different numbers of characters; for example, you could replace *flower* with *daisy*.

The Replace command implements either ***selective replacement***, which lets you examine each occurrence of the character string in context and decide whether to replace it, or ***automatic replacement***, where the substitution is made automatically. Selective replacement is implemented by clicking the Find Next command, then clicking (or not clicking) Replace to make the substitution. Automatic replacement (through the entire document) is implemented by clicking Replace All. This feature can save you a great deal of time if you need to make a replacement throughout a document, but it also can produce unintended consequences. For example, if you substitute the word *text* for *book*, the word *textbook* would become *texttext*, which is not what you had in mind.

The Find and Replace commands can include formatting and/or special characters. This command is helpful in situations where you need to make changes to the way text is formatted, but not necessarily to the text itself. You can, for example, change all italicized text to boldface, as shown in Figure 1.23, or you can change five consecutive spaces to a tab character, which makes it easier to align text. You also can use special characters in the character string, such as the "any character" (consisting of ^?). For example, to find all four-letter words that begin with "f" and end with "l" (such as *fall*, *fill*, or *fail*), search for f^?^?l. (The question mark stands for any character, just like a wildcard in a card game.) You also can search for all forms of a word; for example, if you specify *am*, it will also find *is* and *are*. You can even search for a word based on how it sounds. When searching for *Marion*, for example, check the Sounds like check box, and the search will find both *Marion* and *Marian*.

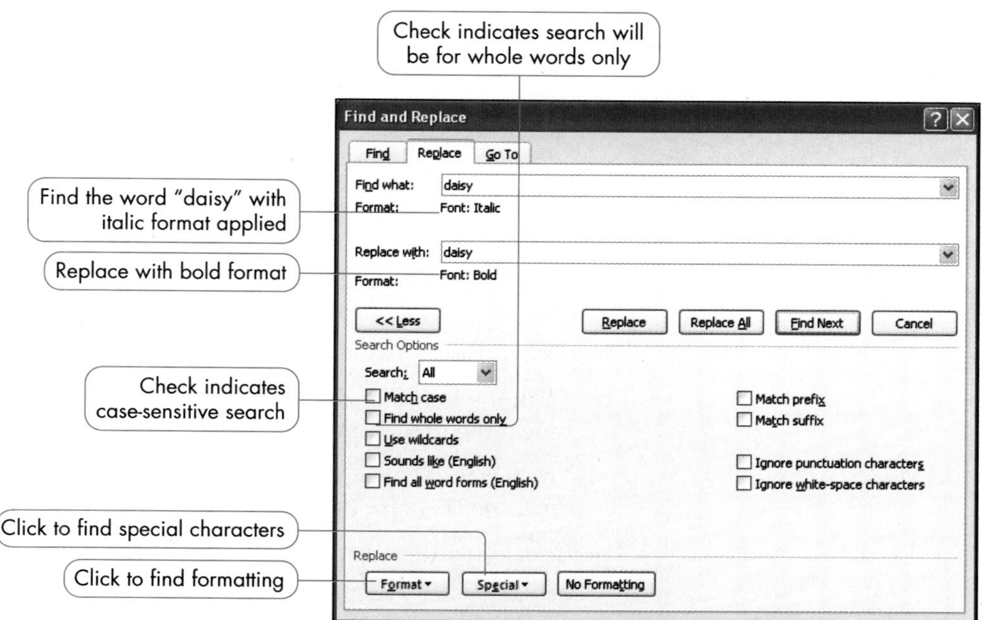

Figure 1.23 The Find and Replace Dialog Box

TIP The Go To Command

The Go To command moves the insertion point to a designated location in the document. The command is accessed by clicking the Find down arrow in the Editing group on the Home tab, by pressing **Ctrl+G**, or by clicking the page number on the status bar. After you activate the command, the Find and Replace dialog box displays the Go To tab in which you enter a page number, section, line, footnote, or other areas in the Go to what list. You also can specify a relative page number—for example, +2 to move forward two pages or –1 to move back one page.

Hands-On Exercises

2 | Document Organization

Skills covered: 1. Set Page Margins and Orientation **2.** Insert a Page Break **3.** Add a Cover Page and Insert a Document Header **4.** Insert a Section Break **5.** Insert a Page Number in the Footer **6.** Use Find, Replace, and Go To

Step 1
Set Page Margins and Orientation

Refer to Figure 1.24 as you complete Step 1.

a. Open the *chap1_ho1_credit_solution* document if you closed it after the last hands-on exercise and save it as **chap1_ho2_credit_solution**.

b. Click the **Page Layout tab** and click **Margins** in the Page Setup group. Click **Custom Margins**.

   The Page Setup dialog box displays.

c. Click the **Margins tab**, if necessary. Type **.75** in the Top margin box. Press **Tab** to move the insertion point to the Bottom margin box. Type **.75** and press **Tab** to move to the Left margin box.

   0.75″ is the equivalent of ¾ of one inch.

d. Click the **Left margin down arrow** to reduce the left margin to **0.5″**, and then repeat the procedure to set the right margin to **0.5″**.

   The top and bottom margins are now set at 0.75″ and the left and right margins are set at 0.5″ (see Figure 1.24).

e. Check that these settings apply to the **Whole document**, located in the lower portion of the dialog box. Click **OK**.

   You can see the change in layout as a result of changing the margins. More text displays on the first three pages, and there is only one line of text remaining on the fourth page.

f. Click **Orientation** in the Page Setup group on the Page Layout tab, and then select **Landscape**.

   The pages now display in landscape orientation. Whereas the document looks fine, we will return to portrait orientation to prepare for the remaining exercises.

g. Click **Undo** on the Quick Access Toolbar. Save the document.

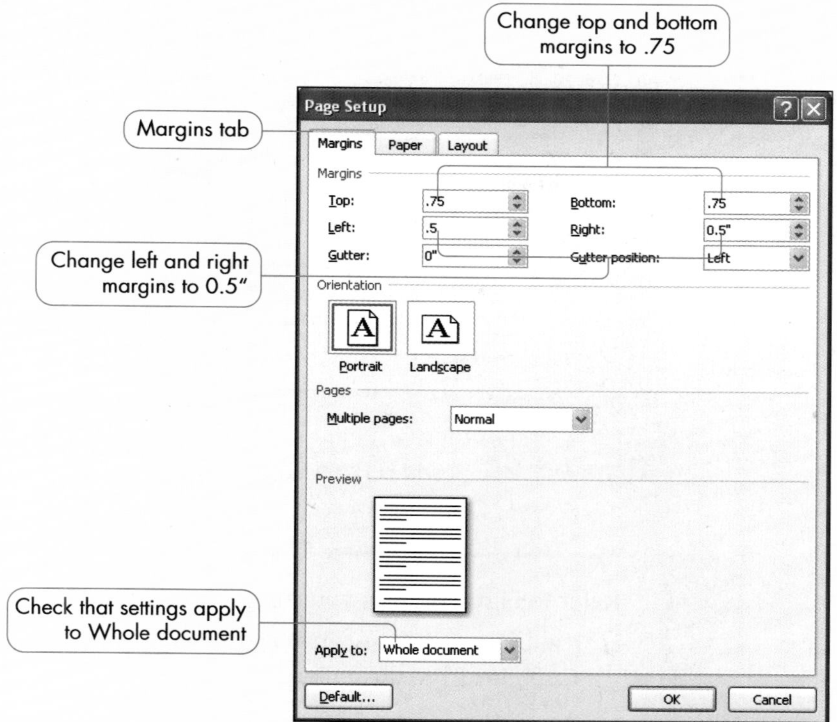

Figure 1.24 Change the Margins

Step 2
Insert a Page Break

Refer to Figure 1.25 as you complete Step 2.

a. Click the **Zoom slider** and increase the zoom to **100%**.

b. Place the insertion point on the left side of the heading *Examples of balance computation methods include the following* on the bottom of the first page.

c. Press **Ctrl+Enter** to insert a page break.

   The heading and paragraph that follows move to the top of the second page. It leaves a gap of space at the bottom of the first page, but you will make other adjustments to compensate for that.

d. Place the insertion point on the left side of the paragraph heading *Prompt Credit for Payment* on the bottom of the second page. Press **Enter** one time.

   The hard returns force the paragraph to relocate to the top of the next page.

e. Click the **Zoom slider** and decrease the zoom to 50%, and then display pages one and two. If necessary, click **Show/Hide ¶** in the Paragraph group on the Home tab to view formatting marks.

   Notice the marks that indicate the Page Break and hard return at the bottom of the first and second pages, as seen in Figure 1.25.

f. Save the document.

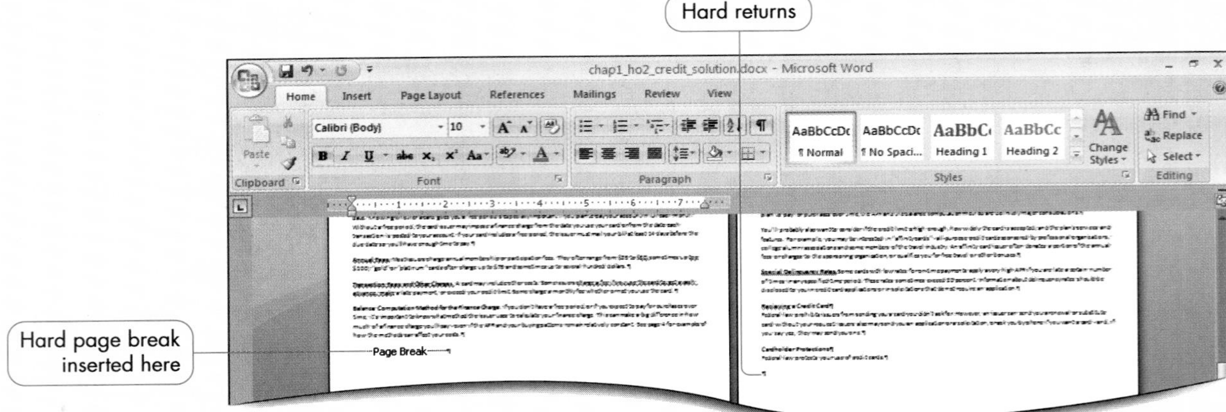

Figure 1.25 Insert a Hard Page Break

Step 3
Add a Cover Page and Insert a Document Header

Refer to Figure 1.26 as you complete Step 3.

a. Click the **Insert tab**, click **Cover Page** in the Pages group, and then click **Cubicles** from the gallery.

   You now have a title page that already displays the report title, and the rest of the document begins at the top of page two. The insertion point does not have to be at the beginning of a document to insert a cover page.

   TROUBLESHOOTING: If the document title does not display automatically, click the Title field and replace the text *Type the document title* with **Choosing and Using Credit Cards**.

b. Right-click the Subtitle field and click **Cut**. Right-click the company name field at the top of the page, and then click **Cut**. Click the Year field and type the current year. If necessary, click the Author Name field and type your name.

   Due to the preset format of the title page, the date 2008 will change to 08 automatically.

c. Click the **Zoom slider** and increase the zoom to **100%**. Click **Header** on the Insert tab and click **Edit Header** at the bottom of the gallery list.

   The Design tab displays and the header area of the page is bordered by a blue line.

d. Look at the status bar on the bottom of the page to determine the page where the insertion point is located. If necessary, place your insertion point in the header of page two. Confirm that the **Different First Page** option is selected in the Design tab's Options group.

   The cover page you created does not require a heading, and this setting prevents the heading from displaying on that page.

e. Press **Tab** two times to move the insertion point to the right side of the footer. Click **Quick Parts** in the Insert group and point to a different **Document Properties**. Click **Title** at the end of the submenu,

   The title of the document, *Choosing and Using Credit Cards*, displays in the header, as seen in Figure 1.26.

f. Scroll down and notice the header on the remaining pages. Click **Close Header and Footer**.

g. Save the document.

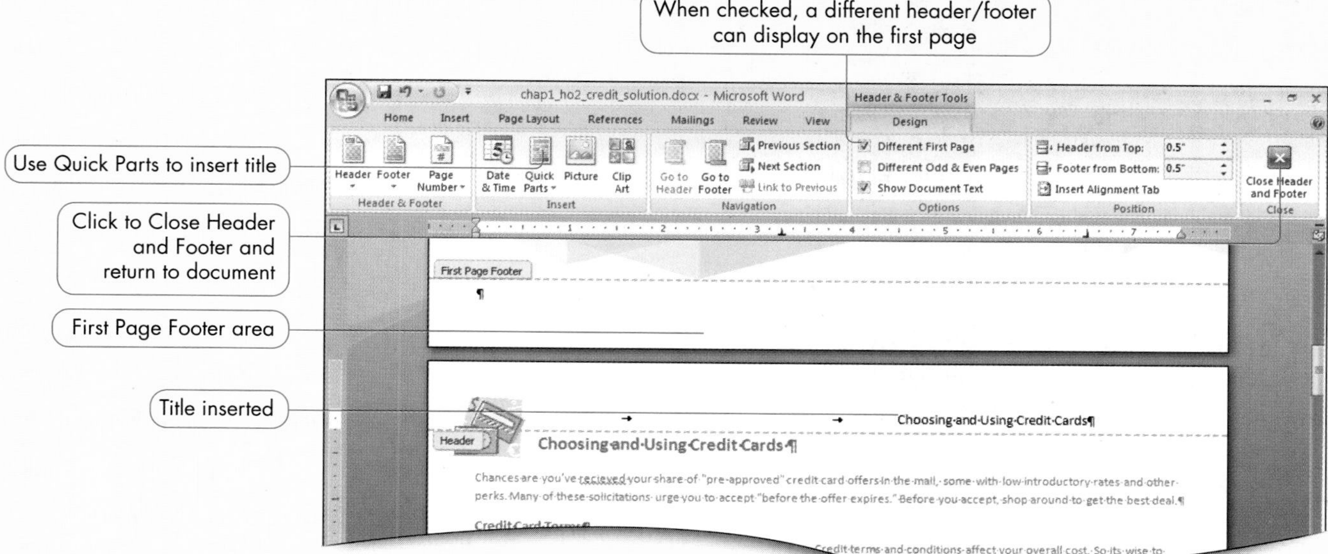
When checked, a different header/footer can display on the first page
Use Quick Parts to insert title
Click to Close Header and Footer and return to document
First Page Footer area
Title inserted

Figure 1.26 Create a Header

Step 4
Insert a Section Break

Refer to Figure 1.27 as you complete Step 4.

a. Press **Ctrl+End** to move to the end of the document, then place the insertion point on the left side of the date. Click the **Page Layout tab,** click **Breaks** in the Page Setup group, and then click **Next Page** under Section Breaks.

By inserting this section break, you are now free to make modifications to the last page without changing the previous pages.

b. Double-click in the header or footer area of the last page to display the Design tab. Click in the header of the last page, and then click **Link to Previous** in the Navigation group to deselect it.

Even though you insert a section break, the header and footer of this page take on the same formatting as the first section. When you remove that link, you can set up an independent header and/or footer.

c. In the header of the last page, type **This project was completed on**, as shown in Figure 1.27.

d. Click **Go To Footer** in the Navigation group. Click **Link to Previous** to toggle it off. In the Position group, click the **Footer from Bottom** up arrow until **.8"** displays.

This footer is now independent from all other document footers, and the page number at the bottom will print in a different location on the page.

e. Click **Close Header and Footer**. Save the document.

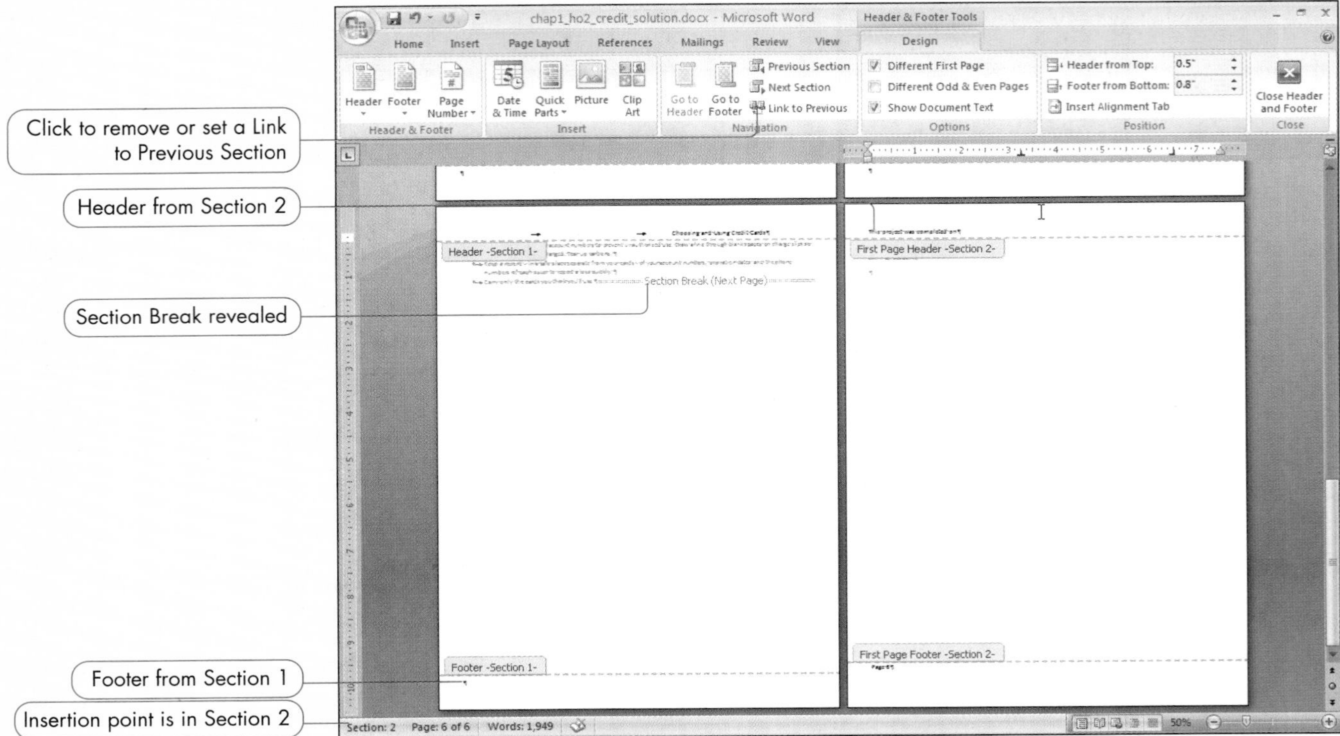

Figure 1.27 Header in Section 2

Step 5
Insert a Page Number in the Footer

Refer to Figure 1.28 as you complete Step 5.

a. Place your insertion point anywhere on the second page. Click the **Insert tab**, if necessary. Click **Page Number** in the Header & Footer group, and then point to **Bottom of Page**. Scroll down to the bottom of the gallery and select **Thick Line**.

A dark line and the page number display on the bottom of each page except the first and last because you changed the Different First Page and Link to Previous options.

TROUBLESHOOTING: If your insertion point was on the first page, the footer will display on that page only. Click Undo on the Quick Access Toolbar, place your insertion point on page two, and repeat the step above to add the footer to the remaining pages.

b. Click **Page Number** in the Header & Footer group of the Design tab and click **Format Page Numbers**.

The Page Number Format dialog box displays.

c. Click **Start at**, then click the down arrow until **0** displays.

If you begin page numbering with zero, the second page, which is the first page of content, displays as page 1.

d. Scroll to the bottom of page 6. Place the insertion point on the left side of the footer area, type **Page,** and then press **Spacebar** one time.

e. Click **Quick Parts** in the Insert group and select **Field**. Click the **Categories drop-down arrow** and select **Numbering**.

   You can insert many different items in your document; use the category option to minimize the number of fields to browse through to find the one you want.

f. Select **Page** in the **Field names** list and select the first option displayed in the Format list, as seen in Figure 1.28. Click **OK**.

   The end result for this operation will be similar to one that you can reach using the Page Number feature; however, this exercise demonstrates the field feature that allows you to use more customization in headers and footers by combining the field with text of your choice.

g. Click **Close Header and Footer**.

h. Save the document.

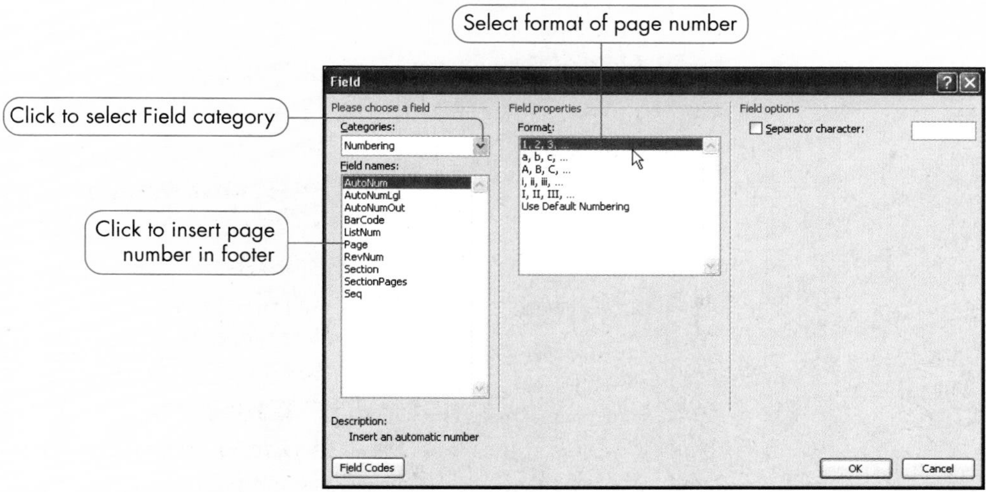

Figure 1.28 Insert a Field in a Footer

Step 6
Use Find, Replace, and Go To

Refer to Figure 1.29 as you complete Step 6.

a. Press **Ctrl+Home** to move to the beginning of the document. Click the **Home tab** and click **Find** in the Editing group.

b. Type **APR** in the *Find what* text box, and then click **Find Next**.

   The first occurrence of the text appears on the second page.

c. Click the **Replace tab** in the Find and Replace dialog box. Type **annual percentage rate** in the *Replace with* box. Click **Replace All**.

   A dialog box displays, indicating seven replacements were made.

d. Click **OK** to remove the dialog box. In the Find what text box, type **$50**. Click **More**, if necessary, then click **Format** and click **Font.** In the Font dialog box, click **Bold** in the *Font style* list, and then click **OK**.

e. In the *Replace with* text box, type **$50**. Click **Format** and click **Font.** In the Font dialog box, click **Regular** in the *Font style* list, and then click **OK**. Compare your window to Figure 1.29.

   TROUBLESHOOTING: If you applied the Bold format to the text in the *Replace with* box instead of the *Find what* box, click **No Formatting** on the bottom of the window, then start again. Be sure the insertion point is in the desired box before you click **Format**.

f. Click **Find Next.**

The bolded occurrence of $50 displays near the bottom of the fourth page.

g. Click **Replace** to remove the formatting from the text, and then click **OK** in the dialog box that informs you Word has finished searching the document.

h. Click the **Go To tab**.

The Go To tab of the Find and Replace dialog box displays, and the insertion point is in the *Enter page number* box.

i. Type **1** in the *Enter page number* box, then click **Go To.**

The top of page 1 displays on your screen, and the Find and Replace dialog box is still onscreen.

j. Click **Section** in the **Go to what** box, type **2** in the *Enter section number* box, and then click **Go To**.

The top of page 6 displays, which is the beginning of the section you added in Step 4.

k. Click **Close**. Save the document.

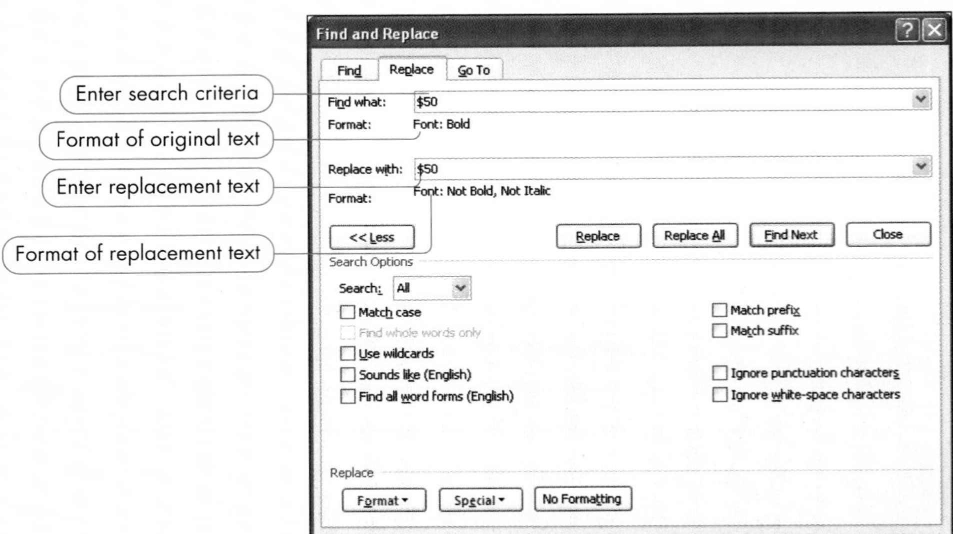

Figure 1.29 Find and Replace Text

The Final Touches

You can create a document that is, for the most part, free of typographical and grammatical errors. Word provides many features that assist in correcting a variety of grammatical mistakes.

As you work on a document, you should save changes frequently. Word even has an option to create backup copies of your work periodically in case of a system failure. When you believe that your document is complete, you should take one last look and run a few diagnostics to check for mistakes in spelling and grammar. If you are sending the document to another person, you also should use the tools that locate compatibility issues your document has with older versions of Word. If you print your document, be sure to use features that avoid wasting paper.

In this section, you check for spelling and grammatical errors. You also revisit the important process of saving files as well as backup options, the Compatibility Checker, and the Document Inspector. You learn different print options, and you learn about the many customization options available in Word 2007.

Checking Spelling and Grammar

You can create a document that is, for the most part, free of typographical and grammatical errors. However, you should always proofread a document at the conclusion of your edits because it is possible the automated spelling and grammar checker did not find every error. Word provides many features that assist in correcting a variety of grammatical mistakes. In the Office Fundamentals chapter, you learned how to use the Spelling and Grammar and the Thesaurus features to assist in writing and proofing. In the following paragraphs, you will learn about other features that help you create error-free documents.

Perform a Spelling and Grammar Check

The ***Spelling and Grammar*** feature looks for mistakes in spelling, punctuation, writing style, and word usage.

The ***Spelling and Grammar*** feature attempts to catch mistakes in spelling, punctuation, writing style, and word usage by comparing strings of text within a document to a series of predefined rules. When located, you can accept the suggested correction and make the replacement automatically, or more often, edit the selected text and make your own changes.

You also can ask the grammar check to explain the rule it is attempting to enforce. Unlike the spell check, the grammar check is subjective, and what seems appropriate to you may be objectionable to someone else. Indeed, the grammar check is quite flexible, and can be set to check for different writing styles; that is, you can implement one set of rules to check a business letter and a different set of rules for casual writing. Many times, however, you will find that the English language is just too complex for the grammar check to detect every error, although it will find many. Depending on your reliance on the grammar check, you can set the option for it to run all the time by marking the selection in the Word Options, Proofing category.

TIP Custom Dictionaries

If you work in a field that uses technical terminology, such as nursing or aviation, you need to include those terms with the existing dictionary in the Spelling and Grammar feature. To use the custom dictionary, click the Office Button, click Word Options, click Proofing, click Custom Dictionary, and then navigate to the location where the dictionary is stored.

Check Contextual Spelling

In addition to spelling and grammar checking, Word 2007 has added a contextual spelling feature that attempts to locate a word that is spelled correctly, but used incorrectly. For example, many people confuse the usage of words such as *their* and *there*, *two* and *too*, and *which* and *witch*. The visual indication that a contextual spelling error occurs is a blue wavy line under the word, as shown in Figure 1.30. By default, this feature is not turned on; to invoke the command, click the Office Button, select Word Options at the bottom, select the Proofing category, then click to select the Use contextual spelling check box.

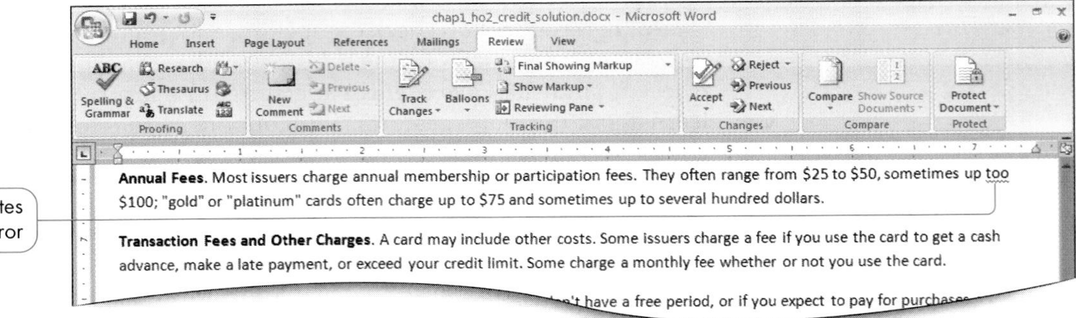

Figure 1.30 Check Contextual Spelling

Using Save and Backup Options

It is not a question of *if* it will happen but *when*. Files are lost, systems crash, and viruses infect a system. That said, we cannot overemphasize the importance of saving your work frequently. Additionally, you should use available resources to provide a backup copy (or two) of your most important documents and back up your files at every opportunity. For example, the Exploring series authors back up all of their manuscript files in case one system crashes. Graduate students periodically back up their lengthy theses and dissertations so that they do not have to recreate these research documents from scratch if one system fails.

Save a Document in Compatible Format

After reading the Office Fundamentals chapter, you know the Save and Save As commands are used to copy your documents to disk and should be used frequently in order to avoid loss of work and data. Because some people may use a different version of Microsoft Word, you should know how to save a document in a format that they can use. People cannot open a Word 2007 document in earlier versions of Word unless they update their earlier version with the Compatibility Pack that contains a converter. If you are not sure if they have installed the Compatibility Pack, it is best to save the document in an older format, such as Word 97–2003.

To save a document so that someone with a different version of Office can open it, click the Office Button and point to the arrow on the right side of the Save As command. The option to save in Word 97–2003 format appears (see Figure 1.31), and after

TIP The Word Compatibility Pack

The Compatibility Pack needed to open files created in Office 2007 can be downloaded from the Microsoft Web site. In addition to the Compatibility Pack, the latest service packs (denoted as SP) for Windows and Office should be installed on the system. The service packs needed to run the Compatibility Pack include Office 2000 SP 3, Office XP SP 3, and Office 2003 SP 1 (even though SP 2 is available). It works on the following operating systems: Windows 2000 SP 4, Windows XP SP 1 (SP 2 is available), and Windows Server 2003 (SP1 is available). If you try to install the Compatibility Pack without updating Windows or Office to the minimum service pack level, a dialog box will direct you to the Web site to download the latest version.

you click it, you can use the Save As dialog box normally. The saved file will have the .doc extension instead of the Word 2007 extension, .docx. Another way to save in the older format is to double-click Save As, then select the Word 97–2003 format from the *Save as type* list in the Save As dialog box.

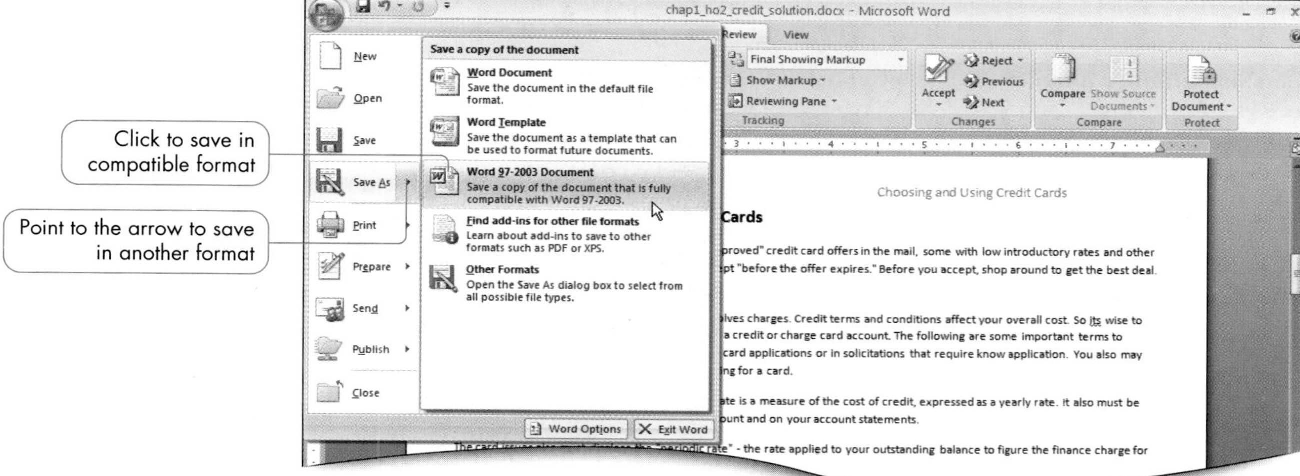

Figure 1.31 Save a File in Compatible Format

If you open a Word document created in an earlier version, such as Word 2003, the title bar will include *(Compatibility Mode)* at the top. You can still work with the document and even save it back in the same format for a Word 97–2003 user. However, some newer features of Word 2007, such as SmartArt and other graphic enhancement options used in the Cover Page and custom headers and footers, are not viewable or available for use in compatibility mode. To remove the file from compatibility mode, click the Office Button and select Convert. It will convert the file and remove the *(Compatibility Mode)* designator, but the .doc extension still displays. The next time you click Save, the extension will change to .docx, indicating that it is converted into a Word 2007 file, and then you can use all of the application features.

Understand Backup Options

Microsoft Word offers several different backup options, the most important of which is to save AutoRecover information periodically. If Microsoft Word crashes, the program will be able to recover a previous version of your document when you restart Word. The only work you will lose is anything you did between the time of the last AutoRecover operation and the time of the crash. The default *Save AutoRecover information every 10 minutes* ensures that you will never lose more than 10 minutes of work.

You also can set Word to create a backup copy in conjunction with every Save. You set these valuable backup and AutoRecover options from the Save and Advanced categories of the Word Options menu. Assume, for example, that you have created the simple document *The fox jumped over the fence* and saved it under the name *Fox*. Assume further that you edit the document to read *The quick brown fox jumped over the fence* and that you saved it a second time. The second Save command changes the name of the original document from *Fox* to *Backup of Fox*, then saves the current contents of memory as *Fox*. In other words, the disk now contains two versions of the document: the current version *Fox* and the most recent previous version *Backup of Fox*.

The cycle goes on indefinitely, with *Fox* always containing the current version and *Backup of Fox* the most recent previous version. So, if you revise and save the document a third time, *Fox* will contain the latest revision while *Backup of Fox* would contain the previous version alluding to the quick brown fox. The original (first) version of the document disappears entirely because only two versions are kept.

The contents of *Fox* and *Backup of Fox* are different, but the existence of the latter enables you to retrieve the previous version if you inadvertently edit beyond repair or accidentally erase the current *Fox* version. Should this situation occur, you can always retrieve its predecessor and at least salvage your work prior to the last save operation. But remember, this process only takes place if you enable the Always create backup copy option in the Advanced category of the Word Options dialog box.

Run the Compatibility Checker

The ***Compatibility Checker*** looks for features that are not supported by previous versions of Word.

The ***Compatibility Checker*** is a feature in Word 2007 that enables you to determine if you have used features that are not supported by previous versions. After you complete your document, click the Office Button, point to Prepare, and then select Compatibility Checker. If the document contains anything that could not be opened in a different version of Word, the Microsoft Office Word Compatibility Checker dialog box will list it. From this dialog box, you also can indicate that you want to always check compatibility when saving this file (see Figure 1.32). If you are saving the document in a format to be used by someone with an earlier version, you will want to make corrections to the items listed in the dialog box before saving again and sending the file.

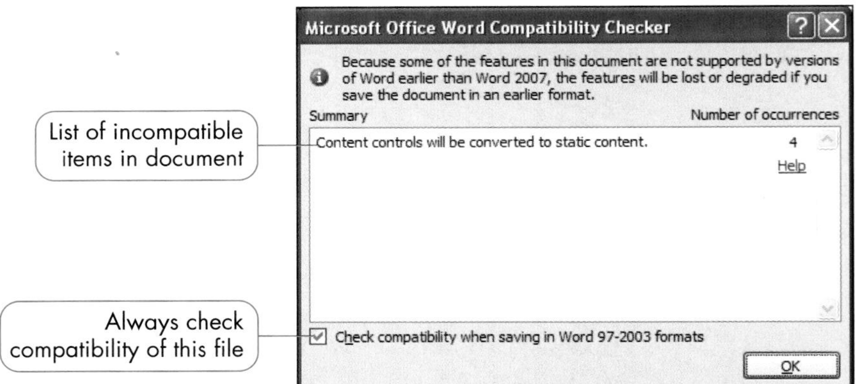

Figure 1.32 The Compatibility Checker

Run the Document Inspector

The ***Document Inspector*** checks for and removes different kinds of hidden and personal information from a document.

Before you send or give a document to another person, you should run the ***Document Inspector*** to reveal any hidden or personal data in the file. For privacy or security reasons, you might want to remove certain items contained in the document such as author name, comments made by one or more persons who have access to the document, or document server locations. Some inspectors are specific to individual Office applications, such as Excel and PowerPoint. Word provides inspectors that you can invoke to reveal different types of information, including:

- Comments, Revisions, Versions, and Annotations
- Document Properties and Personal Information
- Custom XML Data
- Headers, Footers, and Watermarks
- Hidden Text

The inspectors also can locate information in documents created in older versions of Word. Because some information that the Document Inspector might remove cannot be recovered with the Undo command, you should save a copy of your original document, using a different name, just before you run any of the inspectors. After you save the copy, click the Office Button, point to Prepare, and then select the Inspect Document option to run the inspector (see Figure 1.33). When it is complete, it will list the results and enable you to choose whether to remove the information from the document. If you forget to save a backup copy of the document, you can use the Save As command to save a copy of the document with a new name after you run the inspector.

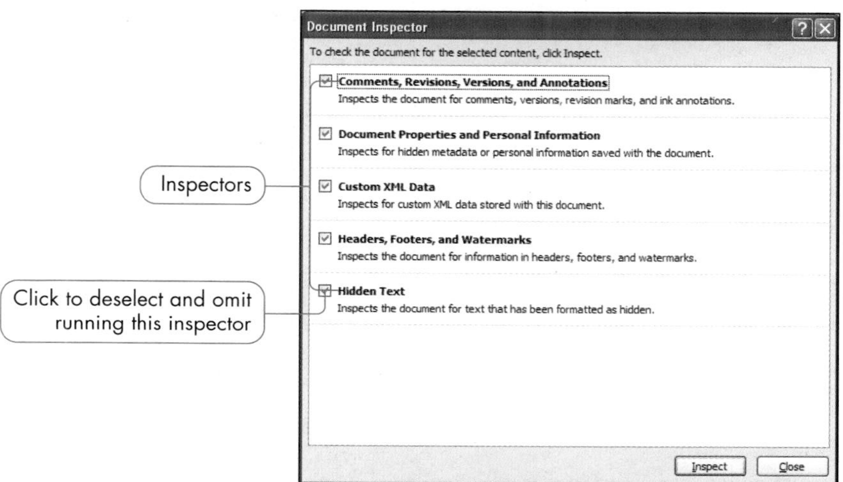

Figure 1.33 The Document Inspector

Selecting Printing Options

People often print an entire document when they want to view only a few pages. All computer users should be mindful of the environment, and limiting printer use is a perfect place to start. Millions of sheets of paper have been wasted because someone did not take a moment to preview his or her work and then had to reprint due to a very minor error that is easily noticed in a preview window.

Click the Office Button and click the Print arrow to see three settings to consider when you are ready to print your work: Print, Quick Print, and Print Preview. You should select the Print Preview option first to see a preview of what the document will look like when you print it. In the Print Preview window, you have several settings that enable you to magnify the page onscreen, display multiple pages, and even make changes to the page layout so you can view the results immediately. If you are satisfied with the document, you can launch the Print dialog box from that window.

The Quick Print option sends a document straight to the printer without prompting you for changes to the printer configuration. If you have only one printer and rarely change printer options, this is an efficient tool.

The final print option is Print, which always displays the Print dialog box and contains many useful options. For example, you can print only the page that contains the insertion point (Current page) or a specific range of pages, such as pages 3–10 (Pages). Furthermore, you can print more than one copy of the document (Number of copies), print miniature copies of pages on a single sheet of paper (Pages per sheet), or adjust the document text size to fit on a particular type of paper (Scale to paper size). If you do not have a duplex printer, you can select the option to print only even numbered pages, flip the paper over and put it back in the printer, then select the option to print only odd pages, as seen in Figure 1.34. This method is used frequently by some of the Exploring authors because they do not own duplex printers and also because they want to conserve paper!

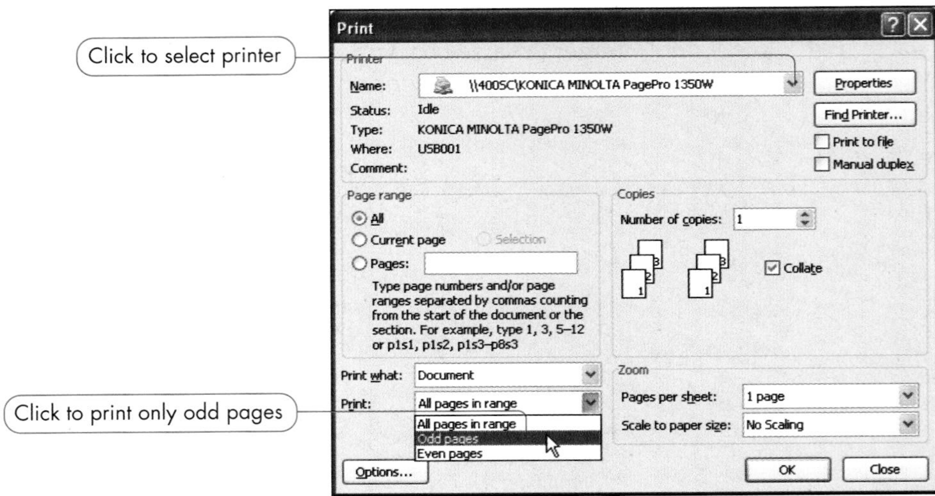

Figure 1.34 Print Options

Customizing Word

As installed, Word is set up to be useful immediately. However, you might find options that you would prefer to customize, add, or remove from the document window. For example, you can add commands to the Quick Access Toolbar (QAT) that do not currently display on any tabs. Or you can add commands that you use so frequently you prefer to access them from the always-visible QAT.

You can customize Word in many ways. To begin the process, or just to view the options available for customization, click the Office Button, then select Word Options. Table 1.2 describes the main categories that you can customize and some of the features in each category. You should take some time to glance through each category as you continue to read this chapter. Keep in mind that if you are working in a school lab, you might not have permission to change options on a permanent basis.

Table 1.2 Word Options

Menu Category	Description	Sample of Options to Change
Popular	Change the most popular options in Word.	Show Mini toolbar; show Enhanced ScreenTips; change color scheme; change user name and initials.
Display	Change how documents are displayed on the screen and in print.	Show white space between pages in Print Layout view; always show formatting marks such as spaces on the screen; print document properties.
Proofing	Modify how Word corrects and formats your text.	Ignore words in uppercase (do not flag as incorrect); use Spellchecker; use contextual spelling (checks for words that sound alike but are spelled differently such as two, too, and to); mark grammatical errors.
Save	Customize how documents are saved.	Default locations and format to save files; AutoRecover file location; Web server location.
Advanced	Specify editing options; cut, copy, and paste options; show document content options; display options; print options; and save options.	Allow text to be dragged and dropped; enable click and type; default paragraph style; show paste option buttons; show smart tags; number of recent documents to show in file menu; print pages in reverse order; always create backup copy; embed smart tags; update automatic links at open; compatibility options.
Customize	Customize the Quick Access Toolbar and other keyboard shortcuts.	Add or remove buttons from the QAT; determine location of QAT; customize keyboard shortcuts.
Add-Ins	View the add-ins previously installed, customize settings for add-ins, and install more add-ins.	View settings for active and inactive application add-ins; manage smart tags, templates, and disabled items.
Trust Center	View online documentation about security and privacy and change settings to protect documents from possible infections.	Enable and disable macros; change ActiveX settings; set privacy options; select trusted publishers and locations.
Resources	Provide links to Microsoft sites where you can find online resources and keep your Office application updated.	Download updates for Office; diagnose and repair problems with Office; contact Microsoft; activate your license for Office; register for free online services; view product specifications.

As you can see, you are able to customize dozens of settings in Word. Table 1.2 mentions only a small sample of them; fortunately, most users do not need to change any settings at all.

Hands-On Exercises

3 | The Final Touches

Skills covered: 1. Perform a Spelling and Grammar Check **2.** Run the Document Inspector and a Compatibility Check **3.** Save in a Compatible Format **4.** Change Word Options **5.** Use Print Preview Features

Step 1
Perform a Spelling and Grammar Check

Refer to Figure 1.35 as you complete Step 1.

a. Open the *chap1_ho2_credit_solution* document if you closed it after the last hands-on exercise and save it as **chap1_ho3_credit_solution**.

b. Press **Ctrl+Home** to move to the beginning of the document. Click the **Review tab** and click **Spelling & Grammar** in the Proofing group.

The Spelling and Grammar dialog box displays with the first error indicated in red text (see Figure 1.35).

c. Click **Change All** to replace all misspellings of the word *recieved* with the correct *received*, then view the next error.

d. Click **Change** to replace *its* with the correct usage, *it's*.

e. Click **Ignore Once** to keep the heading *Annual Percentage Rate*.

Remember that not all grammar usage flagged may be incorrect. Use your best judgment for those occasions.

f. Remove the check from the **Check grammar** option.

Most of the headings in the document will be flagged for incorrect grammar, so this will let you bypass all of them and check the spelling only.

g. Click **Change** to replace the contextual spelling error *too* with *to* near the bottom of the first page. Click **Change** to replace the incorrect spelling of Errors on the third page. Click **OK** in the box that informs you the spelling and grammar check is complete.

h. Save the document.

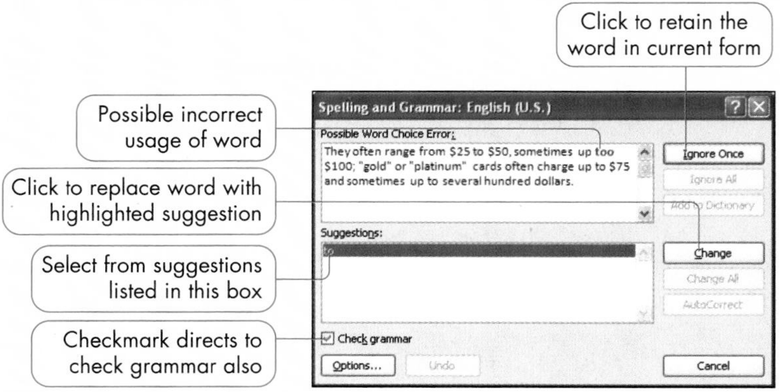

Figure 1.35 Check Spelling and Grammar

Step 2
Run the Document Inspector and a Compatibility Check

Refer to Figure 1.36 as you complete Step 2.

a. Click the **Office Button**, select **Prepare**, and then select **Run Compatibility Checker**.

   A list of any non-compatible items in the document will display in the Microsoft Office Word Compatibility Checker dialog box.

b. Click **OK** after you view the incompatible listings.

c. Click the **Office Button** and select **Save As**. Save the document as **chap1_ho3_credit2_solution**.

   Before you run the Document Inspector you save the document with a different name in order to have a backup.

d. Click the **Office Button**, point to **Prepare**, and then select **Inspect Document**.

   TROUBLESHOOTING: An informational window might display with instructions to save the document before you run the Document Inspector. You should save the document first because the Document Inspector might make changes that you cannot undo.

e. Click to select any inspector check box that is not already checked. Click **Inspect.**

   The Document Inspector results are shown, and Remove All buttons are displayed to remove the items found in each category.

f. Click **Close**; do not remove any items at this time.

g. Save the document as **chap1_ho3_credit_solution**. Click **OK** to overwrite the existing file with the same name.

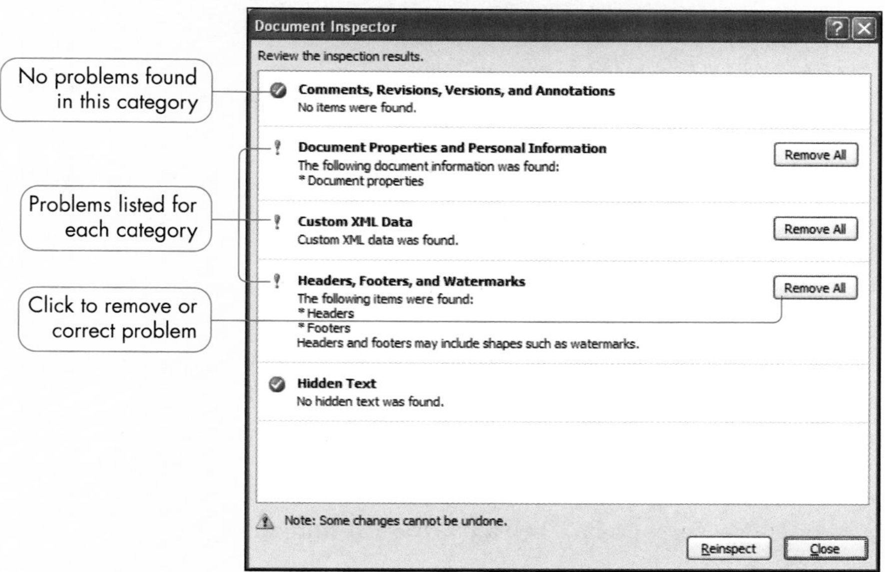

Figure 1.36 Document Inspector Results

Step 3
Save in a Compatible Format

Refer to Figure 1.37 as you complete Step 3.

a. Click the **Office Button**, click the **Save As** arrow, and select **Word 97–2003 Format**.

b. Confirm the *Save as type* box displays **Word 97–2003 document (*.doc)**, then click **Save**.

The Compatibility Checker dialog box displays to confirm the compatibility issues you have seen already.

c. Click **Continue** to accept the alteration.

The title bar displays *(Compatibility Mode)* following the file name. If you set the option to display file extensions on your computer, the document extension .doc displays in the title bar instead of .docx, as shown in Figure 1.37.

d. Click the **Office Button** and select **Convert**.

The Compatibility Mode designation is removed from the title bar. If a dialog box displays stating the document will be converted to the newest file format, click OK. You can check the option that prevents the dialog box from displaying each time this situation occurs.

e. Click **Save** on the Quick Access Toolbar. Click **Save** in the Save As dialog box and click **OK** if the authorization to overwrite the current file displays.

The document extension has been restored to .docx.

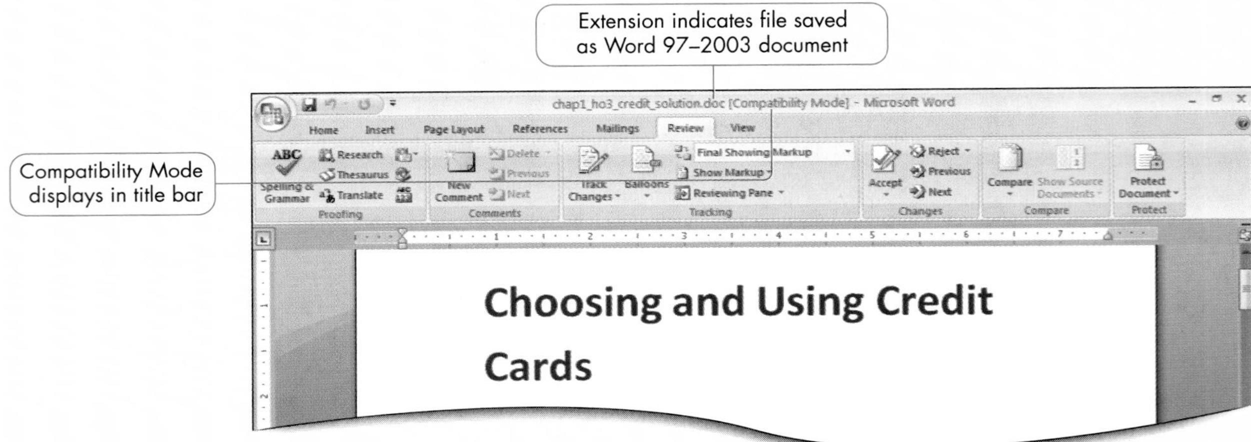

Figure 1.37 File Saved in Word 97–2003 Format

Step 4
Change Word Options

Refer to Figure 1.38 as you complete Step 4.

a. Click the **Office Button**, then click **Word Options** at the bottom of the menu.

b. Click **Customize** on the left side of the Word Options dialog box.

Look at other Word Options also, to view the many different features you can modify.

c. Select **Print Preview** from the *Choose commands from* list and click **Add** in the middle of the dialog box.

Print Preview displays in the Customize Quick Access Toolbar list.

d. Click the *Choose Commands from* drop-down arrow and click **All Commands**. Scroll down the list and click **Inspect Document** from the *Choose commands from* list and click **Add**.

e. Select **Print Preview** from the Customize Quick Access Toolbar list and click **Remove**.

Print Preview no longer displays in the list of icons for the Quick Access Toolbar, as seen in Figure 1.38.

f. Click **OK** at the bottom of the dialog box to return to the document.

The Quick Access Toolbar includes a new icon—the Document Inspector.

TROUBLESHOOTING: If you work in a lab environment, you might not have permission to modify the Word application. Accept any error messages you might see when saving the Word options and proceed to the next step.

g. Click the **Office Button**, click **Word Options** at the bottom of the menu, then click **Customize** on the left side of the Word Options dialog box. Select **Inspect Document** from the Customize Quick Access Toolbar list and click **Remove**. Click **OK** to close the Word Options dialog box.

The Quick Access Toolbar returns to the default setting.

h. Save the document.

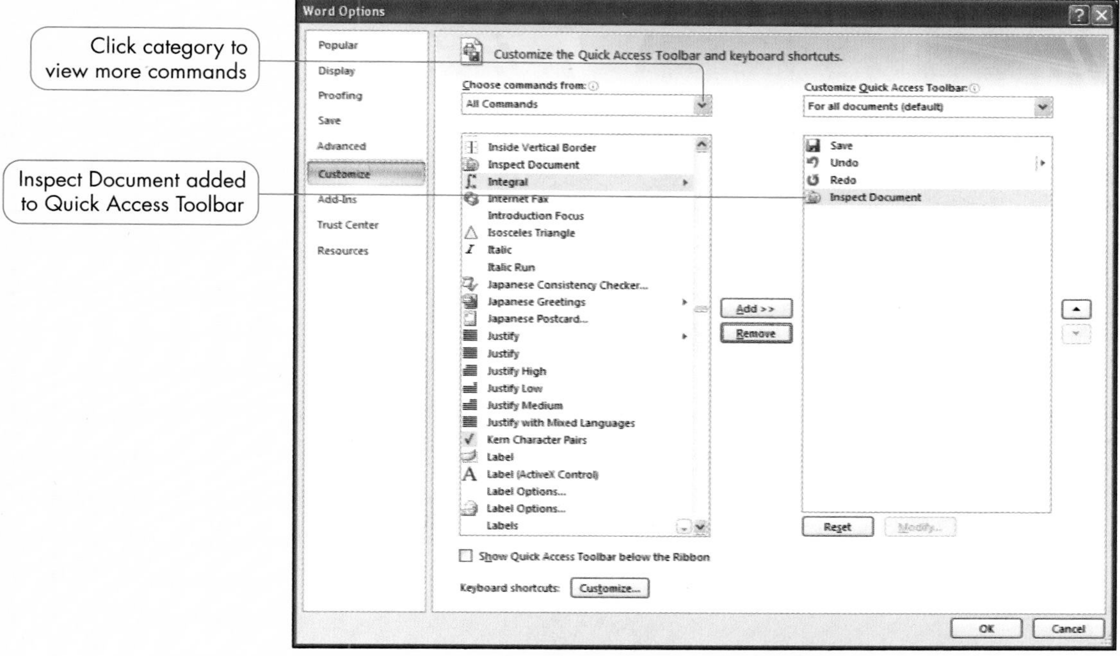

Figure 1.38 Customize the Quick Access Toolbar

Step 5
Use Print Preview Features

Refer to Figure 1.39 as you complete Step 5.

a. Click **Ctrl+Home**, if necessary, to move to the beginning of the document. Click the **Office Button**, click the **Print** arrow, and then select **Print Preview**.

The Print Preview dialog box displays the first page (see Figure 1.39).

b. Click **Two Pages** in the Zoom group to view the first two pages in this document. Click the check box next to **Magnifier** in the Preview group to remove the check mark.

This step removes the magnifying glass displayed on the mouse pointer and displays the insertion point. When you remove the magnifier, you can edit the file in the Print Preview window.

c. Place the insertion point on the left side of your name and type **Presented by:**. Click anywhere on the second page to move the insertion point out of the field.

d. Click **Margins** and select the **Narrow** setting.

   Margins in section one of the document change to .5″ on each side.

e. Click **Next Page** to view each page in the document. Click **Close Print Preview** to return to the document.

f. Save the document and exit Word.

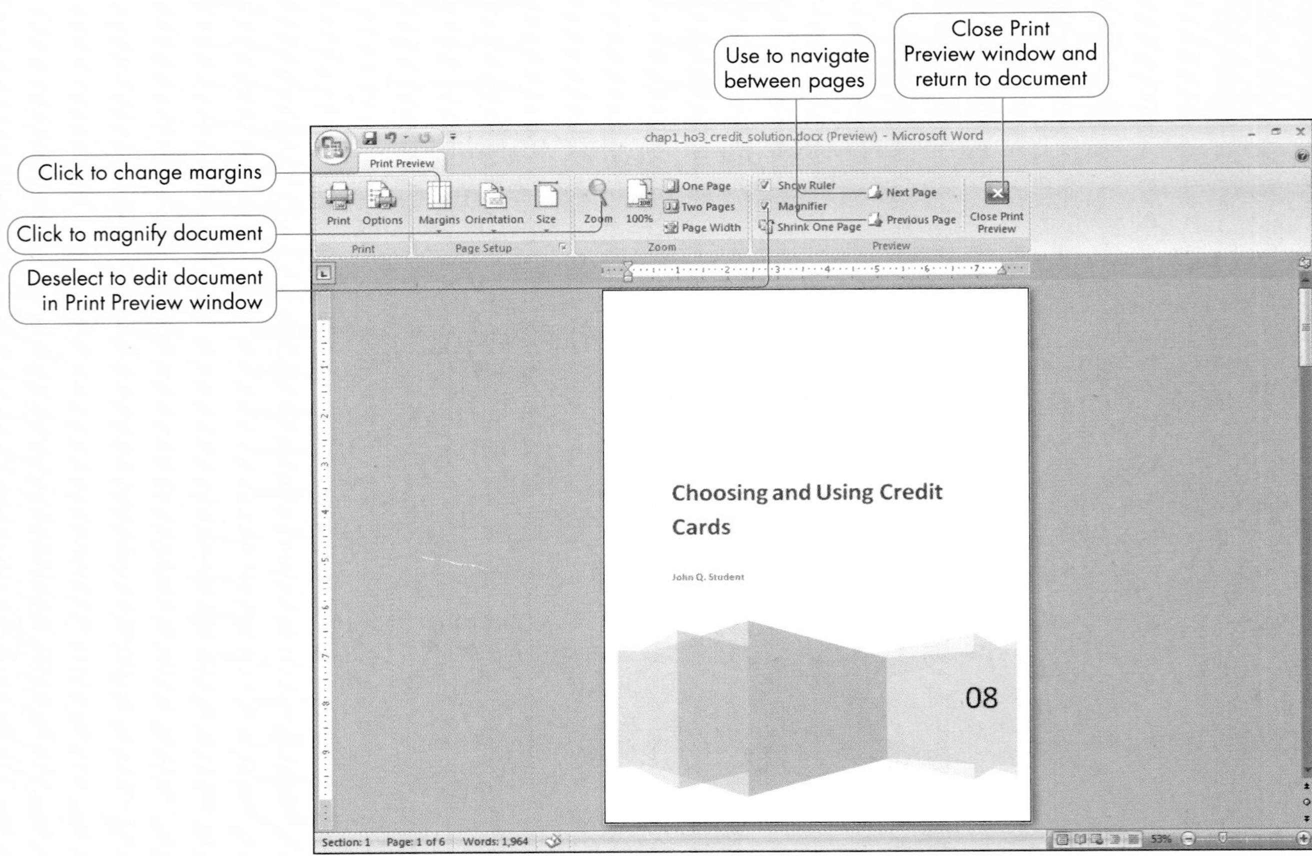

Figure 1.39 Print Preview Options

Summary

1. **Understand Word basics.** A word processing window is made up of several components including the title bar, Quick Access Toolbar, status bar, and the document area. Several tabs contain the commands that you use while working in Word, and the tabs might change according to the current task. As you type in a document, the word wrap feature automatically positions text for you using soft returns; however, you can insert a hard return to force text to the next line. Toggle switches such as the Caps Lock key or Bold feature are often used to alternate between two states while you work. The Show/Hide ¶ feature toggles on to reveal formatting marks in a document. The AutoText feature enables you to quickly insert predefined text or graphics.
2. **Use AutoText.** The AutoText feature substitutes a predefined item for specific text when the user initiates the replacement. Predefined and frequently used items, such as a logo, company name, author name, or return address, are stored as building blocks. You can type a portion of the building block entry, then press F3 to insert the remainder into your document.
3. **View a document.** The View tab provides options that enable you to display a document in many different ways. Views include Print Layout, Full Screen Reading, Web Layout, Outline, and Draft. To quickly change the view, click a button on the status bar in the lower-right corner of the window. You can use the Zoom slider to very quickly change magnification by sliding to a different percentage such as 75%. The Zoom dialog box includes options to change to whole page or multipage view.
4. **Use the Mini toolbar.** The Mini toolbar contains frequently used formatting commands such as Bold, Italic, Underline, Center, and Font Size. It displays faintly when you select text or right-click selected text, but it darkens as you move the mouse pointer closer to it. If you move the mouse pointer away from the Mini toolbar, it becomes fainter; if you do not want to use the Mini toolbar and prefer it disappears from view, press Esc when it displays.
5. **Set margins and specify page orientation.** When you create a document, you should consider how it will look when you print or display it. Margins determine the amount of white space from the text to the edge of the page. Pages can be set to display in portrait or landscape orientation. In portrait orientation, the text runs parallel to the shorter side of the paper. In landscape orientation, the text runs parallel to the longer side of the paper.
6. **Insert page breaks.** Soft page breaks occur when text no longer fits on the current page and automatically wraps to the top of a new page. The break is signified by a hidden marker that you can view using the Show/Hide ¶ feature. Hard page breaks can be used to force text onto a new page. A hard page break is inserted into a document using the Breaks command in the Page Setup group on the Page Layout tab, or Page Break in the Pages group on the Insert tab, but more easily through the Ctrl+Enter keyboard shortcut.
7. **Add page numbers.** Page numbers serve as a convenient reference point and assist in reading through a document. They can appear in the side margins or at the top or bottom of a page and can be left, center, or right aligned. The easiest way to place page numbers into a document is to click Page Number in the Header & Footer group on the Insert tab. When you use this feature, Word not only inserts page numbers but also adjusts automatically the page numbering when you add or delete pages.
8. **Insert headers and footers.** Headers and footers give a professional appearance to a document and are the best location to store page numbers. A header consists of one or more lines that are printed at the top of a page. A footer is printed at the bottom of a page. Footers often contain the page number and the date the document was created. Headers might contain the name of an organization, author, or title of the document. Headers and footers are added from the Insert tab. A simple header or footer also is created automatically by the Insert Page Number command.
9. **Create sections.** A section break is a marker that divides a document into sections, thereby allowing different formatting in each section. You determine where one section ends and another begins by using Breaks in the Page Setup group on the Page Layout tab. By using section breaks, you can change the margins within a multipage letter, where the first page (the letterhead) requires a larger top margin than the other pages in the letter. You also can change the page numbering within a document or even change the number of columns in a newsletter, which may contain a single column at the top of a page for the masthead, then two or three columns in the body of the newsletter.

...continued on Next Page

10. **Insert a cover page.** Word 2007 offers a feature to quickly insert a preformatted cover page in your document. The Cover Page feature includes a gallery with several designs, and each includes building block fields, such as Document Title, Company Name, Date, and Author, which you can personalize.

11. **Use Find and Replace commands.** Find and Replace commands include settings that enable you to look for or replace specific formatting on text. They also include options to conduct a case-sensitive or case-insensitive search. You can also use automatic replacement or selective replacement where you determine on an individual basis whether to replace the text or format. You can search for formatting and special characters. The Go To command moves the insertion point to a designated location in the document. You can go to a page, a section, or specify the number of pages to move forward or backward.

12. **Check spelling and grammar.** The grammar check feature looks for mistakes in punctuation, writing style, and word usage. If it finds an error, it will underline it with a green wavy line. You also can ask the grammar check to explain the rule it is attempting to enforce. When a possible error is found, you can accept the suggested correction, or determine if it is appropriate. The contextual spelling feature attempts to locate a word that is spelled correctly but used incorrectly. For example, it looks for the correct usage of the words *there* and *their*. A contextual spelling error is underlined with a blue wavy line.

13. **Use save and backup options.** To prevent loss of data you should save and back up your work frequently. You also should be familiar with commands that enable you to save your documents in a format compatible with older versions of Microsoft Word. You can use the convert command to alter those files into Word 2007 format, which is more efficient. Several backup options can be set, including an AutoRecover setting you can customize. This feature is useful for recovering a document when the program crashes. You can also require Word to create a backup copy in conjunction with every save operation. Word 2007 includes a compatibility checker to look for features that are not supported by previous versions of Word, and it also offers a Document Inspector that checks for and removes different kinds of hidden or personal information from a document.

14. **Select printing options.** You have three options to consider when you are ready to print your work: Print, Quick Print, and Print Preview. In the Print Preview window, you have several settings that enable you to magnify the page onscreen, display multiple pages, and even make changes to the page layout so you can view the results immediately. The Quick Print option sends a document straight to the printer without prompting you for changes to the printer configuration. The Print dialog box contains many useful options including print only the current page, a specific range of pages, or a specific number of copies.

15. **Customize Word.** After installation, Word is useful immediately. However, many options can be customized. The Word Options dialog box contains nine categories of options you can change including Personalize, Proofing, and Add-Ins. You can add to or remove commands from the Quick Access Toolbar using the Customize section of the Word Options dialog box.

Key Terms

Multiple Choice

1. When entering text within a document, you normally press Enter at the end of every:
   (a) Line
   (b) Sentence
   (c) Paragraph
   (d) Page

2. How do you display the Print dialog box?
   (a) Click the Print button on the Quick Access Toolbar.
   (b) Click the Office Button, and then click the Print command.
   (c) Click the Print Preview command.
   (d) Click the Home tab.

3. Which view removes all tabs from the screen?
   (a) Full Screen Reading
   (b) Print Layout
   (c) Draft
   (d) Print Preview

4. You want to add bold and italic to a phrase that is used several times in a document. What is the easiest way to make this update?
   (a) Use the Go To feature and specify the exact page for each occurrence.
   (b) Use the Find feature, then use overtype mode to replace the text.
   (c) Use the Find and Replace feature and specify the format for the replacement.
   (d) No way exists to automatically complete this update.

5. You are the only person in your office to upgrade to Word 2007. Before you share documents with co-workers you should
   (a) Print out a backup copy.
   (b) Run the Compatibility Checker.
   (c) Burn all documents to CD.
   (d) Have no concerns that they can open your documents.

6. A document has been entered into Word using the default margins. What can you say about the number of hard and soft returns if the margins are increased by 0.5″ on each side?
   (a) The number of hard returns is the same, but the number and/or position of the soft returns increases.
   (b) The number of hard returns is the same, but the number and/or position of the soft returns decreases.
   (c) The number and position of both hard and soft returns is unchanged.
   (d) The number and position of both hard and soft returns decreases.

7. Which of the following is detected by the contextual spell checker?
   (a) Duplicate words
   (b) Irregular capitalization
   (c) Use of the word *hear* when you should use *here*
   (d) Improper use of commas

8. Which option on the Page Layout tab allows you to specify that you are printing on an envelope?
   (a) Orientation
   (b) Margins
   (c) Breaks
   (d) Size

9. You need to insert a large table into a report, but it is too wide to fit on a standard page. Which of the following is the best option to use in this case?
   (a) Put the table in a separate document and don't worry about page numbering.
   (b) Insert section breaks and change the format of the page containing the table to landscape orientation.
   (c) Change the whole document to use landscape orientation.
   (d) Change margins to 0″ on the right and left.

10. What feature adds organization to your documents?
    (a) Print Preview
    (b) Orientation
    (c) Page Numbers
    (d) Find and Replace

Multiple Choice Continued...

11. What might cause you to be unsuccessful in finding a specific block of text in your document?
    (a) You are performing a case-sensitive search.
    (b) You have specified formatting that is not used on the text.
    (c) You are not using wildcard characters even though you are uncertain of the proper spelling of your target.
    (d) All of the above.

12. Which action below is the result of using the AutoText feature?
    (a) When you click the Print button on the Quick Access Toolbar, the document prints.
    (b) When you select text, the Mini toolbar displays.
    (c) When you press Ctrl+F, the Find dialog box displays.
    (d) You start typing the date, a ScreenTip displays the date on the screen, and you press Enter to insert it.

13. If you cannot determine why a block of text starts at the top of the next page, which toggle switch should you invoke to view the formatting marks in use?
    (a) Word wrap
    (b) Show/Hide
    (c) Bold font
    (d) Caps Lock

14. If you use the margins feature frequently, what action should you take to make it more accessible?
    (a) Use the Customization category of Word Options and add Margins to the Quick Access Toolbar.
    (b) Use the Customization category of Word Options and add Margins to the Status bar.
    (c) Use the Personalization category of Word Options and add Margins to the Quick Access Toolbar.
    (d) No way exists to make it more accessible.

15. You are on page 4 of a five-page document. Which of the following is not a way to move the insertion point to the top of the first page?
    (a) Press Ctrl+Home.
    (b) Press Ctrl+G, type 1 in the Enter page number box, and click Go To.
    (c) Press PageUp on the keyboard one time.
    (d) Press Ctrl+F, click the Go To tab, type 1 in the Enter page number box, and click Go To.

16. What visual clue tells you a document is not in Word 2007 format?
    (a) The status bar includes the text (Compatibility Mode).
    (b) The file extension is .docx.
    (c) The title bar is a different color.
    (d) The title bar includes (Compatibility Mode) after the file name.

Practice Exercises

1 Impress a Potential Customer

Chapter 1 introduced you to many of the basic features and abilities of a word processor. In the following steps, you use those tools to make modifications and enhancements to a letter that will be sent to a potential customer. It is important to write in a professional manner, even if the letter is casual. In this case, you use Find and Replace to change a misspelled word. You also insert the date and a page number and observe the AutoCorrect feature as you misspell text while typing.

a. Start Word, if necessary, and open the *chap1_pe1_candle* document. Save the file as **chap1_pe1_candle_solution**.

b. Click **Replace** in the Editing group on the Home tab, and then type **cents** in the *Find what* box and type **Scents** in the *Replace with* box. Click **More**, if necessary, to display additional search options. **Click Find whole words only**, and then click **No Formatting**, if necessary, to remove format settings from the previous Find and Replace operation.

c. Click **Find Next** and click **Replace** when the word is found. Click **OK** to close the dialog box that indicates Word has finished searching the document.

   The first sentence of the first paragraph contains the first occurrence of the word. You must select *Find whole words only* to prevent replacing the occurrences of *Scents* that are spelled correctly.

d. Move the insertion point to the left of the phrase that starts with *Take a look*. Press **Insert** to change into Insert mode, if necessary, and type the sentence **We offer teh above scented candles in four sizes, just right for any room.** As you enter the word *the*, type **teh** instead and watch as the spelling is automatically corrected.

e. Click the **Insert tab** and click **Page Number** in the Header and Footer group. Point to **Bottom of Page** and select **Plain Number 2** from the gallery.

f. Press **Ctrl** + **Home** to move the insertion point to the top of the page. Type the current month, then press **Enter** when the ScreenTip displays the full date.

   TROUBLESHOOTING: If you begin to type the date and the ScreenTip does not display, continue to manually type the current date.

g. Click the **View tab** and select **Full Screen Reading** in the Document Views group. Compare your document to Figure 1.40. Click **Close** to return to Print Layout view.

h. Click **Ctrl+S** to save the document. Click the **Office Button** and select **Close**.

...continued on Next Page

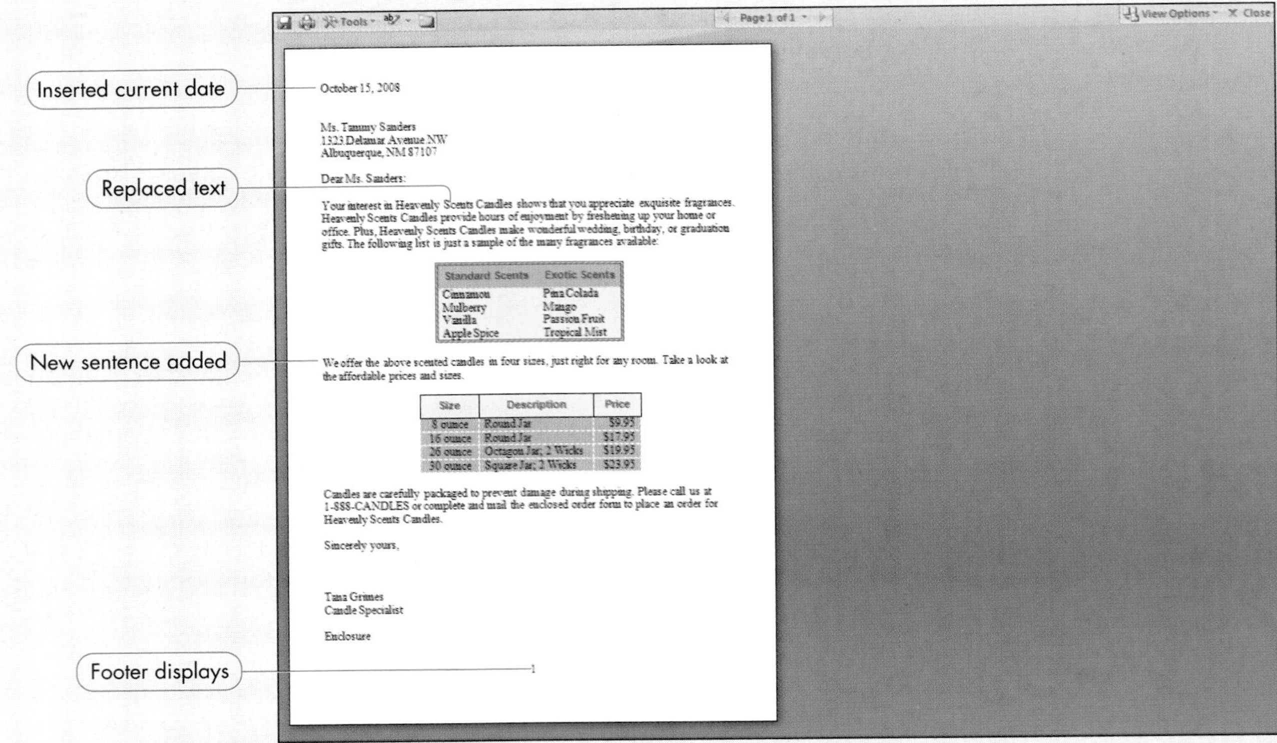

October 15, 2008

Ms. Tammy Sanders
1323 Delamar Avenue NW
Albuquerque, NM 87107

Dear Ms. Sanders:

Your interest in Heavenly Scents Candles shows that you appreciate exquisite fragrances. Heavenly Scents Candles provide hours of enjoyment by freshening up your home or office. Plus, Heavenly Scents Candles make wonderful wedding, birthday, or graduation gifts. The following list is just a sample of the many fragrances available:

Standard Scents	Exotic Scents
Cinnamon	Pina Colada
Mulberry	Mango
Vanilla	Passion Fruit
Apple Spice	Tropical Mist

We offer the above scented candles in four sizes, just right for any room. Take a look at the affordable prices and sizes.

Size	Description	Price
8 ounce	Round Jar	$9.95
16 ounce	Round Jar	$17.95
26 ounce	Octagon Jar; 2 Wicks	$19.95
30 ounce	Square Jar; 2 Wicks	$23.95

Candles are carefully packaged to prevent damage during shipping. Please call us at 1-888-CANDLES or complete and mail the enclosed order form to place an order for Heavenly Scents Candles.

Sincerely yours,

Tana Grimes
Candle Specialist

Enclosure

1

Figure 1.40 Updated Word Processing Document

2 Use Spelling and Grammar Check on a Memo

Mr. McGary, the Human Resources director of a medium-sized company, sends several memos each week to the employees in his company. It is important to communicate effectively with the employees, so he relies heavily on Word to locate errors in spelling, contextual spelling, and grammar as denoted by the wavy red, blue, and green lines, respectively. Even though Word contains these features, some mistakes may go unnoticed by the program. Mr. McGary, as well as anyone who uses a word processor, should always proofread documents carefully in addition to running the electronic spelling and grammar checkers. Your assignment is to correct the document so that it is error free and Mr. McGary can convey his message to employees without the distraction of poor spelling and grammar.

a. Open the *chap1_pe2_memo* document and save it as **chap1_pe2_memo_solution**.
b. Click the **Office Button** and click **Word Options** to display the Word Options dialog box. Click **Proofing** and click **Use contextual spelling**, if necessary, to enable that feature. Click **OK**.
c. Press **Ctrl+Home** to move to the beginning of the document. Click the **Review tab** and click **Spelling & Grammar** to check the document and correct errors. The first error displays in Figure 1.41. Use the following table to validate your corrections.

Error	Correction
Employeees	Employees
As you probably no	As you probably know
seminars are held inn the Cowboy Hat Hotel	seminars are held in the Cowboy Hat Hotel
managers have been instructed too allow employees in their department too attend	managers have been instructed to allow employees in their department to attend
MEntoring	Mentoring
attend..	attend.

...continued on Next Page

d. Right-click the words *These seminars* in the last sentence of the first paragraph. Click **These seminars** to remove the extra space between the words.

e. Click to the right of the letter b in the word *Subrdinate* in the first seminar listed in the table. Type **o** to correct the misspelling of subordinate.

f. Click the **Insert tab** and click **Footer** in the Header and Footer group. Click **Edit Footer** and type **Updated by**, then press **Spacebar** one time. Type your initials, then press **F3** to insert the AutoText entry that contains your name. Click **Close Header and Footer**.

g. Save the document.

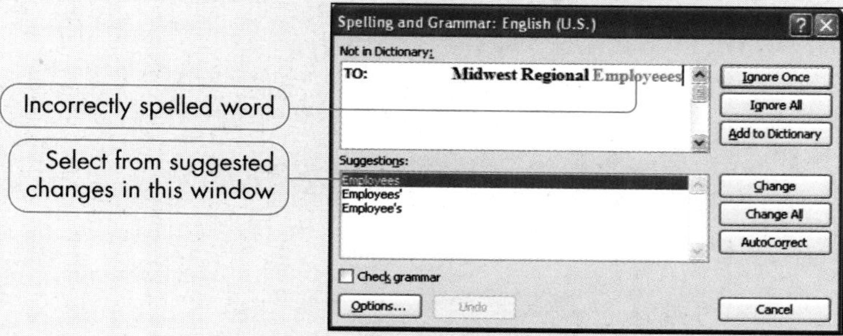

Figure 1.41 The Spell Check Process

3 Keyboard Shortcuts

Keyboard shortcuts are especially useful if you are a good typist because your hands can remain on the keyboard, as opposed to continually moving to and from the mouse. We never set out to memorize the shortcuts; we just learn them along the way as we continue to use Microsoft Office. It is much easier than you think, and the same shortcuts apply to multiple applications, such as Microsoft Excel, PowerPoint, and Access.

a. Open the *chap1_pe3_shortcuts* document. Click the **Office Button** and select **Convert**. Save the document as **chap1_pe3_shortcuts_solution**, paying special attention that it is saved in Word format (*.docx).

b. Click the **Page Layout tab,** click **Margins** in the Page Setup group, and click **Normal**. Click **Orientation**, and then click **Portrait**.

c. Click the **Home tab** and click **Show/Hide ¶** in the Paragraph group, if necessary, to display formatting marks.

   It will be helpful to see the formatting marks when you edit the document in the following steps.

d. Move the insertion point to the left side of the hard return mark at the end of the line containing Ctrl+B. Press **Ctrl+B,** then type the word **Bold**.

e. Move the insertion point to the left side of the hard return mark at the end of the line containing Ctrl+I. Press **Ctrl+I,** then type the word **Italic**.

f. Scroll to the bottom of the first page and place the insertion point on the left side of the title *Other Ctrl Keyboard Shortcuts*. Press **Ctrl+Enter** to insert a hard page break and keep the paragraph together on one page.

g. Click the **Insert tab**, click **Page Number** in the Header & Footer group, point to **Bottom of Page**, and select **Brackets 1** from the gallery.

h. Click **Header** in the Header & Footer group and select **Edit Header**. Click **Different First Page** in the Options group of the Design tab to insert a check mark. Place the insertion point in the header area of the second page and type **Keyboard Shortcuts**.

   Because you selected the *Different First Page* option, the header does not display on the first page as it is not needed there. However, the footer on the first page has been removed, so you will have to reinsert it.

...continued on Next Page

i. Move the insertion point to the first page footer. With the Design tab selected, click **Page Number** in the Header & Footer group, point to **Bottom of Page**, then select **Brackets 1** from the gallery. Click **Close Header and Footer**.

j. Click the **Zoom button** in the status bar, click **Many pages**, then drag to select **1 x 2 pages**. Click **OK** to close the Zoom dialog box. Click **Show/Hide ¶** in the Paragraph group on the Home tab to toggle off the formatting marks. Compare your document to Figure 1.42.

k. Save the document.

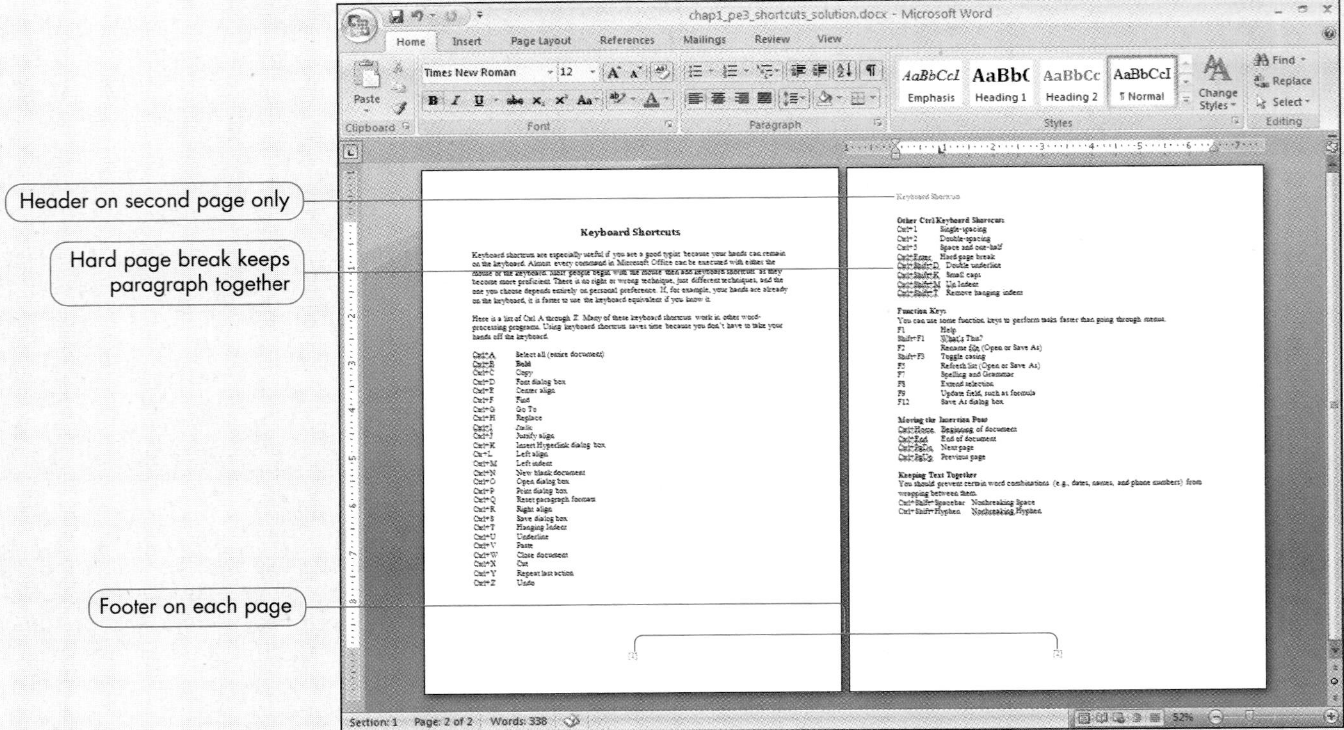

Figure 1.42 Keyboard Shortcut Document

4 Protecting Your System

The document you use in this exercise discusses computer viruses and backup procedures. It is not a question of *if* it will happen, but *when*—hard drives die, removable disks are lost, or viruses may infect a system. You can prepare for the inevitable by creating an adequate backup before the problem occurs. The advice in this document is very important; you should take it very seriously, and then protect yourself and your data.

a. Open the *chap1_pe4_virus* document and save it as **chap1_pe4_virus_solution**.

b. Click **Ctrl+H** to display the Find and Replace dialog box. In the *Find what* box, type **virus**. In the *Replace with* box, type **virus**. Click **More**, if necessary, then click the **Match case** check box.

c. Confirm that the *Replace with* text is selected or that the insertion point is in that box. Click **Format** at the bottom of the window and select **Font**. Click **Bold Italic** under the *Font Style* section, then click **OK**. Click **Replace All**, then click **OK** to confirm 17 replacements in the document. Click **Close** to remove the Find and Replace dialog box.

d. Scroll to the bottom of the first page and place the insertion point on the left side of the title *The Essence of Backup*. Press **Ctrl+Enter** to insert a hard page break.

   This step creates a more appropriate break and keeps the heading and content together on one page.

...continued on Next Page

e. Press **Ctrl+End** to move to the end of the document. Type your name, press **Enter**, type the name of your class, then use the mouse to select it. Click **Quick Parts** in the Text group on the **Insert tab**, then click **Save Selection to Quick Part Gallery**.

   The Create New Building Block dialog box displays, and you will add your name as an AutoText entry.

f. Replace your name in the *Name* box with the word **me**. Change the *Gallery* option to **AutoText**, and then click **OK**.

   Even though you replaced your name in the dialog box, the text that is highlighted in the document will be used when you invoke the AutoText feature.

g. Delete your name at the end of the document. Click **Page Number** in the Header & Footer group on the **Insert tab**, click Bottom of Page, and then click **Circle** from the gallery.

h. The insertion point is on the left margin of the footer. Type **Created by: me** and press **F3**.

   When you click F3, the AutoText entry should replace the text *me* with your name and your class displays on the line below.

i. Click **Close Header and Footer**.

j. Click **Zoom** in the status bar, click **Many pages**, then drag to select **1 × 2 pages**. Click **OK** to close the Zoom dialog box. Click **Show/Hide ¶** in the Paragraph group on the Home tab to toggle off the formatting marks, if necessary. Compare your document to Figure 1.43.

k. Save the document. Click the **Office Button**, click **Prepare**, and then click **Run Compatibility Checker**.

   The results indicate that some text box positioning will change if opened in an older version of Word. It was good to check this before you save the document in Word 97–2003 format.

l. Click **OK** to close the Compatibility Checker window. Click the **Office Button**, click the **Save As arrow**, and select **Word 97–2003 Format**. Confirm the *Save as type* box displays Word 97–2003 document (*.doc), then click **Save**. Click **Continue** when the Compatibility Checker box shows the information you viewed previously.

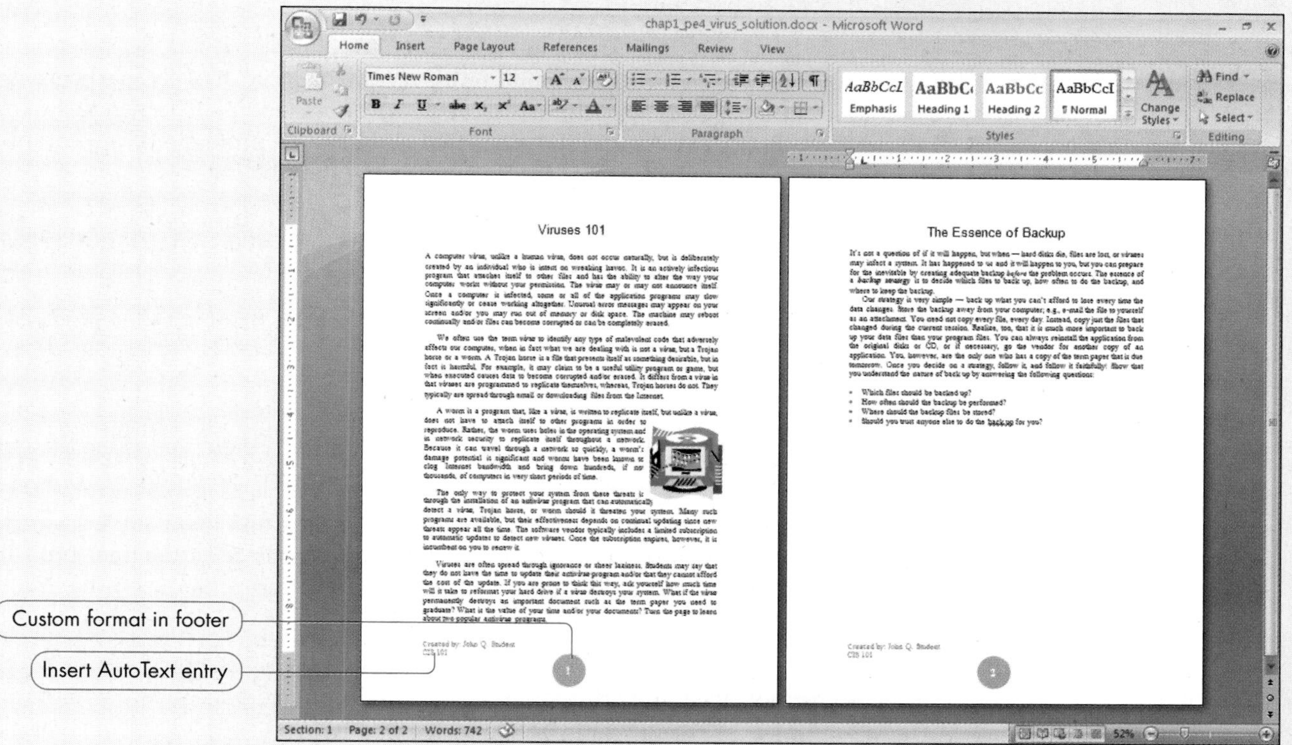

Figure 1.43 Protecting Your System

Mid-Level Exercises

1 Media-Blitz

Media-Blitz is a locally owned store that specializes in both new and used copies of popular music and movies. Its proximity to a local college campus provides a steady flow of customers during the school year. To increase sales during the typically slow summer season, it is offering discounts to students who have already enrolled in classes for the upcoming semester. You are working for the store this summer, and your assistance is needed to put the finishing touches on a flyer it wants to distribute in the area.

a. Open the *chap1_mid1_media* document and save it as **chap1_mid1_media_solution**.

b. Insert hard returns to create a list of discounts using the information below the first paragraph. Use the Mini toolbar to apply Bold and Center formatting to this group of items.

c. Perform a spelling and grammar check on the document to correct errors.

d. Create an AutoText entry for the name and address of the business. Name the entry Blitz. This entry will be useful in other documents you create for the business. Test the entry to make sure it works properly.

e. The school recently changed its name to Greene County Community College. Make appropriate changes in the flyer so each use of the name is updated and bolded.

f. Change to Full Screen Reading view, then change back to Print Layout view.

g. Display the document in the Print Preview window. Change orientation to Landscape.

h. Save and close the document.

2 Training Proposal

All About Training is an established computer training company that actively markets its services to the community. You have the opportunity to preview a document it will be sending to prospective clients and you notice several modifications that would add a professional appearance to the document. Use your skills to make the changes listed in the steps below.

a. Open the *chap1_mid2_proposal* document and save it as **chap1_mid2_proposal_solution**.

b. Insert a section break at the beginning of the document that forces the proposal to start on the second page.

c. Set 1″ margins on all sides of the whole document.

d. At the end of the last page, insert several hard returns, then type a line that says **Last Updated on:** and insert the current date using the AutoText feature.

e. Create a title page, without using the Cover Page feature, that contains a copy of the text *All About Training*. Use a 36 pt bold font and center it on the line. Type **Training Proposal** on the second line; use a 26 pt bold font, and center it on the line. Set 1.5″ margins on all sides for this page.

f. Display page numbers on the side margin. The title page should not display a page number, so page numbering should begin on the second page. (Hint: you must change a setting in the Header and Footer Design tab.)

...continued on Next Page

g. Replace each instance of the company name to display in bold, italic, and red font color. Allow the replacement only when it appears in a paragraph, not in the banner that appears at the top of the document.

h. Perform a spelling and grammar check on the document.

i. Save the document in both Word 2007 and Word 97–2003 formats so it will be available for prospective clients regardless of the version of Word they use. Close all documents.

3 Fundraiser

The organizer of a craft fair has contacted your school to request permission to conduct a fundraiser. Your work in the office of College Relations includes returning the responses from administrators on matters such as this. The response letter has been drafted, and you will complete the letter by adding the recipient's name and address; then you create an envelope in which to mail it.

a. Open a blank document and type your name on a blank line. Use your name to create a Building Block AutoText entry.

b. Open the *chap1_mid3_letter* document and save it as **chap1_mid3_letter_solution**.

c. Move the insertion point to the bottom of the letter and replace the text *Your Name Here* with your name using the AutoText entry you created in the first step.

d. Insert a Next Page Section Break at the end of the letter and apply landscape orientation to the second page.

e. Confirm that the headers and footers in the second section are not linked to the first section. Then use the AutoText entry to insert your name in the header.

f. Use copy and paste to insert the recipient's name and address from the letter in the second section. Center the address so it resembles an envelope.

g. Save and close the document.

4 Heart Disease Prevention

Millions of people suffer from heart disease and other cardiac-related illnesses. Of those people, several million will suffer a heart attack each year. Your mother volunteers for the American Heart Association and has brought you a document that explains what causes a heart attack, the signs of an attack, and what you can do to reduce your risk of having one. The information in the document is very valuable, but she needs you to put the finishing touches on this document before she circulates it in the community.

a. Open the *chap1_mid4_heart* document and save it as **chap1_mid4_heart_solution**.

b. Convert the solution file so it does not open in Compatibility Mode.

c. Create a cover page for the report. Use **Tiles** in the cover page gallery. Add text where necessary to display the report title and subtitle (use *What You Should Know* as the subtitle), and your name as author. Delete any unused fields on the cover page.

d. Change the document margins to .75" on all sides.

e. Create a section break between the cover page and the first page of the report. Set appropriate options to prevent a footer from displaying on the cover page. A page number should display at the bottom of the remaining pages, and you should display the number one on the first page of the report that follows the cover page.

...continued on Next Page

f. Create a header that displays the report title. It should not display on the cover or first page of the report (the page that follows the cover page). Confirm that the headers and footers in the second section are not linked to the first section.

g. Toggle the Show/Hide ¶ feature on, then select Draft view. Remove any page breaks that cause the report data to display on separate pages. Do not remove the page break that immediately follows the cover page. View the document in Print Layout view and insert page breaks where necessary to prevent a paragraph or list from breaking across pages.

h. You are investing a lot of time in this project, so confirm that Word is performing backups every 5 minutes using the Word Options.

i. Save and close the document.

Capstone Exercise

After a hard week of work, you decide to enjoy the great outdoors by taking a canoe trip with your friends. Your friend researched the Buffalo National River and e-mailed you a document that describes the activities and preparations needed before visiting the area. You want to send the information to others who will accompany you on the trip, but the document needs some formatting modifications.

Spelling and Grammar

The first thing you notice about the report is the number of spelling and grammatical errors detected by Word. You will fix those as well as correct all references to the river that omit its status as a National River.

a. Open the *chap1_cap_buffalo* document, found in the Exploring Word folder. Save the document as **chap1_cap_buffalo_solution**.

b. Display the document in Full Screen Reading view. Use the navigation tool to view each page. Return to Print Layout view.

c. Display the Word Options dialog box and engage the Contextual Spelling feature if it is not already in use.

d. Run the spell checker and correct grammar and contextual spelling errors also.

e. Replace all occurrences of *Buffalo River* with **Buffalo National River**. When you make the replacements, add a bold font.

Revise Page Layout

When you zoom out to view multiple pages of the document, you notice that several lines and paragraphs break at odd places. Use formatting tools and page layout options to improve the readability of this file. Take special consideration of the picture on the last page; it seems to be too wide to display on a standard page.

a. Change the Zoom to 50% and determine where the content makes awkward breaks. Click Show/Hide ¶, if necessary, to display formatting marks that will assist you in determining which format options are in use.

b. Remove any unnecessary hard returns that interfere with word wrapping in the first paragraph.

c. Adjust margins to use the Normal setting (1″ on each side). Insert hard page breaks where necessary to keep paragraphs together.

d. Create a footer that displays page numbers. Select the **Annual** format for the page numbers.

e. Insert a Next Page Section break before the picture of the river. Change the orientation of the last page so the whole picture displays on the page.

Save in Multiple Formats

After improving the readability of the document, you remember that it has not yet been saved. Saving work is very important, and you will save it immediately. Since you will be sharing the document with friends, you also decide to save it in a format compatible with older versions.

a. Save the document again as **chap1_ cap_ buffalo2_solution**, then run the Compatibility Checker and Document Inspector, but do not take any suggested actions at this time.

b. Save the document in Word 97–2003 format.

c. Use the Print Preview feature to view the document before printing. Do not print unless instructed to by your teacher.

Mini Cases

Use the rubric following the case as a guide to evaluate your work, but keep in mind that your instructor may impose additional grading criteria or use a different standard to judge your work.

Letter of Appreciation

GENERAL CASE

Have you taken time to think about the people who have helped you get to where you are? For some, parents have provided encouragement and financial assistance so their children can enjoy the privileges of a higher education. Many other students receive the moral support of family but are financing their education personally. Regardless of how your education is funded, there are people who deserve your appreciation. Take this opportunity to write a letter that you can send to those people. In the letter, you can give an update on your classes, tell them about your future plans, and don't forget to express your appreciation for their support. Create an attractive document using skills learned in this chapter, then save your letter as **chap1_mc1_appreciate_solution**.

Performance Elements	Exceeds Expectations	Meets Expectations	Below Expectations
Completeness	Document contains all required elements.	Document contains most required elements.	Document contains elements not specified in instructions.
Page setup	Modified or added at least three Page Layout elements.	Modified or added at least two Page Layout elements.	Did not modify or add any Page Layout elements.
Accuracy	No errors in spelling, grammar, or punctuation were found.	Fewer than two errors in spelling, grammar, or punctuation were found.	More than two errors in spelling, grammar, or punctuation were found.

Animal Concerns

RESEARCH CASE

As the population of family pets continues to grow, it is imperative that we learn how to be responsible pet owners. Very few people take the time to perform thorough research on the fundamental care of and responsibility for animal populations. Open the *chap1_mc2_animal* document and proceed to search the Internet for information that will contribute to this report on animal care and concerns. Compare information from at least three sources. Give consideration to information that is copyrighted and do not reprint it. Any information used should be cited in the document. As you enter the information and sources into the document, you will be reminded of concepts learned in Chapter 1, such as word wrap and soft returns. Use your knowledge of other formatting techniques, such as hard returns, page numbers, and margin settings, to create an attractive document. Create a cover page for the document, perform a spell check, and view the print preview before submitting this assisnment to your instructor. Create headers and/or footers to improve readability. Name your completed document **chap1_mc2_animal_solution**.

Performance Elements	Exceeds Expectations	Meets Expectations	Below Expectations
Research	All sections were completed with comprehensive information and citations.	All sections were updated but with minimal information and no citations.	Sections were not updated, no citations were given.
Page setup	Modified or added at least three Page Layout elements.	Modified or added at least two Page Layout elements.	Did not modify or add any Page Layout elements.
Accuracy	No errors in spelling, grammar, or punctuation were found.	Fewer than two errors in spelling, grammar, or punctuation were found.	More than two errors in spelling, grammar, or punctuation were found.

TMG Newsletter

DISASTER RECOVERY

The *chap1_mc3_tmgnews* document was started by an office assistant, but she quickly gave up on it after she moved paragraphs around until it became unreadable. The document contains significant errors, which cause the newsletter to display in a very disjointed way. Use your knowledge of Page Layout options and other Word features to revise this newsletter in time for the monthly mailing. Save your work as **chap1_mc3_tmgnews_solution**.

Performance Elements	Exceeds Expectations	Meets Expectations	Below Expectations
Page setup	Modified Page Layout options in such a way that newsletter displays on one page.	Few Page Layout modifications applied; newsletter displays on more than one page.	No Page Layout modifications applied; newsletter displays on more than one page.
Accuracy	No errors in spelling, grammar, or punctuation were found.	Fewer than two errors in spelling, grammar, or punctuation were found.	More than two errors in spelling, grammar, or punctuation were found.

chapter 2 | Word

Gaining Proficiency

Editing and Formatting

After you read this chapter, you will be able to:

1. Apply font attributes through the Font dialog box **(page 133)**.
2. Highlight text **(page 136)**.
3. Control word wrapping with nonbreaking hyphens and nonbreaking spaces **(page 137)**.
4. Copy formats with the Format Painter **(page 139)**.
5. Set off paragraphs with tabs, borders, lists, and columns **(page 143)**.
6. Apply paragraph formats **(page 148)**.
7. Create and modify styles **(page 159)**.
8. Create a table of contents **(page 171)**.
9. Create an index **(page 171)**.

Hands-On Exercises

Exercises	Skills Covered
1. CHARACTER FORMATTING (page 140) **Open:** chap2_ho1_description.docx **Save as:** chap2_ho1_description_solution.docx	• Change Text Appearance • Insert Nonbreaking Spaces and Nonbreaking Hyphens • Highlight Text and Use Format Painter
2. PARAGRAPH FORMATTING (page 152) **Open:** chap2_ho1_description_solution.docx (from Exercise 1) **Save as:** chap2_ho2_description_solution.docx (additional modifications)	• Set Tabs in a Footer • Select Text to Format • Specify Line Spacing, Justification, and Pagination • Indent Text • Apply Borders and Shading • Change Column Structure • Insert a Section Break and Create Columns
3. STYLES (page 164) **Open:** chap2_ho3_gd.docx **Save as:** chap2_ho3_gd_solution.docx	• Apply Style Properties • Modify the Body Text Style • Modify the Heading 3 Style • Select the Outline View • Create a Paragraph Style • Create a Character Style • View the Completed Document
4. REFERENCE PAGES (page 173) **Open:** chap2_ho3_gd_solution.docx (from Exercise 3) **Save as:** chap2_ho4_gd_solution.docx (additional modifications)	• Apply a Style • Insert a Table of Contents • Define an Index Entry • Create the Index • Complete the Index • View the Completed Document

CASE STUDY

Treyserv-Pitkin Enterprises

Treyserv, a consumer products manufacturing company, has recently acquired a competitor, paving the way for a larger, stronger company poised to meet the demands of the market. Each year Treyserv generates a corporate annual report and distributes it to all employees and stockholders. You are the executive assistant to the president of Treyserv and your responsibilities include preparing and distributing the corporate annual report. This year the report emphasizes the importance of acquiring Pitkin Industries to form Treyserv-Pitkin Enterprises.

Case Study

As with most mergers or acquisitions, the newly created Treyserv-Pitkin organization will enable management to make significant changes to establish a more strategic and profitable company. Management will focus on reorganizing both companies to eliminate duplication of efforts and reduce expenses; it will reduce long-term debt when possible and combine research and development activities. The annual report always provides a synopsis of recent changes to upper management, and this year it will introduce a new Chair and Chief Executive Officer, Mr. Dewey A. Larson. The company also hired Ms. Amanda Wray as chief financial officer; both positions are very high profile and contribute to the stockholders' impression of the company's continued success. Information about these newly appointed executives and other financial data have been gathered, but the report needs to be formatted attractively before it can be distributed to employees and stockholders.

Your Assignment

- Read the chapter, paying special attention to sections that describe how to apply styles, create a table of contents, and create an index.
- Open the document, *chap2_case_treyserv,* which contains the unformatted report that was provided to you by the president of the company.
- Add format features such as borders and shading, line spacing, justification, paragraph indention, and bullet and number lists to enhance the appearance of information in the report.
- Use tabs or columns, when appropriate, to align information in the report.
- Use predefined styles, such as Heading 1 and Heading 2, to format paragraph headings throughout the document.
- Apply paragraph formats such as widow/orphan control to prevent text from wrapping awkwardly when it spans from one page to the next.
- Add a table of contents and page numbering to assist readers in locating information.
- Save your work in a document named **chap2_case_treyserv_solution**.

Text Formatting

> The ultimate success of any document depends greatly on its appearance. Typeface should reinforce the message without calling attention to itself and should be consistent with the information you want to convey.

The arrangement and appearance of printed matter is called ***typography***. You also may define it as the process of selecting typefaces, type styles, and type sizes. The importance of these decisions is obvious, for the ultimate success of any document depends greatly on its appearance. Typeface should reinforce the message without calling attention to itself and should be consistent with the information you want to convey. For example, a paper prepared for a professional purpose, such as a résumé, should use a standard typeface and abstain from using one that looks funny or cute. Additionally, you want to minimize the variety of typefaces in a document to maintain a professional look.

Typography is the appearance of printed matter.

A ***typeface*** or ***font*** is a complete set of characters.

A ***serif typeface*** contains a thin line at the top and bottom of characters.

A ***sans serif typeface*** does not contain thin lines on characters.

A ***typeface*** or ***font*** is a complete set of characters—upper- and lowercase letters, numbers, punctuation marks, and special symbols. A definitive characteristic of any typeface is the presence or absence of thin lines that end the main strokes of each letter. A ***serif typeface*** contains a thin line or extension at the top and bottom of the primary strokes on characters. A ***sans serif typeface*** (sans from the French for without) does not contain the thin lines on characters. Times New Roman is an example of a serif typeface. Arial is a sans serif typeface.

Serifs help the eye to connect one letter with the next and generally are used with large amounts of text. This book, for example, is set in a serif typeface. A sans serif typeface is more effective with smaller amounts of text such as titles, headlines, corporate logos, and Web pages.

A ***monospaced typeface*** uses the same amount of horizontal space for every character.

A ***proportional typeface*** allocates horizontal space to the character.

Type style is the characteristic applied to a font, such as bold.

A second characteristic of a typeface is whether it is monospaced or proportional. A ***monospaced*** typeface (such as Courier New) uses the same amount of horizontal space for every character regardless of its width. A ***proportional*** typeface (such as Times New Roman or Arial) allocates space according to the width of the character. For example, the lowercase *m* is wider than the lowercase *i*. Monospaced fonts are used in tables and financial projections where text must be precisely lined up, one character underneath the other. Proportional typefaces create a more professional appearance and are appropriate for most documents, such as research papers, status reports, and letters. You can set any typeface in different ***type styles*** such as regular, **bold**, *italic*, or ***bold italic***.

In this section, you apply font attributes through the Font dialog box, change casing, and highlight text so that it stands out. You also control word wrapping by inserting nonbreaking hyphens and nonbreaking spaces between words. Finally, you copy formats using the Format Painter.

Applying Font Attributes Through the Font Dialog Box

In the Office Fundamentals chapter, you learned how to use the Font group on the Home tab to apply font attributes. The Font group contains commands to change the font, font size, and font color; and apply bold, italic, and underline. In addition to applying commands from the Font group, you can display the Font dialog box to give you complete control over the typeface, size, and style of the text in a document. Making selections in the Font dialog box before entering text sets the format of the text as you type. You also can change the font of existing text by selecting the text and then applying the desired attributes from the Font dialog box, as shown in Figure 2.1.

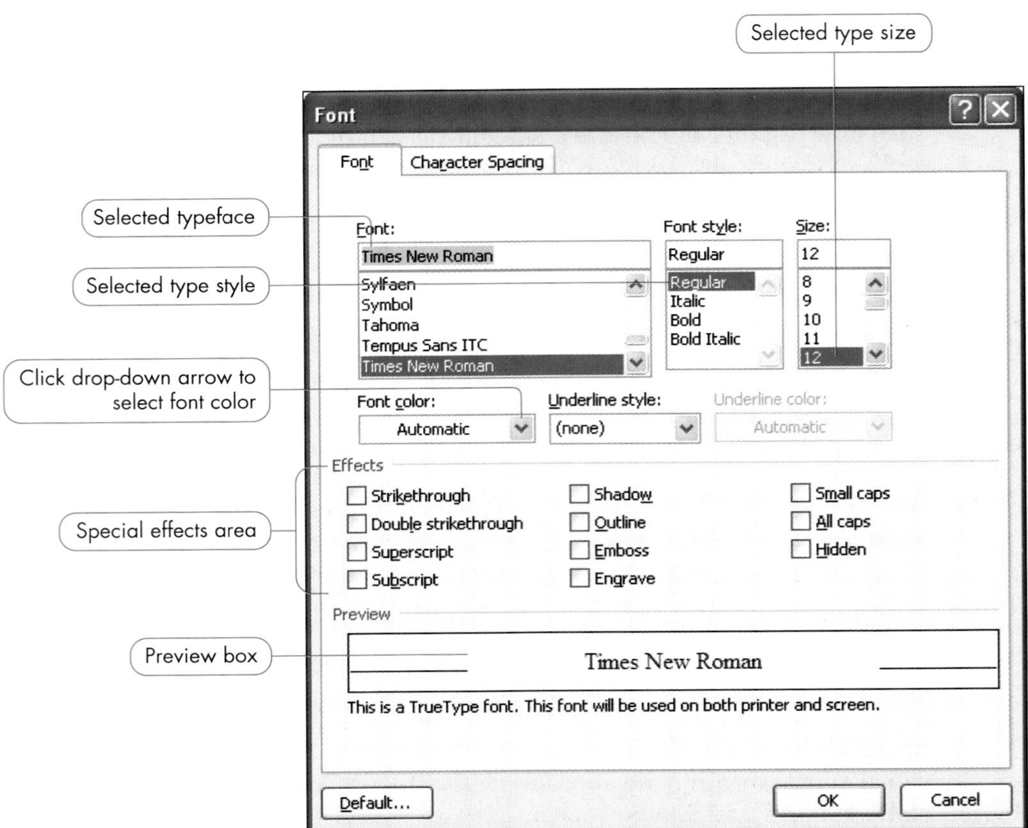

Figure 2.1 Font Dialog Box

Change Text Case (Capitalization)

Use ***Change Case*** to change capitalization of text.

To quickly change the capitalization of text in a document use ***Change Case*** in the Font group on the Home tab. When you click Change Case, the following list of options display:

- **Sentence case.** (capitalizes only the first word of the sentence or phrase)
- **lowercase** (changes the text to lowercase)
- **UPPERCASE** (changes the text to all capital letters)
- **Capitalize Each Word** (capitalizes the first letter of each word; effective for formatting titles, but remember to lowercase first letters of short prepositions, such as *of*)
- **tOGGLE cASE** (changes lowercase to uppercase and uppercase to lowercase)

This feature is useful when generating a list and you want to use the same case formatting for each item. If you do not select text first, the casing format will take effect on the text where the insertion point is located. You can toggle among uppercase, lowercase, and sentence case formats by pressing Shift+F3.

Select Font Options

In addition to changing the font, font style, and size, you can apply other font attributes to text. Although the Font group on the Home tab contains special effects commands such as strikethrough, subscript, and superscript, the *Effects* section in the Font tab in the Font dialog box contains a comprehensive set of options for applying color and special effects, such as SMALL CAPS, ^{superscripts}, or $_{\text{subscripts}}$. Table 2.1 lists and defines more of these special effects. You also can change the underline options and indicate if spaces are to be underlined or just words. You can even change the color of the text and underline.

Table 2.1 Font Effects

Effect	Description	Example
Strikethrough	Displays a horizontal line through the middle of the text	~~strikethrough~~
Superscript	Displays text in a smaller size and raised above the baseline	Super^{script}
Subscript	Displays text in a smaller size and lowered below the baseline	Sub$_{\text{script}}$
Shadow	Displays text with a 3D shadow effect	Shadow
Emboss	Displays text as if it has been raised from the page	Emboss
Engrave	Displays text as if it has been pressed down into the page	Engrave
Small caps	Displays letters as uppercase but smaller than regular-sized uppercase letters	SMALL CAPS

TIP Hidden Text

Hidden text is document text that does not appear on screen, unless you click Show/Hide ¶ in the Paragraph group on the Home tab. You can use this special effect format to hide confidential information before printing documents for other people. For example, an employer can hide employees' Social Security numbers before printing a company roster.

Hidden text does not appear onscreen.

Set Character Spacing

Character spacing is the horizontal space between characters.

Character spacing refers to the amount of horizontal space between characters. Although most character spacing is acceptable, some character combinations appear too far apart or too close together in large-sized text when printed. If so, you might want to adjust for this spacing discrepancy. The Character Spacing tab in the Font dialog box contains options in which you manually control the spacing between characters. The Character Spacing tab shown in Figure 2.2 displays four options for adjusting character spacing: Scale, Spacing, Position, and Kerning.

Scale increases or decreases text as a percentage of its size.

Scale increases or decreases the text horizontally as a percentage of its size; it does not change the vertical height of text. You may use the scale feature on justified text, which does not produce the best-looking results—adjust the scale by a low percentage (90%–95%) to improve text flow without a noticeable difference to the reader.

You may select the *Expanded* option to stretch a word or sentence so it fills more space; for example, use it on a title you want to span across the top of a page. The *Condensed* option is useful to squeeze text closer together, such as when you want to prevent one word from wrapping to another line.

Position raises or lowers text from the baseline.

Kerning allows more even spacing between characters.

Position raises or lowers text from the baseline without creating superscript or subscript size. Use this feature when you want text to stand out from other text on the same line; or use it to create a fun title by raising and/or lowering every few letters. ***Kerning*** automatically adjusts spacing between characters to achieve a more evenly spaced appearance. Kerning primarily allows letters to fit closer together, especially when a capital letter can use space unoccupied by a lowercase letter beside it. For example, you can kern the letters *Va* so the top of the *V* extends into the empty space above the *a* instead of leaving an awkward gap between them.

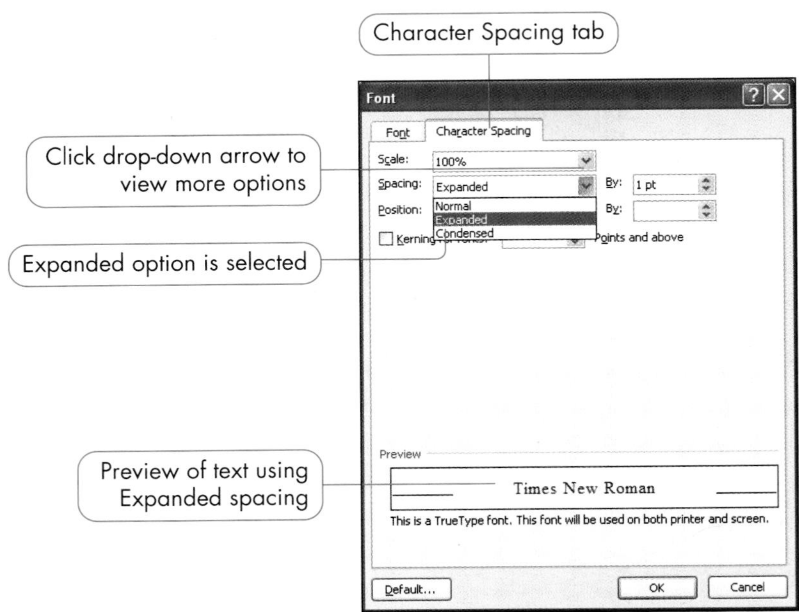

Figure 2.2 Character Spacing Tab in the Font Dialog Box

Highlighting Text

Use the ***Highlighter*** to mark text that you want to locate easily.

People often use a highlighting marker to highlight important parts of textbooks, magazine articles, and other documents. In Word, you use the ***Highlighter*** to mark text that you want to stand out or locate easily. Highlighted text draws the reader's attention to important information within the documents you create, as illustrated in Figure 2.3. The Text Highlight Color command is located in the Font group on the Home tab and also on the Mini toolbar. You can click Text Highlight Color before or after selecting text. When you click Text Highlight Color before selecting text, the mouse pointer resembles a pen that you can click and drag across text to highlight it. The feature stays on so you can highlight additional text. When you finish highlighting text, press Esc to turn it off. If you select text first, click Text Highlight Color to apply the color. To remove highlights, select the highlighted text, click the Text Highlight Color arrow, and choose No Color.

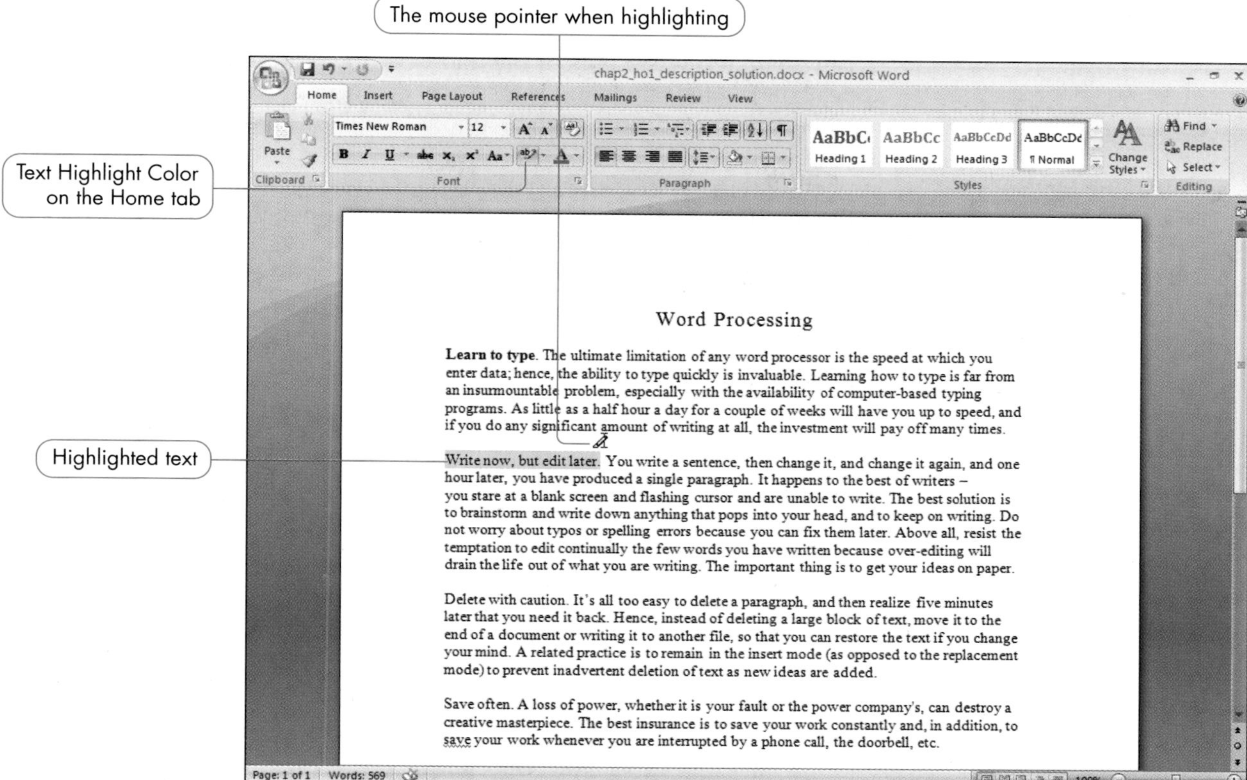

Figure 2.3 The Highlight Tool

If you use a color printer, you see the highlight colors on your printout. If you use a monochrome printer, the highlight appears in shades of gray. Be sure that you can easily read the text with the gray highlight. If not, select a lighter highlight color, and print your document again. You can create a unique highlighting effect by choosing a dark highlight color, such as Dark Blue, and applying a light font color, such as White.

TIP Impose a Time Limit

Word 2007 is supposed to save time and make you more productive. It will do exactly that, provided you use Word for its primary purpose—writing and editing. It is all too easy, however, to lose sight of that objective and spend too much time formatting the document. Concentrate on the content of your document rather than its appearance and remember that the success of a document ultimately depends on its content. Impose a limit on the amount of time you will spend on formatting.

Controlling Word Wrapping with Nonbreaking Hyphens and Nonbreaking Spaces

In Word, text wraps to the next line when the current line of text is full. Most of the time, the way words wrap is acceptable. Occasionally, however, text may wrap in an undesirable location. To improve the readability of text, you need to proofread word-wrapping locations and insert special characters. Two general areas of concern are hyphenated words and spacing within proper nouns.

Insert Nonbreaking Hyphens

A ***nonbreaking hyphen*** prevents a word from becoming separated at the hyphen.

If a hyphenated word falls at the end of a line, the first word and the hyphen may appear on the first line, and the second word may wrap to the next line. However, certain hyphenated text, such as phone numbers, should stay together to improve the readability of the text. To keep hyphenated words together, replace the regular hyphen with a nonbreaking hyphen. A ***nonbreaking hyphen*** keeps text on both sides of the hyphen together, thus preventing the hyphenated word from becoming separated at the hyphen, as shown in Figure 2.4. To insert a nonbreaking hyphen, press Ctrl+Shift+Hyphen. When you click Show/Hide ¶ in the Paragraph group on the Home tab to display formatting symbols, a regular hyphen looks like a hyphen, and a nonbreaking hyphen appears as a wider hyphen. However, the nonbreaking hyphen looks like a regular hyphen when printed.

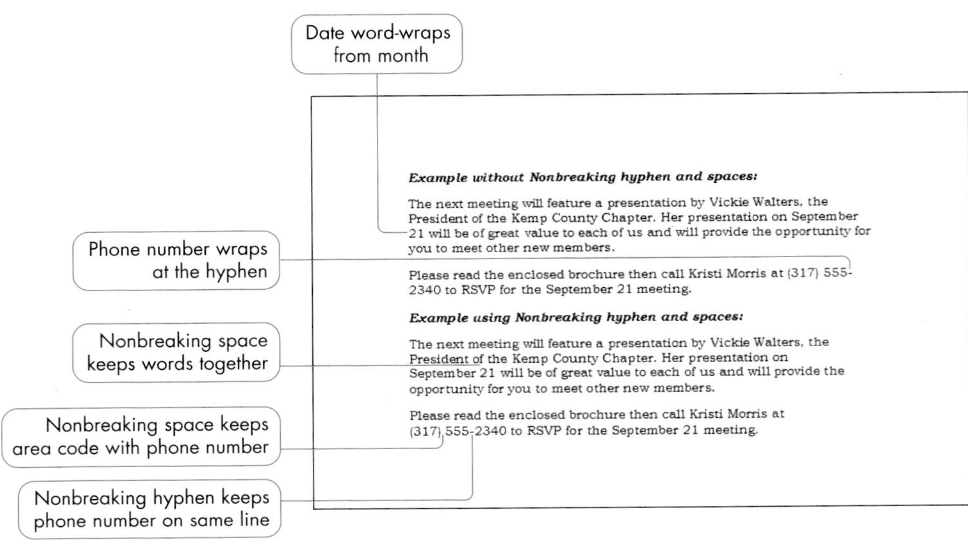

Figure 2.4 Nonbreaking Hyphens and Spaces

Insert Nonbreaking Spaces

A ***nonbreaking space*** keeps two or more words together on a line.

Because text will wrap to the next line if a word does not fit at the end of the current line, occasionally word-wrapping between certain types of words is undesirable; that is, some words should be kept together for improved readability. For example, the date *March 31* should stay together instead of word-wrapping after March. Other items that should stay together include names, such as *Ms. Stevenson*, and page references, such as *page 15*. To prevent words from separating due to the word-wrap feature, you can insert a ***nonbreaking space***—a special character that keeps two or more words together. To insert a nonbreaking space, press Ctrl+Shift+Spacebar between the two words that you want to keep together. If a space already exists, the result of pressing the Spacebar, you should delete it before you insert the nonbreaking space.

Copying Formats with the Format Painter

You should format similar headings and text within a document with the same formatting. However, it is time-consuming to select every heading individually and apply the desired format (such as bold, underline, and font color). You can use the ***Format Painter*** to copy existing text formats to other text to ensure consistency. Using the Format Painter helps you improve your efficiency because you spend less time copying multiple formats rather than applying individual formats to each heading or block of text one at a time. When you single-click Format Painter in the Clipboard group on the Home tab, you can copy the formats only one time, then Word turns off Format Painter. When you double-click Format Painter, it stays activated so you can format an unlimited amount of text. To turn off Format Painter, click Format Painter once or press Esc.

Use the ***Format Painter*** to copy existing text formats to other text.

(You can use Format Painter to . . . ensure consistency . . . and improve your efficiency by spending less time copying multiple formats rather than applying individual formats to each heading or block of text one at a time.)

Display Nonprinting Formatting Marks

As you type text, Word inserts nonprinting marks or symbols. While these symbols do not display on printouts, they do affect the appearance. For example, Word inserts a "code" every time you press Spacebar, Tab, and Enter. The paragraph mark ¶ at the end of a paragraph does more than just indicate the presence of a hard return. It also stores all of the formatting in effect for the paragraph. To preserve the formatting when you move or copy a paragraph, you must include the paragraph mark in the selected text. Click Show/Hide ¶ in the Paragraph group on the Home tab to display the paragraph mark and make sure it has been selected. Table 2.2 lists several common formatting marks. Both the hyphen and nonbreaking hyphen look like a regular hyphen when printed.

Table 2.2 Nonprinting Symbols

Symbol	Description	Create by
•	Regular space	Pressing Spacebar
°	Nonbreaking space	Pressing Ctrl+Shift+Spacebar
-	Regular hyphen	Pressing Hyphen
—	Nonbreaking hyphen	Pressing Ctrl+Shift+Hyphen
→	Tab	Pressing Tab
¶	End of paragraph	Pressing Enter
. . .	Hidden text	Selecting Hidden check box in Font dialog box
↲	Line break	Pressing Shift+Enter

Hands-On Exercises

1 | Character Formatting

Skills covered: 1. Change Text Appearance **2.** Insert Nonbreaking Spaces and Nonbreaking Hyphens **3.** Highlight Text and Use Format Painter

Step 1 Change Text Appearance

Refer to Figure 2.5 as you complete Step 1.

a. Start Word. Open the *chap2_ho1_description* document in the **Exploring Word folder** and save it as **chap2_ho1_description_solution**.

   You must select the text for which you want to adjust the character spacing.

b. Select the heading *Word Processing*, then click the **Font Dialog Box Launcher** in the Font group on the Home tab.

   The Font dialog box displays with the Font tab options.

c. Click the **Character spacing tab** and click the **Spacing drop-down arrow**. Select **Expanded** and notice how the text changes in the preview box. Click **OK**.

   Word expands the spacing between letters in the heading *Word Processing*, as shown in Figure 2.5.

d. Save the document.

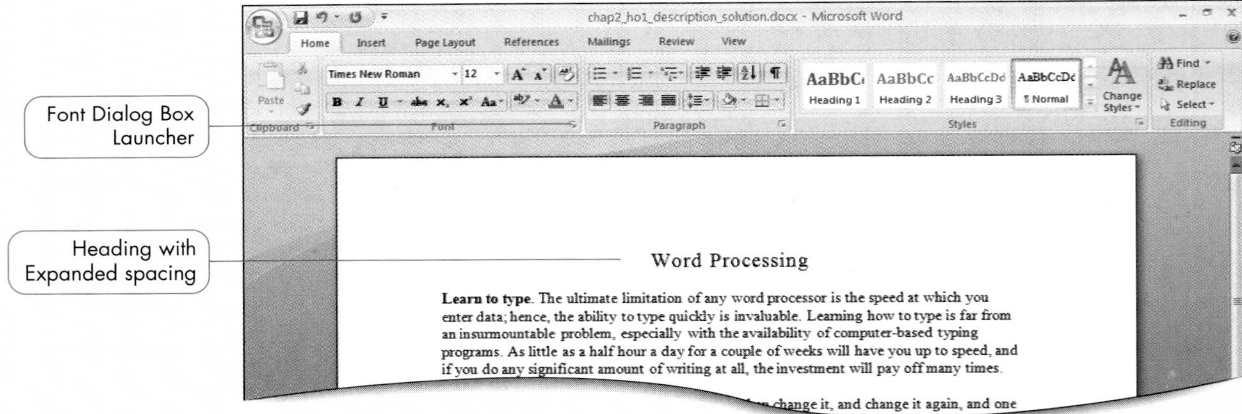

Figure 2.5 Text Formatting

Step 2 Insert Nonbreaking Spaces and Nonbreaking Hyphens

Refer to Figure 2.6 as you complete Step 2.

a. Place the insertion point between the words *you stare* in the third sentence of the second paragraph.

   Before inserting a nonbreaking space, you must position the insertion point between the two words you want to keep together.

b. Delete the existing space, and then press **Ctrl+Shift+Spacebar** to insert a non-breaking space.

   The nonbreaking space keeps the words *you stare* together, preventing word wrapping between the two words.

c. Select the hyphen between the text *five-minute* in the third sentence of the sixth paragraph. Delete the hyphen, and then press **Ctrl+Shift+Hyphen** to insert a nonbreaking hyphen, as shown in Figure 2.6.

TROUBLESHOOTING: If text continues word-wrapping between two words after you insert a nonbreaking space or nonbreaking hyphen, click Show/Hide ¶ in the Paragraph group on the Home tab to display symbols and then identify and delete regular spaces or hyphens that still exist between words.

d. Save the document.

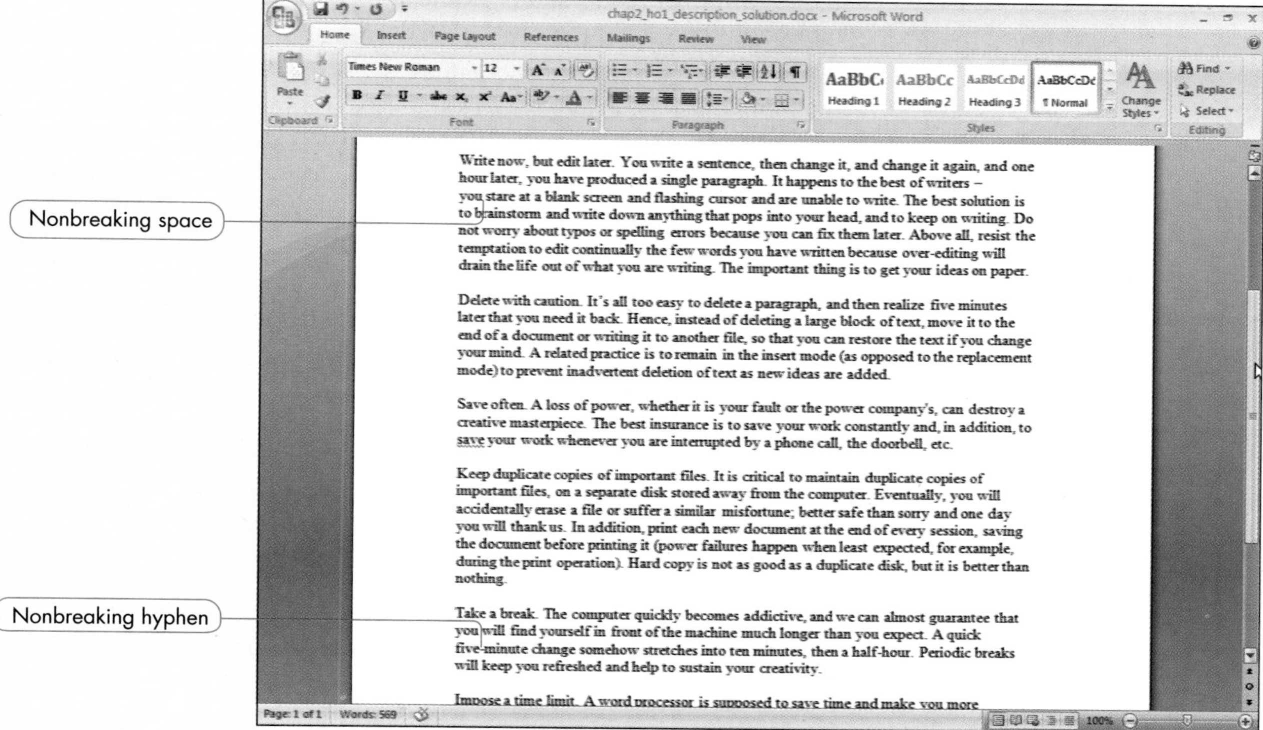

Figure 2.6 Nonbreaking Characters

TIP Another Way to Insert Nonbreaking Spaces and Hyphens

An alternative to using keyboard shortcuts to insert nonbreaking spaces and hyphens is to use the Symbols gallery on the Insert tab. Click **More Symbols** to display the Symbol dialog box, click the Special Characters tab, select the Nonbreaking Hyphen or the Nonbreaking Space character option, and click **Insert** to insert a nonbreaking hyphen or a nonbreaking space, respectively. Close the Symbol dialog box after inserting the nonbreaking hyphen or nonbreaking space.

Step 3

Highlight Text and Use Format Painter

Refer to Figure 2.7 as you complete Step 3.

a. Select the text *Learn to type.* in the first paragraph.

b. Click **Text Highlight Color** in the Font group on the Home tab.

Word highlighted the selected text in the default highlight color, yellow.

TROUBLESHOOTING: If Word applies a different color to the selected text, that means another highlight color was selected after starting Word. If this happens, select the text again, click the Text Highlight Color arrow, and select Yellow.

c. Click anywhere within the sentence *Learn to type*. Double-click **Format Painter** in the Clipboard group on the Home tab. (Remember that clicking the Format Painter button once, rather than double-clicking it, enables you to copy the format only one time.)

The mouse pointer changes to a paintbrush, as shown in Figure 2.7.

d. Drag the mouse pointer over the first sentence in the second paragraph, *Write now, but edit later.*, and release the mouse.

The formatting from the original sentence (bold font and yellow highlight) is applied to this sentence as well.

e. Drag the mouse pointer (in the shape of a paintbrush) over the remaining titles (the first sentence in each paragraph) to copy the formatting. You can click the scroll down arrow on the vertical scroll bar to display the other headings in the document.

f. Press **Esc** to turn off Format Painter after you copy the formatting to the last tip.

g. Save the *chap2_ho1_description_solution* document and keep it onscreen if you plan to continue with the next hands-on exercise. Close the file and exit Word if you will not continue with the next exercise at this time.

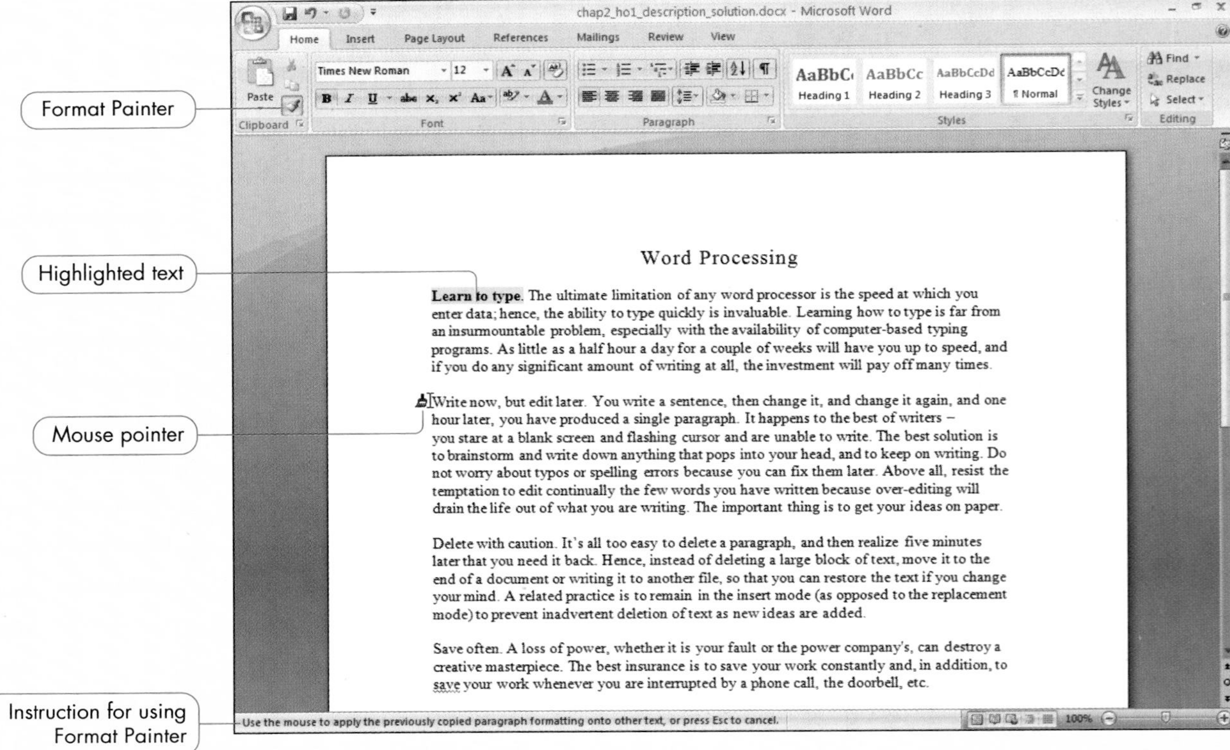

Figure 2.7 The Format Painter

Paragraph Formats

A change in typography is only one way to alter the appearance of a document. You also can change the alignment, indentation, tab stops, or line spacing for any paragraph(s) within the document. You can control the pagination and prevent the occurrence of awkward page breaks by specifying that an entire paragraph must appear on the same page, or that a one-line paragraph (e.g., a heading) should appear on the same page as the next paragraph. You can include borders or shading for added emphasis around selected paragraphs.

Word implements all of these paragraph formats for all selected paragraphs. If no paragraphs are selected, Word applies the formats to the current paragraph (the paragraph containing the insertion point), regardless of the position of the insertion point within the paragraph when you apply the paragraph formats.

> Word implements all of these paragraph formats for all selected paragraphs. If no paragraphs are selected, Word applies the feature to the current paragraph.

In this section, you set tabs, apply borders, create lists, and format text into columns to help offset text for better readability. You also change text alignment, indent paragraphs, set line and paragraph spacing, and control pagination breaks.

Setting Off Paragraphs with Tabs, Borders, Lists, and Columns

Many people agree that their eyes tire and minds wander when they read page after page of plain black text on white paper. To break up long blocks of text or draw attention to an area of a page, you can format text with tabs, borders, lists, or columns. These formatting features enable you to modify positioning, frame a section, itemize for easy reading, order steps in a sequence, or create pillars of text for visual appeal and easy reading. For example, look through the pages of this book and notice the use of bulleted lists, tables for reference points, and borders around TIP boxes to draw your attention and enhance the pages.

Set Tabs

Tabs are markers for aligning text in a document.

Tabs are markers that specify the position for aligning text and add organization to a document. They often are used to create columns of text within a document. When you start a new document, the default tab stops are set every one-half inch across the page and are left aligned. Every time you press Tab, the insertion point moves over ½". You typically press Tab to indent the first line of paragraphs in double-spaced reports or the first line of paragraphs in a modified block style letter.

You access the Tabs feature by first clicking the Paragraph Dialog Box Launcher in the Paragraph group on the Home tab, then click the Tabs button. The Tabs dialog box displays so that you can set left, center, right, decimal, and bar tabs.

A ***left tab*** marks the position to align text on the left.

A ***center tab*** marks where text centers as you type.

A ***right tab*** marks the position to align text on the right.

A ***decimal tab*** marks where numbers align on a decimal point as you type.

A ***bar tab*** marks the location of a vertical line between columns.

- A ***left tab*** sets the start position on the left so as you type, text moves to the right of the tab setting.
- A ***center tab*** sets the middle point of the text you type; whatever you type will be centered on that tab setting.
- A ***right tab*** sets the start position on the right so as you type, text moves to the left of that tab setting and aligns on the right.
- A ***decimal tab*** aligns numbers on a decimal point. Regardless of how long the number, each number lines up with the decimal in the same position.
- A ***bar tab*** does not position text or decimals, but inserts a vertical bar at the tab setting. This bar is useful as a separator for text printed on the same line.

Instead of setting tabs in the Tabs dialog box, you can set tabs on the ruler. First, click the Tabs button to the left of the ruler (refer to Figure 2.8) until you see the tab alignment you want. Then click on the ruler in the location where you want to set the type of tab you selected. To delete a tab, click the tab marker on the ruler, then drag it down and off the ruler.

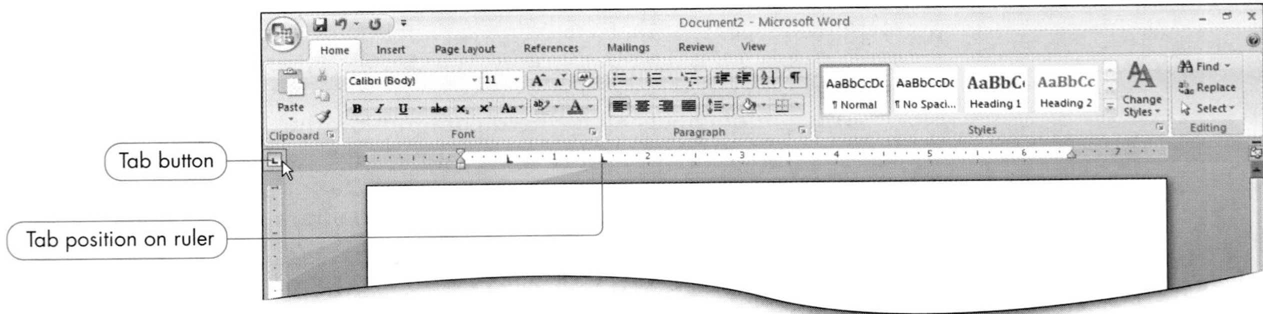

Figure 2.8 Tab Button and Ruler

TIP Deleting Default Tabs

When you set a tab on the ruler, Word deletes all of the default tab settings to the *left* of the tab you set. If you need to delete a single tab setting, click the tab marker on the ruler and drag it down. When you release the mouse, you delete the tab setting.

A ***leader character*** is dots or hyphens that connect two items.

In the Tabs dialog box, you also can specify a ***leader character***, typically dots or hyphens, to draw the reader's eye across the page. For example, in a table of contents you can easily read a topic and the associated page where it is found when tab leaders connect the two, as shown in Figure 2.9. Notice also in Figure 2.9 that the default tab settings have been cleared, and a right tab is set at 5".

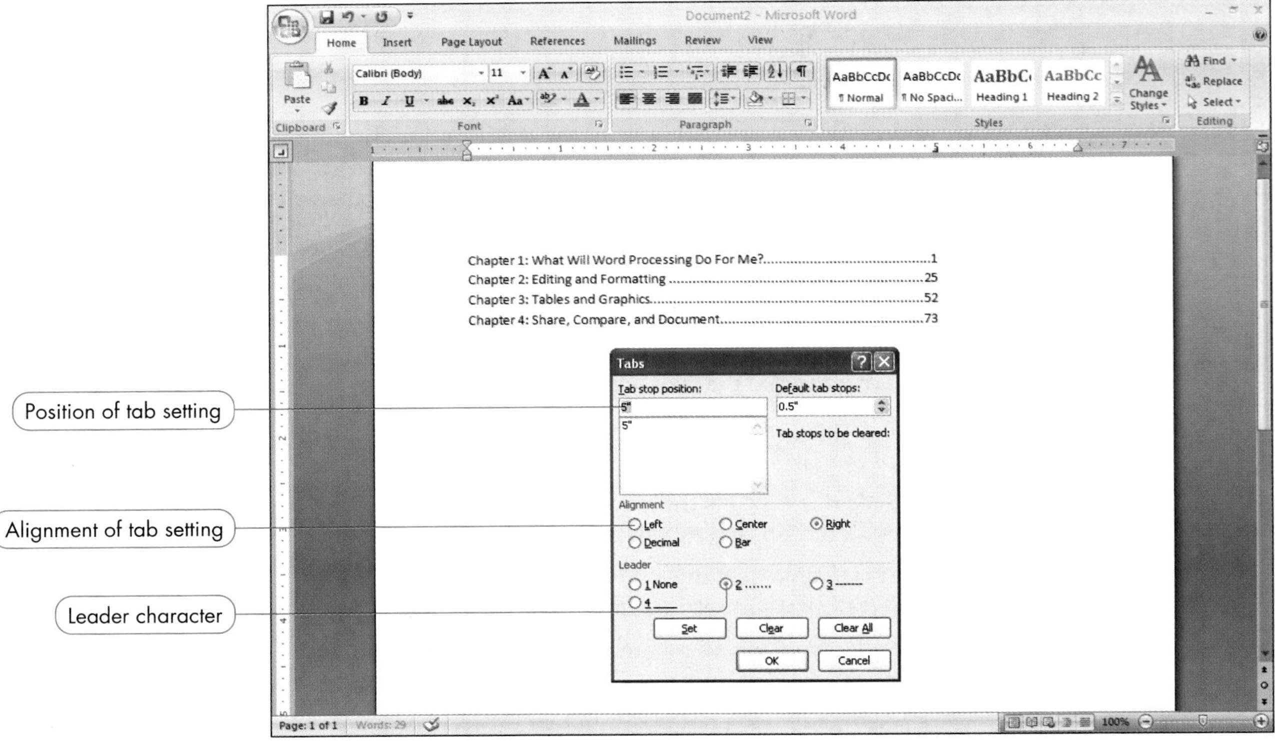

Figure 2.9 The Tabs Dialog Box

Apply Borders and Shading

A **border** is a line that surrounds a paragraph, a page, a table, or an image.

Shading is background color that appears behind text.

You can draw attention to a document or an area of a document by using the Borders and Shading command. A ***border*** is a line that surrounds a paragraph, a page, a table, or an image, similar to how a picture frame surrounds a photograph or piece of art. ***Shading*** is a background color that appears behind text in a paragraph, a page, or a table. You can apply specific borders, such as top, bottom, or outside, from the Border command in the Paragraph group on the Home tab. To allow more customization of borders, open the Borders and Shading dialog box when you click the Borders arrow in the Paragraph group on the Home tab, as shown in Figure 2.10. Borders or shading is applied to selected text within a paragraph, to the entire paragraph if no text is selected, to the entire page if the Page Border tab is selected, and also can be used on tables and images. You can create boxed and/or shaded text as well as place horizontal or vertical lines around different quantities of text. A good example of this practice is used in the *Exploring* series: The TIP boxes are surrounded by a border with dark shading and a white font color for the headings to attract your attention.

You can choose from several different line styles in any color, but remember you must use a color printer to display the line colors on the printed page. Colored lines appear in gray on a monochrome printer. You can place a uniform border around a paragraph (choose Box), or you can choose a shadow effect with thicker lines at the right and bottom. You also can apply lines to selected sides of a paragraph(s) by selecting a line style, then clicking the desired sides as appropriate.

The horizontal line button at the bottom of the Borders and Shading dialog box provides access to a variety of attractive horizontal line designs.

(Use page borders on . . . fliers, newsletters, and invitations, but not on formal documents such as research papers and professional reports.)

The Page Border tab enables you to place a decorative border around one or more selected pages. As with a paragraph border, you can place the border around the entire page, or you can select one or more sides. The page border also provides an additional option to use preselected clip art instead of ordinary lines. Note that it is appropriate to use page borders on documents such as fliers, newsletters, and invitations, but not on formal documents such as research papers and professional reports.

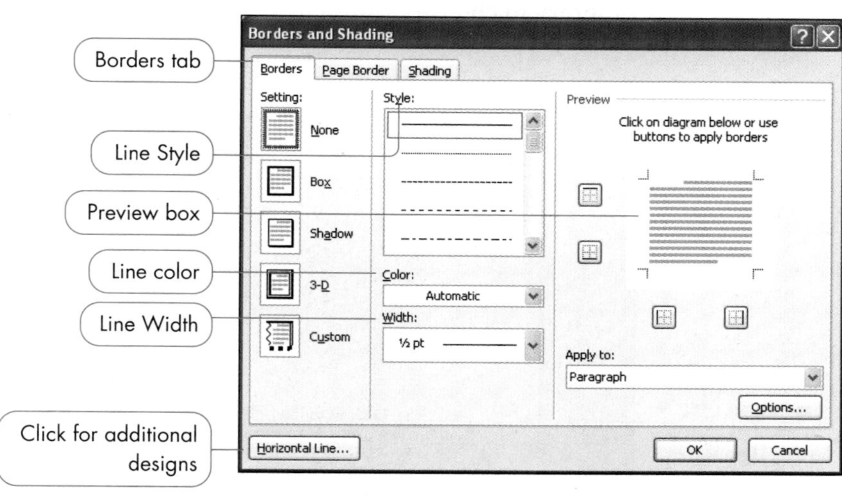

Figure 2.10 Apply a Border Around Text, Paragraphs, or Pages

Shading is applied independently of the border and is accessed from the Borders and Shading dialog box or from Shading in the Paragraph group on the Home tab. Clear (no shading) is the default. Solid (100%) shading creates a solid box where the text is turned white so you can read it. Shading of 10% or 20% generally is most effective to add emphasis to the selected paragraph (see Figure 2.11). The Borders and Shading command is implemented on the paragraph level and affects the entire paragraph unless text has been selected within the paragraph.

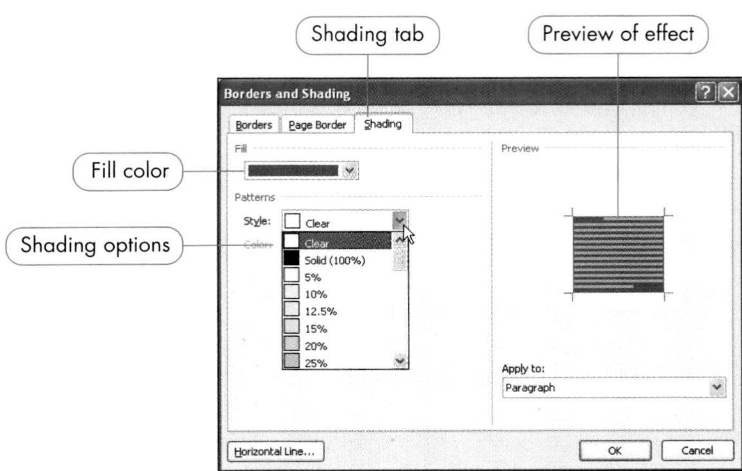

Figure 2.11 Apply Shading to Text or a Paragraph

Create Bulleted and Numbered Lists

A ***bulleted list*** itemizes and separates paragraph text to increase readability.

A ***numbered list*** sequences and prioritizes items.

A ***multilevel list*** extends a numbered list to several levels.

A list helps you organize information by highlighting important topics. A ***bulleted list*** itemizes and separates paragraphs to increase readability. A ***numbered list*** sequences and prioritizes the items and is automatically updated to accommodate additions or deletions. A ***multilevel list*** extends a numbered list to several levels, and it too is updated automatically when topics are added or deleted. You create each of these lists from the Paragraph group on the Home tab.

To apply bullet formatting to a list, click the Bullets arrow and choose one of several predefined symbols in the Bullet library (see Figure 2.12). Position your mouse over one of the bullet styles in the Bullet Library and a preview of that bullet style will display in your document. To use that style, simply click the bullet. If you want to use a different bullet symbol, click the Define New Bullet option below the Bullet Library to choose a different symbol or picture for the bullet.

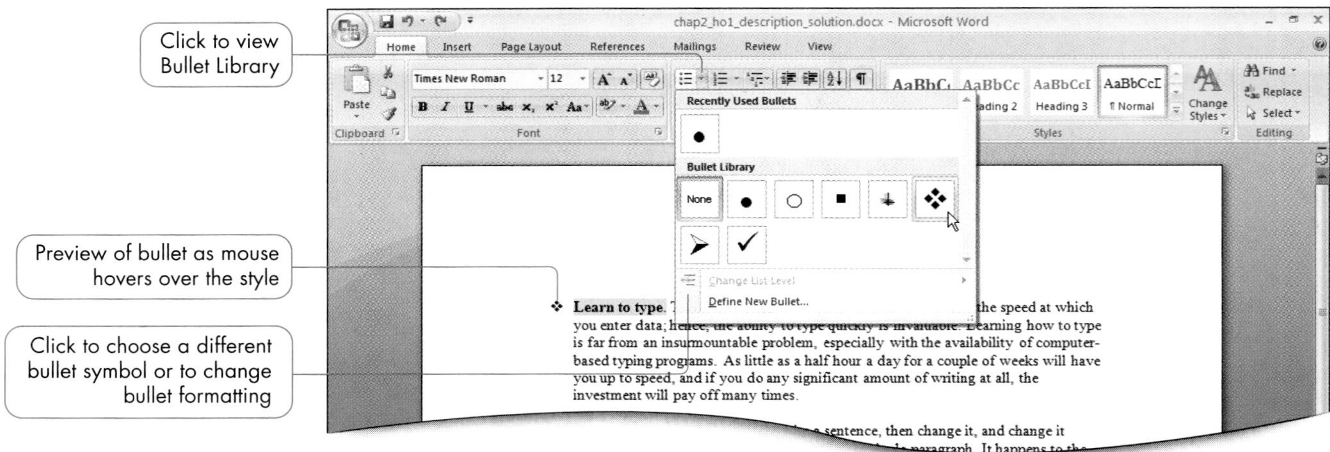

Figure 2.12 Bulleted List Options

Click the Numbering arrow in the Paragraph group to apply Arabic or Roman numerals, or upper- or lowercase letters, for a numbered list. When you position the mouse pointer over a style in the Numbering Library, you see a preview of that numbering style in your document. As with a bulleted list, you can define a new style by selecting the Define New Number Format option below the Numbering Library. Note, too, the options to restart or continue numbering found by selecting the Set Numbering Value option. These become important if a list appears in multiple places within a document. In other words, each occurrence of a list can start numbering anew, or it can continue from where the previous list left off.

The Mulitlevel List command enables you to create an outline to organize your thoughts in a hierarchical structure. As with the other types of lists, you can choose one of several default styles, and/or modify a style through the Define New Multilevel List option below the My Lists gallery. You also can specify whether each outline within a document is to restart its numbering, or whether it is to continue numbering from the previous outline.

Format Text into Columns

Columns format a section of a document into side-by-side vertical blocks.

Columns format a section of a document into side-by-side vertical blocks in which the text flows down the first column and then continues at the top of the next column. The length of a line of columnar text is shorter, enabling people to read through each article faster. To format text into columns, click the Page Layout tab and click Columns in the Page Setup group. From the Columns gallery, you can specify the number of columns or select More Columns to display the Columns dialog box. The Columns dialog box provides options for setting the number of columns and spacing between columns. Microsoft Word calculates the width of each column according to the left and right document margins on the page and the specified (default) space between columns.

The dialog box in Figure 2.13 implements a design of three equal columns. The 2" width of each column is computed based on current 1" left and right document margins and the ¼" spacing between columns. The width of each column is determined by subtracting the sum of the margins and the space between the columns (a total of 2½" in this example) from the page width of 8½". The result of the subtraction is 6", which is divided by 3 columns, resulting in a column width of 2".

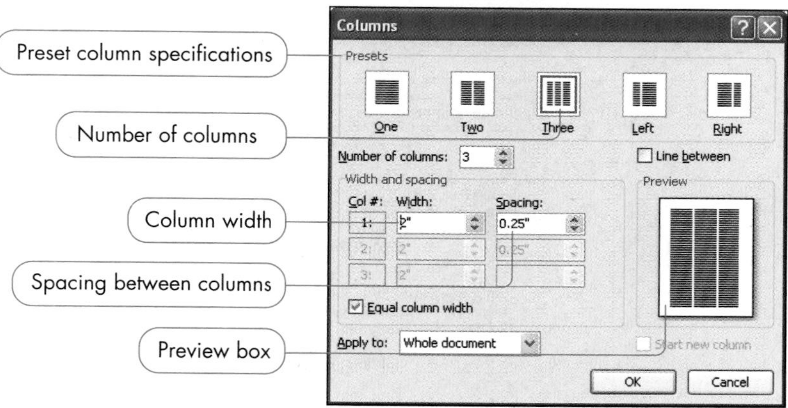

Figure 2.13 The Columns Dialog Box

One subtlety associated with column formatting is the use of sections, which control elements such as the orientation of a page (landscape or portrait), margins, page numbers, and the number of columns. All of the documents you have worked with so far have consisted of a single section, so section formatting was not an issue. It becomes important only when you want to vary an element that is formatted at the section level. You could, for example, use section formatting to create a document that has one column on its title page and two columns on the remaining pages. Creating this type of formatting requires you to divide the document into two sections by inserting a section break. You then format each section independently and specify the number of columns in each section. Table 2.3 guides you in formatting text into columns.

Table 2.3 Formatting with Columns

If your document contains . . .	And you want to apply column formatting to . . .	Do this:
only one section	the entire document	apply column formatting from anywhere within the document
two or more sections	only one section	position the insertion point in that section, and apply column formatting
one or more sections	only part of the document within a section	select the text you want to format, and then apply column formatting

Applying Paragraph Formats

The Paragraph group on the Home tab contains commands to set and control several format options for a paragraph. The options include alignment, indentation, line spacing, and pagination. These features also are found in the Paragraph dialog box. All of these formatting features are implemented at the paragraph level and affect all selected paragraphs. If no paragraphs are selected, Word applies the formatting to the current paragraph—the paragraph containing the insertion point.

Change Text Alignment

Horizontal alignment refers to the placement of text between the left and right margins.

Horizontal alignment refers to the placement of text between the left and right margins. Text is aligned in four different ways as shown in Figure 2.14. Alignment options are justified (flush left/flush right), left aligned (flush left with a ragged right margin), right aligned (flush right with a ragged left margin), or centered within the margins (ragged left and right). The default alignment is left.

We, the people of the United States, in order to form a more perfect Union, establish justice, insure domestic tranquility, provide for the common defense, promote the general welfare, and secure the blessings of liberty to ourselves and our posterity, do ordain and establish this Constitution for the United States of America.

Justified (flush left/flush right)

We, the people of the United States, in order to form a more perfect Union, establish justice, insure domestic tranquility, provide for the common defense, promote the general welfare, and secure the blessings of liberty to ourselves and our posterity, do ordain and establish this Constitution for the United States of America.

Left Aligned (flush left/ragged right)

We, the people of the United States, in order to form a more perfect Union, establish justice, insure domestic tranquility, provide for the common defense, promote the general welfare, and secure the blessings of liberty to ourselves and our posterity, do ordain and establish this Constitution for the United States of America.

Right Aligned (ragged left/flush right)

We, the people of the United States, in order to form a more perfect Union, establish justice, insure domestic tranquility, provide for the common defense, promote the general welfare, and secure the blessings of liberty to ourselves and our posterity, do ordain and establish this Constitution for the United States of America.

Centered (ragged left/ragged right)

Figure 2.14 Horizontal Alignment

Left-aligned text is perhaps the easiest to read. The first letters of each line align with each other, helping the eye to find the beginning of each line. The lines themselves are of irregular length. Uniform spacing exists between words, and the ragged margin on the right adds white space to the text, giving it a lighter and more informal look.

Justified text, sometimes called fully justified, produces lines of equal length, with the spacing between words adjusted to align at the margins. Look closely and you will see many books, magazines, and newspapers fully justify text to add formality and "neatness" to the text. Some find this style more difficult to read because of the uneven (sometimes excessive) word spacing and/or the greater number of hyphenated words needed to justify the lines. But it also can enable you to pack more information onto a page when space is constrained.

Text that is centered or right aligned is usually restricted to limited amounts of text where the effect is more important than the ease of reading. Centered text, for example, appears frequently on wedding invitations, poems, or formal announcements. In research papers, first-level titles often are centered as well. Right-aligned text is used with figure captions and short headlines.

The Paragraph group on the Home tab contains the four alignment options: Align Left, Center, Align Right, and Justify. To apply the alignment, select text, then click the alignment option on the Home tab. You can also set alignment from the Paragraph dialog box; the Indents and Spacing tab contains an Alignment drop-down box in the General section.

TIP Alignment Keyboard Shortcuts

You can quickly apply alignment by using keyboard shortcuts. After you select the text, click Ctrl+L to align left, click Ctrl+E to align center, click Ctrl+R to align right, or click Ctrl+J to justify.

Indent Paragraphs

You can indent individual paragraphs so they appear to have different margins from the rest of a document. Indentation is established at the paragraph level; thus it is possible to apply different indentation properties to different paragraphs. You can indent one paragraph from the left margin only, another from the right margin only, and a third from both the left and right margins. For example, the fifth edition of the *Publication Manual of the American Psychological Association* specifies that quotations consisting of 40 or more words should be contained in a separate paragraph that is indented ½" from the left margin. Additionally, you can indent the first line of any paragraph differently from the rest of the paragraph. And finally, a paragraph may have no indentation at all, so that it aligns on the left and right margins.

Three settings determine the indentation of a paragraph: the left indent, the right indent, and a special indent, if any (see Figure 2.15). The left and right indents are set to 0 by default, as is the special indent, and produce a paragraph with no indentation at all. Positive values for the left and right indents offset the paragraph from both margins.

A ***first line indent*** marks the location to indent only the first line in a paragraph.

A ***hanging indent*** marks how far to indent each line of a paragraph except the first.

The two types of special indentation are first line and hanging. The ***first line indent*** affects only the first line in the paragraph, and you apply it by pressing the Tab key at the beginning of the paragraph or by setting a specific measurement in the Paragr aph dialog box. Remaining lines in the paragraph align at the left margin. A ***hanging indent*** aligns the first line of a paragraph at the left margin and indents the remaining lines. Hanging indents often are used with bulleted or numbered lists and to format citations on a bibliography page.

TIP Decrease Indent and Increase Indent

You can click Decrease Indent in the Paragraph group on the Home tab to decrease (bring text to the left) indented text ½". Click Increase Indent to move text to the right an additional ½".

Set Line and Paragraph Spacing

Line spacing is the space between the lines in a paragraph.

Paragraph spacing is the amount of space before or after a paragraph.

Line spacing determines the space between the lines in a paragraph and between paragraphs. Word provides complete flexibility and enables you to select any multiple of line spacing (single, double, line and a half, and so on). You also can specify line spacing in terms of points (1" vertical contains 72 points). Click the Line spacing command in the Paragraph group on the Home tab to establish line spacing for the current paragraph. You can also set line spacing in the *Spacing* section on the Indents and Spacing tab in the Paragraph dialog box.

Paragraph spacing is the amount of space before or after a paragraph, as indicated by the paragraph mark when you press Enter between paragraphs. Unlike line spacing that controls *all* spacing within and between paragraphs, paragraph spacing controls only the spacing between paragraphs.

Sometimes you need to single-space text within a paragraph but want to have a blank line between paragraphs. Instead of pressing Enter twice between paragraphs, you can set the paragraph spacing to control the amount of space before or after the paragraph. You can set paragraph spacing in the *Spacing* section on the Indents and Spacing tab in the Paragraph dialog box. Setting a 12-point *After* spacing creates the appearance of a double-space after the paragraph even though the user presses Enter only once between paragraphs.

The Paragraph dialog box is illustrated in Figure 2.15. The Indents and Spacing tab specifies a hanging indent, 1.5 line spacing, and justified alignment. The Preview area within the Paragraph dialog box enables you to see how the paragraph will appear within the document.

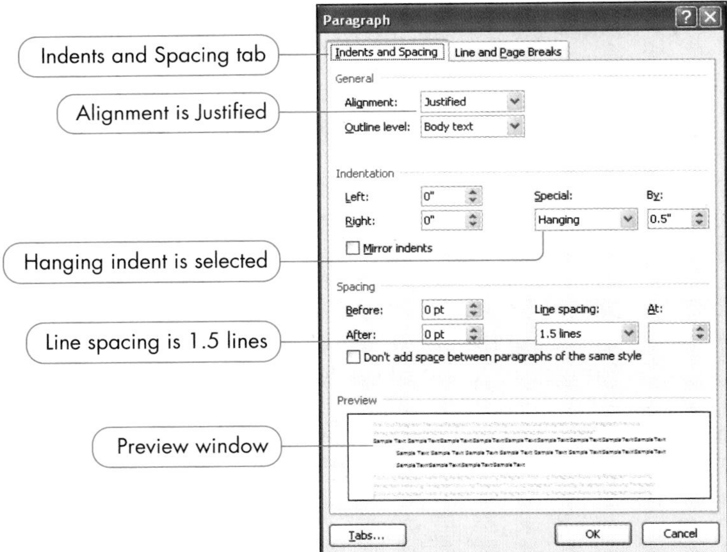

Figure 2.15 Indents and Spacing

Control Widows and Orphans

A ***widow*** is the last line of a paragraph appearing by itself at the top of a page.

An ***orphan*** is the first line of a paragraph appearing by itself at the bottom of a page.

Some lines become isolated from the remainder of a paragraph and seem out of place at the beginning or end of a multipage document. A ***widow*** refers to the last line of a paragraph appearing by itself at the top of a page. An ***orphan*** is the first line of a paragraph appearing by itself at the bottom of a page. You can prevent these from occurring by clicking the *Widow/Orphan control* check box in the *Pagination* section of the Line and Page Breaks tab of the Paragraph dialog box.

To prevent a page break from occurring within a paragraph and ensure that the entire paragraph appears on the same page use the *Keep lines together* option in the *Pagination* section of the Line and Page Breaks tab of the Paragraph dialog box. The paragraph is moved to the top of the next page if it does not fit on the bottom of the current page. Use the *Keep with next* option in the *Pagination* section to prevent a soft page break between the two paragraphs. This option is typically used to keep a heading (a one-line paragraph) with its associated text in the next paragraph. The check boxes in Figure 2.16 enable you to prevent the occurrence of awkward soft page breaks that detract from the appearance of a document.

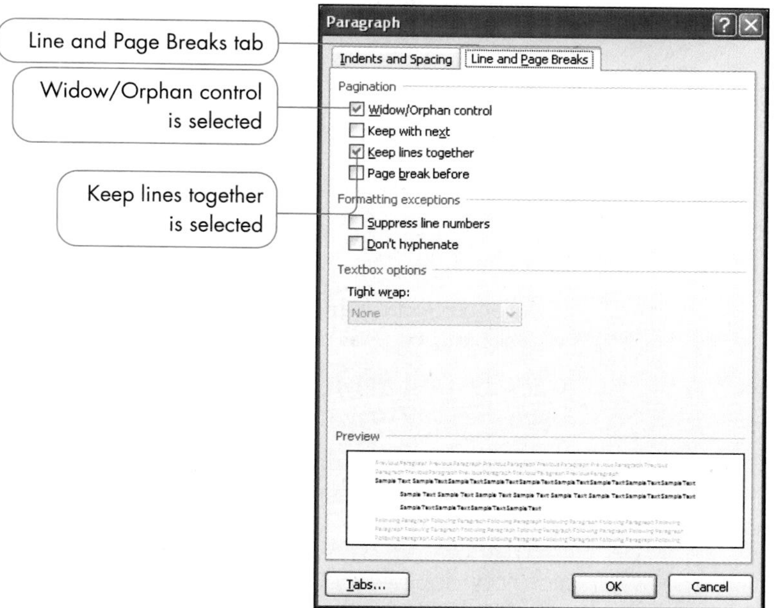

Figure 2.16 Line and Page Breaks

TIP The Section Versus the Paragraph

Line spacing, alignment, tabs, and indents are implemented at the paragraph level. Change any of these parameters anywhere within the current (or selected) paragraph(s) and you change *only* those paragraph(s). Margins, page numbering, orientation, and columns are implemented at the section level. Change these parameters anywhere within a section and you change the characteristics of every page within that section.

Hands-On Exercises

2 | Paragraph Formatting

Skills covered: 1. Set Tabs in a Footer **2.** Select Text to Format **3.** Specify Line Spacing, Justification, and Pagination **4.** Indent Text **5.** Apply Borders and Shading **6.** Change Column Structure **7.** Insert a Section Break and Create Columns

Step 1
Set Tabs in a Footer

Refer to Figure 2.17 as you complete Step 1.

a. Open the *chap2_ho1_description_solution* document if you closed it after the last hands-on exercise and save it as **chap2_ho2_description_solution**.

b. Click the **Insert tab**, and then click **Footer** in the Header & Footer group. Click **Edit Footer** and notice the document text is dimmed except for the footer area.

c. Click the **Home tab**, and then click the **Paragraph Dialog Box Launcher** to display the Paragraph dialog box. Click **Tabs** in the lower-left corner to display the Tabs dialog box.

   This footer contains no tab settings. You will add a 3" center tab that will be used for a page number.

d. Type **3** in the *Tab stop position* box. Click **Center**, and then click **OK**.

e. Click near the bottom of your page to display the footer area, if necessary. Press **Tab** one time, type **Page**, and press **Spacebar** one time.

   You reposition the insertion point to the middle of the footer area using the tab you set and type the text you want to precede the page number.

f. Click the **Design tab** and click **Quick Parts** in the Insert group, then click **Field** to open the Field dialog box. Click **Page** in the *Field Names* box, then click **OK**.

   The actual page number displays in the footer, as shown in Figure 2.17, and will automatically paginate for any additional pages added to your document.

   TROUBLESHOOTING: If the page number is not horizontally centered at the 3" position, double-check the tab settings on the ruler. If tab settings appear to the left of the 3" tab setting, drag the tab markers off the ruler to delete them.

g. Click **Close Header and Footer** in the Close group of the Header and Footer Tools tab.

h. Save the document.

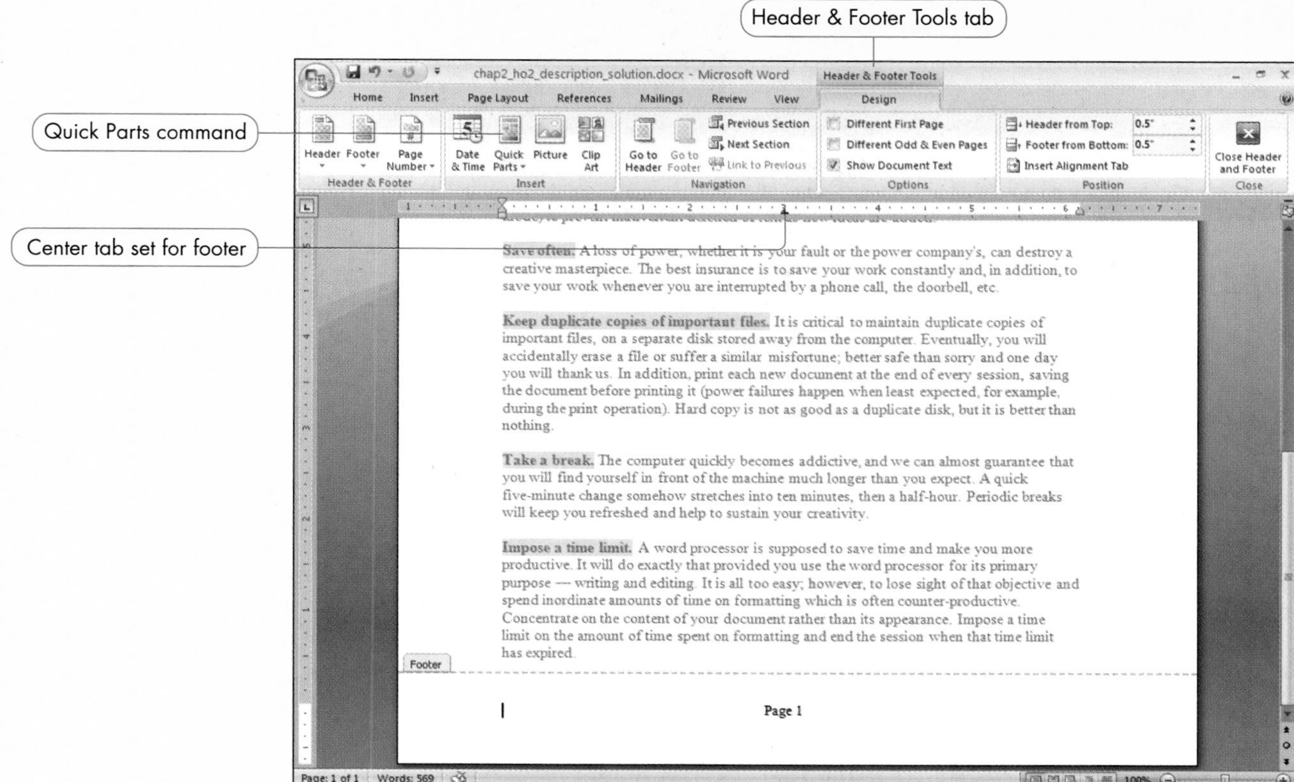

Figure 2.17 Insert Tab in Footer

Step 2
Select Text to Format

Refer to Figure 2.18 as you complete Step 2.

a. Position your insertion point at the end of the title, *Word Processing*, then press **Ctrl+Enter**.

You inserted a manual page break between the title and the list of tips.

b. Click **Zoom** in the status bar to display the Zoom dialog box. Click **Many pages** and drag to select the first two icons that represent two pages, as shown in Figure 2.18. Click **OK**.

You can see the entire document as you select text to format.

c. Select the entire second page.

d. Save the document.

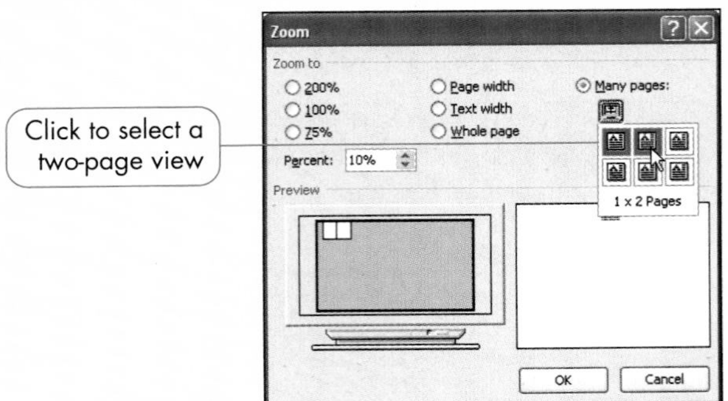

Figure 2.18 Zoom Dialog Box

Step 3
Specify Line Spacing, Justification, and Pagination

Refer to Figure 2.19 as you complete Step 3.

a. Select page 2, if necessary, and then click **Justify** in the Paragraph group on the Home tab.

b. Click **Line Spacing** in the Paragraph group on the Home tab, and then select **1.5**.

   These settings align the text on the right and left margins and add spacing before and after lines of text, making it easier to read.

c. Right-click the selected text and select **Paragraph** on the menu to display the Paragraph dialog box.

d. Click the **Line and Page Breaks tab**. Click the **Keep lines together check box** in the *Pagination* section, if necessary. Click the **Widow/Orphan control check box** in the *Pagination* section, if necessary.

e. Click **OK** to accept the settings and close the dialog box.

   These settings prevent paragraphs from being split at a page break.

f. Click anywhere in the document to deselect the text and see the effects of the formatting changes that were just specified.

   Three paragraphs now display on a third page, and none are split at the page break, as shown in Figure 2.19.

g. Save the document.

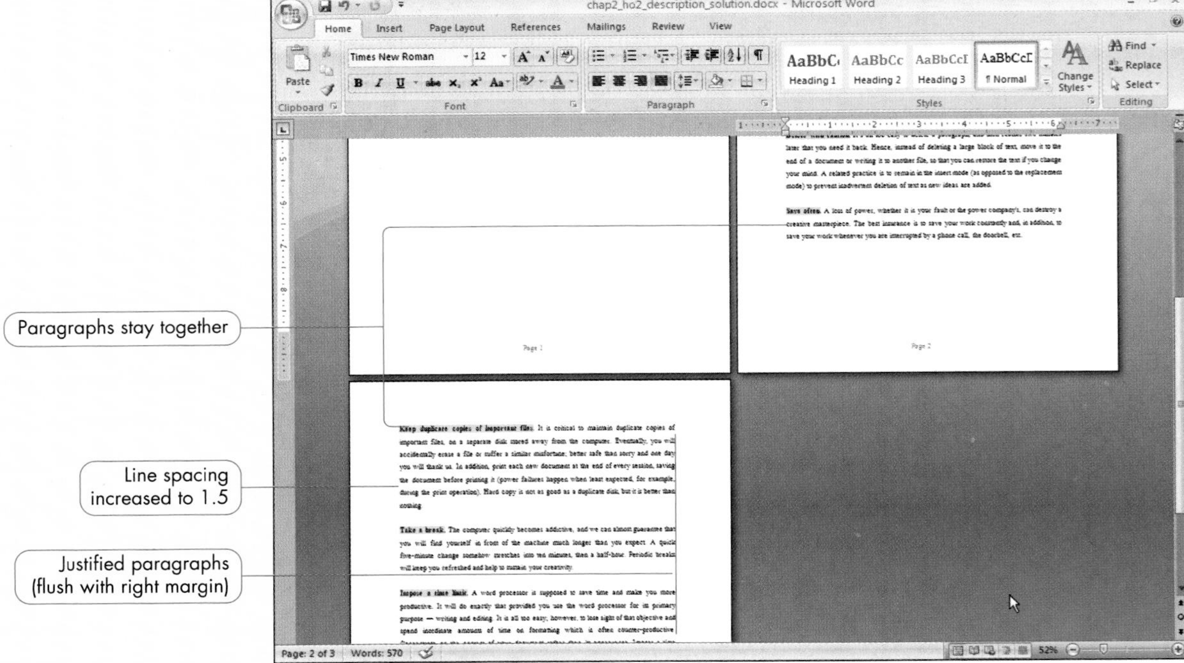

Figure 2.19 Result of Changing Line Spacing, Alignment, and Pagination

Step 4
Indent Text

Refer to Figure 2.20 as you complete Step 4.

a. Click the **Zoom slider** in the status bar and select **100%**. Select the second paragraph, as shown in Figure 2.20.

The second paragraph will not be indented yet.

b. Right-click the selected text and select **Paragraph** from the shortcut menu.

c. If necessary, click the **Indents and Spacing tab** in the Paragraph dialog box.

d. Click the **Left spin box** up arrow to display 0.5" in the *Indentation* section. Set the **Right indention** to 0.5" also. Click **OK**.

Your document should match Figure 2.20.

e. Save the document.

Drag triangle to change right indent

Drag box to change left indent

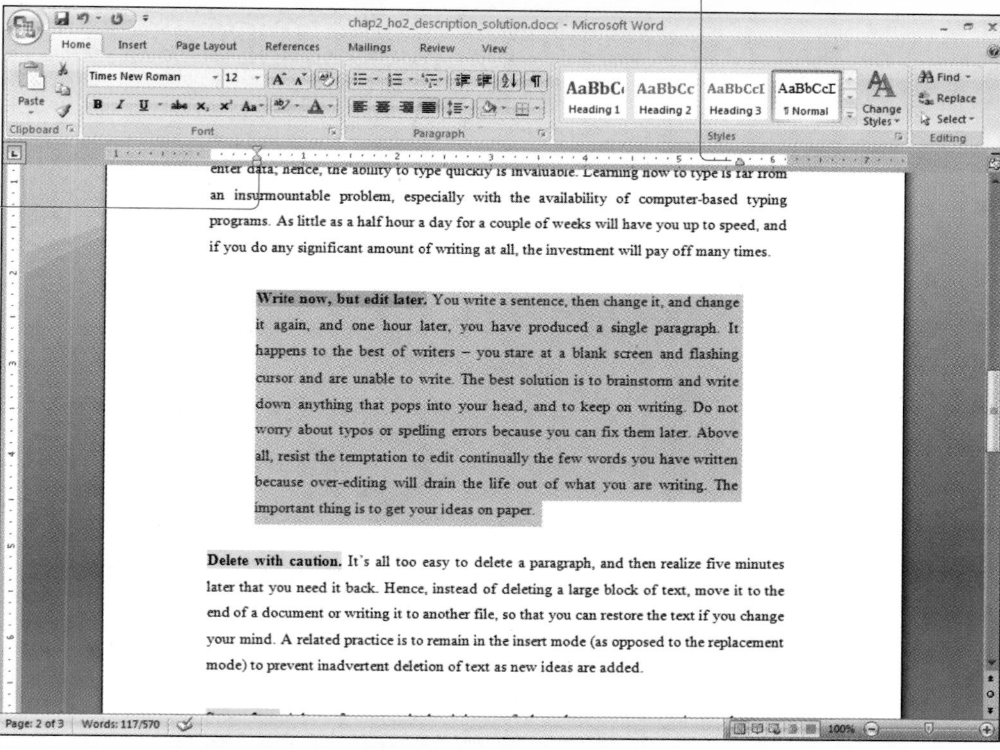

Figure 2.20 Indent

TIP Indents and the Ruler

You can use the ruler to change the special, left, and/or right indents. Select the paragraph (or paragraphs) in which you want to change indents, and then drag the appropriate indent markers to the new location(s) on the ruler. If you get a hanging indent when you wanted to change the left indent, it means you dragged the bottom triangle instead of the box. Click Undo on the Quick Access Toolbar and try again. You can always use the Paragraph dialog box rather than the ruler if you continue to have difficulty.

Step 5
Apply Borders and Shading

Refer to Figure 2.21 as you complete Step 5.

a. Click the **Home tab**, click the **Borders arrow**, and then click **Borders and Shading** to display the Borders and Shading dialog box shown in Figure 2.21.

b. Click the **Borders tab**, if necessary, then click the double line style in the *Style* list. Click **¾ pt** in the *Width* list, then click **Box** in the *Setting* section.

A preview of these settings will display on the right side of the window in the Preview area.

c. Click the **Shading tab**, then click the **Fill drop-down arrow** and select **Dark Blue, Text 2, Lighter 80%** from the palette. It is located in the fourth column from the left and in the second row from the top. Click **OK** to accept the settings for both Borders and Shading.

The paragraph is surrounded by a ¾ point double-line border, and a light blue shading appears behind the text.

d. Click outside the paragraph to deselect it and view your formatting changes.

e. Save the document.

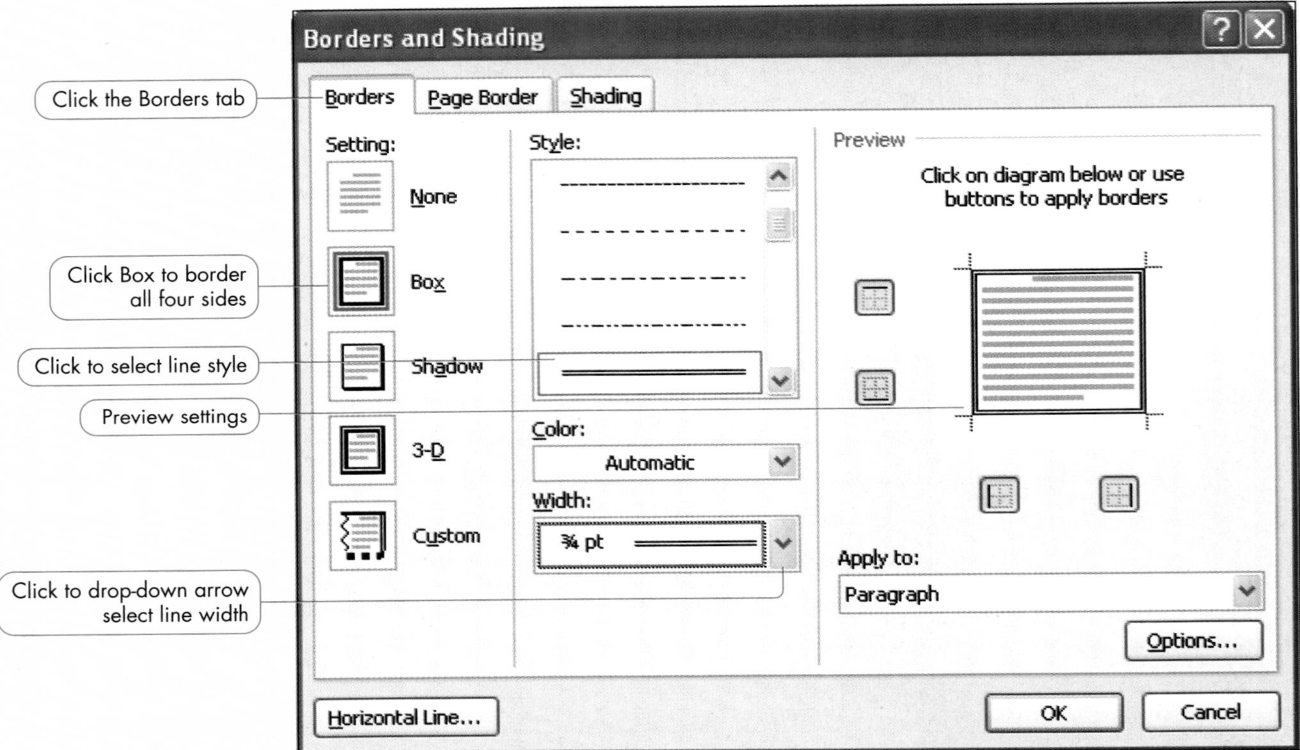

Figure 2.21 Borders and Shading Dialog Box

Step 6
Change Column Structure

Refer to Figure 2.22 as you complete Step 6.

a. Click the **Page Layout tab** and click **Margins** in the Page Setup group. Click **Custom Margins** and select the **Margins tab** if necessary.

b. Click the spin arrows to set **1"** left and right margins. Click **OK**.

The document is now formatted by 1" left, right, top, and bottom margins.

c. Click the **Zoom button** in the status bar, select **Page width,** and then click **OK**. Press **PgUp** or **PgDn** on the keyboard to scroll until the second page comes into view.

d. Click anywhere in the paragraph, *Write now, but edit later*. Right-click and select **Paragraph,** click the **Indents and Spacing tab** if necessary, then change left and right to **0"** in the *Indentation* section. Click **OK**.

These settings prepare your document for the changes you make in the next steps.

e. Click the **Page Layout tab** and click **Columns** in the Page Setup group. Click **More Columns** to display the Columns dialog box.

Because you will change several settings related to columns, you clicked the More Columns option instead of clicking the gallery option to create three columns.

f. Click **Three** in the *Presets* section of the dialog box. The default spacing between columns is 0.5", which leads to a column width of 1.83". Change the spacing to **.25**" in the **Spacing** list, which automatically changes the column width to 2".

g. Click the **Line between column check box**, as shown in Figure 2.22. Click **OK**.

The document is now formatted in three columns with 0.25" space between columns. Vertical lines appear between columns.

h. Save the document.

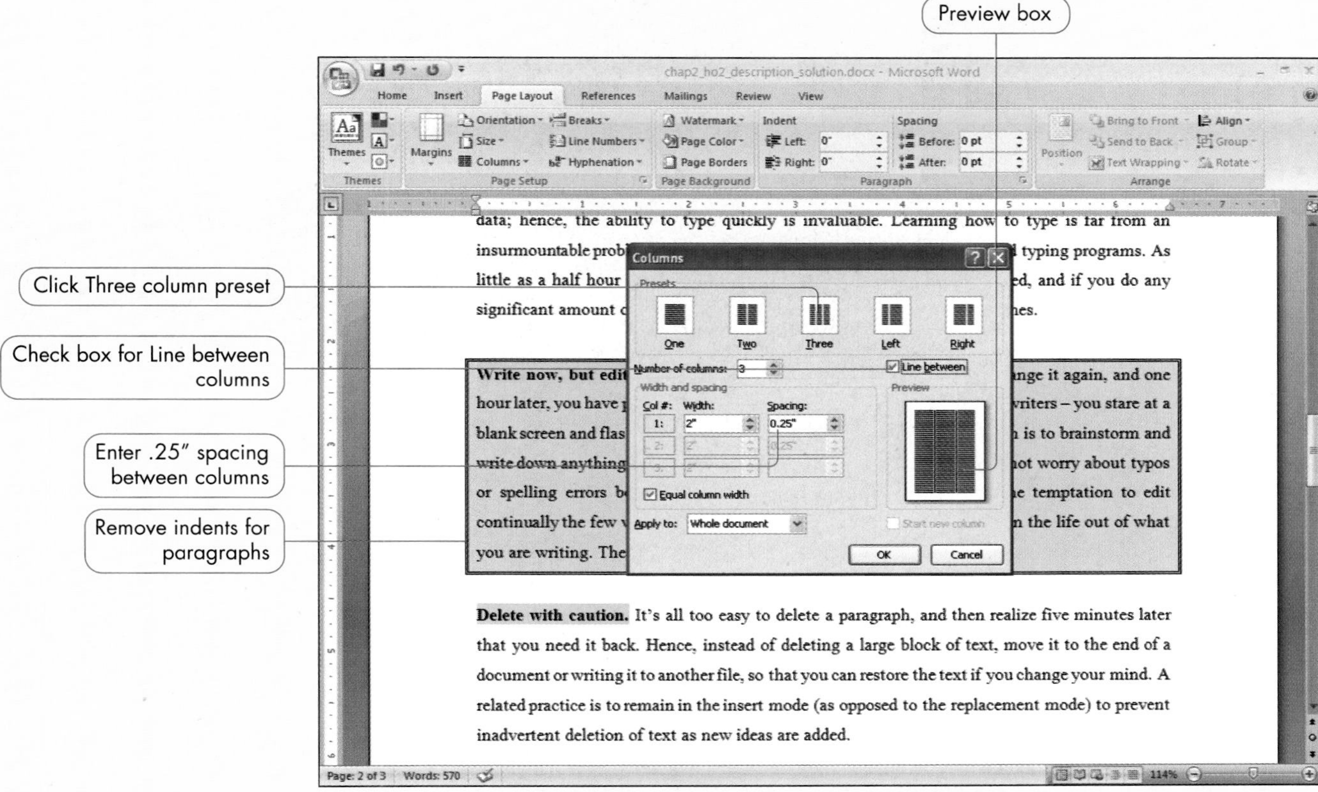

Figure 2.22 Change Column Structure

Step 7
Insert a Section Break and Create Columns

Refer to Figure 2.23 as you complete Step 7.

a. Click **Zoom** on the status bar to display the Zoom dialog box. Click **Many Pages**, drag to select **1x3** pages, and then click **OK**.

The document displays the column formatting.

b. Place the insertion point immediately to the left of the first paragraph on the second page. Click the **Page Layout tab** and click **Breaks** to display the list shown in Figure 2.23. Click **Continuous** under *Section Breaks*.

c. Click anywhere on the title page, above the section break you just inserted. Click **Columns**, then click **One** to display the content in one column.

The formatting for the first section of the document (the title page) should change to one column; the title of the document is centered across the entire page.

d. Save and close the *chap2_ho2_description_solution* document. Exit Word if you will not continue with the next exercise at this time.

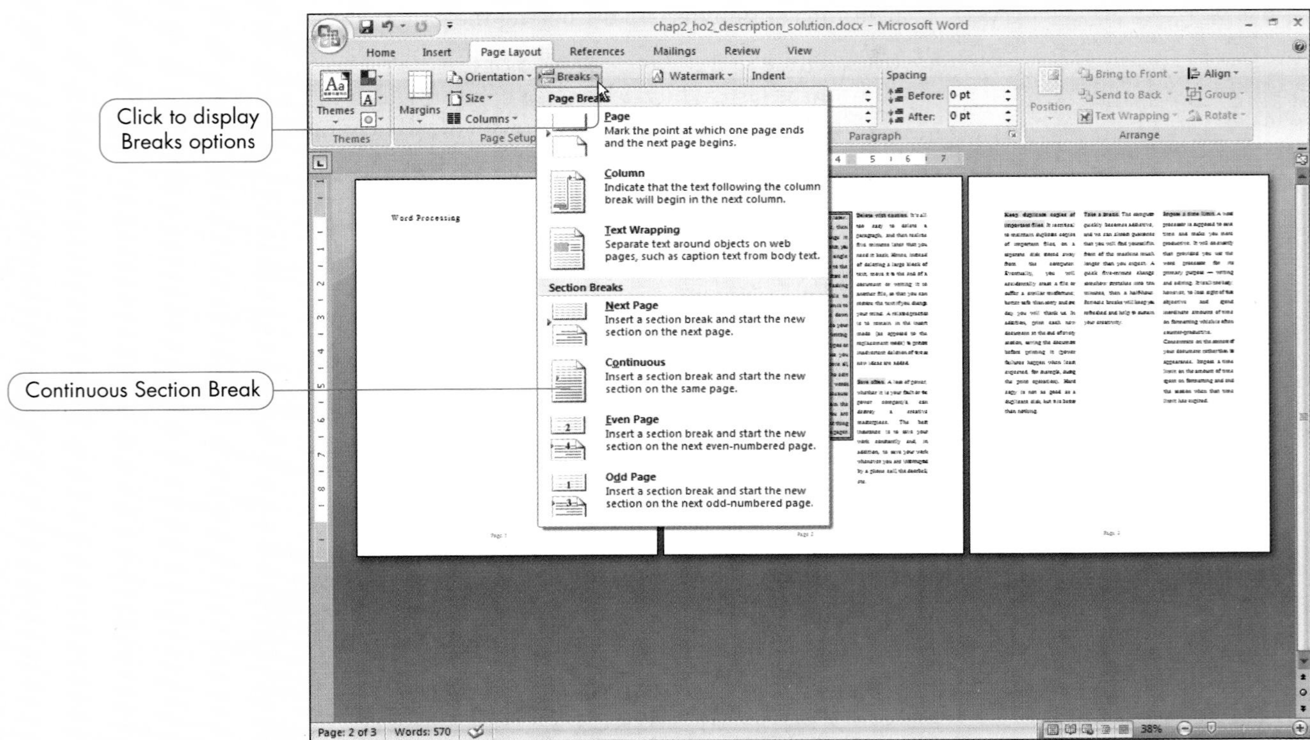

Figure 2.23 Insert a Section Break

Styles and Document References

As you complete reports, assignments, and projects for other classes or in your job, you probably apply the same text, paragraph, table, and list formatting for similar documents. Instead of formatting each document individually, you can create your own custom style to save time in setting particular formats for titles, headings, and paragraphs. Styles and other features in Word then can be used to automatically generate reference pages such as a table of contents and indexes.

In this section, you create and modify styles. You also display a document in the Outline view. Finally, you learn how to use the AutoFormat feature.

Creating and Modifying Styles

(One way to achieve uniformity throughout a document is to store the formatting information as a style. Change the style and you automatically change all text defined by that style.)

One characteristic of a professional document is the uniform formatting that is applied to similar elements throughout the document. Different elements have different formatting. For headings you can use one font, color, style, and size, and then use a completely different format design on text below those headings. The headings may be left aligned, while the text is fully justified. You can format lists and footnotes in entirely different styles.

One way to achieve uniformity throughout the document is to use the Format Painter to copy the formatting from one occurrence of each element to the next, but this step is tedious and inefficient. And if you were to change your mind after copying the formatting throughout a document, you would have to repeat the entire process all over again. A much easier way to achieve uniformity is to store all the formatting information together, which is what we refer to as a ***style***. Styles automate the formatting process and provide a consistent appearance to a document. It is possible to store any type of character or paragraph formatting within a style, and once a style is defined, you can apply it to any element within a document to produce identical formatting. Change the style and you automatically change all text defined by that style.

A ***style*** is a set of formatting options you apply to characters or paragraphs.

Styles are created on the character or paragraph level. A ***character style*** stores character formatting (font, size, and style) and affects only the selected text. A ***paragraph style*** stores paragraph formatting such as alignment, line spacing, indents, tabs, text flow, and borders and shading, as well as the font, size, and style of the text in the paragraph. A paragraph style affects the current paragraph or, if selected, multiple paragraphs. You create and apply styles from the Styles group on the Home tab, as shown in Figure 2.24.

A ***character style*** stores character formatting and affects only selected text.

A ***paragraph style*** stores paragraph formatting of text.

The Normal template contains more than 100 styles. Unless you specify a style, Word uses the Normal style. The Normal style contains these settings: 12-point Calibri, English (U.S.) language, single line spacing, left horizontal alignment, and Widow/Orphan control. You can create your own styles to use in a document, modify or delete an existing style, and even add your new style to the Normal template for use in other documents.

The document in Figure 2.25 is a report about the Great Depression. Each paragraph begins with a one-line heading, followed by the supporting text. The task pane in the figure displays all of the styles used in the document. The Normal style contains the default paragraph settings (left aligned, single spacing, and a default font) and is assigned automatically to every paragraph unless a different style is specified. The Clear Formatting style removes all formatting from selected text. It is the Heading 3 and Body Text styles, however, that are of interest to us, as these styles have been applied throughout the document to the associated elements.

Click to view gallery of styles

Click to apply this Quick Style to selected text

Click to change Quick Styles category

Click to display Styles pane

Styles pane

The Great Depression

1929 - 1933

Introduction

In the late 1920s, the U.S. economy was strong. Many companies were growing and earning money. People bought shares of the companies, called stock. The stocks were traded and bought in the Stock Market.

On October 24, 1929, stock values dropped or became worthless rapidly. This started the most severe economic depression in U.S. history—the Great Depression. Today, that day is still remembered as Black Thursday.

Chapter 1. Black Thursday

In the late 1920s, prices in the stock market soared up, becoming very valuable. For example, in 1928, the price of a common share of the Dupont stock went from $310 to $525 The rising stock values encouraged people to buy stocks in hope of making large profits when the stock exchange increased in the future. Even though experts predicted that the stock prices might fall, people didn't listen. So many investors threw their money into the stock exchange that the plan backfired. Instead of increasing in value, the share prices crashed, becoming worthless. When the stock market crashed on Black Thursday millions of people

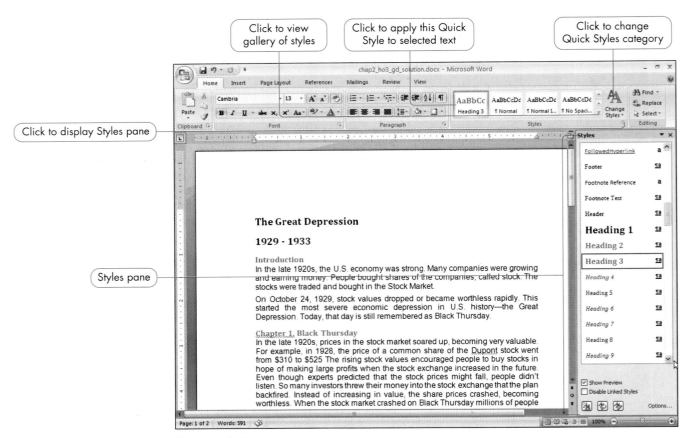

Figure 2.24 The Styles Group

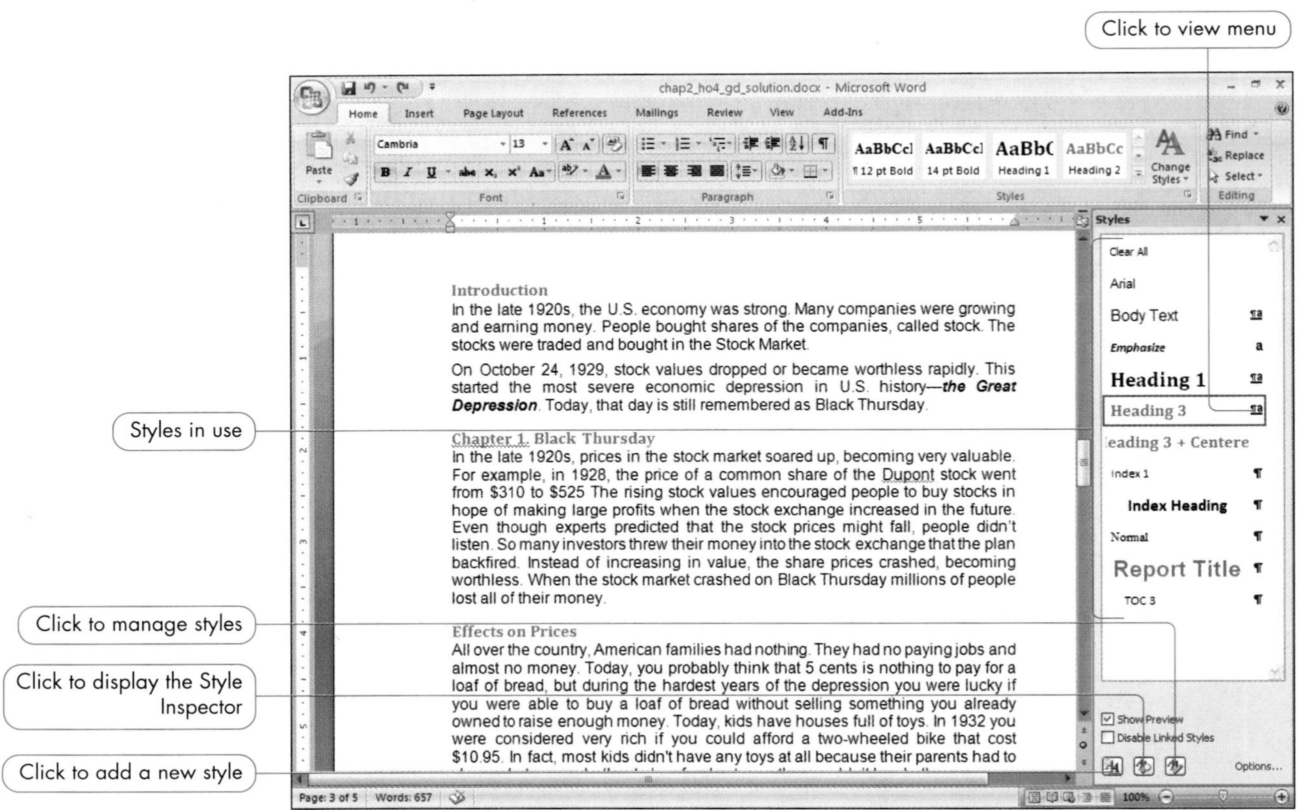

Figure 2.25 Styles Task Pane

You can change the specifications of a style by clicking the down arrow for the particular style, then selecting Modify. The specifications for the Heading 3 style are shown in Figure 2.26. The current settings within the Heading 3 style call for 13-point Cambria bold type using a custom color. There is a 12-point space before the text, and the heading appears on the same page as the next paragraph. The preview frame in the dialog box shows how paragraphs formatted in this style display. Click the Format button in the Modify Style dialog box to select and open other dialog boxes where you modify settings that are used in the style. And, as indicated earlier, any changes to the style are reflected automatically in any text or element defined by that style.

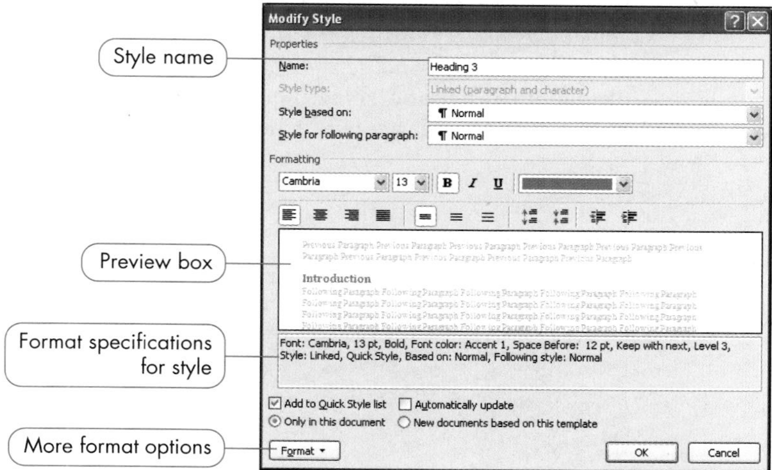

Figure 2.26 Modify a Style

TIP Styles and Paragraphs

A paragraph style affects the entire paragraph; that is, you cannot apply a paragraph style to only part of a paragraph. To apply a style to an existing paragraph, place the insertion point anywhere within the paragraph, click the Styles Dialog Box Launcher on the Home tab to display the Styles pane, then click the name of the style you want to use. The Styles pane can display in several locations. Initially, it might display as a floating window, but you can drag the title bar to move it. Drag to the far left or right side, and it will dock on that side of the window.

Use the Styles Pane Options

When you display the Styles pane in your document, it might contain only the styles used in the document, as in Figure 2.25, or it might list every style in the Word document template. If the Styles pane only displays styles used in the document, you are unable to view or apply other styles. You can change the styles that display in the Styles pane by using the Styles Gallery Options dialog box, which displays when you click *Options* in the lower-right corner of the Styles pane. In the *Select styles to show* box, you select from several options including Recommended, In use, In current document, and All styles. Select *In use* to view only styles used in this document; select *All styles* to view all styles created for the document template as well as any custom styles you create. Other options are available in this dialog box, including how to sort the styles when displayed and whether to show Paragraph or Font or both types of styles. To view the style names with their styles applied, click the *Show Preview* check box near the bottom of the Styles pane.

Reveal Formatting

To display complete format properties for selected text in the document, use the Reveal Formatting task pane, as shown in Figure 2.27. The properties are displayed by Font, Paragraph, and Section, enabling you to click the plus or minus sign next to each item to view or hide the underlying details. The properties in each area are links to the associated dialog boxes. Click Alignment or Justification, for example, within the Paragraph area to open the Paragraph dialog box, where you can change the indicated property. This panel is often helpful for troubleshooting a format problem in a document. To view this pane, click the Styles Dialog Box Launcher on the Home tab, click Style Inspector at the bottom of the Styles pane, then click Reveal Formatting in the Style Inspector pane. If you use this feature often, you can add it to the Quick Access Toolbar. To add it, click the Office Button, then click Word Options; select *Customize* on the left side of the Word Options dialog box, then click the drop-down arrow for *Choose commands from* and select *All Commands*. Scroll down the alphabetical list and select *Reveal Formatting*, then click the Add button displayed between the two large lists. Click OK to save the addition.

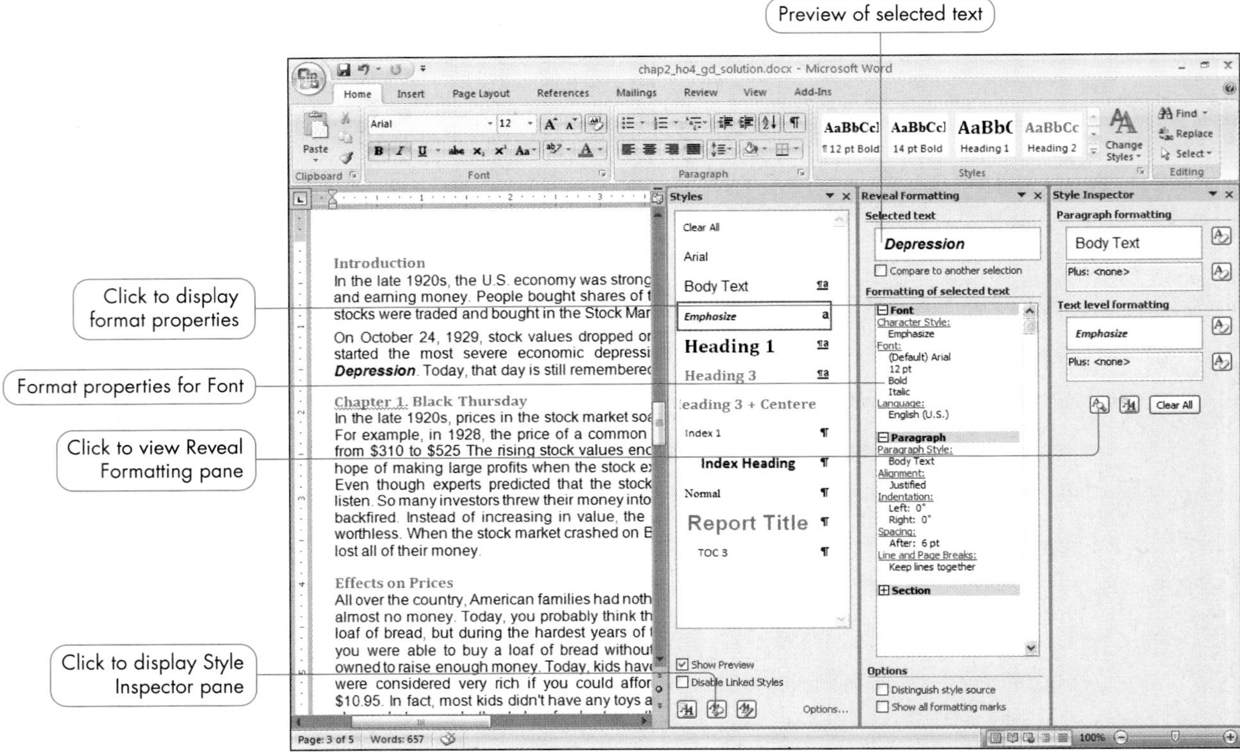

Figure 2.27 Reveal Formatting

Use the Outline View

Outline view is a structural view that displays varying amounts of detail.

One additional advantage of styles is that they enable you to view a document in the Outline view. The ***Outline view*** does not display a conventional outline, but rather a structural view of a document that can be collapsed or expanded as necessary. Consider, for example, Figure 2.28, which displays the Outline view of a report about the Great Depression. The heading for each tip is formatted according to the Heading 3 style. The text of each tip is formatted according to the Body Text style.

The advantage of Outline view is that you can collapse or expand portions of a document to provide varying amounts of detail. We have, for example, collapsed almost the entire document in Figure 2.28, displaying the headings while suppressing the body text. We also expanded the text for two sections (*Introduction* and *The New Deal*) for purposes of illustration.

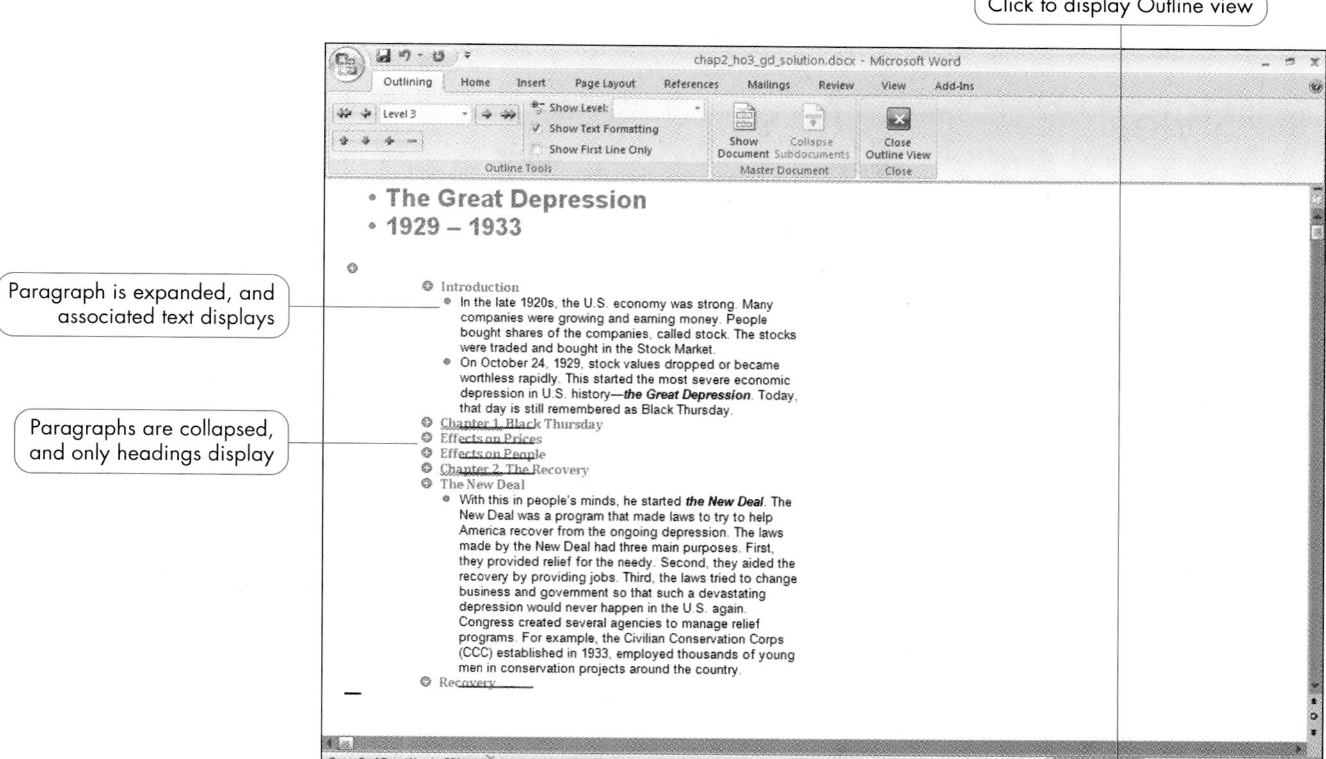

Figure 2.28 The Outline View

Now assume that you want to move one paragraph from its present position to a different position in the document. Without the Outline view, the text might stretch over several pages, making it difficult to see the text of both areas at the same time. Using the Outline view, however, you can collapse what you do not need to see, then simply click and drag headings to rearrange the text within the document. The Outline view is very useful with long documents, but it requires the use of styles throughout the document.

TIP The Outline Versus the Outline View

A conventional outline is created as a multilevel list using the Multilevel List command in the Paragraph group on the Home tab. Text for the outline is entered in the Print Layout view, *not* the Outline view. The latter provides a condensed view of a document that is used in conjunction with styles.

Use the AutoFormat Feature

The ***AutoFormat*** feature analyzes a document and formats it for you.

Styles are extremely powerful. They enable you to impose uniform formatting within a document, and they let you take advantage of the Outline view. What if, however, you have an existing or lengthy document that does not contain any styles (other than the default Normal style, which is applied to every paragraph)? Do you have to manually go through every paragraph in order to apply the appropriate style? Fortunately, the answer is no, because the AutoFormat feature provides a quick solution. The ***AutoFormat*** feature analyzes a document and formats it for you; it evaluates an entire document and determines how each paragraph is used, then it applies an appropriate style to each paragraph. To use the AutoFormat feature, you must add it to the Quick Access Toolbar using the same procedure explained previously in the Reveal Formatting section.

Hands-On Exercises

3 | Styles

Skills covered: 1. Apply Style Properties **2.** Modify the Body Text Style **3.** Modify the Heading 3 Style **4.** Select the Outline View **5.** Create a Paragraph Style **6.** Create a Character Style **7.** View the Completed Document

Step 1 Apply Style Properties

Refer to Figure 2.29 as you complete Step 1.

a. Open the document *chap2_ho3_gd* in the **Exploring Word folder** and save it as **chap2_ho3_gd_solution.**

b. Press **Ctrl+Home** to move to the beginning of the document.

   Notice the headings have been formatted with 14-point and 12-point bold font.

c. Select the first two lines, *The Great Depression* and *1929–1933*, then click **Heading 1** from the Quick Style gallery in the Styles group on the Home tab.

d. Click anywhere in the first paragraph heading, *Introduction*. Click the **Styles Dialog Box Launcher** on the Home tab. Double-click the title bar of the task pane to dock it, if necessary, so it does not float on the screen. Click the down arrow that displays when you hover over the *12 pt Bold* style listed in the Styles pane, then click **Select all 7 instances**.

   All paragraph headings in this document are selected, as shown in Figure 2.29.

e. Click the **More button** on the right side of the **Quick Style** gallery to display more styles, then click the **Heading 3** style.

   When you hover your mouse over the different styles in the gallery, the Live Preview feature displays the style on your selected text but will not apply it until you click on the style.

f. Save the document.

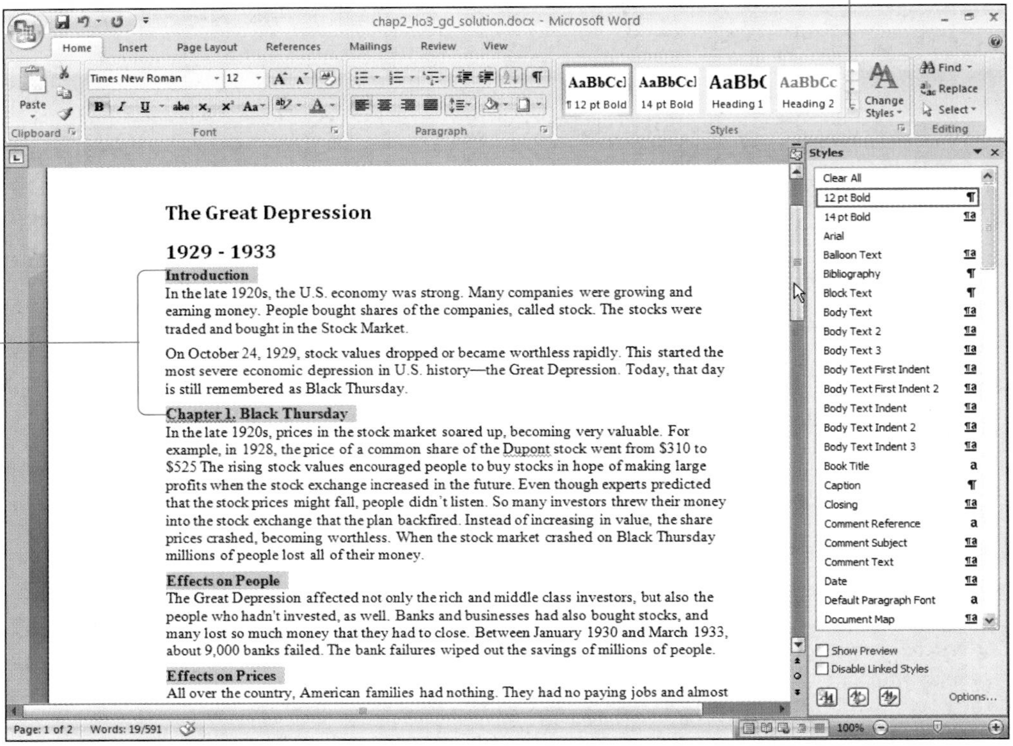

Figure 2.29 View Style Properties

Step 2
Modify the Body Text Style

Refer to Figure 2.30 as you complete Step 2.

a. Press **Ctrl+Home** to move to the beginning of the document. Place the insertion point in the first paragraph, then notice the Body Text style is selected in the Styles pane. Click the down arrow next to the style and click **Modify** to display the Modify Style dialog box.

   TROUBLESHOOTING: If you click the style name instead of the down arrow, you will apply the style to the selected text instead of modifying it. Click Undo on the Quick Access Toolbar to cancel the command. Click the down arrow next to the style name to display the associated menu and click the Modify command to display the Modify Style dialog box.

b. Change the font to **Arial**. Click **Justify** to change the alignment of every paragraph in the document formatted with the *Body Text* style.

c. Click **Format** in the lower-left corner of the window, as shown in Figure 2.30, then click **Paragraph** to display the Paragraph dialog box. If necessary, click the **Line and Page Breaks tab**.

   The box for Widow/Orphan control is checked by default. This option ensures that any paragraph defined by the Body Text style will not be split, leaving a single line of text at the bottom or top of a page.

d. Click the **Keep lines together check box** in the *Pagination* section.

   This option is a more stringent requirement and ensures that the entire paragraph is not split.

e. Click **OK** to close the Paragraph dialog box. Click **OK** to close the Modify Style dialog box.

   All of the multiline paragraphs in the document change automatically to reflect the new definition of the Body Text style, which includes full justification, a new font, and ensuring that a paragraph is not split across pages.

f. Save the document.

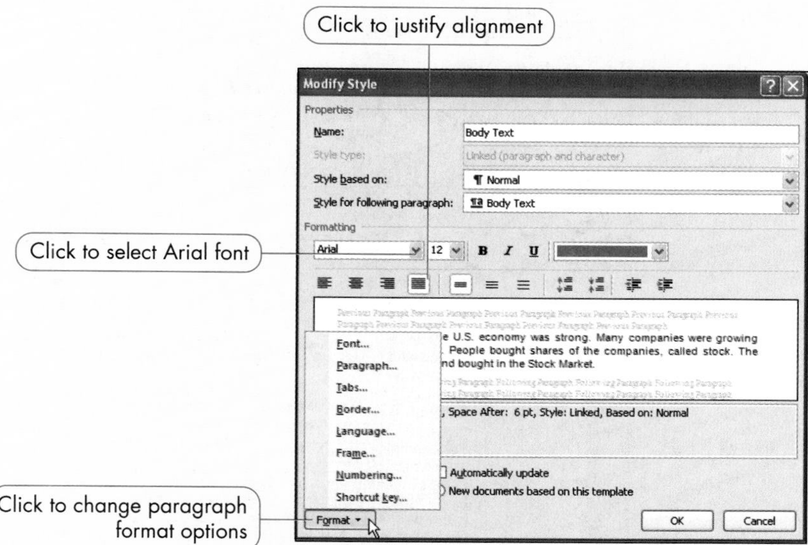

Figure 2.30 Modify the Body Text Style

Step 3
Modify the Heading 3 Style

Refer to Figure 2.31 as you complete Step 3.

a. Place the insertion point in one of the headings that has been formatted with the *Heading 3* style. Scroll, if necessary, to view *Heading 3* in the Styles pane. Hover your mouse over Heading 3, click the down arrow, then click **Modify** to display the Modify Style dialog box.

b. Click the **Font Color drop-down arrow** to display the palette in Figure 2.31. Click **Blue, Accent 1**, the blue color swatch on the first row, to change the color of all of the headings in the document.

   You see a preview of the effect as you hover the mouse over the color, but the change will not take effect until you click *OK* to accept the settings and close the dialog box.

c. Click **Format** at the bottom of the dialog box, then click **Paragraph** to display the Paragraph dialog box. Click the **Indents and Spacing tab**, then change the **Spacing After** to **0**. Click **OK** to accept the settings and close the Paragraph dialog box.

   You modified the style by changing the spacing after the heading to 0, which forces the paragraph text to display closer to the heading.

d. Click **OK** to close the Modify Style dialog box.

   The formatting in your document has changed to reflect the changes in the Heading 3 style.

e. Save the document.

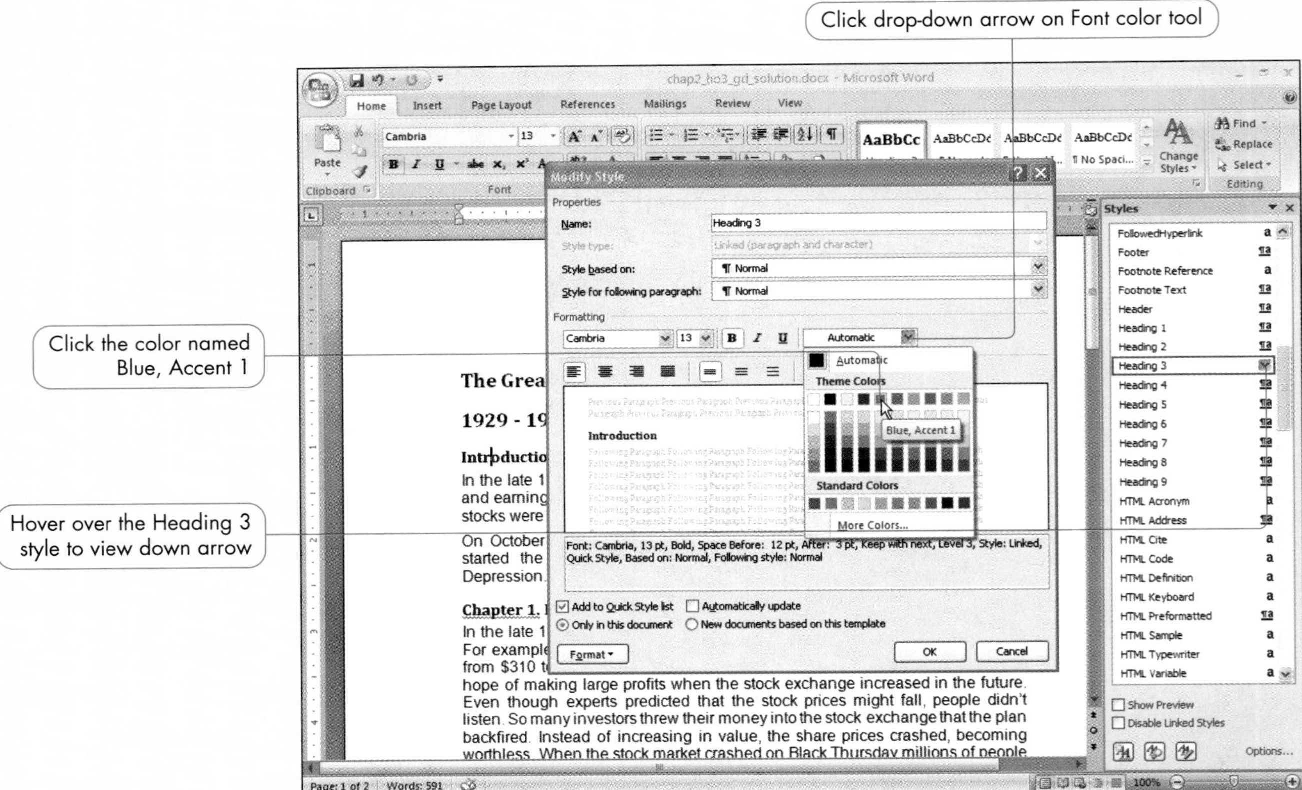

Figure 2.31 Modify the Heading 3 Style

TIP Space Before and After

Within single-spaced text, it is common practice to press the Enter key twice at the end of a paragraph (once to end the paragraph and a second time to insert a blank line before the next paragraph). The same effect is achieved by setting the spacing before or after the paragraph using the Spacing Before or After list boxes in the Paragraph dialog box. The latter technique gives you greater flexibility in that you can specify any amount of spacing (e.g., 6 pt) to leave only half a line before or after a paragraph. It also enables you to change the spacing between paragraphs more easily because the spacing information is stored within the paragraph style.

Step 4
Select the Outline View

Refer to Figure 2.32 as you complete Step 4.

a. Close the Styles pane. Click the **View tab**, then click **Outline** to display the document in Outline view.

b. Place the insertion point to the left of the first paragraph heading, *Introduction*, and select the rest of the document. Click the **Outlining tab**, if necessary, then click **Collapse** in the Outline Tools group.

   The entire document collapses so that only the headings display.

c. Click in the heading titled *The New Deal*, as shown in Figure 2.32. Click **Expand** in the Outline Tools group to see the subordinate items under this heading.

d. Select the paragraph heading *Effects on Prices*, then click **Move Up** on the Outline Tools group.

   You moved the paragraph above the paragraph that precedes it in the outline. Note that you also can drag and drop a selected paragraph.

e. Save the document.

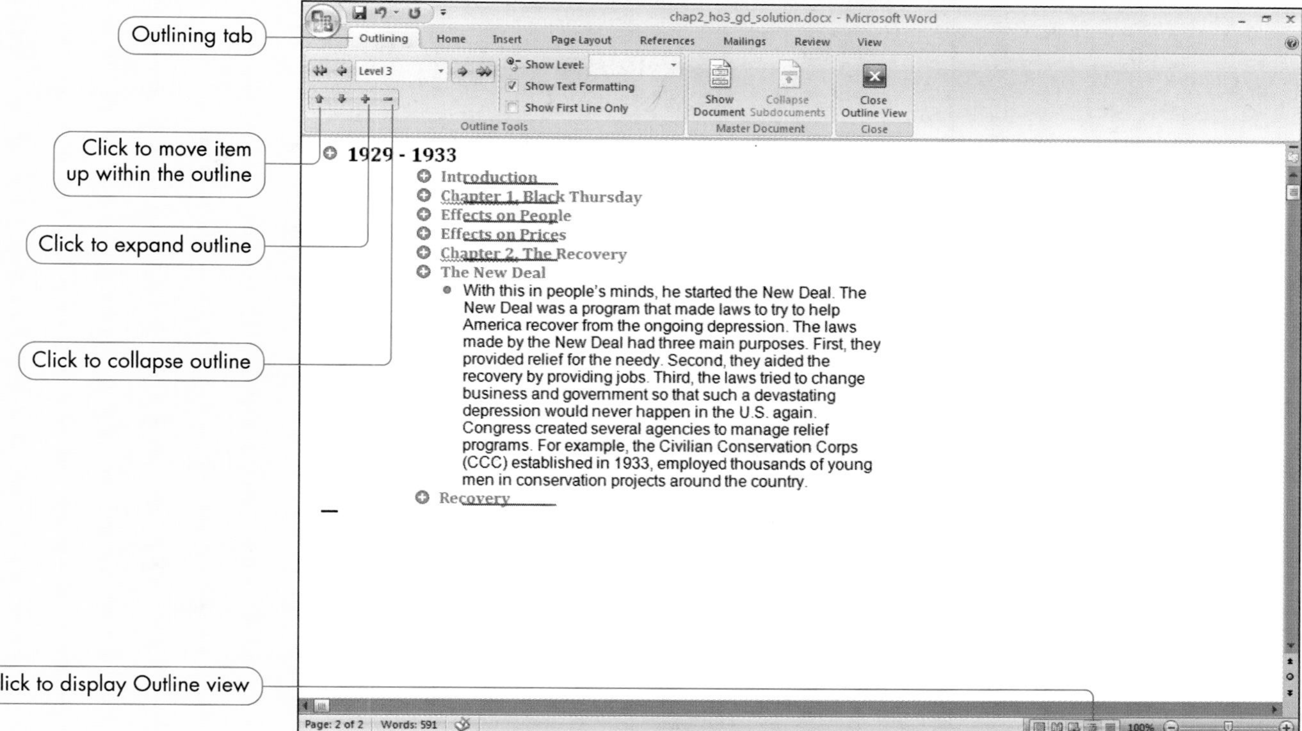

Figure 2.32 The Outline View

Step 5
Create a Paragraph Style

Refer to Figure 2.33 as you complete Step 5.

a. Click Close Outline View to change to return to Print Layout view. Click the **Home tab**, if necessary, and then click the **Styles Dialog Box Launcher** to open the Styles pane.

b. Press **Ctrl+Home** to move the insertion point to the beginning of the document, then place the insertion point to the right of *1933* and press **Ctrl+Enter**.

Inserting a page break creates space where you can add a title page.

c. Press **Ctrl+Home** to move the insertion point to the beginning of the new page, then select both lines on the title page. Scroll up if necessary and click **Clear All** in the Styles pane. Click the **Font arrow** on the Home tab and select **Arial,** then click the **Font Size arrow**, select **24**, and click **Bold** and **Center** in the Paragraph group on the Home tab. Click the **Font Color arrow** and select **Blue, Accent 1** on the color palette (the blue color swatch on the first row) to change the color of the text to blue.

The Styles task pane displays the specifications for the text you just entered. You have created a new style, but the style is not yet named.

d. Point to the description for the title on the Styles pane (you may only be able to see the first or last few format effects such as Bold, Accent 1), hover your mouse over the description to view the down arrow, click the down arrow, as shown in Figure 2.33, and then select **Modify Style** to display the Modify Style dialog box.

e. Click in the **Name text box** in the Properties area and type **Report Title** as the name of the new style. Click **OK**.

f. Save the document.

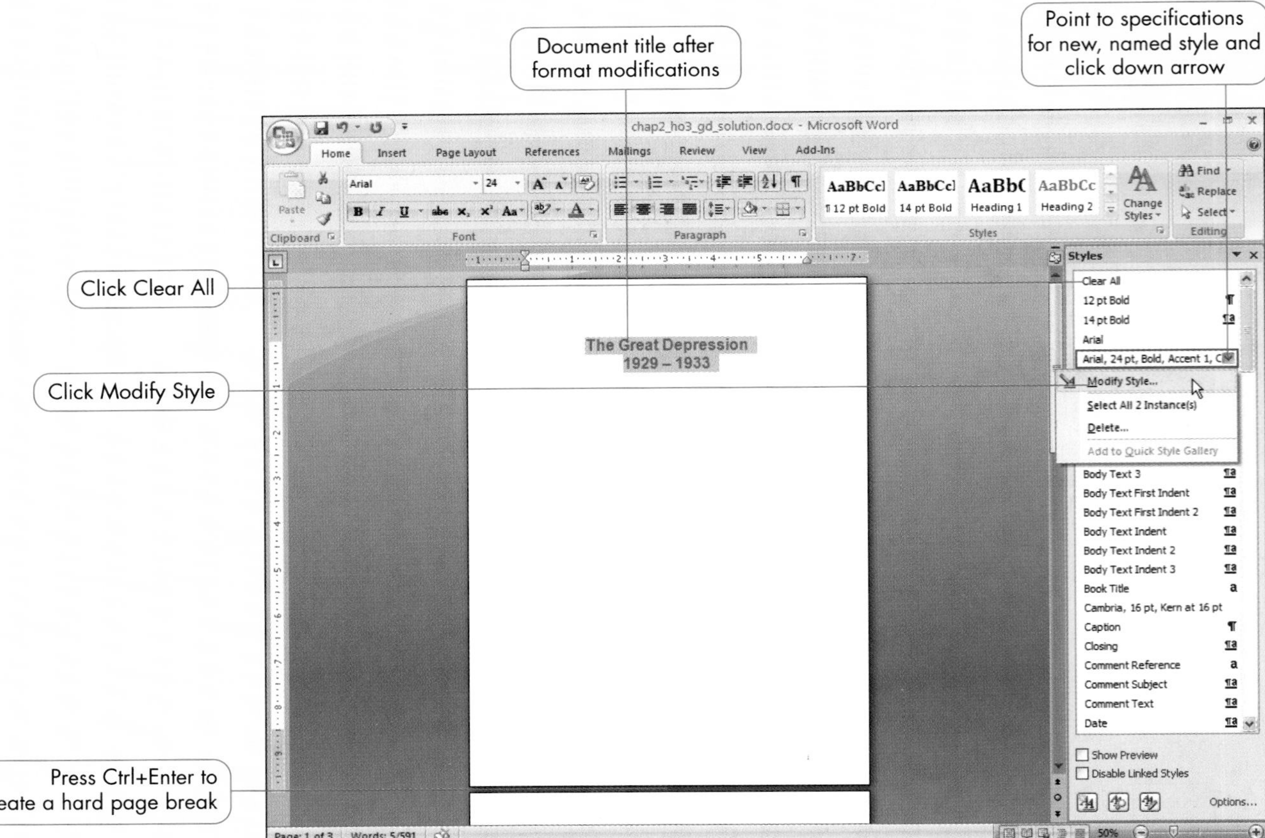

Figure 2.33 Create a Paragraph Style

Step 6
Create a Character Style

Refer to Figure 2.34 as you complete Step 6.

a. Select the words *the Great Depression* (that appear within the second paragraph of the Introduction). Click **Bold** and **Italic** in the Font group on the Home tab.

b. Click **New Style** on the bottom of the Styles pane, and then type **Emphasize** as the name of the style.

c. Click the **Style type drop-down arrow** and select **Character** (see Figure 2.34). Click **OK**.

The style named Emphasize is listed in the Style pane and can be used throughout your document.

d. Select the words *the New Deal* in the first sentence of the *New Deal* section. Click **More** in the Quick Style gallery on the Home tab and apply the newly created *Emphasize* character style to the selected text. Close the Styles task pane.

e. Save the document.

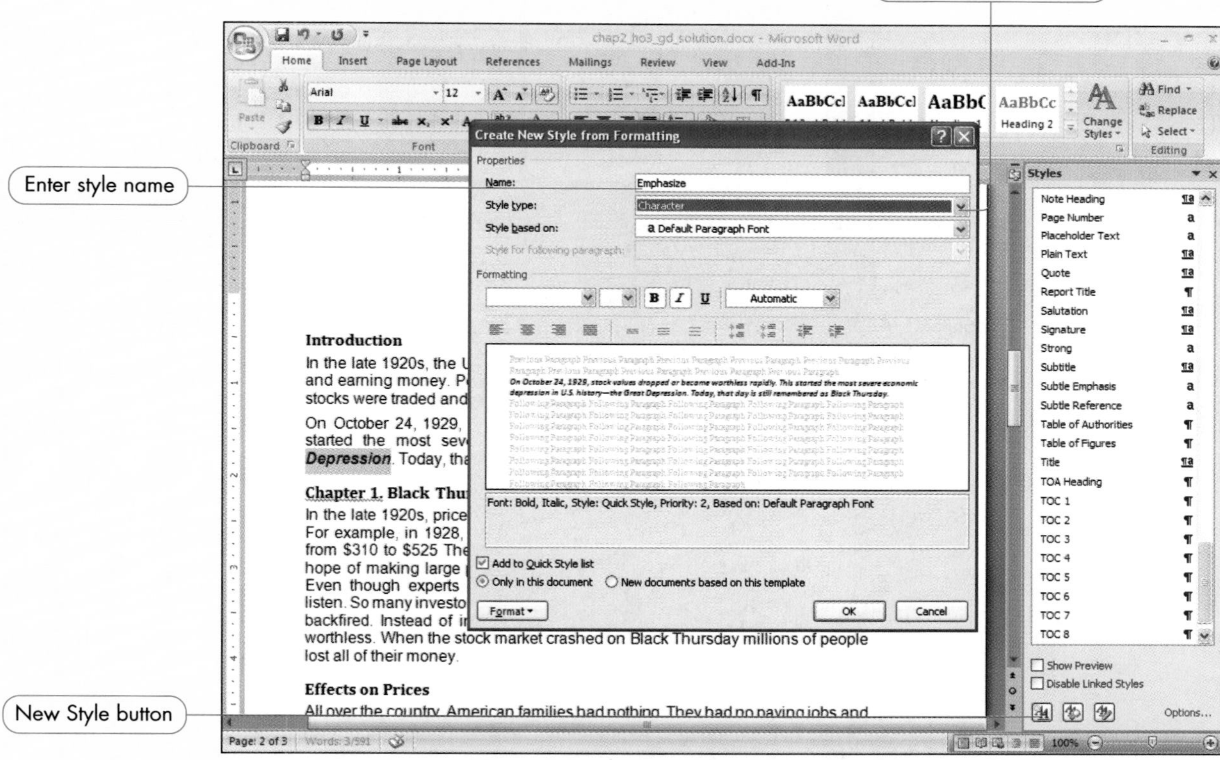

Figure 2.34 Create a Character Style

Step 7
View the Completed Document

Refer to Figure 2.35 as you complete Step 7.

a. Click **Zoom** on the status bar, click **Many Pages**, then click and drag to select 1 x 3 pages. Click **OK**.

You should see a multipage display similar to Figure 2.35. The text on the individual pages is too small to read, but you can see the page breaks and overall document flow. According to the specifications in the Body Text style, the paragraphs should all be justified and each should fit completely on one page without spilling over to the next page.

b. Click to the left of the title on the first page and press **Enter** three times to position the title further down the page.

c. Save the *chap2_ho3_gd_solution* document and keep it onscreen if you plan to continue with the next hands-on exercise. Close the file and exit Word if you will not continue with the next exercise at this time.

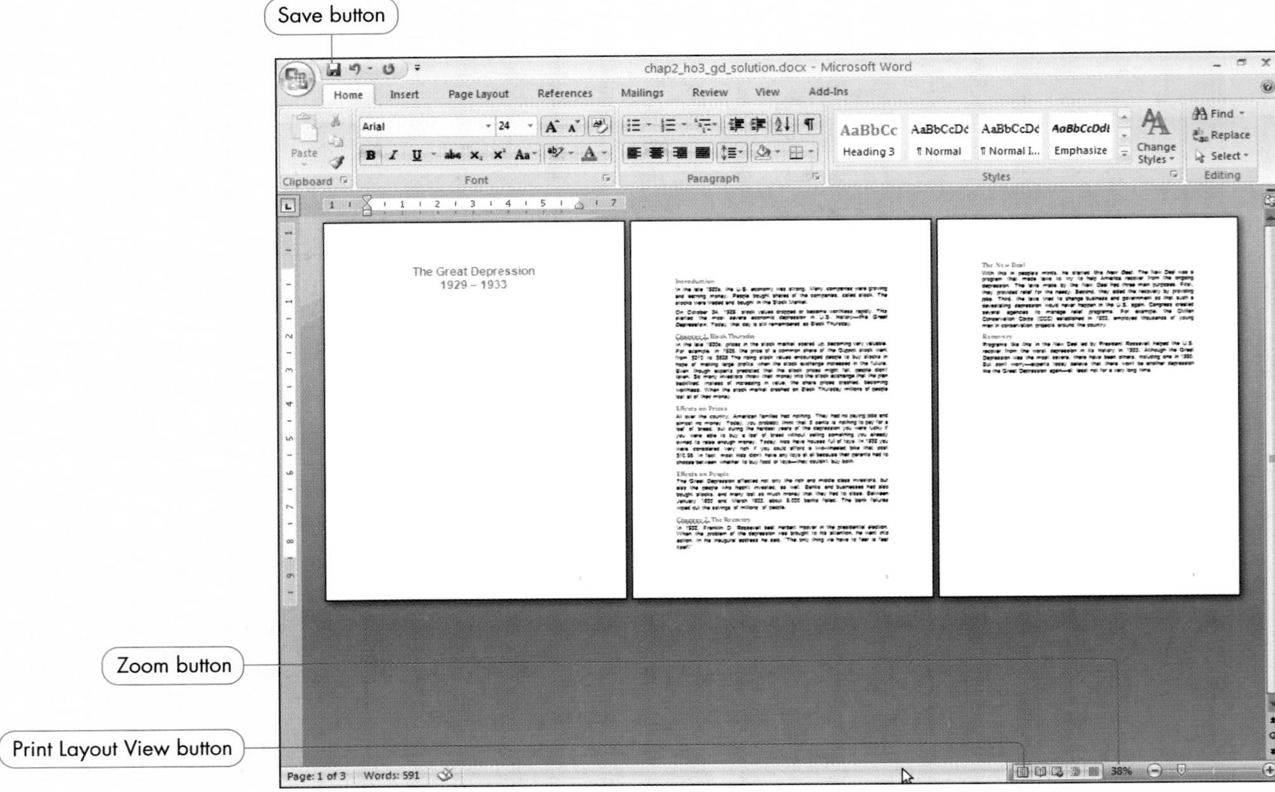

Figure 2.35 The Completed Document

Table of Contents and Indexes

(Well-prepared long documents include special features to help readers locate information easily. You can use Word to help you create these supplemental document components with minimal effort.)

Well-prepared long documents include special features to help readers locate information easily. For example, people often refer to the table of contents or the index in a long document—such as a book, reference manual, or company policy—to locate particular topics within that document. You can use Word to help you create these supplemental document components with minimal effort.

In this section, you generate a table of contents at the beginning of a document. You then learn how to designate text to include in an index and then generate the index at the end of a document.

Creating a Table of Contents

A ***table of contents*** lists headings and the page numbers where they appear in a document.

A ***table of contents*** lists headings in the order they appear in a document and the page numbers where the entries begin. Word can create the table of contents automatically, if you apply a style to each heading in the document. You can use built-in styles, Heading 1 through Heading 9, or identify your own custom styles to use when generating the table of contents. Word also will update the table to accommodate the addition or deletion of headings and/or changes in page numbers brought about through changes in the document.

The table of contents is located on the References tab. You can select from several predefined formats such as Classic and Formal, as well as determine how many levels to display in the table; the latter correspond to the heading styles used within the document. You can determine whether or not to right-align the page numbers; and you also can choose to include a leader character to draw the reader's eyes across the page from a heading to a page number.

Creating an Index

An ***index*** is a listing of topics and the page numbers where the topic is discussed.

An index puts the finishing touch on a long document. The ***index*** provides an alphabetical listing of topics covered in a document, along with the page numbers where the topic is discussed. Typically, the index appears at the end of a book or document. Word will create an index automatically, provided that the entries for the index have been previously marked. This result, in turn, requires you to go through a document, select the terms to be included in the index, and mark them accordingly. It is not as tedious as it sounds. You can, for example, select a single occurrence of an entry and tell Word to mark all occurrences of that entry for the index. You also can create cross-references, such as "see also Internet."

After you specify the entries, create the index by choosing the Insert Index command on the References tab. You can choose a variety of styles for the index, just as you can for the table of contents. Word arranges the index entries in alphabetical order and enters the appropriate page references. You also can create additional index entries and/or move text within a document, then update the index with the click of a mouse.

Table of Contents and Index Styles | Reference

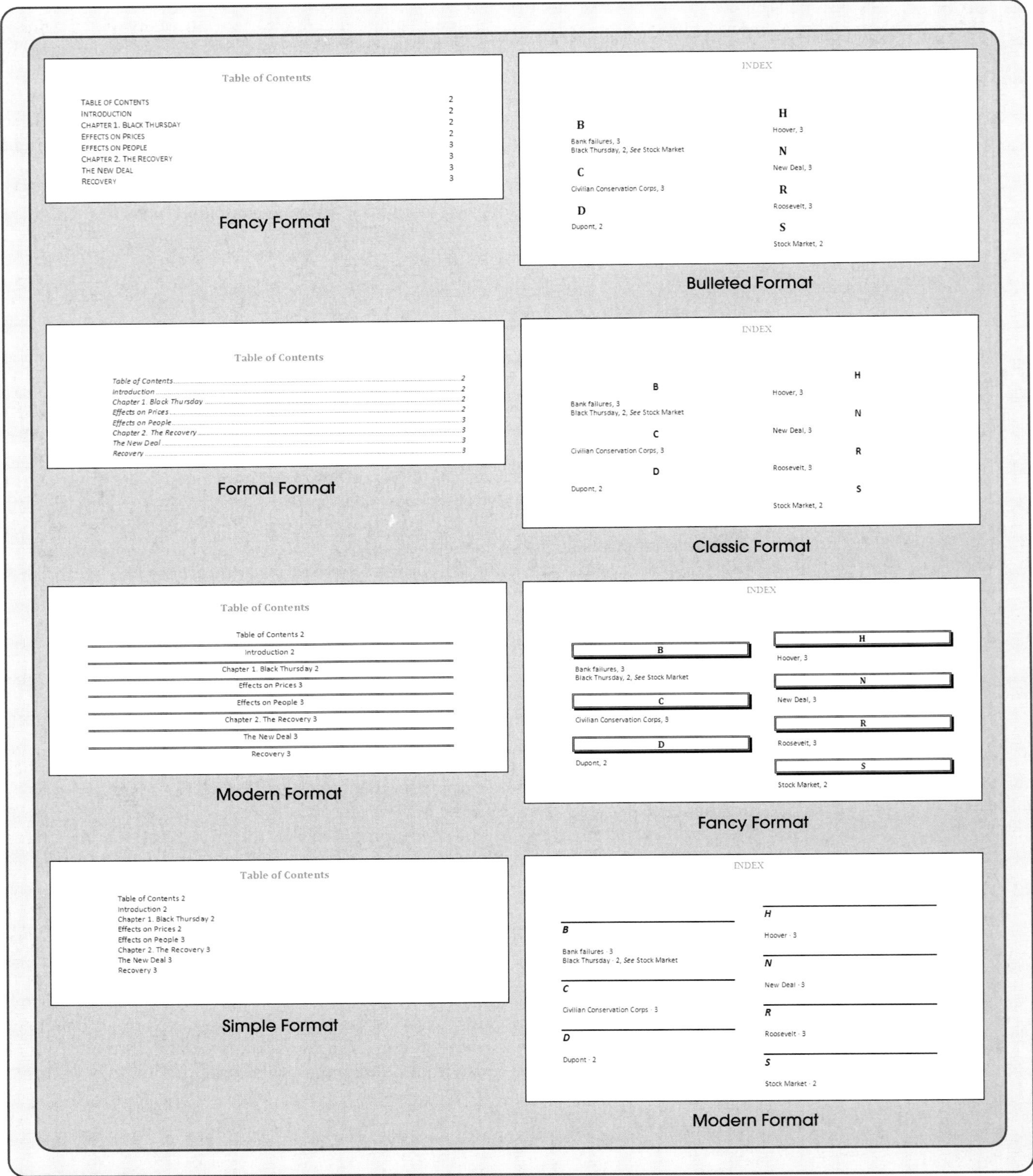

4 | Reference Pages

Skills covered: **1.** Apply a Style **2.** Insert a Table of Contents **3.** Define an Index Entry **4.** Create the Index **5.** Complete the Index **6.** View the Completed Document

Step 1
Apply a Style

Refer to Figure 2.36 as you complete Step 1.

a. Open the *chap2_ho3_gd_solution* document if you closed it after the last hands-on exercise and save it as **chap2_ho4_gd_solution**.

b. Click **Zoom** in the status bar, click **Page Width**, then click **OK**. Scroll to the top of the second page.

c. Click to the left of the *Introduction* title. Type **Table of Contents**, and then press **Enter** two times. Press **Ctrl+Enter** to insert a page break.

   The table of contents displays on a page between the title page and the body of the document using the Heading 3 style you modified in the previous exercise.

d. Click anywhere in the *Table of Contents* heading.

   TROUBLESHOOTING: If the Heading 3 style does not display, click Heading 3 from the Quick Style gallery on the Home tab.

e. Click **Center** in the Paragraph group on the Home tab and compare your document to Figure 2.36.

f. Save the document.

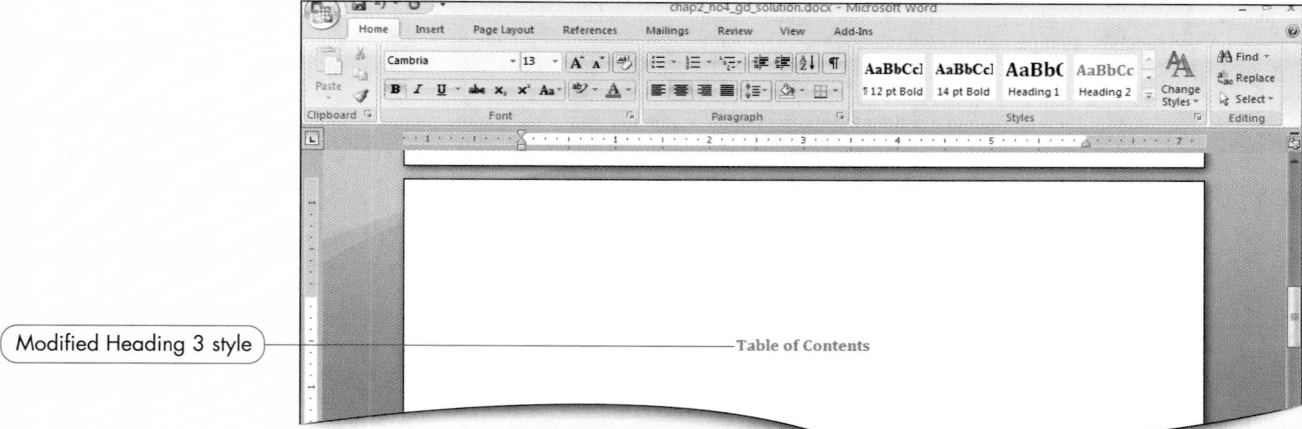

Figure 2.36 Apply a Style to a Heading

Step 2
Insert a Table of Contents

Refer to Figure 2.37 as you complete Step 2.

a. Place the insertion point immediately under the *Table of Contents* title, then click **Zoom** on the status bar. Click **Many Pages**, then click and drag to select 1 x 4 pages. Click **OK**.

The display changes to show all four pages in the document.

b. Click the **References tab**, and then click **Table of Contents** in the Table of Contents group. Select **Insert Table of Contents.**

The Table of Contents dialog box displays (see Figure 2.37).

c. If necessary, click the **Show page numbers check box** and the **Right align page numbers check box**.

d. Click the **Formats drop-down arrow** in the *General* section and select **Distinctive**. Click the **Tab leader drop-down arrow** in the *Print Preview* section and choose a **dot leader**. Click **OK**.

Word takes a moment to create the table of contents, and then displays it in the location of your insertion point.

e. Save the document.

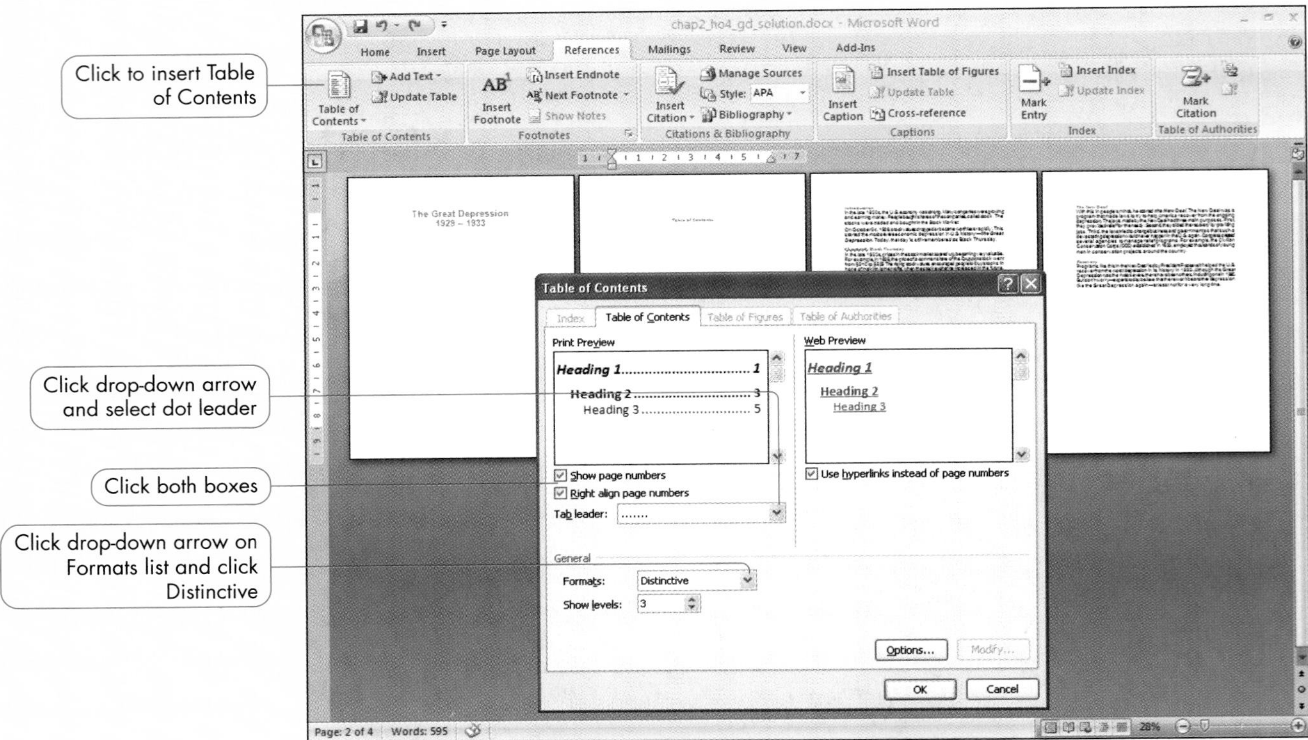

Figure 2.37 Create a Table of Contents

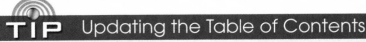

TIP Updating the Table of Contents

You can use a shortcut menu to update the table of contents. Point to any entry in the table of contents, then press the right mouse button to display the menu. Click **Update Field**, click **Update Entire Table**, and then click **OK**. The table of contents is adjusted automatically to reflect page number changes as well as the addition or deletion of any text defined by a style.

Step 3
Define an Index Entry

Refer to Figure 2.38 as you complete Step 3.

a. Press **Ctrl+Home** to move to the beginning of the document. Drag the Zoom Slider on the task bar to 100%. Click the **Home tab**, then click **Find** in the Editing group. Type **Black Thursday** in the *Find what* box, and then click **Find Next** two times.

You click Find Next two times because the first occurrence of *Black Thursday* is in the table of contents, but that is not the occurrence you want to mark for the index.

b. Click **Cancel** to close the Find and Replace dialog box. Click **Show/Hide ¶** in the Paragraph group on the Home tab so you can see the nonprinting characters in the document.

The index entries that were created by the authors appear in curly brackets and begin with the letters XE.

c. Check that the text *Black Thursday* is selected within the document, then press **Alt+Shift+X** to display the Mark Index Entry dialog box, as shown in Figure 2.38.

TROUBLESHOOTING: If you forget the shortcut, click Mark Entry on the References tab.

d. Click **Mark** to create the index entry.

After you create the index entry, you see the field code, {XE "Black Thursday"}, to indicate that the index entry is created. The Mark Index Entry dialog box stays open so that you can create additional entries by selecting additional text.

e. Click the **Cross-reference check box** in the *Options* section. Type **Stock Market** in the Cross-reference text box, then click **Mark**.

f. Click in the document, scroll down to the next paragraph, select the text *Dupont*, then click in the Mark Index Entry dialog box and notice Main entry automatically changes to Dupont. Click **Mark** to create the index entry, then close the Mark Index Entry dialog box.

g. Save the document.

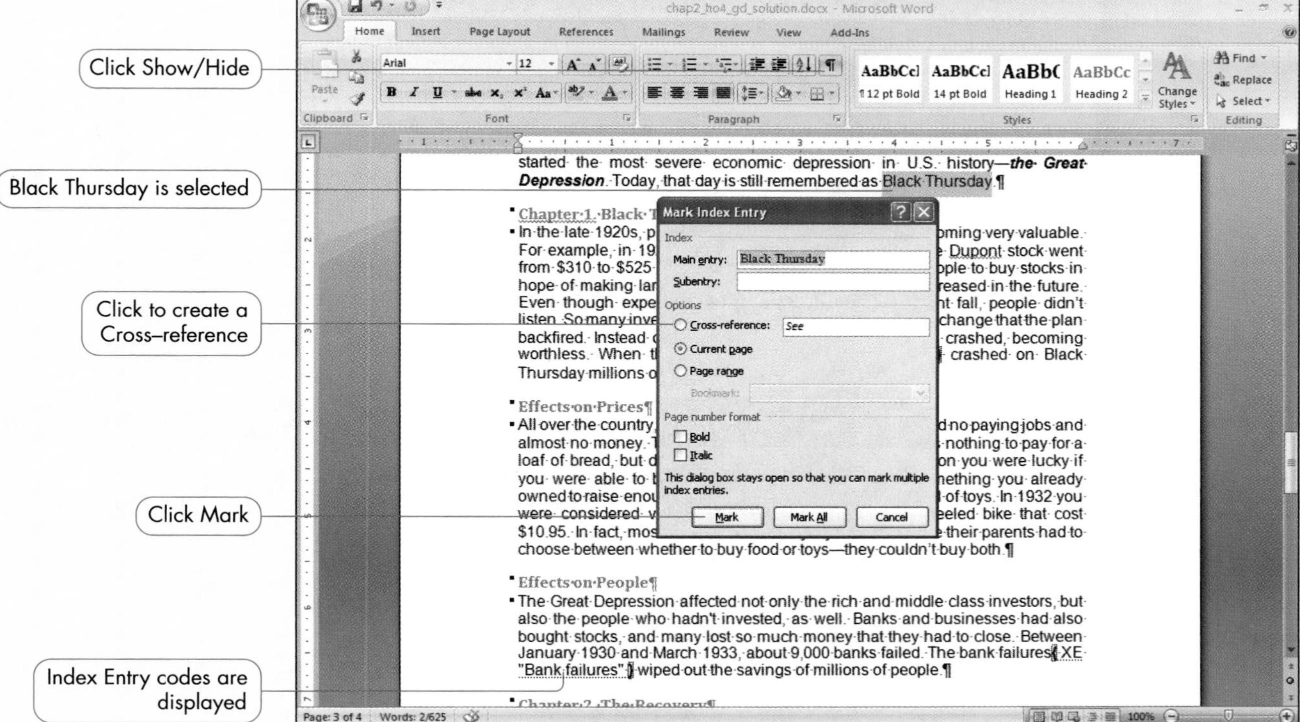

Figure 2.38 Create an Index Entry

Step 4
Create the Index

Refer to Figure 2.39 as you complete Step 4.

a. Press **Ctrl+End** to move to the end of the document, then press **Enter** to begin a new line.

This spot is where you will insert the index.

b. Click the **References tab**, and then click **Insert Index** in the Index group.

The Index dialog box displays, as shown in Figure 2.39.

c. Click the **Formats drop-down arrow** and select **Classic**. If necessary, click the **Columns spin box arrows** until **2** displays. Click **OK** to create the index.

TROUBLESHOOTING: Click Undo on the Quick Access Toolbar if you are not satisfied with the appearance of the index or if it does not display at the end of the document, then repeat the process.

d. Save the document.

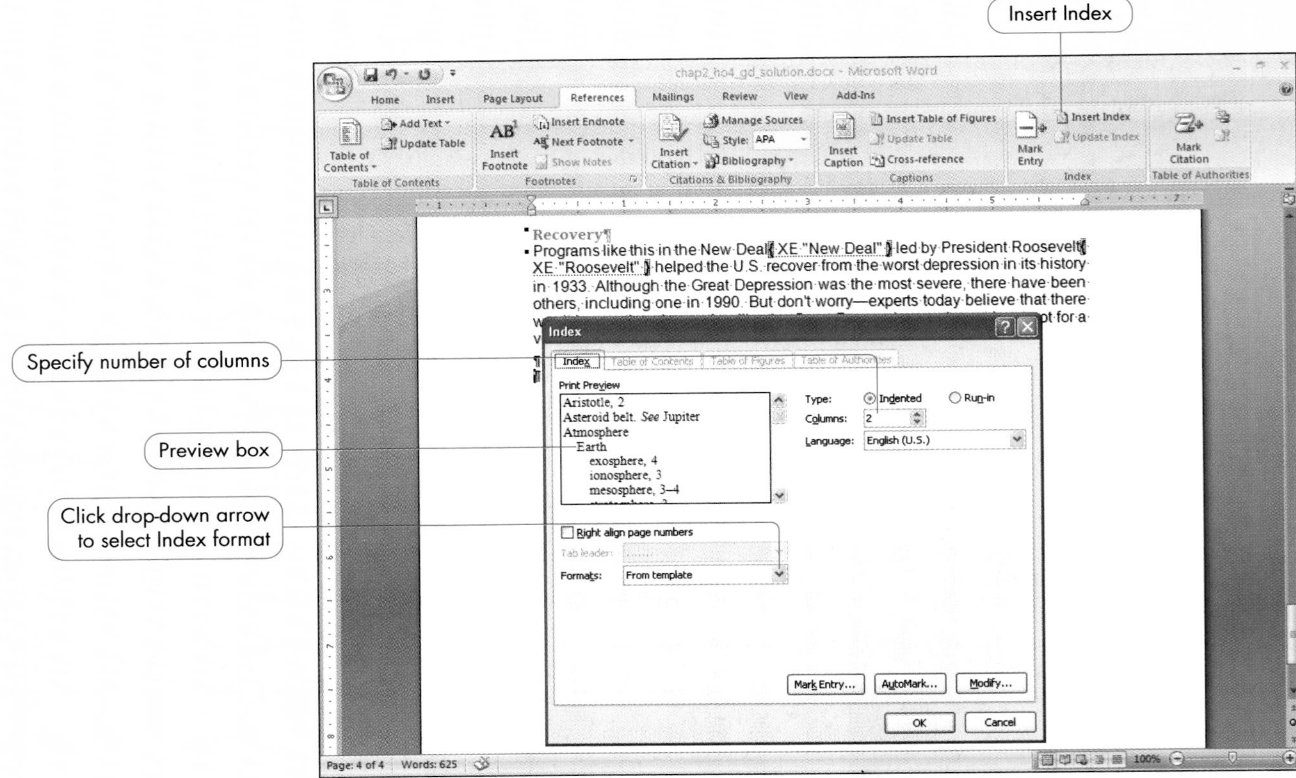

Figure 2.39 Create the Index

TIP AutoMark Index Entries

The AutoMark command will, as the name implies, automatically mark all occurrences of all entries for inclusion in an index. To use the feature, you have to create a separate document that lists the terms you want to reference, then you execute the AutoMark command from the Index dialog box. The advantage is that it is fast. The disadvantage is that every occurrence of an entry is marked in the index so that a commonly used term may have too many page references. You can, however, delete superfluous entries by manually deleting the field codes. Click **Show/Hide ¶** in the Paragraph group of the Home tab if you do not see the entries in the document.

Step 5
Complete the Index

Refer to Figure 2.40 as you complete Step 5.

a. At the beginning of the index click to position the insertion point on the left of the letter "B".

b. Click the **Page Layout tab**, then click **Breaks** and select **Next Page**.

The index moves to the top of a new page.

c. Click the **Insert tab**, click **Page Number** in the Header & Footer group, and then select **Format Page Numbers** to display the Page Number Format dialog box. Click **Continue from previous section**, if necessary, then click **OK**.

d. Click **Header** in the Header & Footer group, and then click **Edit Header** to display the Design tab as shown in Figure 2.40. Click **Link to Previous**.

When you toggle the Link to Previous indicator off, you create a new header for this section that is independent of and different from the header in the previous section. Notice other Header and Footer options that display in the tab.

e. Type **INDEX** in the header. Select *INDEX* then on the Mini toolbar click **Center**. Click **Close Header and Footer** in the Close group to return to the document. Click **Show/Hide ¶** in the Paragraph group on the Home tab to turn off display of field codes.

f. Save the document.

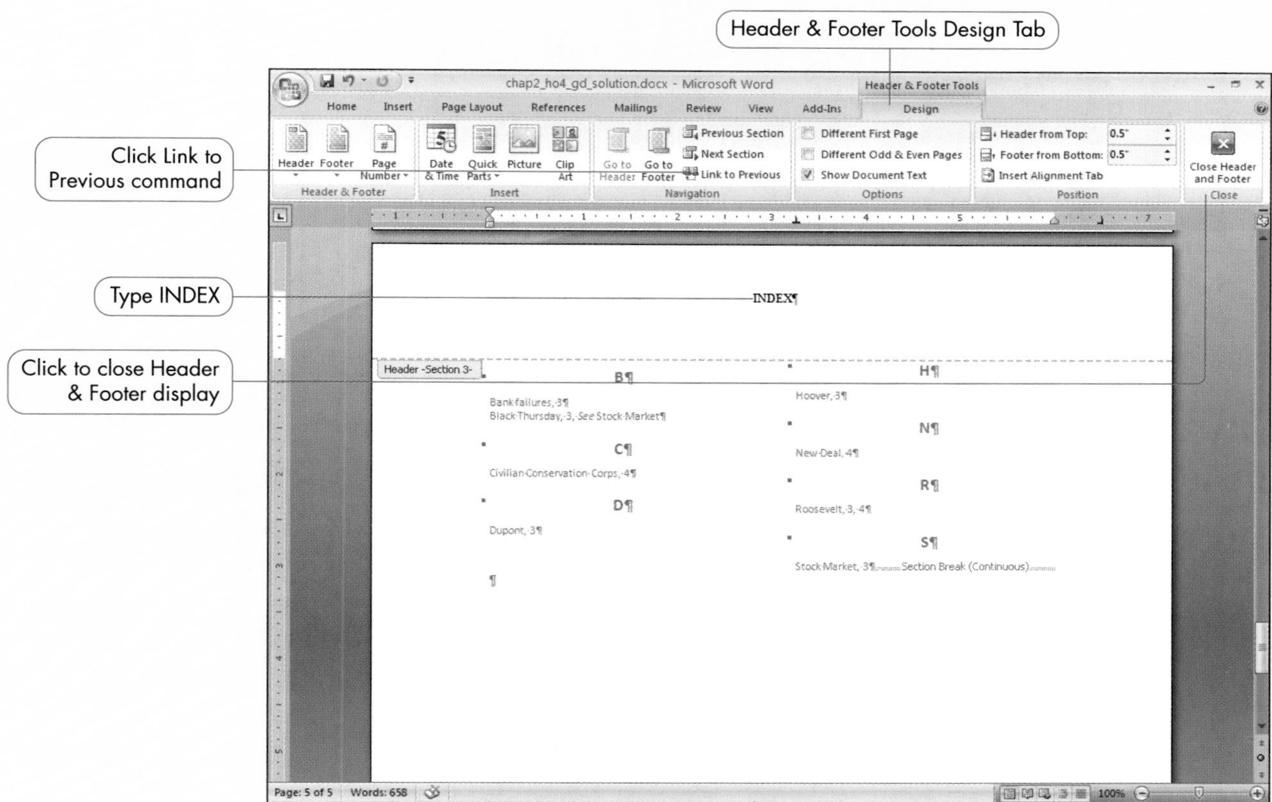

Figure 2.40 Complete the Index

TIP Check the Index Entries

Every entry in the index should begin with an uppercase letter. If this is not the case, it is because the origin entry within the body of the document was marked improperly. Click **Show/Hide ¶** in the Paragraph group on the Home tab to display the indexed entries within the document, which appear within brackets; e.g., {XE "Practice Files"}. Change each entry to begin with an uppercase letter as necessary.

Step 6

View the Completed Document

Refer to Figure 2.41 as you complete Step 6.

a. Click **Zoom** on the status bar. Click **Many pages** and drag to display 2 x 3. Click **OK**.

The completed document is shown in Figure 2.41. The index appears by itself on the last page of the document.

b. Save and close the *chap2_ho4_gd_solution* document.

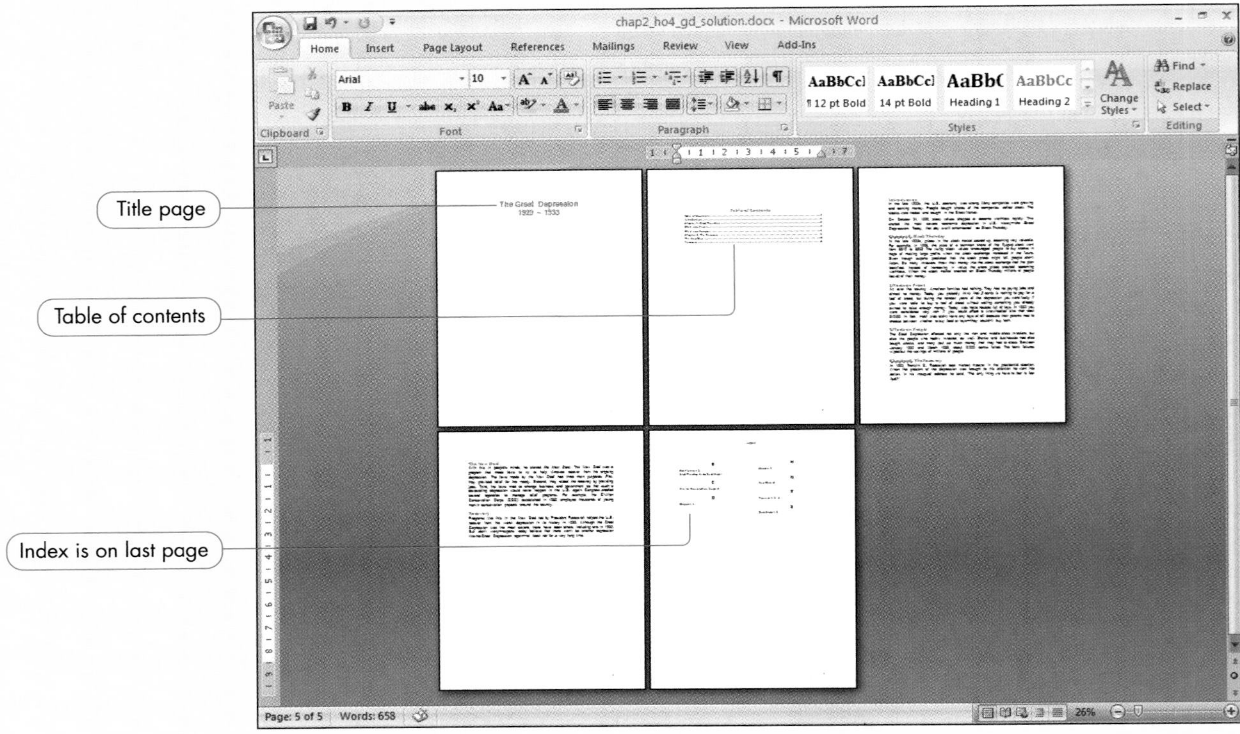

Figure 2.41 The Completed Document

Summary

1. **Apply font attributes through the Font dialog box.** Formatting occurs at the character, paragraph, or section level. The Font dialog box allows you to change spacing of the characters and also provides special formatting options for text that only appears on the screen. Through this dialog box, you can change the font and character spacing attributes including font, font size, font color, underline color, and effects. Use the character spacing options to control horizontal spacing between letters. You also can adjust the scale, position, and kerning of characters.
2. **Highlight text.** The Text Highlight Color command provides the ability to color text on screen so it stands out or resembles highlighting marks you often make in books. The Text Highlight Color command is located on the Home tab and also on the Mini toolbar that appears when you select text.
3. **Control word-wrapping with nonbreaking hyphens and nonbreaking spaces.** Occasionally, text wraps in an undesirable location in your document, or you just want to keep words together for better readability. To keep hyphenated words together on one line, use a nonbreaking hyphen to replace the regular hyphen. You insert a nonbreaking hyphen by pressing Ctrl+Shift+Hyphen in place of a hypen. You also can keep words together on one line by inserting a nonbreaking space instead of using the spacebar. To insert a nonbreaking space, click Ctrl+Shift+Spacebar.
4. **Copy formats with the Format Painter.** Use the Format Painter to copy existing format features to other text for consistency in appearance. The Format Painter uses fewer clicks than formatting from scratch. You can use it one time by single-clicking Format Painter in the Clipboard group on the Home tab, then selecting the text to format. If you double-click Format Painter, it toggles on and you can select many items to format the text. To toggle off the Format Painter, press Esc or click Format Painter again.
5. **Set off paragraphs with tabs, borders, lists, and columns.** You can change the appearance and add interest to documents by using paragraph formatting options. Tabs allow you to set markers in the document to use for aligning text. Borders and shading are set at the character or paragraph level and enable you to use boxes and/or shading to highlight an area of your document. A bulleted or numbered list helps to organize information by emphasizing and/or ordering important topics. Columns add interest to a document by formatting text into side-by-side vertical blocks of text and are implemented at the section level.
6. **Apply paragraph formats.** You can use additional formatting options in the Paragraph dialog box. Paragraph alignment refers to the placement of text between the left and right margins; text can be aligned left, right, centered between, or justified, which allows it to touch both margins. Another option that incorporates the distance from margins is indention. You can specify indention from the left margin, right margin, or both, or use special indents such as hanging or first-line. Line spacing determines the space between lines in a document and can be customized as single, double, or 1.5, for example. You also can specify an amount of space to insert before or after a paragraph, which is more efficient than pressing Enter. Widow/Orphan control prevents a single line from displaying at the top or bottom of a page, separate from the rest of a paragraph.
7. **Create and modify styles.** A style is a set of formatting instructions that has been saved under a distinct name. Styles are created at the character or paragraph level and provide a consistent appearance to similar elements throughout a document. You can modify any existing style to change the formatting of all text defined by that style. You can even create a new style for use in the current or any other document. Styles provide the foundation to use other tools such as outlines and the table of contents. The Outline view displays a condensed view of a document based on styles within the document. Text may be collapsed or expanded as necessary to facilitate moving text within long documents. The Outline view does not display a conventional outline, which is created in Print Layout view using the Multilevel List command on the Home tab.
8. **Create a table of contents.** A table of contents lists headings in the order they appear in a document with their respective page numbers. Word can create it automatically, provided the built-in heading styles were applied previously to the items for inclusion.
9. **Create an index.** Word also will create an index automatically, provided that the entries for the index have been marked previously. This result, in turn, requires you to go through a document, select the appropriate text, and mark the entries accordingly.

Key Terms

AutoFormat 163
Bar tab 143
Border 145
Bulleted list 146
Center tab 143
Change Case 134
Character spacing 135
Character style 159
Columns 147
Decimal tab 143
First line indent 149
Font 133
Format Painter 139
Hanging indent 149
Hidden text 135
Highlighter 136
Horizontal alignment 148
Index 171
Kerning 136
Leader character 144
Left tab 143
Line spacing 150
Monospaced typeface 133
Multilevel list 146
Nonbreaking hyphen 138
Nonbreaking space 138
Numbered list 146
Orphan 151
Outline view 162
Paragraph spacing 150
Paragraph style 159
Position 136
Proportional typeface 133
Right tab 143
Sans serif typeface 133
Scale 135
Serif typeface 133
Shading 145
Style 159
Tabs 143
Table of contents 171
Type style 133
Typeface 133
Typography 133
Widow 151

Multiple Choice

1. Which of the following can be stored within a paragraph style?
   (a) Tabs and indents
   (b) Line spacing and alignment
   (c) Shading and borders
   (d) All of the above

2. What is the easiest way to change the alignment of five paragraphs scattered throughout a document, each of which is formatted with the same style?
   (a) Select the paragraphs individually, then click the appropriate alignment button.
   (b) Select the paragraphs at the same time, then click the appropriate alignment button on the Home tab.
   (c) Change the format of the existing style, which changes the paragraphs.
   (d) Retype the paragraphs according to the new specifications.

3. Which feature analyzes a document and formats it for you?
   (a) Character styles
   (b) AutoFormat
   (c) Multilevel list
   (d) Table of contents

4. Which of the following is used to create a conventional outline?
   (a) A Numbered list
   (b) The Outline view
   (c) A table of contents
   (d) An index

5. A(n) ____________ occurs when the first line of a paragraph is isolated at the bottom of a page and the rest of the paragraph continues on the next page.
   (a) widow
   (b) section break
   (c) footer
   (d) orphan

6. What is the keyboard shortcut to mark an index entry?
   (a) Index entries cannot be marked manually.
   (b) Press Ctrl+Enter
   (c) Ctrl+I
   (d) Alt+Shift+X

7. Which of the following is true regarding the formatting within a document?
   (a) Line spacing and alignment are implemented at the section level.
   (b) Margins, headers, and footers are implemented at the paragraph level.
   (c) Nonbreaking hyphens are implemented at the paragraph level.
   (d) Columns are implemented at the section level.

8. Which tab contains the Table of Contents and Index features?
   (a) Home
   (b) Insert
   (c) View
   (d) References

9. After you create and insert a table of contents into a document,
   (a) any subsequent page changes arising from the insertion or deletion of text to existing paragraphs must be entered manually.
   (b) any additions to the entries in the table arising due to the insertion of new paragraphs defined by a heading style must be entered manually.
   (c) an index can not be added to the document.
   (d) you can right-click, then select Update Field to update the table of contents.

10. Which of the following is a false statement about the Outline view?
    (a) It can be collapsed to display only headings.
    (b) It can be expanded to show the entire document.
    (c) It requires the application of styles.
    (d) It is used to create a conventional outline.

11. What is the best way to create a conventional outline in a Word document?
    (a) Use the Outline view.
    (b) Use the Mulitlevel List command in the Paragraph group in Print Layout view.
    (c) Use the Outlining toolbar.
    (d) All of the above are equally acceptable.

Multiple Choice Continued...

12. Which of the following is not a predefined Word style that is available in every document?
    (a) Normal
    (b) Heading 1
    (c) Body Text
    (d) Special 1

13. What happens if you modify the Body Text style in a Word document?
    (a) Only the paragraph where the insertion point is located is changed.
    (b) All paragraphs in the document will be changed.
    (c) Only those paragraphs formatted with the Body Text style will be changed.
    (d) It is not possible to change a Word default style such as Body Text.

14. Which of the following are not set at the paragraph level?
    (a) Alignment
    (b) Tabs and indents
    (c) Line spacing
    (d) Columns

15. Which of the following is a true statement regarding indents?
    (a) Indents are measured from the edge of the page.
    (b) The left, right, and first line indents must be set to the same value.
    (c) The insertion point can be anywhere in the paragraph when indents are set.
    (d) Indents must be set within the Paragraph dialog box.

16. The default tab stops are set to:
    (a) Left indents every ½".
    (b) Left indents every ¼".
    (c) Right indents every ½".
    (d) Right indents every ¼".

17. The spacing in an existing multipage document is changed from single spacing to double spacing throughout the document. What can you say about the number of hard and soft page breaks before and after the formatting change?
    (a) The number of soft page breaks is the same, but the number and/or position of the hard page breaks is different.
    (b) The number of hard page breaks is the same, but the number and/or position of the soft page breaks is different.
    (c) The number and position of both hard and soft page breaks is the same.
    (d) The number and position of both hard and soft page breaks is different.

18. Which of the following is not a valid use of the Format Painter?
    (a) View formatting codes assigned to a paragraph.
    (b) Copy the font style of a paragraph heading to other paragraph headings.
    (c) Restore character style to a paragraph (whose style was deleted accidentally) using the style from a properly formatted paragraph.
    (d) Copy the format of a paragraph that includes a hanging indent to a paragraph formatted in the Normal style.

19. If you want to be sure the phone number 555-1234 does not word-wrap what should you do?
    (a) Use a nonbreaking hyphen in place of the hyphen.
    (b) Use expanded spacing on the whole number.
    (c) Use a nonbreaking space in place of the hyphen.
    (d) Press Ctrl+Enter before you type the phone number.

Practice Exercises

1 The Purchase of a PC

You can purchase a PC from any number of vendors, each of which offers multiple models and typically enables you to upgrade individual components. You want to remember a few important tips as you shop for your next system. We have provided a few of those tips for you, but the document is difficult to read in its current state. Follow instructions to change the formatting of this document and improve readability. Refer to Figure 2.42 as you complete this exercise.

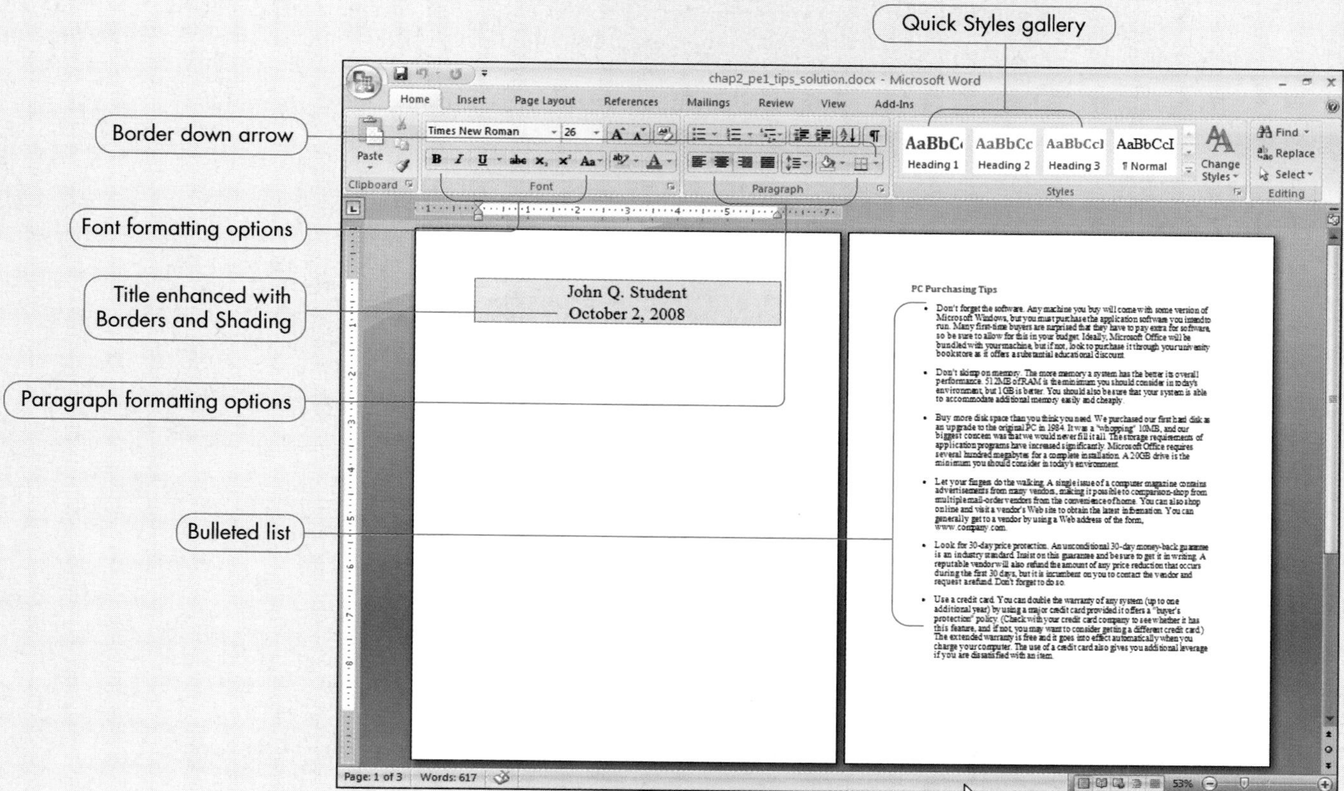

Figure 2.42 PC Purchasing Tips

a. Open the *chap2_pe1_tips* document in the Exploring Word folder and save the document as **chap2_pe1_tips_solution**.

b. Press **Ctrl+Home** to go to the beginning of the document, and then press **Ctrl+Enter** to insert a page break. Press **Ctrl+Home** to move to the beginning of the document and type your name. Press **Enter**, then type today's date. This is your title page.

c. Click the **Home tab**, select your name and date, and then click the **Borders arrow** in the Paragraph group on the Home tab. Select **Borders and Shading** to open the dialog box.

d. In the Borders tab, select **Box** in the *Setting* section. Click the **Color drop-down arrow** and select **Accent 4**, which is purple. Click the **Width drop-down arrow** and select 2¼.

e. Click the **Shading tab**. Click the **Fill drop-down arrow**, then select **Purple, Accent 4** (a shade of purple). Click **OK** to close the Borders and Shading dialog box.

f. Select your name again, if necessary, click the **Font size arrow** in the Font group on the Home tab, and select **26**. Click **Center** in the Paragraph group on the Home tab. Click the **Styles Dialog Box Launcher** to display the Styles Pane, then scroll to find the format applied to your name. Move your mouse over the style, then click the down arrow and select **Modify** to display the Modify Style dialog box. Type **PCTitle** in the Name box, then click **OK**.

g. Select the date, then click **PCTitle** in the Styles pane to apply the style to the second line of your title page. Close the Styles pane.

...continued on Next Page

h. The second page of the document contains various tips that we provide, but it is up to you to complete the formatting. Select the title *PC Purchasing Tips* at the top of this page. Click **Heading 1** in the Quick Styles gallery on the Home tab to format this title.

i. To create a bulleted list for the tips on this page, select all remaining text that has not been formatted, then click the **Bullets arrow** in the Paragraph group on the Home tab. Select a round black circle from the bullet Style gallery.

j. The bullets help differentiate each point, but they are still spaced pretty close together. To make the document easier to read, click the **Paragraph Dialog Box Launcher**, and then click the **After spin box up arrow** until **12 pt** displays. Click the **Don't add space between paragraphs of the same style** check box.

k. One paragraph splits between two pages. To eliminate that split, click the **Line and Page Breaks tab** in the Paragraph dialog box, and then click the **Keep lines together check box**. Click **OK**.

l. Compare your document to Figure 2.42. Save and close the document.

2 Creating a List of Job Descriptions

You work for a major book publisher, and your supervisor asked you to prepare a document that lists key personnel and their job descriptions. This information sheet will be sent to each author on the Microsoft Office 2007 team, so they will know who is responsible for different aspects of the publication process. Refer to Figure 2.43 as you complete this exercise.

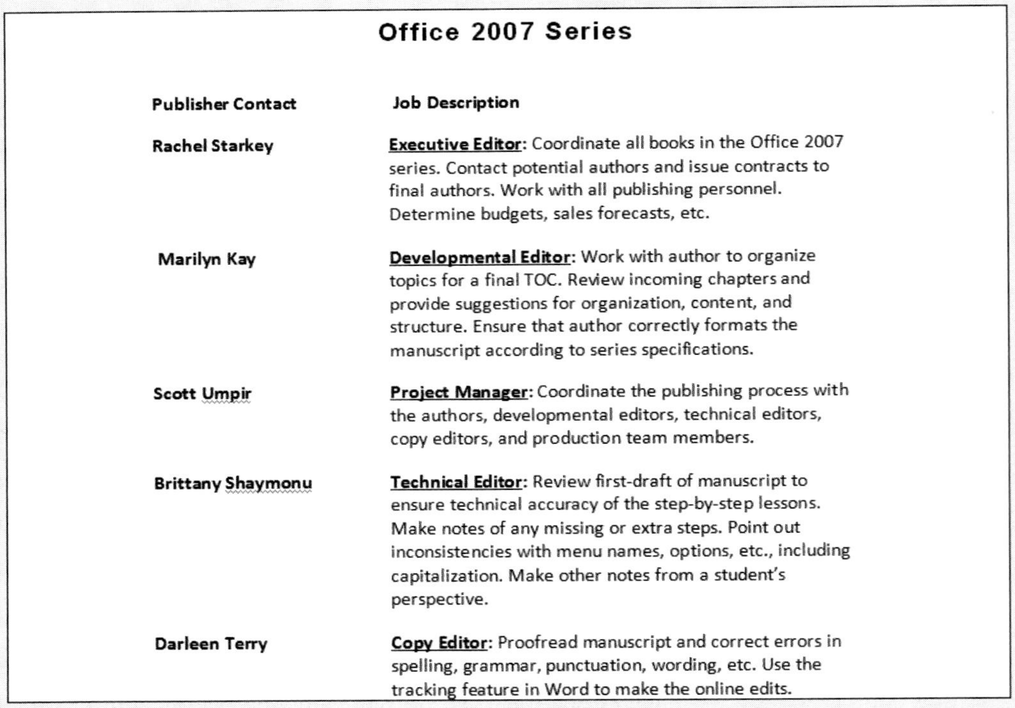

Office 2007 Series

Publisher Contact	Job Description
Rachel Starkey	Executive Editor: Coordinate all books in the Office 2007 series. Contact potential authors and issue contracts to final authors. Work with all publishing personnel. Determine budgets, sales forecasts, etc.
Marilyn Kay	Developmental Editor: Work with author to organize topics for a final TOC. Review incoming chapters and provide suggestions for organization, content, and structure. Ensure that author correctly formats the manuscript according to series specifications.
Scott Umpir	Project Manager: Coordinate the publishing process with the authors, developmental editors, technical editors, copy editors, and production team members.
Brittany Shaymonu	Technical Editor: Review first-draft of manuscript to ensure technical accuracy of the step-by-step lessons. Make notes of any missing or extra steps. Point out inconsistencies with menu names, options, etc., including capitalization. Make other notes from a student's perspective.
Darleen Terry	Copy Editor: Proofread manuscript and correct errors in spelling, grammar, punctuation, wording, etc. Use the tracking feature in Word to make the online edits.

Figure 2.43 Publisher Job Descriptions

a. Click the **Office Button**, click **New**, and then double-click **Blank document** to open a new document. Save as **chap2_pe2_personnel_solution**.

b. Click the **Page Layout tab**, click **Margins** in the Page Setup group, and then click **Custom Margins** to display the Page Setup dialog box. Click the **Top margin spin box up arrow** until **2** displays, and then click **OK**.

...continued on Next Page

c. Type the title shown in Figure 2.43. Press **Enter** three times to triple-space after the title. Select the title, and then on the Mini Toolbar click **Center**, click the **Font arrow** and select **Arial,** click the **Font Size arrow** and select **16**, and click **Bold**.
d. Click the **Font Dialog Box Launcher** on the Home tab and select the **Character Spacing tab**. Click the **Spacing drop-down arrow** and select **Expanded**. Click **OK**. Click on one of the blank lines below the title to deselect it.
e. Click the **View tab** and click the **Ruler check box**, if necessary. The ruler should display at the top of your page.
f. Click on the **2"** mark on the ruler to insert a Left tab. The Left tab mark displays on the ruler.
g. Click the **Home tab**. Click the **Paragraph Dialog Box Launcher**. Click the **Special drop-down arrow** in the *Indention* section and select **Hanging**. Click in the **After text box** in the Spacing section and type **12**. Click **OK**.
h. Type the column heading **Publisher Contact**. Press **Tab** and type the column heading **Job Description**. Press **Enter** to begin on the next line. Select the column headings and on the Mini toolbar, click **Bold**. Finish typing the rest of the columnar text, as shown in Figure 2.43; notice the 12-point After paragraph spacing creates the equivalent of one blank line between rows.
i. Select the first job description, *Executive Editor*, and click **Underline** in the Font group on the Home tab. Double-click **Format Painter** in the Clipboard group on the Home tab, then select the remaining job descriptions to apply the Underline format to each job. After you format the last job description, press **Esc** to turn off the Format Painter.
j. Select the name of each person and apply bold formatting. Save and close the *chap2_pe2_personnel_solution* document.

3 Creating and Updating a Table of Contents and an Index

You have received an ISO 9000 document that lists standards for quality management and assurance and is used by international manufacturing and service organizations. You need to distribute the standards to your employees. It is a multipage document that does not contain a table of contents or index for easy reference. You decide to add each before making copies. After creating the table of contents, you decide only two levels of headings are necessary, so you update it to reflect your changes. After adding the index, you decide to make it more detailed, so you edit and update it as well. Refer to Figure 2.44 as you complete this exercise.

a. Open the *chap2_pe3_iso* document and save it as **chap2_pe3_iso_solution**.
b. Place the insertion point at the end of *ISO 9000* at the top of the first page and press **Ctrl+Enter** to create a hard page break. The page break creates a page for the table of contents.
c. Click the **References tab**, click **Table of Contents** in the Table of Contents group, and then select **Contents Table** from the gallery. Select **Update Entire Table** if the Update Table of Contents dialog box appears.
d. Click to place the insertion point on the left of the heading *I. Introduction* and press **Ctrl+Enter** to create a hard page break.
e. Click one time anywhere in the table of contents to select it, click **Table of Contents** on the References tab, and then click **Insert Table of Contents Field**. Click the **Show Levels spin box down arrow** until **2** displays. Click **OK**, and then click **OK** again at the prompt asking to replace the selected table of contents.
f. Before you insert the index, you must mark several words as entries. Locate, then select the word *quality* in the *Quality Policy* paragraph, and then press **Alt+Shift+X** to display the Mark Index Entry dialog box. Click **Mark** to create the index entry.
g. Locate and select the following words, and then click **Mark** for each one, just as you did in the previous step:

authority	In heading *Responsibility and authority*
procedures	In heading *Quality System Procedures*
supplier	First sentence under heading *Quality System Procedures*
testing	In heading *Inspection and Testing*

...continued on Next Page

h. Press **Ctrl+End** to go to the end of the document. Press **Ctrl+Enter** to insert a new page where you will display the index. Click **Insert Index** from the Index group on the References tab, and then click **OK** to create the Index.

i. You decide your index is incomplete and should include more words. Locate and select the words below. Remember to press **Alt+Shift+X** to display the Mark Index Entry dialog box and click **Mark** to create the index entry.

data control	In heading *Document and Data Control*
training	In heading *Training*
records	In heading *Control of Quality Records*

j. Close the Mark Index Entry dialog box. Position the insertion point anywhere in the index and click **Update index** in the Index group on the References tab. Your additional entries will display in the updated index.

k. Select all entries, then click **Change Case** in the Font group on the Home tab. Select **lowercase** to change the case of all entries.

l. Position the insertion point left of the section break that precedes the first index entry heading and press **Enter** two times. Move the insertion point up to the first empty line and type **INDEX**, and then select it and click **Heading 1** in the Quick Styles gallery on the Home tab.

m. Save the document and compare your results to Figure 2.44.

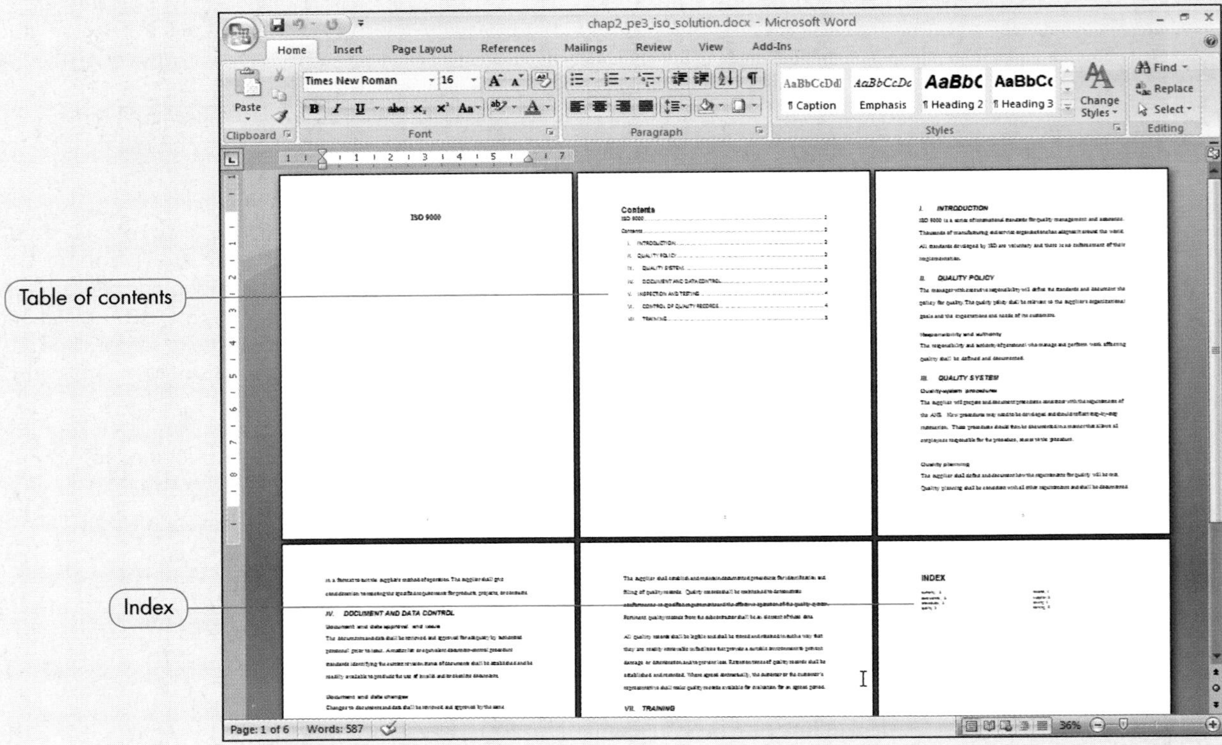

Figure 2.44 Report Including Table of Contents and Index

4 Editing a Memo to the HR Director

Tracey Spears is the training coordinator for a local company, and her responsibilities include tracking employees' continuing education efforts. The company urges employees to pursue educational opportunities that add experience and knowledge to their positions, including taking any certification exams that enhance their credentials. The human resources director has asked Ms. Spears to provide him with a list of employees who have met minimum qualifications to take an upcoming certification exam. In its present state, the memo prints on two pages; you will

...continued on Next Page

format the memo using columns in order to save paper and display the entire list on one page. Refer to Figure 2.45 as you complete this exercise.

a. Open the *chap2_pe4_training* document and save it as **chap2_pe4_training_solution**.
b. Select the word *MEMO*, click **Heading 1** in the Quick Styles gallery on the Home tab, and then click **Center** in the Paragraph group on the Home tab.
c. Several employees have a work conflict and will be unable to sit for the certification exam in October. To specify the people who fall into that category scroll over *Alana Bell* to select her name, and then on the Mini toolbar click **Text Highlight Color** or click **Text Highlight Color** in the Font group on the Home tab. Repeat this process for *Amy Kay Lynn*, *Piau Shing*, and *Ryan Stubbs*.
d. Employees can opt out of the exam for personal reasons, and we need to specify those as well. Hold down **Ctrl** and select the following employees: *Simon Anderson*, *Randall Larsen*, and *Winnifred Roark*. Click the **Font Dialog Box Launcher**, and then click the **Strikethrough check box** in the *Effects* section on the Font tab; click **OK** to return to the memo.
e. Now you list the employees in two columns so you can print the memo on one sheet of paper instead of two. Drag your mouse over the list of employees to select all names. Click the **Page Layout tab**, click **Columns**, and then select **Two**. The names now display in two columns, and the entire memo fits on one page, as shown in Figure 2.45.
f. Save your work and close the document.

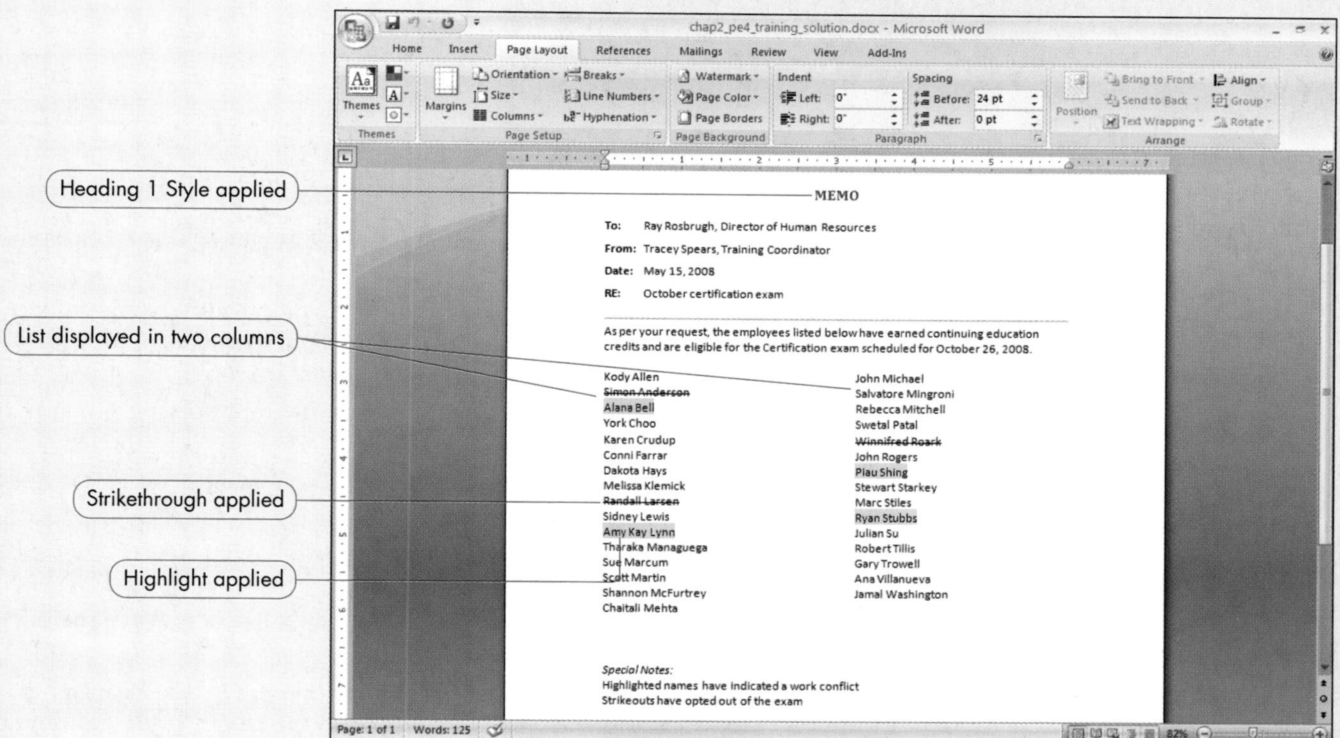

Figure 2.45 The Formatted Memo

Mid-Level Exercises

1 Creating and Applying Styles

You created a status report to inform committee members about an upcoming conference of which you are in charge. You want it to look attractive and professional, and you decide to create and apply your own styles rather than use those already available in Word. You create a paragraph style named Side Heading to format the headings, and then you create a character style named Session to format the names of the conference sessions and apply these formats to document text. You then copy these two styles to the Normal template. Eventually, you delete these two styles from the Normal template. Refer to Figure 2.46 as you complete this exercise.

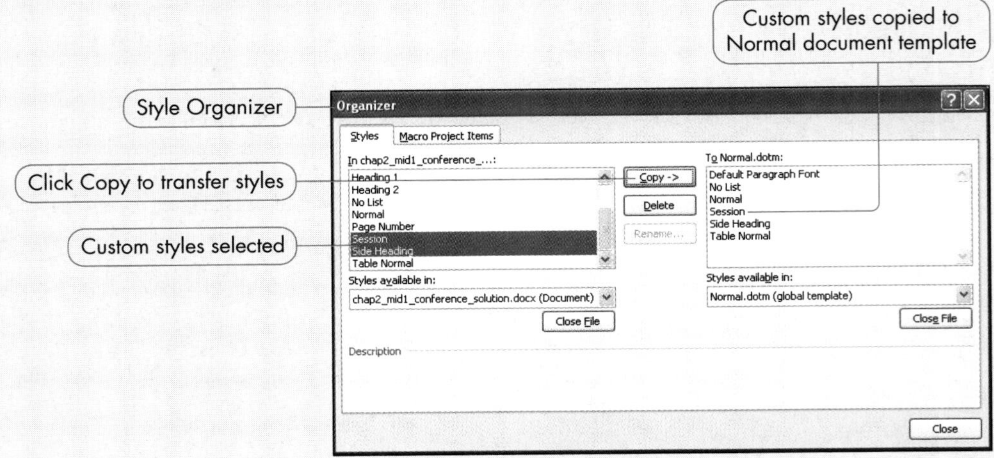

Figure 2.46 Transfer Custom Styles to the Global Template

a. Open the *chap2_mid1_conference* document and save it as **chap2_mid1_conference_solution**.

b. Create a new paragraph style named **Side Heading** using the following properties: Style based on is Normal, Style for following paragraph is Normal. Font properties are Arial, 14-pt, Bold, Red, Accent 2, Darker 50% font color.

c. Set the following paragraph formats: 12-point Before paragraph spacing, 6-point After paragraph spacing.

d. Apply the Side Heading style to the three headings *The Committee, Training Sessions,* and *Training Goal.*

e. Create a new character style named **Session** using the following specifications: Bold and Red, Accent 2, Darker 50% font color.

f. In the bulleted list, apply the Session style to the following: *Word, Web Page Development, Multimedia,* and *Presentations Graphics.*

g. Open the **Manage Styles** dialog box, then click **Import/Export**. In the Organizer dialog box, copy the **Side Heading** and **Session** styles from the **chap2_mid1_conference_solution.docx** list to the **Normal.dotm** list, as shown in Figure 2.46. Close the Organizer dialog box.

h. Save and close *chap2_mid1_conference_solution*.

i. Open a new document. Display the Styles pane, if necessary, then verify that the Session and Side Heading styles are listed. This step proves that you copied the two styles to the Normal template so that they are available for all new documents.

j. Open the **Manage Styles** dialog box, then click the **Import/Export button**. In the Organizer dialog box, delete the two styles from the **In Normal.dotm** list. Click **Yes to All** when prompted. Close the Organizer dialog box.

k. Close the blank document without saving it.

...continued on Next Page

2 Tips for Healthy Living

As a student in the Physician Assistant program at a local university you create a document containing tips for healthier living. The facts have been typed into a Word 2007 document but are thus far unformatted. You will modify it to incorporate styles and add readability as you follow the steps below. Refer to Figure 2.47 as you complete this exercise.

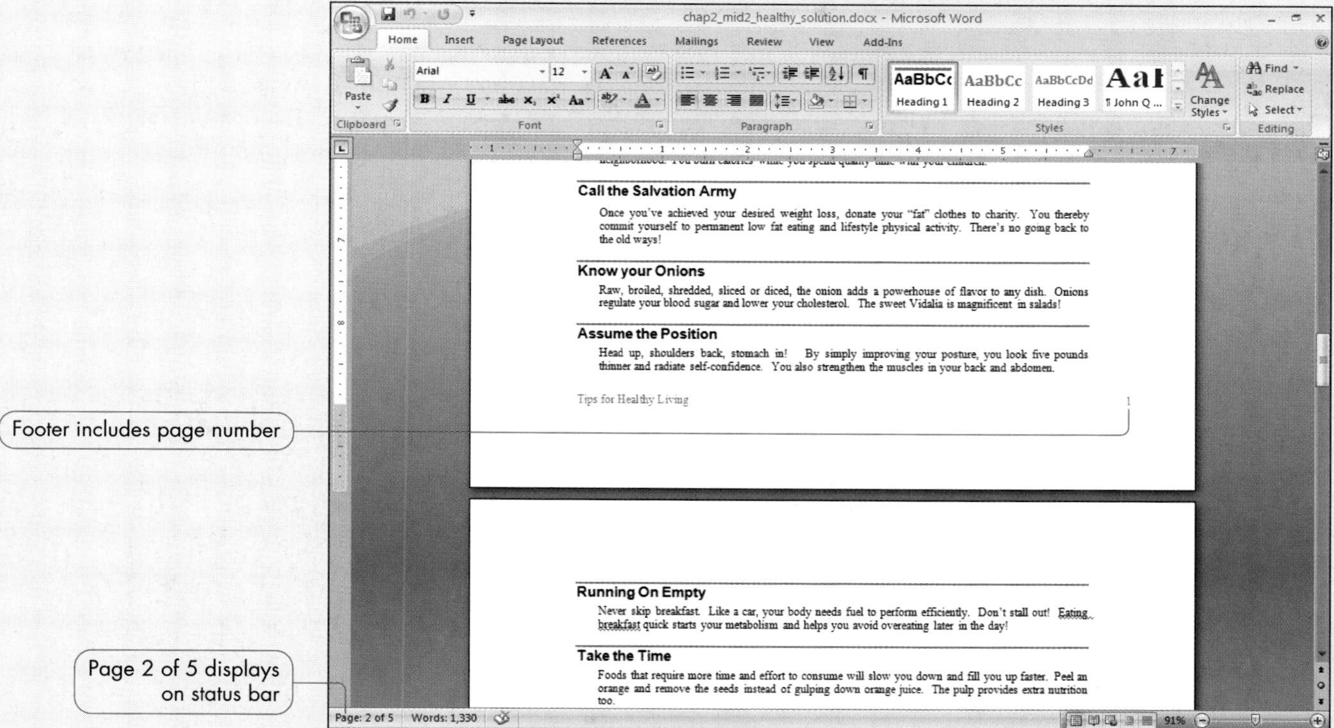

Figure 2.47 Tips for Healthy Living

a. Open the *chap2_mid2_healthy* document and save it as **chap2_mid2_healthy_solution**.

b. Apply the **Heading 1** and **Body Text** styles throughout the document. The Format Painter is a useful tool to copy formats.

c. Change the specifications for the *Body Text* and *Heading 1* styles so that your document matches the document in Figure 2.47. The Heading 1 style is 12-point Arial bold with a blue top border. The Body Text style is 10-point Times New Roman, justified, ¼" left indent, and 12-point spacing After.

d. Create a title page for the document consisting of the title, *Tips for Healthy Living*, and an additional line of text that indicates the document was prepared by you. Format the title page content using a custom style named after yourself. The custom style should contain 28-point Times New Roman font that is bold, centered, and colored in Dark Blue, Text 2 (a blue color).

e. Create a footer for the document consisting of the title, **Tips for Healthy Living,** and a page number. (You can see the footer in Figure 2.47.) The footer should not appear on the title page; that is, page 1 is actually the second page of the document. Look closely at the status bar in Figure 2.47 and you will see that you are on page 1, but that this is the second page of a five-page document.

f. Click Outline View, collapse the text, and view the headings only.

g. Save and close the document.

...continued on Next Page

3 Enhance the Healthy Living Document

Your modifications to the Healthy Living document in the last exercise set it up nicely for the next step in creating a comprehensive document that includes a table of contents and index.

a. Open the *chap2_mid2_healthy_solution* document you created in the last exercise and save it as **chap2_mid3_healthy_solution**. Change the document view to Print Layout so the whole document displays.

b. Create a page specifically for the table of contents, then give the page a title and generate a table of contents using the Healthy Living tip headings. Do not include the custom styles you created for the Title page in the table of contents. You should use a dashed leader to connect the headings to the page numbers in the table.

c. Mark the following text for inclusion in the index: *diet, exercise, metabolism, vegetables, fat*. At the end of your document, create the index and take necessary steps so the index heading displays in the table of contents.

d. Save and close the document.

4 Editing a Welcome Letter

You composed a letter to welcome new members to an organization of which you are president. Now, you need to apply various paragraph formatting, such as alignment, paragraph spacing, and a paragraph border and shading. In addition, you want to create a customized bulleted list that describes plans for the organization. Refer to Figure 2.48 as you complete this exercise.

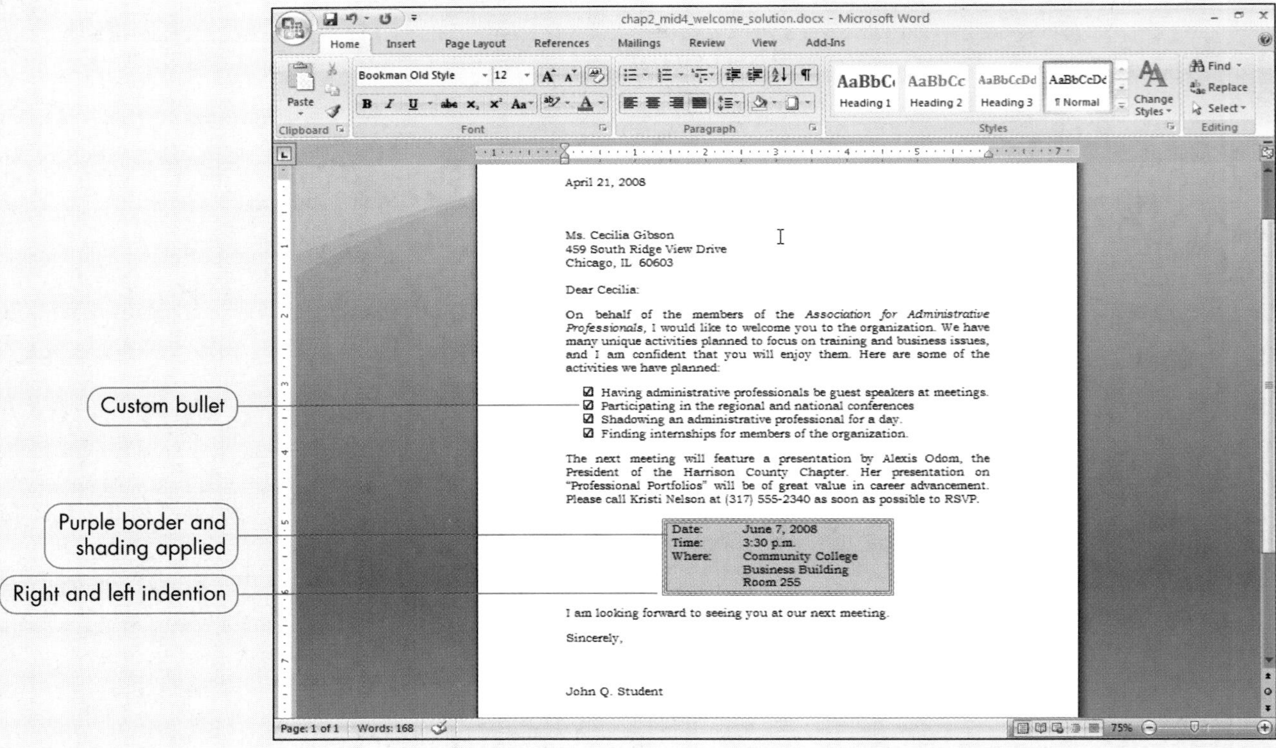

Figure 2.48 Formatted Welcome Letter

...continued on Next Page

a. Open the *chap2_mid4_welcome* document and save it as **chap2_mid4_welcome_solution**. Change Ken's name to your name in the signature block.

b. Apply Justified alignment to the entire document. Delete the asterisk (*) and create a customized bulleted list, selecting a picture bullet of your choice. Type the following items in the bulleted list:

Having administrative professionals be guest speakers at meetings.
Participating in the regional and national conferences.
Shadowing an administrative professional for a day.
Finding internships for members of the organization.

c. Select text from the salutation, *Dear Cecilia*, through the last paragraph that ends with *next meeting*. Set 12-point spacing After paragraph.

d. Select the italicized lines of text and remove the italics. For these lines of text, set 1.5" left and right indents and 0.0-point spacing After paragraph. Apply a triple-line border, Purple, Accent 4 border color, ¾ pt border width, and Purple, Accent 4, Lighter 60% shading color.

e. Click on the line containing the text *Room 255* and set 12-point spacing After paragraph.

f. Select the entire document, and then change the Font to 12-point Bookman Old Style.

g. If needed, delete an extra tab formatting mark to the left of *Community College* to prevent it from word-wrapping. Compare your work to Figure 2.48.

h. Save and close the document.

Capstone Exercise

In this project, you work with a document prepared for managers involved in the hiring process. This report analyzes the validity of the interview process and suggests that selection doesn't depend only on quality information, but on the quality of the interpretation of information. The document requires formatting to enhance readability and important information; you will use skills from this chapter to format multiple levels of headings and figures. To make it easy for readers to locate topics in your document, create and use various supplemental document components such as a table of contents and index.

Adding Style

This document is ready for enhancements, and the styles feature is a good tool that allows you to add them quickly and easily.

a. Open the file *chap2_cap_interview* document and save it as **chap2_cap_interview_solution**.

b. Create a **Title_Page_1** with these formats: 22-point size, Shadow font effect, character spacing expanded by 1 point, horizontally centered, and no Widow/Orphan control. Apply this style to the first line of the title on the title page.

c. Create a paragraph style named **Title_Page_2** based on the first style you created, with these additional formats: 20-point size, custom color 66, 4, 66. Apply this style to the subtitle on the title page.

d. Replace the * at the bottom of the first page with your name. Apply the Heading 3 style to your name and the line that precedes it.

e. Apply the Body Text style to all regular paragraphs.

f. Apply the Heading 2 style to the side headings and the Heading 1 style to the main headings, throughout the document.

Formatting the Paragraphs

Next, you will apply paragraph formatting to the document. These format options will further increase the readability and attractiveness of your document.

a. Select the second paragraph in the *Introduction* section and apply these formats: 0.7" left and right indent, 6-point spacing after the paragraph, boxed 1½-point border with a custom color (31, 73, 125 RGB), and custom shading color (210, 218, 229 RGB).

b. Select the second and third paragraphs in *The Unfavorable Information Effect* section and create a two-column format with a line between the columns.

c. Use Keep Lines Together controls to prevent paragraphs from being separated across pages.

d. Insert nonbreaking spaces and nonbreaking hyphens where appropriate.

e. Apply the arrow bulleted-list format for the five-item list in the *Introduction*.

f. Apply the (1) numbered-list format for the three phases in the *Pre-Interview Impressions* section.

Inserting References

To put the finishing touches on your document, you will add a table of contents and index. These additions enable the reader to quickly locate topics in your document and add a level of professionalism to your work.

a. Create a table of contents based on the styles you applied to paragraph headings; do not include the style you used for the title page.

b. Mark these words as index entries: behavior, favorable, impression, interview, interviewer, perceptions, personal interview, reference, unqualified. Add an index to the end of the document. Use the Classic index format.

c. A page number should display in the footer of the document. Use the **Accent Bar 4** format, but prevent it from displaying on the title page and start numbering on the page that contains the table of contents.

d. Save your changes and close the document.

Mini Cases

Use the rubric following the case as a guide to evaluate your work, but keep in mind that your instructor may impose additional grading criteria or use a different standard to judge your work.

A Fundraising Letter

GENERAL CASE

Each year, you update a letter to several community partners soliciting support for an auction. The auction raises funds for your organization, and your letter should impress your supporters by using several formatting styles and options that give it a very professional look. Open the *chap2_mc1_auction* document and make necessary changes to improve the appearance. Consider the use of columns for auction items, bullets to draw attention to the list of forms, and page borders—and that is just for starters! Your finished document should be saved as **chap2_mc1_auction_solution**.

Performance Elements	Exceeds Expectations	Meets Expectations	Below Expectations
Enhanced document using the following paragraph formatting features: columns, bullets/numbering, borders/shading	Document contains at least three of the paragraph formatting features.	Document contains at least two of the paragraph formatting features.	Document contains one or none of the paragraph formatting features.
Use of character formatting features such as Font, Font Size, Font color, or other attributes from Font dialog box	Used character formatting options throughout entire document.	Used character formatting options in most sections of document.	Used character formatting options on a small portion of document.
Overall appearance of document	Used formatting tools to create a very attractive document that is easy to read.	Some formatting has been applied, but more updates are required for an attractive and readable document.	Minimal formatting has been applied, resulting in a plain and somewhat unattractive document.

The Invitation

RESEARCH CASE

Search the Internet for an upcoming local event at your school or in your community and produce the perfect invitation. You can invite people to a charity ball, a fun run, or to a fraternity party. Your laser printer and abundance of fancy fonts enable you to do anything a professional printer can do. Your finished document should be saved as **chap2_mc2_invitation_solution**.

Performance Elements	Exceeds Expectations	Meets Expectations	Below Expectations
Use of character formatting	Three or more character formats applied to text.	One or two character formats applied to text.	Does not apply character formats to text.
Use of styles	Created custom paragraph or character style.	Used at least two predefined styles.	Used one or no predefined style.
Use of paragraph formatting	Two or more paragraph format options used.	Used one paragraph format option.	Does not use paragraph format options.
Presentation	Invitation is formatted attractively; information is easy to read and understand.	Special formatting has been applied, but information is somewhat cluttered.	Invitation lists basic information with no special formatting for attractiveness.

Tips for Windows XP

DISASTER RECOVERY

Open the *chap2_mc3_wintips* document. The document is formatted, but it contains several errors and problems. For example, the paragraph titles are not all formatted with the same style, so they do not all display in the table of contents. You will notice most of the problems easily and you must fix them before the document can be useful. Your finished document should be saved as **chap2_mc3_wintips_solution**.

Performance Elements	Exceeds Expectations	Meets Expectations	Below Expectations
Paragraph and text formatting	Standardized style used on all paragraph text and headings.	Standardized style used on either text or headings, but not both.	Did not standardize styles on text or headings.
Table of contents	All appropriate paragraph titles are listed in the TOC.	Most paragraph titles are listed; no inappropriate titles are listed.	Some paragraph titles are not listed, and TOC contains some inappropriate titles.
Updated footer	Made all necessary updates to footer.	Made some updates to footer.	Did not update footer.

chapter 3 | **Word**

Enhancing a Document

Tables and Graphics

After you read this chapter, you will be able to:

1. Insert a table **(page 197)**.
2. Format a table **(page 205)**.
3. Sort and apply formulas to table data **(page 207)**.
4. Convert text to a table **(page 210)**.
5. Insert clip art and images into a document **(page 219)**.
6. Format a graphic element **(page 220)**.
7. Insert WordArt into a document **(page 225)**.
8. Insert symbols into a document **(page 226)**.

Hands-On Exercises

Exercises	Skills Covered
1. INSERT A TABLE (page 201) **Open:** Blank document **Save as:** chap3_ho1_vacation_solution.docx	• Create a Table • Insert Rows and Columns • Change Row Height and Column Width • Merge Cells to Create Header Row
2. ADVANCED TABLE FEATURES (page 212) **Open:** chap3_ho1_vacation_solution.docx (from Exercise 1) **Save as:** chap3_ho2_vacation_solution.docx (additional modifications) **Open:** chap3_ho2_expenses.docx (Step 7) **Save as:** chap3_ho2_expenses_solution.docx	• Apply a Table Style • Add Table Borders and Shading • Enter Formulas to Calculate Totals • Add a Row and Enter a Formula • Sort Data in a Table • Align Table and Data • Convert Text to a Table
3. CLIP ART, WORDART, AND SYMBOLS (page 227) **Open:** chap3_ho3_ergonomics.docx **Save as:** chap3_ho3_ergonomics_solution.docx	• Insert a Clip Art Object • Move and Resize the Clip Art Object • Create a WordArt Object • Modify the WordArt Object • Insert a Symbol

CASE STUDY

The Ozarks Science and Engineering Fair

Each spring Luanne Norgren is responsible for coordinating the Science and Engineering Fair at Southwest State University. The premier science event for the Ozarks region, it attracts middle school and high school students from 28 counties. You have been hired to serve as the assistant coordinator for the event and are responsible for communications with school administrators and faculty. You prepared an informational letter that will be sent to each school explaining the event registration procedures and project criteria. At your suggestion, Luanne agreed to let you develop a one-page flyer that can be mailed independently or with the informational letter. The flyer will be an attractive source of information that will encourage participation by faculty and students at the schools.

The event takes place April 4–6, 2008, on the university campus. The students who participate will be entered into either the Junior or Senior division, depending on their grade (7–9 in Junior, 10–12 in Senior). In both divisions students can enter a science project in any of the following categories: Biochemistry, Botany, Chemistry, Computer Science, Earth and Space Sciences, Engineering, Environmental Sciences, Physics, or Zoology.

Your Assignment

- Read the chapter, paying special attention to sections that describe how to insert and format tables and graphics.
- As assistant coordinator in charge of communications, you develop a flyer in Word that can be used as a quick source of information about the event. The flyer must include the date, divisions, and categories listed above, and contact information.
- You consider the use of a table, primarily as a placeholder for other information that you will add. Merge and split cells as necessary to create the effect you want to portray using the flyer. Use table styles to enhance color and readability of data in the table. Use borders and shading where appropriate or to supplement any table style you use.
- Insert clip art or other science-oriented graphics to add emphasis and excitement to the flyer. Use graphic formatting tools as needed to enhance colors, change styles, and compress the graphics.
- Use WordArt to create an exciting heading and in any other place it can be used to enhance the flyer.
- Add a "For more information" section to the flyer and list your contact information, Phone: (555) 111-2222 and e-mail: yourname@swsu.edu.
- Save the document as **chap3_case_science_solution**.

Tables

A ***table*** is a series of columns and rows that organize data.

A ***cell*** is the intersection of a column and row in a table.

A ***table*** is a series of columns and rows that organize data effectively. The columns and rows in a table intersect to form ***cells***. The table feature is one of the most powerful in Word and is an easy way to organize a series of data in a columnar list format such as employee names, inventory lists, and e-mail addresses. The Vacation Planner in Figure 3.1, for example, is actually a 4x9 table (4 columns and 9 rows). The completed table looks impressive, but it is very easy to create once you understand how a table works. In addition to the organizational benefits, tables make an excellent alignment tool. For example, you can create tables to organize data such as employee lists with phone numbers and e-mail addresses. The Exploring series uses tables to provide descriptions for various software commands. Although you can align text with tabs, you have more format control when you create a table. (See the Practice Exercises at the end of the chapter for other examples.)

(The table feature is one of the most powerful in Word and is the basis for an almost limitless variety of documents. It is very easy to create once you understand how a table works.)

Vacation Planner			
Item	Number of Days	Amount per Day (est)	Total Amount
Airline Ticket			449.00
Amusement Park Tickets	4	50.00	200.00
Hotel	5	120.00	600.00
Meals	6	50.00	300.00
Rental Car	5	30.00	150.00
Souvenirs	5	20.00	100.00
TOTAL EXPECTED EXPENSES			**$1799.00**

Figure 3.1 The Vacation Planner

In this section, you insert a table in a document. After inserting the table, you can insert or delete columns and rows if you need to change the structure. Furthermore, you learn how to merge and split cells within the table. Finally, you change the row height and column width to accommodate data in the table.

Inserting a Table

You can create a table from the Insert tab. Click Table in the Tables group on the Insert tab to see a gallery of cells from which you select the number of columns and rows you require in the table, or you can choose the Insert Table command below the gallery to display the Insert Table dialog box and enter the table composition you prefer. When you select the table dimension from the gallery or from the Insert Table dialog box, Word creates a table structure with the number of columns and rows you specify. After you define a table, you can enter text, numbers, or graphics in individual cells. Text wraps as it is entered within a cell so that you can add or delete text without affecting the entries in other cells.

You format the contents of an individual cell the same way you format an ordinary paragraph; that is, you change the font, apply boldface or italic, change the text alignment, or apply any other formatting command. You can select multiple cells and apply the formatting to all selected cells at once, or you can format a cell independently of every other cell.

After you insert a table in your document, use commands in the Table Tools Design and Layout tabs to modify and enhance it. Place the insertion point anywhere in the table, then click either the Design or Layout tab to view the commands. In either tab, just point to a command and a ScreenTip describes its function.

TIP Tabs and Tables

The Tab key functions differently in a table than in a regular document. Press Tab to move to the next cell in the current row or to the first cell in the next row if you are at the end of a row. Press Tab when you are in the last cell of a table to add a new blank row to the bottom of the table. Press Shift+Tab to move to the previous cell in the current row (or to the last cell in the previous row). You must press Ctrl+Tab to insert a regular tab character within a cell.

Insert and Delete Rows and Columns

You can change the structure of a table after it has been created. If you need more rows or columns to accommodate additional data in your table, it is easy to add or insert them using the Rows & Columns group on the Table Tools Layout tab. The Insert and Delete commands enable you to add new or delete existing rows or columns. When you add a column, you can specify if you want to insert it to the right or left of the current column. Likewise, you can specify where to place a new row—either above or below the currently selected row—based on where you need to add the new row.

You can delete complete rows and columns using the commands mentioned above, or you can delete only the data in those rows and columns using the Delete key on your keyboard. Keep in mind that when you insert or delete complete rows or columns those that remain will adjust positioning. For example, if you delete the third row of a 5x5 table, the data in the fourth and fifth rows move up and become the third and fourth rows. If you delete only the data in the third row, the cells would be blank and the fourth and fifth rows would not change at all.

Merge and Split Cells

You can use the Merge Cells command in the Merge group on the Table Tools Layout tab to join individual cells together (merge) to form a larger cell, as was done in the first and last rows of Figure 3.1. People often merge cells to enter a main title at the top of a table. Conversely, you can use the Split Cells command in the Merge group to split a single cell into multiple cells if you find you require more cells to hold data.

Change Row Height and Column Width

Row height is the vertical space from the top to the bottom of a row.

Column width is the horizontal space or length of a column.

When you create a table, Word builds evenly spaced columns. Frequently you need to change the row height or column width to fit your data. ***Row height*** is the vertical distance from the top to the bottom of a row. ***Column width*** is the horizontal space or width of a column. You might increase the column width to display a wide string of text, such as first and last name, to prevent it from wrapping in the cell. You might increase row height to better fit a header that has been enlarged for emphasis.

The table command is easy to master, and as you might have guessed, you will benefit from reviewing the available commands listed in the Design and Layout tabs as shown in the reference pages. You will use many of these commands as you create a table in the hands-on exercises.

Table Tools Layout Ribbon | Reference

Group	Commands	Enables You to
Table	Select ▾ View Gridlines Properties Table	• Select particular parts of a table (entire table, column, row, or cell). • Show or hide the gridlines around the table. • Display the Table Properties dialog box to format the table.
Rows & Columns	Delete ▾ Insert Above Insert Below Insert Left Insert Right Rows & Columns	• Delete cells, columns, rows, or the entire table. • Insert rows and columns. • Display the Insert Cells dialog box.
Merge	Merge Cells Split Cells Split Table Merge	• Merge (join) selected cells together. • Split cells into additional cells. • Split the table into two tables.
Cell Size	0.22" 6.15" AutoFit ▾ Cell Size	• Adjust the row height and column width. • Adjust the column width automatically based on the data in the column. • Display the Table Properties dialog box.
Alignment	Text Direction Cell Margins Alignment	• Specify the combined horizontal and vertical alignment of text within a cell. • Change the text direction. • Set margins within a cell.
Data	Sort Repeat Heading Rows Convert to Text Formula Data	• Sort data within a table. • Repeat heading rows when tables span multiple pages. • Convert tabulated text to table format. • Insert a formula in a table.

Hands-On Exercises

1 | Insert a Table

Skills covered: 1. Create a Table **2.** Insert Rows and Columns **3.** Change Row Height and Column Width **4.** Merge Cells to Create Header Row

Step 1
Create a Table

Refer to Figure 3.2 as you complete Step 1.

a. Start Word and press **Enter** two times in the blank document, then click the **Insert tab**.

The Insert tab contains the Table command.

b. Click **Table** in the Tables group, and then drag your mouse over the cells until you select 3 columns and 7 rows; you will see the table size, 3x7, displayed above the cells, as shown in Figure 3.2. Click the lower-right cell (where the 3rd column and the 7th row intersect) to insert the table into your document.

Word creates an empty table that contains three columns and seven rows. The default columns have identical widths, and the table spans from the left to the right margin.

c. Practice selecting various elements from the table, something that you will have to do in subsequent steps:

- To select a single cell, click inside the left grid line (the pointer changes to a black slanted arrow when you are in the proper position).
- To select a row, click outside the table to the left of the first cell in that row.
- To select a column, click just above the top of the column (the pointer changes to a small black downward pointing arrow).
- To select adjacent cells, drag the mouse over the cells.
- To select the entire table, drag the mouse over the table or click the table selection box that appears at the upper-left corner of the table.

d. Save the document as **chap3_ho1_vacation_solution**.

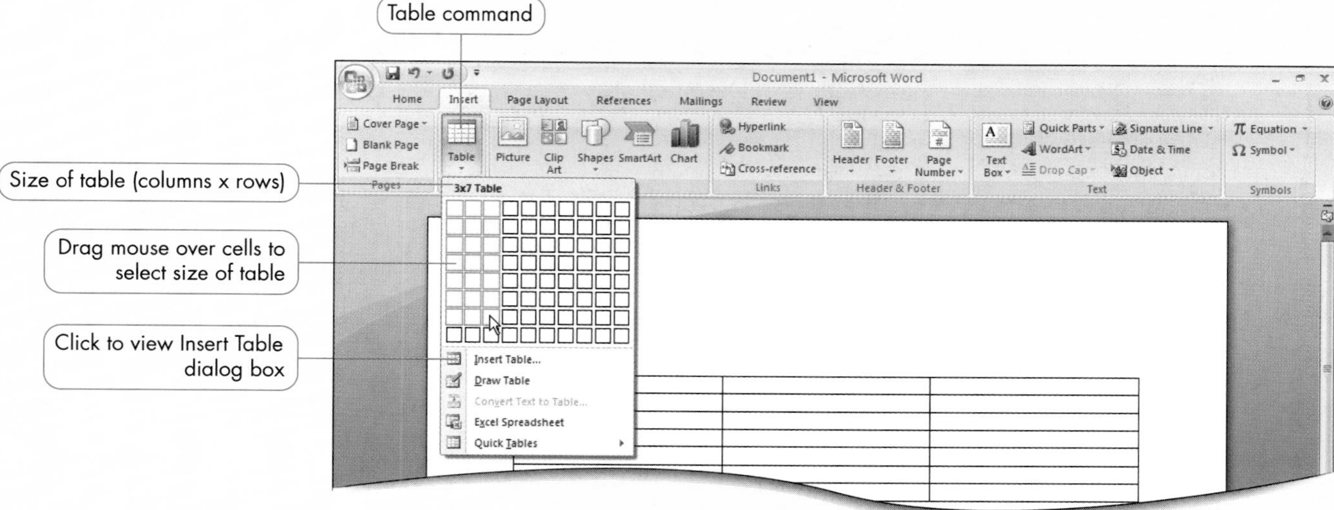

Figure 3.2 Inserting a Table

Step 2
Insert Rows and Columns

Refer to Figure 3.3 as you complete Step 2.

a. Click in the first cell of the first row and type **Vacation Planner**.

b. Click the first cell in the second row and type **Item**. Press **Tab** (or **right arrow**) to move to the next cell. Type **Number of Days**. Press **Tab** to move to the next cell, and then type **Amount per Day (est)**.

Notice you do not have enough columns to add the last heading, *Total Amount*.

c. Click anywhere in the last column of your table, then click the **Layout tab**. Click **Insert Right** in the Rows & Columns group to add a new column to your table. Click in the second row of the new column and type **Total Amount**.

You added a new column on the right side of the table. Notice that the column widths decrease to make room for the new column you just added.

TROUBLESHOOTING: If the column you insert is not in the correct location within the table, click Undo on the Quick Access Toolbar, confirm your insertion point is in the last column, and then click the appropriate Insert command.

d. Select the text *Vacation Planner* in the first row. On the Mini toolbar, click the **Font Size arrow** and click **18**, click **Bold,** and click **Center** to center the heading within the cell.

The table title stands out with the larger font size, bold, and center horizontal alignment.

e. Click outside and left of the second row to select the entire row. On the Mini toolbar, click the **Font Size arrow** and select **16,** and then click **Bold** and **Center**.

f. Enter the remaining data, as shown in Figure 3.3. When you get to the last row and find the table is too small to hold all the data, place the insertion point in the last cell (in the Total Amount column) and press **Tab** to add a row to the end of your table. Then enter the last item and amounts.

g. Save the document.

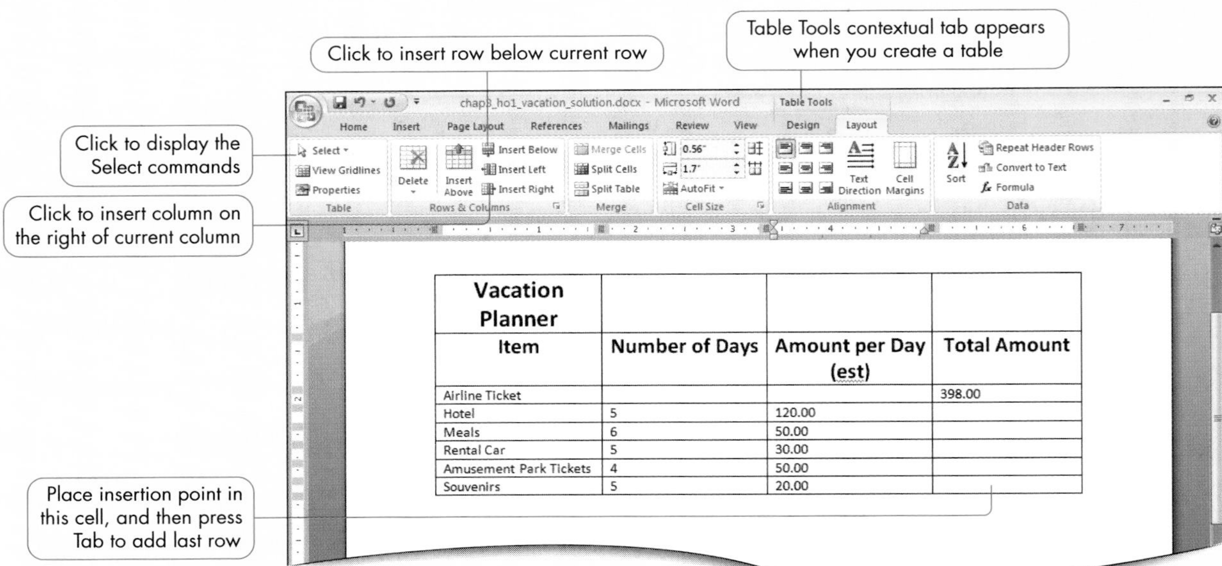

Figure 3.3 Enter the Vacation Planner Data

TIP Other Ways to Select a Table

You can click Select in the Table group on the Layout tab to display commands for selecting a cell, a column, a row, or the entire table. Figure 3.3 shows the location of the Select command.

Step 3

Change Row Height and Column Width

Refer to Figure 3.4 as you complete Step 3.

a. Hold your mouse over the second column of data until the small black arrow appears, then hold down your mouse and drag to the right to select the last three columns of the table.

b. Click the **Layout tab**, then type **1.2** in the **Width** box in the Cell Size group, as shown in Figure 3.4.

You changed the width of the last three columns so that they are each 1.2″ wide. They are now narrower, and the headings wrap even more in the cells.

c. Place the insertion point anywhere in the cell containing the text *Airline Ticket*, then click **Select** in the Table group on the Layout tab. Click **Select Row**, then hold down **Shift** and press the **down arrow** on your keyboard five times to select the remaining rows in the table. Click the **Height spin arrow** in the Cell Size group on the Layout tab to display 0.3″.

You changed the height of some of the rows in the table to 0.3″ tall.

d. Save the document.

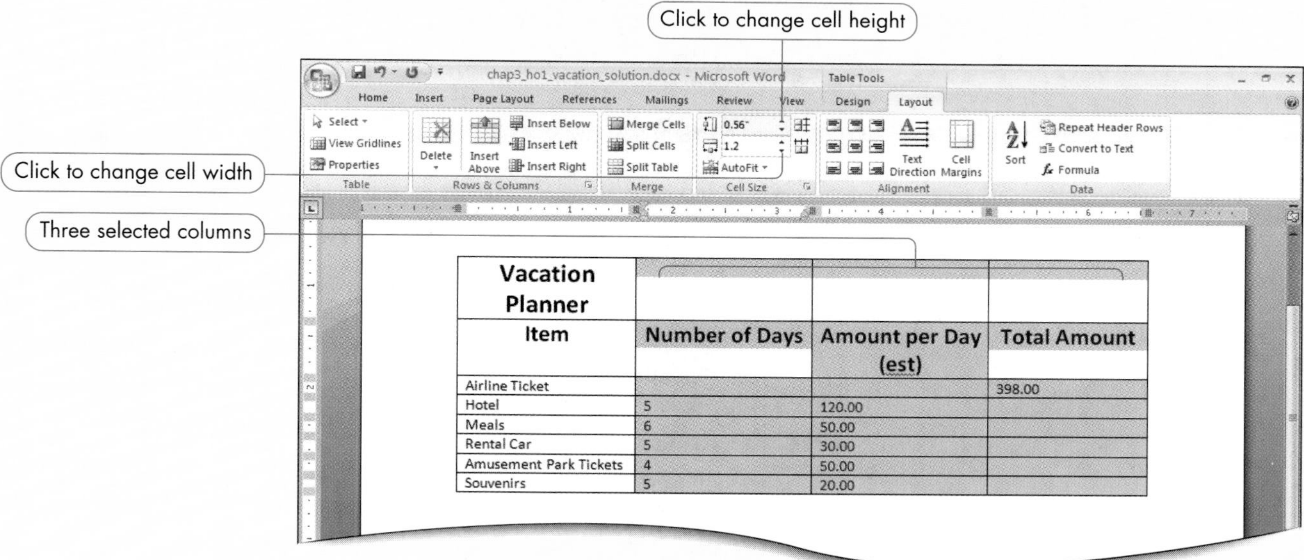

Figure 3.4 Adjust Cell Height and Width

TIP Adjusting Column Width and Row Height

If you are not certain of the exact measurements needed for row height or column width, you can use the mouse to increase or decrease the size. Position the mouse pointer on the gridline that separates the rows (or columns) until the pointer changes to a two-headed arrow. The two-headed arrow indicates you can adjust the height (or width) by clicking and dragging the gridline up or down (right or left) to resize the cell.

Step 4
Merge Cells to Create Header Row

Refer to Figure 3.5 as you complete Step 4.

a. Click outside the table to the left of the first cell in the first row to select the entire first row.

b. Click **Merge Cells** in the Merge group on the Layout tab, as shown in Figure 3.5.

You merged or joined the selected cells. The first row now contains a single cell.

c. Place the insertion point anywhere in the first row, click **Select** in the Table group on the Layout tab, then choose **Select Row**. Click the **Home tab**, click the **Font Size arrow**, and select **24**. Click **Center** in the Paragraph group.

d. Click the **Layout tab**, then click the **Height spin arrow** in the Cell Size group to display **0.5″**.

After increasing the size of the cell contents, you increased the height of the cell so the text is easier to read.

e. Save the *chap3_ho1_vacation_solution* document and keep it onscreen if you plan to continue to the next hands-on exercise. Close the file and exit Word if you do not want to continue with the next exercise at this time.

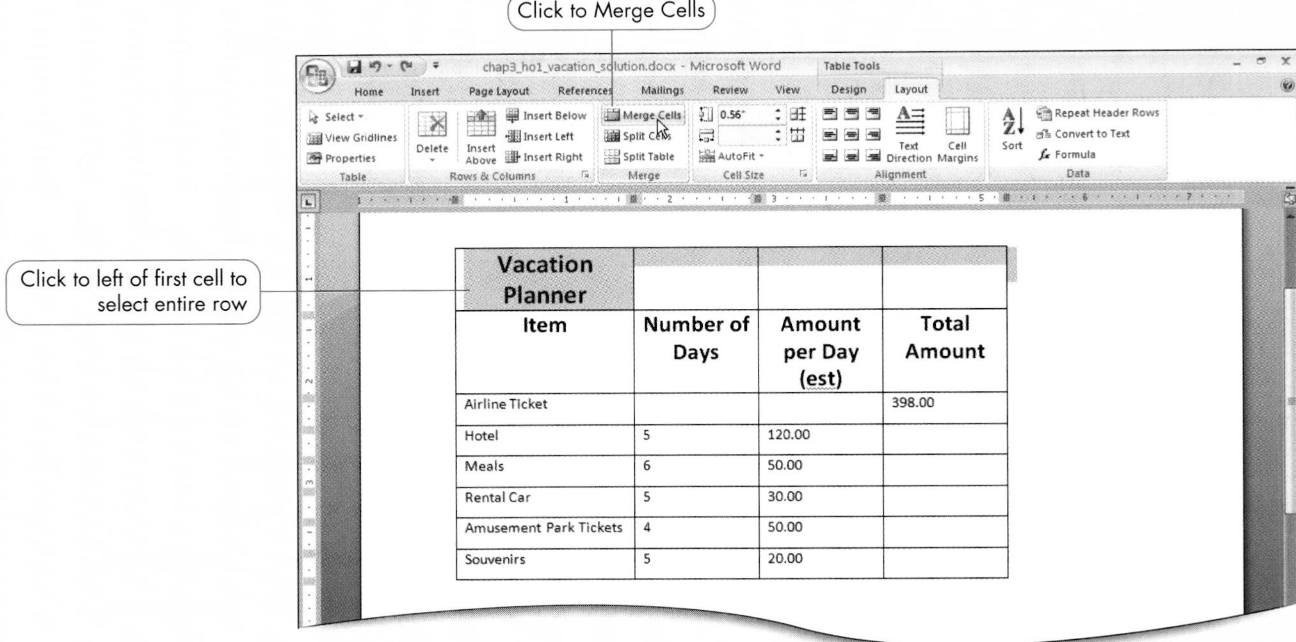

Figure 3.5 Merge First Row Cells

Advanced Table Features

After you create a basic table, you will want to enhance the appearance to create interest for the reader and improve readability. Microsoft Word 2007 provides many predefined styles, which contain borders, shading, font sizes, and other attributes that enhance a table.

You now have a good understanding of the table features and realize there are many uses for them in your Word documents. After you create the basic table, you want to enhance the appearance to create interest for the reader and improve readability. Microsoft Word 2007 includes many tools to assist with these efforts, and you will use several of them to complete the Vacation Planner table.

In this section, you learn how to format a table. Specifically, you apply borders and shading to table cells, apply table styles to the entire table, and select table alignment and position. In addition, you sort data within a table and insert formulas to perform calculations. Finally, you convert text to a table format.

Formatting a Table

Shading affects the background color within a cell.

Border refers to the line style around each cell.

You can use basic formatting options to enhance the appearance of your table. The Borders and Shading commands, for example, offer a wide variety of choices for formatting the table structure. ***Shading*** affects the background color within a cell or group of cells. Table shading is similar to the Highlight feature that places a color behind text. You often apply shading to the header row of a table to make it stand out from the data. ***Border*** refers to the line style around each cell in the table. The default is a single line, but you can choose from many styles to outline a table such as a double, triple, or a wavy line. You can even choose invisible borders if you want only data to display in your document without the outline of a table. Borders and Shading commands are located on the Design tab so you do not have to return to the Home tab to use them.

Apply Table Styles

A ***table style*** contains borders, shading, and other attributes to enhance a table.

When you do not have time to apply custom borders and shading, you will find the Table Styles feature very helpful. Microsoft Word 2007 provides many predefined ***table styles*** that contain borders, shading, font sizes, and other attributes that enhance readability of a table. The custom styles are available in the Table Styles group on the Design tab. To use a predefined table style, click anywhere in your table, and then click a style from the Table Styles gallery. A few styles from the gallery display, but you can select from many others by clicking the down arrow on the right side of the gallery, as shown in Figure 3.6. The Live preview of a style displays on your table when you hover your mouse over it in the gallery. To apply a style, click it one time.

You can modify a predefined style if you wish to make changes to features such as color or alignment. You also can create your own table style and save it for use in the current document or add it to a document template for use in other Word documents. Click More in the Table Styles group to access the Modify Table Style and New Table Style commands.

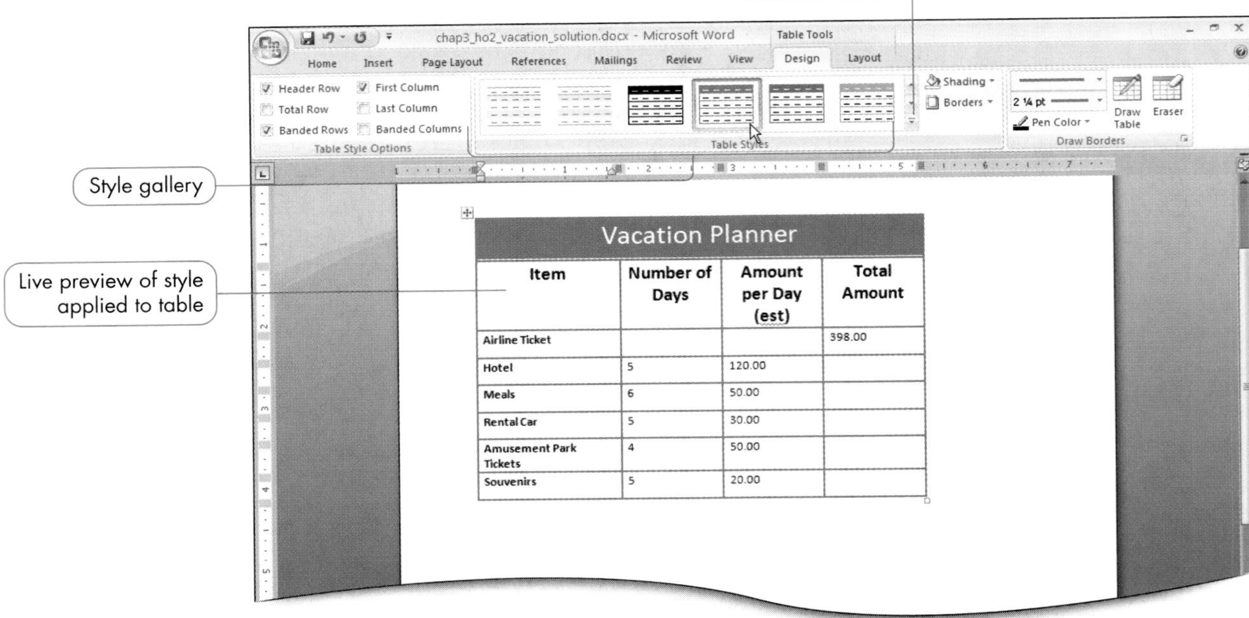

Figure 3.6 Table Styles Command

Select the Table Position and Alignment

Table alignment is the position of a table between the left and right margins.

When you insert a table, Word aligns it at the left margin by default. However, you can click Properties in the Table group on the Layout tab to change the ***table alignment***, the position of a table between the left and right document margins. For example, you might want to center the table between the margins or align it at the right margin.

You also can change alignment of the data in a table separately from the table itself using the Properties dialog box. The Layout tab includes the Alignment group that contains many options to quickly format table data.

Table data can be formatted to align in many different horizontal and vertical combinations. We often apply horizontal settings, such as center, to our data, but using vertical settings also increases readability. For example, when you want your data to be centered both horizontally and vertically within a cell so it is easy to read and does not appear to be elevated on the top or too close to the bottom, click Align Center in the Alignment group to apply that setting.

Text direction refers to the degree of rotation in which text displays.

The default ***text direction*** places text in an upright position. However, you can rotate text so it displays sideways. To change text direction, click Text Direction in the Alignment group on the Layout tab. Each time you click Text Direction, the text rotates. This is a useful tool for aligning text that is in the header row of a narrow column.

Cell margins are the amount of space between data and the cell border in a table.

The ***Cell Margins*** command in the Alignment group on the Layout tab enables you to adjust the amount of white space inside a cell as well as spacing between cells. Use this setting to improve readability of cell contents by adjusting white space around your data or between cells if they contain large amounts of text or data. If you increase cell margins, it prevents data from looking squeezed together.

TIP Right-Click for Table Formatting Options

As an alternative to using the Layout tab, you can find many table options in the context-sensitive menu that displays when you right-click the mouse. The insertion point can be anywhere in the table, and after you right-click you see several table options including Insert, Delete Cells, and Split Cells. You also can change format and alignment of table cells using the Borders and Shading, Cell Alignment, and Text Direction commands in this menu. The Table Properties option is available in the menu if you need to access features such as table alignment and cell spacing.

Sorting and Applying Formulas to Table Data

Sorting is the process of rearranging data.

Because tables provide an easy way to arrange numbers within a document, it is important to know how to use table calculations. This feature gives a Word document the power of a simple spreadsheet. Additional organization of table data is possible by the use of ***sorting***, or rearranging data based on a certain criteria. Figure 3.7 displays the vacation expenses you created previously, but this table illustrates two additional capabilities of the table feature—sorting and calculating.

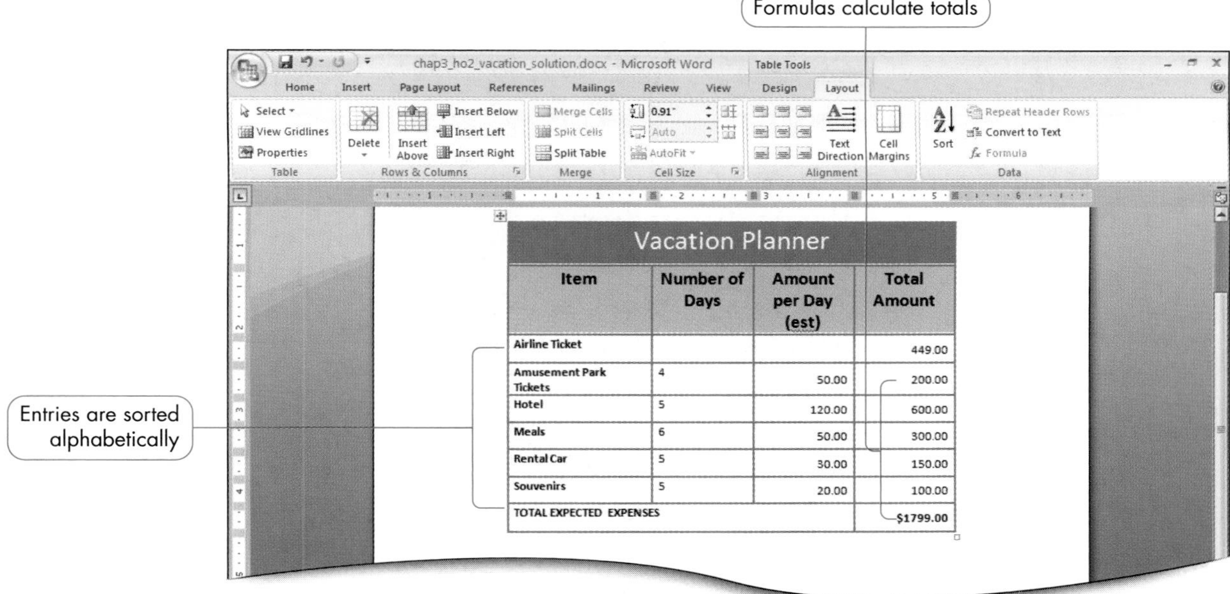

Figure 3.7 The Vacation Planner Table with Enhancements

Calculate Using Table Formulas

In this table, the entries in the Total Amount column consist of formulas that were entered into the table to perform a calculation. The entries are similar to those in a spreadsheet. Thus, the rows in the table are numbered from one to nine while the columns are labeled from A to D. The row and column labels do not appear in the table, but are used in the formulas.

You know that the intersection of a row and column forms a cell. Word uses the column letter and row number of that intersection to identify the cell and to give it an address. Cell D5, for example, contains the entry to compute the total hotel expense by multiplying the number of days (in cell B5) by the amount charged per day (in cell C5). In similar fashion, the entry in cell D6 computes the total expense for meals by multiplying the values in cells B6 and C6, respectively. The formula is not entered (typed) into the cell explicitly, but is created using the Formula command in the Data group on the Layout tab.

Figure 3.8 is a slight variation of Figure 3.7 in which the field codes have been toggled on to display the formulas, as opposed to the calculated values. The cells are shaded to emphasize that these cells contain formulas (fields), as opposed to numerical values. The field codes are toggled on and off by selecting the formula and pressing Shift+F9 or by right-clicking the entry and selecting the Toggle Field Codes command.

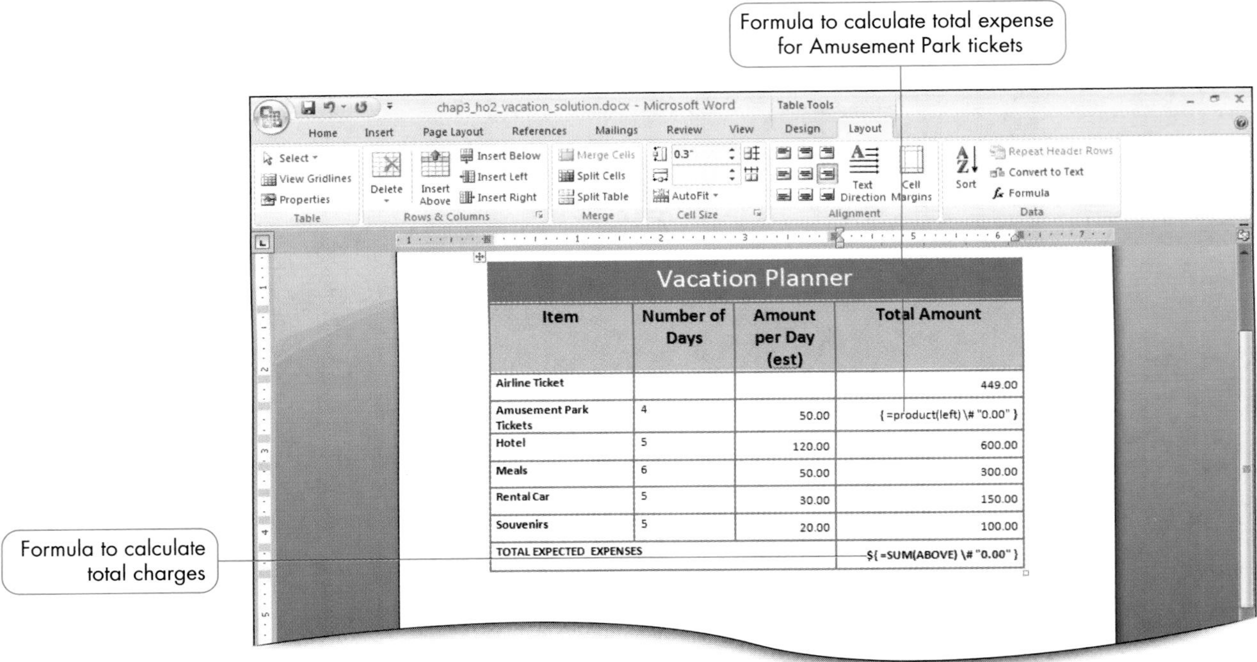

Figure 3.8 The Vacation Planner Table Displaying Formulas

The formula in cell D9 has a different syntax and sums the value of all cells directly above it. You do not need to know the syntax because Word provides a dialog box that supplies the entry for you, but once you use it to create the formula, you will find it easy to understand. It is better to use the Formula command to calculate totals than to type a number because if you add data to the table, you can use formula tools to recalculate for you.

Sort Data in a Table

Ascending order arranges data from lowest to highest.

Descending order arranges data from highest to lowest.

At times, you might need to sort data in a table to enhance order or understand the data. For example, when a list of employees is reviewed, a manager would prefer to view the names in alphabetical order by last name or department. You can sort data according to the entries in a specific column or row of the table. Sort orders include ***ascending order***, which arranges text in alphabetical or sequential order starting with the lowest letter or number and continuing to the highest (A–Z or 0–9). Or you can sort in ***descending order***, where data is arranged from highest to lowest (Z–A or 9–0).

You can sort the rows in a table to display data in different sequences as shown in Figure 3.9, where the vacation items are sorted from lowest to highest expense. You also could sort the data in descending (high to low) sequence according to the Total Amount. In descending order, the hotel (largest expense) displays at the top of the list, and the souvenirs (smallest expense) appear last. The second row of the table contains the field names for each column and is not included in the sort. The next six rows contain the sorted data, while the last row displays the total for all expenses and is not included in the sort.

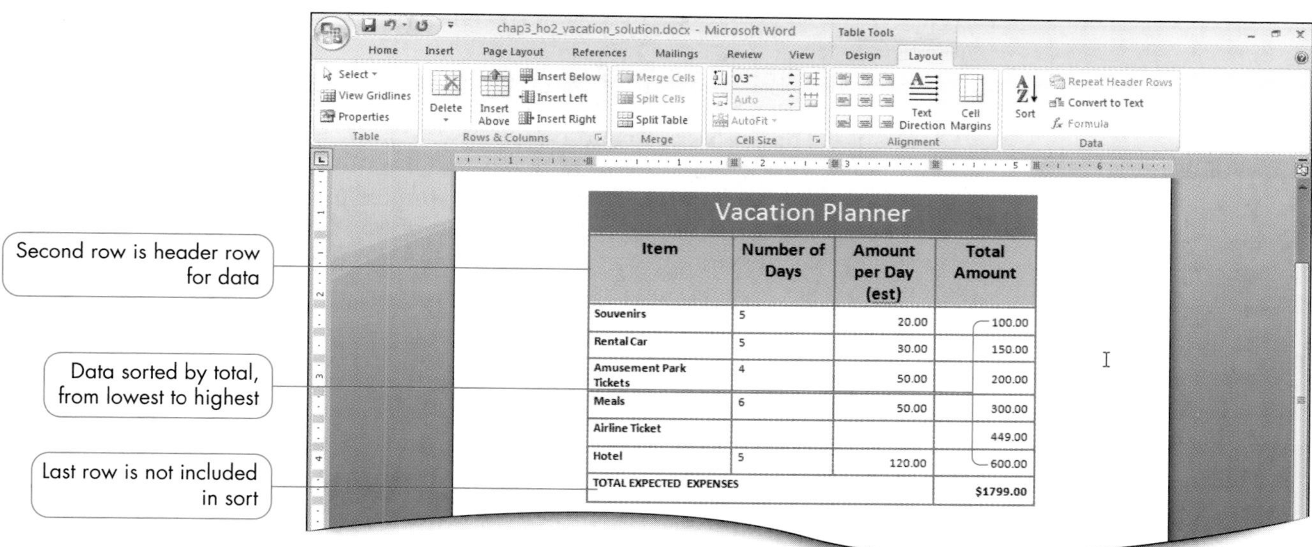

Figure 3.9 Sort the Table Data

Sorting is accomplished according to the select-then-do methodology that is used for many operations in Microsoft Word. You select the rows that are to be sorted, rows three through nine in this example, and then you click Sort in the Data group on the Layout tab. The Sort dialog box displays, as shown in Figure 3.10, which enables you to select the direction and sort criteria.

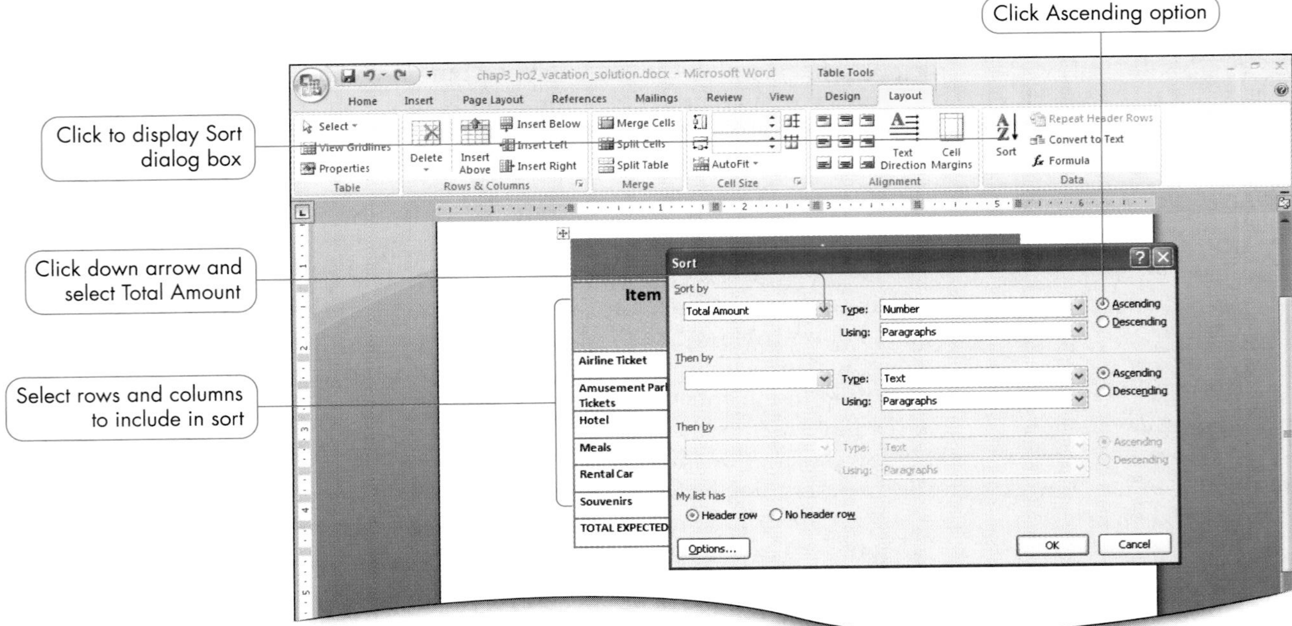

Figure 3.10 The Sort Command

Converting Text to a Table

The tables feature is outstanding. But what if you are given a lengthy list of items—for example, two items per line separated by a tab that should have been formatted as a table? The Table command on the Insert tab includes the Convert Text to Table command, and it can aid you in this transformation. After you select the text and choose this command, the Convert Text to Table dialog box displays and offers several options to assist in a quick conversion of text into a table. The command also works in reverse; you can convert a table to text. You will perform a table conversion in the next set of hands-on exercises.

Table Tools Design Ribbon | Reference

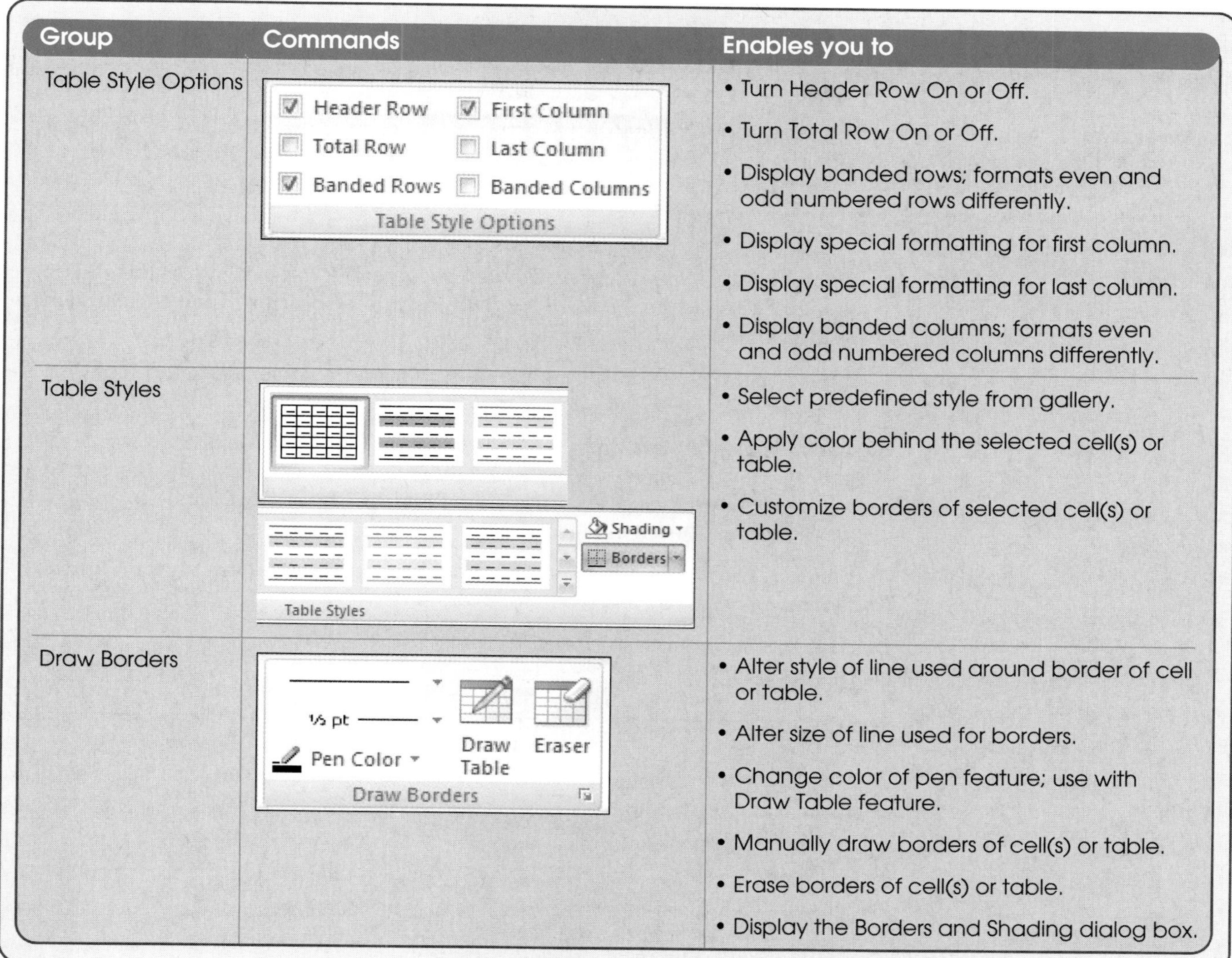

Group	Commands	Enables you to
Table Style Options	Header Row, First Column, Total Row, Last Column, Banded Rows, Banded Columns Table Style Options	• Turn Header Row On or Off. • Turn Total Row On or Off. • Display banded rows; formats even and odd numbered rows differently. • Display special formatting for first column. • Display special formatting for last column. • Display banded columns; formats even and odd numbered columns differently.
Table Styles	Shading, Borders Table Styles	• Select predefined style from gallery. • Apply color behind the selected cell(s) or table. • Customize borders of selected cell(s) or table.
Draw Borders	½ pt, Pen Color, Draw Table, Eraser Draw Borders	• Alter style of line used around border of cell or table. • Alter size of line used for borders. • Change color of pen feature; use with Draw Table feature. • Manually draw borders of cell(s) or table. • Erase borders of cell(s) or table. • Display the Borders and Shading dialog box.

Hands-On Exercises

2 | Advanced Table Features

Skills covered: 1. Apply a Table Style **2.** Add Table Borders and Shading **3.** Enter Formulas to Calculate Totals **4.** Add a Row and Enter a Formula **5.** Sort Data in a Table **6.** Align Table and Data **7.** Convert Text to a Table

Step 1 Apply a Table Style

Refer to Figure 3.11 as you complete Step 1.

a. Open the *chap3_ho1_vacation_solution* document if you closed it at the end of the first exercise and save it as **chap3_ho2_vacation_solution**. Then click anywhere in the table.

The insertion point must be somewhere within the table before the Table Tools tabs display.

b. Click the **Design tab**, and then click **More** on the right side of the Table Styles gallery. Hover your mouse over several styles and notice how the table changes to preview that style. Click once on the **Light List – Accent 1** style to apply it to your table, as shown in Figure 3.11.

Previous cell shading is replaced by the formatting attributes for the **Light List – Accent 1** style.

c. Save the document.

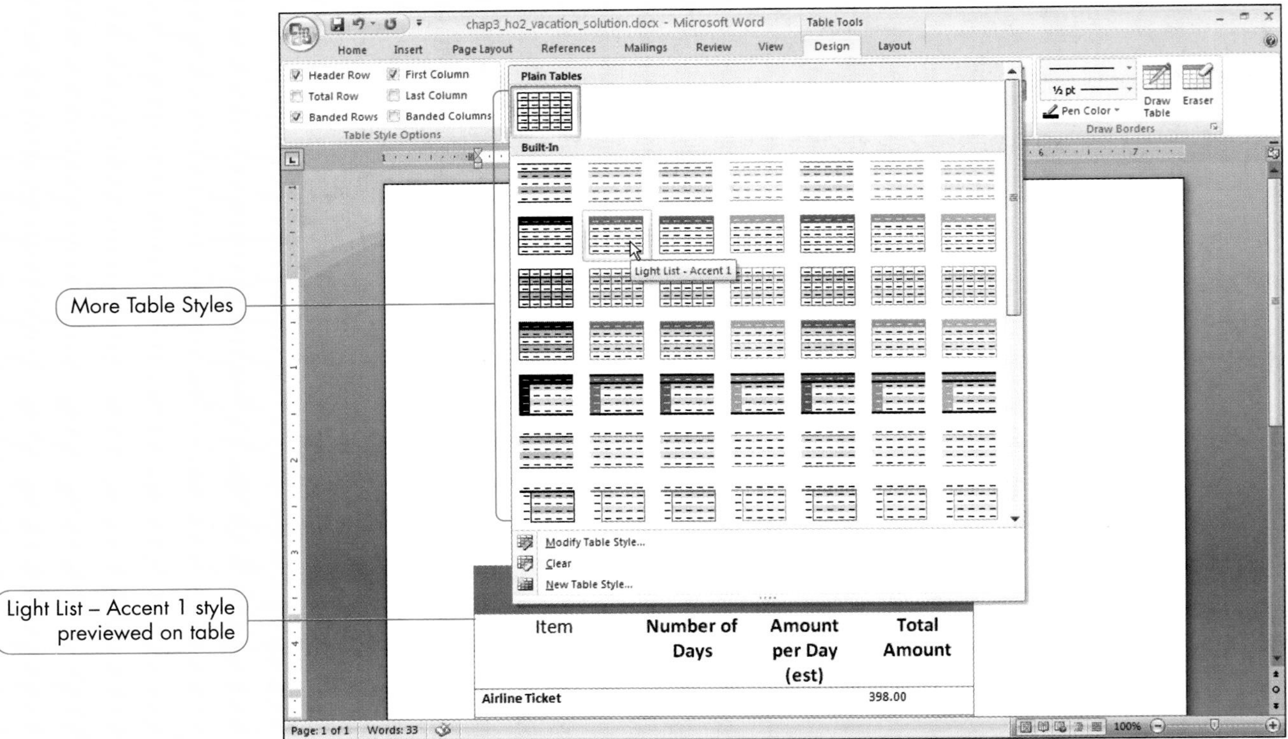

Figure 3.11 Style Applied to Vacation Planner Table

Step 2
Add Table Borders and Shading

Refer to Figure 3.12 as you complete Step 2.

a. Click anywhere in the Vacation Planner table. Click the **Borders arrow** in the Table Styles group and select **Borders and Shading**.

b. Click **All** in the *Setting* section on the left side of the Borders tab. Then click the **Width drop-down arrow** and select 2¼ pt. Click **OK** to close the Borders and Shading box.

   Your table has a darker blue border surrounding each cell.

c. Drag your mouse across the cells in the second row of the table to select them, then click **Shading** in the Table Styles group. Click the swatch in the fourth row of the first column named **White, Background 1, Darker 25%**, as shown in Figure 3.12.

   The table now displays a large, blue title row, a gray colored header row, and blue borders around the remaining data.

d. Save the document.

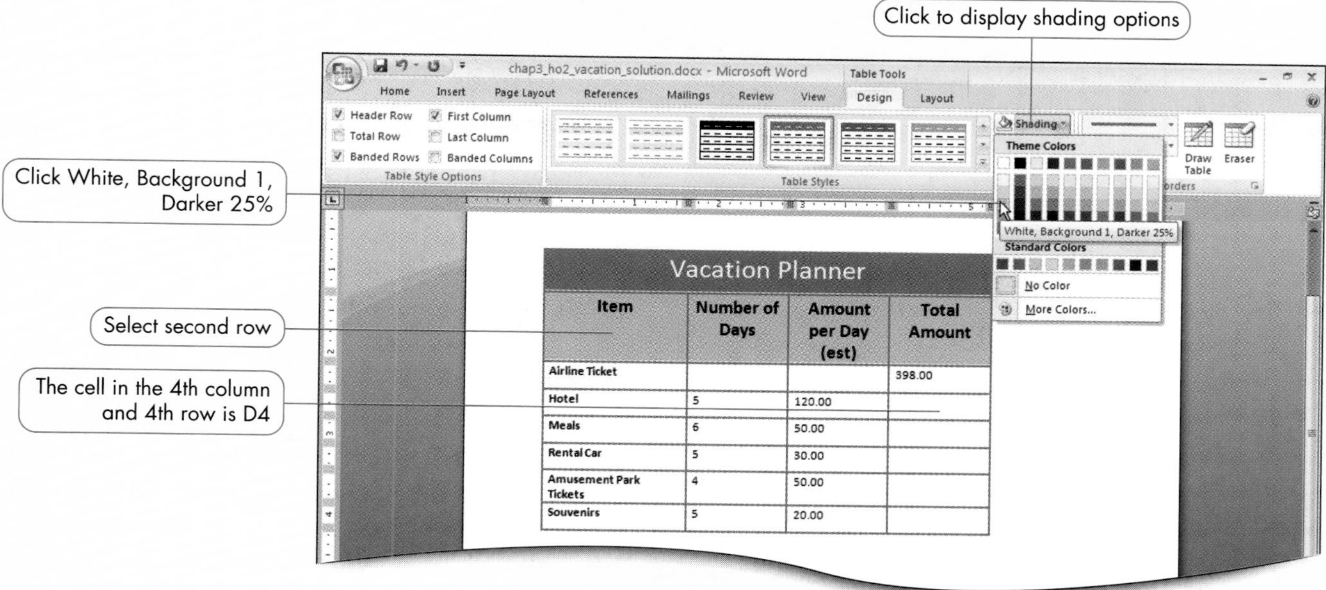

Figure 3.12 Borders and Shading Applied to Table

Step 3
Enter Formulas to Calculate Totals

Refer to Figure 3.13 as you complete Step 3.

a. Click in **cell D4**, the cell in the fourth column and fourth row. Click the **Layout tab** and click **Formula** in the Data group to display the formula box.

b. Click and drag to select the =SUM(ABOVE) function, which is entered by default. Type **=b4*c4**, as shown in Figure 3.13, to replace the existing formula and compute the total hotel expense. Click the **Number format drop-down arrow** and select **0.00**, and then click **OK**.

The formula is not case sensitive; you can type formula references in lowercase or capital letters. The total is computed by multiplying the number of days (in cell B4) by the amount per day (in cell C4). The result, 600, displays in a number format with two decimal places because these numbers represent a monetary value in dollars and cents.

c. Click in **cell D5**, directly below the cell you edited in the last step, then click **Formula**. In the Formula box, click and drag to select SUM(ABOVE) but do not select the equal sign, then press **Delete** to remove the formula. Click the **Paste function drop-down arrow**, and then scroll and select **PRODUCT**. Type **left** between the parentheses where the insertion point is blinking in the Formula box. Click the **Number format drop-down arrow**, select **0.00**, and then click **OK**.

   This formula performs the same function as the one you used in Step B, but it references cells to the left of the current cell instead of using actual cell addresses.

d. Calculate the total expenses for cells D6, D7, and D8 using either formula used in the previous steps.

e. Save the document.

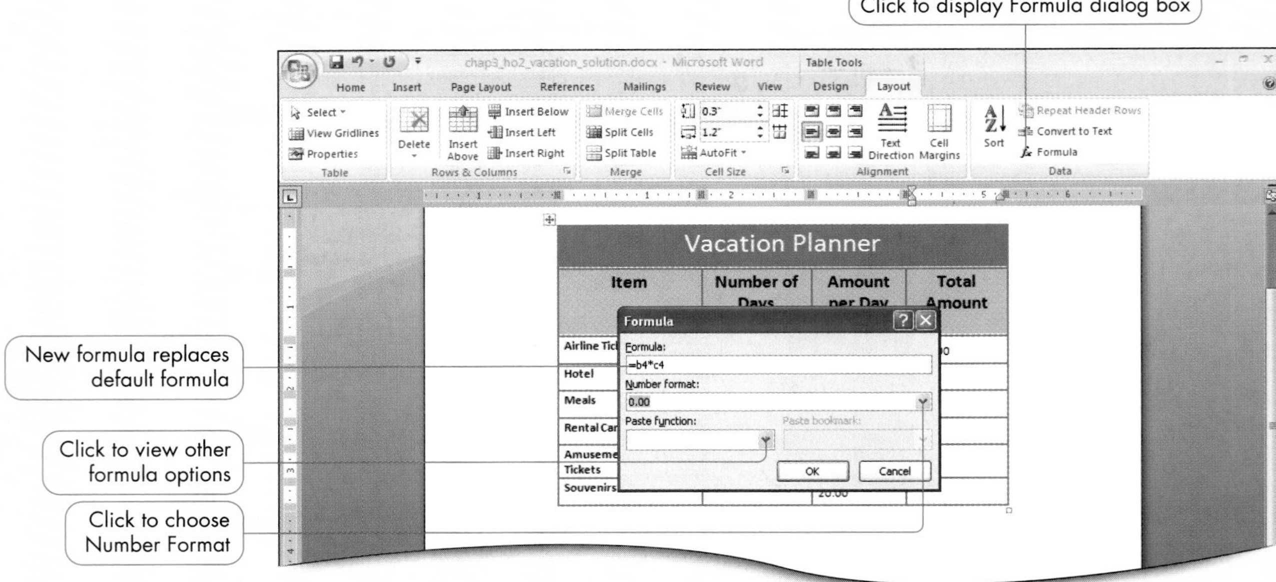

Figure 3.13 Compute a Formula in a Table

Step 4
Add a Row and Enter a Formula

Refer to Figure 3.14 as you complete Step 4.

a. Click the last cell in the table and press **Tab** to add another row to the table. Drag your mouse across all four cells in this row to select them, and then click **Merge Cells** in the Merge group on the Layout tab. Type the words **TOTAL EXPECTED EXPENSES** in the newly merged cell.

b. Click **Split Cells** in the Merge group to display the Split Cells dialog box. If necessary, click the **Number of columns spin box** to display **2**, then click **OK**.

   The last row displays two cells of equal size. You will display the total vacation expense amount in the last cell, but you need to resize it to the same size as cells in the last column so the numbers will align correctly.

c. Hold your mouse over the border between the cells in the last row until a two-headed arrow displays. Then click and drag to the right until the border aligns with the border of the last column in the rows above, as shown in Figure 3.14.

d. Click in the last cell of the table, click **Formula**, click the **Number format drop-down arrow**, select **0.00**, then click **OK** to accept the default formula, =SUM(ABOVE).

   You should see 1748.00 (the sum of the cells in the last column) displayed in the selected cell.

e. Click the number, 1748.00, one time so that it is shaded in grey, then press **Shift+F9** to display the code {=SUM(ABOVE)\#"0.00"}. Press **Shift+F9** a second time to display the actual value.

f. Click in **cell D3** (the cell containing the airfare). Replace 398.00 with **449.00** and press **Tab** to move out of the cell.

   The total expenses are not yet updated in cell D9.

g. Right-click on the number that displays in **cell D9** to display a shortcut menu, then select **Update Field**.

   Cell D9 displays 1799.00, the updated total for all expenses.

h. Save the document.

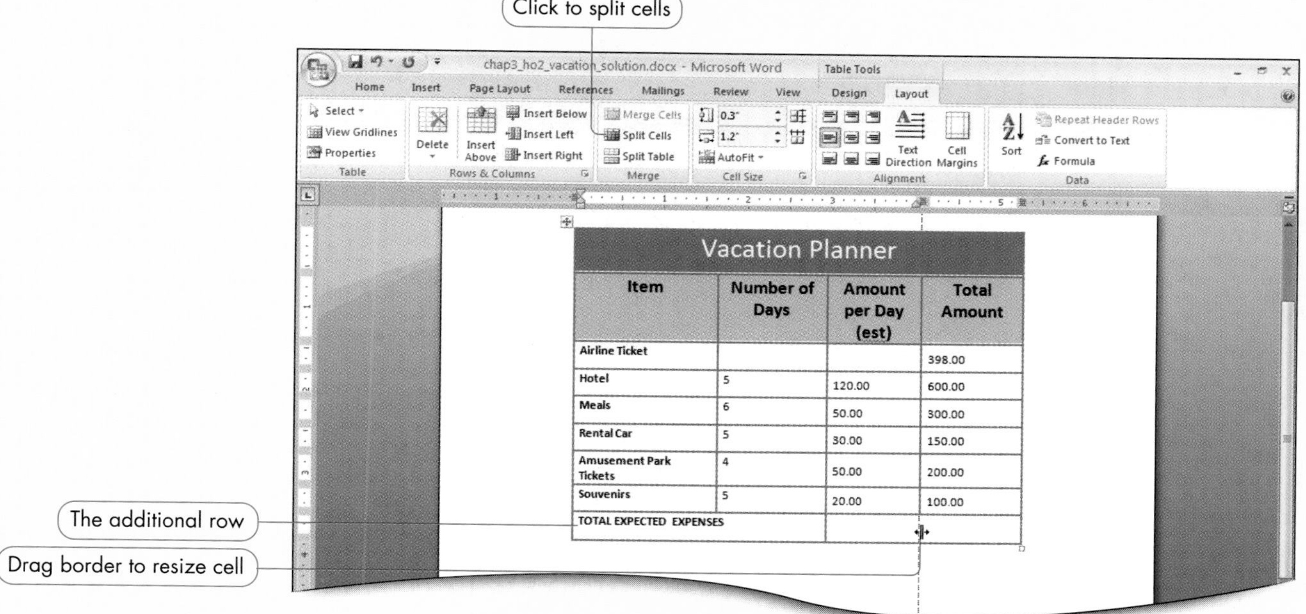

Figure 3.14 Drag to Resize Cell Width

Step 5
Sort Data in a Table

Refer to Figure 3.15 as you complete Step 5.

a. Click and drag to select rows two through eight in the table. Click **Sort** in the Data group on the Layout tab.

b. Click **Header row** in the *My list has* section of the dialog box.

c. If necessary, click the **Sort by drop-down arrow** and select **Item** (the column heading for the first column). The Ascending option is selected by default, as shown in Figure 3.15. Click **OK**.

The entries in the table are rearranged alphabetically according to the entry in the Item column. The Total row remains at the bottom of the table since it was not included in the sort.

TROUBLESHOOTING: If you do not first click Header row, the headings for each column will not display in the Sort by drop-down list; instead, you will see the Column numbers listed. You can sort by Column number (1, 2, 3, or 4), but it is important to click the Header row option before you leave this dialog box so the header row is not included in the sort.

d. Select rows four through six, which have lost formatting along the left and right borders. Click the **Design tab**, click the **Borders arrow** in the Table Styles group, and then select **All Borders**.

The dark blue borders fill the left and right borders of the selected cells, matching the remainder of the table.

e. Save the document.

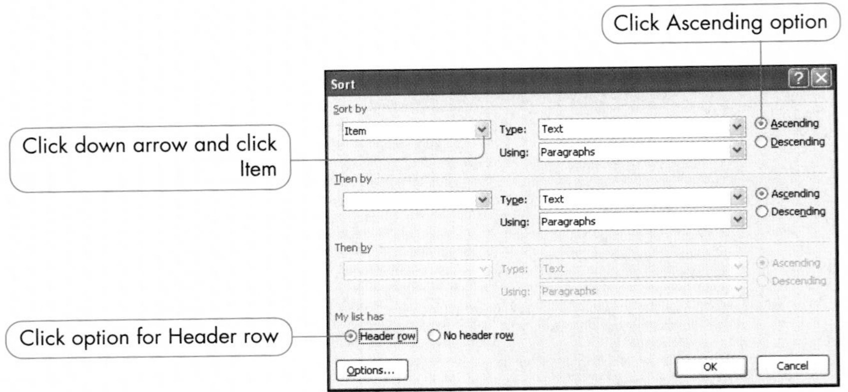

Figure 3.15 Sort Data in a Table

Step 6
Align Table and Data

Refer to Figure 3.16 as you complete Step 6.

a. Click the table selector to select the entire table. Click the **Layout tab**, then click **Properties** in the Table group.

b. Click the **Table tab**, if necessary, and then click **Center** in the *Alignment* section, as shown in Figure 3.16. Click **OK**.

Your table is now centered between the left and right margins.

c. Click anywhere to deselect the whole table, then drag your mouse to select the last two columns of rows three through eight. Select entries listed under Amount Per Day (est) and Total Amount, but do not select data in the header row. Click **Align Center Right** from the Alignment group. Select the last cell in the table and click **Align Center Right** to align it with other data.

Because these columns contain numerical data, you right align them to give the effect of decimal alignment. However, the numbers are not decimal aligned, so if you display an additional digit in a value, it will result in misaligned numbers.

d. Click in the last cell and insert a dollar sign ($) in front of the amount of expected expenses.

e. Save and close the *chap3_ho2_vacation_solution* document.

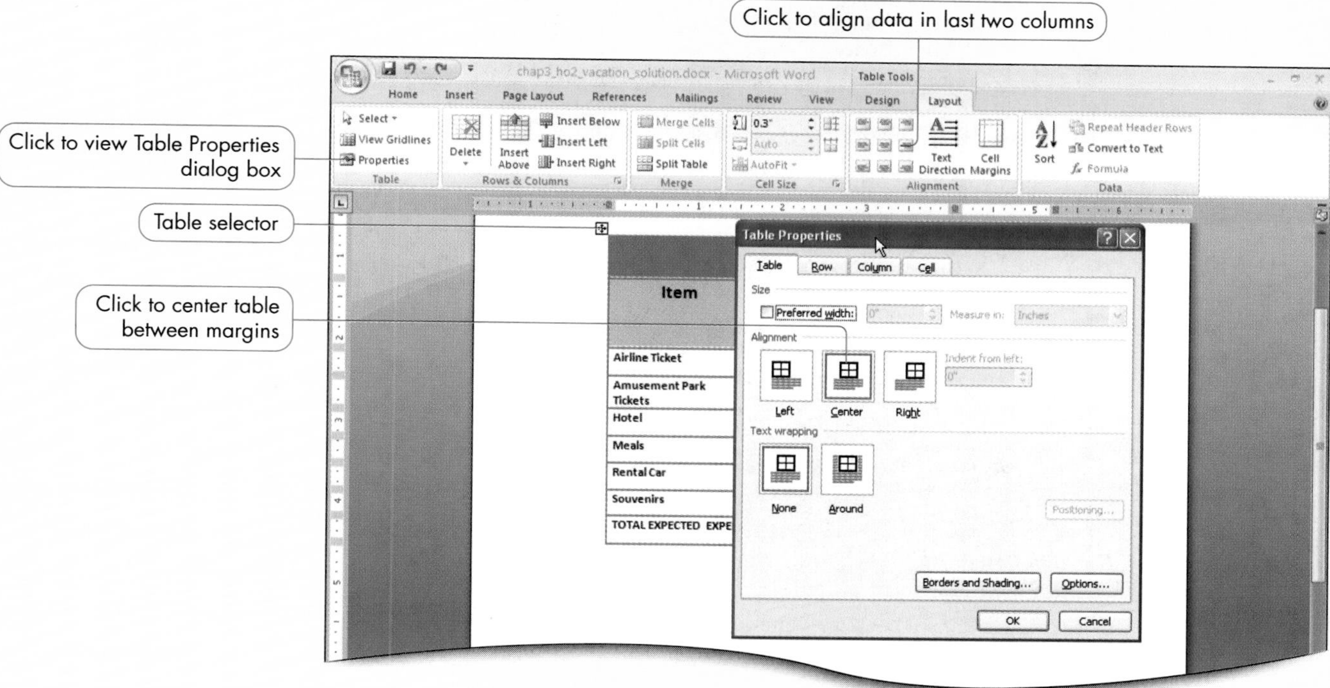

Figure 3.16 Apply Alignment to Vacation Planner Table

Step 7
Convert Text to a Table

Refer to Figure 3.17 as you complete Step 7.

a. Open the *chap3_ho2_expenses* document and save it as **chap3_ho2_expenses_solution**.

b. Press **Ctrl+A** to select all text in this document and then click the **Insert tab**.

c. Click **Table**, and then select **Convert Text to Table**. View the options in the Convert Text to Table dialog box, as shown in Figure 3.17, but do not make any changes at this time. Click **OK**.

The list of items display in a table that can now be sorted and formatted.

d. Save and close the *chap3_ho2_expenses_solution* document.

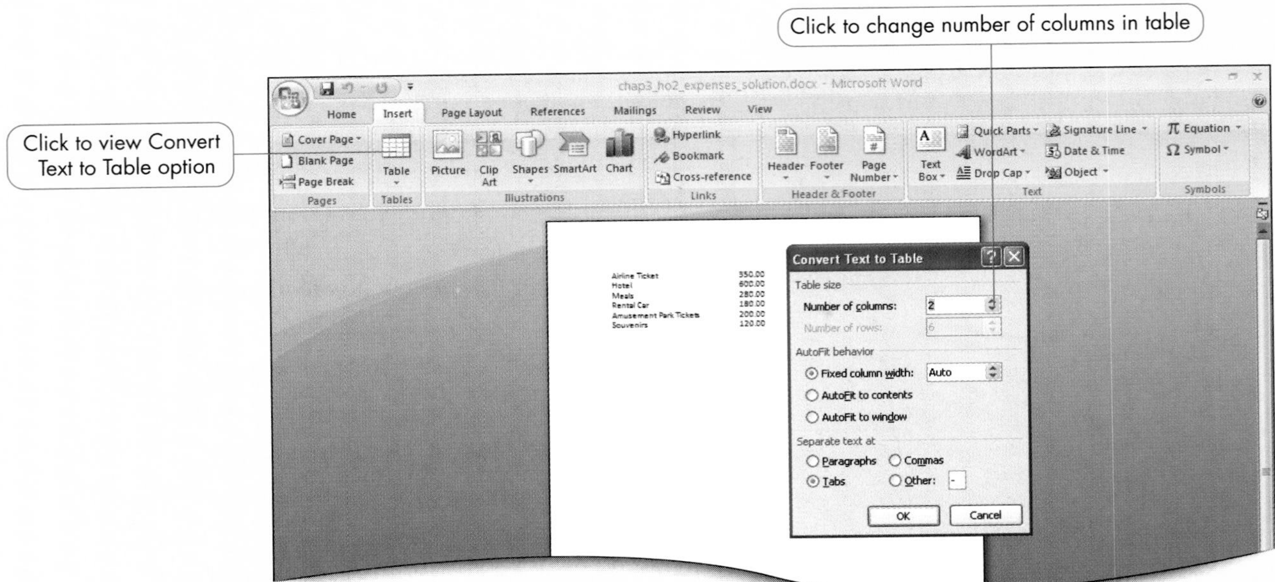

Figure 3.17 Convert Text to Table Dialog Box

Graphic Tools

Clip art is a graphical image, illustration, drawing, or sketch.

One of the most exciting features of Word is its graphic capabilities. You can use clip art, images, drawings, and scanned photographs to visually enhance brochures, newsletters, announcements, and reports. ***Clip art*** is a graphical image, illustration, drawing, or sketch. In addition to inserting clip art in a document, you can insert photographs from a digital camera or scanner, graphically shaped text, and special boxes to hold text. After inserting a graphical image or text, you can adjust size, choose placement, and perform other graphical format options.

(One of the most exciting features of Word is its graphic capabilities. You can use clip art, images, drawings, and scanned photographs to visually enhance brochures, newsletters, announcements, and reports.)

In this section, you insert clip art and an image in a document. Then you format the image by changing the height and width, applying a text-wrapping style, applying a quick style, and adjusting graphic properties. Finally, you insert WordArt and symbols in a document.

Inserting Clip Art and Images into a Document

A **copyright** provides legal protection to a written or artistic work.

Clip art and other graphical images or objects may be stored locally, purchased on a CD at a computer supply store, or downloaded from the Internet for inclusion into a document. Whether you use Microsoft's online clip gallery or purchase clip art, you should read the license agreements to know how you may legally use the images. A ***copyright*** provides legal protection to a written or artistic work, giving the author exclusive rights to its use and reproduction, except as governed under the fair use exclusion. Anything on the Internet should be considered copyrighted unless the document specifically says it is in the public domain. The Fair Use doctrine allows you to use a portion of the work for educational, nonprofit purposes, or for the purpose of critical review or commentary. All such material should be cited through an appropriate footnote or endnote. Using clip art for a purpose not allowed by the license agreement is illegal.

Manage Clips with the Microsoft Clip Organizer

The Clip Art command displays a task pane through which you can search, select, and insert clip art, photographs, sounds, and movies (collectively called clips). The clips can come from a variety of sources. They may be installed locally in the My Collections folder, they may have been installed in conjunction with Microsoft Office in the Office Collections folder, and/or they may have been downloaded from the Web and stored in the Web Collections folder. You can insert a specific clip into a document if you know its location. You also can search for a clip that will enhance the document on which you are working.

The **Microsoft Clip Organizer** catalogs pictures, sounds, and movies stored on your hard drive.

The ***Microsoft Clip Organizer*** brings order out of potential chaos by cataloging the clips, photos, sounds, and movies that are available to you. You enter a keyword that describes the clip you are looking for, specify the collections that are to be searched, and indicate the type of clip(s) you are looking for. The results are returned in the task pane, as shown in Figure 3.18, which displays the clips that are described by the keyword *computer*. You can restrict the search to selected collections but request that all media types be displayed. If you also specify to search for items stored locally, the search is faster than one that searches online as well. When you see a clip that you want to use, click the clip to insert it into your document. For more options, point to the clip, click the down arrow that appears, and then select from the menu.

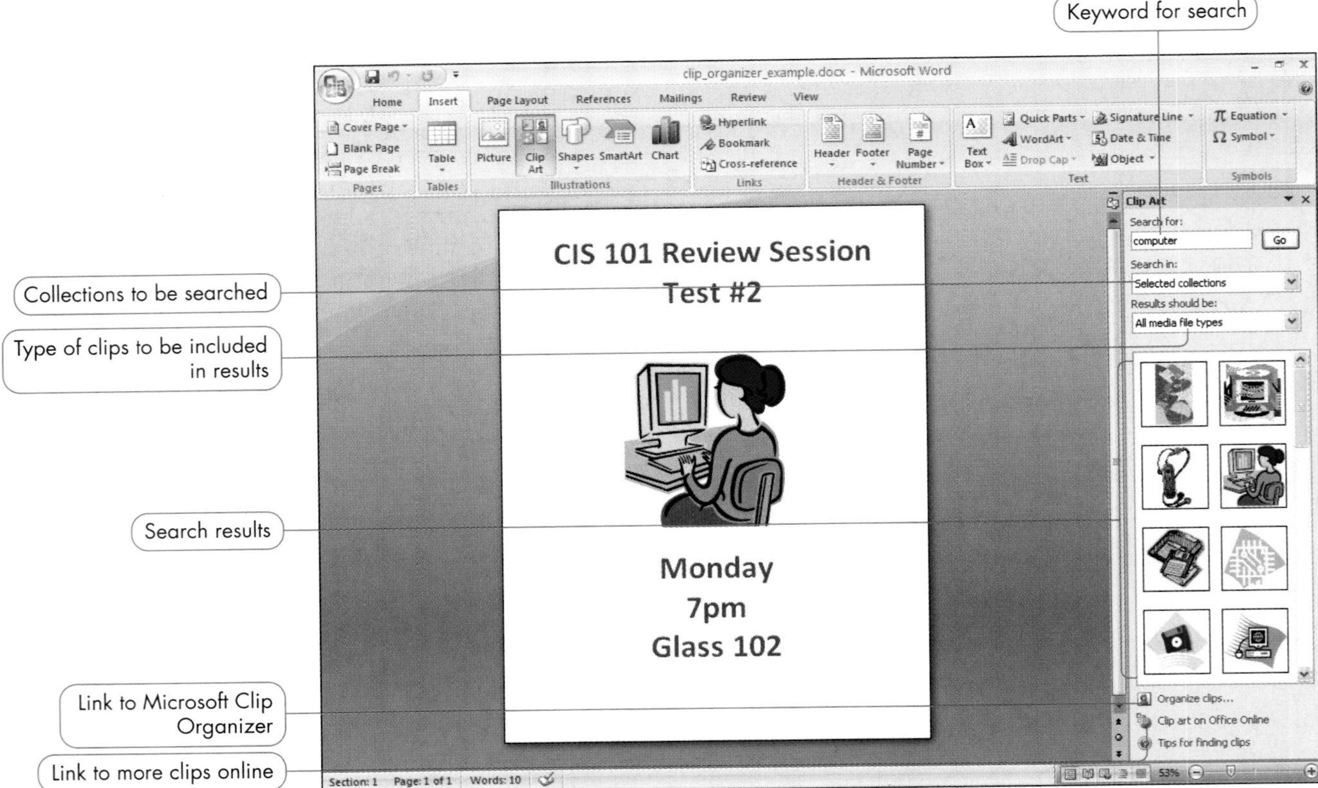

Figure 3.18 The Clip Art Task Pane

You can access the Microsoft Clip Organizer (to view the various collections) by clicking Organize clips at the bottom of the Clip Art task pane. You also can access the Clip Organizer when you are not using Word; click the Start button on the taskbar, click All Programs, Microsoft Office, Microsoft Office Tools, and Microsoft Clip Organizer. Once in the Organizer, you can search through the clips in the various collections, reorganize the existing collections, add new collections, and even add new clips (with their associated keywords) to the collections. The other links at the bottom of the task pane in Figure 3.18 provide access to additional clip art online and tips for finding more relevant clips.

Insert a Picture

In addition to the collection of clip art and pictures that you can access from Word, you also can insert your own pictures into a document. If you have a scanner or digital camera attached to your computer, you can scan or download a picture for use in Word. After you save the picture to your disk, click Picture in the Illustrations group on the Insert tab to locate and insert it in the document. The Insert Picture dialog box opens so that you can navigate to the location where the picture is saved. After you insert the picture, there are many commands you can use to format it. Those commands are discussed in the next section.

Formatting a Graphic Element

> Remember that graphical elements should enhance a document, not overpower it.

When you insert an image in a document, it comes in a predefined size. For example, the clip art image in Figure 3.18 was very large and took up much space on the page before it was resized. Most times, you need to adjust an image's size so it fits within the document and does not greatly increase the document file size. Remember that graphical elements should enhance a document, not overpower it.

Adjust the Height and Width of a Graphic

Sizing handles are the small circles and squares that appear around a selected object and enable you to adjust the height and width of an object.

Word provides different tools you can use to adjust the height or width of an image, depending on how exact you want the measurements. The Picture Tools Format tab contains Height and Width commands that enable you to specify exact measurements. You can use ***sizing handles***, the small circles and squares that appear around a selected object, to size an object by clicking and dragging any one of the handles. When you use the circular sizing handles in the corner of a graphic to adjust the height (or width), Word also adjusts the width (or height) simultaneously. If needed, hold down Shift while dragging the corner sizing handle to maintain the correct proportion of the image. If you use square sizing handles on the right, left, top, or bottom, you adjust that measurement without regard to any other sides.

Adjust Text Wrapping

Text wrapping style refers to the way text wraps around an image.

When you first insert an image, Word treats it as a character in the line of text, which leaves a lot of empty space on the left or right side of the image. You may want it to align differently, perhaps allowing text to display very tightly around the object or even behind the text. ***Text wrapping style*** refers to the way text wraps around an image. Table 3.1 describes the different wrapping options.

Table 3.1 Text Wrapping Styles

Text Wrapping Style	Description
Square	Allows text to wrap around the graphic frame that surrounds the image.
Tight	Allows text to wrap tightly around the outer edges of the image itself instead of the frame.
Through	Select this option to wrap text around the perimeter and inside any open portions of the object.
Top and Bottom	Text wraps to the top and bottom of the image frame, but no text appears on the sides.
Behind Text	Allows the image to display behind the text in such a way that the image appears to float directly behind the text and does not move if text is inserted or deleted.
In Front of Text	Allows the image to display on top of the text in such a way that the image appears to float directly on top of the text and does not move if text is inserted or deleted.
In Line with Text	Graphic displays on the line where inserted so that as you add or delete text, causing the line of text to move, the image moves with it.

Apply Picture Quick Styles

The ***Picture Styles*** gallery contains preformatted options that can be applied to a graphical object.

Word 2007 introduces the ***Picture Styles*** gallery that contains many preformatted picture formats. The gallery of styles you can apply to a picture or clip art is extensive, and you also can modify the style after you apply it. The quick styles provide a valuable resource if you want to improve the appearance of a graphic but are not familiar with graphic design and format tools. For example, after you insert a graphic, with one click you can choose a style from the Quick Styles gallery that adds a border and displays a reflection of the picture. You might want to select a style that changes the shape of your graphic to an octagon, or select a style that applies a 3-D effect to the image. To apply a quick style, select the graphical object, then choose a quick style from the Picture Styles group on the Picture Tools Format tab. Other style formatting options, such as Soft Edges or 3-D Rotation, are listed in Picture Effects on the Picture Styles group, as shown in Figure 3.19.

Adjust Graphic Properties

Crop or Cropping is the process of trimming the edges of an image or other graphical object.

Scale or scaling is the adjustment of height or width by a percentage of the image's original size.

Contrast is the difference between light and dark areas of an image.

Brightness is the ratio between lightness and darkness of an image.

After you insert a graphic or an image, you might find that you need to edit it before using a picture style. One of the most common changes includes ***crop or cropping***, which is the process of trimming edges or other portions of an image or other graphical object that you do not wish to display. Cropping enables you to call attention to a specific area of a graphical element while omitting any unnecessary detail. When you add images to enhance a document, you may find clip art that has more objects than you desire or you may find an image that has damaged edges that you do not wish to appear in your document. You can solve the problems with these graphics by cropping. The cropping tool is located in the Size group on the Format tab.

Instead of cropping unused portions of a graphic, you may need to enlarge or reduce its size to fit in the desired area. The easiest method for sizing is selecting the image and dragging the selection handles. For more exact measurements, however, you could adjust the ***scale or scaling***, which adjusts the height or width of an image by a percentage of its original size. The scale adjustment is located in the Size dialog box, which you display by clicking the Size Dialog Box Launcher on the Format tab.

Other common adjustments to a graphical object include contrast and/or brightness. Adjusting the ***contrast*** increases or decreases the difference in dark and light areas of the image. Adjusting the ***brightness*** lightens or darkens the overall image.

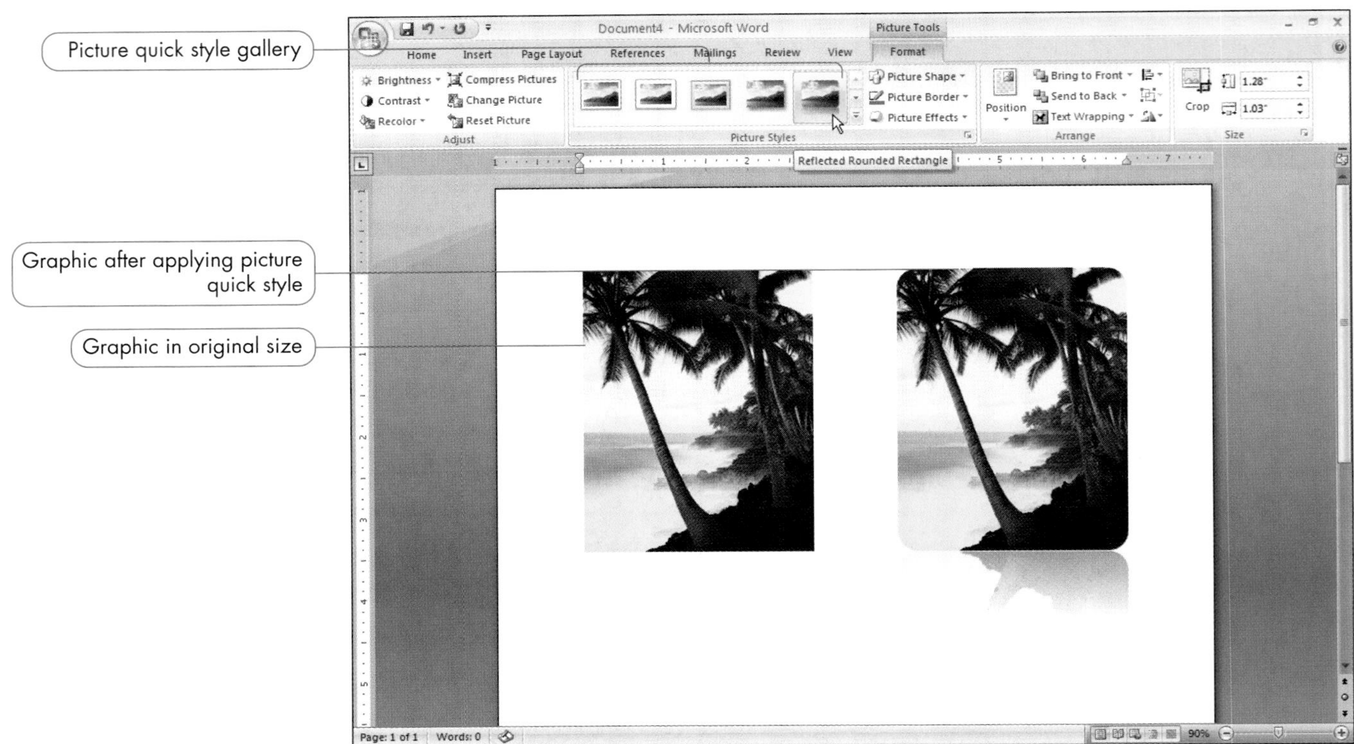

Figure 3.19 The Picture Styles Gallery

These adjustments often are made on a picture taken with a digital camera in poor lighting or if a clip art image is too bright or dull to match other objects in your document. Adjusting contrast or brightness can improve the visibility of subjects in a picture. You may want to increase contrast for a dramatic effect or lower contrast to soften an image. The Brightness and Contrast adjustments are in the Picture Tools group on the Format tab.

Even though graphical objects add a great deal of visual enhancement to a document, they also can increase the file size of the document. If you add several graphics to a document, you should view the file size before you copy or save it to a portable storage device, and then confirm the device has enough empty space to hold the large file. Additional consideration should be given to files you send as e-mail attachments. Many people have space limitations in their mailboxes, and a document that contains several graphics can fill their space or take a long time to download. To decrease the size a graphic occupies, you can use the ***Compress*** feature, which reduces the size of an object. When you select a graphical object, you can click the Compress Pictures command on the Picture Tools group in the Format tab. The Compression Settings dialog box displays, and you can select from options that allow you to reduce the size of the graphical elements, thus reducing the size of the file when you save.

Compress reduces the file size of an object.

The Picture Tools tab offers many additional graphic editing features, which are described on the following reference page.

Graphic Editing Features | Reference

Feature	Button	Description
Height		Height of an object in inches.
Width		Width of an object in inches.
Crop	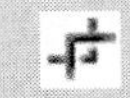	Remove unwanted portions of the object from top, bottom, left, or right to adjust size.
Align		Adjust edges of object to line up on right or left margin or center between margins.
Group		Process of selecting multiple objects so you can move and format them together.
Rotate		Ability to change the position of an object by rotating it around its own center.
Text Wrapping		Refers to the way text wraps around an object.
Position		Specify location on page where object will reside.
Border		The outline surrounding an object; it can be formatted using color, shapes, or width, or can be set as invisible.
Shadow Effects		Ability to add a shadow to an object.
Compress		Reduce the file size of an object.
Brightness		Increase or decrease brightness of an object.
Contrast		Increase or decrease difference between black and white colors of an object.
Recolor		Change object to give it an effect such as washed-out or grayscale.

Inserting WordArt into a Document

Microsoft WordArt creates decorative text for a document.

Microsoft WordArt is a Microsoft Office application that creates decorative text that can be used to add interest to a document. You can use WordArt in addition to clip art, or in place of clip art if the right image is not available. You can rotate text in any direction, add three-dimensional effects, display the text vertically, slant it, arch it, or even print it upside down.

WordArt is intuitively easy to use. In essence, you choose a style from the gallery (see Figure 3.20). Then you enter the specific text in the Edit WordArt Text dialog box, after which the results display (see Figure 3.21). The WordArt object can be moved and sized, just like any object. A WordArt Tools tab provides many formatting features that enable you to change alignment, add special effects, and change styles quickly. It is fun and easy, and you can create some truly unique documents.

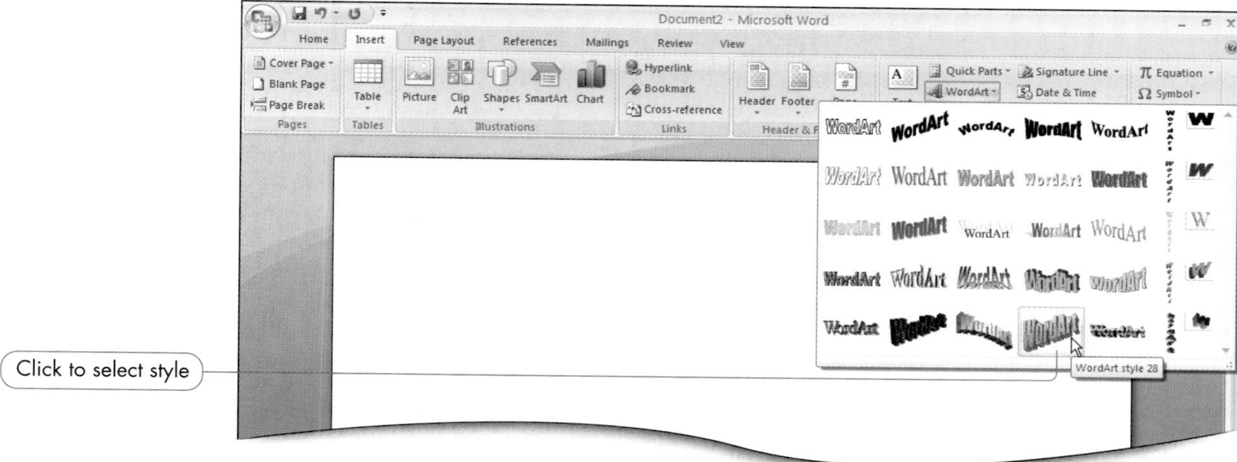

Figure 3.20 The WordArt Gallery

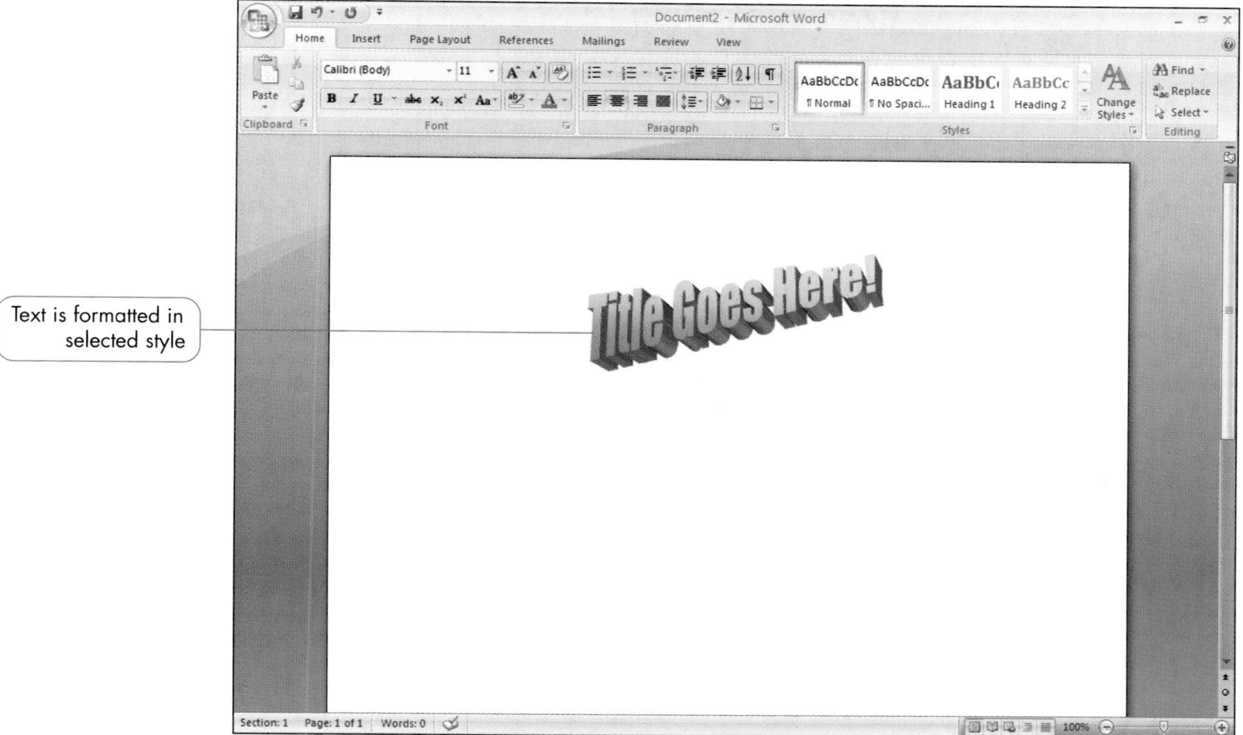

Figure 3.21 The Completed WordArt Object

Inserting Symbols into a Document

The Symbol command enables you to enter typographic symbols and/or foreign language characters into a document in place of ordinary typing—for example, ® rather than (R), © rather than (c), ½ and ¼, rather than 1/2 and 1/4, or é rather than e (as used in the word résumé). These special characters give a document a very professional look.

You may have already discovered that some of this formatting can be done automatically through the AutoCorrect feature that is built in to Word. If, for example, you type the letter "c" enclosed in parentheses, it will automatically be converted to the copyright symbol. You can use the Symbol command to insert other symbols, such as accented letters like the é in résumé or those in a foreign language (e.g., ¿Cómo está usted?).

The installation of Microsoft Office adds a variety of fonts onto your computer, each of which contains various symbols that can be inserted into a document. Selecting "normal text," however, as was done in Figure 3.22, provides access to the accented characters as well as other common symbols. Other fonts—especially the Wingdings, Webdings, and Symbol fonts—contain special symbols, including the Windows logo. The Wingdings, Webdings, and Symbol fonts are among the best-kept secrets in Microsoft Office. Each font contains a variety of symbols that are actually pictures. You can insert any of these symbols into a document as text, select the character and enlarge the point size, change the color, then copy the modified character to create a truly original document.

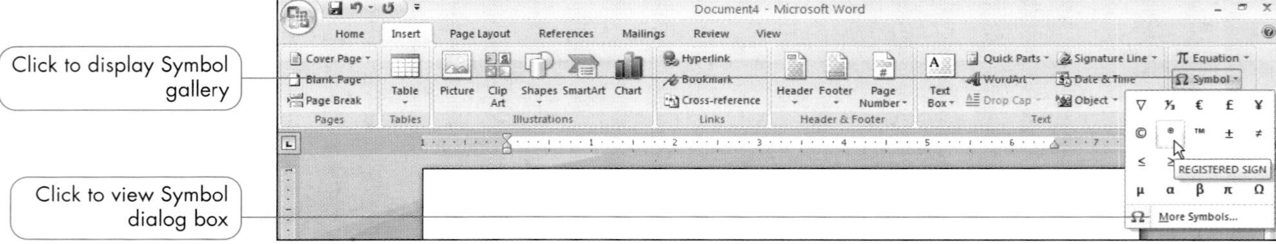

Figure 3.22 Insert Symbol Command

Hands-On Exercises

3 | Clip Art, WordArt, and Symbols

Skills covered: 1. Insert a Clip Art Object **2.** Move and Resize the Clip Art Object **3.** Create a WordArt Object **4.** Modify the WordArt Object **5.** Insert a Symbol

Step 1 Insert a Clip Art Object

Refer to Figure 3.23 as you complete Step 1.

a. Open the *chap3_ho3_ergonomics* document and save it as **chap3_ho3_ergonomics_solution**.

b. Click to move the insertion point to the beginning of the document, if necessary. Click the **Insert tab** and click **Clip Art** in the Illustrations group.

   The Clip Art task pane opens, as shown in Figure 3.23.

c. Type **computer** in the **Search for box** to search for any clip art image that is indexed with this keyword. Click the **Search in drop-down arrow** and click **Office Collections**, then click to deselect My Collections and Web Collections, if necessary. Click **Go**.

   The images display in the task pane.

d. Point to the first image to display a down arrow, and then click the arrow to display a menu.

e. Click **Insert** to insert the image into the document. Do not be concerned about its size or position at this time. Close the task pane.

f. Save the document.

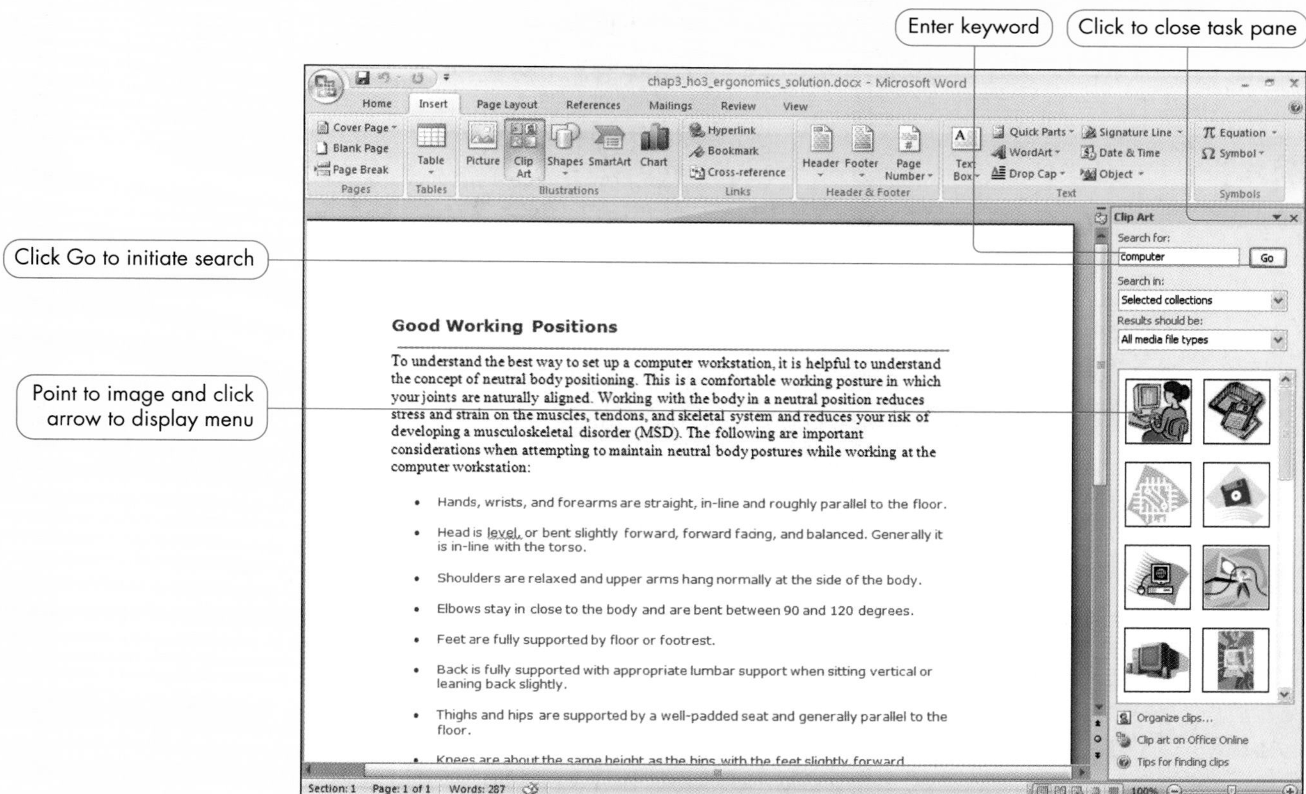

Figure 3.23 Clip Art Task Pane

Step 2
Move and Resize the Clip Art Object

Refer to Figure 3.24 as you complete Step 2.

a. Click once on the clip art object to select it. Click **Text Wrapping** in the Arrange group on the Picture Tools Format tab to display the text wrapping options, and then select **Square**, as shown in Figure 3.24.

You must change the layout in order to move and size the object.

b. Click **Position** in the Arrange group, and then click **More Layout Options.** Click the **Picture Position tab** in the Advanced Layout dialog box, if necessary, then click **Alignment** in the *Horizontal* section. Click the **Alignment drop-down arrow** and select **Right**. Deselect the **Allow overlap check box** in the *Options* section. Click **OK.**

c. Click **Crop** in the Size group, then hold your mouse over the sizing handles and notice how the pointer changes to angular shapes. Click the **bottom center handle** and drag it up. Drag the side handles inward to remove excess space surrounding the graphical object.

d. Click the Shape **Height box** in the Size group and type **2.77**.

Notice the width is changed automatically to retain the proportion.

e. Save the document.

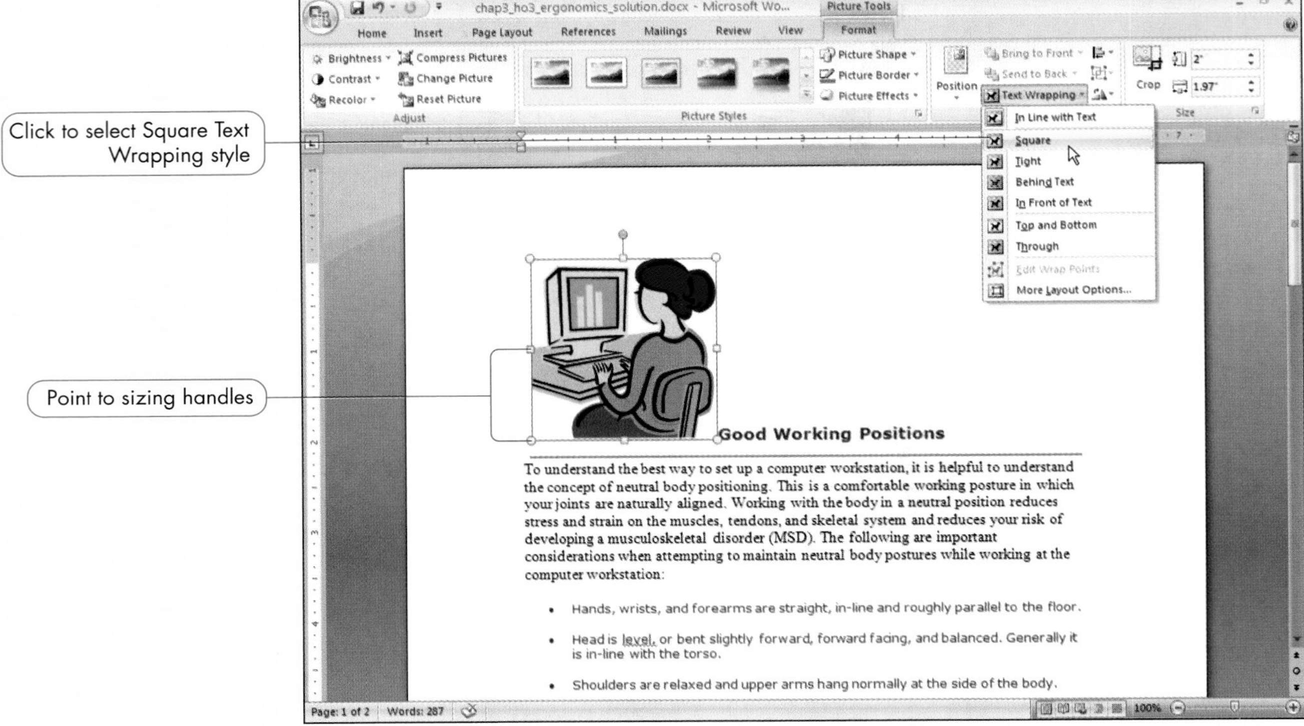

Figure 3.24 Formatting Clip Art

Step 3
Create a WordArt Object

Refer to Figure 3.25 as you complete Step 3.

a. Press **Ctrl+End** to move to the end of the document. Click the **Insert tab**, and then click **WordArt** in the Text group to display the WordArt gallery.

b. Click **WordArt Style 28** on the bottom row of the gallery.

The Edit WordArt Text dialog box displays, as shown in Figure 3.25.

c. Type **WWW.OSHA.GOV**, and then click OK.

The WordArt object appears in your document in the style you selected.

TROUBLESHOOTING: If the WordArt object displays on another page, you can correct it in the next steps.

d. Point to the WordArt object and right-click to display a shortcut menu. Select **Format WordArt** to display the Format WordArt dialog box.

e. Click the **Layout tab** and click **Square** in the *Wrapping style* section. Click **OK**.

It is important to select this wrapping option to facilitate placing the WordArt at the bottom of the first page.

f. Save the document.

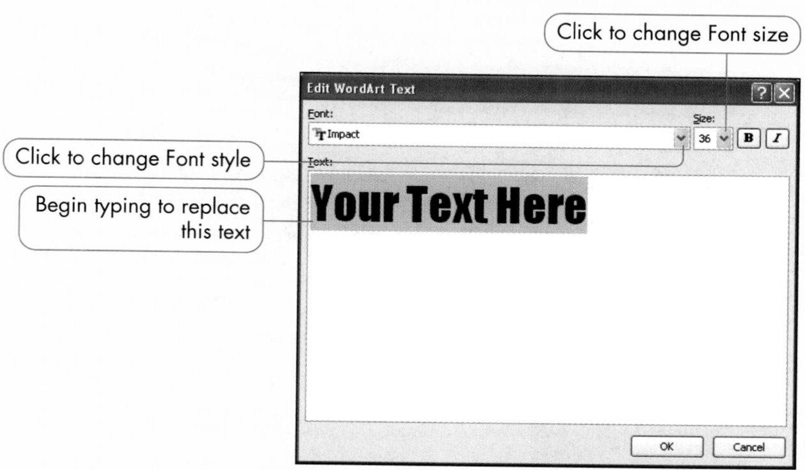

Figure 3.25 Edit WordArt Text Dialog Box

To save time and mouse clicks, you can double-click a WordArt object to quickly display the WordArt Tools Format tab.

Step 4
Modify the WordArt Object

Refer to Figure 3.26 as you complete Step 4.

a. Click and drag the WordArt object to move it to the bottom-right corner of the document, below the text.

The Format WordArt dialog box is not yet visible.

b. Point to the WordArt object, right-click to display a menu, and then click **Format WordArt** to display the Format WordArt dialog box.

Remember that many of the options in this dialog box also are displayed in the WordArt Tools Format tab.

c. Click the **Colors and Lines tab** and click the **Color drop-down arrow** in the *Fill* section to display the color palette. Click **Orange, Accent 6, Lighter 40%**, which is in the last column. Click **OK**.

This action enables you to customize the colors used in the WordArt graphic. In this case, you minimize much of the bright orange tint in the WordArt.

d. Click **3-D Effects** on the Format tab, then click **3-D Effects** to display the 3-D Effects gallery, as shown in Figure 3.26. Click **3-D Style 1** from the Parallel group.

TROUBLESHOOTING: If your monitor uses a high resolution, or if you have a wide monitor, the 3-D Effects gallery might display immediately after you click 3-D Effects the first time. In that case, you will not click 3-D Effects twice, as instructed in Step D.

e. Save the document.

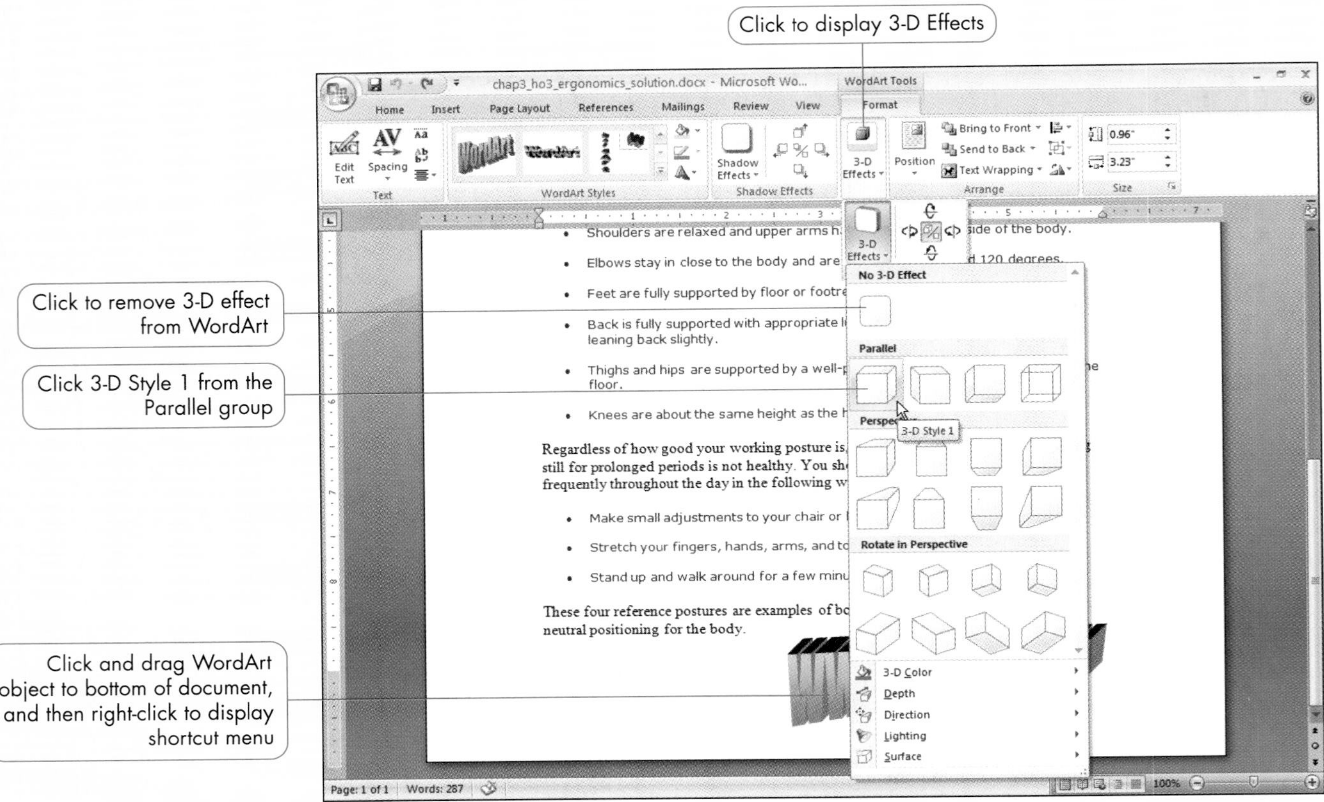

Figure 3.26 3-D Style Gallery for WordArt

Step 5 Insert a Symbol

Refer to Figure 3.27 as you complete Step 5.

a. Select the word *degrees* that displays at the end of the fourth bullet item in the document. Press **Backspace** to remove the word and the space that follows 120.

b. Click the **Insert tab**, click **Symbol** in the Symbols group, and click **More Symbols** to display the Symbol dialog box. Click the **Font** drop-down box, and then select **Verdana** as shown in Figure 3.27. If necessary, click the *Subset* drop-down box and select **Basic Latin**.

c. Click the **Degree symbol** (the last character in the seventh line), click **Insert**, and close the Symbol dialog box.

d. Save the *chap3_ho3_ergonomics_solution* document and close Word if you do not want to continue with the end-of-chapter exercise at this time.

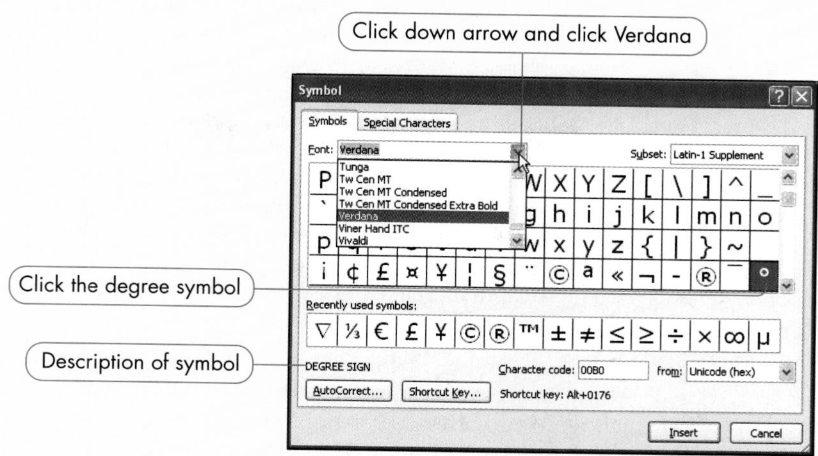

Figure 3.27 The Insert Symbol Command Symbol Dialog Box

Summary

1. **Insert a table.** Tables represent a very powerful capability within Word and are used to organize a variety of data in documents. The Table command is on the Insert tab, and tables are made up of rows and columns; the intersection of a row and column is called a cell. You can insert additional rows and columns if you need to add more data to a table, or you can delete a row or column if you no longer need data in the respective row or column. Individual cells can be merged to create a larger cell. Conversely, you can split a single cell into multiple cells. The rows in a table can be different heights and/or each column can be a different width.
2. **Format a table.** Each cell in a table is formatted independently and may contain text, numbers, and/or graphics. To enhance readability of table data, you can apply a predefined style, which Word provides, or use Borders and Shading tools to add color and enhance it. Furthermore, you can align table data—at the left margin, at the right margin, or centered between the margins. You also can change the text direction within a cell.
3. **Sort and apply formulas to table data.** You can sort the rows in a table to display the data in ascending or descending sequence, according to the values in one or more columns in the table. Sorting is accomplished by selecting the rows within the table that are to be sorted, then executing the Sort command in on the Layout tab. Calculations can be performed within a table using the Formula command in that same tab.
4. **Convert text to a table.** If you have a list of tabulated items that would be easier to manipulate in a table, you can use the Convert Text to Table command. The command also works in reverse, enabling you to remove data from a table and format it as tabulated text.
5. **Insert clip art and images into a document.** You often add graphics to enhance a document. When you click the Clip Art command, Office displays a task pane where you enter a keyword to describe the clip you are looking for. The search is made possible by the Microsoft Clip Organizer, which organizes the media files available to you into collections, then enables you to limit the search to specific media types and/or specific collections. Resources (such as clip art or photographs) can be downloaded from the Web for inclusion in a Word document. Although clip art is often acceptable for educational or nonprofit use, it may not be permitted in some advertising situations. You should always assume a graphic is copyrighted unless noted otherwise.
6. **Format a graphic element.** After you insert the clip art object, you can use a variety of tools to refine the object to fit in your document, such as changing height and width, cropping, rotating, or aligning.
7. **Insert WordArt into a document.** Microsoft WordArt is an application within Microsoft Office that creates decorative text that can be used to add interest to a document. WordArt can be used in addition to clip art or in place of clip art if the right image is not available. You can rotate text in any direction, add three-dimensional effects, display the text vertically down the page, or print it upside down.
8. **Insert symbols into a document.** The Insert Symbol command provides access to special characters, making it easy to place typographic characters into a document. The symbols can be taken from any font and can be displayed in any point size.

Key Terms

Multiple Choice

1. You have created a table containing numerical values and have entered the SUM(ABOVE) function at the bottom of a column. You then delete one of the rows included in the sum. Which of the following is true?
   (a) The row cannot be deleted because it contains a cell that is included in the sum function.
   (b) The sum is updated automatically.
   (c) The sum cannot be updated.
   (d) The sum will be updated provided you right-click the cell and click the Update Field command.

2. Which process below is the best option to change the size of a selected object so that the height and width change in proportion to one another?
   (a) Enter the Height and allow Word to establish the Width.
   (b) Click and drag the sizing handle on the top border, then click and drag the sizing handle on the left side.
   (c) Click and drag the sizing handle on the bottom border, then click and drag the sizing handle on the right side.
   (d) Click only the sizing handle in the middle of the left side.

3. How do you search for clip art using the Clip Organizer?
   (a) By entering a keyword that describes the image you want.
   (b) By selecting the photo album option.
   (c) By clicking the Clip Organizer command on the Insert tab.
   (d) There is no such thing as a Clip Organizer.

4. What guideline should you remember when inserting graphics into a document?
   (a) It is distasteful to insert more than two graphics into a document.
   (b) It is not necessary to consider copyright notices if the document is for personal use.
   (c) WordArt should always be center aligned on a page.
   (d) Graphic elements should enhance a document, not overpower it.

5. Which of the following commands in the Picture Tools Format tab would you use to remove portions of a graphic that you do not wish to see in your document?
   (a) Height
   (b) Position
   (c) Crop
   (d) Reset Picture

6. Which of the following is not an example of how to use the Symbols feature in a document?
   (a) You can type (c) to insert the copyright symbol.
   (b) You can insert WordArt from the Symbol dialog box.
   (c) You can insert the Windows logo from the Symbol dialog box.
   (d) You can insert special characters from the Symbol dialog box.

7. Which of the following is true regarding objects and their associated tabs?
   (a) Clicking a WordArt object displays the WordArt Tools tab.
   (b) Right-clicking on a Picture displays the Picture Tools tab.
   (c) You can only display a tab by clicking the tab across the top of the screen.
   (d) Neither (a) nor (b).

8. Which wrap style allows text to wrap around the graphic frame that surrounds the image?
   (a) Top and Bottom
   (b) Tight
   (c) Behind Text
   (d) Square

9. What provides legal protection to the author for a written or artistic work?
   (a) Copyright
   (b) Public domain
   (c) Fair use
   (d) Footnote

Multiple Choice Continued...

10. Microsoft WordArt cannot be used to:

(a) Arch text, or print it upside down
(b) Rotate text, or add three-dimensional effects
(c) Display text vertically down a page
(d) Insert a copyright symbol

11. What happens when you press Tab from within the last cell of a table?

(a) A Tab character is inserted just as it would be for ordinary text.
(b) Word inserts a new row below the current row.
(c) Word inserts a new column to the right of the current column.
(d) The insertion point appears in the paragraph below the table.

12. What happens when you type more than one line of text into a cell?

(a) The cell gets wider to accommodate the extra text.
(b) The row gets taller as word wrapping occurs to display the additional text.
(c) The other lines are hidden by default.
(d) A new column is inserted automatically.

13. Assume you created a table with the names of the months in the first column. Each row lists data for that particular month. The insertion point is in the first cell on the third row—this row lists goals for April. You realize that you left out the goals for March. What should you do?

(a) Display the Insert tab and click the Table command.
(b) Display the Table Tools Design tab and click the Insert Cell command.
(c) Display the Table Tools Layout tab and click the Insert Left command.
(d) Display the Table Tools Layout tab and click the Insert Above command.

14. You have a list of people who were sent an invitation to a wedding. You are responsible for monitoring their responses to the invitation, whether they will attend or not, and to determine the grand total of those attending. Using skills learned in this chapter what would be a good way to track this information?

(a) Use pen and paper to mark through names of those who decline the invitation and put stars by those who accept.
(b) Convert the list of names to a table; add columns that allow you to mark their response, including the number who will attend, and use a formula to add up the numbers when all responses are received.
(c) Insert wedding clip art in the document so you will know the purpose of the document.
(d) Insert a two-column table beside the names and mark the responses as declined or attending.

15. If cell A1 contains the value 2 and A2 contains the value 4, what value will be displayed if cell A3 contains the formula =PRODUCT(ABOVE)?

(a) 8
(b) 2
(c) 6
(d) This is not a valid formula.

16. What option would you use if you were given a lengthy list of items that are separated by tabs and that would be easier to format in a table?

(a) Insert Table
(b) Convert Table to Text
(c) Convert Text to Table
(d) Insert Text Box

17. Which option should you use to add color to improve the attractiveness and readability of a table?

(a) Text wrapping
(b) Sort
(c) Add column to right
(d) Borders and shading

Practice Exercises

1 The Library Station

While working as a volunteer at the local library, you are asked to create a flyer to advertise the upcoming annual book sale, as shown in Figure 3.28. You are required to use a combination of tables, clip art, WordArt, and symbols to create an informative and attractive flyer. If you are unable to find the exact same graphics, find something as similar as possible; you need not match our flyer exactly.

a. Open a new document and save it as **chap3_pe1_flyer_solution**.
b. Click the **Page Layout tab** and click **Margins** in the Page Setup group. Click **Normal**, if necessary, to set all four margins to 1″.
c. Click the **Insert tab** and click **Table** in the Tables group to insert a table. Click only one cell to insert a **1x1** table.
d. Click the **Home tab**, and then click the **Font Dialog Box Launcher**. Select **Comic Sans MS** in the **Font list**, select **Bold** in the **Font style list**, and select **36** in the **Size list**. Click the **Font color drop-down arrow** and select **Red, Accent 2, Darker 25%** (a shade of red). Click **OK** to close the Font dialog box.
e. Type **Annual Book Sale** in the table. Click **Center** in the Paragraph group to center the text within the table cell.
f. Click the **Design tab**, click the **Borders arrow**, and click **Borders and Shading**. Select **None** in the *Setting* section to remove all current borders around the table. Click the **Color drop-down arrow** and select **Red, Accent 2, Darker 50%** (at the bottom of the red column). Then click the **Width drop-down arrow** and select **3 pt**.
g. Click once on the top of the diagram in the *Preview* section to insert a top border, and then click once on the bottom of the diagram to insert a bottom border. If necessary, click the **Apply to drop-down arrow**, and select **Table**, and click **OK**.
h. Click below the table to move the insertion point. Click the **Home tab**, and then click the **Font Size arrow** and select **28**. Type the date of the sale, **March 1**, and click **Align Right** in the Paragraph group to move the date to the right side of the flyer.
i. Press **Enter** two times to move the insertion point down the page, click the **Insert tab,** and click **WordArt** in the Text group. Click **WordArt style 28** on the bottom row. In the Edit WordArt Text dialog box, type **The Library Station** and click **OK**.
j. The WordArt object needs to be resized and relocated to have a bigger impact on our flyer. Click **Position** in the Arrange group of the Format tab and click **Position in Middle Center with Tight Text Wrapping**.
k. Click the **Height box** and type **2** to increase the height of the object. Click the **Width box** and type **6** to elongate the object. Click the uppermost handle on the top of the object and notice the insertion point changes to a curved arrow. Click this handle and hold down while rotating the object to the left so that it appears similar to Figure 3.28.
l. Click anywhere to deselect the WordArt object. Click the **Insert** tab, and then click **Clip Art**. When the Clip Art task pane displays, type **book** in the **Search for** box, click the **Search in drop-down arrow**, and click **Office Collections**. Deselect My Collections and Web Collections, if necessary, and click **Go**. Click one time on the first object to insert it in your document, then close the Clip Art task pane.
m. Click the clip art object to display the Format tab, if necessary. Click **Text Wrapping** in the Arrange group, and then select **Square**. Now you can move the object anywhere in your document. Move it to the left side above the WordArt object, as it appears in Figure 3.28.
n. Double-click anywhere in the bottom of your document to reposition the insertion point. Click the **Insert tab**, and then click **Table**. Drag your mouse over the cells until **2x3 Table** displays (a 2 column, 3 row table), and click to insert it in the document.
o. Click the table selector in the upper-left corner to select the whole table and click the **Layout** tab. Click **Properties** in the Table group to display the Table Properties dialog box. Click the **Table tab**, and then click the **Preferred width check box**. Type **8** in the **Preferred width box** and click **OK**.
p. Drag your mouse across the two cells in the first row to select it, then right-click and select **Merge Cells**. Type **Hourly Drawings for FREE Books!** in the first row.
q. Click the **Design tab**, and then click **More** in the **Table Styles** group. Scroll to view the **B2 Dark List Accent 2** style. Click once to apply the style to your table.

...continued on Next Page

r. Right-click the table, click **Table Properties**, click **Center** alignment, and click **OK**.
s. Select the two empty cells in the first (left) column of the table, right-click, and click **Merge Cells**. In this column enter the phrase **Discounts of 50% or More**. Select the two empty cells in the right column of the table, right-click, and select **Merge Cells**. In this column, type the phrase **Only at our North Glenstone Location**.
t. Click anywhere in the table, if necessary, and click the **Layout tab**. Click **Cell Margins**, click the **Allow spacing between cells check box**, then type **.1** as the spacing amount. Click **OK** and notice the improvement.
u. Select only the text in the table, but do not click the table selector; on the Mini toolbar, click **Center**.
v. Make minor adjustments to each element as necessary so your flyer looks attractive and spacing is retained. Save and close the document.

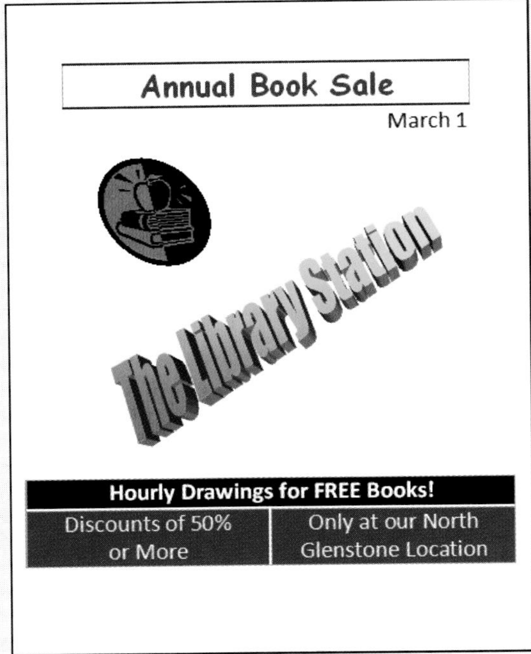

Figure 3.28 The Book Sale Flyer

2 Lost Pet

In an unfortunate mishap, your 3-year-old dog escaped from your fenced yard and is now missing. After calling local shelters and pet stores, you decide to create a flyer to post around the neighborhood and shops so that people will know whom to contact if they see her. Figure 3.29 displays a flyer that is intended to give information about your dog, Dakota, and also provide a tag with contact information that someone can pull from the flyer and take with him or her. The tag displays your name and phone number. Use a table as the basis of this document; you can use the picture of our pet or any other picture you like.

a. Open a new document and save it as **chap3_pe2_lostpet_solution**.
b. Click the **Insert tab** and click **Table** in the Tables group. Drag to select cells to create a table with 10 columns and 4 rows (**10x4 Table**), then click on the last cell to insert the table.
c. Click left of the first cell in the first row to select the entire row. Right-click the selected row and select **Merge Cells** to merge all the cells in the first row. Repeat the step to merge the cells in rows 2, and then the cells in row 3.
d. Click in the first row and enter the text **Lost Pet**. Select the text, and then on the Mini toolbar click the **Font size arrow** and select **26**. The row height will increase automatically to accommodate the larger text. On the Mini toolbar, click **Center** to center the text in the cell.
e. Select the cell in the second row. Click the **Design tab** and click **Shading** in the Table Styles group. Click **Black, Text 1** (the black swatch in the first row), which will place a black background in the cell.

...continued on Next Page

f. Click **Insert tab** and click **Picture** in the Illustrations group. Locate pictures of your pet or pets; we have provided a picture of Dakota, dakota.jpg, in the Exploring Word folder. When you locate the file, double-click to insert the picture. The row height will expand automatically to accommodate the picture. Click once to select the picture, if necessary, and then press **Ctrl+E** to center the picture.

g. Click in the third row and enter text to describe your pet or pets. Feel free to duplicate the information we have provided in Figure 3.29. Select the text, then on the Mini toolbar, click the **Font size arrow**, select **14**, and click **Center**.

h. Type your name and phone number in the first cell of the fourth row. Display the **Layout tab**, and then click **Text Direction** one time to rotate the text (see Figure 3.29). Click **Align Top Center** to align the text vertically on the top of the cell. Right-click the cell and click **Copy**. Select the empty cells on that row, right-click, and click **Paste Cells** to populate the remaining cells with the owner information.

i. Select the entire row, right-click, and select **Borders and Shading**. Click the **Borders** tab, if necessary, and click a dashed line in the **Style list**. Click **OK**.

j. Click the **Height** box in the Cell Size group and increase the size to at least **1.5"**. The contact information now displays correctly.

k. Click **Zoom** in the task bar, click **Whole page**, and click **OK**.

l. Save and close the document.

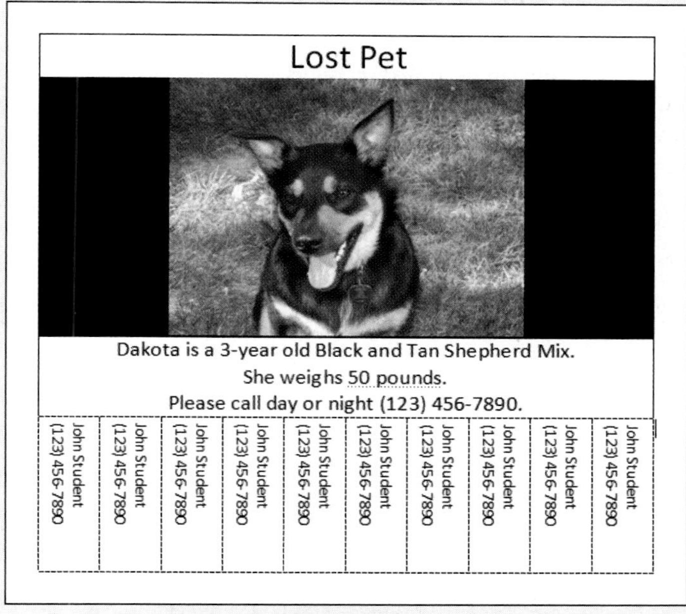

Figure 3.29 The Lost Pet Flyer

3 The Study Schedule

Your midterm grades reveal the need to set up a solid study schedule. The best way to plan your study time is to create a daily schedule, mark the times you are in class or at work, then find the needed study time. Your work in this chapter provided information you can use to create a document that lists days and times and allows you to establish your new study schedule. You can even add colorful borders and shading, as well as graphics, to create a document you can proudly display.

a. Open a new blank document and save it as **chap3_pe3_schedule_solution**.

b. Click the **Page Layout tab**. Click **Margins** in the Page Setup group, and then click **Custom Margins** to display the Page Layout dialog box. Type **.75** in the **Top** and **Bottom** boxes, then type **.5** in the **Left** and **Right** boxes. Click **Landscape** in the *Orientation* section and click **OK**.

...continued on Next Page

c. Click the **Insert tab** and click **Table**. Click **Insert Table** to display the Insert Table dialog box. Type **8** in the **Number of columns** box and type **12** in the **Number of rows** box. Click **OK**.

d. Click left of the first cell in the first row to select the entire first row, then **right-click** and select **Merge Cells**. Click in the merged cell, then type **Weekly Class and Study Schedule**. Select the text you typed. On the Mini toolbar, click the **Font arrow** and select **Arial**, click the **Font size arrow** and select **24**, and click **Bold** and **Center**.

e. Click left of the first cell in the last row to select the entire row, then right-click and select **Merge Cells**. Click in the merged cell, type **Notes:**, then press **Enter** five times. The height of the cell increases to accommodate the blank lines.

f. Select the text you typed. On the Mini toolbar, click the **Font arrow** and select **Arial**, click the **Font size arrow** and select **12**, and click **Bold**.

g. Click the second cell in the second row. Type **Monday**. Press **Tab** (or right arrow key) to move to the next cell. Type **Tuesday**. Continue until the days of the week have been entered. Select the entire row. On the Mini toolbar, click the **Font arrow** and select **Arial**, click the **Font size arrow** and select **10**, and then click **Bold** and **Center**.

h. Click the first cell in the third row. Type **8:00 a.m.** Press the **down arrow key** to move to the first cell in the fourth row. Type **9:00 a.m.** Continue to enter the hourly periods up to **4:00 p.m.**

i. Select the cells containing the hours of the day, and then right-click and select **Table Properties**. Click the **Row tab**, then click the **Specify height check box**. Click the spin button until the height is **0.5"**. Click the **Row height is drop-down arrow** and select **Exactly**.

j. Click the **Cell tab** in the Table Properties dialog box and click **Center** in the *Vertical alignment* section. Click **OK** to accept the settings and close the dialog box.

k. Select the first row, containing the title of your table. Click the **Design tab** and click **Shading**. Click **Orange, Accent 6**, the orange color at the end of the first row.

l. Click and drag to select the first four cells under Sunday, then right-click and select **Merge Cells**. Type **Reserved for services** in the new large cell. Select this text, then click the **Layout tab**. Click **Text Direction** one time to rotate the text, and then click **Align Center** to display the text, as shown in Figure 3.30.

m. Click anywhere in the cell in the last row of the table. Click the **Insert tab** and click **Clip Art** to display the task pane. Type **books** in the **Search for** box, and then click **Go** or press **Enter**. Click the first clip art object to insert it in your table.

n. Click the newly inserted clip art to display the Format tab, if necessary, and click **Text Wrapping** and select **Square**. Click the sizing handle on the upper-right corner, hold down **Shift**, and drag the sizing handle to reduce the size of the object and maintain proportions. Move the object to the lower-right corner of the last row and close the Clip Art task pane.

o. Save and close the document.

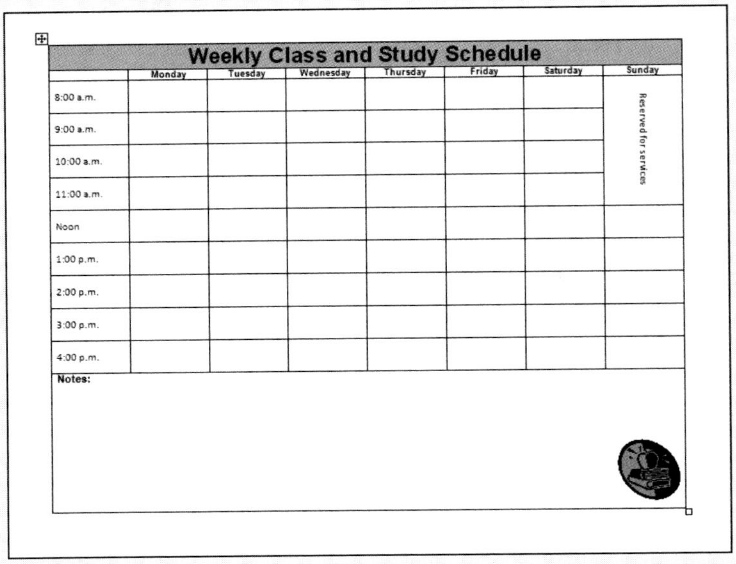

Weekly Class and Study Schedule							
	Monday	**Tuesday**	**Wednesday**	**Thursday**	**Friday**	**Saturday**	**Sunday**
8:00 a.m.							Reserved for services
9:00 a.m.							
10:00 a.m.							
11:00 a.m.							
Noon							
1:00 p.m.							
2:00 p.m.							
3:00 p.m.							
4:00 p.m.							
Notes:							

Figure 3.30 The Completed Study Schedule

...continued on Next Page

4 The Invoice

You work as a bank consultant for a software firm and must bill for services each month. Traditionally, you type the amount of your invoice in the document, but after a discussion with a coworker you discover how to use table formulas and begin to use them to calculate your total fees on the invoice. In this exercise, you develop a professional-looking invoice and use formulas to calculate totals within the table.

a. Open a blank document and save it as **chap3_pe4_invoice_solution**.

b. Click the **Page Layout tab**, click **Margins**, and click **Office 2003 Default**, which sets 1.25″ left and right margins. Click the **Insert tab** and click **Table**. Drag to select eight rows and two columns (**2x8 Table**).

c. Click left of the first cell in the first row to select the entire first row, right-click, and select **Merge Cells**. Click in the merged cell, and then type **Invoice**. Select the text you typed, click the **Home tab**, and click **Heading 1** from the Styles gallery. Click **Center** in the Paragraph group to complete the first row of the table.

d. Select the second and third cells in the first column, and then click the **Layout tab**. Click **Merge Cells**, click the **Height box** in the Cell Size group, and type **1** to increase the size of the cell. In this cell, enter the following text:

TO:
Jack Hendrix Technologies
4999 Garland Street
Fayetteville, AR 72703

e. Select the second and third cells in the right column and click **Merge Cells**. They inherit the size from the cell on their left. Click **Align Top Right** in the Alignment group and type the following text in the cell:

FROM:
John Q. Student
9444 Elton Lane
Tulsa, OK 74129

f. Select the last five cells in the first column, then click the **Width box** in the Cell Size group and type **5**. The cells on the right might extend beyond the borders of the page, but you will fix that next. Select the five cells in the second column, then click the **Width box** and type **1.15**. Now the cells should align with the cells in the first two rows.

g. Type the following text in the third through sixth cells of the two columns, as shown in Figure 3.31:

Description	**Amount**
Consulting Fee for June	**$5640.00**
Travel Expenses	**500.00**
Supplies	**200.00**

h. In the first column of the last row, type **TOTAL**. Click in the second column in the last row and click **Formula** on the Layout tab. Click **OK** to accept the formula, =SUM(ABOVE), which is correct for our calculation. The total is $6340.00.

i. Your invoice is correct, but formatting changes are needed to give it a more professional appearance. Select the third row, which contains the Description and Amount titles, and hold down **Ctrl**, and select the last row of the table. Click the **Design tab**

...continued on Next Page

and click **Shading**. Click **White, Background 1, Darker 15%** from the first column. Do not deselect the rows.

j. While the rows are selected, click the **Home tab** and click **Heading 3** from the Styles gallery. You may need to click the **More button** in the Styles group, select **Apply Styles** from the gallery, type **Heading 3** in the Apply Styles dialog box, and click **Apply**. Click anywhere to deselect the rows and view the format changes.

k. Select the last four cells in the second column, click the **Layout tab**, and click **Align Center Right** on the tab. The result gives the effect of decimal alignment. However, the numbers are not decimal aligned, so if you display an additional decimal place, it will result in misaligned numbers.

l. Select the fourth, fifth, and sixth rows, which contain the items you bill for, then click **Sort** in the Data group. Click **OK**. Deselect the rows to view the newly sorted list.

m. You determine the travel expenses were incorrect; change the amount to **550.00**. Right-click the cell that contains the formula and select **Update Field** to recalculate the total. The new total $6390.00 displays.

n. Save and close the document.

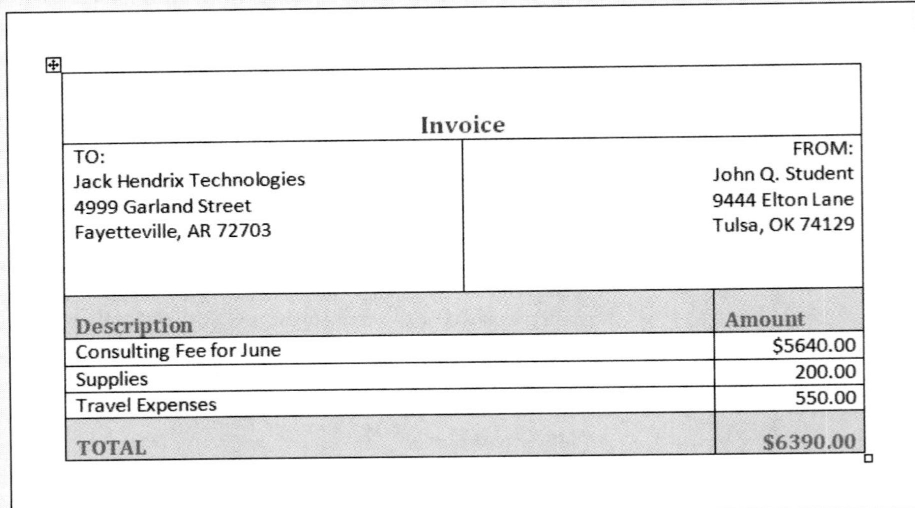

Invoice	
TO: Jack Hendrix Technologies 4999 Garland Street Fayetteville, AR 72703	FROM: John Q. Student 9444 Elton Lane Tulsa, OK 74129
Description	**Amount**
Consulting Fee for June	$5640.00
Supplies	200.00
Travel Expenses	550.00
TOTAL	**$6390.00**

Figure 3.31 The Completed Invoice

Mid-Level Exercises

1 The Résumé

Microsoft Word 2007 includes a Résumé template, but you can achieve an equally good result through the tables feature. In this exercise you create a resume for yourself using the tools learned in this chapter. Follow the instructions below to create a résumé similar to the document in Figure 3.32. Remember that a resume often serves as the first impression between you and a potential employer, so you must include all the information expected by an employer and display it in a manner that is easy to read and follow.

a. Open a new blank document and save it as **chap3_mid1_resume_solution**. Set margins at 1″ on the top and bottom, and 1.25″ on the left and right. Insert a 2-column, 10-row table into your document. Additional rows can be added as needed. Conversely, rows can be deleted at a later time if they are not needed.

b. Merge the two cells in the first row. Type your name in the cell, and then center it. Change the font to Times New Roman, 24 pt, and bold, as shown in Figure 3.32.

c. Enter your addresses in the second row. Type your campus address, telephone number, and e-mail address in the cell on the left and your permanent address and telephone number in the cell on the right. Format the text in Times New Roman, 12 pt. Left align the text in the cell on the left and right align the text in the cell on the right.

d. Enter the categories in the left cell of each row, being sure to include the following categories: **Objective**, **Professional Accomplishments**, **Education**, **Honors**, and **References**. Format the text in Times New Roman, 12 pt, boldface and right align the text in these cells. (Not all of these categories are visible in Figure 3.32.)

e. Enter the associated information in the right cell of each row. Be sure to include all information that would interest a prospective employer. Format the text in Times New Roman, 12 pt. Left align the text in these cells, using boldface and italics where appropriate.

f. Select rows three through ten in the first column, then change the width of the cells to 1.5″. Select the same rows in the second column and increase the width of the cells until they align with the first two rows.

g. Select the entire table and remove the borders surrounding the individual cells. (Figure 3.32 displays gridlines, which—unlike borders—do not appear in the printed document.) For the first row only, set a bottom line border.

h. Save and close the document.

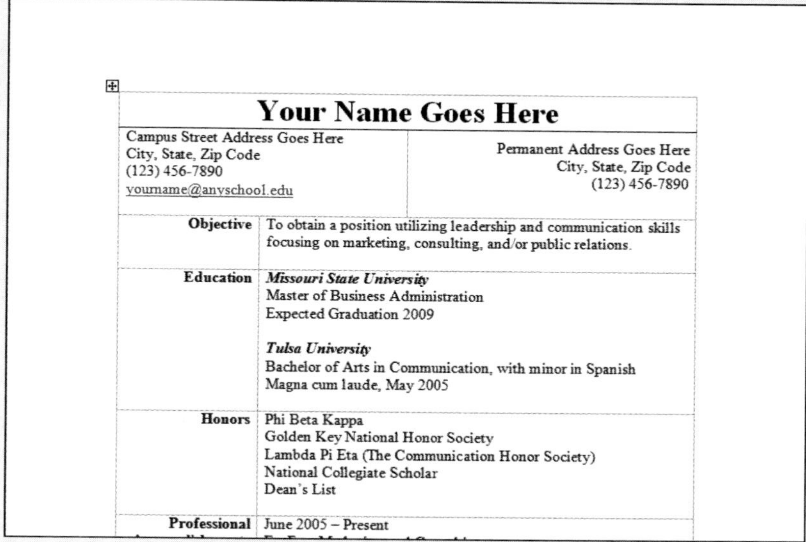

Figure 3.32 The Completed Résumé

...continued on Next Page

2 The Employment Application

You work as an intern for the Human Resources department of a company that offers home health consulting services. Your manager mentions the need for a new employment application form and asks you to create an application form similar to the document in Figure 3.33. Use the skills you recently acquired about the tables feature in Word to follow our design and create the application form. Remember that the Tables and Borders toolbar can be used in place of the Table menu to execute various commands during the exercise. Proceed as follows:

a. Open a blank document and save it as **chap3_mid2_application_solution.**

b. Create a 9 × 3 (nine rows and three columns) table to match our design. Select the entire table after it is created initially. Change the before paragraph spacing to 6 pt. The result will drop the text in each cell half a line from the top border of the cell, and also determine the spacing between paragraphs within a cell.

c. Merge the cells in the first row to create the title for the application. Enter the text for the first line, press **Shift+Enter** to create a line break instead of a paragraph break (to minimize the spacing between lines), then enter the text on the second line. Center the text. Select the first cell, and then shade the cell with the color **Black, Text 1** to create white letters on a dark background. Increase the font size of the title to 22 pt.

d. Enter the text in the next several cells, as shown in Figure 3.33. Select cells individually and adjust the width to create the offsetting form fields.

e. Move down in the table until you can select the cell for the highest degree attained. Enter the indicated text, click and drag to select all four degrees, and create a custom bulleted list using the check box character in the Wingdings font.

f. Merge the cells in row 7, then enter the text that asks the applicant to describe the skills that qualify him or her for the position. Merge the cells in row 8 (these cells are not visible in Figure 3.33) to create a single cell for employment references.

g. Reduce the zoom setting to view the entire document. Change the row heights as necessary so that the completed application fills the entire page.

h. Complete the finished application as though you were applying for a job. Replace the check box next to the highest degree earned (remove the bullet) with the letter X.

i. Save and close the document.

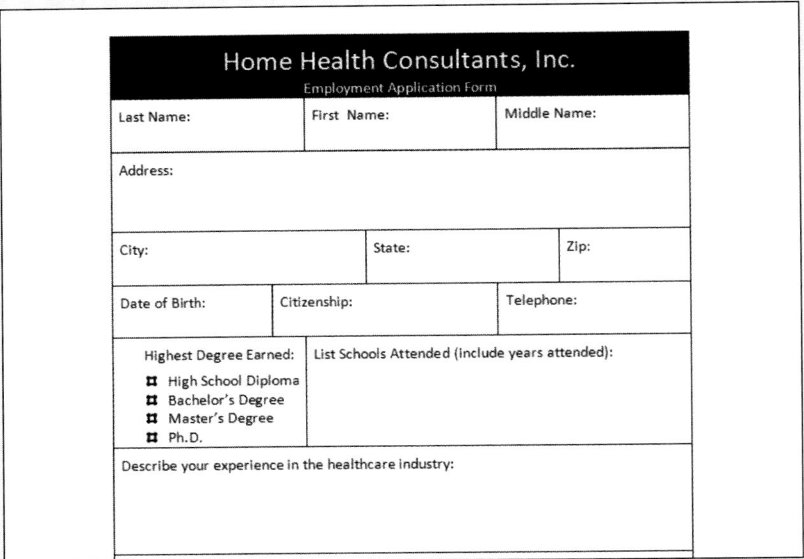

Figure 3.33 The Employment Application

...continued on Next Page

3 Create Company Stationery

You are the marketing manager for a private pilot flight school. Periodically, you perform a review of marketing tools used in the company, then make a list of items that must be changed. In your last review, you noticed the company letterhead is quite dated and should be changed. Since the change is being made, all company stationery will be replaced with the new logo. Figure 3.34 displays an envelope and matching letterhead designed by an intern. Replicate that design as closely as possible, creating both the letterhead and matching envelope.

a. Begin with the stationery. Open a blank document and save it as **chap3_mid3_stationery_solution.**
b. Click the **Narrow** margin setting, which sets 1/2″ margins all around. Enter the company name, address, telephone, and e-mail information at the top of the page. Use a larger font and distinguishing color for your name, then center all of the text at the top of the page.
c. After you type your information, convert the text into a table. Split the table into three columns so you can add a logo to each side of your information.
d. Use the Clip Organizer to locate the clip art image shown in Figure 3.34. (If you cannot find the same clip art image, use one with the same theme.) Use that image as a logo by inserting it in the first column of the table. Click the Square text wrap style. Change the image height to **1″**. Crop the image to decrease width to approximately **1.1″**. Select the clip art, click Copy, then Paste the image in the third column of the table on the right side of the page.
e. Center align the information in each cell both horizontally and vertically. Use the Borders command to add a 3-pt wide horizontal line below the text that contains your address information. Do not extend the border below the clip art images.
f. Insert a new page section break at the beginning of the document. (The result creates a new page as well as a new section. The latter enables you to change the page orientation within a document.)
g. Click on the newly inserted page and select landscape orientation. Change the **Size** to **Envelope #10** (the standard business envelope).
h. Copy the clip art and address information from the letterhead to the envelope. Make adjustments as necessary to align your address beside the logo.
i. Save and close the document.

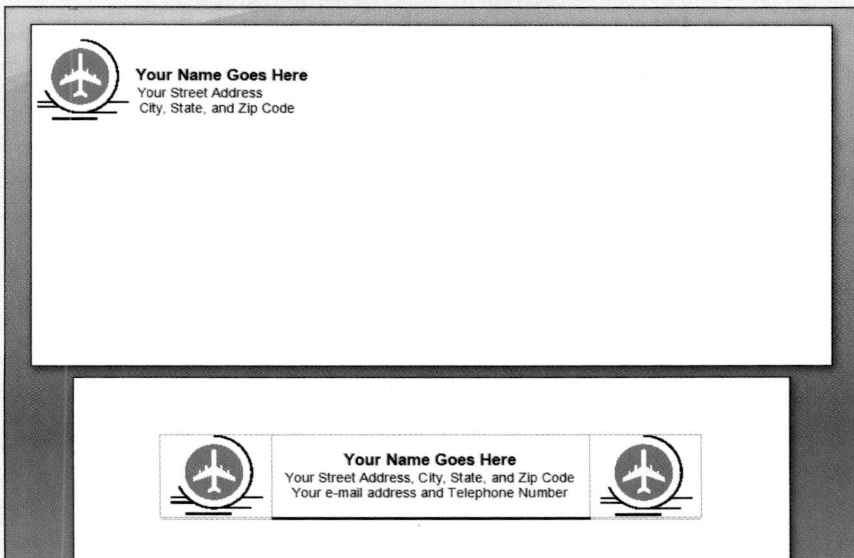

Figure 3.34 Custom Stationery

...continued on Next Page

4 July Fireworks Poster

You work as an intern for the mayor's office in City Hall. The office sponsors a yearly fireworks display near the local airport and posts informational flyers in local businesses prior to the event. The community relations director has asked for your help to create the flyers they will distribute because of your experience using Microsoft Word 2007. You are responsible for creating an exciting and attractive flyer for this year's event using the guidelines below.

a. Open a new blank document and save it as **chap3_mid4_fireworks_solution**.
b. Set the following margins: 0.6″ top, 0.3″ bottom, 0.5″ left, and 0.5″ right. If a warning appears mentioning that the margins are outside the boundary, choose the option to fix the problem.
c. Create a WordArt object with these settings: Click WordArt style 11 in the WordArt gallery. Type **Independence Day Fireworks!** in the WordArt box. Add the **3-D Style 11** effect. Change the Shape Fill, located in the WordArt Styles group of the Format tab, to use the **Linear Down** gradient color scheme. Change the height to **1.5″** and the width to **7″**, then Format the object to use **Square Text Wrapping**, and center it horizontally on the page.
d. Use the Clip Art task pane and search for **fireworks** in the Web Collections. Find and insert the image, as shown in Figure 3.35. Adjust the height to **3″**, then crop the image to trim white space from the top and bottom of the picture. Adjust the brightness to **+20%**. Apply square text wrapping, and then move the object to the right side of the flyer, as shown in Figure 3.35.
e. Place the insertion point on the left side of the document and type **City of Stockton** on the left side of the Clip art object. Format the text in Comic Sans MS, 26-pt size, and change the font color to red.
f. Insert a table to list the events shown in Figure 3.35. Align text on the left and right as displayed. In addition to increasing Cell Margins, insert an extra column to create the gap between columns. Apply a Dark Red Double-line outside border, then left-align the table.
g. Below the table insert the text **Best Small-Town Celebration in the State**, as shown in Figure 3.35. Format the text using Comic Sans MS 18-pt, change the font color to red, and center the text on the page.
h. Save and close the document.

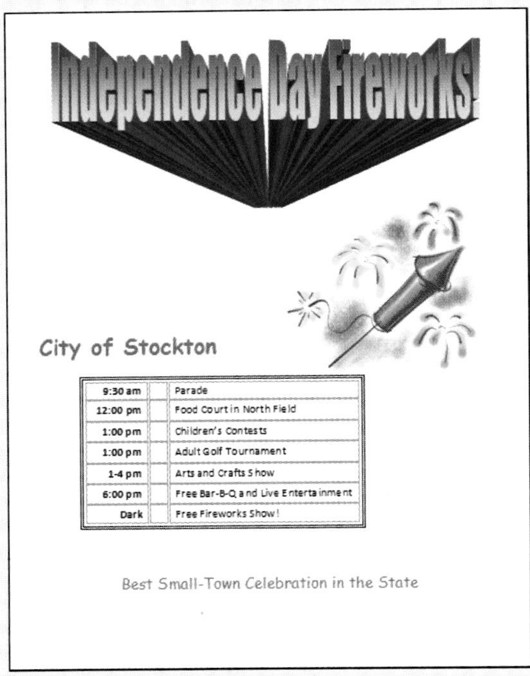

Figure 3.35 Fireworks Announcement Flyer

Capstone Exercise

You are the executive assistant to a general contractor, and your duties include listing the materials that will be used on a home remodeling project. Due to the large number of people who work on the project, from plumbers to electricians to carpenters, it is necessary to keep detailed records of the materials and supplies to use during the remodel. After the first job, you decide to provide the crew with a table of materials that includes pictures. This also might be helpful for any crewmember who does not speak English.

Create the Table

Fortunately, a list of materials has been provided, which will eliminate the need for you to type a list of supplies. However, the preexisting list is weak. You decide to modify the document to increase organization and clarity by putting the list in table format, creating a header row and labels, and also adding visual enhancements with WordArt.

a. Open the *chap3_cap_construction* document and save it as **chap3_cap_construction_solution**. You wisely decide to convert this list to a three-column table so you can organize the list of materials and add more data.

b. Insert two rows at the top to use for a heading and item descriptions.
   - Create a title row on the table by merging cells in the first row.
   - Use WordArt to create a title using the phrase **Supply List**.
   - Use the second row as a header for the columns.
   - Enter an appropriate label for each column.

Format the Table

Your table is functional now, but it would look even better with additional improvements. Enhance the table of materials by aligning the data in columns, sorting the data, and using formulas to calculate costs. Since the table spans more than one page, you also should change the table properties so that the header row repeats on every page.

a. Use the Table Properties dialog box to indicate the first row should repeat as a header row at the top of each page if your table spans more than one page.

b. Align the prices of each item in the third column. The prices should appear to align on the decimal point.

c. Center the data in the second column, which displays the quantity of each item you will use in the project.

d. Sort the data in ascending order by Item.

e. Use the Split cell option to add a column to calculate the total cost of materials.

f. Use a formula to calculate the total cost of any item that has a quantity of 10 or more.

Add Visual Enhancements

Your table is very factual, but to assist members of the crew who need more visual information, you will enhance the table with pictures. Insert pictures from the Clip Organizer and then use formatting tools, when appropriate, to modify the graphics so they will fit into the table cells.

a. Insert a column to the left of the first column.

b. Insert a picture of each item in the first column.
   - Use symbols, clip art, or pictures to visually describe the following materials in your table: Drill, Faucet, Hammer, Paint, Paintbrushes, Screwdriver, Toilet, and Towel holder.
   - You might not be able to locate a graphic for each item, but you should be able to find at least five to use in the table.
   - Crop or resize the graphics as necessary so they do not exceed 2" in height or width.
   - All graphics should align in the center of the cell.

TROUBLESHOOTING: If your Clip Organizer query does not return any results, click Clip art on Office Online. The Online organizer will display in a new Internet Explorer window, but you can return to Word and continue your clip art search. Your search should now return more results.

c. Apply the **Light Grid Accent 1** style to the table. Add a double-line outside border to the table, then center it horizontally on the page. If necessary, click Table Properties and verify that the setting for the first row will repeat as a header row on the top of each page.

d. Save and close the document.

Mini Cases

Use the rubric following the case as a guide to evaluate your work, but keep in mind that your instructor may impose additional grading criteria or use a different standard to judge your work.

Holiday Greetings

GENERAL CASE

After learning how to use the creative tools in Microsoft Word 2007, you decide to create your own holiday greeting card. Your greeting card should include a picture of a family (feel free to use your own or one from the Clip Organizer) and decorative text. Use several editing features on the graphics so the greeting card reflects your personality or sentiment during the holidays. Due to printing constraints for special paper used for cards, design only the cover of your Greeting card. Save the document as **chap3_mc1_greeting_solution**.

Performance Elements	Exceeds Expectations	Meets Expectations	Below Expectations
Use of tables and table formatting	Inserted table; applied two or more table format options.	Inserted table; applied one table format option.	Inserted table; did not apply additional formatting.
Use of graphics	Inserted at least two graphical objects and used at least three formatting options.	Inserted at least one graphical object and applied formatting.	Inserted zero or one graphical object.
Presentation	Greeting card is formatted attractively; information is easy to read and understand.	Special formatting has been applied, but information is somewhat cluttered.	Greeting card lists basic information with no special formatting for attractiveness.

Travel World

RESEARCH CASE

You have been hired at *Let's Go!* Travel Agency and asked to create a flyer to distribute on campus. Search the Internet to find a company that offers cruises to Alaska and sails through the Inside Passage. Then create a flyer that provides information about one of the cruises through the Alaska Inside Passage. You should include your name and e-mail address as the travel agent. Use a combination of clip art, photographs, and/or WordArt to make the flyer as attractive as possible. Use a table to list the Ports of Call in Alaska. Save your work as **chap3_mc2_alaska_solution**.

Performance Elements	Exceeds Expectations	Meets Expectations	Below Expectations
Use of tables and table formatting	Inserted table; applied three or more table formats.	Inserted table; applied one or two table format options.	Inserted table; did not apply additional formatting.
Use of graphics	Inserted at least two graphical objects and applied formatting to objects.	Inserted at least two graphical objects and resized them.	Inserted zero or one graphical object.
Use of research	Two or more pieces of information are included in flyer, reflecting adequate research was performed.	Includes one piece of information reflecting research of topic.	Does not include data that indicate research was performed.
Presentation	Flyer is formatted attractively; information is easy to read and understand.	Special formatting has been applied, but information is somewhat cluttered.	Flyer lists basic information with no special formatting for attractiveness.

Payroll Report

DISASTER RECOVERY

You are assigned the job of proofreading a payroll report before it goes to the department head who issues checks. After looking at the data you find several errors that must be corrected before the report can be submitted. Open the *chap3_mc3_payroll_report* document and correct the errors. Remember to use the keyboard shortcut that reveals formulas in a table. Make further adjustments that enhance your ability to view the information easily and to make the report look more professional. Save your work as **chap3_mc3_payroll_solution**.

Performance Elements	Exceeds Expectations	Meets Expectations	Below Expectations
Use of table formulas	Table formulas applied correctly to all entries.	Table formulas applied correctly to two entries.	Table formulas applied incorrectly to at least one item.
Use of other table formatting options	Used at least three table format options.	Used two table format options.	Does not use table format options.
Presentation	Report is formatted attractively; information is easy to read and understand.	Some report formatting corrections have been applied, but information is somewhat cluttered.	Report contains errors in formatting and presentation is poor.

chapter 1 | Excel

Introduction to Excel

What Can I Do with a Spreadsheet?

Objectives

After you read this chapter, you will be able to:

1. Define worksheets and workbooks **(page 252)**.
2. Use spreadsheets across disciplines **(page 252)**.
3. Plan for good workbook and worksheet design **(page 253)**.
4. Identify Excel window components **(page 255)**.
5. Enter and edit data in cells **(page 260)**.
6. Describe and use symbols and the order of precedence **(page 266)**.
7. Display cell formulas **(page 268)**.
8. Insert and delete rows and columns **(page 269)**.
9. Use cell ranges; Excel move; copy, paste, paste special; and AutoFill **(page 270)**.
10. Manage worksheets **(page 278)**.
11. Format worksheets **(page 279)**.
12. Select page setup options for printing **(page 291)**.
13. Manage cell comments **(page 294)**.

Hands-On Exercises

Exercises	Skills Covered
1. **INTRODUCTION TO MICROSOFT EXCEL (page 262)** **Open:** none **Save as:** chap1_ho1_jake_solution.xlsx	• Plan Your Workbook • Start Microsoft Office Excel 2007 • Enter and Edit Data in Cells • Use the Save As Command and Explore the Worksheet
2. **JAKE'S GYM CONTINUED (page 273)** **Open:** chap1_ho2_jake.xlsx **Save as:** chap1_ho2_jake_solution.xlsx	• Open an Existing Workbook • Use Save As to Save an Existing Workbook • Insert a Row and Compute Totals • Copy the Formulas • Continue the Calculations • Insert a Column
3. **FORMATTING JAKE'S GYM WORKSHEET (page 285)** **Open:** chap1_ho2_jake_solution.xlsx (from Exercise 2) **Save as:** chap1_ho3_jake_solution (additional modifications)	• Manage the Workbook • Apply Number Formats • Apply Font Attributes and Borders • Change Alignment Attributes • Insert an Image
4. **PRINTING JAKE'S GYM WORKSHEET (page 295)** **Open:** chap1_ho3_jake_solution (from Exercise 3) **Save as:** chap1_ho4_ jake_solution (additional modifications)	• Insert a Comment • Insert Custom Header and Footer • Format to Print the Worksheet

CASE STUDY

Weddings by Grace

Grace Galia is a wedding consultant who specializes in all aspects of wedding planning for her clients. Although more and more couples are striving to cut costs by handling most of the planning on their own, Grace is successfully growing her business based on a proven history of superbly run events resulting in many happy newlyweds. She offers her clients a complete wedding package that includes the cocktail hour, dinner, and beverage (including alcohol). The client chooses the type of dinner (e.g., chicken, salmon, filet mignon, or some combination), which determines the cost per guest, and specifies the number of guests, and then the cost of the reception is obtained by simple multiplication.

Grace provides a detailed budget to all of her clients that divides the cost of a wedding into three major categories—the ceremony, the reception (based on the package selected), and other items such as music and photography. She asks each client for their total budget, and then works closely with the client to allocate that amount over the myriad items that will be necessary. Grace promises to take the stress out of planning, and she advertises a turnkey operation, from invitations to thank-you notes. She assures her clients that their needs will be met without the clients overextending themselves financially. Grace has asked you, her manager trainee, to complete her worksheet comparing the two wedding plans she offers her clients.

Your Assignment

- Read the chapter carefully, focusing on spreadsheet formulas and basic spreadsheet commands.
- Open *chap1_case_wedding*, which contains the partially completed worksheet, and save it as **chap1_case_wedding_solution**.
- Insert formulas to calculate the cost of the reception in both options.
- Use appropriate formulas to calculate the difference in cost for each item in the two options.
- Copy the total formula to the difference column.
- Format cells as currency with no decimals. Widen or narrow columns as necessary to conform to good design principles.
- Emphasize totals with borders and separate the categories with a complimentary fill color.
- Merge and center rows 1 and 2 so the headings are centered over the worksheet. Change the font, font color, and font size to match your design.
- Insert an appropriate image in the space indicated. You may have to resize to fit.
- Emphasize the category headings.
- Add your name and today's date to the worksheet.
- Choose the options you need to set from the Page Setup dialog box.

Introduction to Spreadsheets

A ***spreadsheet***, the computerized equivalent of a ledger, contains rows and columns of data.

A ***spreadsheet program*** is a computer application designed to build and manipulate spreadsheets.

After word processing, a spreadsheet program is the second most common software application in use. The most popular spreadsheet program used in businesses and organizations around the world is Microsoft Excel. A ***spreadsheet***, is the computerized equivalent of a ledger. It is a grid of rows and columns enabling users to organize data, recalculate results for cells containing formulas when any data in input cells change, and make decisions based on quantitative data. A ***spreadsheet program*** is a computer application, such as Microsoft Excel, that you use to build and manipulate electronic spreadsheets. The spreadsheet has become a much more powerful tool since the first spreadsheet program, VisiCalc, was introduced in 1979.

Before the introduction of spreadsheet software, people used ledgers to track expenses and other quantitative data. Ledgers have been the basis of accounting for hundreds of years, but the accountant was always faced with the issue of making changes to correct errors or update values. The major issue, however, was the time and work involved in changing the ledger and manually calculating the results again. Figure 1.1 shows an edited ledger page that had to be recalculated. A spreadsheet makes these changes in a significantly shorter period of time and, if the data and formulas are correct, does not make errors. Any area that has numeric data is a potential area of application for a spreadsheet. Herein lies the advantage of the electronic spreadsheet: quicker, more accurate changes than were possible with a manual ledger. Further, the use of formulas and functions in Excel, along with the ability to easily copy these formulas, adds to the program's functionality and power. Figure 1.2 shows an electronic spreadsheet, and Figure 1.3 shows that the results are automatically recalculated after changing the unit price.

> A spreadsheet makes these changes in a significantly shorter period of time and, if the data and formulas are correct, does not make errors.

Changes made manually

		1	2	3	4	5	6	
1	UNIT PRICE		~~20~~ 22					1
2	UNIT SALES		1,200					2
3	GROSS PROFIT		~~240~~ 264 00					3
4								4
5	EXPENSES							5
6	PRODUCTION		10,000					6
7	DISTRIBUTION		1,200					7
8	MARKETING		5,000					8
9	OVERHEAD		3,000					9
10	TOTAL EXPENSES		19,200					10
11								11
12	NET PROFIT		~~48~~ 72 00					12

Figure 1.1 Ledger

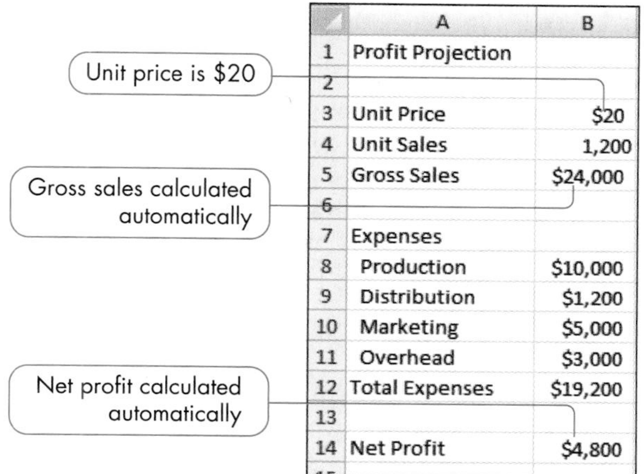

	A	B
1	Profit Projection	
2		
3	Unit Price	$20
4	Unit Sales	1,200
5	Gross Sales	$24,000
6		
7	Expenses	
8	Production	$10,000
9	Distribution	$1,200
10	Marketing	$5,000
11	Overhead	$3,000
12	Total Expenses	$19,200
13		
14	Net Profit	$4,800

Figure 1.2 Original Spreadsheet

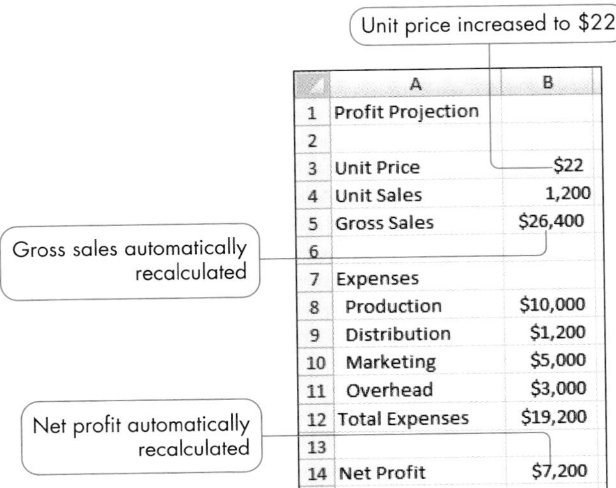

Figure 1.3 Modified Spreadsheet

In this section, you learn about workbooks and worksheets and how spreadsheets are used in various disciplines. You plan good workbook and worksheet design and identify Excel window components prior to creating a spreadsheet.

Defining Worksheets and Workbooks

A ***worksheet*** is a spreadsheet that may contain formulas, functions, values, text, and graphics.

A ***workbook*** is a file containing related worksheets.

A ***worksheet*** is a single spreadsheet consisting of a grid of columns and rows that often contain descriptive labels, numeric values, formulas, functions, and graphics. The terms worksheet and spreadsheet are often used interchangeably. A ***workbook*** is a collection of related worksheets contained within a single file. Storing multiple worksheets within one workbook helps organize related data in one file. In addition, it enables you to perform calculations among the worksheets within the workbook.

Managers often create workbooks to store an organization's annual budget. The workbook may consist of five worksheets, one for each quarter, with the fifth spreadsheet showing summary figures. Alternatively, individuals and families often create a budget workbook of 12 worksheets, one for each month, to store personal income and expenses. Instructors often create a workbook to store a grade book with individual worksheets for each class. On a personal level, you might want to list your DVD collection in one workbook in which you have a worksheet for each category, such as action, comedy, drama, etc. Within each worksheet, you list the DVD title, release date, purchase price, and so on. Regardless of the situation, you can use one workbook to contain many related worksheets.

TIP The Workbook

An Excel workbook is the electronic equivalent of the three-ring binder. A workbook contains one or more worksheets (or chart sheets), each of which is identified by a tab at the bottom of the workbook. The worksheets in a workbook are normally related to one another; for example, each worksheet may contain the sales for a specific division within a company. The advantage of a workbook is that all of its worksheets are stored in a single file, which is accessed as a unit.

Using Spreadsheets Across Disciplines

Students typically think spreadsheets are used solely for business applications. Spreadsheets are used for accounting and business planning using powerful "what-if" functions. These functions enable business planners to project different amounts of profit as other factors change. Even students can use basic "what if" analysis with a budget to determine if they can afford a particular payment or determine if they have sufficient income to buy a new car.

Spreadsheets are, however, used in many other areas. Because of the powerful graphing or charting feature of Excel, geologists and physical scientists use spreadsheets to store data about earthquakes or other physical phenomena, chart the data with a scatter chart, and then plot it on maps to predict where these phenomena might occur. Historians and social scientists have long used spreadsheets for predicting voting behavior or supporting or refuting theses such as Beard's Economic Interpretation of the Constitution. Figure 1.4 shows another use for spreadsheets—a summary of temperatures over time for several cities.

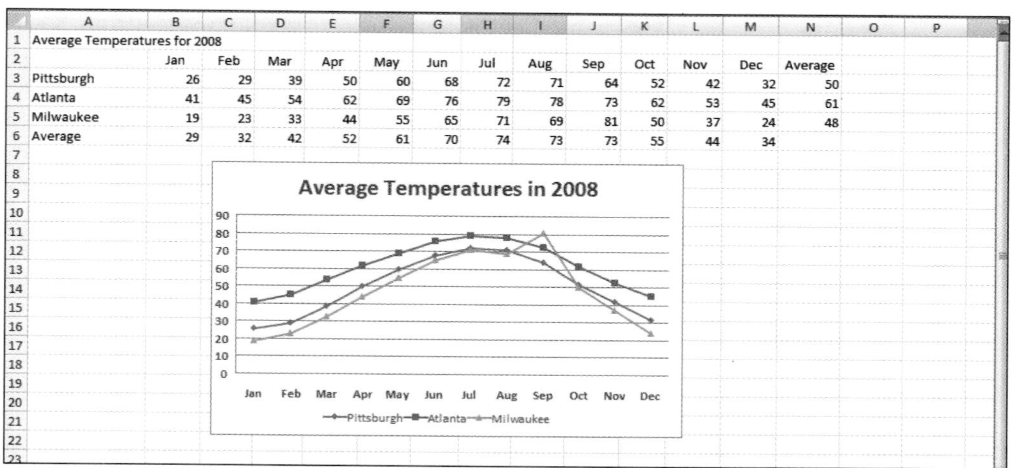

Average Temperatures for 2008													
	Jan	Feb	Mar	Apr	May	Jun	Jul	Aug	Sep	Oct	Nov	Dec	Average
Pittsburgh	26	29	39	50	60	68	72	71	64	52	42	32	50
Atlanta	41	45	54	62	69	76	79	78	73	62	53	45	61
Milwaukee	19	23	33	44	55	65	71	69	81	50	37	24	48
Average	29	32	42	52	61	70	74	73	73	55	44	34	

Figure 1.4 Temperatures over Time by City Example Spreadsheet

Educators at all levels—elementary school teachers through university professors—are increasing their use of electronic spreadsheets. Many Web sites now show literally thousands of examples of how educators are using spreadsheets in their classrooms. Once both students and teachers understand the basics of Excel, the possibilities are endless. As noted, spreadsheets are widely used in education. The most common use of Excel is in creating grade book spreadsheets.

Planning for Good Workbook and Worksheet Design

Figures 1.5, 1.6, and 1.7 show three views of a teacher's grade book. The first figure shows a grade book as a teacher might keep it with paper and pencil. The second figure shows the grade book in a spreadsheet program, and the third figure shows the grade book after some changes are made. The handwritten version of the grade book has the teacher writing in grades and calculating averages with a calculator or on paper. If changes are necessary, out comes the eraser and correction fluid. The second and third examples using the electronic spreadsheet show its simplicity. The teacher can easily enter grades, change grades, use weighted items, and recalculate—that is the power of the spreadsheet. For many teachers the spreadsheet grade book is such an integral part of their work that they have never seen or cannot remember a paper grade book.

You should plan the structure of the spreadsheet before you start entering data into a new worksheet. At times, it may be necessary for you to sit with paper and pencil and create the spreadsheet design on paper. See Figure 1.5 for an example of a handwritten grade book. The steps that are necessary for the design of a workbook and a worksheet include the following:

1. Figure out the purpose of the spreadsheet and how it will be constructed. For example, a professor's purpose is to create an electronic grade book to store student names and scores and to calculate student grades.

2. Make it obvious where data are to be entered. The teacher needs to store student first names, last names, and three test scores for all students in the class. See Figure 1.6 for a sample worksheet.
3. Enter data and set up formulas wherever possible. Never do manually what Excel can do automatically. You could, for example, calculate each student's class average. Furthermore, you can calculate the class average for each test to see if the tests are too easy or too difficult.
4. Test, test, and test again to make sure the results are what you expect. It is easy to make mistakes when entering data and when constructing formulas. Make whatever changes are necessary.
5. Format the worksheet so it is attractive but not so obtrusive that the purpose of the worksheet is lost. Include a title and column headings, and center the headings. Make sure decimal points align. Add bold to headings, increase the font size for readability, and use color to draw attention to important values or to trends.
6. Document the worksheet as thoroughly as possible. Include the current date, your name, class, and semester. Include cell comments describing the formulas so you know what values are used to produce the results.
7. Save and print the finished product. Auditors and teachers may require you to print a second time with cell formulas displayed so they can verify the formulas are correct. We will discuss cell formulas more thoroughly later in the chapter.

Student	Test 1	Test 2	Final	Average
Adams	100	90	81	90.3
Baker	90	76	87	84.3
Glassman	90	78	78	82.0
Moldof	60	60	40	53.3
Walker	80	80	90	83.3
Class Average	84.0	76.8	75.2	

Walker's average grade is 83.3

Walker's final exam grade is 90

Figure 1.5 The Professor's Grade Book

	A	B	C	D	E	F
1	Student	Test 1	Test 2	Final	Average	
2						
3	Adams	100	90	81	90.3	
4	Baker	90	76	87	84.3	
5	Glassman	90	78	78	82.0	
6	Moldof	60	60	40	53.3	
7	Walker	80	80	90	83.3	
8						
9	Class Average	84.0	76.8	75.2		
10						

Walker's final exam grade is 90

Figure 1.6 Original Grades

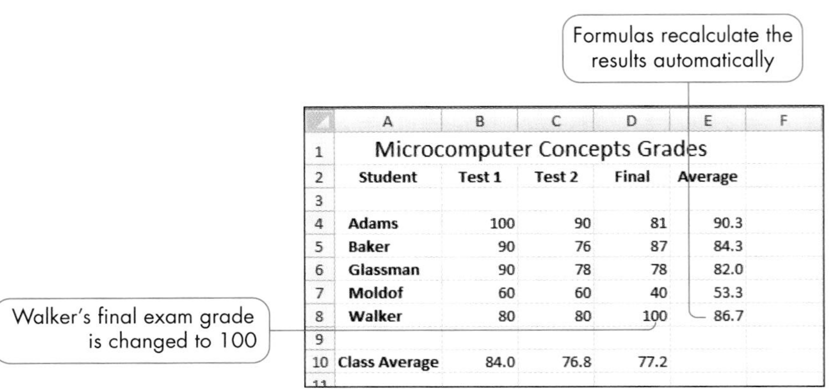

Formulas recalculate the results automatically
Walker's final exam grade is changed to 100

	A	B	C	D	E	F
1	Microcomputer Concepts Grades					
2	Student	Test 1	Test 2	Final	Average	
3						
4	Adams	100	90	81	90.3	
5	Baker	90	76	87	84.3	
6	Glassman	90	78	78	82.0	
7	Moldof	60	60	40	53.3	
8	Walker	80	80	100	86.7	
9						
10	Class Average	84.0	76.8	77.2		

Figure 1.7 Modified Spreadsheet

Identifying Excel Window Components

The ***active cell*** is the cell you are working in, the cell where information or data will be input.

Each window in Excel has its own Minimize, Maximize, and Close buttons. The title bar contains the name of the application (Excel) and the name of the workbook you are using. At the bottom and right of the document window are the vertical and horizontal scroll bars. The ***active cell*** is the cell you are working in, the cell where information or data will be input. Its cell reference appears in the name box, its contents in the formula bar, and it is surrounded by a dark black box. The active cell can be changed by clicking in a different cell or using the arrow keys to move to another cell.

The Excel window includes items that are similar to other Office applications and items that are unique to the Excel application. See Figure 1.8, the Excel window, with the parts of the window identified. The following paragraphs name and describe items in the Excel window.

- **Ribbon**: The Ribbon is made of tabs, groups, and commands.
- **Tab**: Each tab is made up of several groups so that you can see all of its functions without opening menus. The contents of each tab are shown on the reference page. This defines the tabs, the groups they contain, and their general function. You will refer to this page frequently.
- **Office Menu**: The Office menu displays when you click the Office Button in the upper left of the Excel window and contains the following commands, all of which open dialog boxes: New, Open, Save, Save As, Finish, Share, Print, and Close. A list of recently used workbooks and an extensive Excel Options section displays. See Figure 1.9 for the contents of the Office menu.

The ***formula bar*** is used to enter or edit cell contents.

- **Formula Bar**: The formula bar appears below the Ribbon and above the workbook screen and shows the active cell's contents. The ***formula bar*** displays the contents of cells; you can enter or edit cell contents here or directly in the active cell.

The ***name box*** indicates the location or name for the active cell.

- **Name Box**: The ***name box*** is another name for the cell reference of the cell currently used in the worksheet. The name box appears to the left of the formula bar and displays the active cell's address (D4) or a name it has been assigned.

Sheet tabs tell the user what sheets of a workbook are available.

- **Sheet Tabs**: ***Sheet tabs*** are located at the bottom left of the Excel window and tell the user what sheets of a workbook are available. Three sheet tabs, initially named Sheet1, Sheet2, and Sheet3, are included when you open a new workbook in Excel. To move between sheets, click on the sheet you want to work with. You can even rename sheets with more meaningful names. If you create more sheets than can be displayed, you can use the sheet tab scroll buttons to scroll through all sheet tabs.
- **Status Bar**: The status bar is located at the bottom of the Excel window. It is below the sheet tabs and above the Windows taskbar and displays information about a selected command or operation in progress. For example, it displays CAPS when Caps Lock is active and the default setting is On.

The ***Select All button*** is clicked to select all elements of the worksheet.

- **Select All Button**: The ***Select All button*** is the square at the intersection of the rows and column headings, and you can use it to select all elements of the worksheet.

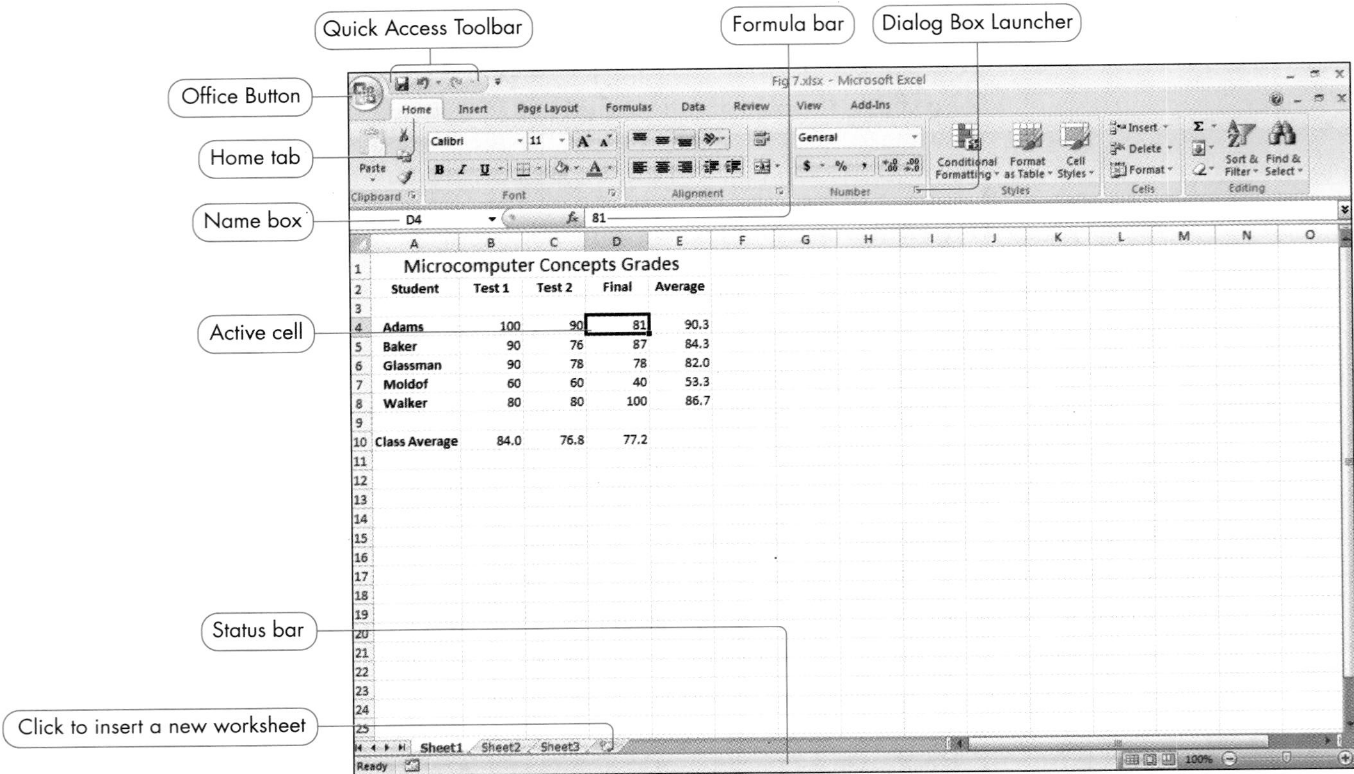

Figure 1.8 The Excel Window

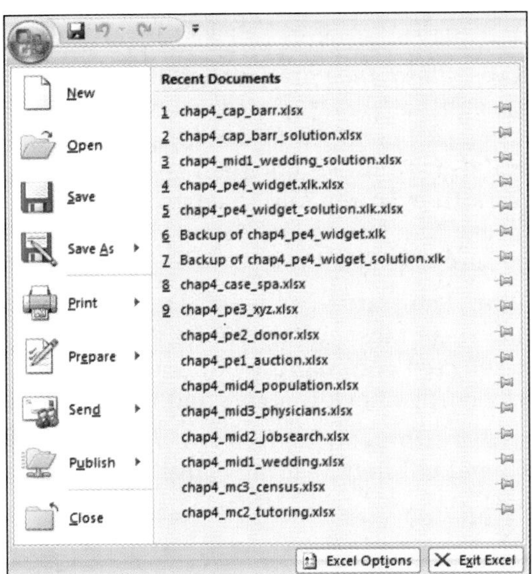

Figure 1.9 The Office Menu

Tab, Group, Description | Reference

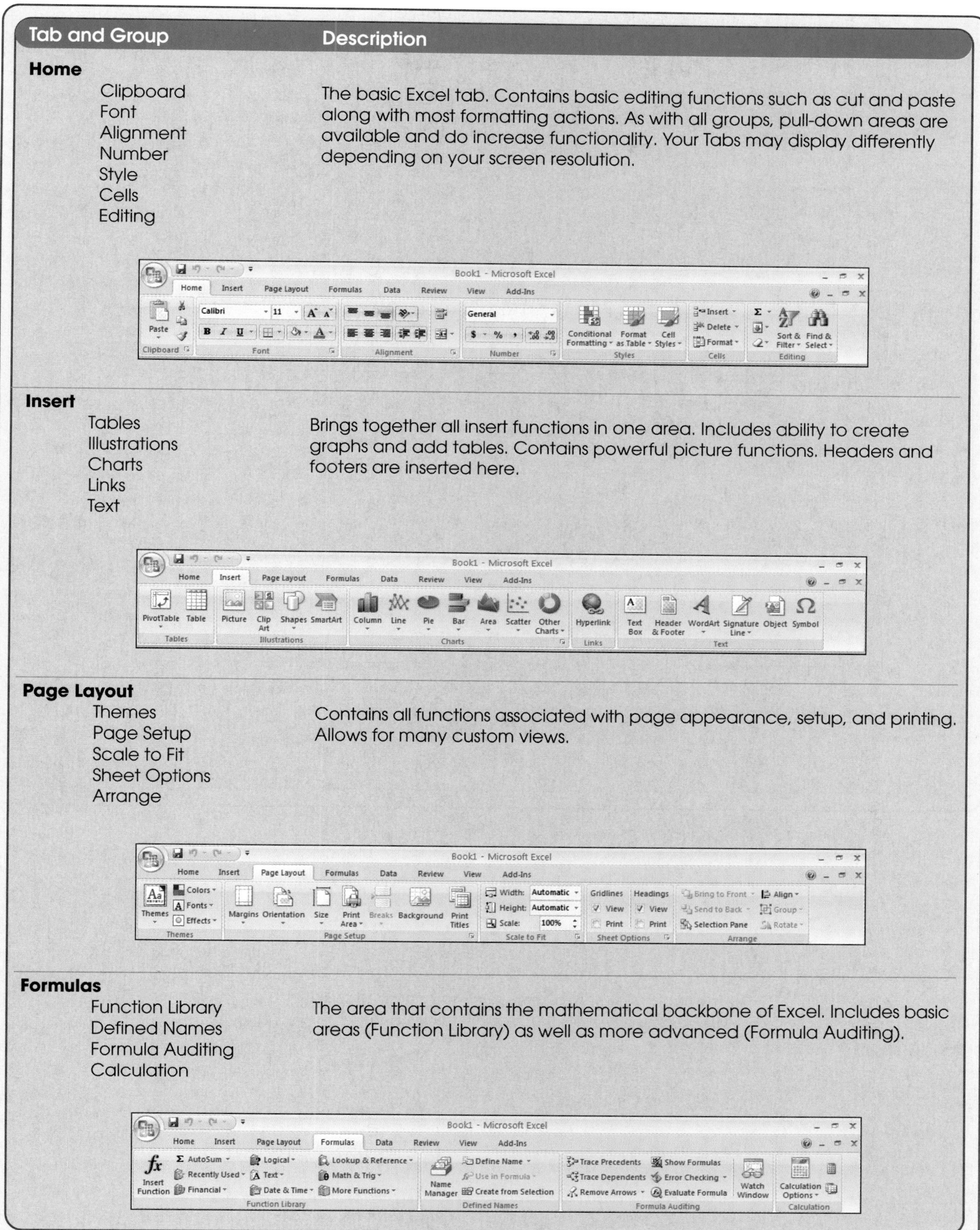

Tab and Group	Description
Home Clipboard Font Alignment Number Style Cells Editing	The basic Excel tab. Contains basic editing functions such as cut and paste along with most formatting actions. As with all groups, pull-down areas are available and do increase functionality. Your Tabs may display differently depending on your screen resolution.
Insert Tables Illustrations Charts Links Text	Brings together all insert functions in one area. Includes ability to create graphs and add tables. Contains powerful picture functions. Headers and footers are inserted here.
Page Layout Themes Page Setup Scale to Fit Sheet Options Arrange	Contains all functions associated with page appearance, setup, and printing. Allows for many custom views.
Formulas Function Library Defined Names Formula Auditing Calculation	The area that contains the mathematical backbone of Excel. Includes basic areas (Function Library) as well as more advanced (Formula Auditing).

Data

Get External Data
Connections
Sort & Filter
Data Tools
Outline

The heart of the database portions of Excel. While not a true relational database, it has much power and includes Goal Seek and Scenario Manager.

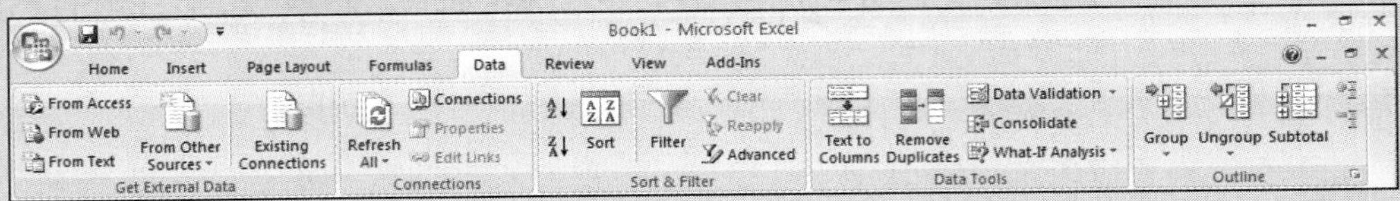

Review

Proofing
Comments
Changes

Contains all reviewing tools in Excel, including such things as spelling, the use of comments, and sharing and protection.

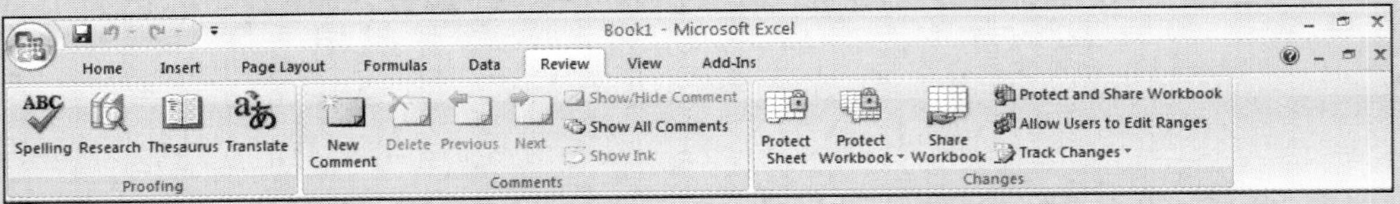

View

Workbook Views
Show/Hide
Zoom
Window
Macros

Contains basic and advanced view settings. Some of these options also appear below the horizontal and vertical scroll bars.

Navigate in Worksheets

Selecting cells to make them active and navigating from cell to cell are basic navigational skills in Excel. Using the mouse is probably the most convenient way to select a cell and navigate. To make a cell active, click on the desired cell. Making another cell active simply involves clicking on another cell. If the cell to be made active is not visible, use the vertical or horizontal scroll bars or the arrow keys to move so the desired cell is visible.

The other way is to use different keys to navigate through the worksheet. Table 1.1 shows keys that can be used to move in a worksheet.

Table 1.1 Keystrokes and Actions

Keystroke	Action
↑	Moves up one cell.
↓	Moves down one cell.
←	Moves left one cell.
→	Moves right one cell.
PgUp	Moves active cell up one screen.
PgDn	Moves active cell down one screen.
Home	Moves active cell to column A of current row.
Ctrl+Home	Moves active cell to cell A1.
Ctrl+End	Moves to the rightmost, lowermost active corner of the worksheet.
F5	Displays the GoTo dialog box to enter any cell address.

Identify Columns, Rows, and Cells

A spreadsheet is divided into columns and rows, with each column and row assigned a heading. Columns are assigned alphabetic headings from column A to Z, continue from AA to AZ, and then from BA to BZ until the last of the 18,278 columns is reached. Rows have numeric headings ranging from 1 to 1,048,576 (the maximum number of rows allowed).

A ***cell*** is the intersection of a column and row.

A ***cell reference*** is designated by a column letter and a row number.

The intersection of a column and row forms a ***cell***, with the number of cells in a spreadsheet equal to the number of columns times the number of rows. Each cell has a unique ***cell reference***, which is the intersection of a column and row designated by a column letter and a row number. For example, the cell at the intersection of column A and row 9 is known as cell A9. The column heading always precedes the row heading in the cell reference.

Start Excel and Create a New Worksheet

The first thing you should do is open Excel. You can do this by taking the following steps:

1. Click the Start button to display the Start menu. Position the mouse pointer over All Programs, select Microsoft Office, and then select Microsoft Office Excel 2007 from its location on the Programs menu.
2. Maximize the Excel program if necessary.

This opens a new Excel workbook with the default three-sheet worksheet tabs. When Excel is already open and you want to open a new workbook, complete the following steps:

1. Click the Office Button.
2. Select New, and then select Blank Workbook.

A new workbook is now open.

Entering and Editing Data in Cells

The three types of data that can be entered in a cell in an Excel worksheet are text, values, and formulas, which also include functions. You can create very sophisticated workbooks and simple worksheets with any combination of text, values, and formulas.

Enter Text

Text includes letters, numbers, symbols, and spaces.

Text is any combination of entries from the keyboard and includes letters, numbers, symbols, and spaces. Even though text entries may be used as data, they are most often used to identify and document the spreadsheet. Text is used to indicate the title of the spreadsheet. Typically text is used for row and column labels. When you need to enter text, click in the cell where the text is to appear, type the text, and either press Enter or click the ✓ on the formula bar.

Sometimes, you may have a long label that does not fit well in the cell. You can insert a line break to display the label on multiple lines within the cell. To insert a line break, press Alt+Enter where you want to start the next line of text within the cell.

Enter Values

A ***value*** is a number that represent a quantity, an amount, a date, or time.

Values are numbers entered in a cell that represent a quantity, an amount, a date, or time. As a general rule, Excel can recognize if you are entering text or values by what is typed. The biggest difference between text and value entries is that value entries can be the basis of calculation while text cannot.

Enter Formulas

A ***formula*** is a combination of numbers, cell references, operators, and/or functions.

Formulas (and their shorthand form, functions) are the combination of constants, cell references, arithmetic operations, and/or functions displayed in a calculation. For Excel to recognize a formula, it must always start with an equal sign (=). You learn about basic formulas in this chapter. Chapter 2 provides a detailed discussion of formulas and functions. At this point, it is sufficient to say that =A2+B2 is an example of a formula to perform addition.

TIP AutoComplete

As soon as you begin typing a label into a cell, Excel searches for and (automatically) displays any other label in that column that matches the letters you typed. AutoComplete is helpful if you want to repeat a label, but it can be distracting if you want to enter a different label that begins with the same letter. To turn the feature on (or off), click the Office Button, click Excel Options, and click the Edit tab. Check (clear) the box to enable (disable) the AutoComplete feature.

Edit and Clear Cell Contents

You have several ways to edit the contents of a cell. You will probably select and stay with one technique that you find most convenient. The first method is to select the cell you want to edit, click in the formula bar, make changes, and then press Enter. The second method requires that you double-click in the cell to be edited, make the edits, and then press Enter. The third method is similar except that you select the cell, press the F2 key, and then make the edit.

You have two options to clear the contents of a cell. First, just click on a cell and press Delete. The second option involves clicking the Clear arrow in the Editing group on the Home tab. This gives you several options as to what will be cleared from the cell (see Figure 1.10).

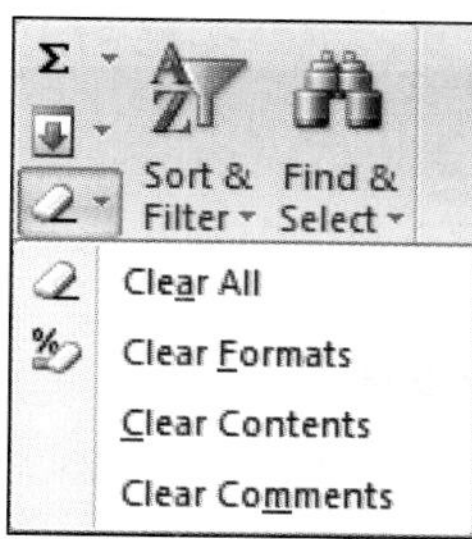

Figure 1.10 Clear Pull-down List

Use Save and Save As

It is basic computer practice that files, including workbooks, should be saved often. If you are using a workbook and you do not want to change its name, the easiest way to save it is to click the Office Button and select Save. If you prefer keyboard shortcuts, press Ctrl+S. You also can click Save on the Quick Access Toolbar.

The first time you save a workbook, you can use the Save command or the Save As command that is located on the Office menu. For an unnamed file, either command displays the Save As dialog box. You can then assign a file name that is descriptive of the workbook (gradebook08, for example), determine the file location, and choose the file type. After selecting the appropriate options, click Save. When you use the Save command after initially saving a workbook, the subsequent changes are saved under the same workbook name and in the same location. If you want to assign a different name to a modified workbook so that you can preserve the original workbook, use the Save As command.

TIP File Management with Excel

Use the Office Button in the Open or Save As dialog box to perform basic file management within any Office application. You can select any existing file or folder, and delete it or rename it. You can also create a new folder, which is very useful when you begin to work with a large number of documents. You can also use the Views button to change the way the files are listed within the dialog box.

Hands-On Exercises

1 | Introduction to Microsoft Excel

Skills covered: 1. Plan Your Workbook **2.** Start Microsoft Office Excel 2007 **3.** Enter and Edit Data in Cells **4.** Use the Save As Command and Explore the Worksheet

Step 1 Plan Your Workbook

Refer to Figure 1.11 as you complete Step 1.

a. Prepare notes before beginning Excel.

Specify or define the problem. What statistics will be produced by your spreadsheet? Do you already have the statistics, or do you need to collect them from another source? Brainstorm about what formulas and functions will be required. Experiment with paper and pencil and a calculator. The first spreadsheet you create will be a sample showing membership sales in a gym. This sample worksheet includes monthly sales by region for both first and second quarters. Also included are the calculations to determine total monthly sales, average monthly sales, total and average sales by region, and increase or decrease in sales between the first and second quarters.

b. Simplify your Excel spreadsheet for those who will enter data.

You should treat your Excel workbook like a Microsoft Word document by doing such things as adding cell comments, giving instructions, and using attractive formatting.

c. Consider these layout suggestions when designing your Excel spreadsheets:

- Reserve the first row for a spreadsheet title.
- Reserve a row for column headings.
- Reserve a column at the left for row headings.
- Do not leave blank rows and columns for white space within the spreadsheet layout.
- Widen the columns and rows and use alignment instead of leaving blank rows or columns.
- Save your work often.

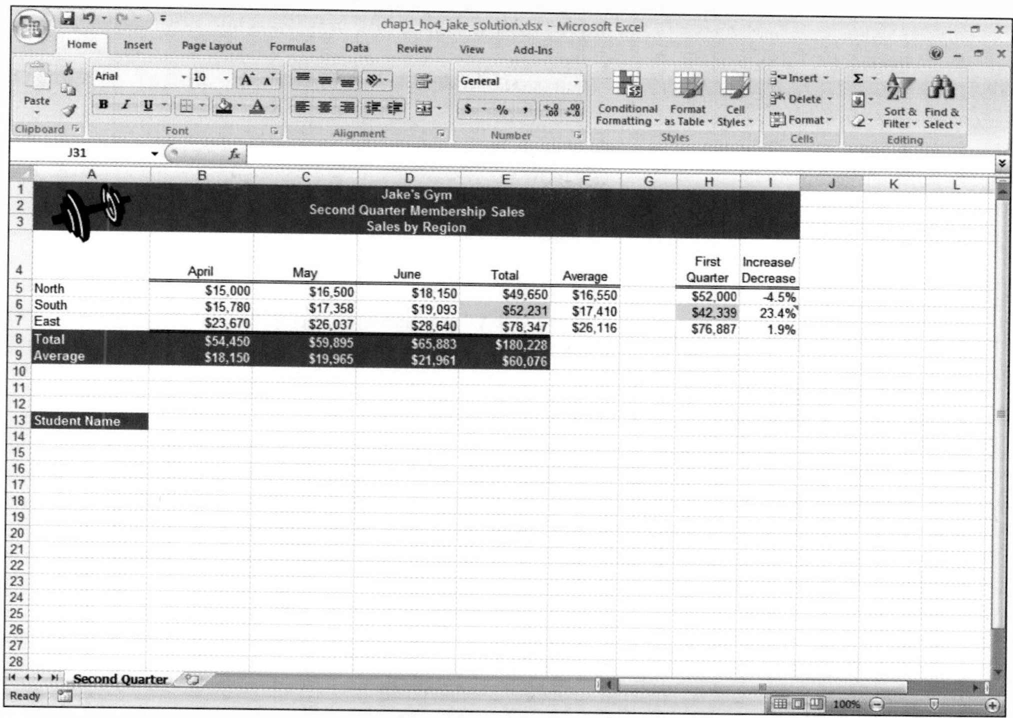

Figure 1.11 Well-Designed Spreadsheet

Step 2
Start Microsoft Office Excel 2007

a. Click the **Start button** to display the Start menu. Click (or point to) **All Programs**, click **Microsoft Office**, and then click **Microsoft Office Excel 2007** to start the program.

You should be familiar with basic file management and very comfortable moving and copying files from one folder to another. If not, you may want to review the Help material for basic file management.

b. If necessary, click the **Maximize** button in the application window so that Excel takes the entire desktop, as shown in Figure 1.11. Click the **Maximize** button in the document window (if necessary) so that the workbook window is as large as possible.

Step 3
Enter and Edit Data in Cells

Refer to Figure 1.12 as you complete Step 3.

a. Click **cell A1**, type **Jake's Gym**, and press **Enter**.

b. Click in **cell A2** and type **Second Quarter Membership Sales**.

c. Click **cell B3**, type the label **April**, and press the **right arrow**.

d. Click in **cell C3**, type the label **May**, and press the **right arrow**. Complete the typing for **cells D3** through **H3** as shown. Do not be concerned if the entire column label is not visible.

D3	June
E3	Total
F3	Average
G3	First Quarter
H3	Increase/Decrease

e. Enter the data for three regions as shown below:

Region	April	May	June	First Quarter
North	15000	16500	18150	31000
South	15780	17358	19093	42339
East	23670	26037	28640	76887

TROUBLESHOOTING: Data entry is important for good spreadsheet use. Verify values as you finish typing them. To change an entry, click on the cell and retype the value. To delete an entry, click on the cell and press Delete.

f. Type **Total** in **cell A7** and type **Average** in **cell A8**.

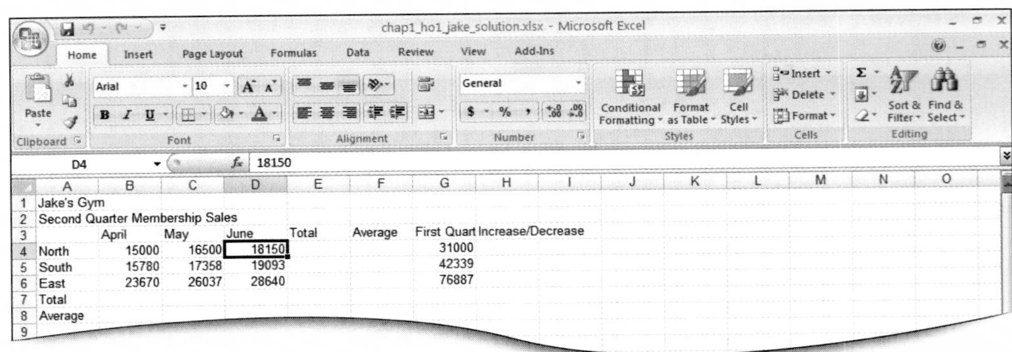

Figure 1.12 Jake's Gym Data

Step 4
Use the Save As Command and Explore the Worksheet

Refer to Figures 1.12 and 1.13 as you complete Step 4. Your Tab may not display exactly as shown because of different screen resolutions.

a. Click the **Office Button** and select **Save As** to display the Save As dialog box shown in Figure 1.13.

b. Type **chap1_ho1_jake_solution** as the name of the new workbook.

A file name may contain up to 255 characters. Spaces, underscores, and commas are allowed in the filename.

c. Navigate to the location of your data files and click the **Save button**.

You should see the workbook in Figure 1.12.

d. Click in **cell D4**, the cell containing 18150 or the North June sales.

Cell D4 is now the active cell and is surrounded by a heavy border. The name box indicates that cell D4 is the active cell, and its contents are displayed in the formula bar.

e. Click in **cell D5** (or press the down arrow key) to make it the active cell.

The name box indicates cell D5.

f. Refer to Table 1.1 as you move around the worksheet.

g. Close the *chap1_ho1_jake_solution* workbook.

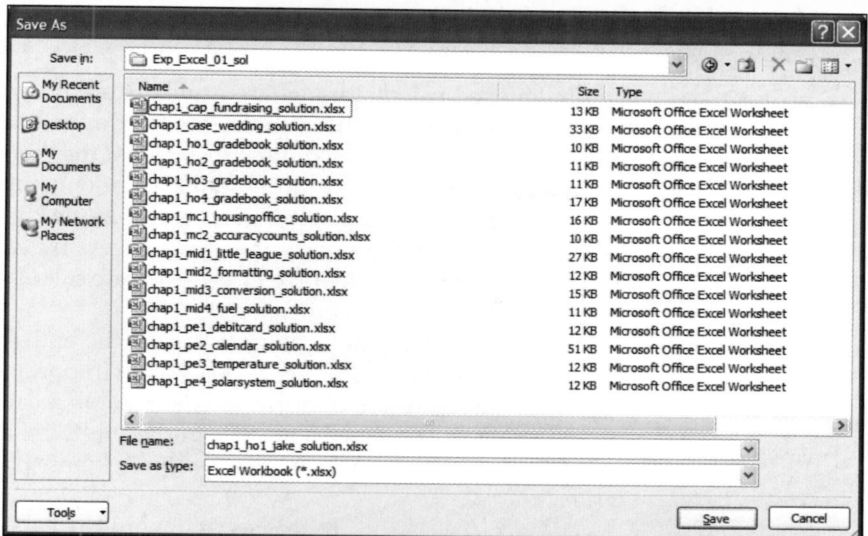

Figure 1.13 Save As Dialog Box

TIP Keyboard Shortcuts—The Dialog Box

Press Tab or Shift+Tab to move forward or backward between fields in a dialog box, or press Alt plus the underlined letter to move directly to an option. You will see underlined letters in words in dialog boxes. These are the letters you use in conjunction with the Alt key. Use the spacebar to toggle check boxes on or off and the up (or down) arrow keys to move between options in a list box. Press Enter to activate the highlighted command and Esc to exit the dialog box without accepting the changes. These are universal shortcuts and apply to any Windows application.

Mathematics and Formulas

You have used calculators where numbers are entered, the correct arithmetic function key is pressed, and the correct answer appears. What is missing though is the knowledge of the process, or how to arrive at the correct answer. These mathematical processes are the key to understanding and using Excel. Without knowing the process and how to apply it in Excel, you are left with just numbers, not answers. Arithmetic and mathematics produce answers by calculating numbers using Excel. You might want to think of Excel as a gigantic calculating program on the most powerful calculator of all, a computer.

With Excel, when any change is made, the entire worksheet is updated based on this new value. This fact brings us back to an important question: Why use Excel when one could just as easily perform calculations on a calculator or on paper? What happens if profit is 4% rather than 5%? In the pre-Excel days, answering these questions required rewriting and retyping the whole business plan using pencil, paper, and typewriter.

In this section, you learn about the mathematical operations that are the backbone of Excel. You also will see that the order these mathematical operations are performed in can have a significant impact on the results. We touch briefly on the construction of mathematical expressions, called ***formulas***, that direct Excel to perform mathematical operations and arrive at a calculated result. Whenever you want Excel to perform a calculation, you must enter an equal sign (=) in the cell where the answer is to appear. For example, if you wanted to calculate the sum of cells C2 and C3 in cell C4, you would do the following:

Formulas can be as simple or as complex as necessary, but always begin with an = sign and contain mathematical operators.

1. Click in cell C4 and type an = sign.
2. Click in cell C2 and type a + sign.
3. Click in cell C3 and press Enter.

This is an extremely simplified example but the principle holds true in all formulas. See Table 1.2 for examples of formulas. Formulas can be as simple or as complex as necessary, but always begin with an = sign and contain mathematical operators.

Table 1.2 Formula Examples

Operation	Formula
Addition	=C1+C2
Subtraction	=C2-C1
Multiplication	=C1*C2
Division	=C1/C2

Describing and Using Symbols and the Order of Precedence

The four mathematical functions—addition, subtraction, multiplication, and division—are the basis of all mathematical operations. Table 1.3 lists the arithmetic operators and their purposes.

Table 1.3 Arithmetic Operators and Symbols

Operation	Common Symbol	Symbol in Excel
Addition	+	+
Subtraction	–	–
Multiplication	X	*
Division	÷	/
Exponentiation	^	^

Enter Cell References in Formulas

If this were all there was to it, Excel would be effortless for all of us, but two other things need to be done if Excel is to perform mathematical functions as it was designed to do. First, rather than entering the numbers that are contained in the cells, Excel works at its full potential if cell references (C5, B2, etc.) are used rather than the numbers themselves. See Figure 1.14 for an example.

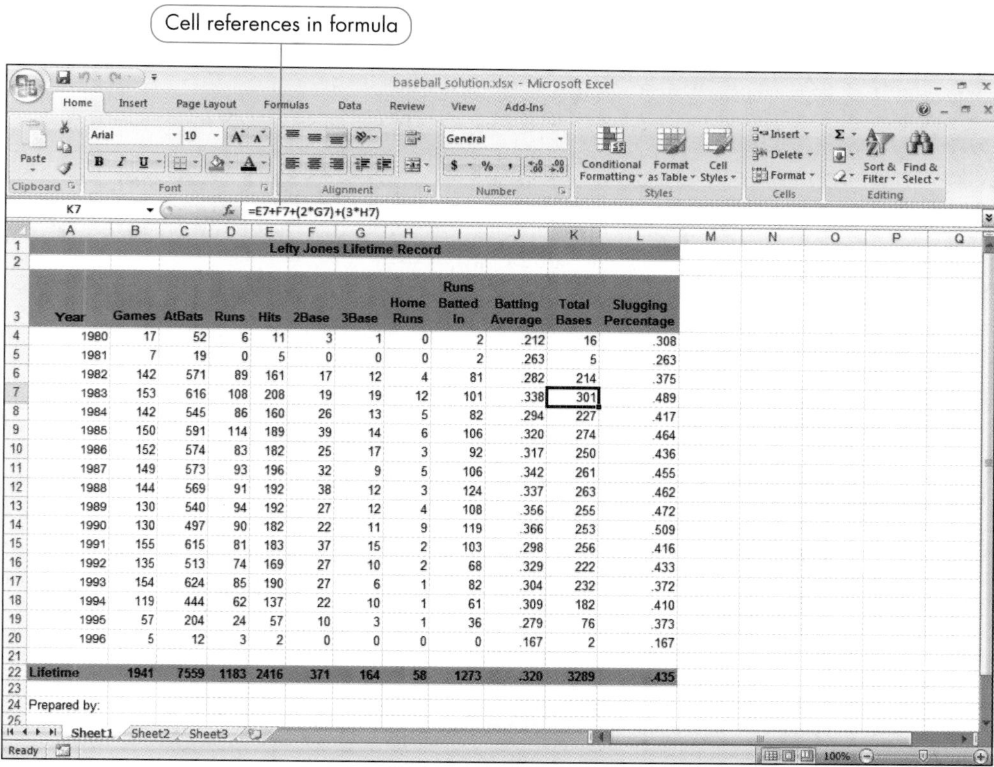

Year	Games	AtBats	Runs	Hits	2Base	3Base	Home Runs	Runs Batted In	Batting Average	Total Bases	Slugging Percentage
1980	17	52	6	11	3	1	0	2	.212	16	.308
1981	7	19	0	5	0	0	0	2	.263	5	.263
1982	142	571	89	161	17	12	4	81	.282	214	.375
1983	153	616	108	208	19	19	12	101	.338	301	.489
1984	142	545	86	160	26	13	5	82	.294	227	.417
1985	150	591	114	189	39	14	6	106	.320	274	.464
1986	152	574	83	182	25	17	3	92	.317	250	.436
1987	149	573	93	196	32	9	5	106	.342	261	.455
1988	144	569	91	192	38	12	3	124	.337	263	.462
1989	130	540	94	192	27	12	4	108	.356	255	.472
1990	130	497	90	182	22	11	9	119	.366	253	.509
1991	155	615	81	183	37	15	2	103	.298	256	.416
1992	135	513	74	169	27	10	2	68	.329	222	.433
1993	154	624	85	190	27	6	1	82	.304	232	.372
1994	119	444	62	137	22	10	1	61	.309	182	.410
1995	57	204	24	57	10	3	1	36	.279	76	.373
1996	5	12	3	2	0	0	0	0	.167	2	.167
Lifetime	1941	7559	1183	2416	371	164	58	1273	.320	3289	.435

Prepared by:

Figure 1.14 Baseball Statistics with Cell References

The first thing to consider is how Excel (or the computer) recognizes that you want to perform a mathematical operation. For example, you decide that you need to add the contents of cells C1 and C2 and place the sum in cell C3. In C1 you have the number 5, and in C2 you have the number 3. If you enter 5+3 and press Enter, the result you see will be "5+3." This is not the answer, however, that you are looking for. You want the result of 8. Anytime you want Excel to perform a mathematical calculation, you must begin by typing =. The equal sign tells Excel "get ready to do some math." One way to get the answer of 8 is by typing =5+3 and pressing Enter to see the sum, 8, in cell C3.

If you then change the number in cell C1 from 5 to 7, you must now change the 5 to a 7 in the formula in cell C3 to calculate the new result. Excel gives you an easier and much more efficient way to update results of calculations so you do not have to change the content of cell C3 every time the values in cells C1 or C2 change. This operation is done by using cell references. Rather than using the expression =5+3 in cell C3 to get a sum, you should enter the expression =C1+C2 in cell C3. This way, even if you change the values of cell C1 or C2, the value in cell C3 remains the sum of cells C1 and C2 because you are using cell references rather than the value in the cells.

Control the Results with the Order of Precedence

The ***order of precedence*** controls the sequence in which arithmetic operations are performed, which affects the result.

Before moving on to formulas, the final mathematics concept you need to know is order of precedence. The ***order of precedence*** are rules that control the order or sequence in which arithmetic operations are performed, which in turn, will change the result reported in Excel. Excel performs mathematical calculations left to right in this order: parentheses, exponentiation, multiplication or division, and finally addition or subtraction.

Review the expressions in Table 1.4 and notice how the parentheses change the value of the expression. In the second expression, the addition inside the parentheses is performed before the multiplication, changing the order of operations. Strictly following the order of mathematical operations eliminates many puzzling results when using Excel.

Table 1.4 Examples of Order of Precedence

Expression	Order to Perform Calculations	Output
= 6 + 6 * 2	Multiply first **and then** add.	18
= (6 + 6) * 2	Add the values inside the parentheses first **and then** multiply.	24
= 6 + 6 ^ 2	Simplify the exponent first: 36=6*6, **and then** add.	42
= 10/2 + 3	Divide first **and then** add.	8
= 10/(2+3)	Add first to simplify the parenthetical expression **and then** divide.	2
= 10 * 2 - 3 * 2	Multiply first **and then** subtract.	14

Displaying Cell Formulas

One of the tools that can be used to document an Excel worksheet is the ability to display cell formulas. When you display formulas, they will appear in the cells instead of the results of the calculation. See Figures 1.15 and 1.16. The quickest way to display cell formulas is to press Ctrl+~. The tilde (~) key is in the upper-left corner of the keyboard, under Esc. Note: you do not press the Shift key with the tilde key to make cell formulas visible in your worksheet.

J9						
	A	B	C	D	E	F
1	Microcomputer Concepts Grades					
2	Student	Test 1	Test 2	Final	Average	
3						
4	Adams	100	90	81	90.3	
5	Baker	90	76	87	84.3	
6	Glassman	90	78	78	82.0	
7	Moldof	60	60	40	53.3	
8	Walker	80	80	100	86.7	
9						
10	Class Average	84.0	76.8	77.2		

Figure 1.15 Spreadsheet with Values Displayed

	A	B	C	D	E
1	Microcomputer Concepts Grades				
2	Student	Test 1	Test 2	Final	Average
3					
4	Adams	100	90	81	=AVERAGE(B4:D4)
5	Baker	90	76	87	=AVERAGE(B5:D5)
6	Glassman	90	78	78	=AVERAGE(B6:D6)
7	Moldof	60	60	40	=AVERAGE(B7:D7)
8	Walker	80	80	100	=AVERAGE(B8:D8)
9					
10	Class Average	=AVERAGE(B4:B9)	=AVERAGE(C4:C9)	=AVERAGE(D4:D9)	

Figure 1.16 Spreadsheet with Formulas Displayed

Inserting and Deleting Rows and Columns

After you construct a worksheet, it is often necessary to add or delete columns or rows of information. For example, in a grade book kept by a professor, names are constantly added or deleted. This process typically involves the use of the Insert command that adds cells, rows, or columns or the Delete command that deletes cells, rows, or columns. When you use either command, the cell references in existing cells are adjusted automatically to reflect the insertion or deletion. These commands also allow sheets to be added or deleted from the workbook.

To insert a row, click in the row below where you want a row inserted (rows are always inserted above, and columns are always inserted to the left of, the selected cell), and then click the Insert down arrow in the Cells group on the Home tab. You would then select Insert Sheet Rows. To insert a column, the user would select Insert Sheet Columns. For example, if the active cell is E4, row 4 is the current row. The row added is inserted above. If a column is inserted, it is inserted to the left of E4. The process is similar for deleting rows and columns, except you begin by choosing the Delete pull-down arrow in the Cells group. The row above the row selected is deleted, and the column to the left of the selected column is deleted.

TIP Inserting and Deleting Individual Cells

In some situations, you may need to insert and delete individual cells instead of inserting or deleting an entire row or column. To insert a cell, click in the cell where you want the new cell, click the Insert pull-down arrow in the Cells group on the Cells tab, and then click Insert Cells to display the Insert dialog box. Click the appropriate option to shift cells right or down and click OK (see Figure 1.17). To delete a cell or cells, select the cell(s), click the Delete arrow in the Cells group on the Cells tab, and then click Delete Cells to display the Delete dialog box. Click the appropriate option to shift cells right or down and click OK (see Figure 1.18).

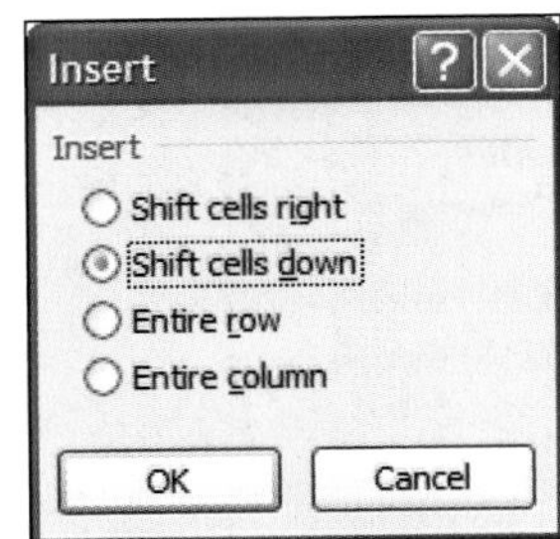

Figure 1.17 Insert Dialog Box

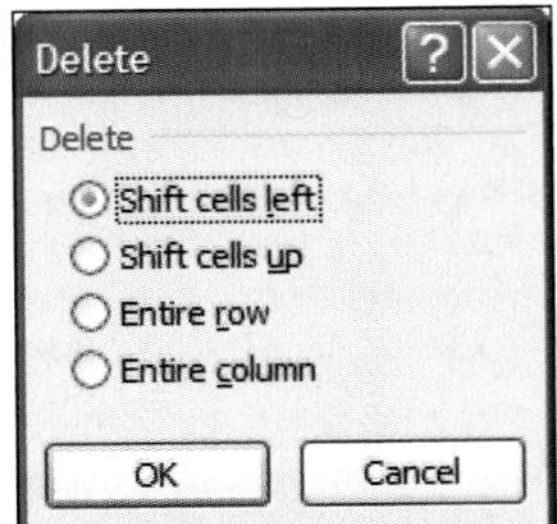

Figure 1.18 Delete Dialog Box

Using Cell Ranges; Excel Move; Copy, Paste, Paste Special; and AutoFill

Each of these topics is a basic editing function in Excel. They will be discussed in detail here, and you will be able to show your proficiency with them in Hands-On Exercise 2.

Select a Range

A ***range*** is a rectangular group of cells.

Every command in Excel applies to a rectangular group of cells known as a ***range***. A range may be as small as a single cell or as large as the entire worksheet. It may consist of a row or part of a row, a column or part of a column, or multiple rows or columns. The cells within a range are specified by indicating the diagonally opposite corners, typically the upper-left and lower-right corners of the rectangle. Many different ranges could be selected in conjunction with the worksheet shown in Figure 1.19. For example, the 1980 Player data is contained in the range B4:I4. The Lifetime Totals are found in the range B22:L22. The Batting Averages are found in the range J4:J20.

(A range may be as small as a single cell or as large as the entire worksheet.)

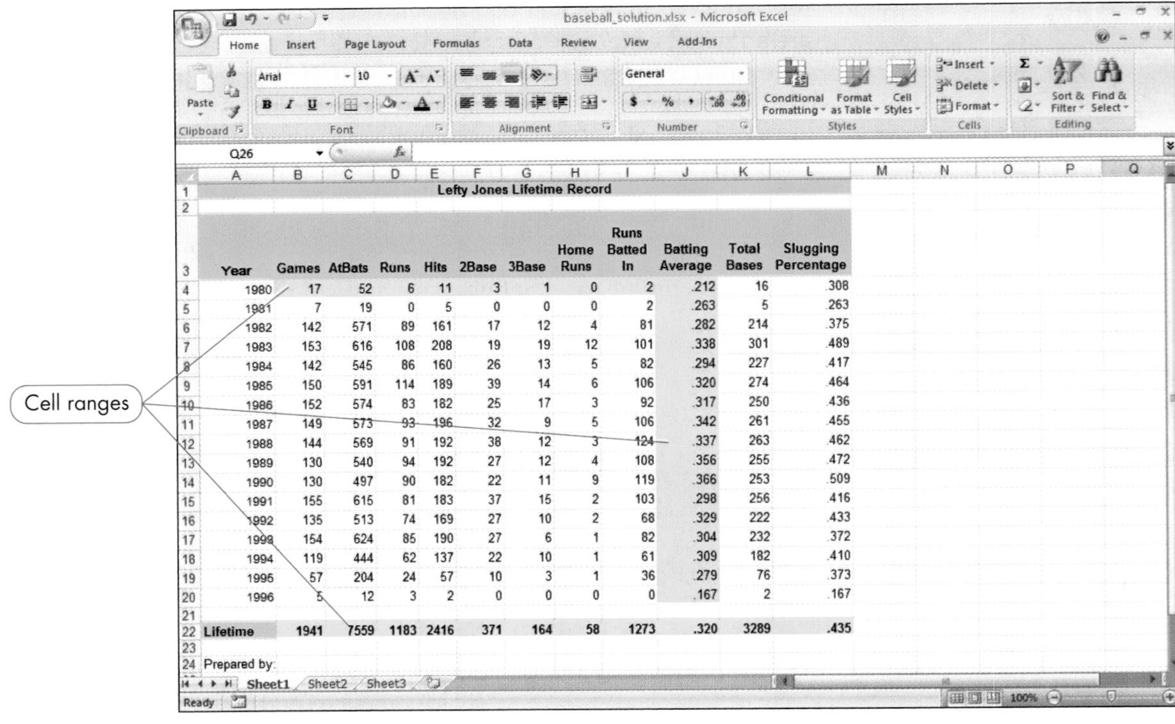

Year	Games	AtBats	Runs	Hits	2Base	3Base	Home Runs	Runs Batted In	Batting Average	Total Bases	Slugging Percentage
1980	17	52	6	11	3	1	0	2	.212	16	.308
1981	7	19	0	5	0	0	0	2	.263	5	.263
1982	142	571	89	161	17	12	4	81	.282	214	.375
1983	153	616	108	208	19	19	12	101	.338	301	.489
1984	142	545	86	160	26	13	5	82	.294	227	.417
1985	150	591	114	189	39	14	6	106	.320	274	.464
1986	152	574	83	182	25	17	3	92	.317	250	.436
1987	149	573	93	196	32	9	5	106	.342	261	.455
1988	144	569	91	192	38	12	3	124	.337	263	.462
1989	130	540	94	192	27	12	4	108	.356	255	.472
1990	130	497	90	182	22	11	9	119	.366	253	.509
1991	155	615	81	183	37	15	2	103	.298	256	.416
1992	135	513	74	169	27	10	2	68	.329	222	.433
1993	154	624	85	190	27	6	1	82	.304	232	.372
1994	119	444	62	137	22	10	1	61	.309	182	.410
1995	57	204	24	57	10	3	1	36	.279	76	.373
1996	5	12	3	2	0	0	0	0	.167	2	.167
Lifetime	1941	7559	1183	2416	371	164	58	1273	.320	3289	.435

Figure 1.19 Defined Ranges

The easiest way to select a range is to click and drag—click at the beginning of the range and then press and hold the left mouse button as you drag the mouse to the end of the range, where you release the mouse. To select an entire column, click the column letter. To select an entire row, click the row number. Once selected, the range is highlighted, and its cells will be affected by any subsequent command. The range remains selected until another range is defined or until you click another cell anywhere on the worksheet.

Move a Cell's Contents

The ***move operation*** transfers the content of a cell or cell range from one location to another, with the cells where the move originated becoming empty.

The ***move operation*** transfers the content of a cell or cell range from one location in the worksheet to another, with the cells where the move originated becoming empty. The use of the move command can be confusing when you copy a cell containing a formula. The cell references within formulas are not changed when a cell containing a formula is moved. Excel does, however, adjust all of the cells making up the formula when a cell containing a formula is moved. You can use the drag-and-drop technique to move a range of cells or the cut and paste method. To use the cut and paste method:

1. Select the range of cells to be moved.
2. Pick Cut in the Clipboard group on the Home tab.
3. Select the range the cells will be moved to.
4. Click Paste in the Clipboard group on the Home tab.

The ***delete operation*** removes all content from a cell or from a selected cell range.

The ***delete operation*** removes all content from a cell or from a selected cell range. While there are several ways to execute the delete operation, the most simple is to select a cell or range of cells and press Delete to remove the information from the cell(s).

Copy, Paste, Paste Special

The Copy, Paste, and Paste Special operations are essential editing operations in any Microsoft Office 2007 application. The Copy command enables you to begin to duplicate information in a cell or range of cells into another cell or range of cells. In order to copy material, you select the cell(s) to be copied and click Copy in the Clipboard group on the Home tab. The Paste operation enables you to duplicate cell contents that you have copied to a new location. Once the contents of a cell or range of cells have been copied, select the location on the worksheet where the material is to be copied to and click Paste in the Clipboard group on the Home tab. The Paste Special operation provides several different options when pasting material (see Figure 1.20). The power of the Copy and Paste operation is enhanced with the use of Paste Special in Excel.

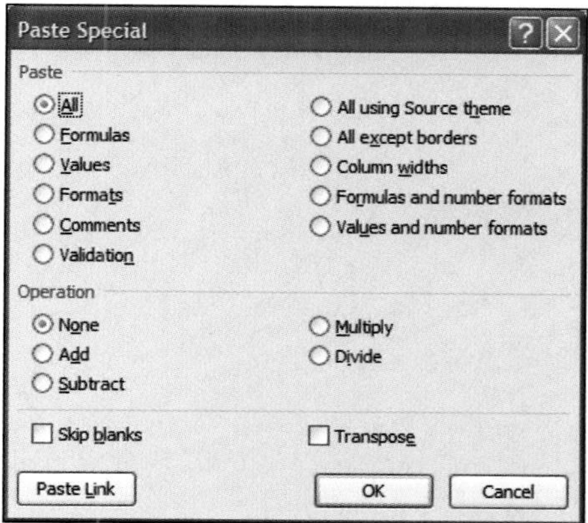

Figure 1.20 Paste Special Dialog Box

AutoFill enables you to copy the content of a cell or a range of cells by dragging the fill handle over an adjacent cell or range of cells.

The **fill handle** is a small black square appearing in the bottom-right corner of a cell.

Use AutoFill

AutoFill is an Excel operation that enables you to copy the content of a cell or a range of cells by dragging the ***fill handle*** (a small black square appearing in the bottom-right corner of a cell) over an adjacent cell or range of cells. AutoFill can be used in two different ways. First, you can use it to repetitively copy the contents of one cell. To do this, click the cell and use the fill handle to repeat the content. This operation is valuable for copying formulas, because the cell references are updated automatically during the AutoFill process. AutoFill also can be used to complete a sequence. For example, if you enter January in a cell, you can use AutoFill to enter the rest of the months of the year.

You can complete the quarters of a year by typing Qtr 1 in a cell and using AutoFill to fill in Qtr 2, Qtr 3, and Qtr 4 in sequence. Other sequences you can complete are weekdays and weekday abbreviations by typing the first item and using AutoFill to complete the other entries. For numeric values, however, you must specify the first two values in sequence. For example, if you want to fill in 5, 10, 15, and so on, you must enter the first two values in two cells, select the two cells, and then use AutoFill so that Excel knows to increment by 5.

TIP Two Different Clipboards

The Office Clipboard holds a total of up to 24 objects from multiple applications, as opposed to the Windows Clipboard, which stores only the results of the last Cut or Copy command. Thus, each time you execute a Cut or Copy command, the contents of the Windows Clipboard are replaced, whereas the copied object is added to the objects already in the Office Clipboard. To display the Office Clipboard, click the Home tab and click the arrow to the right of the word Clipboard. Leave the Clipboard open as you execute multiple cut and copy operations to observe what happens.

Hands-On Exercises

2 | Jake's Gym Continued

Skills covered: 1. Open an Existing Workbook **2.** Use Save As to Save an Existing Workbook **3.** Insert a Row and Compute Totals **4.** Copy the Formulas **5.** Continue the Calculations **6.** Insert a Column

Step 1 Open an Existing Workbook

Refer to Figures 1.21 and 1.22 as you complete Step 1.

a. Click the **Office Button** and select **Open**.

You should see the Open dialog box, similar to Figure 1.21.

b. Click the **Views drop-down arrow**, and then select **Details**.

You changed the file list to a detailed list view, which shows more information.

c. Click the arrow on the **Look In** list box and click the appropriate drive depending on the location of your data.

You are navigating to the file you want to open.

d. Click the scroll arrow if necessary in order to select *chap1_ho2_jake*. Click **Open** to open the workbook shown in Figure 1.22.

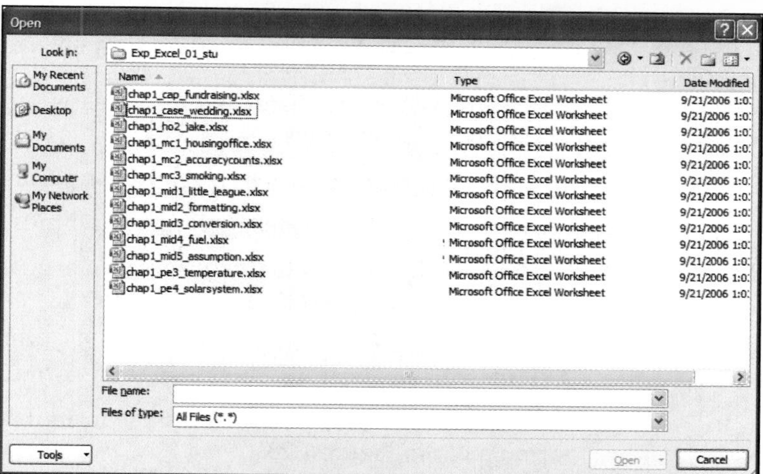

Figure 1.21 Open Dialog Box

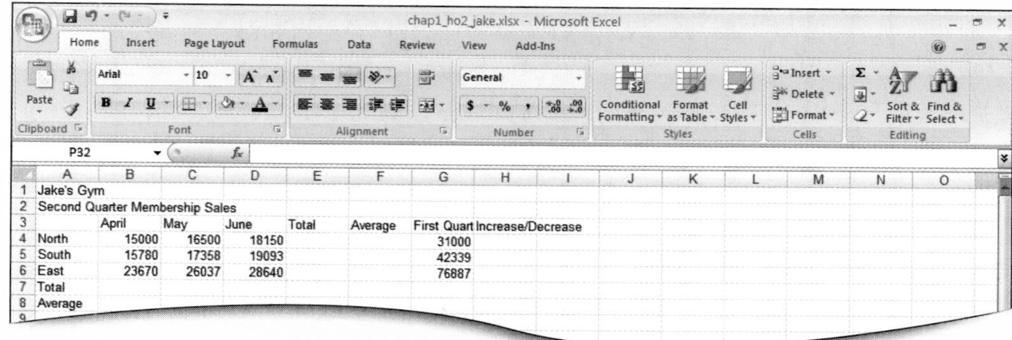

Figure 1.22 Original Jake's Gym Spreadsheet

Step 2
Use Save As to Save an Existing Workbook

a. Click the **Office Button** and select **Save As** to display the Save As dialog box.

b. Type **chap1_ho2_jake_solution** as the name of the new workbook.

   A file name may contain up to 255 characters. Spaces, underscores, and commas are allowed in the file name.

c. Click the **Save** button.

   Two identical copies of the file exist on disk, *chap1_ho2_jake* and *chap1_ho2_jake_solution*, which you just created. The title bar shows the latter name, which is the workbook currently in memory. You will work with *chap1_ho2_jake_solution* workbook but can always return to the original *chap1_ho2_jake* workbook if necessary.

TIP Create a New Folder

Do you work with a large number of different workbooks? If so, it may be useful to store those workbooks in different folders, perhaps one folder for each subject you are taking. Click the Office Button, select Save As to display the Save As dialog box, and then click the Create New Folder button to display the associated dialog box. Enter the name of the folder, and then click OK. After you create the folder, use the *Look in* box to change to that folder the next time you open that workbook.

Step 3
Insert a Row and Compute Totals

Refer to Figure 1.23 as you complete Step 3.

a. Select **row 3**, click the **Insert arrow** in the Cells group on the Home tab, and select **Insert Sheet Rows**.

   You have inserted a new row between rows 2 and 3.

b. Click in **cell A3**. Type **Sales by Region** and press **Enter**.

c. Click in **cell E5**, the cell that will contain the quarterly sales total for the North region. Type **=B5+C5+D5** and press **Enter**.

   The border appearing around cells B5, C5, and D5 indicates they are part of the formula you are creating. You entered the formula to compute a total.

d. Click in **cell E5**, check to make sure the formula matches the formula in the formula bar in Figure 1.23.

   If necessary, click in the formula box in the formula bar and make the appropriate changes so that you have the correct formula in cell E5.

e. Click in **cell F5**, the cell that will contain the average sales for the North region for the second quarter. Type **=E5**.

   You have begun to create the formula to calculate the average for the second quarter.

f. Type **=E5/3** to calculate the average for the second quarter by dividing the total by 3, the number of months in the quarter. Press **Enter**.

   Total sales, 49650, is the second quarter total, and 16550 is the average quarterly sales.

   TROUBLESHOOTING: If you type an extra arithmetic symbol at the end of a formula and press Enter, Excel will display an error message box suggesting a correction. Read the message carefully before selecting Yes or No.

g. Click in **cell F5** and verify that the formula **=E5/3** is correct.

h. Type your name in **cell A13** and click **Save** on the Quick Access Toolbar to save the workbook.

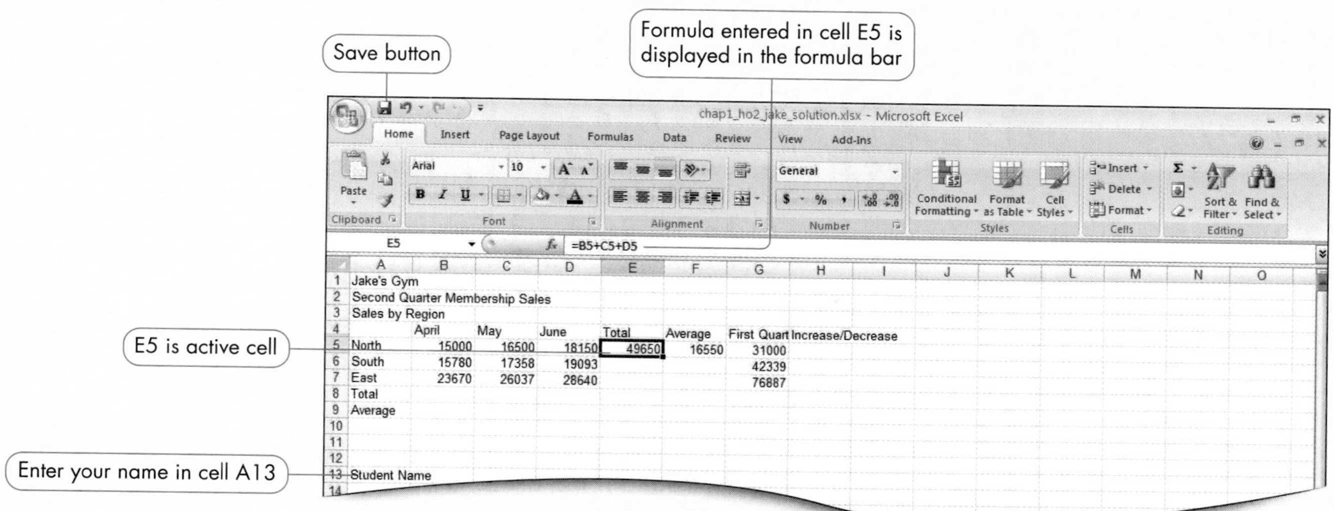
Save button
Formula entered in cell E5 is displayed in the formula bar
E5 is active cell
Enter your name in cell A13

Figure 1.23 Insert Name and Compute Totals

Step 4
Copy the Formulas

Refer to Figure 1.24 as you complete Step 4.

a. Click **cell E5**.

   Point to the fill handle in the lower-right corner of cell E5. The mouse pointer changes to a thin crosshair.

b. Drag the fill handle to **cell E7** (the last cell in the region total column).

   A light gray color appears as you drag the fill handle, as shown in Figure 1.24.

c. Release the mouse to complete the copy operation.

   The formulas for region totals have been copied to the corresponding rows for the other regions. When you click in cell E7, the cell displaying the total for the East region, you should see the formula: =B7+C7+D7.

d. Click **cell F5** and drag the fill handle to **cell F7** to copy the average sales formula down the column.

e. Save the workbook.

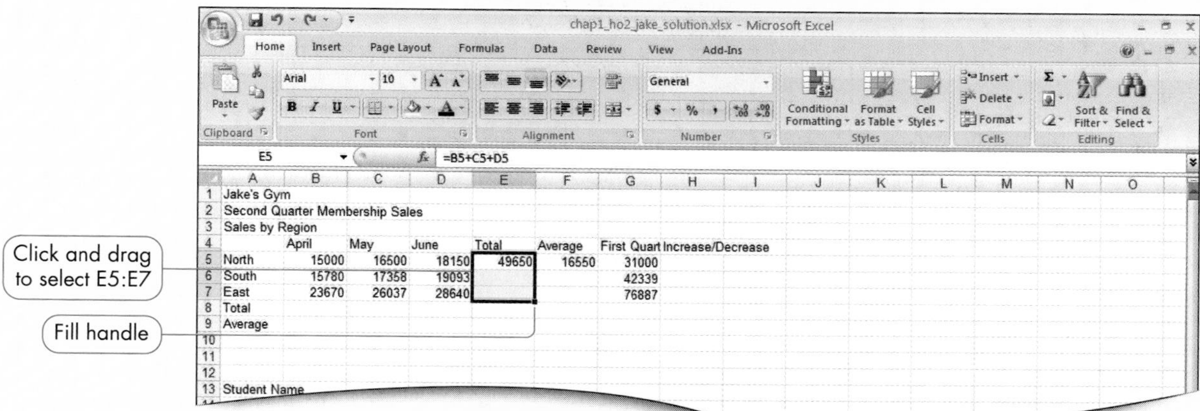
Click and drag to select E5:E7
Fill handle

Figure 1.24 Copy the Formulas

Step 5

Continue the Calculations

Refer to Figure 1.25 as you complete Step 5.

a. Click **cell H5**, the cell that will contain the quarterly sales increase or decrease.

b. Type **=(E5–G5)/G5** and press **Enter**.

   You should see 0.601613 as the increase in sales from the first quarter to the second quarter for the North region. If this result is not correct, click cell H5 and verify that the formula =(E5-G5)/G5 is correct. Correct it in the formula bar if necessary.

c. Click **cell H5** and use the fill handle to copy the formula down the column to **cell H7**.

d. Click in **cell B8**. Type **=B5+B6+B7** and press **Enter**.

e. Click in **cell B9** to begin the formula to calculate the average sales for April. Type **=(B5+B6+B7)/3** and press Enter.

   If the formula is entered correctly, you will see 18150 in cell B9. This is an awkward method of creating a formula to determine an average of values, and you will learn to use another method in Chapter 2. However, this formula illustrates the use of parentheses to control the order of precedence.

   TROUBLESHOOTING: The parentheses used in the formula force the addition before the division and must be used to calculate the correct value.

f. Click **cell B8** and drag through **cell B9** to select both cells. Drag the fill handle in the lower-right corner of cell B9 across through **cell E9** to copy the formulas.

   You copied the formulas to calculate both the monthly sales totals and averages for columns B through E.

g. Click in **cell G5** and type **52000**, then press **Enter**. See Figure 1.25.

   Updated information shows that the first-quarter earnings in the North region were misreported. The new number, 52000, represents a decrease in sales between the first and second quarters in the North region.

h. Save the workbook.

   You entered the formulas to calculate the appropriate totals and averages for all regions for the second quarter. You also entered the formula to determine the increase or decrease in sales from the first quarter to the second quarter.

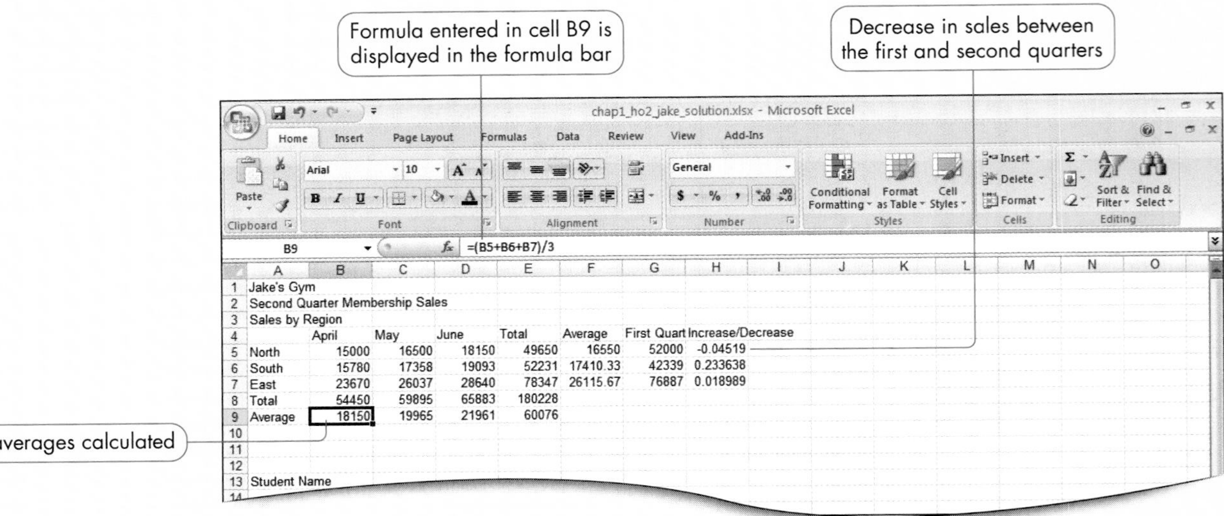

Figure 1.25 Continue the Calculations

Step 6
Insert a Column

Refer to Figure 1.26 as you complete Step 6.

a. Click the **column letter G**, the column to the left of where you want to insert a column.

When you insert a column, it appears to the left of your initial selection, and the columns are moved to the right.

b. Click on the **Insert down arrow** in the Cells group on the Home tab.

Figure 1.26 shows the Insert options in the Cells group.

c. Select **Insert Sheet Columns**.

You inserted a blank column to the left of the First Quarter column or column G.

d. Save the *chap1_ho2_jake_solution* workbook and keep it onscreen if you plan to continue to the next hands-on exercise. Close the workbook and exit Excel if you do not want to continue with the next exercise at this time.

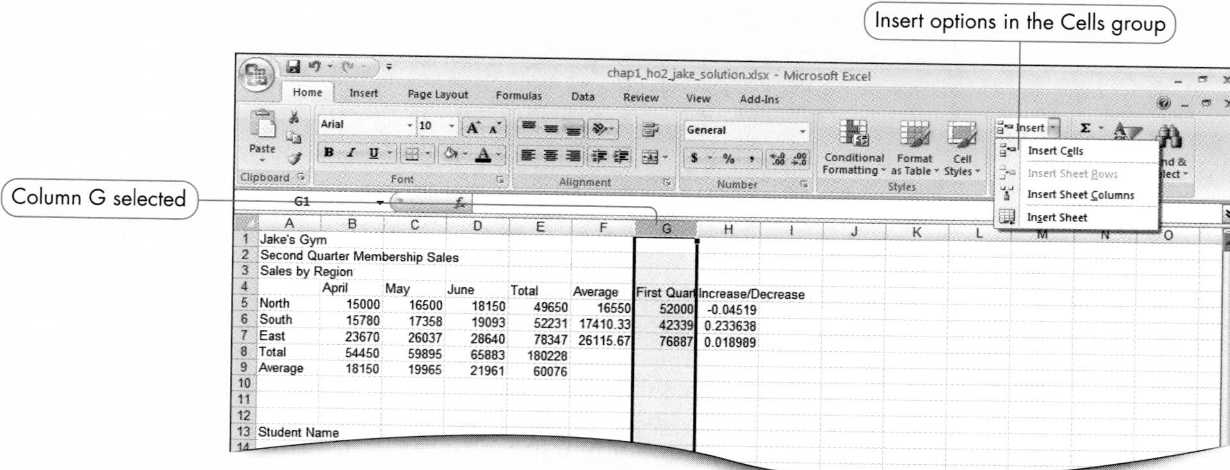

Figure 1.26 Insert a Column

TIP Using a Shortcut Menu

Another method to insert a row or column is to right-click anywhere on a row or column to show a shortcut menu. Click Insert to insert a row or a column and then select the appropriate option from the dialog box. Rows are inserted above the active cell, and columns are inserted to the left of the active cell.

Workbook and Worksheet Enhancements

At the beginning of this chapter, you learned that a worksheet or spreadsheet is a grid containing columns and rows to store numerical data. Further, you learned that a workbook is a single file that contains one or more related worksheets. So far, you have created one worksheet within a workbook. However, as you continue using Excel to develop workbooks for personal and professional use, you need to learn how to manage multiple worksheets.

In this section, you learn how to manage worksheets. Specifically, you rename worksheets and change worksheet tab colors. Furthermore, you learn how to insert, delete, add, and move worksheets.

Managing Worksheets

When you start a new blank workbook in Excel, the workbook contains three worksheets by default. These worksheets are called Sheet1, Sheet2, and Sheet3. You can insert additional worksheets if you need to store related worksheet data in the same workbook, or you can delete worksheets that you do not need. Furthermore, you can rename worksheets, rearrange the sequence of worksheets, or change the color of the worksheet tabs.

Rename Worksheets

As you have learned, it is a simple matter to move among sheets in a workbook by clicking on the appropriate sheet tab at the bottom of the worksheet window. You also learned that the default names of sheets in a new workbook are Sheet1, Sheet2, etc. To give workbook sheets more meaningful names, you will want to rename them. For example, if your budget workbook contains worksheets for each month, you should name the worksheets by month, such as *January* and *February*. A teacher who uses a workbook to store a grade book for several classes should name each sheet by class name or number, such as *MIS 1000* and *MIS 2450*. Follow these steps to rename a worksheet tab:

1. Right-click a sheet tab to show a shortcut menu.
2. Select Rename and the sheet tab name is highlighted.
3. Type the new sheet tab name and press Enter.

Change Worksheet Tab Color

The sheet tabs are blue in color by default. The active worksheet tab is white. When you use multiple worksheets, you might find it helpful to add a color to sheet tabs in order to make the tab stand out or to emphasize the difference between sheets. For example, you might want the January tab to be blue, the February tab to be red, and the March tab to be green in a workbook containing monthly worksheets. Changing the color of the tabs in workbooks when sheets have similar names helps to identify the tab you want to work with. Follow these steps to change the worksheet tab color:

1. Right-click the Sheet1 tab.
2. Select Tab Color.
3. You select Theme Colors, Standard Colors, No Color, or More Colors.

Move, Delete, Copy, and Add Worksheets

The fastest way to move a worksheet is to click and drag the worksheet tab. To delete a worksheet in a workbook, right-click on the sheet tab and select Delete from the shortcut menu. You can copy a worksheet in similar fashion by pressing and holding

Ctrl as you drag the worksheet tab. Move, Copy, and Delete worksheet operations also are accomplished by right-clicking the desired sheet tab and selecting the needed option from the shortcut menu.

To add a new blank worksheet, right-click any sheet tab, and select Worksheet from the Insert dialog box, and click OK.

You might want to move a worksheet to reorder existing sheets. For example, January is the first budget sheet, but at the end of January you move it after December so February is the sheet that opens first. If a professor is no longer teaching a course, she might delete a grade book sheet. Once a grade book sheet is created, it can be copied, modified, and used for another course.

TIP Moving, Copying, and Renaming Worksheets

The fastest way to move a worksheet is to click and drag the worksheet tab. You can copy a worksheet in similar fashion by pressing and holding Ctrl as you drag the worksheet tab. To rename a worksheet, double-click its tab to select the current name, type the new name, and press Enter.

Formatting Worksheets

Formatting worksheets allows you to change or alter the way numbers and text are presented. You can change alignment, fonts, the style of text, and the format of values, and apply borders and shading to cells, for example. These formatting procedures allow you to prepare a more eye-appealing worksheet. You format to draw attention to important areas of the worksheet, and you can emphasize totals or summary area values.

(. . . formatting procedures allow you to prepare a more eye-appealing worksheet.)

Merge and Center Labels

The ***merge and center cells*** option centers an entry across a range of selected cells.

You may want to place a title at the top of a worksheet and center it over the material contained in the worksheet. Centering helps to unify the information on the worksheet. The best way to do this is to ***merge and center cells*** into one cell across the top of the worksheet and center the content of the merged cell. See Figure 1.27, the before, and Figure 1.28, the after. The merged cells are treated as one single cell. This is a toggle command and can be undone by clicking Merge & Center a second time. To merge cells and center a title across columns A through L you would:

1. Enter the title in cell A1.
2. Select cells A1:L1.
3. Click Merge & Center in the Alignment group on the Home tab.

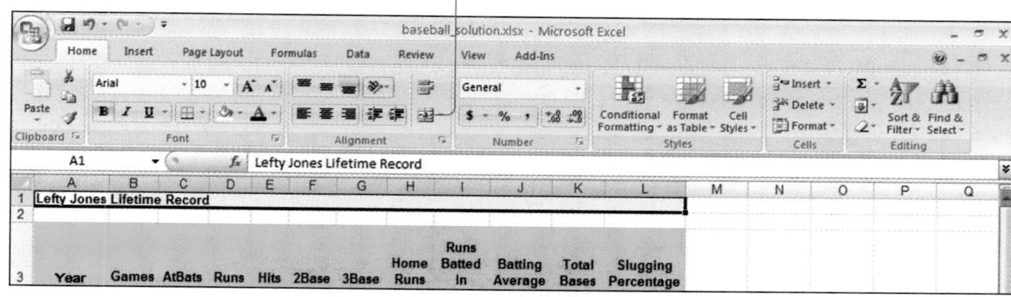

Figure 1.27 Merge and Center Title

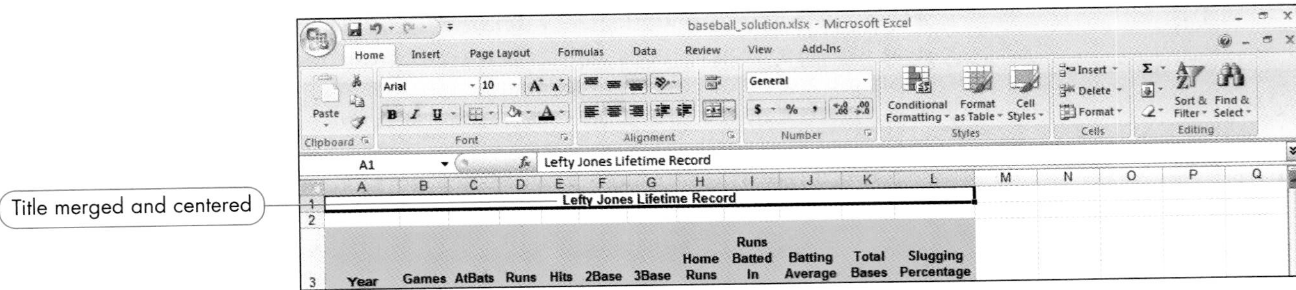

Figure 1.28 Merged and Centered Title

Adjust Cell Height and Width

It often is necessary to change the height and/or width of a cell so all of its contents are visible. When labels are longer than the cell width, they are displayed in the next cell if it is empty. If the adjacent cell is not empty, the label is truncated. Numbers appear as a series of pound signs (######) when the cell is not wide enough to display the complete number. To widen a column, drag the border between column headings to change the column width.

For example, to increase or decrease the width of column A, point to the border, and you will see a two-headed arrow. Drag the border between column headings A and B to the right or left. You also can double-click the right boundary of a column heading to change the column width to accommodate the widest entry in that column.

To increase or decrease the width of row 1, drag the border between row headings 1 and 2 up or down. You can also double-click the bottom boundary of a row heading to change the row height to accommodate entries in their entirety. Alternatively, right-click on the row number to show a shortcut menu and select Row Height. Enter an integer and click OK.

AutoFit automatically adjusts the height and width of cells.

AutoFit is an important command used when formatting a spreadsheet to automatically adjust the height and width of cells. You can choose from two types of AutoFit commands available in Format in the Cells group on the Home tab (see Figure 1.29). The AutoFit Column Width changes the column width of the selected columns to fit the contents of the column. AutoFit Row Height changes the row height of the selected row to fit the contents of the row.

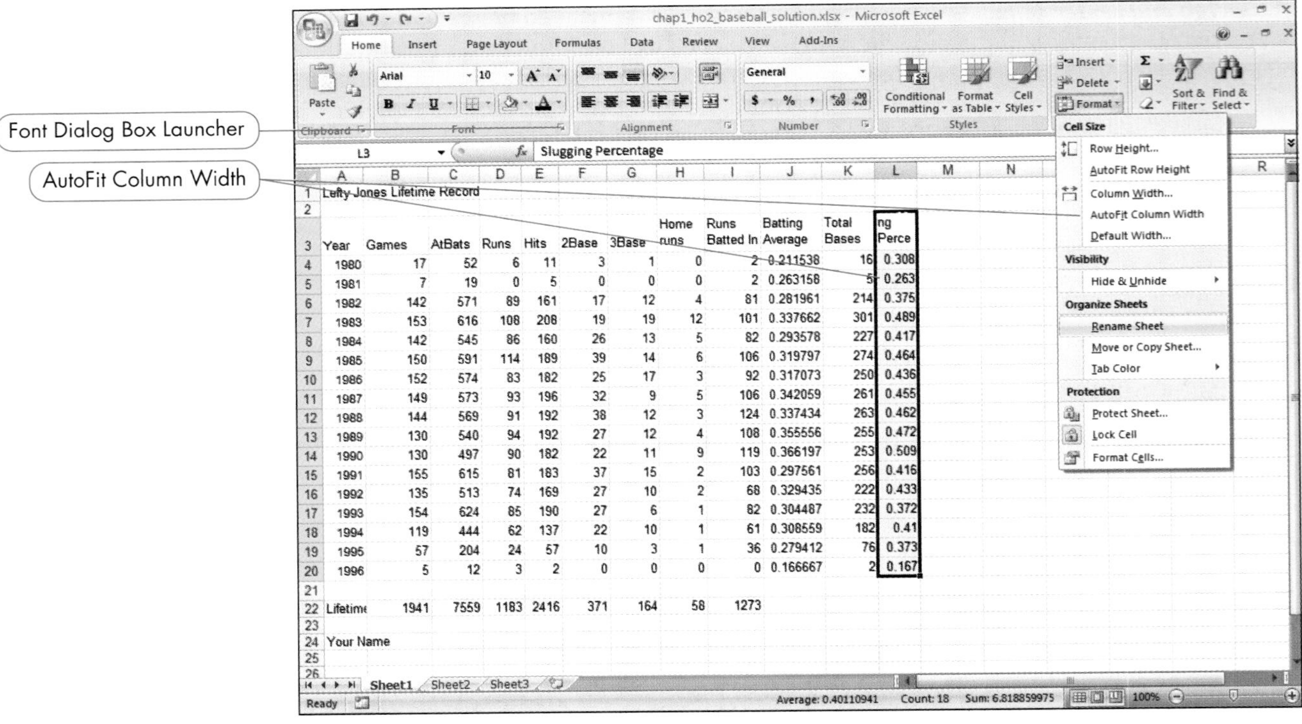

Figure 1.29 AutoFit

TIP Multiple Row Height/Column Width

To change the row height of many rows at one time, select the multiple rows and right-click to show the shortcut menu. Select Row Height and enter a number in the Row Height dialog box, as shown in Figure 1.30. Click OK. To change the column width of many columns at one time, select the multiple columns and right-click to show the shortcut menu. Select Column Width and enter a number in the Column Width dialog box. Click OK.

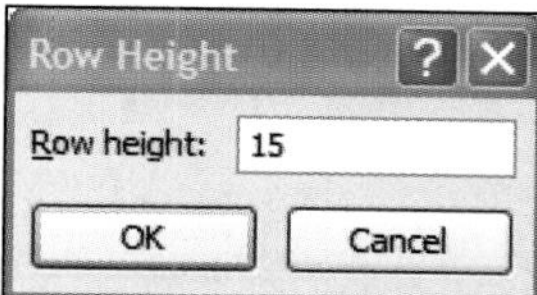

Figure 1.30 Row Height Dialog Box

Apply Borders and Shading

You have several options to choose from when adding borders to cells or applying a shade to cells. You can select a cell border from Borders in the Font group on the Home tab or you can use the Border tab in the Format Cells dialog box. Either way, you can create a border around a cell (or cells) for additional emphasis. Click the Font Dialog Box Launcher in the Font group on the Home tab (see Figure 1.29), and then click the Border tab. Figure 1.31 shows the Border tab in the Format Cells dialog box. Select (click) the line style at the left of the dialog box, and then click the left, right, top, and/or bottom border. It is possible to outline the entire cell or selected cells, or choose the specific side or sides; for example, thicker lines on the bottom and right sides produce a drop shadow, which can be very effective. Also, you can specify a different line style and/or a different color for the border, but a color printer is needed to see the effect on the printed output.

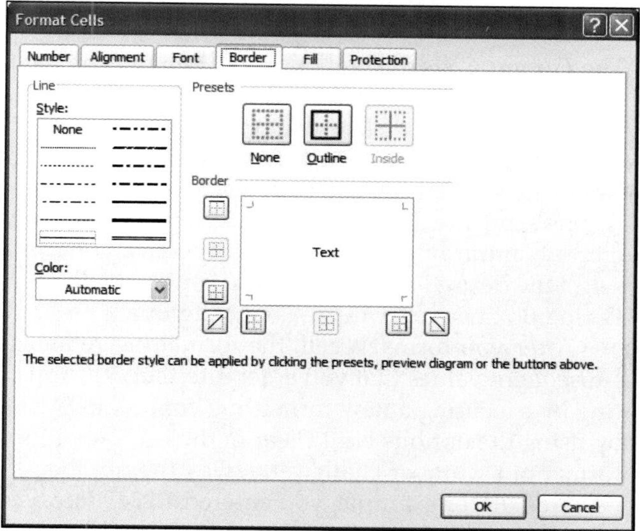

Figure 1.31 Border Tab on the Format Cells Dialog Box

You can add a shade to a cell from Fill Color in the Font group on the Home tab or you can use the Fill tab in the Format Cells dialog box. The Fill tab and Fill Color enable you to choose a different color in which to shade the cell and further emphasize its contents. The Pattern Style drop-down list lets you select an alternate pattern, such as dots or slanted lines. Click OK to accept the settings and close the dialog box. Figure 1.32 shows the Fill tab of the Format Cells dialog box.

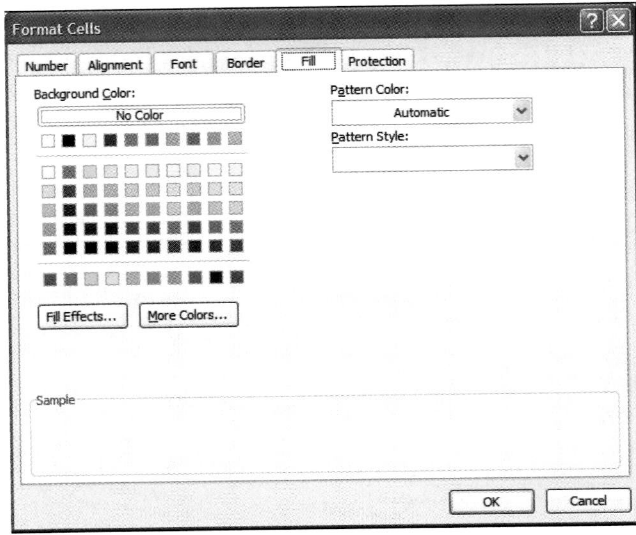

Figure 1.32 Fill Tab on the Format Cells Dialog Box

Insert Clip Art

A good way to enhance the appearance of a spreadsheet is to insert a clip art image. These images can represent the subject of the spreadsheet, the company preparing the spreadsheet, or even the personal interests of the person preparing the spreadsheet. You should use caution when inserting clip art because they can be distracting to the user of the spreadsheet or can take large amounts of disk space and slow operations on the spreadsheet. If you want to insert clip art, click Clip Art in the Illustrations group on the Insert tab to open the Clip Art task pane. Type a keyword in the Search for text box and click Go to begin the search for images matching your keyword. When you find an appropriate image, double-click it to place it in your spreadsheet. You can now move and resize the image as desired.

Format Cells

The ***Format Cells*** operation controls formatting for numbers, alignment, fonts, borders, colors, and patterns.

The ***Format Cells*** dialog box and commands on the Home tab control the formatting for numbers, alignment, fonts, borders, colors, and patterns. Execution of the command produces a tabbed dialog box in which you choose the particular formatting category, and then enter the desired options. All formatting is done within the context of select-then-do. You can select the cells to which the formatting is to apply and then execute the Format Cells command. If you want to apply the same formats to an entire column or row, click the respective column letter or row number, and then select the desired format. You can display the Format Cells dialog box by clicking the Dialog Box Launcher in the Font, Alignment, or Number group.

After you format a cell, the formatting remains in the cell and is applied to all subsequent values that you enter into that cell. You can, however, change the formatting by executing a new formatting command. Also, you can remove the formatting by using the options with Clear in the Editing group on the Home tab. Changing the format of a number changes the way the number is displayed, but does not change its value. If, for example, you entered 1.2345 into a cell, but displayed the number as 1.23, the actual value (1.2345) would be used in all calculations involving that cell. The numeric formats are shown and described in Table 1.5. They are accessed by clicking the Number Format down arrow in the Number group on the Home tab. The tabbed Format Cells dialog box is displayed by selecting More.

Table 1.5 Formatting Definitions

Format Style	Definition
General	The default format for numeric entries and displays a number according to the way it was originally entered. Numbers are shown as integers (e.g., 123), decimal fractions (e.g., 1.23), or in scientific notation (e.g., 1.23E+10) if the number exceeds 11 digits.
Number	Displays a number with or without the 1000 separator (e.g., a comma) and with any number of decimal places. Negative numbers can be displayed with parentheses and/or can be shown in red.
Currency	Displays a number with the 1000 separator and an optional dollar sign (which is placed immediately to the left of the number). Negative values can be preceded by a minus sign or displayed with parentheses, and/or can be shown in red.
Accounting	Displays a number with the 1000 separator, an optional dollar sign (at the left border of the cell, vertically aligned within a column), negative values in parentheses, and zero values as hyphens.
Date	Displays the date in different ways, such as March 14, 2009, 3/14/09, or 14-Mar-09.
Time	Displays the time in different formats, such as 10:50 PM or the equivalent 22:50 (24-hour time).
Percentage	Shows when the number is multiplied by 100 for display purposes only, a percent sign is included, and any number of decimal places can be specified.
Fraction	Displays a number as a fraction, and is appropriate when there is no exact decimal equivalent. A fraction is entered into a cell by preceding the fraction with an equal sign—for example, =1/3. If the cell is not formatted as a fraction, you will see the results of the formula.
Scientific	Displays a number as a decimal fraction followed by a whole number exponent of 10; for example, the number 12345 would appear as 1.2345E+04. The exponent, +04 in the example, is the number of places the decimal point is moved to the left (or right if the exponent is negative). Very small numbers have negative exponents.
Text	Left aligns the entry and is useful for numerical values that have leading zeros and should be treated as text, such as ZIP codes.
Special	Displays a number with editing characters, such as hyphens in a Social Security number.
Custom	Enables you to select a predefined customized number format or use special symbols to create your own customized number format.

Use Fonts

You can use the same fonts in Excel as you can in any other Windows application. All fonts are WYSIWYG (What You See Is What You Get), meaning that the worksheet you see on the monitor will match the printed worksheet.

Any entry in a worksheet may be displayed in any font, style, or point size, as indicated in the Font group on the Home tab, as shown in Figure 1.33. The example shows Arial, Bold, Italic, and 14 points. Special effects, such as subscripts or superscripts, are also possible. You can even select a different color, but you will need a color printer to see the effect on the printed page.

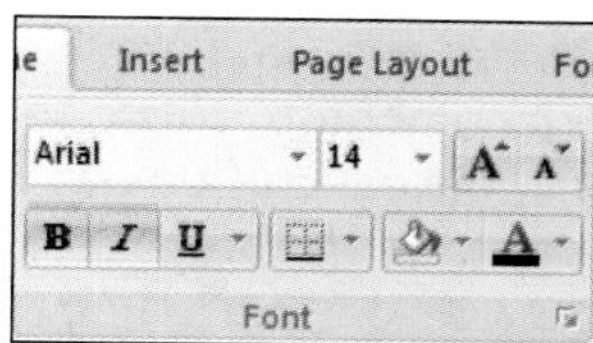

Figure 1.33 Font Group on the Home Tab

Alignment of Cell Contents

The Alignment tab in the Format Cells dialog box and the Alignment group on the Home tab together give you a wealth of options to choose from. Changing the orientation of cell contents is useful when labels are too long and widening columns is not an option. Wrapping text in a cell also reduces the need to widen a column when space is at a premium. Centering, right aligning, or left aligning text can be done for emphasis or to best display cell contents in columns. When the height of rows is changed, it is necessary to vertically adjust alignment for ease of reading. Figure 1.34 shows both the Alignment group and the Format Cells dialog box with the Alignment tab visible.

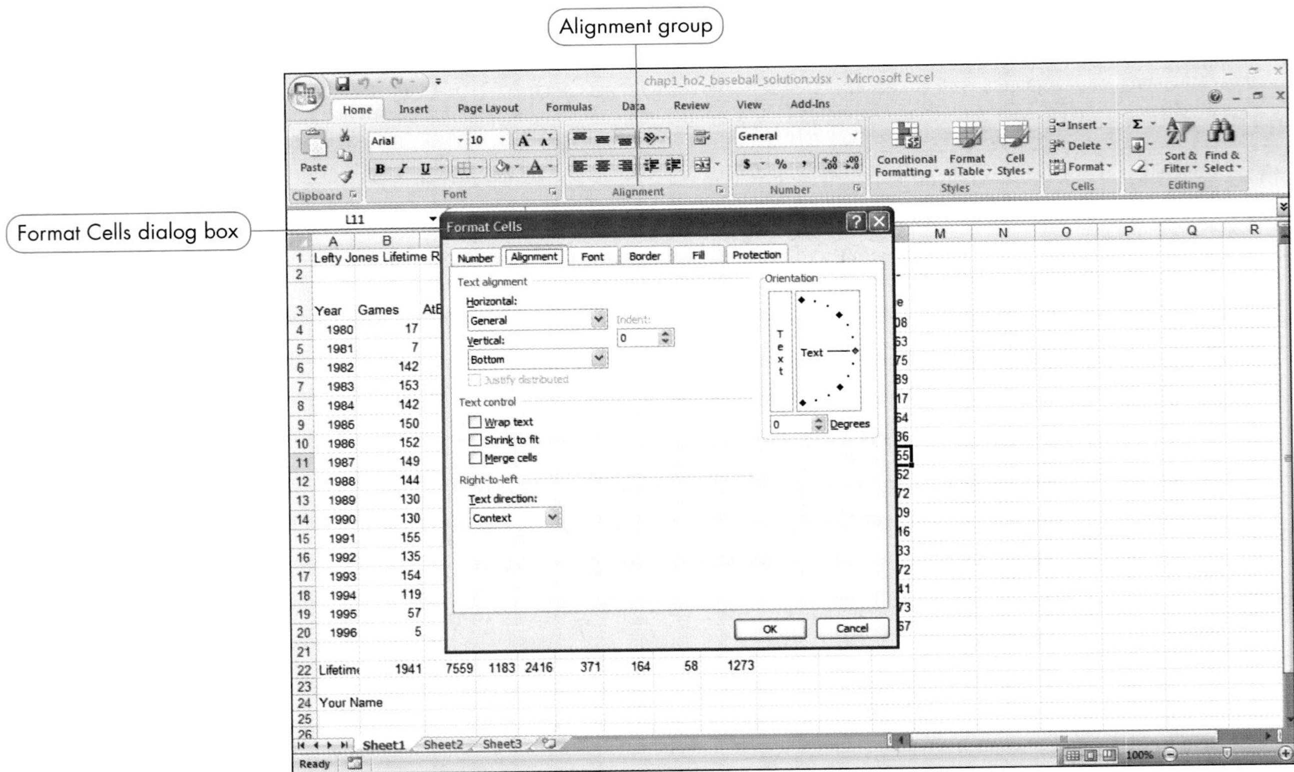

Figure 1.34 Alignment Group and Alignment Tab

TIP Use Restraint

More is not better, especially in the case of too many typefaces and styles, which produce cluttered worksheets that impress no one. Limit yourself to a maximum of two typefaces per worksheet, but choose multiple sizes or styles within those typefaces. Use boldface or italics for emphasis, but do so in moderation, because if you emphasize too many elements, the effect is lost. Figure 1.37 shows locations of number format commands.

Hands-On Exercises

3 | Formatting Jake's Gym Worksheet

Skills covered: 1. Manage the Workbook **2.** Apply Number Formats **3.** Apply Font Attributes and Borders **4.** Change Alignment Attributes **5.** Insert an Image

Step 1 Manage the Workbook

Refer to Figure 1.35 as you complete Step 1.

a. If necessary, open the *chap1_ho2_jake_solution* workbook and save it as **chap1_ho3_jake_solution**.

b. Right-click **Sheet1 tab** at the bottom of the worksheet and select **Rename** from the shortcut menu.

You selected the generic Sheet1 tab so you can give it a more meaningful name.

c. Type **Second Quarter** and press **Enter**.

d. Right-click on the **Second Quarter** sheet tab and select **Tab Color**.

e. Select **Accent 5** color from the Theme Colors gallery.

You applied a color to the Second Quarter sheet tab to make it more distinctive.

f. Right-click the **Sheet2 tab** and click **Delete**.

g. Right-click the **Sheet3 tab** and click **Delete**.

You have deleted the unused worksheets from the workbook.

h. Save the workbook.

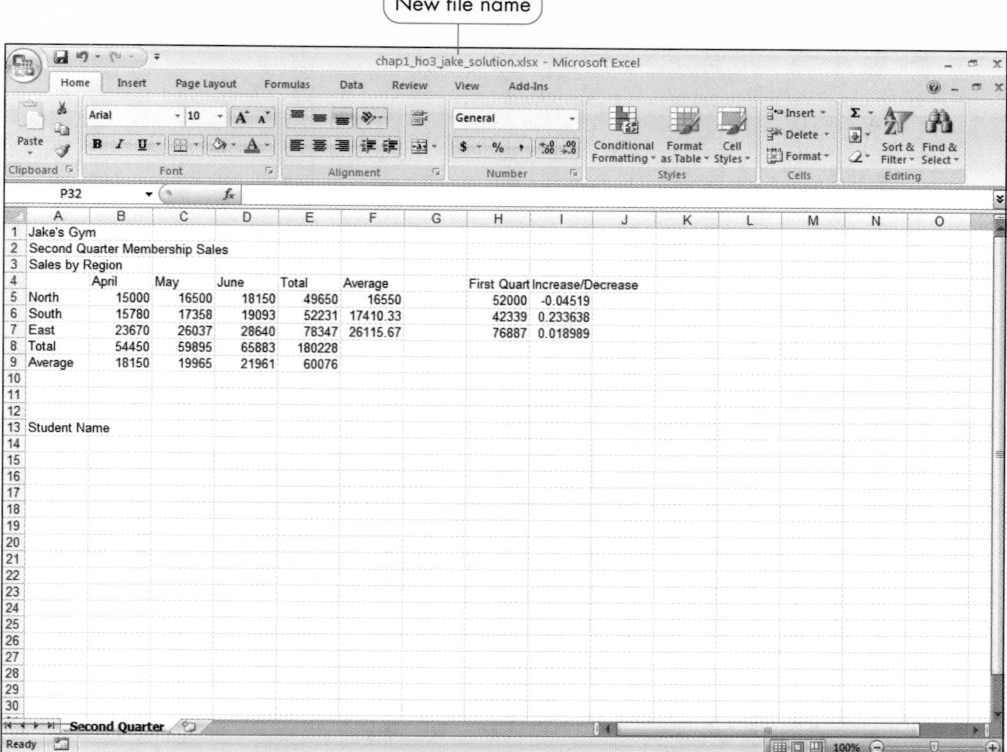

Figure 1.35 Workbook Management

Step 2
Apply Number Formats

Refer to Figure 1.36 as you complete Step 2.

a. Click in **cell I5**, and then click and drag to select the **range I5:I7**.

   You selected the range of cells to be formatted.

b. Click the **Home tab** and click the **Number Dialog Box Launcher** in the Number group.

   The Format Cells dialog box shown in Figure 1.36 is now displayed on your screen.

c. Click the **Number tab** and select **Percentage** from the *Category* list.

d. Type **1** in the Decimal places box. Click **OK** to close the dialog box.

   You formatted the increase or decrease in sales as a percentage with 1 decimal place.

e. Click and drag to select the **range B5:H9**.

f. Click the **Number Dialog Box Launcher** in the Number group.

g. Click the **Number tab** and select **Currency** from the *Category* list.

h. Type **0** for the Decimal places box. Click **OK** to close the dialog box.

   You formatted the remaining values as currency with 0 decimal places.

i. Save the workbook.

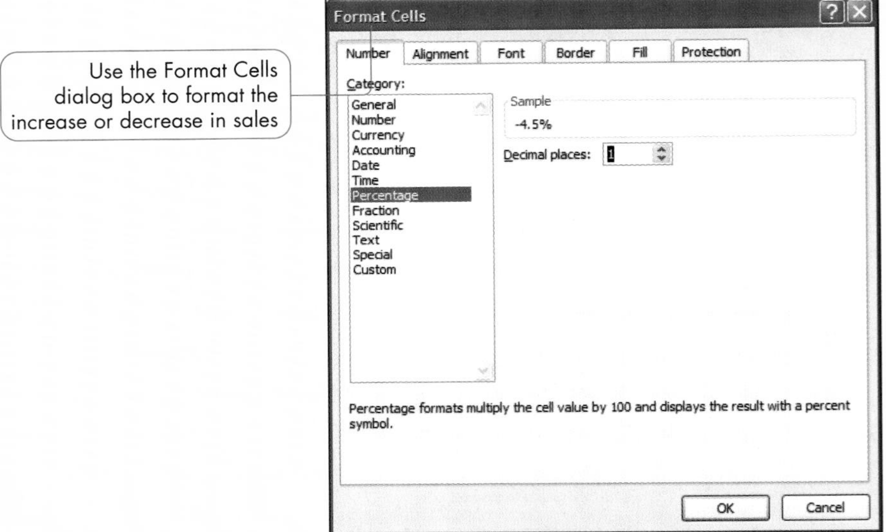

Figure 1.36 Apply Number Format

TIP Number Formats

You can change some number formats in the Number group on the Home tab. For example, you can click Accounting Number Format to display dollar signs and align decimal points for monetary amounts. You can click the Number down arrow to select various number formats, such as Number, Accounting, Date, Percentage, and Fraction. The Number group also contains commands to increase or decrease the number of decimal points. Figure 1.37 shows locations of number format commands.

Step 3
Apply Font Attributes and Borders

Refer to Figure 1.37 as you complete Step 3. Your screen display may be different despending on your screen resolution.

a. Click and drag to select the **range A1:I3**.

b. Press and hold **Ctrl** while selecting the **range A8:E9**. Continue to press and hold Ctrl while clicking **cell A13** to select it.

   You selected several ranges of noncontiguous cells and you can now apply multiple formats to these ranges.

c. Click the **Fill Color** arrow in the Font group and select the color **Purple**.

d. Click the **Font Color** arrow in the Font group and select **White**.

   TROUBLESHOOTING: If you apply a format and change your mind, just apply another format or clear the formatting using Clear in the Editing group on the Home tab.

e. Click **Bold** in the Font group to make the text stand out.

   You formatted parts of the worksheet by using a color fill, a font color, and a font enhancement. You want to draw attention to these areas of the worksheet.

f. Select the **range B4:F4**, then press and hold **Ctrl** while selecting the **ranges H4:I4** and **B7:E7**.

g. Click **More Borders** in Font group and click **Bottom Double Border**.

   You again selected noncontiguous ranges of cells and then applied a double border to the bottom of the cells.

h. Select **cell E6**, press and hold **Ctrl** while selecting **cell H6,** and select **Yellow** from **Fill Color** in the Font group.

   This highlights the large increase in sales in the South region between the first and second quarter.

i. Save the workbook.

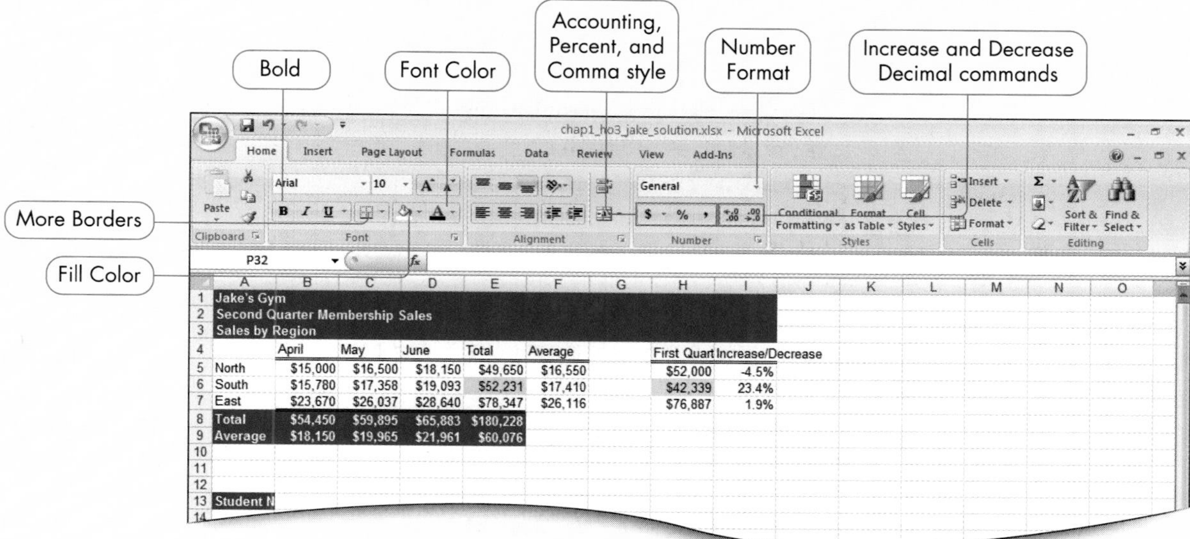

Figure 1.37 Continue Formatting Attributes and Borders

Step 4
Change Alignment Attributes

Refer to Figure 1.38 as you complete Step 4.

a. Click on the **Home tab** if it is not already active.

b. Click and drag to select the **range A1:I1**.

c. Click **Merge & Center** in the Alignment group on the Home tab.

d. Click and drag to select the **range A2:I2**.

e. Click **Merge & Center** in the Alignment group on the Home tab.

f. Click and drag to select the **range A3:I3**.

g. Click **Merge & Center** in the Alignment group on the Home tab.

   You have now merged cells and centered the title and two subtitles in single cells. You cannot select more than one row and merge into a single cell.

h. Click and drag to select the **range A4:I4**.

i. Right-click on the selected cell range to display a shortcut menu, then select **Format Cells** to display the dialog box.

j. Click the **Alignment tab**, and then click the **Wrap text check box** in the *Text control* section.

k. Click the **Horizontal drop-down arrow** in the *Text alignment* section, select **Center**, and click **OK** to accept the settings and close the dialog box.

   You used the shortcut menu to open the dialog box and made two enhancements to the selected text. It is more efficient to make multiple changes using a dialog box.

   TROUBLESHOOTING: If your monitor is set for a high resolution or if you have a wide screen monitor, you may see text by some of the command icons. For example, you might see the words *Wrap Text* by the Wrap Text command in the Alignment group. If you want your screen to have the same resolution as the figures shown in this textbook, change your resolution to 1024 × 768.

TIP Split a Cell

If you merge too many cells or decide you no longer want cells to be merged, you can split the merged cell into individual cells again. To do this, select the merged cell and click Merge & Center in the Alignment group or deselect Merge cells on the Alignment tab in the Format Cells dialog box.

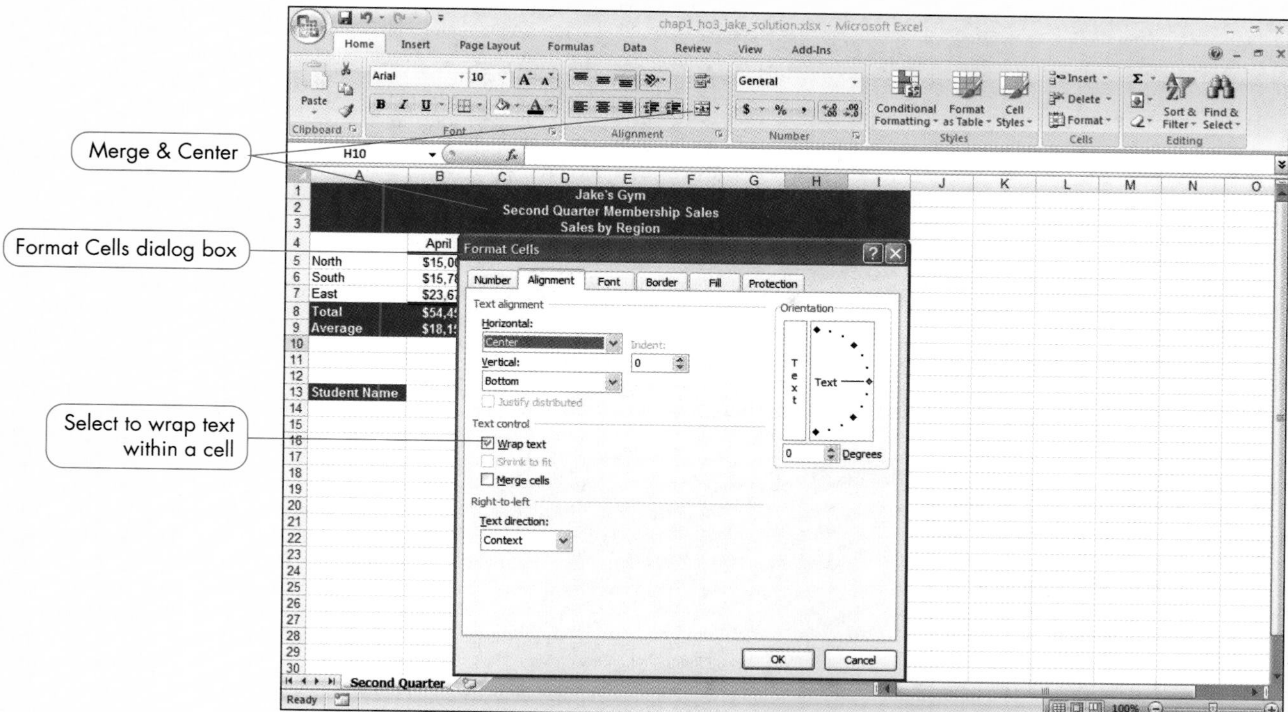

Figure 1.38 Change Alignment Attributes

Step 5
Insert an Image

Refer to Figure 1.39 as you complete Step 5.

a. Click in **cell A1**, click the **Insert tab**, and click **Clip Art** in the Illustrations group. A Clip Art task pane opens. Type **exercise** in the **Search for** box and click **Go**.

   You are going to insert a clip art image in the worksheet but must first search for an appropriate image.

b. Click to insert the image shown in Figure 1.39. Click the image to select it and drag the lower-right sizing handle to resize the image to fit the worksheet.

   When working with images, it is necessary to resize the images and widen columns or change row height.

c. Save the *chap1_ho3_jake_solution* workbook and keep it onscreen if you plan to continue to the next hands-on exercise. Close the workbook and exit Excel if you do not want to continue with the next exercise at this time.

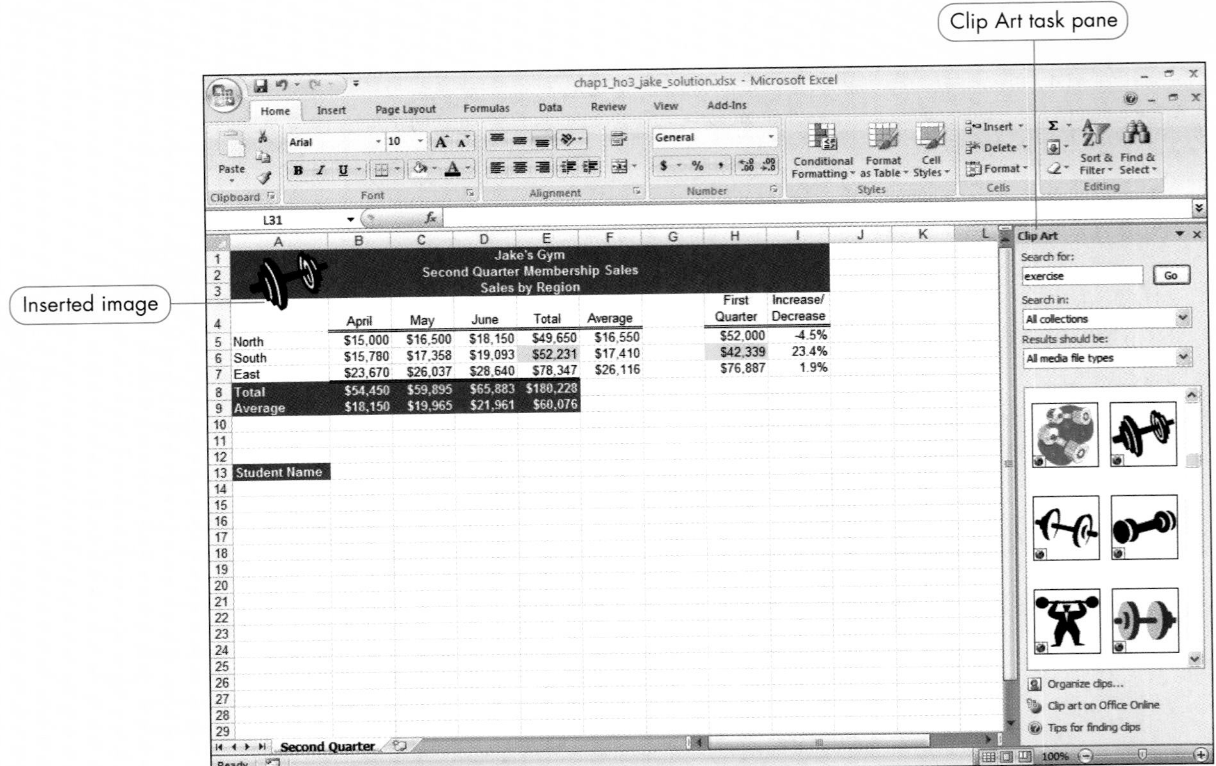

Figure 1.39 Continue to Format the Worksheet

Page Setup and Printing

The Page Setup command gives you complete control of the printed worksheet. Many of the options may not appear significant now, but you will appreciate them as you develop larger and more complicated worksheets later in the text. Workbooks and worksheets become part of auditor's reports in organizations' annual reports and quarterly reports. Spreadsheets are part of dissertations and grade books, and are the basis for budgeting both for personal use and corporate use. As you can see, printing workbooks and worksheets is an important function.

(The Page Setup command gives you complete control of the printed worksheet.)

In this section, you select options in the Page Setup dialog box that will help make your printouts look more professional.

Selecting Page Setup Options for Printing

The key to selecting correct settings to print lies within the Page Setup dialog box. This dialog box contains four tabs. You will make selections from each to indicate the printing settings for the worksheet you want to print. The Page Setup dialog box also contains the Print Preview button. This appears on each tab, and you will use the preview feature to view your selections from each tab. Print preview is a handy and efficient way to see how the printed output will appear without wasting paper. To launch the Print Dialog box, you click the Page Setup Dialog Box Launcher from the Page Setup group on the Page Layout tab. This dialog box is shown in Figure 1.40.

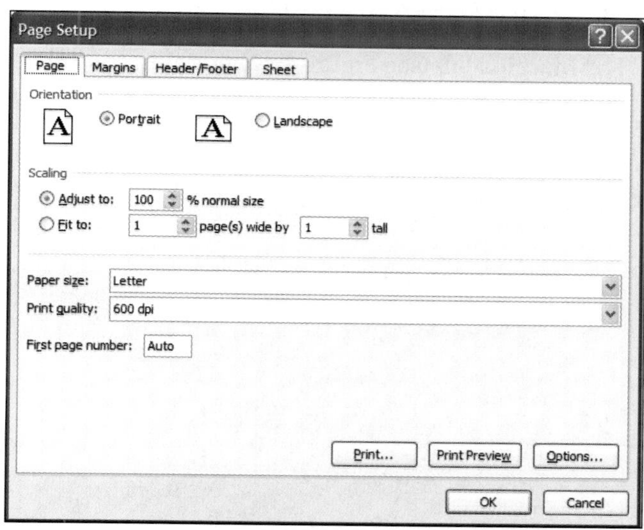

Figure 1.40 Page Setup Dialog Box

Specify Page Options with the Page Tab

The first tab that is open in the Page Setup dialog box is the Page tab, as shown in Figure 1.41. Note that you can use the Print Preview button from any of the Page Setup dialog box tabs and that the Options button takes the user to settings for the particular printer he or she is using. The Print Preview command shows you how the worksheet will appear when printed and saves you from having to rely on trial and error.

Portrait orientation prints vertically down the page.

Landscape orientation prints horizontally across the page.

The Page orientation options determine the orientation and scaling of the printed page. ***Portrait orientation*** (8.5 × 11) prints vertically down the page. ***Landscape orientation*** (11 × 8.5) prints horizontally across the page and is used when the worksheet is too wide to fit on a portrait page. Changing the page orientation to landscape is often an acceptable solution to fit a worksheet on one page. The other option, scaling, can produce uneven results when you print a workbook consisting of multiple worksheets.

Scaling option buttons are used to choose the scaling factor. You can reduce or enlarge the output by a designated scaling factor, or you can force the output to fit on a specified number of pages. The latter option is typically used to force a worksheet to fit on a single page. The Paper size and Print quality lists present several options for the size paper your printer is using and the dpi (Dots Per Inch) quality of the printer.

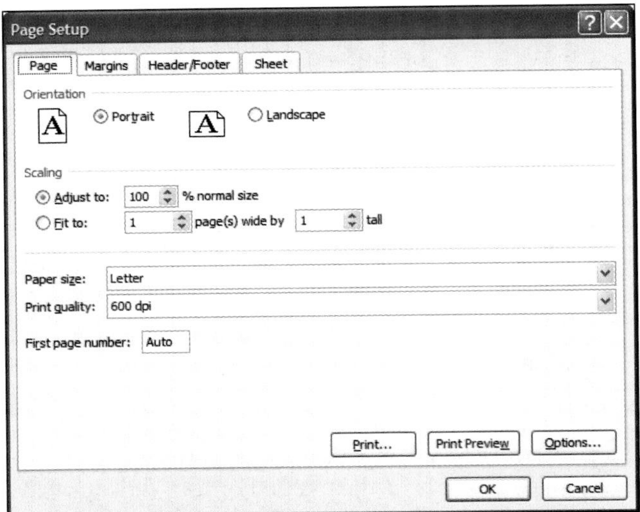

Figure 1.41 Page Tab

Use the Margins Tab to Set Margins

The Margins tab (see Figure 1.42) not only controls the margins, but is used to center the worksheet horizontally or vertically on the page. The Margins tab also determines the distance of the header and footer from the edge of the page. You must exercise caution in setting the margins as not all printers can accept very small margins (generally less than .25 inches). Worksheets appear more professional when you adjust margins and center the worksheet horizontally and vertically on a page.

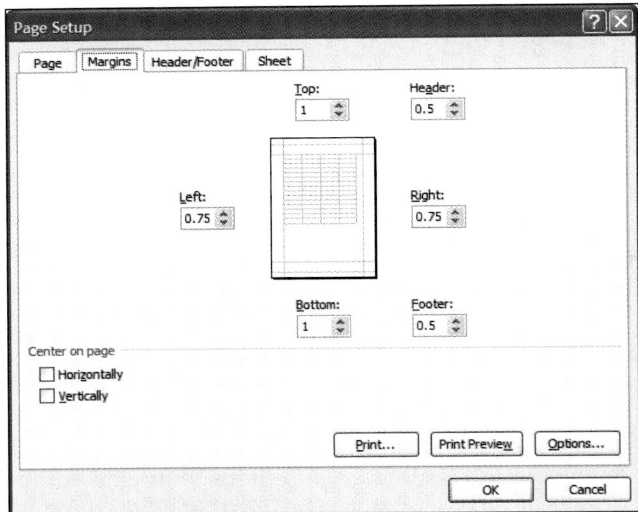

Figure 1.42 Margins

Create Headers and Footers with Header/Footer Tab

The Header/Footer tab, shown in Figure 1.43, lets you create a header and/or footer that appears at the top and/or bottom of every page. The pull-down list boxes let you choose from several preformatted entries, or alternatively, you can click the Custom Header or Custom Footer button, and then click the appropriate formatting button to customize either entry. Table 1.6 below shows a summary of the formatting buttons for headers and footers. You can use headers and footers to provide additional information about the worksheet. You can include your name, the date the worksheet was prepared, and page numbers, for example.

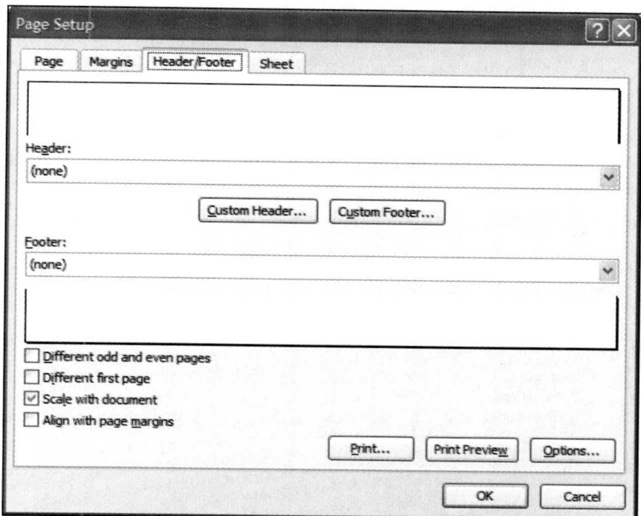

Figure 1.43 Headers and Footers

Table 1.6 Header/Footer Button Summary

Button	Name	Code Entered	Result
	Format Text	None	Sets font, size, and text style.
	Insert Page Number	&(Page)	Inserts page number.
	Insert Number of Pages	&(Pages)	Indicates total number of pages.
	Insert Date	&(Date)	Inserts the current date.
	Insert Time	&(Time)	Inserts the current time.
	Insert File Path	&(Path)&(File)	Indicates path and file name.
	Insert File Name	&(File)	Indicates the file name.
	Insert Sheet Name	&(Tab)	Shows the name of the active worksheet.
	Insert Picture	&(Picture)	Inserts an image file.
	Format Picture	None	Opens the Format Picture dialog box.

Select Sheet Options from the Sheet Tab

The Sheet tab contains several additional options, as shown in Figure 1.44. The Gridlines option prints lines to separate the cells within the worksheet. The Row and Column Headings option displays the column letters and row numbers. Both options should be selected for most worksheets. Just because you see gridlines on the screen does not mean they print. You must intentionally select the options to print both gridlines and row and column headings if you want them to print.

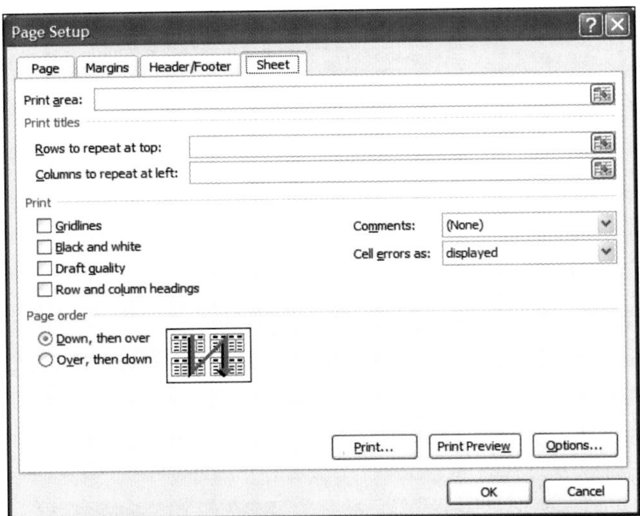

Figure 1.44 Sheet Tab

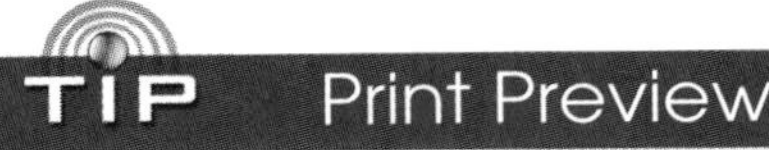

The Print Preview button is on all tabs of the Page Setup dialog box. This button is used to verify options as you make your page setup choices. Print Preview is a paper-saving feature because you can preview before printing. The Print button is located on all tabs of the Page Setup dialog box.

Managing Cell Comments

A ***comment*** adds documentation to a cell.

The use of cell ***comments*** in Excel is an important yet simple way to provide documentation to others who may view the file. Comments add documentation to a cell and are inserted in a cell to explain the preparer's thoughts to or define formulas for those using the workbook. Often, the creator of a file will want to provide information about a cell or cells in a worksheet without them always being visible. Inserting comments will accomplish this result. A red triangle appears in the cell containing the comment, and the comment is visible when you point at the cell. See Figure 1.45. To create a cell comment:

1. Click the cell requiring a comment.
2. On the Review tab, in the Comments group, click New Comment.
3. Enter the comment.
4. Click any other cell to complete the process.
5. Or right-click on the cell requiring a comment and select Insert Comment from the shortcut menu.

Hands-On Exercises

4 | Printing Jake's Gym Worksheet

Skills covered: 1. Insert a Comment **2.** Insert Custom Header and Footer **3.** Format to Print the Worksheet

Step 1
Insert a Comment

Refer to Figure 1.45 as you complete Step 1.

a. Open the *chap1_ho3_jake_solution* workbook and save it as **chap1_ho4_jake_solution**.

b. Click in **cell I6**.

You will type a descriptive comment in the selected cell.

c. Click the **Review tab** and click **New Comment** in the Comments group.

The name in the comment box will be different depending on how the application was registered.

d. Type **The largest percent of increase**.

e. Click any other cell to complete the process.

You can right-click the cell requiring a comment and select Insert Comment from the shortcut menu.

TROUBLESHOOTING: You can print your comments by first clicking in the cell containing a comment, and then clicking Show All Comments in the Comments group of the Review tab. Then select As displayed on sheet from the Comments list in the Sheet tab of the Page Setup dialog box.

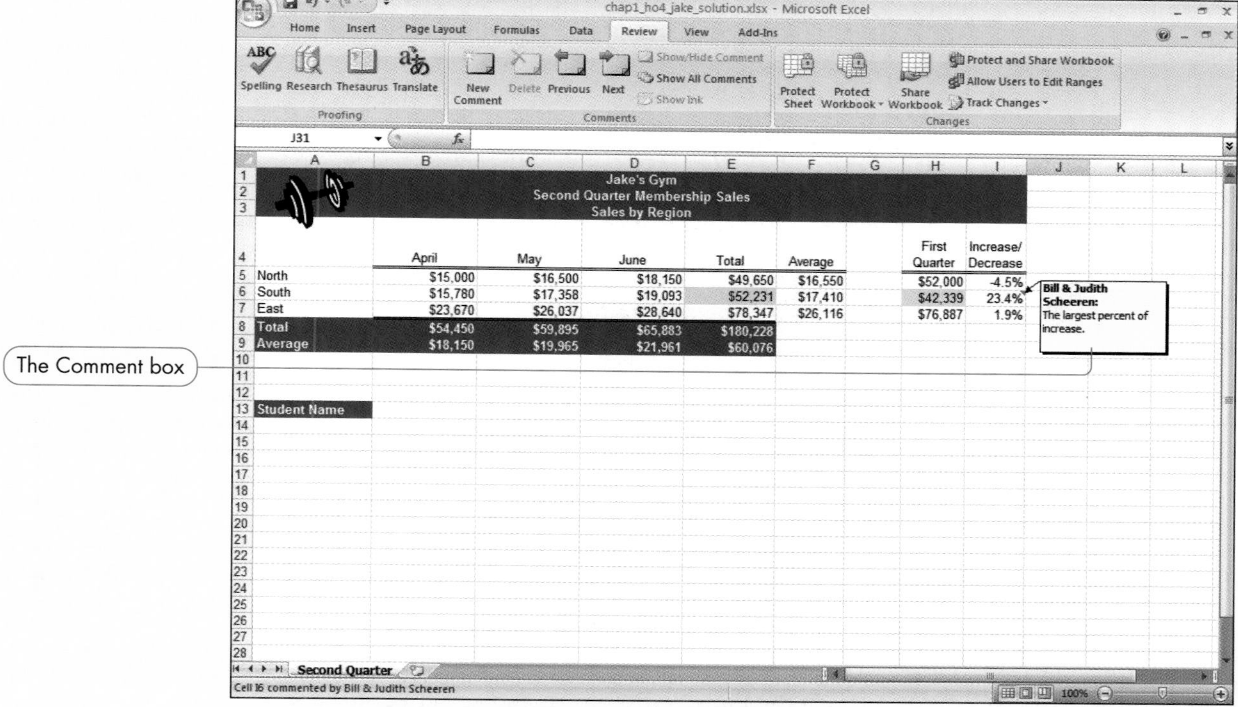

Figure 1.45 Insert a Comment

Step 2
Insert Custom Header and Footer

Refer to Figure 1.46 as you complete Step 2.

a. Click the **Page Layout tab** and click the **Page Setup Dialog Box Launcher** in the Page Setup group.

   You opened the Page Setup box so you can make several selections at one time.

b. Click the **Header/Footer tab**.

c. Click **Custom Header** and type your name in the left section.

d. Click in the right section and click **Insert Page Number**. Click **OK**.

   You created a header so your name and page number will display at the top of the spreadsheet page.

e. Click **Custom Footer** and click in the center section. Type your instructor's name.

f. Click in the right section, click **Insert Date**, and click **OK**.

   You created a footer so your instructor's name and the date will print at the bottom of the spreadsheet page.

g. Click **Print Preview**.

   You use the preview feature to verify the accuracy and placement of your header and footer information. You can also determine how much of the worksheet will print on a page.

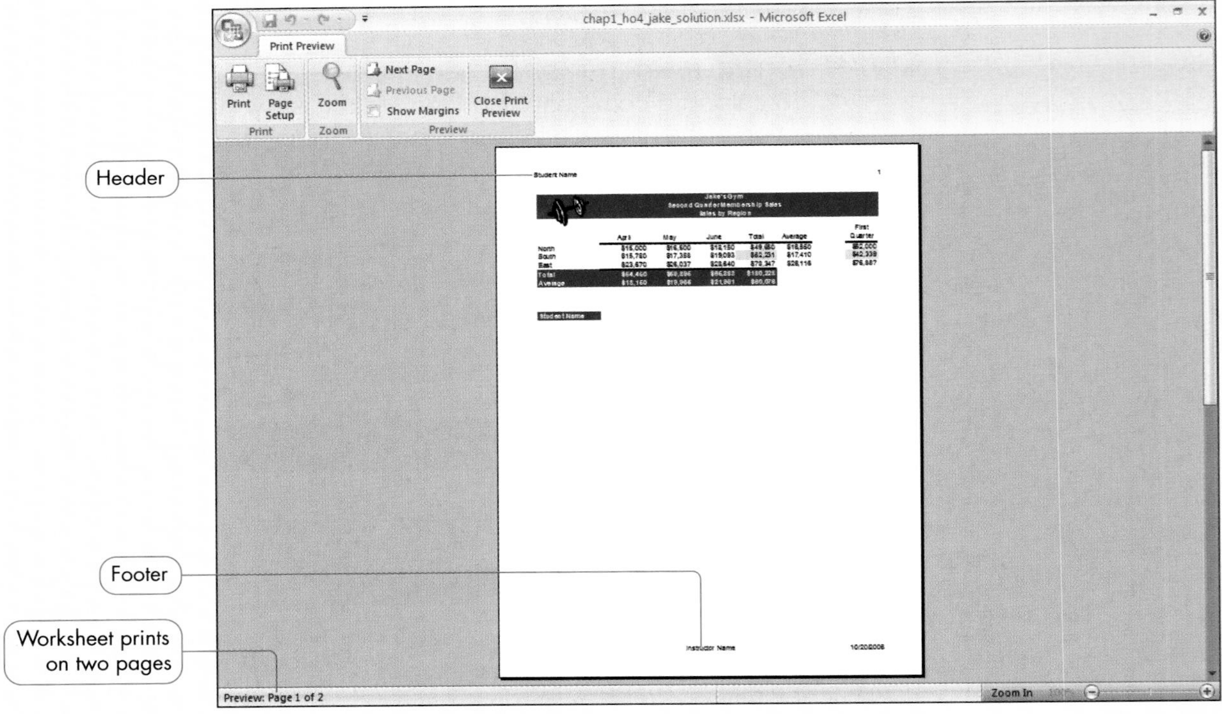

Figure 1.46 Insert a Custom Header and Footer

Step 3
Format to Print the Worksheet

Refer to Figure 1.47 as you complete Step 3.

a. Click the **Page Layout tab** if it is not the active tab. Click the **Orientation** arrow in the Page Setup group and select **Landscape**.

You changed from portrait to landscape as one method to make sure the worksheet prints on one page.

b. Click the **Size** arrow in the Page Setup group, select **More Paper Sizes**, and click the **Fit to 1 page option** in the *Scaling* section.

   You opened the Page Setup dialog box and selected *Fit to 1 page* to force the worksheet to print on a single page, another method to print the worksheet on one page. You will continue to make selections from the Page Setup dialog box.

c. Click the **Margins tab** in the Page Setup dialog box and click the **Horizontally** and **Vertically check boxes** in the *Center on page* section.

   Printing a worksheet that is centered both horizontally and vertically results in a Professional-appearing document.

d. Click the **Sheet tab** in the Page Setup dialog box and click the **Row and column headings** and **Gridlines check boxes** in the *Print* section. Click the **Print Preview button**.

   Row and column headings and gridlines facilitate reading the data in a worksheet.

e. Click **Print** to print the worksheet.

f. Save the workbook and press **Ctrl+~** to show the cell formulas rather than the displayed values. See Figure 1.47. Adjust the column widths as necessary to print on one page and then print the worksheet a second time.

   Displaying and printing cell formulas is one of the more important tasks associated with worksheet creation. Formulas are the basis of many values, and it is necessary to verify the accuracy of the values. Analyzing the formulas and perhaps manually calculating the formulas is one way to verify accuracy. Printing with formulas displayed is part of worksheet documentation.

g. Close the workbook. Do not save the changes unless your instructor tells you to save the worksheet.

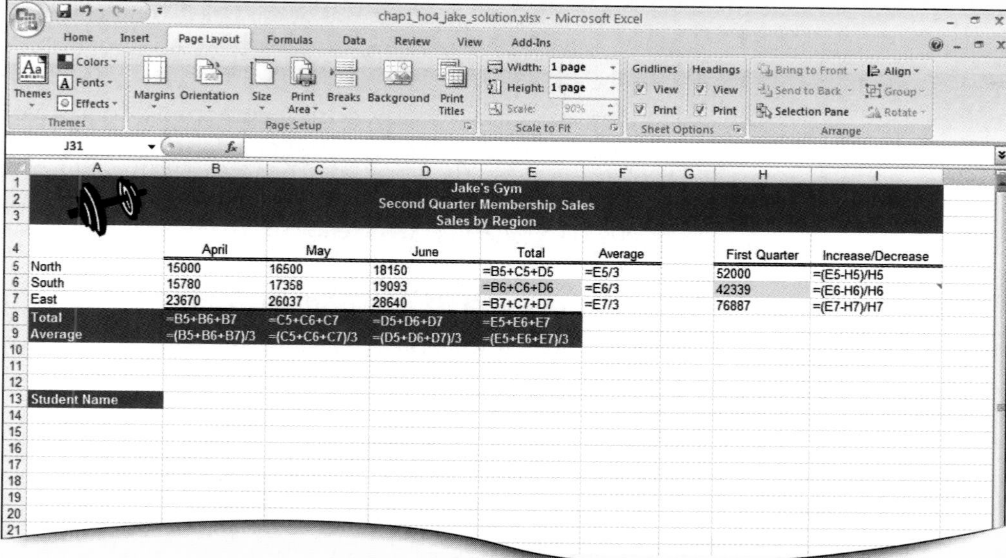

Figure 1.47 Displayed Cell Formulas

TIP Quit Without Saving

At times, you may not want to save the changes to a workbook—for example, when you have edited it beyond recognition and wish you had never started. Click the Office Button, click the Close command, and then click No in response to the message asking whether to save the changes. Click the Office Button, click the file's name at the right of the menu to reopen the file, and then begin all over.

Summary

1. **Define worksheets and workbooks.** A spreadsheet is the computerized equivalent of an accountant's ledger. It is divided into rows and columns, with each row and column assigned a heading. The intersection of a row and column forms a cell. Spreadsheet is a generic term. Workbook and worksheet are Excel specific. An Excel workbook contains one or more worksheets.
2. **Use spreadsheets across disciplines.** Spreadsheets are used in many areas other than business. Because of the powerful graphing or charting feature of Excel, geologists and physical scientists use spreadsheets to store data about earthquakes or other physical phenomena and then graph it. Historians and social scientists have long used the power of spreadsheets for such uses as predicting voting behavior.
3. **Plan for good workbook and worksheet design.** Planning a spreadsheet before entering data into it is a necessary activity. The more prior planning that is done, the better the spreadsheet will appear, and it also will ensure that the spreadsheet shows what it is supposed to.
4. **Identify Excel window components.** The elements of the Excel window include the ribbon, tabs, and groups. There are also quick buttons above the tabs to simplify some functions. The formula bar, sheet tabs, the status bar, and the Select All button are parts of the Excel window.
5. **Enter and edit data in cells.** You can enter three types of data in an Excel worksheet. They are text, values, and formulas. Each of these types of data has different uses in Excel.
6. **Describe and use symbols and the order of precedence.** Mathematical symbols are the base of all calculations in Excel. Understanding the order of precedence also helps clarify how mathematical calculations occur in Excel.
7. **Display cell formulas.** One of the tools that can be used to document an Excel worksheet is the ability to display cell formulas. When this tool is used, the formulas that appear in cells are shown rather than the results of the calculation.
8. **Insert and delete rows and columns.** This feature typically involves the use of the Insert command that adds cells, rows, or columns or the Delete command that deletes cells, rows, or columns. When either of these commands is used, the cell references in existing cells are automatically adjusted to reflect the insertion or deletion.
9. **Use cell ranges; Excel move; copy, paste, paste special; and AutoFill.** Each of these topics is a basic editing function in Excel. Every command in Excel applies to a rectangular group of cells known as a *range*. The Move operation transfers the content of a cell or cell range from one location on the worksheet to another with the cells where the move originated becoming empty. The Delete operation removes all content from a cell or from a selected cell range. The Copy command enables users to begin to duplicate information in a cell or range of cells into another cell or range of cells. The Paste operation enables the user to duplicate cell contents that have been copied to a new location. The Paste Special operation enables users several different options when pasting material. AutoFill is an Excel operation that enables users to copy the content of a cell or a range of cells by dragging the fill handle over another cell or range of cells.
10. **Manage worksheets.** These are operations that users of Excel should be familiar with in order to make worksheets more attractive and also to understand some basic operations that can assist in the construction of worksheets.
11. **Format worksheets.** Formatting is done within the context of select-then-do; that is, select the cell or range of cells, then execute the appropriate command. The Format Cells command controls the formatting for numbers, alignment, fonts, borders, and patterns (colors). The Formatting toolbar simplifies the formatting process. As you format a worksheet to improve its appearance, you might want to insert clip art as well.
12. **Select page setup options for printing.** The Page Setup command provides complete control over the printed page, enabling you to print a worksheet with or without gridlines or row and column headings. The Page Setup command also controls margins, headers and footers, centering the worksheet on a page, and orientation. The Print Preview command shows the worksheet as it will print and should be used prior to printing.
13. **Manage cell comments.** The use of comments in Excel is an important, yet simple, way to provide documentation to others who may view the file. Often the creator of a file will want to provide information about a cell or cells in a worksheet without them always being visible.

Key Terms

Active cell 255
AutoFill 272
AutoFit 280
Cell 259
Cell reference 259
Comment 294
Delete operation 271
Fill handle 272
Format Cells 282
Formula bar 255
Formula 260
Landscape orientation 291
Merge and center cells 279
Move operation 271
Name box 255
Order of precedence 268
Portrait orientation 291
Range 270
Select All button 255
Sheet tabs 255
Spreadsheet 251
Spreadsheet program 251
Text 260
Value 260
Workbook 252
Worksheet 252

Multiple Choice

1. Which of the following is true?
   (a) A worksheet contains one or more workbooks.
   (b) A workbook contains one or more worksheets.
   (c) A spreadsheet contains one or more worksheets.
   (d) A worksheet contains one or more spreadsheets.

2. The cell at the intersection of the second column and third row is cell:
   (a) B3
   (b) 3B
   (c) C2
   (d) 2C

3. Which options are mutually exclusive in the Page Setup menu?
   (a) Portrait and landscape orientation
   (b) Cell gridlines and row and column headings
   (c) Left and right margins
   (d) Fit to page and Adjust to normal size

4. Which of the following is not a symbol for a mathematical operation in Excel?
   (a) +
   (b) –
   (c) C
   (d) *

5. Which command enables you to change the margins for a printed worksheet?
   (a) View
   (b) Edit
   (c) Page Setup
   (d) Options

6. What is the effect of typing F5+F6 into a cell without a beginning equal sign?
   (a) The entry is equivalent to the formula =F5+F6.
   (b) The cell will display the contents of cell F5 plus cell F6.
   (c) The entry will be treated as a text entry and display F5+F6 in the cell.
   (d) The entry will be rejected by Excel, which will signal an error message.

7. The Save command:
   (a) Brings a workbook from disk into memory.
   (b) Brings a workbook from disk into memory and then erases the workbook on disk.
   (c) Stores the workbook in memory on disk.
   (d) Stores the workbook in memory on disk and then erases the workbook from memory.

8. Which of the following is not a basic mathematical operation?
   (a) Parentheses
   (b) Division
   (c) Multiplication
   (d) Subtraction

9. Given the formula =B5*B6+C3/D4^2, which expression would be evaluated first?
   (a) B5*B6
   (b) D4^2
   (c) C3/D4
   (d) It is impossible to determine.

10. If you see the term "C3" used in relation to Excel, this refers to what?
    (a) Absolute reference
    (b) Cell reference
    (c) Worksheet reference
    (d) Mixed reference

11. Which of the following is the correct order of mathematical operations?
    (a) Parentheses, multiplication or division, addition or subtraction
    (b) Parentheses, exponents, multiplication or division, addition or subtraction
    (c) Parentheses, exponents, addition or subtraction, multiplication or division
    (d) Multiplication or division, addition or subtraction, parentheses, exponents

12. What is the answer to =10+4*3?
    (a) 42
    (b) 22
    (c) 34
    (d) 17

Multiple Choice Continued...

13. What is the answer to =(6*5)+4?

(a) 34
(b) 44
(c) 26
(d) 54

14. The fill handle is used to:

(a) Copy
(b) Paste
(c) Cut
(d) Select

15. The small black square in the bottom-right corner of a cell is called what?

(a) Pointer
(b) Fill handle
(c) Cross hair
(d) Select box

16. A red triangle in a cell indicates which of the following:

(a) A cell is locked.
(b) The cell contains an absolute reference.
(c) The cell contains a comment.
(d) The cell contains numeric data.

17. Which of the following is entered first when creating a formula?

(a) The equal sign
(b) A mathematical operator
(c) A function
(d) A value

18. What is the end result of clicking in a cell and then clicking Italic on the Home tab twice in a row?

(a) The cell contents are displayed in italic.
(b) The cell contents are not displayed in ordinary (non-italicized) type.
(c) The cell contents are unchanged and appear exactly as they did prior to clicking the Italic button twice in a row.
(d) Impossible to determine.

19. Which option is not available when creating a custom header or custom footer?

(a) Format Text
(b) Insert Formula
(c) Insert Number of Pages
(d) Format Picture

Practice Exercises

1 Verifying a Debit Card

One of the more common challenges beginning college students face is keeping track of their finances. The worksheet in this problem is one that you could use to verify your weekly debit card expenditures. Failure to track your debit card correctly could lead to financial disaster, as you are charged for overdrafts and could get a bad credit rating. You will use the data shown in the table below to create the worksheet. Refer to Figure 1.48 as you complete this exercise.

a. Start Excel and select **New** to display a blank workbook. Save the workbook as **chap1_pe1_debitcard_solution**.
b. Click in **cell A1** and type **Your Name Debit Card**. Do not worry about formatting at this time. Enter the labels as shown in the table below:

Cell Address	Label
A2	Item #
B2	Date
C2	Description
D2	Amount
E2	Deposit
F2	Balance

c. Click in **cell F3** and type the initial balance of **1000**. You will format the values later. Use the table below to enter the data for the first item:

Cell Reference	Data
A4	100
B4	6/2
C4	Rent
D4	575

d. Click in **cell F4** and type the formula **=F3-D4+E4** to compute the balance. The formula is entered so that the balance is computed correctly. It does not matter if an amount or deposit is entered as the transaction because Excel treats the blank cells as zeros.
e. Enter data in rows 5 through 8, as shown in Figure 1.48. Type **Weekly Verification** in cell C8. Click in **cell F4** and use the fill handle to copy the formula to **cells F5:F7**.
f. Insert a new row above row 8 by right-clicking in row 8, selecting **Insert** from the shortcut menu, clicking **Entire row** in the Insert dialog box, and then clicking **OK**.
g. Click in **cell D9** to enter the formula to total your weekly expenditure amount. Type **= D4+D6+D7** and press **Enter**. If the formula is entered correctly, you will see 670.43 in cell D9.
h. Click in **cell E9** and type **=E5** to enter the formula to total your weekly deposit. If the formula is entered correctly, you will see 250 as the total first week deposit.
i. To verify your balance, click in **cell F9,** and type **=F3-D9+E9,** and press **Enter.** If you entered the formula correctly, you will see 579.57 as the balance.
j. Right-click **cell F9** and select **Insert Comment**. Type the following comment: **Balance is equal to the initial balance minus the amounts and ATM withdrawals plus the deposits.**
k. Format the completed worksheet, as shown in Figure 1.48. Click in **cell D3**, and then click and drag to select the **range D3:F9**. Click the **Home tab** and click the **Number Format down arrow** in the Number group. Click **Currency** from the Number Format gallery.
l. Click and drag to select the **range B4:B7**. Click the **Number Format down arrow** in the Number group. Click **Short Date** from the Number Format gallery. Select the **range**

...continued on Next Page

A4:A7; press and hold **Ctrl** while dragging to select the **range A2:F2**. Click **Center** in the Alignment group on the Home tab.

m. Click and drag to select the **range A1:F2**. Click the **Fill Color arrow** in the Font group and select the color **Orange**. Click the **Font Color arrow** in the Font group and select **Blue**. Click **Bold** in the Font group and **select 16** from **Font Size** list to make the text stand out. Click **More Borders** in the Font group and click **Top and Thick Bottom Border**.

n. Widen columns A through F so all text is visible by dragging the right border of each column to the right.

o. Click and drag to select the **range A1:F1**. Click **Merge & Center** in the Alignment group on the Home tab.

p. Click the **Page Layout tab** and click the **Page Setup Dialog Box Launcher** in the Page Setup group. Click the **Header/Footer tab**, click **Custom Header**, and type **Your Name** in the *Left section*. Click in the *Right section* and click **Insert Page Number**. Click **OK**.

q. Click **Custom Footer** and click in the *Center section*. Type **Your Instructor's Name**. Click in the *Right section*, click **Insert Date**, and click **OK**. Click **Print Preview**. Click **Page Setup** on the Print Preview tab.

r. Click the **Margins tab** in the Page Setup dialog box and click the **Horizontally** and **Vertically check boxes** in the *Center on page* section. Click the **Sheet tab** and click the **Row and column headings** and **Gridlines check boxes** in the *Print* section. Click **OK**. Click **Close Print Preview** on the Print Preview tab.

s. Click **Save** on the Quick Access Toolbar to save the workbook. Click the **Office Button**, select **Print**, and select **Quick Print** to print the worksheet.

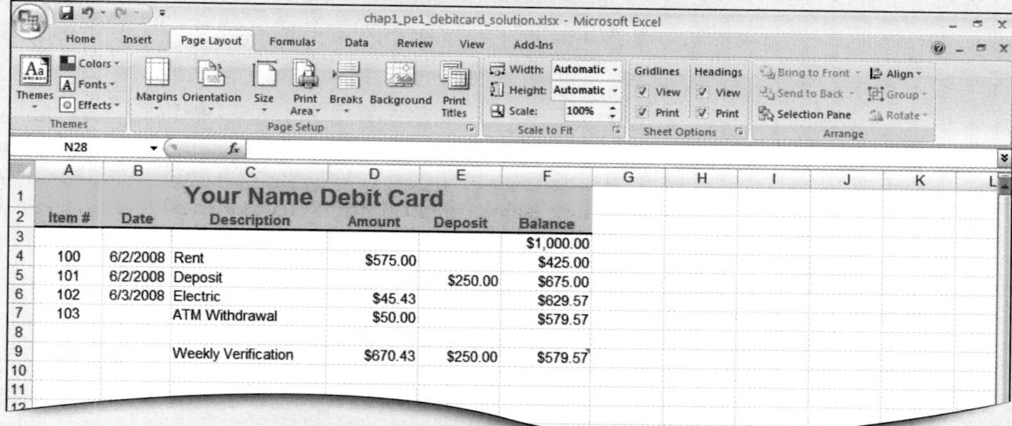

Figure 1.48 Verify Your Debit Card

2 Formatting—Create a Calendar

Excel is a spreadsheet application that gives you a row column table to work with. In this exercise, you will use the row column table to create a calendar worksheet that also demonstrates the formatting capabilities available in Excel. You will insert images representing a variety of activities in a particular month. Review Figure 1.49 to see a sample calendar page.

a. Start Excel to display a blank workbook and save it as **chap1_pe2_calendar_solution**.

b. In **cell D1**, enter the month for which you will create the calendar—July, for example. Click and drag to select **cells D1:F1**, then click **Merge & Center** in the Alignment group on the Home tab. Use the Font group to select **Comic Sans MS** font and **26** for the font size. Type **Your Name** in **cell D2** and press **Enter**. Click and drag to select **cells D2:F2** and merge and center as described above. Use the Font group to select **Comic Sans MS** font and **14** for the font size.

c. Right-click **row 1**, select **Row Height** from the shortcut menu, and type **39** in the Row Height dialog box to increase the row height. In similar fashion, right-click **row 2** and verify the row height is **21**.

d. Select **columns B** through **H**, right-click, select **Column Width** from the shortcut menu, and type **16** to change the width of the selected columns.

...continued on Next Page

e. Press and hold **Ctrl** while selecting the **ranges B1:H3**, **B4:B8**, and **H4:H8**. Click the **Fill Color** arrow in the Font group and select the color **Blue**. Click the **Font Color** arrow in the Font group and select **White**. Click **Bold** in the Font group to make the text stand out.

f. Click in **cell B3**, type **Sunday**, and press **Enter**. Click **cell B3** to make it the active cell. Click and drag the fill handle from **cell B3** to **H3** to automatically enter the remaining days of the week.

g. Keeping cells B3:H3 selected, click **Center** in the Alignment group on the Home tab. Increase the row height by right-clicking **row 3**, selecting **Row Height** and typing **23.25** in the Row Height dialog box, and then clicking **OK**.

h. Click **cell D4** and type **1** for the first day of the month. Type numbers for the remaining 30 days of the month in rows **4** through **8**. Increase the row height in rows 4 through 8 to **65**. Select rows **4** through **8**, click **Top Align**, and click **Align Text Left** in the Alignment group on the Home tab. Click and drag to select **cells B4:G8**, then select **Arial, 14 point**, and **Bold** in the Font group on the Home tab. Click and drag to select **cells B3:H8**, right-click the selected cells, select **Format Cells** to open the Format cells dialog box. Click **Border**, and then click both **Outline** and **Inside** in the *Presets section*. Click **OK**.

i. Click **Clip Art** in the Illustrations group on the Insert tab and type **Fourth of July** in the **Search for** text box. Insert and resize the images, as shown in Figure 1.49. Search for **Cardinal**, insert, and resize the image shown in Figure 1.49.

j. Right-click on the **Sheet1 tab**, select **Rename**, and type **July**. Right-click the July tab, select **Tab Color**, and select **Red**. Delete the remaining sheets by right-clicking the sheet tab and selecting **Delete**.

k. Click the **Page Layout tab** and click the **Page Setup Dialog Box Launcher** in the Page Setup group. Click the **Header/Footer tab**. Click **Custom Footer** and type **Your Name** in the *Left section*. Click in the *Right section* and type your instructor's name. Click **OK**.

l. Click the **Margins tab** in the Page Setup dialog box and click the **Horizontally** and **Vertically check boxes** in the *Center on page* section. Click the **Page tab**, click **Landscape** in the *Orientation section*, and click **OK**.

m. Click **Save** on the Quick Access Toolbar to save the workbook. Click the **Office Button**, select **Print**, and select **Quick Print** to print the worksheet.

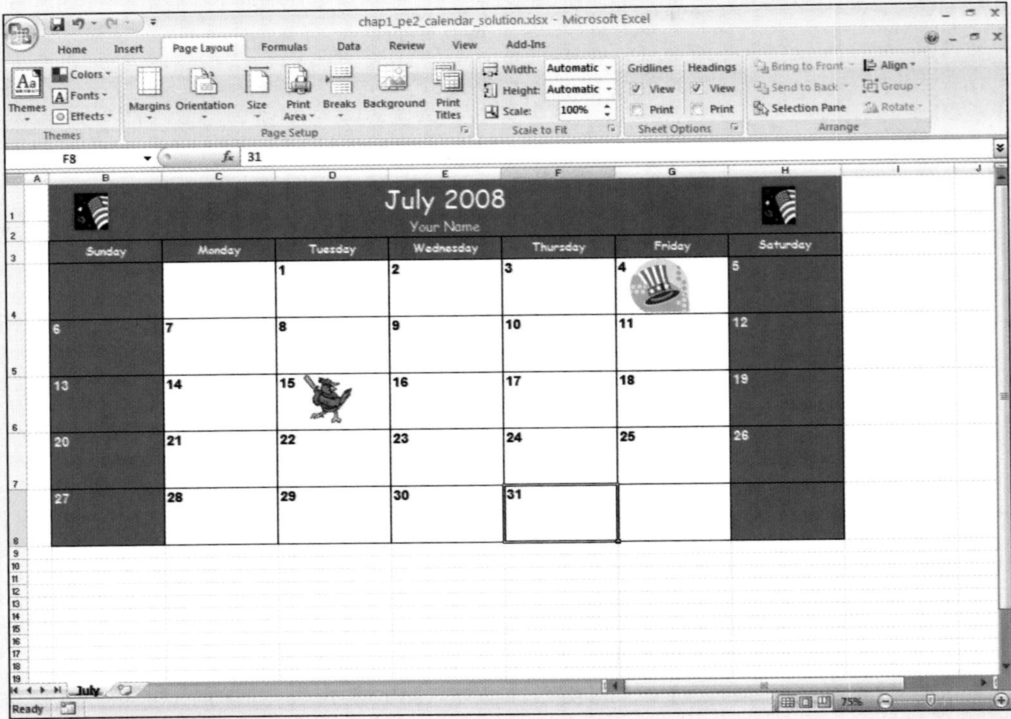

Figure 1.49 Create a Calendar

...continued on Next Page

3 Temperature Data

Your hobby is collecting, recording, and monitoring metrological data to track trends in temperature. Figure 1.50 displays the average temperature for summer in three American cities. Working with the partially completed workbook, you will create formulas, copy and paste a portion of a spreadsheet, and format both worksheets in an attractive and readable manner.

a. Open the *chap1_pe3_temperature* workbook and save it as **chap1_pe3_temperature_solution** so that you can return to the original workbook if necessary.
b. Click in **cell E3**, type **=(B3+C3+D3)/3**, and press **Enter**. You entered the formula to calculate the average summer temperature for Pittsburgh. Click in **cell E3** and use the fill handle to copy the formula to **cells E4:E5**.
c. Click in **cell A6** and type **Monthly Averages**. Enter the formula to calculate the average temperature for June by clicking in **cell B6** and typing **=(B3+B4+B5)/3**, then pressing **Enter**. Click in **cell B6** and use the fill handle to copy the formula to **cells C6:D6**.
d. Click in **cell E9** and type **=(B9+C9+D9)/3**, then press **Enter** to calculate the average temperature by city for the winter months. Click in **cell E9** and use the fill handle to copy the formula to **cells E10:E11**.
e. Click in **cell A12** and type **Monthly Averages**. Click in **cell B12** and type **=(B9+B10+B11)/3**, then pressing **Enter** to calculate the average temperature for December. Click in **cell B12** and use the fill handle to copy the formula to **cells C12:D12**.
f. Format numbers in column E and rows 6 and 12 with 2 decimals by pressing and holding **Ctrl** while selecting **cells E3:E5, E9:E11, B6:D6,** and **B12:D12**. Click the **Number Format arrow** in the Number group on the Home tab and select **Number**. Widen **column A** to **18**, and **columns B** through **E** to **11**.
g. Insert a blank row above row 1 by right-clicking the row number and selecting **Insert** from the shortcut menu. Type the title **Temperature Comparison** in **cell A1**.
h. Select **cells A1:E1** and click **Merge & Center** in the Alignment group. Repeat for cells **A2:E2** and cells **A8:E8**. Press and hold **Ctrl** while selecting **A1:E2** and **A8:E8**, and then select **Light Blue** from **Fill Color** and **White** from **Font Color** in the Font group. Change the title font and size by selecting **cells A1:E1** and then selecting **Comic Sans MS** from the **Font** drop-down list and **18** from the **Font Size** drop-down list in the Font group.
i. Press and hold **Ctrl** while selecting **cells B3:E3** and **B9:E9** and clicking **Center** in the Alignment group.
j. Press and hold **Ctrl** while selecting **cells A1:E3, A7:E9,** and **A13:E13** and click **Bold** in the Font group.
k. Press and hold **Ctrl** while selecting **A4:A6** and **A10:A12** and clicking **Increase Indent** in the Alignment group.
l. Type **Your Name** in **cell G1** to identify the worksheet as yours.
m. You will move your winter temperature data, as well as the title to a new sheet, and then rename and change the color of both sheet tabs and delete Sheet3. Select **cell A1** and click **Copy** in the Clipboard group on the Home tab.
n. Click the **Sheet2 tab**, make sure cell A1 is the active cell, and click the **Paste down arrow** in the Clipboard group, and select **Paste Special**. Select **All** from the *Paste* section of the Paste Special dialog box, and then click **OK** to paste the formatted title in cell A1. Immediately open the Paste Special dialog box again and select **Column Widths** from the *Paste* section. When you click **OK** to close, you will see the correct column widths.
o. Click the **Sheet1 tab**, press **Esc** to cancel the previous selected range, select **cells A8:E13**, and click **Copy** in the Clipboard group. Click the **Sheet2 tab**, make sure **cell A2** is the active cell, click the **Paste down arrow** in the Clipboard group, and select **Paste Special**. Select **All** from the *Paste* section of the Paste Special dialog box, and then click **OK** to paste the formatted portion of the worksheet in cell A2. Click **Sheet1** and delete the winter portion of the worksheet by right-clicking and selecting **Delete** from the shortcut menu. Select **Shift cells up** and click **OK**. Right-click the **Sheet1 tab**, select **Rename**, and type **Summer**. Right-click the **Sheet2 tab**, select **Rename**, and type **Winter**. Right-click the **Sheet3 tab** and select **Delete**. Right-click the **Summer tab** and select **Red** from the **Tab color palette**. Repeat but choose **Blue** for the **Winter tab**.

...continued on Next Page

p. Click the **Page Layout tab** and click the **Page Setup Dialog Box Launcher** in the Page Setup group. Click the **Header/Footer tab**. Click **Custom Header** and type **Your Name** in the *Left section*. Click in the *Right section* and type your course name. Click **OK**.

q. Click the **Margins tab** in the Page Setup dialog box, click **Horizontally** and **Vertically check boxes** in the *Center on page* section, and click **OK**.

r. Print the worksheet two ways, to show both displayed values and cell formula. Save the workbook.

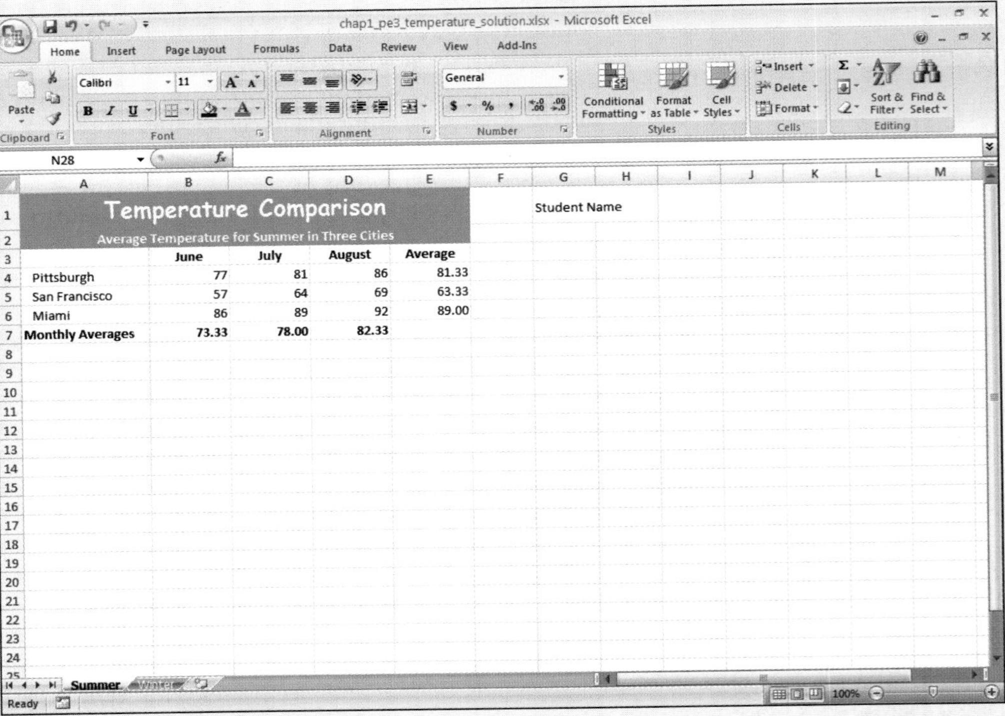

Figure 1.50 Temperature Data

4 Astronomy Lab

The potential uses of a spreadsheet are limited only by your imagination, as shown by Figure 1.51, which displays a spreadsheet with information about our solar system. Your astronomy professor asked you to complete the worksheet as part of your lab assignment. You will open the partially completed version of the workbook and complete the worksheet by developing the formulas for the first planet, copying those formulas to the remaining rows in the worksheet, and then formatting the worksheet for your professor.

a. Open the *chap1_pe4_solarsystem* workbook and save it as **chap1_pe4_solarsystem_solution** so that you can return to the original workbook if necessary.

b. Click in **cell C15** and enter your weight in pounds on Earth. Click in cell **C16** and enter **Pi=3.141597**, which is the value of Pi for this worksheet.

c. Click in **cell D4** and enter the formula to compute the diameter of the first planet (Mercury). The diameter of a planet is equal to twice its radius. Type **Pi=2*B4** and press **Enter**.

d. Click in **cell E4** and enter the formula to compute the circumference of a planet. The circumference is equal to the diameter times Pi. Type **pi=3.141597*D4** and press enter.

e. Click in **cell F4** and enter the formula to compute the surface area, which is equal to four times Pi times the radius squared. This is the formula to compute the surface area of a sphere, which is different from the formula to compute the area of a circle. Type **Pi=4*pi=3.141597*B4^2** and press **Enter**.

...continued on Next Page

f. Click in **cell G4** and enter the formula to compute your weight on Mercury, which is your weight on Earth times the relative gravity of Mercury compared to that of Earth. Type **=150*C4** and press **Enter**. The weight in the example is 150, but you will enter your weight and the result will be different.

g. To copy the formulas, select **cells D4:G4** and use the **fill handle** to copy the formula to **cells D4:G11**.

h. Click in **cell E14** and type **Your Name**. Format the worksheet appropriately making sure to do the following:

- Merge and center the cells in **row 1**.
- Format numbers in columns **B**, **D**, **E**, and **F** as Number with 0 decimal places
- Last selection in custom list is a time format. This is not a good format for numbers. Format it with number, no decimal places.
- Widen columns as necessary.
- Bold rows **1**, **3**, and **13**.
- Use **Green Navy** fill and **White** font color for cell ranges **A1:G3**, **A13:C13**, and **E13:F13**.

i. Use the Page Setup command to specify:

- **Landscape** orientation and appropriate **scaling** so that the entire worksheet fits on a single page.
- Create a custom header that includes the name of your institution and the current date.
- Display gridlines and row and column headings.
- **Center** the worksheet **horizontally** on the page.

j. Print the worksheet two ways in order to show both displayed values and cell formulas.

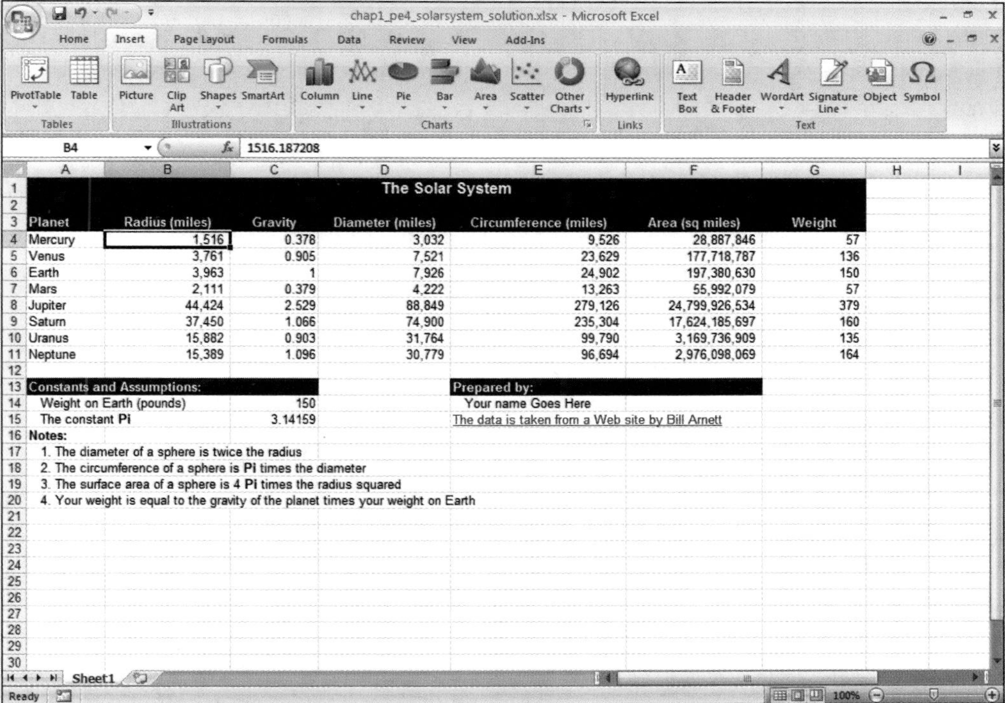

	A	B	C	D	E	F	G
1				The Solar System			
2							
3	Planet	Radius (miles)	Gravity	Diameter (miles)	Circumference (miles)	Area (sq miles)	Weight
4	Mercury	1,516	0.378	3,032	9,526	28,887,846	57
5	Venus	3,761	0.905	7,521	23,629	177,718,787	136
6	Earth	3,963	1	7,926	24,902	197,380,630	150
7	Mars	2,111	0.379	4,222	13,263	55,992,079	57
8	Jupiter	44,424	2.529	88,849	279,126	24,799,926,534	379
9	Saturn	37,450	1.066	74,900	235,304	17,624,185,697	160
10	Uranus	15,882	0.903	31,764	99,790	3,169,736,909	135
11	Neptune	15,389	1.096	30,779	96,694	2,976,098,069	164
12							
13	Constants and Assumptions:				Prepared by:		
14	Weight on Earth (pounds)		150		Your name Goes Here		
15	The constant Pi		3.14159		The data is taken from a Web site by Bill Arnett		
16	Notes:						
17	1. The diameter of a sphere is twice the radius						
18	2. The circumference of a sphere is PI times the diameter						
19	3. The surface area of a sphere is 4 PI times the radius squared						
20	4. Your weight is equal to the gravity of the planet times your weight on Earth						

Figure 1.51 Astronomy Lab

Mid-Level Exercises

1 Little League Statistician

Your mother has appointed you the family statistician for your siblings throughout their Little League career. Figure 1.52 displays the completed worksheet showing the statistical data from the last two seasons. Your task is to enter the formulas, format, and print the worksheet for your mother. You will calculate batting averages, totals for statistical data, and family totals.

a. Open the *chap1_mid1_little_league* workbook and save it as **chap1_mid1_little_league_solution** so that you can return to the original workbook if necessary.

b. Click in **cell B16** and type **Your Name**. Enter the formula to compute totals in cells **C7:I7** and **C14:I14**. Click in **cell J4** and enter a formula to compute batting average, Hits/At Bats.

c. Click and drag to select the formula in **cell J4** and copy the formula to **cells J5:J7**. Enter the formula to determine the Batting Average and copy it for the 2007 season.

d. Click in **cell A18** and type **Family Batting Average**. Enter a formula in **cell B18** to calculate the family batting average. Hint: Parentheses are important here.

e. Format the worksheet exactly as shown in Figure 1.52.

f. Print the worksheet twice, once to show displayed values and once to show the cell formulas. Use **landscape** orientation and be sure that the worksheet fits on one sheet of paper.

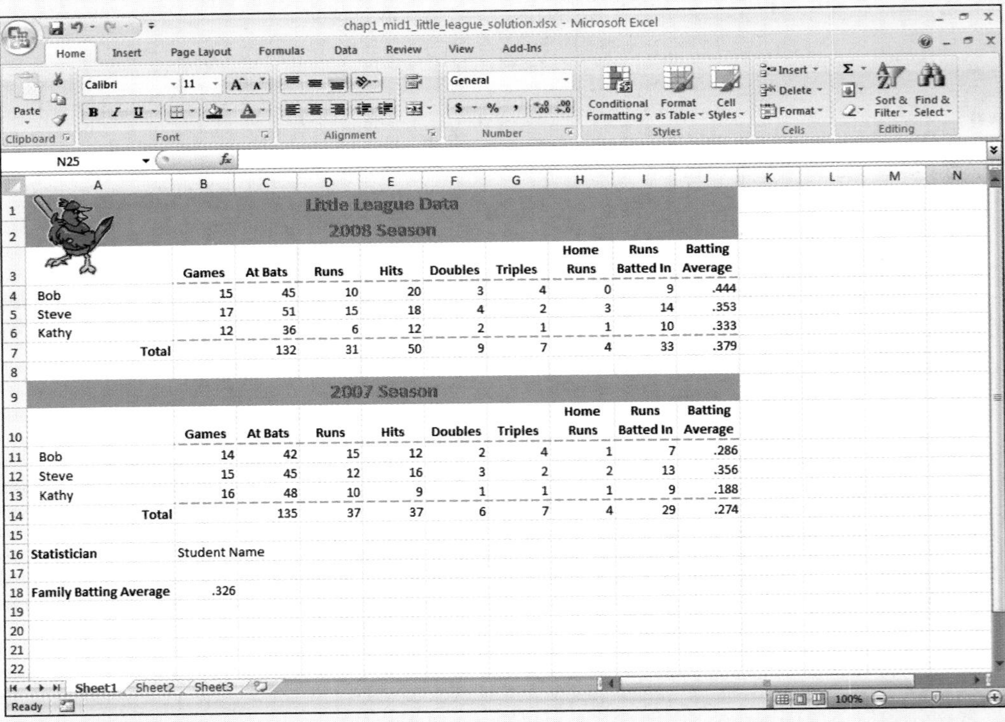

	Games	At Bats	Runs	Hits	Doubles	Triples	Home Runs	Runs Batted In	Batting Average
Little League Data									
2008 Season									
Bob	15	45	10	20	3	4	0	9	.444
Steve	17	51	15	18	4	2	3	14	.353
Kathy	12	36	6	12	2	1	1	10	.333
Total		132	31	50	9	7	4	33	.379
2007 Season									
Bob	14	42	15	12	2	4	1	7	.286
Steve	15	45	12	16	3	2	2	13	.356
Kathy	16	48	10	9	1	1	1	9	.188
Total		135	37	37	6	7	4	29	.274
Statistician	Student Name								
Family Batting Average	.326								

Figure 1.52 Little League Statistician

...continued on Next Page

2 Exploring Formatting Options

Your computer professor has determined that you need more practice with basic formatting and cell operations in Excel. The workbook in Figure 1.53 offers this practice for you. Remember to start in cell A1 and work your way down the worksheet, using the instructions in each cell.

a. Open the *chap1_mid2_formatting* workbook and save it as **chap1_mid2_formatting_solution** so that you can return to the original workbook if necessary. Click in **cell A1** and type your name, then change the formatting as indicated. Merge and center **cells A1** and **B1** into a single cell.

b. Change the width of column A to **53**.

c. Move to **cell A3** and format the text as indicated in the cell. Move to **cell B3** and double underline the text in Green.

d. Format **cells A4:B7** according to the instructions in the respective cells.

e. Follow the instructions in cells A8 to A14 to format the contents of cells **B8 to B14**. Click in **cell B4**, click the Format Painter tool, and then click and drag **cells A8:A14** to apply the formatting from **cell B4**.

f. Click in **cell A15**, then deselect the Merge & Center command to split the merged cell into two cells. Follow the instructions in the cell to wrap and center the text. Cell B15 should be blank when you are finished.

g. Right-click in **cell A16**, select Insert from the shortcut menu, click to shift cells down, and then click **OK**. You have inserted a new cell A16, but the contents in cell B16 should remain the same. Format **cell B16**.

h. Merge cells **A17** and **B17**, and then complete the indicated formatting.

i. Use the Page Setup command to display gridlines and row and column headings. Change to landscape orientation and center the worksheet horizontally on the page. Add a custom footer that contains your name and the date and time you completed the assignment. Print the completed workbook.

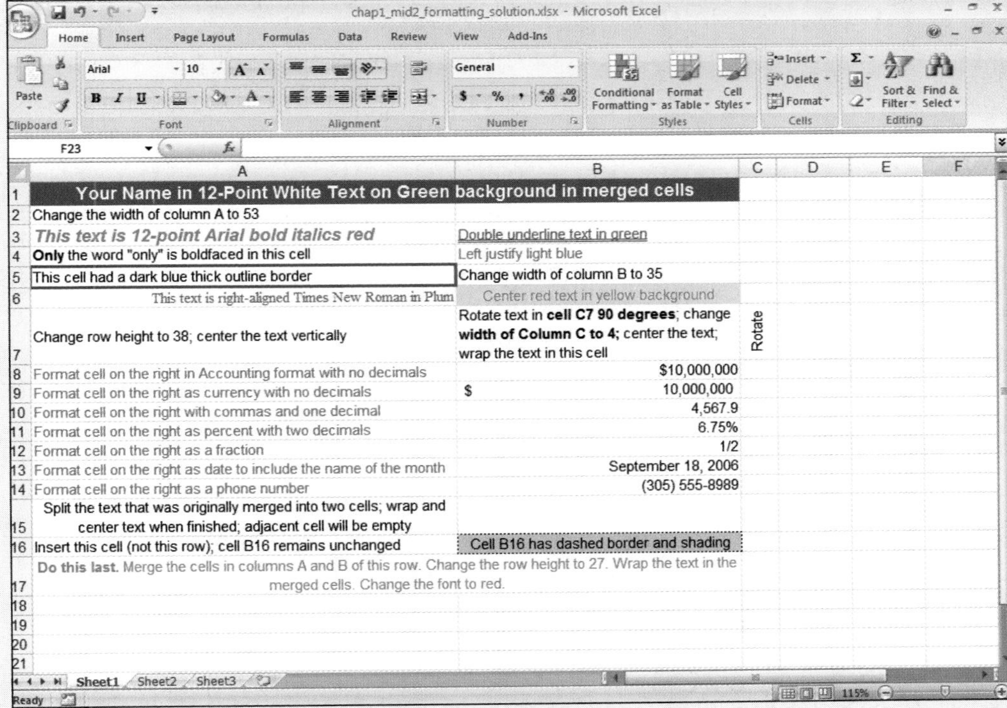

Figure 1.53 Exploring Formatting Options

...continued on Next Page

3 Measurement Conversions

You work in a testing lab for a major industrial company, and your supervisor has asked you to prepare a table of conversion factors and a table of equivalencies. You will use this as a "crib sheet" during your work and in the preparation of reports, so you want to make it as complete and as accurate as possible. The workbook in Figure 1.54 provides practice with formulas, formatting, and basic cell operations. You do have to match the formatting exactly and you must enter the identical values into column G.

a. Open the *chap1_mid3_conversion* workbook and save it as **chap1_mid3_conversion_solution** so that you can return to the original workbook if necessary. Click in **cell E8** and type the formula **=1/E7**. Cell E7 contains the value to convert inches to centimeters; the reciprocal of that value will convert centimeters to inches. Enter the appropriate formula into **cell E19** to convert kilograms to pounds.

b. A kilobyte is mistakenly thought of as 1,000 bytes, whereas it is actually 1,024 (2^{10}) bytes. In similar fashion, a megabyte and a gigabyte are 2^{20} and 2^{30} bytes. Use this information to enter the appropriate formulas to display the conversion factors in cells **E21, E22,** and **E23.**

c. Enter the formulas for the first conversion into row 7. Click in **cell H7** and type **=C7.** Click in **cell J7** and type **=E7*G7**. Click in **cell K7** and type **=D7**. Copy the formulas in row 7 to the remaining rows in the worksheet. The use of formulas for columns H through K builds flexibility into the worksheet; that is, you can change any of the conversion factors on the left side of the worksheet and the right side will be updated automatically.

d. Enter a set of values in column G for conversion; for example, type 12 in **cell G7** to convert 12 inches to centimeters. The result should appear automatically in **cell** J7.

e. Type your name in **cell G3**. Use Aqua as the fill color in cells **G7:G23** and other ranges of cells, as shown in Figure 1.54.

f. Use the Merge & Center command as necessary throughout the worksheet to approximate the formatting in Figure 1.54. Change the orientation in column B so that the various labels are displayed as indicated.

g. Display the border around the groups of cells, as shown in Figure 1.54.

h. Print the displayed values and the cell formulas. Be sure to show the row and column headings as well as the gridlines. Use landscape orientation to be sure the worksheet fits on a single sheet of paper.

...continued on Next Page

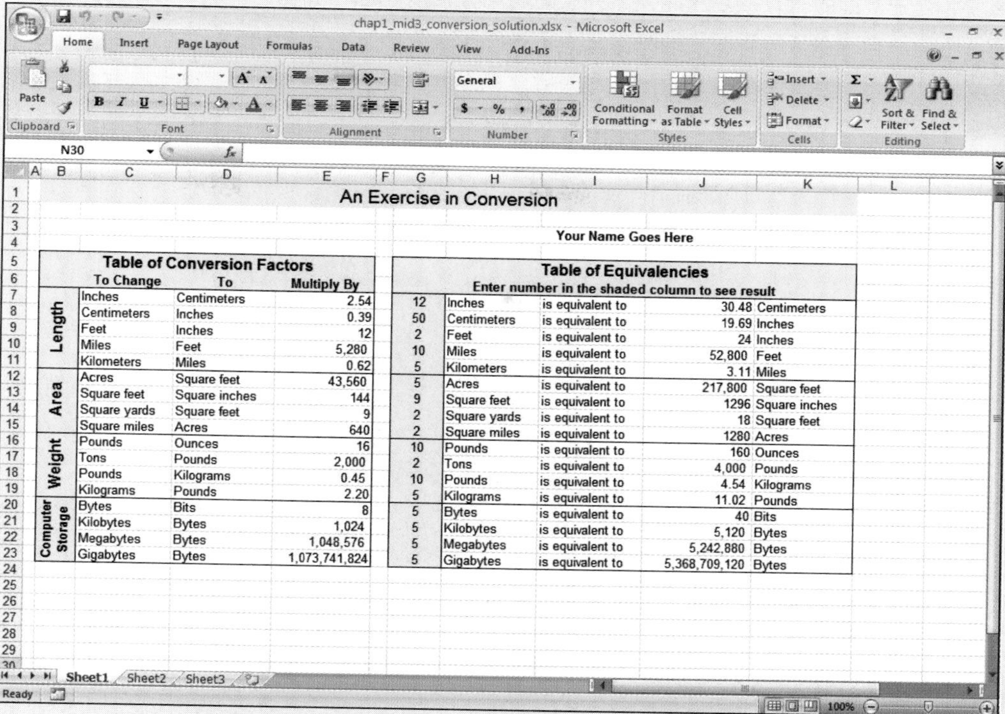

Figure 1.54 Measurement Conversions

4 Fuel Efficiency

Your summer vacation involved traveling through several states to visit relatives and to view the scenic attractions. While traveling, you kept a travel log of mileage and gasoline purchases. Now that the vacation is over, you want to determine the fuel efficiency of your automobile. The partially completed worksheet in Figure 1.55 includes the beginning mileage for the vacation trips and the amount of fuel purchased. This exercise provides practice with formulas, formatting, copying, and basic cell operations.

a. Open the *chap1_mid4_fuel* workbook and save it as **chap1_mid4_fuel_solution** so that you can return to the original workbook if necessary. Click in **cell C12** and change the gallons to **9.2** because you are correcting a typing error.

b. Insert a new column between columns B and C and type **Miles Driven** in **cell C3**.

c. Select **cells A5:A12**, copy the selected range, and paste it in **cells B4:B11**. This ensures that the ending mileage for one trip is the same as the beginning mileage for the next trip. Click **cell B12** and type **34525**, the mileage at the end of the last trip.

d. Use cell references and create the formula to calculate the miles driven for each trip. Use cell references and create the formula to calculate the miles per gallon for each trip.

e. Select **cells A1:E1** and apply the Dark Blue fill color. Apply the following formats to **cell A1**: Times New Roman, 16 point, Bold, White font color. Merge and center the title over columns A through E.

f. Word-wrap the contents of **cells C3** and **E3**. Bold and center horizontally the headings in row 3. Apply the following number formats to the values in columns A and B: whole numbers, no decimals, comma format.

...continued on Next Page

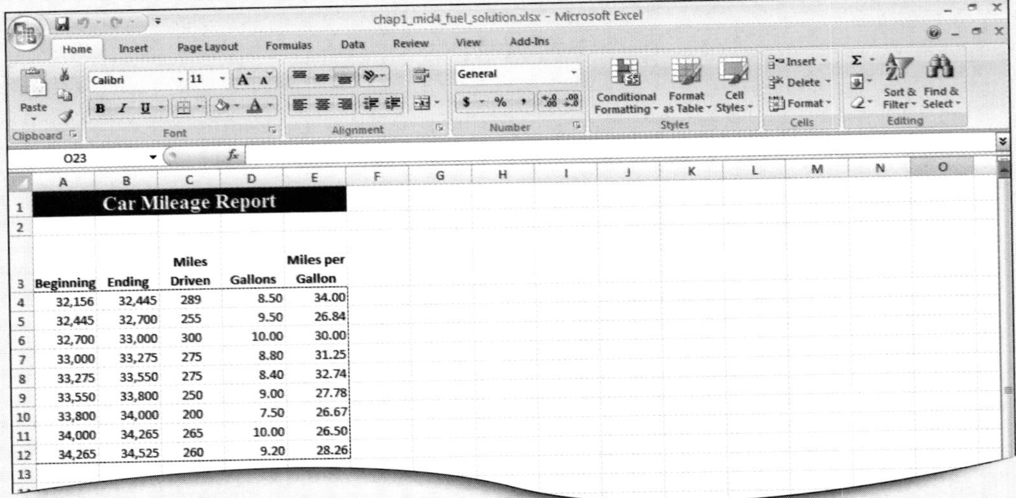

Figure 1.55 Fuel Efficiency

g. Format the last two columns of values as whole numbers with two decimals. Center the values in the third column. Display a border around **cells A4:E12**, as shown in Figure 1.55.

h. Use the Page Setup command to display gridlines and row and column headings. Change to landscape orientation and center the worksheet horizontally on the page. Add a custom footer that contains your name and the date and time you completed the assignment. Print the completed workbook.

5 Freshman Seminar Grade Book

Figure 1.56 displays your instructor's sample grade book complete with a grading scheme. Students take three exams worth 100 points each, submit a term paper and various homework assignments worth 50 points each, and then receive a grade for the semester based on their total points. The maximum number of points is 400. Your semester average is computed by dividing your total points by the maximum total points. You will complete the Freshman Seminar Grade Book worksheet so the displayed values match Figure 1.56.

a. Open the *chap1_mid5_assumption* workbook and save it as **chap1_mid5_assumption_solution** so that you can return to the original workbook if necessary.

b. Click in **cell A6** and type **Your Name**. Enter your test scores: **98, 87, and 99**. The term paper is worth **46** and the homework **24**. Insert a column between columns D and E. Type **Exam Total** in **cell E3**. Click in **cell E4** and enter a formula to compute Smith's exam total points. Click in **cell H4** and enter a formula that will compute Smith's total points for the semester. Click in **cell I4** and enter a formula to compute Smith's semester average.

c. Click and drag to select the formula in **cell E4**. Copy this formula through **E6**. Click and drag to select the formulas in **cells H4:I4** and copy the formulas through **I6**.

d. Click in **cell B7** and enter a formula that will compute the class average on the first exam. Copy this formula to cells **C7:H7**.

e. Insert a column between columns C and D and type **Percent Change in Exams** in **cell D3**. Click in **cell D4** and enter the formula to calculate the change in exam scores between the first and second exam.

f. Format the worksheet appropriately, as shown in Figure 1.56.

...continued on Next Page

g. Add your name as the grading assistant, then print the worksheet twice, once to show displayed values and once to show the cell formulas. Use landscape orientation and be sure that the worksheet fits on one sheet of paper.

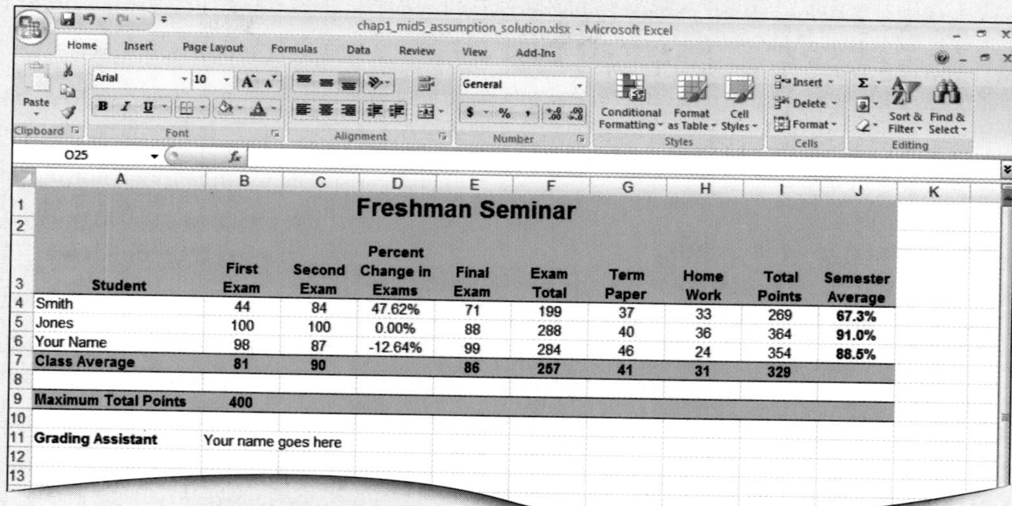

	A	B	C	D	E	F	G	H	I	J
1	**Freshman Seminar**									
2										
3	**Student**	**First Exam**	**Second Exam**	**Percent Change in Exams**	**Final Exam**	**Exam Total**	**Term Paper**	**Home Work**	**Total Points**	**Semester Average**
4	Smith	44	84	47.62%	71	199	37	33	269	**67.3%**
5	Jones	100	100	0.00%	88	288	40	36	364	**91.0%**
6	Your Name	98	87	-12.64%	99	284	46	24	354	**88.5%**
7	**Class Average**	**81**	**90**		**86**	**257**	**41**	**31**	**329**	
8										
9	**Maximum Total Points**	**400**								
10										
11	**Grading Assistant**	Your name goes here								

Figure 1.56 Freshman Seminar Grade Book

Capstone Exercise

You are the new assistant to the band director for the Upper Saddle River Marching Band and you must prepare a report showing the status of the marching band fund-raising event for the board of trustees. The report will summarize sales of all items and include the total profit to date with the amount remaining to reach the profit goal. You will open the partially completed workbook, create formulas, and format for presentation to the board of trustees.

Open and Save Worksheet

You must open a worksheet that has the fundraising sales information in it and complete the worksheet.

a. Open the *chap1_cap_fundraising* workbook.

b. Save it as **chap1_cap_fundraising_solution**.

c. Type your name in **cell A20**.

Calculate Values

You are to create the formulas used to calculate profit per item and profit based on the number of items sold. You create a formula to calculate total profit to date and the remaining profit needed to reach the goal.

a. Enter the profit per item formula in **column C**. The profit per item is 50% of the sales price.

b. Enter the profit formula in **column E**. The profit is the profit per item multiplied by the number items sold.

c. Copy all appropriate formulas.

d. Enter a formula to calculate the total profit to date in **cell E15**.

e. The formula for calculating the remaining profit to reach the goal is the goal minus the total profit to date. Enter the formula in **cell E16**.

Format the Worksheet

Now that you have finished the calculations, you must format the worksheet in a professional manner and suitable for presentation to the board of trustees of the college.

a. Insert a comment in **cell E16** and explain the formula in **cell E16**.

b. Format all money figures as currency with two decimals. Format the profit with no decimals.

c. Center and merge rows 1 and 2.

d. Change the font to Arial and increase font size in rows 1, 2, and 3, increasing row height as needed.

e. Change font color in rows 1, 2, 3, 5, 15, and 16.

f. Place borders at the top and bottom of **cells A4:E4**. Place a border at the bottom of **cells A14:E14**.

g. Change the fill color for **cells E4:E4**.

h. Search for the keyword **marching band** in the Clip Art task pane. Insert the bass drums image in **cell E2**, resizing as necessary.

Lay Out the Worksheet

Now that you have finished the major formatting, you must lay out the worksheet to further separate and define areas of the worksheet. This step makes the worksheet more aesthetically pleasing and easier to read.

a. Insert new rows above **row 4** and **row 16**.

b. Delete sheet tabs 2 and 3.

c. Change the color of Sheet1 to **purple**.

d. Rename Sheet1 as **Fundraising**.

Print the Report

Before printing the report, you see it is missing the standard headers and should be printed in landscape orientation to fit on one page. You also want to show and print the cell formulas.

a. Create a custom header with your name on the left and your instructor's name on the right.

b. Change the page orientation to landscape.

c. Print the worksheet with displayed values.

d. Print the worksheet again with cell formulas but make sure to fit the worksheet on one page.

e. Save your changes and exit Excel.

Mini Cases

Use the rubric following the case as a guide to evaluate your work, but keep in mind that your instructor may impose additional grading criteria or use a different standard to judge your work.

Housing Office

GENERAL CASE

Your supervisor in the student housing office has asked for your help in preparing a workbook for her annual budget. Open the partially completed *chap1_mc1_housingoffice* workbook and save it as **chap1_mc1_housingoffice_solution**. This workbook is intended to compute the revenue for the dorms on campus. The revenue includes the income from single rooms, double rooms, and the associated meal plans. Your assignment is to complete the workbook. If you do the assignment correctly, the total revenue for Douglass Hall should be $5,325,000. Note that each double room has two students, each of whom is required to pay for the meal plan. Format the completed worksheet as appropriate. Place your name somewhere in the worksheet and print the worksheet two ways in order to show both displayed values and cell formulas. Be sure to use the Page Setup command to specify landscape orientation and appropriate scaling so that the entire worksheet fits on a single page.

Performance Elements	Exceeds Expectations	Meets Expectations	Below Expectations
Create formulas	All formulas work and most efficiently stated.	Formulas are correct.	No formulas, numbers entered.
Attractive, appropriate format	Well formatted and easy to read.	Adequately formatted, difficult to read.	No formatting.
Print formulas and values	Prints both formulas and values.	Prints ether formulas or values.	No printout.

The Cost of Smoking

RESEARCH CASE

Smoking is hazardous to your health as well as your pocketbook. A one-pack-a-day habit, at $4.50/pack, will cost you more than $1,600 per year. Use the Web to find the current price for the items listed in the worksheet that you could purchase in one year. Open the partially completed *chap1_mc2_smoking* workbook, save it as **chap1_mc2_smoking_solution**, and compute the number of various items that you could buy over the course of a year in lieu of cigarettes. The approximate prices have been entered already, but you need not use these numbers and/or you can substitute additional items of your own. Place your name somewhere in the worksheet and print the worksheet two ways to show both displayed values and cell. Be sure to use the Page Setup command to specify landscape orientation and appropriate scaling so that the entire worksheet fits on a single page.

Performance Elements	Exceeds Expectations	Meets Expectations	Below Expectations
Research current prices	Prices current within 30 days.	Prices current within 3 months.	Prices more than 3 months old.
Create formulas	All formulas work and most efficiently stated.	Formulas are correct.	No formulas, numbers entered.
Format for one sheet	Formatted correctly and easy to read.	Adequately formatted, difficult to read.	Not formatted for one sheet.
Print values and cell formulas	Values and formulas both printed.	Values or formulas printed.	No print.

Accuracy Counts

DISASTER RECOVERY

The *chap1_mc3_accuracycounts* workbook was the last assignment completed by your predecessor prior to his unfortunate dismissal. The worksheet contains a significant error, which caused your company to underbid a contract and assume a subsequent loss of $200,000. As you look for the error, do not be distracted by the attractive formatting. The shading, lines, and other touches are nice, but accuracy is more important than anything else. Write a memo to your instructor describing the nature of the error. Include suggestions in the memo on how to avoid mistakes of this nature in the future. Open the *chap1_mc3_accuracycounts* workbook and save it as **chap1_mc3_accuracycounts_solution**.

Performance Elements	Exceeds Expectations	Meets Expectations	Below Expectations
Identify and correct the error	Error correctly identified within 10 minutes.	Error correctly identified within 20 minutes.	Error not identified.
Explain the error	Complete and correct explanation of the error.	Explanation is too brief to fully explain the error.	No explanation.
Describe how to prevent the error	Prevention description correct.	Prevention description too brief to be of any value.	No prevention description.

chapter 2 | Excel

Formulas and Functions

Math Basics for Spreadsheet Use

After you read this chapter, you will be able to:

1. Create and copy formulas **(page 319)**.
2. Use relative and absolute cell addresses **(page 320)**.
3. Use AutoSum **(page 327)**.
4. Insert basic statistical functions **(page 328)**.
5. Use date functions **(page 330)**.
6. Use the IF function **(page 337)**.
7. Use the VLOOKUP function **(page 338)**.
8. Use the PMT function **(page 346)**.
9. Use the FV function **(page 347)**.

Hands-On Exercises

Exercises	Skills Covered
1. **SMITHTOWN HOSPITAL RADIOLOGY DEPARTMENT PAYROLL (PAGE 322)** **Open:** chap2_ho1_payroll.xlsx **Save as:** chap2_ho1_payroll_solution.xlsx	• Compute the Gross Pay • Complete the Calculations • Copy the Formulas with the Fill Handle
2. **COMPLETING THE SMITHTOWN HOSPITAL RADIOLOGY DEPARTMENT PAYROLL (PAGE 332)** **Open:** chap2_ho1_payroll_solution.xlsx (from Exercise 1) **Save as:** chap2_ho2_payroll_solution.xlsx (additional modifications)	• Compute the Totals • Using Other General Functions • Apply Number Formatting • Apply Font and Alignment Formatting • Insert a Comment to Complete the Worksheet
3. **ATHLETIC DEPARTMENT ELIGIBILITY GRADEBOOK (PAGE 341)** **Open:** chap2_ho3_gradebook.xlsx **Save as:** chap2_ho3_gradebook_solution.xlsx	• Use the IF Function • Use the VLOOKUP Function • Copy the IF and VLOOKUP Functions • Apply Page Setup Options and Print the Worksheet
4. **PURCHASING A VAN FOR THE SCHOOL FOR EXCEPTIONAL CHILDREN (PAGE 348)** **Open:** New workbook **Save as:** chap2_ho4_van_solution.xlsx	• Create the Worksheet • Insert the PMT Function • Format the Worksheet • Complete the Worksheet

CASE STUDY

West Transylvania College Athletic Department

The athletic department of West Transylvania College has reached a fork in the road. A significant alumni contingent insists that the college upgrade its athletic program from NCAA Division II to Division I. This process will involve adding sports, funding athletic scholarships, expanding staff, and coordinating a variety of fundraising activities.

Tom Hunt, the athletic director, wants to determine if the funding support is available both inside and outside the college to accomplish this goal. You are helping Tom prepare the five-year projected budget based on current budget figures. The plan is to increase revenues at a rate of 10% per year for five years while handling an estimated 8% increase in expenses over the same five-year period. Tom feels that a 10% increase in revenue versus an 8% increase in expenses should make the upgrade viable. Tom wants to examine how increased alumni giving, increases in college fees, and grant monies will increase the revenue flow. The Transylvania College's Athletic Committee and its Alumni Association Board of Directors want Tom to present an analysis of funding and expenses to determine if the move to NCAA Division I is feasible. As Tom's student assistant this year, it is your responsibility to help him with special projects. Tom prepared the basic projected budget spreadsheet and has asked you to finish it for him.

Your Assignment

- Read the chapter carefully and pay close attention to mathematical operations, formulas, and functions.
- Open *chap2_case_athletics*, which contains the partially completed, projected budget spreadsheet.
- Study the structure of the worksheet to determine what type of formulas you need to complete the financial calculations. Identify how you would perform calculations if you were using a calculator and make a list of formulas using regular language to determine if the financial goals will be met. As you read the chapter, identify formulas and functions that will help you complete the financial analysis. You will insert formulas in the revenue and expenditures sections for column C. Use appropriate cell references in formulas. Do not enter constant values within a formula; instead enter the 10% and 8% increases in an input area. Use appropriate functions for column totals in both the revenue and expenditures sections. Insert formulas for the Net Operating Margin and Net Margin rows. Copy the formulas.
- Review the spreadsheet and identify weaknesses in the formatting. Use your knowledge of good formatting design to improve the appearance of the spreadsheet so that it will be attractive to the Athletic Committee and the alumni board. You will format cells as currency with 0 decimals and widen columns as needed. Merge and center the title and use an attractive fill color. Emphasize the totals and margin rows with borders. Enter your name and current date. Create a custom footer that includes a page number and your instructor's name. Print the worksheet as displayed and again with cell formulas displayed. Save the workbook as **chap2_case_athletics_solution**.

Formula Basics

A ***formula*** performs mathematical operations that produce a calculated result.

Mathematical operations are the backbone of Excel. The order in which these mathematical operations are performed has a significant impact on the answers that are arrived at. We touched briefly on the construction of mathematical expressions or ***formulas*** that direct Excel to perform mathematical operations and arrive at a calculated result. A formula also may be defined as the combination of constants, cell references, and arithmetic operations displayed in a calculation. Formulas can be as simple or as complex as necessary, but they always begin with an = sign and contain mathematical operators. In this section, you learn how to use the pointing method to create formulas and the fill handle to copy formulas. Finally, you learn how to prevent a cell reference from changing when you copy a formula to other cells.

(Formulas can be as simple or as complex as necessary, but they always begin with an = sign and contain mathematical operators.)

Creating and Copying Formulas

As you recall, whenever you want Excel to perform a calculation, you must enter an equal sign (=) in the cell where the answer is to appear. The equal sign indicates within Excel that a mathematical calculation is about to begin. Previously, you created formulas by typing in the cell references. Here in Chapter 2, you enter cell references to create a formula in a more efficient, straightforward way.

Point to Create a Formula

(Rather than typing a cell address . . . as you construct a formula, you can use an alternative method that involves *minimal* typing.)

Pointing uses the mouse or arrow keys to select the cell directly when creating a formula.

As previously discussed, the creation of formulas in Excel is the mathematical basis for the program and the use of cell references is integral in the creation of formulas. However, rather than typing a cell address, such as C2, as you construct a formula, you can use an alternative method that involves *minimal* typing. ***Pointing*** uses the mouse or arrow keys to select the cell directly when creating a formula. To use the pointing technique to create a formula:

1. Click on the cell where the formula will be entered.
2. Type an equal sign (=) to start a formula.
3. Click on the cell with the value to be entered in the formula.
4. Type a mathematical operator.
5. Continue clicking on cells and typing operators to finish the formula.
6. Press Enter to complete the formula.

While the formulas may be more complex than indicated in this example, the steps are the same.

Copy Formulas with the Fill Handle

The ***fill handle*** is a small black square in the bottom-right corner of a selected cell.

Another powerful copying tool in Excel is the ***fill handle***, which is a small black solid square in the bottom-right corner of a selected cell. Using the fill handle provides another, more clear-cut alternative method for copying the contents of a cell. You can use the fill handle to duplicate formulas. To copy and paste using the fill handle:

1. Click on the cell (or drag through the cells) to be copied.
2. Position the mouse pointer directly over the fill handle on the cell or cells to be copied. The pointer changes to a thin crosshair.
3. Click and hold down the left mouse button while dragging over the destination cells. Note that using the fill handle only works with contiguous or adjacent cells.

4. Release the mouse button. If the cell to be copied contained a formula, the formula is copied, the cell references are changed appropriately, and Excel performs the calculations.

TIP Contiguous Cells

In addition to using the fill handle to copy formulas, you can also use the fill handle to finish a text series. For example, you can use the fill handle to complete the days of the week, the four quarters of a year, and the month names to simplify the data-entry process. Type January in a cell, select the cell, click on the fill handle, drag to cover a total of 12 cells. Figure 2.1 shows before and after using the fill handle to complete the January through December series.

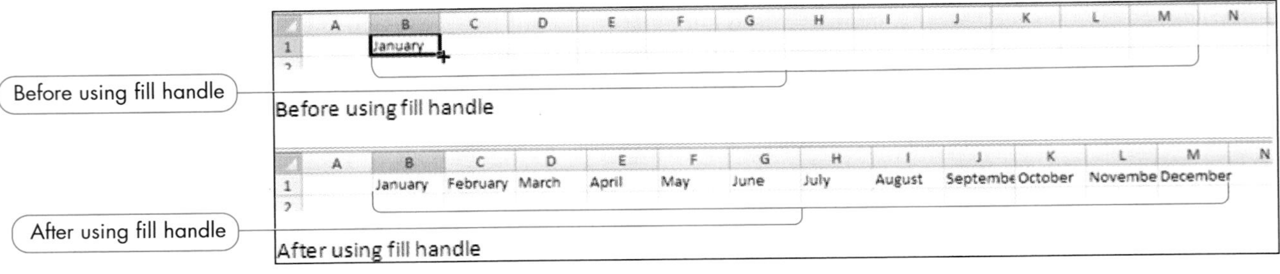

Figure 2.1 Fill Handle

Using Relative and Absolute Cell Addresses

Excel uses three different ways to express a reference to a cell in a formula. These references are relative, absolute, and mixed, and each affects copying cell references in different ways.

A ***relative cell reference*** is a typical cell reference that changes when copied.

An ***absolute cell reference***, indicated by dollar signs before the column letter and row number, stays the same regardless of where a formula is copied.

A ***relative cell reference*** within a formula is a cell reference that changes *relative to* the direction in which the formula is being copied. It is expressed in the form C13 (column letter, row number) and is adjusted or changed according to the direction and relative distance it is copied. When you copy a formula containing a relative cell reference over multiple columns, the column letter changes. When you copy a formula containing a relative cell reference down multiple rows, the row number changes. For example, if you copy the contents of cell C5, =C3+C4, to cell E5, the formula becomes =E3+E4. If you copy the contents of cell C5, =C3+C4, to cell E6, the formula becomes =E4+E5.

> A benefit of an absolute cell reference is that if an input value changes, . . . you type the new input value in only one cell and Excel recalculates . . . all the formulas. You do not have to individually edit cells containing formulas. . . .

An ***absolute cell reference*** in a formula, on the other hand, is one that stays the same no matter where you copy a formula. An absolute cell reference appears with dollar signs before both the column letter and row number ($C$13). Absolute cell references are used when the value in the cell seldom changes but the formula containing the absolute cell reference is copied. An example would be in a payroll spreadsheet that includes a calculation for state income tax using a constant tax rate. The reference to the cell that contains the state income rate (C13) would therefore be expressed as an absolute cell reference when used in a formula (=$C$13*D26). The absolute address prevents the cell reference from changing when you copy the formula to calculate the amount of state income tax for the other employees. A benefit of an absolute cell reference is that if an input value changes, for example if the state income tax rate changes from 14% to 15.5% in this example, you type the new input value in only one cell and Excel recalculates the amount of state tax for all the formulas. You do not have to individually edit cells containing formulas to change the tax rate value because the formulas contain an absolute cell reference to the cell containing the state tax rate.

The ***mixed cell reference*** combines an absolute reference with a relative reference.

The third type of cell reference, the ***mixed cell reference***, occurs when you create a formula that combines an absolute reference with a relative reference ($C13 or C$13). As a result, either the row number or column letter does not change when the cell is copied. Using the relative cell reference C13, it would be expressed as a mixed reference either as $C13 or C$13. In the first case, the column C is absolute and the row number is relative; in the second case, the row 13 is absolute and the column C is relative.

TIP The F4 Key

The F4 key toggles through relative, absolute, and mixed references. Click on any cell reference within a formula on the formula bar; for example, click on B4 in the formula =B4+B5. Press F4, and B4 changes to an absolute reference, $B$4. Press F4 a second time, and $B$4 becomes a mixed reference, B$4; press F4 again, and it is a different mixed reference, $B4. Press F4 a fourth time, and the cell reference returns to the original relative reference, B4.

In the first hands-on exercise, you calculate the gross pay for employees in the Smithtown Radiology Department using the pointing method. You perform other payroll calculations, and then use the fill handle to copy the formulas for the remaining employees.

Hands-On Exercises

1 | Smithtown Hospital Radiology Department Payroll

Skills covered: 1. Compute the Gross Pay **2.** Complete the Calculations **3.** Copy the Formulas with the Fill Handle

Step 1
Compute the Gross Pay

Refer to Figure 2.2 as you complete Step 1.

a. Start Excel. Open the *chap2_ho1_payroll* workbook to display the worksheet shown in Figure 2.2.

b. Save the workbook as **chap2_ho1_payroll_solution** so that you can return to the original workbook if necessary.

c. Click in **cell F4**, the cell that will contain gross pay for Dwyer. Press = on the keyboard to begin pointing, click **cell C4** (producing a moving border around the cell), press the **asterisk key** (*), and then click **cell D4**.

You have entered the first part of the formula to compute the gross pay.

d. Press the **plus sign** (+), click **cell E4**, press *, click **cell C4**, press *, click **cell D20**, press **F4** to change the cell reference to **$D$20**, and then press **Enter**.

The formula, =C4*D4+E4*C4*$D$20, calculates the gross pay for employee Dwyer by multiplying the $8 hourly wage by 40 regular hours. This amount is added to the 8 overtime hours, multiplied by the $8 hourly wage, multiplied by the 1.5 overtime rate. Note the use of the absolute address ($D$20) in the formula. You should see 416 as the displayed value in cell F4.

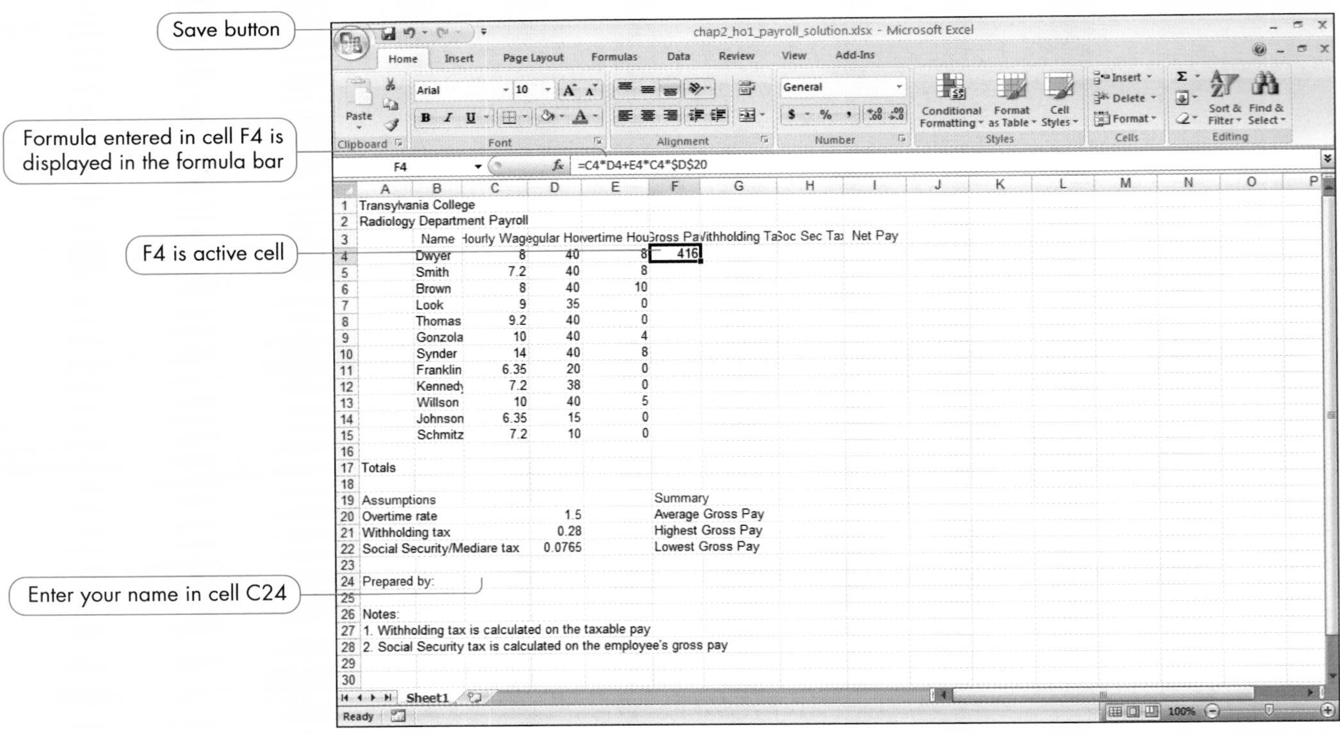

Figure 2.2 Compute the Gross Pay with Absolute Reference

e. Click in **cell F4** to be sure that the formula you entered matches the formula shown in the formula bar in Figure 2.2. If necessary, click in the formula bar and make the appropriate changes so the formula is correct in cell F4.

f. Enter your name in **cell C24** and save the workbook.

Step 2
Complete the Calculations

a. Click in **cell G4**, the cell that will contain the withholding tax for Dwyer. Press = to begin pointing, and then click **cell F4**, the cell containing the gross pay cell. Press the * and click **cell D21**, the withholding tax.

Cell G4 now contains the formula =F4*D21 that calculates Dwyer's withholding tax. However, if you were to copy the formula now, the copied formula would be =F5*D22, which is not quite correct. If a cell address is not made explicitly absolute, Excel's default relative address mode will automatically change a cell address when a formula is copied.

b. Verify that the insertion point is within or immediately behind cell reference D21 and press **F4.**

Pressing F4 changes the cell reference to $D$21 and explicitly makes the cell address an absolute reference. The formula can be copied and will calculate the desired result.

c. Press **Enter.**

The value in cell G4 should be 116.48. This amount is Dwyer's withholding tax.

d. Use the pointing method to enter the remaining formulas for Dwyer. Click in **cell H4** and enter the formula **=F4*$D$22.**

The formula calculates the employee's Social Security tax, which is 7.65% of the gross pay. The formula uses an absolute reference ($D$22) so the cell reference will not change when you copy the formula for the other employees. The value in cell H4 should be 31.824, and this is Dwyer's Social Security tax.

e. Click in **cell I4**, and enter the formula **=F4–(G4+H4)**. Press **Enter** when you finish.

The formula adds the withholding tax and Social Security tax, and then subtracts the total tax from the gross pay. The formula uses only relative cell addresses because you want the copied formulas to refer to the appropriate gross pay and tax cells for each respective employee. The value in cell I4 should be 267.696, and this amount is Dwyer's net pay.

f. Save the workbook.

Step 3
Copy the Formulas with the Fill Handle

Refer to Figure 2.3 as you complete Step 3.

a. Click and drag to select **cells F4:I4**, as shown in Figure 2.3. Point to the fill handle in the lower-right corner of **cell I4**. The mouse pointer changes to a thin crosshair.

You have selected the range containing formulas that you want to copy. Pointing to the fill handle triggers the display of the thin crosshair.

b. Drag the fill handle to **cell I15**, the lower-right cell in the range of employee calculations, and release the mouse to complete the copy operation.

The formulas for Dwyer have been copied to the corresponding rows. You can use Excel to calculate the gross pay, withholding tax, Social Security tax, and net pay for each employee.

c. Click in **cell F5**, the cell containing the gross pay for Smith.

   You should see the formula =C5*D5+E5*C5*$D$20.

d. Click in **cell G5**, the cell containing the withholding tax for Smith.

   You should see the formula =F5*$D$21, which contains a relative reference (F5) that is adjusted from one row to the next, and an absolute reference ($D$21) that remains constant from one employee to the next.

e. Save the *chap2_ho1_payroll_solution* workbook and keep it onscreen if you plan to continue to the next hands-on exercise. Save the workbook. Close the workbook and exit Excel if you do not want to continue with the next exercise at this time.

   TROUBLESHOOTING: If you double-click a cell that contains a formula, Excel will display the formula, highlight the components, and allow for editing in the cell. If you double-click a cell that contains values or text, you can edit the data directly in the cell.

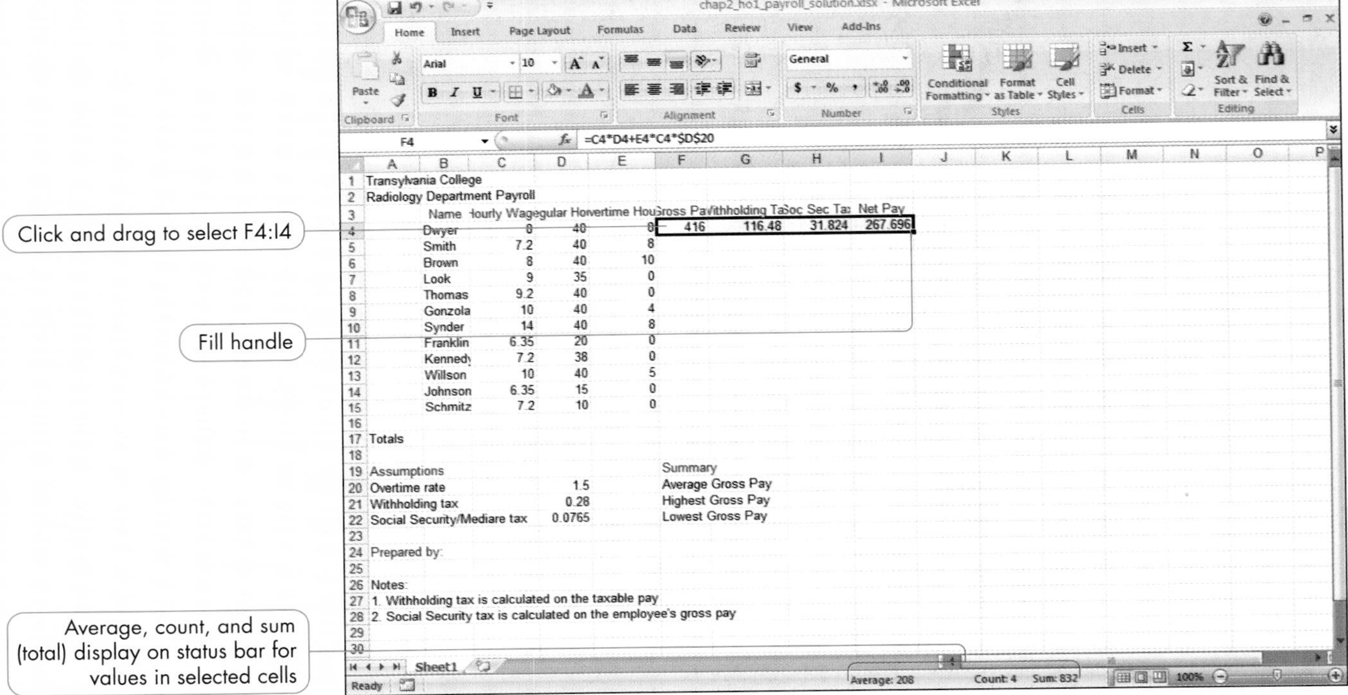

Figure 2.3 Copy the Formulas

TIP Isolate Assumptions

The formulas in a worksheet should always be based on cell references rather than specific values—for example, C25 or $C$25 rather than .07. The cells containing the values are clearly labeled and set apart from the rest of the worksheet. You can vary the inputs (or assumptions on which the worksheet is based) to see the effect within the worksheet. The chance for error is minimized because you are changing the contents of just a single cell instead of multiple formulas that reference those values. Excel automatically recalculates formulas when values change.

Function Basics

SUM Function | Reference

SUM(number1,number2,. . .)

A ***function*** is a preconstructed formula that makes difficult computations less complicated.

The ***SUM function***, represented by Σ or sigma, adds up or sums the numeric entries within a range of cells.

You also can construct formulas by using a *function*, a preconstructed formula that makes difficult computations less complicated. But keep in mind that functions CANNOT replace all formulas. Functions take a value or values, perform an operation, and return a value or values. The most often used function in Excel is the ***SUM function***, represented by Σ or sigma. It adds or sums numeric entries within a range of cells, and then displays the result in the cell containing the function. This function is so useful that the SUM function has its own command in the Function Library group on the Formulas tab. In all, Excel contains more than 325 functions, which are broken down into categories, as shown in Table 2.1.

Syntax refers to the rules for constructing the function.

Arguments are values as input that perform an indicated calculation, and then return another value as output.

When you want to use a function, keep two things in mind. The first is the ***syntax*** of the function or, more simply put, the rules for constructing the function. The second is the function's ***arguments***, which are values as input that perform an indicated calculation, and then return another value as output or the data to be used in the function. While users often type functions such as =SUM(C7:C14), it also is possible to click Insert Function in the Function Library group on the Formulas tab to display the Insert Function dialog box. Using the Insert Function dialog box enables you to select the function to be used (such as MAX, SUM, etc.) from the complete list of functions and specify the arguments to be used in the function. Using Insert Function greatly simplifies the construction of functions by making it easier to select and construct functions. Clicking Insert Function in the Function Library group on the Formulas tab (see Figure 2.4) displays the Insert Function dialog box shown in Figure 2.5. Use the Insert Function dialog box to do the following:

(Using Insert Function greatly simplifies the construction of functions. . . .)

Table 2.1 Function Category and Descriptions

Category Group	Description
Cube	Works with multi-dimensional data stored on an SQL server.
Database	Analyzes data stored in Excel.
Date and Time	Works with dates and time.
Financial	Works with financial-related data.
Information	Determines what type of data is in a cell.
Logical	Calculates yes/no answers.
Lookup and Reference	Provides answers after searching a table.
Math and Trigonometry	Performs standard math and trig functions.
Statistical	Calculates standard statistical functions.
Text	Analyzes labels.

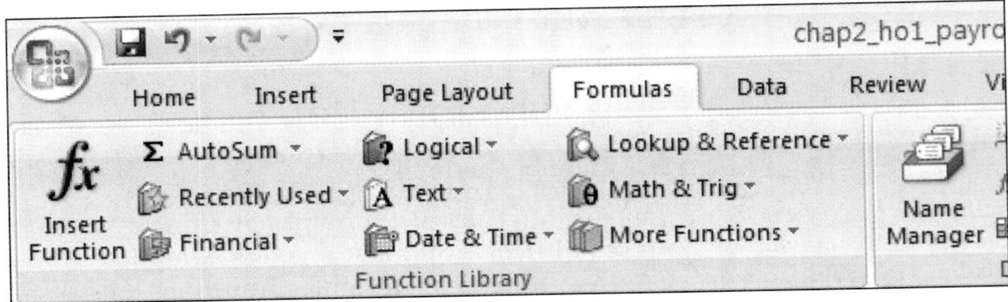

Figure 2.4 Function Library

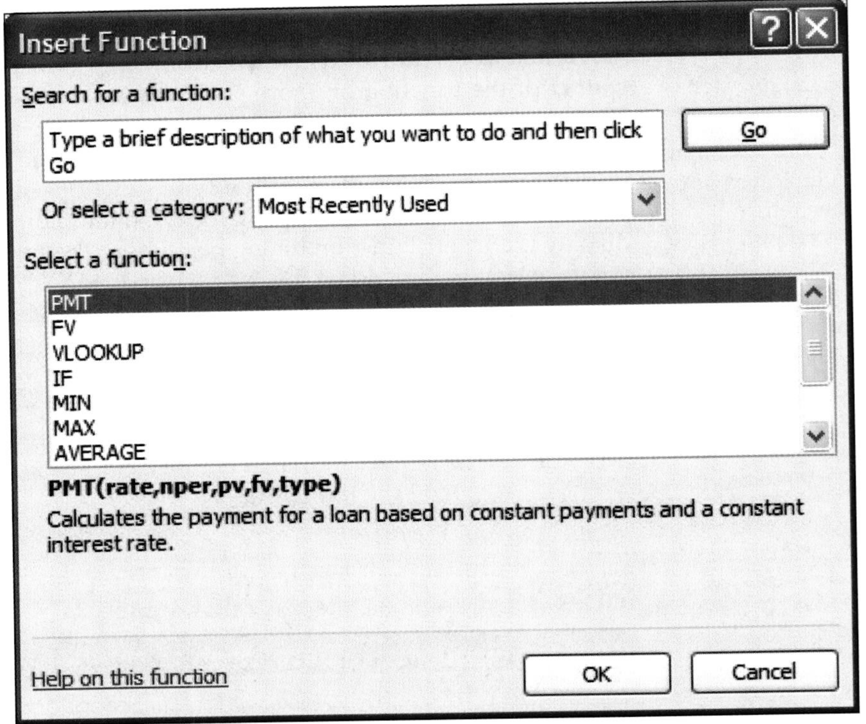

Figure 2.5 Insert Function Dialog Box

1. Search for a function by typing a brief description of what you want the function to do.
2. Select a function from the *Most Recently Used* list, by function category displayed in alphabetical order, or from an alphabetical list of *All* functions.
3. Click the function name to see the syntax and description or double-click the function name to see the function and the Function Arguments dialog box for help with adding the correct arguments. Figure 2.6 shows the Function Arguments dialog box for the SUM function.

If you know the category of the function you want to use, you can click the appropriate command in the Function Library group on the Formulas tab. Select the function and use the Function Arguments dialog box to add the arguments. See Figure 2.4 for the Function Library group.

Function Arguments

SUM

Number1 C4:E4 = {8,40,8}

Number2 = number

= 56

Adds all the numbers in a range of cells.

Number1: number1,number2,... are 1 to 255 numbers to sum. Logical values and text are ignored in cells, included if typed as arguments.

Formula result = 472

Help on this function

OK Cancel

Figure 2.6 Function Arguments Box

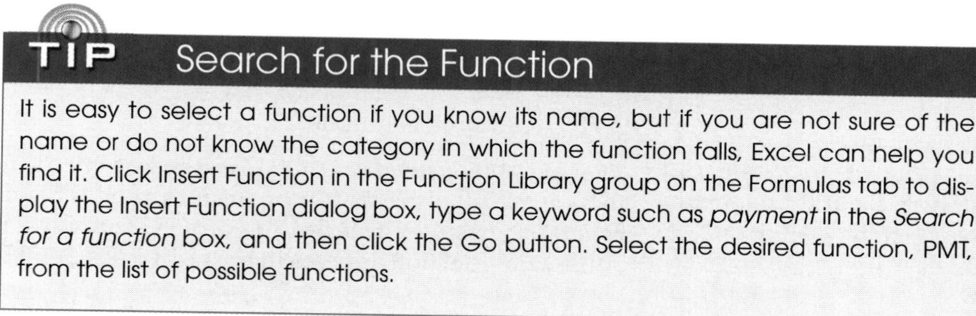

TIP Search for the Function

It is easy to select a function if you know its name, but if you are not sure of the name or do not know the category in which the function falls, Excel can help you find it. Click Insert Function in the Function Library group on the Formulas tab to display the Insert Function dialog box, type a keyword such as *payment* in the *Search for a function* box, and then click the Go button. Select the desired function, PMT, from the list of possible functions.

In this section, you insert a variety of commonly used functions, such as the SUM function.

Using AutoSum

In this chapter, you will examine several different commonly used functions, beginning with the SUM function. You can create formulas in different ways. For example, if you want to add the contents of cells C4 through C10, the formula would be written =C4+C5+C6+C7+C8+C9+C10. However, creating this type of formula manually is time-consuming and increases the probability of entering an inaccurate cell address. This process would be especially problematic if you had to add values stored in several hundred cells. Using the SUM function simplifies this operation and improves the accuracy of the addition. To create the same formula using the SUM function, you can type **=SUM(C4:C10)**. The C4:C10 represents the cell range containing the values to be summed. Rather than typing this entire formula, you can also type **=SUM(**, and then click and drag to select the range of cells containing values to be summed, then type the closing parenthesis. Alternatively, you can click Σ (AutoSum) in the Function Library group on the Formulas tab. To use the AutoSum, click the cell where you want to see the results, and then click AutoSum. Drag to select the cell range or values to be summed and press Enter to see the total.

TIP Avoiding Functions for Basic Formulas

Good spreadsheet design includes using function syntax appropriately. Therefore, you should use functions for their intended purpose, not to encapsulate basic formulas not intended by the function. For example, although =SUM(B4/C4) produces the same result as =B4/C4, the SUM function is not needed to perform the basic arithmetic division. Therefore, you should use the most appropriate, clear-cut formula, =B4/C4.

Inserting Basic Statistical Functions

The use of the SUM function, the most basic statistical function, already has been discussed. Now you will learn several other commonly used statistical functions. These functions perform a variety of calculations to identify key values to help people make decisions. For example, you can use functions to calculate how much you spend on average per month on DVD rentals, what your highest electric bill is to control spending, and what your lowest test score is so you know what you have to study for the final exam. You can use the statistical functions to create or monitor your budget. Climatologists use statistical functions to compare rainfall averages over time in specific geographic areas.

Calculate an Average with the AVERAGE Function

AVERAGE Function | Reference

AVERAGE(number1,number2,. . .)

The ***AVERAGE function*** calculates the arithmetic mean, or average, for the values in an argument list.

The ***AVERAGE function*** calculates the arithmetic mean, or average, for the values in a range of cells. This function can be used for such calculations as the average of several scores on a test or the average score for a number of rounds of golf. The AVERAGE function appears in the form =AVERAGE(C6:C24).

Identify the Lowest Value with the MIN Function

MIN Function | Reference

MIN(number1,number2,. . .)

The ***MIN function*** determines the smallest value of all cells in a list of arguments.

The ***MIN function*** determines the smallest value of all cells in a list of arguments. An application of the MIN might be to determine the lowest score on a test. The function typically appears as =MIN(C6:C24). Although you could manually inspect a range of values to identify the lowest value, doing so is inefficient, especially in large spreadsheets. The MIN function increases your efficiency by always identifying the lowest value in the range. If you change values in the range, the MIN function will identify the new lowest value and display this value in the cell containing the MIN function.

Identify the Highest Value with the MAX Function

MAX Function | Reference

MAX(number1,number2,. . .)

The ***MAX function*** determines the highest value of all cells in a list of arguments.

The ***MAX function*** is the opposite of the MIN function in that it analyzes an argument list to determine the highest value, as in the highest score on a test or the highest points a basketball player scored in a game in a season. This function appears as =MAX(C6:C24). Like the MIN function, when the values in the range change, the MAX function will display the new highest value within the range of cells. Generally the MIN and MAX statistical functions are discussed in concert with the AVERAGE function. These three functions are typically beginning statistical functions and are used together as a start point for more sophisticated analysis. They also are commonly used educational statistics in gradebooks and in analysis of test scores.

Identify the Total Number with the COUNT and COUNTA Functions

COUNT Function | Reference

COUNT(value1,value2,. . .)

COUNTA Function | Reference

COUNTA(value1,value2,. . .)

The ***COUNT function*** counts the number of cells in a range that contain numerical data.
The ***COUNTA function*** counts the number of cells in a range that are not blank.

The two basic count functions, COUNT and COUNTA, enable a user to count the cells in a range that meet a particular criterion. The ***COUNT function*** counts the number of cells in a range that contain numerical data. This function is expressed as =COUNT(C6:C24). The ***COUNTA function*** counts the number of cells in a range that are not blank. This function is expressed as =COUNTA(C6:C24). These functions might be used to verify data entry; for example, you may need to verify that the correct type of data has been entered into the appropriate number of cells. The COUNT function is used to verify that cells have numbers in them and the COUNTA function is used to make sure data are in every cell.

Determine the Midpoint Value with the MEDIAN Function

MEDIAN Function | Reference

MEDIAN(number1,number2,. . .)

The ***MEDIAN function*** finds the midpoint value in a set of values.

Another easy basic statistical function often overlooked is the ***MEDIAN function*** that finds the midpoint value in a set of values. It is helpful to identify at what value ½ of the population is above or below. The median shows that half of the sample data are above a particular value and half are below that value. The median is particularly useful because the AVERAGE function often is influenced by extreme numbers. For example, if 10 grades are between 90 and 100 and the eleventh grade is 0, the extreme value of 0 distorts the overall average as an indicator of the set of grades. See Table 2.2 for this example. Note that 86 is the average and 95 is the median.

Table 2.2 Compare Average and Median

Scores	
99	
98	
97	
96	
95	
95	**Midpoint Score (half the scores above and half the scores below this score)**
93	
92	
91	
90	
0	
86	**Average Score (Equal to the sum of the values divided by the number of values)**
95	**Median (midpoint) Score**

TIP Average, Count, and Sum

When you select a range of cells containing values, Excel displays the average, count, and sum of those values on the status bar. See Figure 2.3 at the end of Hands-On Exercise 1 for an example.

Using Date Functions

Before electronic spreadsheets, you could spend hours trying to figure out pay dates for the next year or when a new employee's probation period was up. Excel enables you to increase your productivity by using date and time functions. These functions help in two ways: by efficiently handling time-consuming procedures and by helping you analyze data related to the passing of time. For example, you can use the date and time functions to calculate when employees are eligible for certain benefits or how many days it takes to complete a project. You also can use the date functions to help you calculate if an account is 30, 60, or more days past due. Excel converts and stores dates as numbers. Using date functions allows you to calculate the difference between dates, add or subtract days from a given date, and so on.

TODAY Function | Reference

TODAY( )

The ***TODAY function*** displays the current date in a cell.

The ***TODAY function*** is a date-related function that places the current date in a cell. The function is expressed as =TODAY(). This function is updated when the worksheet is calculated or the file is opened. Unlike the statistical functions you just learned about, some date functions like TODAY() do not require cell references or data as arguments. However, you must still include the parentheses for the function to work.

NOW Function | Reference

NOW( )

The ***NOW function*** uses the computer's clock to display the current date and time side by side in a cell.

The ***NOW function*** uses the computer's clock to display the current date and time side by side in a cell. It returns the time the workbook was last opened, so the value will change every time the workbook is opened. The Now function does the same thing as the Today function, except the result is formatted to display the current time as well as the current date. Both of these functions will display the current date/time when the spreadsheet file is opened. Thus, date/time is always current; it is not the date/time when the function was first entered in the cell. The NOW function is expressed as =NOW(). Note that failure to insert the parentheses will cause Excel to return an error message.

TIP Function AutoComplete

Use Function AutoComplete to quickly create and edit functions, minimizing typing and syntax errors. Type an = and the beginning letters of the desired function, and Excel will display a drop-down list of valid functions, names, and text strings matching the letters. Double-click the appropriate function from the list to complete the function name automatically.

Functions Used | Reference

Name	Syntax	Definition
SUM	SUM(number1,number2, . . .)	The ***SUM function***, represented by Σ or sigma, adds up or sums the numeric entries within a range of cells.
AVERAGE	AVERAGE(number1,number2, . . .)	The ***AVERAGE function*** calculates the arithmetic mean, or average, for the values in an argument list.
MIN	MIN(number1,number2, . . .)	The ***MIN function*** determines the smallest value of all cells in a list of arguments.
MAX	MAX(number1,number2, . . .)	The ***MAX function*** determines the highest value of all cells in a list of arguments.
COUNT	COUNT(value1,value2, . . .)	The ***COUNT function*** counts the number of cells in a range that contain numerical data.
COUNTA	COUNTA(value1,value2, . . .)	The ***COUNTA function*** counts the number of cells in a range that are not blank.
MEDIAN	MEDIAN(number1,number2, . . .)	The ***MEDIAN function*** finds the midpoint value in a set of values.
NOW	NOW( )	The ***NOW function*** uses the computer's clock to display the current date and time side by side in a cell.
TODAY	TODAY( )	The ***TODAY function*** displays the current date in a cell.
IF	IF(logical_test,value_if_true,value_if_false)	The ***IF function*** is the most basic logical function in that it returns one value when a condition is met and returns another value when the condition is not met.
VLOOKUP	VLOOKUP(lookup_value,table_array, col_index_num,range_lookup)	The ***VLOOKUP function*** allows the Excel user to look up an answer from a table of possible answers.
PMT	PMT(rate,nper,pv,fv,type)	The ***PMT function*** calculates the payment on a loan.
FV	FV(rate,nper,pmt,pv,type)	The ***FV function*** returns the future value of an investment

Hands-On Exercises

2 | Completing the Smithtown Hospital Radiology Department Payroll

Skills covered: 1. Compute the Totals **2.** Using Other General Functions **3.** Apply Number Formatting **4.** Apply Font and Alignment Formatting **5.** Insert a Comment to Complete the Worksheet

Step 1
Compute the Totals

Refer to Figure 2.7 as you complete Step 1.

a. Open the *chap2_ho1_payroll_solution* workbook if you closed it after the last hands-on exercise and save it as **chap2_ho2_payroll_solution**.

b. Click in **cell F17**, the cell that will contain the total gross pay for all employees. Click the **Formulas tab**, click **AutoSum** in the Function Library group, and click and drag over **cells F4:F15** to select the correct range.

c. Press **Enter** to complete the formula.

Cell F17 displays the value 4144.25 and if you click in **cell F17**, you will see the function =SUM(F4:F15) in the formula bar. You have entered the SUM function to calculate the total gross pay.

d. Click and drag the fill handle in **cell F17** to **cell I17**, the remaining cells in the row. Complete the copy operation by releasing the mouse.

Cell I17 now displays 2666.825, which is the total net pay for all employees.

e. Save the workbook.

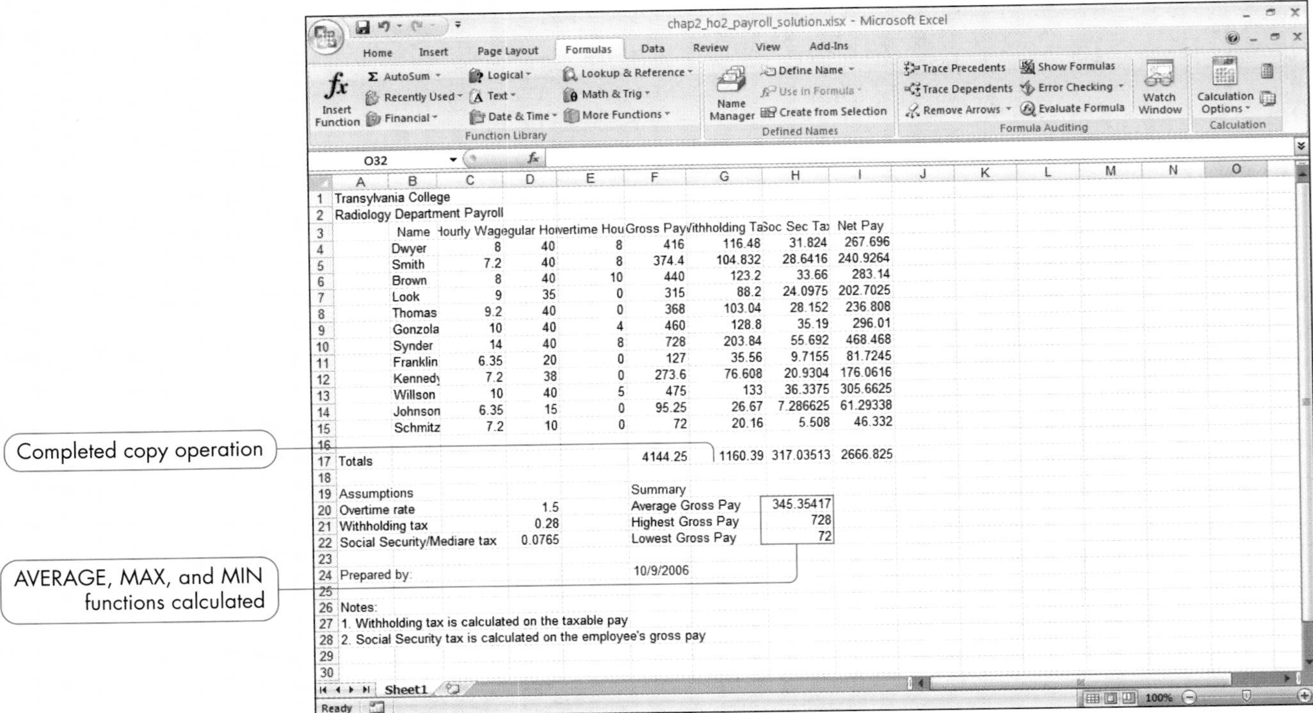

Figure 2.7 Using Functions

Step 2
Using Other General Functions

Refer to Figure 2.7 as you complete Step 2.

a. Click in **cell H20**. This cell will contain the average gross pay for all employees.

b. Type **=AVERAGE(F4:F15)** and press **Enter**.

Cell H20 displays 345.35417, which is the average gross pay for all radiology department employees.

c. Click in **cell H21**.

d. Type **=MAX(** and move the mouse pointer to cell **F4**. Click and drag to select **cells F4:F15**. The dashed line indicates the cells selected as you drag the mouse. Release the mouse, type **)**, and press **Enter**.

Cell H21 displays the value 728, which is the highest gross pay for any employee of the radiology department.

e. Click in **cell H22**.

This cell will display the lowest gross pay of any radiology department employee.

f. Type **=MIN(** and move the mouse pointer to **cell F4**. Click and drag to select **cells F4:F15**. Release the mouse, type **)**, and press **Enter**.

Cell H22 displays the value 72, which is the lowest gross pay for any employee of the radiology department.

g. Click in **cell F24**, type **=TODAY()**, and press **Enter**. The current date displays in cell F24. Widen the column if necessary. Save the workbook.

Step 3
Apply Number Formatting

Refer to Figure 2.7 as you complete Step 3.

a. Select **cells C4:C15**. Press and hold **Ctrl** as you click and drag to select **cells F4:I15**, **cells F17:I17**, and **cells H20:H22**. Click the **Home tab**, click the **Number Format arrow** in the Number group, and then click **Currency**.

b. Click and drag to select **cells D21:D22**. Click **Percent Style** in the Number group on the Home tab and click **Increase Decimal** twice in the Number group to format each number to two decimal places.

c. Save the workbook.

Step 4
Apply Font and Alignment Formatting

Refer to Figure 2.8 as you complete Step 4.

a. Select **cells A3:I3**. Press and hold **Ctrl** as you click and drag to select **cells A19:I19**. Continue to hold **Ctrl** as you click and drag to select **cells A24:I24**.

This action will produce three rows of non-adjacent selected cells.

b. Click the **Fill Color arrow** in the Font group and select **Black** as the fill color. Click the **Font Color arrow** in the Font group and select **White** as the text color. Click **Bold** in the Font group so the text stands out.

c. Click and drag to select **cells A3:I3**, which also will deselect the cells in rows 19 and 24. Click **Wrap Text** in the Alignment group on the Home tab.

The column heading text is now centered and wraps in cells.

TROUBLESHOOTING: Excel may not automatically increase row height after you wrap text. You may have to increase the height of row 3 manually if necessary. Click and drag the dividing line between rows 3 and 4 to increase the height of row 3.

d. Click and drag to select **cells A1:I1**.

- Click **Fill Color** in the Font group to apply the last fill color, which is black.
- Click **Font Color** in the Font group to apply the last font color, which is white.
- Click **Bold** in the Font group so the text stands out.
- Click **Merge and Center** in the Alignment group on the Home tab.

The title, *Smithtown Hospital*, is now bold, white, and centered in a black box over the nine columns in the worksheet.

e. Click and drag to select **cells A2:I2** and apply the same four formats that you did in Step 3d.

The subtitle, *Radiology Department Payroll*, is now bold, white, and centered in a black box over the columns in the worksheet.

f. Save the workbook.

TIP The Format Painter

The Format Painter copies the formatting of the selected cell to other cells in the worksheet. Click the cell whose formatting you want to copy, then double-click Format Painter in the Clipboard group on the Home tab. The mouse pointer changes to a paintbrush to indicate that you can copy the current formatting; just click and drag the paintbrush over the cells that you want to assume the formatting of the original cell. Repeat the painting process as often as necessary, then click Format Painter a second time to return to normal editing.

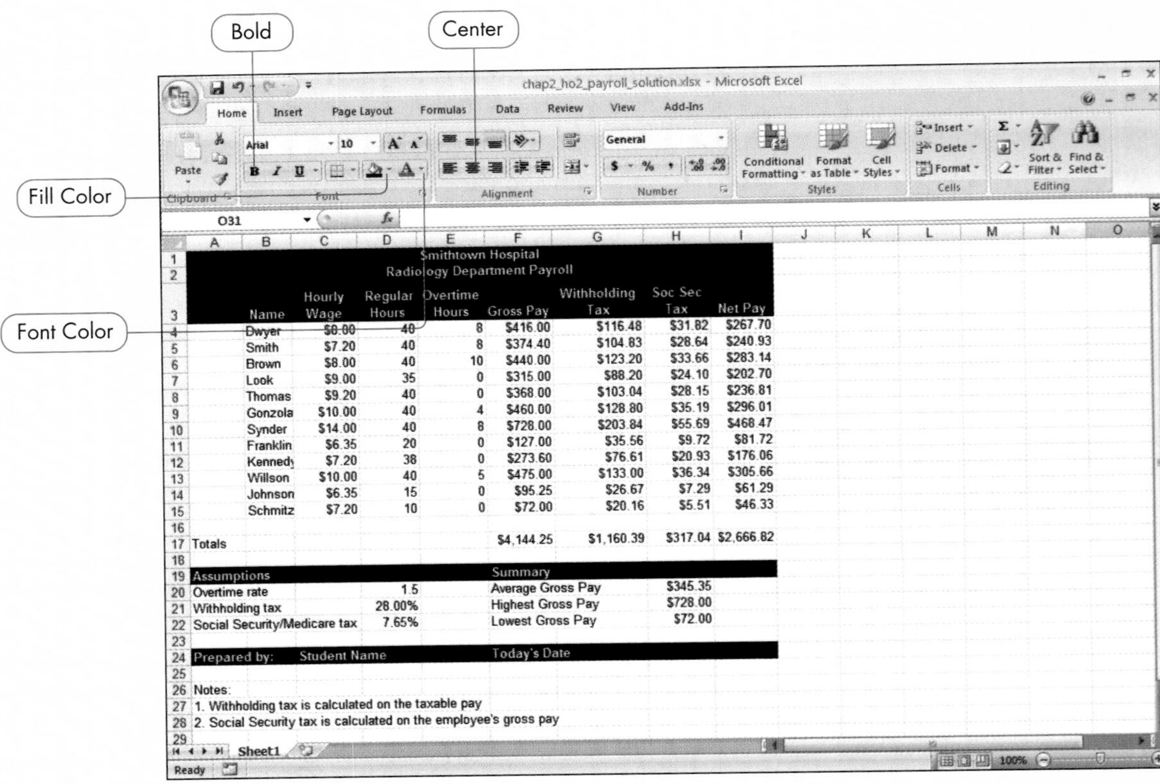

Name	Hourly Wage	Regular Hours	Overtime Hours	Gross Pay	Withholding Tax	Soc Sec Tax	Net Pay
Dwyer	$8.00	40	8	$416.00	$116.48	$31.82	$267.70
Smith	$7.20	40	8	$374.40	$104.83	$28.64	$240.93
Brown	$8.00	40	10	$440.00	$123.20	$33.66	$283.14
Look	$9.00	35	0	$315.00	$88.20	$24.10	$202.70
Thomas	$9.20	40	0	$368.00	$103.04	$28.15	$236.81
Gonzola	$10.00	40	4	$460.00	$128.80	$35.19	$296.01
Synder	$14.00	40	8	$728.00	$203.84	$55.69	$468.47
Franklin	$6.35	20	0	$127.00	$35.56	$9.72	$81.72
Kennedy	$7.20	38	0	$273.60	$76.61	$20.93	$176.06
Willson	$10.00	40	5	$475.00	$133.00	$36.34	$305.66
Johnson	$6.35	15	0	$95.25	$26.67	$7.29	$61.29
Schmitz	$7.20	10	0	$72.00	$20.16	$5.51	$46.33
Totals				$4,144.25	$1,160.39	$317.04	$2,666.82

Assumptions		Summary	
Overtime rate	1.5	Average Gross Pay	$345.35
Withholding tax	28.00%	Highest Gross Pay	$728.00
Social Security/Medicare tax	7.65%	Lowest Gross Pay	$72.00

Prepared by: Student Name | Today's Date

Notes:
1. Withholding tax is calculated on the taxable pay
2. Social Security tax is calculated on the employee's gross pay

Figure 2.8 Complete the Formatting

Step 5

Insert a Comment to Complete the Worksheet

Refer to Figure 2.9 as you complete Step 5.

a. Click in **cell D21**. Click the **Review tab**, click **New Comment** in the Comments group, and type **The exercise uses a constant value for simplicity sake.**, as shown in Figure 2.9.

   TROUBLESHOOTING: The name in the Comment box will be different on your system. The name or initials entered when registering the Microsoft Office 2007 software will appear in the comment box as the author of the comment. Use Help to learn how to change the name or initials for yourself.

b. Click any cell.

   Clicking another cell after you finish entering the comment closes the comment box. The text of the comment is no longer visible, but a tiny triangle is visible in cell D21. When you point to cell D21, you will see the text of the comment.

c. Click the **Page Layout tab**, click **Orientation** in the Page Setup group, and click **Landscape**. Click **Size** and select **More Paper Sizes**.

   Clicking More Paper Sizes displays the Page Setup dialog box.

TIP Displaying the Page Setup Dialog Box

You also can click the Page Setup Dialog Box Launcher in the lower-right corner of the Page Setup group to display the Page Setup dialog box.

d. Click the **Page tab**, if necessary, in the Page Setup dialog box and click **Fit to 1 page** in the *Scaling* section.

e. Click the **Margins tab** and click the **Horizontally check box** in the *Center on page* section.

   This option centers worksheet data between the left and right margins.

f. Click the **Sheet tab**, click the **Row and column headings check box**, and click the **Gridlines check box** in the *Print* section. Click **OK**.

   You changed the orientation of the spreadsheet for printing as well as selected the option to force the spreadsheet on one piece of paper. The spreadsheet also will be centered horizontally with row/column headings and gridlines printed.

g. Print the worksheet. Save the *chap2_ho2_payroll_solution* workbook.

h. Press **Ctrl + ~** (to the left of the number 1 key) to show the cell formulas rather than the displayed values. Adjust the column widths as necessary and print the worksheet a second time.

   To view the underlying formulas in your worksheet, press and hold down Ctrl while pressing ~ (tilde). This key is located above Tab on the keyboard.

i. Close the workbook without saving the view of the formulas. Exit Excel if you do not want to continue with the next exercise at this time.

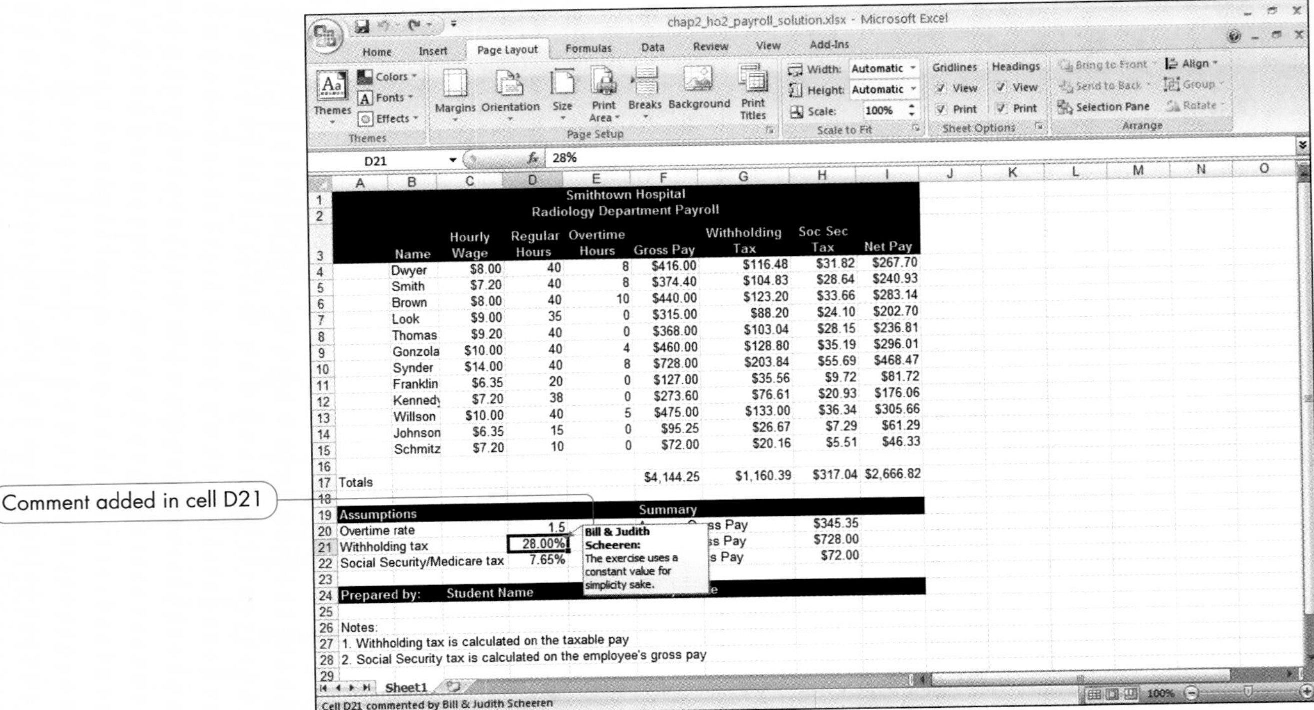

Figure 2.9 Comments and Formatting

Logical and Lookup Functions

> (. . . mathematics is the problem; thinking is the solution. . . .)

Several functions in Excel are designed to return an answer when a particular condition is met. These logical functions are very useful for decision-making. Excel also contains functions that search for or "look up" information in a table. These lookup functions use a designated worksheet area or table and search row by row for a match. Just remember that mathematics is the problem; thinking is the solution as you work with these functions. In this section, you use one major logical function and one major lookup function.

Using the IF Function

IF Function | Reference

IF(logical_test,value_if_true,value_if_false)

The ***IF function*** returns one value when a condition is met and returns another value when the condition is not met.

In the set of logical functions, the ***IF function*** is the most basic in that it returns one value when a condition is met and returns another value when the condition is not met. For example, you may have a display of student GPAs and want to determine if the students are eligible for the Dean's List. If the range of student GPAs were C6 through C24, the IF function would appear in cell D6 as =IF(C6>3.5, "Dean's List", "No"). This function then would be copied to cells D7 through D24. The IF function supports the decision-making capability that is used in a worksheet. The IF function has three arguments:

1. a condition that is tested to determine if it is either true or false,
2. the resulting value if the condition is true, and
3. the resulting value if the condition is false.

This function can be illustrated as:

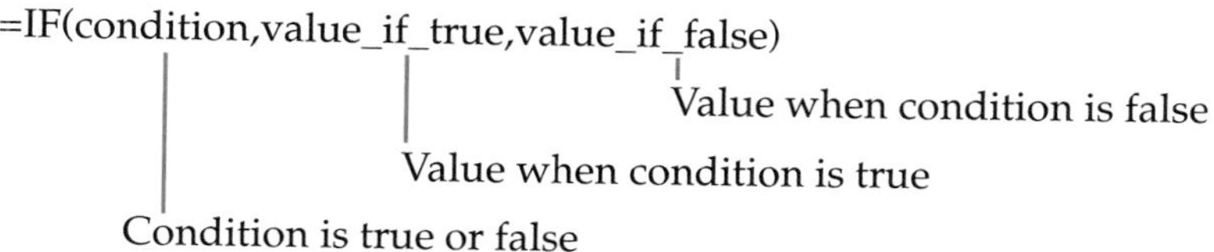

An IF function returns either the second or third argument, depending if the condition is true or false. The value_if_true and value_if_false parameters can contain text, a value, a formula, or a nested function. For example, an IF function used in a gradebook might award a bonus for a student whose homework is "OK," while others do not get the bonus.

=IF(H4= "OK",G4=$H$19,G4)

Value if condition is false

Value if condition is true

Condition is true or false

Note that when you want to compare the contents of a cell to specific text, you must enclose the comparison text in quotation marks. You also can return text in the value_if_true and value_if_false parameters by enclosing the text (but not the commas) in quotation marks.

The condition in the IF function includes one of the six comparison operators shown in Table 2.3.

Table 2.3 Comparison Operators

Operator	Description
=	Equal to
<>	Not equal to
<	Less than
>	Greater than
<=	Less than or equal to
>=	Greater than or equal to

The small sample worksheet, Figure 2.10, shows the data the IF function uses to create the examples in Table 2.4. Arguments may be numeric, cell references to display cells' contents, a formula, a function, or a text entry. Review Table 2.4 to see how Excel evaluates conditions and the results.

	A	B	C	D	E
1	10	15	April		
2	10	30	May		
3					

Figure 2.10 IF Data

Table 2.4 IF Function, Evaluation, and Result

IF Function	Evaluation	Result
=IF(A1=A2,1000,2000)	10 is equal to 10, TRUE	1000
=IF(A1<>A2,1000,2000)	10 is not equal to 10, FALSE	2000
=If(A1<>A2,B1,B2)	10 is not equal to10, FALSE	30
=IF(A1<B2,MAX(B1:B2),MIN(B1:B2))	10 is less than 30, TRUE	30
=IF(A1<A2,B1+10,B1-10)	10 is less than 10, FALSE	5
=IF(A1=A2,C1,C2)	10 is equal to 10, TRUE	April

Using the VLOOKUP Function

VLOOKUP Function | Reference

VLOOKUP(lookup_value,table_array,col_index_num,range_lookup)

The ***VLOOKUP function*** looks up an answer from a vertical table of possible answers.

When you order something on the Web or by catalog, you look up the shipping costs for your order. You find the information you want because you look up a specific piece of information (the total amount of your order) to find the associated information (the shipping cost). The VLOOKUP function works the same way. You can use the VLOOKUP function to find a company's specific tax rate from a table or look up your own tax rate. The ***VLOOKUP function*** evaluates a value and looks up this value in a vertical table to return a value, text, or formula. Use VLOOKUP to search for exact matches or for the nearest value that is less than or equal to the search value (such as assigning a shipping cost of $15.25 to an order of $300.87). Or use the VLOOKUP function to assign a B grade for an 87% class average.

Understand the VLOOKUP Function Syntax

The VLOOKUP function has three arguments:

1. a lookup value stored in a cell,
2. a range of cells containing a lookup table, and
3. the number of the column within the lookup table that contains the value to return.

One use of a VLOOKUP function is the assignment of letter grades in a gradebook based on numeric values. Figure 2.11 shows a portion of a worksheet with a Grading Criteria Table that associates letter grades with the numerical value earned by a student. The first student's overall class average is 76.3. You can use the VLOOKUP function to identify the cell containing the student's numerical average and use that value to look up the equivalent letter grade in a table. To determine the letter grade in cell J4 based on a numeric value in cell I4, you would use the following:

=VLOOKUP(I4,$I$20:$J$24,2)

- Column number with the grade
- Range of the table
- Value to lookup (semester average)

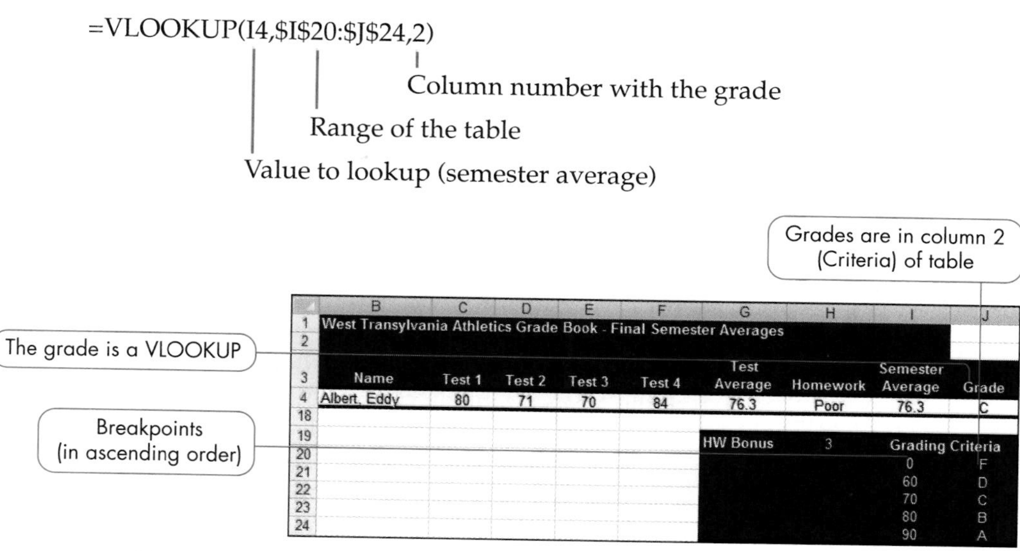

Figure 2.11 VLOOKUP Table Data

The ***lookup value*** is the value to look up in a reference table.

The ***lookup table*** is a range of cells containing the reference table.

The ***column index number*** is the column number in the lookup table that contains return values.

Cell I4 is the ***lookup value*** that represents the cell containing the value to look up in a table. In this example, the lookup value is 76.3. The table that Excel searches using a lookup function is called a ***lookup table***. In this example, the lookup table is stored in the range $I$20:$J$24. Note that an absolute reference is used so the address is not changed when the formula is copied to other cells. The ***column index number***, indicated by col_index_num in the function, refers to the number of the column in the lookup table that contains the return values. In the example, the col_index_num of 2 returns the value in the second column in the lookup table that corresponds to the value being looked up.

Structure the Lookup Table

The VLOOKUP function searches the left column of a table for a specific value and returns a corresponding value from the same row but a different column. You set up the table to include unique values in the left column (for example, ranges of total amounts or numeric ranges to assign letter grades), and then Excel retrieves the associated information (for example, shipping cost or letter grade) from another column. In Figure 2.11, the lookup table extends over two columns, I and J, and five rows, 20 through 24. The table is located in the range I20:J24.

You should set up the lookup table before using the VLOOKUP function. The left column, known as the lookup column, of the table includes the reference data used to look up information in the table, such as customer number, income, grade points, or the total amount range of the order. The other columns include information related to the first column, such as customer credit limit, tax rate, letter grades, or shipping cost. The values in the left or lookup column must be sorted in ascending order, from lowest to highest value. However, instead of typing an entire range, such as 80–89, for the range of B grades, you enter breakpoints only. The ***breakpoint*** is the lowest numeric value for a specific category or in a series of a lookup table to produce a corresponding result to return for a lookup function. Breakpoints are listed in ascending order in the first column of the lookup table. For example, the breakpoints in the gradebook lookup table represent the lowest numerical score to earn a particular letter grade. The breakpoints are listed in column I, and the corresponding letter grades are found in column J.

A ***breakpoint*** is the lowest numeric value for a category or series in a lookup table to produce a corresponding result for a lookup function.

Understand How Excel Processes the Lookup

The VLOOKUP function works by searching in the left column of the lookup table until it finds an exact match or a number that is larger than the lookup value. If Excel finds an exact match, it returns the value stored in the column designated by the index number on that same row. If the table contains breakpoints for ranges rather than exact matches, when Excel finds a value larger than the lookup value, it returns the next lower value in the column designated by the col_index_num. To work accurately, the reference column must be in ascending order.

For example, the VLOOKUP function to assign letter grades works like this: Excel identifies the lookup value (76.3 stored in I4) and compares it to the values in the lookup table (stored in I20:J24). It tries to find an exact match; however, the table contains breakpoints rather than every conceivable numeric average. Because the lookup table is in ascending order, it notices that 76.3 is not equal to 80, so it goes back up to the 70 row. Excel then looks at the column index number of 2 and returns the letter grade of C, which is located in the second column of the lookup table. The returned grade of C is then stored in the cell J4, which contains the VLOOKUP function.

TIP HLOOKUP Function

The VLOOKUP function is arranged vertically in a table, while its counterpart, the HLOOKUP function, is arranged horizontally. Use the HLOOKUP function when your comparison values are located in a row across the top of a table of data and you want to look down a specified number of rows.

Hands-On Exercises

3 | Athletic Department Eligibility Gradebook

Skills covered: 1. Use the IF Function **2.** Use the VLOOKUP Function **3.** Copy the IF and VLOOKUP Functions **4.** Apply Page Setup Options and Print the Worksheet

Step 1
Use the IF Function

Refer to Figure 2.12 as you complete Step 1.

a. Open the *chap2_ho3_gradebook* workbook and save it as **chap2_ho3_gradebook_solution** so that you can return to the original workbook if necessary.

   The partially completed gradebook contains student test scores and their respective test averages. You need to create an IF function to determine if students have completed their homework. If they did, they receive a 3-point bonus added to their semester average. Those students who did not complete homework receive no bonus, so their semester average is the same as their test average.

b. Click in **cell I4**. Click the **Formulas tab** and click **Insert Function** in the Function Library group. Select the **IF** function from the *Select a function* list. Click **OK** to close the Insert Function dialog box and display the Function Argument dialog box.

   You will use the Function Arguments dialog box to build the IF function.

c. Click in the **Logical_test** box, keep the Function Arguments dialog box open but drag it down to see cell H4, click **cell H4** in the worksheet, and type **="OK"** to complete the logical test.

d. Click in the **Value_if_true** box, keep the Function Arguments dialog box open, click **cell G4** in the worksheet, type **+**, and click **cell H19**. Press **F4** to change H19 to an absolute cell reference.

e. Click in the **Value_if_false** box, keep the Function Arguments dialog box open, and click **cell G4** in the worksheet.

   TROUBLESHOOTING: Text values used in arguments must be enclosed in quotes.

f. Click **OK** to insert the function into the worksheet. Save the workbook.

   Because Eddy's homework was "Poor," he did not earn the 3-point bonus. His semester average is the same as his test average, which is 76.3 in cell I4.

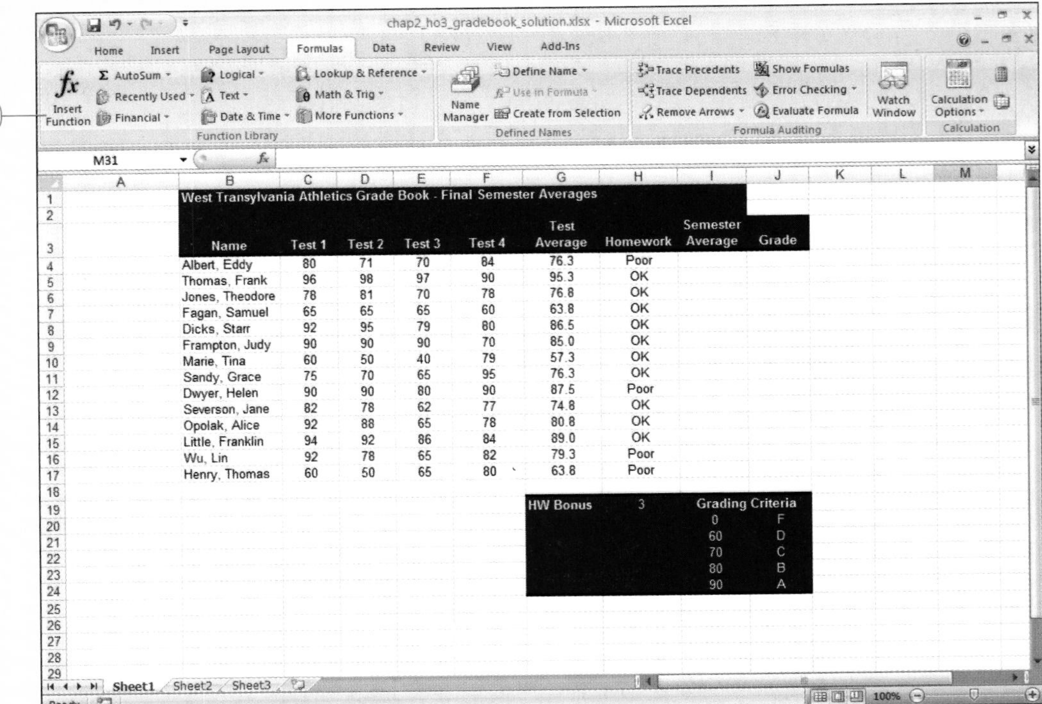

Figure 2.12 Athletics Gradebook

Step 2
Use the VLOOKUP Function

Refer to Figure 2.11 as you complete Step 2.

a. Click in **cell J4** and click the **Lookup & Reference arrow** in the Function Library group on the Formulas tab. Select **VLOOKUP**.

You will create a VLOOKUP function using the semester average stored in column I to determine the letter grade for each student.

b. Click in the **Lookup_value** box and click **cell I4** in the worksheet.

The first student's semester average, which is stored in cell I4, is the value to look up.

c. Click in the **Table_array** box. Click **cell I20** and drag to **cell J24**, and then press **F4** to convert the entire range reference to absolute ($I$20:$J$24).

The table containing the letter grade equivalents is stored in I20:J24. You made the reference absolute so that the cell addresses do not change when you copy the function for the remaining student athletes.

d. Click in the **Col_index_num** box and type **2**.

e. Click **OK** to insert the function into the worksheet and save the workbook.

The first student's letter grade is C because his semester average of 76.3 is over 70 but less than 80.

TROUBLESHOOTING: Make sure to use an absolute reference with the table in the VLOOKUP function. You will see inaccurate results if you forget to use absolute references.

Step 3
Copy the IF and VLOOKUP Functions

Refer to Figure 2.13 as you complete Step 3.

a. Copy the IF and VLOOKUP Functions by selecting **cells I4:J4**, point to the fill handle in the lower-right corner of **cell J4**, and drag the fill handle over cells **I5:J17**.

   You just copied the original IF and VLOOKUP functions for the rest of the students.

b. Check that the semester averages are formatted to one decimal place.

c. Click **cell A19** and enter your name. Click **cell A1** and type **=TODAY()** to enter today's date.

d. Click **cell A1** and hold **Ctrl** as you click **cell A19**. Click the **Home tab** and click **Bold** in the Font group. Save the workbook.

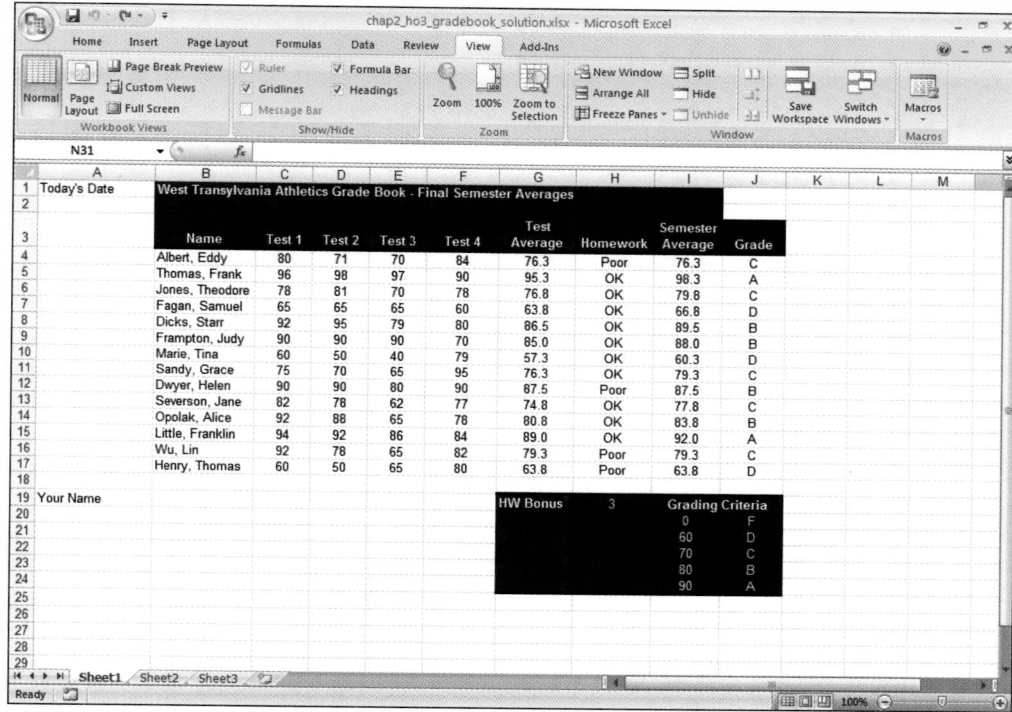

	A	B	C	D	E	F	G	H	I	J
1	Today's Date	West Transylvania Athletics Grade Book - Final Semester Averages								
2										
3		Name	Test 1	Test 2	Test 3	Test 4	Test Average	Homework	Semester Average	Grade
4		Albert, Eddy	80	71	70	84	76.3	Poor	76.3	C
5		Thomas, Frank	96	98	97	90	95.3	OK	98.3	A
6		Jones, Theodore	78	81	70	78	76.8	OK	79.8	C
7		Fagan, Samuel	65	65	65	60	63.8	OK	66.8	D
8		Dicks, Starr	92	95	79	80	86.5	OK	89.5	B
9		Frampton, Judy	90	90	90	70	85.0	OK	88.0	B
10		Marie, Tina	60	50	40	79	57.3	OK	60.3	D
11		Sandy, Grace	75	70	65	95	76.3	OK	79.3	C
12		Dwyer, Helen	90	90	80	90	87.5	Poor	87.5	B
13		Severson, Jane	82	78	62	77	74.8	OK	77.8	C
14		Opolak, Alice	92	88	65	78	80.8	OK	83.8	B
15		Little, Franklin	94	92	86	84	89.0	OK	92.0	A
16		Wu, Lin	92	78	65	82	79.3	Poor	79.3	C
17		Henry, Thomas	60	50	65	80	63.8	Poor	63.8	D
18										
19	Your Name						HW Bonus	3	Grading Criteria	
20									0	F
21									60	D
22									70	C
23									80	B
24									90	A

Figure 2.13 Athletics Gradebook

Step 4
Apply Page Setup Options and Print the Worksheet

a. Click the **Page Layout tab** and click **Margins** in the Page Setup group. Click **Custom Margins** to display the Margins tab in the Page Setup dialog box.

b. Click the **Horizontally check box** in the *Center on page* section to center the worksheet between the left and right margins.

c. Click the **Sheet tab**. Click the **Gridlines check box** and click the **Row and column headings check box** in the *Print* section.

d. Click **OK**. Save the workbook.

e. Click the **Office Button** and select **Print**. Click the **Preview button** to see how the workbook will print.

TROUBLESHOOTING: If the worksheet previews as two pages in the Print Preview window, close the Print Preview window, display the Page Setup dialog box, and decrease the scaling. Display the worksheet in Print Preview again to make sure the worksheet fits on one page.

f. Click the **Print button**, and then click **OK** to print the worksheet.

g. Press **Ctrl + ~** to show the cell formulas rather than the values. Adjust the column width as necessary and print the worksheet a second time. Close the workbook without saving.

Financial Functions

A spreadsheet is a tool used for decision-making. Many decisions typically involve financial situations: payments, investments, interest rates, and so on. Excel contains several financial functions to help you perform calculations with monetary values.

Review Figures 2.14, 2.15, 2.16, and 2.17 to see how a worksheet might be applied to the purchase of a car. You need to know the monthly payment, which depends on the price of the car, the down payment, and the terms of the loan. In other words:

> Can you afford the monthly payment on the car of your choice?

- Can you afford the monthly payment on the car of your choice?
- What if you settle for a less expensive car and receive a manufacturer's rebate?
- What if you work next summer to earn money for a down payment?
- What if you extend the life of the loan and receive a better interest rate?
- Have you accounted for additional items such as insurance, gas, and maintenance?

The answers to these and other questions determine whether you can afford a car, and if so, which car, and how you will pay for it. The decision is made easier by developing the worksheet in Figure 2.14, and then by changing the various input values as indicated.

The availability of the worksheet lets you consider several alternatives. You realize that the purchase of a $14,999 car, as shown in Figure 2.15, is prohibitive because the monthly payment is almost $476.96. Settling for a less expensive car, coming up with a substantial down payment, and obtaining a manufacturer's rebate in Figure 2.16 help, but the $317.97 monthly payment is still too high. Extending the loan to a fourth year

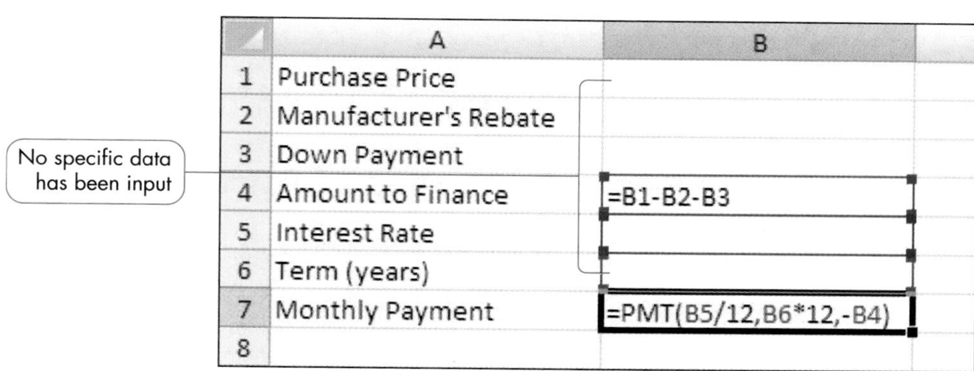

	A	B
1	Purchase Price	
2	Manufacturer's Rebate	
3	Down Payment	
4	Amount to Finance	=B1-B2-B3
5	Interest Rate	
6	Term (years)	
7	Monthly Payment	=PMT(B5/12,B6*12,-B4)
8		

Figure 2.14 Spreadsheets for Decision-Making

	A	B	C	D
1	Purchase Price	$14,999		
2	Manufacturer's Rebate			
3	Down Payment			
4	Amount to Finance	$14,999		
5	Interest Rate	9%		
6	Term (years)	3		
7	Monthly Payment	**$476.96**		
8				

Data entered

Figure 2.15 Spreadsheets for Decision-Making

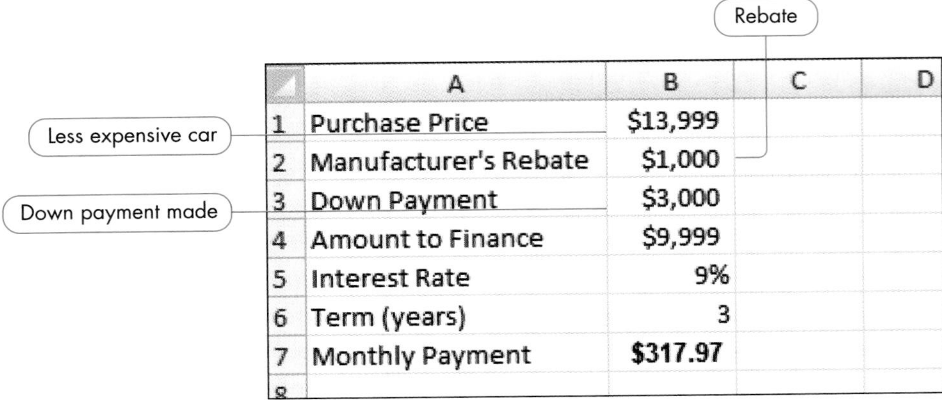

	A	B	C	D
1	Purchase Price	$13,999		
2	Manufacturer's Rebate	$1,000		
3	Down Payment	$3,000		
4	Amount to Finance	$9,999		
5	Interest Rate	9%		
6	Term (years)	3		
7	Monthly Payment	**$317.97**		
8				

Figure 2.16 Spreadsheets for Decision-Making

	A	B	C	D
1	Purchase Price	$13,999		
2	Manufacturer's Rebate	$1,000		
3	Down Payment	$3,000		
4	Amount to Finance	$9,999		
5	Interest Rate	8%		
6	Term (years)	4		
7	Monthly Payment	**$244.10**		
8				

Lower interest rate
Longer term
Lower monthly payment

Figure 2.17 Spreadsheets for Decision-Making

at a lower interest rate, as in Figure 2.17, reduces the monthly payment to $244.10, which is closer to your budgeted amount.

Using the PMT Function

PMT Function | Reference

PMT(rate,nper,pv,fv,type)

The ***PMT function*** calculates the payment on a loan.

The ***PMT function*** calculates payments for a loan that is paid off at a fixed amount at a periodic rate. The PMT function requires three arguments: the interest rate per period, the number of periods, and the amount of the loan, from which it computes the associated payment on a loan. The arguments are placed in parentheses and are separated by commas. Consider the PMT function as it might apply to Figure 2.15:

=PMT(.09/12,36,–14999)

Amount of loan (as a *negative* amount)

Number of periods (3 years × 12 months/year)

Interest rate per period (annual rate divided by 12)

Instead of using specific values, however, you should use cell references in the PMT function arguments, so that you can easily change the input values in the individual cells instead of editing the values in the function itself. The PMT function is entered as =PMT(B5/12,B6*12,–B4) to reflect the terms of a specific loan whose arguments are in cells B4, B5, and B6. You must divide the 9% annual percentage rate (APR) by 12 months to obtain the monthly *periodic* rate. Next, you must multiply the

3-year term by the number of payments per year. Because you will make monthly payments, you multiply 3 by 12 months to calculate the total number of months in the term, which is 36. The amount of the loan is a minus figure because it is a debt. The loan is considered a negative because it is an outflow of cash or an expense. The amount of the loan is entered as a negative amount so the worksheet will display a positive value after calculations.

Using the FV Function

FV Function | Reference

FV(rate,nper,pmt,pv,type)

The ***FV function*** returns the future value of an investment.

The ***FV function*** returns the future value of an investment if you know the interest rate, the term, and the periodic payment. You can use the FV function to determine how much an IRA would be worth in a particular period of time. This function would be expressed as =FV(rate,nper,payment).

Assume that you plan to contribute $3,000 a year to an IRA, that you expect to earn 7% annually, and that you will be contributing for 40 years. The future value of that investment—the amount you will have at age 65—would be $598,905! You would have contributed $120,000 ($3,000 a year for 40 years). The difference, more than $470,000, results from compound interest you will earn over the life of your investment of $120,000!

(. . . more than $470,000, results from compound interest you will earn over the life of your investment of $120,000!)

The FV function has three arguments—the interest rate (also called the rate of return), the number of periods (how long you will pay into the IRA), and the periodic investment (how much you will invest into the IRA per year). The FV function corresponding to the earlier example would be:

Amount at retirement =FV(Rate of return, Term, Periodic payment)

Rate of return: 7%
Term: 40 years
Periodic payment: $3,000

Computed value becomes $598,905

It is more practical, however, to enter the values into a worksheet and then use cell references within the FV function. If, for example, cells A1, A2, and A3 contained the rate of return, term, and annual contribution, respectively, the resulting FV function would be =FV(A1,A2,–A3). The periodic payment is preceded by a minus sign, just as the principal in the PMT function.

These financial functions as well as the other examples of functions provide you with the tools to perform sophisticated mathematical, statistical, and financial calculations.

Hands-On Exercises

4 | Purchasing a Van for the School for Exceptional Children

Skills covered: 1. Create the Worksheet **2.** Insert the PMT Function **3.** Format the Worksheet **4.** Complete the Worksheet

Step 1 Create the Worksheet

Refer to Figure 2.18 as you complete Step 1.

a. Start a new blank workbook. Click in **cell B1** and type the title **School for Exceptional Children**. Enter the remaining labels for column B, as shown in Figure 2.18.

As the transportation director, one of your responsibilities is to purchase vehicles for the school's use. You will create a worksheet, use the PMT function, and format a worksheet to show the proposed purchase price.

b. Increase the column widths to accommodate the widest entry, as necessary (other than cell B3). Enter the following as indicated below. Include the dollar sign and the percent sign as you enter the data to automatically format the cell.

Cell	Value
C4	$26,000
C5	$1,000
C6	$3,000
C8	9%
C9	3

The loan parameters have been entered into the worksheet, and you are ready to work with the PMT function.

c. Enter the formula to caculate the Amount to Finance in cell C7 by clicking in **cell C7** and typing **=C4−(C5+C6)**. Press **Enter**.

Although parentheses are not required for order of precedence, they may be used to help for understandability. You could also enter the formula **=C4−C5−C6** as an alternative.

d. Save the workbook as **chap2_ho4_van_solution**.

Step 2 Insert the PMT Function

a. Click the **Formulas tab**. Click **cell C10**, click **Financial** in the Function Library group, and click the **PMT** function. Click in the **Rate** box, click **cell C8** of the worksheet, then type **/12**.

The Rate box contains C8/12 because interest is calculated monthly.

b. Click in the **Nper** box, click **cell C9** of the worksheet, and type ***12**.

The Nper box contains C9*12 to calculate the total number of payment periods in the loan.

c. Click in the **Pv** box, type a minus sign (–), and click **cell C7**. Click **OK** to close the Function Arguments dialog box.

The monthly payment of $699.59 is now displayed in cell C10.

d. Save the workbook.

TROUBLESHOOTING: Divide the interest rate by 12 because the rate is requested as a percentage per period. Multiply the years by 12 because the term of the loan is stated in years.

Step 3 Format the Worksheet

a. Click the **Home tab**, select cells **B1** and **C1**, and click **Merge and Center** in the Alignment group.

b. Click the **Font size arrow** in the Font group and click **12**. Click **Bold** in the Font group to boldface the title.

c. Click **cell B3**, press and hold **Ctrl** as you click **cells B10:C10**, and click **Bold**.

d. Click and drag to select **cells B4:B9**. Click **Increase Indent** in the Alignment group to indent the labels.

e. Click in **cell A12** and enter your name. Click **cell A1** and use the **TODAY** function to enter today's date. Click **cell A1** and hold **Ctrl** as you click **cell A12**. Click **Bold**. Save the workbook.

Step 4 Complete the Worksheet

a. Click the **Page Layout tab** and click **Margins** in the Page Setup group. Click **Custom Margins** to display the Page Setup dialog box.

b. Click the **Horizontally check box** in the *Center on page* section.

c. Click the **Sheet tab**, click the **Gridlines check box**, and click the **Row and column headings check box** in the *Print* section.

You used the Page Layout options to print gridlines as well as row and column headings and centered the worksheet horizontally.

d. Click **OK**. Save the workbook.

e. Click the **Office Button**, select **Print**, and click **Preview** to see how the workbook will print. Click the **Print button**, and then **OK** to print the worksheet.

f. Press **Ctrl + ~** to show the cell formulas rather than the values. Adjust the column width as necessary and print the worksheet a second time. Close the workbook.

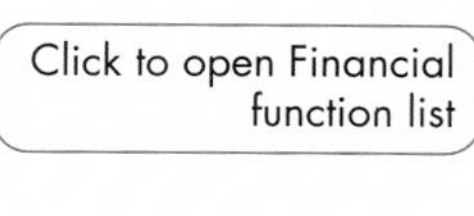

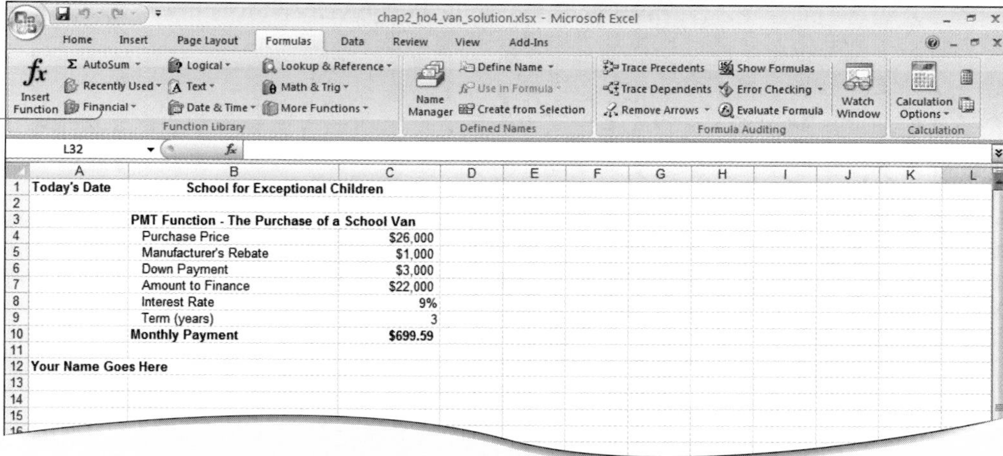

Figure 2.18 School for Exceptional Children Van

Summary

1. **Create and copy formulas.** When constructing formulas in Excel, it is more efficient to enter cell references in formulas rather than the cell contents. Entering cell references means that an addition formula should be stated as =A2+B2 rather than =1+2. By using cell references rather than cell contents, the formula does not have to be changed when the cell content changes. Pointing and using the fill handle are techniques that make the development of an Excel spreadsheet easier. The fill handle is a small black square at the lower-right corner of a selected cell(s). It is the efficient way to copy cell formulas to adjacent cells.
2. **Use relative and absolute cell addresses.** A relative reference (such as C4) changes both row and column when the cell containing the reference is copied to other worksheet cells. An absolute cell reference, such as $C$4, stays the same during the copy process. A mixed reference, such as $C4 or C$4, modifies the row or column during the copy. The use of relative and absolute references is common in the design and construction of most spreadsheets.
3. **Use AutoSum.** The AutoSum is the most often used statistical function in Excel. It is represented by the sigma and automatically sums values contained in a range of cells.
4. **Insert basic statistical functions.** Statistical functions discussed include SUM, which returns the sum of an argument list, and AVERAGE, MEDIAN, MAX, and MIN, which return the average value, the midpoint of a range of values, the highest value, and lowest value, respectively, in an argument list. The COUNT function displays the number of cells with numeric entries and the COUNTA function displays the number of cells with numeric and/or text entries.
5. **Use date functions.** The NOW function uses the computer's clock to display the current date and time side by side in a cell. The TODAY function is another date-related function that places the current date in a cell.
6. **Use the IF function.** In the set of logical functions, the IF is the most basic. It returns one value when a condition is met and returns another value when the condition is not met. The IF function allows decision-making to be used within a worksheet. IF functions have three arguments: the condition, the result when true, and the result when false.
7. **Use the VLOOKUP function.** You can use VLOOKUP to look up an answer from a table of possible answers. The table that Excel searches using a lookup function is called a lookup table, and the value being used to search the lookup table is called a lookup value.
8. **Use the PMT function.** You can use the PMT function to calculate payments for a loan that is paid off at a fixed amount at a periodic rate. The PMT function requires three arguments: the interest rate per period, the number of periods, and the amount of the loan, from which it computes the associated payment on a loan. The arguments are placed in parentheses and are separated by commas.
9. **Use the FV function.** If you know the interest rate, the term, and the periodic payment, then you can use the FV function to return the future value of an investment. You can use the FV function to determine how much an investment would be worth at the end of a defined period of time.

Key Terms

Absolute cell reference 320
Arguments 325
AVERAGE function 328
Breakpoint 340
Column index number 339
COUNT function 329
COUNTA function 329
Fill handle 319
Formula 319
Function 325
FV function 347
IF function 337
Lookup table 339
Lookup value 339
MAX function 328
MEDIAN function 329
MIN function 328
Mixed cell reference 321
NOW function 330
PMT function 346
Pointing 319
Relative cell reference 320
SUM function 325
Syntax 325
TODAY function 330
VLOOKUP function 338

Multiple Choice

1. After entering numbers and using the SUM function to sum the numbers, when is the function updated if one of the numbers changes?
   (a) When the file is saved
   (b) When you refresh the worksheet
   (c) When you close the file
   (d) At once

2. Which of the following returns the system date?
   (a) The Date() function
   (b) The Today() function
   (c) Date arithmetic
   (d) The Insert Date command

3. If you see the term "C3" used in relation to Excel, it refers to what?
   (a) Absolute reference
   (b) Cell reference
   (c) Worksheet reference
   (d) Mixed reference

4. The entry =PMT(C5/12,C6*12,C7):
   (a) Is invalid because the cell reference C7 is not absolute
   (b) Computes an annual payment
   (c) Divides the interest rate in C5, multiplies the number of periods in C6, and C7 is the loan amount
   (d) Is invalid because the value in C7 is negative

5. Pointing is a technique to:
   (a) Select a single cell
   (b) Select a range of contiguous cells
   (c) Select ranges of noncontiguous cells
   (d) All of the above

6. The small black square in the bottom-right corner of a cell is called what?
   (a) Pointer
   (b) Fill handle
   (c) Crosshair
   (d) Select box

7. Given the function =VLOOKUP(C6,D12:F18,3):
   (a) The entries in cells D12 through D18 are in ascending order.
   (b) The entries in cells D12 through D18 are in descending order.
   (c) The entries in cells F12 through F18 are in ascending order.
   (d) The entries in cells F12 through F18 are in descending order.

8. Which of the following must be entered when creating a formula?
   (a) The equal sign
   (b) A mathematical operator
   (c) A function
   (d) Nothing special is required.

9. Which of the following is an example of an absolute cell reference?
   (a) C4
   (b) $C$4
   (c) =C4
   (d) $C4

10. If you wanted the contents of only a column to stay the same throughout the copy process, you would use which of the following?
    (a) Relative reference
    (b) Mixed reference
    (c) Absolute reference
    (d) This is not possible

11. Which of the following references would indicate that the column would not change during the copy process?
    (a) $C$4
    (b) =C4
    (c) $C4
    (d) C$4

12. The Σ indicates which of the following functions?
    (a) AVERAGE
    (b) MAX
    (c) MIN
    (d) SUM

Multiple Choice Continued...

13. Which function will return the number of nonempty cells in the range A2 through A6, when the cells contain text as well as numeric entries?

(a) =COUNT(A2:A6)

(b) =COUNTA(A2:A6)

(c) =COUNT(A2,A6)

(d) =COUNTA(A2,A6)

14. The MAX function is an example of what type of function?

(a) Database

(b) Statistical

(c) Logical

(d) Lookup

15. If you want to determine the future value of an investment, what function would you use?

(a) PV

(b) FV

(c) VLOOKUP

(d) IF

Practice Exercises

1 West Transylvania Women's Basketball Season Statistics

You are the statistician for the West Transylvania Women's basketball team. You have entered basic statistics into a worksheet for the 2007–08 season. The coach wants to expand the statistics so that she can compare production for different seasons. Complete the worksheet as directed using Figure 2.19 as a guide.

a. Open the *chap2_pe1_basketball* workbook and save it as **chap2_pe1_basketball_solution** so that you can return to the original workbook if necessary.
b. The first calculation will be total points (TP). Click in **cell I5**, the cell that will contain the total points for Adams. Type = on the keyboard to begin pointing, then click **cell C5** to enter the first part of the formula to calculate total points.
c. Type **+(** and click **cell F5**, then type ***2)+(** and click **cell H5**. Type ***3)**. You should see 84 as the displayed value for cell I5. Enter your name in **cell I22**. Save the workbook.
d. Click in **cell D5**, the cell that contains Adams's free throw percentage (FT%). Type = and click **cell C5**. Type / and click **cell B5**. Press **Enter**. You should see .8 in cell D5.
e. To calculate two-point field goal percentage (2-Pt FG%), click in **cell G5**, type =, click **cell F5**, type /, and click **cell E5**. Press **Enter** to see .36364 in cell G5.
f. To calculate points per game (PPG), type =. Click **cell I5**, type /, and click **cell C22**. Press **F4** to set cell C22 as absolute ($C$22) and press **Enter**. You should see 7 in cell J5.
g. To calculate rebounds per game (RPG), click **cell L5** and type =. Click **cell K5**, type /, click **cell C22**, and press **F4** to make C22 an absolute reference ($C$22). Press **Enter** and you will see 4.58333 in cell L5. Save the workbook.
h. Click in **cell D5**. Point to the fill handle in the lower-right corner of cell D5; the mouse pointer changes to a thin crosshair. Drag the fill handle to **cell D14**.
i. Release the mouse to complete the copy operation. The formula for FT% has been copied to the corresponding rows for the other players. Repeat the above two steps for columns G, I, J, and L to complete all players' statistics.
j. Use statistical functions to complete the summary area below the player statistics. Click in **cell B18**, type **=AVERAGE(**, and click and drag **cells B5:B14**. Type **)** and press **Enter**. Click in **cell B19**, type **=MAX(**, and click and drag cells **B5:B14**. Type **)** and press **Enter**. Click in **cell B20**, type **=MIN(**, and click and drag cells **B5:B14**. Type **)** and press **Enter**.
k. To copy the formulas across the worksheet, click and drag over **cells B18:B20**. Point to the fill handle in the lower-right corner of cell B20; the mouse pointer changes to a thin crosshair. Drag the fill handle to **cell L20**.
l. To calculate totals in row 17, click in **cell B17**, click **AutoSum** in the Function Library group on the Formulas tab, and then click and drag **cells B5:B14**. Press **Enter** to finish the function. To copy, click **cell B17** and click **Copy** in the Clipboard group on the Home tab. Click in **cell C17** and click **Paste** in the Clipboard group on the Home tab. Click and **Paste** in **cells E17, F17, H17, I17,** and **K17** to paste the formula in the appropriate cells. Enter **=TODAY()** in **cell I23** for today's date. Verify your calculations and format the worksheet, as shown in Figure 2.19.
m. Format columns D and G as **Percent Style** with **1** decimal place. Format columns J and L as **Number** with **1** decimal place. Replace **Your Name** with your name in **cell I22** and use a **date function** to retrieve today's date in **cell I5**. Verify your calculations and format the worksheet, as shown in Figure 2.19.
n. Click the **Page Layout tab**. Click **Orientation** and click **Landscape** in the Page Setup group. Click **Size**, select **More Paper Sizes**, and click **Fit to 1 page** in the *Scaling* section. Click the **Margins tab**, and then click the **Horizontally check box** in the *Center on page* section. Click the **Sheet tab**, click the **Gridlines check box**, and click the **Row and column headings check box** in the *Print* section. Click **OK**. Print the worksheet.
o. Save the workbook. Press **Ctrl + ~** to show the cell formulas rather than the displayed values. Adjust the column widths as necessary and print the worksheet a second time. Save and close the workbook.

...continued on Next Page

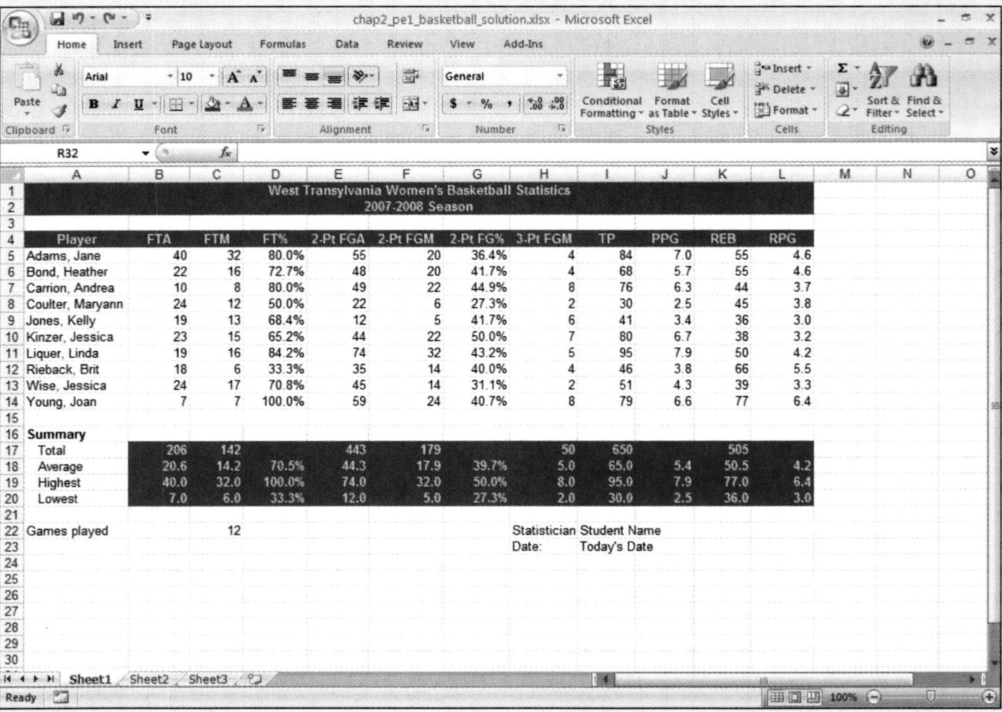

West Transylvania Women's Basketball Statistics
2007-2008 Season

Player	FTA	FTM	FT%	2-Pt FGA	2-Pt FGM	2-Pt FG%	3-Pt FGM	TP	PPG	REB	RPG
Adams, Jane	40	32	80.0%	55	20	36.4%	4	84	7.0	55	4.6
Bond, Heather	22	16	72.7%	48	20	41.7%	4	68	5.7	55	4.6
Carrion, Andrea	10	8	80.0%	49	22	44.9%	8	76	6.3	44	3.7
Coulter, Maryann	24	12	50.0%	22	6	27.3%	2	30	2.5	45	3.8
Jones, Kelly	19	13	68.4%	12	5	41.7%	6	41	3.4	36	3.0
Kinzer, Jessica	23	15	65.2%	44	22	50.0%	7	80	6.7	38	3.2
Liquer, Linda	19	16	84.2%	74	32	43.2%	5	95	7.9	50	4.2
Rieback, Brit	18	6	33.3%	35	14	40.0%	4	46	3.8	66	5.5
Wise, Jessica	24	17	70.8%	45	14	31.1%	2	51	4.3	39	3.3
Young, Joan	7	7	100.0%	59	24	40.7%	8	79	6.6	77	6.4
Summary											
Total	206	142		443	179		50	650		505	
Average	20.6	14.2	70.5%	44.3	17.9	39.7%	5.0	65.0	5.4	50.5	4.2
Highest	40.0	32.0	100.0%	74.0	32.0	50.0%	8.0	95.0	7.9	77.0	6.4
Lowest	7.0	6.0	33.3%	12.0	5.0	27.3%	2.0	30.0	2.5	36.0	3.0

Games played 12

Statistician Student Name
Date: Today's Date

Figure 2.19 Women's Basketball Statistics

2 Predicting Retirement Income

Retirement might be years away, but it is never too soon to start planning. The Future Value function enables you to calculate the amount of money you will have at retirement, based on a series of uniform contributions. Once you reach retirement, you do not withdraw all of the money immediately, but withdraw it periodically, perhaps as a monthly pension. Your assignment is to create a new worksheet similar to the one in Figure 2.20.

a. In a new blank workbook, enter the data for the accrual phase as shown in the following table (begin in cell A3):

Annual salary	$60,000
Employee contribution	6.20%
Employer contribution	6.20%
Total contribution	
Interest rate	6%
Years contributing	45

b. The first calculation will be the total contribution per year. Click in **cell B7**, type =, click **cell B4**, and type * and (. Click **cell B5**, type +, and click **cell B6**. Type). The total contribution in **cell B7** is a formula based on a percentage of your annual salary, plus a matching contribution from your employer. The 6.2% in the figure corresponds to the percentages that are currently in effect for Social Security.

c. The future value of your contributions (i.e., the amount of your "nest egg") depends on the assumptions on the left side of the worksheet. The 6% interest rate is conservative and can be achieved by investing in bonds, as opposed to equities. The

...continued on Next Page

45 years of contributions corresponds to an individual entering the work force at age 22 and retiring at 67 (the age at which today's worker will begin to collect Social Security). To calculate the future value of your nest egg, type **Future Value** in **cell A10**. Click in **cell B10**, where the future value will be calculated. Enter the FV function as follows:

- Click the **Formulas tab**, click **Financial** in the Function Library group, and click **FV**.
- Click in the **Rate** box, and then click **cell B8**.
- Click in the **Nper** box and click **cell B9**.
- Click in the **Pmt** box, type a minus sign (–), and click **cell B7**.
- Click **OK** to close the Function Arguments dialog box. The future value of your nest egg is $1,582,812.

d. The pension phase uses the PMT function to determine the payments you will receive in retirement. The formula in cell E4 is a reference to the amount accumulated in cell B10. The formula in cell E7 uses the PMT function to compute your monthly pension based on your nest egg, the interest rate, and the years in retirement. Note that accrual phase uses an *annual* contribution in its calculations, whereas the pension phase determines a *monthly* pension.

- Click **cell D3** and type **Pension Phase**. Enter the data shown below beginning in cell D4

The size of your "nest egg"	=B10
Interest rate	6%
Years in retirement	25

- Click in **cell D7** and type **Monthly Pension**. Click in **cell E7** to begin to enter the PMT function.
- Click **Financial** in the Function Library group on the Formulas tab, and then click **PMT**.
- Click in the **Rate** box, click **cell E5**, and type **/12**.
- Click in the **Nper** box, click **cell E6**, and type ***12**.
- Click in the **Pv** box, type a minus sign (–), and click **cell E4**.
- Click **OK** to close the Function Arguments dialog box. The monthly pension is $10,198.

e. Click in **cell D10** and enter your name. Enter **=TODAY()** in **cell D11** for today's date. Verify your calculations and format the worksheet, as shown in Figure 2.20.

f. Click the **Page Layout tab**, click **Orientation** in the Page Setup group, and click **Landscape**. Click **Size**, click **More Paper Sizes**, and click **Fit to 1 page** in the *Scaling* section. Click the **Margins tab** and click the **Horizontally check box** in the *Center on page* section. Click the **Sheet tab**, click the **Gridlines check box**, and click the **Row and column headings check box** in the *Print* section. Click **OK**. Print the worksheet.

g. Save the workbook as **chap2_pe2_retirement_solution.xlsx**. Press **Ctrl + ~** to show the cell formulas rather than the displayed values. Adjust the column widths as necessary and print the worksheet a second time.

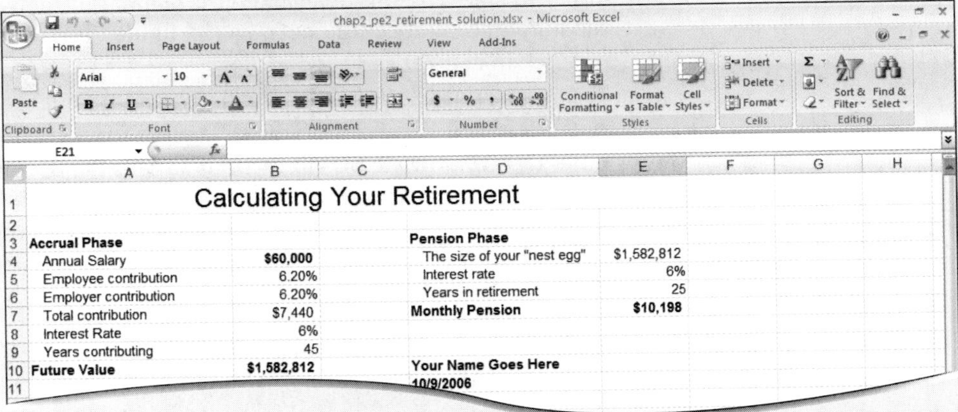

Figure 2.20 Predicting Retirement Income

...continued on Next Page

3 Election Trends

The presidential election has come and gone, but it is interesting to analyze the results of both the popular and electoral votes. You want to compare total votes and votes by state. You will find a partially completed version of the workbook shown in Figure 2.21 and enter functions to help identify election trends.

a. Open the *chap2_pe3_election* workbook and save it as **chap2_pe3_election_solution**.

b. Enter an appropriate IF function in cells D9 and F9 to determine the number of electoral votes for each candidate. The electoral votes are awarded on an all-or-nothing basis; that is, the candidate with the larger popular vote wins all of that state's electoral votes. The other candidate gets zero votes.
   - Click in **cell D9** to begin the first IF function. Click the **Formulas tab** and click **Insert Function** in the Function Library group.
   - Click **IF** to select the IF function.
   - Click in the **Logical test** box in the Function Arguments dialog box and type **C9>E9**.
   - Click in the **Value_if_true** box and click **cell B9**.
   - Click in the **Value_if_false** box and **type ""** (quotes are needed to make empty cells).
   - Click **OK** to finish the IF function and close the dialog box.
   - Click **cell F9** to begin the second IF function.
   - Click **Insert Function** in the Function Library on the Formulas tab and click **IF** to select the IF function.
   - Click in the **Logical test** box, type **E9>C9**.
   - Click in the **Value_if_true** box and click **cell B9**.
   - Click in the **Value_if_false** box and **type ""** (quotes are needed to make empty cells).
   - Click **OK** to finish the IF function and close the dialog box.

c. You will now copy the entries in cells D9 and F9 to the remaining rows in the respective columns. You also will format these columns to display red and blue values, for Mr. Bush and Mr. Kerry, respectively.
   - Click in **cell D9** and drag the fill handle through **D59** to copy the formula.
   - To format the columns select **cells C8:D59**. Click the **Home tab**, click the **Font Color arrow** in the Font group, and click **Red**.
   - Adapt the previous two bulleted list instructions for columns E and F, substituting the appropriate column letters and applying **Blue** font color.

d. Enter a formula into cell G9 to determine the difference in the popular vote between the two candidates. The result will appear as a positive number and you will use an absolute value function. Copy this formula to the remaining rows in the column.
   - Click in **cell G9** and type **=ABS(**.
   - Click in **cell C9**, type minus (–), click in **cell E9**, type **)**, and press **Enter**.
   - Click in **cell G9** and drag the fill handle through **G59** to copy the formula.

e. You will calculate the percentage differential in the popular vote. This differential is the difference in the number of votes, divided by the total number of votes.
   - Click in **cell H9** and type **=G9/(**.
   - Click in **cell C9**, type **+**, click **cell E9**, and type **)**.
   - Click in **cell H9** and drag the fill handle through **H59** to copy the formula.

f. Enter the appropriate SUM functions in cells B4, B5, C4, and C5 to determine the electoral and popular vote totals for each candidate.
   - To calculate the total in cell B4, click in **cell B4**, click **AutoSum** in the Function Library on the Formulas tab, click and drag **cells C9:C59**, and press **Enter**.
   - To calculate the total in cell B5, click in **cell B5**, click **AutoSum** on the Formulas tab, click and drag **cells D9:D59**, and press **Enter**.
   - Repeat the first two bulleted instructions in Step f for **cells C4** and **C5** using the appropriate cell ranges.

...continued on Next Page

g. Add your name as indicated. Click the **Page Layout tab**, click **Margins** in the Page Setup group, and click **Custom Margins**. Type **0.75** in the **Top** and **Bottom** boxes to ensure the worksheet fits on one page. Adjust the column widths as necessary. Create a custom footer that shows the **date** the worksheet was printed. Print the displayed values, and then print the worksheet a second time to show the cell formulas. Save and close the workbook.

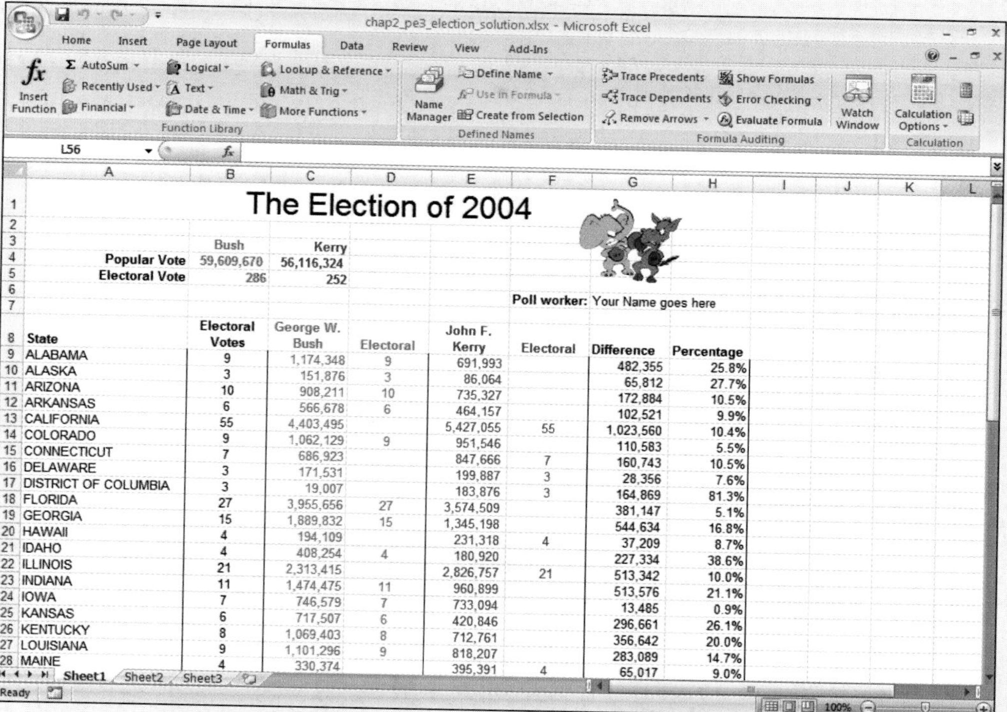

Figure 2.21 Election Trends

4 Expanded Payroll

You will revisit the payroll completed earlier in this chapter in the hands-on exercises but revise it to use a VLOOKUP function to determine the withholding tax amount based on a tax bracket, rather than a flat tax rate. Use Figure 2.22 for reference to complete the expanded payroll example. Be sure to use the appropriate combination of relative and absolute addresses so the formula in column G may be copied to the remaining rows in the worksheet.

a. Open the *chap2_pe4_exppayroll* workbook and save it as **chap2_pe4_exppayroll_solution**.

b. Click in **cell G4**, click the **Formulas tab**, click **Insert Function** in the Function Library group, and click **VLOOKUP** from the *Select a function* list. Click **OK** to close the Insert Function dialog box and display the **Function Arguments** dialog box.
   - Click in the **Lookup_value** box and click **cell F4**.
   - Click in the **Table_array** box, drag through **cells J20:K24**, and press **F4** to make the table references absolute.
   - Click in the **Col_index_num** box and type **2**.
   - Click **OK** to finish the VLOOKUP function and close the Function Argument box.
   - Click after the closing parenthesis for the VLOOKUP function in the formula bar, type ***F4**, and press **Enter**.

c. Click in **cell G4** and drag the fill handle through **G15** to copy the formula.

...continued on Next Page

d. To calculate the Social Security withholding tax, click **cell H4**, and type **=F4***

e. Click **cell D21**, press **F4**, and then press **Enter**.

f. Click **cell H4** and drag the fill handle through **H15** to copy the formula.

g. Calculate the net pay by clicking **cell I4** and type **=F4–(**.

h. Click **cell G4**, type **+**, click **cell H4**, type **)**, and press **Enter**.

i. Click in **cell I4** and drag the fill handle through **I15** to copy the formula.

j. Format columns G, H, and I as **currency** with two decimal places. Replace **Your Name** with your name and use a **date function** to retrieve today's date. Verify your calculations and format the worksheet, as shown in Figure 2.22.

k. Click the **Page Layout tab**, click **Orientation** in the Page Setup group, and click **Landscape**. Click **Size**, select **More Paper Sizes**, and click **Fit to 1 page** in the *Scaling* section. Click the **Margins tab** and click the **Horizontally check box** in the *Center on page* section. Click the **Sheet tab**, click the **Gridlines check box**, and click the **Row and column headings check box** in the *Print* section. Click **OK**. Print the worksheet.

l. Save the workbook. Press **Ctrl + ~** to show the cell formulas rather than the displayed values. Adjust the column widths as necessary and print the worksheet a second time.

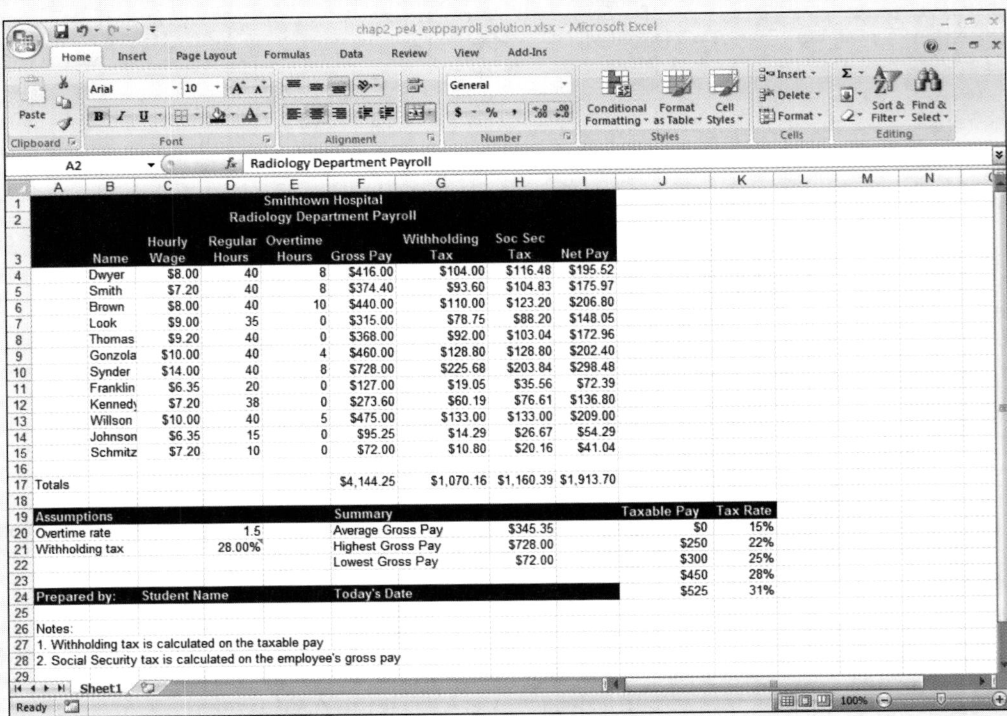

	A	B	C	D	E	F	G	H	I	J	K
1						Smithtown Hospital					
2						Radiology Department Payroll					
3		Name	Hourly Wage	Regular Hours	Overtime Hours	Gross Pay	Withholding Tax	Soc Sec Tax	Net Pay		
4		Dwyer	$8.00	40	8	$416.00	$104.00	$116.48	$195.52		
5		Smith	$7.20	40	8	$374.40	$93.60	$104.83	$175.97		
6		Brown	$8.00	40	10	$440.00	$110.00	$123.20	$206.80		
7		Look	$9.00	35	0	$315.00	$78.75	$88.20	$148.05		
8		Thomas	$9.20	40	0	$368.00	$92.00	$103.04	$172.96		
9		Gonzola	$10.00	40	4	$460.00	$128.80	$128.80	$202.40		
10		Synder	$14.00	40	8	$728.00	$225.68	$203.84	$298.48		
11		Franklin	$6.35	20	0	$127.00	$19.05	$35.56	$72.39		
12		Kennedy	$7.20	38	0	$273.60	$60.19	$76.61	$136.80		
13		Willson	$10.00	40	5	$475.00	$133.00	$133.00	$209.00		
14		Johnson	$6.35	15	0	$95.25	$14.29	$26.67	$54.29		
15		Schmitz	$7.20	10	0	$72.00	$10.80	$20.16	$41.04		
16											
17	Totals					$4,144.25	$1,070.16	$1,160.39	$1,913.70		
18											
19	Assumptions					Summary				Taxable Pay	Tax Rate
20	Overtime rate			1.5		Average Gross Pay		$345.35		$0	15%
21	Withholding tax			28.00%		Highest Gross Pay		$728.00		$250	22%
22						Lowest Gross Pay		$72.00		$300	25%
23										$450	28%
24	Prepared by:	Student Name				Today's Date				$525	31%
25											
26	Notes:										
27	1. Withholding tax is calculated on the taxable pay										
28	2. Social Security tax is calculated on the employee's gross pay										

Figure 2.22 Expanded Payroll

Mid-Level Exercises

1 Banquet Room Inventory

Managing or tracking inventory is an important way for businesses to control operating costs. During semester breaks you work as an assistant to the manager of a banquet room facility and are responsible for updating the inventory workbook. You will create formulas and functions to illustrate how Excel is used for inventory control. Refer to Figure 2.23 as you complete the worksheet.

a. Open the *chap2_mid1_banquet* workbook. Save it as **chap2_mid1_banquet_ solution** so that you can return to the original workbook if necessary.

b. The cost is calculated by multiplying number purchased by purchase price (e.g., 200 chairs * $186.00). The total cost of inventoried items is the sum of all values. Use the **SUM function** to compute the total cost.

c. Enter the **MAX** and **MIN functions** where appropriate to determine the most and least expensive items in inventory. Use the **COUNTA function** to determine the number of categories of items in inventory.

d. Replace Student Name with Your Name. Add an appropriate Clip art image somewhere in the worksheet using the same technique as in any Microsoft Office 2007 application. Use an appropriate date function to get today's date in your worksheet and format it as **mm/dd/yyyy**.

e. Format the worksheet in an attractive fashion, making sure to format dollar figures as currency with two decimal places. Wrap the column heading text to increase readability.

f. Print the completed worksheet twice, once with displayed values, and once to show the cell formulas. Use Page Setup for the cell formulas to switch to landscape orientation and force the output onto one page. Print gridlines and row and column headings. Save and close the workbook.

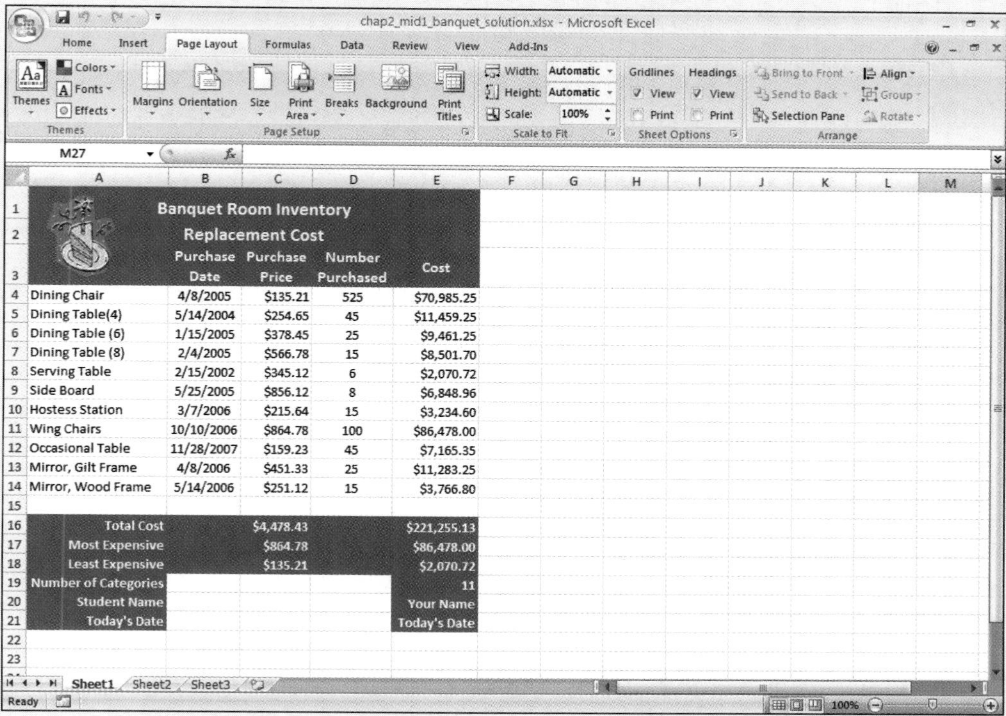

	A	B	C	D	E
1		Banquet Room Inventory			
2		Replacement Cost			
3		Purchase Date	Purchase Price	Number Purchased	Cost
4	Dining Chair	4/8/2005	$135.21	525	$70,985.25
5	Dining Table(4)	5/14/2004	$254.65	45	$11,459.25
6	Dining Table (6)	1/15/2005	$378.45	25	$9,461.25
7	Dining Table (8)	2/4/2005	$566.78	15	$8,501.70
8	Serving Table	2/15/2002	$345.12	6	$2,070.72
9	Side Board	5/25/2005	$856.12	8	$6,848.96
10	Hostess Station	3/7/2006	$215.64	15	$3,234.60
11	Wing Chairs	10/10/2006	$864.78	100	$86,478.00
12	Occasional Table	11/28/2007	$159.23	45	$7,165.35
13	Mirror, Gilt Frame	4/8/2006	$451.33	25	$11,283.25
14	Mirror, Wood Frame	5/14/2006	$251.12	15	$3,766.80
15					
16	Total Cost		$4,478.43		$221,255.13
17	Most Expensive		$864.78		$86,478.00
18	Least Expensive		$135.21		$2,070.72
19	Number of Categories				11
20	Student Name				Your Name
21	Today's Date				Today's Date

Figure 2.23 Banquet Room Inventory

...continued on Next Page

2 Real Estate Sales

The real estate market is booming, and electronic methods are necessary to keep up with the rapidly changing field. As an intern with the Duke Real Estate company, you have prepared the worksheet shown in Figure 2.24. It shows how the Duke Real Estate company uses Excel to track monthly sales and sales commissions. You will complete the Real Estate worksheet so that the displayed values match Figure 2.24.

The price per square foot is calculated by dividing the selling price by size. The percent of list price is calculated by dividing the selling price by the list price. Use an absolute reference to determine sales commission so the formula can be copied to other rows.

a. Open the *chap2_mid2_rls* workbook and save it as **chap2_mid2_rls_solution** so that you can return to the original workbook if necessary.

b. Enter the **SUM function** in **cell B14** to compute the total square feet. Copy the formula to the remaining cells in the row. Use the appropriate functions to calculate the values in the summary area.

c. Format the worksheet in an attractive manner, making sure to display all dollar amounts with the currency symbol and no decimal places. Display percentages with the percent symbol and one decimal place. Use a date function to display the current date in the cell below the heading.

d. Enter Your Name in **cell A17** and print the worksheet twice, once with displayed values, and once to show cell formulas. Use the Page Setup command to switch to landscape orientation and force the output onto one page. Print gridlines and row and column headings. Save and close the workbook.

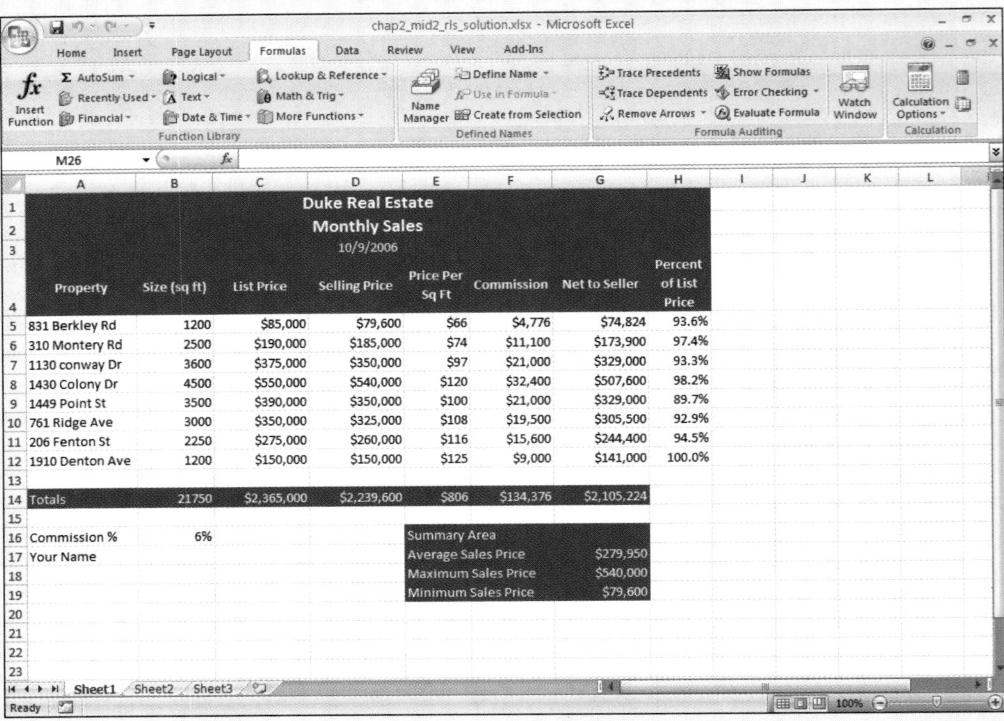

Duke Real Estate
Monthly Sales
10/9/2006

Property	Size (sq ft)	List Price	Selling Price	Price Per Sq Ft	Commission	Net to Seller	Percent of List Price
831 Berkley Rd	1200	$85,000	$79,600	$66	$4,776	$74,824	93.6%
310 Montery Rd	2500	$190,000	$185,000	$74	$11,100	$173,900	97.4%
1130 conway Dr	3600	$375,000	$350,000	$97	$21,000	$329,000	93.3%
1430 Colony Dr	4500	$550,000	$540,000	$120	$32,400	$507,600	98.2%
1449 Point St	3500	$390,000	$350,000	$100	$21,000	$329,000	89.7%
761 Ridge Ave	3000	$350,000	$325,000	$108	$19,500	$305,500	92.9%
206 Fenton St	2250	$275,000	$260,000	$116	$15,600	$244,400	94.5%
1910 Denton Ave	1200	$150,000	$150,000	$125	$9,000	$141,000	100.0%
Totals	21750	$2,365,000	$2,239,600	$806	$134,376	$2,105,224	

Commission %	6%
Your Name	

Summary Area	
Average Sales Price	$279,950
Maximum Sales Price	$540,000
Minimum Sales Price	$79,600

Figure 2.24 Real Estate Sales

...continued on Next Page

3 High School Art Collection

The Greater Latrobe School District is well known for its 70-year-old art collection. One of your duties as a summer intern is to help ready the collection for a traveling exhibition. You will use the IF function and the VLOOKUP function in Excel to determine costs associated with this art exhibition. You will complete the Greater Latrobe School District worksheet so that displayed values match Figure 2.25.

a. Open the *chap2_mid3_glsd* workbook and save it as **chap2_mid3_glsd_solution** so that you can return to the original workbook if necessary.

b. The cost of insurance is based on the value of the artwork. If the value is greater than $500, then the insurance is 25% of the value; otherwise, the insurance is 10% of the value of the painting. Enter an **IF function** in G6 to compute the cost of insurance and copy the formula to the remaining cells in the column.

c. Cubic footage is calculated by multiplying height by width and dividing by 144. Enter the formula in cell H6 and copy the formula to the remaining cells.

d. The cost of the box is determined by looking up the value in a lookup table. The shipping cost also is determined by looking up the value in a lookup table. Use the table at **cells H23:J28** with a **VLOOKUP function** to determine the cost of a box. Remember to use absolute references for the table and copy the formula to the remaining cells in the column.

e. Use the table at **cells H23:J28** with a **VLOOKUP function** to determine the shipping cost. Remember to use absolute references for the table and copy the formula to the remaining cells in the column. Save and close the workbook.

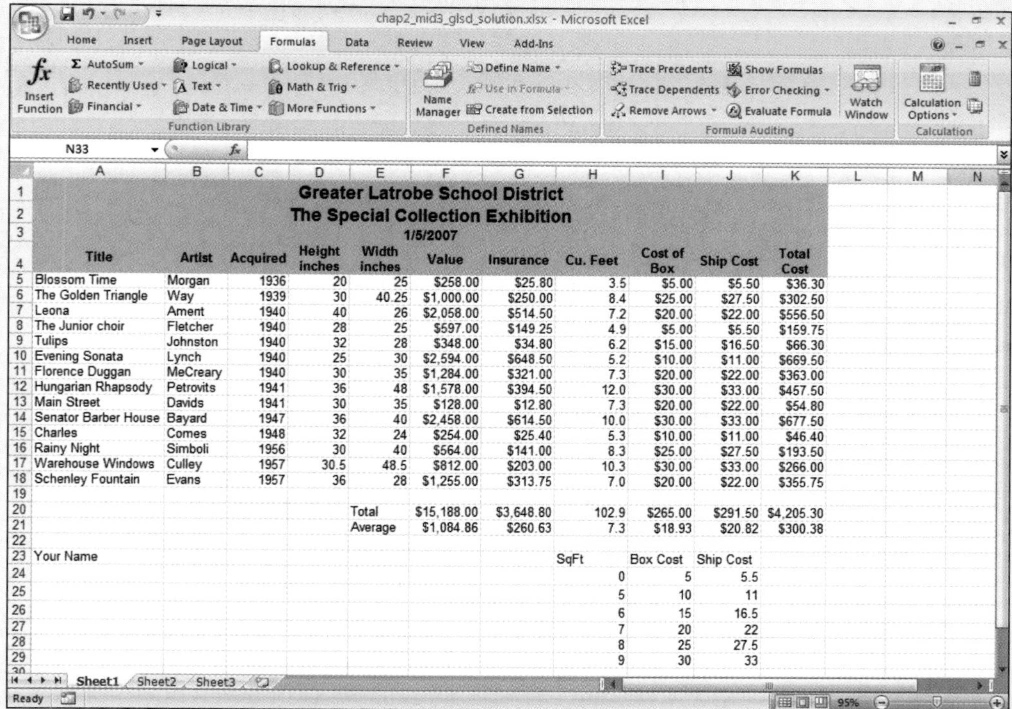

Greater Latrobe School District
The Special Collection Exhibition
1/5/2007

	A	B	C	D	E	F	G	H	I	J	K
4	Title	Artist	Acquired	Height inches	Width inches	Value	Insurance	Cu. Feet	Cost of Box	Ship Cost	Total Cost
5	Blossom Time	Morgan	1936	20	25	$258.00	$25.80	3.5	$5.00	$5.50	$36.30
6	The Golden Triangle	Way	1939	30	40.25	$1,000.00	$250.00	8.4	$25.00	$27.50	$302.50
7	Leona	Ament	1940	40	26	$2,058.00	$514.50	7.2	$20.00	$22.00	$556.50
8	The Junior choir	Fletcher	1940	28	25	$597.00	$149.25	4.9	$5.00	$5.50	$159.75
9	Tulips	Johnston	1940	32	28	$348.00	$34.80	6.2	$15.00	$16.50	$66.30
10	Evening Sonata	Lynch	1940	25	30	$2,594.00	$648.50	5.2	$10.00	$11.00	$669.50
11	Florence Duggan	MeCreary	1940	30	35	$1,284.00	$321.00	7.3	$20.00	$22.00	$363.00
12	Hungarian Rhapsody	Petrovits	1941	36	48	$1,578.00	$394.50	12.0	$30.00	$33.00	$457.50
13	Main Street	Davids	1941	30	35	$128.00	$12.80	7.3	$20.00	$22.00	$54.80
14	Senator Barber House	Bayard	1947	36	40	$2,458.00	$614.50	10.0	$30.00	$33.00	$677.50
15	Charles	Comes	1948	32	24	$254.00	$25.40	5.3	$10.00	$11.00	$46.40
16	Rainy Night	Simboli	1956	30	40	$564.00	$141.00	8.3	$25.00	$27.50	$193.50
17	Warehouse Windows	Culley	1957	30.5	48.5	$812.00	$203.00	10.3	$30.00	$33.00	$266.00
18	Schenley Fountain	Evans	1957	36	28	$1,255.00	$313.75	7.0	$20.00	$22.00	$355.75
19											
20					Total	$15,188.00	$3,648.80	102.9	$265.00	$291.50	$4,205.30
21					Average	$1,084.86	$260.63	7.3	$18.93	$20.82	$300.38
22											
23	Your Name							SqFt	Box Cost	Ship Cost	
24								0	5	5.5	
25								5	10	11	
26								6	15	16.5	
27								7	20	22	
28								8	25	27.5	
29								9	30	33	

Figure 2.25 Art Collection

...continued on Next Page

f. Use the **SUM function** in **cell F20** to compute the total value of the art collection. Copy the formula to the remaining cells in the row. Use the **AVERAGE function** in **cell F21** to compute the average value of a painting. Copy the formula to the remaining cells in the row.

g. Format the worksheet in an attractive manner but similar to Figure 2.25, making sure to display all dollar amounts with the currency symbol and two decimal places. Display height, width, and cubic feet with one decimal place. Use a date function to display the current date in **cell A3**.

h. Enter **Your Name** in **cell A23** and print the worksheet twice, once with displayed values, and once to show cell formulas. Use the Page Setup command to switch to landscape orientation and force the output onto one page. Print gridlines and row and column headings. Save and close the workbook.

4 Financial Functions

Your accounting professor has asked you to create a worksheet that compares interest rates and monthly payments over different time periods. Figure 2.26 is an example of how Excel is used to compare interest rates and monthly payments over different time periods. You will create this worksheet and use financial functions with relative, absolute, and mixed references.

a. Begin a new workbook by typing the following in the cells indicated:

Cell	Value
A1	Amount Borrowed
A2	Starting Interest
A5	Interest
B5	30 Years
C5	15 Years
D5	Difference
D1	100000
D2	.075
A13	Assumptions
A14	30 years
A15	15 years
B14	30
B15	15
A16	Financial Consultant
A17	Your Name

b. Save the workbook as **chap2_mid4_financial_solution.**

c. To copy the interest rate and then use it in a formula, enter the formula **=D2** in **cell A6** and enter the formula **=A6+.01** in **cell A7**. Copy the formula into **cells A8:A11.**

d. Calculate the payment for 30 years in **cell B6**. Make sure to use an absolute reference for **B14**. Copy the formula down the column, **B7:B11.**

e. Calculate the payment for 15 years in **cell C6**. Remember to use an absolute reference for **B15** and copy the formula down the column, **C7:C11**. If any cell displays a series of #####, use AutoFit to quickly widen the selection.

...continued on Next Page

f. Calculate the difference between 15 years and 30 years and copy the formula down the column, **D7:D11**.

g. Format the worksheet in an attractive manner but similar to Figure 2.26, making sure to display all dollar amounts with the currency symbol and two decimal places. Use a date function to display the current date in **cell A19.**

h. Print the worksheet twice, once with displayed values, and once to show cell formulas. Use the Page Setup command to switch to landscape orientation and force the output onto one page. Print gridlines and row and column headings. Save the changes.

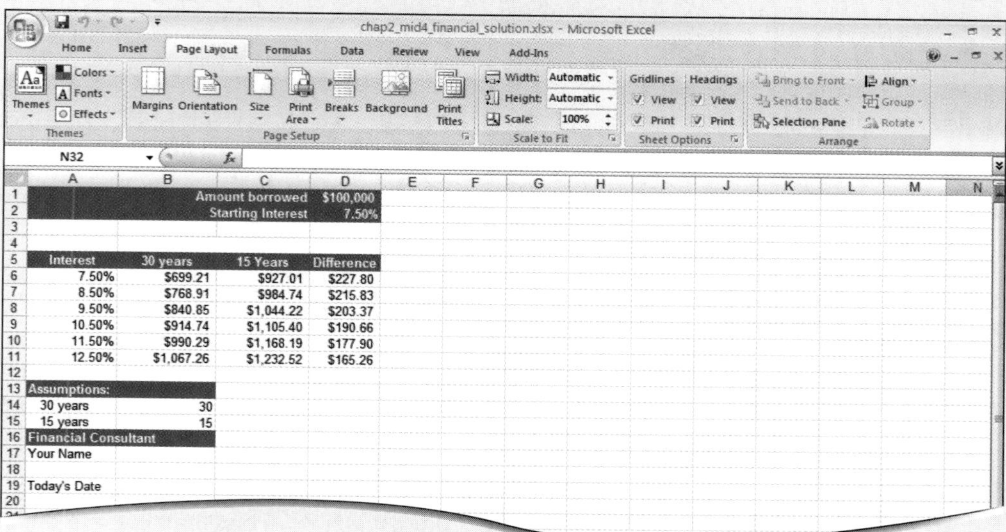

Figure 2.26 Financial Functions

Capstone Exercise

You are an intern at the First National Bank working in the loan department, and your boss has asked you to prepare the monthly "New Loan Report" for the Board of Directors. This analysis report will clearly list and summarize all new loans for residential housing in the past month. The summary area includes the loan statistics as labeled in the data file. The format of the report is appropriate for the Board of Directors for the First National Bank.

Open and Save Worksheet

You must open a worksheet that lists housing sales and finish it to complete the capstone exercise.

a. Open the file *chap2_cap_housing*.

b. Save it as **chap2_cap_housing_solution**.

c. Enter your name in **cell B28**.

Calculate Values

Functions are used to calculate the interest rate, down payment, monthly payment, and average selling price for each residential home in the worksheet. You need to create a formula to determine the down payment. Finish the calculations by using the appropriate functions to complete the Loan Statistics summary area of the worksheet.

a. Use a VLOOKUP function to determine the interest rates in column D.

b. Calculate the down payment by multiplying the results of a VLOOKUP function by the selling price. Enter the formula in column E.

c. Calculate the amount financed by subtracting the down payment from the selling price. Enter the formula in column F.

d. Use a PMT function to determine the monthly payment in column G.

e. Copy all formulas as appropriate.

f. Use an AVERAGE function to calculate the average selling price in **cell B13**.

g. Use appropriate functions to determine the statistics in **cells C22:C26**.

Format the Worksheet

Now that you have finished the calculations, you must format the worksheet in a professional manner and suitable for presentation to the Board of Directors of the bank.

a. Format all money figures as currency with two decimal places. Remember the Loan Statistics summary figures.

b. Format the interest rates in percent style with two decimal places. Format column D and the data table columns used in the VLOOKUP functions as percent with two decimals.

c. Insert an image appropriate for a bank and representative of the housing market.

d. Widen columns to display the headings but wrap the text in columns F and G. Center all column headings.

e. Merge and center the title of the report. Apply dark blue font color to the title and headings.

Print the Report

Before printing the report, you see it is missing the standard headers and should be printed in the landscape orientation to fit on one page.

a. Create a custom header with your name on the left and your instructor's name on the right.

b. Change the page orientation to landscape.

c. Print the worksheet with displayed values.

d. Print the worksheet again with cell formulas but make sure to fit the worksheet on one sheet.

e. Save your changes and close the workbook.

Mini Cases

Use the rubric following the case as a guide to evaluate your work, but keep in mind that your instructor may impose additional grading criteria or use a different standard to judge your work.

Corporate Salary Summary

GENERAL CASE

As a recent graduate and newly hired employee at the JAS Corporation, you are asked to complete the Annual Salary Summary Report. You are to open the *chap2_mc1_salary* workbook, save it as **chap2_mc1_salary_solution**, and complete the worksheet. You will AutoFill the months as headings, and calculate deductions, totals, and net salaries for each month. Format the worksheet for the corporate environment, making sure to use currency, no decimal places, and commas as well as percent symbols with two decimal places. Include your name in the worksheet and print displayed values and cell formulas.

Performance Elements	Exceeds Expectations	Meets Expectations	Below Expectations
Create formulas	All formulas work and most efficiently stated.	Formulas are correct.	No formulas, numbers entered.
Use functions	All functions entered correctly.	One function incorrectly used.	No functions used, numbers entered.
Attractive, appropriate format	Well formatted and easy to read.	Adequately formatted, difficult to read.	No formatting.
Printing	Printed correct range and widened columns for cell formulas.	Printed correct range but did not widen columns.	Printed once (missing formula copy or worksheet copy).

Investment Club

RESEARCH CASE

As treasurer of your investment club, you must update the monthly statement for the members. Open the *chap2_mc2_investment* workbook, save it as **chap2_mc2_investment_solution**, and use the Web to find the current price per share for each of the listed stocks. Complete the worksheet, formatting as appropriate to fit on one sheet. Enter your name as treasurer, the current date as a function formatted as mm/dd/yyyy, and print displayed values as well as cell formulas, making sure to fit on one page.

Performance Elements	Exceeds Expecations	Meets Expectations	Below Expectations
Research current price	All current stock prices found.	Missing two current prices.	No current prices.
Create formulas and functions	All formulas and functions correctly applied.	Two or more formulas and functions incorrectly applied.	No formulas or functions applied.
Format attractively for analysis use	Easy to read and analyze date on single sheet.	Difficult to read; lining up multiple sheets.	Lack of formatting hinders analysis.
Print values and cell formulas on one sheet	Printed correct range and widened columns for cell formulas.	Printed correct range but did not widen columns.	Printed once (missing formula copy or worksheet copy).

Peer Tutoring

DISASTER RECOVERY

As part of your service-learning project, you volunteered to tutor students in Excel. Open the spreadsheet *chap2_mc3_tutoring*, save it as **chap2_mc3_tutoring_solution**, and find five errors. Correct the errors and explain how the errors might have occurred and how they can be prevented. Include your explanation in the cells below the spreadsheet.

Performance Elements	Exceeds Expectations	Meets Expectations	Below Expectations
Identify five errors	Identified all five errors.	Identified four errors.	Identified three or fewer errors.
Correct five errors	Corrected all five errors.	Corrected four errors.	Corrected three or fewer errors.
Explain the error	Complete and correct explanation of each error.	Explanation is too brief to fully explain errors.	No explanations.
Prevention description	Prevention description correct and practical.	Prevention description but obtuse.	No prevention description.

chapter 3 | **Excel**

Charts

Delivering a Message

After you read this chapter, you will be able to:

1. Choose a chart type **(page 369)**.
2. Create a chart **(page 376)**.
3. Modify a chart **(page 388)**.
4. Enhance charts with graphic shapes **(page 391)**.
5. Embed charts **(page 397)**.
6. Print charts **(page 398)**.

Hands-On Exercises

Exercises	Skills Covered
1. **THE FIRST CHART (page 381)** **Open:** chap3_ho1_sales.xlsx **Save as:** chap3_ho1_sales_solution.xlsx	• Use AutoSum • Create the Chart • Complete the Chart • Move and Size the Chart • Change the Worksheet • Change the Chart Type • Create a Second Chart
2. **MULTIPLE DATA SERIES (page 392)** **Open:** chap3_ho1_sales_solution.xlsx (from Exercise 1) **Save as:** chap3_ho2_sales_solution.xlsx (additional modifications)	• Rename the Worksheet • Create Chart with Multiple Data Series • Copy the Chart • Change the Source Data • Change the Chart Type • Insert a Graphic Shape and Add a Text Box
3. **EMBEDDING, PRINTING, AND SAVING A CHART AS A WEB PAGE (page 400)** **Open:** chap3_ho2_sales_solution.xlsx (from Exercise 2), chap3_ho3_memo.docx **Save as:** chap3_ho3_sales.solution.xlsx (additional modifications), chap_ho3_memo_solution.docx	• Embed a Chart in Microsoft Word • Copy the Worksheet • Embed the Data • Copy the Chart • Embed the Chart • Modify the Worksheet • Update the Links • Print Worksheet and Chart • Save and View Chart as Web Page

CASE STUDY

The Changing Student Population

Congratulations! You have just been hired as a student intern in the Admissions Office. Helen Dwyer, the dean of admissions, has asked you to start tomorrow morning to help her prepare for an upcoming presentation with the Board of Trustees in which she will report on enrollment trends over the past four years. Daytime enrollments have been steady, whereas enrollments in evening and distance (online) learning are increasing significantly. Dean Dwyer has asked for a chart(s) to summarize the data. She also would like your thoughts on what impact (if any) the Internet and the trend toward lifelong learning have had on the college population. The dean has asked you to present the information in the form of a memo addressed to the Board of Trustees with the data and graph embedded onto that page.

Case Study

Dean Dwyer will be presenting her findings on "The Changing Student Population" to the Board of Trustees in two weeks. She will speak briefly and then open the floor for questions and discussion among the group. She has invited you to the meeting to answer specific questions pertaining to these trends from a student's perspective. This is an outstanding opportunity for you to participate with a key group of individuals who support the university. Be prepared to present yourself appropriately!

Your Assignment

- Read the chapter carefully and pay close attention to sections that demonstrate chart creation, chart formatting, and chart printing.
- Open the workbook *chap3_case_enrollment*, which has the enrollment statistics partially completed. You will save your workbook as **chap3_case_enrollment_solution**.
- When you review the workbook, think about the mathematical operations, formulas, and functions you would use to complete the worksheet. You will create formulas and functions to calculate annual totals and type of course totals. You also will format cells appropriately: use numbers with commas, merge and center the title, use an attractive fill color, and increase font sizes for improved readability.
- As you read the chapter, pay particular attention to the types of charts that are discussed. Some are more appropriate for presenting enrollment data than others. You will use your understanding of chart methods to determine the most appropriate charts used with the enrollment data. You will create charts to emphasize enrollment data on separate sheets. Remember to format the charts for a professional presentation that includes titles, legends, and data labels.
- As part of your presentation, you also must consider the preparation of a memo describing the enrollment information presented both in the worksheet and in the chart. The worksheet and the charts will be embedded in the final memo. The memo in Microsoft Word will summarize your enrollment data findings and include the embedded worksheet and charts.
- Remember that you will present the information to the university Board of Trustees, and the trustees will expect a professional, polished report. Save the memo as **chap3_case_enrollment_solution** after creating custom footers that include the page number, your name, and your instructor's name. Print the memo, the worksheet, and the charts.

A Picture Is the Message

A ***chart*** is a graphic representation of data.

A picture really is worth a thousand words. Excel makes it easy to create a ***chart***, which is a graphic or visual representation of data. Once data is displayed in a chart, the options to enhance the information for more visual appeal and ease of analysis are almost unlimited. Because large amounts of data are available, using graphical analysis is valuable to discover what messages are hidden in the data.

In this chapter, you learn the importance of determining the message to be conveyed by a chart. You select the type of chart that best presents your message. You create and modify a chart, enhance a chart with a shape, plot multiple sets of data, embed a chart in a worksheet, and create a chart in a separate chart sheet. You enhance a chart by creating lines, objects, and 3-D shapes. The second half of the chapter explains how to create a compound document, in which a chart and its associated worksheet are dynamically linked to a memo created in Word.

Choosing a Chart Type

Managers know that a graphic representation of data is an attractive, clear way to convey information. Business graphics are one of the most exciting Windows applications, where charts (graphs) are created in a straightforward manner from a worksheet with just a few keystrokes or mouse clicks.

In this section, you learn chart terminology and how to choose a chart type based on your needs. For example, you learn when to use a column chart and when to use a pie chart. You select the range of cells containing the numerical values and labels from which to create the chart, choose the chart type, insert the chart, and designate the chart's location.

A ***data point*** is a numeric value that describes a single item on a chart.

A ***data series*** is a group of related data points.

A ***category label*** describes a group of data points in a chart.

A chart is based on numeric values in the cells called ***data points***. For example, a data point might be the database sales for Milwaukee. A group of related data points that appear in row(s) or column(s) in the worksheet create a ***data series***. For example, a data series might be a collection of database data points for four different cities. In every data series, exactly one data point is connected to a numerical value contained in a cell. Textual information, such as column and row headings (cities, months, years, product names, etc.), are used for descriptive entries called ***category labels***.

The worksheet in Figure 3.1 is used throughout the chapter as the basis for the charts you create. As you can see from the worksheet, the company sells different types of software programs, and it has sales in four cities. You believe that the sales numbers are more easily grasped when they are presented graphically instead of only relying on the numbers. You need to develop a series of charts to convey the sales numbers.

1	Transylvania Software Sales					
2						
3		Milwaukee	Buffalo	Harrisburg	Pittsburgh	Total
4	Word Processing	$50,000	$67,500	$200,000	$141,000	$458,500
5	Spreadsheets	$44,000	$18,000	$11,500	$105,000	$178,500
6	Database	$12,000	$7,500	$6,000	$30,000	$55,500
7	Total	$106,000	$93,000	$217,500	$276,000	

Figure 3.1 Worksheet for Charts

The sales data in the worksheet can be presented several ways—for example, by city, by product, or by a combination of the two. Determine which type of chart is best suited to answer the following questions:

- What percentage of the total revenue comes from each city? What percentage comes from each product?
- How much revenue is produced by each city? What is the revenue for each product?

- What is the rank of each city with respect to sales?
- How much revenue does each product produce in each city?

. . . you cannot create an effective chart unless you are sure of what that message is.

In every instance, realize that a chart exists only to deliver a message and that *you cannot create an effective chart unless you are sure of what that message is.* The next several pages discuss various types of charts, each of which is best suited to a particular type of message. After you understand how charts are used conceptually, you will create various charts in Excel.

Create Column Charts

A ***column chart*** displays data comparisons vertically in columns.

The ***X or horizontal axis*** depicts categorical labels.

The ***Y or vertical axis*** depicts numerical values.

The ***plot area*** contains graphical representation of values in data series.

The ***chart area*** contains the entire chart and all of its elements.

A ***column chart*** displays data vertically in a column formation and is used to compare values across different categories. Figure 3.2 shows total revenue by geographic area based on the worksheet data from Figure 3.1. The category labels represented by cities stored in cells B3:E3 are shown along the ***X or horizontal axis***, whereas the data points representing total monthly sales stored in cells B7:E7 are shown along the ***Y or vertical axis***. The height of each column represents the value of the individual data points. The ***plot area*** of a chart is the area containing the graphical representation of the values in a data series. The ***chart area*** contains the entire chart and all of its elements.

	A	B	C	D	E	F
3		Milwaukee	Buffalo	Harrisburg	Pittsburgh	Total
4	Word Processing	$50,000	$67,500	$200,000	$141,000	$458,500
5	Spreadsheets	$44,000	$18,000	$11,500	$105,000	$178,500
6	Database	$12,000	$7,500	$6,000	$30,000	$55,500
7	Total	$106,000	$93,000	$217,500	$276,000	

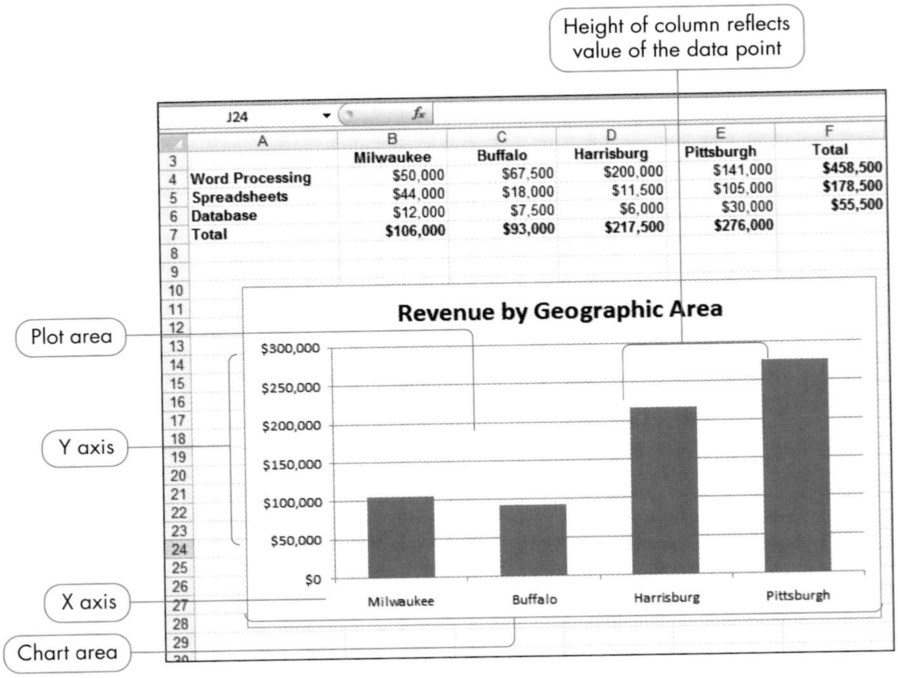

Figure 3.2 Column Chart Depicting Revenue by Geographic Area

Different types of column charts can be created to add interest or clarify the data representation. Figure 3.3 is an example of a three-dimensional (3-D) column chart. The 3-D charts present a more dynamic representation of data, as this chart demonstrates. However, the 3-D column chart is sometimes misleading. Professors often discourage students from using 3-D charts because the charts do not clearly communicate the data—the third dimension distorts data. In 3-D column charts, some columns appear taller than they really are because they are either somewhat behind or at an angle to other columns. See Figure 3.3 for an example of this.

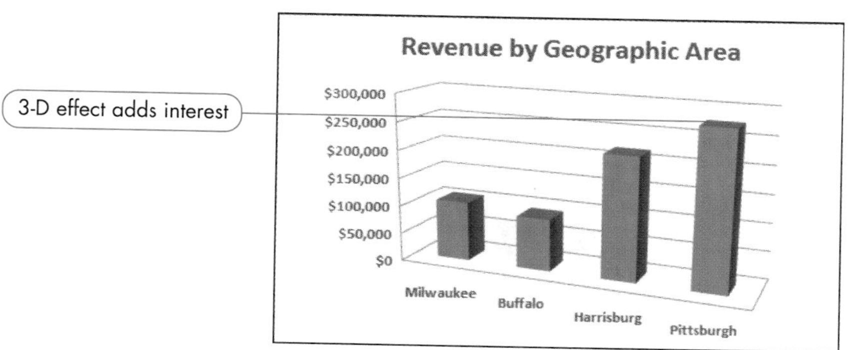

Figure 3.3 Three-Dimensional Column Chart

A ***multiple data series*** compares two or more sets of data in one chart.

Another example of the use of column charts is to compare ***multiple data series***—two or more data series—on the same chart. The concept of charting multiple data series will be discussed at some length later in the chapter, but this concept involves the use of clustered column charts.

The choice of clustered versus stacked column charts depends on the intended message. If you want the audience to see the individual sales in each city or product category, the clustered column chart in Figure 3.4 is more appropriate. If, on the other hand, you want to emphasize the total sales for each city or product category, the stacked columns are preferable. The advantage of the stacked column is that the totals are shown clearly and can be compared easily. The disadvantage is that the segments within each column do not start at the same point, making it difficult to determine the actual sales for the individual categories. ***Clustered column charts*** group similar data together in columns making visual comparison of the data easier to determine. ***Stacked column charts*** place similar data in one column with each data series a different color. The effect emphasizes the total of the data series.

A ***clustered column chart*** groups similar data in columns, making visual comparison easier to determine.

A ***stacked column chart*** places (stacks) data in one column with each data series a different color for each category.

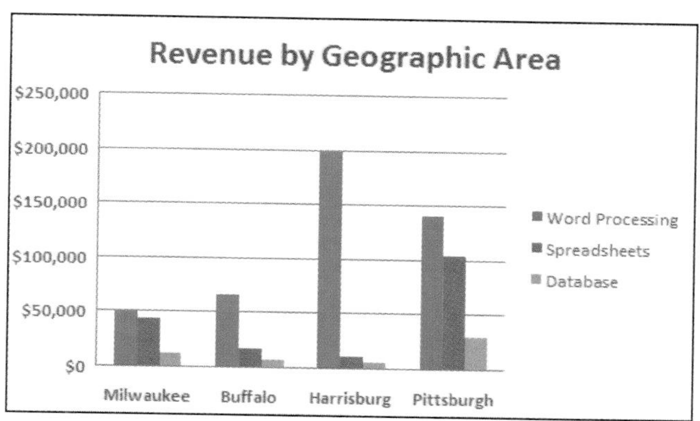

Figure 3.4 Clustered Column Chart

The scale on the Y axis is different for charts with clustered columns versus charts with stacked columns. The clustered columns in Figure 3.4 show the sales of each product category and so the Y axis goes to $250,000. The stacked columns in Figure 3.5 reflect the total sales for all products in each city, and thus the scale goes to $300,000. For a stacked column chart to make sense, its numbers must be additive. You would not convert a column chart that plots units and dollar sales side by side to a stacked column chart, because units and dollars are not additive, that is, you cannot add products and revenue. The chart in Figure 3.5 also displays a legend on the right side of the chart. A ***legend*** identifies the format or color of the data used for each series in a chart.

A ***legend*** identifies the format or color of each data series.

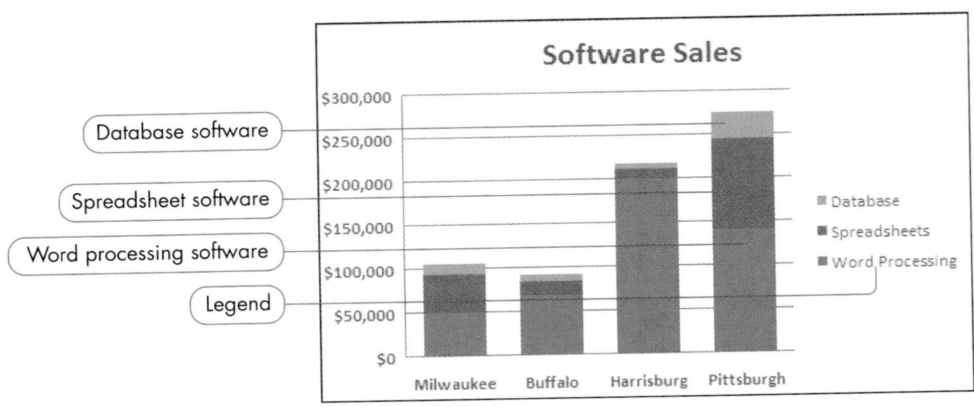

Figure 3.5 Stacked Columns

Column charts are most effective when they are limited to small numbers of categories—generally seven or fewer. If more categories exist, they end up being plotted so close together that reading and labeling become difficult or impossible.

Create a Bar Chart

A ***bar chart*** is a column chart that has been given a horizontal orientation.

A ***bar chart*** is basically a column chart that has a horizontal orientation, as shown in Figure 3.6. Many people prefer this representation because it emphasizes the difference between items. Further, long descriptive labels are easier to read in a bar chart than in a column chart. Sorting the data points either from lowest to highest or highest to lowest makes a bar chart even more effective. The most basic bar chart is a clustered bar chart.

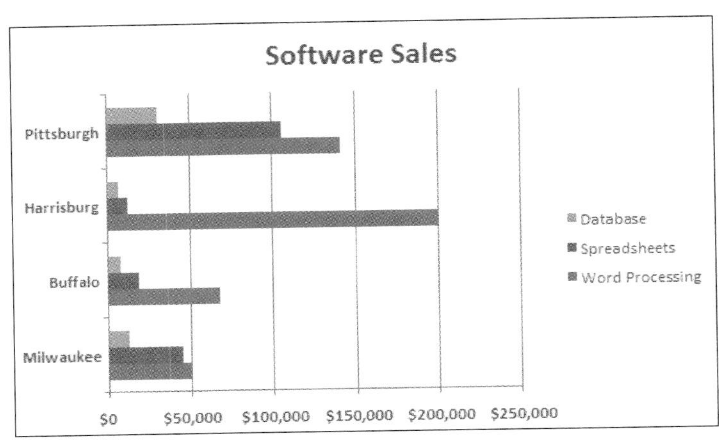

Figure 3.6 Clustered Bar Chart

TIP Keep It Simple

This rule applies to both your message and the means of conveying that message. Excel makes it easy to change fonts, styles, the shape of columns, type sizes, and colors, but such changes often detract from rather than enhance a chart. More is not necessarily better, and you do not have to use a feature just because it is there. A chart must ultimately succeed based on content alone.

Create a Pie Chart

A ***pie chart*** displays proportional relationships.

A ***pie chart*** is the most effective way to display proportional relationships. It is the type of chart to select whenever words like *percentage* or *market share* appear in the message to be delivered. The pie, or complete circle, denotes the total amount. Each slice of the pie corresponds to its respective percentage of the total.

The pie chart in Figure 3.7 divides the pie representing total sales into four slices, one for each city. The size of each slice is proportional to the percentage of total sales in that city. The chart depicts a single data series, which appears in cells B7:E7 on the associated worksheet. The data series has four data points corresponding to the total sales in each city. The data labels are placed in the wedges if they fit. If they do not fit, they are placed outside the wedge with a line pointing to the appropriate wedge.

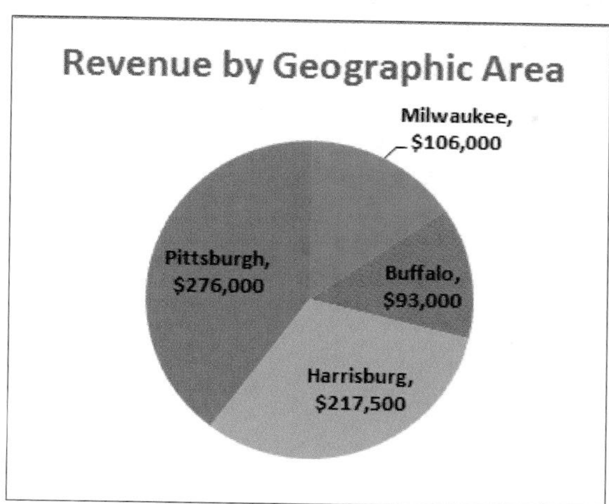

Figure 3.7 Pie Chart Showing Values

To create the pie chart, Excel computes the total sales ($692,000 in our example), calculates the percentage contributed by each city, and draws each slice of the pie in proportion to its computed percentage. Pittsburgh's sales of $276,000 account for 40% of the total, so this slice of the pie is allotted 40% of the area of the circle.

An ***exploded pie chart*** separates one or more slices of the pie chart for emphasis.

An ***exploded pie chart,*** shown in Figure 3.8, separates one or more slices of the pie for emphasis. Another way to achieve emphasis in a chart is to choose a title that reflects the message you are trying to deliver. The title in Figure 3.7, *Revenue by Geographic Area*, is neutral and leaves the reader to develop his or her own conclusion about the relative contribution of each area. In contrast, the title in Figure 3.8, *Buffalo Accounts for Only 13% of the Revenue*, is more suggestive and emphasizes the problems in this office. The title could be changed to *Pittsburgh Exceeds 40% of Total Revenue* if the intent were to emphasize the contribution of Pittsburgh.

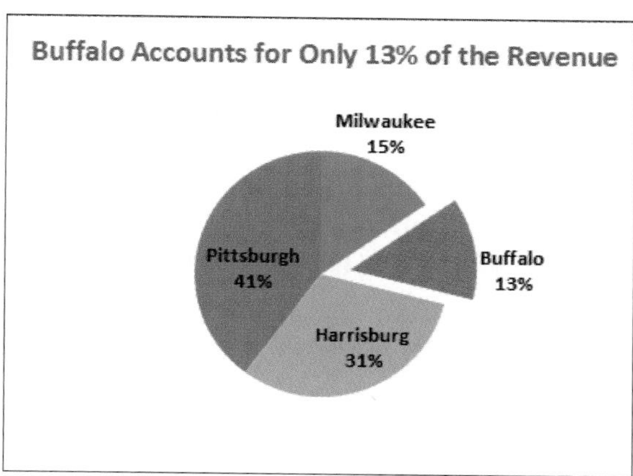

Figure 3.8 Pie Chart Showing Percentages

A ***three-dimensional pie chart*** is a pie chart that contains a three-dimensional view.

Three-dimensional pie charts may be created in exploded or unexploded format. See Figure 3.9 for an example of an unexploded pie chart. The 3-D chart is misleading because it appears as though the Harrisburg slice is larger than the Pittsburgh slice. This difference is why 3-D charts are seldom used. A pie chart is easiest to read when the number of slices is small (for example, not more than six or seven), and when small categories (percentages less than five) are grouped into a single category called *Other*.

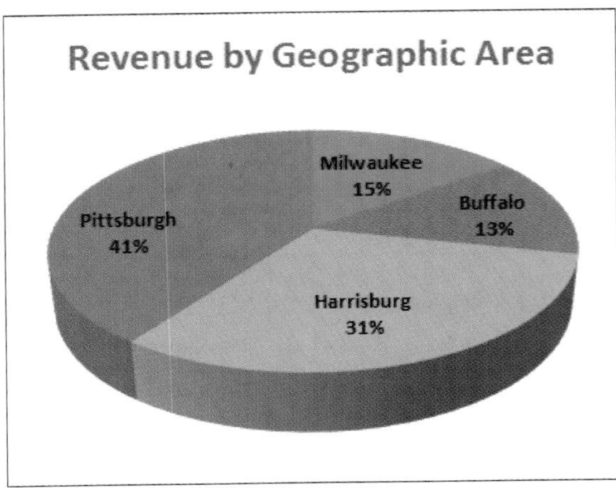

Figure 3.9 Three-Dimensional Pie Chart

Create a Line Chart

A *line chart* uses a line to connect data points in order to show trends over a long period of time.

A ***line chart*** shows trends over a period of time. A line connects data points. A line chart is used frequently to show stock market or economic trends. The X axis represents time, such as ten-year increments, whereas the vertical axis represents the value of a stock or quantity. The line chart enables a user to easily spot trends in the data. Figure 3.10 shows a line chart with yearly increments for four years.

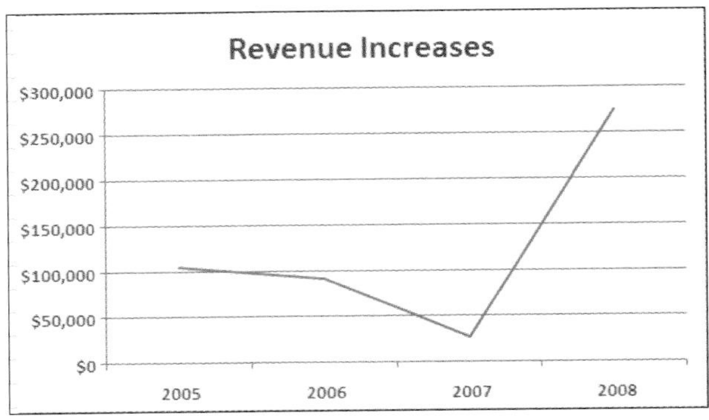

Figure 3.10 Line Chart

Create Other Chart Types

A *doughnut chart* displays values as percentages of the whole.

The ***doughnut chart*** is similar to a pie chart in that it shows relationship of parts to a whole, but the doughnut chart can display more than one series of data, and it has a hole in the middle (see Figure 3.11). Chart designers sometimes use the doughnut hole for titles. Each ring represents a data series. Note, however, the display of the data series in a doughnut chart can be confusing.

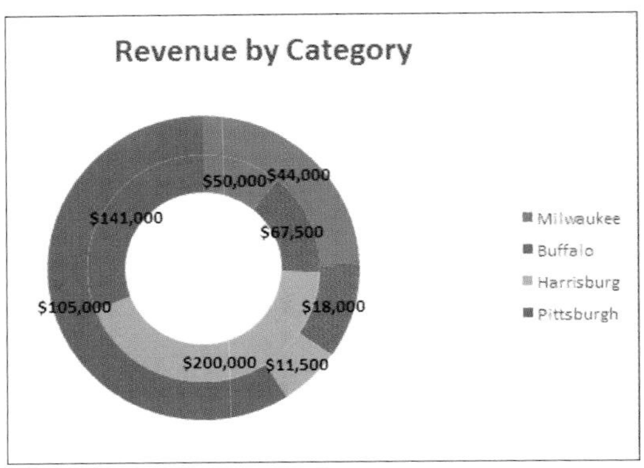

Figure 3.11 Doughnut Chart

A *scatter (XY) chart* shows a relationship between two variables.

A *scatter (XY) chart* shows a relationship between two variables. Scatter charts are used to represent the data from scientific or educational experiments that demonstrate relationships. A scatter chart is essentially the plotted dots without any connecting line. A scatter chart is used to determine if a relationship exists between two different sets of numerical data. If you plot people's wages and educational levels, you can see if a relationship between wages and education levels exists. Figure 3.12 shows a comparison of temperature over time. As the month of April passes, the temperatures rise. However, higher- and lower-than-normal temperatures affect the trend.

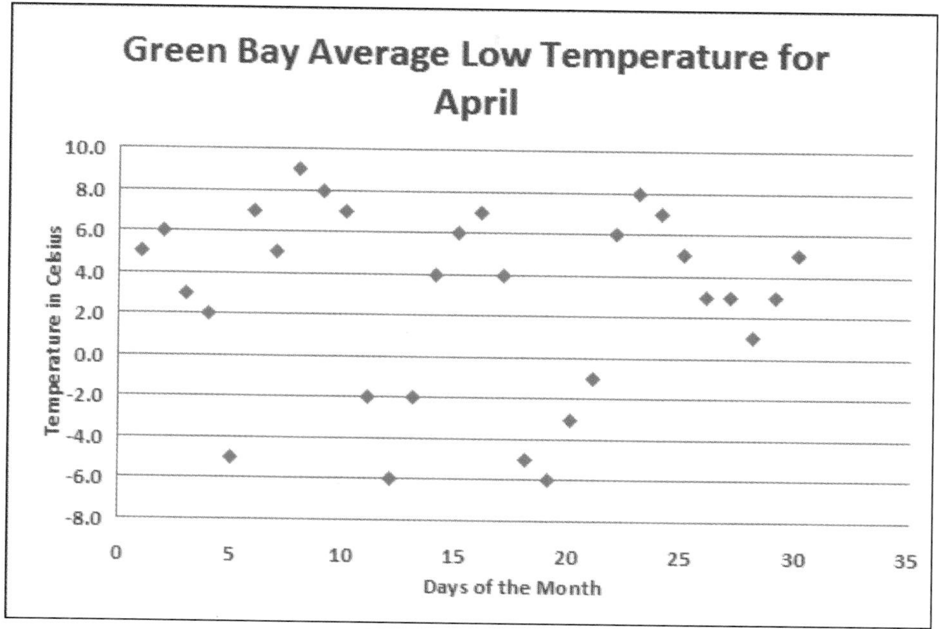

Figure 3.12 Scatter Chart

A *stock chart* shows the high, low, and close prices for individual stocks over a period of time.

Stock charts have only one major purpose: to show the high, low, and close prices for individual stocks over a period of time. While stock charts may have some other uses, such as showing a range of temperatures over a period of time, they usually are used to show stock prices. Figure 3.13 shows a stock chart that displays opening stock price, high stock price, low stock price, and closing stock price over time.

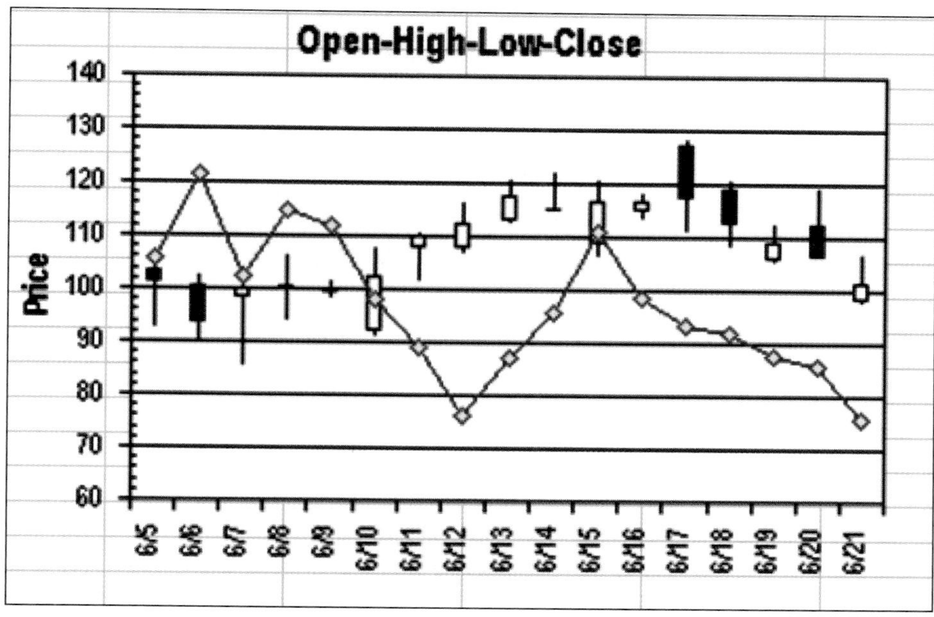

Figure 3.13 Stock Chart

Creating a Chart

Creating a chart in Excel is quick. Excel provides a variety of chart types that you can use when you create a chart. The main types of charts are described above. The six main steps to create a chart are the following:

1. Specify the data series.
2. Select the range of cells to chart.
3. Select the chart type.
4. Insert the chart and designate the chart location.
5. Choose chart options.
6. Change the chart location and size.

Specify the Data Series

For most charts, such as column and bar charts, you can plot the data in a chart that you have arranged in rows or columns on a worksheet. Some chart types, however, such as a pie chart, require a specific data arrangement. On the worksheet, arrange the data that you want to plot in a chart for the type of chart you will select.

The charts presented so far in the chapter displayed only a single data series, such as the total sales by location or the total sales by product category. Although such charts are useful, it is often more informative to view multiple data series, which are ranges of data values plotted as a unit in the same chart. Figure 3.14 displays the worksheet we have been using throughout the chapter. Figure 3.4 displays a clustered column chart that plots multiple data series that exist as rows (cells B4:E4, B5:E5, and B6:E6) within the worksheet. Figure 3.14 displays a chart based on the same data when the series are in columns (cells B4:B6, C4:C6, D4:D6, and E4:E6).

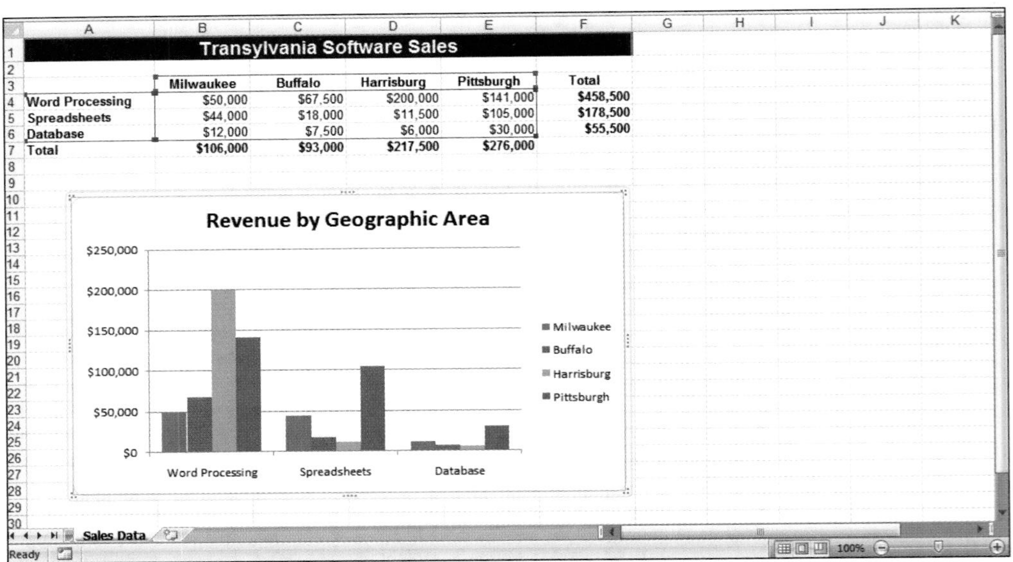

Transylvania Software Sales

	Milwaukee	Buffalo	Harrisburg	Pittsburgh	Total
Word Processing	$50,000	$67,500	$200,000	$141,000	$458,500
Spreadsheets	$44,000	$18,000	$11,500	$105,000	$178,500
Database	$12,000	$7,500	$6,000	$30,000	$55,500
Total	$106,000	$93,000	$217,500	$276,000	

Figure 3.14 Clustered Column with Multiple Data Series as Columns

Both charts plot a total of 12 data points (three product categories for each of four locations), but they group the data differently. Figure 3.4 displays the data by city in which the sales of three product categories are shown for each of four cities. Figure 3.14 is the reverse and groups the data by product category. This time, the sales in the four cities are shown for each of three product categories. The choice between the two charts depends on your message and whether you want to emphasize revenue by city or by product category. You should create the chart according to your intended purpose.

Figure 3.15 shows two charts. The one on the left plots data series in the cells B4:E4, B5:E5, and B6:E6, whereas the chart on the right plots the same data series but

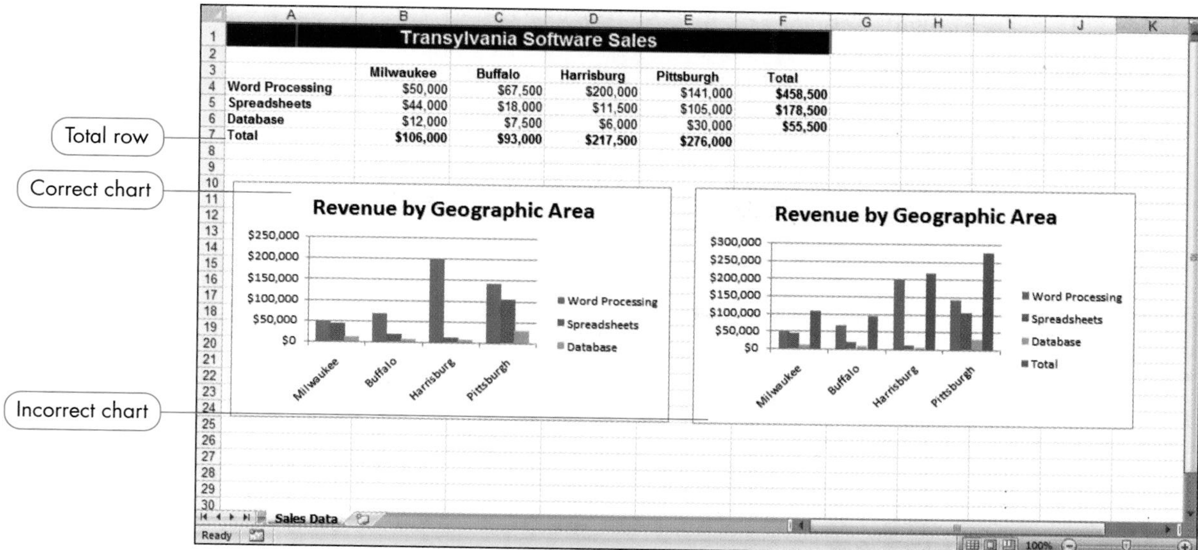

Figure 3.15

includes B7:E7, which is the total for all products. Including the total row figures (or column total figures) dramatically skews the chart, presents a misleading picture, and indicates you have selected an incorrect range for your chart. Do NOT include totals and individual data points on the same chart.

Select the Range to Chart

Too often Excel users do not put any thought into the data they select for a chart. Selecting the correct data goes hand-in-hand with having a plan for what a chart should display. For example, a user would not want to show totals in column totals that represent only several months. Even though it is a simple process to deselect cells once they have been selected, users should have a plan before selecting cells for a chart.

Table 3.1 describes different techniques for selecting cells.

Select the Chart Type

After you select the range of cells that you want to chart, your next step is to select the type of chart you want to create. Each type of chart is designed to visually illustrate a particular type of data. Table 3.2 lists the different types of charts and their purposes. Use this table as a guide for selecting the type of chart you want to use for the worksheet data.

In the Charts group on the Insert tab, do one of the following:

1. Click the chart type, and then click a chart subtype that you want to use.
2. To see all available chart types, click a chart type, and then click All Chart Types to display the Create Chart dialog box.
3. Click the arrows to scroll through all available chart types and chart subtypes, and then click the one that you want to use.

Insert the Chart and Designate the Chart Location

Excel places the chart as an embedded object on the current worksheet. You can leave the chart on the same worksheet as the worksheet data used to create the chart, or you can place the chart in a separate chart sheet. If you leave the chart in the same worksheet, you can print the worksheet and chart on the same page. If you want to print a full-sized chart, you can move the chart to its own chart sheet.

Table 3.1 Cell Selection Techniques

To Select	Do This
A single cell	Click the cell or press the arrow keys to move to the cell.
A range of cells	Click the first cell in the range, and then drag to the last cell, or hold down Shift while you press the arrow keys to extend the selection. You also can select the first cell in the range, and then press F8 to extend the selection by using the arrow keys. To stop extending the selection, press F8 again.
A large range of cells	Click the first cell in the range, and then hold down Shift while you click the last cell in the range. You can scroll to make the last cell visible.
All cells on a worksheet	Click the Select All button. To select the entire worksheet, you also can press Ctrl+A.
Nonadjacent cells or cell ranges	Select the first cell or range of cells, and then hold down Ctrl while you select the other cells or ranges. You also can select the first cell or range of cells, and then press Shift+F8 to add another nonadjacent cell or range to the selection. To stop adding cells or ranges to the selection, press Shift+F8 again.
An entire row or column	Click the row or column heading. You also can select cells in a row or column by selecting the first cell and then pressing Ctrl+Shift+Arrow key (Right Arrow or Left Arrow for rows, Up Arrow or Down Arrow for columns).
Adjacent rows or columns	Drag across the row or column headings. Or select the first row or column, then hold down Shift while you select the last row or column.
Noncontiguous rows or columns	Click the column or row heading of the first row or column in your selection, then hold down Ctrl while you click the column or row headings of other rows or columns that you want to add to the selection.

Table 3.2 Chart Types and Purposes

Chart Type	Purpose
Column	Compares categories, shows changes over time.
Bar	Shows comparison between independent variables. Not used for time or dates.
Pie	Shows percentages of a whole. Exploded pie emphasizes a popular category.
Line	Shows change in a series over categories or time.
Doughnut	Compares how two or more series contribute to the whole.
Scatter	Shows correlation between two sets of values.
Stock	Shows high-low stock prices.

To change the location of a chart:

1. Click the embedded chart or the chart sheet to select it and to display the chart tools.
2. Click Move Chart in the Location group on the Design tab.
3. In the *Choose where you want the chart to be placed* section, do one of the following:
   - Click *New sheet* to display the chart in its own chart sheet.
   - Click *Object in*, click the drop-down arrow, and select a worksheet to move the chart to another worksheet.

Choose Chart Options

When you create a chart, the Chart Tools contextual tab is available. The Design, Layout, and Format tabs are displayed in Chart Tools. You can use the commands on these tabs to modify the chart. For example, use the Design tab to display the data series by row or by column, make changes to the source data of the chart, change the location of the chart, change the chart type, save a chart as a template, or select predefined layout and formatting options. Use the Layout tab to change the display of chart elements such as chart titles and data labels, use drawing tools, or add text boxes and pictures to the chart. Use the Format tab to add fill colors, change line styles, or apply special effects. Review the Reference Page for examples of the contextual chart tools tab with the Design, Layout, and Design tabs depicted.

Chart Tools | Reference

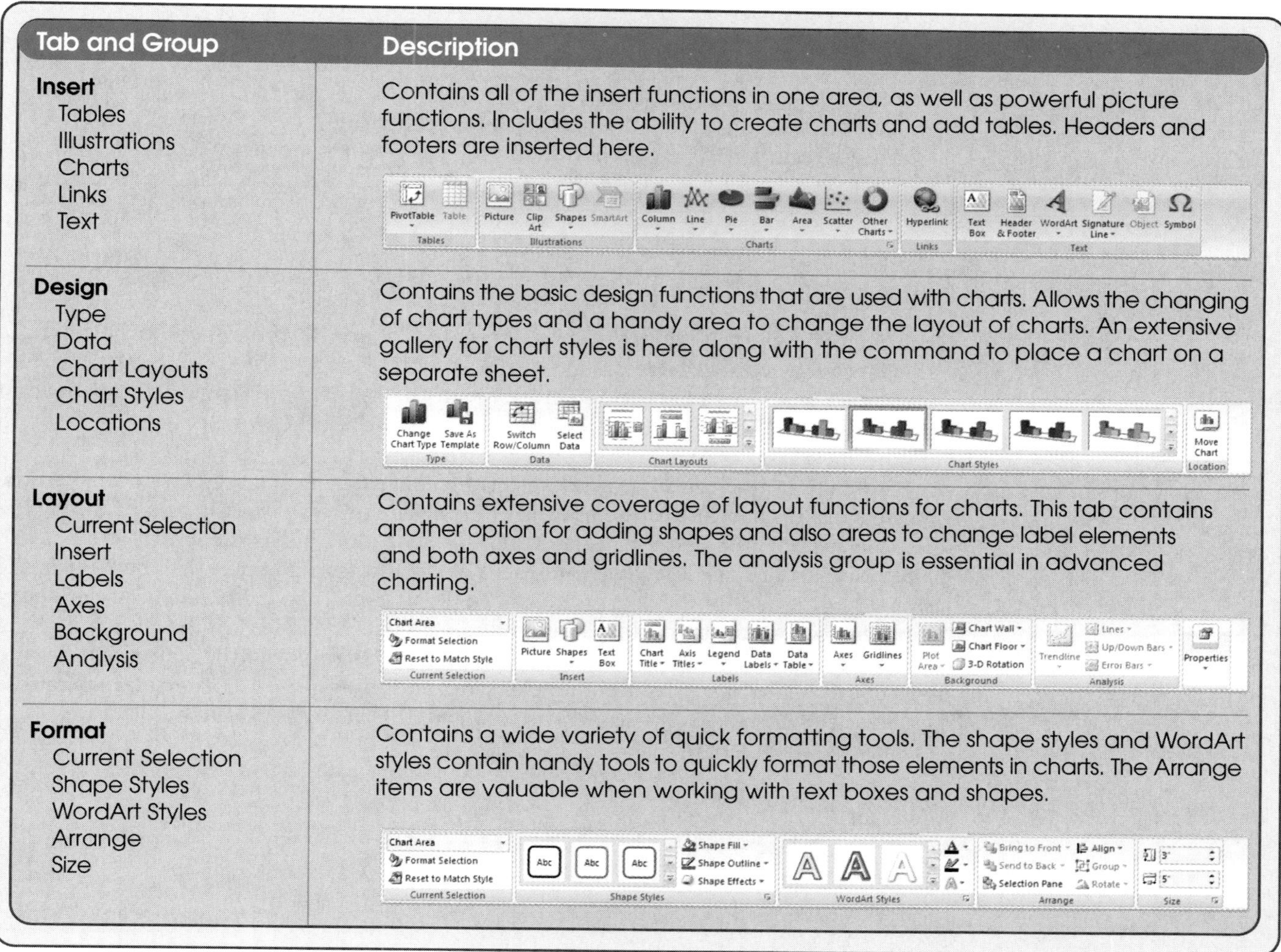

Tab and Group	Description
Insert Tables Illustrations Charts Links Text	Contains all of the insert functions in one area, as well as powerful picture functions. Includes the ability to create charts and add tables. Headers and footers are inserted here.
Design Type Data Chart Layouts Chart Styles Locations	Contains the basic design functions that are used with charts. Allows the changing of chart types and a handy area to change the layout of charts. An extensive gallery for chart styles is here along with the command to place a chart on a separate sheet.
Layout Current Selection Insert Labels Axes Background Analysis	Contains extensive coverage of layout functions for charts. This tab contains another option for adding shapes and also areas to change label elements and both axes and gridlines. The analysis group is essential in advanced charting.
Format Current Selection Shape Styles WordArt Styles Arrange Size	Contains a wide variety of quick formatting tools. The shape styles and WordArt styles contain handy tools to quickly format those elements in charts. The Arrange items are valuable when working with text boxes and shapes.

Add Graphics in Charts

You may want to add graphics, such as company logos or representative clip art, to charts to personalize the charts or make them more distinctive. In either case, the procedure is simple. Again, this is a case where less is sometimes more. Be sparing in the use of graphics that can change the message being conveyed.

To add a graphic to a chart:

1. In the Illustrations section on the Insert tab, select the medium where the graphic will come from (Picture, Clip Art, or Smart Art).
2. Search for and insert the graphic.
3. Size and move the graphic on the chart as desired.

TIP Set a Time Limit

You can customize virtually every aspect of every object within a chart. That is the good news. It is also bad news because you can spend inordinate amounts of time for little or no gain. It is fun to experiment, but set a time limit and stop when you reach the allocated time. The default settings are often adequate to convey your message, and further experimentation might prove counterproductive.

Change the Chart Location and Size

Whether the chart is embedded on the worksheet with the data or on a separate sheet, at times you will need to move a chart or to change its size. To move a chart on any sheet, click the chart to select it. When the pointer appears as a four-headed arrow while on the margin of the chart, click and drag the chart to another location on the sheet.

To change the size of a chart, select the chart. Sizing handles are located in the corners of the chart and at the middle of the edge borders. Clicking and dragging the middle left or right sizing handle of the edge borders adjusts the width of the chart. Drag the sizing handle away from the chart to stretch or widen the chart; drag the sizing handle within the chart to decrease the width of the chart. Clicking and dragging the top or bottom middle sizing handle adjusts the height of the chart. Drag the sizing handle away from the chart to increase its height; drag the sizing handle into the chart to decrease its height. Clicking and dragging a corner sizing handle increases or decreases the height and width of the chart proportionately.

Hands-On Exercises

1 | The First Chart

Skills covered: 1. Use AutoSum **2.** Create the Chart **3.** Complete the Chart **4.** Move and Size the Chart **5.** Change the Worksheet **6.** Change the Chart Type **7.** Create a Second Chart

Step 1 Use AutoSum

Use Figure 3.16 as a guide as you work through the steps in the exercise.

a. Start Excel. Open the *chap3_ho1_sales* workbook and save it as **chap3_ho1_sales_solution**.

b. Click and drag to select **cells B7:E7** (the cells that will contain the total sales for each location). Click **AutoSum** in the Editing group on the Home tab to compute the total for each city.

c. Click and drag to select **cells F4:F6**, and then click **AutoSum**.

The SUM function is entered automatically into these cells to total the entries to the left of the selected cells.

d. Click and drag to select **cells B4:F7** and format these cells with the currency symbol and no decimal places.

e. Bold the row and column headings and the totals. Center the entries in **cells B3:F3**.

f. Save the workbook.

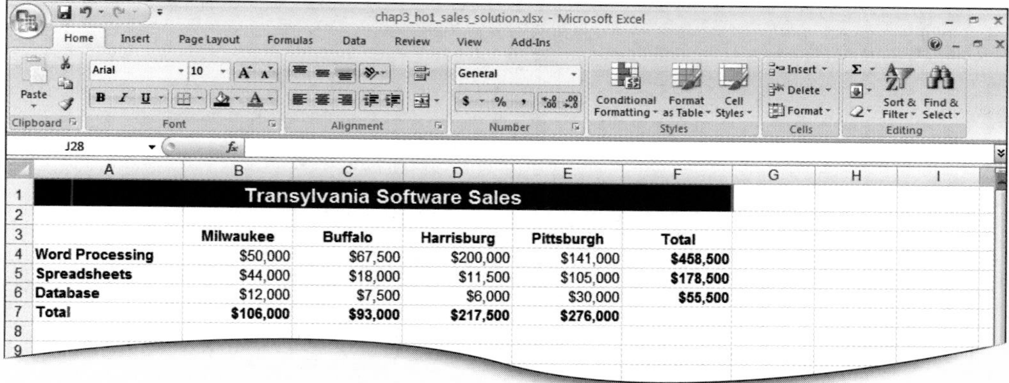

	Milwaukee	Buffalo	Harrisburg	Pittsburgh	Total
Word Processing	$50,000	$67,500	$200,000	$141,000	$458,500
Spreadsheets	$44,000	$18,000	$11,500	$105,000	$178,500
Database	$12,000	$7,500	$6,000	$30,000	$55,500
Total	$106,000	$93,000	$217,500	$276,000	

Figure 3.16 Formatted Worksheet with Totals

Step 2 Create the Chart

Refer to Figure 3.17 as you complete Step 2. Note that the colors displayed in figures may not match your screen display.

a. Select **cells B3:E3** to select the category labels (the names of the cities). Press and hold **Ctrl** as you drag the mouse over **cells B7:E7** to select the data series (the cells containing the total sales for the individual cities).

You have selected the cities that will become the X axis in your chart. You selected B7 through E7 as the values that will become the data series.

b. Check that **cells B3:E3** and **cells B7:E7** are selected. Click the **Insert tab** and click **Column** in the Chart group.

You should see the Column Chart palette, as shown in Figure 3.17. When the Column chart type and Clustered column subtype are selected, the chart appears on Sheet1. Note that your default colors may differ from those displayed in your textbook.

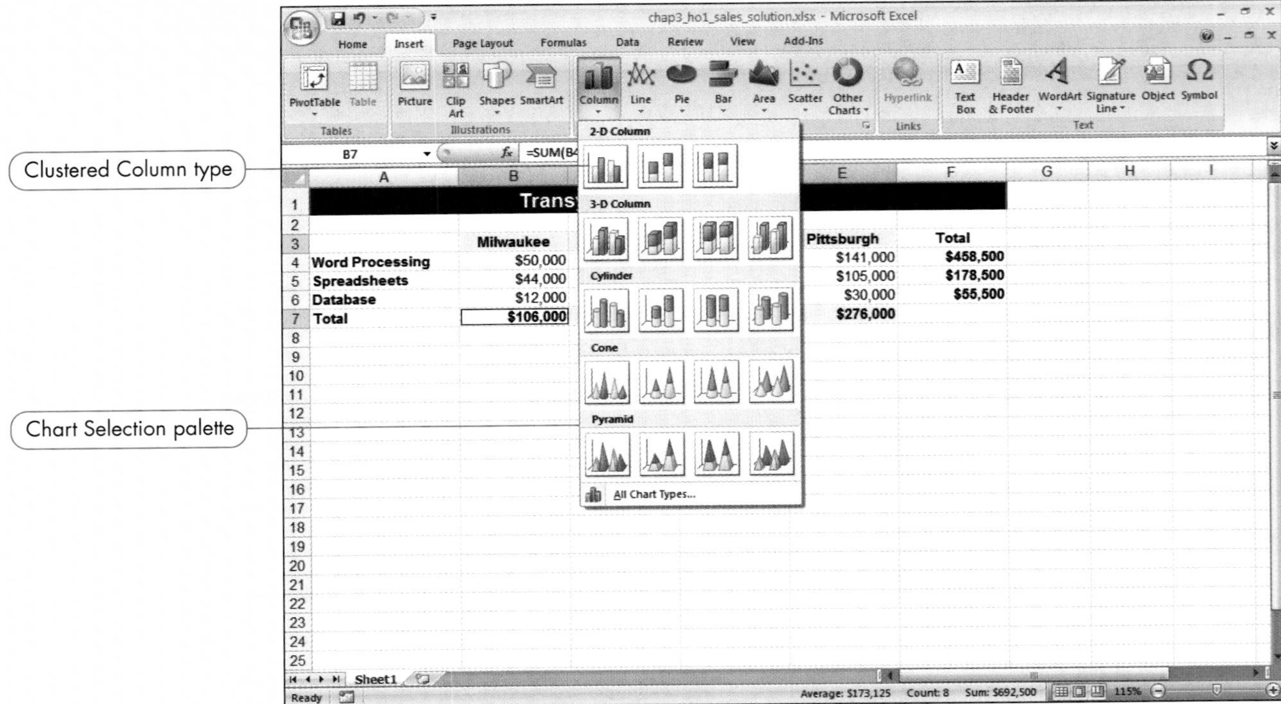

Figure 3.17 Gallery of Chart Types

TROUBLESHOOTING: If you select too little or too much data for charting purposes, you can change your data ranges. Make the Design tab active, then click Edit Data Source to open the Edit Data Source dialog box. Click Edit and select the correct data range.

c. Click **Clustered Column** in the *2-D Column* section to insert a chart.

As you move the mouse over the palette, a ScreenTip appears that indicates the name of the chart type.

TIP The F11 Key

The F11 key is the fastest way to create a chart in its own sheet. Select the worksheet data, including the legends and category labels, and then press F11 to create the chart. The chart displays according to the default format built into the Excel column chart. After you create the chart, you can use the Chart Tools tabs, Mini toolbars, or shortcut menus to choose a different chart type and customize the formatting.

Step 3 Complete the Chart

Refer to Figure 3.18 as you complete Step 3.

a. Click the chart object to make the chart active. Click the **Layout tab**, click **Chart Title** in the Labels group, and then click **Above Chart** to create a title for the chart.

You selected the chart, and then selected the placement of the chart title using the Chart Tools tabs.

b. Type **Revenue by Geographic Area** for the title and press **Enter**.

c. Click **Legend** in the Labels group of the Layout tab and select **None** to delete the legend.

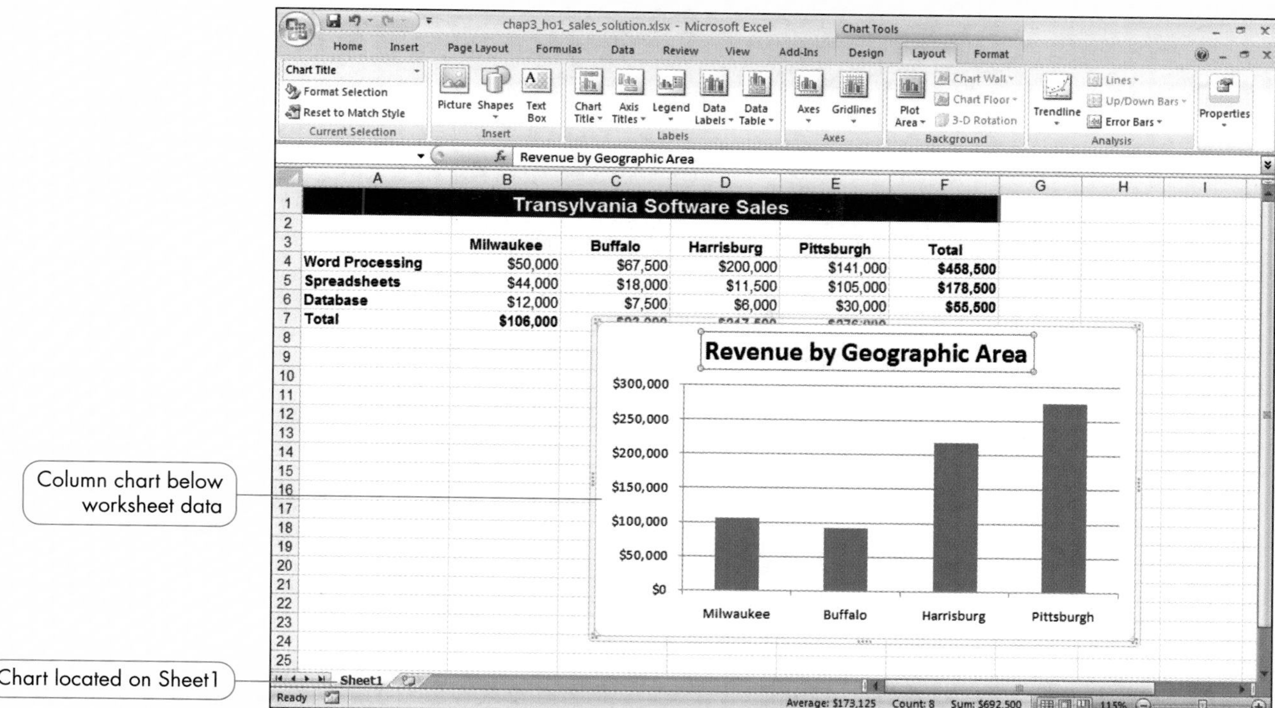

Figure 3.18 Column Chart with Title

Step 4
Move and Size the Chart

Refer to Figure 3.19 as you complete Step 4.

a. Move and size the chart just as you would any other Windows object.

You should see the completed chart in Figure 3.19. When you click the chart, the sizing handles indicate the chart is selected and will be affected by subsequent commands.

1. Click the chart border to select the chart, then click on the highlighted outline of the chart and drag (the mouse pointer changes to a four-sided arrow) to move the chart so that the top left side of the chart starts in **cell A9**.

2. Drag a corner handle (the mouse pointer changes to a double arrow) to change the length and width of the chart simultaneously so that the chart covers the **range A9:G29**.

b. Click outside the chart to deselect it. The sizing handle is no longer visible.

When working with any graphic object in Excel, you can resize it by making it active and dragging sizing handles that appear at the corners and on the perimeter of the object.

c. Save the workbook.

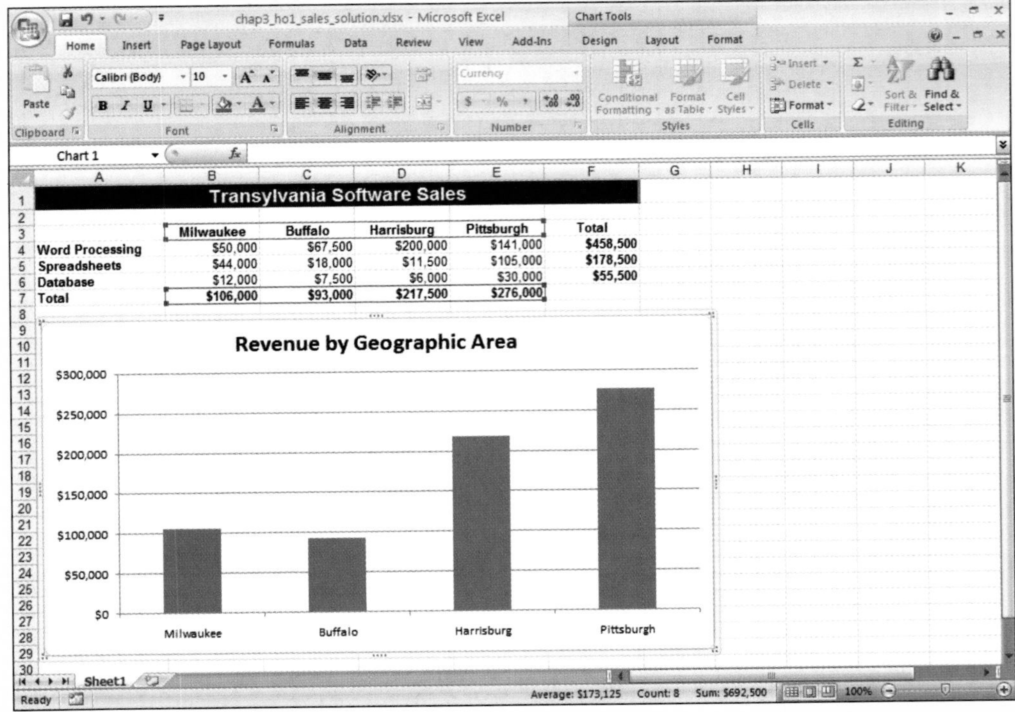

Figure 3.19 Chart Size and Location Changed

TIP Embedded Charts

An embedded chart is treated as an object that can be moved, sized, copied, or deleted just as any other Windows object. To move an embedded chart, click the border of the chart to select the chart and drag it to a new location in the worksheet. To size the chart, select it and then drag any of the eight sizing handles in the desired direction. To delete the chart, select it and press Delete. To copy the chart, select it, click Copy in the Clipboard group on the Home tab to copy the chart to the clipboard, click elsewhere in the workbook where you want the copied chart to go, and click Paste.

Step 5
Change the Worksheet

Refer to Figure 3.20 as you complete Step 5.

a. Click in **cell B4**. Change the entry to **$225,000** and press **Enter**.

   Any changes in a worksheet are automatically reflected in the associated chart. The total sales for Milwaukee in cell B7 change automatically to reflect the increased sales for word processing. The column for Milwaukee also changes in the chart and is now larger than the column for Pittsburgh.

b. Click in **cell B3**. Change the entry to **Chicago** and press **Enter**.

   The category label on the X axis changes automatically to reflect the new city name (see Figure 3.20).

c. Click **Undo** twice on the Quick Access Toolbar.

   You changed the worksheet and chart back to Milwaukee and $50,000 by clicking Undo twice. The worksheet and chart are restored to their earlier values.

d. Save the workbook.

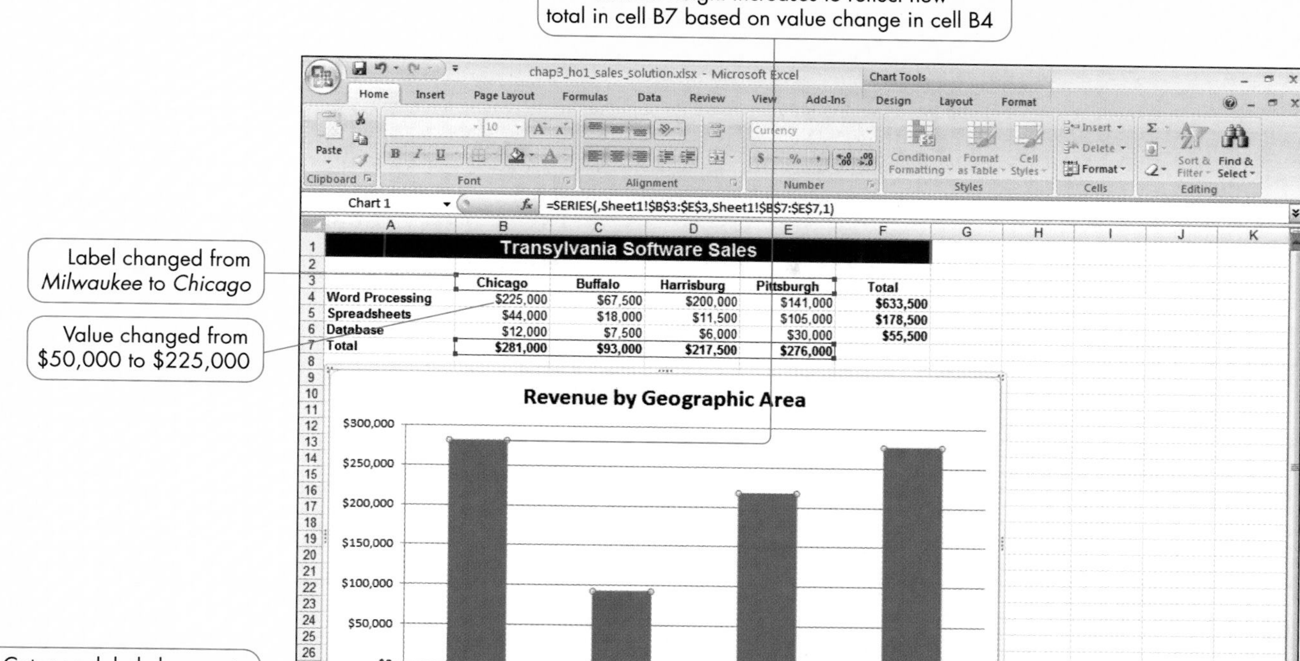

Figure 3.20 Temporary Data Changes Affect Chart

Step 6
Change the Chart Type

Refer to Figure 3.21 as you complete Step 6.

a. Click the chart border area to select the chart, click **Change Chart Type** in the Type group on the Design tab, click the **Pie** type, and then click **Pie** (the first button in the Pie row). Click **OK**, and the chart changes to a pie chart.

   You used the Design tab to change the type of chart. The following steps will guide you through adding data labels to the chart area, and formatting those data labels as percentages.

b. Point to any pie wedge, click the right mouse button to display a shortcut menu, and click **Add Data Labels**.

c. Right-click the mouse button on any pie wedge to display a shortcut menu and select **Format Data Labels** to display the Format Data Labels dialog box. Make sure **Label Options** in the left column is selected, and then click the **Category Name** and **Percentage** check boxes to format the data labels. Remove the checks from the **Value** and **Show Leader Lines** check boxes.

d. Change the values in the data labels to percentages by clicking **Number** below *Label Options* on the left side of the dialog box, click **Percentage** in *Category* list, type **0** in the **Decimal places** box, and click **Close** to accept the settings and close the dialog box.

   The pie chart now displays data labels as percentages. The Number format is the default when initially inserting data labels.

e. Modify each component as necessary:

   1. Click the plot area to select the chart. Click and drag the sizing handles to increase the size of the plot area within the embedded chart.

   2. Click a label to select all data labels. Click the **Home tab**, click the **Font Size down arrow** in the Font group, and select **12**.

f. Save the workbook.

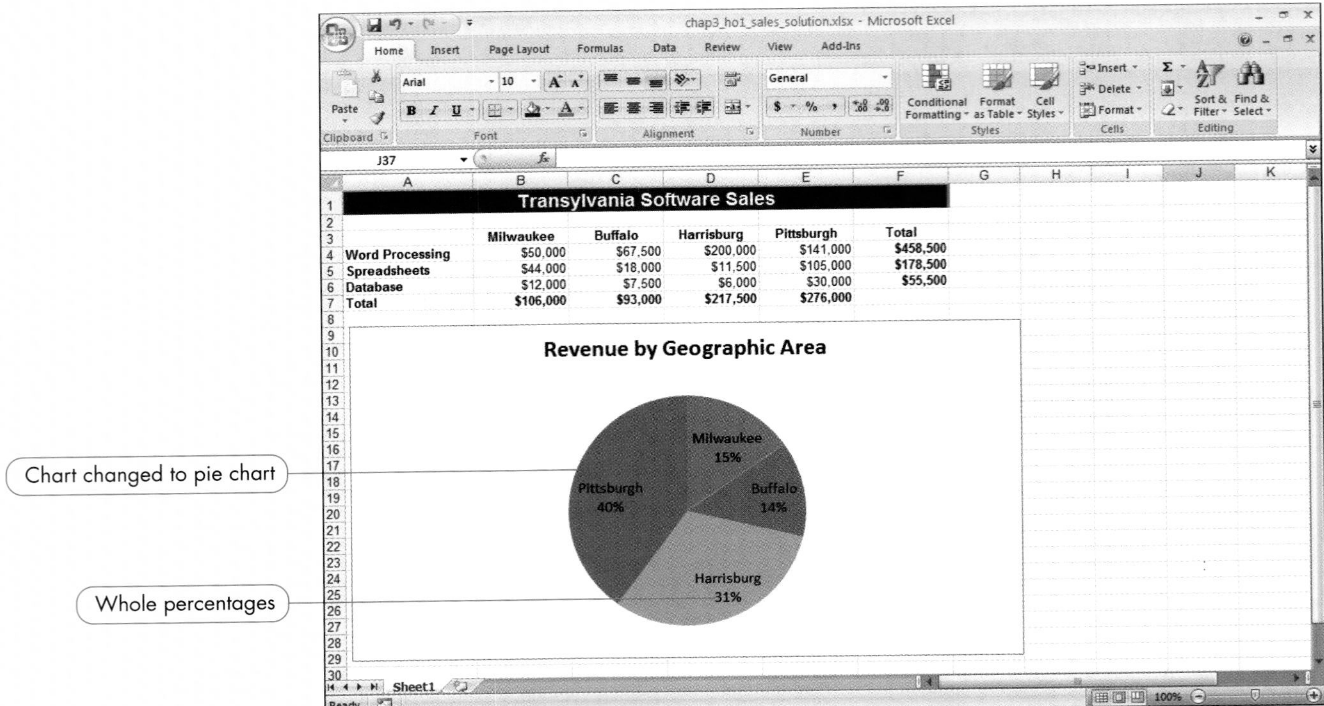

Figure 3.21 Chart Changed to Pie Chart

Step 7
Create a Second Chart

Refer to Figure 3.22 as you complete Step 7.

a. Click and drag to select **cells A4:A6** in the worksheet. Press and hold **Ctrl** as you drag the mouse to select **cells F4:F6**.

b. Click the **Insert tab**, click **Column** in the Chart group, and select **3-D Clustered Column.**

   When the Column chart type and 3-D Clustered Column subtype are selected, the chart appears on Sheet1. The values (the data being plotted) are in cells F4:F6. The category labels for the X axis are in cells A4:A6.

c. Click **Chart Title** in the Labels group on the Layout tab and select **Centered Overlay Title.**

d. Type **Revenue by Product Category** for the title. Click **Legend** in the Labels group on the Layout tab and select **None** to delete the legend.

   You have created a title for your 3-D clustered column chart. You deleted the legend because you have only one data series.

e. Click the **Design tab** and click **Move Chart** in the Location group. Click **New sheet**, and then click **OK** to display the chart on a new sheet and close the Move Chart dialog box.

   The 3-D column chart has been created in the chart sheet labeled Chart1, as shown in Figure 3.22.

f. Save the workbook. Exit Excel if you do not want to continue with the next exercise at this time.

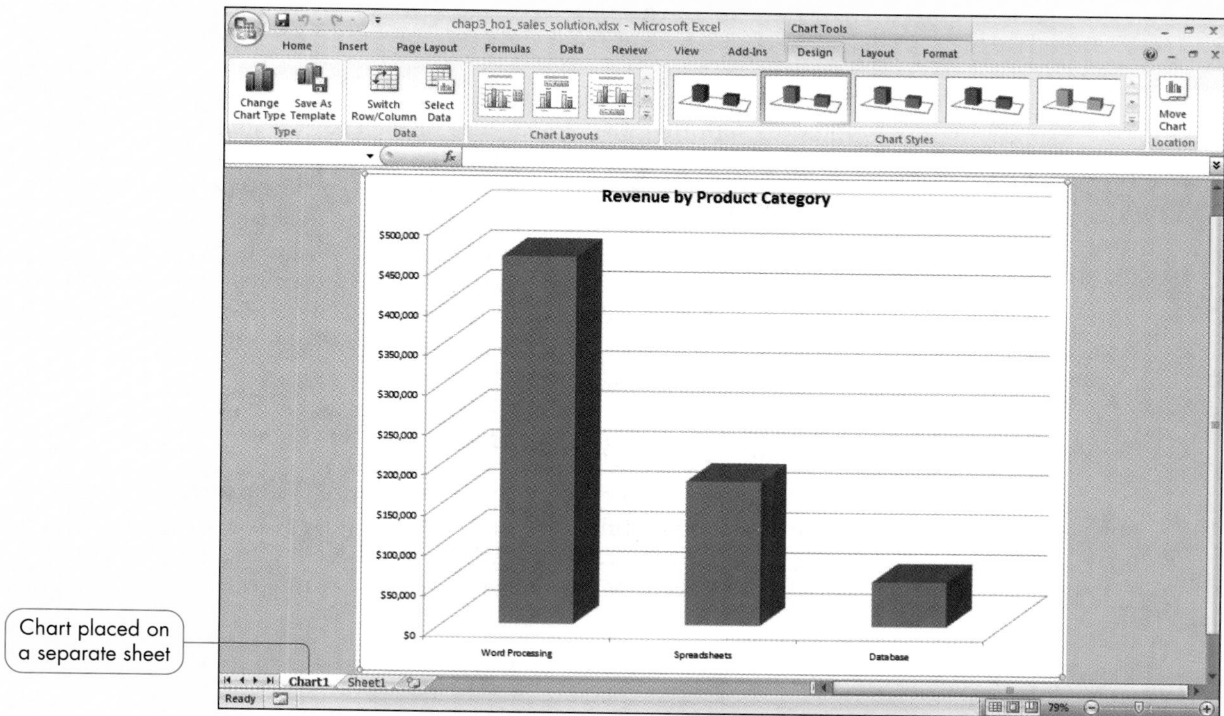

Figure 3.22 Chart Moved to Chart1 Sheet

Chart Enhancements

Now that you already have created a chart by selecting the appropriate values and labels, you must improve the appearance of the chart. Adding and editing chart elements enhance the information value of a chart. For example, you can draw attention to a specific bar using an arrow shape that includes an appropriate text phrase. Charts are used to express information visually, and subtle visual enhancements improve comprehension while presenting a more powerful message.

Charts are used to express information visually, and subtle visual enhancements improve comprehension while presenting a more powerful message.

In this section, you modify a chart. Specifically, you change and edit chart elements, format a chart, add data labels, and change the fill color for chart elements. Then you enhance charts by adding shapes.

Modifying a Chart

You can modify any chart element to enhance the chart and improve its appearance. Some of the most common chart modifications include the following properties: size, color, font, format, scale, or style just by selecting the element and choosing from a variety of options. Mini toolbars and shortcut menus appear as needed for you to make your selections.

TIP Anatomy of a Chart

A chart is composed of multiple components (objects), each of which can be selected and changed separately. Point to any part of a chart to display a ScreenTip indicating the name of the component, then click the mouse to select that component and display the sizing handles. You can then click and drag the object within the chart and/or right-click the mouse to display a Mini toolbar and shortcut menu with commands pertaining to the selected object.

Change and Edit Chart Elements

It is often necessary to change chart elements such as titles and axes. For example, you might need to change the title of the chart or adjust the font size of the title to balance the title text and the chart size. You can change these elements to reflect different words or edit the elements to reflect formatting changes.

On a chart, do one of the following:

- To edit the contents of a title, click the chart or axis title that you want to change.
- To edit the contents of a data label, click twice on the data label that you want to change.
- Click again to place the title or data label in editing mode, drag to select the text that you want to change, type the new text or value, and then press Enter.

To format the text, select it, and then click the formatting options that you want on the Mini toolbar. You can also use the formatting buttons in the Font group on the Home tab. To format the entire title or data label, right-click the selected text, select Format Chart Title, Format Axis Title, or Format Data Labels on the shortcut menu, and then select the formatting options that you want.

Format a Chart

The options for formatting a chart may be approached in two ways, either by using the tabs or by selecting the chart and then right-clicking and using the various format commands on the shortcut menu. Table 3.3 shows the different tabs and the formatting capabilities available with each. Figures 3.23 through 3.26 show these tabs as defined in Table 3.3.

Table 3.3 Tab and Format Features

Tab	Format Features
Insert	Insert shapes, insert illustrations, create and edit WordArt and textboxes, insert symbols.
Design	Change chart type, edit the data sources, change the chart style and layout, and change the location of the chart.
Layout	Again allows the insertion of shapes, graphics, and text boxes. Add or change chart title, axis title, legend, data labels, and data table. Format axis and change the background.
Format	Deals with more sophisticated control of WordArt, shapes, and arrangement.

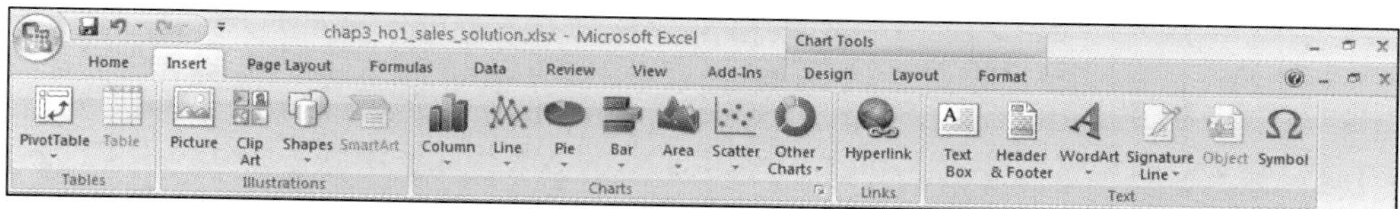

Figure 3.23 Insert Tab

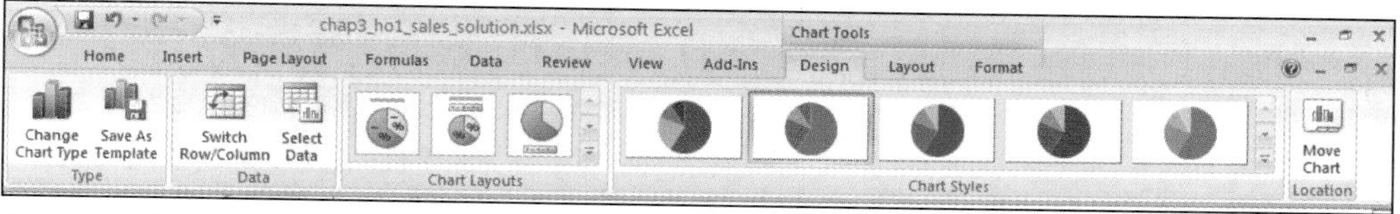

Figure 3.24 Design Tab

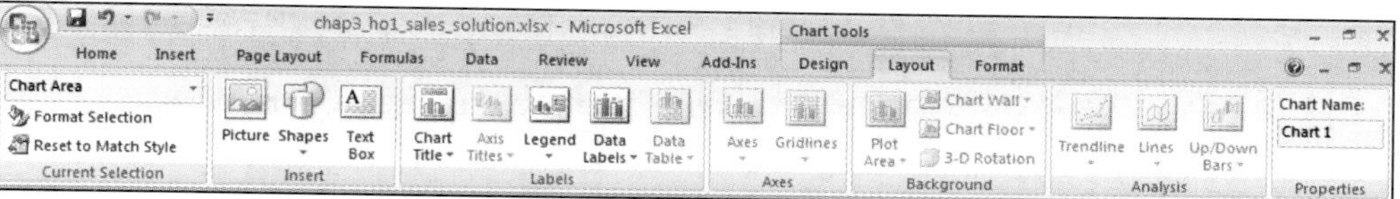

Figure 3.25 Layout Tab

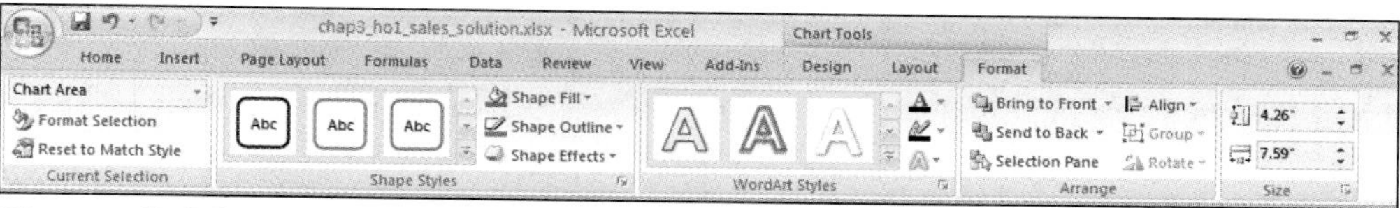

Figure 3.26 Format Tab

Add Data Labels

A ***data label*** is the value or name of a data point.

One of the features of Excel charting that does much to enhance charts is the use of ***data labels***, which are the value or name of a data point. The exact values of data shown by charts are not always clear, particularly in 3-D charts, as well as scatter charts and some line charts. It assists the readers of your charts if you label the data points with text and their values. These labels amplify the data represented in the chart by providing their numerical values on the chart. To add data labels to a chart:

1. Select the chart that will have data labels added.
2. Click on the Data Labels list in the Labels group on the Layout tab.
3. Select the location for the data labels on the chart.

Change the Fill Color for Chart Elements

Another component you can change is the color or fill pattern of any element in the chart. Colors are used to accentuate data presented in chart form. Colors also are used to underplay data presented in chart form. Charts often are used in Microsoft PowerPoint for presentation, so you must pay attention to contrast and use appropriate colors for large screen display. Remember also that color blindness and other visual impairments can change how charts are viewed. To change the color of a data series in a column chart:

1. Right-click on any column to open the shortcut menu.
2. Select Format Data Series.
3. Select Fill from the Series Options and select a color from the Color list.
4. Click Close.

To change the color of the plot area, right-click on the plot area to open the shortcut menu and select Format Plot area. Repeat Steps 3 and 4 above.

Another unique feature you can use to enhance a chart and make the data more meaningful is to use an image in the data series. See Figure 3.27 for an example of a chart using an image of an apple to represent bushels of apples. To use an image as a data series, select the data series, click the Shape Fill down arrow in the Shape Styles group on the Format tab, and select Picture. From the Insert Picture dialog box, select the image and click Insert.

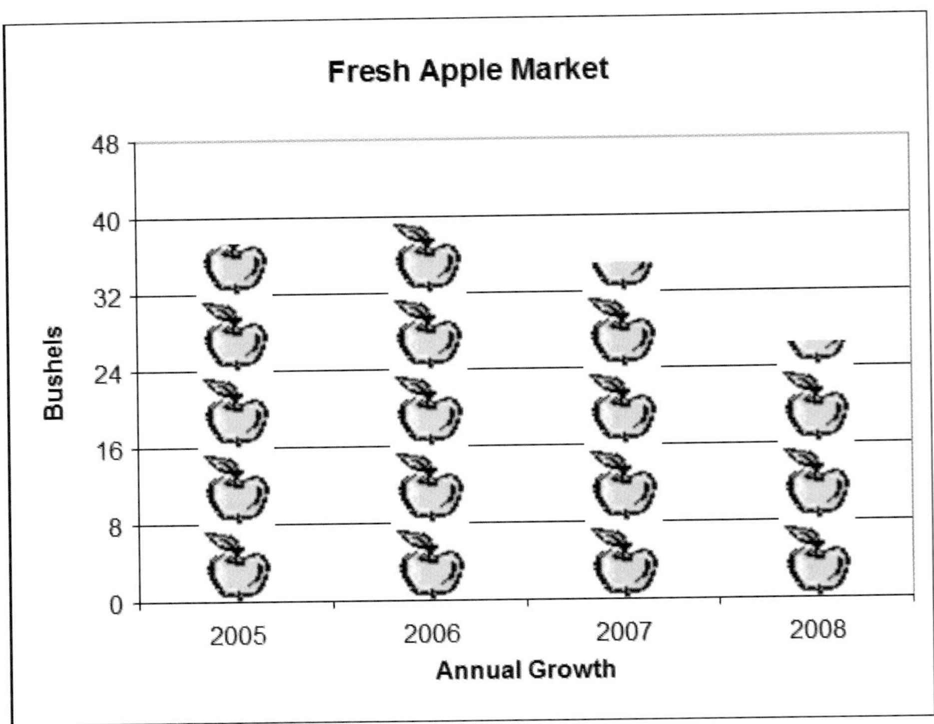

Figure 3.27 Images in Charts

Quick Layout

Excel enables you to instantly change the look of a chart. After creating a chart, quickly apply a predefined layout to the chart. Choose from a variety of useful predefined layouts and then manually customize the layout of individual chart elements if desired. Select the chart before formatting. This action displays Chart Tools tab, adding the Design, Layout, and Format tabs. On the Design tab, in the Quick Layout group, click the chart layout that you want to use. To see all available layouts, click More.

Shape Fill

As an alternative to right-clicking a chart element to change a fill color, you can select the specific chart element, such as one data series and click the Shape Fill down arrow in the Shape Styles group on the Format tab. You can choose specific colors, such as **Red, Accent 2, Lighter 60%** in the *Theme Colors* section, or you can select a regular color from the *Standard Colors* section.

Enhancing Charts with Graphic Shapes

Using shapes is a technique that lets you add pre-made graphics to a chart to emphasize the content of a part of a chart. Ready-made shapes come in forms such as rectangles, circles, arrows, lines, flowchart symbols, and callouts. Words also can be placed in shapes using text boxes.

Shapes can be inserted either from the Insert tab or from the Layout tab. You want to experiment with both techniques and decide which you prefer. To insert a shape using the Layout tab:

1. Click the Shapes pull-down menu on the Layout tab.
2. Click on the shape you want to insert.
3. Place the crosshair pointer over the location on the chart where the graphic is to be located and drag the pointer to place the shape. To constrain the drawing element to the proportion illustrated in the shapes palette, hold Shift while you drag the pointer to place the shape.
4. Release the mouse button.
5. To resize a shape, select the shape and use one of the nine selection handles to change its size.
6. Rotate the graphic by clicking the green rotation handle and dragging to rotate the shape.
7. Change the shape of the graphic by clicking the yellow diamond tool and dragging.

Hands-On Exercises

2 | Multiple Data Series

Skills covered: 1. Rename the Worksheet **2.** Create Chart with Multiple Data Series **3.** Copy the Chart **4.** Change the Source Data **5.** Change the Chart Type **6.** Insert a Graphic Shape and Add a Text Box

Step 1
Rename the Worksheet

Refer to Figure 3.28 as you complete Step 1.

a. Open the *chap3_ho1_sales_solution* workbook if you closed it at the end of the previous exercise. Save the workbook as **chap3_ho2_sales_solution**.

b. Point to the workbook tab labeled Sheet1, right-click the mouse to display a shortcut menu, and then click **Rename**.

   The name of the worksheet (Sheet1) is selected.

c. Type **Sales Data** to change the name of the worksheet to the more descriptive name. Press **Enter**. Right-click the worksheet tab a second time, select **Tab Color**, then change the color to the **Blue, Accent 1** theme shade. Click **OK**.

   You renamed the worksheet and will now change the color of the sheet tab.

d. Change the name of the Chart1 sheet to **Column Chart**. Change the tab color to the **Red, Accent 2** theme shade. Save the workbook.

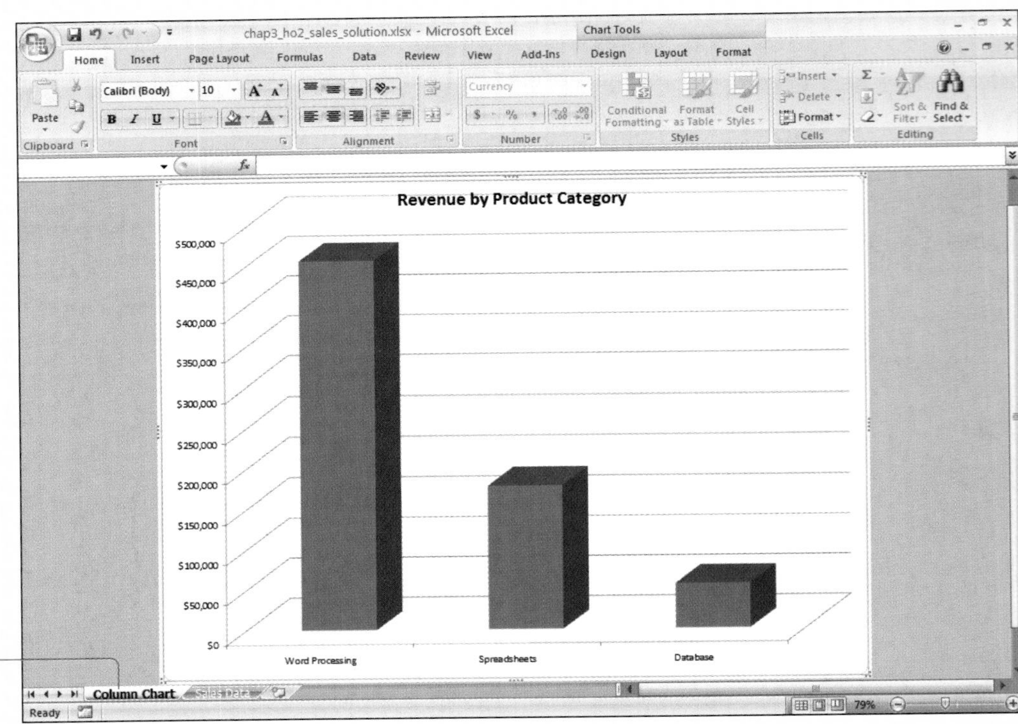

Figure 3.28 Renamed Worksheet

Step 2
Create Chart with Multiple Data Series

Refer to Figure 3.29 as you complete Step 2.

a. Click the **Sales Data tab**, then click and drag to select **cells A3:E6**.

b. Click the **Insert tab**, click the **Column** list in the Chart group, and select **Clustered Column** as the subtype from the gallery of column chart types.

   This type of chart is best for displaying multiple data series.

c. Click **Chart Title** in the Labels group on the Layout tab and select **Above Chart** to create a title for the chart.

d. Type **Revenue by City** for the chart title and press **Enter**.

   Using appropriate chart titles is essential as no chart should appear without a title. Viewers of your chart need to be able to quickly identify the subject of the chart.

e. Click **Move Chart** in the Location group on the Design tab. Click **New sheet**, and then click **OK**.

   You have moved the chart from the Sales Data sheet to a new chart sheet.

f. Change the name of the Chart2 sheet to **Revenue by City**. Your sheet name for the chart may differ. Change the tab color to theme shade **Orange, Accent 6**. Save the workbook.

   After changing both the tab name and tab color, your chart should be similar to Figure 3.29.

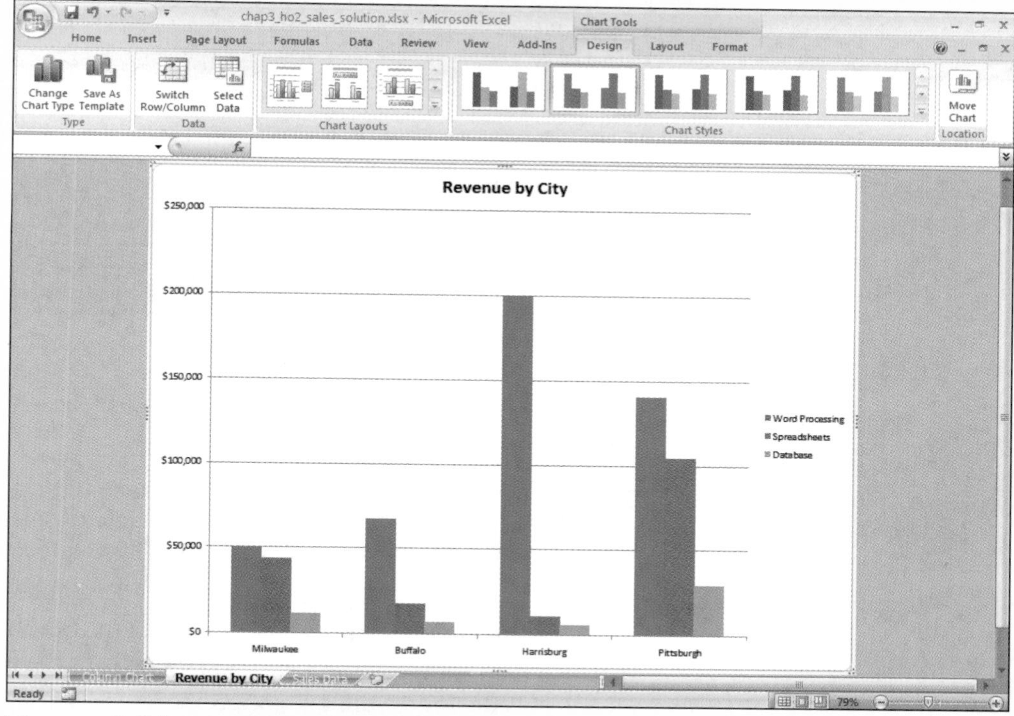

Figure 3.29 Multiple Data Series

Step 3
Copy the Chart

Refer to Figure 3.30 as you complete Step 3.

a. Click anywhere in the chart title to select the title. Click the **Font Size** list box on the Home tab and change to **24-point** type to enlarge the title.

   You changed the font size of the title to make it easier to read.

b. Point to the worksheet tab named **Revenue by City** and click to select it if it is not already selected. Then click **Format** in the Cells group of the Home tab. Click **Move or Copy sheet** to display the dialog box shown in Figure 3.30.

c. Click **Sales Data** in the Before Sheet list box. Check the box to **Create a copy**. Click **OK**.

d. A duplicate worksheet called Chart 4 (your sheet tab name may vary) is created and appears before or to the left of the Sales Data worksheet.

   You have now created a copy of the original chart and can enhance it without having to replot the data.

   TROUBLESHOOTING: The appearance of the Chart Tools tabs will change depending on the type of chart created and the location of the chart.

e. Double-click the newly created worksheet tab to select the name. Type **Revenue by Product** as the new name and save the workbook.

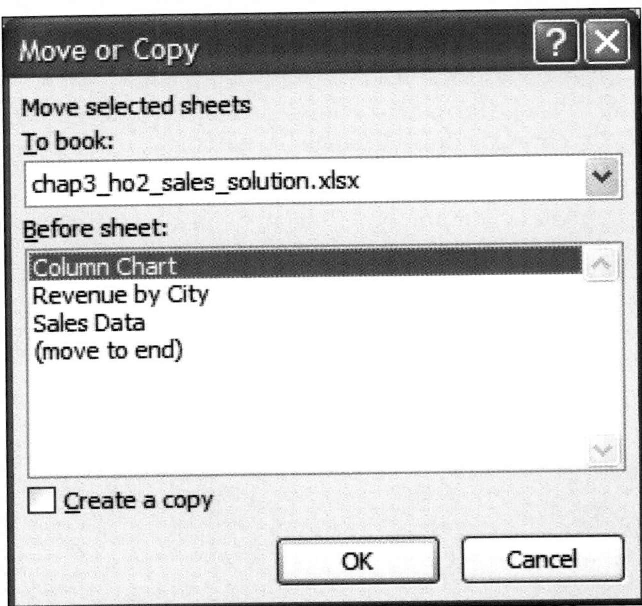

Figure 3.30 Move or Copy Dialog Box

Step 4
Change the Source Data

Refer to Figure 3.31 as you complete Step 4.

a. Click the **Revenue by Product tab** to make it the active sheet if it is not already active. Click anywhere in the title of the chart, select the word *City*, and then type **Product Category** to replace the selected text. Click outside the title to deselect it.

   You edited the title of the chart to reflect the new data source.

b. Click the **Design tab** and click **Select Data** in the Data group to display the Select Data Source dialog box, as shown in Figure 3.31.

c. Click the **Switch Row/Column button**. Click **OK** to close the Select Data Source dialog box.

   Your original chart plotted the data in rows. The chart originally contained three data series, one series for each product. Your new chart plots the data in columns. The chart contains four data series, one for each city.

d. Save the workbook.

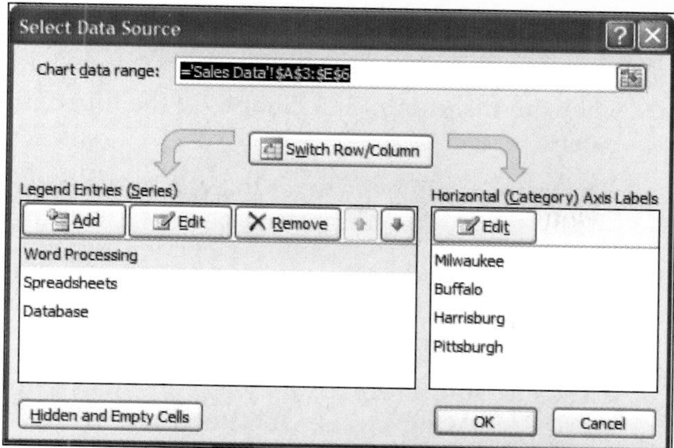

Figure 3.31 Edit Data Source Dialog Box

Step 5
Change the Chart Type

Refer to Figure 3.32 as you complete Step 5.

a. Click the chart border area to select the chart, click **Change Chart Type** in the Type group on the Design tab, and click the **Stacked Column** (the second from the left in the top row of the column chart gallery). Click **OK**.

   The chart changes to a stacked column chart.

b. Right-click the legend and select 14 points font size from the Mini toolbar.

   You increased the font size of the legend to make it more readable. Your chart should be similar to Figure 3.32.

c. Save the workbook.

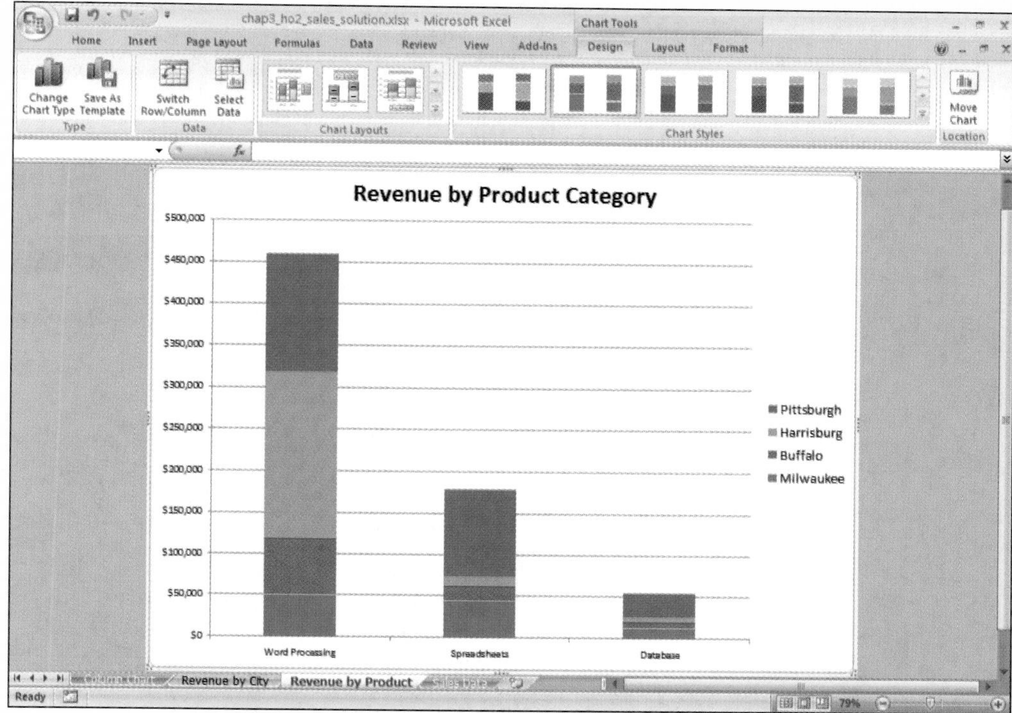

Figure 3.32 Stacked Column Chart

Step 6

Insert a Graphic Shape and Add a Text Box

Refer to Figure 3.33 as you complete Step 6.

a. Click the **Insert tab**, click **Shapes** in the Illustrations group to view the Shapes palette, and click the **Left Arrow**.

   The mouse pointer changes to a thin crosshair that you will drag to "draw" the arrow shape. The crosshair appears when you click in the chart.

b. Click and drag to create a thick arrow that points to the Word Processing column. Release the mouse. The arrow is selected, and you are viewing the **Format** tab.

c. Click **Text Box** in the Insert Shapes group on the Format tab to insert a text box. Click and drag a text box on top of the thick arrow. Release the mouse. Type **Word Processing Leads All Categories.**

   You can use shapes to draw attention to significant trends or changes in date. The text in the shape describes the trend or change.

d. Select the text you just typed, then right-click to display a shortcut menu and Mini toolbar. Use the Mini toolbar to change the font to **12-point** bold white.

   TROUBLESHOOTING: Should you have difficulty selecting the text box, right-click on the text itself to reshow the shortcut menu and Mini toolbar.

e. Click the title of the chart and you will see sizing handles around the title to indicate it has been selected. Click the **Font Size down arrow** on the Home tab. Click **24** to increase the size of the title. Your chart will be similar to Figure 3.33.

   Increasing the size of the title enables your viewers to quickly see the subject of the chart.

f. Save the workbook, but do not print it. Exit Excel if you do not want to continue with the next exercise at this time.

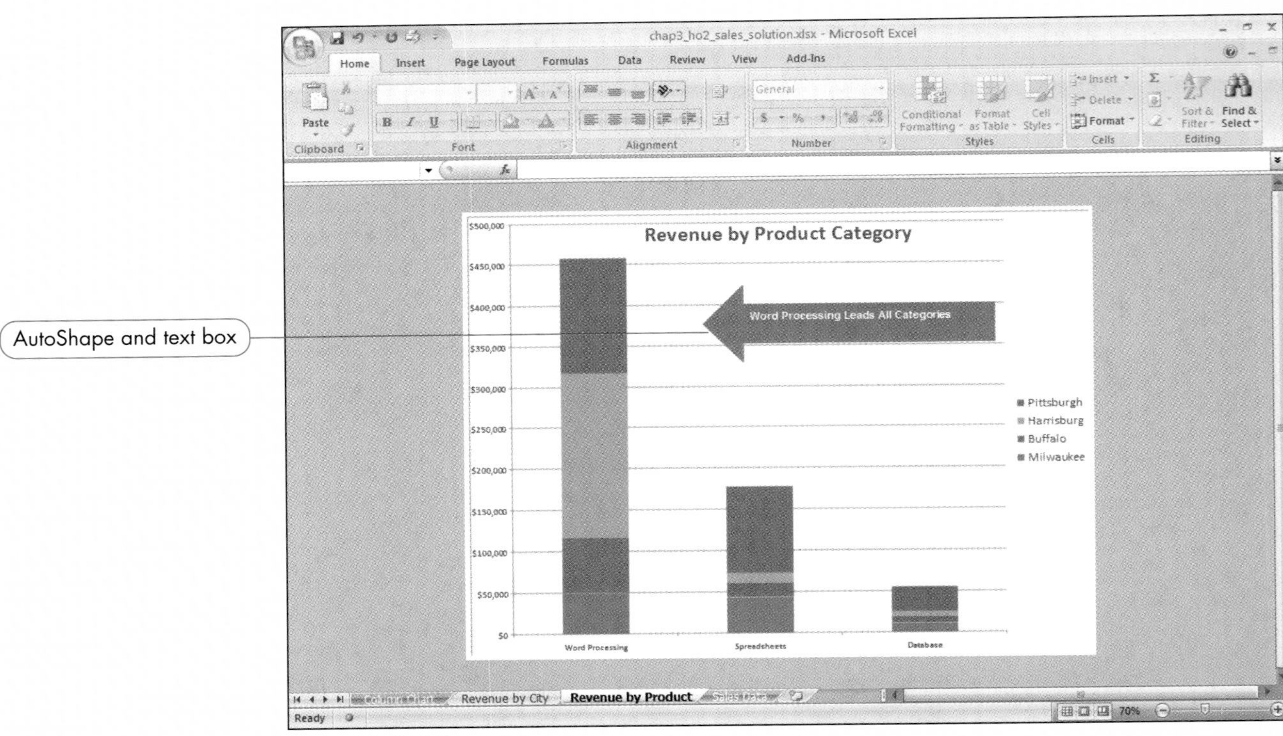

Figure 3.33 Chart with AutoShape and Text Box

Chart Distribution

(You can create visual information masterpieces that could be shared with others.)

You can create visual information masterpieces that could be shared with others. Charts are used as documentation in Web pages, memos, reports, research papers, books, and a variety of other types of documents. Therefore, it is important to experience how charts are transferred to these documents.

In this section, you embed Excel charts in other Microsoft Office applications. Then you learn how to print the chart within a worksheet or by itself. Finally, you learn how to save a chart as a Web file.

Embedding Charts

Microsoft Excel 2007 is just one application in the Microsoft Office 2007 suite. The applications are integrated and enable for data sharing. It is straightforward to copy worksheets and charts and paste in Word and PowerPoint. You can then format the objects in Word or PowerPoint.

Export to Other Applications

Microsoft Office 2007 enables you to create a file in one application that contains data (objects) from another application. The memo in Figure 3.34, for example, was created in Word, and it contains an object (a chart) that was developed in Excel. The Excel object is linked to the Word document, so that any changes to the Excel workbook data are automatically reflected in the Word document. Formatting of the object

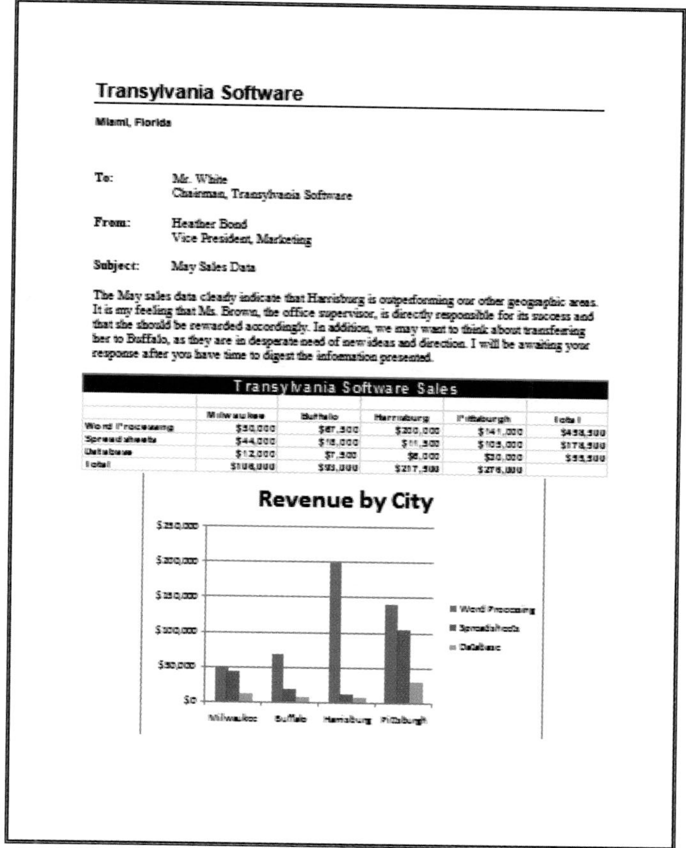

Transylvania Software

Miami, Florida

To: Mr. White
Chairman, Transylvania Software

From: Heather Bond
Vice President, Marketing

Subject: May Sales Data

The May sales data clearly indicate that Harrisburg is outperforming our other geographic areas. It is my feeling that Ms. Brown, the office supervisor, is directly responsible for its success and that she should be rewarded accordingly. In addition, we may want to think about transferring her to Buffalo, as they are in desperate need of new ideas and direction. I will be awaiting your response after you have time to digest the infomation presented.

Transylvania Software Sales					
	Milwaukee	Buffalo	Harrisburg	Pittsburgh	Total
Word Processing	$50,000	$67,500	$200,000	$141,000	$458,500
Spreadsheets	$44,000	$18,000	$11,500	$105,000	$178,500
Database	$12,000	$7,500	$6,000	$30,000	$55,500
Total	$106,000	$93,000	$217,500	$276,000	

Figure 3.34 Memo in Microsoft Office Word

in Excel after it is placed in the Word document will not be seen in the Word document. The steps to embed a chart in a Word (or PowerPoint) document are:

1. Click on the chart in Excel to select it.
2. Click Copy in the Clipboard group on the Home tab.
3. Open the appropriate Word or PowerPoint document.
4. Click Paste in the Clipboard group on the Home tab.

Remember that changes to the worksheet data made in Excel will automatically update the chart in Excel and the other application, but changes in formatting will not be updated in the other application.

TIP Hiding and Unhiding a Worksheet

A chart delivers a message more effectively than the corresponding numeric data, and thus it may be convenient to hide the associated worksheet on which the chart is based. Click the Home tab. Then click Format in the Cells group, click Hide & Unhide, and then Hide Sheet the worksheet you want to hide. Repeat the selecting Unhide Sheet to make the worksheet visible again.

Printing Charts

Printing charts is a straightforward operation but requires that you closely observe the Print Preview window in the Print group on the Office menu. You have to see what will print to make sure this is what you want to print. Printing is an output that many Excel users prefer because the chart is often part of a report, research paper, or some other paper document.

Print an Object in a Worksheet

If the chart is contained on the same worksheet page as the data, you have two options, either to print only the chart or only the data table, or to print both. To print only the chart, click on the chart to ensure it is selected. You then select Print Preview from the Print group on the Office menu. Verify that only the chart is selected for printing. Then select the Page Setup options that best show the printed chart, and then print the chart.

If you want to print both the chart and the data table, the above steps are followed except you must ensure that the chart is deselected. This is a case where the use of the Print Preview command is essential to ensure the correct items are being printed.

Print a Full-Page Chart

The options above can be difficult to use if a full-page printing of a chart is desired. The easier option is to place the chart on a separate sheet in the workbook and print it from there.

1. Click to select the chart.
2. Click Move Chart in the Location group on the Design tab.
3. Click the New Sheet option.
4. Move to the sheet added in Step 3.
5. Use Print Preview to ensure the chart will be displayed properly when printed.
6. Select the appropriate Page Setup options and print the chart.

TIP Print Only What You Need

Why print an entire workbook if you need only a single worksheet? Press and hold the Ctrl key as you click the tab(s) of the worksheet(s) that you want to print. Open the Office Button and select Print. If it is not already selected, click Active Sheet(s) in the Print What area, and then click OK. (You also can print selected cells within a worksheet by selecting the cells, and then clicking the Selection option.)

Save as a Web Page

Excel users can place an Excel chart (and sometimes entire workbooks) on the World Wide Web. The first step to placement on the Web is to save the worksheet as a Web page. To do this:

1. Click the Office Button and select Save As.
2. Select Web Page (*.htm; *.html) from the *Save as Type* menu.
3. Title the file appropriately and save it to the desired location.
4. You can preview the chart or workbook by opening your browser, navigating to the location of the Web page, and opening it.

Hands-On Exercises

3 | Embedding, Printing, and Saving a Chart as a Web Page

Skills covered: 1. Embed a Chart in Microsoft Word **2.** Copy the Worksheet **3.** Embed the Data **4.** Copy the Chart **5.** Embed the Chart **6.** Modify the Worksheet **7.** Update the Links **8.** Print Worksheet and Chart **9.** Save and View Chart as Web Page

Step 1
Embed a Chart in Microsoft Word

Refer to Figure 3.35 as you complete Step 1.

a. Start Word and if necessary, click the **Maximize** button in the application window so that Word takes up the entire screen.

b. Click the **Office Button** and select **Open**.

   1. Open the *chap3_ho3_memo* document.

   2. Save the document as **chap3_ho3_memo_solution**.

c. Click **Print Layout** on the status bar to change to the Print Layout view, and then set the **Zoom slider** to **100%**.

   The software memo is open on your desktop.

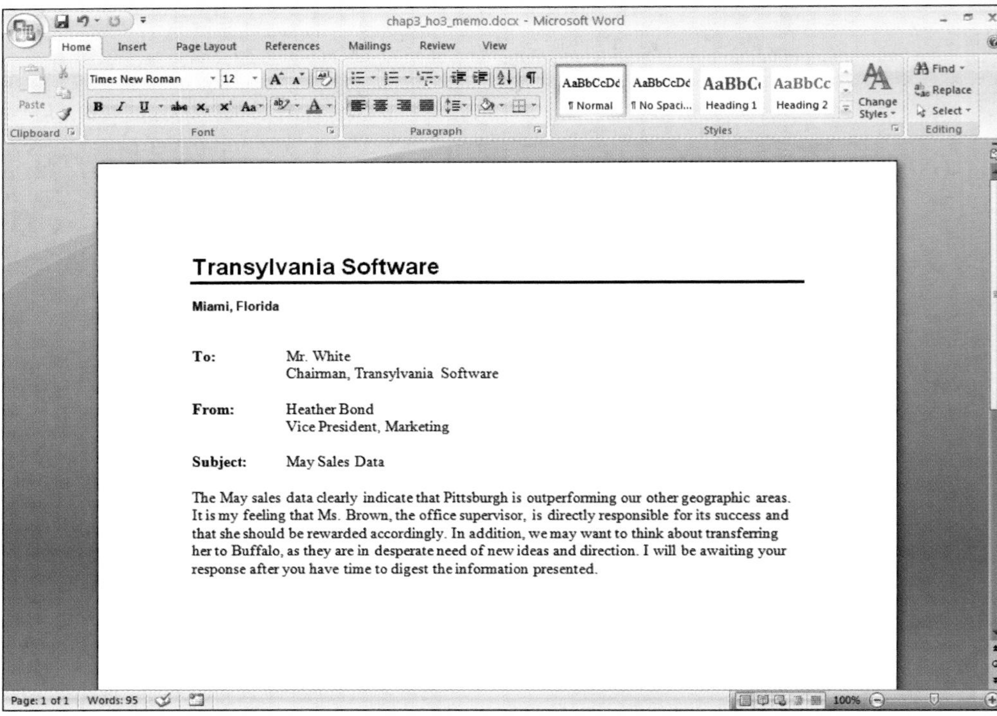

Figure 3.35 Memo in Word

Step 2
Copy the Worksheet

Refer to Figure 3.36 as you complete Step 2.

a. Open the *chap3_ho2_sales_solution* workbook from the previous exercise.

- If you did not close Microsoft Excel at the end of the previous exercise, you will see its button on the taskbar. Click the **Microsoft Excel button** to return to the *chap3_ho2_sales_solution* workbook.
- If you closed Microsoft Excel, start Excel again, and then open the *chap3_ho2_sales_solution* workbook.

b. Save the workbook as **chap3_ho3_sales_solution**.

The taskbar contains a button for both Microsoft Word and Microsoft Excel. You can click either button to move back and forth between the open applications. End by clicking the Microsoft Excel button to make it the active application.

c. Click the **Sales Data tab**. Click and drag to select **cells A1:F7** to select the entire worksheet, as shown in Figure 3.36.

d. Right-click the selected area and select **Copy** from the shortcut menu.

A moving border appears around the entire worksheet, indicating that it has been copied to the clipboard.

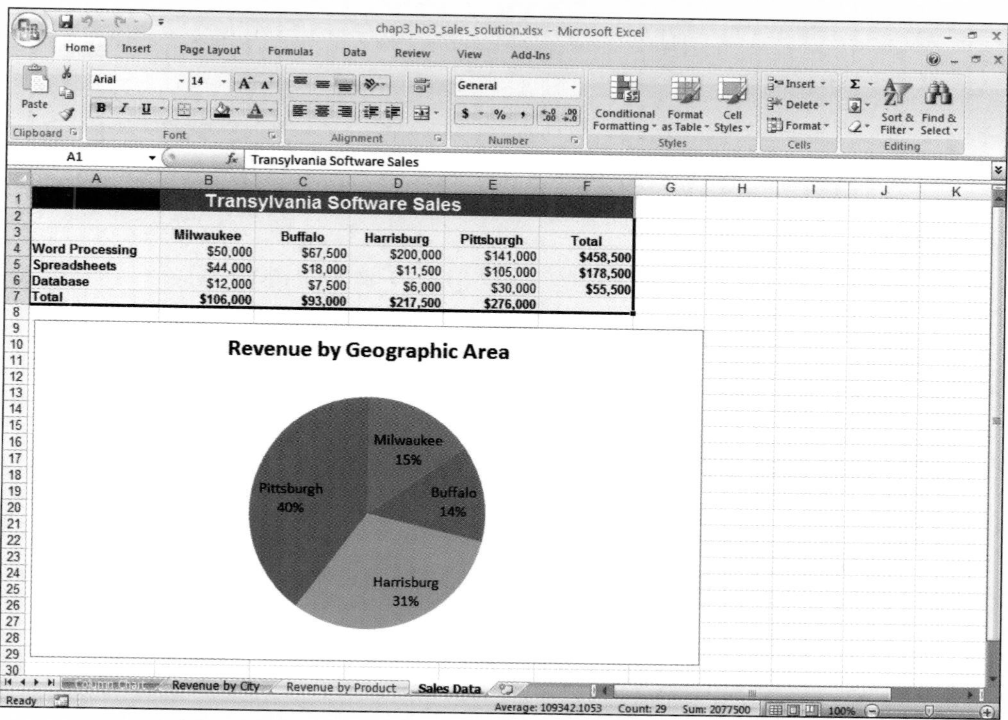

Figure 3.36 Worksheet Data to Copy

Step 3
Embed the Data

Refer to Figure 3.37 as you complete Step 3.

a. Click the **Microsoft Word button** on the taskbar to display the *chap3_ho3_memo_solution* document. Press **Ctrl+End** to move to the end of the memo, which is where you will insert the Excel worksheet.

Microsoft Word is the active window, and the insertion point is at the end of the Memo document.

b. Open the **Paste** list in the Clipboard group on the Home tab and select **Paste Special** to display the dialog box shown in Figure 3.37.

c. Click **Microsoft Office Excel Worksheet Object** in the As list. Click **Paste link.** Click **OK** to insert the worksheet into the document.

Using the Paste Special option gives you the opportunity to paste the object and establish the link for later data editing in Excel.

d. Right-click the worksheet, select **Format Object** on the shortcut menu to display the associated dialog box, and click the **Layout tab.**

TROUBLESHOOTING: If you paste the spreadsheet only, it becomes a table in Word, not an object. You cannot format it because it is not an object with a link to Excel. You must use the Paste Special option to make sure the worksheet link is created.

e. Choose **Square** in the *Wrapping Style* section and click **Center**. Click **OK** to accept the settings and close the dialog box. Click anywhere outside the table to deselect it. Save the *chap3_ho3_memo_solution* document.

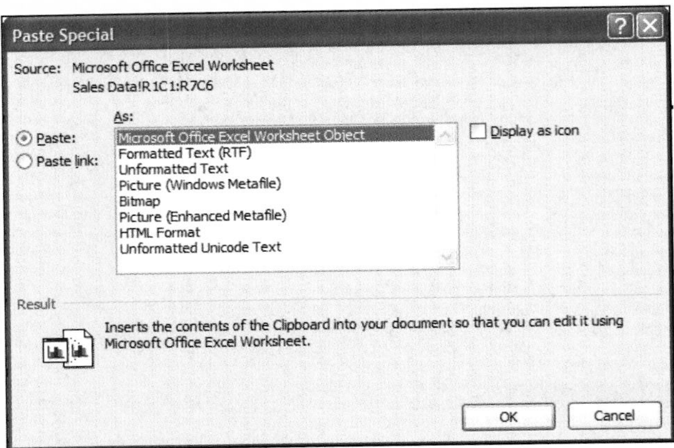

Figure 3.37 Paste Special Dialog Box

Step 4
Copy the Chart

a. Click the **Microsoft Excel button** on the taskbar to return to the worksheet.

b. Click outside the selected area to deselect the cells. Press **Esc** to remove the moving border.

c. Click the **Revenue by City tab** and click the chart area to select the chart.

The chart is selected when you see the sizing handles on the border of the chart area.

d. Click **Copy** in the Clipboard group on the Home tab.

Step 5
Embed the Chart

Refer to Figure 3.38 as you complete Step 5.

a. Switch to **Word**, open the **Paste** list in the Clipboard group on the Home tab, and select **Paste Special** to display the dialog box.

b. Click **Microsoft Office Graphic Object** in the As list. **Paste** option is already selected. Click **OK** to insert the chart into the document.

You pasted the chart object into your Memo. As an object, it will be updated when the spreadsheet data is updated. The object, created with the Paste Special option, permits chart formatting within the Word document.

TROUBLESHOOTING: If the object moves to another page, use the resize handles to shrink the object until it fits on the previous page.

c. Click **Center** in the Paragraph group on the Home tab to center the chart.

d. Click the **Office Button**, select **Print**, and then select **Print Preview**.

Your document should be similar to Figure 3.38. You use Print Preview to view your document to verify that the elements fit on one page.

e. Save the document.

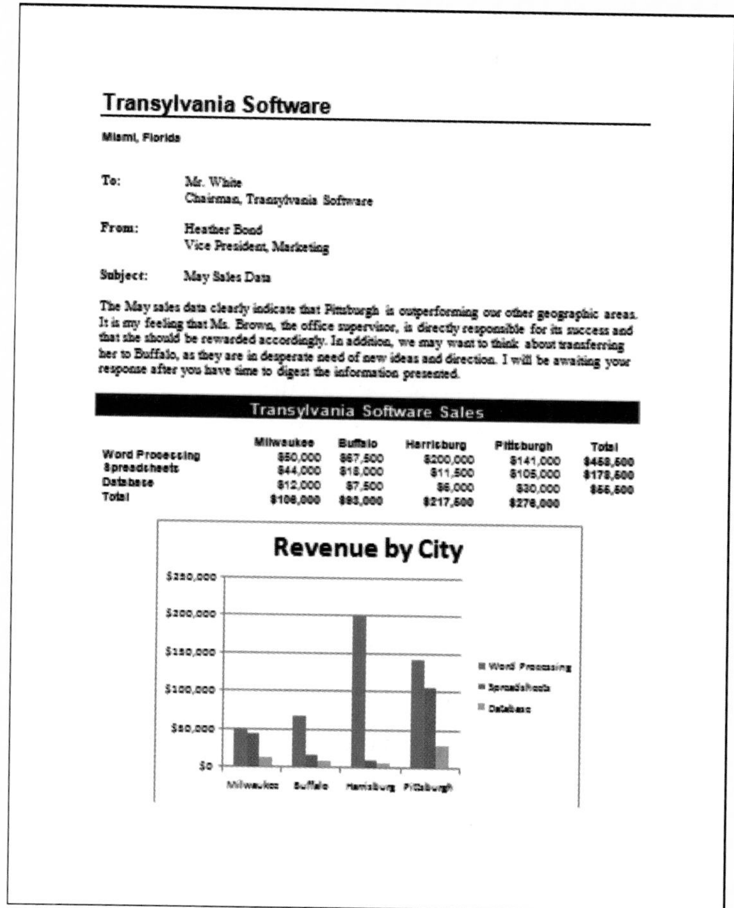

Transylvania Software

Miami, Florida

To: Mr. White
Chairman, Transylvania Software

From: Heather Bond
Vice President, Marketing

Subject: May Sales Data

The May sales data clearly indicate that Pittsburgh is outperforming our other geographic areas. It is my feeling that Ms. Brown, the office supervisor, is directly responsible for its success and that she should be rewarded accordingly. In addition, we may want to think about transferring her to Buffalo, as they are in desperate need of new ideas and direction. I will be awaiting your response after you have time to digest the information presented.

Transylvania Software Sales

	Milwaukee	Buffalo	Harrisburg	Pittsburgh	Total
Word Processing	$50,000	$67,500	$200,000	$141,000	$458,500
Spreadsheets	$44,000	$18,000	$11,500	$105,000	$178,500
Database	$12,000	$7,500	$6,000	$30,000	$55,500
Total	$106,000	$93,000	$217,500	$276,000	

Figure 3.38 Chart Embedded in Memo

Step 6
Modify the Worksheet

Refer to Figure 3.39 as you complete Step 6.

a. Working in the Word document, click anywhere in the worksheet to select the worksheet and display the sizing handles.

The status bar indicates that you can double-click to edit the worksheet.

b. Double-click the worksheet to start Excel so you can change the data.

Excel starts and reopens the *chap3_ho3_sales_solution* workbook.

c. Click **Maximize** to maximize the Excel window, if needed.

d. Click the **Sales Data tab** within the workbook, if needed. Click in **cell B4**. Type **$150,000** and press **Enter**.

The wedge for Milwaukee shows the increase in the chart.

e. Click the **Revenue by City tab** to select the chart sheet. Save the workbook.

The chart reflects the increased sales for Milwaukee.

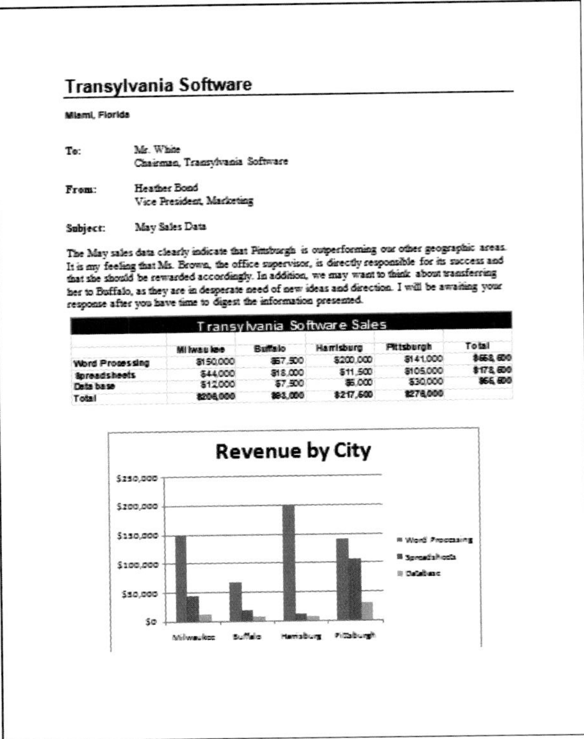

Transylvania Software

Miami, Florida

To: Mr. White
Chairman, Transylvania Software

From: Heather Bond
Vice President, Marketing

Subject: May Sales Data

The May sales data clearly indicate that Pittsburgh is outperforming our other geographic areas. It is my feeling that Ms. Brown, the office supervisor, is directly responsible for its success and that she should be rewarded accordingly. In addition, we may want to think about transferring her to Buffalo, as they are in desperate need of new ideas and direction. I will be awaiting your response after you have time to digest the information presented.

Transylvania Software Sales					
	Milwaukee	Buffalo	Harrisburg	Pittsburgh	Total
Word Processing	$150,000	$67,500	$200,000	$141,000	$558,500
Spreadsheets	$44,000	$18,000	$11,500	$105,000	$178,500
Data base	$12,000	$7,500	$6,000	$30,000	$56,500
Total	$206,000	$93,000	$217,500	$276,000	

Figure 3.39 Modified Worksheet Changes Reflected in Word Document

Step 7
Update the Links

a. Click the **Microsoft Word button** on the taskbar to display the *chap3_ho3_solution* document.

   The worksheet and chart update automatically to reflect $150,000 for word processing sales in Milwaukee.

   TROUBLESHOOTING: If the worksheet and chart do not automatically update, then point to the sheet object and click the right mouse button. Select Update Link from the shortcut menu.

b. Zoom to the **Whole Page** to view the completed document. Click and drag the worksheet or the chart within the memo to make any last-minute changes.

c. Save the memo again and close Word.

Step 8
Print Worksheet and Chart

Refer to Figure 3.40 as you complete Step 8.

a. Click on the **Sales Data tab** to make the Sales Data sheet active. Click the chart area to select it. Click **Move Chart** on the Design tab to display the dialog box. Click **New Sheet** and click **OK** to close the dialog box.

   The chart has been moved from below the spreadsheet to a new page and is displayed as full-screen view.

b. Click the **Office Button** and select **Print Preview** from the Print menu. Click **Show Margins** on the **Print Preview** toolbar to toggle the display of the margins on and off. Click **Close Print Preview** to return to the chart.

   You used Print Preview and the Show Margins option to verify that the chart displays properly before printing.

c. Click **Page Setup** on the Page Layout tab. Click the **Page tab** in the Page Setup dialog box. Verify that **Landscape** is selected.

   Changing the print option to Landscape enables you to see more of the chart.

d. Click the **Header/Footer tab** in the Page Setup dialog box, and then click **Custom Footer** to display the Footer dialog box.

e. Click the text box for the left section and enter your name. Click the text box for the center section and enter your instructor's name.

   Headers and footers provide documentation on each page for any worksheet and chart.

f. Click the text box for the right section. Click the **Date** button, press **Spacebar**, and then click the **Time** button. Click **OK** to accept these settings and close the Footer dialog box. Click **OK** to close the Page Setup dialog box.

   You used the Page Setup options to change to landscape mode and create a custom header and footer on the page with the chart.

g. Print the workbook. Close the workbook without saving.

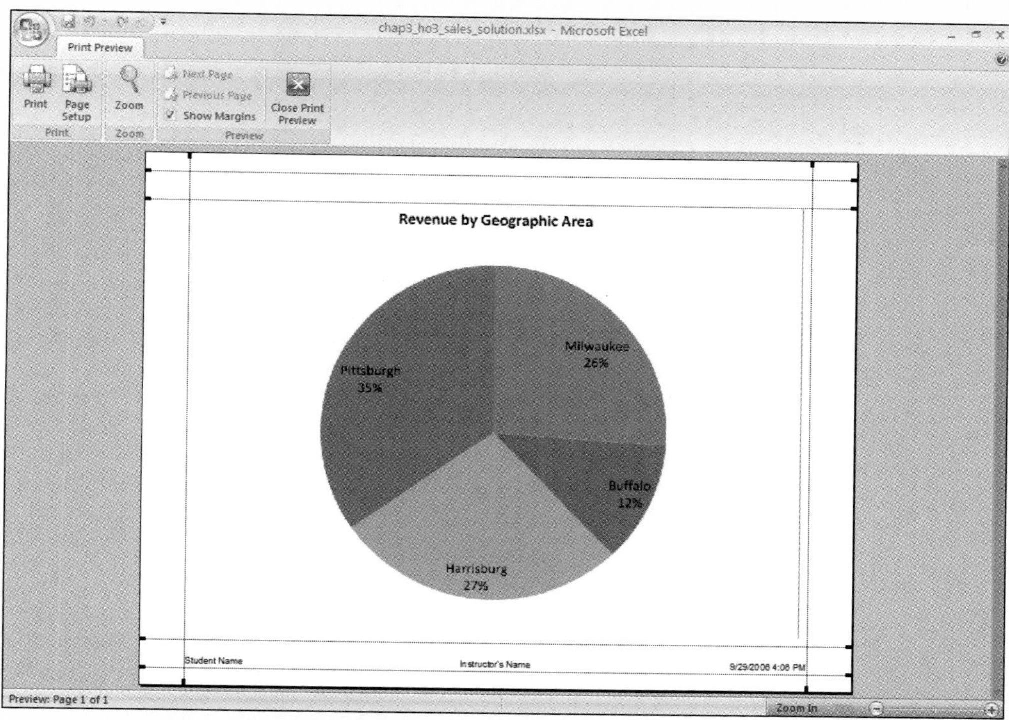

Figure 3.40 Print Preview of Chart with Custom Footers and Margin

Step 9
Save and View Chart as Web Page

a. Start Excel and open the *chap3_ho3_sales_solution* workbook.

b. Click on the **Revenue by Product tab** to make it the active sheet. Click the **Office Button** and select **Save As**.

c. Select **Web Page** from the *Save as type* list. Click **Selection: Chart**. Title the file appropriately and save it to the desired location.

d. You can preview the chart or workbook by opening your browser, navigating to the location of the Web page, and opening it.

Summary

1. **Choose a chart type.** A chart is a graphic representation of data in a worksheet. The type of chart chosen depends on the message to be conveyed. A pie chart is best for proportional relationships. A column or bar chart is used to show actual numbers rather than percentages. A line chart is preferable for time-related data. The choice between a clustered and a stacked column chart depends on the intended message. A clustered chart shows the contribution of each data point, but the total for each series is not as clear as with a stacked column chart. The stacked column chart, on the other hand, shows the totals clearly, but the contribution of the individual data points is obscured because the segments do not start at zero. It is important that charts are created accurately and that they do not mislead the reader. Stacked column charts should not add dissimilar quantities such as units and dollars.
2. **Create a chart.** Using the Insert tab is an effortless way to create charts. The title of a chart can help to convey the message. A neutral title such as "Revenue by City" leaves the reader to draw his or her own conclusion. Using a different title such as "Boston Leads All Cities" or "New York Is Trailing Badly" sends a very different message.
3. **Modify a chart.** Once created, a chart can be enhanced with arrows and text boxes. Multiple data series may be specified in either rows or columns. If the data are in rows, the first row is assumed to contain the category labels, and the first column is assumed to contain the legend. Conversely, if the data are in columns, the first column is assumed to contain the category labels, and the first row the legend.
4. **Enhance charts with graphic shapes.** These objects can be moved or sized and/or modified with respect to their color and other properties. The chart itself can also be modified using various tabs.
5. **Embed charts.** A chart may be embedded in a worksheet or created in a separate chart sheet. An embedded chart may be moved within a worksheet by selecting it and dragging it to its new location. An embedded chart may be sized by selecting it and dragging any of the sizing handles in the desired direction. Object embedding enables the creation of a compound document containing data from multiple applications. The essential difference between linking and embedding is whether the object is stored within the compound document (embedding) or in its own file (linking). An embedded object is stored in the compound document, which in turn becomes the only user (client) of that object. A linked object is stored in its own file, and the compound document is one of many potential users of that object. The same chart can be linked to a Word document and a PowerPoint presentation.
6. **Print charts.** Several options exist for printing charts. Users can print one chart, several charts, or a combination of the worksheet and the charts. Placing a chart on a separate sheet enables the user to print the chart in full-page format. Charts and worksheets can be saved as Web pages in HTML format and then be published to the World Wide Web (WWW).

Key Terms

Bar chart 372
Category label 369
Chart 369
Chart area 370
Clustered column chart 371
Column chart 370
Data label 389
Data point 369
Data series 369
Doughnut chart 374
Exploded pie chart 373
Legend 371
Line chart 374
Multiple data series 371
Pie chart 372
Plot area 370
Scatter (XY) chart 375
Stacked column chart 371
Stock chart 375
Three-dimensional pie chart ..373
X or horizontal axis 370
Y or vertical axis 370

Multiple Choice

1. Which type of chart is best to portray proportion or market share?
   (a) Pie chart
   (b) Line chart
   (c) Column chart
   (d) Combination chart

2. Which of the following chart types is *not* suitable to display multiple data series?
   (a) Pie chart
   (b) Horizontal bar chart
   (c) Column chart
   (d) All of the above are equally suitable.

3. Which of the following is best to display additive information from multiple data series?
   (a) A column chart with the data series stacked one on top of another
   (b) A column chart with the data series side by side
   (c) A scatter chart with two data series
   (d) A pie chart with five to ten wedges

4. A workbook can contain:
   (a) A separate chart sheet for every workbook
   (b) A separate workbook for every chart sheet
   (c) A sheet with both a workbook and chart
   (d) A separate chart sheet for every worksheet

5. Which of the following is true regarding an embedded chart?
   (a) It can be moved elsewhere within the worksheet.
   (b) It can be made larger or smaller.
   (c) Both (a) and (b).
   (d) Neither (a) nor (b).

6. Which of the following will produce a shortcut menu?
   (a) Pointing to a workbook tab and clicking the right mouse button
   (b) Pointing to an embedded chart and clicking the right mouse button
   (c) Pointing to a selected cell range and clicking the right mouse button
   (d) All of the above

7. Which of the following is done *prior* to beginning to create a chart?
   (a) The data series are selected.
   (b) The location of the embedded chart within the worksheet is specified.
   (c) The workbook is saved.
   (d) The worksheet is formatted.

8. Which of the following will display sizing handles when selected?
   (a) An embedded chart
   (b) The title of a chart
   (c) A text box or arrow
   (d) All of the above

9. How do you switch between open applications?
   (a) Click the appropriate button on the taskbar.
   (b) Click the Start button in the taskbar.
   (c) Use Shift+Tab to cycle through the applications.
   (d) Use Crtl+~ to cycle through the applications.

10. To represent multiple data series on the same chart:
    (a) The data series must be in rows, and the rows must be adjacent to one another on the worksheet.
    (b) The data series must be in columns, and the columns must be adjacent to one another on the worksheet.
    (c) The data series may be in rows or columns so long as they are adjacent to one another.
    (d) The data series may be in rows or columns with no requirement to be next to one another.

11. If multiple data series are selected and rows are specified:
    (a) The first row will be used for the category labels.
    (b) The first row will be used for the legend.
    (c) The first column will be used for the legend.
    (d) The first column will be used for the category labels.

Multiple Choice Continued...

12. If multiple data series are selected and columns are specified:
    (a) The first column will be used for the category (X axis) labels.
    (b) The first row will be used for the legend.
    (c) Both (a) and (b).
    (d) Neither (a) nor (b).

13. Which of the following is true about the scale on the Y axis in a column chart that plots multiple data series clustered versus one that stacks the values one on top of another?
    (a) The scale for the stacked columns chart contains larger values than the clustered chart.
    (b) The scale for the clustered columns contains larger values than the stacked columns.
    (c) The values on the scale will be the same for both charts.
    (d) The values will be different, but it is not possible to tell which chart has higher values.

14. A workbook includes a revenue worksheet with two embedded charts. The workbook also includes one chart in its own worksheet. How many files does it take to store this workbook?
    (a) 1
    (b) 2
    (c) 3
    (d) 4

15. You have created a Word document and embedded an Excel worksheet in that document. You make a change to the worksheet. What happens to the worksheet in the Word document?
    (a) It will be updated when you select the Refresh Data command.
    (b) It is unchanged.
    (c) It is automatically updated to reflect the changes.
    (d) You cannot change the worksheet because you have embedded it in a Word document.

16. You have selected cells B5:B10 as the data series for a chart and specified the data series are in columns. Which of the following is the legend text?
    (a) Cells B5 through F5
    (b) Cells C6 through F10
    (c) Cells B5 through B10
    (d) It is impossible to determine from the information given.

17. The same data range is used as the basis for an embedded pie chart, as well as a column chart in a chart sheet. Which chart(s) will change if you change the values in the data range?
    (a) The column chart
    (b) The pie chart
    (c) Both the pie chart and the column chart
    (d) Neither the pie chart nor the column chart

Practice Exercises

1 Vacation Park Admissions

Your summer job is with the professional organization representing theme parks across the country. You have gathered data on theme park admissions in four areas of the country. In this exercise, you will finish the worksheet and create charts. The completed version of the worksheet is shown in Figure 3.41.

a. Open the *chap3_pe1_vacation* workbook and save it as **chap3_pe1_vacation_solution.**

b. Select **cells B8:E8**. Click **AutoSum** in the Editing group on the Home tab to compute the total for each quarter. Select **cells F4:F8**, and then click **AutoSum.**

c. Select **cells B4:F8** and format these cells as **Number with Commas**. Bold the row and column headings and the totals. Center the entries in **cells B3:F3**. Select **cells A1:F1**, then click **Merge and Center** in the Alignment group on the Home tab to center the title. With the same cells selected, choose the **Blue, Accent 1** theme color from the **Fill color** list. Increase the title font size to **14 points** and change the Font color to **white.** Select **cells B3:F3** and change the Font color to the same theme color used in row 1. Similarly, change **cell A8**. Save the workbook.

d. Complete the substeps to create a column chart that shows the number of admissions for each region and for each quarter within each region and insert the graphic, as shown in Figure 3.41:

- Select **cells A3:E7**. Click the **Insert tab** and click **Column** in the Chart group. When the Column chart type and Clustered column subtype are selected, the chart appears on Admissions Data worksheet.
- Click the outline of the chart to select it. Using the four-headed arrow, drag the chart into position under the worksheet.
- Right-click the legend and select **Bold** and **Italic** to format the legend.
- Click the **Insert tab** and click the left facing arrow in the Shapes group. Click and drag to create a thick arrow that points to the **1st Quarter South** column. Release the mouse. The arrow is selected, and you are viewing the Format tab.
- Click **Text Box** in the Insert Shapes group on the Format tab to insert a text box. Click and drag a text box on top of the thick arrow. Release the mouse. Enter text by typing **South First-Quarter Admissions High**. Select the text you just typed and use the Mini toolbar to change the font to **9-point** bold white.

e. Complete the substeps to create a pie chart, in its own sheet, that shows the percentage of the total number of admissions in each region:

- Select **cells A4:A7**, then press and hold **Ctrl** while selecting **cells F4:F7**.
- Click the **Insert tab** to make it active. Click **Pie** in the Chart group and the pie chart appears on the Admissions Data sheet. Click **Move Chart** on the Design tab, click the **New Sheet** option, and click **OK**. Right-click the **Chart 1 tab** just created and select **Rename** from the shortcut menu. Type **Pie Chart** and press **Enter**.
- Right-click any pie wedge and select **Add Data Labels** to add data labels to the chart area. Right-click any pie wedge and select **Format Data Labels** to display the Format Data Labels dialog box. Click **Label Options**, and then click the **Category Name** and **Percentage check boxes** to format the data labels. Remove the check from the **Value** check box.
- Change the values in the data labels to percentages by clicking **Number** in Label options, click **Percentage** in **Category** options and click **Close** to accept the settings and close the dialog box. Right-click any data label and increase the font size to **14-point** italic.

...continued on Next Page

- Click **Legend** in the Labels group on the Layout tab and select **None** to delete the legend.
- Click **Chart Title** in the Labels group on the Layout tab and select **Centered Overlay Title**. Type **Vacation Park Admissions by Region**.

f. Complete the substeps to create a stacked column chart, in its own sheet, showing the number of admissions for each quarter and for each region within each quarter:

- Select **cells A3:E7**. Click the **Insert tab** and click **Column** in the Chart group. When the Column chart type and Stacked Column in 3-D subtype are selected, the chart appears on Sheet1.
- Click **Move Chart** on the Design tab, click the **New sheet** option, and click **OK.** Right-click the **Chart-2 tab** just created and select **Rename**. Type **Stacked Column** and press **Enter.**
- Click in the outline of the chart to select the entire chart. Click the **Data Labels** list in the Labels group on the Layout tab and select **Show**. Click **Chart Title** in the **Labels** group on the **Layout** tab and select **Centered Overlay Title**. Type **Admissions by Quarter and Region Within Quarter**. Change the color of each worksheet tab to **Accent 1**.

g. Click the **Stacked Column tab** to make it the active sheet. Click the **Office Button** and select **Save As**. Select **Web Page** from the *Save as type* list. Click **Selection: Chart.** Click **Change Title** and type **Vacation Web Page**, then click **OK** and save it. You can preview the chart by opening your Internet browser, navigating to the location of the Web page, and opening it.

h. Create a custom header for the worksheet that includes your name, your course, and your instructor's name. Create a custom footer for the worksheet that includes the name of the worksheet. Print the entire workbook, consisting of the worksheet in Figure 3.41, plus the additional sheets you created. Use portrait orientation for the **Admissions Data** worksheet and landscape orientation for the other worksheets. Save and close the workbook.

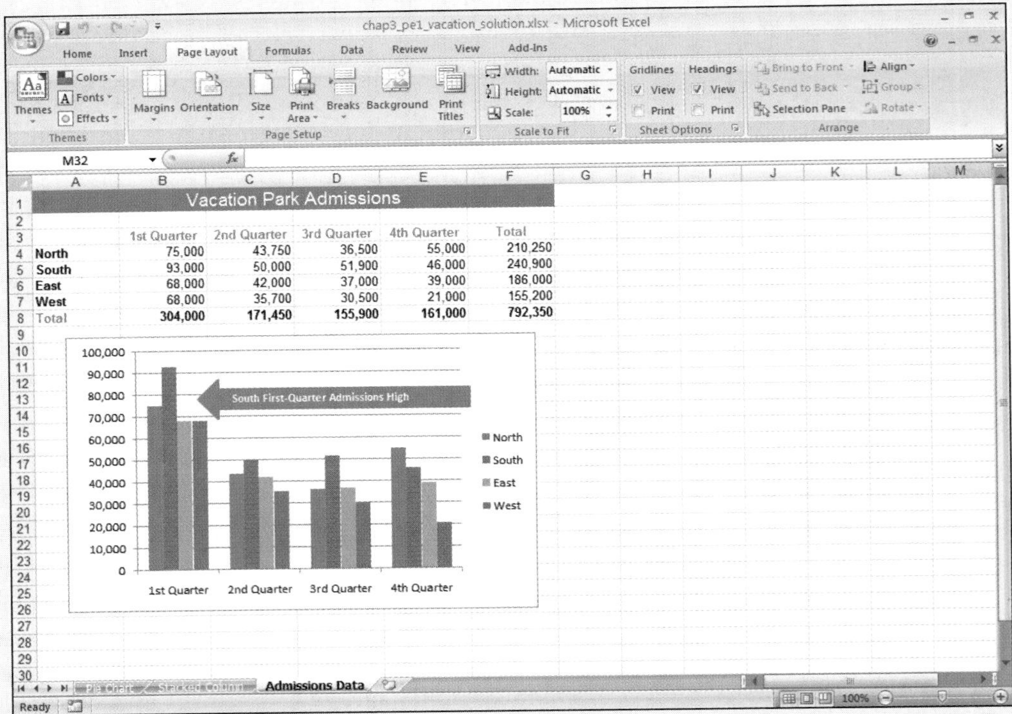

Figure 3.41 Vacation Park Charts

...continued on Next Page

2 AnytimeTalk, Inc.—Chart Formatting

The worksheet shown in Figure 3.42 shows third-quarter revenues for each salesperson at AnytimeTalk, Inc., the cellular company where you will do your internship this summer. One of your assigned duties is to complete the Fourth-Quarter Revenue worksheet and create a column chart showing a comparison of each salesperson's total sales for the fourth quarter. The chart is to be formatted for a professional presentation.

a. Open the *chap3_pe2_talk* workbook and save it as **chap3_pe2_talk_solution**.
b. Click and drag to select **cells E3:E7**. Click **AutoSum** in the Editing group on the Home tab to compute the total for each salesperson. Click and drag to select **cells B8:E8**, and then click **AutoSum** to compute the totals for each month and the total for the quarter.
c. Click and drag to select **cells B3:E8** and format these cells as **Currency with no decimals**. Bold the row and column headings and the totals. Center the entries in **cells B2:E2**.
d. Select **cells A1:E1**, then click **Merge and Center** in the Alignment group on the Home tab to center the title. With the same cells selected, choose **Orange, Accent 6** from the theme colors in the **Fill color** list. Increase the title font size to **18 points** and change the Font color to **Orange, Accent 6, Darker 50%**.
e. Increase the height of row 1 as necessary to display the title. Select **cells A2:E2** and change the Font color to the same theme color used in row 1.
f. Select **cells A4:E4** and use Fill color in the Font group on the Home tab to highlight the cells with a theme shade. Similarly, change **cell A8**. Save the workbook.
g. Select **cells A3:A7**, and while holding **Ctrl**, select **cells E3:E7**. Click the **Insert tab** and click **Column** in the Chart group. When the Column chart type and Clustered Cylinder column subtype are selected, the chart appears on the Sales Data sheet.
h. Click the white background of the chart to select it and using the four-headed arrow, drag the chart into position below the worksheet data. Right-click the legend and select **Delete** to delete the legend.
i. Right-click any cylinder and select **Add Data Labels** to add data labels to the chart area. Right-click any cylinder and select **Format Data Labels** to display the Format Data Labels dialog box.
j. Triple-click the second column to select just this column. Right-click the selected column, select **Format Data Point**, click the **Fill** option in the associated dialog box, click **Gradient Fill**, and then change the color of this column to the coordinating theme shade. Select **Close** to close the dialog box.
k. Click in **cell A4** and enter your name. The value on the X axis changes automatically to reflect the entry in cell A4. Open the **Chart Title** menu in the Labels group on the Layout tab. Click **Above Chart** and type **Fourth-Quarter Revenues** as the title of the chart.
l. Click the **Insert tab**. Click **Line Callout 1** in the Shapes group. Click and drag to create a callout that points to your cylinder. Release the mouse. The callout is selected, and you are viewing the Format tab. Change the Shape Fill color and the Shape Outline color by selecting appropriate theme colors from the **Shape Fill** list and the **Shape Outline** list in the Shape Styles group on the Format tab.
m. Click **Text Box** in the Insert Shapes group on the Format tab to insert a text box. Click and drag a text box on top of the callout. Release the mouse. Enter text by clicking **Text Fill** in the WordArt group of the Format tab and type the words **This Cylinder Represents My Data**. Select the text you just typed, right-click the selected text, and change the font to **10 point** from the Mini toolbar.
n. Right-click the border of the chart, select **Format Chart Area**, then change the border to include rounded corners with a shadow effect. Use the Border Styles and Shadow options to make the changes.
o. Save the workbook and print the completed worksheet. Close the workbook.

...continued on Next Page

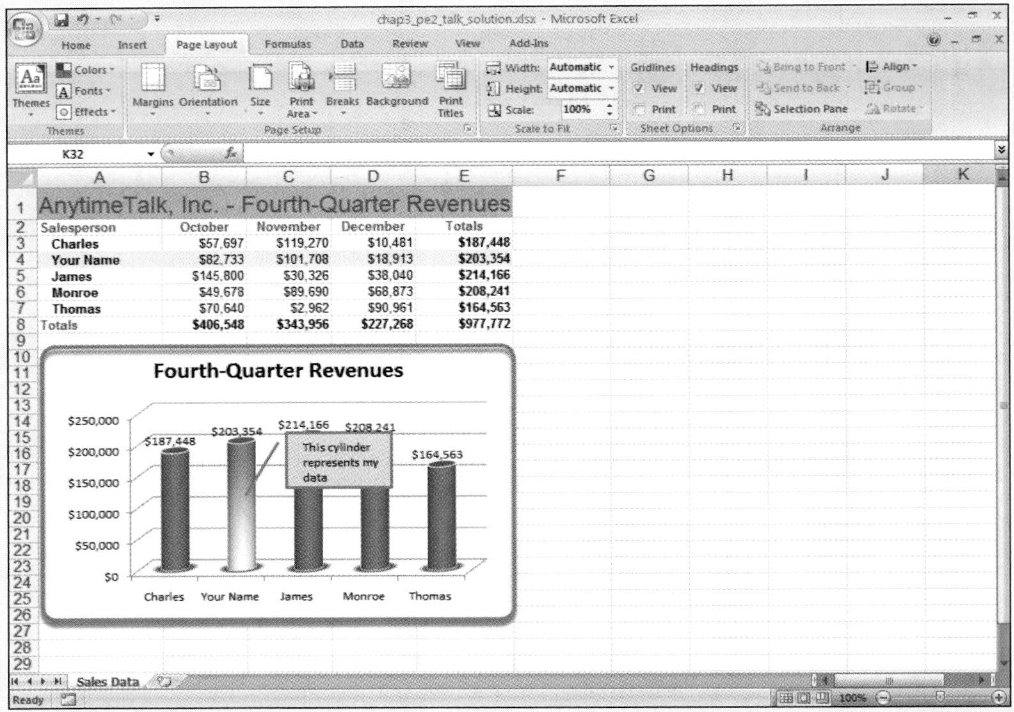

Figure 3.42 AnytimeTalk, Inc.

3 Printing Charts

Your sister asked you to chart weekly sales from her chain of mystery bookstores. As shown in Figure 3.43, stores are in four cities, and you must plot four product lines. You will create the charts as embedded objects on the worksheet. Do not be concerned about the placement of each chart until you have completed all four charts. The first chart is a clustered column and emphasizes the sales in each city (the data are in rows). The second chart is a stacked column version of the first chart. The third chart (that begins in column H of the worksheet) is a clustered column chart that emphasizes the sales in each product line (the data are in columns). The fourth chart is a stacked column version of the third chart. Figure 3.43 shows a reduced screen view of the four charts.

a. Open the *chap3_pe3_print* workbook and save it as **chap3_pe3_print_solution**.

b. Select **cells A2:E6** and click the **2-D Column** area of **Column** in the Charts group on the Insert tab to embed a clustered column chart. With the chart selected, click **Style 16** in the Chart Styles group on the Design tab. To add a chart title, click **Layout 1** in the Chart Layouts group on the Design tab. To change the default title, click the words *Chart Title* to select the words and type **Weekly Sales by Location and Product Line.** Right-click the already selected title and change the font size to 14 points. Drag the chart into position below the workbook. Save the workbook.

c. Select the chart, click the **Home tab**, click **Copy** in the Clipboard group to copy the chart, click in **cell A27**, and click **Paste** in the Clipboard group on the Home tab. With the chart selected, click the **Design tab** and click **Change Chart Type** in the Type group. Click **Stacked Column** in the Column area of the Change Chart Type dialog box and click **OK**. Save the workbook.

d. Select the **first** chart, click the **Home tab**, click in **cell H2**, and click **Paste**. With the chart selected, click the **Design tab** and click **Switch Row and Column** in the Data group. Save the workbook.

e. Select the chart, click the **Home tab**, click **Copy** to copy the chart, click in **cell H19**, and click **Paste** on the Home tab. With the chart selected, click the **Design tab** and click **Change Chart Type** in the Type group. Click the **Stacked Column** in the Column area of the Change Chart Type dialog box and click **OK**. Save the workbook.

...continued on Next Page

f. Click **Page Break Preview** in the Workbook Views group on the View tab. Your screen should be similar to Figure 3.43. You will see one or more dotted lines that show where the page breaks will occur. You will also see a message indicating that you can change the location of the page breaks. Click **OK** after you have read the message.
g. Remove any existing page breaks by clicking and dragging the solid blue line that indicates the break. (You can insert horizontal or vertical page breaks by clicking the appropriate cell, clicking **Breaks** in the Page Setup group on the Page Layout **tab**, and selecting **Page Break**.) To return to Normal view, click **Normal** in the Workbook Views group on the View tab.
h. Print the worksheet and four embedded charts on one page. Change to landscape orientation for a more attractive layout. Open the **Orientation** list in the Page Setup group on the Page Layout tab and select **Landscape**. Click the **Page Layout tab** and use the Page Setup dialog box to create a custom header with your name, your course, and your instructor's name. Create a custom footer that contains today's date, the name of the workbook, and the current time. Click **OK** to close the dialog box. Print the worksheet. Save and close the workbook.
i. Write a short note to your instructor that describes the differences between the charts. Suggest a different title for one or more charts that helps to convey a specific message.

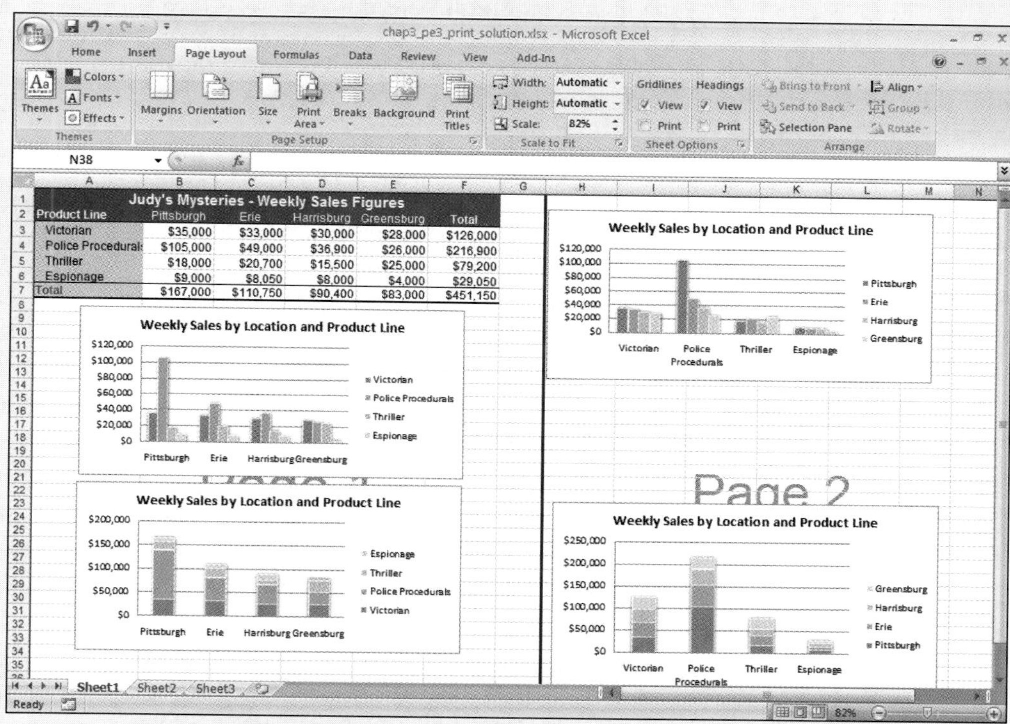

Figure 3.43 Printing Charts

4 Stock Price Comparisons

Figure 3.44 contains a combination chart to display different kinds of information on different scales for multiple data series. You start by creating a clustered column chart for the revenue and profits, and then you create a second data series to chart the stock prices as a line. Two different scales are necessary because the magnitudes of the numbers differ significantly. Your investment club asked you to make a recommendation about the purchase of the stock based on your analysis.

a. Open the *chap3_pe4_stock* workbook and save it as **chap3_pe4_stock_solution**.
b. Select **cells A1:F4**. Click the **Insert tab** and click **Column** in the Charts group. Then select **Clustered Column** from the 2-D Column row.

...continued on Next Page

c. Click chart outline to select the chart and using the four-headed arrow, drag the chart into position under the worksheet. Right-click the legend and select **Format Legend**. In the *Legend Options* section, click **Bottom** as the legend position and click **Close**.

You are now going to add a secondary vertical axis to display Stock Price because the size of the numbers differs significantly from Revenue and Profit.

d. Click the chart to make it active. Click the **Format tab**. Click the **Chart Elements down arrow** in the Current Selection group and select **Series "Stock Price"** as the data series to plot on the secondary axis.

e. Click **Format Selection** in the Current Selection group and click **Secondary Axis** in *Series Options* in the Format Data Series dialog box. Click **Close** to close the dialog box. Click the **Layout tab**, click **Axes** in the Axes group, select **Secondary Vertical Axis**, and select **Show Default Axis**.

f. Change the data series to a line chart to distinguish the secondary axis. Click the **Format tab**, click the **Chart Elements down arrow** in the Current Selection group, and select **Series "Stock Price."** Click the **Design tab**, click **Change Chart Type** in the Type group, select **Line** as the chart type, and then click the first example of a line chart. Click **OK** to view the combination chart.

g. Right-click on the chart but above the plot area, select **Format Chart Area**, click **Border Styles**, check **Rounded Corners** and increase the width to 1.5 pts, click **Border Color**, click **Solid Line**, and choose a coordinating theme color from the color selection menu. Click **Shadow** and select an appropriate shadow from the **Presets** list. Click **Close** to see the customized border around the chart.

h. Deselect the chart. Click the **Page Layout tab** and open the *Page Setup* dialog box. Click **Landscape** for orientation, click the **Margins tab**, and click the **Horizontally** and **Vertically check boxes** to center the worksheet and chart on the page. Click the **Header/Footer tab** create a custom header for the worksheet that includes **your name**, **your course name**, and **your instructor's name**. Create a custom footer that contains the name of the **file** in which the worksheet is contained, **today's date**, and the **current time**. Save the workbook and print your worksheet. Close the workbook.

i. What do you think should be the more important factor influencing a company's stock price, its revenue (sales) or its profit (net income)? Could the situation depicted in the worksheet occur in the real world? Summarize your thoughts in a brief note to your instructor. Print the document.

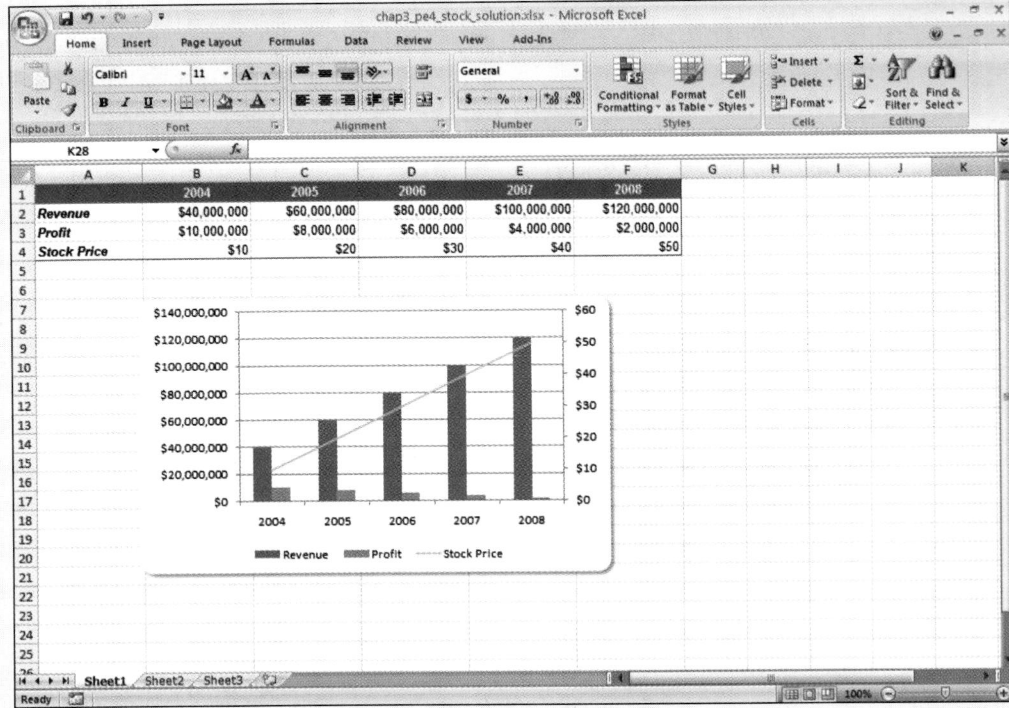

Figure 3.44 Stock Price Comparison

Mid-Level Exercises

1 The Next Car You Purchase

The Word document in Figure 3.45 displays descriptive information about a car you are interested in purchasing, a picture of the car, and a hyperlink to the Web site where the information was obtained. In addition, the document is linked to an Excel workbook that computes the car payment for you, based on the loan parameters that you provide. Your assignment is to create a similar document based on any car you choose.

a. Open the *chap3_mid1_auto* document and save it as **chap3_mid1_auto_solution**.

b. Locate a Web site that contains information about the car you are interested in. You can go to the Web site of the manufacturer, or you can go to a general site such as carpoint.msn.com, which contains information about all makes and models. Select the car you want and obtain the retail price of the car.

c. Enter the price of the car, a hypothetical down payment, the interest rate of the car loan, and the term of the loan in the indicated cells. The monthly payment will be determined automatically by the PMT function that is stored in the workbook. Use Help if needed to review the PMT function. Save the workbook.

d. Select **cells A3:B9** (the cells that contain the information you want to insert into the Word document) and copy the selected range to the Clipboard.

e. Open the partially completed *chap3_mid1_auto* Word document. Use the Paste Special option to paste the worksheet data. Save the Word document as **chap3_mid1_auto solution**.

f. Use the taskbar to return to the Excel workbook. Change the amount of the down payment to **$8,500** and the interest rate for your loan to **6%**. Save the workbook. Close Excel. Return to the Word document, which should reflect the updated loan information.

g. Return to the Web page that contains the information about your car. Right-click the picture of the car that appears within the Web page and select **Save As** to save the picture of the car to your computer. Use the **Insert** command to insert the picture that you just obtained.

h. Complete the Word document by inserting some descriptive information about your car. Print the completed document. Save and close the document.

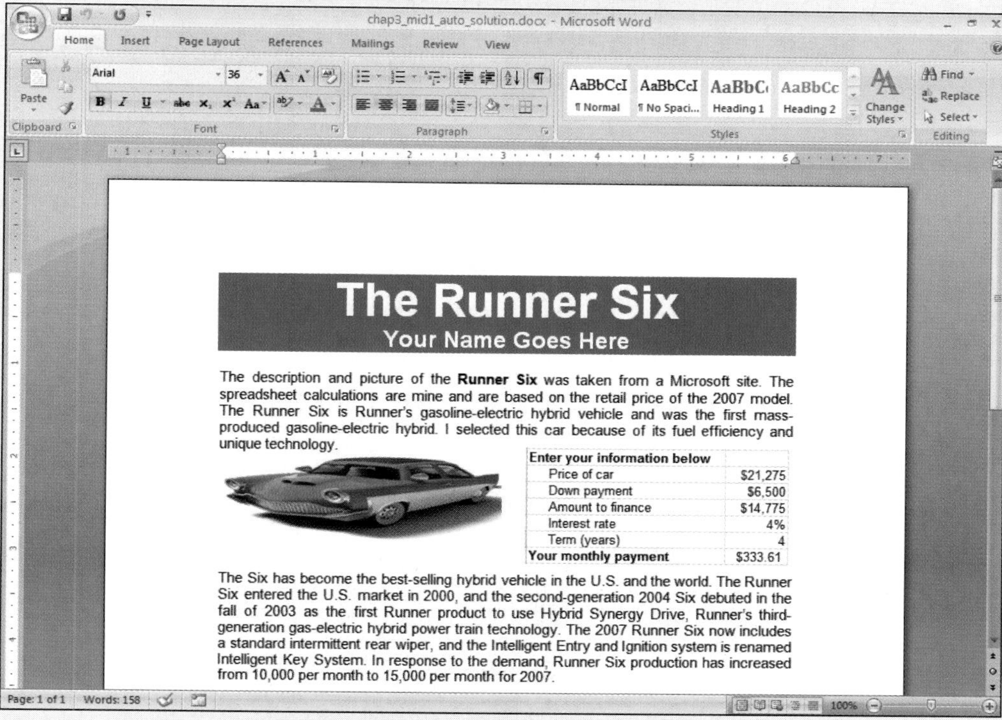

Figure 3.45 The Next Car You Purchase

...continued on Next Page

2 Comparison of Rows and Columns

Figure 3.46 displays a worksheet with two similar charts detailing annual visits to different exhibits at the local Petting Zoo, one that plots data by rows and the other by columns. The distinction depends on the message you want to deliver. Both charts are correct. You collected the data at your summer job at the Petting Zoo and must now plot it for your intern supervisor as part of the analysis of the most popular animals at the zoo. You will create both charts shown and for comparison purposes create two more charts on a new sheet to determine the best presentation of data.

a. Open the *chap3_mid2_zoo* workbook and save it as **chap3_mid2_zoo_solution**.

b. Use **AutoSum** to compute the total number of visits for each animal category and each quarter. Rename the Sheet1 tab as **Side by Side Columns**. Format the worksheet in an attractive manner by matching the formatting shown in Figure 3.46.

c. Create each of the charts in Figure 3.46 as embedded charts on the current worksheet. The first chart specifies that the data series are in columns. The second chart specifies the data series are in rows.

d. Change to landscape orientation when the chart is printed. Create a custom header that includes your name, your course, and your instructor's name. Create a custom footer with the name of the worksheet, today's date, and the current time. Specify that the worksheet will be printed at 110% to create a more attractive printed page. Be sure, however, that the worksheet and associated charts fit on a single page.

e. Copy the worksheet and name the duplicate worksheet as **Stacked Columns**.

f. Select the first chart in the newly created Stacked Columns worksheet. Change the chart type to Stacked Columns. Change the chart type of the second chart to Stacked Columns as well. Repeat step d for the Stacked Columns worksheet.

g. Print the completed workbook (both worksheets). Add a short note that summarizes the difference between plotting data in rows versus columns and between clustered column charts and stacked column charts. Save and close the workbook.

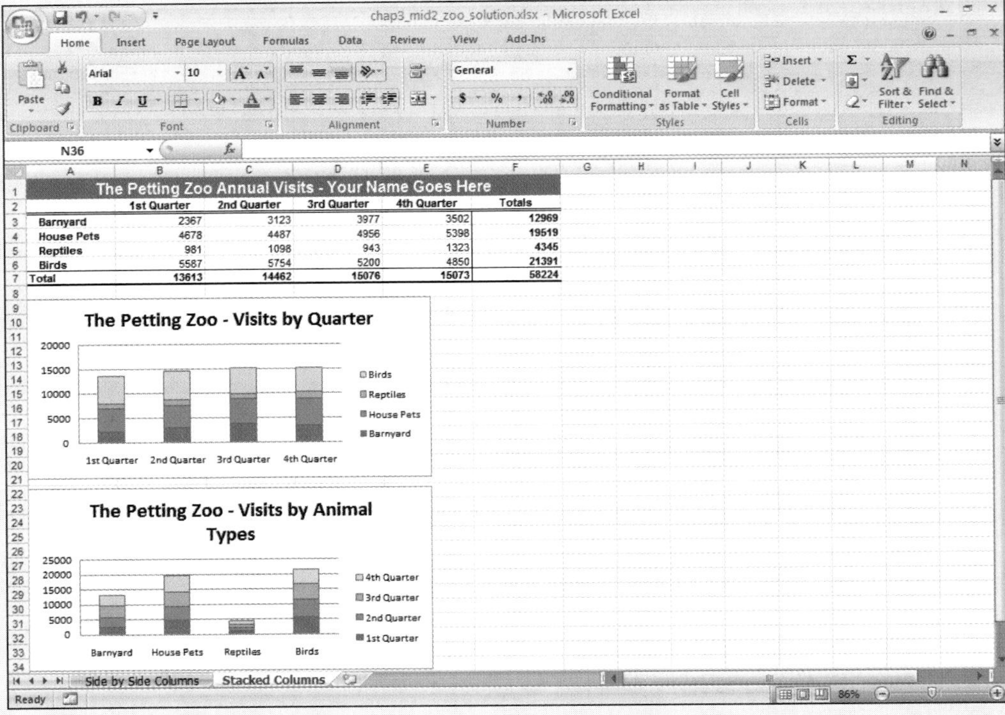

Figure 3.46 Comparison of Rows and Columns

...continued on Next Page

3 Home Arts

Your first job is as a management trainee at the Needlework Nook, a store specializing in home arts. The store manager has asked you to examine sales for the four quarters of the current year in five categories. She also has asked you to chart the sales figures. Complete the partially completed version of the spreadsheet in Figure 3.47 and create a chart that highlights quarterly product sales for the current year.

a. Open the *chap3_mid3_homearts* workbook and save it as **chap3_mid3_homearts_solution**.

b. Use the **AutoSum** command to compute the totals for the quarters and categories of products. Format the completed worksheet in an attractive manner duplicating the formatting exactly as shown. Rename sheet 1 as **Current Year**.

c. Create a stacked column chart based on the data in **cells A2:E7**. Specify that the data series are in rows so that each column represents total sales for each quarter. Display the legend on the right side of the chart. Save the chart in its own sheet called **Graphical Analysis**.

d. Experiment with variations of the chart created. Change the chart type from a stacked column to a clustered column and change the orientation of the data series from rows to columns. Choose the chart most appropriate to show the sales by quarter and category. Also experiment with the placement of the legend by moving to the bottom and the top. After experimenting with the placement of the legend, place it to the right of the chart.

e. Add data labels to the stacks on the Graphical Analysis sheet. Change the color of the worksheet tabs to **Aqua Accent 5** for the Current Year tab and **Aqua, Accent 5, Darker 50%** for the Graphical Analysis tab.

f. Use the Page Setup dialog box to display gridlines and row and column headings. Create a custom header that includes your name, your course, and your instructor's name. Create a custom footer with the name of the worksheet, today's date, and the current time.

g. Print the completed workbook consisting of two worksheets. Save and close the workbook.

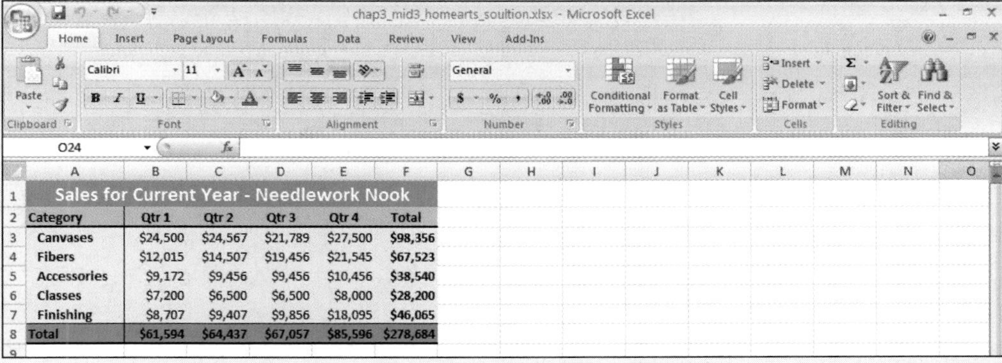

Sales for Current Year - Needlework Nook					
Category	Qtr 1	Qtr 2	Qtr 3	Qtr 4	Total
Canvases	$24,500	$24,567	$21,789	$27,500	$98,356
Fibers	$12,015	$14,507	$19,456	$21,545	$67,523
Accessories	$9,172	$9,456	$9,456	$10,456	$38,540
Classes	$7,200	$6,500	$6,500	$8,000	$28,200
Finishing	$8,707	$9,407	$9,856	$18,095	$46,065
Total	$61,594	$64,437	$67,057	$85,596	$278,684

Figure 3.47 Home Arts

...continued on Next Page

4 Study Analysis

Your sociology professor wants to know the correlation between time spent studying for quizzes and quiz scores, if any. You recorded the time spent studying for 10 quizzes and asked two friends to do the same thing. Now you must plot the data in a scatter chart and complete the analysis. Use the worksheet shown in Figure 3.48 and chart your data.

a. Open the *chap3_mid4_scatter* workbook and save it as **chap3_mid4_scatter_solution**.

b. Insert a row above the worksheet and type the title **Test Analysis**. Center the title above the worksheet. Format the completed worksheet in an attractive manner. You do not have to duplicate our formatting exactly.

c. Create a scatter chart based on the data in **cells A2:E12**. Display the legend to the right of the chart.

d. Insert a chart title **Study Time and Quiz Scores.** Add an X-axis title **Time in Hours** and a Y-axis title **Test Score**.

e. Change the chart type to **Scatter with Smooth Lines and Markers**. Change the chart style so the colors are more vibrant.

f. Remember to add your analysis of the correlation between study time and quiz scores below the chart.

g. Delete the Sheet2 and Sheet3 tabs and rename Sheet1 as **Test Scores**. Add a tab color, Red, to the Test Scores tab.

h. Use the Page Setup dialog box to display gridlines and row and column headings. Create a custom header that includes your name, your course, and your instructor's name. Create a custom footer with the name of the worksheet, today's date, and the current time.

i. Print the completed workbook making sure the worksheet, chart, and analysis fit on one page. Save and close the workbook.

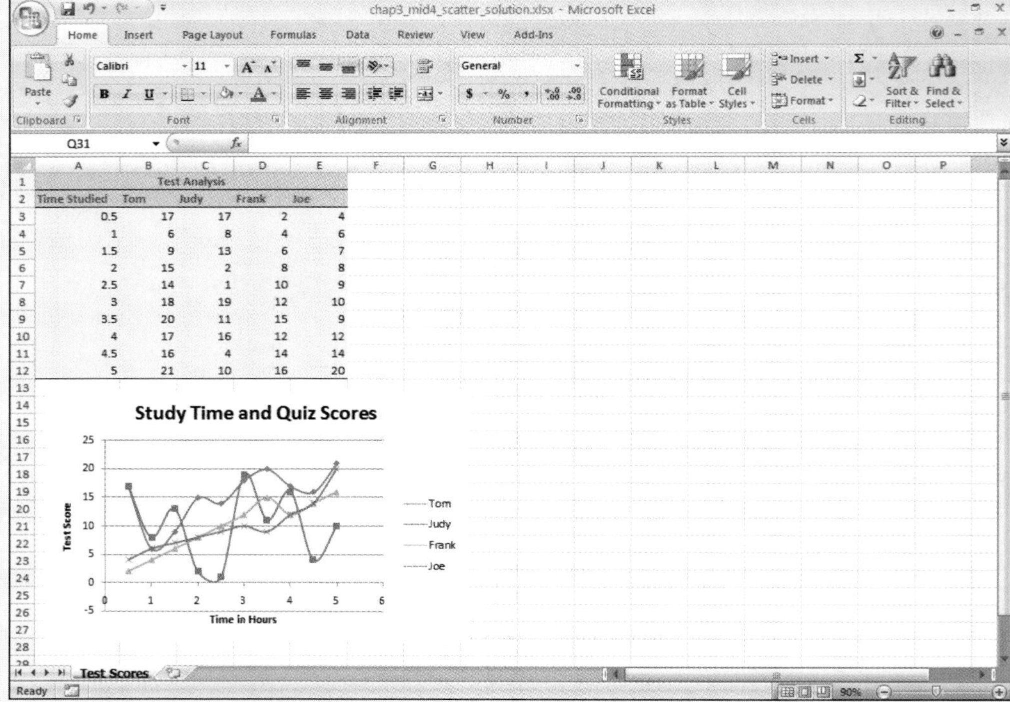

Test Analysis

Time Studied	Tom	Judy	Frank	Joe
0.5	17	17	2	4
1	6	8	4	6
1.5	9	13	6	7
2	15	2	8	8
2.5	14	1	10	9
3	18	19	12	10
3.5	20	11	15	9
4	17	16	12	12
4.5	16	4	14	14
5	21	10	16	20

Figure 3.48 Study Analysis

...continued on Next Page

5 Computer Sales Analysis

Your computer professor has asked you to provide a comparison of computer sales across the country. Complete the worksheet shown in Figure 3.49 but include three charts to show the sales in a variety of ways. Include a summary indicating the most effective chart and why you consider it the most effective for comparing sales data.

a. Open the *chap3_mid5_computer* workbook and save it as **chap3_mid5_computer_solution.**

b. Use **AutoSum** to compute the totals for the corporation in column F and row 6.

c. Format **cells B3:F6** as currency, zero decimal. Center the title above the worksheet. Format the completed worksheet in an attractive manner. You do not have to duplicate our formatting exactly.

d. Use the completed worksheet as the basis for a stacked column chart with the data plotted in rows.

e. Create a pie chart showing total sales by city, placing it on a separate sheet. Rename the sheet as **Sales by City**.

f. Make a cluster column chart, placing it on a separate sheet and renaming the sheet **Sales by Product**. Include a legend below the chart, a chart title, axes titles, and a shape to draw attention to the city with the highest notebook sales. Include an appropriate text message on the shape.

g. Use the Page Setup dialog box to display gridlines and row and column headings. Create a custom footer that contains your name, the name of the worksheet, and today's date. Print the entire workbook. Save and close the workbook.

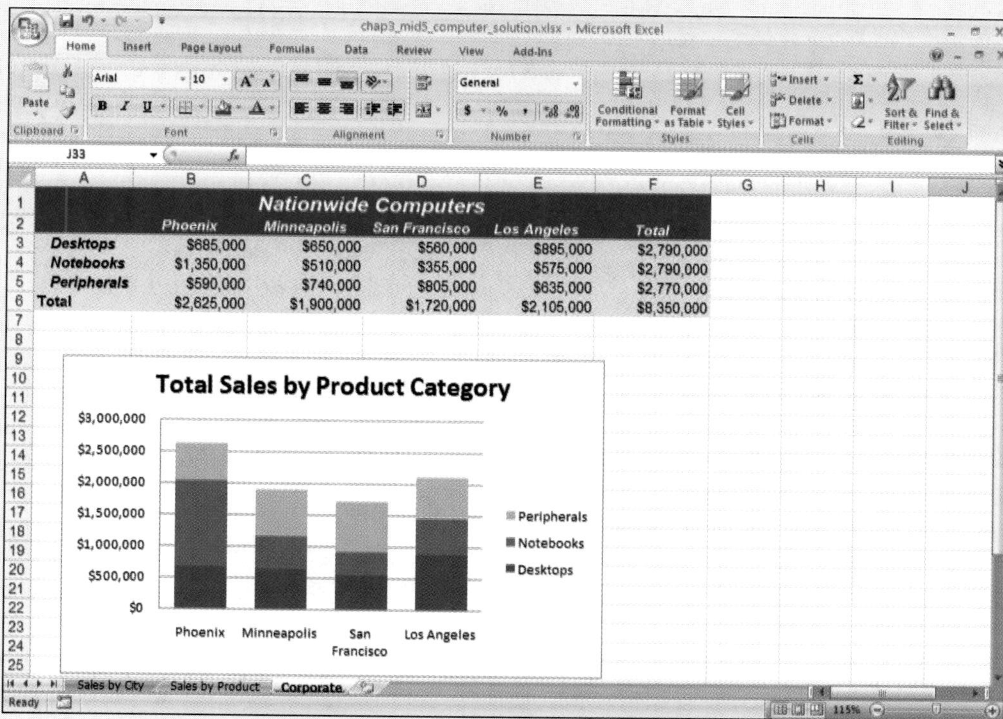

Figure 3.49 Computer Sales Analysis

Capstone Exercise

What if people split a dinner check using the principles of the progressive income tax that is central to our tax code? Five lifelong friends of various means meet once a week for dinner and split the $100 check according to their ability to pay. Tom, Dick, and Harry are of relatively modest means and pay $1, $4, and $9, respectively. Ben and Ken are far more prosperous and pay $18 and $68, respectively.

The friends were quite satisfied with the arrangement until the owner offered a rebate. "You are excellent customers, and I will reduce the cost of your meal by $15." The question became how to divide the $15 windfall to give everyone his fair share? The proprietor suggested that they allocate the savings according to the amount each contributed to the original check. He made a quick calculation, and then rounded each person's share to an integer. For example, Tom's new bill should have been 85 cents, but it was decided he would eat for free. In similar fashion, Dick now owes $3, Harry $7, Ben $15, and Ken $60. (Ken, the most prosperous individual, made up the difference with respect to the cents that were dropped.) The new total is $85, and everyone saves money.

Once outside the restaurant, the friends began to compare their savings. Tom and Dick each complained that they saved only $1. Harry grumbled that he saved only $2. Ben thought it unfair that Ken saved more than the other four friends combined. Everyone continued to pick on Ken. The next week, Ken felt so uncomfortable that he did not show up, so his former friends ate without him. But when the bill came, they were $60 short.

Create the Worksheet

You will create the worksheet that is the basis for the charts. The first sheet, which you will name Numerical Analysis, contains the labels and data described below.

a. Enter a title in row 1. In row 3, enter the following labels: **Person**, **% Paid**, **Amount**, **Projected Saving**, **New Amount**, **Actual Saving**, **% Saving**. Type **Total** in **cell A9** and type **The Original Total** in **cell A11** and **Reduction in Bill** in **cell A12**.

b. Type the names, the percent paid, and the amounts in **cells A4:C8**. This data is in the description of the problem.

Calculations and Formatting

The analysis includes calculations and formatting necessary for presentation. You will create the formulas and select appropriate formatting options.

a. Calculate the projected savings for each individual in column D, the new account in column E, the actual savings in column F, and the percent savings in column G.

b. Calculate appropriate totals in **cells B9:G9**.

c. Calculate the original total in **cell C11** and the reduction in bill in **cell C12**.

d. Format columns B through G as appropriate for the values displayed.

e. Format the remainder of the worksheet with appropriate colors, borders, fonts, and font size.

Create the Charts

You will create the charts based on the worksheet values. The charts provide information visually and help you to analyze that information. You will create three charts: a pie chart, a clustered column chart, and a combination chart.

a. Create a pie chart on a separate sheet that shows the percentage of the bill each individual pays before the refund. Include descriptive titles and labels.

b. Create a column chart on a separate sheet showing the amount each individual saves. Include data labels below the chart and an overlay showing the percentage of savings.

c. Add a shape with text box describing the results depicted on the chart. Include descriptive titles.

d. Create a clustered column chart on a separate sheet showing the new amount of the bill and the actual savings for each individual. Include data labels below the chart and a legend to the right of the chart.

e. Include a shape with a text box describing the data depicted in the chart. Include descriptive titles and labels.

Footers and Printing

Your instructor requires documentation for assignments. You will print the data sheet and the three chart sheets with your name, page numbers, and your instructor's name.

a. Create a custom footer that includes the page number, instructor's name, and your name.

b. Print the worksheet and charts in landscape format to ensure that all charts print on separate pages.

c. Save the workbook as **chap3_cap_dinner_solution**.

Mini Cases

Use the rubric following the case as a guide to evaluate your work, but keep in mind that your instructor may impose additional grading criteria or use a different standard to judge your work.

Designer Clothing

GENERAL CASE

This assignment asks you to complete a worksheet and create an associated chart for a designer clothing boutique, and then link these Excel objects to an appropriate memo. Open the partially completed *chap3_mc1_design* workbook; compute the sales totals for each individual salesperson as well as the totals for each quarter, then format the resulting worksheet in an attractive fashion. Include your name in the title of the worksheet (cell A1). We have started the memo for you and have saved the text in the *chap3_mc1_design* Word document. Open the Word document, and then link the Excel worksheet to the Word document. Repeat the process to link the Excel chart to the Word document. Print the completed document for your instructor. Save as **chap3_mc1_design_solution.**

Performance Elements	Exceeds Expectations	Meets Expectations	Below Expectations
Compute totals	Totals all correct.	Inconsistent use of SUM function.	Typed in the number.
Attractive, appropriate format	Very attractive.	Adequate.	Ugly.
Embed sheet	Sheet embedded correctly.	Sheet embedded but not in correct location.	No embedded sheet.
Embed chart	Chart embedded correctly.	Sheet embedded but not in correct location.	No embedded sheet.

The Convention Planner

RESEARCH CASE

Your first task as a convention planner is to evaluate the hotel capacity for the host city in order to make recommendations as to which hotels should host the convention. The data form can be found in the *chap3_mc2_convention* workbook, which contains a single worksheet. You are to select a city for the convention and research six different hotels in that city. For each hotel, determine the number of standard and deluxe rooms and the rate for each. Insert this information into the worksheet. Complete the worksheet by computing the total number of rooms in each category. Format the worksheet in an attractive way. Create a stacked column chart that shows the total capacity for each hotel. Create a second chart that shows the percentage of total capacity for each hotel. Store each chart in its own worksheet, and then print the entire workbook for your instructor. Save the workbook as **chap3_mc2_convention_solution**.

Performance Elements	Exceeds Expectations	Meets Expectations	Below Expectations
Research hotel information	Found six hotels and data.	Found six hotels but incomplete data.	Found fewer than six hotels with incomplete data.
Create totals	Totals all correct.	Inconsistent use of SUM function.	Typed in the number.
Format attractive	Very attractive.	Adequate.	Ugly.
Create stacked column chart	Chart created correctly.	Incorrect data used for chart.	No chart.
Create second chart	Chart created correctly.	Incorrect data used for chart.	No chart.
Charts on separate sheets	Both charts on separate sheets.	One chart on separate sheet.	No chart.
Printing	Three printed sheets.	Two printed sheets.	No printed output.

Peer Tutoring

DISASTER RECOVERY

As part of your service learning project you volunteer tutoring students in Excel, you will identify and correct six separate errors in the chart. Your biggest task will be selecting the correct type of chart to show the data most clearly. Open the spreadsheet *chap3_mc3_peer* and find six errors. Correct the errors and explain how the errors might have occurred and how they can be prevented. Include your explanation in the cells below the embedded chart. Save as **chap3_mc3_peer_solution.**

Performance Elements	Exceeds Expectations	Meets Expectations	Below Expectations
Identify six errors	Finds all six errors.	Finds four errors.	Finds three or fewer errors.
Explain the error	Complete and correct explanation of each error.	Explanation is too brief to fully explain error.	No explanations.
Prevention description	Prevention description correct and practical.	Prevention description but obtuse.	No prevention description.

Introduction to Access

Finding Your Way Through a Database

After you read this chapter, you will be able to:

1. Explore, describe, and navigate among the objects in an Access database **(page 425)**.
2. Understand the difference between working in storage and memory **(page 432)**.
3. Practice good file management **(page 433)**.
4. Back up, compact, and repair Access files **(page 434)**.
5. Create filters **(page 443)**.
6. Sort table data on one or more fields **(page 446)**.
7. Know when to use Access or Excel to manage data **(page 448)**.
8. Use the Relationship window **(page 456)**.
9. Understand relational power **(page 457)**.

Hands-On Exercises

Exercises	Skills Covered
1. **INTRODUCTION TO DATABASES (page 435)** **Open:** chap1_ho1-3_traders.accdb **Copy, rename, and backup as:** chap1_ho1-3_traders_solution.accdb and chap1_ho1_traders_solution.accdb	• Create a Production Folder and Copy an Access File • Open an Access File • Edit a Record • Navigate an Access Form and Add Records • Recognize the Table and Form Connectivity and Delete a Record • Back Up and Compact the Database
2. **DATA MANIPULATION: FILTERS AND SORTS (page 450)** **Open:** chap1_ho1-3_traders_soution.accdb (from Exercise 1) **Copy, rename, and backup as:** chap1_ho1-3_traders_solution.accdb (additional modifications), chap1_ho2_traders_solution.docx, and chap1_ho2_traders_solution.accdb	• Use Filter by Selection with an Equal Setting • Use Filter by Selection with a Contains Setting • Use Filter by Form with an Inequity Setting • Sort a Table
3. **INTRODUCTION TO RELATIONSHIPS (page 459)** **Open:** chap1_ho1-3_traders_solution.accdb (from Exercise 2) **Copy, rename, and backup as:** chap1_ho1-3_traders_solution.accdb (additional modifications)	• Examine the Relationships Window • Discover that Changes in Table Data Affect Queries • Use Filter by Form with an Inequity Setting and Reapply a Saved Filter • Filter a Report • Remove an Advanced Filter

CASE STUDY

Medical Research—The Lifelong Learning Physicians Association

Case Study

Today is the first day of your information technology internship appointment with the *Lifelong Learning Physicians Association*. This medical association selected you for the internship because your résumé indicates that you are proficient with Access. Bonnie Clinton, M.D., founded the organization with the purpose of keeping doctors informed about current research and to help physicians identify qualified study participants. Dr. Clinton worries that physicians do not inform their patients about study participation opportunities. She expressed further concerns that the physicians in one field, e.g., cardiology, are unfamiliar with research studies conducted in other fields, such as obstetrics.

Because the association is new, you have very little data to manage. However, the system was designed to accommodate additional data. You will need to talk to Dr. Clinton on a regular basis to determine the association's changing information needs. You may need to guide her in this process. Your responsibilities as the association's IT intern include many items.

Your Assignment

- Read the chapter, paying special attention to learning the vocabulary of database software.
- Copy the *chap1_case_physicians.accdb* file to your production folder, rename it **chap1_case_physicians_solution.accdb**, and enable the content.
- Open the Relationships window and examine the relationships among the tables and the fields contained within each of the tables to become acquainted with this database.
- Open the Volunteers table. Add yourself as a study participant by replacing record **22** with your own information. You should invent data about your height, weight, blood pressure, and your cholesterol. Examine the values in the other records and enter a realistic value. Do not change the stored birthday.
- Identify all of the volunteers who might be college freshmen (18- and 19-year-olds). After you identify them, print the table listing their names and addresses. Use a filter by form with an appropriately set date criterion to identify the correctly aged participants.
- Identify all of the physicians participating in a study involving cholesterol management.
- Open the *Studies and Volunteers Report*. Print it.
- Compact and repair the database file.
- Create a backup of the database. Name the backup **chap1_case_physicians_backup.accdb**.

Data and Files Everywhere!

You probably use databases often. Each time you download an MP3 file, you enter a database via the Internet. There, you find searchable data identifying files by artist's name, music style, most frequently requested files, first lines, publication companies, and song titles. If you know the name of the song but not the recording artist or record label, you generally can find it. The software supporting the Web site helps you locate the information you need. The server for the Web site provides access to a major database that contains a lot of data about available MP3 files.

> Each time you download an MP3 file, you enter a database via the internet.

You are exposed to other databases on a regular basis. For example, your university uses a database to support the registration process. When you registered for this course, you entered a database. It probably told you how many seats remained but not the names of the other students. In addition, Web-based job and dating boards are based on database software. Organizations rely on data to conduct daily operations, regardless of whether the organization exists as a profit or not-for-profit environment. The organization maintains data about employees, volunteers, customers, activities, and facilities. Every keystroke and mouse click creates data about the organization that needs to be stored, organized, and analyzed. Microsoft Access provides the organizational decision-maker a valuable tool facilitating data retrieval and use.

In this section, you explore Access database objects and work with table views. You also learn the difference between working in storage and memory to understand how changes to database objects are saved. Finally, you practice good file management techniques by backing up, compacting, and repairing databases.

Exploring, Describing, and Navigating Among the Objects in an Access Database

A ***field*** is a basic entity or data element, such as the name of a book or the telephone number of a publisher.

A ***record*** is a complete set of all of the data (fields) about one person, place, event, or idea.

A ***table*** is a collection of records. Every record in a table contains the same fields in the same order.

A ***database*** consists of one or more tables and the supporting objects used to get data into and out of the tables.

To understand database management effectively and to use Access productively, you should first learn the vocabulary. A ***field*** is a basic entity, data element, or category, such as book titles or telephone numbers. The field does not necessarily need to contain a value. For example, a field might store fax numbers for a firm's customers. However, some of the customers may not have a fax machine so the Fax field is blank for that record. A ***record*** is a complete set of all of the data (fields) about one person, place, event, or idea. For example, your name, homework, and test scores constitute your record in your instructor's grade book. A ***table***, the foundation of every database, is a collection of related records that contain fields to organize data. If you have used Excel, you will see the similarities between a spreadsheet and an Access table. Each column represents a field, and each row represents a record. Every record in a table contains the same fields in the same order. An instructor's grade book for one class is a table containing records of all students in one structure. A ***database*** consists of one or more tables and the supporting objects used to get data into and out of the tables.

Prior to the advent of database management software, organizations managed their data manually. They placed papers in file folders and organized the folders in multiple drawer filing cabinets. You can think of the filing cabinet in the manual system as a database. Each drawer full of folders in the filing cabinet corresponds to a table within the database. Figure 1.1 shows a college's database system from before the information age. File drawers (tables) contain student data. Each folder (record) contains facts (fields) about that student. The cabinet also contains drawers (tables) full of data about the faculty and the courses offered. Together, the tables combine to form a database system.

TIP Data Versus Information

Data and information are not synonymous, although, the terms often are used interchangeably. Data is the raw material and consists of the table (or tables) that comprise a database. Information is the finished product. Data is converted to information by selecting (filtering) records, by sequencing (sorting) the selected records, or by summarizing data from multiple records. Decisions in an organization are based on information compiled from multiple records, as opposed to raw data.

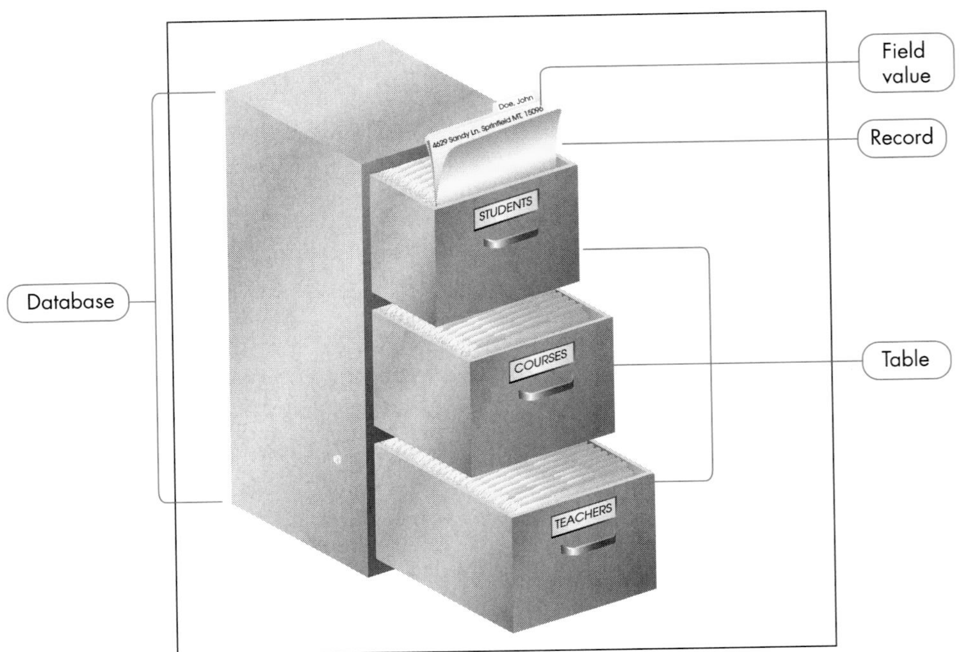

Figure 1.1 Primitive Database

Identify Access Interface Elements

Figure 1.2 shows how Microsoft Access appears onscreen. It contains two open windows—an application window for Microsoft Access and a document (database) window for the open database. Each window has its own title bar and icons. The title bar in the application window contains the name of the application (Microsoft Access) and the Minimize and Maximize (or Restore) icons. The title bar in the document (database) window contains the name of the object that is currently open (Employees table). Should more than one object be open at a time, the top of the document window will display tabs for each open object. The Access application window is maximized; therefore, Restore is visible.

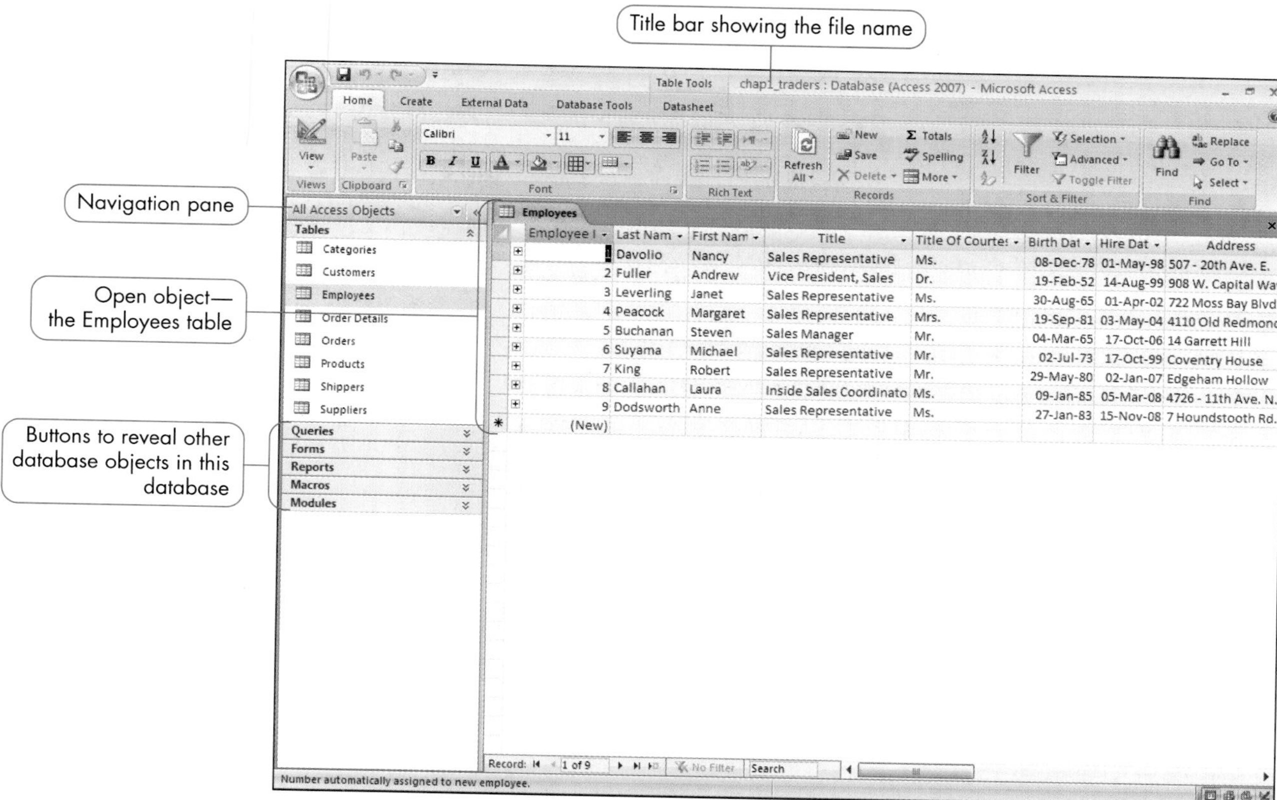

Figure 1.2 An Access Database

Let us look at an example of a database for an international food distribution company—The Northwind Traders. This firm sells specialty food items to restaurants and food shops around the world. It also purchases the products it sells from diversely located firms. The Northwind Traders Company database contains eight tables: Categories, Customers, Employees, Order Details, Orders, Products, Shippers, and Suppliers. Each table, in turn, consists of multiple records, corresponding to the folders in the file cabinet. The Employees table, for example, contains a record for every employee. Each record in the Employees table contains 17 fields—where data about the employee's education, address, photograph, position, and so on are stored. Occasionally, a field does not contain a value for a particular record. One of the employees, Margaret Peacock, did not provide a picture. The value of that field is missing. Access provides a placeholder to store the data when it is available. The Suppliers table has a record for each vendor from whom the firm purchases products, just as the Orders table has a record for each order. The real power of Access is derived from a database with multiple tables and the relationships that connect the tables.

An Access ***object*** contains the basic elements of the database.

The database window displays the various objects in an Access database. An Access ***object*** stores the basic elements of the database. Access uses six types of objects—tables, queries, forms, reports, macros, and modules. Every database must contain at least one table, and it may contain any, all, or none of the other objects. Each object type is accessed through the appropriate tab within the database window. Because of the interrelationships among objects, you may either view all of the objects of a type in a single place or view all of the related objects in a way that demonstrates their inner-connectivity. You select an object for viewing using the Navigation pane. The Navigation pane on the left side groups related objects.

The Reference page describes the tabs and groups on the Ribbon in Access 2007. You do not need to memorize most of these tabs and groups now. You will learn where things are located as you explore using the features.

Reference Page | Access Ribbon

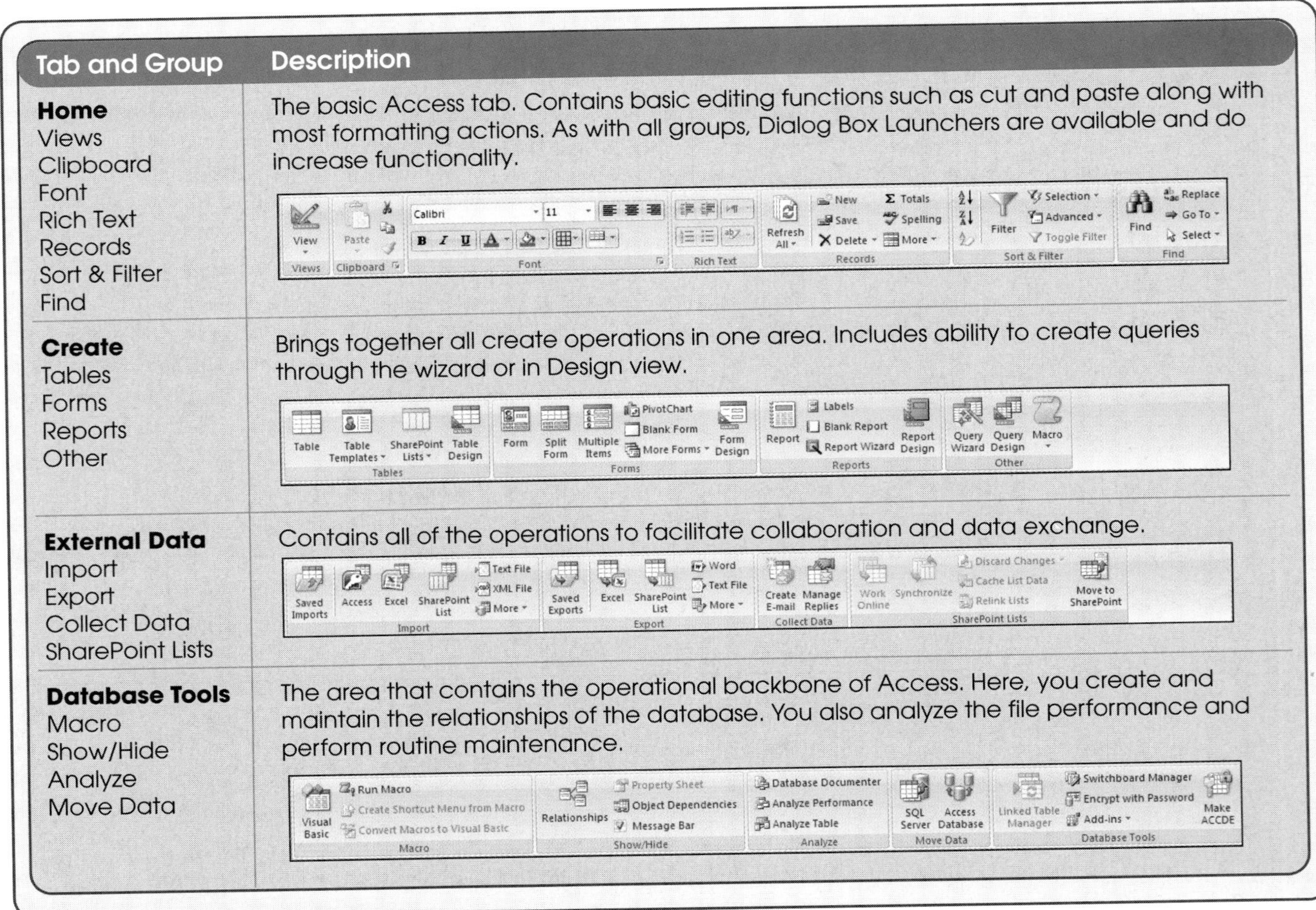

Tab and Group	Description
Home Views Clipboard Font Rich Text Records Sort & Filter Find	The basic Access tab. Contains basic editing functions such as cut and paste along with most formatting actions. As with all groups, Dialog Box Launchers are available and do increase functionality.
Create Tables Forms Reports Other	Brings together all create operations in one area. Includes ability to create queries through the wizard or in Design view.
External Data Import Export Collect Data SharePoint Lists	Contains all of the operations to facilitate collaboration and data exchange.
Database Tools Macro Show/Hide Analyze Move Data	The area that contains the operational backbone of Access. Here, you create and maintain the relationships of the database. You also analyze the file performance and perform routine maintenance.

Work with Table Views

The ***Datasheet view*** is a grid where you add, edit, and delete the records of a table.

The ***Design view*** is a different grid where you create and modify the properties of the table.

Access provides different ways in which to view a table and most other objects. The ***Datasheet view*** is a grid containing columns (fields) and rows (records). You can view, add, edit, and delete records of a table in the Datasheet view. You can use the ***Design view*** to create and modify the table by specifying the fields it will contain and their associated properties. The field type (for example, text or numeric data) and the field length are examples of field properties. If you need the values stored in a particular field to display as currency, you would modify the property of that field to ensure all values display appropriately.

Figure 1.3 shows the Datasheet view for the Customers table. The first row in the table displays the field names. Each additional row contains a record (the data for a specific customer). Each column represents a field (one fact about a customer). Every record in the table contains the same fields in the same order.

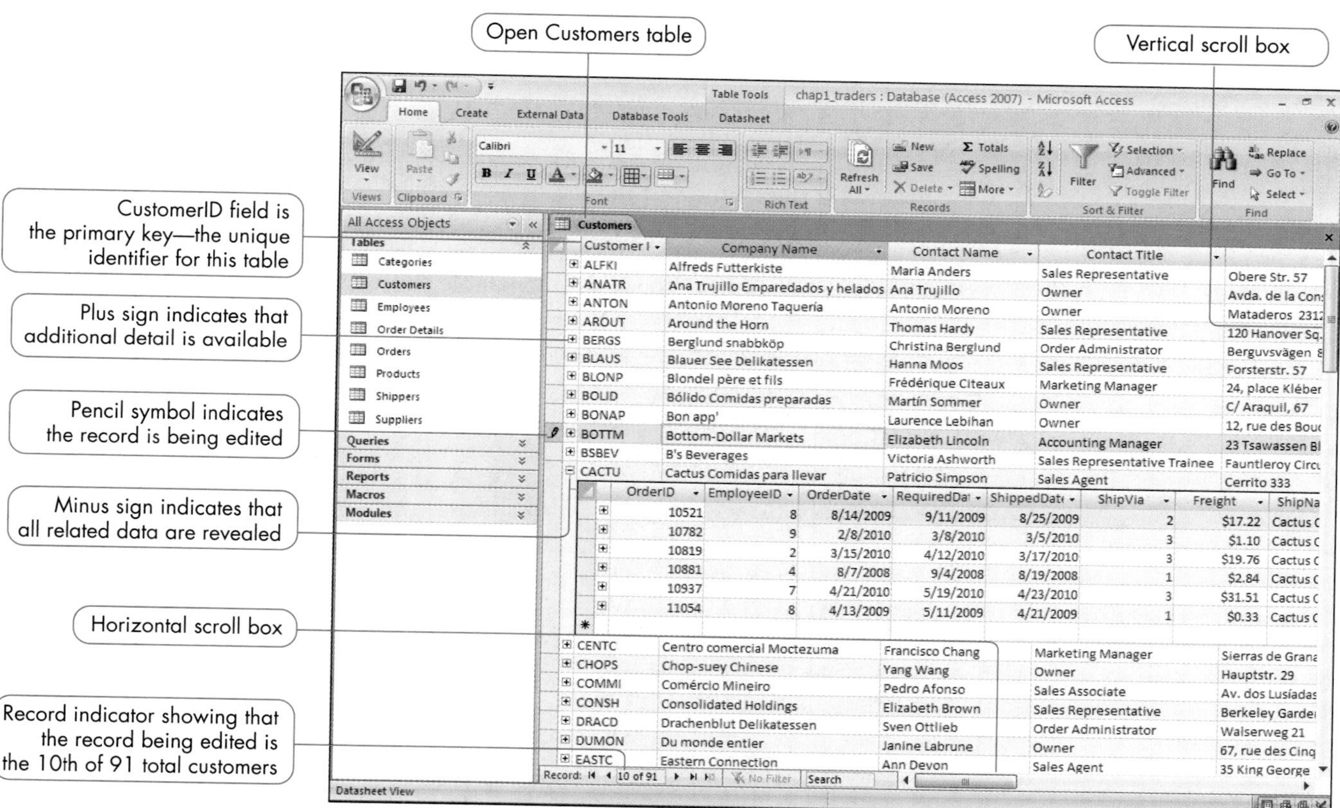

Figure 1.3 The Customers Table and Related Order Information

The ***primary key*** is the field that makes each record in a table unique.

The ***primary key*** is the field (or combination of fields) that makes each record in a table unique. The CustomerID is the primary key in the Customers table; it ensures that every record in a table is different from every other record, and it prevents the occurrence of duplicate records. Primary key fields may be numbers, letters, or a combination of both. In this case the primary key is text (letters).

The Navigation bar at the bottom of Figure 1.3 shows a table with 91 records and record number 10 as the current record. You can work on only one record at a time. The vertical scroll bar at the right of the window shows that more records exist in the table than you can see at one time. The horizontal scroll bar at the bottom of the window indicates that you cannot see an entire record.

The pencil icon at the left of the record indicates that the data in the current record are being edited and that the changes have not yet been saved. The pencil icon disappears after you complete the data entry and move to another record, because Access saves data automatically as soon as you move from one record to the next.

Figure 1.4 displays the navigation buttons that you use to move within most Access objects. You may navigate using commands to go to the last and first records, advance and go back one record, and add a new record.

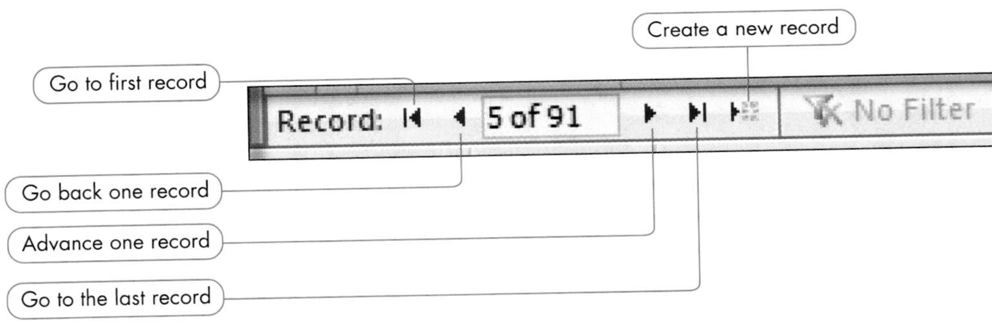

Figure 1.4 Navigation Buttons

Use Forms, Queries, and Reports

As previously indicated, an Access database is made up of different types of objects together with the tables and the data they contain. A table (or set of tables) is at the heart of any database because it contains the actual data. The other objects in a database—such as forms, queries, and reports—are based on an underlying table. Figure 1.5 displays a form based on the Customers table shown earlier.

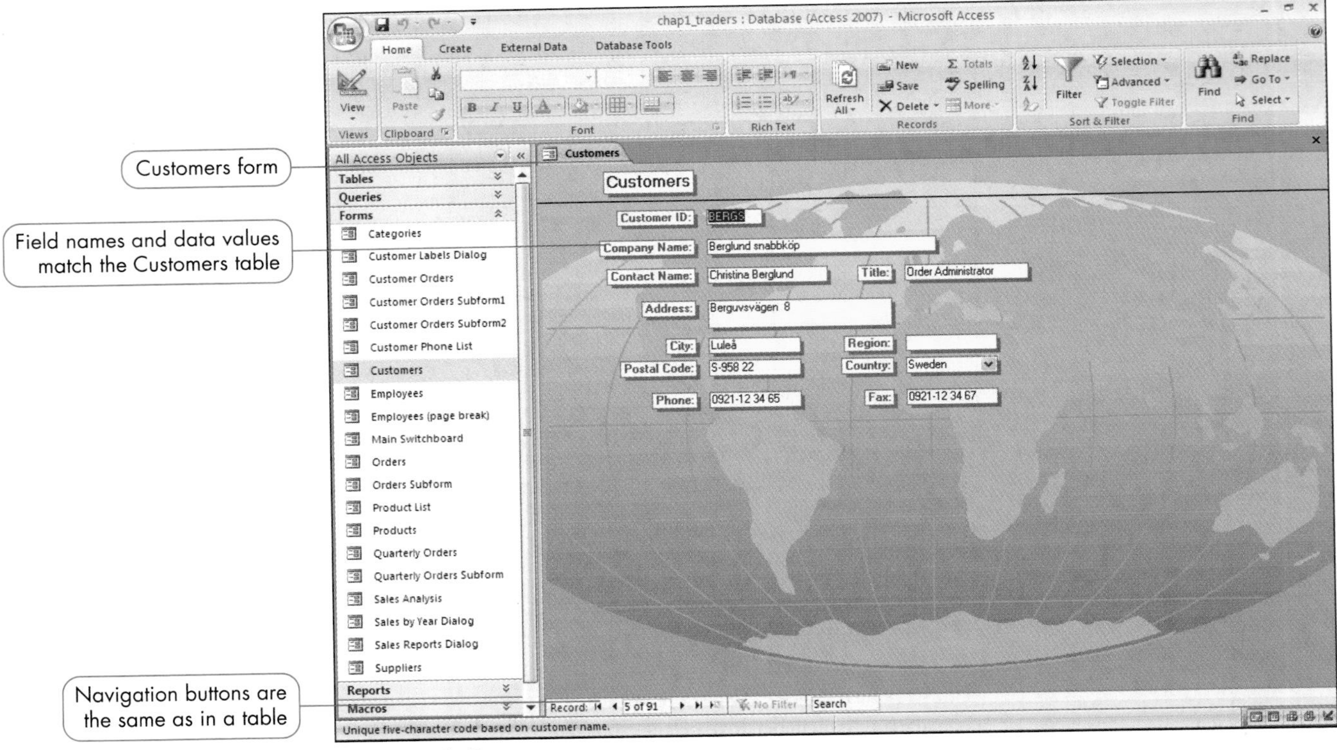

Figure 1.5 Customers Form

A ***form*** is an interface that enables you to enter or modify record data.

A ***form*** is an interface that enables you to enter or modify record data. Commands may appear in the form to add a new record, print a record, or close the form. The form provides access to all of the data maintenance operations that are available through a table. The status bar and navigation buttons at the bottom of the form are similar to those that appear at the bottom of a table. You use the form in Datasheet view, but create and edit the form structure in Design view.

A ***query*** provides information that answers a question.

Figure 1.6 displays a query that lists the products that the firm purchases from a particular supplier. A ***query*** provides information that answers a question based on the data within an underlying table or tables. The Suppliers table, for example, contains records for many vendors, but the query in Figure 1.6 shows only the products that were supplied by a specific supplier. If you want to know the details about a specific supplier, you establish a criterion to specify which supplier you need to know about. A ***criterion*** (***criteria***, pl) is a rule or norm that is the basis for making judgments. If you need the names of all the suppliers in New York, you set a criterion to identify the New York suppliers. The results would yield only those suppliers from New York. Query results are similar in appearance to the underlying table, except that the query contains selected records and/or selected fields for those records. The query also may list the records in a different sequence from that of the table. (You also can use a query to add new records and modify existing records.) If you have a query open and notice an error in an address field, you can edit the record, and the edited value would immediately and permanently transfer to the table storing that record. Queries may be opened in Datasheet view or Design view. You use the Datasheet view to examine the query output and use the Design view to specify which fields and records to include in the query.

A ***criterion*** (***criteria***, pl) is a rule or norm that is the basis for making judgments.

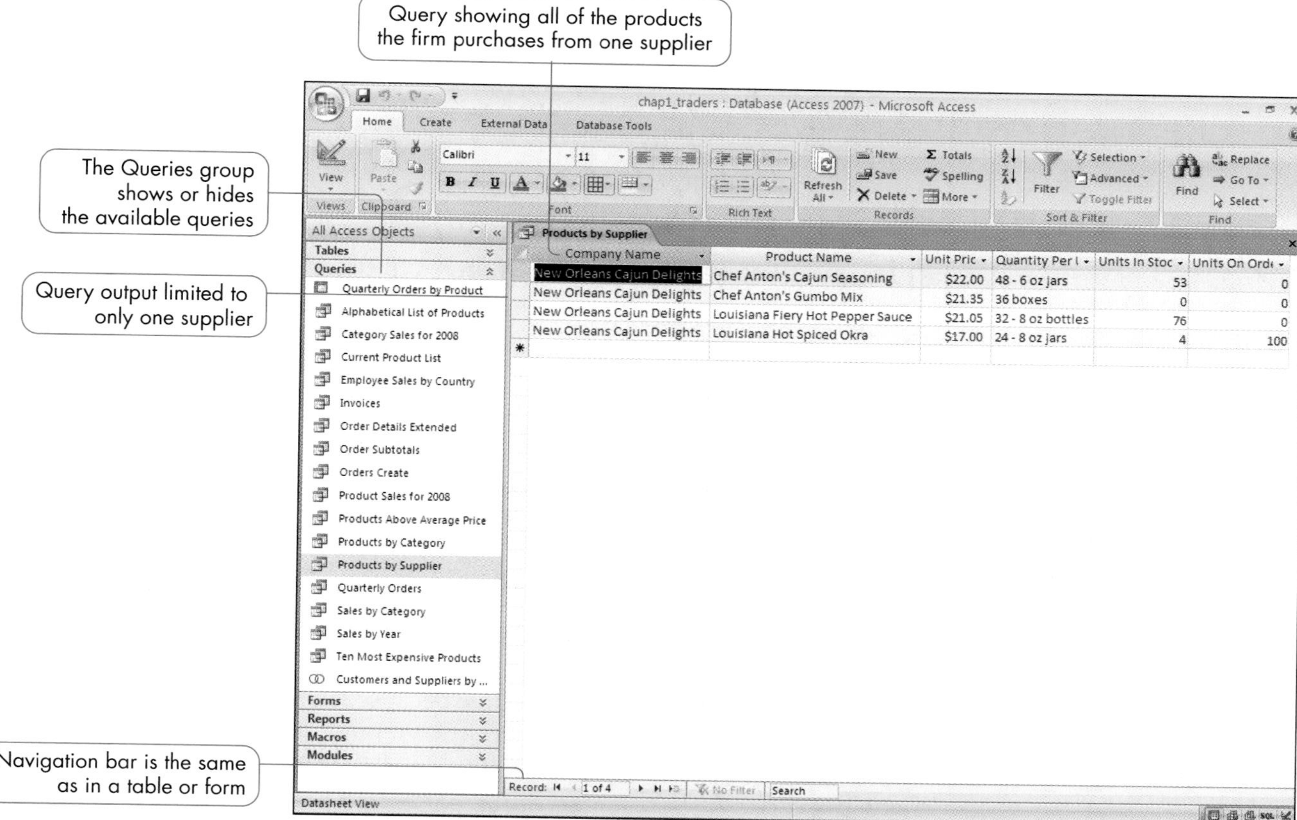

Figure 1.6 Results of a Query Shown in Datasheet View

A ***report*** presents database information professionally.

Figure 1.7 displays a report that contains the same information as the query in Figure 1.6. A ***report*** contains professionally formatted information from underlying tables or queries. Because the report information contains a more enhanced format than a query or table, you place database output in a report to print. Access provides different views for designing, modifying, and running reports. Most Access users use only the Print Preview, Print Layout, and Report views of a report.

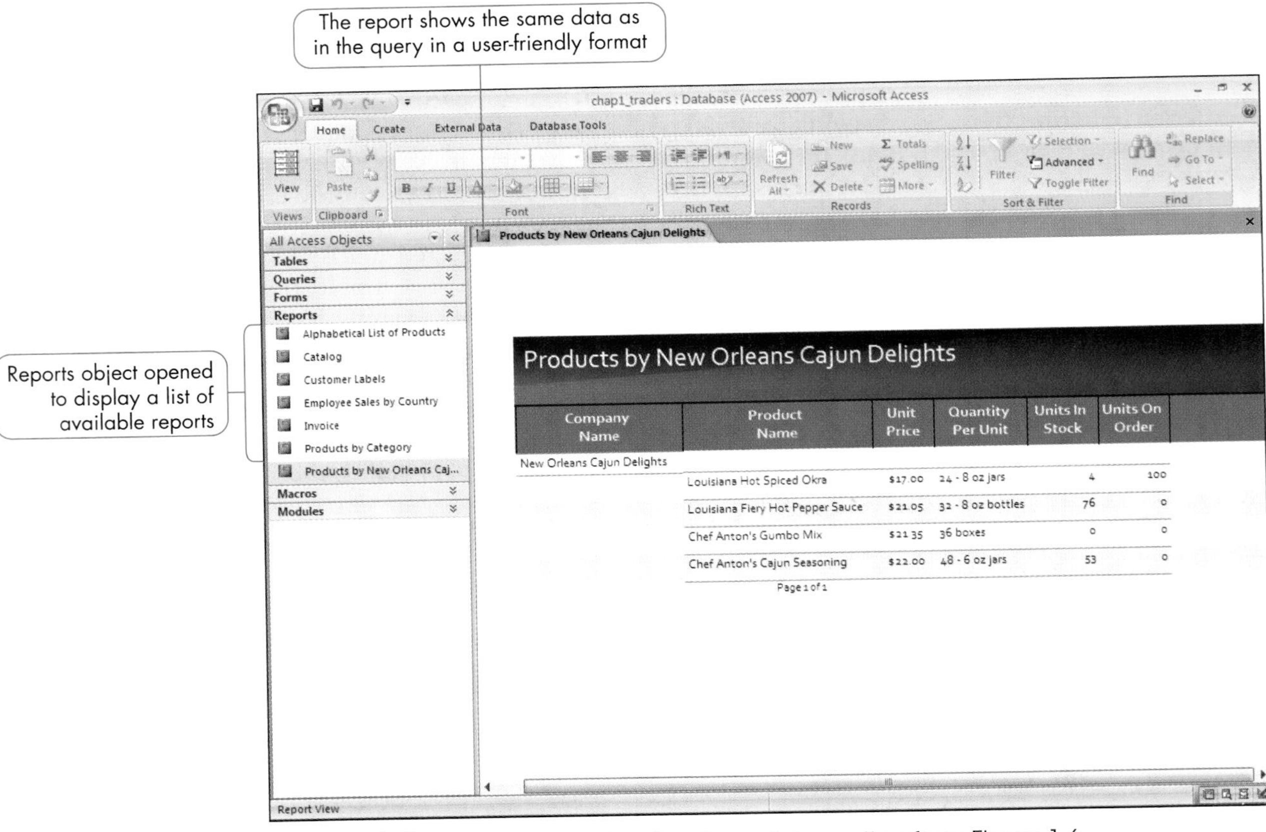

Figure 1.7 Report Displaying the Query Information from Figure 1.6

Understanding the Difference Between Working in Storage and Memory

Access is different from the other Microsoft Office applications. Word, Excel, and PowerPoint all work primarily from memory. In those applications you can easily reverse mistakes by using Undo. You make a change, discover that you dislike it, and click Undo to restore the original. These actions are possible because you work in memory (RAM) most of the time while in the other Microsoft Office applications; changes are not saved automatically to the file immediately after you make the changes. These actions are also possible because, generally, you are the only user of your file. If you work on a group project, you might e-mail the PowerPoint file to the others in the group, but you are the primary owner and user of that file. Access is *different*.

(Access is different from the other Microsoft Office applications.)

Access works primarily from storage. When you make a change to a field's content in an Access table (for example, changing a customer's area code), Access saves your changes as soon as you move the insertion point to a different record; you do not need to click Save. You can click Undo to reverse several editing changes (such as changing an area code and a contact name) for a single record **immediately** after making the changes to that record. However, unlike other Office programs that let you continue

Undoing actions, you cannot use Undo to reverse edits to more than the last record you edited or to restore a field if you delete it.

Multiple users can work on the database simultaneously. As long as no two users attempt to interact with the same record at the same time, the system updates as it goes. This also means that any reports extracting the information from the database contain the most up-to-date data. The only time you need to click Save is when you are creating or changing a structural element, such as a table, query, form, or report.

TIP **Save Edits While Keeping a Record Active**

When you want to save changes to a record you are editing while staying on the same record, press Shift+Enter. The pencil icon, indicating an editing mode, disappears, indicating that the change is saved.

Be careful to avoid accidentally typing something in a record and pressing Enter. Doing so saves the change, and you can retrieve the original data if you are lucky enough to remember to click Undo immediately before making or editing other records. Because Access is a relational database, several other related objects (queries, reports, or forms) could also be permanently changed. In Access, one file holds everything. All of the objects—tables, forms, queries, and reports—are saved both individually and as part of the Access collection.

TIP **Data Validation**

No system, no matter how sophisticated, can produce valid output from invalid input. Thus, good systems are built to anticipate errors in data entry and to reject those errors prior to saving a record. Access will automatically prevent you from adding records with a duplicate primary key or entering invalid data into a numeric or date field. The database developer has the choice whether to require other types of validation, such as requiring the author's name.

Practicing Good File Management

You must exercise methodical and deliberate file management techniques to avoid damaging data. Every time you need to open a file, this book will direct you to copy the file to your production folder and rename the copied file. Name the production folder with **Your Name Access Production**. You would not copy a real database and work in the copy often. However, as you learn, you will probably make mistakes. Following the practice of working in a copied file will facilitate mistake recovery during the learning process.

Further, it matters to which type of media you save your files. Access does not work from some media. Access runs best from a hard or network drive because those drives have sufficient access speed to support the software. Access speed measures the time it takes for the storage device to make the file content available for use. If you work from your own computer, create the production folder in the My Documents folder on the hard drive. Most schools lock their hard drives so that students cannot permanently save files there. If your school provides you with storage space on the school's network, store your production folder there. The advantage to using the network is that the network administration staff backs up files regularly. If you have no storage on the school network, your next best storage option is a thumb drive, also known as USB jump drive, flash drive, Pen drive, or stick drive.

Access speed measures the time it takes for the storage device to make the file content available for use.

TIP Do Not Use This Media

Because storage space is limited, you should not use floppy disks or Zip disks. Furthermore, you should not use CDs or DVDs because Access must constantly save changes to the file, a process that does not work with storage media that have slow access speed or limited write privileges. ***Access speed*** measures the time it takes for the storage device to locate the file, open it, and transfer it to memory so that the file content is available for use. However, you may back up your work or archive it to these storage devices.

All of the objects in an Access database are stored in a single file. You can open a database from within Windows Explorer by double-clicking the file name. You also can open the database from within Access through the Recent Documents list or by clicking the Microsoft Office Button (noted as Office Button only in this textbook) and selecting Open from the Office menu. The individual objects within a database are opened from the database window.

Backing Up, Compacting, and Repairing Access Files

Data is the lifeblood of any organization. Imagine what would happen to a firm that loses the records of the orders placed but not shipped or the charity that loses the list of donor contribution records or the hospital that loses the digital records of patient X-rays. What would happen to the employee who "accidentally" deleted mission-critical data? What would happen to the other employees who did not lose the mission-critical data? Fortunately, Access recognizes how critical backup procedures are to organizations and makes backing up the database files easy.

Back Up a Database

You back up an Access file (and all of the objects it contains) with just a few mouse clicks. To back up files, click the Office Button and select Manage from the Office menu. When you select Backup, a dialog box, much like a Save As dialog box in the other applications, opens. You may use controls in the Backup dialog box to specify storage location and file name. Access provides a default file name that is the original file name followed by the date. In most organizations, this step is useful because the Information Technology department backs up every database each day.

Compact and Repair a Database

All databases have a tendency to expand with use. This expansion will occur without new information being added. Simply using the database, creating queries and running them, or applying and removing filters may cause the file to store inefficiently. Because the files tend to be rather large to start with, any growth creates problems. Access provides another utility, Compact and Repair, under the Manage submenu in the Office menu that addresses this issue. The Compact and Repair utility acts much like a disk defragmenter utility. It finds related file sectors and reassembles them in one location if they become scattered from database use. You should compact and repair your database each day when you close the file. This step often will decrease file size by 50% or more. Access closes any open objects during the compact and repair procedure, so it is a good idea to close any objects in the database prior to compacting so that you will control if any design changes will be saved or not.

In the next hands-on exercise, you will work with a database from an international gourmet food distributor, the Northwind Traders. This firm purchases food items from suppliers and sells them to restaurants and specialty food shops. It depends on the data stored in the Access database to make daily decisions.

Hands-On Exercises

1 | Introduction to Databases

Skills covered: 1. Create a Production Folder and Copy an Access File **2.** Open an Access File **3.** Edit a Record **4.** Navigate an Access Form and Add Records **5.** Recognize the Table and Form Connectivity and Delete a Record **6.** Back Up and Compact the Database

Step 1
Create a Production Folder and Copy an Access File

Refer to Figure 1.8 as you complete Step 1.

a. Right-click **My Computer** on the desktop and select **Explore** from the shortcut menu.

   This step opens the Explore utility in a two-pane view that facilitates transferring materials between folders.

b. Determine where your production folder will reside and double-click that location. For example, double-click the **My Documents** folder if that is where your files will reside.

   For the remainder of this book, it is assumed that your production folder resides in the My Document folder on the hard drive. Your folder may actually exist on another drive. What is important is that you (1) create and use the folder and (2) remember where it is.

c. Right-click anywhere on a blank spot in the right pane of the Exploring window. Select **New**, and then select **Folder** from the shortcut menu.

   A new folder is created with the default name, New Folder, selected and ready to be renamed.

d. Type **Your Name Access Production** and press **Enter**.

e. Open the folder that contains the student data files that accompany this textbook.

f. Find the file named *chap1_ho1-3_traders.accdb*, right-click the file, and select **Copy** from the shortcut menu.

g. Go to the newly created production folder named with your name. Right-click a blank area in the right side of the Exploring window and select **Paste**.

   You have created a copy of the original *chap1_ho1-3_traders.accdb* file. You will work with the copy. In the event that you make mistakes, the original remains intact in the student data folder. You can recopy it and rework the exercise if necessary.

h. Rename the newly copied file **your_name_chap1_ho1-3_traders_solution.accdb**.

   You need to remember to rename all of the solution files with your name. If your instructor requests that you submit your work for evaluation using a shared folder on the campus network, each file must have a unique name. You risk overwriting another student's work (or having someone overwrite your work) if you do not name your files with your name and the file designation.

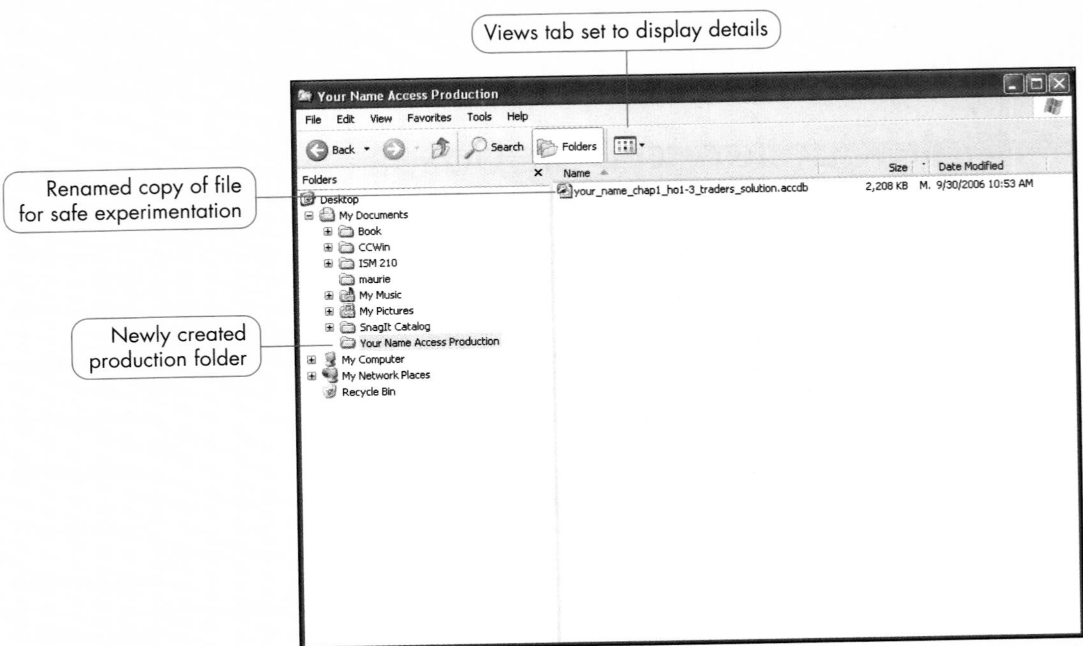

Figure 1.8 Production Folder Created Showing Copied and Renamed File

Step 2
Open an Access File

Refer to Figure 1.9 as you complete Step 2.

a. Double-click the *your_name_chap1_ho1-3_traders_solution* file to open it.

This step launches Access and opens the Explore file. From now on, this book will refer to the files without the *your_name* prefix.

b. Click **Options** on the Security Warning toolbar. See Figure 1.9.

Each time you open an Access file for the remainder of the class, you will need to enable the content. Several viruses and worms may be transmitted via Access files. You may be reasonably confident of the trustworthiness of the files in this book. However, if an Access file arrives as an attachment from an unsolicited e-mail message, you should not open it. Microsoft warns all users of Access files that a potential threat exists every time the file is opened.

c. Click **Enable this content**, and then click **OK**.

The Microsoft Office Security Options dialog box closes and the Security Warning toolbar disappears.

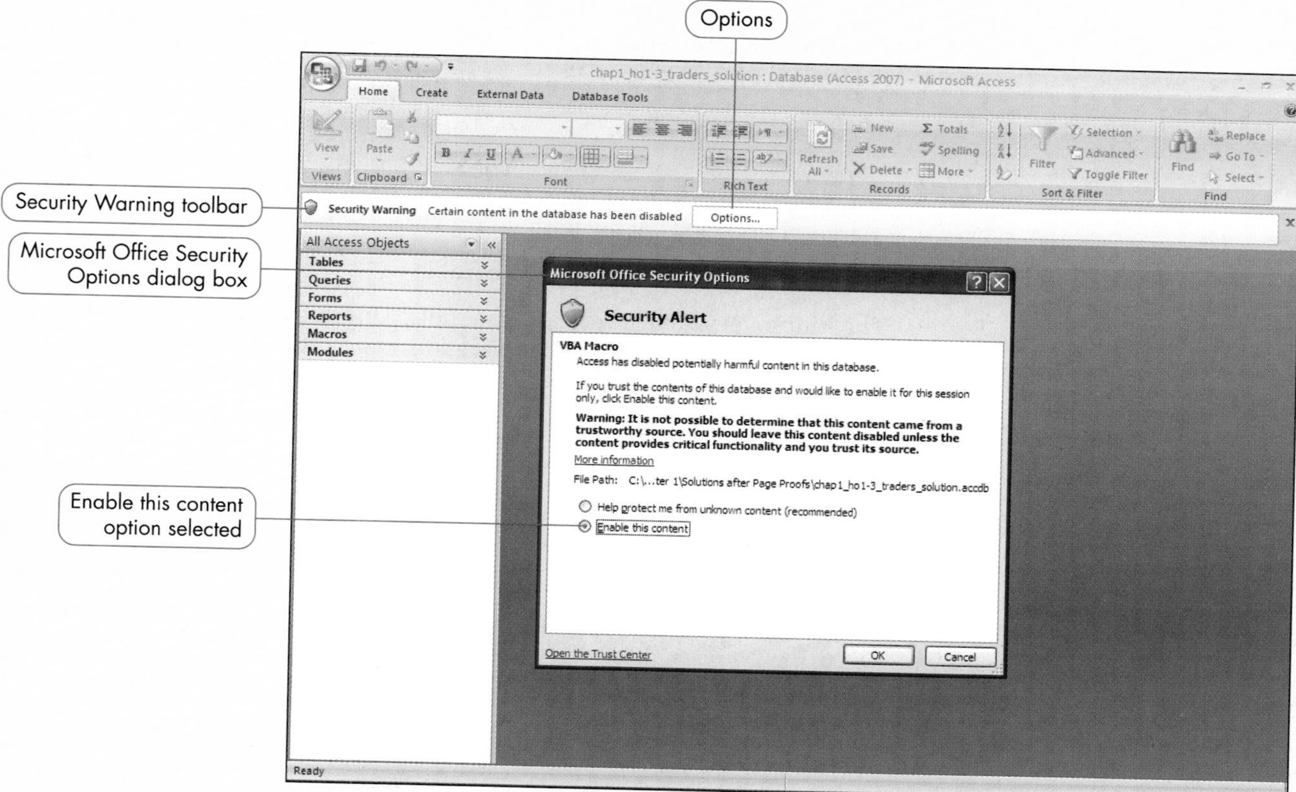

Figure 1.9 Microsoft Office Security Options Dialog Box

Step 3
Edit a Record

Refer to Figure 1.10 as you complete Step 3.

a. Click **Tables** in the Navigation pane to expand the list of available tables.

   The list of tables contained in the database file opens.

b. Double-click the **Employees table** to open it. See Figure 1.10.

c. Click the insertion point in the fourth row. Double-click *Peacock* in the LastName field. The entire name highlights. Type **your last name** to replace *Peacock*.

d. Press **Tab** to move to the next field in the fourth row. Replace *Margaret* with **your first name**.

   You have made changes to two fields in the same record (row); the pencil displays in the row selector box.

e. Click **Undo** on the Quick Access Toolbar.

   Your first name reverts back to Margaret because you have not yet left the record.

f. Type your name again to replace *Margaret* with **your first name**. Press **Enter**.

   You should now be in the Title field and your title, *Sales Representative,* is selected. The pencil icon still displays in the row selector.

g. Click anywhere in the third row where Janet Leverling's data are stored.

   The pencil icon disappears; your changes to the table have been saved.

h. Click the address field in the first record, the one for Nancy Davolio. Type **4004 East Morningside Dr**. Click your insertion point into Andrew Fuller's name field.

i. Click **Undo**.

   Nancy's address changes back to *20th Ave. E*. However, the Undo command is now faded. You can no longer undo the change that you made replacing Margaret Peacock's name with your own.

j. Click **Close** to close the Employees table.

   The Employees table closes. You are not prompted about saving your changes, because they have already been saved for you. If you reopen the Employees table, you will find your name, not Margaret's, because Access works in storage, not memory.

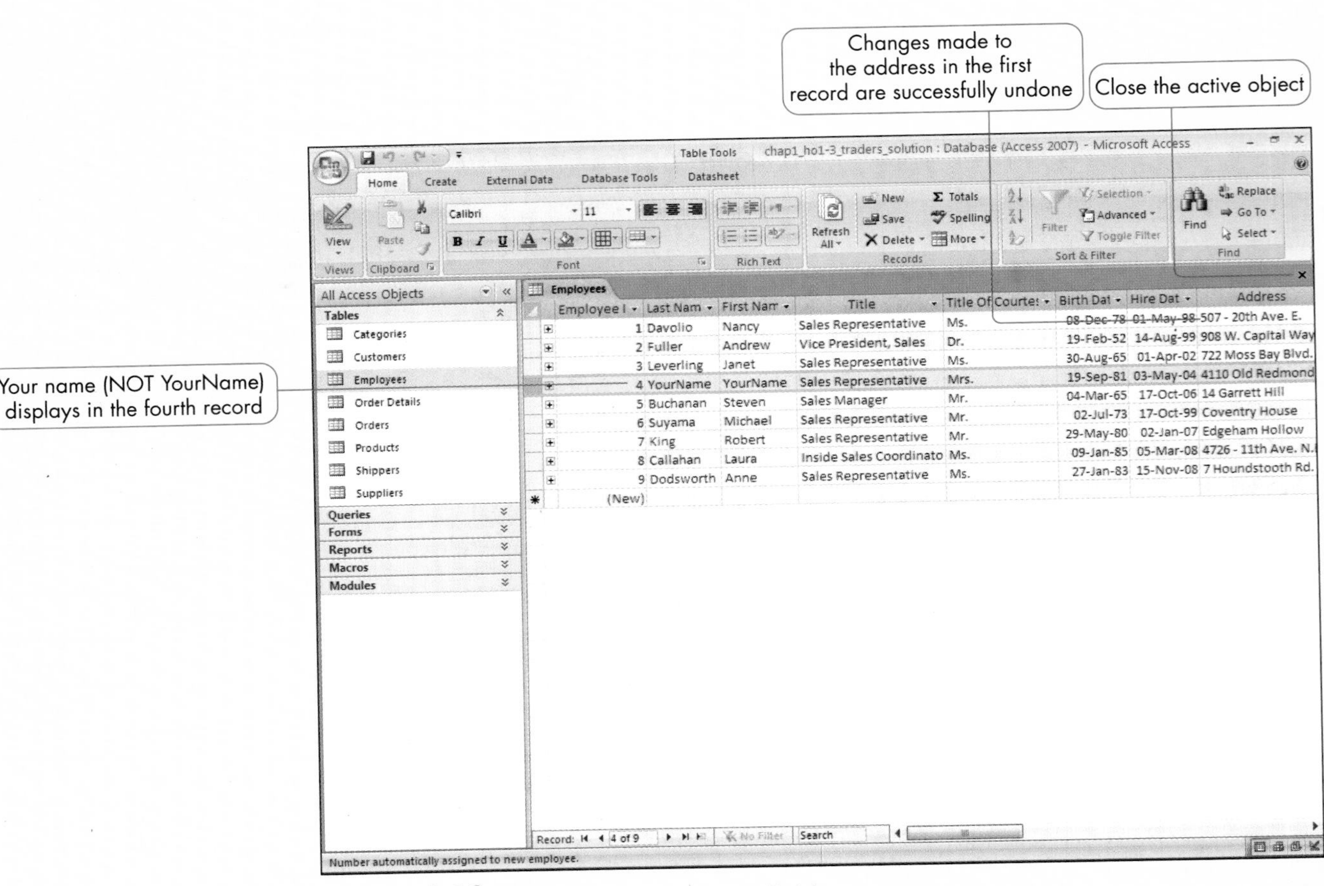

Figure 1.10 The Edited Employees Table

Step 4
Navigate an Access Form and Add Records

Refer to Figure 1.11 as you complete Step 4.

a. Click **Tables** in the Navigation pane to close it.

   The list of available tables collapses.

b. Click **Forms** in the Navigation pane to expand it.

c. Double-click the **Products form** to open it.

d. Practice with the navigation buttons above the status bar to move from one record to the next. Click **Next record**, and then click **Last record**.

e. Click **Find** in the Find group on the Home tab.

The Find command is an ideal way to search for specific records within a table, form, or query. You can search a single field or the entire record, match all or part of the selected field(s), move forward or back in a table, or specify a case-sensitive search. The Replace command can be used to substitute one value for another. Be careful, however, about using the Replace All option for global replacement because unintended replacements are far too common.

f. Type **ikura** in the *Find What* section of the Find and Replace dialog box. Check to make sure that the *Look In* option is set to **Product Name** and the *Match* option is set to **Whole Field**. The *Search* option should be set to **All**. Click **Find Next.**

You should see the information about *ikura*, a seafood supplied by Tokyo Traders.

g. Type **Grandma** in the *Find What* box, click the **Match drop-down arrow**, and select **Any Part of Field**. Click **Find Next**.

You should see information about Grandma's Boysenberry Spread. Setting the match option to any part of the field will return a match even if it is contained in the middle of a word.

h. Close the Find and Replace dialog box.

i. Click **New (blank) record** located on the Navigation bar.

j. Enter the following information for a new product. Press **Tab** to navigate the form.

Field Name	Value to Type
Product Name	Your Name Pecan Pie
Supplier	Grandma Kelly's Homestead (Note, display the drop-down list to enter this information quickly)
Category	Confections (Use the drop-down box here, too)
Quantity Per Unit	1
Unit Price	25.00
Units in Stock	18
Units on Order	50
Reorder Level	20

As soon as you begin typing in the product name box, Access assigns a Product ID, in this case 78, to the record. The Product ID is used as the primary key in the Products table.

k. Close the Products form.

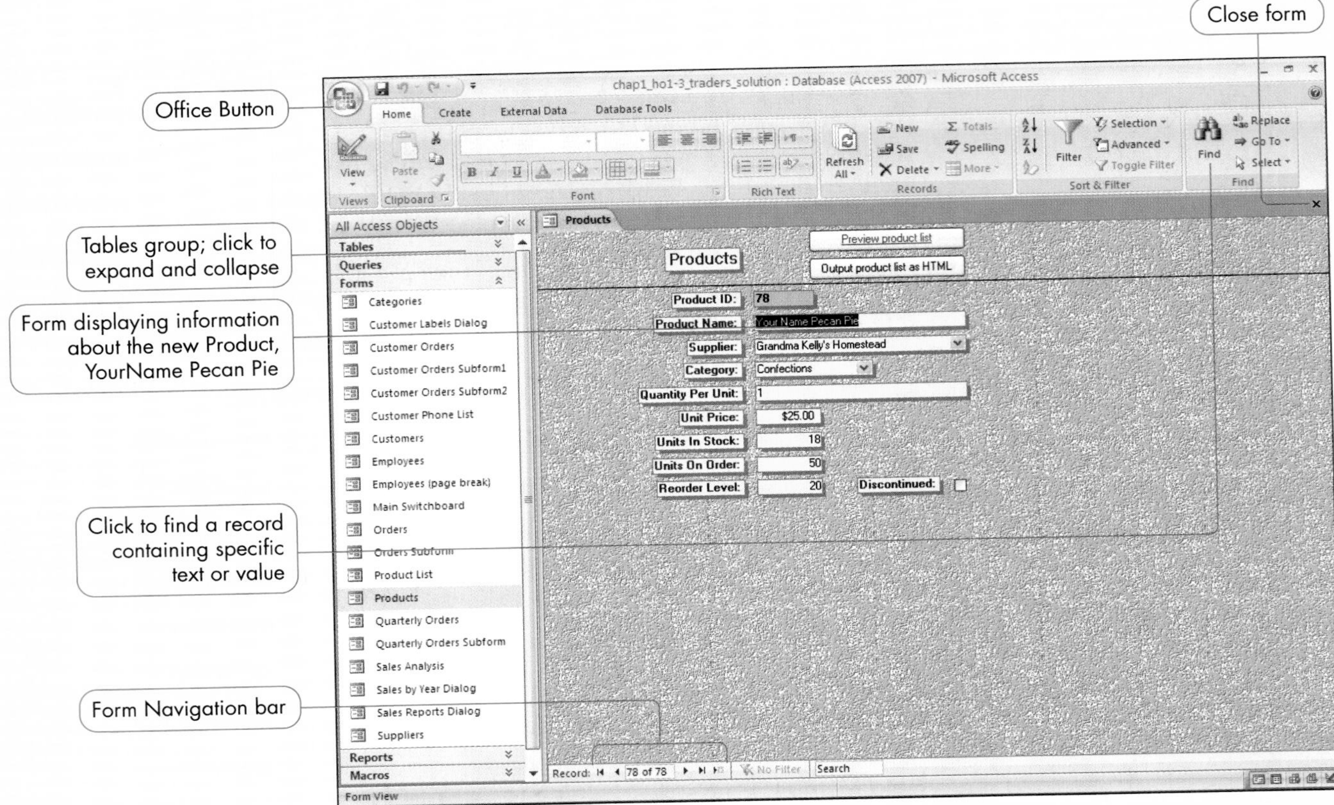

Figure 1.11 The Newly Created Record in the Products Form

Step 5

Recognize the Table and Form Connectivity and Delete a Record

Refer to Figure 1.12 as you complete Step 5.

a. Click **Forms** in the Navigation pane to close it.

The list of available forms collapses.

b. Click **Tables** in the Navigation pane to expand it.

The list of available tables expands. You need to assure yourself that the change you made to the Products form will transfer to the Products table.

c. Double-click the **Products table** to open it.

d. Click **Last record** on the Navigation bar.

The Products form was designed to make data entry easier. It is linked to the Products table. Your newly created record about the Pecan Pie product name is stored in the Products table even though you created it in the form.

e. Navigate to the fifth record in the table, *Chef Anton's Gumbo Mix*.

f. Use the horizontal scroll bar to scroll right until you see the *Discontinued* field.

The check mark in the Discontinued check box tells you that this product has been discontinued.

g. Click the row selector box at the left of the window (see Figure 1.12).

The row highlights with a gold-colored border.

h. Press **Delete**.

An error message appears. It tells you that you cannot delete this record because the table, Order Details, has related records. Even though the product is now discontinued and none of it is in stock, it cannot be deleted from the table because related records are connected to it. A customer in the past ordered this product. If you first deleted all of the orders in the Order Details table that referenced this product, you would be permitted to delete the product from the Products table.

i. Read the error message. Click **OK**.

j. Navigate to the last record. Click the *row selector* to highlight the entire row.

k. Press **Delete**. STOP. Read the error message.

   A warning box appears. It tells you that this action cannot be undone. This product can be deleted because it was just created. No customers have ever ordered it so no related records are in the system.

l. Click **No**. You do not want to delete this record.

   TROUBLESHOOTING: If you clicked Yes and deleted the record, return to Step 4j. Reenter the information for this record. You will need it later in the lesson.

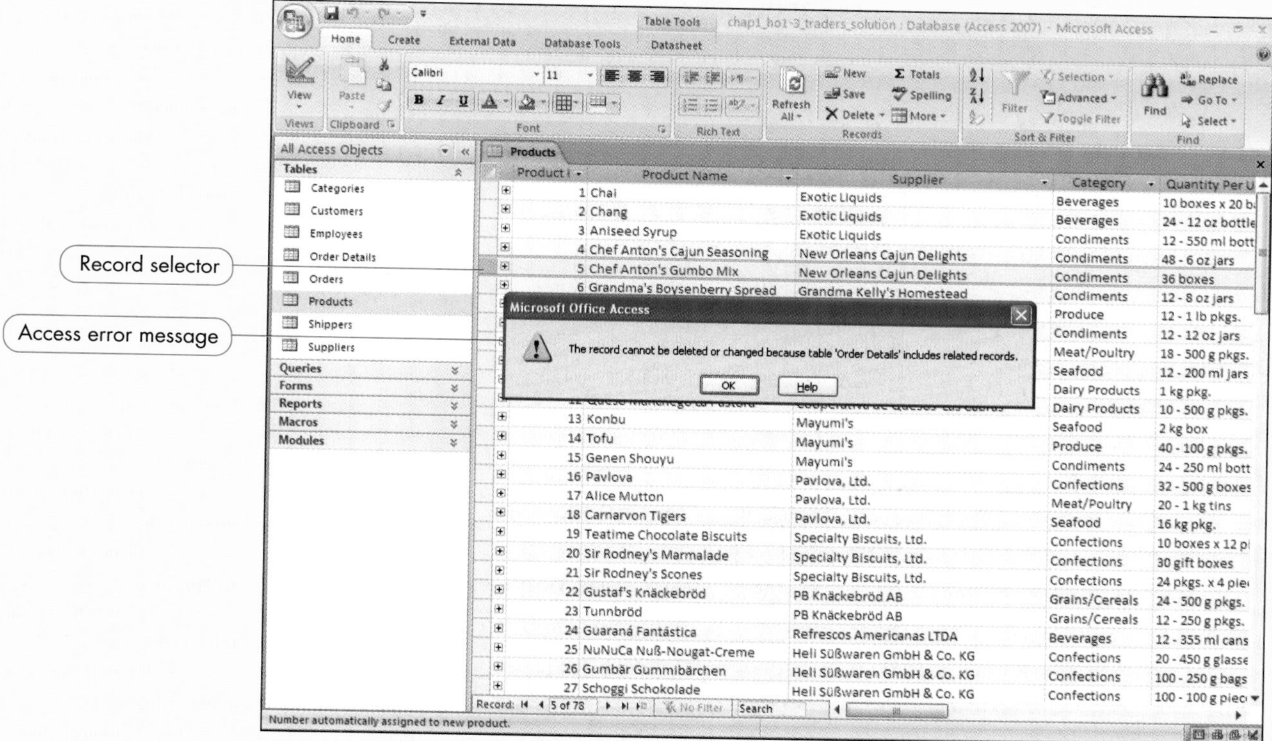

Figure 1.12 How Databases Work to Protect Data

Step 6
Back Up and Compact the Database

Refer to Figure 1.13 as you complete Step 6.

a. Click the **Office Button** and select **Manage**.

The Manage menu gives you access to three critically important tools.

b. Select **Compact and Repair Database**.

Databases tend to get larger and larger as you use them. This feature acts as a defragmenter and eliminates wasted space. As it runs, it closes any open objects in the database.

c. Click the **Office Button**, select **Manage**, and then select **Back Up Database**.

The Save As dialog box opens. The backup utility assigns a default name by adding a date to your file name.

d. Type **chap1_ho1_traders_solution** and click **Save**.

You just created a backup of the database after completing the first hands-on exercise. The original database *chap1_ho1-3_traders_solution* remains onscreen. If you ruin the original database as you complete the second hands-on exercise, you can use the backup file you just created.

e. Close the file and exit Access if you do not want to continue with the next exercise at this time.

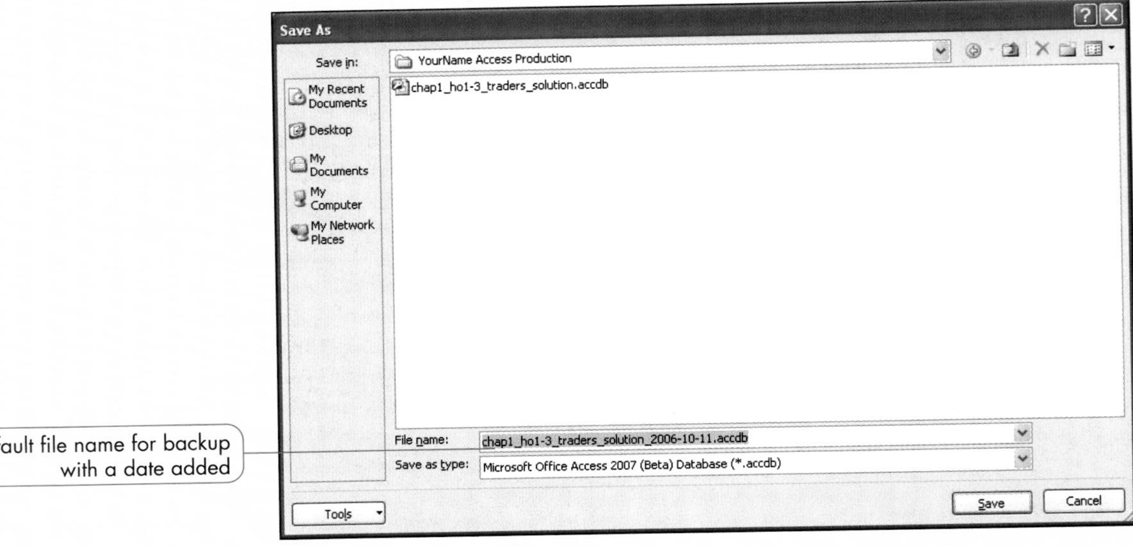

Figure 1.13 Save As Dialog Box to Back Up a Database

Filters, Sorts, and Access Versus Excel

Microsoft Office provides you with many tools that you may use to identify and extract only the records needed at the moment. For example, you might need to know which suppliers are located in New Orleans or which customers have not ordered any products in the last 60 days. You might use that information to identify possible disruptions to product deliveries or customers who may need a telephone call to see if all is well. Both Access and Excel contain powerful tools that enable you to sift through data and extract the information you need and arrange it in a way that makes sense to you. An important part of becoming a proficient computer user is recognizing when to use which tool to accomplish a task.

In this section, you learn how to create filters to examine records and organize these records by sorting table data. You also will examine the logic of Access and Excel in more detail. You will investigate when to use which application to complete a given task.

Creating Filters

A ***filter*** lets you find a subset of data meeting your specifications.

In the first hands-on exercise, you used data from an existing table to obtain information from the database. You created new records and saw that the changes made in a form update data in the associated table data. You found the pecan pie, but you also saw lots of other products. When all of the information needed is contained in a single table, form, report, or query, you can open the object in the Datasheet view, and then apply a filter to display only the records of interest to you. A ***filter*** displays a subset of records; from the object according to specified criteria. You use filters to examine data. Applying a filter does not delete any records; it simply hides extraneous records from your view.

Figure 1.14 displays a Customers table with 91 records. The records in the table are displayed in sequence according to the CustomerID, which is also the primary key (the field or combination of fields that uniquely identifies a record). The status bar indicates that the active record is the sixth in the table. Let's explore how you would retrieve a partial list of those records, such as records of customers in Germany only.

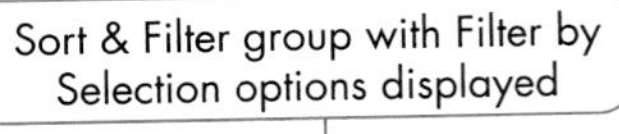

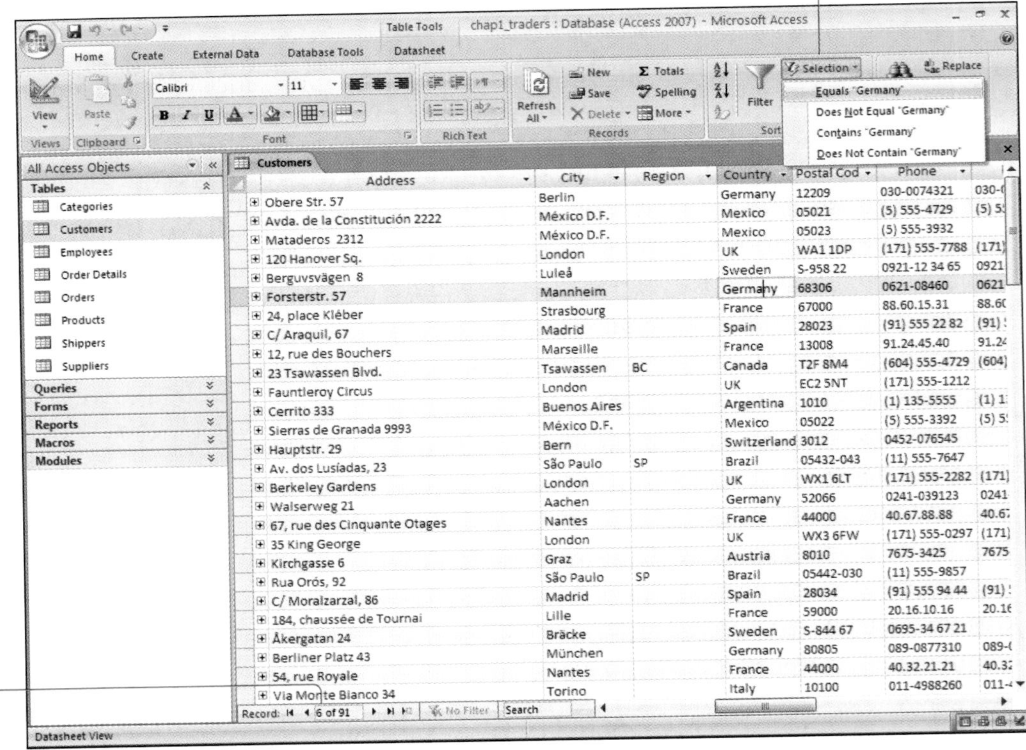

Record Status indicator

Figure 1.14 Unfiltered Table with Appropriate Sort Options Selected

Figure 1.15 displays a filtered view of the same table in which we see only the customers in Germany. The Navigation bar shows that this is a filtered list and that the filter found 11 records satisfying the criteria. (The Customers table still contains the original 91 records, but only 11 records are visible with the filter applied.)

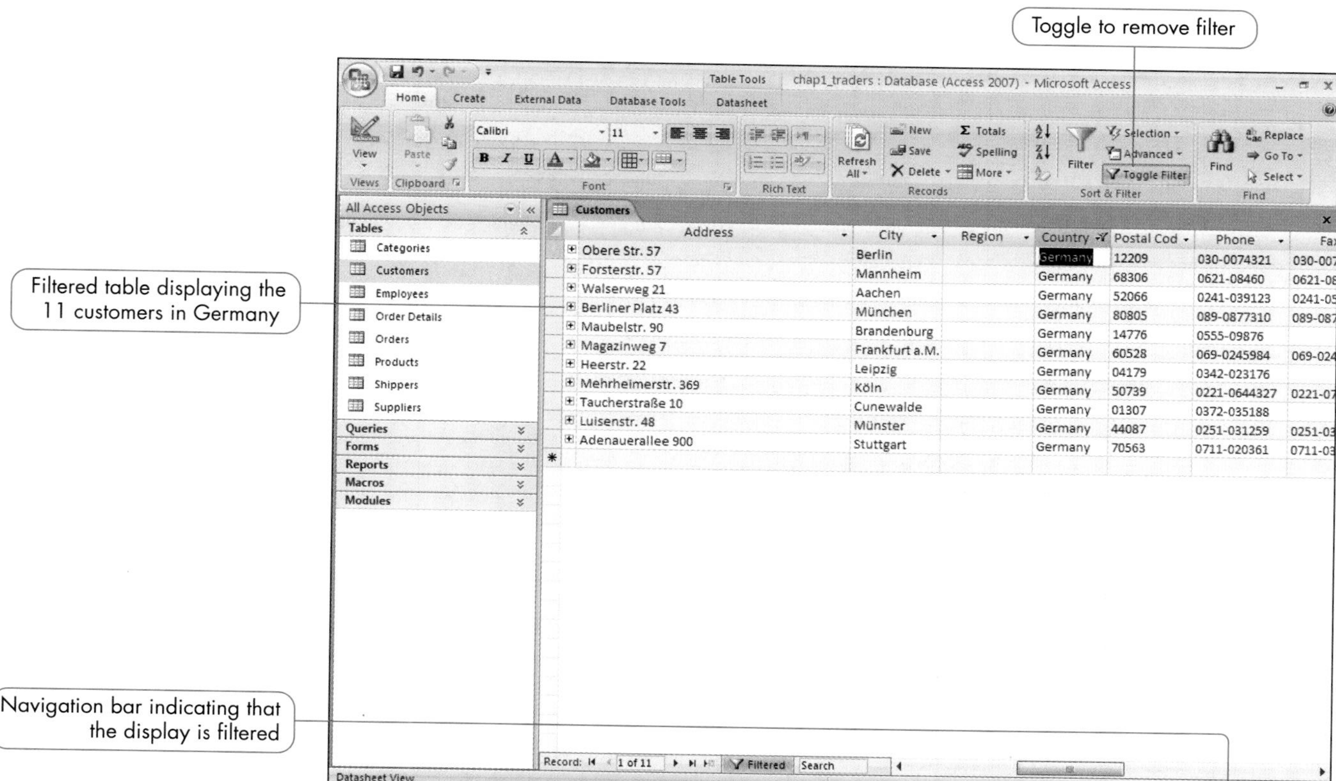

Figure 1.15 Filtered Table with Appropriate Sort Options Selected

TIP Use Quick Keyboard Shortcuts

Look for underlined letters in Access menus. They indicate the letters to use for the keyboard shortcuts. For example, when you click in a field and click the Selection down arrow in the Sort & Filter group, you can click the Equals "London" menu selection or simply type the letter e because the letter E in Equals is underlined, indicating a shortcut key.

Filter by Selection selects only the records that match the pre-selected criteria.

Filter by Form permits selecting criteria from a drop-down list or applying multiple criteria.

An ***inequity*** examines a mathematical relationship such as equals, not equals, greater than, less than, greater than or equal to, or less than or equal to.

The easiest way to implement a filter is to click in any cell that contains the value of the desired criterion (such as any cell that contains *Account Rep* in the Title field), then click Filter by Selection in the Sort & Filter group. ***Filter by Selection*** selects only the records that match the pre-selected criteria.

Figure 1.16 illustrates an alternate and more powerful way to apply a filter. ***Filter by Form*** permits selecting the criteria from a drop-down list and/or applying multiple criteria simultaneously. However, the real advantage of the Filter by Form command extends beyond these conveniences to two additional capabilities. First, you can specify relationships within a criterion; for example, you can use an inequity setting to select products with an inventory level greater than (or less than) 30. An ***inequity*** examines a mathematical relationship such as equals, not equals, greater than, less than, greater than or equal to, or less than or equal to. Filter by Selection, on the other hand, requires you to specify criteria equal to an existing value. Figure 1.16 shows the filtered query setup to select Beverages with more than 30 units in stock.

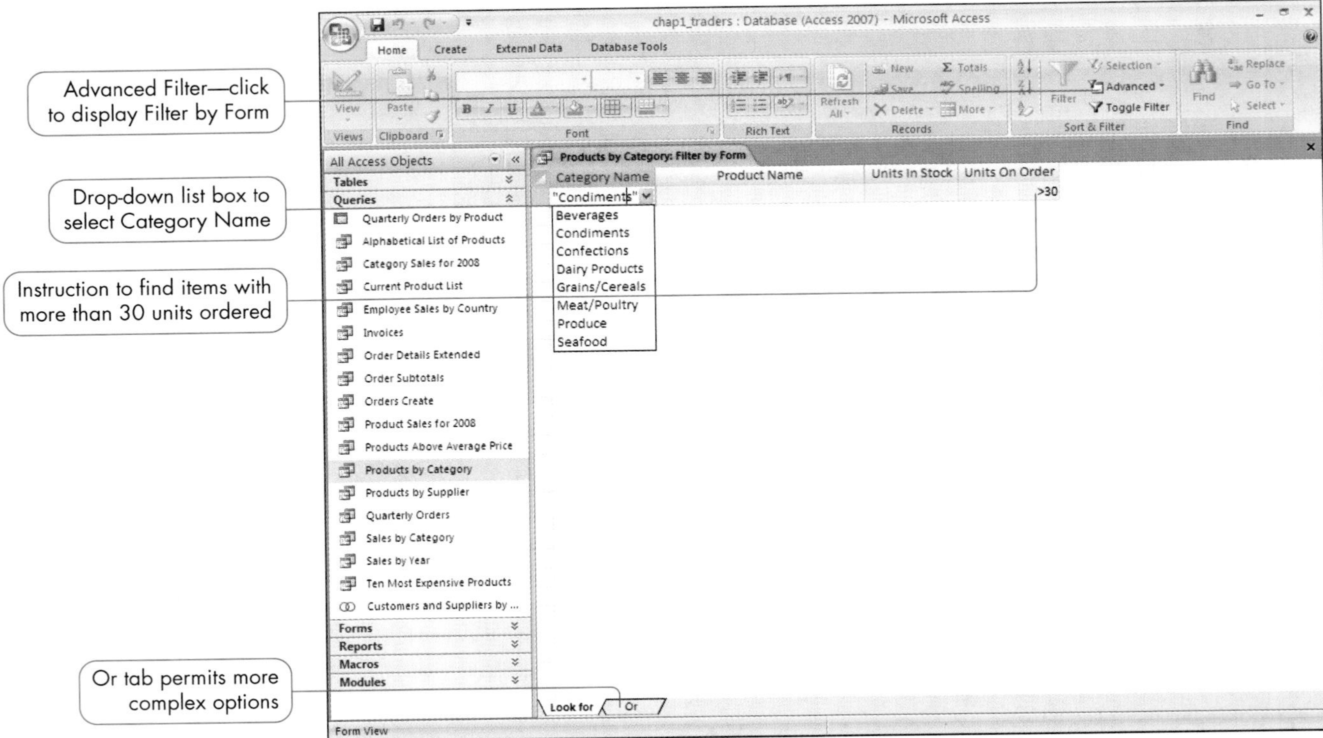

Figure 1.16 Filter by Form Design Grid

A second advantage of the Filter by Form command is that you can specify alternative criteria (such as customers in Germany or orders for over 30 units) by clicking the Or tab. (The latter capability is not implemented in Figure 1.16.) However, the availability of the various filter and sort commands enables you to obtain information from a database quickly and easily without creating a query or report.

Sorting Table Data on One or More Fields

A ***sort*** lists those records in a specific sequence, such as alphabetically by last name.

Sort Ascending provides an alphabetical list of text data or a small to large list of numeric data.

Sort Descending displays records with the highest value listed first.

You also can change the order of the information by sorting by one or more fields. A ***sort*** lists those records in a specific sequence, such as alphabetically by last name or by EmployeeID. To sort the table, click in the field on which you want to sequence the records (the LastName field in this example), then click Sort Ascending in the Sort & Filter group on the Home tab. ***Sort Ascending*** provides an alphabetical list of text data or a small to large list of numeric data. ***Sort Descending*** is appropriate for numeric fields such as salary, if you want to display the records with the highest value listed first. Figure 1.17 shows the Customers table sorted in alphabetical order by country. You may apply both filters and sorts to table or query information to select and order the data in the way that you need to make decisions.

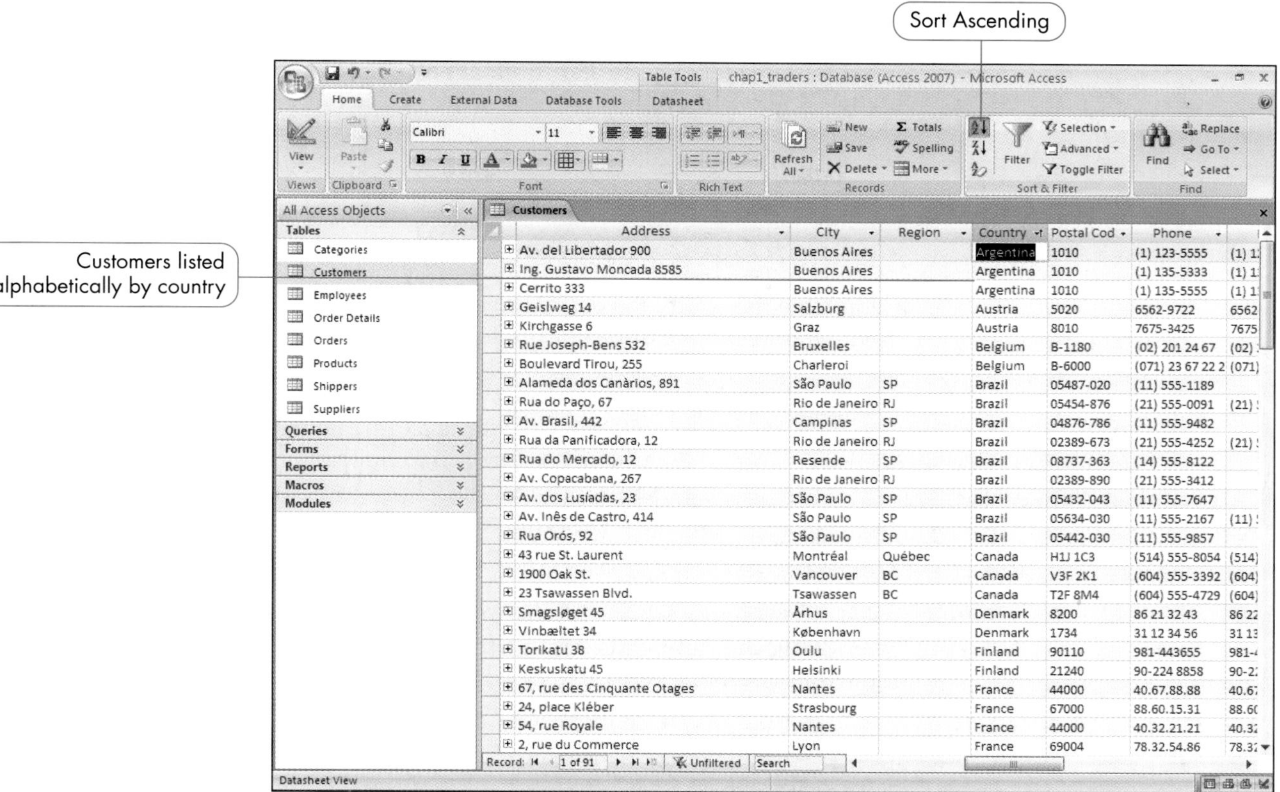

Figure 1.17 Customers Table Sorted by Country

The operations can be done in any order; that is, you can filter a table to show only selected records, then you can sort the filtered table to display the records in a different order. Conversely, you can sort a table, and then apply a filter. It does not matter which operation is performed first, and indeed, you can go back and forth between the two. You can also filter the table further, by applying a second (or third) criterion; for example, click in a cell containing *USA* and apply a Filter by Selection. Then click in a record for Oregon (OR) and apply a Filter by Selection a second time to display the customers from Oregon. You also can click Toggle Filter at any time to display all of the records in the table. Filters are a temporary method for examining subsets of data. If you close the filtered table or query and reopen it, all of the records display.

TIP The Sort or Filter—Which Is First?

It doesn't matter whether you sort a table, and then apply a filter or filter first, and then sort. The operations are cumulative. Thus, after you sort a table, any subsequent display of filtered records for that table will be in the specified sequence. Alternatively, you can apply a filter, and then sort the filtered table by clicking in the desired field and clicking the appropriate sort command. Remember, too, that all filter commands are cumulative and hence, you must remove the filter to see the original table.

You may be familiar with applying a filter, sorting data, or designing a form using Excel. The fact is, Excel can accomplish all of these activities. You need to examine your data needs and think about what your future data requirements may be to decide whether to use Access or Excel.

Knowing When to Use Access or Excel to Manage Data

If you have the ability to control data and turn it into useful information, you possess a marketable skill. It does not matter whether you are planning to become a social worker, a teacher, an engineer, an entrepreneur, a radiologist, a marketer, a day care worker, a musician, or an accountant. You will need to collect, store, maintain, manage, and protect data as well as convert it into information used to make strategic decisions. A widely used program that you probably already know is Excel. This course will help you become familiar with Access. You can accomplish many of the same things in either software. Although the two packages have much in common, they each have advantages. So, how do you choose whether to use Access or Excel?

If you have the ability to control data and turn it into useful information, you possess a marketable skill.

Making the right choice is critical if you want to find and update your information with maximum performance and accuracy. Ideally, your data needs and the type and amount of data used will determine how to pick the program that will work best. Sometimes organizations use Access when they probably would be better served with Excel and vice versa. The answer to the question of which to use may depend on who you ask. An accountant probably will use Excel. The information technology professional probably will use a more sophisticated database software like Oracle, but not Access. The middle manager in the marketing or manufacturing department will probably use Access. The question remains.

Select the Software to Use

A contacts list is an example of flat data. Each column of data (names, addresses, and phone numbers) is logically related to the others. If you can store your data logically in a single table or worksheet, then do. Update your data in the same type of file. Data contained in a single page or sheet (not multiple) are called ***flat*** or ***non-relational data***. You would never store your friend's last name on a different sheet from the sheet containing the friend's cell phone number.

Data contained in a single page or sheet (not multiple) are called ***flat*** *or* ***non-relational data***.

Suppose you had a spreadsheet of club members' names and contact information. Your club decides to sell cookies as a fundraiser. You might create a new worksheet listing how many boxes of which type of cookie each member picked up to sell. Your third worksheet might show how much money each member has turned in from the cookie sales. These data are different. They are not flat. Can you imagine needing to know someone's phone number or how many cookie boxes he or she promised to sell while looking at the worksheet of data about how much money has been turned in? These data are multi-dimensional and need to be stored in more than one worksheet or table. This describes relational data. Each table holds a particular type of data (number of boxes collected, contact information, funds turned in). Relational data are best stored in Access. In this example, you would create a database with three tables. You need to adhere to the following rules about assigning data to the appropriate table.

Assign table data so that each table:

- Represents only a single subject
- Has a field(s) that uniquely identifies each record
- Does not contain duplicate fields
- Has no repetition of the same type of value
- Has no fields belonging in other tables

As the quantity and complexity of data increase, the need to organize it efficiently also increases. Access affords better data organization than Excel. Access accomplishes the organization through a system of linkages among the tables. Each record (row) should be designated with a primary key—a unique identifier that sets it apart from all of the other records in the table. The primary key might be an account number, a student identification number, or an employee access code. All data in Excel have a unique identifier—the cell address. In life, you have a Social Security Number. It is the best unique identifier you have. Ever notice how, when at the doctor's office or applying for college admission, you are asked for your Social Security Number as well as your name? Your record in its database system probably uses your Social Security Number as a unique identifier.

You still need to answer the question of when to use Access and when to use Excel.

Use Access

You should use Access to manage data when you:

- Require a relational database (multiple tables or multi-dimensional tables) to store your data or anticipate adding more tables in the future.

  For example, you may set your club membership contact list in either software, but if you believe that you also will need to keep track of the cookie sales and fund collection, use Access.
- Have a large amount of data.
- Rely on external databases to derive and analyze the data you need.

  If you frequently need to have Excel exchange data to or from Access, use Access. Even though the programs are compatible, it makes sense to work in Access to minimize compatibility issues.
- Need to maintain constant connectivity to a large external database, such as one built with Microsoft SQL Server or your organization's Enterprise Resource Planning system.
- Need to regroup data from different tables in a single place through complex queries.

  You might need to create output showing how many boxes of cookies each club member picked up and how much money they turned in along with the club member's name and phone number.
- Have many people working in the database and need strong options to update the data.

  For example, five different clerks at an auto parts store might wait on five different customers. Each clerk connects to the inventory table to find out if the needed part is in stock and where in the warehouse it is located. When the customer says, "Yes, I want that," the inventory list is instantly updated and that product is no longer available to be purchased by the other four customers.

Use Excel

You should use Excel to manage data when you:

- Require a flat or non-relational view of your data (you do not need a relational database with multiple tables).

  This idea is especially true if that data is mostly numeric—for example, if you need to maintain an expense statement.
- Want to run primarily calculations and statistical comparisons on your data.
- Know your dataset is manageable in size (no more than 15,000 rows).

In the next exercise, you will create and apply filters, perform sorts, and develop skills to customize the data presentation to answer your questions.

Hands-On Exercises

2 | Data Manipulation: Filters and Sorts

Skills covered: 1. Use Filter by Selection with an Equal Setting **2.** Use Filter by Selection with a Contains Setting **3.** Use Filter by Form with an Inequity Setting **4.** Sort a Table

Step 1
Use Filter by Selection with an Equal Setting

Refer to Figure 1.18 as you complete Step 1.

a. Open the *chap1_ho1-3_traders_solution* file if necessary, and click **Options** on the Security Warning toolbar, click the **Enable this content option** in the Microsoft Office Security Options dialog box, and click **OK**.

TROUBLESHOOTING: If you create unrecoverable errors while completing this hands-on exercise, you can delete the *chap1_ho1-3_traders_solution* file, copy the *chap1_ho1_traders_solution* backup database you created at the end of the first hands-on exercise, and open the copy of the backup database to start the second hands-on exercise again.

b. Open the **Customers table**; navigate to record 4 and replace *Thomas Hardy's* name with **your name** in the **Contact Name field.**

c. Scroll right until the **City field** is visible. Look through the record values of the field form until you locate a customer in **London**, for example, the fourth record. Click in the field box to select it.

The word *"London"* will have a gold colored border around it to let you know that it is active.

d. Click **Selection** in the Sort & Filter group on the Home tab.

e. Choose **Equals "London"** from the menu.

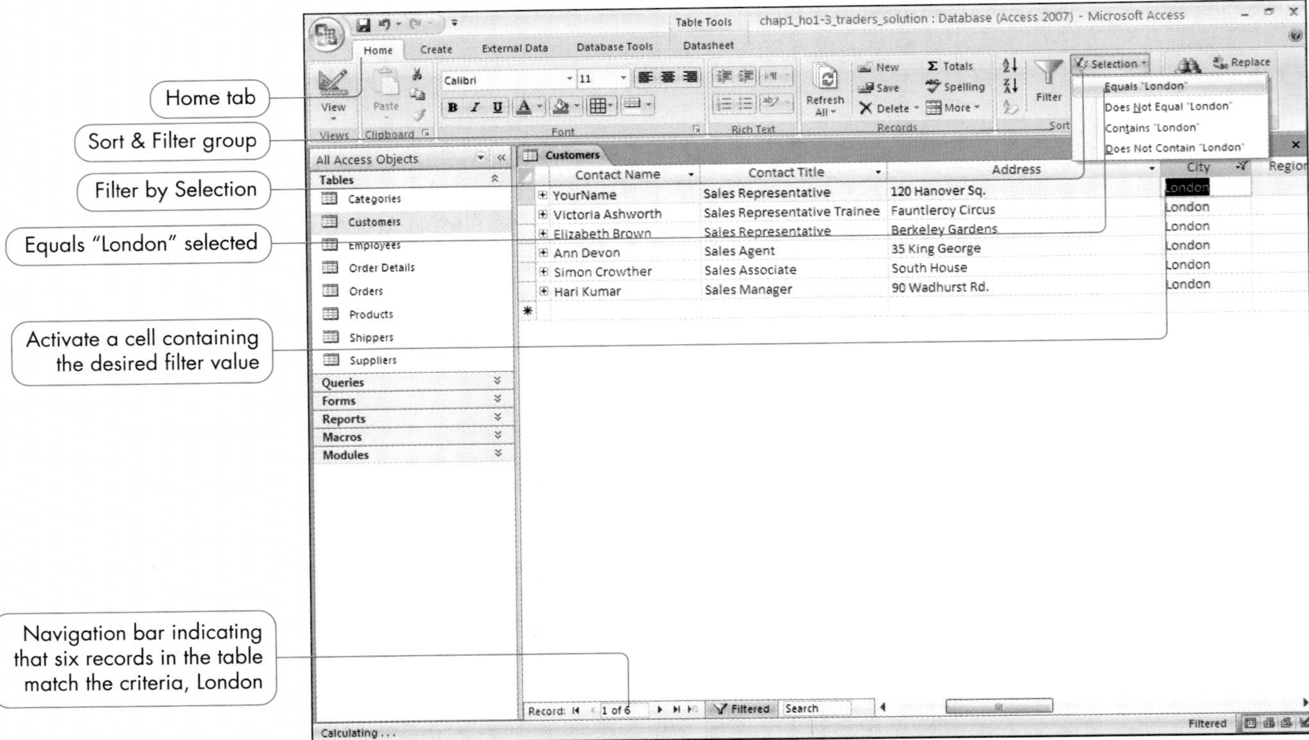

Figure 1.18 Customers Table Filtered to Display London Records Only

Step 2
Use Filter by Selection with a Contains Setting

Refer to Figure 1.19 as you complete Step 2.

a. Find a record with the value **Sales Representative** in the **Contact Title field**. Click your insertion point to activate that field. The first record has a value of *Sales Representative* for the Contact Title field.

   Sales Representative will have a gold colored border around it to let you know that it is activated.

b. Click **Selection** on the Sort & Filter group located on the Home tab.

c. Click on **Contains "Sales Representative"** (or type t).

   You have applied a second layer of filtering to the customers in London. The second layer further restricts the display to only those customers who have the words Sales Representative contained in their title.

d. Scroll left until you see your name. Compare your results to those shown in Figure 1.19.

e. Click the **Office Button**, select **Print**, and then select **Quick Print**.

f. Click **Toggle Filter** in the Sort & Filter group to remove the filters.

g. Close the Customers table. Click **No** if a dialog box asks if you want to save the design changes to the Customers table.

TIP Removing Versus Deleting a Filter

Removing a filter displays all of the records that are in a table, but it does not delete the filter because the filter is stored permanently with the table. To delete the filter entirely is more complicated than simply removing it. Click Advanced on the Sort & Filter group and select the Clear All Filters option from the drop-down list box. Deleting unnecessary filters may reduce the load on the CPU and will allow the database manager to optimize the database performance.

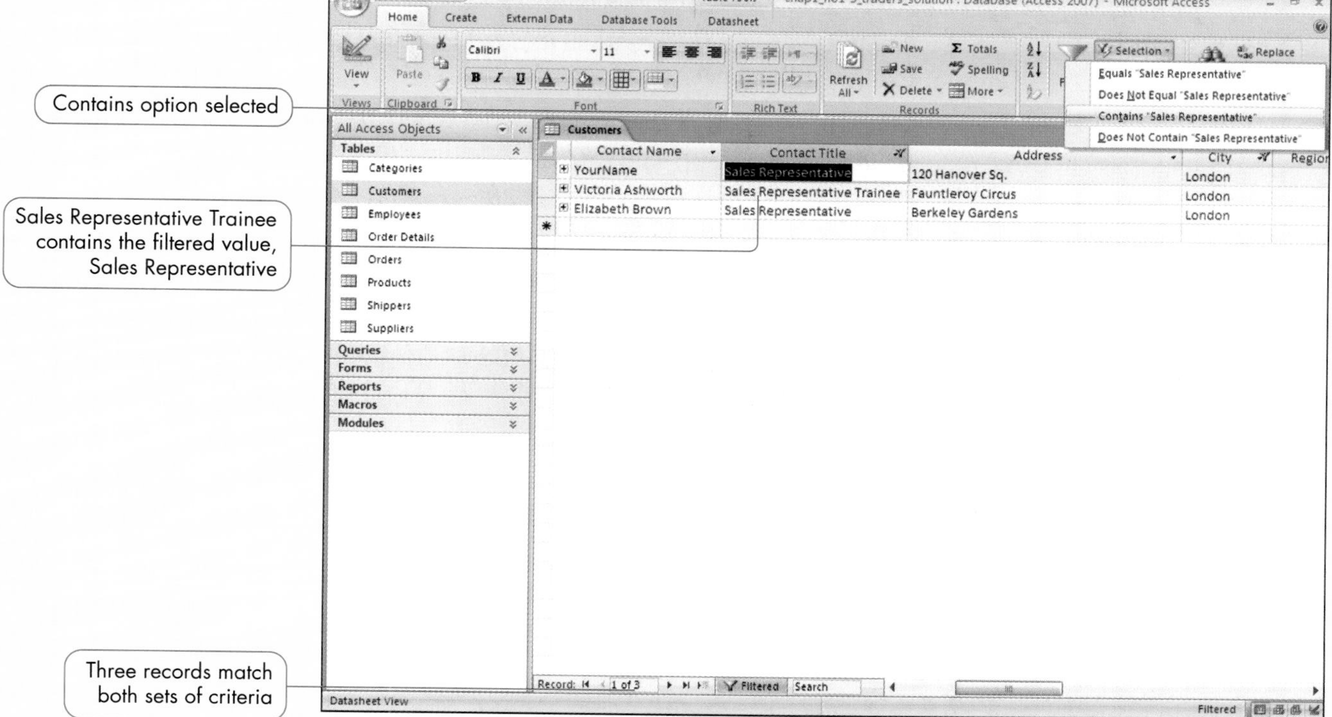

Figure 1.19 Customers Table Filtered to Display London and Sales Representative Job Titles

Step 3
Use Filter by Form with an Inequity Setting

Refer to Figure 1.20 as you complete Step 3.

a. Click **Tables** in the Navigation pane to collapse the listed tables.

b. Click **Queries** in the Navigation pane to expand the lists of available queries.

c. Locate and double-click the **Order Details Extended** query to open it.

   This query contains information about orders. It has fields containing information about the salesperson, the Order ID, the product name, the unit price, quantity ordered, the discount given, and an extended price. The extended price is a term used to total order information.

d. Click **Advanced** in the Sort & Filter group on the Home tab.

   The process to apply a filter by form is identical in a table or a query.

e. Select **Filter By Form** from the list.

   All of the records seem to vanish and you see only a list of field names.

f. Click in the **first row** under the **First Name** field.

   A down arrow appears at the right of the box.

g. Click the **First Name down arrow**. A list of all available first names appears.

   Your name should be on the list. It may be in a different location than that shown in Figure 1.20 because the list is in alphabetical order.

   TROUBLESHOOTING: If you do not see your name and you do see Margaret on the list, you probably skipped Steps 3c and 3d in Hands-On Exercise 1. Close the query without saving changes, turn back to the first hands-on exercise, and rework it, making sure not to omit any steps. Then you can return to this spot and work the remainder of this hands-on exercise.

h. Select **your first name** from the list.

i. Click in the *first row* under the *Last Name field* to turn on the drop-down arrow. Locate and select **your last name** by clicking it.

j. Scroll right until you see the Extended Price field. Click in the *first row* under the Extended Price field and type **<50**.

   This will select all of the items ordered where the total was under $50. You ignore the drop-down arrow and type the expression needed.

k. Click **Toggle Filter** in the Sort & Filter group.

   You have specified which records to include and have executed the filtering by clicking Toggle Filter. You should have 31 records that match the criteria you specified.

l. Click the **Office Button**, and then select **Print**. In the Print dialog box, locate the **Pages** control in the *Print Range* section. Type **1** in the *From* box and again in the *To* box. Click **OK**.

   You have instructed Access to print the first page of the filtered query results.

m. Close the query. Click **No** when asked if you want to save the design changes.

TIP Deleting Filter by Form Criterion

The Filter by Form command has all of the capabilities of the Filter by Selection command and provides two additional capabilities. First, you can use relational operators such as >, >=, <, or <= as opposed to searching for an exact value. Second, you can search for records that meet one of several conditions (the equivalent of an "Or" operation). Enter the first criterion as you normally would, then click the Or tab at the bottom of the window to display a second form in which you enter the alternate criteria. (To delete an alternate criterion, click the associated tab, and then click Delete on the toolbar.)

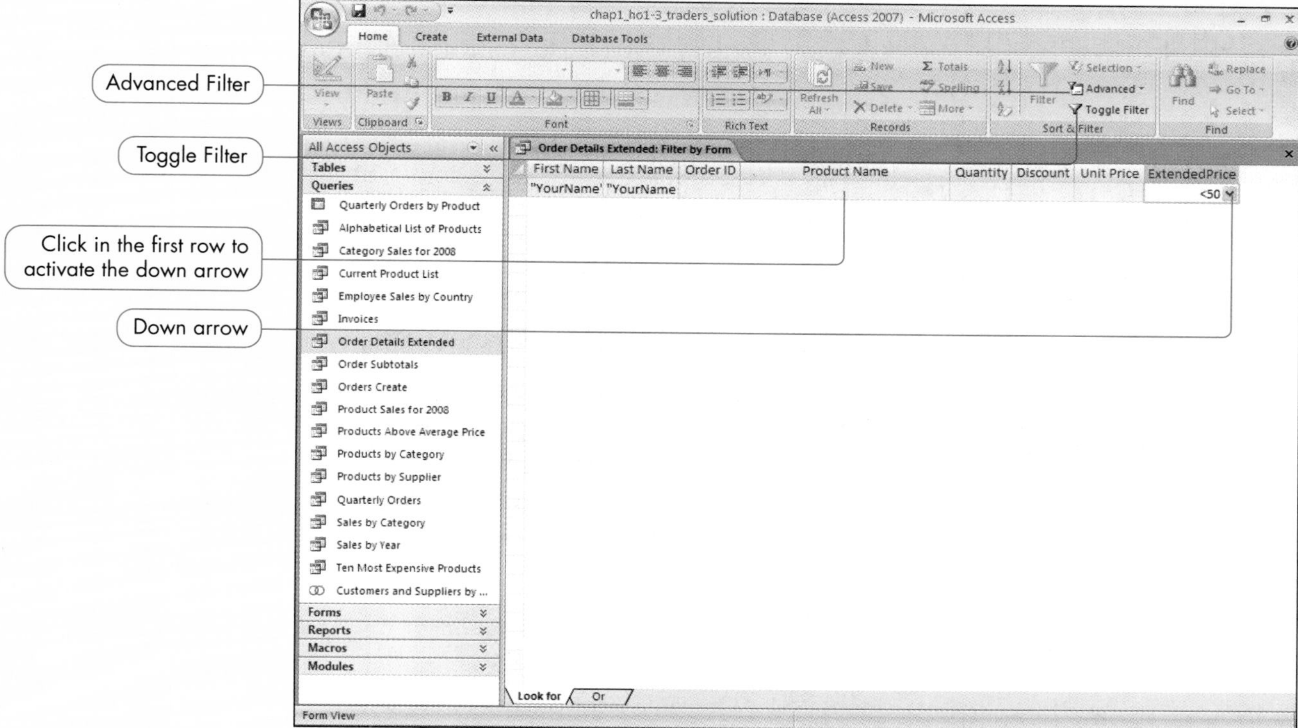

Figure 1.20 Filter by Selection Criteria Settings

Step 4
Sort a Table

Refer to Figure 1.21 as you complete Step 4.

a. Click **Queries** in the Navigation pane to collapse the listed queries.

b. Click **Tables** in the Navigation pane to expand the lists of available tables.

c. Locate and double-click the **Customers table** to open it.

This table contains information about customers. It is sorted in ascending order by the Customer ID field. Because this field contains text, the table is sorted in alphabetical order.

d. Click any value in the **Customer ID field**. Click **Sort Descending** in the Sort & Filter group on the Home tab.

Sorting in descending order on a character field produces a reverse alphabetical order.

e. Scroll right until you can see both the **Country** and **City fields**.

You will sort the customers by country and then by city within the countries. You can sort on more than one field as long as you sort on the primary field (in this case the country) last.

f. Click the field name for **Country**.

The entire column selects.

g. Click the **Country field name box** and hold the left mouse down.

A thick dark blue line displays on the left edge of the Country field column.

h. Check to make sure that you see the thick blue line. When you do, drag the country field to the **left**. When the thick black line moves to between the *Address and City* fields, release the mouse and the Country field position moves to the left of the City field.

i. Click any city name in the **City field** and click **Sort Ascending**.

j. Click any country name in the **Country field** and click **Sort Ascending**.

The countries are sorted in alphabetical order. The cities within each country also are sorted alphabetically. For example, the customer in Graz, Austria, is listed before the one in Saltzburg.

k. Scroll down until you see the *UK* customers listed.

l. Scroll to the left until the *Contact Name* is the first field in the left of the screen.

m. Press **PrntScrn** located somewhere in the upper right of your keyboard.

You have captured a picture of your screen. If nothing seemed to happen, it is because the picture was saved to the Clipboard. You must retrieve the picture from the Clipboard in order to see it.

TROUBLESHOOTING: Some notebook computers have Print Screen as a function. If the words Print Screen on the key are a different color, you must press **Fn+Print Screen**.

n. Launch Word, open a *new blank document*, and type **your name and section number** on the first line. Press **Enter**.

o. Press **Ctrl+V** to paste your picture of the screenshot into the Word document. Save the document as **chap1_ho2_traders_solution.docx**. Print the Word document.

p. Close the **Customers table**. Do not save the changes.

q. Click the **Office Button**, select **Manage**, and then select **Compact and Repair Database**.

r. Click the **Office Button** again, select **Manage**, and then select **Back Up Database**. Type **chap1_ho2_traders_solution** as the file name and click **Save**.

You just created a backup of the database after completing the second hands-on exercise. The original database *chap1_ho1-3_traders_solution* remains onscreen. If you ruin the original database as you complete the third hands-on exercise, you can use the backup file you just created.

s. Close the file and exit Access if you do not want to continue with the next exercise at this time.

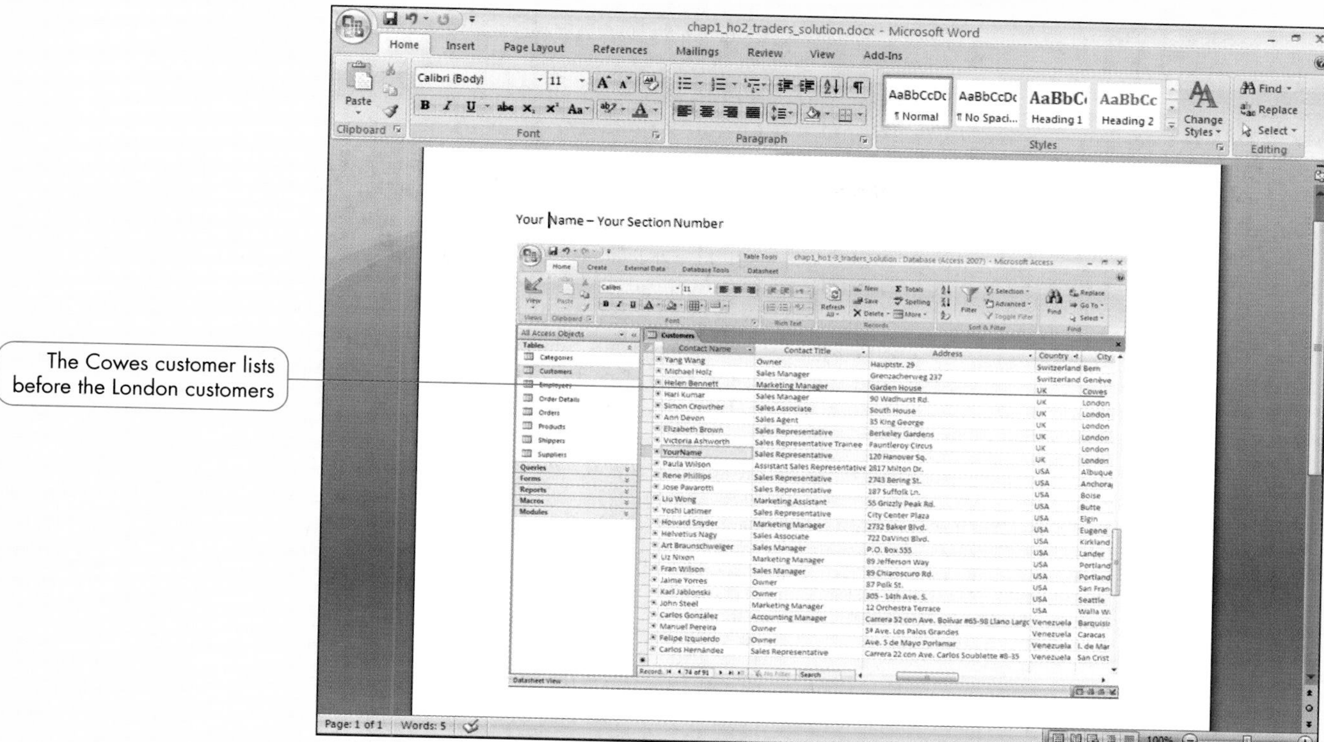
The Cowes customer lists before the London customers
Your Name – Your Section Number

Figure 1.21 The Customers Table Sorted by Country and Then by City in Word

The Relational Database

A ***relational database management system*** is one in which data are grouped into similar collections, called tables, and the relationships between tables are formed by using a common field.

In the previous section, you read that you should use Access when you have multidimensional data. Access derives power from multiple tables and the relationships among those tables. A ***relational database management system*** is one in which data are grouped into similar collections called tables, and the relationships between tables are formed by using a common field. The design of a relational database system is illustrated in Figure 1.22. The power of a relational database lies in the software's ability to organize data and combine items in different ways to obtain a complete picture of the events the data describe. Good database design connects the data in different tables through a system of linkages. These links are the relationships that give relational databases the name. Look at Figure 1.1. The student record (folder) contains information about the student, but also contains cross-references to data stored in other cabinet drawers, such as the advisor's name or a list of courses completed. If you need to know the advisor's phone number, you can open the faculty drawer, find the advisor's record, and then locate the field containing the phone number. The cross-reference from the student file to the faculty file illustrates how a relationship works in a database. Figure 1.22 displays the cross-references between the tables as a series of lines connecting the common fields. When the database is set up properly, the users of the data can be confident that if they search a specific customer identification number, they will be given accurate information about that customer's order history and payment balances, and his/her product or shipping preferences.

(The power of a relational database lies in the software's ability to organize data and combine items in different ways to obtain a complete picture of the events the data describe.)

In this section, you will explore the relationships among tables, learn about the power of relational integrity, and discover how the software protects the organization's data.

Using the Relationship Window

The relationship (the lines between the tables in Figure 1.22) is like a piece of electronic string that travels throughout the database, searching every record of every table until it finds the data satisfying the user's request. Once identified, the fields and records of interest will be tied to the end of the string, pulled through the computer and reassembled in a way that makes the data easy to understand. The first end of the string was created when the primary key was established in the Customers table. The primary key is a unique identifier for each table record. The other end of the string will be tied to a field in a different table. If you examine Figure 1.22, you will see that the CustomerID is a foreign field in the Orders table. A ***foreign key*** is a field in one table that also is stored in a different table as a primary key. Each value of the CustomerID can occur only once in the Customers table because it is a primary key. However, the CustomerID may appear multiple times in the Orders table because one customer may make many different purchases. The CustomerID field is a foreign key in the Orders table but the primary key in the Customers table.

A ***foreign key*** is a field in one table that also is stored in a different table as a primary key.

Examine Referential Integrity

Referential integrity is the set of rules that ensure that data stored in related tables remain consistent as the data are updated.

The relationships connecting the tables will be created using an Access feature that uses referential integrity. Integrity means truthful or reliable. When ***referential integrity*** is enforced, the user can trust the "threads" running through the database and "tying" related items together. The sales manager can use the database to find the names and phone numbers of all the customers who have ordered Teatime Chocolate Biscuits (a specific product). Because referential integrity has been enforced, it will not matter that the order information is in a different table from the customer data. The invisible threads will keep the information accurately connected. The threads also provide a method of ensuring data accuracy. You cannot enter a record in the Orders table that references a ProductID or a CustomerID that does not exist elsewhere in the system. Nor can you easily delete a record in one table if it has related records in related tables.

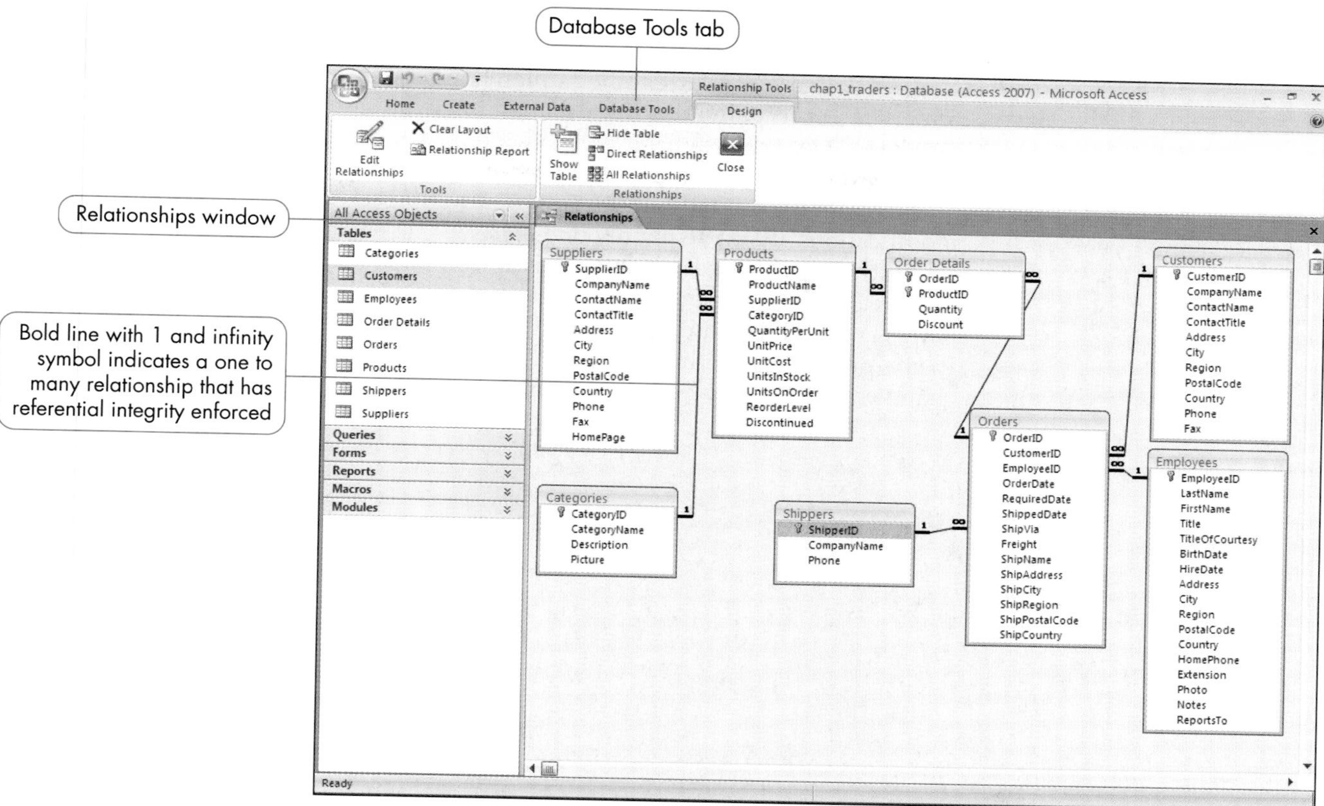

Figure 1.22 The Relationships Window Displaying Table Connections

If this were a real organization's data system, the files would be much, much larger and the data more sophisticated. When learning database skills, you should start with smaller, more manageable files. The same design principles apply regardless of the database size. A small file gives you the ability to check the tables and see if your results are correct. Even though the data amounts are small, you need to develop the work practices needed to manage large amounts of data. With only a handful of records, you can easily count the number of employees at the Washington state office. In addition to learning how to accomplish a task, you also should begin to learn to anticipate the computer's response to an instruction. As you work, ask yourself what the anticipated results should be and then verify. When you become skilled at anticipating output correctly, you are surprised less often.

(As you work, ask yourself what the anticipated results should be and then verify. When you become skilled at anticipating output correctly, you are surprised less often.)

Understanding Relational Power

In the previous section, you read that you should use Access when you have multidimensional data. Access derives power from multiple tables and the relationships between those tables. This type of database is known as a relational database and is illustrated in Figure 1.22. This figure describes the database structure. Examine some of the connections. The Employee ID is a foreign field in the Orders table. For example, you can produce a document displaying the history of each order a customer had placed and the employee's name (from the Employees table) that entered the order. The Orders table references the Order Details table where the OrderID is a foreign field. The ProductID relates to the Products table (where it is the primary key). The Category ID is the primary key in the Categories table, but shows up as a foreign field in the Products table. The table connections, even when more than one table is involved, provide the decision-maker power. This feature gives the manager the ability to find out sales by category. How many different beverages were shipped last week? What was the total revenue generated from seafood orders last year?

Suppose a customer called to complain that his orders were arriving late. Because the Shipper ID is a foreign field in the Orders table, you could look up which shipper delivered that customer's merchandise, and then find out what other customers received deliveries from that shipper the same month. Are the other orders also late? Does the firm need to reconsider its shipping options? The design of a relational database enables us to extract information from multiple tables in a single query or report. Equally important, it simplifies the way data are changed in that modifications are made in only one place.

In the previous hands-on exercises, you have made modifications to table data. You created a new product, you changed an employee and customer name to your name, and you sorted data. You will trace through some of those changes in the next hands-on exercise to help you understand the power of relationships and how a change made to one object travels throughout the database file structure.

Hands-On Exercises

3 | Introduction to Relationships

Skills covered: 1. Examine the Relationships Window **2.** Discover that Changes in Table Data Affect Queries **3.** Use Filter by Form with an Inequity Setting and Reapply a Saved Filter **4.** Filter a Report **5.** Remove an Advanced Filter

Step 1 Examine the Relationships Window

Refer to Figure 1.23 as you complete Step 1.

a. Open the *chap1_ho1-3_traders_solution* file if necessary, click **Options** on the *security warning* toolbar, click the **Enable this content option** in the Microsoft Office Security Options dialog box, and click **OK**.

TROUBLESHOOTING: If you create unrecoverable errors while completing this hands-on exercise, you can delete the *chap1_ho1-3_traders_solution* file, copy the *chap1_ho2_traders_solution* database you created at the end of the second hands-on exercise, and open the copy of the backup database to start the third hands-on exercise again.

b. Click the **Database Tools tab** and click **Relationships** in the Show/Hide group.

Examine the relationships that connect the various tables. For example, the Products table is connected to the Suppliers, Categories, and Order Details tables.

c. Click **Show Table**.

The Show Table dialog box opens. It tells you that there are eight available tables in the database. If you look in the Relationship window, you will see that all eight tables are in the relationship diagram.

d. Click the **Queries tab** in the Show Table dialog box.

You could add all of the queries to the Relationships window. Things might become cluttered, but you could tell at a glance where the queries get their information.

e. Close the Show Table dialog box.

f. Click the **down arrow** in the All Access Objects bar of the Navigation pane.

g. Click **Tables and Related Views**.

You can now see not only the tables, but also the queries, forms, and reports that connect to the table data. If a query is sourced on more than one table, it will appear multiple times in the Navigation pane. This view provides an alternate method of viewing the relationships connecting the tables.

h. Close the Relationships window. Save the changes.

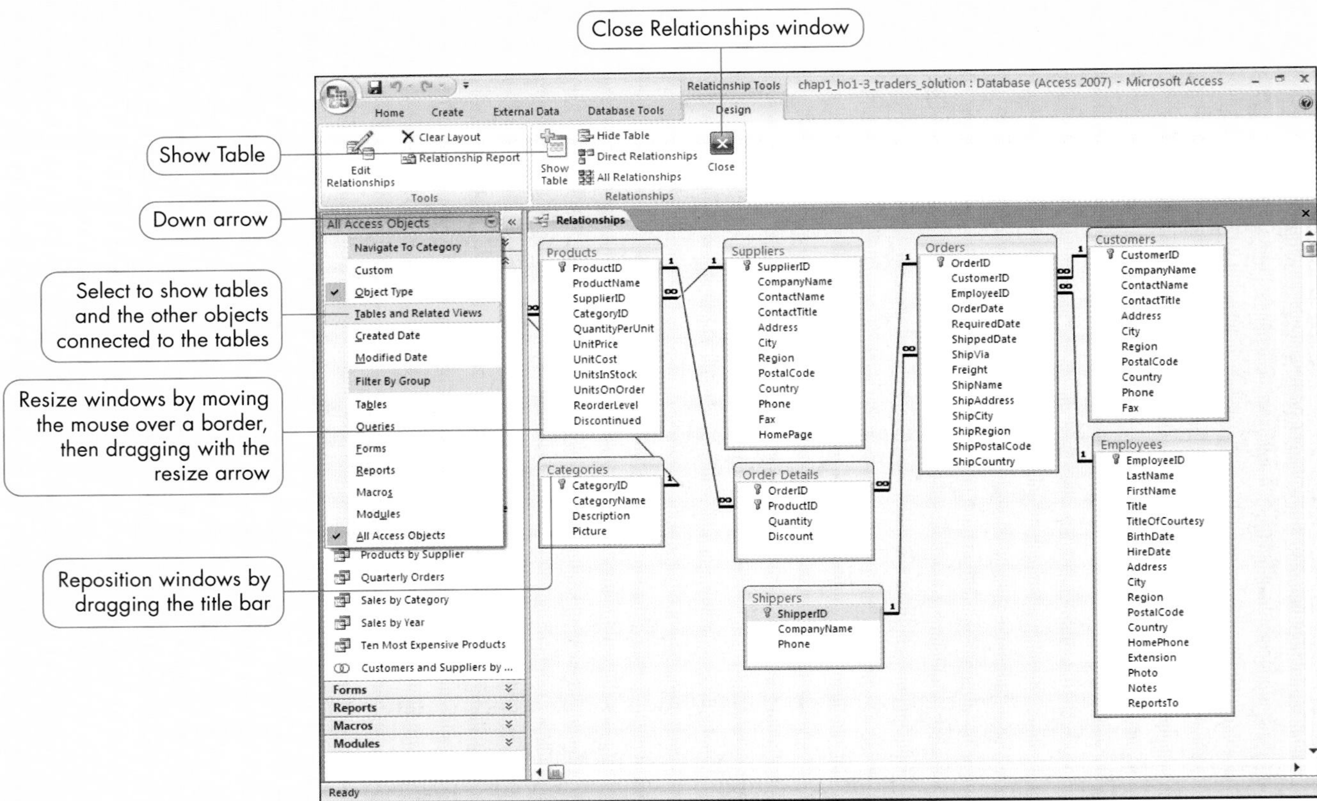
Close Relationships window
Show Table
Down arrow
Select to show tables and the other objects connected to the tables
Resize windows by moving the mouse over a border, then dragging with the resize arrow
Reposition windows by dragging the title bar

Figure 1.23 The Relationships Window Displaying the Northwind Table Relationships

Step 2
Discover that Changes in Table Data Affect Queries

Refer to Figure 1.24 as you complete Step 2.

a. Scroll in the Navigation pane until you see the *Products table and Related Objects*. Locate and double-click the **Order Details Extended query**.

b. Examine the icons on the left edge of the Navigation pane. Figure 1.24 identifies the object type for each of the objects.

c. Find an occurrence of *your last name* anywhere in the query (record 7 should show your name) and click it to make it active.

   The query contains your name because in Hands-On Exercise 1 you replaced Margaret Peacock's name in the Employees table with your name. The Employees table is related to the Orders table, the Orders table to the Order Details table, and the Order Details table to the Products table. Therefore, any change you make to the Employees table is carried throughout the database via the relationships.

d. Click **Filter by Selection** in the Sort & Filter group. Select **Equals "YourName"** from the selection menu.

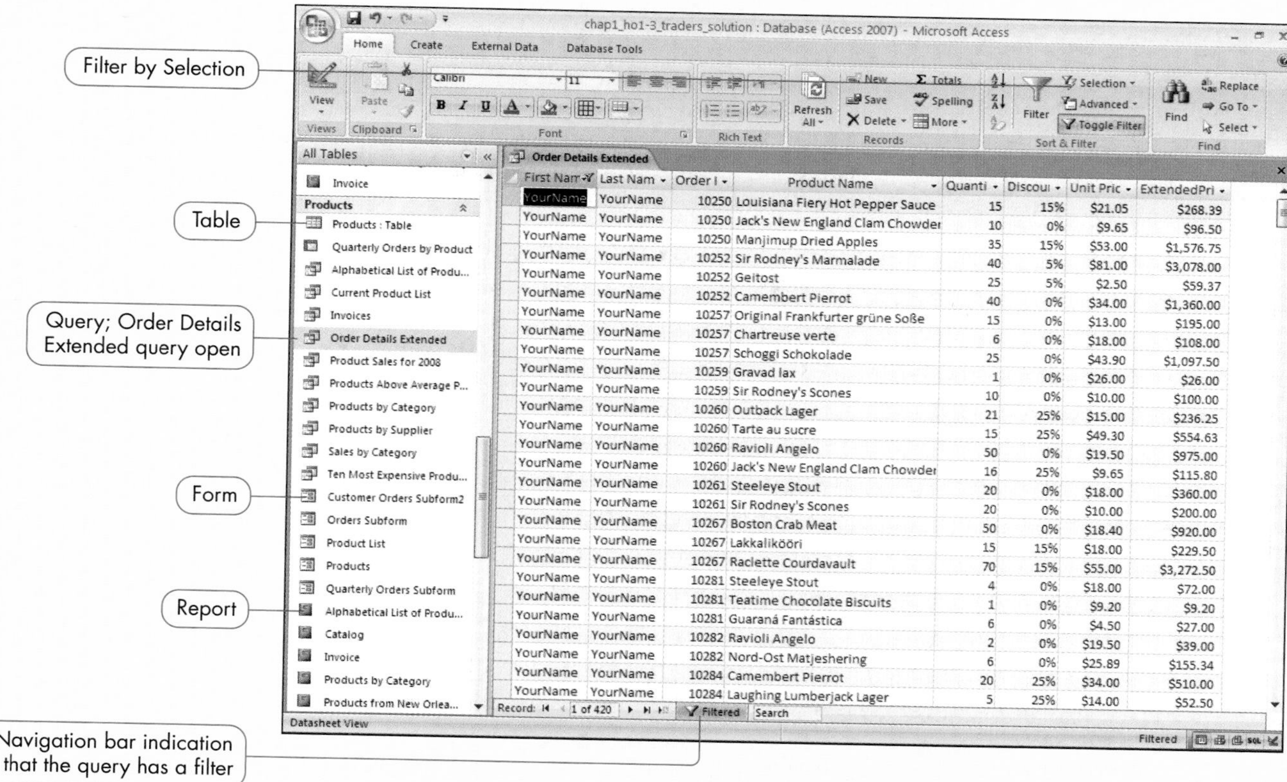

Figure 1.24 Filtered Query Results

Step 3
Use Filter by Form with an Inequity Setting and Reapply a Saved Filter

Refer to Figure 1.25 as you complete Step 3.

a. Click **Advanced Filter options**.

b. Select **Filter By Form** from the drop-down list.

Because you already applied a filter to these data, the Filter By Form design sheet opens with one criterion already filled in. Your name displays in the selection box under the Last Name field.

c. Scroll right (or press **Tab**) until the Extended Price field is visible. Click the insertion point in the **first row** under the Extended Price field.

d. Type **>2000**.

The Extended Price field shows the purchased amount for each item ordered. If an item sold for $15 and a customer ordered 10, the Extended Price would display $150.

e. Click **Toggle Filter** in the Sort & Filter group. Examine the filtered results.

Your inequity instruction, >2000, identified the items ordered where the extended price exceeded $2,000.

f. Press **Ctrl+S** to save the query. Close the query by clicking the X in the object window.

g. Open the **Order Details Extended query**.

The filter disengages when you close and reopen the object. However, your filtering directions have been stored with the query design. You may reapply the filter at any time by clicking the Toggle Filter command.

h. Click **Toggle Filter** in the Sort & Filter group.

i. Compare your work to Figure 1.25. If it is correct, close the query.

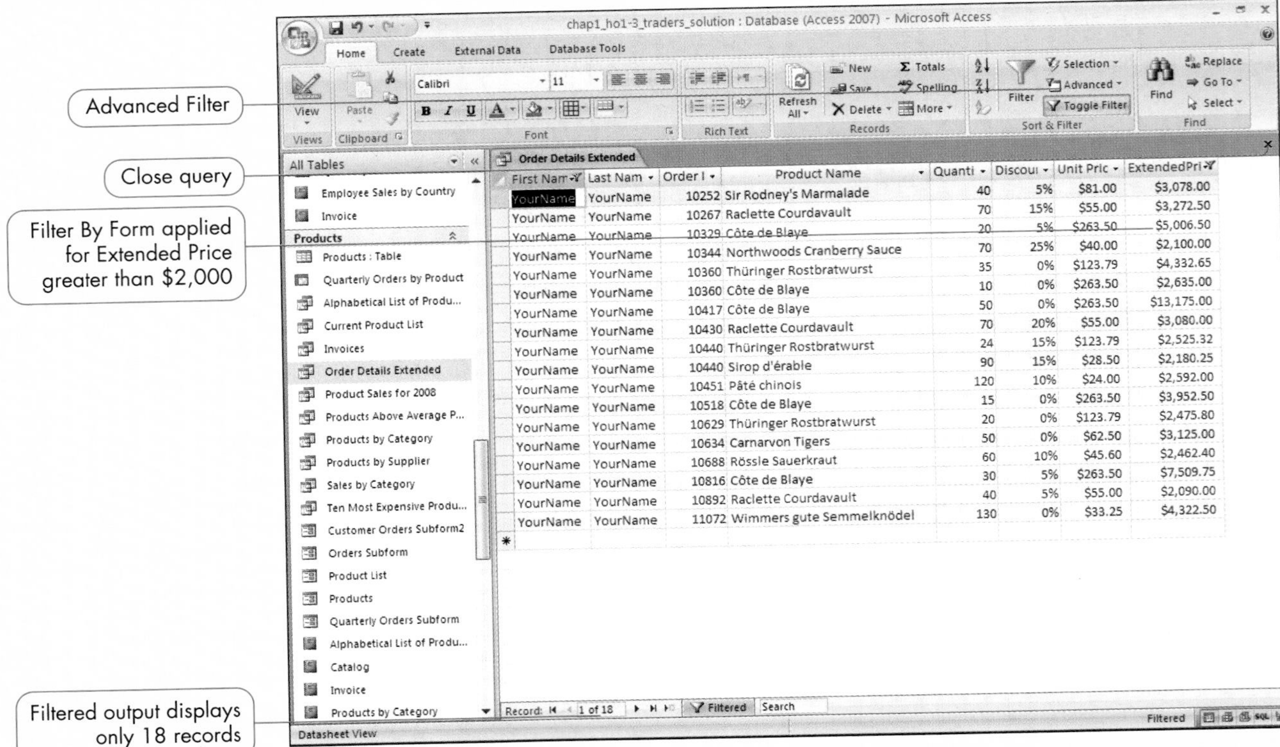

Advanced Filter
Close query
Filter By Form applied for Extended Price greater than $2,000
Filtered output displays only 18 records

Figure 1.25 Filtered Query Results After Limiting Output to Extended Prices over $2,000

Step 4
Filter a Report

Refer to Figure 1.26 as you complete Step 4.

a. Open the **Products by Category report** located in the Navigation pane under the Products group. You may need to scroll down to locate it.

   The report should open in Print Preview with a gray stripe highlighting the report title. The Print Preview displays the report exactly as it will print. This report was formatted to display in three columns.

   TROUBLESHOOTING: If you do not see the gray stripe and three columns, you probably opened the wrong object. The database also contains a Product by Category query. It is the source for the Products by Category report. Make sure you open the report (shown with the green report icon) and not the query. Close the query and open the report.

b. Examine the Confections category products. You should see **Your Name Pecan Pie**.

   You created this product by entering data in a form in Hands-On Exercise 1. You later discovered that changes made to a form affect the related table. Now you see that other related objects also change when the source data changes.

c. Right-click the **gold report tab**. Select **Report View** from the shortcut menu.

   The Report view displays the information a little differently. It no longer shows three columns. If you clicked the Print command while in Report view, the columns would print even though you do not see them. The Report view permits limited data interaction (for example, filtering).

d. Scroll down in the report until you see the title *Category: Confections*. **Right-click** the word **Confections** in the title. Select **Equals "Confections"** from the shortcut menu.

Right-clicking a selected data value in an Access table, query, form, or report activates a shortcut to a Filter by Selection menu. Alternatively, you can click the selected value, in this case, Confections, and then click the Filter by Selection command in the Sort & Filter group.

e. Right-click the **gold report tab**. Select **Print Preview** from the shortcut menu.

You need to print this report. Always view your reports in Print Preview prior to printing.

f. Click the **Office Button**, select **Print**, and then select **Quick Print** to produce a printed copy of the filtered report. Click **OK**.

The Quick Print command sends your work to the default printer as soon as you click it. You can use this safely when you have already viewed your work in Print Preview.

g. Save and close the report.

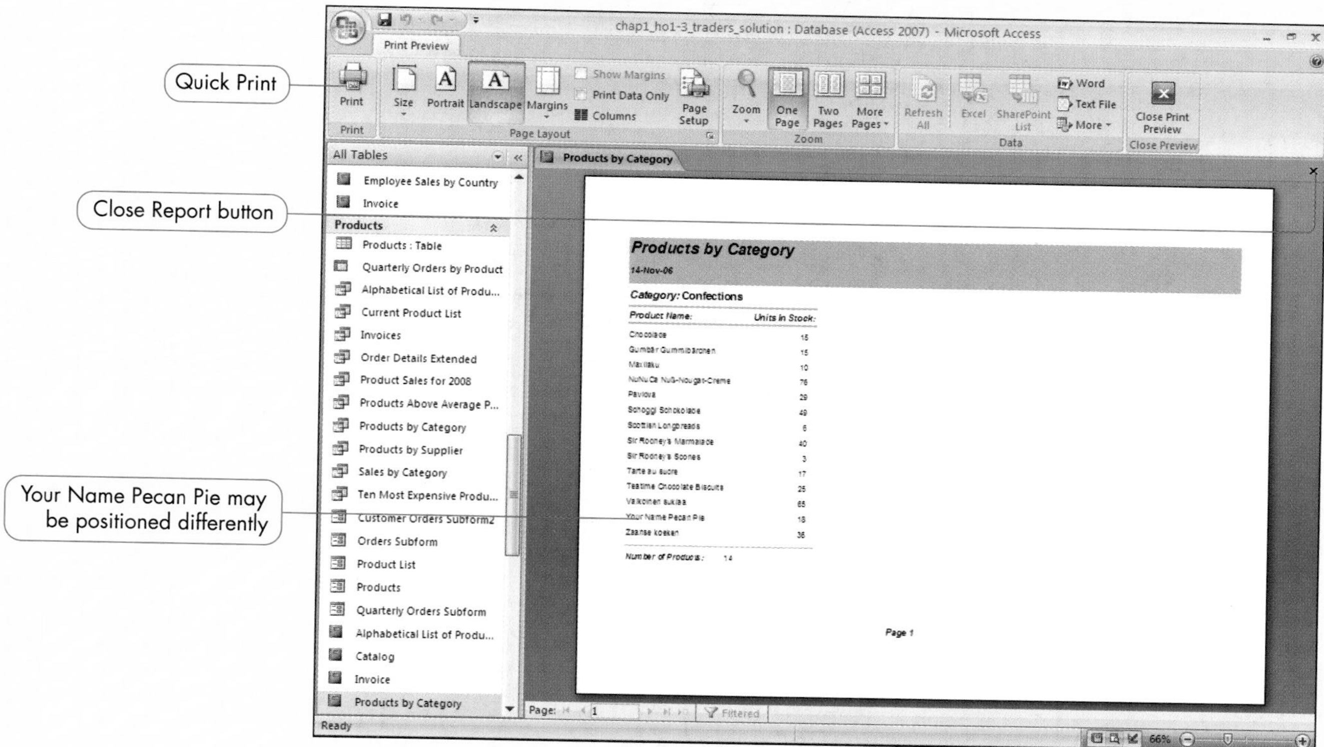

Figure 1.26 Filtered Report Results

Step 5
Remove an Advanced Filter

Refer to Figure 1.27 as you complete Step 5.

a. Open the **Order Details Extended query**.

All 2,155 records should display in the query. You have unfiltered the data. However, the filter still exists.

b. Click **Toggle Filter** in the Sort & Filter group.

You will see the same 18 filtered records that you printed in Step 3.

c. Click **Advanced** in the Sort & Filter group and click **Clear All Filters**.

d. Close the query. A dialog box opens asking if you want to save changes. Click **Yes**.

e. Open the **Order Details Extended query**.

f. Click **Advanced Filter Options** in the Sort & Filter group.

g. Check to ensure the *Clear All Filters* option is dim. Save and close the query.

h. Click the **Office Button**, select **Manage**, and select **Compact and Repair Database**. Close the file and exit Access.

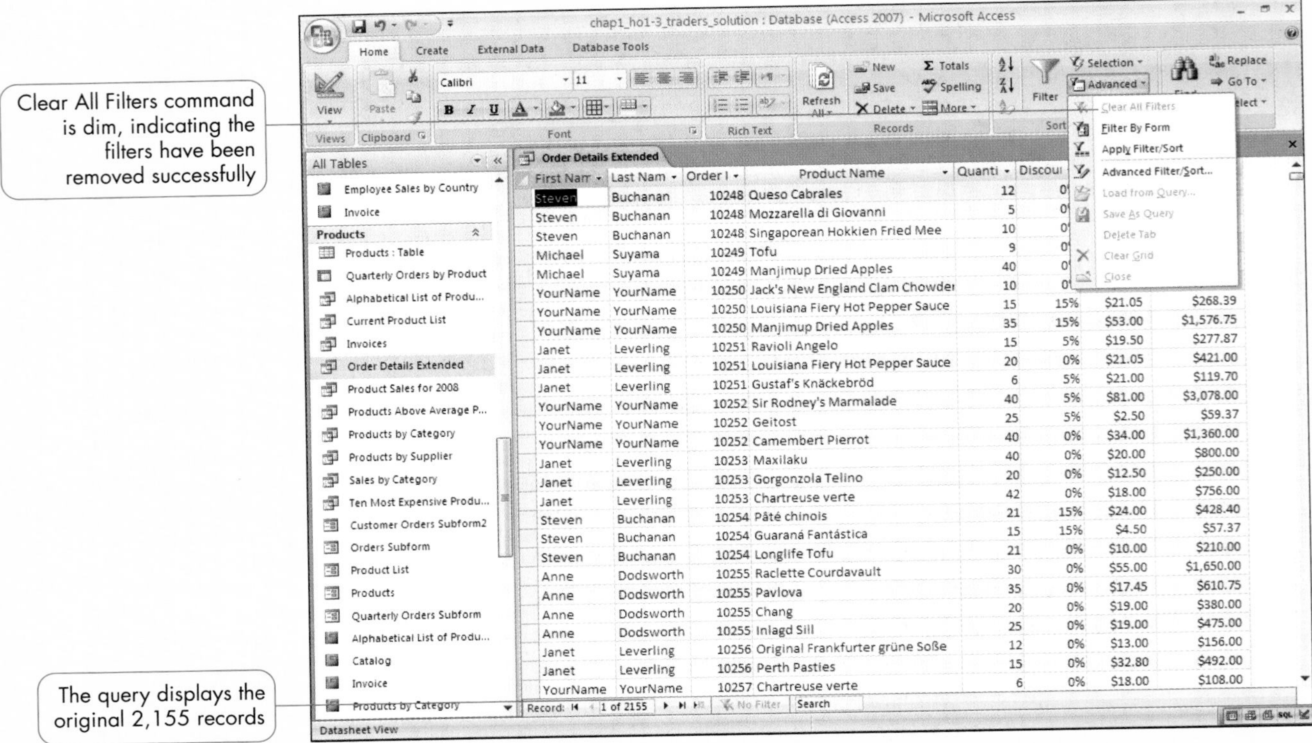

Clear All Filters command is dim, indicating the filters have been removed successfully
The query displays the original 2,155 records

Figure 1.27 Query Results with Filters Removed

Summary

1. **Explore, describe, and navigate among objects in an Access database.** An Access database has six types of objects: tables, forms, queries, reports, macros, and modules. The database window displays these objects and enables you to open an existing object or create new objects. You may arrange these objects by type or by relationship views. The relationship view provides a listing of each table and all other objects in the database that use that table as a source. Thus, one query or report may appear several times, listed once under each table from which it derives information. Each table in the database is composed of records, and each record is in turn composed of fields. Every record in a given table has the same fields in the same order. The primary key is the field (or combination of fields) that makes every record in a table unique.
2. **Understand the difference between working in storage and memory.** Access automatically saves any changes in the current record as soon as you move to the next record or when you close the table. The Undo Current Record command cancels (undoes) the changes to the previously saved record.
3. **Practice good file management.** Because organizations depend on the data stored in databases, database users need to be intentional about exercising good file management practices. You need to be intentional about where you save your files. As you learn new Access skills, you need to make a copy of the database file and practice on the copy. This practice provides a recovery point should you make data-damaging errors.
4. **Back up, compact, and repair Access files.** Because using a database tends to increase the size of the file, you should always close any database objects and compact the database prior to closing the file. This step may reduce the storage requirement by half. Adequate backup is essential when working with an Access database (or any other Office application). A duplicate copy of the database should be created at the end of every session and stored off-site (away from the computer).
5. **Create filters.** A filter is a set of criteria that is applied to a table to display a subset of the records in that table. Microsoft Access lets you Filter by Selection or Filter by Form. The application of a filter does not remove the records from the table, but simply suppresses them from view.
6. **Sort table data on one or more fields.** The records in a table can be displayed in ascending or descending order by clicking the appropriate command on the Home tab.
7. **Know when to use Access or Excel to manage data.** Excel data typically is flat. All of the needed information easily presents in a one-dimensional spreadsheet. Use Excel when the data are primarily numeric. Access handles multi-dimensional data more effectively. Use Access when you need to exchange data with other databases, for large amounts of data, or if your data needs are likely to expand.
8. **Use the Relationship window.** The Relationships window provides a summarizing overview of the database design. Use it to discover which fields are stored in what table. It displays the system of linkages among the table data. The Relationships window provides an excellent tool for you to become acquainted with a new database quickly.
9. **Understand relational power.** A relational database contains multiple tables and enables you to extract information from those tables in a single query. The related tables must be consistent with one another, a concept known as referential integrity. Thus, Access automatically implements additional data validation to ensure the integrity of a database. No system, no matter how sophisticated, can produce valid output from invalid input. Changes made in one object travel through the database and affect other, related objects. The relationships are based on linking primary and foreign key fields between tables.

Key Terms

Multiple Choice

1. Which sequence represents the hierarchy of terms, from smallest to largest?
   (a) Database, table, record, field
   (b) Field, record, table, database
   (c) Record, field, table, database
   (d) Field, record, database, table

2. Which of the following is not true regarding movement within a record (assuming you are not in the first or last field of that record)?
   (a) Press Tab or the right arrow key to move to the next field.
   (b) Press Spacebar to move to the next field to the right.
   (c) Press Shift+Tab or the left arrow key to return to the previous field.
   (d) Press the Enter key and move to the next record.

3. You are performing routine maintenance on a table within an Access database. When should you execute the Save command?
   (a) Immediately after you add, edit, or delete a record
   (b) Periodically during a session—for example, after every fifth change
   (c) Once at the end of a session
   (d) None of the above since Access automatically saves the changes as they are made

4. Which of the following objects are not contained within an Access database?
   (a) Tables and forms
   (b) Queries and reports
   (c) Macros and modules
   (d) Web sites and worksheets

5. You have opened an Access file. The left pane displays a table with forms, queries, and reports listed under the table. Then another table and its objects display. You notice some of the object names are repeated under different tables. Why?
   (a) The database has been set to Object Type View. The object names repeat because a query or report is frequently based on multiple tables.
   (b) The database has been set to Tables and Related View. The object names repeat because a query or report is frequently based on multiple tables.
   (c) The database has been set to Most Recently Used View. The object names repeat because an object has been used frequently.
   (d) The database objects have been alphabetized.

6. Which of the following is not true of an Access database?
   (a) Every record in a table has the same fields as every other record. The fields are in the same order in each record.
   (b) Every table contains the same number of records as every other table.
   (c) Every record in a table has the same fields as every other record. The fields may be ordered differently depending on the record.
   (d) All records contain the same data as all other records.

7. Which of the following is true regarding the record selector symbol?
   (a) A pencil indicates that the current record already has been saved.
   (b) An empty square indicates that the current record has not changed.
   (c) An asterisk indicates the first record in the table.
   (d) A gold border surrounds the active record.

8. You have finished an Access assignment and wish to turn it in to your instructor for evaluation. As you prepare to transfer the file, you discover that it has grown in size. It is now more than double the original size. You should:
   (a) Zip the database file prior to transmitting it to the instructor.
   (b) Turn it in; the size does not matter.
   (c) Compact and repair the database file prior to transmitting it to the instructor.
   (d) Delete extra tables or reports or fields to make the file smaller.

9. Which of the following will be accepted as valid during data entry?
   (a) Adding a record with a duplicate primary key
   (b) Entering text into a numeric field
   (c) Entering numbers into a text field
   (d) Omitting an entry in a required field

10. In a Replace command, the values for the Find and Replace commands must be:
    (a) The same length
    (b) The same case
    (c) Any part of a word
    (d) Either the same or a different length and case

Multiple Choice Continued...

11. Which of the following capabilities is available through Filter by Selection?
    (a) The imposition of a relational condition
    (b) The imposition of an alternate (OR) condition
    (c) The imposition of an Equal condition
    (d) The imposition of a delete condition

12. You open an Access form and use it to update an address for customer Lee Fong. You exited the record and closed the form. Later you open a report that generates mailing labels. What will the address label for Lee Fong show?
    (a) The new address
    (b) The old address
    (c) The new address if you remembered to save the changes made to the form
    (d) The old address until you remember to update it in the report

13. You have created a Filter by Form in an Order Total field. You set the criterion to >25. Which of the following accurately reflects the instruction given to Access?
    (a) All orders with an Order Total of at least 25
    (b) All orders with an Order Total of less than 25
    (c) All orders with an Order Total over 25
    (d) All orders with an Order Total of 25 or less

14. You have used Find and Replace to find all occurrences of the word "his" with "his/her." You typed only his in the Find box and only his/her in the Replace box. What will the result be?
    (a) History will become His/Herstory
    (b) This will become This/Her
    (c) His will become His/Her
    (d) All of the above
    (e) None of the above

15. You are looking at an Employees table in Datasheet view. You want the names sorted alphabetically by last name and then by first name, e.g., Smith, Andrea is listed before Smith, William. To accomplish this, you must:
    (a) First sort ascending on first name, and then on last name
    (b) First sort descending on first name, and then on last name
    (c) First sort ascending on last name, and then on first name
    (d) First sort ascending on last name, and then on first name

Practice Exercises

1 Comfort Insurance

The Comfort Insurance Agency is a midsized company with offices located across the country. You are the human resource director for the company. Your office is located in the home office in Miami. Each employee receives an annual performance review. The review determines employee eligibility for salary increases and the performance bonus. The employee data are stored in an Access database. This database is used by the Human Resource department to monitor and maintain employee records. Your task is to identify the employees who have a performance rating of excellent and a salary under $40,000 per year (if any). Once you identify the appropriate records, you need to sort them alphabetically by the employee's last name. Verify your work by examining Figure 1.28.

a. Copy the partially completed file in *chap1_pe1_insurance.accdb* from the Exploring Access folder to your production folder. Rename it **chap1_pe1_insurance_solution**. Double-click the file name to open it. Enable the security content by clicking the **Options** command in the Security Warning bar. Select **Enable this content**, and then click **OK**.
b. Click the **Database Tools tab** and click **Relationships** in the Show/Hide group. Examine the table structure, relationships, and fields. Once you are familiar with the database, close the Relationships window.
c. Double-click the **Raises and Bonuses query** in the Navigation pane to open it. Find *Debbie Johnson*'s name in the seventh record. Double-click *Debbie* and type your **first name**. Double-click *Johnson* and type your **last name**. Click on a different record to save your change.
d. Examine the number of records in the query and remember it for future reference.
e. Find a record that has a value of *Excellent* in the *Performance field*. The record for Johnny Park (sixth record) is one. Click your insertion point in that field on the word **Excellent**.
f. Activate the **Filter by Selection** in the Sort & Filter group. Select **Equals "Excellent"** from the menu. Examine the number of records in the query and remember it for future reference.
g. Click **Advanced Filter** in the Sort & Filter group and select **Filter By Form**.
h. Position the insertion point in the first row in the *Salary field*. Type **<40000**. (Make sure you apply this number to the Salary field and not the NewSalary field.)
i. Click **Toggle Filter** in the Sort & Filter group. Examine the number of records in the query and remember it for future reference. As you add additional criteria, the number of filtered results should decrease.
j. Click the **first record** in the *LastName* field. Click **Sort Ascending** in the Sort & Filter group on the Home tab to sort the filtered output by the employee's last name alphabetically.
k. Compare your results with Figure 1.28. Your name will be sorted into the list so your results may not match exactly. The number of records should exactly match.
l. Click the **Office Button** and select **Print**. Select **Quick Print** and click OK. Save the query.
m. Click the **Office Button**, select **Manage**, and select **Compact and Repair Database**. Close the file.

...continued on Next Page

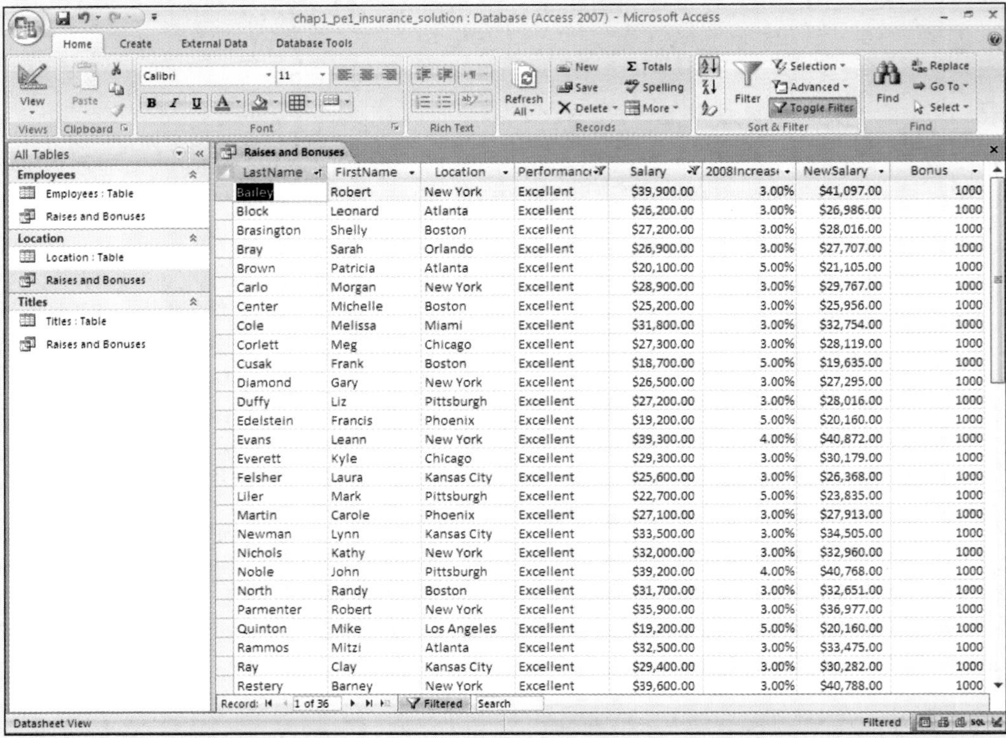

LastName	FirstName	Location	Performanc	Salary	2008Increas	NewSalary	Bonus
Bailey	Robert	New York	Excellent	$39,900.00	3.00%	$41,097.00	1000
Block	Leonard	Atlanta	Excellent	$26,200.00	3.00%	$26,986.00	1000
Brasington	Shelly	Boston	Excellent	$27,200.00	3.00%	$28,016.00	1000
Bray	Sarah	Orlando	Excellent	$26,900.00	3.00%	$27,707.00	1000
Brown	Patricia	Atlanta	Excellent	$20,100.00	5.00%	$21,105.00	1000
Carlo	Morgan	New York	Excellent	$28,900.00	3.00%	$29,767.00	1000
Center	Michelle	Boston	Excellent	$25,200.00	3.00%	$25,956.00	1000
Cole	Melissa	Miami	Excellent	$31,800.00	3.00%	$32,754.00	1000
Corlett	Meg	Chicago	Excellent	$27,300.00	3.00%	$28,119.00	1000
Cusak	Frank	Boston	Excellent	$18,700.00	5.00%	$19,635.00	1000
Diamond	Gary	New York	Excellent	$26,500.00	3.00%	$27,295.00	1000
Duffy	Liz	Pittsburgh	Excellent	$27,200.00	3.00%	$28,016.00	1000
Edelstein	Francis	Phoenix	Excellent	$19,200.00	5.00%	$20,160.00	1000
Evans	Leann	New York	Excellent	$39,300.00	4.00%	$40,872.00	1000
Everett	Kyle	Chicago	Excellent	$29,300.00	3.00%	$30,179.00	1000
Felsher	Laura	Kansas City	Excellent	$25,600.00	3.00%	$26,368.00	1000
Liler	Mark	Pittsburgh	Excellent	$22,700.00	5.00%	$23,835.00	1000
Martin	Carole	Phoenix	Excellent	$27,100.00	3.00%	$27,913.00	1000
Newman	Lynn	Kansas City	Excellent	$33,500.00	3.00%	$34,505.00	1000
Nichols	Kathy	New York	Excellent	$32,000.00	3.00%	$32,960.00	1000
Noble	John	Pittsburgh	Excellent	$39,200.00	4.00%	$40,768.00	1000
North	Randy	Boston	Excellent	$31,700.00	3.00%	$32,651.00	1000
Parmenter	Robert	New York	Excellent	$35,900.00	3.00%	$36,977.00	1000
Quinton	Mike	Los Angeles	Excellent	$19,200.00	5.00%	$20,160.00	1000
Rammos	Mitzi	Atlanta	Excellent	$32,500.00	3.00%	$33,475.00	1000
Ray	Clay	Kansas City	Excellent	$29,400.00	3.00%	$30,282.00	1000
Restery	Barney	New York	Excellent	$39,600.00	3.00%	$40,788.00	1000

Figure 1.28 Sorted and Filtered Query Results

2 Member Rewards

The Prestige Hotel chain caters to upscale business travelers and provides state of the art conference, meeting, and reception facilities. It prides itself on its international, four-star cuisines. Last year, it began a member rewards club to help the marketing department track the purchasing patterns of its most loyal customers. All of the hotel transactions are stored in the database. Your task is to update a customer record and identify the customers who had weddings in St. Paul. Verify your work by examining Figure 1.29.

a. Copy the partially completed file in *chap1_pe2_memrewards.accdb* from the Exploring Access folder to your production folder. Rename it **chap1_pe2_memrewards_solution**. Double-click the file name to open it. Enable the security content by clicking the **Options** command in the Security Warning bar. Select **Enable this content** and then click **OK**.

b. Open the **Members Form form** and click **New (blank) record** in the Navigation bar. (It has a yellow asterisk.)

c. Enter the information below in the form. Press **Tab** to move from field to field.

Field Name	Value
MemNumber	1718
LastName	Your Last Name
FirstName	Your First Name
JoinDate	7/30/2008
Address	124 West Elm Apt 12
City	Your hometown
State	Your state (2 character code)
Zip	00001

...continued on Next Page

Phone	9995551234
Email	Your e-mail
OrderID	9325
ServiceDate	8/1/2008
ServiceID	3
NoInParty	2
Location	20

d. Click **Close form** in the database window (X) to close the form.

e. Double-click the **Members table** in the Navigation pane. Find Boyd Pegel in the first and last name field and replace his name with **your name**.

f. Double-click the **Member Service by City query** in the Navigation pane. Find a record that displays **St Paul** as the value in the *City field*. Click **St Paul** to select that data entry.

g. Select **Filter by Selection** in the Sort & Filter group on the Home tab. Click **Equals "St Paul"**.

h. Find a record that displays **Wedding** as the value in the *ServiceName* field. Click **Wedding** to select that data entry.

i. Select **Filter by Selection** in the Sort & Filter group on the Home tab. Click **Equals "Wedding"**.

j. Click any value in the **FirstName** field. Click **Sort Ascending** in the Sort & Filter group on the Home tab. Click any value in the **LastName** field. Click **Sort Ascending** in the Sort & Filter group on the Home tab.

k. Click the **Office Button**, select **Print**, and click **OK** to print the sorted and filtered query.

l. Save and close the query.

m. Click the **Office Button**, select **Manage**, and then select **Compact and Repair Database**. Close the file.

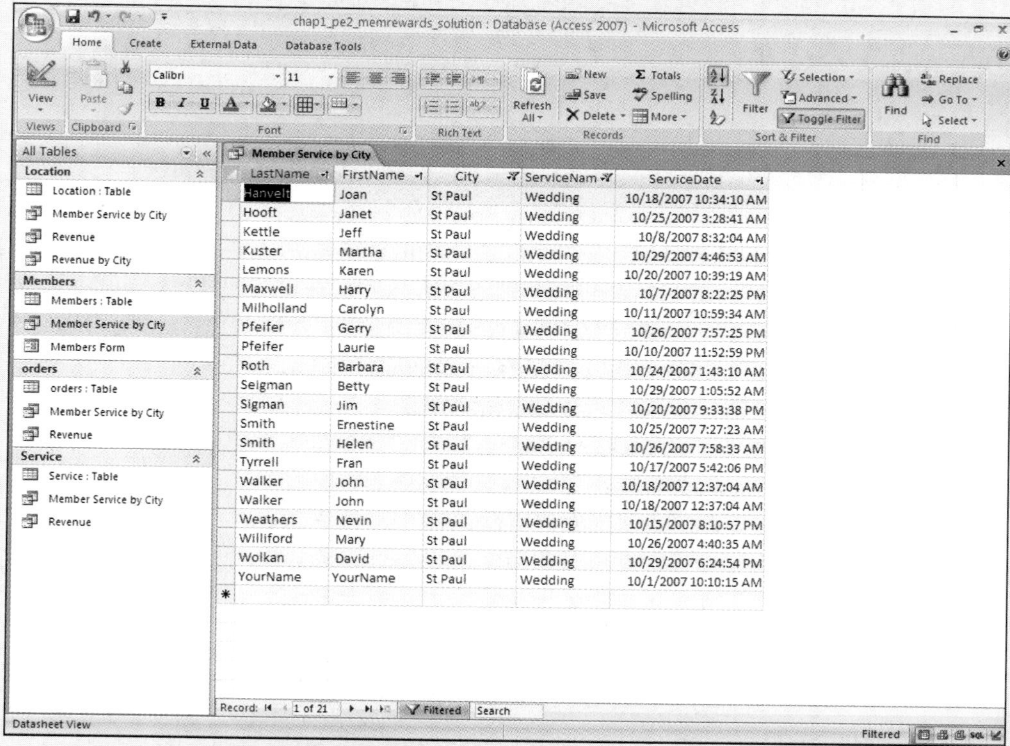

Figure 1.29 Sorted and Filtered Query Results

...continued on Next Page

3 Vancouver Preschool

The Vancouver Preschool is a dynamic and exciting educational environment for young children. It launches each school year with a fundraiser that helps provide classroom supplies. Patrons are asked to donate goods and services, which are auctioned at a welcome-back-to-school dinner for students, parents, grandparents, and friends. All of the data about the donations are contained in an Access file. Your task is to make some modifications to the data and print a form and a report. Verify your work by comparing it to Figure 1.30. The report in the figure is displayed at a higher zoom percentage so that you can read the report easily. Your report may appear as a full page.

a. Copy the partially completed file *chap1_pe3_preschool.accdb* from the Exploring Access folder to your production folder. Rename it **chap1_pe3_preschool_solution.accdb**. Double-click the file name to open it. Click **Options** on the Security Warning bar, click **Enable this content**, and then click **OK**.

b. Open the **Donors form**. Navigate to a **new blank record** by clicking the navigation button with the yellow asterisk on it.

c. Enter the information below in the form.

Field Name	Value
DonorID	(New)
FirstName	Your First Name
LastName	Your Last Name
Address	124 West Elm Apt 12
City	Your hometown
State	Your state
Zip	00001
Phone	9995551234
Notes	Your e-mail
Item Donated	Car wash and hand wax
Number Attending	2
Item Value	100
Category	Service

d. Click **Print Record**. Close the form.

e. Open the **Items for Auction** report. Check to ensure that the *car wash and hand wax* donation is listed. If it is, print the report. Close Print preview.

f. Click the **Office Button**, select **Manage**, and select **Compact and Repair Database**.

g. Click the **Office Button**, select **Manage**, and select **Back Up Database**. Use the default backup file name.

h. Close the file.

...continued on Next Page

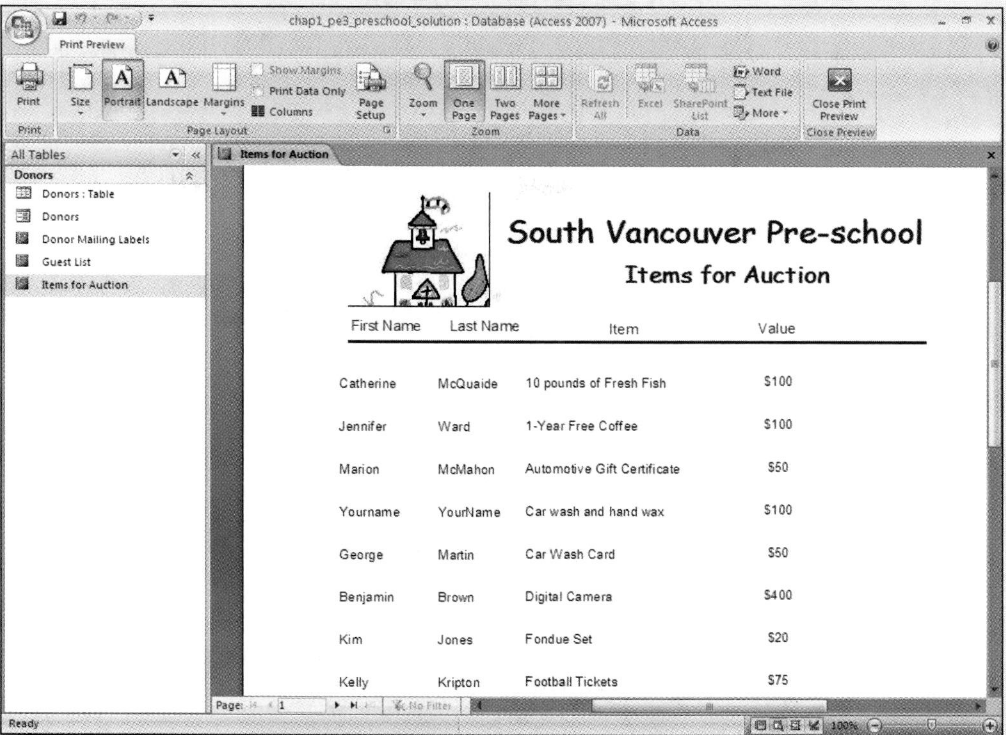

Figure 1.30 Report

4 Custom Coffee

The Custom Coffee Company is a small service organization that provides coffee, tea, and snacks to offices. Custom Coffee also provides and maintains the equipment for brewing the beverages. Although the firm is small, its excellent reputation for providing outstanding customer service has helped it grow. Part of the customer service is determined through a database the firm owner set up to organize and keep track of customer purchases. Verify your work by comparing it to Figure 1.31. The report in the figure is displayed at a higher zoom percentage so that you can read the report easily. Your report may appear as a full page.

a. Copy the partially completed file *chap1_pe4_coffee.accdb* from the Exploring Access folder to your production folder. Rename it **chap1_pe4_coffee_solution.accdb**. Double-click the file name to open the file. Click **Options** in the Security Warning bar, click **Enable this content**, and then click **OK**.
b. Click the **Navigation pane down arrow** to change the object view from Tables and Related Views to **Object Type**.
c. Examine the other objects, reports, forms, and queries in the database. Click the **Navigation pane down arrow** and restore the **Tables and Related Views** method of looking at the objects.
d. Double-click the **Sales Reps table** to open it. Replace *YourName* with **your name**. Close the table by clicking Close in the database window.
e. Double-click the **Customers Form** to open it. Navigate to a **new blank record** by clicking the navigation button with the yellow asterisk on it. Use **your name** for the *Customer* and *Contact* fields. Invent an address, phone, and e-mail. Type **Miami** for the city and **FL** for the state fields. The *Service Start Date* is **01/17/2005**. The *Credit Rating* is **A**. Type a **2** for the *Sales Rep ID*. It will convert to *S002* automatically.
f. Close the Customers Form.
g. Double-click the **Orders form** to open it. Navigate to a new blank record by clicking the navigation button with the yellow asterisk on it.
h. Type **16** as the *Customer ID*. The database will convert it to *C0016*. In the *Payment Type*, type **Cash**.

...continued on Next Page

i. Type **4** in the *Product ID box* and **2** in *Quantity*. In the next row, type **6** and **1** for *Product ID* and *Quantity*. The Product IDs will convert to P0004 and P0006. Close the form, saving changes if requested.

j. Open the **Order Details Report**. Scroll down to verify that your name appears both as a customer and as a sales rep. Right-click **your name** in the SalesRep field and select **Equals "Your Name"** from the shortcut menu. Right click **Miami** in the City field and select **Equals "Miami"** from the shortcut menu.

k. Click the **Office Button**, select **Print**, and select **Print Preview**. Click **Print**.

l. Click the **Office Button**, select **Manage**, and then select **Compact and Repair Database**.

m. Click the **Office Button**, select **Manage**, and then select **Back Up Database**. Use the default backup file name. Close the file.

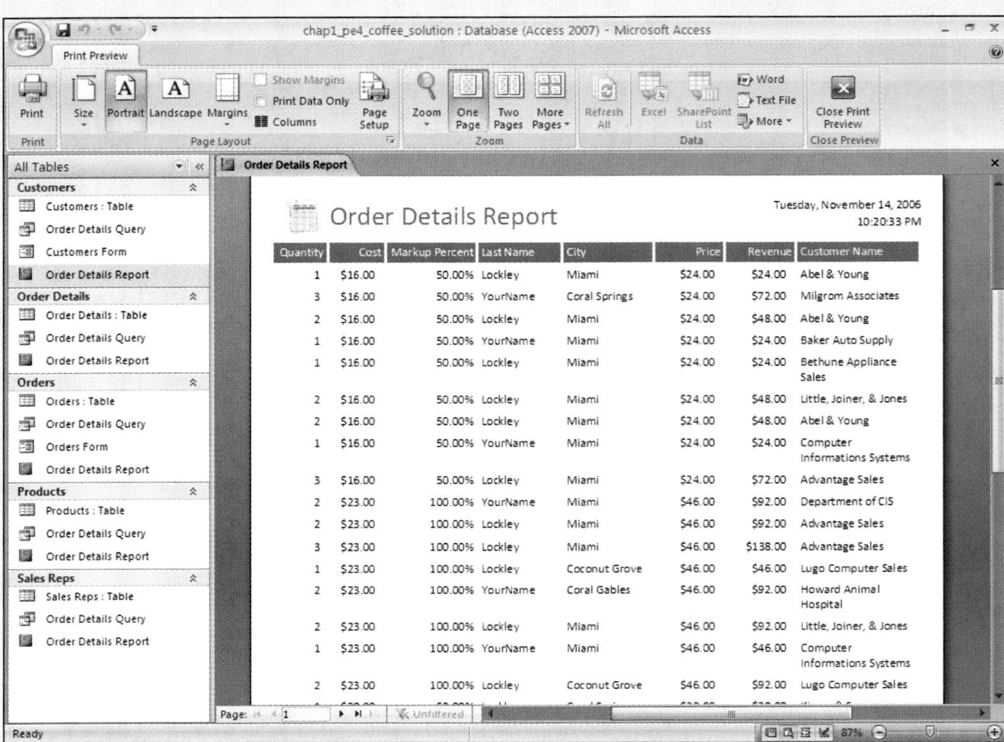

Figure 1.31 Report Showing Changes Made to Forms

Mid-Level Exercises

1 Object Navigation, Data Entry, and Printing Database Objects

Your little sister lives to play soccer. She told her coach that you have become a computer expert. Coach (who is also the league director) called you to ask for help with the Access database file containing all of the league information. You agreed, and he promptly delivered a disc containing a copy of the league's database. The file contains information on the players, the coaches, and the teams. Players are classified by skill and experience level, with the best players described as "A." The Coaches table classifies coaching status as level 1 (head coaches) or 2 (assistant coaches). Coach asks that you add new players to the database and then identify all of the players not yet assigned to teams. He also needs you to identify the teams without coaches, the unassigned coaches, and asks that you assign each team a head and an assistant coach. Finally, Coach convinces you to volunteer as a coach in the league. Verify your work by looking at Figure 1.32.

a. Locate the file named *chap1_mid1_soccer.accdb*, copy it to your working folder, and rename it **chap1_mid1_soccer_solution.accdb**. Open the file and enable the content.

b. Open the Relationships window and examine the tables, the relationships, and the fields located in each table. Close the Relationships window.

c. Examine all of the objects in the database and think about the work Coach asked you to do. Identify which objects will assist you in accomplishing the assigned tasks.

d. Open the **Players form** and create a new record. Use your name, but you may invent the data about your address and phone. You are classified as an "A" player. Print the form containing your record. Close the form.

e. Open the **Coaches table**. Replace record 13 with **your instructor's name**. Add **yourself** as a new record. You are a *coach status* **1**.

f. Identify the players not assigned to teams. Assign each player to a team while balancing skill levels. (You would not want one team in the league to have all of the "A" skill level players because they would always win.)

g. Identify the teams without coaches and the coaches not assigned to teams. Assign a head coach and an assistant coach to each team. You may need to assign a person with head coaching qualifications to an assistant position. If you do, change his or her *status* to **2**.

h. After you assign all of the players and coaches to teams, open and print the **Master Coaching List report**.

i. After you assign all of the players and coaches to teams, open and print the **Team Rosters report**. Close the database.

...continued on Next Page

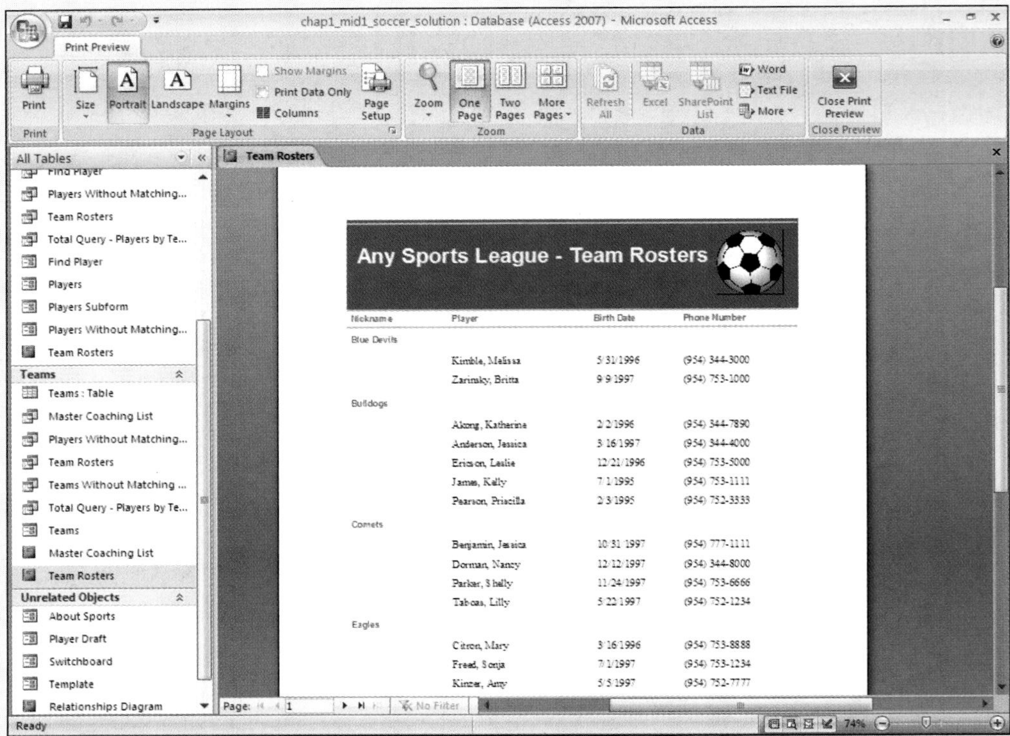

Figure 1.32 Team Roster Report

2 Sorting and Filtering Table Data Using Advanced Filters

You are the senior partner in a large, independent real estate firm that specializes in home sales. Although you still represent buyers and sellers in real estate transactions, you find that most of your time is spent supervising the agents who work for your firm. This fact distresses you because you like helping people buy and sell homes. There is a database containing all of the information on the properties your firm has listed. You believe that by using the data in the database more effectively, you can spend less time supervising the other agents and spend more time doing the part of your job that you like doing the best. Your task is to determine how many three-bedroom, two-bathroom, and garage properties your firm has listed for sale with a listing price under $400,000. Finally, you need to sort the data by list price in descending order. Refer to Figure 1.33 to verify that your results match the results shown.

a. Locate the file named *chap1_mid2_realestate.accdb*; copy it to your working folder and rename it **chap1_mid2_realestate_solution.accdb**. Open the file and enable the content. Open the *Agents* table. Find and replace *YourName* with **your name** in the first and last name fields.

b. Create a filter by form on the data stored in the *Under 400K query*. Set the criteria to identify **three or more bedrooms**, **two or more bathrooms**, and **garage** properties you have listed for sale with a listing price **under $400,000**.

c. Sort the filtered results in **descending** order by the **ListPrice** field.

d. After you are sure that your results are correct, save the query.

e. Capture a screenshot of the sorted and filtered Under 400K query. With the sorted and filtered table open on your computer, press **PrintScrn**. Open Word; launch a new blank document, type **your name and section number**, and press **Enter**. Press **Ctrl+V** or

...continued on Next Page

click Paste. Print the word document. Save it as **chap1_mid2_realestate_solution.docx**. Close the Word document.

f. Compact, repair, and back up the database. Name the backup **chap1_mid2_realestate_backup.accdb**. Close the database.

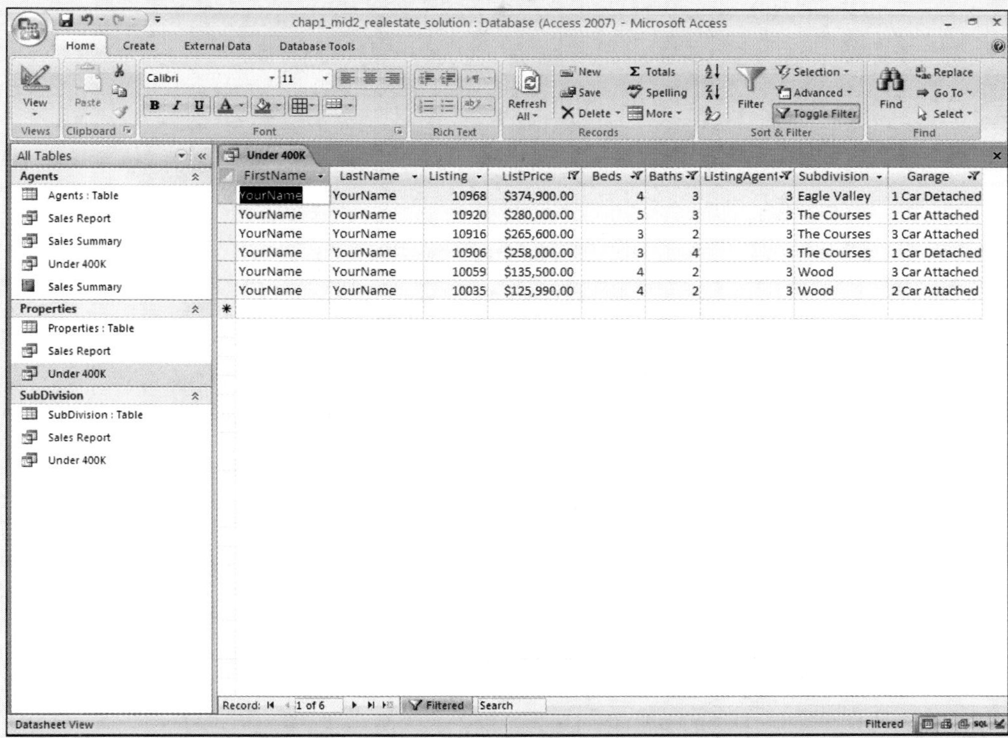

Figure 1.33 Sorted, Filtered Table

3 Sorting and Filtering Table Data Using Advanced Filters, Printing a Report

You work for the Office of Residence Life at your university as a work/study employee. The dean of student affairs, Martha Sink, Ph.D., placed you in this position because your transcript noted that you were enrolled in a computing class covering Microsoft Access. Dr. Sink has a special project for you. Each year, the Association of Higher Education hosts a national conference to share new ideas and best practices. Next year, the conference will be held on your campus, and the Office of Residence life has the responsibility of planning and organizing the events, speakers, and physical meeting spaces. To facilitate the work, the IT department has created a database containing information on the rooms, speakers, and sessions. Dr. Sink needs your assistance with extracting information from the database. Examine Figure 1.34 to verify your work.

a. Locate the file named *chap1_mid3_natconf.accdb*; copy it to your working folder and rename it **chap1_mid3_natconf_solution.accdb**. Open the file and enable the content. Open the **Speakers table**. Find and replace *YourName* with **your name**. Close the Speakers table.

...continued on Next Page

b. Open the **Speaker - Session Query** and apply a filter to identify the sessions where you or Holly Davis are the speakers. Use Filter by Form and engage the Or tab.

c. Sort the filtered results in descending order by the RoomID field.

d. Capture a screenshot of the sorted and filtered Speaker Session query. With the sorted and filtered query open on your computer press **PrintScrn**. Open Word, launch a new blank document, type **your name and section number**, and press **Enter**. Press **Ctrl+V** or click **Paste**. Print the Word document. Save it as **chap1_mid3_natconf_solution.docx**. Close the Word document.

e. Open the **Master List – Sessions and Speakers report** in Report View. Apply a filter that limits the report to sessions where you are the speaker. Print the report.

f. Compact, repair, and back up the database. Name the backup **chap1_mid3_natconf_backup.accdb**. Close the database.

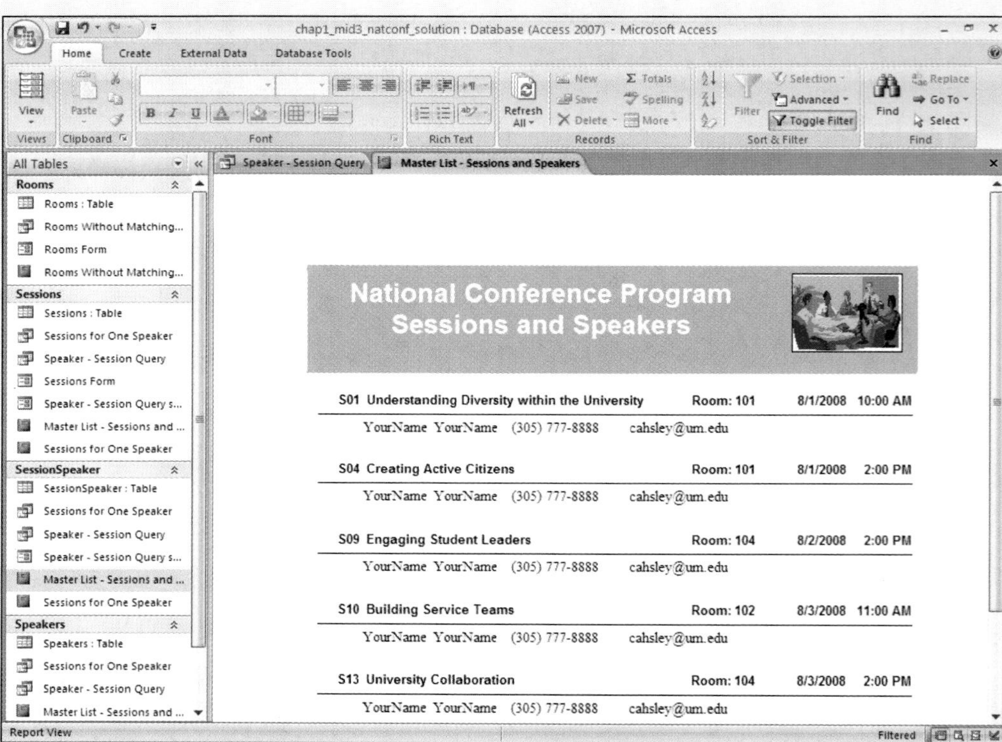

Figure 1.34 Master Sessions and Speakers Report

Capstone Exercise

Your boss expressed a concern about the accuracy of the inventory reports in the bookstore. He needs you to open the inventory database, make modifications to some records, and determine if the changes you make carry through to the other objects in the database. You will make changes to a form and then visit those changes in a table, a query, and a report. When you have verified that the changes update automatically, you will compact and repair the database and make a backup of it.

Database File Setup

You need to copy an original database file, rename the copied file, and then open the copied database to complete this capstone exercise. After you open the copied database, you will replace an existing employee's name with your name.

a. Locate the file named *chap1_cap_bookstore.accdb* and copy it to your working folder.

b. Rename the copied file as **chap1_cap_bookstore_solution.accdb**.

c. Open the *chap1_cap_bookstore_solution.accdb* file and enable the content.

d. Open the **Author Form** form.

e. Navigate to record 7 and replace *YourName* with **your name**.

f. Add a new *Title*, **Computer Wisdom II**. The *ISBN* is **0-684-80416-5**, the *PubID* is **SS**, the *PublDate* is **2007**, the *Price* is **$28.00** (just type 28, no $, period, or zeros), and *StockAmt* is **27** *units*.

g. Navigate to record 6 (or any other record). Close the form.

h. Open the **Author Form** again and navigate to record 7. The changes are there because Access works from storage, not memory. Close the form.

Sort a Query and Apply a Filter by Selection

You need to reorder a detail query so that the results are sorted alphabetically by the publisher name.

a. Open the **Publishers, Books, and Authors Query**.

b. Click in any record in the PubName field and sort the field in alphabetical order.

c. Check to make sure that two books list you as the author.

d. Click *your name* in the Author field and filter the records to show your books.

e. Close the query without saving the changes.

View a Report

You need to examine the Publishers, Books, and Authors report to determine if the changes you made to the Author form carried through to the report.

a. Open the **Publishers, Books, and Authors Report**.

b. Check to make sure that the report shows two books listing you as the author.

c. Print the report.

d. Close the report.

Filter a Table

You need to examine the Books table to determine if the changes you made to the Author form carried through to the related table. You also will filter the table to display books published after 2004 with fewer than 30 copies in inventory.

a. Open the **Books** table.

b. Click **Advanced** in the Sort & Filter group, and then select **Filter by Form** from the drop-down list.

c. Create the criteria that will identify all records with fewer than 30 items in stock.

d. Apply the filter.

e. Print the filtered table.

f. Close the table. Do not save the design changes.

Compact, Repair, and Back Up a Database

Now that you are satisfied that any changes made to a form, table, or query carry through the database, you are ready to compact, repair, and back up your file.

a. Select the option to compact and repair your database.

b. Select the option to create a backup copy of your database, accept the default file name, and save it.

c. Close the file.

Mini Cases

Use the rubric following the case as a guide to evaluate your work, but keep in mind that your instructor may impose additional grading criteria or use a different standard to judge your work.

Applying Filters, Printing, and File Management

GENERAL CASE

The *chap1_mc1_safebank.accdb* file contains data from a small bank. Copy the *chap1_mc1_safebank.accdb* file to your working storage folder, name it **chap1_mc1_safebank_solution.accdb**, and open the copied file. Use the skills from this chapter to perform several tasks. Open the Customer table, replace YourName with your name, and sort the data in alphabetical order by LastName. Print the Customer table. Open the Branch table and make yourself the manager of the Campus branch. Close both tables. Open the Branch Customers query and filter it to show only the accounts at the Campus branch with balances over $1,500.00. Print the filtered query results. Compact, repair, and backup your work.

Performance Elements	Exceeds Expectations	Meets Expectations	Below Expectations
Sort and print table data	Printout displays data sorted in requested order.	The table was successfully printed, but the order is incorrect.	Output missing or corrupted.
Apply filters and print query data	Appropriate filters successfully created and printed.	One of the requested filters but not both work correctly. Output created.	Output missing or corrupted.
Data entry	Data were entered correctly.	Some but not all of the requested data were entered correctly, or other data were overwritten.	Output missing or corrupted.
File management	Database was correctly compacted, repaired, and backed up.	The database was successfully compacted but not backed up or vice versa.	Files not submitted.

Combining Name Fields

RESEARCH CASE

This chapter introduced you to the power of using Access filters and setting criteria, but you have much more to explore. Copy the file named *chap1_mc2_traders.accdb* to your production folder and rename it **chap1_mc2_traders_solution.accdb**. Open the file and enable the content. Open the Employees table and replace YourName with your first and last names. Open the Revenue report and switch to the appropriate view. Use the tools that you have learned in this chapter to filter the report. You wish to limit the output to only your sales of Seafood. You may need to use Access Help to get the filters to work. Once the report is filtered, print it. Write your instructor a letter explaining how you accomplished this step. Use a letter template in Word, your most professional writing style, and clear directions that someone could follow in order to accomplish this task. Attach the printout of the name list to the letter. Turn the printouts in to the instructor if instructed to do so. Back up, compact, and repair your database.

Performance Elements	Exceeds Expectations	Meets Expectations	Below Expectations
Use online help	Appropriate articles located, and letter indicates comprehension.	Appropriate articles located, but letter did not demonstrate comprehension.	Articles not found.
Report filtered to display only your sales of seafood	Printed list attached to letter in requested format.	Printed list is attached, but the filter failed to screen one or more salespeople or categories.	List missing or incomprehensible.
Summarize and communicate	Letter clearly written and could be used as directions.	Letter text indicates some understanding but also weaknesses.	Letter missing or incomprehensible.
File management	Database was correctly compacted, repaired, and backed up.	Database was successfully compacted but not backed up or vice versa.	Files not submitted.
Esthetics	Letter template correctly employed.	Template employed but signed in the wrong place or improperly used.	Letter missing or incomprehensible.

Coffee Revenue Queries

DISASTER RECOVERY

A co-worker called you into his office and explained that he was having difficulty with Access 2007 and asked you to look at his work. Copy the *chap1_mc3_coffee.accdb* file to your working storage folder, rename it **chap1_mc3_coffee_solution.accdb**, and open the file. Your co-worker explains that the report is incorrect. It shows that Lockley is the sales representative for "Coulter Office Supplies" and the "Little, Joiner, and Jones" customers, when in fact, you are those customers' sales representative. Make sure your name replaces YourName in the Sales Reps table. Find the source of the error and correct it. Run and print the report and turn the printout and file in to your instructor if instructed to do so. Compact, repair, and backup your database.

Performance Elements	Exceeds Expectations	Meets Expectations	Below Expectations
Error identification	Correct identification and correction of all errors.	Correct identification of all errors and correction of some errors.	Errors neither located nor corrected.
Reporting	Report opened, run, and printed successfully.	Printout submitted, but with errors.	No printout submitted for evaluation.
File management	Database was correctly compacted, repaired, and backed up.	Database was successfully compacted but not backed up or vice versa.	Files not submitted.

chapter 1 | **PowerPoint**

Introduction to PowerPoint

Presentations Made Easy

After you read this chapter, you will be able to:

1. Identify PowerPoint user interface elements **(page 489)**.
2. Use PowerPoint views **(page 494)**.
3. Open and save a slide show **(page 499)**.
4. Get Help **(page 502)**.
5. Create a storyboard **(page 507)**.
6. Use slide layouts **(page 510)**.
7. Apply design themes **(page 510)**.
8. Review the presentation **(page 512)**.
9. Add a table **(page 519)**.
10. Insert clip art **(page 519)**.
11. Use transitions and animations **(page 521)**.
12. Run and navigate a slide show **(page 530)**.
13. Print with PowerPoint **(page 532)**.

Hands-On Exercises

Exercises	Skills Covered
1. **INTRODUCTION TO POWERPOINT (page 503)** **Open:** chap1_ho1_intro.pptx **Save as:** chap1_ho1_intro_solution.pptx	• Start PowerPoint • Open an Existing Presentation • Type a Speaker's Note • View the Presentation • Save the Presentation with a New Name • Locate Information Using Help
2. **CREATING A PRESENTATION (page 513)** **Open:** none **Save as:** chap1_ho2_content_solution.pptx	• Create a New Presentation • Add Slides • Check Spelling and Use the Thesaurus • Modify Text and Layout • Reorder Slides • Apply a Design Theme
3. **STRENGTHENING A PRESENTATION (page 524)** **Open:** chap1_ho2_content _solution.pptx (from Exercise 2) **Save as:** chap1_ho3_content_solution.pptx (additional modifications)	• Add a Table • Insert, Move, and Resize Clip Art • Apply a Transition • Animate Objects
4. **NAVIGATING AND PRINTING (page 535)** **Open:** chap1_ho3_content_solution.pptx (from Exercise 3) **Save as:** chap1_ho4_content_solution.pptx (additional modifications)	• Display a Slide Show • Navigate to Specific Slides • Annotate a Slide • Print Audience Handouts

CASE STUDY

Be a Volunteer

Case Study

While watching television one evening, you see a public service announcement on the volunteer organization Big Brothers Big Sisters. The Big Brothers Big Sisters organization seeks to help children ages 6 through 18 reach their potential by providing mentors through their growing years. The organization matches "Bigs" (adults) with "Littles" (children) in one-on-one relationships with the goal of having the mentor make a positive impact on the child's life. Being intrigued, you attend an informational open house where volunteers and board members give an overview of the program and share personal experiences. At the open house you discover that the organization has been helping at-risk children for more than 100 years and that in 2003 Big Brothers Big Sisters was selected by *Forbes Magazine* as one of its top ten charities that it believes are worthy of donor consideration.

You choose to answer Big Brothers Big Sisters' call to "Be a friend. Be a mentor. Just be there." You call the local organization for further information and you are invited to come in and meet representatives, introduce yourself, and complete an application. Because "Bigs" and "Littles" are matched by interests, you decide to create a presentation to introduce you and give information about your interests. Your assignment is to create a PowerPoint slide show about yourself to use in your presentation. You may want to include a slide about a mentor who has positively impacted your life. Forget modesty at this point—toot your own horn!

Your Assignment

- Read the chapter, paying special attention to how to create and enhance a presentation.
- Create a new presentation with a title slide that includes your name. Save the presentation as **chap1_case_introduction_solution**.
- Storyboard a presentation that includes four to six slides that introduce you, your background, and your interests. Include an introduction slide and a summary or conclusion slide as well as your main point slides introducing you.
- Use the storyboard to create a PowerPoint slide show about you.
- Apply a design theme and add a transition to at least one slide.
- Insert at least one clip art image in an appropriate location.
- Display your slide show to at least one class member, or to the entire class if asked by your instructor.
- Print handouts, four slides per page, framed.

Introduction to PowerPoint

This chapter introduces you to PowerPoint 2007, one of the major applications in Microsoft Office 2007. PowerPoint enables you to create a professional presentation without relying on others, and then lets you deliver that presentation in a variety of ways. You can show the presentation from your computer, on the World Wide Web, or create traditional overhead transparencies. You can even use PowerPoint's Package for CD feature to package your presentation with a viewer so those without PowerPoint may still view your presentation.

A PowerPoint presentation consists of a series of slides such as those shown in Figures 1.1–1.6. The various slides contain different elements (such as text, images, and WordArt), yet the presentation has a consistent look with respect to its overall design and color scheme. Creating this type of presentation is relatively easy, and that is the power in PowerPoint. In essence, PowerPoint enables you to concentrate on the content of a presentation without worrying about its appearance. You supply the text and supporting elements and leave the formatting to PowerPoint. If, however, you wish to create your own presentation design, PowerPoint provides you with powerful tools to use in the design process.

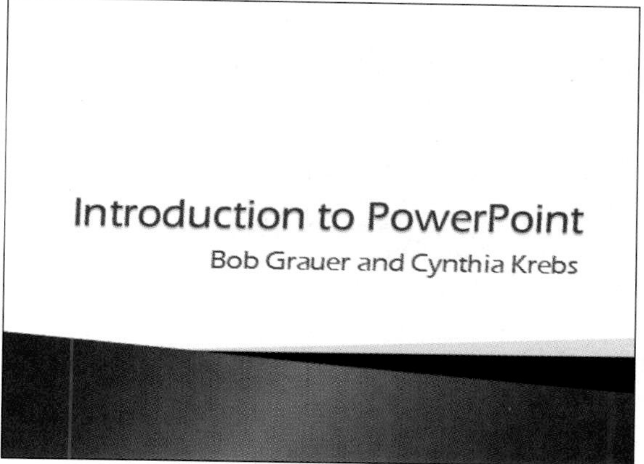

Figure 1.1 Title Slide

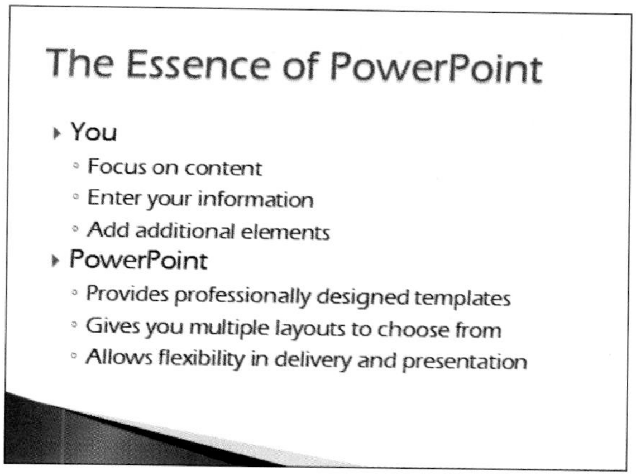

The Essence of PowerPoint

- You
  - Focus on content
  - Enter your information
  - Add additional elements
- PowerPoint
  - Provides professionally designed templates
  - Gives you multiple layouts to choose from
  - Allows flexibility in delivery and presentation

Figure 1.2 Title and Content Slide

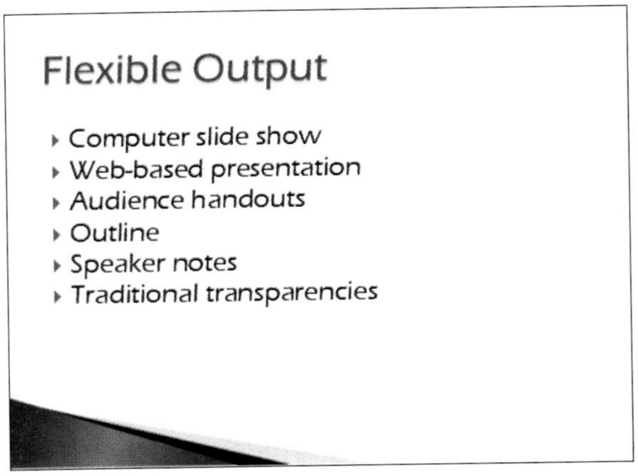

Flexible Output

- Computer slide show
- Web-based presentation
- Audience handouts
- Outline
- Speaker notes
- Traditional transparencies

Figure 1.3 Title and Content Slide

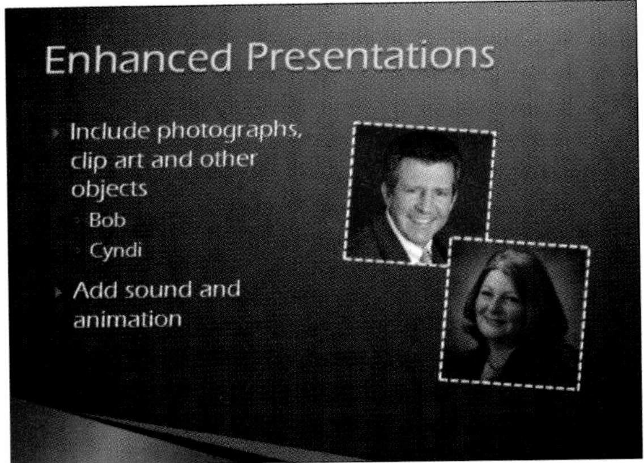

Figure 1.4 Title and Two Content Slides with Images

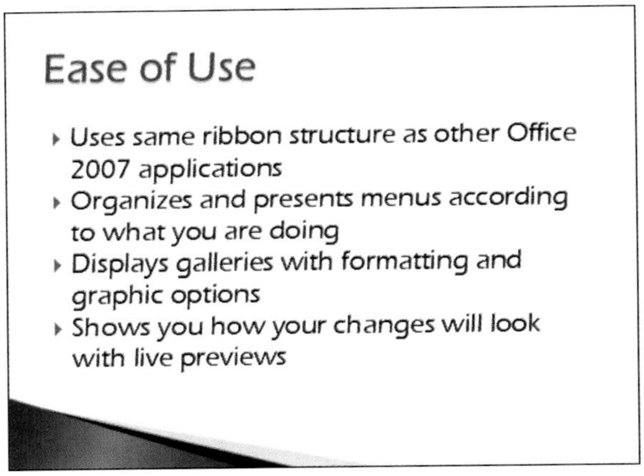

Ease of Use

- Uses same ribbon structure as other Office 2007 applications
- Organizes and presents menus according to what you are doing
- Displays galleries with formatting and graphic options
- Shows you how your changes will look with live previews

Figure 1.5 Title and Content Slide

Figure 1.6 Title Slide with WordArt

In addition to helping you create the presentation, PowerPoint provides a variety of ways to deliver it. You can show the presentation on a computer monitor as a slide show or Web presentation, or you can project the slide show onto a screen or a wall for an audience. You can include sound and video in the presentation, provided your system has a sound card and speakers. You can automate the presentation and display it at a convention booth or kiosk. If you cannot show the presentation on a computer with a monitor or projector, you can easily convert it to overhead transparencies or print the presentation in various ways to distribute to your audience.

In this section, you start your exploration of PowerPoint by viewing a previously completed presentation so that you can better appreciate what PowerPoint is all about. You examine the PowerPoint interface and various views to discover the advantages of each view. You modify and save an existing presentation, and then you create your own. Finally, you use Help to obtain assistance within PowerPoint.

Reference

Practice the following delivery tips to gain confidence and polish your delivery:

- Look at the audience, not at the screen, as you speak and you will open communication and gain credibility. Use the three-second guide: look into the eyes of a member of the audience for three seconds and then scan the entire audience. Continue doing this throughout your presentation. Use your eye contact to keep members of the audience involved.
- Do not read from a prepared script or your PowerPoint Notes. Know your material thoroughly. Glance at your notes infrequently. Never post a screen full of small text, and then torture your audience by saying "I know you cannot read this so I will…"
- Practice or rehearse your presentation with your PowerPoint at home until you are comfortable with the material and its corresponding slides.
- Speak slowly and clearly and try to vary your delivery. Show emotion or enthusiasm for your topic. If you do not care about your topic, why should the audience?
- Pause to emphasize key points when speaking.
- Speak to the person farthest away from you to be sure the people in the last row can hear you.
- Do not overwhelm your audience with your PowerPoint animations, sounds, and special effects. These features should not overpower you and your message, but should enhance your message.
- Arrive early to set up so you do not keep the audience waiting while you manage equipment. Have a backup in case the equipment does not work: overhead transparencies or handouts work well. Again, know your material well enough that you can present without the slide show if necessary.
- Prepare handouts for your audience so they can relax and participate in your presentation rather than scramble taking notes.
- Thank the audience for their attention and participation. Leave on a positive note.

TIP Polish Your Delivery

The speaker is the most important part of any presentation, and a poor delivery will ruin even the best presentation. Remember that a PowerPoint slide show is a tool to aid YOU in your presentation and that YOU are the key to a good presentation. Do not use a PowerPoint slide show as a crutch for lack of preparation for a presentation. A PowerPoint presentation should not be like "karaoke," where you read your information word for word from the screen!

Identifying PowerPoint User Interface Elements

If you have completed the Exploring Series Office Fundamentals chapter on Office 2007, many of the PowerPoint 2007 interface features will be familiar to you. If this is your first experience with an Office 2007 application, you will quickly feel comfortable in PowerPoint, and because the interface is core to all of the Office 2007 applications, you will quickly be able to apply the knowledge in Word, Excel, Access, and Outlook. In Office 2007, Microsoft organizes features and commands to correspond directly to the common tasks people perform, making it possible for you to find the features you need quickly.

Normal view is the tri-pane default PowerPoint view.

In PowerPoint 2007, you work with two windows: the PowerPoint application window and the document window for the current presentation. The PowerPoint application window contains the Minimize, Maximize (or Restore), and Close buttons. The PowerPoint application window also contains the title bar, which indicates the file name of the document on which you are working and the name of the application (Microsoft PowerPoint). Figure 1.7 shows the default PowerPoint view, the ***Normal view***, with three panes that provide maximum flexibility in working with the presentation. The pane on the left side of the screen shows either thumbnails or an outline of the presentation, depending on whether you select the Slides tab or the Outline tab. The Slide pane on the right displays the currently selected slide in your presentation. The final pane, the Notes pane, is located at the bottom of the screen where you enter notes pertaining to the slide or the presentation.

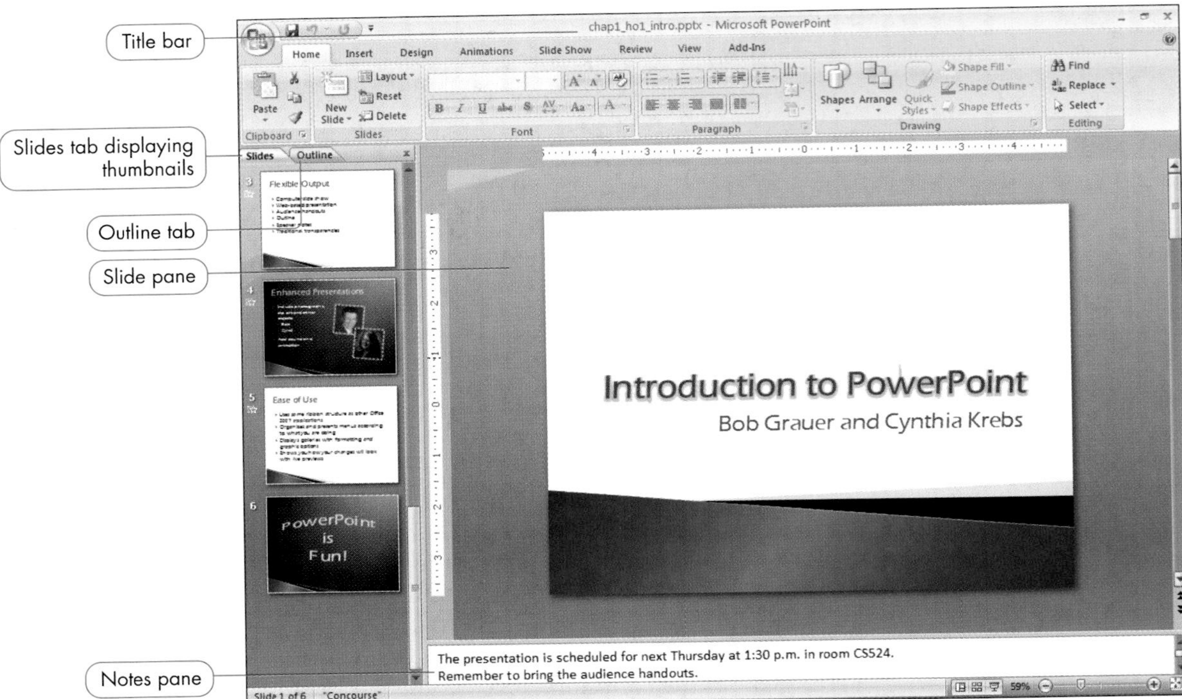

Figure 1.7 The Default PowerPoint View (Normal View)

Refer to Figure 1.8 to see the Microsoft Office Button, hereafter referred to as the Office Button, displayed below the title bar. This button provides you with an easy way to access commands for saving and printing, and includes features for finalizing your work and sharing your work with others. To the right of the Office Button is the Quick Access Toolbar, which gives you quick access to the commands that you may need at any time: Save, Undo, and Redo. You also can add other commands to the Quick Access Toolbar.

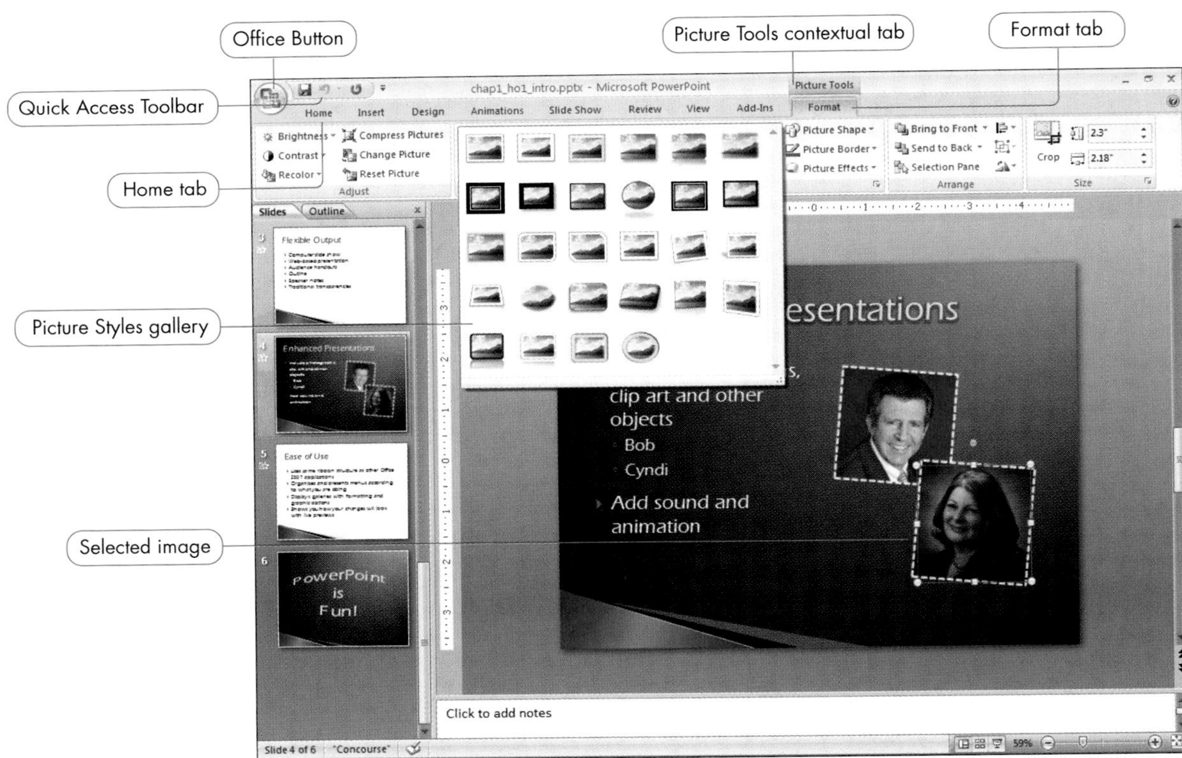

Figure 1.8 PowerPoint's Interface

The ***Ribbon*** is a command center that organizes commands into groups accessed from tabs.

Beneath the Office Button and the Quick Access Toolbar is the ***Ribbon***, a command center that organizes commands into groups. The Ribbon makes it easy for you to find the features you need. Locate the Ribbon in Figure 1.8.

TIP View Hidden Commands

If, when you look at your PowerPoint screen, it does not show all of the commands, your monitor could be set to display at a low resolution. For example, a resolution of 800 by 600 pixels used with small notebooks and older 13" CRT screens will not show all the commands. To see the hidden commands, click the ▶ on the vertical bar on the far right of the Ribbon. The remaining commands will appear. Changing your resolution to 1026 by 768 pixels or a higher resolution will allow all commands to display.

A ***tab*** sits above the Ribbon and is used to organize or group like features for quick access.

A ***tab*** sits above the Ribbon and organizes commands by grouping the most commonly used features related to your task for quick access. Once you select a tab based on the task you wish to perform, the commands that relate to one another when working on that task appear together in groups. For example, when you click the Home tab, the core PowerPoint commands appear in groups such as Clipboard, Slides, Font, Paragraph, Drawing, and Editing. PowerPoint has seven tabs: Home, Insert, Design, Animations, Slide Show, Review, and View. You may see an additional tab, Add-Ins, if you have any supplemental programs that add features to Microsoft Office. The author installed a supplemental image-capturing program, so all figures in this text display the Add-Ins tab. Table 1.1 lists each of the tabs, the groups that appear when the tab is selected, and a general description of the available commands.

TIP Minimize the Ribbon

To increase the size of the working area on your screen, you can minimize the Ribbon by clicking any active tab, located above the Ribbon. To restore the Ribbon, click any tab. As an alternative, use the keyboard shortcut by pressing **Ctrl+F1**.

An ***object*** is any type of information that can be inserted in a slide.

A ***contextual tab*** is a specialty tab that appears only when certain types of objects are being edited.

When you add text, a graphic, a table, a chart, or any other form of information to a slide, you are adding an ***object*** to the slide. When you select certain types of objects for editing, ***contextual tabs*** containing commands specific to that object appear. The contextual tabs appear above the Ribbon and, when clicked, open a tab containing multiple tools you need. For example, in Figure 1.8, because the image of Cyndi is selected for editing, the Picture Tools contextual tab displays. Clicking the Picture Tools tab opened the Format tab. The Format tab is organized into groups related to specific tasks (Picture Tools, Picture Styles, Arrange, and Size).

(Microsoft . . . "pick and click" formatting . . . gives you results that look good without much design effort.)

As you examine Figure 1.8, notice the large box that appears on top of the Ribbon, showing a wide variety of styles that could be applied to a picture. This is the Picture Styles gallery, one of many galleries within PowerPoint. A ***gallery*** provides you with a set of visual options to choose from when working with your presentation. You click an option, and the styles in that option are applied to your object. Microsoft refers to this feature as "pick and click" formatting. "Picking and clicking" gives you results that look good without much design effort.

A ***gallery*** displays a set of predefined options that can be clicked to apply to an object.

Table 1.1 Tab, Group, and Description

Tab and Group	Description
Home Clipboard Slides Font Paragraph Drawing Editing	The core PowerPoint tab. Contains basic editing functions such as cut and paste, and finding and replacing text. Includes adding slides and changing slide layout. Formatting using font, paragraph, and drawing tools is available.
Insert Tables Illustrations Links Text Media Clips	Contains all insert functions in one area. Includes ability to create tables and illustrations. Hyperlinks, text boxes, headers and footers, WordArt, and media clips are inserted here.
Design Page Setup Themes Background	Contains all functions associated with slide design including themes and backgrounds. Change page setup and slide orientation here.
Animations Preview Animations Transition To This Slide	Controls all aspects of animation including transitions, advanced options, and customizing.
Slide Show Start Slide Show Set Up Monitors	Includes slide show setup, monitor set up, and timing. Options for starting the slide show available.
Review Proofing Comments Protect	Contains all reviewing tools in PowerPoint, including such things as spelling and the use of comments.
View Presentation Views Show/Hide Zoom Color/Grayscale Window Macros	Contains Presentation Views. Advanced view options include showing or hiding slides, zooming, and available color choices. Set window arrangement here. Enables macro creation.
Add-Ins Custom Toolbars	Displays programs added to system that extend PowerPoint functionality. Does not display if supplemental programs are not installed.

A ***ScreenTip*** is a small window that describes a command.

Figure 1.9 shows a ***ScreenTip***, or small window that appears when the mouse pointer moves over a command. The ScreenTip states the name or more descriptive explanation of a command. Enhanced ScreenTips also contain an icon that you can click to get more assistance from Help. ScreenTips can be invaluable when you need to identify a selected style. In this case, the ScreenTip gives the name of a WordArt choice, Fill–Accent 2, Warm Matte Bevel, and a preview of how it would look if selected. In some instances, an Enhanced ScreenTip provides brief description of the feature and includes a link to a Help topic relating to the command.

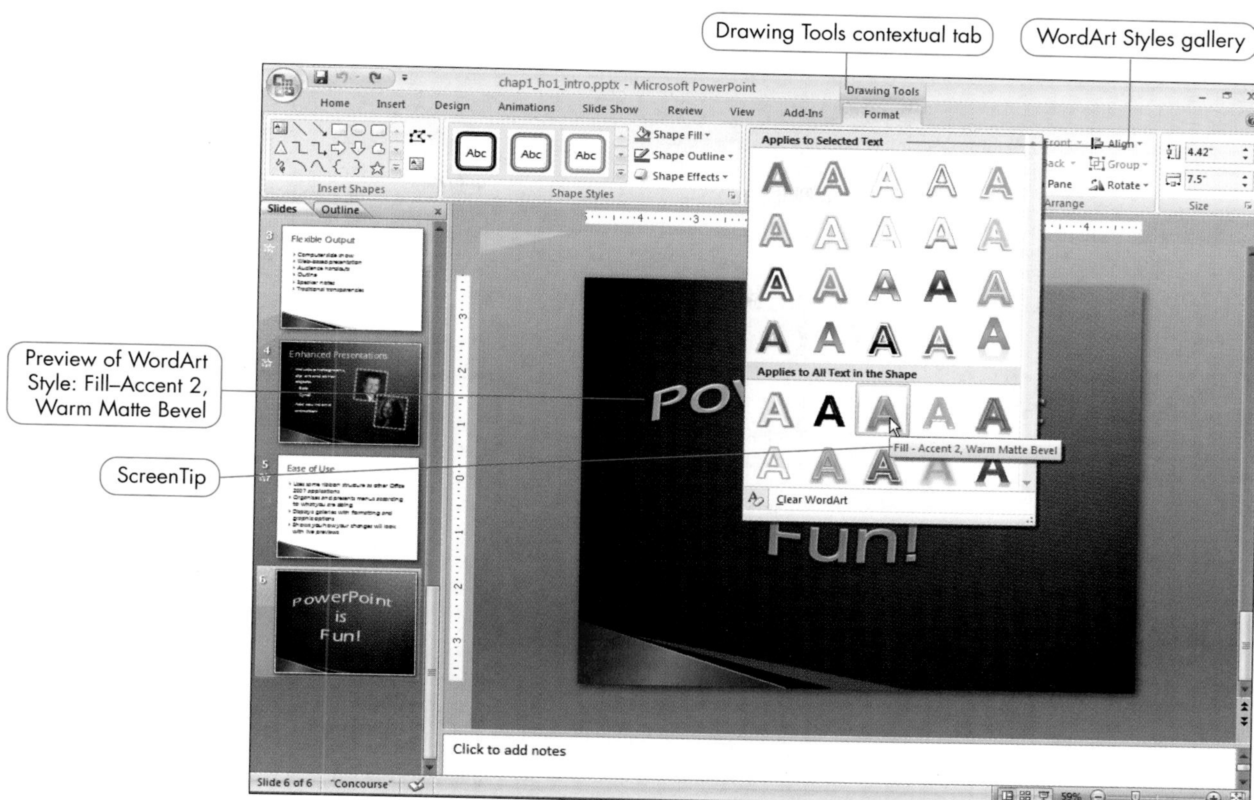

Figure 1.9 WordArt Gallery with ScreenTip

The ***Mini toolbar*** is a small, semitransparent toolbar that you can use to format text.

The ***Mini toolbar*** is a small semitransparent toolbar that appears above selected text (see Figure 1.10) and gives you quick and easy access to the formatting commands commonly applied to text (such as font, font styles, font size, text alignment, text color, indent levels, and bullet features). Because the Mini toolbar appears above the selected text, you do not have to move the mouse pointer up to the Ribbon. When you first select text, the Mini toolbar appears as a semitransparent image, but if you move the mouse pointer over the toolbar, it fades in and becomes active for your use. As the mouse pointer moves away from the toolbar, or if a command is not selected, the Mini toolbar disappears.

The ***status bar*** is a bar that contains the slide number, the Design Theme name, and view options.

Figure 1.10 also shows PowerPoint's unique ***status bar***, a bar that contains the slide number, the design theme name, and options that control the view of your presentation: view buttons, the Zoom level button, the Zoom Slider, and the *Fit slide to current window* button. The status bar is located at the bottom of your screen, and can be customized. To customize the status bar, right-click on the bar and then click the options you want displayed from the Customize Status Bar list.

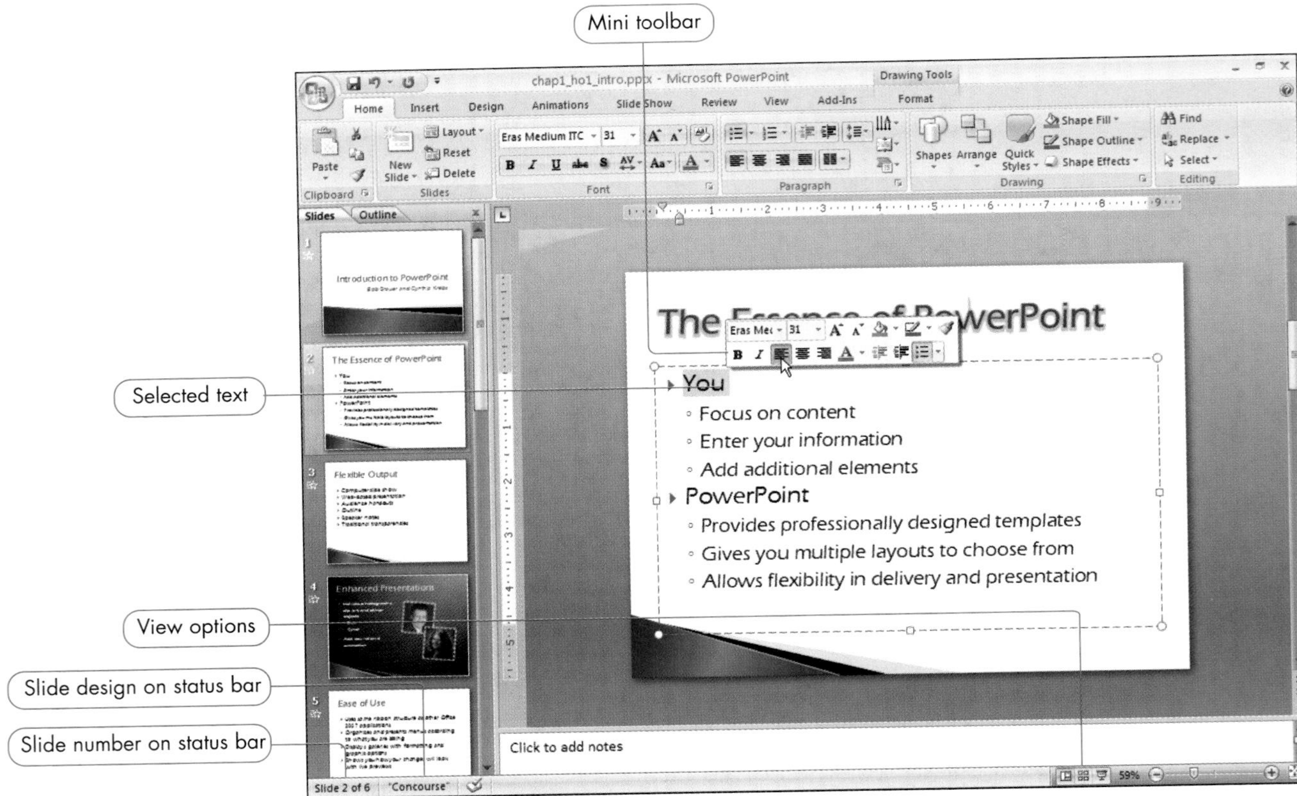

Figure 1.10 Mini Toolbar and Status Bar

Using PowerPoint Views

PowerPoint offers four primary views in which to create, modify, and deliver a presentation: Normal, Slide Sorter, Notes Page, and Slide Show. Each view represents a different way of looking at the presentation and each view has unique capabilities. (You will find some redundancy among the views in that certain tasks can be accomplished from multiple views.) The View tab gives you access to the four primary views, plus three additional views for working with masters. If you prefer, you may use the view buttons on the status bar to switch from one view to another, but only three views are available from the status bar: Normal, Slide Sorter, and Slide Show.

You looked at the default Normal view earlier in the chapter (refer to Figure 1.7), but you will examine it in more detail now and compare it to other PowerPoint views. Knowing the benefits of each view enables to you work more efficiently. Figure 1.11 shows Normal view with the screen divided into three panes: the Outline tab pane showing the text of the presentation, the Slide pane displaying an enlarged view of one slide, and the Notes pane showing a portion of any associated speaker notes for the selected slide. The Outline tab pane provides the fastest way to type or edit text for the presentation. You type directly into the outline pane and move easily from one slide to the next. You also can use the outline pane to move and copy text from one slide to another or to rearrange the order of the slides within a presentation. The outline pane is limited, however, in that it does not show graphic elements that may be present on individual slides. Thus, you may want to switch to the Normal view that shows the Slides tab containing ***thumbnail*** images (slide miniatures) rather than the outline. In this view, you can change the order of the slides by clicking and dragging a slide to a new position. The Outline and Slides tabs let you switch between the two variations of the Normal view.

A ***thumbnail*** is a miniature of a slide that appears in the Slides tab.

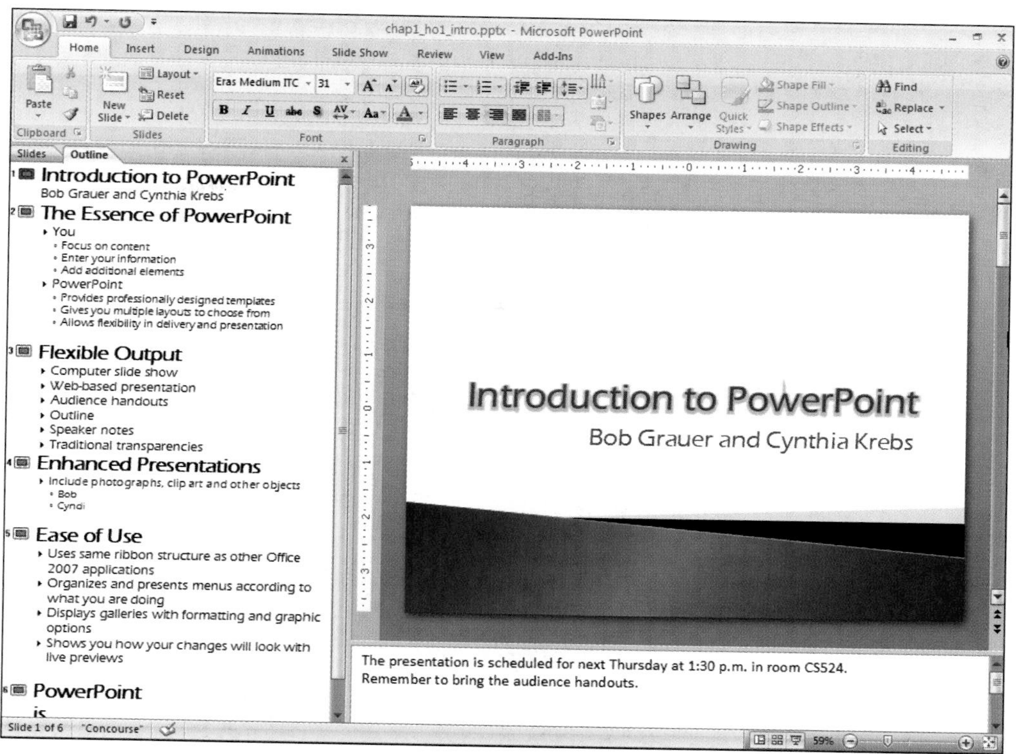

Figure 1.11 Normal View with Outline Tab Selected

The Normal view also provides access to the individual slides and speaker notes, each of which appears in its own pane. The Slide pane is the large pane on the right of the window. The Notes pane displays on the bottom of the window. You can change the size of these panes by dragging the splitter bar (border) that separates one pane from another. Figure 1.12 shows the Slides tab selected, the size of the Slide pane reduced, and the size of the Notes pane enlarged to allow for more space in which to create speaker notes.

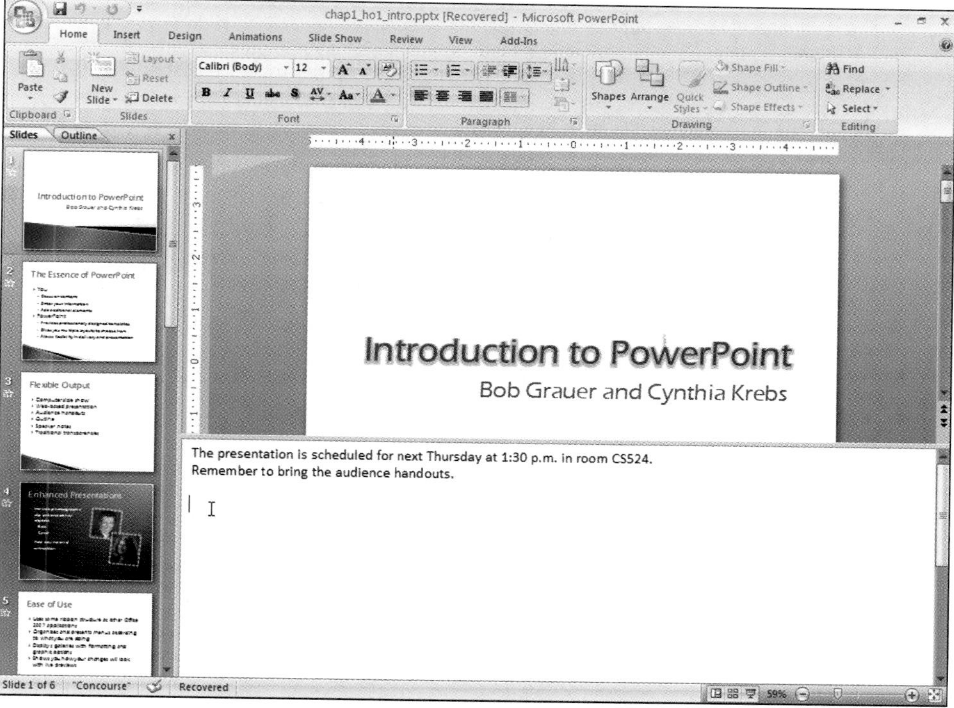

Figure 1.12 Normal View with Resized Panes

The Normal view is probably all that you need, but some designers like to close the left pane completely to see just an individual slide. This variation of the Normal view enlarges the individual slide so you can see more detail. Because the individual slide is where you change or format text, add graphical elements, or apply various animation effects an enlarged view is helpful. Figure 1.13 shows the individual slide in Normal view with the left pane closed. If you close the left pane, you can restore the screen to its usual tri-pane view by clicking the View tab, and then clicking Normal in the Presentation Views group.

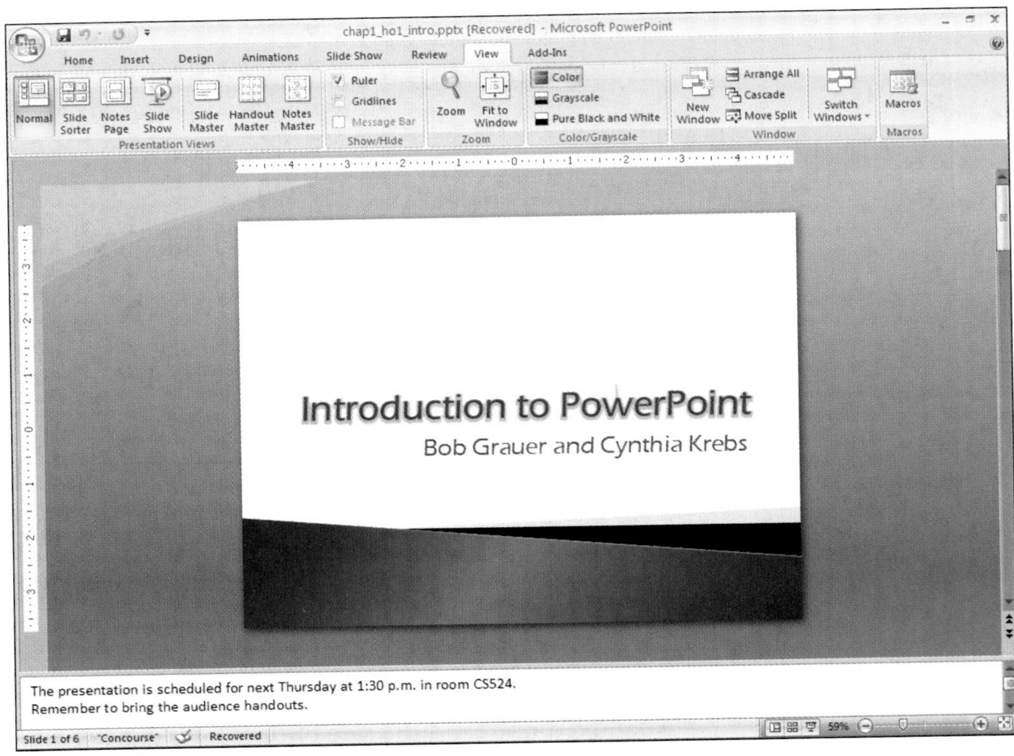

Figure 1.13 Individual Slide View

The ***Notes Page view*** is used for entering and editing large amounts of text that the speaker can refer to when presenting.

Rather than create speaker notes in the small pane available in the Normal view, you can work in the ***Notes Page view***, a view specifically created to enter and edit large amounts of text that the speaker can refer to when presenting. If you have a large amount of technical detail in the speaker notes, you also may want to print audience handouts of this view since each page contains a picture of the slide plus the associated speaker notes. The notes do not appear when the presentation is shown, but are intended to help the speaker remember the key points about each slide. To switch from Normal view to Notes Page view, click the View tab, and then click Notes Page view in the Presentation Views group. Figure 1.14 shows an example of the Notes Page view.

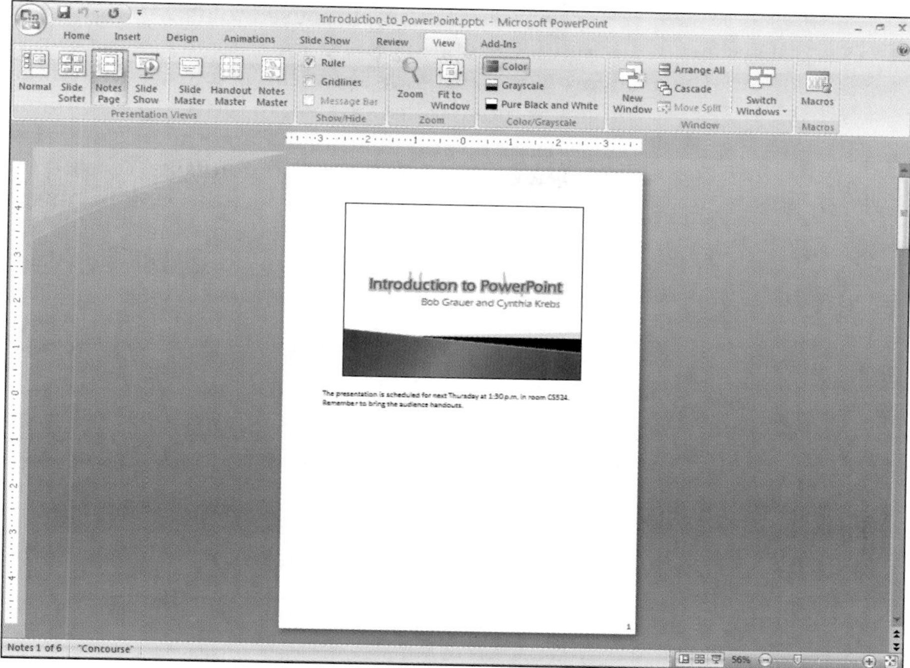

Figure 1.14 Notes Page View

The ***Slide Sorter view*** displays thumbnails of slides.

The ***Slide Sorter view*** enables you to see miniatures of your presentation slides to view multiple slides simultaneously (see Figure 1.15). This view is helpful when you wish to reorder the slides in a presentation. It also provides a convenient way to delete one or more slides. It lets you set transition effects for multiple slides. Any edit that you perform in one view is automatically updated in the other views. If, for example, you change the order of the slides in the Slide Sorter view, the changes automatically are reflected in the outline or thumbnail images within the Normal view. To switch to Slide Sorter view, click the View tab, and then click Slide Sorter in the Presentation Views group. If you are in Slide Sorter view and double-click a thumbnail, PowerPoint returns to the Normal view.

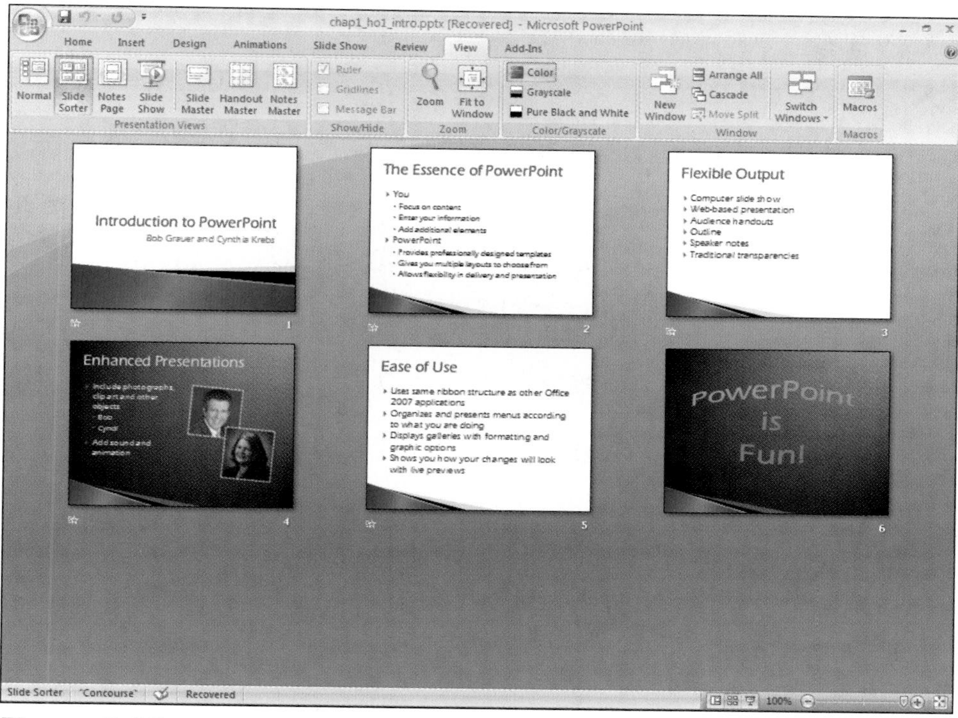

Figure 1.15 Slide Sorter View

The ***Slide Show view*** displays a full-screen view of a presentation.

The ***Slide Show view*** is used to deliver the completed presentation full screen to an audience, one slide at a time, as an electronic presentation on the computer (see Figure 1.16). The slide show can be presented manually, where the speaker clicks the mouse to move from one slide to the next, or automatically, where each slide stays on the screen for a predetermined amount of time, after which the next slide appears. A slide show can contain a combination of both methods for advancing. You can insert transition effects to impact the look of how one slide moves to the next. To view the presentation in Slide Show view, click the View tab and then click Slide Show in the Presentation Views group. This step begins the show with Slide 1. To end the slide show, press Escape on the keyboard.

TIP Start the Slide Show

To choose whether you start a slide show from the beginning, Slide 1, or from the current slide, click the Slide Show tab, and then click either From Beginning or From Current Slide in the Start Slide Show group.

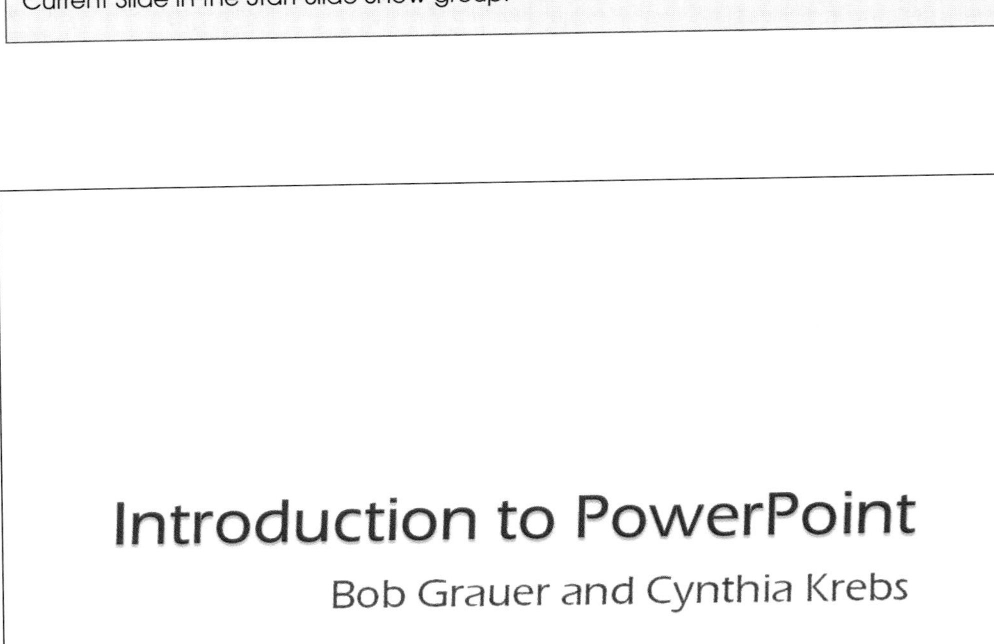

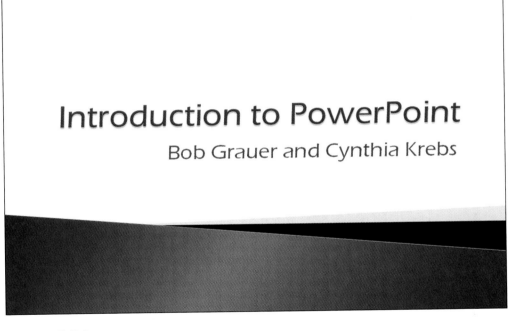

Figure 1.16 Slide Show View

Have you been in an audience watching a presenter use PowerPoint to deliver an electronic presentation? Did the presenter look professional at all times? While this is the desired scenario, consider another real-life scenario—the presenter holds a remote in one hand, printed speaker notes in the other hand, and is wearing a watch. The presenter is conscious of the time allotted for the presentation and attempts to look at the watch to see how much time has elapsed. Using the remote, the presenter attempts to slide a long sleeve up and reveal the watch. The remote catches on the printed speaker notes, the notes start to fall, the presenter grabs to catch them . . . and chaos results. Presenter Fumble lives! You can avoid "Presenter Fumble" by using Presenter view.

(. . . avoid "Presenter Fumble" by using Presenter view!)

Presenter view delivers a presentation on two monitors simultaneously.

Presenter view delivers a presentation on two monitors simultaneously. Typically, one monitor is a projector that delivers the full-screen presentation to the audience and one monitor is a laptop or computer at the presenter's station. Having two monitors enables your audience to see your presentation at the same time you are seeing a special view of the presentation that includes the slide, speaker notes, slide thumbnails so you can jump between slides as needed, navigation arrows that advance your slide or return to the previous slide, options to enable a marking on the slide, and a timer that displays the time elapsed since you began. Figure 1.17 shows the audience view on the left side of the figure and the Presenter view on the right side.

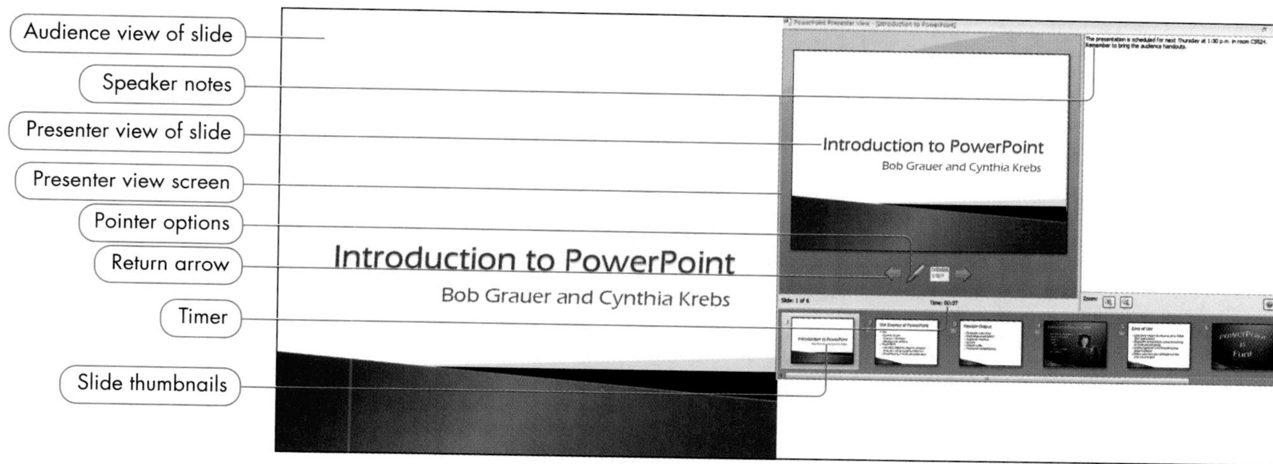

Figure 1.17 Presenter View

In order to use Presenter view, you must use a computer that has multiple monitor capability, and multiple monitor support must be turned on. If you need information about how to enable multiple monitor support, see Microsoft Windows Help. After you enable multiple monitor support, click Show Presenter View in the Monitors group on the Slide Show tab, and then click from Beginning in the Start Slide Show group under the same tab.

Opening and Saving a Slide Show

The Office Button gives you access to an important menu. The available options include the New command so that you can create a new document; in this case, a presentation that is blank or that is based upon a template. You use the Open command to retrieve a presentation saved on a storage device and place it in the RAM memory of your computer so you can work on it. The Print command opens a dialog box so that you may choose print settings and then print. The Close command closes the current presentation but leaves PowerPoint open. To exit PowerPoint, click the X located on the top right of the application window.

While you are working on a previously saved presentation, it is being saved in the temporary memory or RAM memory of your computer. The Save As command copies the presentation that you are working on to the hard drive of your computer or to a storage device such as a flash drive. When you activate the Save As command, the Save As dialog box appears (see Figure 1.18). The dialog box requires you to specify the drive or folder in which to store the presentation, the name of the presentation, and the type of file you wish the presentation to be saved as. All subsequent executions of the Save command save the presentation under the assigned name, replacing the previously saved version with the new version. If you wish to change the name of the presentation, use Save As again. Pressing Ctrl+S also displays the Save As dialog box if it is the first time you are saving the slide show.

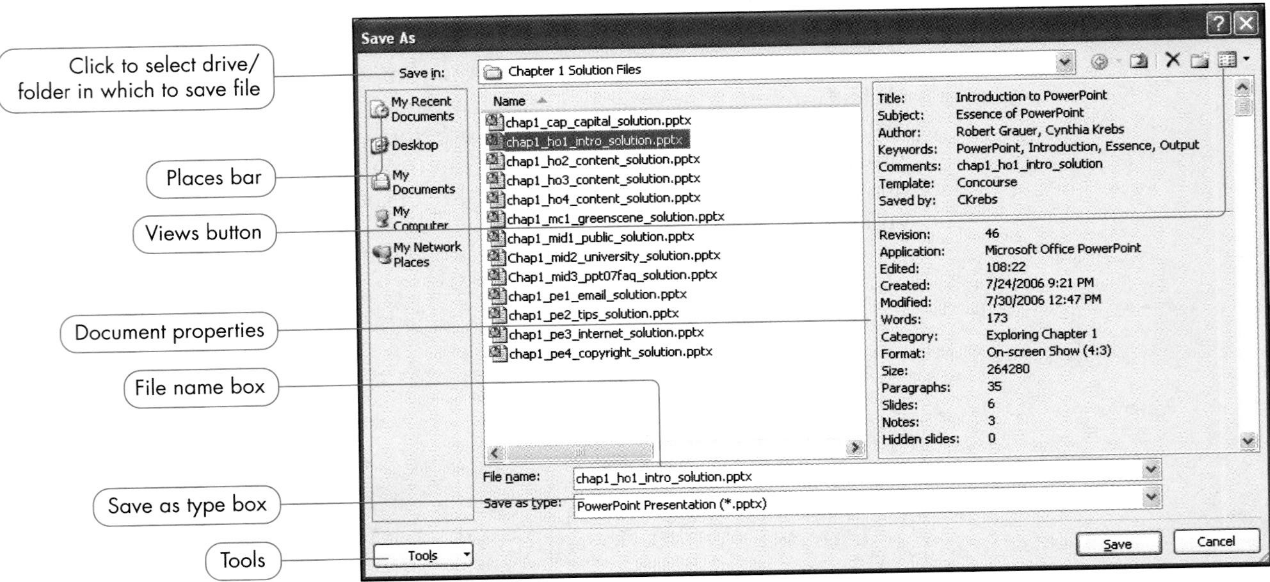

Figure 1.18 Save As Dialog Box

The file name (e.g., chap1_ho1_intro_solution) can contain up to 255 characters including spaces, commas, and/or periods. Periods are discouraged, however, since they are too easily confused with the file extensions explained in the next paragraph. Click the *Save in* drop-down arrow to select the drive and the folder in which the presentation file will be saved.

The file type defaults to a PowerPoint presentation. You can save to other formats including a Web page. When you save a PowerPoint file, it is assigned a .pptx extension. This file type is an XML (eXtensible Markup Language) format. This file format compresses data, which greatly reduces file sizes, thereby saving storage space on your hard drive or storage device. Another benefit of using the XML file format is that it reduces the chance of file corruption and helps you recover corrupted documents. This file format also provides increased security. One caution must be noted, however: Files created in the XML format cannot be opened in earlier versions of Office software unless the Microsoft Compatibility Pack is installed. Your colleagues who share files with you should download the Compatibility Pack on all computers that may be used to open your XML files.

TIP New Folder Creation

By default, all Office documents are stored in the My Documents folder. It is helpful, however, to create additional folders, especially if you work with a large number of different documents. You can create one folder for school and another for personal work, or you can create different folders for different applications. To create a folder, click the Office Button, select Save As, and then click the Create New Folder button to display the New Folder dialog box. Type the name of the folder, and then click OK to create the folder. The next time you open or save a presentation, use the *Look in* or *Save in* box to navigate to that folder. For this class, you may wish to create a folder with your assignment solutions for each chapter so you can quickly locate them.

The Open command retrieves a copy of an existing presentation into memory, enabling you to work with that presentation. The Open command displays the Open dialog box in which you specify the file name, the drive (and optionally, the folder) that contains the file, and the file type. PowerPoint will then list all files of that type on the designated drive (and folder), enabling you to open the file you want. To aid you in selecting the correct file, click the Views button. The Preview view shows the first slide in a presentation, without having to open the presentation.

TIP Use the Tools Button for File Management

Both the Open and the Save As dialog boxes contain a Tools button on the bottom left of their dialog boxes. Once you select any existing file and click the Tools button, you can perform basic file management functions. You can delete or rename the file. You also are able to print the file.

Metadata is data that describes other data.

Document properties is the collection of metadata.

The Properties view shows the document ***metadata***, or the data that describes the document data. The collection of metadata is referred to as the ***document properties***. Author name, keywords, and date created are all examples of metadata displayed in the Properties view. Figure 1.19 shows the Open dialog box in Properties view with the document properties of our sample slideshow displayed.

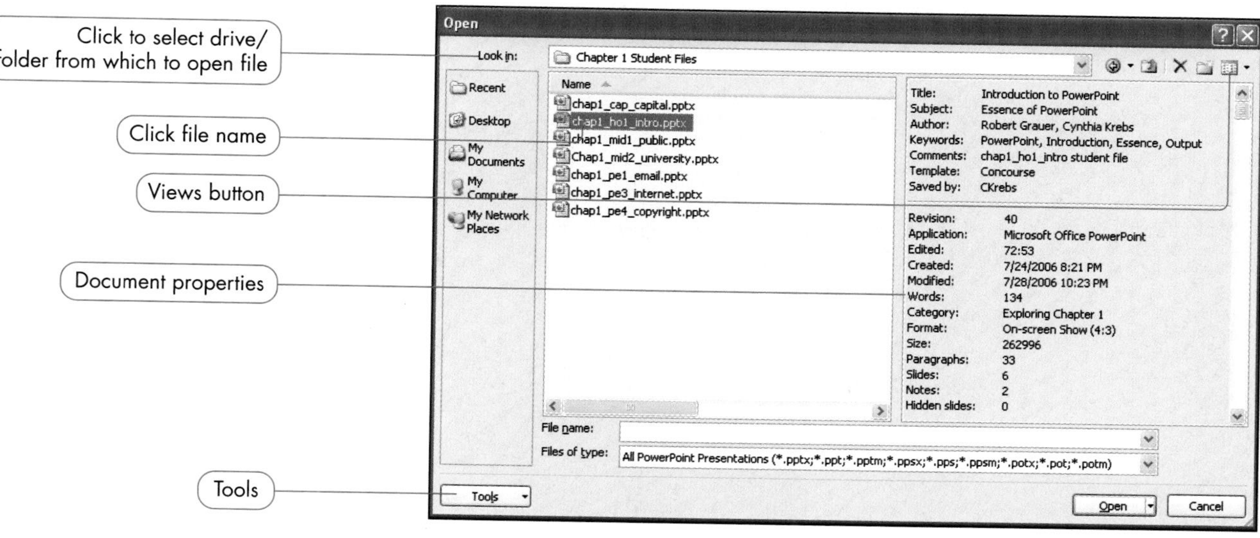

Figure 1.19 Open Dialog Box

TIP Sort by Name, Date, or File Size

The files in the Save As and Open dialog boxes can be displayed in ascending or descending sequence by name, size, file type, or date modified. Change to the Details view, then click the heading of the desired column; for example, click the Modified column to list the files according to the date they were last changed. Click the column heading a second time to reverse the sequence—that is, to switch from ascending to descending, and vice versa.

Getting Help

Microsoft Help is designed to give you all the information you need, whether it is locating information about a specific feature, troubleshooting to solve a problem, searching for software updates, finding a template, or receiving additional training. Help is installed on your computer system at the same time your Office software applications are installed. You can use Help online or offline, depending on whether you are connected to the Internet.

To access Help, you click the Microsoft Office PowerPoint Help button located at the top right of the screen below the Close button. Or, if you prefer, you can use the Help keyboard shortcut by pressing F1. The Help window will appear. This window is designed to make Help easier for you to use. You can navigate and locate information by clicking one of the hyperlinked Help topics, or you can enter a topic in the Search box. The bottom portion of the Help Window gives you access to Office Online where you can obtain clip art, download templates or training, or read articles. Clicking the *Get up to speed with Microsoft Office 2007* hyperlink and then reading the resulting Help screen will help you review the information covered thus far.

Hands-On Exercises

1 | Introduction to PowerPoint

Skills covered: **1.** Start PowerPoint **2.** Open an Existing Presentation **3.** Type a Speaker's Note **4.** View the Presentation **5.** Save the Presentation with a New Name **6.** Locate Information Using Help

Step 1
Start PowerPoint

a. Click **Start** on your Windows taskbar, and then click **All Programs**.

b. Click **Microsoft Office**, and then click **Microsoft Office PowerPoint 2007**.

You should see a blank PowerPoint presentation in Normal view.

Step 2
Open an Existing Presentation

Refer to Figure 1.20 as you complete Step 2.

a. Click the **Office Button** and select **Open**.

The Open dialog box will appear. Do not be concerned that your file list does not match Figure 1.20.

b. Click the **Look in drop-down arrow**, and then click the appropriate drive depending on the storage location of your data.

c. Double-click the **Exploring PowerPoint folder** to make it active.

This is the folder from which you will retrieve files and into which you will save your assignment solutions.

TROUBLESHOOTING: If you do not see an Exploring PowerPoint folder, it is possible that the student files for this text were saved to a different folder for your class. Check with your instructor to find out where to locate your student files.

d. Click the **Views button** repeatedly to cycle through the different views.

As you cycle through the various views, in the Open dialog box observe the differences in each view. Identify a reason you might use each view. Figure 1.20 is displayed in Preview view.

e. Double-click the *chap1_ho1_intro* presentation.

The slide show opens to the *Introduction to PowerPoint* title slide.

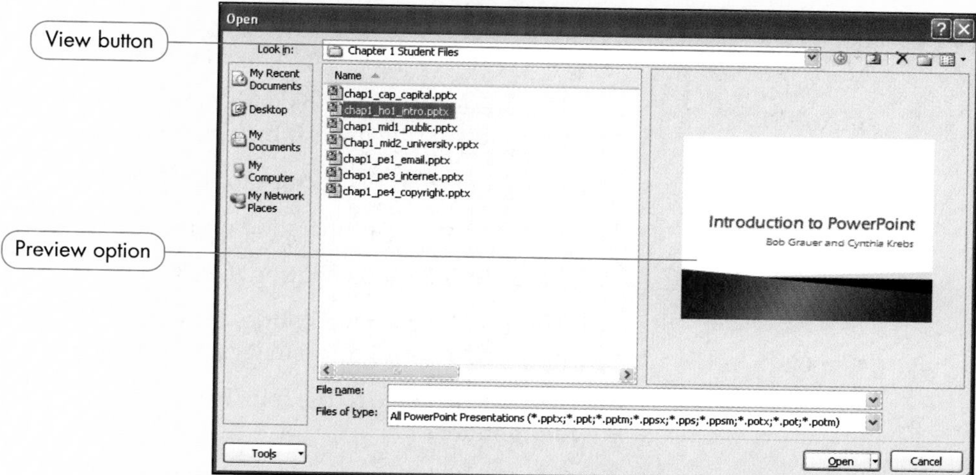

Figure 1.20 Open Dialog Box

Step 3
Type a Speaker's Note

Refer to Figure 1.21 as you complete Step 3.

a. Click the **Slide 4 thumbnail** in the Slides tab.

   Slide 4 is selected and the slide appears in the Slide pane.

b. Drag the splitter bar between the Slide Pane and the Notes pane upward to create more room in the Notes pane area.

c. Type the following information in the Notes pane: **Among the objects that can be inserted into PowerPoint are tables, clip art, diagrams, charts, hyperlinks, text boxes, headers and footers, movies, sound, and objects from other software packages.**

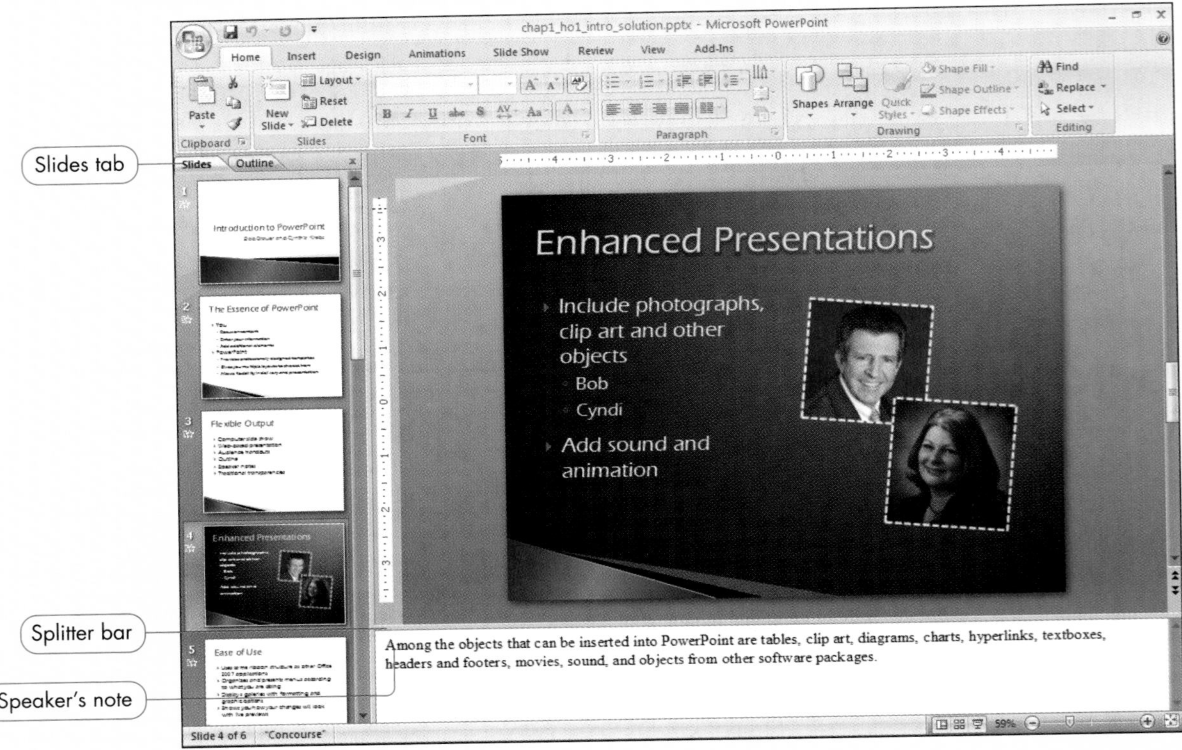

Figure 1.21 Speaker's Note

Step 4
View the Presentation

a. Click **From Beginning** in the Start Slide Show group on the Slide Show tab.

   The presentation begins with the title slide, the first slide in all slide shows. The title and subtitle have animations assigned, so they come in automatically.

b. Press **Spacebar** to advance to the second slide.

   The text on the second slide wipes down and creates each bullet point.

c. Click the left mouse button to advance to the third slide.

   The text on the third slide, and all following slides, has the same animation applied to create consistency in the presentation.

d. Click to advance to the fourth slide, which has sound added to the image animations.

e. Continue to view the show until you come to the end of the presentation.

f. Press **Esc** to return to the PowerPoint Normal view.

Step 5
Save the Presentation with a New Name

Refer to Figure 1.22 as you complete Step 3.

a. Click the **Office Button**, and then select **Save As**.

b. Click the **Save in drop-down arrow**.

c. Click the appropriate drive, depending on where you are storing your data.

d. Double-click the *Exploring PowerPoint* folder to make it the active folder.

If you have created a different folder to store your solutions, change to that folder.

e. Type **chap1_ho1_intro_solution** as the file name for the presentation.

f. Click **Save**.

TIP Change the Default Folder

The default folder is where PowerPoint goes initially to open an existing presentation or to save a new presentation. You may find it useful to change the default folder if you are working on your own computer and not in a classroom lab. Click the Office Button, and then select Application Settings, which enables you to modify your document settings and customize how PowerPoint behaves by default. Click Saving from the frame on the left side. Click in the box that contains the default file location, enter the new drive or the new folder where you wish your files to be saved, and click OK. The next time you open or save a file, PowerPoint will go automatically to that location. This feature may not work in a classroom lab, however, if the lab has a "deep freeze" program to ensure students work from default settings.

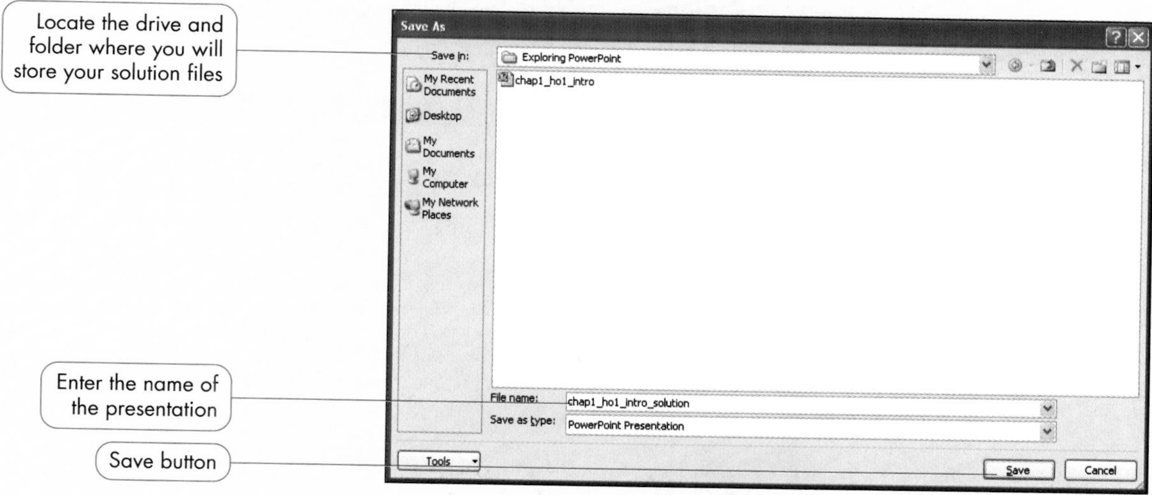

Figure 1.22 Save the Presentation with a New Name

Step 6
Locate Information Using Help

Refer to Figure 1.23 as you complete Step 6.

a. Click **Microsoft Office PowerPoint Help** on the top right side of the screen.

   The PowerPoint Help window opens.

   TROUBLESHOOTING: If you do not see the same Help viewer, as displayed in Figure 1.23, you may not have an active Internet connection. If you do not have an active Internet connection, the Help feature retrieves the Help information that was installed on your computer. Also, because Help Online is a dynamic feature, Microsoft frequently adds content. Each time you open a Help Online topic, you are asked to give Microsoft feedback on the value of the topic. Due to this feature, topics may be added and links changed.

b. Click the *What's New* hyperlink, and then click the *Use the Ribbon* hyperlink.

c. Scroll to the bottom of the Help window until the *See Also* box is visible. Click *Use the keyboard to work with Ribbon programs*, and then read the article on using access keys with the Ribbon.

d. Close Help, and then press **F1** on the keyboard.

   F1 is the shortcut for opening Help.

e. Type **print preview** in the Search box, and then click Search.

f. Click *Print a Help topic* and read the article.

g. Close Help, and then close the *chap1_ho1_intro_solution* presentation.

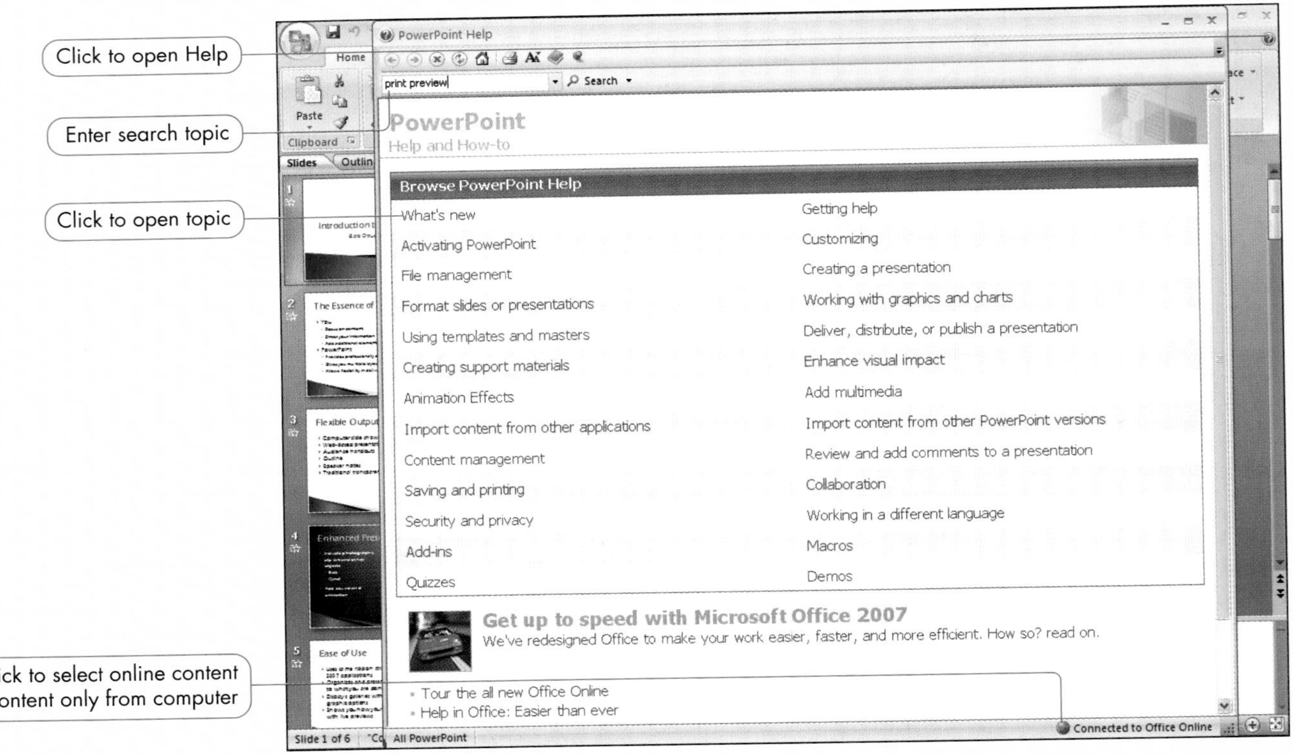

Figure 1.23 The Help Window

Presentation Creation

You are ready to create your own presentation, a process that requires you to develop its content and apply the formatting through the use of a template or design specification. You can do the steps in either order, but by starting with the content, you can concentrate on your message and the structure of your message without getting distracted by the formatting and design of the presentation.

> Before you start the presentation in PowerPoint, you can complete several tasks that could make your presentation more effective and save you time.

Before you start the presentation in PowerPoint, you can complete several tasks that could make your presentation more effective and save you time. While you know the topic you are going to present, the way you present it should be tailored to your audience. Research your audience—determine who makes up your audience, what their needs are, and what their expectations are. By tailoring your presentation to the audience, you will have a much more interesting presentation and an involved audience. After researching your audience, begin brainstorming on how to deliver your information and message to the audience. Sketch out your thoughts to help you organize them.

After you have sketched out your thoughts, enter them into the PowerPoint presentation and apply a theme to give your presentation a polished look. Review the presentation for spelling errors and word choice problems so your presentation is professional.

In this section, you create a visual plan known as a storyboard. You learn how to change layouts, apply design themes, and use the Spell Check and the Thesaurus to review your presentation for errors.

Creating a Storyboard

A ***storyboard*** is a visual plan that displays the content of each slide in the slideshow.

A ***storyboard*** is a visual plan for your presentation. It can be a very rough draft you sketch out while brainstorming, or it can be an elaborate plan that includes the text and objects drawn as they would appear on a slide. The complexity of your storyboard is your choice, but the key point is that the storyboard helps you plan the direction of your presentation. Remember the old adage, "If you don't know where you are going, you are going to end up somewhere else!"

A simple PowerPoint storyboard is divided into sections representing individual slides. The first block in the storyboard is used for the title slide. The title slide should have a short title that indicates the purpose of the presentation and introduces the speaker. Try to capture the title in two to five words. The speaker introduction information is usually included in a subtitle and can include the speaker's name and title, the speaker's organization, the organization's logo, and the date of the presentation.

While a title slide may serve as the introduction, having a separate introduction sets a professional tone for the presentation. The introduction should get the audience's attention and convince them your presentation will be worth their time. Creating an agenda showing the topics to be covered in the presentation can serve as an introduction because as you review the agenda with the audience you start them thinking about the topics. Often, presenters use a thought-provoking quotation or question as the introduction, and pause for a short time to give the audience time to think. An image can be particularly moving if it relates to the topic and is displayed in silence for a moment. The presenter may then introduce the idea behind the image or question the audience to extract the meaning of the image from them, thereby inducing the audience to introduce the topic.

Following the title slide and the introduction, you have slides containing the main body of information you want your audience to have. Each key thought deserves a slide, and on that slide, text bullets or other objects should develop that key thought. When preparing these slides, ask yourself what you want your audience to know that they did not know before. Ask yourself what it is you want them to remember. Create the slides to answer these questions and support these main points on the slides with facts, examples, charts or graphs, illustrations, images, or video clips.

Finally, end your presentation with a summary or conclusion. This is your last chance to get your message across to your audience. It should review main points, restate the purpose of the presentation, or invoke a call to action. The summary will solidify your purpose with the audience. Remember the old marketing maxim, "Tell 'em what you're going to tell 'em, tell 'em, then tell 'em what you told 'em,"—or in other words, "Introduction, Body, Conclusion."

After you create the storyboard, review what you wrote. Now is a good time to edit your text. Shorten complete sentences to phrases. As you present, you can expand on the information shown on the slide. The phrases on the slide help your audience organize the information in their minds. Edit phrases to use as bullet points. Review and edit the phrases so they begin with an active voice when possible to involve the user. Active voice uses action verbs—action verbs ACT! Passive verbs can be recognized by the presence of linking verbs (is, am, are, was, were).

TIP The "7 x 7" Guideline

Keep the information on your slide concise. The slide is merely a tool to help your audience "chuck into memory" the information you give. Your delivery will cover the detail. To help you remember to stay concise, follow the 7 x 7 guideline that suggests you limit the words on a visual to no more than seven words per line and seven lines per slide. This guideline gives you a total of 49 or fewer words per slide. While you may be forced to exceed this guideline on occasion, follow it as often as possible.

After you complete your planning, you are ready to prepare your PowerPoint presentation. Now instead of wasting computer time trying to decide what to say, you spend your computer time entering information, formatting, and designing. Figure 1.24 shows a working copy of a storyboard for planning presentation content. The storyboard is in rough draft form and shows changes made during the review process. The PowerPoint presentation (Figure 1.25) incorporates the changes.

Presentation Storyboard

Purpose of Presentation: Educational presentation

Audience: IAAP membership **Location:** Marriott Hotel **Date:** 9/20/08

Content	Layout	Visual Element(s)
Title Slide (Title slide) Planning ~~Before Creating~~ Presentation Content	Title Slide	O Shapes O Chart O Table O WordArt O Picture O Movie O Clip Art O Sound O SmartArt O ______ *Description:*
Introduction (Key Points, Quote, Image, Other) (Introduction) "If you don't know where you are going, you might end up someplace else." Casey Stengel	Section Header	O Shapes O Chart O Table O WordArt O Picture O Movie ☒ Clip Art O Sound O SmartArt O ______ *Description:* Stengel pic ~~confusion image~~
Support for Key Point #1 (Key topics with main points) Identify Purpose ~~Selling~~ (E-Commerce), Persuading, Informing, Advertising, ~~Building Good Will~~ Entertaining, Educating, Motivation	Two Content	O Shapes O Chart O Table O WordArt O Picture O Movie O Clip Art O Sound O SmartArt O ______ *Description:*
Support for Key Point #2 Define Audience Who is ~~going to be in the audience~~? What are the ~~audience's~~ expectations? How much do they ~~does the audience~~ already know?	Title & Content	O Shapes O Chart O Table O WordArt ☒ Picture O Movie O Clip Art O Sound O SmartArt O ______ *Description:* Audience pic
Support for Key Point #3 Develop the Content Brainstorm ~~and write ideas down~~, Research ~~the topic and take notes~~, Storyboard ~~a rough draft and then refine~~,	Title & Content	O Shapes O Chart O Table O WordArt O Picture O Movie O Clip Art O Sound O SmartArt O ______ *Description:* SmartArt
Support for Key Point #4 Edit the Content ~~Shorten the text from sentences to phrases~~ make ~~it~~ text concise. Make bullets parallel + use active verbs	Title & Content	O Shapes O Chart O Table O WordArt O Picture O Movie O Clip Art O Sound O SmartArt O ______ *Description:*
Summary (Restatement of Key Points, Quote, Other) (Conclusion) The key to an effective presentation is planning ahead.	Title	O Shapes O Chart O Table O WordArt O Picture O Movie ☒ Clip Art O Sound O SmartArt O ______ *Description:* Key

Figure 1.24 Rough Draft Storyboard

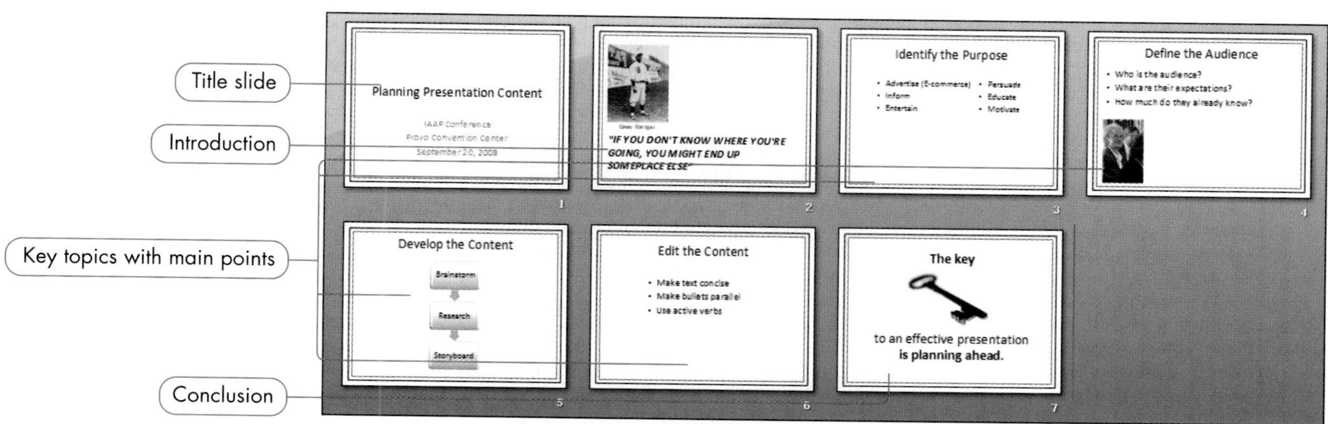

Figure 1.25 Presentation from Storyboard

TIP Storyboard Template

A sample storyboard template, *chap1_storyboard.docx*, is available in the PowerPoint Chapter 1 data files folder for you to use to help you plan your presentations.

Using Slide Layouts

When you first begin a new slide show, PowerPoint presents you with a slide for use as a title slide. New slides from that point on are typically created as content slides, consisting of a slide title and a defined area for content. You can enter content in the defined area or add new elements manually. If the slide arrangement does not meet your needs, you can change it by changing the slide layout.

A slide ***layout*** determines the position of objects containing content on the slide.

A ***placeholder*** is a container that holds content and is used in the layout to determine the position of objects on the slide.

PowerPoint provides a set of predefined slide ***layouts*** that determine the position of the objects or content on a slide. Slide layouts contain any number and combination of placeholders, and are available each time you click New Slide on the Home tab. When you click New Slide, the gallery of layouts is displayed for you to choose from. All of the layouts except the Blank layout include placeholders. ***Placeholders*** hold content and determine the position of the objects, or content, on the slide. After you select the layout, you simply click the appropriate placeholder to add the content you desire. Thus, you would click on the placeholder for the title and enter the text of the title as indicated. In similar fashion, you click the placeholder for text and enter the associated text. By default, the text appears as bullets. You can change the size and position of the placeholders by moving the placeholders just as you would any object.

Applying Design Themes

A ***theme*** is a set of design elements that gives the slide show a unified, professional appearance.

PowerPoint enables you to concentrate on the content of a presentation without concern for its appearance. You focus on what you are going to say, and then utilize PowerPoint features to format the presentation attractively. The simplest method to format a slide show is to select a design theme. A design ***theme*** is a collection of formatting choices that includes colors, fonts, and special theme effects such as shadowing or glows. PowerPoint designers have created beautiful design themes for your use, and the themes are available in other Office applications, which lets you unify all of the documents you create.

When you apply a theme, the formatting implements automatically. To select and apply a theme, click the Design tab and click the More button in the Themes group. From the Themes gallery that appears, choose the theme you like. PowerPoint formats the entire presentation according to the theme you choose. Do not be afraid to apply new themes. As you gain experience with PowerPoint and design, you can rely less on PowerPoint and more on your own creativity for your design. Figures 1.26–1.29 show a title slide with four different themes applied. Note the color, font, and text alignment in each theme.

Figure 1.26 Opulent Theme

Figure 1.27 Urban Theme

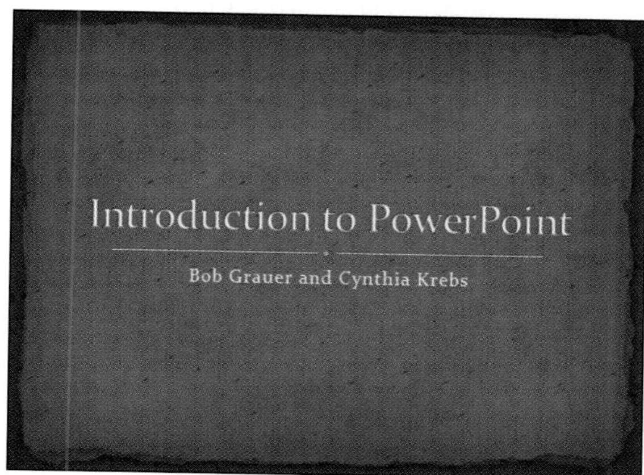

Figure 1.28 Paper Theme

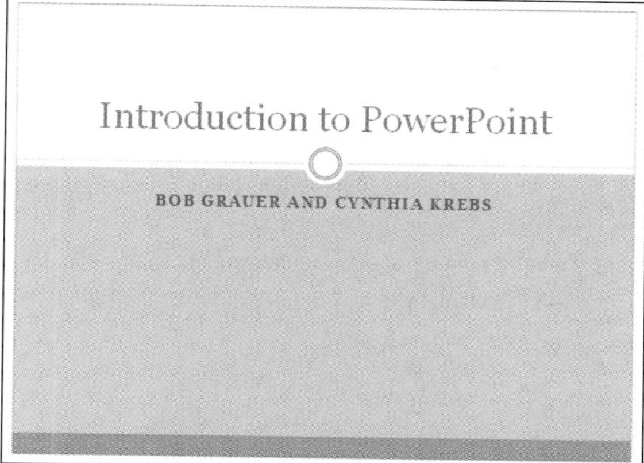

Figure 1.29 Civic Theme

Reviewing the Presentation

After you create the presentation, check for spelling errors and incorrect word usage. This step can be done before or after you apply the design theme, but sometimes applying the theme before checking for spelling errors helps you see errors you did not see before. It gives you a fresh look at the slide, which helps you revisualize what is displaying.

Check Spelling

The first step to checking your spelling is to visually check the slide after you create the text in the placeholders. A red wavy line under a word indicates that a word is misspelled. In the case of a proper name, the word may be spelled correctly but is not in the standard dictionary shared by the software in the Microsoft Office suite. In either event, point to the underlined word and click the right mouse button to display a shortcut menu. Select the appropriate spelling from the list of suggestions. If the word does not appear in the list of suggestions, you can add the word to the ***custom dictionary***, a supplemental dictionary Microsoft Office uses to store items such as proper names, acronyms, or specialized words for your business or industry.

A ***custom dictionary*** is a supplemental dictionary Microsoft Office uses to store items such as proper names, acronyms, or specialized words.

After you complete the presentation and have visually checked each slide, use PowerPoint's Spelling feature to check the entire presentation again. Click the Review tab, and then click Spelling in the Proofing group. If a word does not appear in the dictionary, the Spelling dialog box appears. Use the options on the right side to choose whether you wish to accept the word and resume spell checking, ignore all occurrences of the word, change the word to one of the listed choices, add the word to your custom dictionary, look at other suggested spellings, add the word to AutoCorrect, or close the dialog box.

Finally, display the presentation in Slide Show view and read each word on each slide out loud. Reading the words in the Slide Show view eliminates the distractions in PowerPoint's creation screen and allows you to concentrate fully on the text. Although the Spelling feature is a valuable tool, it does **NOT** catch commonly misused words like to, too, and two, or for, fore, and four. While proofreading three times may seem excessive to you, if you ever flash a misspelled word before an audience in full Slide Show view, you will wish you had taken the time to proofread carefully. Nothing is more embarrassing and can make you seem less professional than a misspelled word enlarged on a big screen for your audience so they cannot miss it.

Use the Thesaurus

As you proofread your presentation, or even while you are creating it, you may notice that you are using one word too often. Perhaps you find a word that does not seem right, but you cannot think of another word. The Thesaurus, which gives you synonyms or words with the same meaning, is ideal to use in these situations. Click the Review tab and click Thesaurus in the Proofing group. The Research task pane appears on the right side of the screen and displays synonyms for the selected word. Point to the desired replacement key, click the drop-down arrow to display a menu, and click Insert to replace the word. Click Undo on the Quick Access Toolbar to return to the original text if you prefer the original word.

TIP The Research Task Pane

Microsoft Office 2007 brings the resources of the Web directly into the application. Click Research in the Proofing group on the Review tab. Type the entry you are searching for, click the down arrow to choose a reference book, and then click the green arrow to initiate the search. You have access to reference, research, business, and financial sites. You even have an online bilingual dictionary. Research has never been easier.

Hands-On Exercises

2 | Creating a Presentation

Skills covered: 1. Create a New Presentation **2.** Add Slides **3.** Check Spelling and Use the Thesaurus **4.** Modify Text and Layout **5.** Reorder Slides **6.** Apply a Design Theme

Step 1
Create a New Presentation

Refer to Figure 1.30 as you complete Step 1.

a. Click the **Office Button**, select **New**, and then click **Blank Presentation**.

   PowerPoint opens with a new blank presentation.

b. Click inside the placeholder containing the *Click to add title* prompt, and then type the presentation title **Creating Presentation Content**.

c. Click inside the placeholder containing the *Click to add subtitle* prompt and enter your name.

   Type your name as it shows on the class roll. Do not enter a nickname or the words *Your Name*.

d. Click in the Notes pane and type today's date and the name of the course for which you are creating this slide show.

e. Save the presentation as **chap1_ho2_content_solution**.

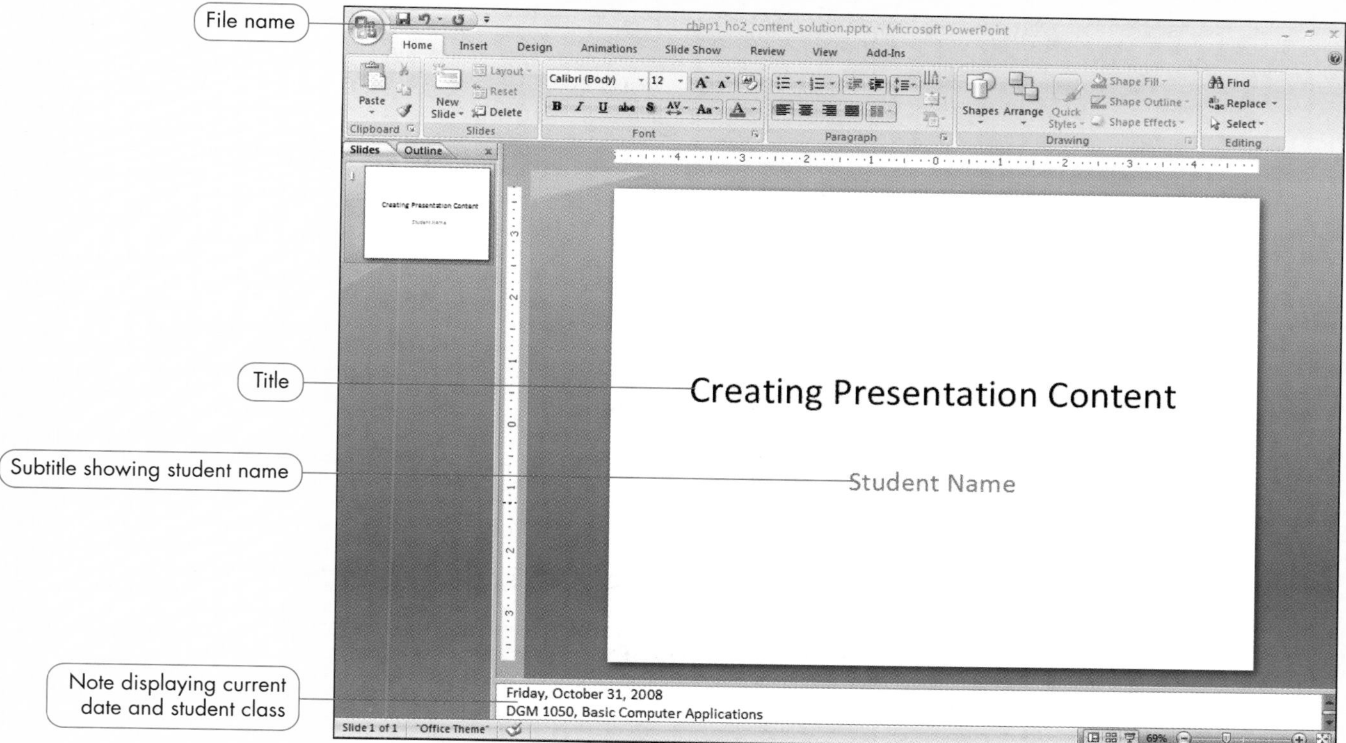

Figure 1.30 Creating Presentation Content Title Slide

Step 2
Add Slides

Refer to Figure 1.31 as you complete Step 2.

a. Click **New Slide** in the Slides group on the Home tab.

b. Select the **Title and Content** layout from the gallery.

   Slide 2 is created with two placeholders: one for the title and one for body content. You can insert an object by clicking on the bar in the center of the content placeholder, or you can enter bullets by typing text in the placeholder.

c. Type **Simplify the Content** in the title placeholder.

d. Click in the content placeholder and type **Use one main concept per slide**, and then press **Enter**.

e. Type **Use the 7 x 7 guideline** and press **Enter** again.

f. Click **Increase List Level** in the Paragraph group on the Home tab.

   Clicking Increase List Level creates a new bullet level that you can use for detail related to the main bullet. If you wish to return to the main bullet level, click Decrease List Level.

g. Type **Limit slide to seven or fewer lines** and press **Enter**.

h. Type **Limit lines to seven or fewer words**.

i. Save the *chap1_ho2_content_solution* presentation.

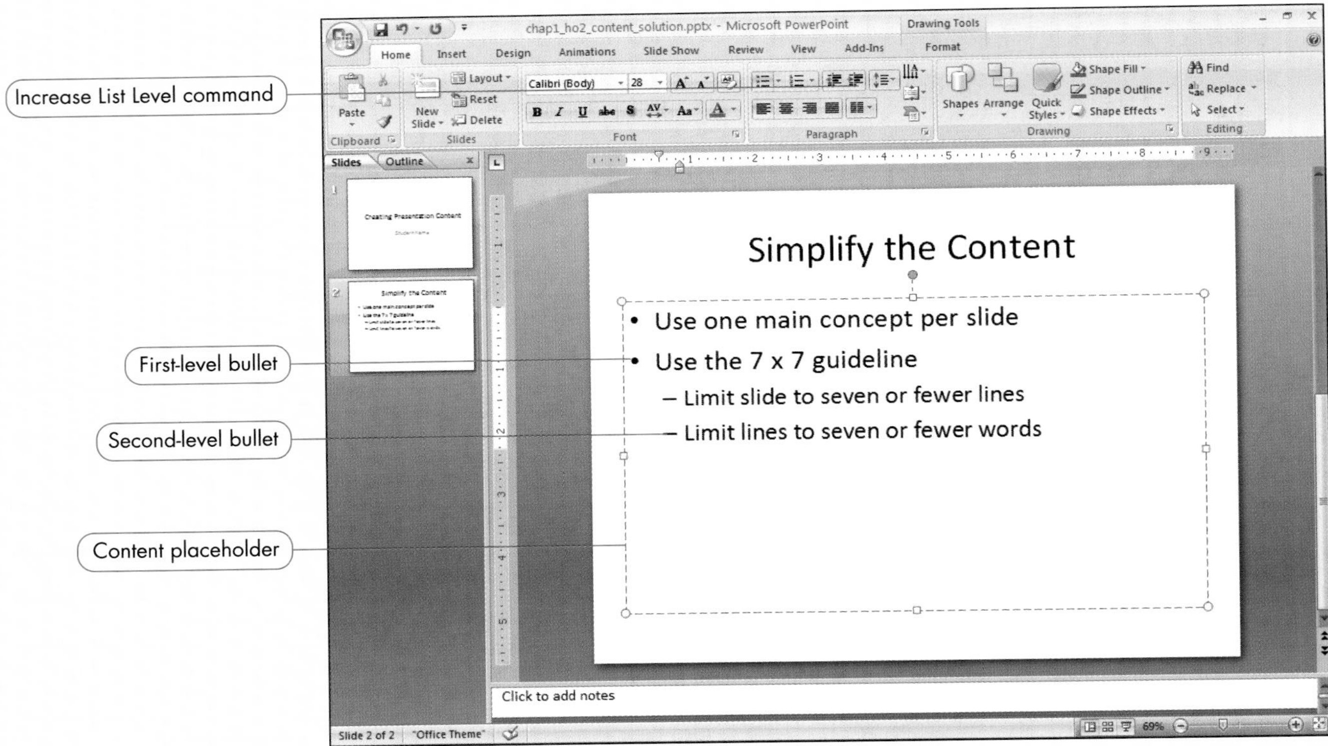

Figure 1.31 New Slide

Step 3
Check Spelling and Use the Thesaurus

Refer to Figure 1.32 as you complete Step 3.

a. Use the **New Slide** command to create four more slides with the Title and Content layout.

b. Type the following text in the appropriate slide.

Slide	Slide Title	Level 1 Bullets	Level 2 Bullets
3	Define the Audience	Who is the audience? What are their needs? What are their expectations? How much do they already know? How can you help them understand message?	
4	Develop the Content	Identify purpose Research topic Brainstorm Create storyboard	Title slide Introduction Key points Conclusion
5	Edit the Content	Make text concise Use consistent verb tense Utilize strong active verbs Eliminate excess adverbs and adjectives Use few prepositions	
6		The key to an effective presentation is planning ahead!	

c. Click **Spelling** in the Proofing group on the Review tab.

The result of the spelling check depends on how accurately you entered the text of the presentation. If the spell checker locates a word not in its dictionary, you will be prompted to resume checking, change the word, ignore the word in that occurrence or in all occurrences, or add the word to your dictionary so it is not identified as misspelled in the future. Select one of these options, and then continue checking the presentation for spelling errors, if necessary.

d. Move to **Slide 2** and click anywhere within the word *main*.

e. Click **Thesaurus** in the Proofing group on the Review tab.

The Research task pane opens and displays a list of synonyms from which to choose a replacement word.

f. Point to the word *key*, click the drop-down arrow, and click **Insert**.

The word *main* is replaced with the word *key*.

TROUBLESHOOTING: If you click the replacement word in the Research pane list instead of clicking the drop-down arrow and choosing Insert, the replacement word you clicked will replace the original word in the Search for box and the Research pane changes to display the synonyms of the replacement word. The word in your presentation will not change.

g. Save the *chap1_ho2_content_solution* presentation.

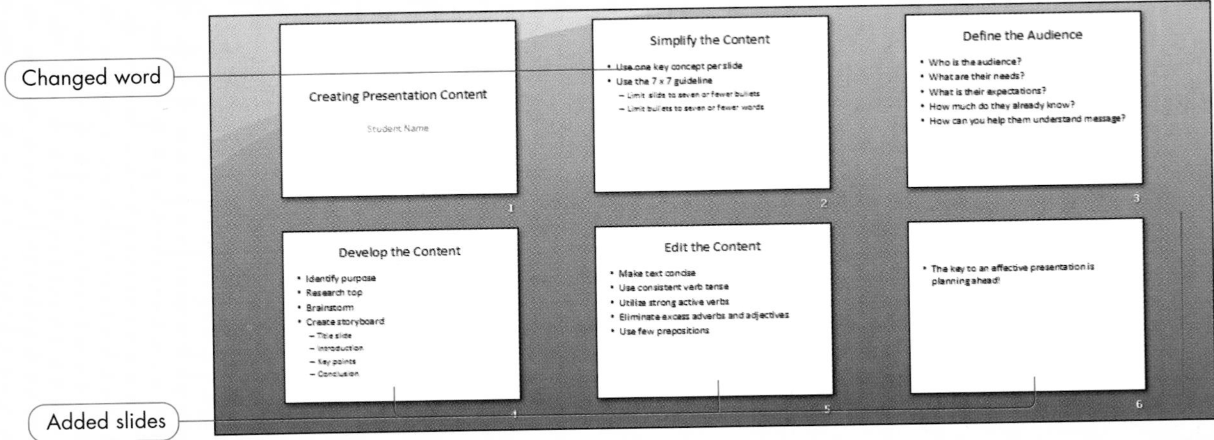

Figure 1.32 Proofed Slide Show

Step 4 Modify Text and Layout

Refer to Figure 1.33 as you complete Step 4.

a. Click the **Slide 6 thumbnail** in the Slide tab pane.

   You wish to end the slide show with a statement emphasizing the importance of planning. You created the statement in a content placeholder in a slide using the Title and Content layout. You decide to modify the text and layout of the slide to give the statement more emphasis.

b. Click the **Home tab** and click **Layout** in the Slides group.

c. Click **Title Slide**.

   The layout for Slide 6 changes to the Title Slide layout. Layouts can be used on any slide in a slide show if their format meets your needs.

d. Click the border of the Title placeholder, press **Delete** twice on the keyboard, and then drag the Subtitle placeholder containing your text upward until it is slightly above the center of your slide.

   The layout in Slide 6 has now been modified.

e. Drag across the text in the subtitle placeholder to select it, and then move your pointer upwards until the Mini toolbar appears.

f. Click **Bold**, and then click **Italic** on the Mini toolbar.

   Using the Mini toolbar to modify text is much faster than moving back and forth to the commands in the Font group on the Home tab to make changes.

g. Save the *chap1_ho2_content_solution* presentation.

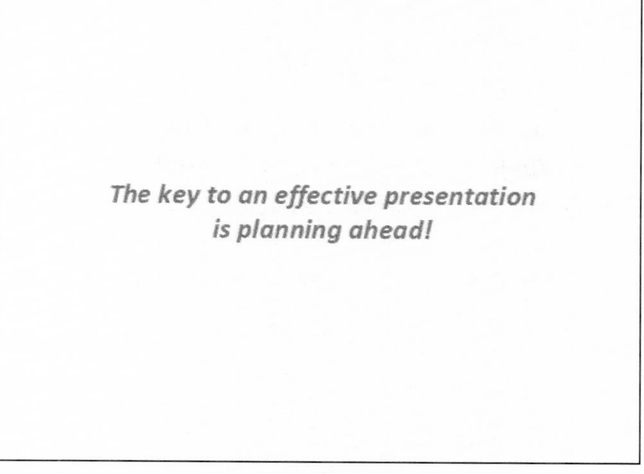

Figure 1.33 Slide with Modified Text and Layout

Step 5
Reorder Slides

Refer to Figure 1.34 as you complete Step 5.

a. Click the **View tab** and click **Slide Sorter** in the Presentation Views group.

   The view changes to thumbnail views of the slides in the slide show with the current slide surrounded by a heavy border to indicate it is selected. Your view may differ from Figure 1.34 depending on what your zoom level is set at. Notice that the slides do not follow logical order. The Slide Sorter view is ideal for checking the logical sequence of slides and for changing slide position if necessary.

b. Select **Slide 2**, and then drag it so that it becomes Slide 5, the slide before the summary slide.

   As you drag Slide 2 to the right, the pointer becomes a move cursor and a vertical bar appears to indicate the position of the slide when you drop it. After you drop the slide, all slides renumber.

c. Double-click **Slide 6**.

   Double-clicking a slide in the Slide Sorter view returns you to Normal view.

d. Save the *chap1_ho2_content_solution* presentation.

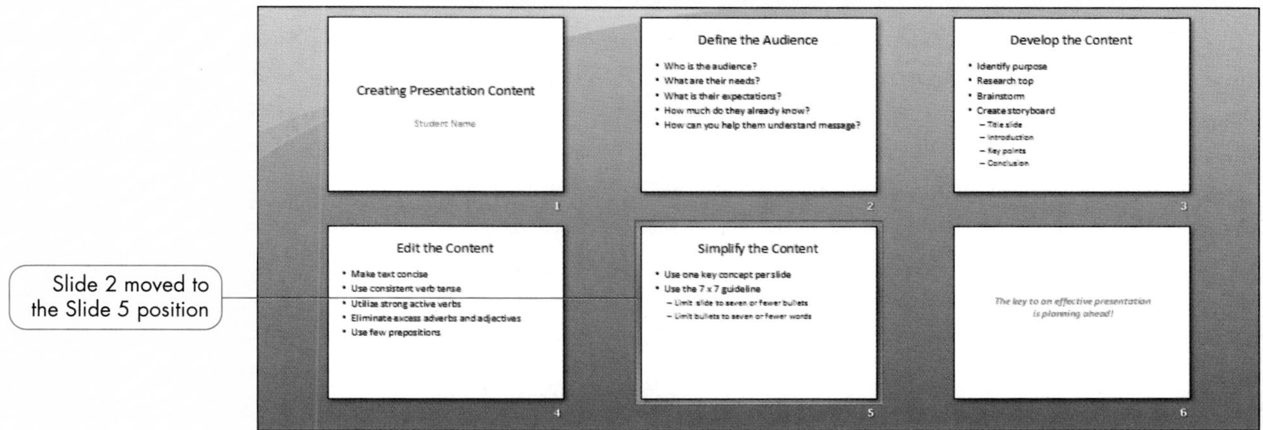

Figure 1.34 Reordered Slide Show

Step 6
Apply a Design Theme

Refer to Figure 1.35 as you complete Step 6.

a. Click the **Design tab** and click the **More button** in the Themes group.

   Point at each of the themes that appear in the gallery and note how the theme formatting impacts the text in Slide 6.

b. Click **Urban** to apply the theme to the presentation.

   The Urban theme is characterized by a clean, simple background with a business-like color scheme, making it a good choice for this presentation.

c. Drag the Title placeholder down and to the left, and then resize it so that it contains three lines.

   When you add the Urban theme, the background of the theme hides the text in the placeholder. You adjust the placeholder location and size to fit the theme.

d. Save the *chap1_ho2_content_solution* presentation. Close the file and exit PowerPoint if you do not want to continue to the next exercise at this time.

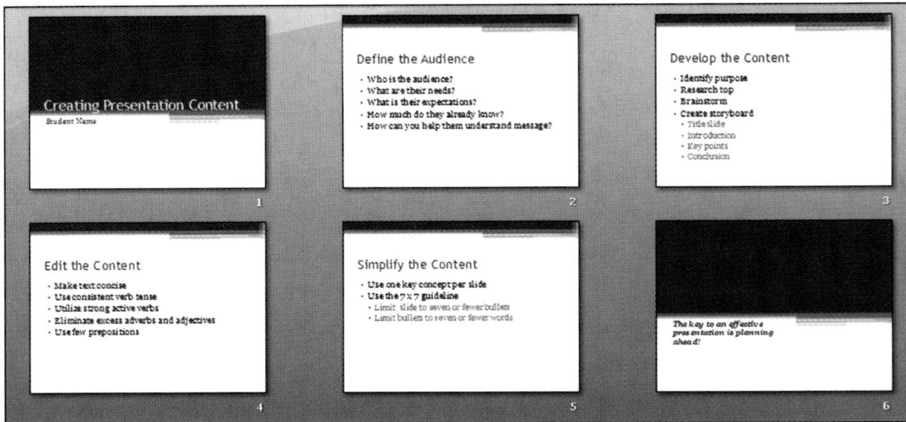

Figure 1.35 Slide Show with Urban Theme Applied

Presentation Development

Thus far, our presentation is strictly text. You can strengthen your slide show by adding objects that relate to the message. PowerPoint enables you to include a variety of visual objects to add impact to your presentation. You can add clip art, images, WordArt, sound, animated clips, or video clips to increase your presentation's impact. You can add tables, charts and graphs, and diagrams to provide more information for the audience. These objects can be created in PowerPoint, or you can insert objects that were created in other applications, such as a chart from Microsoft Excel or a table from Microsoft Word.

> . . . clip art, images, WordArt, sound, animated clips, or video clips . . . increase your presentation's impact.

In this section, you add a table to organize data in columns and rows. Then you insert clip art objects that relate to your topics. You move and resize the clip art to position it attractively on the slide. Finally, you apply transitions to your slide to control how one slide changes to another, and you apply animations to your text and clip art to help maintain your audience's attention.

Adding a Table

A ***table*** is an illustration that places information in columns and rows.

A ***table*** is an illustration that places information in columns and rows. Tables are a great way for you to present related information in an orderly manner. Tables can be simple and include just words or images, or they can be complex and include a great deal of structured numerical data. Because tables organize information for the viewer, they are a great way to augment your presentation.

You can add a table to your presentation by creating it in PowerPoint or by reusing a table created in Word or Excel. In this chapter, you create a basic table in PowerPoint. To create a table, you can select the Title and Content layout and then click the Table icon on the Content bar, or you can select the Title Only layout and click the Insert tab and then click Table in the Tables group. These two options create the table with slightly different sizing, however. Figure 1.36 shows the same data entered into tables created in each of these ways.

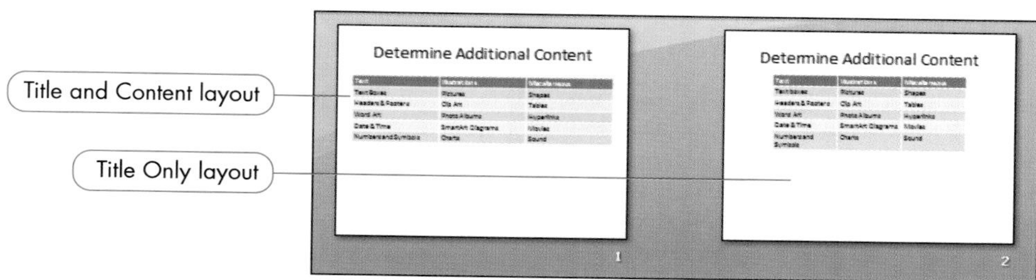

Figure 1.36 Table Layout

Inserting Clip Art

In addition to inserting tables from the Insert tab, you can insert other objects and media in your presentation. From the Illustrations group, click Picture and browse to locate a picture or image that has been saved to a storage device, click Clip Art to insert clip art from the Microsoft Clip Organizer, click Photo Album to create a photo album from images you have saved, click Shape to insert a shape, click SmartArt to insert a diagram, or click Chart to insert a chart.

A ***clip*** is any media object that you can insert in a document.

In this chapter, you concentrate on adding clip art from the Microsoft Clip Organizer, although inserting other types of clips uses the same procedure. The Microsoft Clip Organizer contains a variety of ***clips***, or media objects such as clip art, photographs, movies, or sounds, that may be inserted in a presentation. The Microsoft Clip Organizer brings order by cataloging the clips that are available to you. Clips installed locally are cataloged in the My Collections folder; clips installed in conjunction with Office are cataloged in the Office Collections folder; and clips downloaded from the Web are cataloged in the Web Collections folder. If you are connected to the Internet, clips located in Microsoft Online also display in the Clip Organizer. You can insert a specific clip into your presentation if you know its location, or you can search for a clip that will enhance your presentation.

To search for a clip, you enter a keyword that describes the clip you are looking for, specify the collections that are to be searched, and indicate the type of clip(s) you are looking for. The results are displayed in the Clip Art task pane, as shown in Figure 1.37. This figure shows clips that were located using the keyword *key*. The example searches all collections for all media types to return the greatest number of potential clips. When you point to a clip displaying in the gallery, the clip's keywords, an indication if the clip is scaleable, the clip's file size, and file format appear. When you see the clip that you want to use, point to the clip, click the drop-down arrow, and then click the Insert command from the resulting menu. You also can click the clip to insert it in the center of the slide, or drag the clip onto the slide.

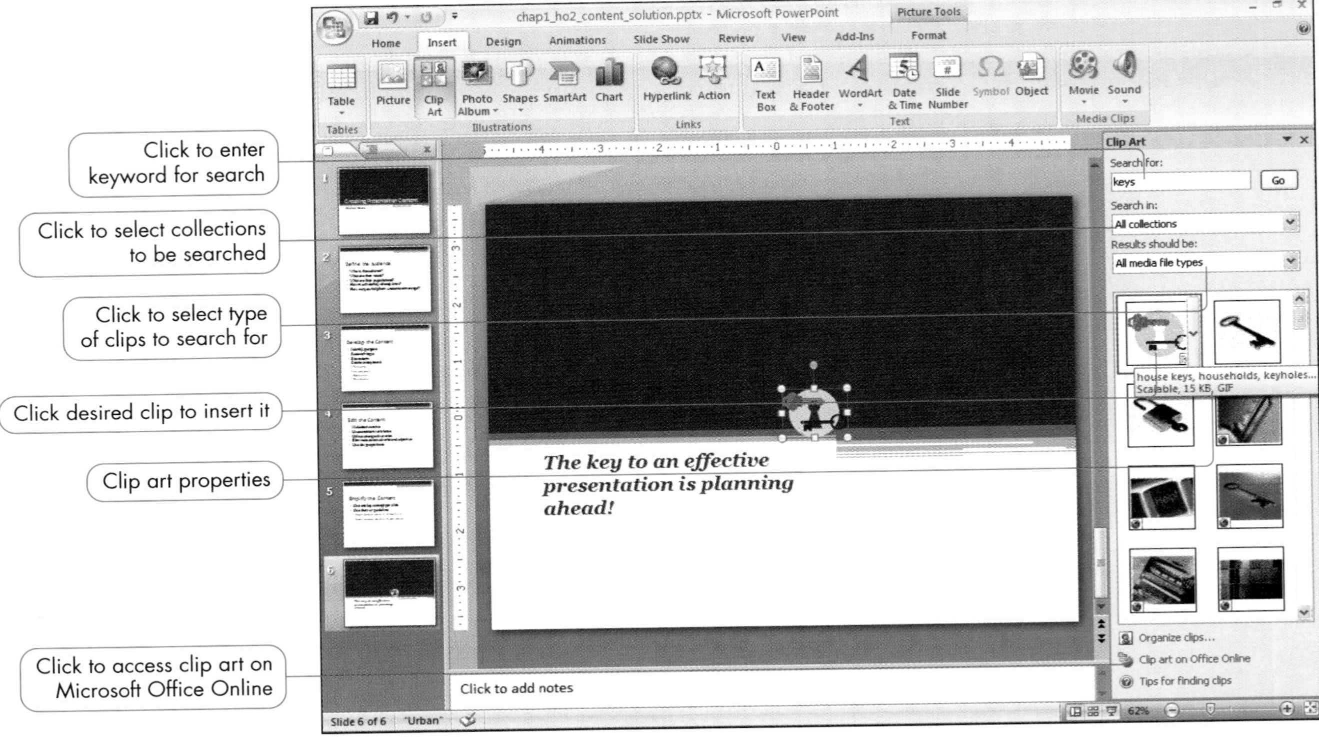

Figure 1.37 Clip Art Task Pane

TIP Reorganizing Clip Collections

You can access the Microsoft Clip Organizer (to view the various collections) by clicking the Organize clips link at the bottom of the task pane. You also can access the Clip Organizer outside of PowerPoint by clicking the Start button on the task bar, and then clicking All Programs, Microsoft Office, Microsoft Office Tools, and Microsoft Clip Organizer. Once in the Organizer, you can search through the clips in the various collections, reorganize the existing collections, add new collections, and even add new clips (with their associated keywords) to the collections.

Move and Resize Clip Art

Just like any Windows object, clip art can be moved and sized. When you click the clip art, the clip art displays editing handles. Position the mouse pointer inside the boundaries of the handles, and it will change to a four-headed arrow. While the pointer has this shape, you can drag the clip art image to a new location. When you position the mouse pointer on one of the editing handles, a double-headed arrow appears. Use this arrow to resize the image. Dragging one of the corner handles resizes the image and keeps it in proportion. Dragging one of the interior handles distorts the image's width or height. Figure 1.38 shows the clip dragged to a new position.

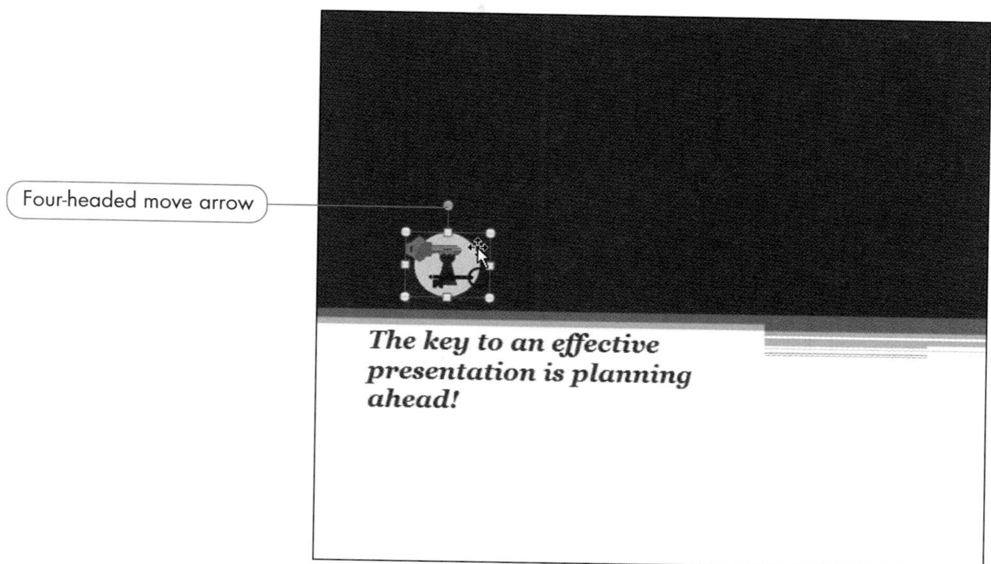

Figure 1.38 Repositioned Clip Art

Using Transitions and Animations

A ***transition*** is a movement special effect that takes place as one slide replaces another in Slide Show view.

An ***animation*** is movement applied to individual elements on a single slide.

You have successfully created a PowerPoint presentation, but the most important step is yet to come—the delivery of the presentation to an audience. Typically, the slide show is projected on a screen through a projection device. While the slide show is being displayed, the slides change. This process can be enhanced through the use of ***transitions***, or movement special effects that take place as you move from slide to slide while in Slide Show view.

While transitions apply to the slide as a whole and control the way a slide moves onto the screen, ***animations*** are movements that control the entrance, emphasis, path, and/or exit of individual objects on a single slide. Multiple animations can be applied to a single object. Animating objects can help focus the audience's attention on an important point, can control the flow of information on a slide, and can help you keep the audience's attention.

Apply Transitions and Animations

Transition special effects include fades and dissolves, wipes, push and cover, stripes and bars, and random effects. The gallery in Figure 1.39 displays the available transition effects. The Transition Gallery contains 58 transitions. To display the Transitions Gallery, click the More button in the Transitions To This Slide group on the Animations tab. To see the effect of a transition on the slide, point to a transition in the Transitions Gallery to see the Live Preview, which shows how the change will affect the slide show before you select the transition.

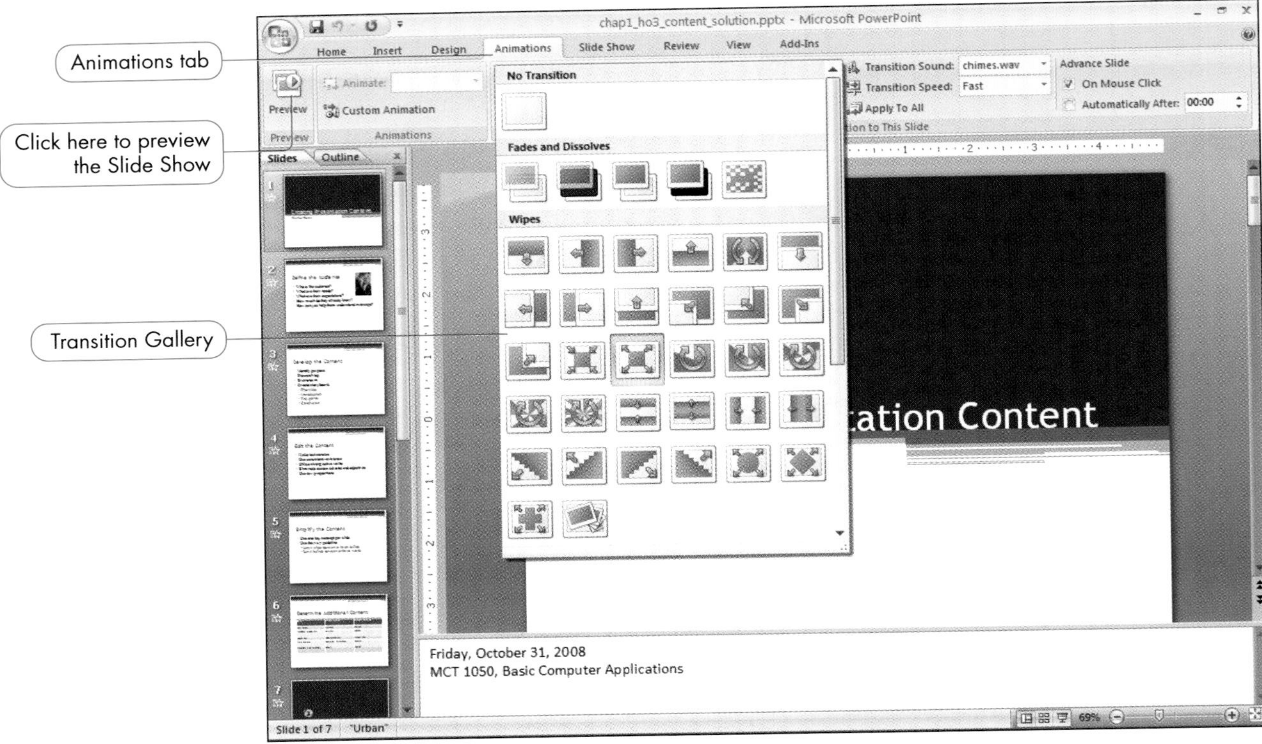

Figure 1.39 The Transitions Gallery

After you choose the effect you desire, you can select a sound to play when the transition takes effect and you can select a speed for the transition. If you wish the transition to impact all slides, click Apply to All in the Transition to This Slide group on the Animations tab. Click Preview Slide Show in the Preview group on the Animations tab to move directly to the show and see what you have accomplished. (Transition effects also can be applied from the Slide Sorter view, where you can apply the same transition to multiple slides by selecting the slides prior to applying the effect.)

Another determination you must make is how you want to start the transition process. Do you want to manually click or press a key to advance to the next slide or do you want the slide to automatically advance after a specified number of seconds? The Advance Slide options in the Transition To This Slide group enable you to determine if you want to mouse click to advance or if you want the slide to advance automatically. You set the number of seconds for the slide to display in the same area.

TIP Effectively Adding Media Objects

When you select your transitions, sounds, and animations, remember that a presentation is not a high-speed music video. Too many transition and animation styles are distracting. The audience wonders what is coming next rather than paying attention to your message. Transitions that are too fast or too slow can lose the interest of the audience. Slow transitions will bore your audience while you stand there saying, "The next slide will load soon." Too many sound clips can be annoying. Consider whether you need to have the sound of applause with the transition of every slide. Is a typewriter sound necessary to keep your audience's attention or will it grate on their nerves if it is used on every set. Ask a classmate to review your presentation and let you know if there are annoying or jarring elements.

Animate Objects

An ***animation scheme*** is a built-in, standard animation.

A ***custom animation*** is an animation where the user determines the animation settings.

You can animate objects such as text, clip art, diagrams, charts, sound, and hyperlinks. You can apply a preset ***animation scheme***, which is a built-in, standard animation created by Microsoft to simplify the animation process, or you can apply a ***custom animation*** where you determine the animation effect, the speed for the effect, the properties of the effect, and the way the animation begins. The properties available with animations are determined by the animation type. For example, if you choose a wipe animation effect, you can determine the direction property. If you choose a color wave effect, you can determine the color to be added to the object.

To apply an animation scheme, select the object you want to animate, click the Animations tab, and then click the Animate down arrow in the Animations group. A list of animation schemes opens. If you have text selected, options will appear for you to choose how you wish the text to animate.

To apply a custom animation to an object, select the object that you want to animate, and then click Custom Animation in the Animations group on the Animations tab. In the Custom Animation task pane, click Add Effect. Point to Entrance, Emphasis, Exit, or Motion Paths. Select an effect from the resulting list. Once the effect has been selected, you can determine the start, property, and speed of the transition. In this chapter, you will apply an animation scheme and a basic custom animation.

The slide in Figure 1.40 shows an animation effect added to the title and the subtitle. The title will animate first, because it was selected first. A tag with the number one is attached to the placeholder to show it is first. The subtitle animates next, and a tag with the number 2 is attached to the subtitle placeholder. Examine the Custom Animation task pane and note the effect that was added to the subtitle, the way it will start, the direction and the speed of the animation.

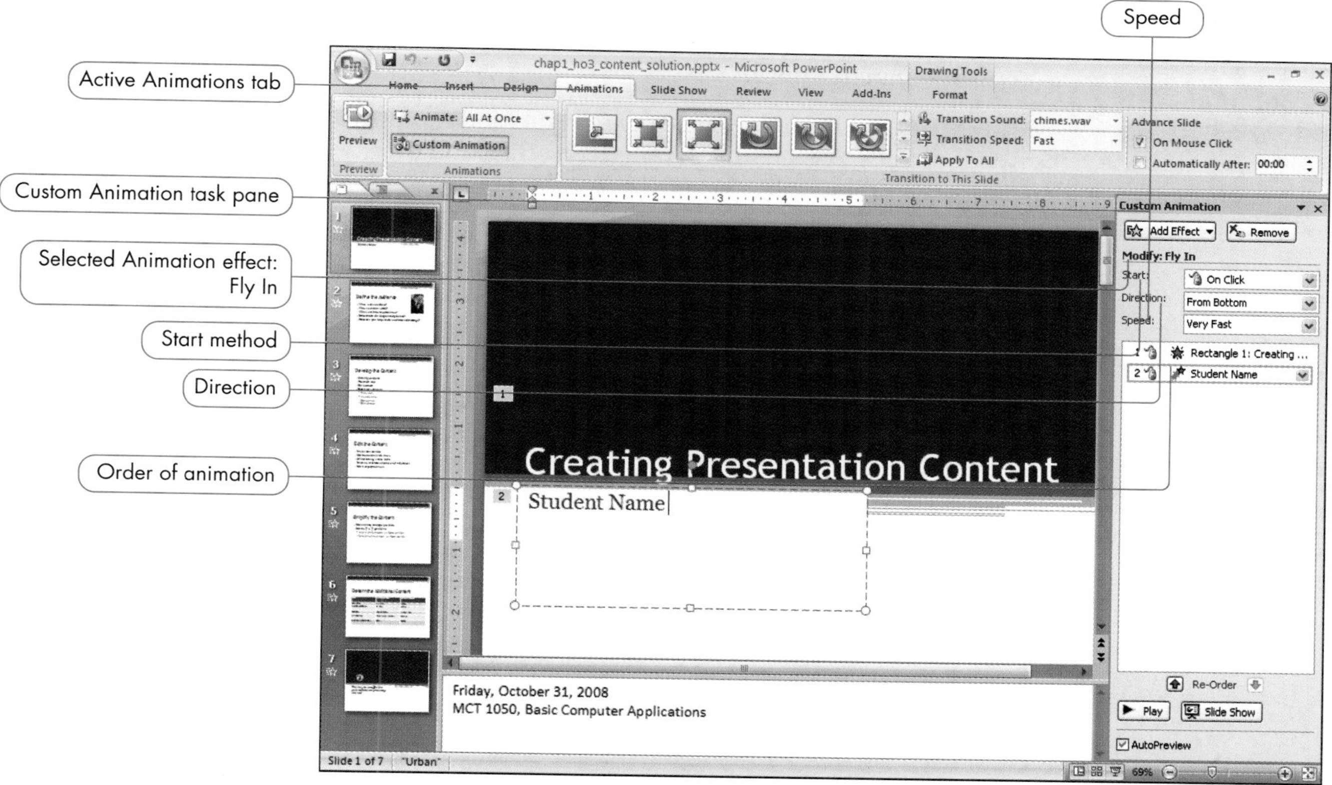

Figure 1.40 The Custom Animation Task Pane

Hands-On Exercises

3 | Strengthening a Presentation

Skills covered: **1.** Add a Table **2.** Insert, Move, and Resize Clip Art **3.** Apply a Transition **4.** Animate Objects

Step 1
Add a Table

Refer to Figure 1.41 as you complete Step 1.

a. Open the *chap1_ho2_content_solution* presentation if you closed it after the last exercise, and then save it as **chap1_ho3_content_solution**.

b. Move to **Slide 5**, click the **Home tab**, and click **New Slide** in the Slides group.

c. Click the **Title and Content** layout.

A new slide with the Title and Content layout is inserted after Slide 5.

d. Click inside the title placeholder and type **Determine Additional Content**.

e. Click the **Table icon** on the toolbar in the center of the content placeholder.

The Insert Table dialog box appears for you to enter the number of columns and the number of rows you desire.

f. Type **3** for the number of columns and **6** for the number of rows.

PowerPoint creates the table and positions it on the slide. The first row of the table is formatted differently from the other rows so that it can be used for column headings.

g. Click in the top left cell of the table and type **Text**. Press **Tab** to move to the next cell and type **Illustrations**. Press **Tab**, and then type **Miscellaneous** in the last heading cell.

h. Type the following text in the remaining table cells.

Text Boxes	Pictures	Shapes
Headers & Footers	Clip Art	Tables
WordArt	Photo Albums	Hyperlinks
Date & Time	SmartArt Diagrams	Movies
Symbols	Charts	Sound

i. Save the *chap1_ho3_content_solution* presentation.

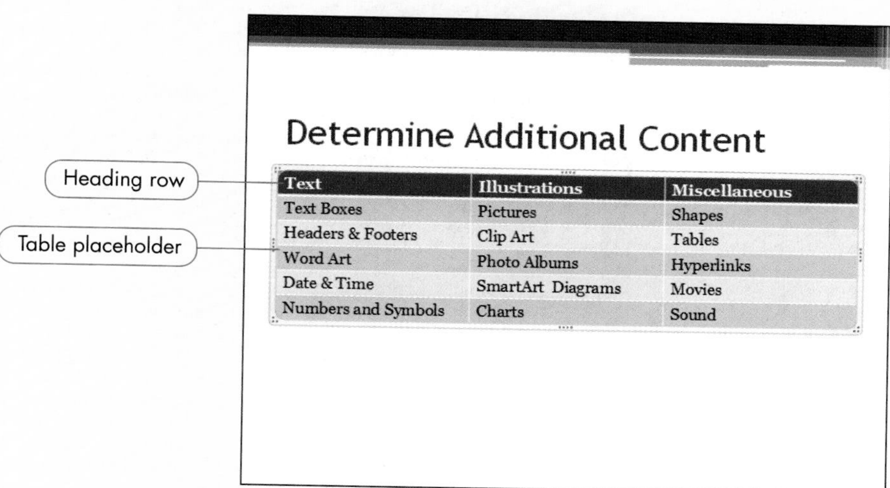

Figure 1.41 PowerPoint Table

Step 2
Insert, Move, and Resize Clip Art

Refer to Figure 1.42 as you complete Step 2.

a. Move to **Slide 2**, click the **Insert tab**, and click **Clip Art** in the Illustrations tab.

b. Type **groups** in the Search for box. Make sure the Search In box is set to All collections.

c. Click the down arrow next to *Results should be*, deselect all options except Photographs, and then click **Go**.

d. Refer to Figure 1.42 to determine the group image to select, and then click the image to insert it in Slide 2.

   If you cannot locate the image in Figure 1.42, select another group photograph that looks like an audience.

e. Position your pointer in the center of the image and drag the image to the top right of the slide so that the top of the image touches the bars.

f. Position your pointer over the bottom-left sizing handle of the image and drag inward to reduce the size of the photograph.

   The photograph is too large. Not only is it overpowering the text, it is blocking text so that it cannot be read. As you drag the sizing handle inward, all four borders are reduced equally so the photograph no longer touches the bars.

g. If necessary, reposition the clip art image so that it is positioned attractively on the slide.

h. Move to **Slide 7**, change the keyword to **keys**, change the results to show **All media types**, and then click **OK**.

i. Refer to Figure 1.42 to determine the keys clip to select, and then click the image to insert it in Slide 7. Close the Clip Art task pane.

j. Reposition the clip so that it is over the word *key* but do not resize it.

   This clip is an animated move clip. If it is enlarged, the image will become pixelated and unattractive.

k. Save the *chap1_ho3_content_solution* presentation.

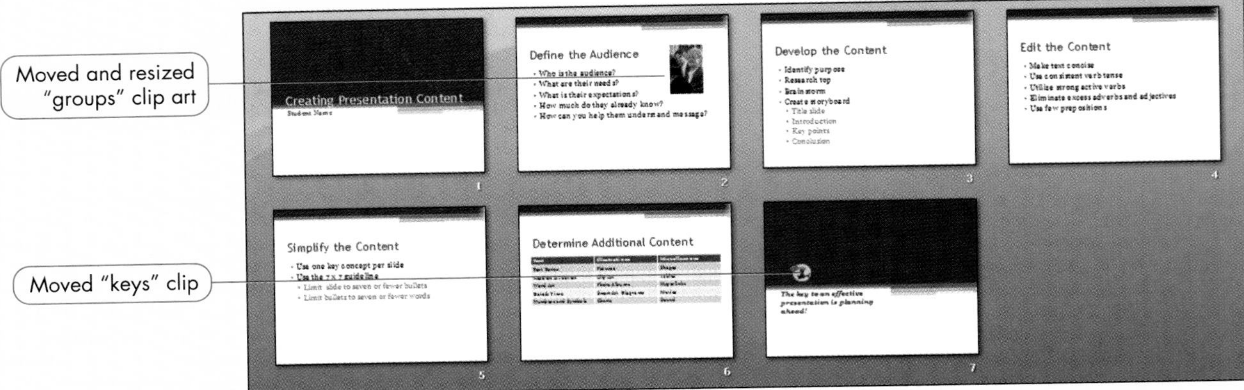

Figure 1.42 Inserted Clip Art

Step 3
Apply a Transition

Refer to Figure 1.43 as you complete Step 3.

a. Click the **Animations tab** and click **More** in the Transitions To This Slide group.

b. Point at several of the transition effects to see how they impact the slide, and then click the **Box Out** wipe transition.

c. Click **Apply To All** in the Transitions To This Slide group on the Animation tab.

The Apply To All will apply the transition set for the current slide to all slides in the slide show.

d. Move to **Slide 1**, click the **Transition Sound down arrow** in the Transitions To This Slide group on the Animations tab, and then click **Chimes**.

The Chimes sound will play as Slide 1 enters. Presenters often use a sound or an audio clip to focus the audience's attention on the screen as the presentation begins.

e. Click **Preview** in the Preview group on the Animations tab.

Because Slide 1 is active, you hear the chimes sound as the Box Out transition occurs.

TROUBLESHOOTING: If you are completing this activity in a classroom lab, you may need to plug in headphones or turn on speakers to hear the sound.

f. Click the **View tab** and click **Slide Sorter** in the Presentation Views group.

Notice the small star beneath each slide. The star indicates a transition has been applied to the slide.

g. Click on any of the stars to see a preview of the transition applied to that slide.

h. Save the *chap1_ho3_content_solution* presentation.

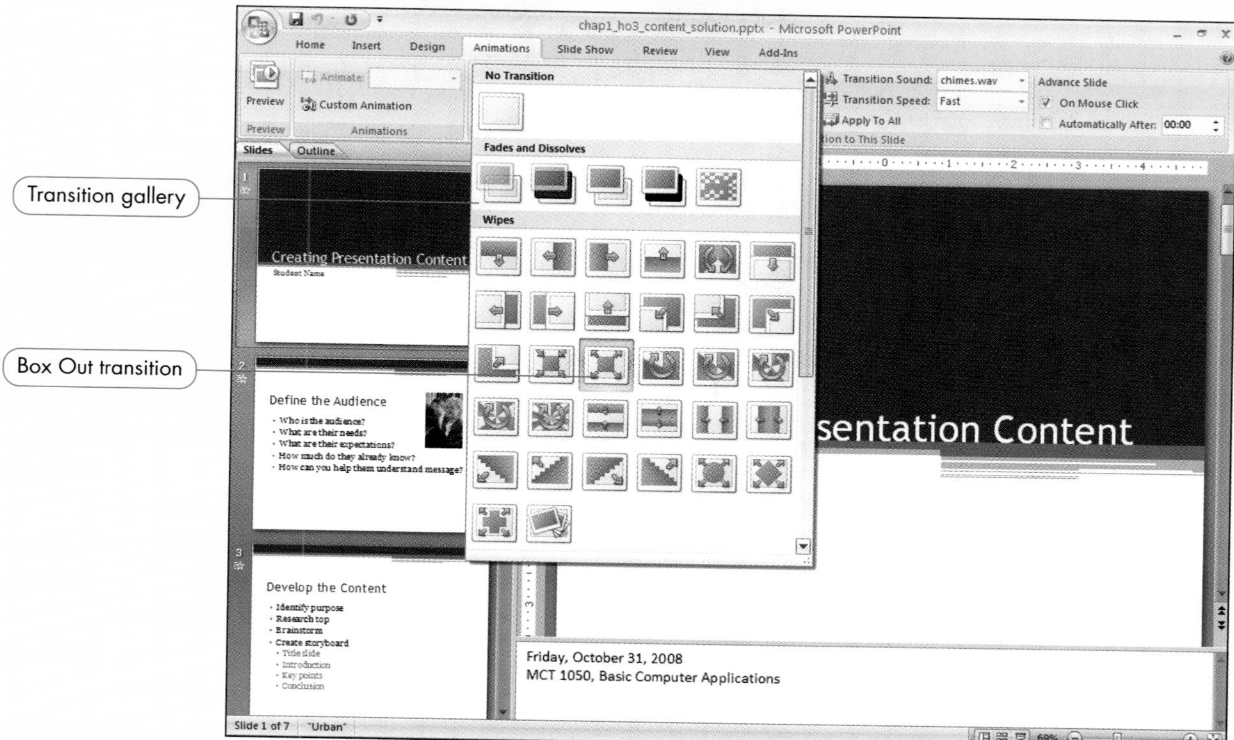

Figure 1.43 The Transition Gallery

Step 4
Animate Objects

Refer to Figure 1.44 as you complete Step 4.

a. Double-click **Slide 1** to open it in Normal view, and then select the Title placeholder.

b. Click the **Animations tab** and click the **Animate down arrow** in the Animations group.

c. Click **Fade**.

The Fade animation scheme is applied to the Title placeholder. The title placeholder dissolves into the background until it is fully visible.

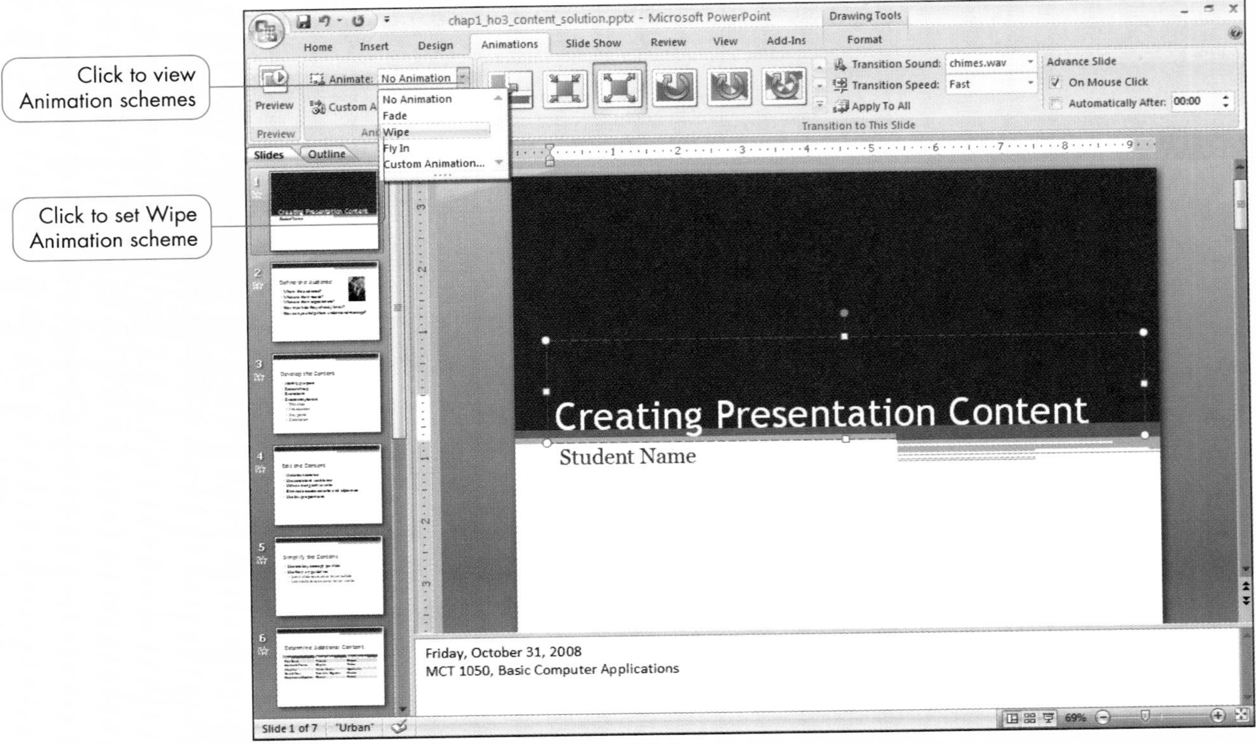

Figure 1.44 Object Animation schemes

d. Select the Subtitle placeholder on Slide 1, and then click the **Animate drop-down arrow** in the Animations group on the Animations tab.

e. Click the **All at once** button located under Fly In.

f. Move to **Slide 2** and select the photograph.

   You decide to use a custom animation on the photograph so that you can have more animation choices and can control the speed with which the photograph animates.

g. Click **Custom Animation** in the Animations group on the Animations tab.

   The Custom Animation task pane opens, which enables you to add an animation effect to the selected object.

h. Click the **Add Effect button**, point at **Entrance**, and then click **More Effects** from the animation list.

   The Add Entrance Effect dialog box appears. The animation effects are separated into categories: Basic, Subtle, Moderate, and Exciting.

i. Scroll down and select **Curve Up** in the Exciting category.

   A preview of the Curve Up animation plays, but the dialog box remains open so that you can continue previewing animations until you find the one you like. Experiment with the Entrance Effects so you can see the impact they will have.

j. Select **Boomerang**, and then click **OK**.

k. Click the drop-down arrow for the **Start** box, and then select **After Previous**.

You can choose to start the animation with a mouse click, or by having the animation start automatically. If you wish to begin the animation automatically, you can choose to have it begin at the same time as a previous animation by selecting Start With Previous, or having it begin after a previous animation by selecting Start After Previous.

l. Click the drop-down arrow for the **Speed** box, and then click **Medium**.

m. Save the *chap1_ho3_content_solution* presentation. Close the file and exit PowerPoint if you do not want to continue to the next exercise at this time.

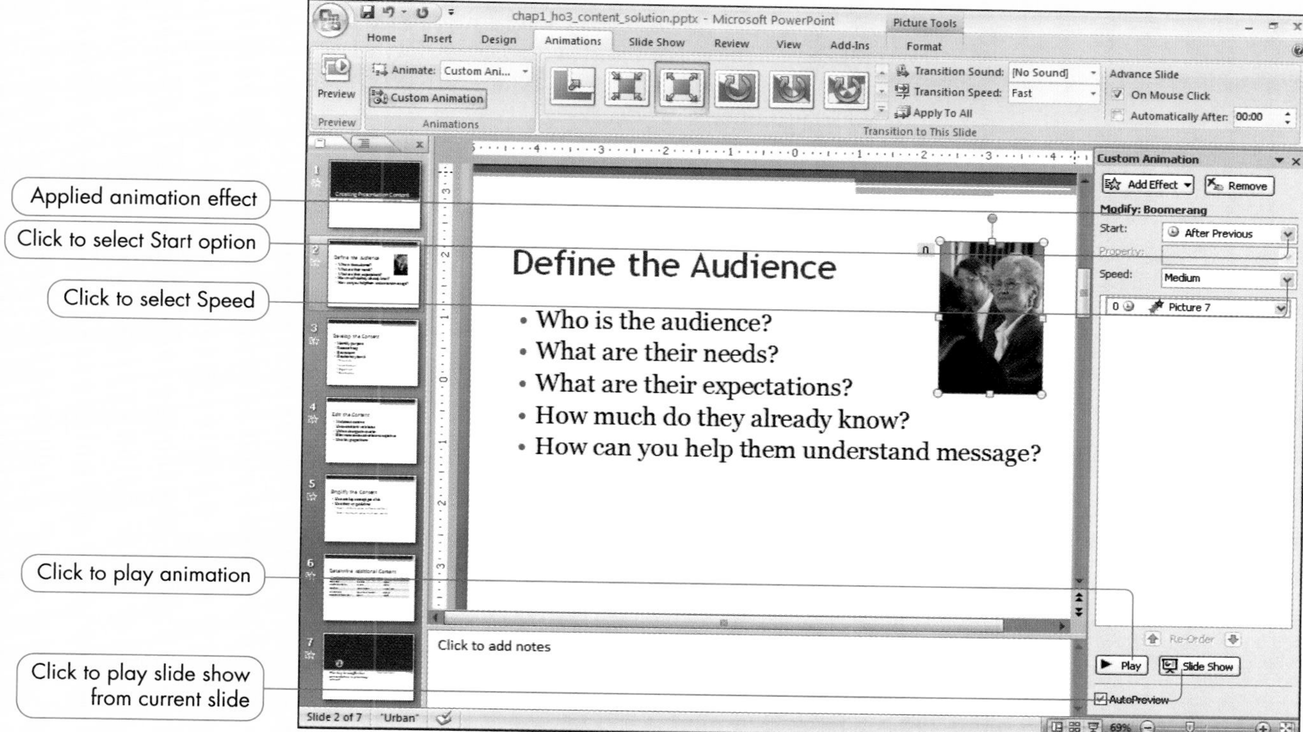

Figure 1.45 Custom Animation Task Pane

Navigation and Printing

In the beginning of this chapter, you opened a slide show and advanced one by one through the slides by clicking the mouse button. This task is possible because PowerPoint is, by default, a linear software tool that advances each slide one after another in a straight line order. Audiences, however, are seldom comfortable with a linear slide show. If they are involved in the presentation, they want to ask questions. As you respond to the questions, you may find yourself needing to jump to a previous slide or needing to move to a future slide. PowerPoint's navigation options allow you to do this maneuver.

> A variety of options are available for audience handouts . . . be aware of the options and choose the one that best suits your audience's needs.

To help your audience follow your presentation, you can choose to provide them with a handout. You may give it to them at the beginning of your presentation for them to take notes on, or you tell them you will be providing them with notes and let them relax and enjoy your slide show. A variety of options are available for audience handouts. All you need do is be aware of the options and choose the one that best suits your audience's needs.

In this section, you run a slide show and navigate within the show. You will practice a variety of methods for advancing to new slides or returning to previously viewed slides. You will annotate slides during a presentation, and change from screen view to black-screen view. Finally, you print the slide show.

Running and Navigating a Slide Show

PowerPoint provides multiple methods you can use to advance through your slide show. You also can go backwards to a previous slide, if desired. Use Table 1.2 to identify the navigation options, and then experiment with each method for advancing and going backwards. Find the method that you are most comfortable using and stay with that method. That way you will not get confused during the slide show and advance to a new slide before you mean to do so.

Table 1.2 Navigation Options

Navigation Option	Navigation Method
To Advance Through the Slide Show	Press the Spacebar
	Press Page Down
	Press the letter **N** or **n** for next
	Press the right arrow or down arrow
	Press Enter
To Return to a Previous Slide or Animation	Right-click and choose Previous from the Popup menu
	Press the Page Up button
	Press the letter **P** or **p** for previous
	Press the left arrow or up arrow
	Press Backspace
To End the Slide Show	Press Esc on the keyboard
	Press the hyphen key
To Go to a Specific Slide	Type Slide number and press Enter
	Right-click, click Go to Slide, then click the slide desired

TIP Slide Show Controls

You can press F1 at any time during your presentation to see a list of slide show controls. Familiarize yourself with these controls before you present to a group for maximum effectiveness.

When an audience member asks a question that is answered in another slide on your slide show, you can go to that specific slide in the slide show by using the Popup menu. Right-clicking while displaying the slide show brings up a handy menu of options. Pointing to the Go to Slide command and then clicking the slide you wish to go to allows you to move to that slide. This pop-up menu also lets you end the slide show.

After the last slide in your slide show displays, the audience sees a black slide. This slide has a two-fold purpose. It enables you to end your show without having your audience see the PowerPoint design screen and it cues the audience to expect the room lights to brighten. If you need to bring up the lights in the room while in your slide show, you can type the letter **B** or **b** for black on the keyboard and the screen blackens. Be careful though—if you blacken the screen, you must bring up the lights. Do not stand and present in complete darkness. When you are ready to launch your slide show again, simply type the letter **B** or **b** again.

If you prefer bringing up a white screen, you can accomplish the same thing by using the letter **W** or **w** for white. White is much harsher on your audience's eyes, however, and can be very jarring. Only use white if you are in an extremely bright room and the bright white screen is not too great of a difference in lighting. Whether using black or white, however, you are enabling the audience to concentrate on you, the speaker, without the slide show interfering.

Annotate the Slide Show

An ***annotation*** is a note that can be written or drawn on a slide for additional commentary or explanation.

You may find it helpful to add ***annotations***, or notes, to your slides. You can write or draw on your slides during a presentation. To do so, right-click to bring up the shortcut menu, and then click Pointer Options to select your pen type. You can change the color of the pen from the Popup menu, too. To create the annotation, hold down the left mouse button as you write or draw on your slide. To erase what you have drawn, press the letter **E** or **e** on the keyboard. Keep in mind that the mouse was never intended to be an artist's tool. Your drawings or added text will be clumsy efforts at best, unless you use a tablet and pen. The annotations you create are not permanent unless you save the annotations when exiting the slide show and then save the changes upon exiting the file.

TIP Annotating Shortcuts

Press Ctrl+P to change the mouse pointer to a point, then click and drag on the slide during the presentation, much the same way your favorite football announcer diagrams a play. Use the PgDn and PgUp keys to move forward and back in the presentation while the annotation is in effect. The annotations will disappear when you exit the slide show unless you elect to keep them permanently when prompted at the end of the show. Press Ctrl+A to return the mouse pointer to an arrow.

Printing with PowerPoint

A printed copy of a PowerPoint slide show is very beneficial. It can be used by the presenter for reference during the presentation. It can be used by the audience for future reference, or as backup during equipment failure. It can even be used by students as a study guide. A printout of a single slide with text on it can be used as a poster or banner.

Print Slides

Use the Print Slides option to print each slide on a full page. One reason to print the slides as full slides is to print the slides for use as a backup. You can print the full slides on overhead transparencies that could be projected with an overhead projector during a presentation. You will be extremely grateful for the backup if your projector bulb blows out or your computer quits working during a presentation. Using the Print Slides option also is valuable if you want to print a single slide that has been formatted as a sign or a card.

If you are printing the slides on transparencies, or on paper smaller than the standard size, be sure to set the slide size and orientation before you print. By default PowerPoint sets the slides for landscape orientation, or printing where the width is greater than the height (11 x 8.5″). If you are going to print on a transparency for an overhead projector, however, you need to set PowerPoint to portrait orientation, or printing where the height is greater than the width (8.5 x 11″).

To change your slide orientation, or to set PowerPoint to print for a different size, click the Design tab and click Page Setup in the Page Setup group to open the Page Setup dialog box. Click in the *Slides sized for* list to select the size or type of paper on which you will print. To print overhead transparency, you click Overhead. You also can set the slide orientation in this dialog box. If you wish to create a custom size of paper to print, enter the height and width. Figure 1.46 displays the Page Setup options. Note that the slide show we have been creating has been changed so that it can be printed on overhead transparencies.

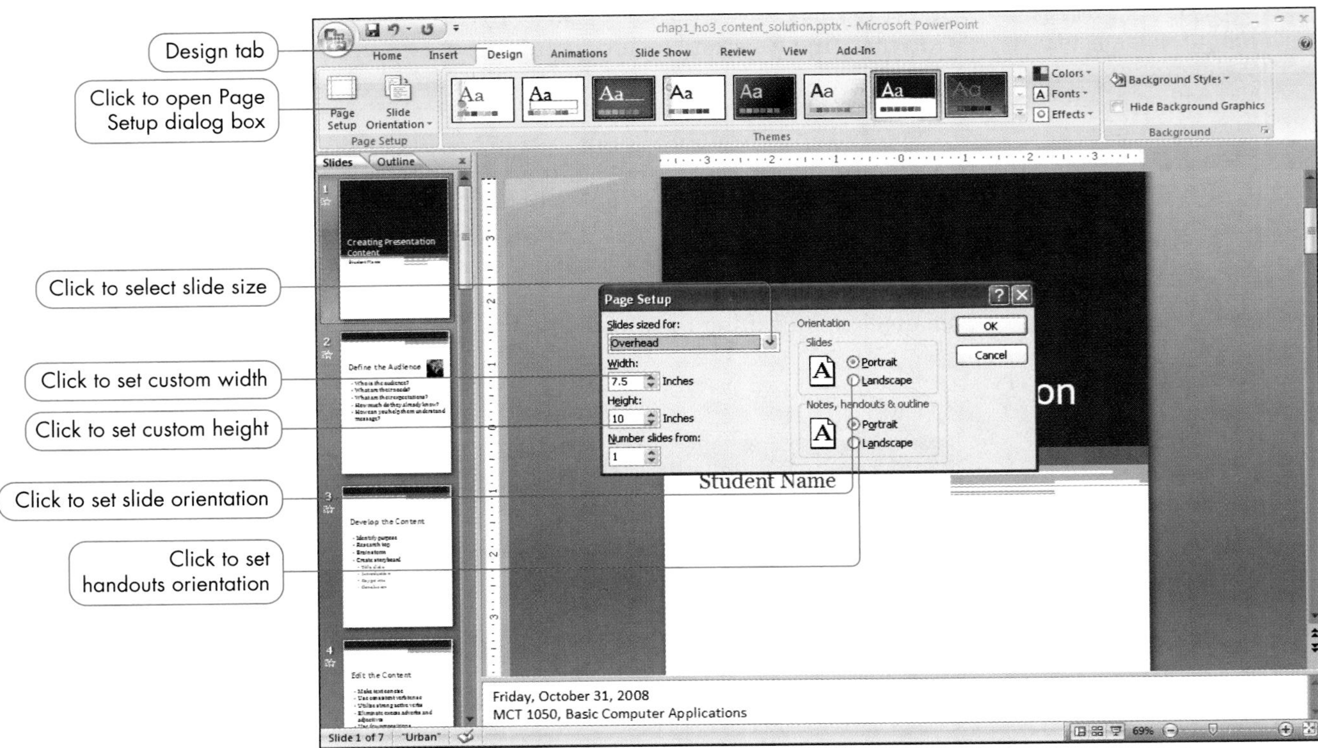

Figure 1.46 Page Setup Options

Once you have determined your page setup, you are ready to print the slides. To print, click the Office Button, select Print, and then select Print in the submenu. The Print dialog box opens so that you can select your printer, your print range, and number of copies—options available to all Office applications. In addition to the standard print options, PowerPoint has many options that tailor the printout to your needs. You can click the *Print what* drop-down arrow and select whether you want to print slides, handouts, notes pages, or outlines.

You can determine the color option with which to print. Selecting Color prints your presentation in color if you have a color printer or grayscale if you are printing on a black-and-white printer. Selecting the Grayscale option prints in shades of gray, but be aware that backgrounds do not print when using the Grayscale option. By not printing the background, you make the text in the printout easier to read and you save a lot of ink or toner. Printing with the Pure Black and White option prints with no gray fills. Try using Microsoft clip art and printing in Pure Black and White to create coloring pages for children.

If you have selected a custom size for your slide show, or if you have set up the slide show so that is it larger than the paper you are printing on, be sure to check the *Scale to fit paper* box. Doing so will ensure that each slide prints on one page. The Frame slides option puts a back border around the slides in the printout, giving the printout a more polished appearance. If you have applied shadows to text or objects, you may want to check the *Print shadows* option so that the shadows print. The final two options, *Print comments and ink markup* and *Print hidden slides*, are only active if you have used these features.

Print Handouts

The principal purpose for printing handouts is to give your audience something they can use to follow during the presentation and give them something on which to take notes. With your handout and their notes, the audience has an excellent resource for the future. Handouts can be printed with one, two, three, four, six, or nine slides per page. Printing three handouts per page is a popular option because it places thumbnails of the slides on the left side of the printout and lines on which the audience can write on the right side of the printout. Figure 1.47 shows the *Print what* option set to Handouts and the Slides per page option set to 3.

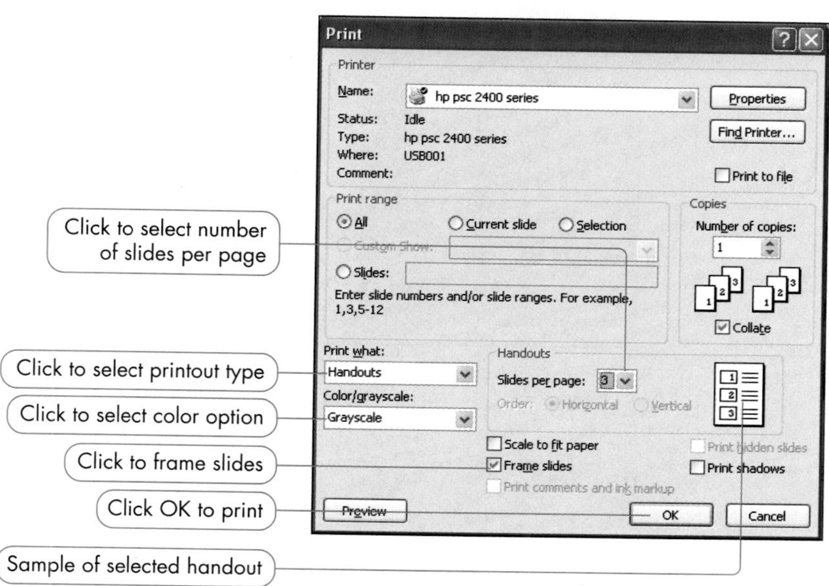

Figure 1.47 Page Setup Options

Print Notes Pages

In the first exercise in this chapter, you created a note in the Notes pane. If you include charts or technical information in your notes, you will want to print the notes for reference. You also may want to print the detailed notes for your audience, especially if your notes contain references. To print your notes, click the Office Button, select Print, select Print from the submenu, and then click Notes Pages in the *Print what* box.

Print Outlines

You may print your presentation as an outline made up of the slide titles and main text from each of your slides. This is a good option if you only want to deal with a few pages instead of a page for each slide as is printed for Notes pages. The outline generally gives you enough detail to keep you on track with your presentation.

You can print the outline following the methods discussed for the other three printout types, but you also can preview it and print from the preview screen. To preview how a printout will look, click the Office Button, and then point to the arrow next to Print. In the list that displays, click Print Preview. Click the arrow next to the *Print what* box, and then click Outline View. If you decide to print, click Print. Figure 1.48 shows the outline for the presentation we have been creating in Print Preview.

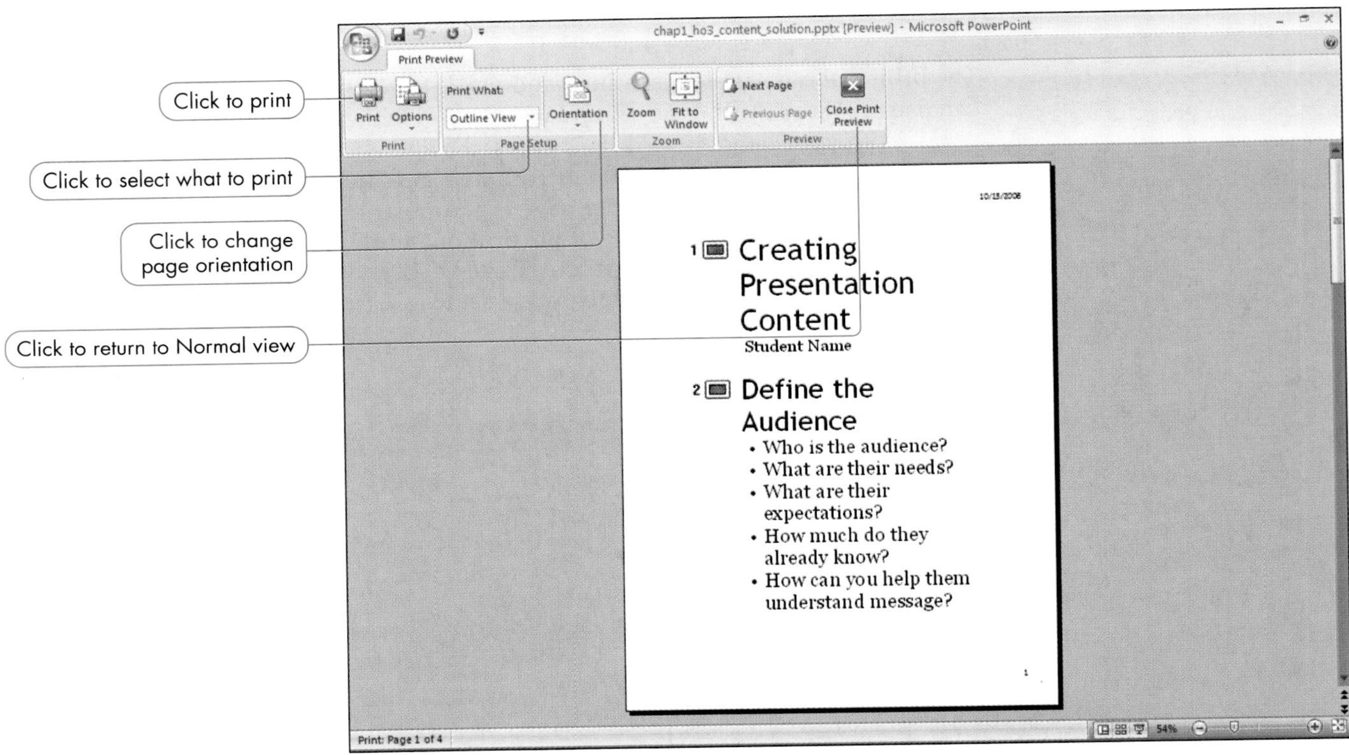

Figure 1.48 Outline View in Print Preview

Hands-On Exercises

4 | Navigating and Printing

Skills covered: 1. Display a Slide Show **2.** Navigate to Specific Slides **3.** Annotate a Slide **4.** Print Audience Handouts

Step 1
Display a Slide Show

a. Open the *chap1_ho3_content_solution* presentation if you closed it after the last exercise, and then save it as **chap1_ho4_content_solution**. Type your class under your name in the title placeholder.

b. Click the **Slide Show tab** and click **From Beginning** in the Start Slide Show group.

Note the transition effect and sound you applied in Hands-On Exercise 3.

c. Press **Spacebar** to animate the title, press **Spacebar** again to animate the subtitle.

Pressing Spacebar advances to the next animation or the next slide.

d. Click to advance to Slide 2.

Note that the photograph animation plays automatically.

e. Press **Page Down** to advance to Slide 3.

f. Press **Page Up** to return to Slide 2.

g. Press **Enter** to advance to Slide 3.

h. Press **N** on the keyboard to advance to Slide 4.

i. Press **Backspace** to return to Slide 3.

Step 2
Navigate to Specific Slides

a. Right-click, select **Go to Slide**, and then select **5 Simply the Content**.

Slide 5 displays.

b. Press the number **3** on the keyboard, and then press **Enter**.

Slide 3 displays.

c. Press **F1** and read the Slide Show Help menu showing the shortcut tips that are available during the display of a slide show.

d. Close the Help menu.

Step 3
Annotate a Slide

a. Press **Ctrl + P**.

The mouse pointer becomes a pen.

b. Circle and underline several words on the slide.

c. Press the letter **E**.

The annotations erase.

d. Press the letter **B**.

The screen blackens.

e. Press the letter **B** again.

   The slide show displays again.

f. Press **Esc** to end the slide show.

Step 4
Print Audience Handouts

a. Click the **Office Button** and select **Print**.

b. Click the **Print what drop-down arrow**, and then click **Handouts**.

c. Specify **4** slides per page, and then click **OK** to print the presentation.

d. Save the *chap1_ho4_content_solution* presentation and close it.

Summary

1. **Identify PowerPoint user interface elements.** PowerPoint features are designed to aid you in creating slide shows in support of presentations you give. Slide shows are electronic presentations that enable you to advance through slides containing content that will help your audience understand your message. PowerPoint 2007 is one of the four main applications in the Office 2007 Suite that uses a new interface designed for easier access to features. PowerPoint has different views, each with unique capabilities. The Normal view is a tri-pane view that displays either thumbnail images or an outline in one pane, the slide in one pane, and a Notes pane. The Slide Sorter view displays thumbnails of multiple slides. The Notes view shows a miniature of the slide and the associated speaker notes. The Slide Show view.
2. **Use PowerPoint views.** PowerPoint contains multiple views to fit the user's needs. The default view is the Normal view—a tri-pane view used predominantly for slideshow creation. The Slide Sorter view enables the user to quickly reorder or delete slides to enhance organization. The Notes Page view displays a thumbnail of the slide and the notes the user has entered for that slide. The Slide Show view displays the slide show in full-screen view for an audience. If a presenter has multiple monitors, the Presenter's view gives the presenter options for greater control of the playback.
3. **Open and save a slide show.** Previously created slide shows can be opened so that they can be modified. After editing, they can be saved with the same file name using the Save feature, or saved with a new file name using the Save As feature. When slide shows are saved, they are assigned an extension of .pptx, indicating they are in XML (eXtensible Markup Language) file format.
4. **Get Help.** PowerPoint's Help can be used to locate information about a specific feature, to troubleshoot, to search for software updates, to find a template, or to locate additional training. Help is available online or offline.
5. **Create a storyboard.** Before creating your slide show you should spend a considerable amount of time analyzing your audience, researching your message, and organizing your ideas. Organize your ideas on a storyboard, and then create your presentation in PowerPoint. After completing the slide show, you should spend a considerable amount of time practicing your presentation so that you are comfortable with your slide content and the technology you will use to present it with.
6. **Use slide layouts.** PowerPoint provides a set of predefined slide layouts that determine the position of the objects or content on a slide. Slide layouts contain any number and combination of placeholders. Placeholders hold content and determine the position of the objects on the slide.
7. **Apply design themes.** PowerPoint themes enable you to focus on the content of a presentation. You create the text and supporting elements, and then you apply a design theme to give the presentation a consistent look. The theme controls the font, background, layout, and colors.
8. **Review the presentation.** To ensure there are no typographical errors or misspelled words in a presentation, use the Check Spelling feature to complete an initial check for errors. You also need to review each slide yourself because the Check Spelling feature does not find all errors. An example of an error that the Check Spelling feature does not find is the misuse of the word "to" or "two" when the correct word is "too." Use the Thesaurus to locate synonyms for overused words in the slide show.
9. **Add a table.** Tables can be created to help organize information needed in the slide show. PowerPoint's table features can be used to specify the number of columns and rows needed in the table. Tables can be inserted from the Content bar in the Content placeholder or through the Insert tab.
10. **Insert clip art.** A variety of clips can be added to slides. Clips are media objects such as clip art, images, movies, and sound. The Microsoft Clip Organizer contains media objects you can insert, or you can locate clips and insert them through the Insert tab. Clips you gather can be added to the Microsoft Clip Organizer to help you locate them more easily.
11. **Use transitions and animations.** Transitions and animations show in Slide Show view. Transitions control the movements of slides as one slide changes to another, while an animation controls the movement of an object on the slide. Both features can aid in keeping the attention of the audience, but animations are especially valuable in directing attention to specific elements you wish to emphasize.

...continued on Next Page

12. **Run and navigate a slide show.** While displaying the slide show, you need flexibility in moving between slides. Various navigation methods advance the slide show, return to previously viewed slides, or go to specific slides. Slides can be annotated during a presentation to add emphasis or comments to slides.

13. **Print with PowerPoint.** PowerPoint has four ways to print the slideshow, each with specific benefits. The Slides method of printing prints each slide on a full page. The Handouts method prints miniatures of the slides in 1, 2, 3, 4, 6, or 9 per page format. The Notes Pages method prints each slide on a separate page and is formatted to display a single thumbnail of a slide with its associated notes. The Outline method prints the titles and main points of the presentation in outline format.

Key Terms

Animation 521
Animation scheme 523
Annotation 531
Clip 519
Contextual tab 491
Custom animation 523
Custom dictionary 512
Document properties 501
Gallery 491
Layout 510
Metadata 501
Mini toolbar 493
Normal view 489
Notes Page view 496
Object 491
Placeholder 510
Presenter view 499
Ribbon 491
ScreenTip 492
Slide Show view 498
Slide Sorter view 497
Status bar 493
Storyboard 507
Tab 491
Table 519
Theme 510
Thumbnail 494
Transition 521

Multiple Choice

1. Which of the following methods does not save changes in a PowerPoint presentation?
   (a) Click the Office Button, and then click the Save As command.
   (b) Click the Save button on the Quick Access toolbar.
   (c) Press Ctrl+S.
   (d) Press F1.

2. The Quick Access Toolbar, containing commands you may need at any time regardless of what tab is active, includes which of the following commands?
   (a) Cut and Paste
   (b) Undo and Redo
   (c) Find and Replace
   (d) Spelling and Grammar

3. You have created a very complex table with great detail on a slide. You want to give the audience a printout of the slide showing all the detail so they can review it with you during your presentation. Which of the following print methods would show the necessary detail?
   (a) Audience handout, 4 per page
   (b) Outline
   (c) Notes page
   (d) Full slide

4. While displaying a slide show, which of the following will display a list of shortcuts for navigating?
   (a) F1
   (b) F11
   (c) Ctrl+Enter
   (d) Esc

5. The predefined slide formats in PowerPoint are:
   (a) Layout views
   (b) Slide layouts
   (c) Slide guides
   (d) Slide displays

6. If you need to add an object such as clip art or a picture to a slide, which tab would you select?
   (a) Add-ins
   (b) Design
   (c) Slide
   (d) Insert

7. The Open command:
   (a) Brings a presentation from a storage device into RAM memory
   (b) Removes the presentation from the storage device and brings it into RAM memory
   (c) Stores the presentation in RAM memory to a storage device
   (d) Stores the presentation in RAM memory to a storage device, and then erases the presentation from RAM memory

8. The Save command:
   (a) Brings a presentation from a storage device into RAM memory
   (b) Removes the presentation from the storage device and brings it into RAM memory
   (c) Stores the presentation in RAM memory to a storage device
   (d) Stores the presentation in RAM memory to a storage device, and then erases the presentation from RAM memory

9. Which of the following provides a ghost image of a toolbar for use in formatting selected text?
   (a) Styles command
   (b) Quick Access Toolbar
   (c) Formatting Text gallery
   (d) Mini toolbar

10. Which of the following is a true statement?
    (a) A design theme must be applied before slides are created.
    (b) The design theme can be changed after all of the slides have been created.
    (c) Design themes control fonts and backgrounds but not placeholder location.
    (d) Placeholders positioned by a design theme cannot be moved.

11. Microsoft Clip Organizer searches:
    (a) May be limited to a specific media type
    (b) Locate clips based on keywords
    (c) May be limited to specific collections
    (d) All of the above

12. Which of the following views is best for reordering the slides in a presentation?
    (a) Presenter view
    (b) Slide Show view
    (c) Reorder view
    (d) Slide Sorter view

Multiple Choice Continued...

13. Normal view contains which of the following components?
    (a) The slide sorter pane, the tabs pane, and the slide pane
    (b) The tabs pane, the slide pane, and the slide sorter pane
    (c) The tabs pane, the slide pane, and the notes pane
    (d) The outline pane, the slide pane, and the tabs pane

14. Which of the following cannot be used to focus audience attention on a specific object on a slide during a slide show?
    (a) Apply a transition to the object
    (b) Apply an animation to the object
    (c) Use the pen tool to circle the object
    (d) Put nothing on the slide but the object

15. What is the animation effect that controls how one slide changes to another slide?
    (a) Custom animation
    (b) Animation scheme
    (c) Transition
    (d) Advance

Practice Exercises

1 Introduction to E-Mail

The presentation in Figure 1.49 reviews the basics of e-mail and simultaneously provides you with practice opening, modifying, and saving an existing PowerPoint presentation. The presentation contains two slides on computer viruses and reminds you that your computer is at risk whenever you receive an e-mail message with an attachment. Notes containing explanations are included for some slides. You create a summary of what you learn and enter it as a note for the last slide.

a. Click the **Office Button** and select **Open**. Click the **Look in drop-down arrow**, and then locate the drive and folder where your student files are saved. Select the *chap1_pe1_email* presentation, and then click **Open**.
b. Click the **Slide Show tab** and click **From Beginning** in the Start Slide Show group. Read each of the slides by pressing **Spacebar** to advance through the slides. Press **Esc** to exit the Slide Show View.
c. Click in the **Slide 1 title placeholder**, and then replace the words *Student Name* with your name as it appears on the instructor's rolls. Replace *Student Class* with the name of the class you are taking.
d. Click in the **Slide 10 Notes pane**, and then type a short note about what you learned regarding e-mail by reviewing this slide show.
e. Click the **Slide 4 thumbnail** in the Tabs pane to move to Slide 4. Select the sample e-mail address, and then type your e-mail address to replace the sample.
f. Move to **Slide 3** and then click inside the content placeholder. Type **Inbox**, and then press **Enter**. Continue typing the following bullet items: **Outbox, Sent items, Deleted items, Custom folders.**
g. Move to **Slide 8**, select the first protocol, *POP Client – Post Office Protocol Client*, and then move your pointer slightly upward until the Mini toolbar appears. Apply **Bold** and **Italics** to the first protocol. Repeat the process for the second protocol, *IMAP – Internet Message Access Protocol*.
h. Click the **Design tab** and click the **More button** in the Themes group.
i. Click **Technic** to apply the Technic theme to all slides in the slide show.
j. Move to **Slide 1** and adjust the size of the Title placeholder so the complete title fits on one line.
k. Click the **Office Button**, point to **Print**, and then click **Print** in the submenu. Click **Current slide** option in the *Print range* section. Click the **Frame slides check box** to activate it, and then click **OK**. Slide 1 will print for your use as a cover page.
l. Open the Print dialog box again, and then click the **Slides** option in the *Print range* section. Type the slide range **2–10**.
m. Click the **Print what drop-down arrow**, and then select **Handouts**. Click the **Slides per page drop-down arrow** in the *Handouts* section, and then select **3**.
n. Click the **Frame slides check box** to activate it, and then click **OK**. Slides 2–10 will print 3 per page with lines for audience note taking. Staple the cover page to the handouts, and then submit it to your instructor if requested to do so.
o. Click the **Office Button** and select **Save As**. Click the **Save in drop-down arrow** and locate the drive and folder where you are saving your file solutions. Type **chap1_pe1_email_solution** as the file name for the presentation. Click **Save**.

...continued on Next Page

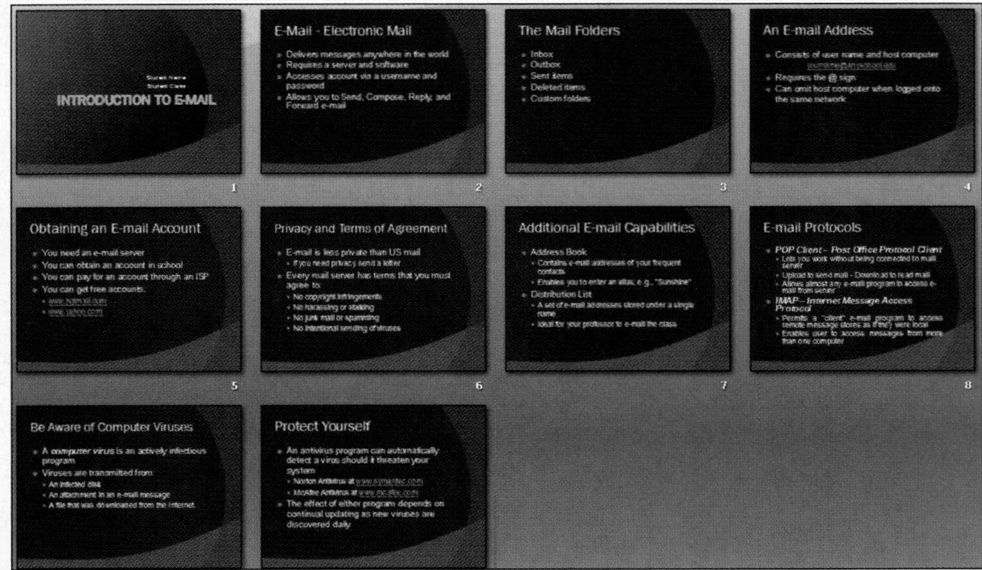

Figure 1.49 Introduction to E-Mail Presentation

2 Successful Presentations

Your employer is a successful author who often presents to various groups. He has been asked by the local International Association of Administrative Professionals (IAAP) to give the group tips for presenting successfully using PowerPoint. He created a storyboard of his presentation and has asked you to create the presentation from the storyboard. Refer to Figure 1.50 as you complete this assignment.

a. Click the **Office Button**, select **New**, click **Blank**, and then click **Create**.
b. Click the **Office Button** and select **Save As**. Click the **Save in drop-down arrow** and locate the drive and folder where you are saving your file solutions. Type **chap1_pe2_tips_solution** as the file name for the presentation. Click **Save**.
c. Click in the **Slide 1 title placeholder**, and then type **Successful Presentations**. Click in the subtitle placeholder and type **Robert Grauer and your name** as it appears on the instructor's rolls.
d. Click the **Home tab**, click the **New Slide down arrow** in the Slides group, and click **Title Only**.
e. Click in the title placeholder and type **Techniques to Consider**.
f. Click **Table** in the Tables group on the Insert tab, and then drag the grid to highlight two columns and five rows.
g. Type the following information in the table cells. Press **Tab** to move from cell to cell.

Feature	**Use**
Rehearse Timings	Helps you determine the length of your presentation
Header/Footer	Puts information on the top and bottom of slides, notes, and handouts
Hidden Slides	Hides slides until needed
Annotate a Slide	Write on the slide

h. Click the **Home tab**, click the **New Slide down arrow** in the Slides group, and then click **Title and Content**. Type **The Delivery is Up to You**.
i. Click in the content placeholder and type the following bullet text: **Practice makes perfect, Arrive early on the big day, Maintain eye contact, Speak slowly, clearly, and with sufficient volume, Allow time for questions**.
j. Click the **Home tab**, click the **New Slide down arrow** in the Slides group, and then click **Title and Content**. Type **Keep Something in Reserve**.

...continued on Next Page

k. Click in the content placeholder and type the following bullet text: **Create hidden slides to answer difficult questions that might occur, Press Ctrl+S to display hidden slides.**

l. Click the **Home tab**, click **New Slide** in the Slides group, and then click **Title and Content**. Type **Provide Handouts.**

m. Click in the content placeholder and type the following bullet text: **Allows the audience to follow the presentation, Lets the audience take the presentation home.**

n. Click the **Review tab** and click **Spelling** in the Proofing group.

o. Correct any misspelled words Check Spelling locates. Proofread the presentation and correct any misspelled words Check Spelling missed.

p. Click the **Design tab** and click the **More button** in the Themes group.

q. Click **Oriel**.

r. Click the **Slide Show tab** and click **From Beginning** in the Start Slide Show group. Press **Page Down** to advance through the slides.

s. When you reach the end of the slide show, press the number **2**, and then press **Enter** to return to Slide 2. Press **Esc**.

t. Press **Ctrl+S** to save the *chap1_pe2_tips_solution* presentation and close.

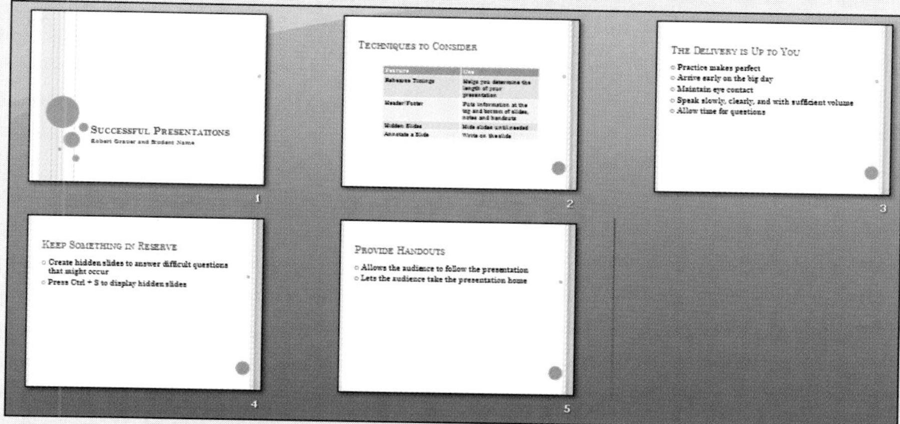

Figure 1.50 Successful Presentations Slide Show

3 Introduction to the Internet

You have been asked to give a presentation covering the basics of the Internet. You created a storyboard and entered the content in a slide show. After viewing the slide show, you realize the slides are text intensive and that transitions and animations would make the show more interesting. You modify the slide show and remove some of the detail from the slides. You put the detail in the Notes pane. You add a transition and apply it to all slides, and you apply custom animations to two images. You print the Notes for you to refer to as you present.

a. Click the **Office Button** and select **Open**. Click the **Look in drop-down arrow**, and then locate the drive and folder where your student files are saved. Click the *chap1_pe3_internet* presentation, and then click **Open**.

b. Click in the **Slide 1** title placeholder and replace the words *Your Name* with your name as it appears on the instructor's rolls. Replace *Your Class* with the name of the class you are taking.

c. Click in the **Slide 2 content placeholder** and modify the text so that it is shortened to brief, easy-to-remember chunks, as displayed in Figure 1.51.

...continued on Next Page

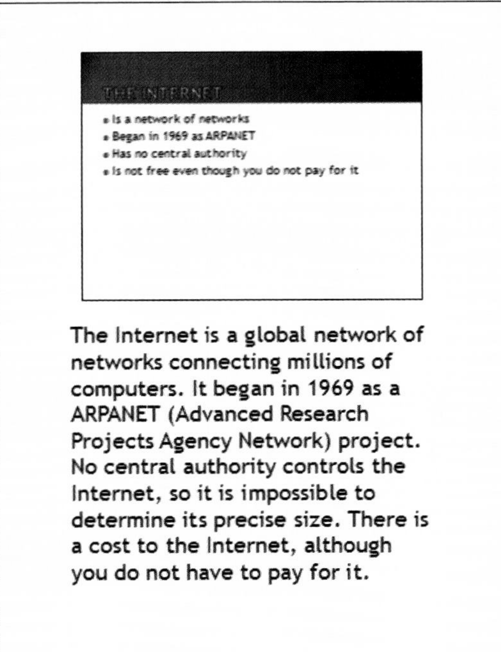

Figure 1.51 Internet Slide 2 Modifications

d. Click the **View tab**. Click **Notes Page** in the Presentation Views group, and then using Figure 1.51 as a guide, enter the notes in the Notes placeholder, which provides the appropriate place for the text omitted in the previous step.
e. Click **Normal** in the Presentation Views group on the View tab, and then move to **Slide 3**. Click in the content placeholder and modify the text so that it is shortened to brief, easy-to-remember chunks, as displayed in Figure 1.52.

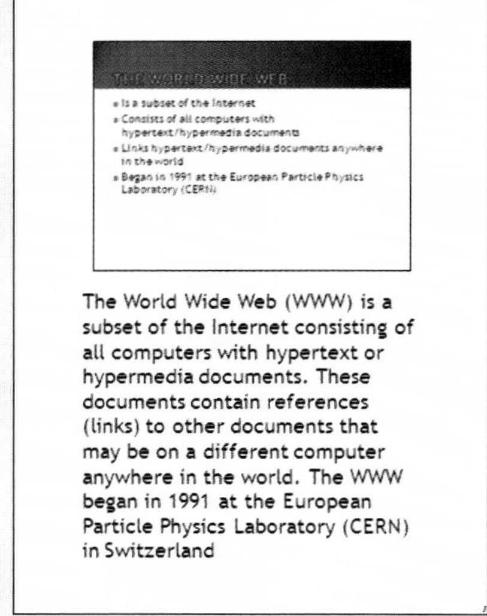

Figure 1.52 Internet Slide 3 Modifications

...continued on Next Page

f. Click the **View tab**, click **Notes Page** in the Presentation Views group, and then using Figure 1.52 as a guide, enter the notes in the Notes placeholder.
g. Click **Normal** in the Presentation Views group, and then click the **Animations tab**. Click the **More button** in the Transition To This Slide group.
h. Click the **Cover Right-Down** option and click **Apply To All**.
i. Move to **Slide 5**, and then click the image of the computer network to select it.
j. Click the down arrow next to **Animate** in the Animations group on the Animations tab, and then click **Fly In**. Repeat this process for the image of the modem and telephone.
k. Click the **View tab**, click **Slide Show** in the Presentation Views group, and then advance through the slide show. Press **Esc** to end the slide show after you have viewed the last slide.
l. Click the **Office Button**, select **Print**, and then select **Print Preview**.
m. Select **Notes Pages** from the Print what list, and then press **Page Down** on the keyboard to advance through the slides. If your instructor asks you to print the Notes Pages, click **Print** in the Print group on the Print Preview tab. Click **Close Print Preview** in the Preview group on the Print Preview tab.
n. Click the **Office Button**, and then select **Save As**. Click the **Save in drop-down arrow** and locate the drive and folder where you are saving your file solutions. Type **chap1_pe3_internet_solution** as the file name for the presentation. Click **Save**.

4 Copyright and the Law

The ethics and values class you are taking this semester requires a final presentation to the class. Although a PowerPoint slide show is not required, you feel it will strengthen your presentation. You create a presentation to review basic copyright law and software licensing and add clip art, a transition, and an animation.

a. Click the **Office Button** and select **Open**. Click the **Look in drop-down arrow**, and then locate the drive and folder where your student files are saved. Select the *chap1_pe4_copyright* presentation, and then click **Open**.
b. Click the **Slide Show tab**, and then click **From Beginning** in the Start Slide Show group. Read each of the slides and note the length of some bullets. Press **Esc** to return to Normal view.
c. Click the **Design tab**, click the **More button** in the Themes group, and select the **Flow theme**.
d. Click in the **Slide 1 title placeholder**, if necessary, and then replace the words *Your Name* with your name as it appears on the instructor's rolls. Replace *Your Class* with the name of the class you are taking.
e. Click the **Insert tab** and click **Clip Art** in the Illustrations group. Type **copyright** in the **Search for** box. Select the animated copyright symbol and drag it to the title slide next to your name. Refer to Figure 1.53 to help you identify the copyright logo.

TROUBLESHOOTING: If the animated copyright clip does not appear when you search for the copyright keyword, change the keyword to **law**, and then select an image that relates to the presentation content and uses the same colors.

f. Click the **Animations tab** and click the **More button** in the Transition To This Slide group.
g. Click the **Fade Through Black** option, and then click **Apply To All**.
h. Move to **Slide 6**, and then select the blue object containing text located at the bottom of the slide.
i. Click **Custom Animation** in the Animations group on the Animations tab.
j. Click **Add Effect** in the Custom Animations task pane, click **More Effects** at the bottom of the Entrance group, and then choose **Faded Zoom** from the Subtle category.
k. Click the **Start** drop-down arrow, and then click **After Previous**.

...continued on Next Page

l. Click **Play** at the bottom of the Custom Animation task pane to see the result of your custom animation.
m. Move to the last slide in the slide show, **Slide 9**, click the **Home tab**, and then click **New Slide** in the Slides group.
n. Click **Section Header** from the list of layouts.
o. Click in the title placeholder and type **Individuals who violate copyright law and/or software licensing agreements may be subject to criminal or civil action by the copyright or license owners**. Press **Ctrl + A** to select the text and change the font size to 40 pts.
p. Click on the border of the subtitle placeholder and press **Delete**.
q. Drag the title placeholder downward until all of the text is visible and is centered vertically on the slide.
r. Select the text, move your pointer upward until the Mini toolbar appears, and then click the **Center Align** button.
s. Click the **Office Button** and select **Save As**. Click the **Save in drop-down arrow** and locate the drive and folder where you are saving your file solutions. Type **chap1_pe4_copyright_solution** as the file name for the presentation. Click **Save**.

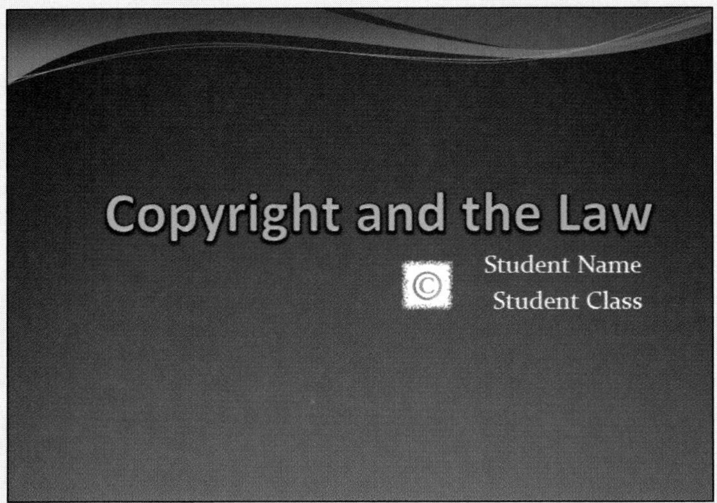

Figure 1.53 Copyright and the Law Presentation

Mid-Level Exercises

1 Public Speaking 101

PowerPoint will help you to create an attractive presentation, but the delivery is still up to you. It is easier than you think, and you should not be intimidated at the prospect of facing an audience. You can gain confidence and become an effective speaker by following the basic tenets of good public speaking. Refer to Figure 1.54 as you complete this exercise.

a. Open the *chap1_mid1_public* presentation and save it as **chap1_mid1_public_solution**.

b. Add your name and e-mail address to the title slide. Add your e-mail address to the summary slide as well.

c. Print the notes for the presentation, and then view the slide show while looking at the appropriate notes for each slide. Which slides have notes attached? Are the notes redundant, or do they add something extra? Do you see how the notes help a speaker to deliver an effective presentation?

d. Which slide contains the phrase, "Common sense is not common practice"? In what context is the phrase used within the presentation?

e. Which personality said, "You can observe a lot by watching?" In what context is the phrase used during the presentation?

f. Join a group of three or four students, and then have each person in the group deliver the presentation to his or her group. Were they able to follow the tenets of good public speaking? Share constructive criticism with each of the presenters. Constructive criticism means you identify both positive aspects of their presentations and aspects that could be improved with practice. The goal of constructive criticism is to help one another improve.

g. Summarize your thoughts about this exercise in an e-mail message to your instructor.

h. Save the *chap1_mid1_public_solution* presentation and close.

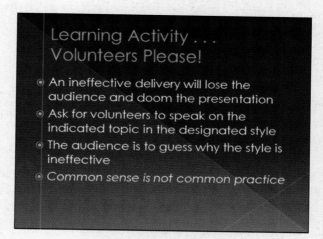

Figure 1.54 Public Speaking 101

...continued on Next Page

2 University Housing

The Provost's Office at your university manages policies and practices that affect the academic life of the university as a whole. The new provost, Dr. Richard Shaw, has asked the housing office administrator to meet with him and update him about the purpose and goals of the housing office. As a work-study student employed by the housing office, you have been asked to take the administrator's notes and prepare a presentation for the provost. Refer to Figure 1.55 as you complete this exercise.

a. Open the *chap1_mid2_university* presentation and save it as **chap1_mid2_university_solution**.

b. Add your name and the name of the class you are taking to the title slide.

c. Insert a new slide using the Title and Content layout as the second slide in the presentation. Type **Mission** as the title.

d. Type the mission in the content placeholder: **The mission of the University Housing Office is to provide a total environment that will enrich the educational experience of its residents. It seeks to promote increased interaction between faculty and students through resident masters, special programs, and intramural activities.**

e. Move to the end of the presentation and insert a new slide with the Blank layout. Insert two photograph clips related to college life from the Microsoft Clip Organizer or Office Online.

f. Move to **Slide 4** and create a table using the following information:

Dorm Name	Room Revenue	Meal Revenue	Total Revenue
Ashe Hall	$2,206,010	$1,616,640	$3,822,650
Memorial	$1,282,365	$934,620	$2,216,985
Ungar Hall	$2,235,040	$1,643,584	$3,878,624
Merrick Hall	$1,941,822	$1,494,456	$3,346,278
Fort Towers	$1,360,183	$981,772	$2,341,955
Totals	$9,025,420	$6,581,072	$15,606,492

g. Select the cells containing numbers, and then use the Mini toolbar to right-align the numbers Select the cells containing the column titles, and then use the Mini toolbar to center-align the text..

h. Apply the Cut transition theme to all slides in the slide show.

i. Add the Curve Up custom animation to each of the images on Slide 6. Curve Up is located in the Exciting category of Entrance Effects. Set the animations so that they start automatically after the previous event.

j. Print the handouts, 3 per page, framed.

k. Save the *chap1_mid2_university_solution* presentation and close.

...continued on Next Page

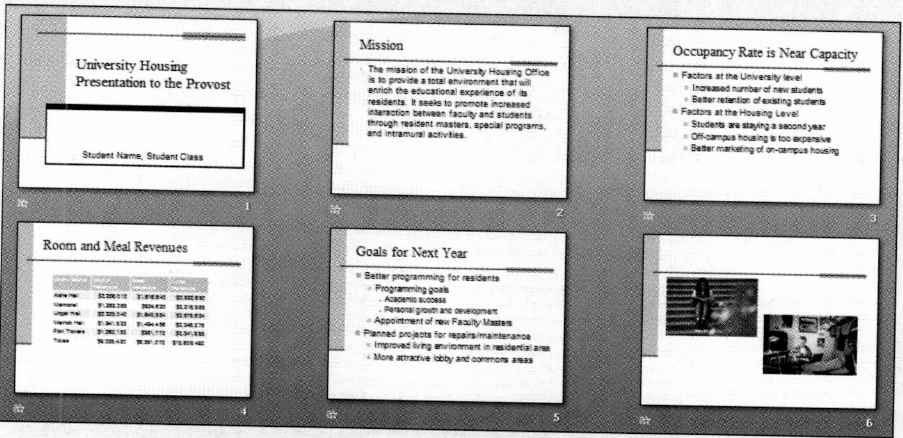

Figure 1.55 University Housing

3 PowerPoint FAQ

As a volunteer in the computer room at the local library, you get a barrage of questions about PowerPoint 2007. To help library personnel and library patrons and to reduce having to repeatedly answer the same questions, you decide to create a PowerPoint FAQ (Frequently Asked Questions) slide show that people can watch when needed. You use Help to help you prepare the FAQ slide show, and as you navigate through Help and read the associated articles, you summarize what you learn in the FAQ slide show. Refer to Figure 1.56 as you complete this exercise.

a. Create a new slide show and save it as **chap1_mid3_ppt07faq_solution**.

b. Type **PowerPoint 2007 Frequently Asked Questions** as the presentation title, and then add your name and the name of the class you are taking to the title slide.

c. Create a new slide for each of the following PowerPoint interfaces using these titles:
   - What is the Microsoft Office Button?
   - What is the Quick Access Toolbar?
   - What is the Ribbon?
   - What is a Gallery?

d. Move to **Slide 2** and open Help. Type **Office Button** as the keyword for the search and then conduct the search. When the results page displays, click the link for *What and where is the Microsoft Office Button?*

e. Read the resulting article and close the Help dialog box. In the content placeholder, enter a summary of what you learned. For example, *The Office Button provides access to the basic commands such as open, save, and print, and replaces the File menu.*

f. Use Help to find information about the remaining features, and then enter a summary about each feature in the content placeholder of each slide.

g. Apply the **Origin** design theme to your slide show.

h. Apply the **Fade Smoothly** transition theme to all slides in the slide show.

i. Check the spelling in your presentation, and then proofread carefully to catch any errors that Spelling may have missed.

j. Print the handouts as directed by your instructor.

k. Save the *chap1_mid3_ppt07faq_solution* presentation and close.

...continued on Next Page

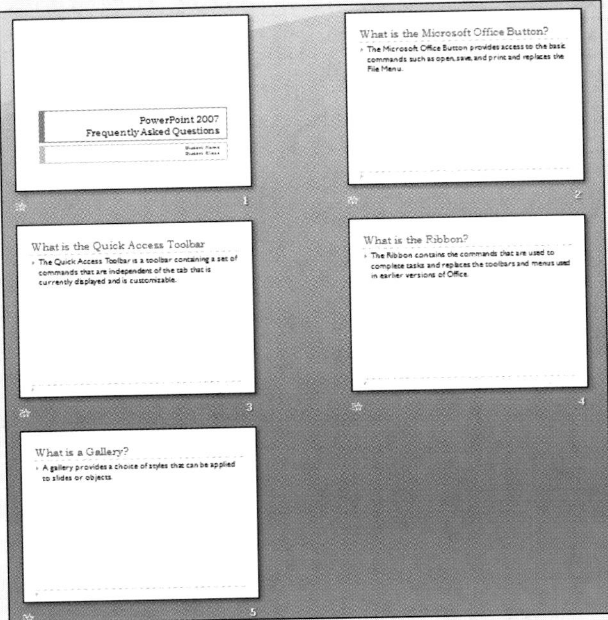

Figure 1.56 FAQ Presentation

Capstone Exercise

Definitely Needlepoint is a successful retail store owned by four close friends. One of them is your mother. The store has been in operation for three years and has increased its revenue and profit each year. The partners are looking to expand their operation by requesting venture capital. They have an important meeting scheduled next week. Help your mother prepare a PowerPoint slide show to help them present their case.

Presentation Setup

You need to open the presentation that you already started, rename the file, and save it. You add your name to the title slide and then you apply a design theme.

a. Locate the file named *chap1_cap_capital*, and then save it as **chap1_cap_capital_solution**.

b. Replace *Your Name* with your name as it appears on your instructor's roll book in the title placeholder of Slide 1.

c. Apply the **Metro** design theme.

Create a Mission Statement Slide

You need to create a slide for the Definitely Needlepoint mission statement. The mission statement created by the four owners clearly reflects their personality and their attitude about their customers. This attitude is a clear factor in the success of the business, so you decide it should be preeminent in the presentation and use it as the introduction slide.

a. Insert a new slide after Slide 1 with the Title Only layout.

b. Type the following mission statement in the title placeholder: **Definitely Needlepoint provides a friendly and intimate setting in which to stitch. Our customers are not just customers, but friends who participate in a variety of social and educational activities that encourage and develop the art of needlepoint.**

c. Select the text, use the Mini toolbar to change the Font size to **28 pts**, and then apply **Italics**.

d. Reposition the placeholder so that the entire statement fits on the slide.

e. Save the *chap1_cap_capital_solution* presentation.

Create Tables

You create tables to show the increase in sales from last year to this year, the sales increase by category, and the sales increase by quarters.

a. Move to **Slide 4**, click the **Insert tab**, and then click **Table** in the Tables group.

b. Create a table with four columns and seven rows. Type the following data in your table:

Category	Last Year	This Year	Increase
Canvases	$75,915	$115,856	$39,941
Fibers	$47,404	$77,038	$29,634
Accessories	$31,590	$38,540	$6,950
Classes	$19,200	$28,200	$9,000
Finishing	$25,755	$46,065	$20,310
Totals	$199,864	$305,699	$105,835

c. Use the Mini toolbar to right-align the numbers and to bold the bottom row of totals.

d. Reposition the table on the slide so that it does not block the title.

e. Move to **Slide 5** and insert a table of six columns and three rows.

f. Type the following data in your table:

Year	Canvases	Fibers	Accessories	Classes	Finishing
Last Year	$75,915	$47,404	$31,590	$19,200	$25,755
This Year	$115,856	$77,038	$38,540	$28,200	$46,065

g. Use the Mini toolbar to change the text font to 16 points and then right-align the numbers.

h. Reposition the table on the slide so that it does not block the title.

i. Move to **Slide 6** and insert a table of five columns and three rows.

j. Type the following data in your table:

...continued on Next Page

Year	Qtr 1	Qtr 2	Qtr 3	Qtr 4
Last Year	$37,761	$51,710	$52,292	$58,101
This Year	$61,594	$64,497	$67,057	$112,551

k. Spell-check the presentation, check the presentation for errors not caught by spell checking, and then carefully compare the numbers in the tables to your text to check for accuracy.

l. Save the *chap1_cap_capital_solution* presentation.

Insert Clip

Definitely Needlepoint uses a needle and thread as its logo. You decide to use a needle and thread clip on the title slide to continue this identifying image.

a. Move to **Slide 1** and open the Clip Organizer.

b. Type **stitching** in the Search for box and press **Go.**

c. Refer to Figure 1.57 to aid you in locating the needle and thread image.

d. Insert the needle and thread image and position it so that the needle is above the word *Needlepoint* and the tread appears to wrap in and out of the word.

e. Save the *chap1_cap_capital_solution* presentation.

Add Custom Animation

To emphasize the profits that Definitely Needlepoint has made over the last two years, you created two text boxes on Slide 4. You decide to animate these text boxes so that they fly in as you discuss each year. You create custom animations for each box.

a. Move to **Slide 4** and click to select the *Our first year was profitable* text box.

b. Open the Custom Animation task pane and apply a Fly In animation from the Entrance category.

c. Keep the text box selected and click the Add Effect button again. Apply a Fly Out animation from the Exit category. Note the non-printing tags now appear on the text box placeholder indicating the order of the animations.

d. Select the *Our second year was significantly better* text box and then apply a Fly In animation from the Entrance category.

e. Change the Start option to **With Previous,** which will cause this text box to fly in as the other text box flies out.

f. Save the *chap1_cap_capital_solution* presentation.

View and Print the Presentation

You view the presentation to proofread it without the distraction of the PowerPoint creation tools and to check to see if the transitions and animations are applied correctly. When you have proofed the presentation, you print a handout with 4 slides per page to give to the owners so they can see how the presentation is progressing.

a. Click the **Slide Show tab,** and then advance through the presentation. When you get to the table slides, compare the figures with the figures in your text to ensure there are no typographical errors.

b. Exit the slide show and correct any errors.

c. Print handouts in Grayscale, 4 slides per page, and framed.

d. Save the *chap1_cap_capital_solution* presentation and close.

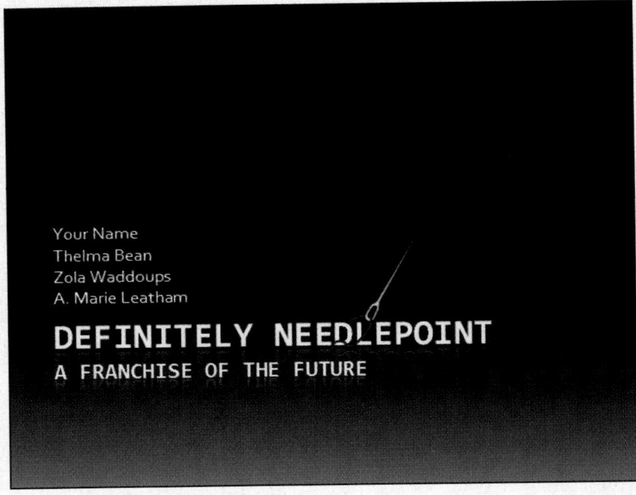

Figure 1.57 Definitely Needlepoint Title Slide

Mini Cases

Use the rubric following the case as a guide to evaluate your work, but keep in mind that your instructor may impose additional grading criteria or use a different standard to judge your work.

Green Scene Lawn Service

GENERAL CASE

You create a yard care service to help supplement your income while going to school. You name the yard service "Green Scene." You decide that one way to get your message out to potential customers is to create a presentation about your services and burn it to a CD. You'll deliver the CD to homes around your neighborhood, knowing that by delivering your message in this format, you are most likely to catch the interest of people with technological savvy—those who are busy spending their time in front of a computer instead of doing yard work.

You provide multiple services that customers can choose from. You mow once a week and cut the lawn one-third of its length at a time, you trim and edge along the foundation of the home and any fence lines, and you use a blower to remove the debris left from the trimming. You aerate the lawn in the spring to relieve soil compaction and increase water infiltration. You fertilize using natural-based, granular fertilizers and include lawn, tree, and shrub fertilization. You apply broadleaf weed control and include a surface insect control when this service is ordered. In the spring, you remove winter debris, dethatch the lawn, and restock mulch beds. In the fall you remove fall leaves and you seed and mulch bare soil patches. Your tree and shrub service includes trimming and removing of trees and shrubs as well as stump removal. You treat the shrubs and trees to protect them from disease.

Create a title slide for your presentation that includes the name of your company and your name. Save your file as **chap1_mc1_greenscene_solution**. Do not worry about burning the presentation to a CD.

Slide 2 should be an introduction slide listing your services:

- Lawn Mowing, Trimming, and Edging
- Aeration, Fertilization,Weed Control
- Spring and Fall Clean-up
- Tree and Shrub Service

Create a slide for each of these topics using the Title and Content layout. The titles for the slides should match the above bullets. Use the case study introductory material to create the content for each slide. Create a summary slide using the Title Slide layout and type **Call today for a free estimate!** in the title placeholder. Include your name and telephone number in the subtitle placeholder. Insert several appropriate clips throughout the presentation, and then resize and position the clips as desired. Apply the design theme of your choice. Reposition, placeholders and modify text as desired. Apply a transition of your choice to all slides.

Performance Elements	Exceeds Expectations	Meets Expectations	Below Expectations
Organization	Presentation is easy to follow because information is presented in a logical interesting sequence.	Presentation is generally easy to follow.	Presentation cannot be understood because there is no sequence of information.
Visual aspects	Presentation background, themes, clip art, and animation are appealing and enhance the understanding of presentation purpose and content. There is a consistent visual theme.	Clip art is related to the topic. Animation enhances the presentation.	The background or theme is distracting to the topic. Clip art does not enhance understanding of the content or is unrelated.
Layout	The layout is visually pleasing and contributes to the overall message with appropriate use of headings, subheadings, bullet points, clip art, and white space.	The layout shows some structure, but placement of some headings, subheadings, bullet points, clip art, and/or white space can be improved.	The layout is cluttered and confusing. Placement of headings, subheadings, bullet points, clip art, and/or white space detracts from readability.
Mechanics	Presentation has no errors in spelling, grammar, word usage, or punctuation. No typographical errors present. Bullet points are parallel.	Presentation has no more than one error in spelling, grammar, word usage, or punctuation. Bullet points are inconsistent in no more than one slide.	Presentation readability is impaired due to repeated errors in spelling, grammar, word usage, or punctuation. Most bullet points are not parallel.

The National Debt

RESEARCH CASE

The national debt is staggering—more than $8 trillion, or approximately $28,000 for every man, woman, and child in the United States. The annual budget is approximately $2 trillion. Use the Internet to obtain exact figures for the current year, then use this information to create a presentation about the national debt. A good place to start your research is the Web site for the United States Department of the Treasury (http://www.treas.gov) where entering National Debt in the FAQ (Frequently Asked Questions) search box brings up several interesting hyperlinks to information that you can use to develop your presentation.

Do some additional research and obtain the national debt for the years 1945 and 1967. The numbers may surprise you. For example, how does the debt for the current year compare to the debt in 1967 (at the height of the Vietnam War)? To the debt in 1945 (at the end of World War II)? Include your references on a Reference slide at the end of your presentation. Save the presentation as **chap1_mc2_debt_solution**.

Performance Elements	Exceeds Expectations	Meets Expectations	Below Expectations
Organization	Presentation indicates accurate research and significant facts. Evidence exists that information has been evaluated and synthesized showing an understanding of the topic.	Presentation indicates some research has taken place and that information was included in the content.	Presentation demonstrates a lack of research or understanding of the topic. Content misinterpreted or incorrect.
Visual aspects	Presentation background, themes, clip art, and animation are appealing and enhance the understanding of presentation purpose and content. There is a consistent visual theme.	Clip art is related to the topic. Animation is not distracting.	The background or theme is distracting to the topic. Clip art does not enhance understanding of the content or is unrelated.
Layout	The layout is visually pleasing and contributes to the overall message with appropriate use of headings, subheadings, bullet points, clip art, and white space.	The layout shows some structure, but placement of some headings, subheadings, bullet points, clip art, and/or white space can be improved.	The layout is cluttered and confusing. Placement of headings, subheadings, bullet points, clip art, and/or white space detracts from readability.
Mechanics	Presentation has no errors in spelling, grammar, word usage, or punctuation. Bullet points are parallel.	Presentation has no more than one error in spelling, grammar, word usage, or punctuation. Bullet points are inconsistent in one slide.	Presentation readability is impaired due to repeated errors in spelling, grammar, word usage, or punctuation. Most bullet points are not parallel.

Planning for Disaster

DISASTER RECOVERY

This case is perhaps the most important case of this chapter as it deals with the question of backup. Do you have a backup strategy? Do you even know what a backup strategy is? This is a good time to learn, because sooner or later you will need to recover a file. The problem always seems to occur the night before an assignment is due. You accidentally erased a file, are unable to read from a storage device like a flash drive, or worse yet, suffer a hardware failure in which you are unable to access the hard drive. The ultimate disaster is the disappearance of your computer, by theft or natural disaster.

Use the Internet to research ideas for backup strategies. Create a title slide and three or four slides related to a backup strategy or ways to protect files. Include a summary on what you plan to implement in conjunction with your work in this class. Choose the design theme, transition, and animations. Save the new presentation as **chap1_mc3_disaster_solution**.

Performance Elements	Exceeds Expectations	Meets Expectations	Below Expectations
Organization	Presentation indicates accurate research and significant facts. Evidence exists that information has been evaluated and synthesized showing an understanding of the topic.	Presentation indicates some research has taken place and the information was included in the content.	Presentation demonstrates a lack of research or understanding of the topic. Content misinterpreted or incorrect.
Visual aspects	Presentation background, themes, clip art, and animation are appealing and enhance the understanding of presentation purpose and content. There is a consistent visual theme.	Clip art is related to the topic. Animation is not distracting.	The background or theme is distracting to the topic. Clip art does not enhance understanding of the content or is unrelated.
Layout	The layout is visually pleasing and contributes to the overall message with appropriate use of headings, subheadings, bullet points, clip art, and white space.	The layout shows some structure, but placement of some headings, subheadings, bullet points, clip art, and/or white space can be improved.	The layout is cluttered and confusing. Placement of headings, subheadings, bullet points, clip art, and/or white space detracts from readability.
Mechanics	Presentation has no errors in spelling, grammar, word usage, or punctuation. Bullet points are parallel.	Presentation has no more than one error in spelling, grammar, word usage, or punctuation. Bullet points are inconsistent in no more than one slide.	Presentation readability is impaired due to repeated errors in spelling, grammar, word usage, or punctuation. Most bullet points are not parallel.

chapter 1 | **Window XP**

Getting Started with Windows XP

After you read this chapter, you will be able to:

1. Identify components on the Windows desktop **(page 559)**.
2. Work with windows and menus **(page 562)**.
3. Identify dialog box components **(page 566)**.
4. Use the Help and Support Center **(page 567)**.
5. Work with folders **(page 572)**.
6. Manage folders and files in Windows Explorer **(page 574)**.
7. Delete items and manage the Recycle Bin **(page 576)**.
8. Change the display settings **(page 584)**.
9. Change computer settings using the Control Panel **(page 585)**.
10. Create shortcuts on the desktop and Quick Launch toolbar **(page 589)**.
11. Use Windows Desktop Search **(page 591)**.

Hands-On Exercises

Exercises	Skills Covered
1. INTRODUCTION TO WINDOWS XP (page 569)	• Turn On the Computer and Select a Username • Modify the Start Menu • Move, Size, and Close a Window • Get Help
2. FILE AND FOLDER MANAGEMENT (page 579)	• Change a Window View • Create and Rename a Folder • Move and Delete a Folder • Create and Save a File
3. CUSTOMIZING YOUR SYSTEM (page 593)	• Customize the Desktop • Create a Desktop Shortcut • Use Windows Desktop Search to Locate Files • Use Control Panel to Customize System Settings • Add a User Account • Add a Shortcut to the Quick Launch Toolbar

CASE STUDY

Virginia Beach Properties

Case Study

Jessica and Brian Street own Virginia Beach Properties, a property management company specializing in managing vacation and long-term rental homes. It is a small and very successful business, due to the business acumen of its owners. Jessica recently graduated with an MBA; Brian has an MIS degree. Both love living and working out of their home on the beach. Brian is in charge of maintaining their database, which contains information about the rental homes and their owners, existing tenants, and pending rental requests. It is an elaborate, user-friendly system that is backed up daily. The backup files are stored onsite for easy access.

The idea for the business stemmed from Jessica's initial experience renting her family's beach home. Her parents were unable to enjoy the home as often as they would like but they were reluctant to sell. They wanted to keep the property in the family and wanted the additional income it could provide. Jessica and Brian started with one property and built the business from there. That was five years ago, and the business has prospered. No major problems existed until the day that Hurricane Isabel came to town.

Brian backed up his files regularly. He assured Jessica that they were protected against computer crashes, viruses, lost files, and so on. He never anticipated a hurricane. Their home was completely destroyed, and the backup media were lost in the ensuing flood damage. Brian was stunned. All he could say to Jessica as they sifted through the wreckage was, "It should not have happened."

Your Assignment

- Read the chapter, paying special attention to the topic of file management.
- Think about how the owners of this business could have avoided the disaster had an appropriate backup strategy been in place.
- Summarize your thoughts in a one-page report, describing the elements of a basic backup strategy. Refer to the Windows XP Help and Support Center for specific information on backing up files and include that research in your report.
- In your report, give several other examples of unforeseen circumstances that can cause data to be lost.
- Save your report as **chap1_case_report_solution.docx**.

Basics of Windows XP

Windows XP is the primary operating system for personal computers.

Windows XP is a popular version of the very successful series of Windows operating systems. Although ***Windows Vista*** is newer and more powerful, you will continue to see Windows XP utilized on many home and business computers for quite some time. Windows XP looks slightly different from earlier versions, but it maintains the conventions of its various predecessors. You have seen the Windows interface many times, but do you really understand it? Can you move and copy files with confidence? Do you know how to back up the Excel spreadsheets, Access databases, and other documents that you work so hard to create? If not, now is the time to learn.

(You have seen the Windows interface many times, but do you really understand it?)

Windows Vista is the newest version of the Windows operating system.

Windows XP Home Edition focuses on entertainment and home use.

Windows XP Professional Edition is designed to support business systems.

Windows XP Media Center Edition coordinates multimedia elements.

Windows XP is available in several versions. ***Windows XP Home Edition*** is intended for entertainment and home use. It includes a media player, support for digital photography, and an instant messenger. ***Windows XP Professional Edition*** has all of the features of the Home Edition plus additional security to encrypt files and protect data. It includes support for high-performance multiprocessor systems. It also lets you connect to your computer from a remote station. ***Windows XP Media Center Edition*** enables you to enjoy video, audio, pictures, and television on your computer monitor. Along with a remote control, the simple layout and intuitive menus enhance the multimedia experience.

A login screen is displayed when the computer is powered on initially or when you switch from one user account to another. Windows XP makes it possible to create several user accounts, each with unique privileges. As the primary user of your computer, your account possesses administrative privileges, enabling you to create other user accounts and maintain your system. Individual ***user accounts*** retain individual desktop settings, a lists of favorite and recently visited Web sites, and other customized Windows settings (such as desktop background). Multiple users can be logged on simultaneously through a feature known as ***fast user switching***.

Fast user switching is a Windows feature that enables you to quickly move from one user account to another.

In this section, you begin by identifying components on the Windows desktop and taskbar. Then you learn how to work with windows. In particular, you learn how to move and size windows, use menus within windows, and identify components of a dialog box.

Identifying Components on the Windows Desktop

The ***desktop*** contains icons and a taskbar. It is displayed when a computer first boots up.

An ***icon*** is a pictorial element representing a program, file, Web site, or shortcut.

Windows XP creates a working environment for your computer that parallels the working environment at home or in an office. You work at a desk. Windows operations take place on the ***desktop***. You can place physical objects, such as folders, a dictionary, a calculator, or a phone, on a desk. The computer equivalents of those objects appear as ***icons*** (pictorial symbols) on the desktop. Each object on a real desk has attributes (properties) such as size, weight, and color. In similar fashion, Windows assigns properties to every object on its desktop. And just as you can move objects on a real desk, you can rearrange the objects on the Windows desktop. The Windows XP desktop (see Figure 1.1) contains standard elements that enable you to access files and other system resources.

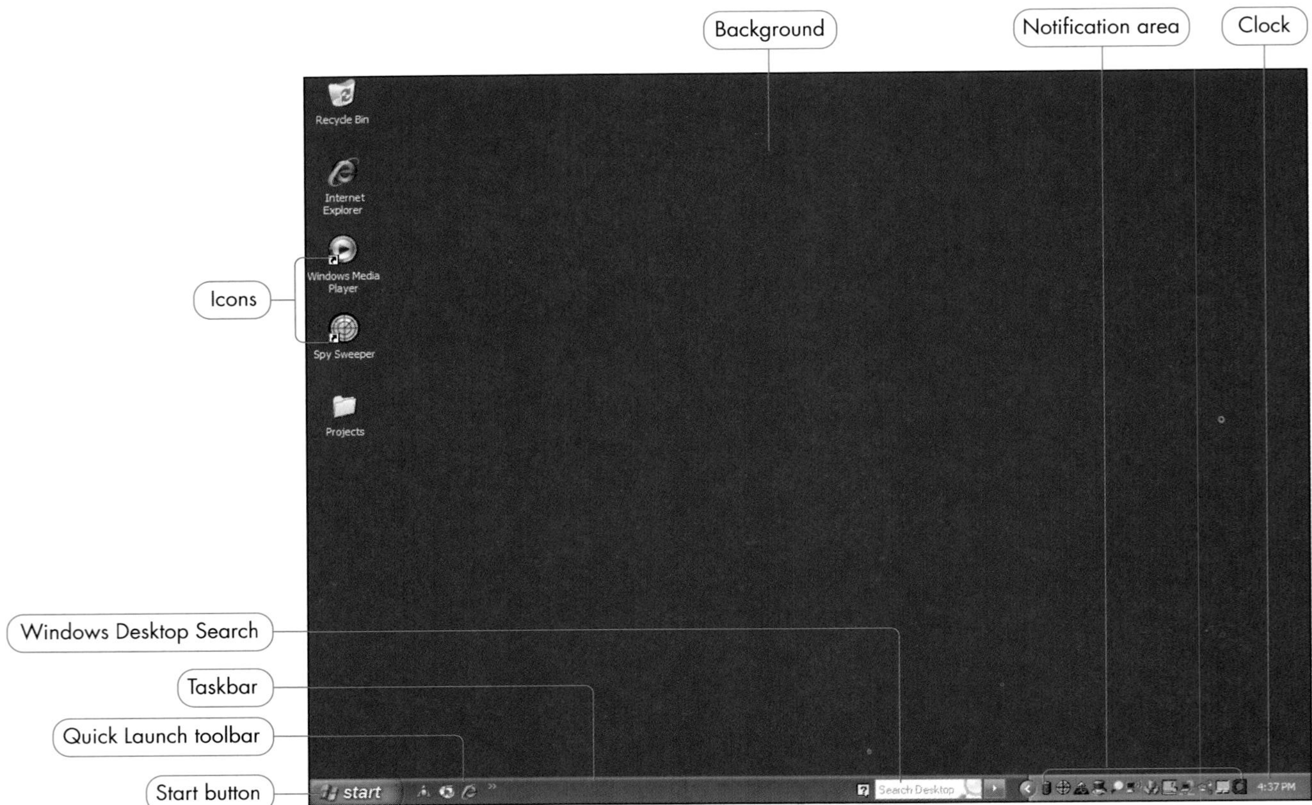

Figure 1.1 The Windows XP Desktop

Your desktop may contain different icons or may be arranged differently than desktops on other computers. That is because each computer has different programs, and each desktop can be customized to suit a user's preferences. Moreover, you are likely to work on different systems—at school, at work, or at home—so desktops are likely to be different. What is important is that you recognize the common functionality that is present on all desktops.

Use the Taskbar

The ***taskbar*** is the horizontal bar that enables you to move among open windows and provides access to system resources.

The ***Start button*** provides access to programs and other system resources.

The ***Start menu*** is displayed when you click the Start button.

At the bottom of the desktop is the ***taskbar***, a horizontal strip that contains the Start button, the Quick Launch toolbar, button area, Windows Desktop Search, and the Notification area. These taskbar sections are discussed in the following paragraphs.

The ***Start button***, as its name suggests, is where you begin. Click Start to see a menu of programs and other functions. The ***Start menu*** is divided into two columns (see Figure 1.2). The left column displays the pinned items list, typically an Internet browser program and an e-mail program that are "pinned" to the top of the column, and a list of the most recently used programs. As you work with programs, the recently used program list changes based on the frequency of usage. The bottom of the left column also contains the All Programs option. Position the mouse over All Programs to see a list of all programs installed on your computer. The right column of the Start menu provides access to Windows folders such as My Music, My Documents, and My Pictures. The right column also contains entries for the Control Panel, Help and Support, and Search.

Although the Windows XP Start menu is typically a two-column display, you can modify the menu so that it appears as only one column. Right-click an empty area of the taskbar and select Properties. Click the Start menu tab in the Taskbar and Start Menu Properties dialog box. Click the Classic Start menu option and click OK.

Figure 1.2 The Windows XP Start Menu

TIP Displaying the Start Menu from the Keyboard

Instead of clicking the Start button to display the Start menu, you can press the Windows button on the keyboard.

The ***Quick Launch toolbar*** contains program icons, making it possible to open programs with a single click.

The ***Notification area***, found at the right side of the taskbar, displays icons for background programs and system processes.

Windows Desktop Search helps you find anything on your computer.

The ***Quick Launch toolbar*** is located just to the right of the Start button. Each button on the Quick Launch toolbar represents a program that you can quickly launch with a single click. For example, the Quick launch toolbar in Figure 1.2 contains icons that you can click to quickly launch America Online and Internet Explorer. If the Quick Launch toolbar is not visible on your taskbar, you can right-click a blank area of the taskbar, select Toolbars from the shortcut menu, and then select Quick Launch.

The third section of the taskbar displays buttons for all open programs. In Figure 1.1, the button area is empty because no programs are open. The clock at the far right side of the taskbar displays the time. If your mouse pointer hovers over the time, you also will see the day of the week and the current date. To the left of the clock is the ***Notification area*** that displays buttons for such items as volume control, wireless network connections, Windows updates, and background programs (programs that are active when your computer is on, like anti-virus software). It also provides a button that enables you to safely remove hardware, such as a flash (USB) drive (described later in this chapter). If you have installed ***Windows Desktop Search***, the search bar will appear to the left of the Notification area. Using Desktop Search, you can quickly find files, folders, programs, e-mail, and calendar appointments.

Working with Windows and Menus

A ***window*** is an enclosed rectangular area representing a program or data.

Multitasking is the ability to run more than one program at a time.

Each ***window*** displays a program or a folder that is currently in use. Figure 1.3 displays a desktop with four open program windows. The ability to run several programs at the same time is known as ***multitasking***, and it is a major benefit of the Windows environment. For example, you can create a document using a word processor in one window, create a spreadsheet in a second window, surf the Internet in a third window, play a game in a fourth window, and so on. You can work in a program as long as you want and then change to a different program by clicking its window or clicking its button on the taskbar.

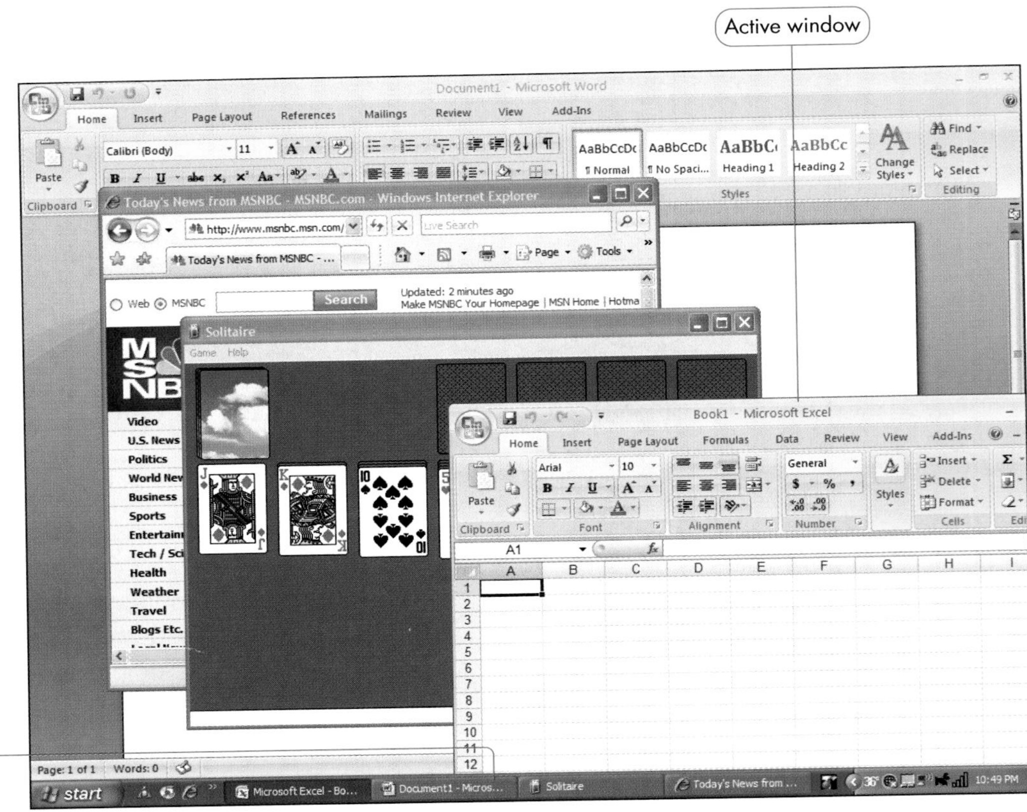

Figure 1.3 Multiple Windows

Move and Size a Window

At times, you will need to resize or move a window. Perhaps you need to resize a window so that you can see icons on the desktop. Or maybe you just want to move a window because part of it appears off screen and you cannot see a critical component. To resize a window, point to any border (the pointer changes to a double arrow) and drag the border in the direction you want to go—inward to shrink the window or outward to enlarge it. You also can drag a corner, instead of a border, to change both dimensions at the same time. To move a window, click and drag the title bar (the shaded bar at the top of the window) to a new position on the desktop. When you release the mouse button, the window moves to its new location.

Identify the Anatomy of a Window

The ***task pane*** is a bar that provides support for a currently selected item or window.

All Windows applications share a common user interface and exhibit a consistent command structure. That means that every Windows application works essentially the same way, providing a sense of familiarity from one application to another. In other words, once you learn the basic concepts and techniques in one application, you can apply that knowledge to every other application.

The My Computer window in Figure 1.4 displays the storage drives on a particular computer system. The computer has one hard drive and a DVD/CD-RW drive. The ***task pane***, displayed at the left of the window, provides easy access to various commands such as viewing system information and adding or removing programs.

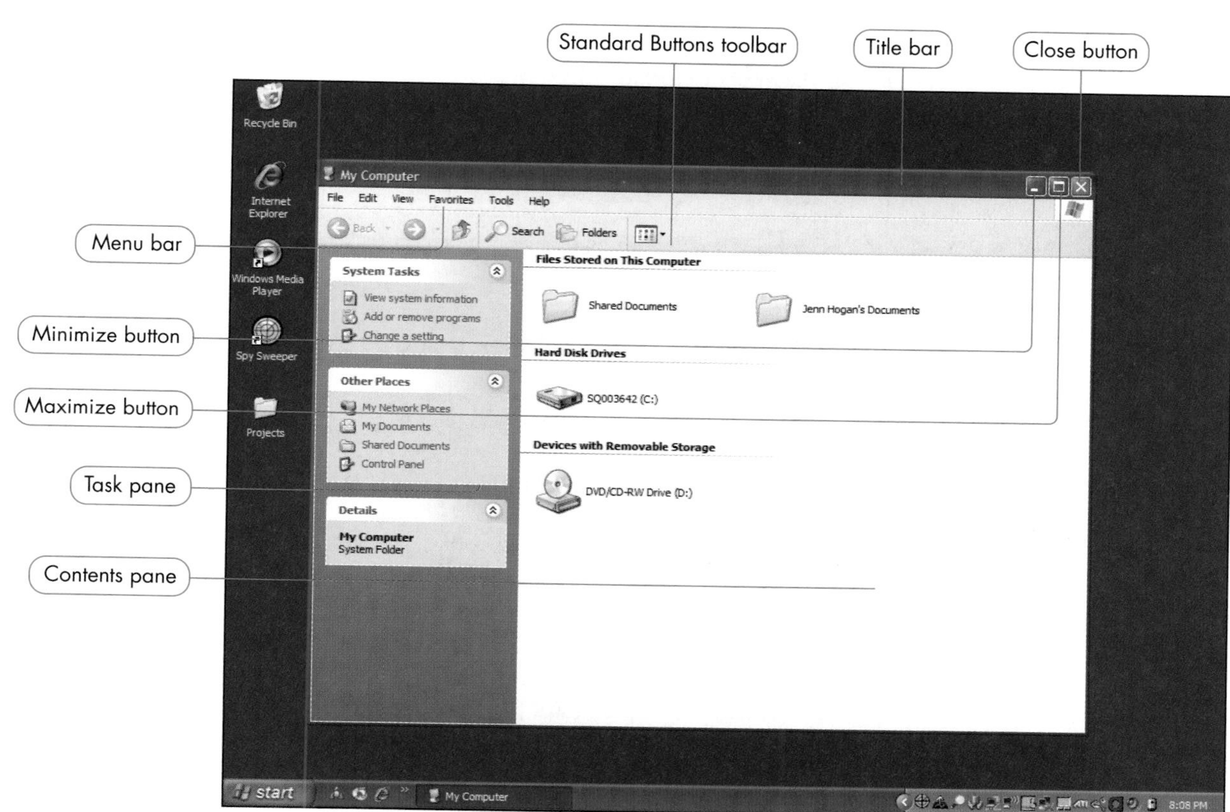

Figure 1.4 My Computer

The ***title bar*** is the shaded bar at the top of every window.

The ***Minimize button*** removes a window from view but not from memory.

The ***Maximize button*** causes a window to fill the screen.

The ***Restore Down button*** returns a window to the size it was before it was maximized.

The ***title bar*** appears at the top of every window, displaying the name of the folder or application. The icon at the extreme left of the title bar identifies the window and also provides access to a control menu with operations relevant to the window, such as moving it or sizing it. Three buttons appear at the right of the title bar. The ***Minimize button*** shrinks the window to a button on the taskbar but leaves the window open in memory. The ***Maximize button*** enlarges the window so that it fills the entire desktop. The ***Restore Down button*** (not shown in Figure 1.4) appears instead of the Maximize button after a window has been maximized, displaying the window in its previous size. The ***Close button*** closes the window and removes it from memory and the desktop.

The **_Close button_** removes a window from memory.

A **_drop-down menu_** displays more selections pertaining to the menu item.

A **_menu bar_** is a horizontal bar at the top of a window containing options to enable you to work with an application.

A **_toolbar_**, usually found at the top or side of a window, contains buttons that are accessed more quickly than menu selections.

A **_status bar_** displays summary information about the selected window or object.

A **_scroll bar_** enables you to control which part of a window is in view at any time.

The **_menu bar_** appears immediately below the title bar. When you click an item on the menu bar, you will see a **_drop-down menu_** with more selections pertaining to the menu item. One or more **_toolbars_** appear below the menu bar and let you execute a command by clicking a button, as opposed to selecting from a menu. Figure 1.4 includes a Standard Buttons toolbar.

The **_status bar_** at the bottom of a window, as shown in Figure 1.5, displays information about the entire window or about a selected object within a window. A vertical (or horizontal) **_scroll bar_** appears at the right (or bottom) border of a window when the window's contents are not completely visible. The scroll bar provides access to unseen areas. The vertical scroll bar along the right border of the contents pane in Figure 1.5 implies that additional items are available that are not currently visible. A horizontal scroll bar does not appear because the display of objects in the currently selected folder extends out of view vertically, but not horizontally, on the screen.

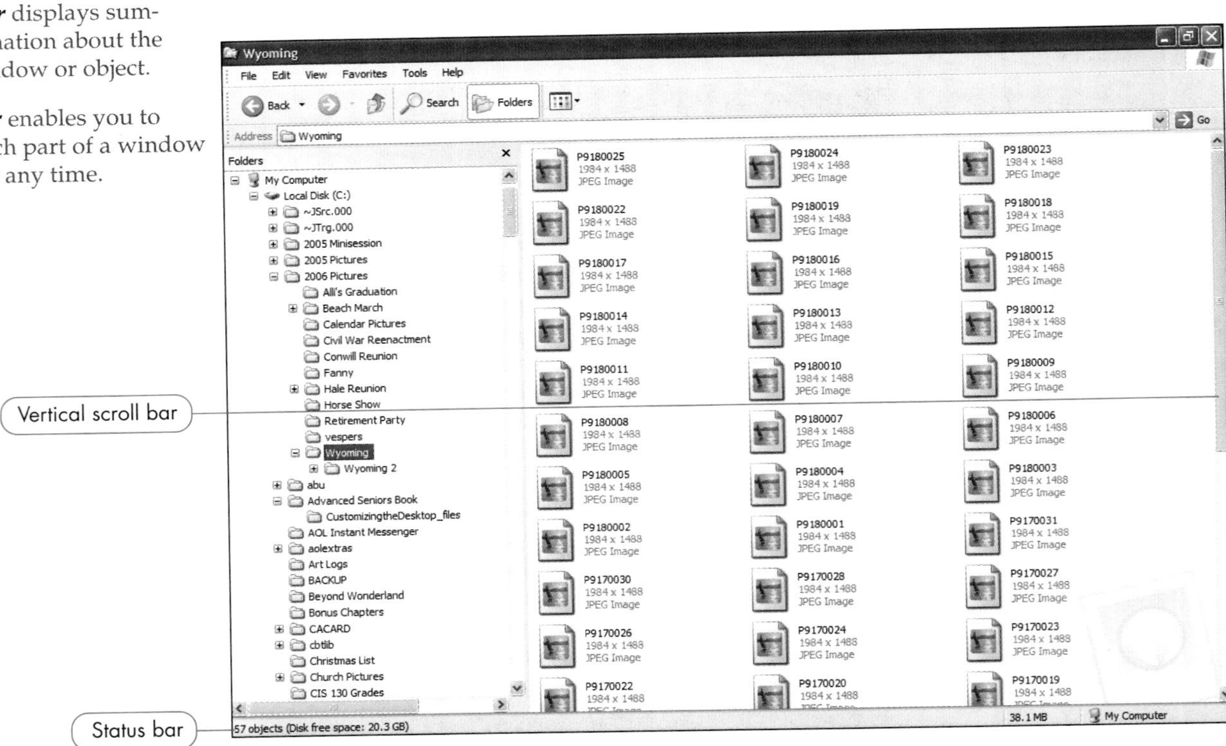

Figure 1.5 Common Window Elements (Status Bar and Scroll Bar)

Display Menus

The menu bar provides access to commands within an application (program). When you click a menu bar item, a drop-down menu appears, listing commands that relate to the menu name. You also can activate a menu bar item by pressing the Alt key plus the underlined letter in the menu name; for example, press Alt+V to select from the View menu.

From a drop-down menu, you can make a selection by clicking a command or by typing the underlined letter. Figure 1.6 shows the menu that results from clicking Edit on the menu bar. From the menu, you can click a selection or you can bypass the menu entirely if you know the equivalent shortcuts shown to the right of the command in the menu. For example, the shortcut key combinations Ctrl+X, Ctrl+C, and Ctrl+V respectively cut, copy, and paste. A dimmed (ghosted) command, such as the Paste command, means that the command is not currently available and that some additional action has to be taken for the command to become available. In the case of the Paste command, you would first have to copy an item or text before it could be pasted.

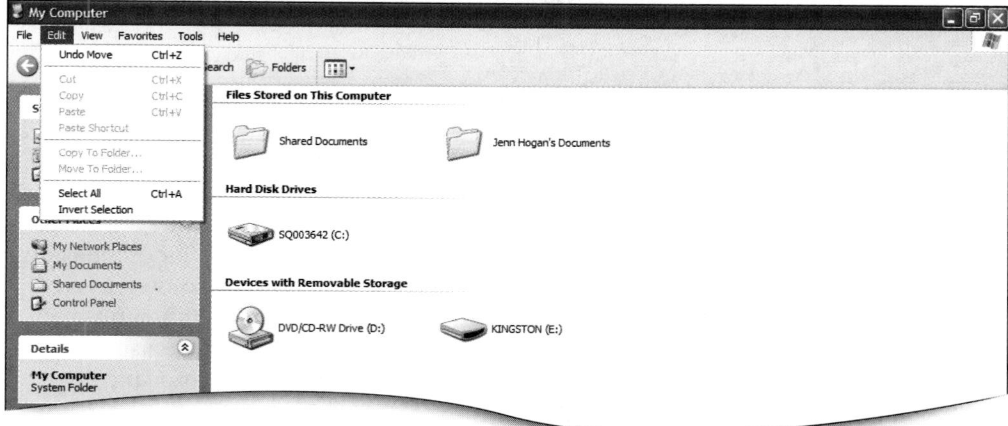

Figure 1.6 Edit Menu

An ellipsis (. . .) following a menu selection indicates that additional information is required to execute the command. For example, if you select Format from the File menu (after having selected a disk drive), as shown in Figure 1.7, you will have to provide or confirm additional information about the formatting process, such as which disk to format. A dialog box, which is a special window that enables you to change settings or make selections, appears after such a menu item is selected.

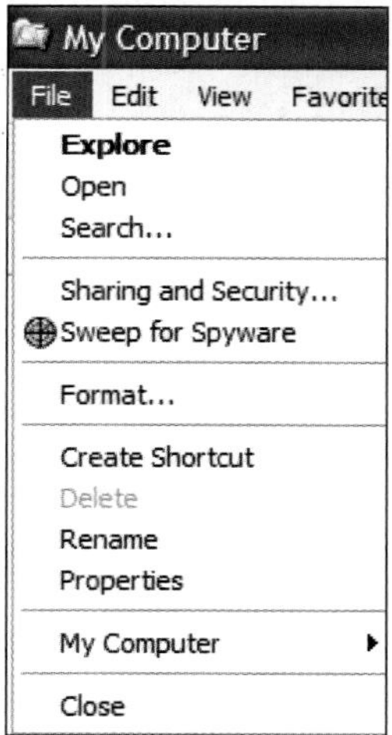

Figure 1.7 File Menu

A check next to a menu command is a toggle switch indicating whether the command is on or off. Figure 1.8 shows a check next to Status Bar in the View menu, which means that the status bar is displayed. Click Status Bar and the check disappears suppressing the display of the status bar. Click the command a second time and the check reappears, as does the status bar in the associated window.

Figure 1.8 View Menu

A **thumbnail** is a miniature display of a folder or page.

A bullet next to an item, such as Tiles in the View menu, indicates a selection from a set of mutually exclusive choices. Click a different option within the group, such as ***thumbnails***, and the bullet will move from the previous selection (Tiles) to the new selection (Thumbnails), providing a different view.

An arrow after a command, like the one beside Arrange Icons by in the View menu, indicates that a submenu (also known as a cascaded menu) will display additional menu options. To access such a submenu, you do not actually have to click the main selection (Arrange Icons by, in this case). Simply pointing to it with the mouse pointer should cause the submenu to appear.

Identify Dialog Box Components

A ***dialog box*** is a special window that requests input or presents information.

A ***dialog box*** appears when additional information is necessary to execute a command. Figure 1.9 shows a typical dialog box, displayed when you are printing a document. The dialog box requests information about precisely what to print and how to print it. The information is entered into the dialog box in different ways, depending on the type of information that is required.

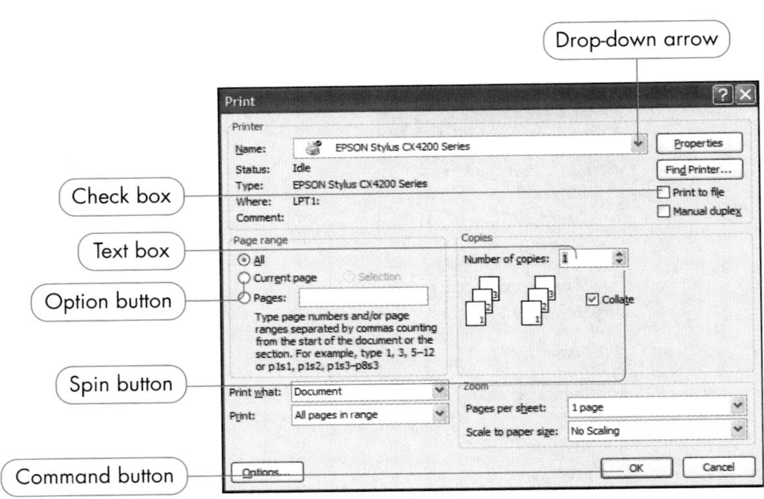

Figure 1.9 Print Dialog Box

An ***option button***, or ***radio button***, is a mutually exclusive selection in a dialog box.

A ***text box*** enables you to give an instruction by typing in a box.

Option buttons, sometimes called ***radio buttons***, indicate mutually exclusive choices, one of which *must* be chosen, such as the page range. In this example you can print all pages, the selection (if it is available), the current page, or a specific set of pages (such as pages 1–4), but you can choose *one and only one* option. Any time you select (click) an option, the previous option is automatically deselected.

A ***text box***, such as the one shown beside the *Pages* option in Figure 1.9, enables you to enter specific information. In this case, you could type *1–5* in the text box if

A ***spin button*** is a dialog box feature with an up or down arrow to increase or decrease a value.

you wanted only the first five pages to print. A ***spin button*** is a common component of a dialog box, providing a quick method of increasing or decreasing a setting. For example, clicking the spin button (or spinner) beside *Number of copies* enables you to increase or decrease the number of copies of the document to print. You also can enter the information explicitly by typing it into the text box beside the spin button.

A ***check box*** enables you to select one or more items that are not mutually exclusive.

A ***list box*** presents several items, any of which can be selected.

Check boxes are used instead of option buttons if the choices are not mutually exclusive. The Collate check box in Figure 1.9 is checked; Print to file is not. You can select or clear options by clicking the appropriate check box, which toggles the operation on and off. A ***list box*** (not shown in Figure 1.9) displays some or all of the available choices, any of which can be selected by clicking the list item.

The Help button (a question mark at the right end of the title bar) provides help for any item in the dialog box. Click the button, and then click the item in the dialog box for which you want additional information. The Close button (the X at the extreme right of the title bar) closes the dialog box without accepting any changes that you might have made.

A ***command button*** is a dialog box item that you click to accept or cancel selections.

All dialog boxes also contain one or more ***command buttons*** that provide options to either accept or cancel your selections. The OK button in Figure 1.9, for example, initiates the printing process. The Cancel button does just the opposite. It ignores (cancels) any changes made to the settings and closes the dialog box.

Using the Help and Support Center

The ***Help and Support Center*** provides assistance on Windows topics.

The ***Help and Support Center*** combines such traditional features as a search function and an index of help topics. It also lets you request remote help from other Windows XP users, or you can access the Microsoft Knowledge Base on the Microsoft Web site. Access Help and Support by clicking Start and Help and Support. As shown in Figure 1.10, Help and Support combines a toolbar, a Search bar, and basic information, some of which is updated daily.

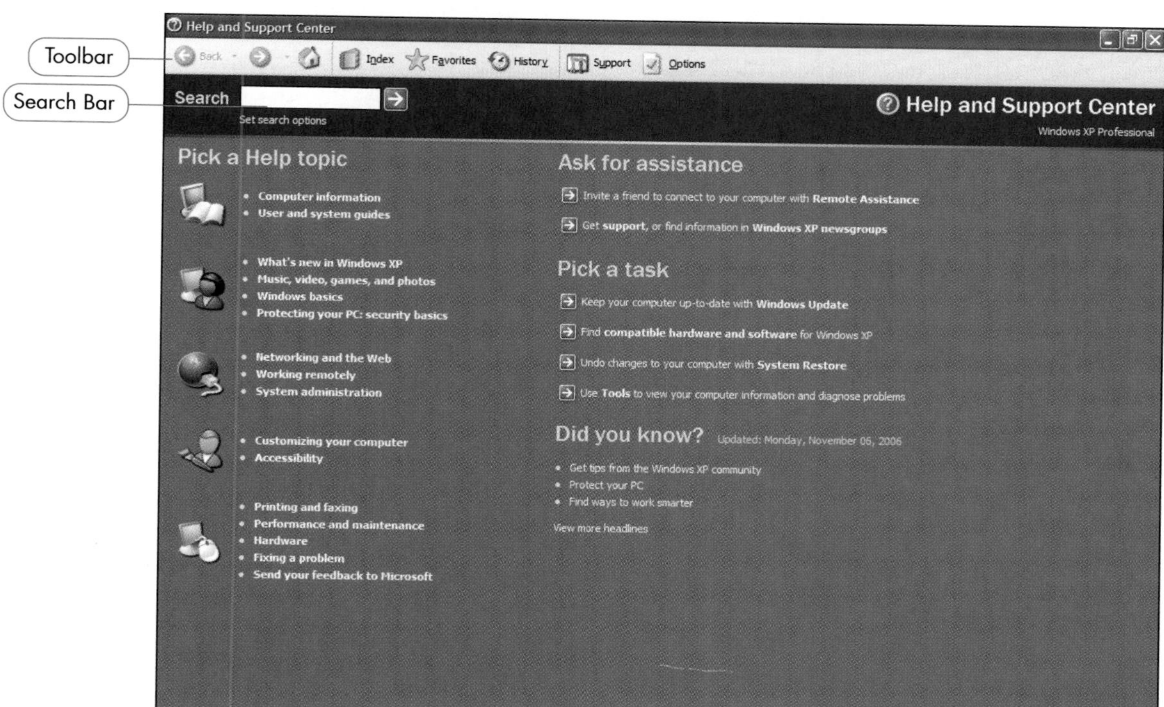

Figure 1.10 Help and Support Center

Windows provides several ways to obtain help on a particular topic. To get quick assistance with a Windows topic, you can use the index feature. Click Index on the toolbar and type a topic in the "Type in the keyword to find" text box. As you type, the Help center narrows the results to match your text. By the time you finish typing, you should see a list of subtopics, if any are available. If you see none, you might try rephrasing the search topic in the index box. You might think, for example, that there is not much to know about the mouse, except how to click and double-click. However, take a look at Figure 1.11, which shows resulting subtopics from an index search on *mouse*. Just about everything you would ever want to know about the mouse is there!

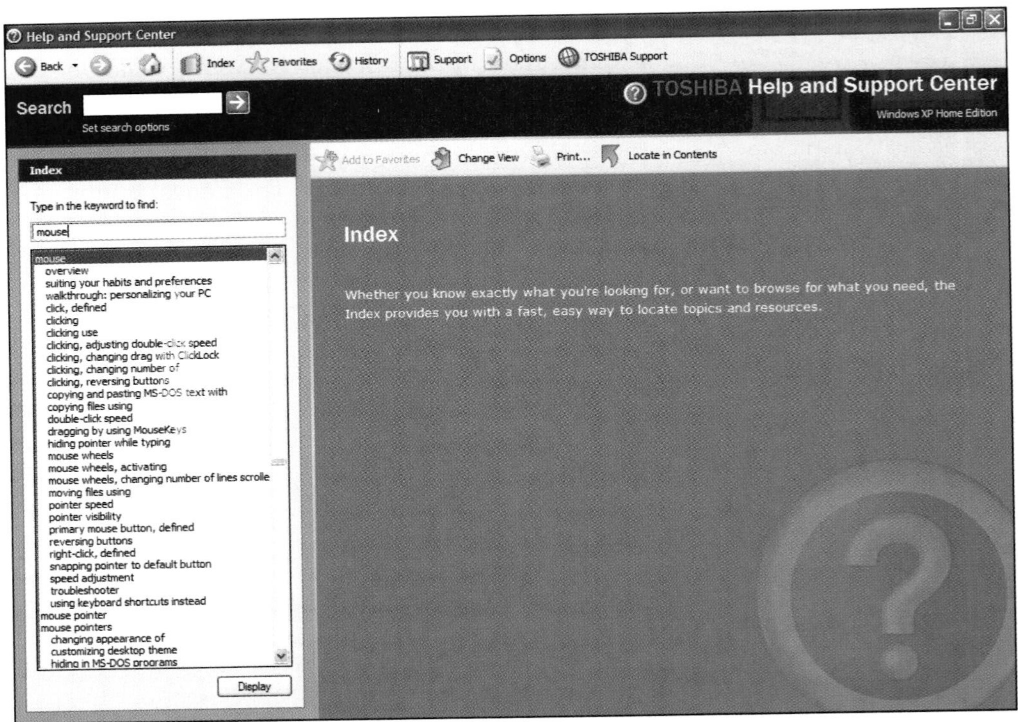

Figure 1.11 Mouse Subtopics

Help and Support also provides a broader search tool that includes information from the Microsoft Knowledge Base, a collection of support on Microsoft tools. Type a topic in the *Search* box and click the green arrow to the right. Results are presented in order of relevance, with the most relevant shown first.

The toolbar at the top of the window contains several buttons that make it easy to navigate through Help and Support. The Back and Forward buttons enable you to move through the various pages that were viewed in the current session. The Favorites button displays a list of previously saved Help topics from previous sessions. The History button shows all pages that were visited in this session. The Support button enables you to get help from a friend or a support professional. You can customize your view of the Help and Support Center through the Options button.

Hands-On Exercise

1 | Introduction to Windows XP

Skills covered: 1. Turn On the Computer and Select a Username **2.** Modify the Start Menu **3.** Move, Size, and Close a Window **4.** Get Help

Step 1 Turn on the Computer and Select a Username

Refer to Figure 1.12 as you complete Step 1.

a. Power on the computer by pressing the power switch.

b. If presented with a choice of one or more user accounts, click the appropriate account. Respond to a password request if prompted.

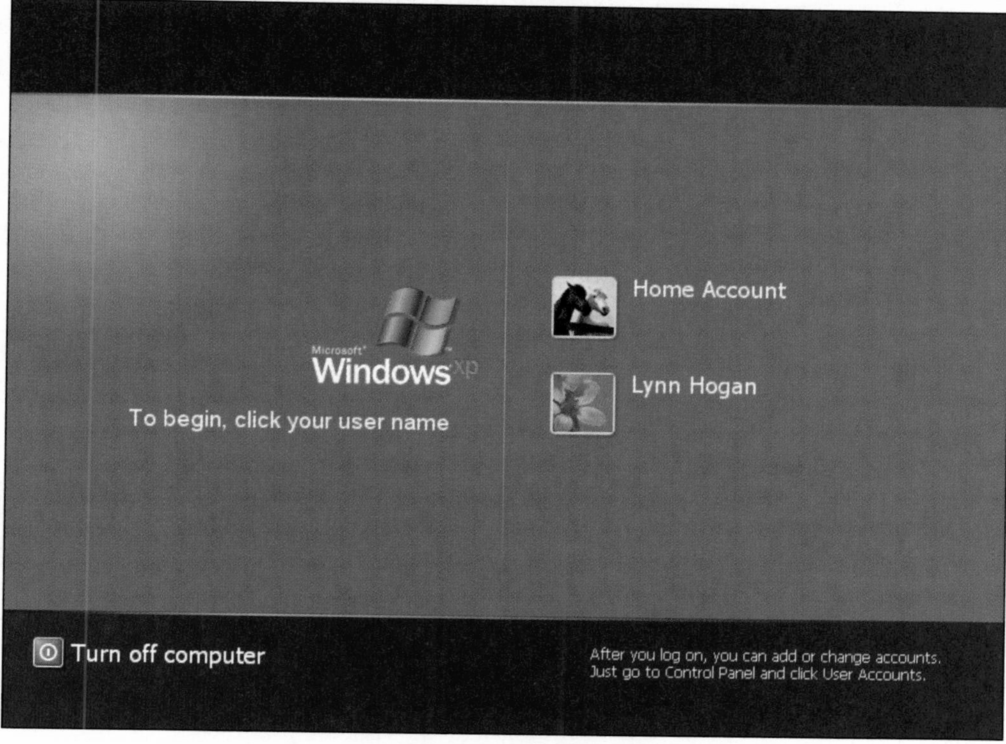

Figure 1.12 User Accounts

Step 2 Modify the Start Menu

Refer to Figure 1.13 as you complete Step 2.

a. Right-click a blank area of the taskbar and select **Properties**.

   The Taskbar and Start Menu Properties dialog box appears.

b. Click the **Start Menu tab**, click the **Classic Start menu option**, and then click **OK**.

   The Start menu will display in the standard one-column Classic view instead of the Windows XP view.

   TROUBLESHOOTING: If you do not see a menu containing the Properties option, you right-clicked an occupied area of the taskbar instead of an empty part. Try the procedure again, this time being careful to click an unoccupied area.

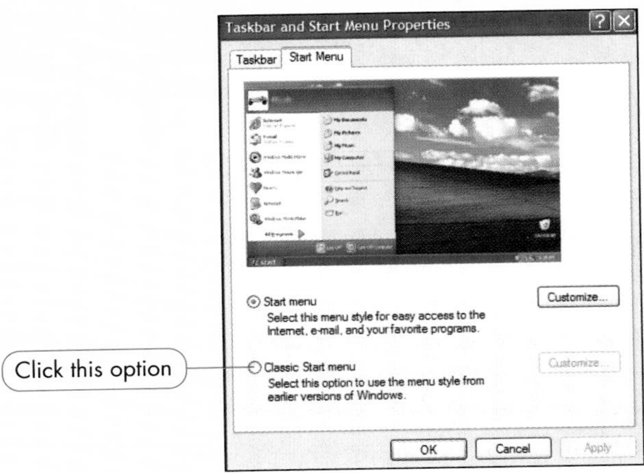

Figure 1.13 Taskbar and Start Menu Properties

c. Change the Start menu back to the Windows XP view by repeating the directions given in Steps 1a and b, but click the **Start menu option**.

The Start menu now displays in the two-column Windows XP view.

Step 3
Move, Size, and Close a Window

Refer to Figure 1.14 as you complete Step 3.

a. Click the **Start button**, and then click **My Computer**. Move and size the window to match that shown in Figure 1.14.

TROUBLESHOOTING: The My Computer window may open as a maximized window. In that case, you cannot move or resize it. You must first Restore Down by clicking the middle control button before you can move or resize it.

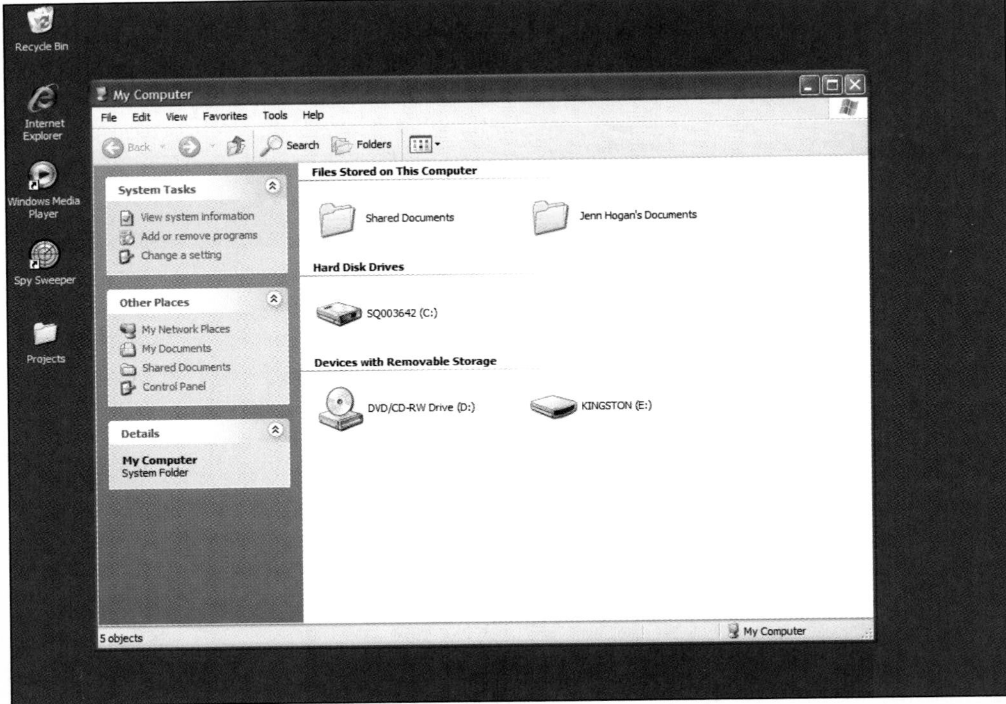

Figure 1.14 Moving and Resizing a Window

To move a window, click and drag the title bar. To resize a window, click and drag a border or corner of the window.

b. Click the **Minimize button** to minimize the window.

My Computer is still open, although you no longer see the window. You should see a button on the taskbar letting you know the window is still open.

c. Click **My Computer** on the taskbar to display the window on the desktop again.

d. Click the **Maximize button** to expand the My Computer window.

e. Click the **Restore Down button** to return the window to its previous size.

f. Click the **Close button** to close My Computer.

Step 4
Get Help

Refer to Figure 1.15 as you complete Step 4.

a. Click **Start** and click **Help and Support**.

b. Click **Index**. The insertion point appears in a text box where you can enter a search topic. Type **mouse** to see an immediate list of topics that relate to *mouse*.

Suppose that you are left-handed and are seeking help for adjusting the mouse so that the buttons are reversed. You can use Help and Support to get assistance.

c. Find and click the *reversing buttons* topic. Click the **Display** button at the bottom of the task pane. Your results should be similar to Figure 1.15.

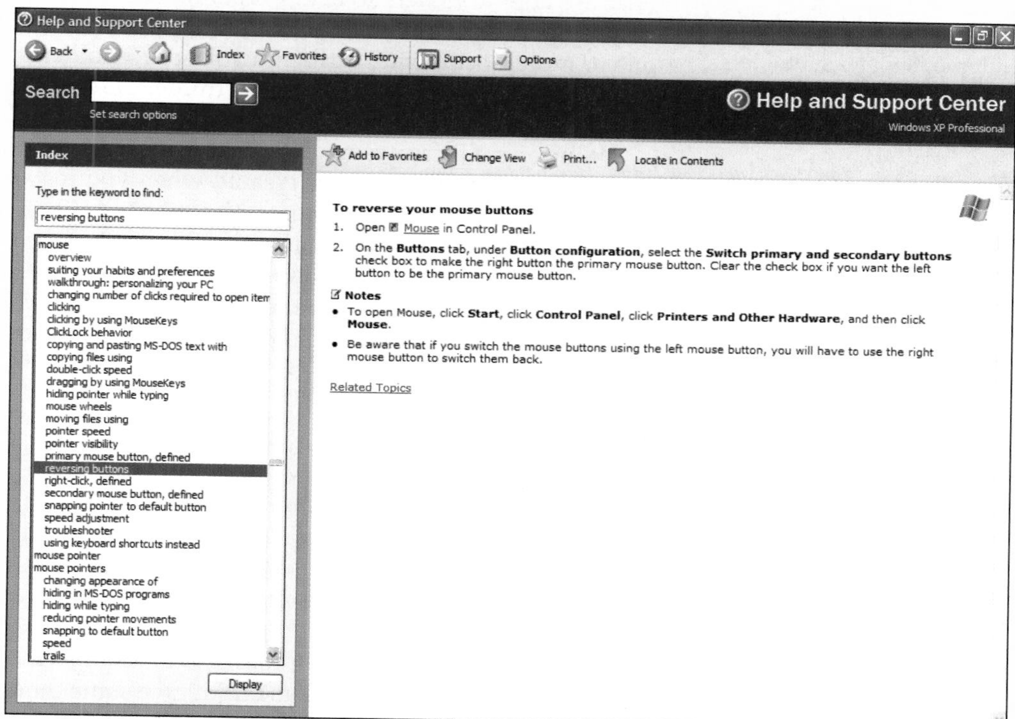

Figure 1.15 Help with Reversing Mouse Buttons

d. Click **Print** to print the Help topic.

e. Click the **Close button** to close Help and Support.

Files and Folders

A ***file*** is a collection of data or information that has a name.

A ***program file*** is part of a software program, such as Microsoft Word.

A ***data file*** is an item that you create and to which you give a name, such as a document.

A ***file name*** is an identifier that you give a file when you save it.

A ***file*** is a set of instructions or data that has been given a name and stored. Two basic types of files exist: ***program files*** and ***data files***. Microsoft Word and Microsoft Excel are examples of program files. The documents and workbooks that you create using these programs are called data files. A program file is executable; it contains instructions that tell the computer what to do. A data file is not executable; it can be used only in conjunction with a specific program. In other words, by using a program file, such as Microsoft Word, you can create data files, like documents that are important to you.

Every file has a ***file name*** that identifies it to the operating system. The file name can contain up to 255 characters and may include spaces and other punctuation. File names cannot contain the following characters: \, /, :, *, ?, ", <, >, and | . Rather than remember the characters to avoid, you might find it easier to limit the characters in a file name to letters, numbers, and spaces. In the Exploring series, underlines are used rather than spaces.

It is important that you learn to work with folders so that you can better organize your storage devices.

In this section, you work with folders. Specifically, you learn how to create, rename, and delete folders. Then you learn how to change the view of folder contents. It is important that you learn to work with folders so that you can better organize your storage devices. Just as you can design your own method of organizing folders in a filing cabinet, you also can design folder structure on your hard drive or another storage medium.

Working with Folders

A ***folder*** is an object or container that can hold multiple files and subfolders.

Files are kept in ***folders*** to better organize the thousands of files on a typical system. A computer folder is similar to a file folder that you might keep in your office to hold one or more documents. Although your office folder probably is kept in a filing cabinet, Windows stores its files in electronic folders that are located on a hard drive, CD, flash drive, or other storage device.

Windows XP creates many folders automatically, such as My Computer or My Documents. Other folders are created when you install new software. You can even create folders to hold documents and other files that you develop. You might, for example, create a folder for your word processing documents and a second folder for your spreadsheets. You could create a folder to hold all of your work for a specific class, which in turn might contain a combination of word processing documents and spreadsheets. Remember, a folder can contain program files, data files, or even other folders.

Create, Rename, and Delete Folders

As you create files, such as letters or worksheets, you will want to save them so that you can easily find them later. The key is to create and name folders appropriately, so that your files are categorized in a system that makes sense to you. Creating, renaming, and deleting folders is a simple process and one with which you should become very familiar.

The first step in creating a folder is to identify the storage device on which you plan to place the folder. You also might give some thought to any subfolders that will be necessary. For example, if you are saving assignments for all classes in which you are enrolled this semester, you might create a folder named Spring Semester on your flash drive. Within the Spring Semester folder, you could include a separate folder for each class, such as English Composition and Biology. To create a folder, open My Computer by clicking Start and then My Computer. Click the Folders button on the Standard buttons toolbar to display a folder hierarchy in the left (folders) pane. Click My Computer (in the left pane) to expand the folder view. You should see all of the storage devices on your system. Because you want to place the Spring Semester folder on your flash drive, click the drive letter that corresponds with your flash drive, such as Removable Disk (E:). Click File in the menu bar and point to New. When a cascaded menu appears, select Folder. You will see a New Folder icon. Type a folder name, such as Spring Semester, and press Enter. You now have a folder named Spring Semester. Although the folder does not yet contain any files, the folder is available. As you create subsequent folders and subfolders, remember to first click the drive or folder under which you want the new folder to appear before creating the folder.

At times, a folder may be named inappropriately. Perhaps you misspelled a word, or the folder's purpose has changed so that a new name is necessary. Renaming a folder is a simple process. First, open My Computer and change the view to Folders by clicking Folders on the Standard buttons toolbar. Expand My Computer by clicking it (in the left pane) and navigate to the folder that you want to rename. When you locate the folder, right-click it and select Rename on the shortcut menu. Type the folder's new name and press Enter.

TIP Using F2 to Rename Folders

You can rename a folder by clicking it, and then pressing F2 on the keyboard. Type the new folder name, and press Enter.

When you delete a folder, the folder and all of its subfolders and files are removed. It is important, therefore, to be certain that you no longer need a folder or its contents before you delete it. To delete a folder, right-click the folder and select Delete from the shortcut menu. You also will have to respond to a dialog box asking if you are certain that you want to remove the folder. If you later decide that you need the folder, you can recover it from the Recycle Bin if you deleted it from the hard drive. However, if it was deleted from a CD or other storage medium, you cannot retrieve it. The Recycle Bin is discussed in a later section of this chapter.

Change Folder Views

Figure 1.16 displays the contents of a folder containing two documents. The folder contents are displayed in Tiles view. Figure 1.17 displays the same folder in Details view, which shows the date the files were created or last modified, along with other file information. Both views display a file icon next to each file to indicate the file type or application that was used to create the file. *Introduction to E-mail*, for example, is a PowerPoint presentation. *Basic Financial Documents* is an Excel workbook. Other views include Icons, which is much like Tiles except only the file name is displayed, and List, which presents folder contents in a columnar format with the file name and a small icon for each file. If the files are digital photos or other graphics, you might like to view them in either Filmstrip, or Thumbnails view. Filmstrip which is only an option if the selected folder contains picture files, shows a miniature image of each file along with a large display of the currently selected (or first in line) image. Similarly, Thumbnails shows a miniature image of each graphic, but does not enlarge a selected file.

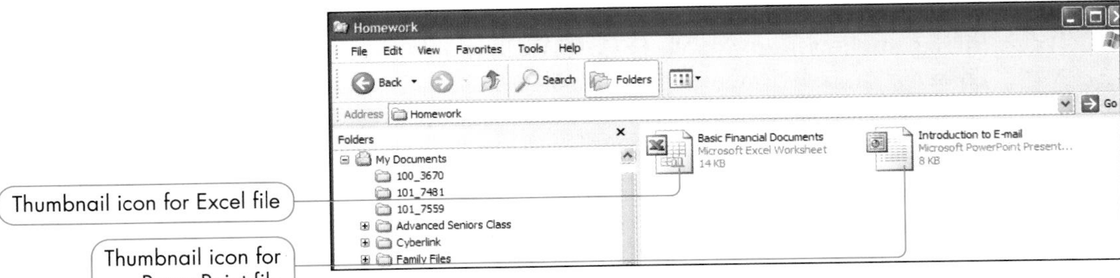

Figure 1.16 Tiles View

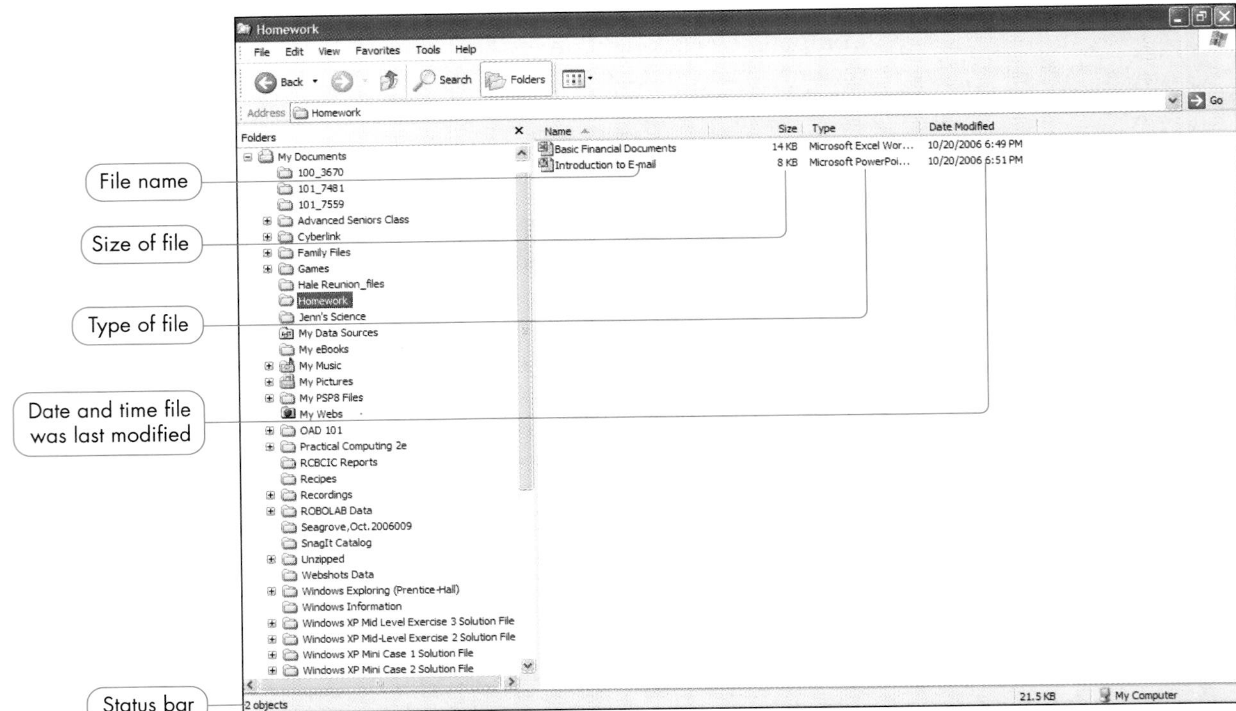

Figure 1.17 Details View

Figures 1.16 and 1.17 have more similarities than differences, such as the name of the folder (*Homework*), which appears in the title bar of the open folder. The Minimize, Restore Down, and Close buttons are found at the right of the title bar. A menu bar appears below the title bar. The Standard buttons toolbar is shown below the menu, with the Address bar (indicating the drive and folder) appearing below the toolbar. A status bar is shown at the bottom of the folder window, giving summary information about the *Homework* folder. For a review of the parts of a window, see Figure 1.4 earlier in this chapter.

Managing Folders and Files in Windows Explorer

Windows Explorer displays a tree structure of the devices and folders on your computer.

Windows Explorer is a program that displays a hierarchical (tree) structure of the devices and folders on your computer. Figure 1.18 displays the contents of the Reports folder (on drive F, which is a removable USB drive). The folder structure is displayed in the left pane, while the contents of the selected object (the Reports folder) are shown in the right pane. To open Windows Explorer, click Start, All Programs, Accessories, Windows Explorer.

Although by default, Windows Explorer displays folders in the left pane, you occasionally might see the left pane used as a task pane, which does not display folder hierarchy. To display the folder structure, click Folders in the toolbar. Alternatively, if the folder structure displays, but you want to work with the task pane (which contains tasks appropriate to a selected item), click Folders. The Folders button is a toggle button that switches back and forth between task pane and folders views.

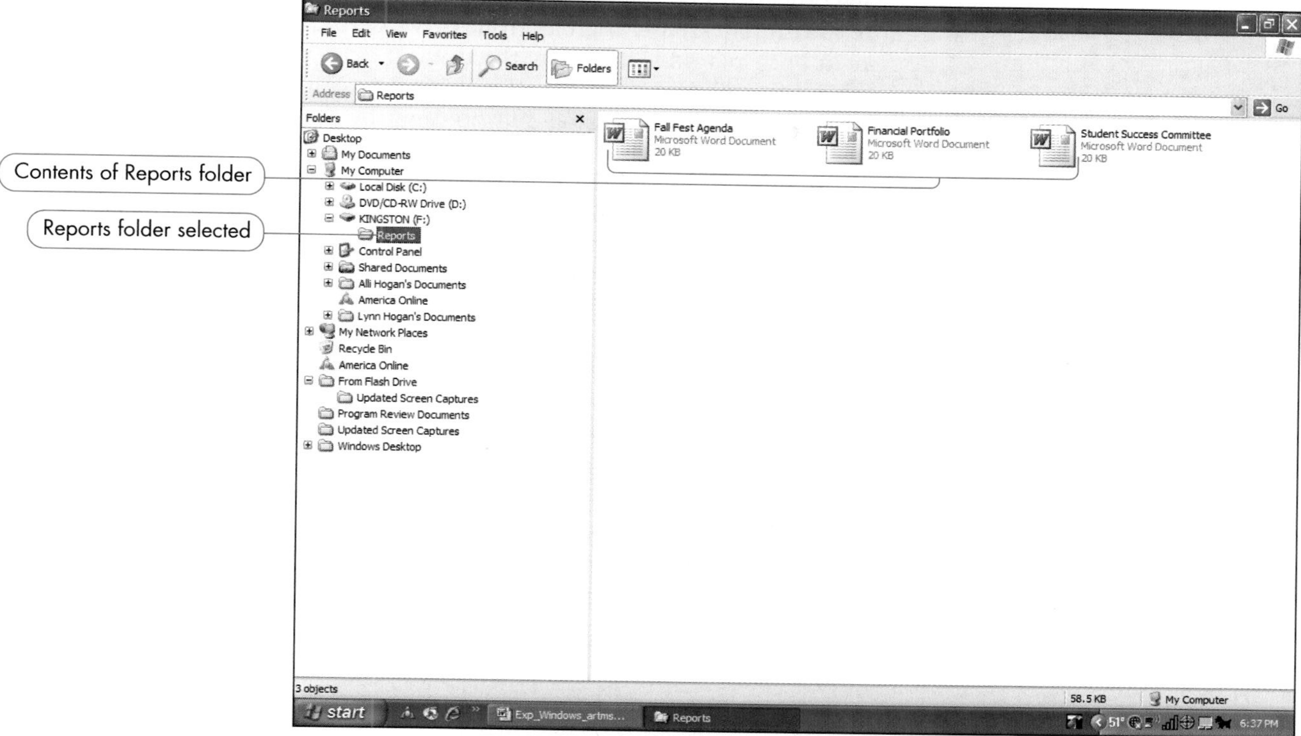

Figure 1.18 A Folder and Its Contents

Take a look at the folders pane (left pane). A plus sign appears beside the icon for My Documents to indicate that the folder has not been expanded to show its subfolders. Clicking the plus sign will expand My Documents to show more detail. The contents of drive C (the hard drive) also are not visible. Look closely and you see that both drive F and drive C are indented under My Computer, which in turn is indented under the desktop. In other words, the desktop is at the top of the hierarchy, containing the My Computer folder, which in turn contains drive F and drive C. The desktop also contains the My Documents folder, but the plus sign next to My Documents indicates the folder is collapsed. My Computer, on the other hand, has a minus sign indicating the folder is expanded. You can see its contents, which consist of the drives on your system as well as other special folders (Control Panel and Shared Documents).

Look at the icon next to the Reports folder in the left pane of Figure 1.18. The icon is an open folder, indicating that the Reports folder is the active folder. The folder's name also is shaded, and it appears in the title bar and address bar. Only one folder can be active at a time, with its contents displayed in the right pane. If you want to work with a document in the Reports folder, you could double-click the document to open it, or click to select it so that you could rename, move, copy, or delete the document. To see the contents of a different folder, such as My Documents, you would select the icon for that folder in the left pane (which automatically closes the Reports folder). The contents of My Documents would then appear in the right pane.

Move and Copy a File or Folder

Basic file management involves moving and copying a file or folder from one location to another. This can be done in various ways. The method of copying and moving files is the same as that for folders. The easiest way to copy or move is to click and drag the file icon from the source drive or folder to the destination drive or folder within Windows Explorer. Whether a file is moved or copied, however, depends on whether the source and destination are on the same or different drives. Dragging a file from one folder to another folder on the same drive moves the file. When you drag a file to a folder on a different drive, you create a copy of the file.

This process is not as arbitrary as it seems. Windows assumes that if you drag an item to a different drive, such as from drive C to drive E, you want the object to appear in both places. Therefore, the default action when you click and drag an object to a different drive is to *copy* the object. You can, however, override the default and move the object by pressing and holding the Shift key as you drag. When you make a copy of an item, the copy is usually on another disk drive, for backup purposes. You might copy a file from the hard drive to a CD or USB drive.

Windows also assumes that you do not want two copies of an object on the same drive, as that would result in wasted disk space. Thus, the default action when you click and drag an item to a different folder on the same drive is to *move* the object. You can override the default and copy the object by pressing and holding Ctrl on the keyboard as you drag the file from one location to another.

A ***shortcut menu*** displays a list of commands when you right-click an item or screen element.

Fortunately, you have an alternative to learning the rules related to clicking and dragging (whether a file is moved or copied). Simply right-click and drag a file to another location, regardless of whether the new location is on the same drive as the original file. When you release the mouse button, you will respond to a ***shortcut menu*** choosing to either *copy* or *move* the file. Using this method, you do not have to remember when, or if, to hold down Shift or Ctrl.

If the disk to which you are copying or moving is a removable media, such as a USB drive, you should follow a few safety tips before removing the drive. When you are ready to disconnect the drive, click the Safely Remove Hardware icon in the Notification area. To identify the Safely Remove Hardware icon, place the pointer over each icon and wait for a ScreenTip to appear, informing you of each icon's purpose. When you find the Safely Remove Hardware icon, click it and select the device from the list of hardware devices. Click the Stop button and the OK button. When the Safe to Remove Hardware screen tip displays, remove the drive. Close the Safely Remove Hardware dialog box.

Backup Files

A ***backup*** is a copy of a file.

It is not a question of *if* it will happen, but *when* it will happen. Hard drives die, files are lost, or viruses infect a system. You certainly do not want to lose any files, but you should be especially attentive to your data files, creating backup copies on different drive media so that you can always recover your work. The essence of a good ***backup*** strategy is to decide which files to back up, how often to copy them, and where to keep the backup.

Your strategy should be very simple—copy what you cannot afford to lose, do so on a regular basis, and store the backup away from your computer. You need not copy every file, every day. Instead, copy just the files that changed during the current session. Realize, too, that it is much more important to copy your data files than your program files. You can always reinstall program files from the original CD, or if necessary, locate another copy of an application. You, however, are the only one who has a copy of the term paper that is due tomorrow. Once you decide on a strategy, follow it, and follow it on a regular basis.

Deleting Items and Managing the Recycle Bin

Deleting a file or folder is a very easy task. In Windows Explorer, you can simply click to select the item and then press Delete on the keyboard. Alternatively, you can right-click the file or folder and select Delete. If you are deleting an item from the hard drive, you can recover it later because it is actually only moved to the Recycle Bin. However, files and folders deleted from a removable disk, such as a CD/RW or USB drive, are not placed in the Recycle Bin and cannot be recovered.

The ***Recycle Bin*** holds files and folders deleted from the hard drive.

The ***Recycle Bin*** is a special folder on the hard drive that contains files and folders that have been deleted from a hard drive. Think of the Recycle Bin as similar to the wastebasket in your room. You throw out (delete) a report by tossing it into a wastebasket. You can still get it back by taking it out of the wastebasket as long as the basket has not been emptied. The Recycle Bin works the same way. Files are not actually removed from the hard drive, but they are instead moved to the Recycle Bin. You can retrieve discarded files and restore them to their original locations as long as it has not been emptied. To view the contents of the Recycle Bin, double-click the Recycle Bin on the desktop. Figure 1.19 shows an open Recycle Bin.

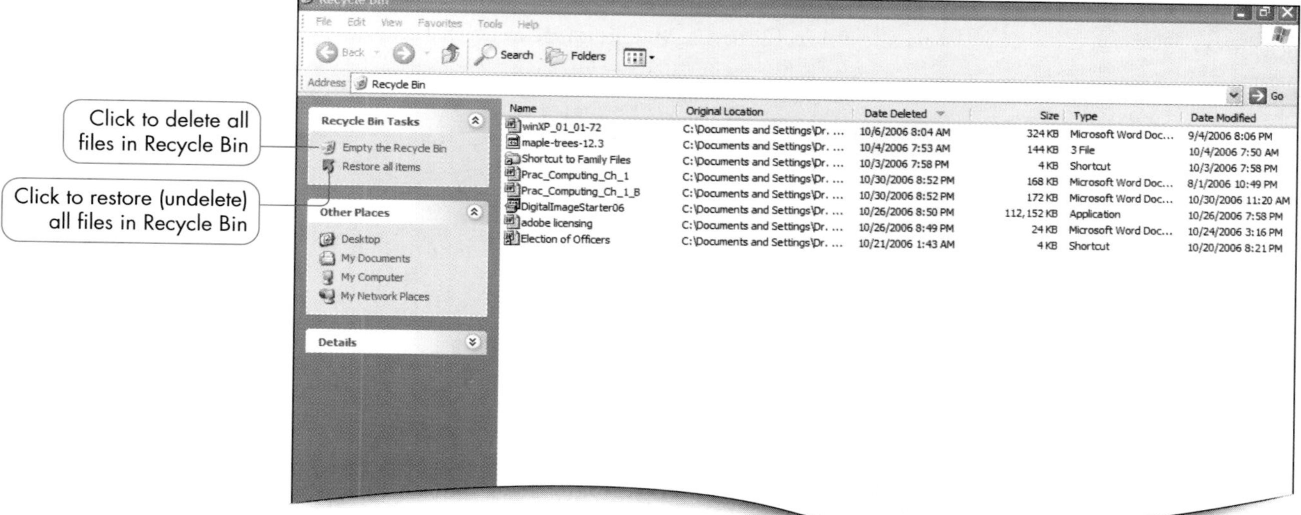

Figure 1.19 Recycle Bin

Windows provides several ways to place a file or folder in the Recycle Bin. In Windows Explorer, you can simply click a file or folder and press Delete. Or you can right-click the item and select Delete. In either case, you will be asked to confirm the deletion. You also can click and drag a file or folder to the Recycle Bin. If you can see the Recycle Bin in the left folders pane of Windows Explorer, simply click and drag the file or folder to the Recycle Bin. If you do not see the Recycle Bin in the left pane, you must click Folders in the Standard buttons toolbar to change the left pane view to folders. You also can drag items to the Recycle Bin on the desktop.

Remember that only items removed from the hard drive are placed in the Recycle Bin, not files deleted from removable media. The Recycle Bin is a type of safety net—if you later decide that you want to recover a deleted item, you can recover it from the Recycle Bin, as long as the Recycle Bin is not full. Because the Recycle Bin reserves 10% of your hard drive space for deleted files, it is very likely that a file will still be there if you retrieve it within a few weeks of removing it. To retrieve a deleted file or folder, open the Recycle Bin by double-clicking the icon on the desktop. If you want to recover all files and folders, click *Restore all items*. If, however, you are retrieving only one item, click it and click *Restore this item*.

The Recycle Bin is an area of hard drive space reserved for deleted items. Therefore, when you delete an item, you are not actually freeing hard drive space, but are instead simply moving an item from one location to another. If your goal is to remove unnecessary items from the hard drive, and you are certain that you will not need them later, you can empty the Recycle Bin. To do so, open the Recycle Bin and click Empty the Recycle Bin. You also can simply right-click the Recycle Bin and click Empty Recycle Bin. If you want to delete some items permanently, but retain others in the Recycle Bin, open the Recycle Bin, right-click any item to be deleted, and select Delete. Remember, when the file or folder is deleted, it is permanently removed and cannot be recovered.

Given the ever-increasing sizes of hard drives, you might determine that the Recycle Bin is requiring too much of that space. At 10% of your hard drive space, the reserved area for deleted files could be excessive. You can adjust the Recycle Bin properties to decrease the amount of space reserved. Right-click the Recycle Bin and click Properties. Click and drag the slider to adjust the percentage of space reserved, as shown in Figure 1.20. Click OK to accept the new settings.

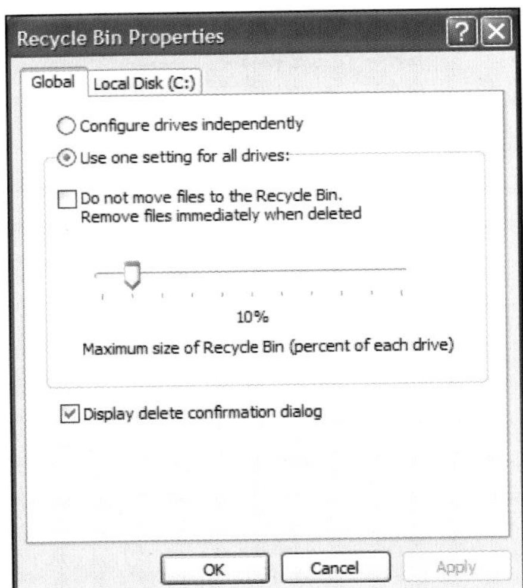

Figure 1.20 Recycle Bin Properties

Hands-On Exercises

2 | File and Folder Management

Skills covered: 1. Change a Window View **2.** Create and Rename a Folder **3.** Move and Delete a Folder **4.** Create and Save a File.

Step 1
Change a Window View

Refer to Figure 1.21 as you complete Step 1.

a. Click **Start**, point to **All Programs**, point to **Accessories**, and then click **Windows Explorer**.

   Windows Explorer enables you to view files and folders saved on your computer. You can modify the view to display large, tiled, or detailed icons. If you are viewing picture files, the *Thumbnails* or *Filmstrip* view provides a preview of each picture.

b. Click **View**. On the menu, Status Bar should be checked. Select **Status Bar** to clear the check mark.

   The status bar is no longer displayed at the bottom of the window. The status bar, which can be displayed or hidden, is shown along the lower edge of the Windows Explorer window, giving additional information about the selected item.

c. Click **View** and check to see which option has a small black circle to the left. That option is the selected icon display. Select **Tiles** (even if it already has a black dot to the left).

   The icons display in a tiled format.

d. Click **View** and point to **Toolbars**. From the submenu that appears, make sure a check mark appears beside both **Standard Buttons** and **Address Bar**. If either is not selected, click to select that option.

e. Click **Folders** on the Standard Buttons toolbar to toggle (change) the contents of the left pane. Click **Folders** again to display the folder structure. End with Windows Explorer displayed, as shown in Figure 1.21.

f. Close Windows Explorer.

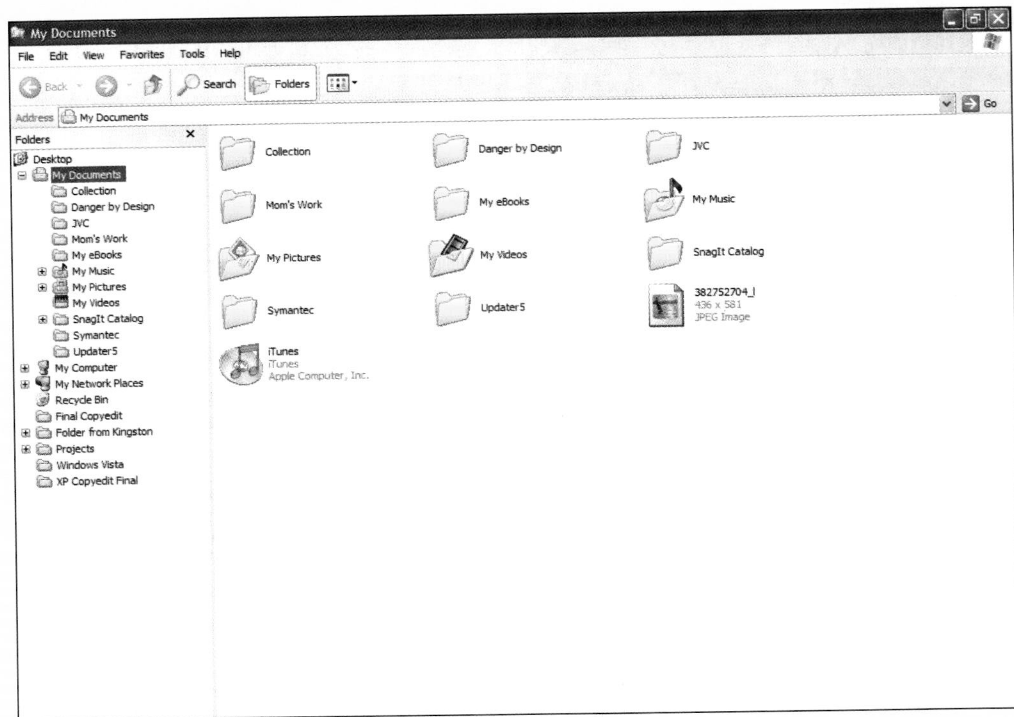

Figure 1.21 Windows Explorer

Step 2
Create and Rename a Folder

Refer to Figure 1.22 as you complete Step 2.

a. Connect your USB (flash) drive to a USB port. Wait a few seconds. Close any dialog box that appears.

When a flash drive, DVD, or CD is identified, Windows XP displays a dialog box providing suggestions for opening or otherwise accessing the new unit. You can either select an option, or close the dialog box.

b. Click **Start**, point to **All Programs**, point to **Accessories**, and then click **Windows Explorer**. Scroll the left pane up or down, if necessary, to locate My Computer. Click the **My Computer +** to expand the view. Click the removable drive (probably drive E or F). Check the contents displayed in the right pane. Depending on what the drive has been used for, you may or may not see folders and files.

c. Select **File**, select **New**, and then select **Folder**. Type **Computer Class** and press **Enter**.

You should see a new folder named Computer Class in the right pane to store assignments for your computer class. Giving the folder an appropriate name and saving it to a removable drive make it easy to take class work to and from class.

TROUBLESHOOTING: Instead of the name that you intend to give it, your renamed folder might be called **New Folder** because you clicked or pressed a key before typing the new name. To correct this problem, you can rename the folder by right-clicking it, clicking **Rename**, and typing the correct name. Or select it and press F2.

d. Right-click **Computer Class** (in either the right or left pane). Select **Rename** from the shortcut menu. Type **CIS 100** and press **Enter**.

Because you are taking a couple of computer classes this term, you want to differentiate between them by using course numbers, instead of generic identification.

e. Click the removable drive. Select **File**, select **New**, and then select **Folder**. Type **CIS 150** and press **Enter**.

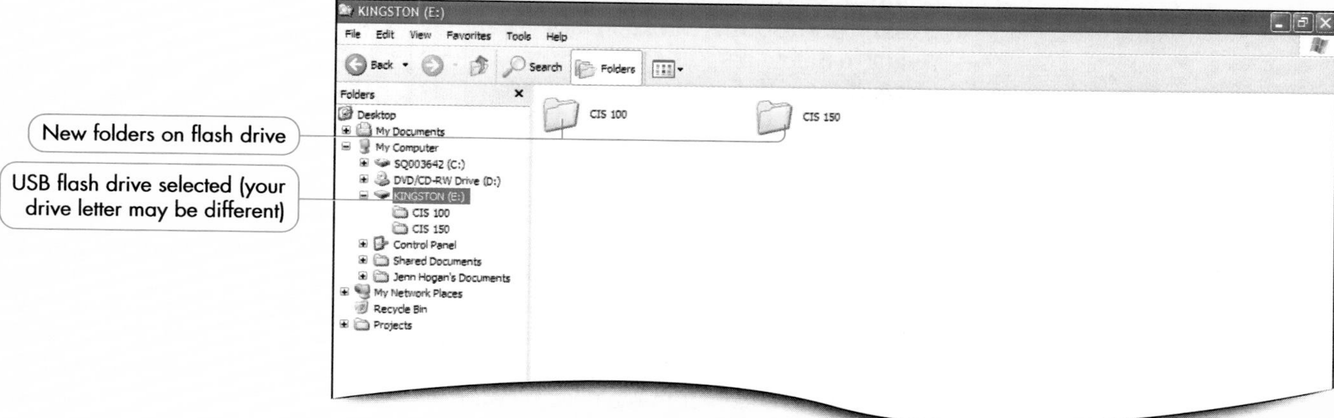

Figure 1.22 Creating New Folders

Step 3
Move and Delete a Folder

Refer to Figure 1.23 as you complete Step 3.

a. Click the removable drive in the left pane. Select **File**, select **New**, and then select **Folder**. Type **Computer Classes** and press **Enter**.

Since you have two computer classes, you plan to create a folder called Computer Classes, in which to place the two folders from Step 1.

b. Right-click and drag **CIS 100** to **Computer Classes** (in either the left or right pane). Click **Move Here**.

c. Move the **CIS 150** folder to the **Computer Classes** folder by repeating Step b. Click "+" beside **Computer Classes**, if necessary, to expand the folder view. Your folder structure should appear, as shown in Figure 1.23.

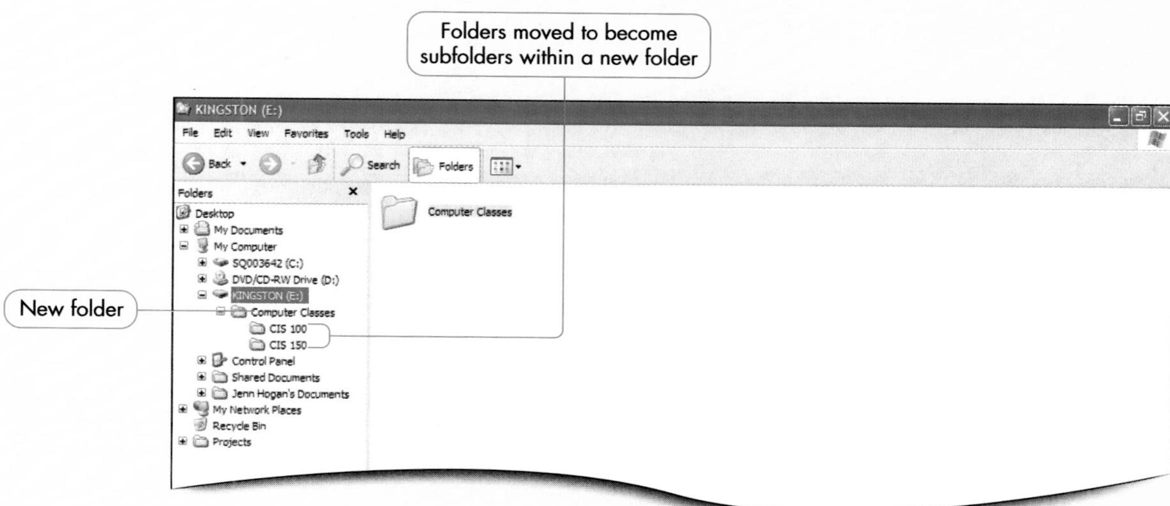

Figure 1.23 Computer Class Folders

d. Right-click the **CIS 150 folder** (in either the right or left pane) and then select **Delete**. Confirm the deletion by clicking **Yes**.

Unfortunately, you have overloaded your schedule this semester and find it necessary to drop the CIS 150 class. Therefore, you no longer need the folder and want to delete it.

e. Close Windows Explorer.

Step 4
Create and Save a File

Refer to Figure 1.24 as you complete Step 4.

a. Click **Start**, point to **All Programs**, point to **Accessories**, and then click **WordPad**.

Your first assignment for the CIS 100 class is to use WordPad to type a paragraph about your favorite vacation place. WordPad is a word processing accessory program included in Windows installations. You will create the document using WordPad and save it in the CIS 100 folder.

b. Type a paragraph about your favorite vacation destination. Do not press Enter, but enable WordPad to automatically wrap lines for you. Include a description of the destination and explain why it is special to you. So that the file can be used in a later hands-on exercise, include the word *vacation* somewhere in the document.

c. Click **File** and select **Save**. Click **My Computer** in the left frame of the Save As dialog box. Double-click the removable drive.

d. Double-click **Computer Classes**. Double-click **CIS 100**. Click in the File name box and type **chap1_ho2_assignment2_solution**. Click **Save**.

e. Close WordPad.

f. Click **Start**, click **All Programs**, click **Accessories**, and click **Windows Explorer**. Click **My Computer**. (You might have to scroll down slightly to find **My Computer**.) Click the removable drive. Click **Computer Classes**. Click **CIS 100**.

Look to the right. You should see *chap1_ho2_assignment2_solution*.

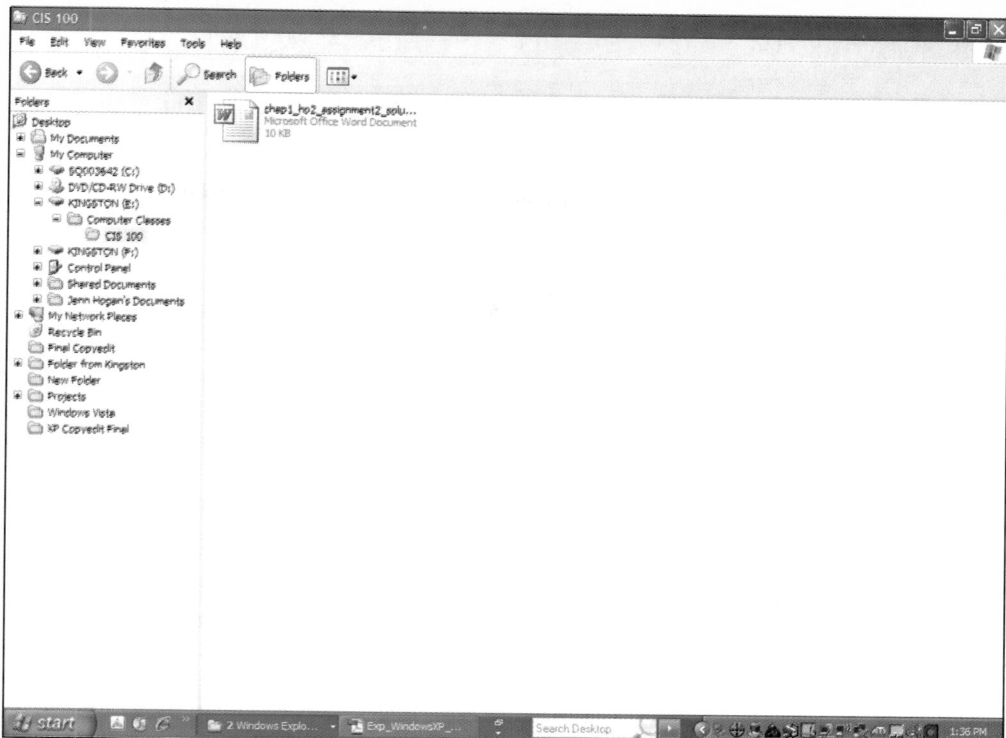

Figure 1.24 File Saved in CIS 100 Folder

g. Right-click **chap1_ho2_assignment2_solution**, select **Open With**, and select **WordPad**. After checking the assignment, click the **Close button** to close WordPad.

h. Close Windows Explorer.

i. Double-click the **Safely Remove Hardware** icon in the Notification area of the taskbar. Select the device, click the Stop button and OK. When the Safe to Remove Hardware ScreenTip appears, remove the USB drive, and close the Safely Remove Hardware dialog box. Disconnect the USB drive.

Windows Customization

You are likely to spend a great deal of time enjoying a computer and using it in the workplace. Windows XP not only enables you to access programs, but it also enables you to customize your Windows experience. What that means is that you can change the appearance of the desktop, create and manage user accounts, select a screen saver, change printer and mouse settings, and use the Control Panel to uninstall programs. As you begin to customize your system, you will identify even more ways to fine-tune Windows settings so that you get the most from your computer.

In this section, you change display settings. Specifically, you learn how to change the background and activate a screen saver. Then you learn how to use the Control Panel to customize Windows settings. You learn how to install and uninstall programs, change the mouse settings, and manage user accounts. Then you learn how to create shortcuts on the desktop and Quick Launch toolbar.

Changing the Display Settings

One of the first things that you will want to do is to modify your display settings. You can change such things as desktop theme, background, screen saver, and screen resolution through the Display Properties dialog box. A simple way to access display settings is to right-click an empty area of the desktop. From the shortcut menu, select Properties. Figure 1.25 shows the Display Properties dialog box. As you can see, tabs at the top of the dialog box enable you to change various display settings.

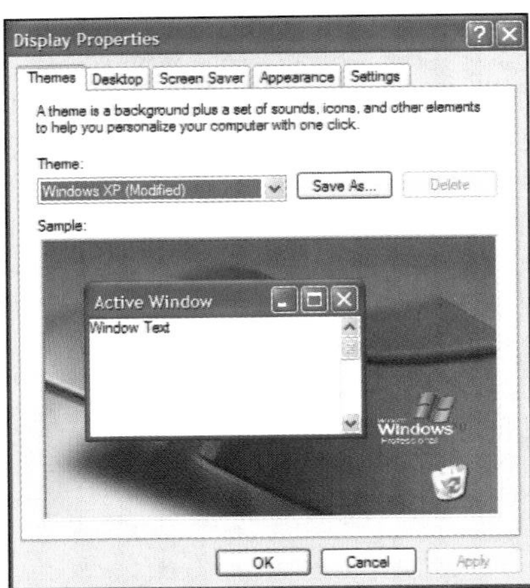

Figure 1.25 Changing the Desktop Background

Change the Background

The ***background*** is the area of a display screen behind the desktop icons.

The desktop ***background*** is the graphic or color that appears behind the icons on the desktop. The background is not displayed in windows or dialog boxes—only on the desktop. Although you can select a favorite photograph as your background, Windows XP has many pre-designed backgrounds from which you can choose. Click Start and click Control Panel. Next, click Appearance and Themes. Click Change the desktop background. Scroll among the background choices, clicking any that look interesting. A sample screen above the background area displays your choice. If your selection does not fill the screen, or if it appears in a checkerboard pattern, click the drop-down arrow beside Position and click Stretch. If you like the background, click OK. Otherwise, make another selection.

To include a favorite photograph saved to your hard drive, click Browse. Navigate through the folder structure to locate the photograph. Double-click the file. Click OK.

Select a Screen Saver

A **_screen saver_** is a moving graphic or image that takes over the display screen when the user is idle.

A ***screen saver*** is a moving pattern or image that occupies your desktop when you are idle for a specified period of time. Originally, screen savers were designed to keep static images from "burning" into the monitor, which they were prone to do with earlier monitors. However, now screen savers are popular because they are entertaining and because they provide a level of security. If you set a password on your screen saver, no one can stop the screen saver by moving the mouse or by pressing a key unless he or she knows the password. You can step away from your computer without the risk of leaving it open for anyone to work with.

Windows XP includes several screen savers from which you can choose. You also can buy screen savers or build them yourself from digital photographs. To select a screen saver, right-click an empty part of the desktop. Click Properties. Click the Screen Saver tab. Click the Screen saver drop-down arrow and make a selection, as shown in Figure 1.26. The screen saver will appear in miniature on the sample screen. To adjust the "wait" time, which is the amount of time that you must be idle before the screen saver displays, click the spinner beside Wait and modify the selected time. To view the screen saver in full-screen size, click Preview. Move the mouse or press any key to stop the screen saver. If you like your selection, click OK.

If you have included favorite photographs in the My Pictures folder and want to use them as your screen saver, visit the screen saver settings dialog box, as described in the previous paragraph. Click the Screen saver drop-down arrow and select My Pictures Slideshow. Click OK to accept the new screen saver.

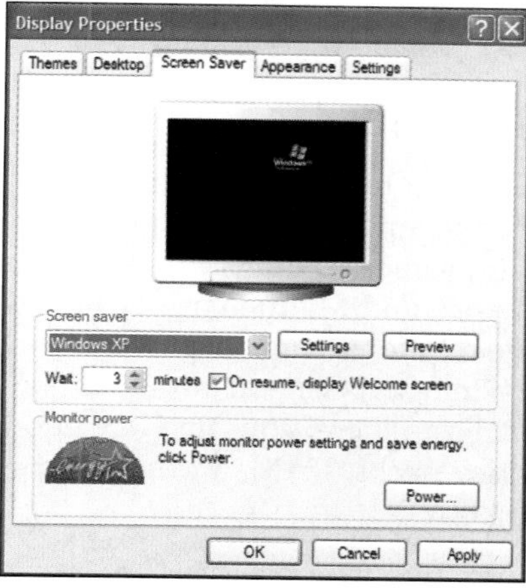

Figure 1.26 Selecting a Screen Saver

Changing Computer Settings Using the Control Panel

The **_Control Panel_** enables you to change system settings.

The ***Control Panel*** enables you to change system settings, such as your background, screen saver, screen fonts, and accessibility options. It also provides information about system configuration and hardware performance. You can, for example, change the way your mouse behaves by switching the function of the left and right mouse buttons and/or by replacing the standard mouse pointers with animated icons that move across the screen. Working with the Control Panel, you can customize your computer system and Desktop to reflect your preferences.

The Control Panel can be organized as categories or as folders; the Category View is shown in Figure 1.27. Point to any category to display a ScreenTip that describes the specific tasks within that category. Appearance and Themes, for example, lets you select a screen saver or customize the Start menu and taskbar. You can switch to the Classic view by clicking the appropriate link in the Task pane. The Classic view displays all tools in a single screen.

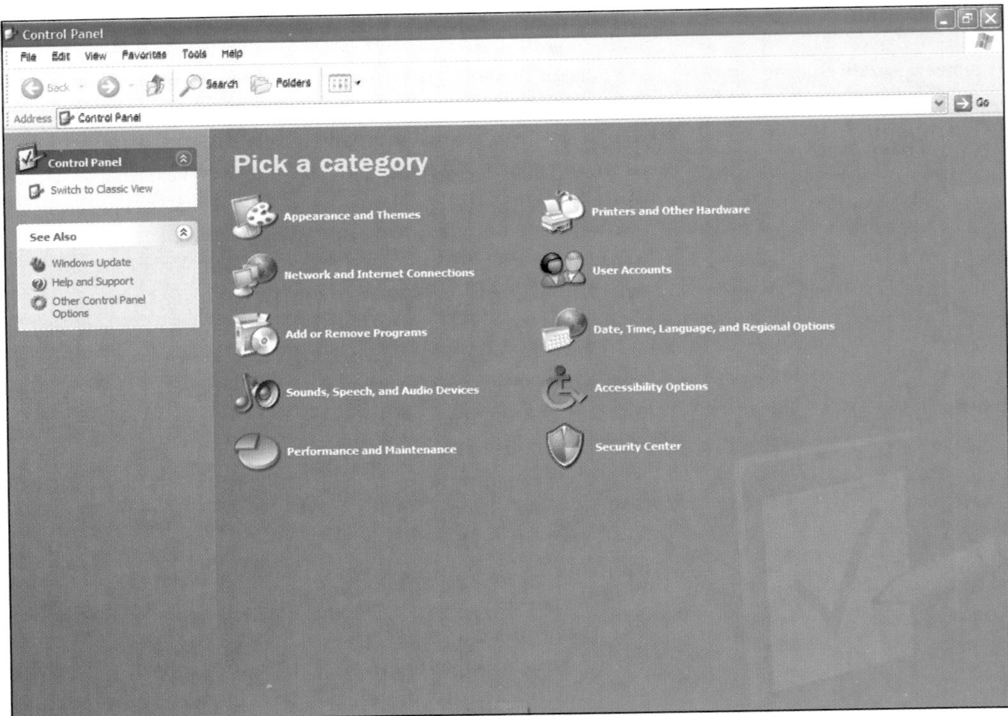

Figure 1.27 Control Pane in Category View

Check System Settings

The Control Panel is also a tool for checking your system settings—displaying your operating system version, amount of RAM, processor speed, power settings, and other performance and maintenance readings. To view those settings, click Start and Control Panel. Click Performance and Maintenance. Click System to view general computer settings, or click Power Options to adjust power settings such as stand-by and hibernation. After clicking System, the General tab should be selected, displaying a dialog box similar to Figure 1.28. From there, you can view information related to your operating system and any service packs, RAM, and processor speed. Figure 1.29 displays the Power Options dialog box.

Figure 1.28 System Settings

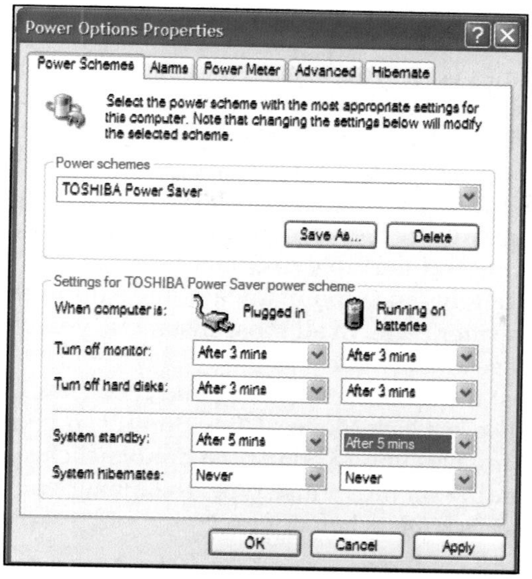

Figure 1.29 Power Options

Install and Uninstall Programs

A ***wizard*** is a set of guided instructions.

When you visit the software aisle of an office supply store, you will likely find many titles in which you have an interest. Software, or programs, must be installed on your computer before you can enjoy them. Luckily, installation is usually very simple. As you open the software package, you will find a CD. Place the CD in your CD drive and wait for onscreen instructions. Most software opens in an installation ***wizard***, which is a step-by-step guided set of instructions. Most often, simply clicking Next and being affirmative to requests for input result in successful installation. Once installed, evidence of the software appears in several locations. It always will be listed as a program on your program list, accessible by clicking Start, All Programs. Sometimes, it also is installed as an icon on your desktop so that you can simply double-click the icon to run the program. Less often, it also is placed as an icon on the Quick Launch toolbar.

Uninstalling software is a relatively simple task, but one with which you should become familiar so that you can maintain your computer. Undoubtedly, you will find that a program you once enjoyed immensely has become unnecessary. Hard drive space is limited, so you may elect to remove software that you no longer need. To uninstall software, click Start, and Control Panel. Click Add or Remove Programs. In a few seconds, you will see a list of all software installed on your computer (Figure 1.30). Find the program that you want to uninstall and click it. Click Remove. Respond affirmatively to any prompts. The software will be completely removed from your system. If you have the original software CD, you can always reinstall it later.

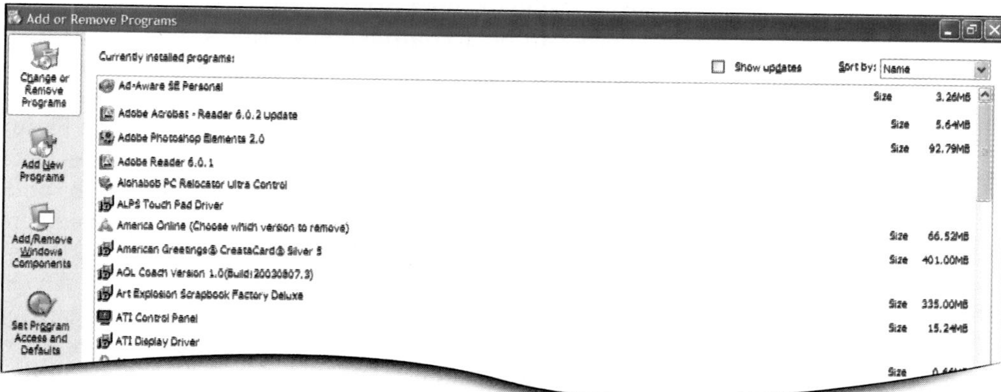

Figure 1.30 Uninstalling Software in Control Panel

Manage the Mouse and Printers

There are times when you will need to make adjustments to your mouse and printer. If you are left-handed, you might want to reverse the mouse buttons so that you can use the mouse effectively with your left hand. If the speed at which you have to double-click is a little fast you can slow it down slightly to make using the mouse more comfortable. As you send documents to the printer, they are buffered (placed in a holding area until they can all be printed) and printed. Sometimes, you might unknowingly send multiple documents to the printer and then find it necessary to cancel printing because too many are lined up in the buffer and the printer is producing page after page. In all those instances, you can use the Control Panel to manage the mouse and printer.

To adjust the mouse, click Start, and then click Control Panel. Click Printers and Other Hardware. Click Mouse. Click Buttons, if necessary. The dialog box shown in Figure 1.31 enables you to adjust the double-click speed and reverse the mouse buttons. Depending on the mouse type, the dialog box may not be exactly as shown in Figure 1.31. Click OK when done.

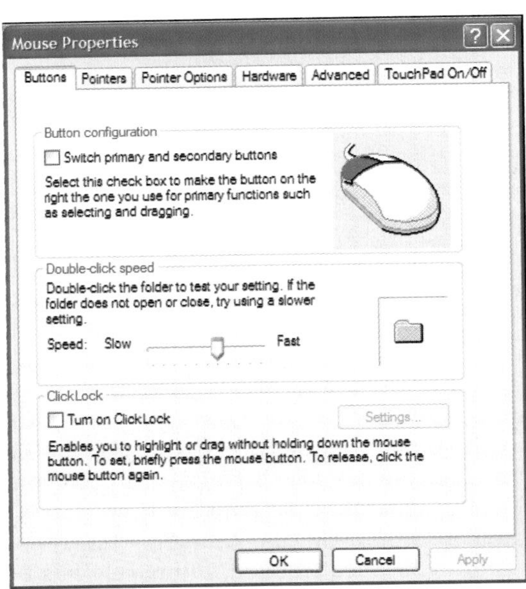

Figure 1.31 Adjusting Mouse

If you are working with more than one printer, you will need to direct the print to the correct printer. One printer will be identified as the default printer, which means that print jobs will be automatically sent to that printer unless you specify otherwise. You might want to change the default printer. Finally, you might need to cancel one or more print jobs if the printer is printing too many pages. All of these tasks can be accomplished through the Control Panel. Click Start, and then click Control Panel. Click Printers and Other Hardware. Click Printers and Faxes. One of the printers listed (if more than one is listed) will have a check mark beside its icon, identifying it as the default printer, as shown in Figure 1.32. To select another printer as the default, right-click another and click Set as Default Printer. If a printer is printing continually and you want to cancel print jobs and stop printing, double-click the printer. A printer dialog box opens, listing all current print jobs. To cancel all print jobs and pause printing, click Printer. From the subsequent menu, click Pause Printing to stop the printer and/or click Cancel All Documents to remove them from the buffer. Be aware, however, that when you pause printing, two things will happen. First, the printer will not immediately stop, since it has some printing left in the buffer. Second, when the printer stops after you have paused printing, it will not begin again until you click to remove the check beside Pause Printing. It is a toggle switch.

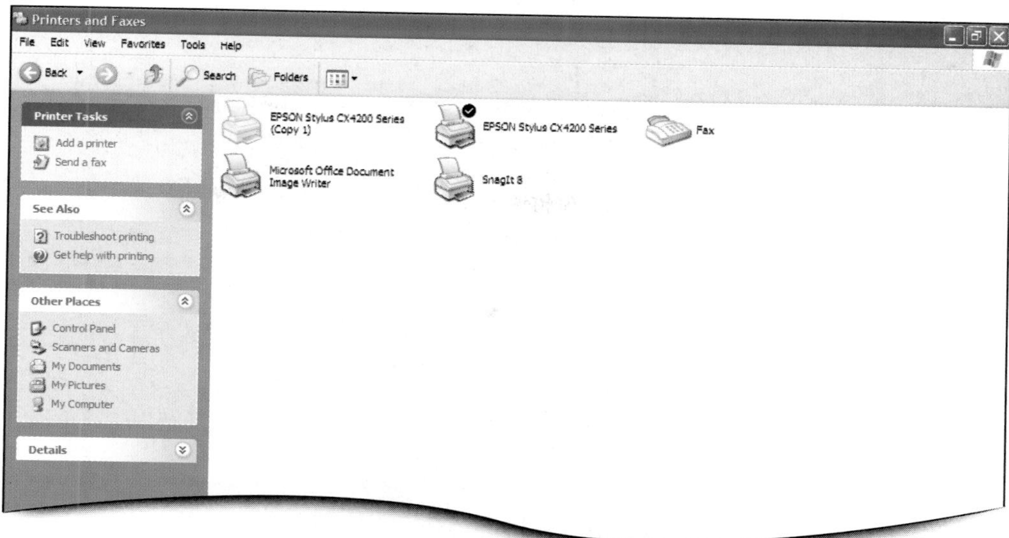

Figure 1.32 Setting a Default Printer

Create and Manage User Accounts

A ***user account*** specifies a user's settings, permissions, and customizations.

Windows XP includes a ***user accounts*** feature. Several people can use the same computer but with different accounts and varying privileges. What that means is that each person can have a customized desktop, personal folders, and even password protection in his account. Setting up user accounts is done easily through the Control Panel.

To create a new user account, click Start and Control Panel. Click User accounts. Click Create a new account. Type an account name and click Next. Select either Administrator or Limited. A limited account can only view and work with files created by this user, customize this user's desktop, and change this user's own password, while an administrator can create accounts, make system-wide changes, and install programs. Click Create Account to finalize the user account. As the administrator, you can also change user accounts, deleting them or changing the status.

Creating Shortcuts on the Desktop and Quick Launch Toolbar

A ***shortcut*** is a special type of file that points to another file or device.

A ***shortcut*** is a link to any object on your computer, such as a program, file, folder, disk drive, or Web page. Shortcuts can appear anywhere, but most often they are placed on the desktop or on the Start menu. The desktop in Figure 1.33 contains several shortcuts; shortcut icons are identified by a small arrow in the corner. If you double-click the shortcut to *Election of Officers*, for example, the document will open in Word (because it was created in Word). In similar fashion, you might double-click the shortcut for a Web page, folder, or disk drive to open the object and display its contents.

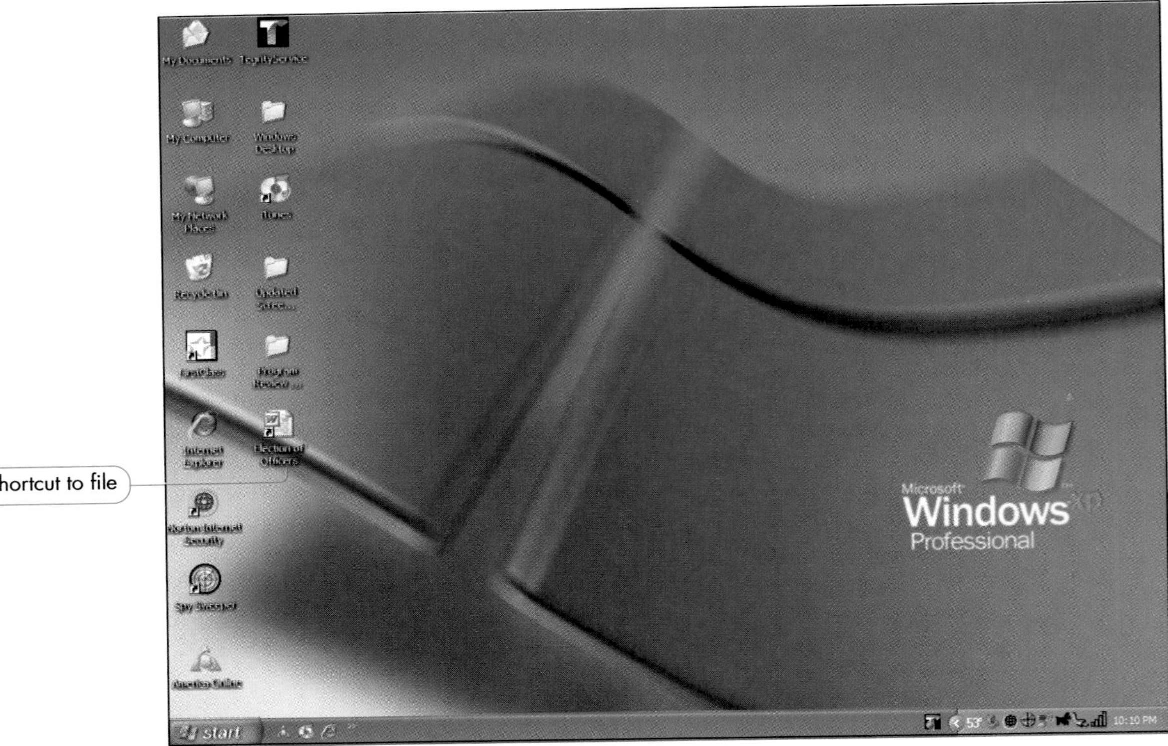

Figure 1.33 Desktop with Shortcuts

Creating a shortcut is a two-step process. First, locate the object, such as a file, folder, or disk drive to which you want to create a shortcut. The object might be in a Windows Explorer view, on the Start menu, or in a Windows Desktop Search result (as described later in this chapter). Then select the object, right-click and drag it to the desktop, and click Create Shortcuts Here. You also can right-click and select Send To, Desktop (create shortcut).

In order to see both the desktop and the window in which the object appears (such as Windows Explorer) at the same time, you probably will need to either Restore Down or otherwise resize the window so that a portion of the desktop appears behind it. After dragging the object to the desktop, a shortcut icon will appear on the desktop with the phrase *Shortcut to* as part of the name. You can create as many shortcuts as you like, and you can place them anywhere on the desktop or in individual folders. You also can right-click a shortcut to change its name. Since a shortcut is simply a pointer to the software or object, deleting the shortcut does not remove the software or item to which it directs. Many people make the mistake of thinking that if they remove a program shortcut from the desktop, the software is removed. The best way to remove software is to uninstall in Control Panel. Removing the shortcut does not uninstall software.

Several shortcuts are found in the Quick Launch toolbar that appears to the right of the Start button. Your Quick Launch toolbar might or might not appear, depending on the settings on your computer. To display the Quick Launch toolbar, right-click an empty area of the taskbar, click Toolbars, and Quick Launch. Click any icon on the Quick Launch toolbar, and the associated program will open.

Another location for shortcuts is the Start menu. Windows XP intuitively adds to the Start menu shortcuts to programs that you frequently access. You can manually add a program shortcut to the Start menu or Quick Launch toolbar by right-clicking and dragging the program to the Start button or to the Quick Launch toolbar.

Using Windows Desktop Search

Search Companion is a search tool option in Windows XP.

Sooner or later you will create a file and then forget where (in which folder) you saved it. Or you may create a document and forget its name, but remember a key word or phrase in the document. You might want to locate all files of a certain type—for example, all of the sound files on your system. You can use either Windows Desktop Search or the ***Search Companion*** to locate such items.

If you have installed Microsoft Office 2007, you might have chosen to install Windows Desktop Search (WDS). You also can download Windows Desktop Search from the Microsoft Web site. If you have not installed WDS, you will work with the Search Companion instead. Because WDS is a more current and complete search tool, however, you will probably want to select it as your primary search tool. WDS appears on the taskbar (see Figure 1.34). To search for an item, click in the WDS text box and type as much as you can remember of the file name or any text that might appear in the file. As you type, WDS begins searching for matches. Figure 1.34 illustrates a search for any documents containing the word *Picture* either in the file name or within file contents. Once a file is found, you can open it by clicking the file name.

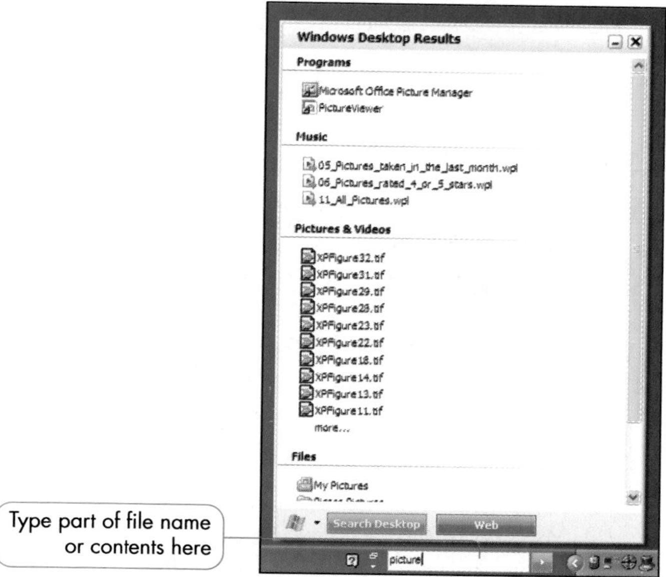

Figure 1.34 Windows Desktop Search

Windows Desktop Search creates a complete index of the files and folders on your system, along with any calendar appointments, contacts, tasks, and e-mails stored in Outlook. That means that you can find items almost instantly, much like a Web search. In fact, as you type an item in the search bar, WDS immediately begins to narrow the results, displaying those that match the text typed so far. Windows Desktop Search can be customized to better reflect your search needs. To explore customization options, click the Deskbar search box. Click the Windows icon (in the bottom-left corner of the Windows Desktop Results box). Click Deskbar Options. In the left pane, click Indexing (see Figure 1.35). In the right pane, you can choose what you want to index and whether you want to automatically run Windows Desktop Search when you log on to Windows.

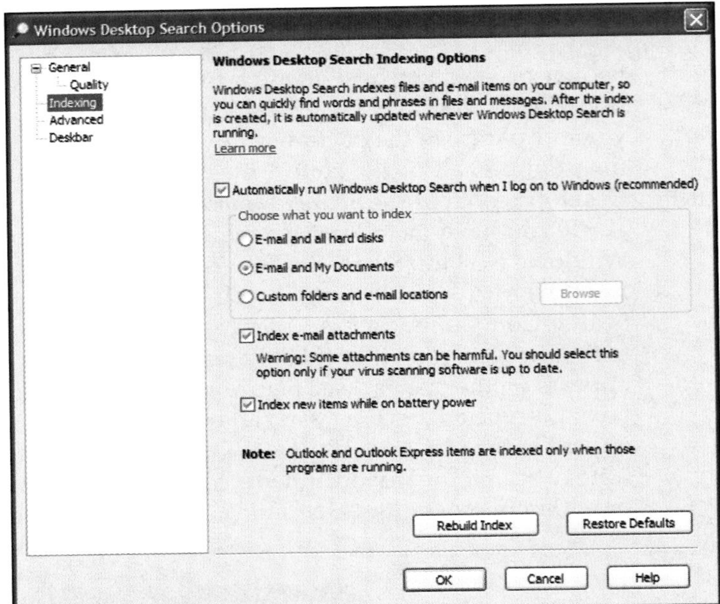

Figure 1.35 Windows Desktop Search Options

TIP Using Search Companion

If you are accustomed to using the Search Companion instead of Windows Desktop Search, you can still use it. To use Search Companion as a default search tool, click the Desktop Search text box on the taskbar. Click the window icon. Click Deskbar Options. Click General. Click Use Search Companion instead of Desktop Search.

You can initiate a search in one of two ways. Either click the WDS box and type what you can remember of the file name or contents, or click Start Search. If you click Start Search, you will be able to respond to categories that narrow the search. If you scroll to the bottom of the left pane, you can select Click here to use Search Companion instead of WDS if you prefer it.

Hands-On Exercises

3 | Customizing Your System

Skills covered: 1. Customize the Desktop **2.** Create a Desktop Shortcut **3.** Use Windows Desktop Search to Locate Files **4.** Use Control Panel to Customize System Settings **5.** Add a User Account **6.** Add a Shortcut to the Quick Launch Toolbar

Step 1 Customize the Desktop

Refer to Figure 1.36 as you complete Step 1.

a. Point to an empty area of the desktop and right-click to display a shortcut menu. Select **Properties**. Click the **Themes tab**, if necessary. Click the drop-down arrow beside **Theme** and click **Windows XP**. Click **OK**.

This step modifies the Theme and Background of your desktop. Before attempting this step, check with your instructor to see if you are allowed to modify the desktop. If you are not able to change settings, move to Step 2.

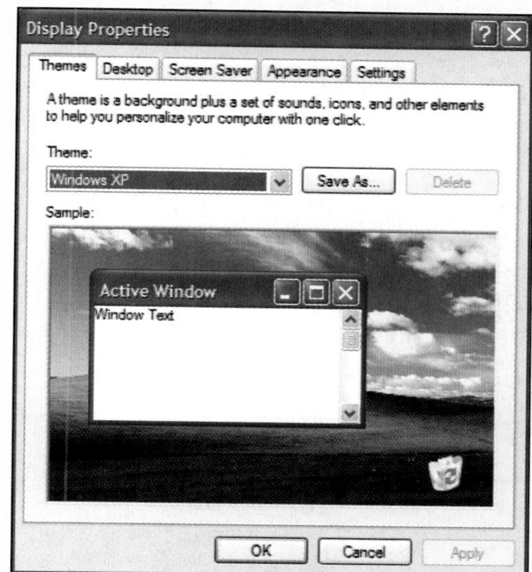

Figure 1.36 Display Properties

b. Right-click an empty part of the desktop, then select **Properties**. Click the **Desktop tab**, select **None** in the Background list box, and click **OK**. The background disappears.

TROUBLESHOOTING: If you do not see None as a choice of background, you might have to scroll up slightly to find the selection.

Step 2
Create a Desktop Shortcut

Refer to Figure 1.37 as you complete Step 2.

a. Click **Start**, click **All Programs**, and click **Accessories**.

Because you often use Windows Explorer, you find it cumbersome to go through the Programs menu structure each time you access the program. Therefore, you want to create a Windows Explorer shortcut on the desktop so that you simply double-click the shortcut to open the program.

b. Right-click and drag **Windows Explorer** to the desktop (visible behind the Programs menu). Click **Copy Here**. A *Shortcut to Windows Explorer* icon displays on the desktop.

c. Connect your USB drive to the USB port on your computer. Wait a few seconds and close any dialog box that appears.

d. Double-click the **Windows Explorer icon** on your desktop. Click "+" beside **My Computer** in the left pane (you might have to scroll the left pane up or down slightly to find My Computer).

TROUBLESHOOTING: If, instead of the folders pane, you see the task pane on the left, click **Folders** in the Standard toolbar. Then repeat Step b.

e. Click the removable drive. Click **Computer Classes**. Click **CIS 100**. To the right, you should see *chap1_ho2_assignment2*.

You will create a shortcut to *chap1_ho2_assignment2* on the desktop. That way, you can quickly open the file at any time by double-clicking the file on the desktop.

f. Return to the Folders pane. Find *Desktop* in the left pane (you might have to scroll the left pane up or down slightly to find Desktop). Do not click it; just locate it. You may have to scroll up to see it. You should still see *chap1_ho2_assignment2* in the right pane. Right-click and drag *chap1_ho2_assignment2* to Desktop. From the shortcut menu, click **Create Shortcuts Here**.

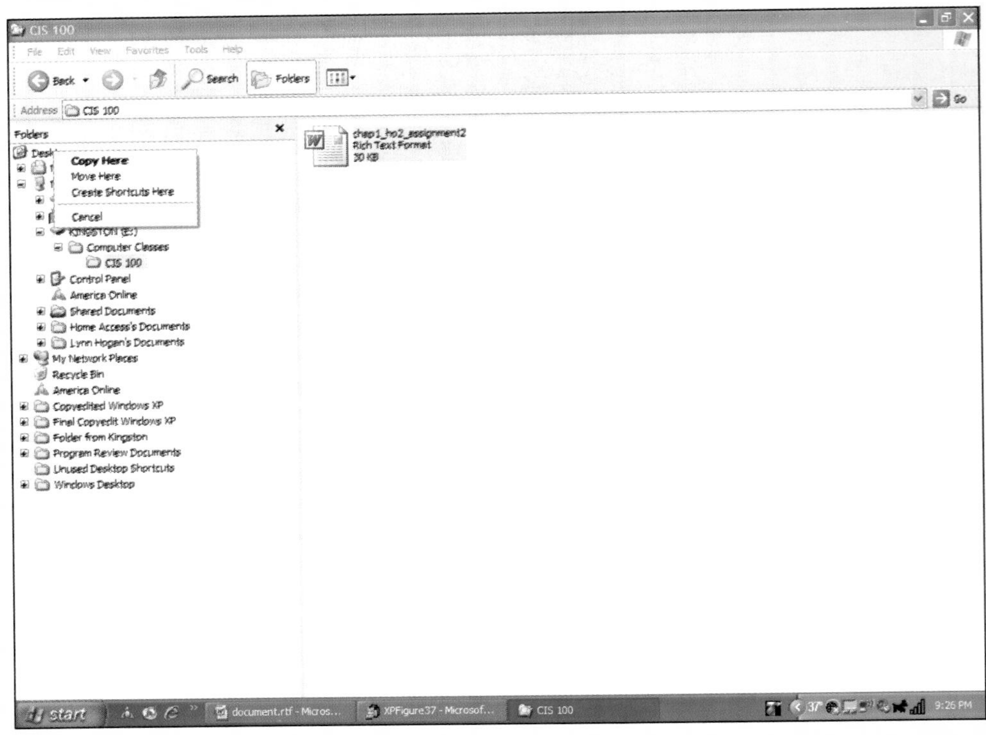

Figure 1.37 Creating a Shortcut

g. Close **Windows Explorer**. Close any open windows. On the desktop, locate the *chap1_ho2_assignment2* shortcut. Right-click the file, select **Open With**, and select **WordPad**. After viewing the file, close WordPad.

h. Right-click Windows Explorer and click **Delete** to remove the Windows Explorer shortcut from the desktop. Confirm the deletion by clicking **Yes**. In similar fashion, remove the *chap1_ho2_assignment2* shortcut from the desktop.

Step 3 Use Windows Desktop Search to Locate Files

Refer to Figure 1.38 as you complete Step 3.

a. Click in the Windows Desktop Search bar on the taskbar. Type **document**.

   You will search the hard drive for all files and folders containing the word **document**.

b. Click **My Documents**, a folder that should have displayed as a result of your search.

c. Close the resulting **My Documents** window as well as any remaining open windows.

   You will use the Search Companion to search for the document on your USB drive containing the word **vacation** (from Step 4 of Hands-On Exercise 2: File and Folder Management).

d. Click **Start** and click **Search**. Maximize the **Desktop Search** window. Scroll to the bottom of the left pane and click **Click here to use Search Companion**.

e. Click **Documents (word processing, spreadsheet, etc.)**. Maximize the Search Results window.

f. Click **Use advanced search options**. Click the box beneath **A word or phrase in the document**. Type **vacation** (because you remember that your document contained the word "vacation").

g. Scroll down slightly to view the *Look in* area. Click the drop-down arrow beside the disk drive selection and click to select your removable drive.

h. Click **Search**.

   Because *chap1_ho2_assignment2* contains the text, *vacation*, the file should be displayed in the right pane, as shown in Figure 1.38. To open the file, you could double-click it.

i. Close all open windows.

j. Double-click the **Safely Remove Hardware** icon in the Notification area of the taskbar. Select the device, click the Stop button and OK. When the Safe to Remove Hardware ScreenTip appears, remove the USB drive and close the Safely Remove Hardware dialog box.

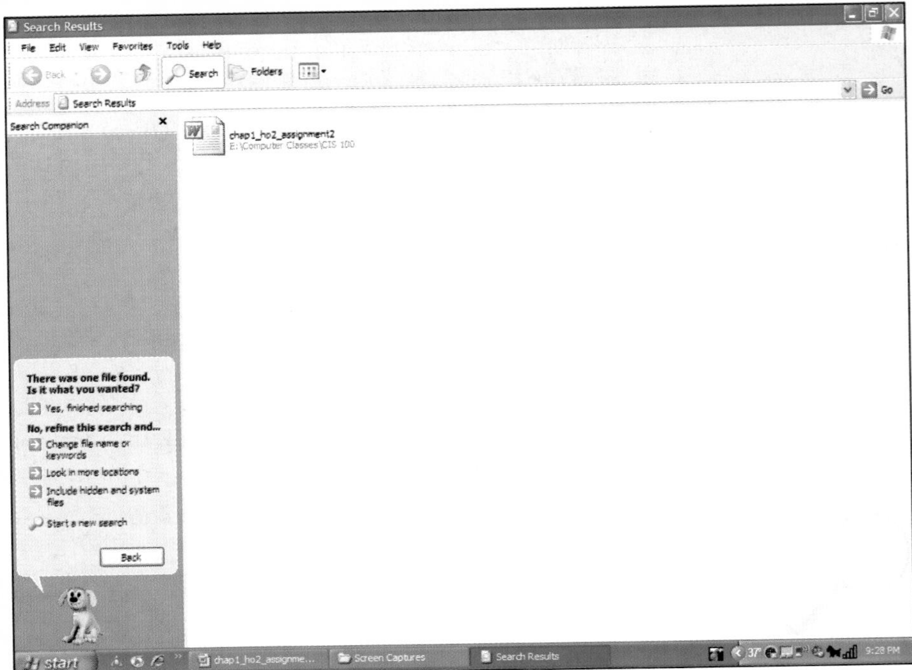

Figure 1.38 Finding a File

Step 4
Use Control Panel to Customize System Settings

Refer to Figure 1.39 as you complete Step 4.

a. Click **Start** and click **Control Panel**.

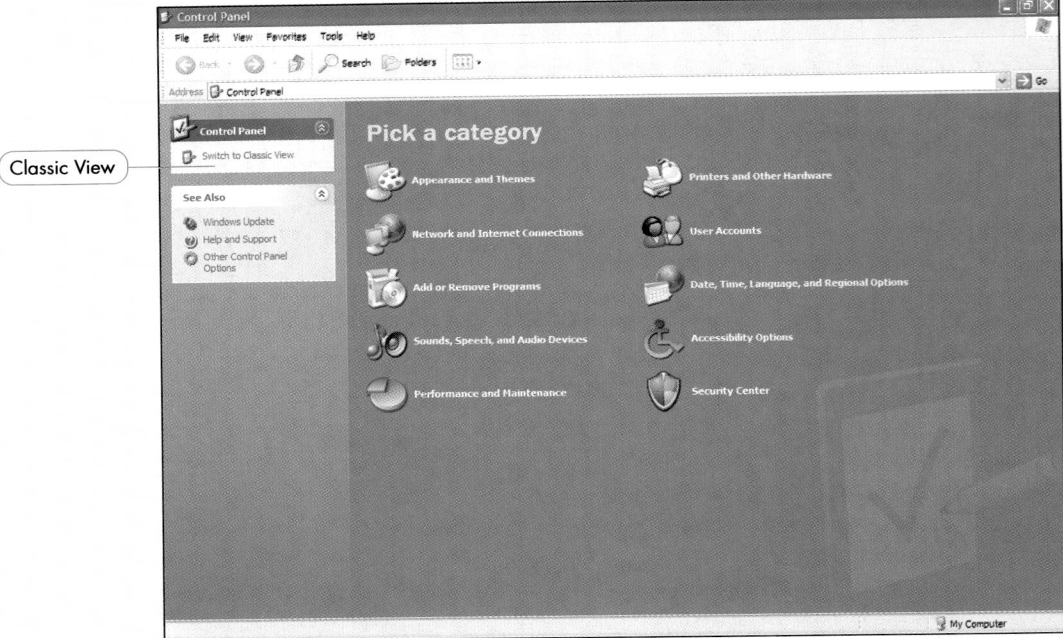

Figure 1.39 Control Panel

TROUBLESHOOTING: The Control Panel might open in the Classic View instead of the Windows XP Category view shown in Figure 1.39. Change to the Windows XP view by clicking **Switch to Category View** in the task pane.

b. Click **Date**, **Time**, **Language**, and **Regional Options**.

c. Click **Change the date and time**.

d. Double-click the **minutes** portion of the time displayed below the clock. When minutes are selected (shaded), type a new minutes setting. Click **OK**.

e. In the Control Panel, click **Back**.

f. Click **Performance and Maintenance**.

g. Click **See basic information about your computer**. Click the **General tab**, if necessary. You should see information including the version of Windows and amount of RAM.

h. Click **Cancel**. Click **Back**.

i. Click **Appearance and Themes**. Click **Choose a screen saver**.

j. Click the drop-down arrow beside the screen saver area. Click 3D Flower Box. Click Preview. If necessary, click to end the preview. If you want to keep the screen saver, click OK. However, if you are in a classroom or lab setting, click Cancel.

k. Close the Control Panel.

Step 5
Add a User Account

Refer to Figure 1.40 as you complete Step 5.

a. Click **Start**, click **Control Panel**, and then click **User Accounts**.

If you are in a computer lab, you might not be allowed to work with user accounts. Please check with your instructor before completing this exercise.

b. Click **Create a New Account**.

c. Type **Home Access** in the "type a name for the new account" text box and click **Next**.

d. Click the **Limited option** to grant only basic privileges to the new account.

e. Click **Create Account**. Figure 1.40 displays the new account. From the User Accounts window, you can change an existing account or create another.

f. Click **Home Access**. You can easily remove an account, but be aware that the user might also lose some data and personal information.

g. Click **Delete the Account**. Click **Delete Files**. Click **Delete Account**. Close all open windows.

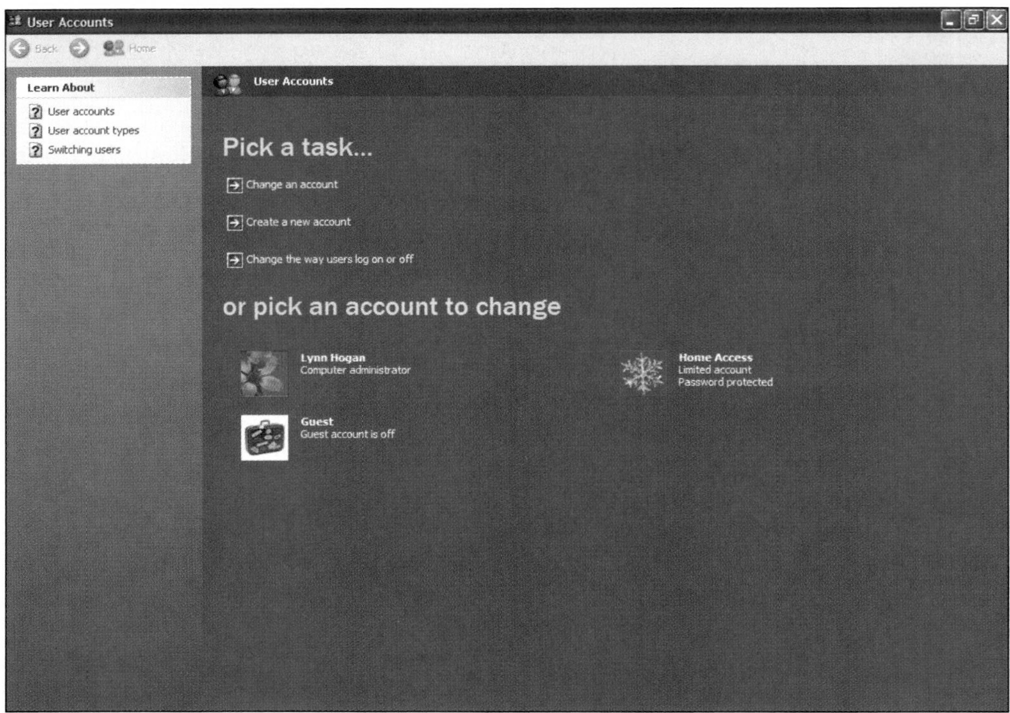

Figure 1.40 User Accounts

Step 6
Add a Shortcut to the Quick Launch Toolbar

a. Right-click an empty area of the taskbar. Point to **Toolbars**. If there is no check mark beside Quick Launch, click **Quick Launch**. If a check mark already appears, click outside the menu to close it.

b. Click and drag the Recycle Bin icon to the Quick Launch toolbar. When a small black vertical line appears on the toolbar, release the mouse button.

c. Click **Recycle Bin** on the taskbar. Does the Recycle Bin open? Close the Recycle Bin.

d. Right-click the **Recycle Bin icon** on the Quick Launch toolbar. Click **Delete**. When asked to confirm the deletion, click **Yes**.

   Remember that removing a shortcut icon only deletes the pointer, not the actual program. Therefore, the Recycle Bin is only removed from the **Quick Launch** toolbar, not the desktop.

Summary

1. **Identify components on the Windows desktop.** The desktop is displayed when the computer is first powered on. Just like a normal desktop that you might use at home, the computer desktop is an area to hold projects, software, and files (in bordered areas called windows). Icons on the desktop represent software, files, Web sites, and shortcuts. You can maintain your computer desktop, keeping clutter to a minimum and customizing the background and other settings.
2. **Work with windows and menus.** A window can be minimized, maximized, resized, moved, and closed. Menus organize commands within an application and enable you to make selections relevant to the current task.
3. **Identify dialog box components.** A dialog box is a window that presents options for the user to select to process instructions. An option button enables you to select only one option in a group. A text box enables you to type information. A spin button enables you to increase or decrease a value. A check box enables you to select one or more items in a group. A list box displays a list of items from which to select. Clicking a command button processes a command to accept or cancel changes or displays another dialog box.
4. **Use the Help Support Center.** Although no printed reference manuals are packaged with Windows XP, there is a wealth of information in the Help and Support Center. Available as a Start menu selection, Help and Support is an indexed tool whereby you can search for information on just about any Windows-related topic.
5. **Work with folders.** A folder is a storage area on a disk in which you can place files and subfolders. You can use My Computer or Windows Explorer to create folders. You can organize folders in any way that you like.
6. **Manage folders and files in Windows Explorer.** Windows XP provides tools that assist you in managing files and folders. Windows Explorer is a program that enables you to view the contents of disks as well as to create folders and move or copy items into them. When you copy an item, a duplicate is saved in another folder or on another drive. When you move an item, the file or folder is removed from its original location and placed in another. The easiest way to move or copy items is to right-click and drag them from one area to another in Windows Explorer.
7. **Delete items and manage the Recycle Bin.** The Recycle Bin is a holding area for items that have been deleted from the hard drive. It does not, however, retain items removed from other media, such as CDs or USB drives. If you decide that you want to retrieve a deleted item, you can open the Recycle Bin, click the item, and click **Restore this item**.
8. **Change the display settings.** As you work with a computer, you probably will want to change the display to a more colorful or personal background. You also might select a screen saver and adjust the screen resolution. All of those activities are possible by working with the Display Properties dialog box.
9. **Change computer settings using the Control Panel.** The Control Panel is a Windows feature that enables you to change certain computer settings, such as the desktop background, screen saver, mouse buttons and pointers, and clock. Through the Control Panel, you also can view system settings, create user accounts, uninstall software, and manage printers and other peripheral devices.
10. **Create shortcuts on the desktop and Quick Launch toolbar.** A shortcut is a file that points to another file or device. You might want to create a shortcut on the desktop so that you can simply double-click it when you want to open the program to which the shortcut points. Shortcuts are most often placed on the desktop by right-clicking and dragging the file to the desktop. Similarly, you can create shortcuts on the Quick Launch toolbar by clicking and dragging items to the toolbar.
11. **Use Windows Desktop Search.** In a perfect world, you would never lose files or misplace them. Realistically, though, you are very likely to create a file and misplace it or download an item from the Internet and not pay attention to where it is saved on your system. Windows Desktop Search makes it easy to find a lost item if you know anything about it, such as part of the file name or file content. Windows Desktop Search indexes files, folders, and e-mail so that items can be found quickly.

Key Terms

Background 584
Backup 576
Check box 567
Close button 564
Command button 567
Control Panel 585
Data file 572
Desktop 559
Dialog box 566
Drop-down menu 564
Fast user switching 559
File 572
File name 572
Folder 572
Help and Support Center ..567
Icon 559
List box 567
Maximize button 563
Menu bar 564
Minimize button 563
Multitasking 562
Notification area 561
Option button 566
Program file 572
Quick Launch toolbar 561
Radio button 566
Recycle Bin 577
Restore Down button 563
Screen saver 585
Scroll bar 564
Search Companion 591
Shortcut 589
Shortcut menu 576
Spin button 567
Start button 560
Start menu 560
Status bar 564
Task pane 563
Taskbar 560
Text box 566
Thumbnail 566
Title bar 563
Toolbar 564
User account 589
Window 562
Windows Desktop Search ...561
Windows Explorer 574
Windows Vista 559
Windows XP 559
Windows XP Home Edition ..559
Windows XP Media Center Edition ...559
Windows XP Professional Edition ...559
Wizard 587

Multiple Choice

1. Which of the following is true regarding a dialog box?
   (a) Option buttons indicate mutually exclusive choices
   (b) Check boxes imply that multiple options may be selected
   (c) Both A and B
   (d) Neither A nor B

2. Which of the following is the first step in sizing a window?
   (a) Point to the title bar.
   (b) Pull down the View menu to display the toolbar.
   (c) Point to any corner or border.
   (d) Pull down the View menu and change to large icons.

3. Which of the following is the first step in moving a window?
   (a) Point to the title bar.
   (b) Pull down the View menu to display the toolbar.
   (c) Point to any corner or border.
   (d) Pull down the View menu and change to large icons.

4. Which button appears immediately after a window has been maximized?
   (a) Close
   (b) Minimize
   (c) Maximize
   (d) Restore Down

5. What happens to a window that has been minimized?
   (a) The window is still visible but it no longer has a Minimize button.
   (b) The window shrinks to a button on the taskbar.
   (c) The window is closed and the application is removed from memory.
   (d) The window is still open but the application has been removed from memory.

6. What is the significance of a faded (dimmed) command in a drop-down menu?
   (a) The command is not currently accessible.
   (b) A dialog box appears if the command is selected.
   (c) A Help window appears if the command is selected.
   (d) There are no equivalent keystrokes for the particular command.

7. The Recycle Bin enables you to restore a file that was deleted from:
   (a) The CD drive
   (b) Drive C
   (c) Both A and B
   (d) Neither A nor B

8. Which of the following is suggested as essential to a backup strategy?
   (a) Back up all program files at the end of every session
   (b) Store backup files at another location
   (c) Both A and B
   (d) Neither A nor B

9. A shortcut may be created for:
   (a) An application or a document
   (b) A folder or a drive
   (c) Both A and B
   (d) Neither A nor B

10. What happens if you click the Folders button (on the Standard Buttons toolbar in the My Computer folder) twice in a row?
    (a) The left pane displays a task pane with commands for the selected object.
    (b) The left pane displays a hierarchical view of the devices on your system.
    (c) The left pane displays either a task pane or the hierarchical view depending on what was displayed prior to clicking the button initially.
    (d) The left pane displays both the task pane and a hierarchical view.

11. Windows Desktop Search can:
    (a) Locate all files containing a specified phrase
    (b) Locate all files of a certain type
    (c) Both A and B
    (d) Neither A nor B

12. Which views display miniature images of photographs within a folder?
    (a) Tiles view and Icons view
    (b) Thumbnails view and Filmstrip view
    (c) Details view and List view
    (d) All views display a miniature image

13. Which of the following statements is true?

(a) A plus sign next to a folder indicates that its contents are hidden.
(b) A minus sign next to a folder indicates that its contents are hidden.
(c) A plus sign appears next to any folder that has been expanded.
(d) A minus sign appears next to any folder that has been collapsed.

14. To create a screen saver using your own pictures, the pictures must be saved in what folder?

(a) My Documents
(b) Favorites
(c) My Photos
(d) My Pictures

15. When is a file permanently deleted?

(a) When you delete the file from Windows Explorer
(b) When you empty the Recycle Bin
(c) When you turn the computer off
(d) All of the above

Practice Exercises

1 Lakeview Heritage Day

Lakeview High School is sponsoring Lakeview Heritage Day, a day of activities and entertainment honoring the heritage of the 50-year-old high school. Your class is coordinating activities for alumni who are 60 years old or older. An alumni survey of students in that age group indicated an interest in basic computer training. Your computer instructor asked you to test some training materials for a class introducing Windows XP to the older alumni, and gave you a suggested outline. Pretend to be a "senior student" and go through the activities given below.

a. Turn on the computer and select an account (entering a password, if necessary).
b. To make sure icons are set to auto-arrange, right-click an empty area of the desktop. Point to **Arrange Icons by**. If a check mark does not appear beside **Auto Arrange**, click **Auto Arrange**.
c. Click **Start** and **Control Panel**. Click **Appearance and Themes**. Click **Change the desktop background**. Select the Windows XP background and click **OK**. Close the Control Panel.
d. Click **Start**, select **All Programs**, select **Accessories**, and then **Calculator**. Practice a calculation: **2025/15**, which is 2025 divided by 15 (the slash is the division operator). You can either type the calculation or use the mouse to enter the calculation. Then press **Enter** or click **=**. What is the result? Close the calculator.
e. Double-click the **Recycle Bin** icon on the desktop. If the window opens as a maximized window (filling the screen), click the **Restore Down button** (the middle button). Your window should be less than full size. Make the window smaller by clicking and dragging a border or corner. Move the window by clicking and dragging the title bar. Click the **Close button** to close the Recycle Bin.
f. Get help. You have heard about hibernation and wonder what that has to do with a computer! Click **Start**, select **Help and Support**, and select **Index**. Click in the Type in the keyword to find text box and type *hibernation*. In the index, click **overview**. Click **Display**. Compare to Figure 1.41. Close Help and Support.

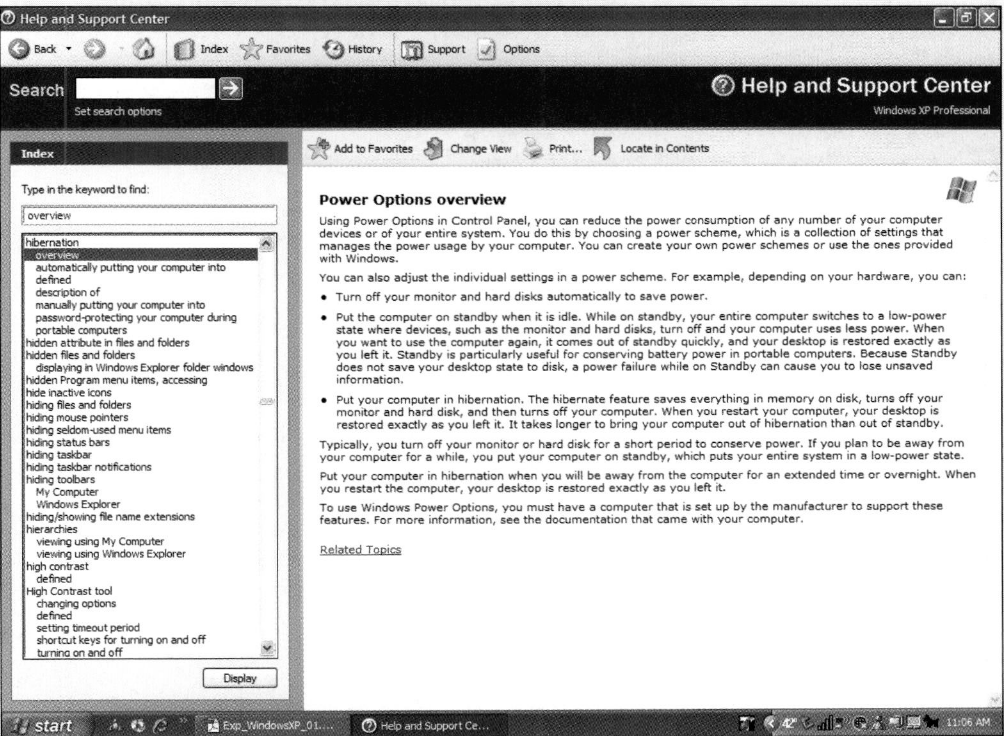

Figure 1.41 Index Keyword

...continued on Next Page

g. Find all pictures on your system. You think there may be some appropriate photographs that you could use for publicizing the computer class. To find all pictures, click the **Windows Desktop Search bar on the taskbar**. Type ***.jpg**. (The * is a wildcard character that represents any file name, while .jpg narrows results to picture files.) All pictures will be displayed. To preview a picture, click it. The picture will appear in the preview pane to the right. Close all open windows.

2 Friends of the Library

As a community service, you have volunteered to work with *Friends of the Library*, a group of people dedicated to raising money for the local public library. A benefactor donated a computer, but it needs to be cleaned up—unnecessary icons should be removed and an appropriate background selected. You also need to take a look at the computer and identify the operating system in use and the configuration of disk drives and programs.

a. To assure a relatively "clean" desktop, you will isolate those desktop icons that are not used often. Right-click an empty area of the desktop. Click **Properties**. Click the **Desktop tab**. Click **Customize Desktop**. Click **Clean Desktop Now**. Click **Next**. Take a look at the icons that are to be placed in an *Unused Desktop Shortcuts* folder. If you are in a classroom or lab setting, check with your instructor, or click **Cancel** to end the activity. If you are at home, or if your instructor approves, click **Next**, and click **Finish**. Close all open windows.
b. Right-click an empty area of the desktop and select **Properties**. Click **Desktop**. Select Tulips. Click **OK**.
c. Click **Start** and click **Control Panel**. Click **Performance and Maintenance**. Click **System**. What operating system is installed on the computer? How much memory (RAM) is available? Close all open windows. Compare to Figure 1.42.

Figure 1.42 System Properties

...continued on Next Page

d. Click **Start** and click **My Computer**. What type of disk drives do you see? How much free space is available on the hard drive? Place your mouse pointer over the local drive to check the availability.
e. Because the computer will be in a public space, you want to set a screen saver so that when the computer is idle, a moving image obscures the screen. Click **Start** and click **Control Panel**. Click **Appearance and Themes**. Click **Choose a screen saver**. Click the **Screen saver drop-down arrow** and select **Starfield**. Change the wait time to 8 minutes. Click **OK**. Close all open windows.
f. You are not sure what programs are already installed on the system so you want to display a complete list. Click **Start** and **Control Panel**. Click **Add or Remove Programs**. Wait a few seconds for the list to appear. Scroll through the list, familiarizing yourself with the programs. You will not remove any programs, but if you were actually working with a donated computer, you could click any program to uninstall and click **Remove**. Close all open windows.

3 College Bound

This is your first semester in college, and you are determined to be as organized as possible. Since most of your instructors require electronic submission of assignments in the form of Word documents and PowerPoint presentations, you will create a folder for each class and its assignments.

a. Click **Start**, click **All Programs**, click **Accessories**, and click **Windows Explorer**. If you do not see the folder hierarchy in the left pane, but instead see the task pane, click **Folders** in the Standard toolbar. Click "+" beside **My Computer** to expand the folders structure. Click **Local Disk (C:)**.
b. Because you plan to be in college for a few years, you will identify your assignments not only by class, but by semester. With the local hard drive selected (shaded) in the left pane, click **File**, **New**, and **Folder**. Type **Fall 2008** and press **Enter**. You should see the new folder in the right pane as well as underneath the local drive in the left pane. If you do not see it in the left pane, click "+" beside **Local Disk (C:)** to display it.
c. You are registered for two classes this term—*Speech 101* and *Biology 100*. Click **Fall 2008** in the left pane. Select **File**, select **New**, and select **Folder**. Type **Speech 101** and press **Enter**. Click **Fall 2008** in the left pane. Select **File**, select **New**, and select **Folder**. Type **Biology 101** and press **Enter**. In the left pane, you should see the two new folders underneath **Fall 2008**, as shown in Figure 1.43. If you do not see the folders, click "+" beside **Fall 2008** to expand the view. If you make a mistake with naming or placing a folder, right-click the folder, click **Rename**, type the correct name, and press **Enter**. To remove a folder that is in the wrong place, right-click the folder and click Delete. Confirm the deletion. Close Windows Explorer.

...continued on Next Page

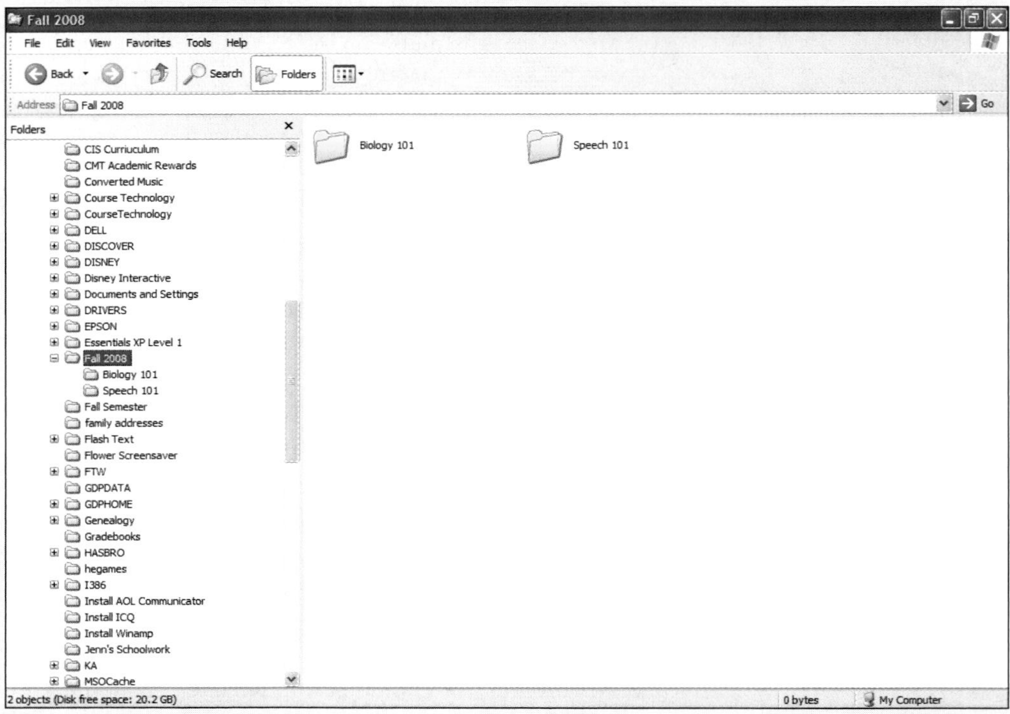

Figure 1.43 Folder Hierarchy

d. Your first Speech assignment is to write a short paragraph about your career goals and save it in WordPad. Click **Start**, select **All Programs**, select **Accessories**, and then select **WordPad**. Type a paragraph, describing your career goals. Click **File** and **Save**. Click **My Computer** in the left frame of the dialog box. Double-click **Local Disk (C:)**. Double-click **Fall 2008**. Double-click **Speech 101**. Click in the **File name** box and type **chap1_pe3_career_solution**. Click **Save**. Close WordPad.
e. To make sure your career paragraph was saved correctly, open Windows Explorer. If necessary, click **Folders** to display the folder structure in the left pane. If **My Computer** is not expanded (showing folders below), click "+" beside **My Computer**. If a "+" appears beside **Local Disk (C:)**, click it. Click **Fall 2008**. Click **Speech 101**. You should see your career goals assignment in the right pane. Right-click the file. Click **Open With**. Click **WordPad**. Close WordPad.
f. Since you probably are working on a school computer, you need to delete the folders that you just created. If you delete a major folder, such as **Fall 2008**, all subfolders and all files also will be removed. Therefore, you will remove **Fall 2008**. In the left pane of Windows Explorer, right-click **Fall 2008**. Click **Delete**. When asked if you want to place the folder in the Recycle Bin, click **Yes**. Confirm that the folder no longer shows in Windows Explorer. Close Windows Explorer.
g. Double-click **Recycle Bin**. Do you see **Fall 2008**? If you ever want to restore the folder and its contents, click the folder and click **Restore this item**. Close the Recycle Bin.
h. For one-click access to the Recycle Bin, you will drag it to the Quick Launch toolbar. First, make sure the Quick Launch toolbar is open on the taskbar. If not, right-click an empty area of the taskbar and point to **Toolbars**. Click **Quick Launch** (if a check mark is not already beside it). Right-click and drag the Recycle Bin to the Quick Launch toolbar. Click **Create shortcuts here**.
i. Right-click the **Recycle Bin icon** on the Quick Launch toolbar, select **Delete**, and confirm the deletion.

Mid-Level Exercises

1 Read-It-Again Bookstore

The Read-It-Again Bookstore is a new business venture in your community. It stocks new and used books in a unique coffee shop setting so that patrons can enjoy coffee and coffee blends while perusing the book collection. Obviously, maintaining accurate records of inventory is important. Your aunt has just purchased the bookstore and has asked for your help in setting up and maintaining a computer for her store records. You will first become familiar with the computer and change a few basic settings.

a. Customize the computer by selecting the Bliss background and the 3D FlowerBox screen saver.

b. Make sure the clock on the taskbar is correct. If not, adjust it.

c. Display the Quick Launch toolbar if it is not already displayed.

d. Open **My Computer**. Maximize the window if it does not fill the screen. Make sure the left pane displays the folder structure of your system. Click **My Documents**. Click **My Pictures**. (You might have to work your way through the folder structure of **My Documents** to find the **My Pictures** folder.) Change the view to **Thumbnails**.

e. Select **My Documents**. Create a folder for an inventory of used books. At the same level (underneath **My Documents**), create a folder for an inventory of new books.

f. Create a shortcut on the Quick Launch toolbar for the Recycle Bin.

g. Get help on copying files and folders to a CD-RW. Because you plan to use a CD-RW for backing up the inventory files, you need to know the proper procedure of copying. In the Help and Support window, you might begin with the keyword **CD-RW** and narrow the search from there. If a printer is installed, print the help screen that explains how to copy files and folders to a CD-RW.

h. Close all open windows.

2 Fitness Challenge

Several people in your neighborhood are interested in forming a fitness group. Having done a good bit of Internet research, you are aware of several weight maintenance and fitness programs that can be customized for the group. You have summarized the programs in Word documents. You plan to print and distribute them for the group to consider. You also have a PowerPoint presentation in mind to further motivate members during the group's first meeting. In preparing the material, you will create and modify some files and folders on your computer.

a. You want to know what Windows can tell you about searching the Internet. In the Help and Support window, click in the **Search** bar and type **Web Search**. Do you find any results on searching the Internet? Close Help and Support.

b. Using Windows Explorer, create a folder as a subfolder of **My Documents** to contain the Word documents that you have created. Name the folder Fitness Resources. Close Windows Explorer.

...continued on Next Page

c. Using WordPad, create a document outlining suggestions for warming up before exercise. Save the file in your new folder as *chap1_mid2_warmups_solution*. Close WordPad.

d. Using Windows Explorer, right-click and drag the folder that you created in Step b to the Desktop to create a shortcut there. Close Windows Explorer.

e. Suppose that you cannot find the *chap1_mid2_warmups_solution* file. Using Windows Desktop Search, search for and locate the file. Close any open windows.

f. You have found some software containing fitness exercises and tips. The software requires a minimum of 10 MB space to install and 256 MB RAM. Check your system to assure that you have enough space for the software.

g. Click **My Documents** and navigate to the folder that you created in Step b. Delete the folder.

h. Close all open windows.

3 Job Search

Nearing graduation from college, you are preparing for a job search. Your first interview includes not only an oral presentation, but a computer skills test to evaluate your preparedness in that area. Although you have completed the required computer literacy component of your degree, you want to refresh your memory and get a little practice before you go for that all-important evaluation. The following skills review should help.

a. Choose the 3D Pipes screen saver. Set the wait time to 5 minutes.

b. Auto Arrange the icons on your desktop.

c. If a Quick Launch toolbar appears on the taskbar, remove it. If it is not there, open it. Be sure to leave the taskbar as you found it by reversing your previous action.

d. Search for help on pausing printing.

e. Create a shortcut to WordPad on the desktop.

f. Change the desktop background to Wind.

g. Open Windows Explorer. Select the **My Pictures** folder (a subfolder of **My Documents**). Change the view to Thumbprints or **Filmstrip**.

h. Connect your USB drive to a USB port. Wait a few seconds for a dialog box to appear. Close the dialog box. Create a folder on the USB drive called **Sample Folder**.

i. Create a subfolder of **Sample Folder** called **Subfolder A**. Create another subfolder of **Sample Folder** called **Subfolder B**.

j. Suppose you place a music selection in the **My Music** folder on the hard drive, but cannot find the **My Music** folder. Using Windows Desktop Search, find the **My Music** folder.

k. Close all open windows.

Mini Cases

Use the rubric following the case as a guide to evaluate your work, but keep in mind that your instructor may impose additional grading criteria or use a different standard to judge your work.

Paint and WordPad

GENERAL CASE

Paint and WordPad are programs included as Accessories in Windows XP. Paint is a graphics program that enables you to create graphics and work with clip art and photographs at an elementary level. WordPad is a basic word processor that is capable of producing text-based documents, but it does not incorporate graphics. Use WordPad to create an invitation to a cookout at your home. Using Paint, you will create a map of your neighborhood. Finally, you will create a folder on your USB (flash) drive to store files related to the cookout. Find and open Paint. Explore the toolbar and determine how to draw a map. *Hint: As you learn to work with Paint, you probably will want to erase your effort and begin anew. Click* ***File, New*** *and indicate that you do not want to save changes to open a new Paint screen.* Save the map to the newly created folder on the USB drive. Save the file as **chap1_mc1_cookout_solution**. Similarly, open WordPad and create an invitation to your home. Explore WordPad text and alignment features in creating the document. Save it to the same folder as your map, calling the file **hap1_mc1_invitation_solution**.

Performance Elements	Exceeds Expectations	Meets Expectations	Below Expectations
Organization	Files are saved in an appropriately named folder. They are complete and would serve the purpose of a mailed invitation.	Files are adequate, but do not appear neat or finished. The end result is not a polished product that could be sent to friends; however, it is recognizable as a map and invitation to a cookout.	Files are poorly designed with incomplete elements. The folder is either inappropriately named or is missing.
Visual aspects	The theme of the map and invitation is consistent, resulting in a pleasing presentation. The invitation contains no errors, and the map is bright, informative, and appealing.	Either the invitation or the map contains elements that are difficult to read or are not related to the topic. There seems to be very little connection between the two files.	The cookout map is not visually appealing and does not take full advantage of Paint's tools. The WordPad invitation includes obvious typos and lack of attention to formatting detail.
Mechanics	The folder is appropriately named and placed. The files are in the folder and are named correctly. The Paint file utilizes at least three different tools and is very readable. The WordPad file contains no mistakes or misspellings.	The folder is not named in a way that suggests its purpose. The Paint file utilizes at least one, but fewer than three tools. The WordPad file contains a mistake.	The folder is missing. The Paint file is a very simple drawing, utilizing little or no color and very few tools. The WordPad document is very short and not informative. The invitation contains multiple errors.

Searching the Internet

RESEARCH CASE

Windows XP enables you to access Web information by entering a URL in the address bar of either **My Computer** or **Windows Explorer**. Open **My Computer**. Click in the address bar and type www.microsoft.com/windowsxp. Press Enter or click Go. In the left frame, click your edition of Windows (**Home Edition**, **Media Center Edition**, or **Professional**). Following relevant links, find as much information as you can about your product, including system requirements, package options (student or academic versions, etc.), and general features. Create a folder called **Windows XP Cases** on a USB drive. Use WordPad or Word to create a one-page report, summarizing your findings. Save the report as **chap1_mc2_report_solution** in the Windows XP Cases folder.

Performance Elements	Exceeds Expectations	Meets Expectations	Below Expectations
Organization	The report is well researched, with findings outlined in a very readable manner. Complete coverage includes a product overview, system requirements, and purchasing options.	Although the basic required elements of the report are included, they are not presented in a coherent fashion. The report may be shorter than one full page.	The report is very short, with an obvious lack of preparation. There is little or no coverage of product details, system requirements, and/or purchasing options.
Visual aspects	The report is well developed, with appropriate paragraph divisions and no typos.	The report contains a few mistakes, but the basic elements are presented in a readable manner.	There is little or no paragraph structure, and it is difficult to identify the major points of the report. Obvious mistakes detract from the subject matter.
Mechanics	The report is saved in the folder on the required storage drive. Both the file and folder are named as directed in the mini case. All required elements are present in the report.	The report is saved in the folder on the required storage drive. However, the file contains several spelling and formatting mistakes and/or the folder and file are not named as required.	The folder is missing or named incorrectly. The report contains multiple mistakes and is very poorly prepared with regard to sentence and paragraph structure.

Glossary

All key terms appearing in this book (in bold italic) are listed alphabetically in this Glossary for easy reference. If you want to learn more about a feature or concept, use the Index to find the term's other significant occurrences.

Absolute cell reference A cell reference that stays the same no matter where you copy a formula.

Access speed Measures the time it takes for the storage device to make the file content available for use.

Active cell The cell you are working in; the cell where information or data will be input.

Animation Movement applied to individual elements on a single slide.

Animation scheme A built-in, standard animation effect.

Annotation A note that can be written or drawn on a slide for additional commentary or explanation.

Argument A necessary input component required to produce the output for a function.

Ascending order Arranges data in alphabetical or sequential order from lowest to highest.

AutoFill An Excel operation that enables users to copy the content of a cell or a range of cells by dragging the fill handle over an adjacent cell or range of cells.

AutoFit The command used when formatting a spreadsheet to automatically adjust the height and width of cells.

AutoFormat A feature that evaluates an entire document, determines how each paragraph is used, then it applies an appropriate style to each paragraph.

Automatic replacement Makes a substitution automatically.

AutoText A feature that substitutes a predefined item for specific text but only when the user initiates it.

AVERAGE function The function that determines the arithmetic mean, or average, for the values in a range of cells.

Background The area of a display screen found behind the desktop icons.

Backup A copy of a file.

Bar chart A chart with a horizontal orientation that compares categories; useful when categorical labels are long.

Bar tab Does not position text or decimals, but inserts a vertical bar at the tab setting; useful as a separator for text printed on the same line.

Border A line that surrounds a paragraph, a page, a table, or an image, similar to how a picture frame surrounds a photograph or piece of art.

Breakpoint The lowest numeric value for a specific category or in a series of a lookup table to produce a corresponding result to return for a lookup function.

Brightness The ratio between lightness and darkness of an image.

Building Blocks Document components used frequently, such as disclaimers, company addresses, or a cover page.

Bulleted list Itemizes and separates paragraph text to increase readability.

Case-insensitive search Finds a word regardless of any capitalization used.

Case-sensitive search Matches not only the text but also the use of upper- and lowercase letters.

Category label Textual information, such as column and row headings (cities, months, years, product names, etc.), used for descriptive entries.

Cell The intersection of a column and row in a table or in an Excel spreadsheet.

Cell margin The amount of space between data and the cell border in a table.

Cell reference The intersection of a column and row designated by a column letter and a row number.

Center tab Sets the middle point of the text you type; whatever you type will be centered on that tab setting.

Change Case Feature that enables you to change capitalization of text to all capital letters, all lowercase letters, sentence case, or toggle case.

Character spacing The horizontal space between characters.

Character style Stores character formatting (font, size, and style) and affects only the selected text.

Chart A graphic or visual representation of data.

Chart area The entire chart and all of its elements.

Check box Enables you to select one or more items that are not mutually exclusive in a dialog box.

Clip Any media object that you can insert in a document.

Clip art A graphical image, illustration, drawing, or sketch.

Clipboard A memory location that holds up to 24 items for you to paste into the current document, another file, or another application.

Close button Removes a window from memory.

Clustered column chart A chart that groups similar data together in columns making visual comparison of the data easier to determine.

Column Formats a section of a document into side-by-side vertical blocks in which the text flows down the first column and then continues at the top of the next column.

Column chart A chart that displays data vertically in a column formation and is used to compare values across different categories.

Column index number A number, indicated by col_index_num in the function, that refers to the number of the column in the lookup table that contains the return values.

Column width The horizontal space or width of a column in a table or in a spreadsheet.

Command An icon on the Quick Access Toolbar or in a group on the Ribbon that you click to perform a task. A command can also appear as text on a menu or within a dialog box.

Command button A dialog box item that you click to accept or cancel selections.

Comment A private note, annotation, or additional information to the author, another reader, or to yourself.

Compatibility checker Looks for features that are not supported by previous versions of Word, Excel, PowerPoint, or Access.

Compress The process of reducing the file size of an object.

Contextual tab A specialty tab that appears on the Ribbon only when certain types of objects are being edited.

Contrast The difference between the darkest and lightest areas of a image.

Control Panel Windows control center that enables you to change system settings, such as your background, screen saver, screen fonts, and accessibility options.

Copy The process of making a duplicate copy of the text or object leaving the original intact.

Copyright The legal protection afforded to a written or artistic work.

COUNT function The function that counts the number of cells in a range that contain numerical data.

COUNTA function The function that counts the number of cells in a range that are not blank.

Criterion (criteria, pl) A rule or norm that is the basis for making judgments.

Cropping Process of reducing an image size by eliminating unwanted portions of an image.

Custom animation An animation where the user determines the animation settings.

Custom dictionary A supplemental dictionary Microsoft Office uses to store items such as proper names, acronyms, or specialized words.

Cut Process of removing the original text or an object from its current location.

Data file An item that you create and to which you give a name, such as a document.

Data label The value or name of a data point in a chart.

Data point A numeric value that describes a single item on a chart.

Data series A group of related data points that appear in row(s) or column(s) in the worksheet.

Database A file that consists of one or more tables and the supporting objects used to get data into and out of the tables.

Datasheet view A grid containing columns (fields) and rows (records) where you add, edit, and delete records in an Access database table.

Decimal tab Marks where numbers align on a decimal point as you type.

Delete operation The operation that removes all content from a cell or from a selected cell range.

Descending order Arranges data in alphabetical or sequential order from highest to lowest.

Design view Displays the infrastructure of a table, form, or report without displaying the data.

Desktop Contains icons and a taskbar. It is displayed when a computer first boots up.

Dialog box A window that provides an interface for a user to select commands.

Dialog Box Launcher A small icon that, when clicked, opens a related dialog box.

Document Inspector Checks for and removes different kinds of hidden and personal information from a document.

Document properties The collection of metadata associated with a file.

Doughnut chart A chart that displays values as percentages of the whole.

Draft view Shows a simplified work area, removing white space and other elements from view.

Drop-down menu Lists commands that relate to the menu name.

Duplex printer A printing device that prints on both sides of the page.

Enhanced ScreenTip Displays when you rest the pointer on a command on the Quick Access Toolbar or Ribbon.

Exploded pie chart A chart that separates one or more slices of the pie for emphasis.

Fast user switching A Windows feature that enables you to quickly move from one user account to another.

Field A basic entity, data element, or category, such as a book title or telephone number.

File A collection of data or information that has a name.

File name An identifier that you give a file when you save it.

Fill handle A small black solid square in the bottom-right corner of a selected cell. It is used to duplicate formulas.

Filter Condition that helps you find a subset of data meeting your specifications.

Filter by Form Permits selecting the criteria from a drop-down list, or applying multiple criterion.

Filter by Selection Selects only the records that match the pre-selected criteria.

Find Locates a word or group of words in a file.

First line indent Marks the location to indent only the first line in a paragraph.

Flat or non-relational Data contained in a single page or sheet (not multiple).

Folder An object that can hold multiple files and subfolders.

Font A complete set of characters—upper- and lowercase letters, numbers, punctuation marks, and special symbols with the same design.

Footer Information printed at the bottom of document pages.

Foreign key A field in one table that also is stored in a different table as a primary key.

Form An interface that enables you to enter or modify record data.

Format Cells Operations that control the formatting for numbers, alignment, fonts, borders, colors, and patterns in a particular cell.

Format Painter Feature that enables you to copy existing text formats to other text to ensure consistency.

Formatting text Changes an individual letter, a word, or a body of selected text.

Formula The combination of constants, cell references, arithmetic operations, and/or functions displayed in a calculation.

Formula bar The area used to enter or edit cell contents.

Full Screen Reading view Eliminates tabs and makes it easier to read your document.

Function A preconstructed formula that makes difficult computations less complicated.

FV function The function that returns the future value of an investment if you know the interest rate, the term, and the periodic payment.

Gallery Displays a set of predefined options that can be clicked to apply to an object or to text.

Go To Moves the insertion point to a specific location in the file.

Group Categories that organize similar commands together within each tab on the Ribbon.

Hanging indent Aligns the first line of a paragraph at the left margin and indents the remaining lines.

Hard page break Forces the next part of a document to begin on a new page.

Hard return Created when you press Enter to move the insertion point to a new line.

Header Information printed at the top of document pages.

Help and Support Center Provides assistance on Windows topics.

Hidden text Document text that does not appear onscreen.

Highlight tool Background color used to mark text that you want to stand out or locate easily.

Horizontal alignment The placement of text between the left and right margins.

Icon A pictorial element representing a program, file, Web site, or shortcut.

IF function, Excel The function that returns one value when a condition is met and returns another value when the condition is not met.

Index An alphabetical listing of topics covered in a document, along with the page numbers where the topic is discussed.

Inequity Examines a mathematical relationship such as equals, not equals, greater than, less than, greater than or equal to, or less than or equal to.

Insert The process of adding text in a document, spreadsheet cell, database object, or presentation slide.

Insertion point The blinking vertical line in the document, cell, slide show, or database table designating the current location where text you type displays.

Kerning Automatically adjusts spacing between characters to achieve a more evenly spaced appearance.

Key Tip The letter or number that displays over each feature on the Ribbon and Quick Access Toolbar and is the keyboard equivalent that you press. Press Alt by itself to display Key Tips.

Landscape orientation Page orientation is wider than it is long, resembling a landscape scene.

Layout Determines the position of objects containing content on a slide, form, report, document, or spreadsheet.

Leader character Typically dots or hyphens that connect two items, to draw the reader's eye across the page.

Left tab Sets the start position on the left so as you type, text moves to the right of the tab setting.

Legend The area that identifies the format or color of the data used for each series in a chart.

Line chart A chart that uses a line to connect data points in order to show trends over a long period of time.

Line spacing The vertical space between the lines in a paragraph and between paragraphs.

List box Presents several items, any of which can be selected.

Live Preview A feature that provides a preview of how a gallery option will affect the current text or object when the mouse pointer hovers over the gallery option.

Lookup table The table that Excel searches using a lookup function

Lookup value The location in a table that represents the cell containing the value to look up the result in a table.

Macro Small program that automates tasks in a file.

Manual duplex Operation that enables you to print on both sides of the paper by printing first on one side and then on the other.

Margin The amount of white space around the top, bottom, left, and right edges the page.

MAX function The function that determines the highest value of all cells in a list of arguments.

Maximize button Causes a window to fill the screen.

MEDIAN function The function that finds the midpoint value in a set of values.

Menu bar A horizontal bar at the top of a window containing options that enable you to work with an application.

Merge and center cells The action that merges the content of several cells into one cell and centers the content of the merged cell.

Metadata Data that describes other data.

Microsoft Clip Organizer Catalogs pictures, sounds, and movies stored on your hard drive.

Microsoft WordArt An application within Microsoft Office that creates decorative text that can be used to add interest to a document.

MIN function The function that determines the smallest value of all cells in a list of arguments.

Mini toolbar A semitransparent toolbar of often-used font, indent, and bullet commands that displays when you position the mouse over selected text and disappears when you move the mouse away from the selected text.

Minimize button Removes a window from view, but not from memory.

Mixed cell reference References that occur when you create a formula that combines an absolute reference with a relative reference ($C13 or C$13). As a result, either the row number or column letter does not change when the cell is copied.

Monospaced typeface Uses the same amount of horizontal space for every character.

Move operation The operation that transfers the content of a cell or cell range from one location in the worksheet to another with the cells where the move originated becoming empty.

Multilevel list Extends a numbered list to several levels, and is updated automatically when topics are added or deleted.

Multiple data series Series that compare two or more sets of data in one chart.

Multitasking The ability to run more than one program at a time.

Name box Displays the cell reference of the active cell in Excel.

Nonbreaking hyphen Keeps text on both sides of the hyphen together, thus preventing the hyphenated word from becoming separated at the hyphen.

Nonbreaking space A special character that keeps two or more words together.

Normal view The tri-pane default PowerPoint view.

Notes Page view Used for entering and editing large amounts of text that the speaker can refer to when presenting.

Notification area Found at the right side of the taskbar; displays icons for background programs and system processes.

NOW function The function that uses the computer's clock to display the current date and time side by side in a cell.

Numbered list Sequences and prioritizes the items and is automatically updated to accommodate additions or deletions.

Object, Access An entity that contains the basic elements of the database. Access uses six types of objects—tables, queries, forms, reports, macros, and modules.

Object, PowerPoint Any type of information that can be inserted in slide.

Office Button Icon that, when clicked, displays the Office menu.

Office menu List of commands (such as New, Open, Save, Save As, Print, and Options) that work with an entire file or with the specific Microsoft Office program.

Option button A mutually exclusive selection in a dialog box.

Order of precedence Rules that establish the sequence by which values are calculated.

Orphan The first line of a paragraph appearing by itself at the bottom of a page.

Outline view Displays varying amounts of detail; a structural view of a document that can be collapsed or expanded as necessary.

Overtype mode Replaces the existing text with text you type character by character.

Paragraph spacing The amount of space before or after a paragraph.

Paragraph style Stores paragraph formatting such as alignment, line spacing, indents, as well as the font, size, and style of the text in the paragraph.

Paste Places the cut or copied text or object in the new location.

Picture style A gallery that contains preformatted options that can be applied to a graphical object.

Pie chart A chart that is the most effective way to display proportional relationships.

Placeholder A container that holds content and is used in the layout to determine the position of objects on the slide.

Plot area The area containing the graphical representation of the values in a data series.

PMT function Calculates a periodic loan payment given a constant interest rate, term, and original value.

Pointing The use of the mouse or arrow keys to select a cell directly when creating a formula.

Portrait orientation Page orientation is longer than it is wide—like the portrait of a person.

Position Raises or lowers text from the baseline without creating superscript or subscript size.

Presentation graphics software A computer application, such as Microsoft PowerPoint, that is used primarily to create electronic slide shows.

Presenter view Delivers a presentation on two monitors simultaneously.

Primary key The field that makes each record in a table unique.

Print Layout view The default view that closely resembles the printed document.

Program file Part of a software program, such as Microsoft Word.

Proportional typeface Allocates horizontal space to the character.

Query A database object that enables you to ask questions about the data stored in a database and returns the answers in the order from the records that match your instructions.

Quick Access Toolbar A customizable row of buttons for frequently used commands, such as Save and Undo.

Quick Launch toolbar Contains program icons, making it possible to open programs with a single click.

Radio button A mutually exclusive selection in a dialog box.

Range A rectangular group of cells. A range may be as small as a single cell or as large as the entire worksheet.

Record A complete set of all of the data (fields) about one person, place, event, or idea.

Recycle Bin Holds files and folders deleted from the hard drive.

Redo Command that reinstates or reserves an action performed by the Undo command.

Referential integrity The set of rules that ensure that data stored in related tables remain consistent as the data are updated.

Relational Database Management System Data are grouped into similar collections, called tables, and the relationships between tables are formed by using a common field.

Relational database software A computer application, such as Microsoft Access, that is used to store data and convert it into information.

Relative cell reference A cell reference that changes relative to the direction in which the formula is being copied.

Repeat Provides limited use because it repeats only the last action you performed. The Repeat icon is replaced with the Redo icon after you use the Undo command.

Replace The process of finding and replacing a word or group of words with other text.

Report A printed document that displays information professionally from a database.

Restore Down button Returns a window to the size it was before it was maximized.

Ribbon The Microsoft Office 2007 GUI command center that organizes commands into related tabs and groups.

Right tab Sets the start position on the right so as you type, text moves to the left of that tab setting and aligns on the right.

Row height The vertical space from the top to the bottom of a row in a table or in a spreadsheet.

Sans serif typeface A typeface that does not contain thin lines on characters.

Scale or scaling Increases or decreases text or a graphic as a percentage of its size.

Scatter (XY) chart A chart that shows a relationship between two variables.

Screen saver A moving graphic or image that takes over the display screen when the user is idle.

ScreenTip A small window that describes a command.

Scroll bar Enables you to control which part of a window is in view at any time.

Search Companion Helps you locate files.

Section break A marker that divides a document into sections thereby allowing different formatting in each section.

Select All button The square at the intersection of the rows and column headings used to select all elements of the worksheet.

Selective replacement Lets you decide whether to replace text.

Serif typeface A typeface that contains a thin line or extension at the top and bottom of the primary strokes on characters.

Shading A background color that appears behind text in a paragraph, a page, a table, or a spreadsheet cell.

Sheet tabs The tabs located at the bottom left of the Excel window that tell the user what sheets of a workbook are available.

Shortcut A special type of file that points to another file or device.

Shortcut menu A list of commands that appears when you right-click an item or screen element.

Show/Hide feature Reveals where formatting marks such as spaces, tabs, and returns are used in the document.

Sizing handle The small circles and squares that appear around a selected object and enable you to adjust the height and width of a selected object.

Slide Show view Used to deliver the completed presentation full screen to an audience, one slide at a time, as an electronic presentation on the computer.

Slide Sorter view Displays thumbnails of slides.

Soft page break Inserted when text fills an entire page then continues on the next page.

Soft return Created by the word processor as it wraps text to a new line.

Sort Lists those records in a specific sequence, such as alphabetically by last name or rearranges data based on a certain criteria.

Sort Ascending Provides an alphabetical list of text data or a small-to-large list of numeric data.

Sort Descending Arranges the records with the highest value listed first.

Sorting The action that arranges records in a table by the value of one or more fields within a table.

Spelling and Grammar Feature that attempts to catch mistakes in spelling, punctuation, writing style, and word usage by comparing strings of text within a document to a series of predefined rules.

Spin button A dialog box feature whereby you can click an up or down arrow to increase or decrease a selection.

Spreadsheet The computerized equivalent of a ledger that is a grid of rows and columns enabling users to organize data, recalculate formulas when any changes in data are made, and make decisions based on quantitative data.

Spreadsheet program A computer application, such as Microsoft Excel, that is used to build and manipulate electronic spreadsheets.

Stacked column chart A chart that places (stacks) data in one column with each data series a different color for each category.

Start button Provides access to programs and other system resources.

Start menu Displayed when you click the Start button.

Status bar The horizontal bar at the bottom of a Microsoft Office application that displays summary information about the selected window or object and contains View buttons and the Zoom slider. The Word status bar displays the page number and total words, while the Excel status bar displays the average, count, and sum of values in a selected range. The PowerPoint status bar displays the slide number and the Design Theme name.

Stock chart A chart that shows the high, low, and close prices for individual stocks over a period of time.

Storyboard A visual plan that displays the content of each slide in the slideshow.

Style A set of formatting options you apply to characters or paragraphs.

SUM function The function that adds or sums numeric entries within a range of cells and then displays the result in the cell containing the function.

Syntax The set of rules by which the words and symbols of an expression are correctly combined.

Tab Looks like a folder tab and divides the Ribbon into task-oriented categories.

Tab, Word Markers that specify the position for aligning text and add organization to a document.

Table A series of rows and columns that organize data effectively.

Table, Access A collection of records. Every record in a table contains the same fields in the same order.

Table alignment The position of a table between the left and right document margins.

Table of contents Lists headings in the order they appear in a document and the page numbers where the entries begin.

Table style Contain borders, shading, font sizes, and other attributes that enhance readability of a table.

Task pane A bar that provides support for a currently selected item or window.

Taskbar The horizontal bar that allows you to move among open windows and provides access to system resources.

Template A file that incorporates a theme, a layout, and content that can be modified.

Text Any combination of entries from the keyboard and includes letters, numbers, symbols, and spaces.

Text box An object that enables you to place text anywhere on a slide or in a document or within a dialog box.

Text direction The degree of rotation in which text displays.

Text wrapping style The way text wraps around an image.

Theme A set of design elements that gives the slide show a unified, professional appearance.

Three-dimensional pie chart A type of pie chart that contains a three-dimensional view.

Thumbnail A miniature display of an image, page, or slide.

Title bar The shaded bar at the top of every window; often displays the program name and filename.

TODAY function The function that is a date-related function that places the current date in a cell.

Toggle switch Causes the computer to alternate between two states. For example, you can toggle between the Insert mode and the Overtype mode.

Toolbar Usually found at the top or side of a window, contains buttons that are accessed more quickly than menu selections.

Transition A movement special effect that takes place as one slide replaces another in Slide Show view.

Typeface A complete set of characters—upper- and lowercase letters, numbers, punctuation marks, and special symbols.

Typography The arrangement and appearance of printed matter.

Undo Command cancels your last one or more operations.

User account A relationship between a user and a com puter (requiring a username and password) defining individual desktop settings and file storage.

User interface The meeting point between computer software and the person using it.

Value Number entered in a cell that represent a quantity, an amount, a date, or time.

Virus checker Software that scans files for a hidden program that can damage your computer.

VLOOKUP function The function that evaluates a value and looks up this value in a vertical table to return a value, text, or formula.

Web Layout view View to display how a document will look when posted on the Web.

Widow The last line of a paragraph appearing by itself at the top of a page.

Window An enclosed rectangular area representing a program or data.

Windows Desktop Search Helps you find anything on your computer by simply typing one or more keywords.

Windows Explorer Displays a tree structure of the devices and folders on your computer.

Windows Vista The newest version of the Windows operating system.

Windows XP The primary operating system (OS) for personal computers.

Windows XP Home Edition Focuses on entertainment and home use.

Windows XP Media Center Edition Coordinates multimedia elements.

Windows XP Professional Edition Designed to support business systems.

Wizard A set of guided instructions.

Word processing software A computer application, such as Microsoft Word, that is used primarily with text to create, edit, and format documents.

Word wrap The feature that automatically moves words to the next line if they do not fit on the current line.

Workbook A collection of related worksheets contained within a single file.

Worksheet A single spreadsheet consisting of columns and rows that may contain formulas, functions, values, text, and graphics.

X or horizontal axis The axis that depicts categorical labels.

Y or vertical axis The axis that depicts numerical values.

Zoom slider Enables you to increase or decrease the magnification of the file onscreen.

Multiple Choice Answer Keys

Office Fundamentals, Chapter 1

1. b
2. c
3. d
4. a
5. d
6. c
7. b
8. c
9. d
10. a
11. c
12. d
13. c
14. a
15. d

Word 2007, Chapter 1

1. c
2. b
3. a
4. c
5. b
6. a
7. c
8. d
9. b
10. c
11. d
12. d
13. b
14. a
15. c
16. d

Word 2007, Chapter 2

1. d
2. c
3. b
4. a
5. d
6. d
7. d
8. d
9. d
10. d
11. b
12. d
13. c
14. d
15. c
16. a
17. b
18. a
19. a

Word 2007, Chapter 3

1. d
2. a
3. a
4. d
5. c
6. b
7. a
8. d
9. a
10. d
11. b
12. b
13. d
14. b
15. a
16. c
17. d

Excel 2007, Chapter 1

1. b
2. a
3. a
4. c
5. c
6. c
7. c
8. a
9. b
10. b
11. b
12. b
13. a
14. a
15. b
16. c
17. a
18. c
19. b

Excel 2007, Chapter 2

1. d
2. b
3. b
4. c
5. d
6. b
7. a
8. a
9. b
10. b
11. c
12. d
13. b
14. b
15. b

Excel 2007, Chapter 3

1. a
2. a
3. a
4. d
5. c
6. d
7. a
8. d
9. a
10. d
11. a
12. c
13. a
14. a
15. c
16. d
17. c

Access 2007, Chapter 1

1. b
2. b
3. d
4. d
5. b
6. b
7. b
8. c
9. c
10. c
11. c
12. a
13. c
14. d
15. a

PowerPoint 2007, Chapter 1

1. d
2. b
3. d
4. a
5. b
6. d
7. a
8. c
9. d
10. b
11. d
12. d
13. c
14. a
15. c

Windows XP, Chapter 1

1. c
2. c
3. a
4. d
5. b
6. a
7. b
8. b
9. c
10. c
11. c
12. b
13. a
14. d
15. b

Index

A

B

C

D

E

F

G

H

I

J

K

L

M

N

O

P

Q

R

S

T

U

V

W

Z